Ten Cool Things To Do Witl

Just because Fedora is a serious operating system doesn't mean it can't be fun too. Here is a list of ten fun and useful things to do with Fedora.

1. **Set Up a Personal Online Desktop:** Use the new GNOME Online Desktop to connect your desktop to your friends, multimedia content, and online applications from Google, Facebook, Yahoo!, and others. Click right on the desktop to immediately get you all your favorite content. (See Chapter 3.)

2. **Launch the new KDE 4 Plasma Desktop:** The next generation KDE desktop lets you add widgets, called plasmoids, to multiple places on your desktop. Find files, Web pages or other items quickly with new search tools. (See Chapter 3.)

3. **Play Commercial Audio/Video:** Licensing restrictions keep many popular codecs from inclusion with Fedora. With the new Codeina feature, Fedora helps you grab the codecs you need to play Windows Media (Audio, Video and MMS), MP3 audio, MPEG-2 and MPEG-4 video decoding, and others. (See Chapter 8.)

4. **Manage music collections:** Launch Rhythmbox to gather, organize, and play music from your hard disk, CDs, or network file systems. You can even select from thousands of free songs from Magnatune and Jamendo online music services. (See Chapter 8.)

5. **Create presentations:** Start up OpenOffice.org Impress to create presentations from scratch or using templates. Tailor presentations to display as slide shows, view on screen, or print on paper. (See Chapter 6.)

6. **Share an Internet connection:** Fedora can be set up as a router and a firewall. With a home or small office LAN set-up, you can use Fedora to share an Internet connection among multiple Linux, Windows, or Mac systems. Then set up a firewall in Fedora to protect your LAN from intruders. (See Chapters 14, 15, and 16.)

7. **Play free games:** As always, Fedora includes dozens of simple card games and board games. The Fedora repository, includes a ton of games, including fun first-person shooter games such as Doom, strategy games such as fantasy game Wesnoth, and online battle games such as BZFlag. (See Chapter 7.)

8. **Run Windows applications:** By adding the wine software packages, you can run many Windows applications right from a Fedora desktop. (See Chapter 5.)

9. **Create an Internet server:** Learn to configure a Web server (Chapter 21), FTP server (Chapter 20) and a mail server (Chapter 19). Then gather that knowledge to create your own public Internet server (Chapter 25). Your server can run from your home Internet connection.

10. **Share over the Internet:** Share your personal videos, software, or other content with friends over the Internet, using Bittorrent swarming network transfer software. While you're at it, instant message your thoughts using Pidgin (formerly GAIM), video-conference your looks (Ekiga), and e-mail your party invitations (Evolution). (See Chapter 7.)

Fedora® 9
and
Red Hat® Enterprise Linux®
Bible

Christopher Negus

WILEY

Wiley Publishing, Inc.

Fedora® 9 and Red Hat® Enterprise Linux® Bible

Published by
Wiley Publishing, Inc.
10475 Crosspoint Boulevard
Indianapolis, IN 46256
www.wiley.com

Published simultaneously in Canada

ISBN: 978-0-470-37362-0

Printed in the United States of America.

10 9 8 7 6 5 4 3 2 1

Library of Congress Cataloging in Publication Data available upon request.

For general information on our other products and services or to obtain technical support, please contact our Customer Care Department within the U.S. at (800) 762-2974, outside the U.S. at (317) 572-3993 or fax (317) 572-4002.

Wiley also publishes its books in a variety of electronic formats. Some content that appears in print may not be available in electronic books.

About the Author

Christopher Negus has been working with UNIX systems, the Internet, and (most recently) Linux systems for more than two decades. During that time, Chris worked at AT&T Bell Laboratories, UNIX System Laboratories, and Novell, helping to develop the UNIX operating system. Features from many of the UNIX projects Chris worked on at AT&T have found their way into Red Hat Enterprise Linux, Fedora, and other Linux systems.

Chris is the author of all editions of what started out as *Red Hat Linux Bible*, which because of the name changes of Red Hat's Linux projects has evolved into the book you are holding. Most recently, Chris co-authored four books in the Linux Toolbox series: *Fedora Linux Toolbox*, *Ubuntu Linux Toolbox*, *SUSE Linux Toolbox, and BSD UNIX Toolbox* (Wiley Publishing).

Before that, Chris authored *Linux Bible 2008 Edition* and co-wrote *Linux Troubleshooting Bible* and *Linux Toys II* for Wiley Publishing. For Prentice Hall, Chris authored *Live Linux CDs* and co-authored the *Official Damn Small Linux Book*, as part of the Negus Live Linux Series.

At home, Chris enjoys spending time with his wife, Sheree, and his boys, Caleb and Seth. His hobbies include soccer, singing, and exercising with Sheree.

As always, I dedicate this book to my wife, Sheree. This book would never have happened without her love and support.

Credits

Acquisitions Editor
Jenny Watson

Development Editor
Sara Shlaer

Production Editor
Debra Banninger

Technical Editor
Tim Boronczyk

Production Manager
Tim Tate

Editorial Manager
Mary Beth Wakefield

**Vice President and
Executive Group Publisher**
Richard Swadley

Vice President and Executive Publisher
Joseph B. Wikert

Project Coordinator
Bill Ramsey

Indexer
Johnna VanHoose Dinse

Media Development Project Manager
Laura Moss-Hollister

Media Assistant Producer
Kit Malone

Media Quality Control
Shawn Patrick

Preface

With the Fedora Linux operating system and the instructions in this book, you can transform your PC into a safe, powerful, and free computer system. Starting with Fedora, you can simply replace (or coexist with) Microsoft Windows on your everyday desktop computer. You can also configure your computer to share your files, printers, Web pages, or directory services to other computers. Then, if you choose, you can transition your skills to manage anything from a small office to a large, corporate Red Hat Enterprise Linux computer installation.

This book tells you how and gives you all the software you need to do it.

Who Are You?

You don't need to be a programmer to use this book. You may be someone who just wants to use Linux (to run programs, access the Internet, and so on). Or you may simply want to know how to administer a Linux system in a workgroup or on a network.

I assume that you are somewhat computer literate but have little or no experience with Linux (or UNIX). You may be migrating from Microsoft operating systems to Linux because of its networking and multiuser features. You may be looking to start a career as a computer technician or network administrator and find that spending a few dollars for an entire operating system and book is more economical than taking those technical classes offered on late-night television. Or you might just think a "free" operating system is cool.

In any case, after you peruse this book you should have a good idea of how to run applications, set up a small network, connect to the Internet, and configure a variety of server types (Web servers, print servers, file servers, and so on). This book represents a great first few steps toward your becoming someone who can set up a home network or a small office network and maintain a group of computers.

This Book's Learn-Through-Tasks Approach

The best way to learn a computer system is to get your hands on it. To help you learn Linux, this book takes a task-oriented approach. Where possible, I step you through the process of working with a feature, such as setting up a network or configuring your desktop.

When you are done with a task, you should have a good, basic setup of the feature that it covers. After that, I often provide pointers to further information on tweaking and tuning the feature.

Instead of assuming that you already know about cryptic topics such as troff, NFS, and TCP/IP, I ease you into those features with headings such as "Publishing with Fedora and RHEL," "Setting up a File Server," and "Connecting to the Internet." Heck, if you already knew what all those things were and how to get them working, you wouldn't need me, would you?

When many tools can be used to achieve the same results, I usually present one or two examples. In other words, I don't describe six different Web browsers, twelve different text editors, and three different news servers. I tell you how to get one or two similar tools really working and then note the others that are available.

What You Need

This book covers two different Linux systems: Fedora 9 and Red Hat Enterprise Linux 5. Because Fedora is most recently released and is included on the media with this book, examples primarily focus on Fedora. However, because Fedora technology feeds into distributions besides RHEL, such as CentOS (www.centos.org), StartCom (www.startcom.org), White Box Enterprise Linux (www.whiteboxlinux.org) and Oracle's Unbreakable Linux (www.oracle.com/technologies/linux), you can use this book to learn about those distributions as well.

To follow along with this book, you can install the complete Fedora 9 software found on the accompanying DVD. If you don't have a DVD drive, you can use the CD that comes with this book to try out Fedora and install a desktop Fedora system to your hard disk. Or you can follow along with your CentOS system (which is free) or Red Hat Enterprise Linux 5 system, (which you can obtain with a subscription from Red Hat, Inc.).

To install Fedora 9 with the media that come with this book, you need a PC with the following general configuration:

- An Intel Pentium or compatible CPU, 200MHz Pentium or better (for text mode); 400MHz Pentium II or better (for GUI mode). Fedora 9 has been optimized for Pentium 4 processors. (Intel 486 computers will not work with Fedora 9.)

- At least 64MB of RAM (text-based install) or 128MB of RAM (graphical install). To run the GNOME or KDE desktop 192MB are needed, although the Fedora Project recommends at least 512MB. (For low RAM systems, try the Xfce desktop described in Chapter 2.)

- At least 620MB of hard disk space (you have to select a minimal install). You need 2.3GB of hard disk space for a personal desktop install, 3.0GB for a typical workstation installation, or at least 1.1GB of space for a server installation.

- A DVD or CD drive. This is recommended for installation (because we give you the installation DVD), although you can install from CD (we provide a live CD that can also be installed to hard disk), over a network, or from a local hard disk instead. For network and hard disk installs, booting installation from a 3.5-inch floppy disk drive is no longer supported. Chapter 2 describes methods of launching installation if you don't have a bootable DVD drive: Once the install is started, you need either an extra hard disk partition or another computer (that can be reached over the network) that has packages or images of the Fedora distribution on it. (I tell you how to do that later, in case you're interested.)

Not every piece of PC hardware works with Fedora. While there is no official hardware compatibility list as there is for Red Hat Enterprise Linux (available at http:// bugzilla.redhat.com/hwcert/), overall hardware support should be improved in Fedora 9. In fact, wireless LAN cards, FireWire devices, and some other components have seen improved support in Fedora 9.

There are versions of Fedora available for other computer architectures as well. If you have a Power PC or X86 64-bit computer, you can download official install and live CDs and DVDs from the Fedora project (http://fedoraproject.org/en/get-fedora.html). Likewise, you can get X86 and X86 64-bit versions of CentOS from that project's site (http://mirror.centos.org/).

Fedora 9 and Red Hat Enterprise Linux Bible Improvements

Fedora® 9 and Red Hat® Enterprise Linux® Bible represents the continuing development of *Red Hat Linux Bible*, which I began in 1999. About every six months since Red Hat Linux 6.1, I've followed new versions of Red Hat Linux with updates of this book.

Red Hat, Inc. split its Red Hat Linux development efforts into two tracks: the Fedora Project and the Red Hat Enterprise Linux (RHEL) product. This book now covers the latest of those two Linux distributions: Fedora 9 and RHEL 5. By learning the features in Fedora 9, you will also be preparing yourself for future releases of RHEL.

The foundation for Fedora, RHEL, and this book rests on the tradition begun with Red Hat Linux. The enhancements included in this edition reflect that foundation, plus some bold new cutting-edge Linux technology.

The overall theme of this edition focuses on improvements to the desktop and some ease-of-use desktop applications. The new KDE 4 desktop offers some striking new features for working with widgets and searches. The GNOME desktop has a new Cheese application for grabbing webcam photos and snapshots. NetworkManager continues to make it easier to connect to wired and wireless networks. PackageKit makes upgrading and adding packages easier. Of course, there are lots of other features of Fedora 9 described in this book as well.

The following list describes new features of this book over the previous edition:

- **Fedora 9 (Nearly) Everything Install DVD** — We provide Fedora 9 on DVD with this edition. You get nearly the entire Fedora 9 distribution. Because the Fedora software repository has grown beyond the 8GB size we can fit on a dual-layer DVD, a handful of packages (mostly those not associated with any installation group) from that repository did not make it on to the DVD. However, those packages will still appear on your PackageKit window, allowing you to easily install them from the Internet.

- **Fedora 9 KDE Desktop Live/Install CD** — Before you install Fedora, you can try out a desktop-oriented live version of Fedora 9 by booting the CD that comes with this book.

For this edition, we decided to use the KDE and not the GNOME live CD because of the new KDE 4 desktop. While that CD is running, you can use it to prepare your computer to do a permanent installation. The contents of that CD can also be installed directly to your hard disk.

- **Preupgrade** — When you prepare to install Fedora 9 from Fedora 8, you have the option of running the new preupgrade program. Preupgrade does tasks like downloading packages and checking dependencies needed for Fedora 9 while Fedora 8 is still running. Check Chapter 2 for information on using preupgrade.

- **Graphical login** — The graphical login screen (GNOME display manager or GDM) was changed to include some security features and better fast user switching. Some behavioral changes associated with the updated GDM features are covered in Chapter 2.

- **Removable media settings** — Settings related to what happens when CDs, DVDs, or USB flash drives start up have moved to the Nautilus file manager preferences page. Descriptions in Chapter 3 tell how to find those settings and change them.

- **KDE 4** — Descriptions of the K Desktop Environment (KDE 4) in Chapter 3 have been overhauled to reflect this major revision of the desktop. Besides describing the new Plasma desktop shell and widget facility, several new KDE applications are covered as well. The new Dolphin file manager, KRunner application launcher, and other applications are described in Chapter 3. The chapter also describes the new System Settings window.

- **Xfce desktop** —Although not a new feature, I decided to add a description of the Xfce desktop to Chapter 3 because it's a good choice to run on computers that have less RAM and processing power.

- **PackageKit** — Because PackageKit is now the default graphical tool in Fedora 9 for adding and updating software, I added a description to Chapter 5.

- **PulseAudio Volume Control** — Although PulseAudio sound system was added to Fedora 8, I decided to add a description of the PulseAudio Volume Control (which lets you control audio levels for different applications independently) to Chapter 8.

- **Cheese webcam application** — In Chapter 8, I describe how to use the new GNOME Cheese application to take snapshots and videos from your webcam.

- **Firefox 3 web browser** — The new Firefox 3 Web browser is included with Fedora 9. Some of the new Firefox 3 features highlighted in this book include neat new ways to work with bookmarks and security warnings from the browser location box. (See Chapter 9 for details.)

- **SELinux** — Features in SELinux continue to evolve and improve. Descriptions in Chapter 10 note how SELinux Troubleshooter now warns you in real time from a desktop icon and how the SELinux Administration window can be used to modify a variety of SELinux features.

- **Firewall Configuration** — The Firewall Configuration window not only makes it easier to manage a simple firewall (opening or closing a few ports) but now also includes features for creating trusted interfaces, IP masquerading, port forwarding and custom rules. (Refer to Chapter 14.)

- **freeIPA Identity Management** — The freeIPA project aims to provide a framework for managing an organization's identity, policy, and auditing information. For this first release of freeIPA that is included with Fedora, the identity portion of that goal has been implemented. Chapter 14 describes some of the features available with this developing technology.

- **NetworkManager** — With an icon in the desktop panel and automatic detection of wired and wireless networks, NetworkManager is designed to make connecting to and managing your network interfaces as easy as possible. For this release it seems that NetworkManager is stable enough to use as your primary means of setting up network connections. Descriptions of using NetworkManager to connect to wired networks, wireless networks, and virtual private networks was added to Chapter 15.

- **OpenVPN** — A description of how to set up an openvpn virtual private network server was added to Chapter 16. These descriptions can be used to set up a VPN connection between two Fedora systems (using NetworkManager on the client) or other clients that support openvpn.

- **Red Hat Enterprise Linux 5.1** — I added a small section on new features in RHEL 5.1 to Appendix C.

In addition to new features just described, procedures throughout the book have been tested and corrected to match changes that have occurred to Fedora 9 software in this version.

Conventions Used in This Book

Throughout the book, special typography indicates code and commands. Commands and code are shown in a monospaced font:

```
This is how code looks.
```

In the event that an example includes both input and output, the monospaced font is still used, but input is presented in bold type to distinguish the two. Here's an example:

```
$ ftp ftp.handsonhistory.com
Name (home:jake): jake
Password: ******
```

The following boxes are used to call your attention to points that are particularly important.

> **NOTE:** A Note box provides extra information to which you need to pay special attention.

> **TIP:** A Tip box shows a special way of performing a particular task.

> **CAUTION:** A Caution box alerts you to take special care when executing a procedure, or damage to your computer hardware or software could result.

> **CROSS-REFERENCE:** A Cross-Reference box refers you to further information on a subject that you can find outside the current chapter.

How This Book Is Organized

The book is organized into four parts.

Part I: Getting Started in Fedora and RHEL

Part I consists of Chapters 1 through 4. Chapters 1 and 2 contain brief descriptions of the Linux technology and tell you what you need to get the operating system installed. Chapter 1 serves as an introduction to the Linux OS and to Fedora in particular. I also pay special attention to the division Red Hat, Inc., makes between the Fedora Project and Red Hat Enterprise Linux. Chapter 2 discusses what you need to install Fedora and how to make the decisions you'll be faced with during installation. It includes procedures for installing from DVD, CD-ROM, hard disk, or network connection (NFS, FTP, or HTTP servers).

In Chapter 3, you learn about the GNOME, KDE, and Xfce desktop environments, as well as the X Window system. These GUIs provide graphical means of using Fedora and RHEL. Chapter 4 describes ways of exploring and understanding Fedora and RHEL, primarily from the Linux shell command interpreter. You learn how to use the bash shell, the vi text editor, and the commands for moving around the Linux file system.

Part II: Using Fedora and RHEL

Part II consists of Chapters 5 through 9, which include information for the average user who wants to use Linux to run applications and access the Internet.

Chapter 5 contains information on obtaining, installing, and running Linux applications. It also helps you run applications from other operating systems in Linux. Chapter 6 describes both old-time publishing tools and new, graphical word processors that are available with Fedora and RHEL. Old tools include the troff and TeX text processing tools, whereas newer publishing software includes OpenOffice.org utilities (included on the DVD) and StarOffice (commercially available).

GNOME and KDE games that run in Fedora and RHEL are described in Chapter 7. This chapter also describes how to run commercial Windows games using Cedega, and commercial Linux games, such as Civilization: Call to Power and Myth II, some of which have demo versions available. Chapter 8 describes how to use audio and video players, as well as how to configure sound cards and CD burners. Chapter 9 describes tools for browsing the Web (such as the Firefox browser) and related tools (such as e-mail clients and newsreaders).

Part III: Administering Fedora and RHEL

Part III consists of Chapters 10 through 14, which cover general setup and system maintenance tasks, including how to set up user accounts, automate system tasks, and back up your data. Chapter 10, in which you learn what you need to know about basic system administration, describes the root login, administrative commands, configuration files, SELinux, and log files. Chapter 11 describes how to set up and provide support for multiple users on your Fedora or RHEL system.

In Chapter 12 you learn to create shell scripts and to use the cron facility to automate a variety of tasks on your Fedora and RHEL system. Techniques for backing up your system and restoring files from backup are described in Chapter 13. Chapter 14 describes issues related to securing your computing assets in Fedora and RHEL.

Part IV: Fedora and RHEL Network and Server Setup

Part IV consists of Chapters 15 through 26, which describe step-by-step procedures for setting up a variety of server types. Simple configurations for what might otherwise be complex tasks are contained in each chapter. Learn to arrange, address, and connect your Linux computers to a local area network (LAN) in Chapter 15. Chapter 16 describes techniques for connecting your Linux computer and LAN to the Internet, using features such as Point-to-Point Protocol (PPP), IP forwarding, IP masquerading, routing, and proxy servers.

Chapter 17 describes how to set up different types of print server interfaces, including Samba (to share with Windows systems) and native Linux CUPS printing. Chapter 18 describes file servers, such as Network File System (NFS) servers and Samba file servers. Chapter 19 describes how to configure sendmail or postfix e-mail servers.

Chapter 20 describes how to configure and secure an FTP server, as well as how to access the server using FTP client programs. Chapter 21 teaches you how to set up Fedora or RHEL as a Web server, focusing on the popular Apache server software. Chapter 22 explains how to use LDAP to create a shared address book. Chapter 23 describes how to set up a DHCP server to distribute information to client workstations on the network.

Chapter 24 describes how to set up and use a MySQL database server in Linux. Chapter 25 takes you through the process of making the servers you configured in the other chapters available on the Internet. Setting up a Domain Name System (DNS) server is also described in Chapter 25. Chapter 26 describes how to set up Fedora or RHEL to be a Macintosh file and printer server. It also describes how to install Fedora on a new Intel-based Mac, so you can dual boot between Mac OS X and Fedora.

Appendixes

This book contains three appendixes. Appendix A describes the contents of the companion media. Appendix B provides an overview of setting up and running network services. Appendix C covers features in Red Hat Enterprise Linux 5.

About the Companion Media

The Fedora 9 DVD that accompanies this book provides the software you need for a complete working Fedora system. With this software, you can install sets of software packages that result in an installation from a few hundred megabytes to up to well over 10 gigabytes of software.

We also include a Fedora 9 KDE Desktop Live/Install CD. That CD can be booted to run a live Fedora KDE desktop system, without touching the contents of your hard disk. You can install the contents of the live CD to your hard disk, to use that desktop system permanently from your hard disk.

This book describes how to configure and use the software for those different media.

About the Companion Web Site

A feature of the Fedora and RHEL Bible Companion Web site for this release is an advanced links page, specially geared toward helping you overcome common problems with Fedora. If you are not finding the answers you need in this book, go to the book's Web site at www.wiley.com/go/fedora9bible and see if some new information on the subject is available.

Even in a book that pushes the 1,000-page boundary, a few topics don't seem to make the cut. The companion Web site contains some bonus material on topics such as using the X Window system, finding neat add-on software, exploring alternative administrative interfaces, Logsentry, and Portsentry.

With the LILO bootloader now gone from the Fedora distribution for several releases, I decided to move descriptions of LILO out of this book and to the Web site. Other topics moved to the Web site from previous editions of this book includes information on using legacy UNIX remote commands (rlogin, rcp, and the like), running Tripwire to manage system security, running a NetWare server in Linux (mars_nwe) and using crack and other password protection tools. Features moved from the immediately preceding edition include descriptions of the wu-FTPd FTP server, INN news server, and the sendmail.cf file.

Reach Out

If you have any questions or comments about this book, feel free to contact me by e-mail at chris@linuxtoys.net. I get busy sometimes, but I'll do my best to help.

Acknowledgments

A special acknowledgment goes to the people at Red Hat, Inc. and members of the Fedora Project. In particular, Paul Frields (new Fedora Project leader), Max Spevack (outgoing Fedora Project leader) and Greg DeKoenigsberg (Fedora Community leader) deserve praise for their leadership in producing a consistently high-quality Linux distribution.

Special thanks to Jesse Keating (Red Hat release engineer for Fedora) for helping me use his excellent Pungi tools to produce the 8GB Fedora DVD that comes with this book. Also special thanks to these members of the Fedora Project who answered my questions during the development of this edition: Christopher Aillon, Rahul Sundaram, Seth Vidal, Ian Weller, Dan Williams, and David Zeuthen.

At Wiley, I'd like to thank Jenny Watson, Colleen Hauser, and Laura Moss-Hollister for helping work out issues related to the publicity, media, and covers for this book. Thanks to Sara Shlaer for her continued great editing and production work on this book, and for keeping me on schedule so we could bring this book to you on time.

Thanks to Debra Banninger for shepherding the book through the final stages of production. Tim Boronczyk provided a thorough technical editing pass. Thanks also to Margot Maley Hutchison and the others at Waterside Productions for bringing me this project.

Thanks, as always, to my dear family for helping me through this project.

Finally, a special thanks goes to those of you who bought this and earlier editions of *Red Hat Linux Bible*. Go out and become a force for Linux in your work, home, and community. If you feel like expanding your Linux horizons, try some of these other books I've written:

- *Linux Bible 2008 Edition* — Contains 16 different bootable and installable Linux distributions on DVD and CD, along with descriptions characterizing those and other popular and interesting Linux distributions.

- *Fedora Linux Toolbox* with François Caen — Includes 1000+ command lines to help Fedora, RHEL, and CentOS power users get the most out of Linux. To try other similar distributions, check out *Ubuntu Linux Toolbox*, *SUSE Linux Toolbox* and *BSD UNIX Toolbox* by the same authors.

- *Linux Troubleshooting Bible* with Thomas Weeks — Goes beyond this book to help you safely deploy and troubleshoot Linux systems.

- *Linux Toys II* — If you're looking for something fun to do with Linux, this book contains nine fun projects you can build with a PC and open source software.

Contents

Downloading a whole Web site 407

Continuing a download..407

Using ssh for remote login/remote execution 408

Using scp for remote file copy..408

Using the "r" commands: rlogin, rcp, and rsh 409

Summary 409

Part III: Administering Fedora and RHEL **411**

Chapter 10: Understanding System Administration... **413**

Using the root user account 414

Becoming Super User (The su Command)..414

Learning about Administrative GUI Tools, Commands, Configuration Files, and Log Files.......416

Using graphical administration tools 416

Becoming Super User in X 417

Administrative commands..421

Administrative configuration files..421

Administrative log files..426

Using other administrative logins...426

Understanding administrative logins 427

Using sudo for assigning administrative privilege...................................427

Administering Your Linux System 429

Configuring Hardware...429

Checking your hardware 430

Reconfiguring hardware with kudzu 430

Configuring modules 431

Listing loaded modules...431

Loading modules 433

Removing modules 433

Managing File Systems and Disk Space...434

Mounting file systems 437

Supported file systems..437

Using the fstab file to define mountable file systems 439

Using the mount command to mount file systems 441

Using the umount command to unmount a file system..........................444

Using the mkfs command to create a file system 444

Adding a hard disk..445

Using RAID disks..448

Checking system space..450

Checking Disk Space with Disk Usage Analyzer....................................450

Displaying system space with df..450

Checking disk usage with du 451

Finding disk consumption with find 452

Monitoring System Performance..452

Watch computer usage with System Monitor..453

Part I

Getting Started in Fedora and RHEL

Chapter 1: An Overview of Fedora and
Red Hat Enterprise Linux

Chapter 2: Installing Fedora

Chapter 3: Getting Started with the Desktop

Chapter 4: Using Linux Commands

Chapter 1

An Overview of Fedora
and Red Hat Enterprise Linux

In This Chapter

- Introducing Fedora and RHEL
- What is Linux?
- Linux's roots in UNIX
- Common Linux features
- Primary advantages of Linux
- What is Fedora?
- Why choose Fedora?
- The culture of free software

Linux was a phenomenon waiting to happen. The computer industry suffered from a rift. In the 1980s and 1990s, people had to choose between inexpensive, market-driven PC operating systems from Microsoft and expensive, technology-driven operating systems such as UNIX. Free software was being created all over the world, but lacked a common platform to rally around. Linux has become that common platform.

For several years, Red Hat Linux was the most popular commercial distribution of Linux. In 2003, Red Hat, Inc. changed the name of its distribution from Red Hat Linux to Fedora Core (later changing the name to simply Fedora) and moved its commercial efforts toward its Red Hat Enterprise Linux products. It then set up Fedora to be:

- Sponsored by Red Hat
- Supported by the Linux community
- Inclusive of high-quality, cutting-edge open source technology
- A proving ground for software slated for commercial Red Hat deployment and support

Red Hat Enterprise Linux, on the other hand, became the basis for Red Hat's fully supported product line, geared toward big companies with the need to set up and manage many Linux systems. After taking its software through about a year and a half of Fedora releases (about once every six to nine months), a commercial Red Hat Enterprise Linux (RHEL) product line is released that includes:

- Subscription service to RHEL that offers stable, tested software (mostly the same software in Fedora that has gone through rigorous testing)
- Multiple support programs, ranging from an online knowledge base to assistance with custom deployment, engineering, and software development
- Official documentation, training, and certification programs

Fedora itself has become a respected and active Linux distribution that thousands of people use worldwide as a desktop, server, or programming workstation. It is the best way to get the latest Linux software that is being built on a foundation for enterprise-quality systems.

Using Fedora is a great way to get a head start learning the features of upcoming RHEL releases. The latest Fedora Linux operating system (referred to as Fedora 9) is included on the DVD that comes with this book. The book also includes a Fedora Live CD with a desktop Linux system that can be installed directly to your hard disk when you are ready.

Introducing Fedora 9 and Red Hat Enterprise Linux

With the split between community (Fedora) and commercial (Red Hat Enterprise Linux) versions of what was Red Hat Linux, Red Hat has created a model that can suit the fast-paced changes in the open source software world, while still meeting the demands for a well-supported commercial Linux distribution.

Technical people have chosen Red Hat Enterprise Linux because of its reputation for solid performance. With the Fedora Project, Red Hat has created an environment where open source developers can bring high-quality software packages to a freely distributed, community-oriented Linux system.

More than 9800 individual software packages (compared to just over 600 in Red Hat Linux 6.2) are included in the single, massive Fedora 9 software repository. The Fedora 9 software repository represents a merging of the basic Fedora system (Fedora Core) and community-contributed software packages (Fedora Extras) that took more than a year ago. These packages contain features that would cost you thousands of dollars to duplicate if you bought them as separate commercial products. These features let you:

- Connect your computers to a LAN or the Internet.
- Create documents and publish your work on paper or on the Web.
- Work with multimedia content to manipulate images, play music files, view video, and even master and burn your own CDs and DVD.

- Play games individually or over a network.
- Communicate over the Internet using a variety of Web tools for browsing, chatting, transferring files, participating in newsgroups, and sending and receiving e-mail.
- Protect your computing resources by having Fedora or RHEL act as a firewall or a router to protect against intruders coming in through public networks.
- Configure a computer to act as a network server, such as a print server, Web server, file server, mail server, news server, and a database server.

This is just a partial list of what you can do with Fedora or RHEL. Using this book as your guide, you will find that there are many more features built into Fedora and RHEL as well.

Support for new video cards, network cards, printers, and storage devices is being added every day. Linux programmers around the world are no longer the only ones creating hardware drivers. Every day more hardware vendors are creating their own Linux drivers, so they can sell products to the growing Linux market. New applications are being created to cover everything from personal productivity tools to programs that access massive corporate databases.

Remember that old Pentium computer in your closet? Don't throw it away! Just because a new release of Fedora is out doesn't mean that you need all new hardware for it to run. Support for many old computer components get carried from one release to the next. With a Minimal install, you could use Fedora as a router (to route data between your LAN and the Internet), firewall (to protect your network from outside intrusion), or file server (to store shared files on your LAN) — with maybe an Ethernet card or an extra hard disk added.

At this point, you may feel that Linux is something you want to try out. This brings us to the basic question: What is Linux?

What Is Linux?

Linux is a free operating system that was created by Linus Torvalds when he was a student at the University of Helsinki in 1991. Torvalds started Linux by writing a *kernel* — the heart of the operating system — partly from scratch and partly by using publicly available software. (For the definition of an operating system and a kernel, see the sidebar "What Is an Operating System?" later in this chapter.) Torvalds then released the system to his friends and to a community of "hackers" on the Internet and asked them to work with it, fix it, and enhance it. It took off.

> **NOTE:** I make the distinction here between hackers (who just like to play with computers) and crackers (who break into computer systems and cause damage).

Today, there are thousands of software developers around the world contributing software to the free and open source software (FOSS) community that feeds the Linux initiative. Because the source code for the software is freely available, anyone can work on it, change it, or enhance it. Developers are encouraged to pass their fixes and improvements back into the community so that Linux can continue to grow and improve.

On top of the Linux kernel effort, the creators of Linux also drew on a great deal of system software and applications that are now bundled with Linux distributions from the GNU project (GNU stands for "GNU is Not UNIX"), which is directed by the Free Software Foundation (www.gnu.org). There is a vast amount of software that can be used with Linux, making it an operating system that can compete with or surpass features available in any other operating system in the world.

If you have heard Linux described as a free version of UNIX, there is good reason for it. Although much of the code for Linux started from scratch, the blueprint for what the code would do was created to follow POSIX (Portable Operating System Interface for UNIX) standards. POSIX is a computer industry operating system standard that every major version of UNIX complied with. In other words, if your operating system was POSIX-compliant, it was UNIX. Today, Linux has formed its own standards and services organizations to help interoperability among Linux systems, including the Linux Foundation, which supports such efforts as the Linux Standard Base (www.linux-foundation.org/en/LSB).

Linux's Roots in UNIX

Linux grew within a culture of free exchange of ideas and software. Like UNIX — the operating system on which Linux is based — the focus was on keeping communications open among software developers. Getting the code to work was the goal and the Internet was the primary communications medium. Keeping the software free and redistributable was a means to that goal. What, then, were the conditions that made the world ripe for a computer system such as Linux?

In the 1980s and 1990s, while Microsoft flooded the world with personal computers running DOS and Windows operating systems, power users demanded more from an operating system. They ached for systems that could run on networks, support many users at once (multiuser), and run many programs at once (multitasking). DOS (Disk Operating System) and Windows didn't cut it.

UNIX, on the other hand, grew out of a culture where technology was king and marketing people were, well, hard to find. Bell Laboratories in Murray Hill, New Jersey, was a think tank where ideas came first and profits were somebody else's problem. A quote from Dennis Ritchie, co-creator of UNIX and designer of the C programming language, in a 1980 lecture on the evolution of UNIX, sums up the spirit that started UNIX. He was commenting on both his hopes and those of his colleagues for the UNIX project after a similar project called Multics had just failed:

> *What we wanted to preserve was not just a good environment in which to do programming, but a system around which a fellowship could form. We knew from experience that the essence of communal computing as supplied by*

> *remote-access, time-shared machines, is not just to type programs into a*
> *terminal instead of a keypunch, but to encourage close communication.*

In that spirit, the first source code of UNIX was distributed free to universities. Like Linux, the availability of UNIX source code made it possible for a diverse population of software developers to make their own enhancements to UNIX and share them with others.

What Is an Operating System?

An operating system is made up of software instructions that lie between the computer hardware (disks, memory, ports, and so on) and the application programs (word processors, Web browsers, spreadsheets, and so on). At the center is the kernel, which provides the most basic computing functions (managing system memory, sharing the processor, opening and closing devices, and so on). Associated with the kernel are a variety of basic services needed to operate the computer, including:

- **File systems** — The file system provides the structure in which information is stored on the computer. Information is stored in files, primarily on hard disks inside the computer, but also on removable media such as CDs and DVDs. Files are organized within a hierarchy of directories. The Linux file system holds the data files that you save, the programs you run, and the configuration files that set up the system.

- **Device drivers** — These provide the interfaces to each of the hardware devices connected to your computer. A device driver enables a program to write to a device without needing to know details about how each piece of hardware is implemented. The program opens a device, sends and receives data, and closes a device.

- **User interfaces** — An operating system needs to provide a way for users to run programs and access the file system. Linux has both graphical and text-based user interfaces. GNOME and KDE provide graphical user interfaces, whereas shell command interpreters (such as bash) run programs by typing commands and options.

- **System services** — An operating system provides system services, many of which can be started automatically when the computer boots. In Linux, system services can include processes that mount file systems, start your network, and run scheduled tasks. In Linux, many services run continuously, enabling users to access printers, Web pages, files, databases, and other computing assets over a network.

Without an operating system, an application program would have to know the details of each piece of hardware, instead of just being able to say, "open that device and write a file there."

By the early 1980s, UNIX development moved from the organization in Murray Hill to a more commercially oriented development laboratory in Summit, New Jersey (a few miles down the road). During that time, UNIX began to find commercial success as the computing system of choice for applications such as AT&T's telephone switching equipment, for supercomputer applications such as modeling weather patterns, and for controlling NASA space projects.

Major computer hardware vendors licensed the UNIX source code to run on their computers. To try to create an environment of fairness and community to its OEMs (original equipment manufacturers), AT&T began standardizing what these different ports of UNIX had to be able to do to still be called UNIX. To that end, compliance with POSIX standards and the AT&T UNIX System V Interface Definition (SVID) were specifications UNIX vendors could use to create compliant UNIX systems. Those same documents also served as road maps for the creation of Linux.

Elsewhere, the UNIX source code that had been distributed to universities had taken on a life of its own. The Berkeley Software Distribution (BSD) began life in the late 1970s as patches to the AT&T UNIX source code from students and staff at the University of California at Berkeley. Over the years, the AT&T code was rewritten and BSD became freely distributed, with offshoot projects such as FreeBSD, OpenBSD, and NetBSD still available.

Linux has been described as a UNIX-like operating system that reflects a combination of SVID, POSIX, and BSD compliance. Linux continues to aim toward POSIX compliance, as well as compliance with standards set by the new owner of the UNIX trademark, The Open Group (www.unix.org). Much of the direction of Linux today comes from the Linux Foundation (www.linux-foundation.org), which was founded in 2007 by a merger of the Free Standards Group and the Open Source Development Labs.

Common Linux Features

No matter what version of Linux you use, the piece of code common to all is the Linux kernel. Although the kernel can be modified to include support for the features you want, every Linux kernel can offer the following features:

- **Multiuser** — Not only can you have many user accounts available on a Linux system, you can also have multiple users logged in and working on the system at the same time. Users can have their own environments arranged the way they want: their own home directory for storing files and their own desktop interface (with icons, menus, and applications arranged to suit them). User accounts can be password-protected, so that users can control who has access to their applications and data.

- **Multitasking** — In Linux, it is possible to have many programs running at the same time, which means that not only can you have many programs going at once, but that the Linux operating system can itself have programs running in the background. Many of these system processes make it possible for Linux to work as a server, with these background processes listening to the network for requests to log in to your system, view a Web page, print a document, or copy a file. These background processes are referred to as *daemons*.

- **Hardware support** — You can configure support for almost every type of hardware that can be connected to a computer. There is support for floppy disk drives, CD-ROMs, removable disks (such as DVDs and USB flash drives), sound cards, tape devices, video cards, and most anything else you can think of. As device interfaces, such as USB and FireWire, have been added to computers, support for those devices has been added to Linux as well.

  For Linux to support a hardware device, Linux needs a driver, a piece of software that interfaces between the Linux kernel and the device. Drivers are available in the Linux kernel to support hundreds of computer hardware components that can be added or removed as needed.

> **NOTE:** Most hardware manufacturers don't provide Linux drivers with their peripheral devices and adapter cards. Although most popular hardware will be supported eventually in Linux, it can sometimes take a while for a member of the Linux community to write a driver. Also, some outdated hardware may not be updated to work with the latest Linux kernels.

- **Networking connectivity** — To connect your Linux system to a network, Linux offers support for a variety of local area network (LAN) cards, modems, and serial devices. In addition to LAN protocols, such as Ethernet (both wired and wireless), all the most popular upper-level networking protocols can be built-in. The most popular of these protocols is TCP/IP (used to connect to the Internet). Other protocols, such as IPX (for Novell networks) and X.25 (a packet-switching network type that is popular in Europe), are also available.

- **Network servers** — Providing networking services to the client computers on the LAN or to the entire Internet is what Linux does best. A variety of software packages are available that enable you to use Linux as a print server, file server, FTP server, mail server, Web server, news server, or workgroup (DHCP or NIS) server.

To make a Linux distribution useful, components need to be added on top of the Linux kernel. For humans to access a Linux system, they can enter commands to a shell or use graphical interfaces to open menus, windows, and icons. Then you need actual applications to run. In particular, a useful Linux desktop system includes the following:

- **Graphical user interface (X Window System)** — The powerful framework for working with graphical applications in Linux is referred to as the X Window System (or simply X). X handles the functions of opening X-based graphical user interface (GUI) applications and displaying them on an X server process (the process that manages your screen, mouse, and keyboard).

  On top of X, you use an X-based desktop environment to provide a desktop metaphor and window manager to provide the look-and-feel of your GUI (icons, window frames, menus, and colors, or a combination of those items called *themes*). There are a few desktop environments and and even more desktop managers to choose from. (Fedora and RHEL focus on the GNOME and KDE desktop environments, but also have several other desktop environments and window managers available.)

- **Application support** — Because of compatibility with POSIX and several different application programming interfaces (APIs), a wide range of free and open source software is available for Linux systems. Compatibility with the GNU C libraries is a major reason for the wide-ranging application support. Often, making an open source application available to a particular version of Linux can be done by simply recompiling the source code to run on that Linux version.

Primary Advantages of Linux

When compared to different commercially available operating systems, Linux's best assets are its price, its reliability, and the freedom it gives you. With the latest 2.6 Linux kernel, you can also argue that scalability is one of its greatest assets.

Most people know that its initial price is free (or at least under $50 when it comes in a box or with a book). However, when people talk about Linux's affordability, they are usually thinking of its total cost, which includes no (or low) licensing fees, the ability to reuse any of the code as you choose, and the capability of using inexpensive hardware and compatible free add-on applications. Although commercial operating systems tend to encourage upgrading to more powerful hardware, Linux doesn't require that (although faster hardware and larger disks are nice to have).

In terms of reliability, the general consensus is that Linux is comparable to many commercial UNIX systems but more reliable than most desktop-oriented operating systems. This is especially true if you rely on your computer system to stay up because it is a Web server or a file server. (You don't have to reboot every time you change something, unless you've replaced the kernel itself.)

This reliability also extends into the realm of safety. While there have been exploits aimed at Linux software, Linux users are for the most part safe from the culture of malware and viruses that plague Windows users. Large-scale Linux deployments don't need to install anti-virus software, a situation you would never allow with Windows in a corporate setting. Furthermore, when people install anti-virus software on Linux, it is usually to scan files and e-mail messages for Windows viruses, to help the distraught users of Windows.

Because you can get the source code, you are free to change any part of the Linux system, along with any open source software that comes with it, in any way that you choose. Unlike many self-contained commercial products, open source software tends to be built in pieces that are meant to interact with other pieces, so you are free to mix and match components to suit your tastes. As I mentioned earlier, Linux is a culture that encourages interoperability. For example, if you don't like a window manager, you can plug in a different one because so many were built to operate within the same framework.

Another advantage of using Linux is that help is always available on the Internet. There is probably someone out there in a Linux newsgroup or mailing list willing to help you get around your problem. Because the source code is available, if you need something fixed you can even patch the code yourself! On the other hand, I've seen commercial operating system vendors sit on reported problems for months without fixing them. Remember that the culture of Linux is one that thrives on people helping other people.

What Are Red Hat Enterprise Linux and Fedora?

Having directories of source code floating extraneously around the Internet was not a bad way for hackers to share software. However, for Linux to be acceptable to a less technical population of computer users, it needed to be simple to install and use. Likewise, businesses that were thinking about committing their mission-critical applications to a computer system would want to know that this system had been carefully tested and well supported.

To those ends, several companies and organizations began gathering and packaging Linux software together into usable forms called *distributions*. The main goal of a Linux distribution is to make the hundreds (or even thousands) of unrelated software packages that make up Linux work together as a cohesive whole. Popular Linux distributions include Debian, Ubuntu, openSUSE, SUSE Linux Enterprise, Slackware, Damn Small Linux, Gentoo, and Mandriva. For many years, the most popular commercial distribution was Red Hat Linux.

In September 2003, Red Hat, Inc. changed its way of doing business. That change resulted in the formation of the Red Hat–sponsored Fedora Project to take the development of Red Hat Linux technology into the future. But what does that mean to individuals and businesses that have come to rely on Red Hat Linux?

Red Hat forms the Fedora Project

With the latest Fedora and Red Hat Enterprise Linux distributions, the promises Red Hat made to the open source community and to Red Hat's commercial customers have begun to solidify. The Red Hat Enterprise Linux product offering is looking like a solid, reliable system for mass deployment of Linux in large organizations. With the Fedora Project merging its Fedora Core and Fedora Extras repositories, a massive number of high-quality software packages is available to Fedora users.

A few years ago, things didn't look so rosy.

The announcement of the Fedora Project by Red Hat, Inc. at first prompted more questions than answers about the future direction of the company and its flagship Red Hat Linux product. In fact, it seemed that nothing named Red Hat Linux even existed anymore. Instead, what *was* Red Hat Linux would be reflected by Linux distributions coming from two paths:

- **Fedora Project** (www.fedoraproject.org) — An open source project, beginning from a Red Hat Linux 9 base, that produces its own Linux distribution. While the project is sponsored by Red Hat, Inc., there is no official support for the Linux distribution (simply called Fedora) that the project produces.

- **Red Hat Enterprise Linux** (www.redhat.com/rhel) — An official set of commercial Linux products from Red Hat, Inc. that are offered on an annual subscription basis. Red Hat backs up its Enterprise product line with technical support, training, and documentation.

The primary results of the Fedora Project are sets of binary and source code packages (distributed as DVD or CD images) containing the Linux distribution referred to as Fedora. Before its name was changed to Fedora, that distribution was being tested simply as the next in the series of Red Hat Linux distributions (presumably, Red Hat Linux 10). The software packages included on the DVD and CD that come with this book are distributed as the official ninth release of that software: Fedora 9.

The name change from Red Hat Linux to Fedora Core (and later to just Fedora) wasn't the only difference between Fedora and Red Hat Enterprise Linux, however. Red Hat, Inc. also changed its association with Fedora in the following ways:

- **No boxed sets** — Red Hat decided to not sell Fedora through retail channels. The ever-shortening release cycle was making it difficult to manage the flow of boxed sets to and from retail channels every few months, and Red Hat believed that early adopters of Linux technology were clever enough to get the software themselves.

- **Short guaranteed update cycle** — Critical fixes and security patches will be available for each Fedora release for a much shorter period of time than on RHEL products. As a result, users will have to upgrade or reinstall the system more often.

- **No technical support offerings** — There are no technical support programs available from Red Hat for Fedora.

- **No Red Hat documentation** — The set of manuals that came with the previous Red Hat Linux product was not brought over to Fedora. Instead, a series of small task-oriented documents are being collected for the project in article format. The Fedora Documentation project (http://fedoraproject.org/wiki/DocsProject) is, however, following a path to release Red Hat documentation under an open source licence so that the Fedora Project can develop and distribute that documentation.

By not creating a whole support industry around Fedora, that project is free to produce software release on a much shorter schedule (usually a six-month release cycle). This allows Fedora users to always have the latest software features and fixes included with a recent version of the operating system. But the Fedora Project is more than just the Fedora Linux release. It is really a collection of projects (http://fedoraproject.org/wiki/Projects) that also includes the following:

- **One Laptop Per Child (OLPC)** — The Fedora Project is working with Red Hat, Inc. and the OLPC project (`www.laptop.org`) to provide laptops to children around the world. Fedora software is being used as the foundation for the software part of OLPC.

- **Fedora Ambassadors and Marketing** — Focuses on spreading the word about Fedora to the world. Ambassadors have been assigned to different parts of the U.S. and to countries around the world to represent Fedora to their areas. The marketing project is helping to encourage presentations, developer conferences, and other initiatives to publicize Fedora.

- **Fedora Live CD Tools** — The Fedora Live CD initiative centers on a set of tools under the name livecd-creator. Using livecd-creator, the Fedora Project produces its own official Fedora live CDs. A live CD provides a means of running a Linux system on a computer without installing it to hard disk. It offers a great way to try out Fedora without disturbing anything installed on your hard disk. Because livecd-creator is itself an open source project, you can use the tools to create your own live CDs. Many advances to the live CD technology have occurred in this release of Fedora, including liveUSB versions and integration with kickstart files.

- **Fedora Artwork** — Creates the graphics used with Fedora (backgrounds, logos, login screens, and so on), primarily using tools that are distributed with Fedora.

- **Fedora Documentation** — Besides seeking to release Red Hat documentation under an open source license and maintaining it publicly with the Fedora Project, the Fedora Documentation Project is pursuing other initiatives. Those include assigning beat writers (to cover various software topics) and editors (to clean up and manage documentation contributions).

For information on the status of these and other Fedora projects, you can refer to the Fedora Weekly News (`http://fedoraproject.org/wiki/FWN`). If you are interested in contributing to any of the Fedora projects, the Fedora Projects page mentioned earlier is a good place to start.

In the past year or so, there has been an extraordinary upsurge of software being made available to run on Fedora. That upsurge has been due in large part to strong Fedora community contributions to Fedora Extras. The Fedora Extras effort has now been merged into the main Fedora repository and the whole repository continues to grow in size and quality, supported by solid packaging guidelines and oversight by the Fedora Engineering Steering Committee (FESCo).

Third-party repositories for Fedora containing software packages that Red Hat won't distribute due to licensing or patent issues have also grown and stabilized lately. (See the descriptions of software repositories in Chapter 5.)

In the area of support, Red Hat has endorsed the `FedoraForum.org` site as the end-user forum of choice for Fedora users. That site already has more than 114,000 members and over 1,300,000 posts you can search for answers to your questions.

Red Hat shifts to Red Hat Enterprise Linux

The major shift of attention to Red Hat Enterprise Linux as the focus of Red Hat, Inc.'s commercial efforts has been on the horizon for some time. Some characteristics of Red Hat Enterprise Linux are:

- **Longer release intervals** — Instead of offering releases every 6 months or so, Enterprise software will have closer to an 18-month update cycle. Customers can be assured of a longer support cycle without having to upgrade to a later release.

- **Multiple support options** — Customers will have the choice of purchasing different levels of support. All subscriptions will include the Update Module, which allows easy access to updates for Red Hat Enterprise Linux systems. The Management Module lets customers develop custom channels and automate management of multiple systems. The Monitoring Module allows customers to monitor and maintain an entire infrastructure of systems.

- **Documentation and training** — Manuals and training courses will center on the Red Hat Enterprise Linux distribution.

Red Hat Enterprise Linux products include offerings for both Server and Desktop operating systems. The base RHEL server system is designed for small server deployment, while RHEL Advanced Platform aims at large installations that can benefit from features such as storage virtualization and high-availability clustering. Standard desktop and workstation versions of RHEL Desktop are available.

Each system in the Red Hat Enterprise Linux family is meant to be compatible with the others. There are Basic, Standard, and Premium editions of these Enterprise systems. While Basic offers only software downloads, standard and premium editions offer hard copy documentation and additional technical support.

For a detailed look at RHEL product features, see Appendix C.

Choosing between Fedora and Enterprise

If you bought this book to try out Linux for the first time, rest assured that what you have on the DVD and CDs with this book is a solid, battle-tested operating system. There is still a lot of overlap between Fedora and Red Hat Enterprise Linux. However, many of the newest features of Fedora 9 provide a way to test out much of the software that is slated to go in later editions of Red Hat Enterprise Linux.

Although Fedora may not be right for everyone, Fedora is great for students, home users, most small businesses, and anyone just wanting to try out the latest Linux technology. Larger businesses should seriously consider the implications on support, training, and future upgrade paths before choosing whether to go the Fedora route or sign on with Red Hat Enterprise Linux. Also, businesses should be willing to deal with more frequent upgrades, because release and support cycles are much shorter with Fedora than with RHEL.

Despite its lack of formal support, however, Fedora is being used today in many businesses, schools, and homes around the world. In whatever way you plan to ultimately use Fedora, it is without a doubt a good way to learn and use the latest Linux technology as it is released to the Linux community and before it makes its way to Red Hat Enterprise Linux.

Many companies and organizations don't choose between Fedora and RHEL, but instead offer a mixed environment. The most critical servers may run Red Hat Enterprise Linux, with a full support contract with Red Hat. In the same location, Fedora may be used for desktop systems or office print and file servers. Organizations that want the stability of RHEL, without the cost of the product, can use CentOS (which is a rebuild of RHEL code). As someone learning to use Fedora with this book, you can likewise scale your use of this technology as far as you want to go.

Why Choose Fedora or Red Hat Enterprise Linux?

To distinguish itself from other versions of Linux, each distribution adds some extra features. Because many power features included in most Linux distributions come from established open source projects (such as Apache, Samba, KDE, and so on), often enhancements for a particular distribution exist to make it easier to install, configure, and use Linux. Also, because there are different software packages available to do the same jobs (such as window managers or a particular server type), a distribution can distinguish itself by which packages it chooses to include and feature with its default installations.

Fedora is continuing the Red Hat Linux tradition by offering many features that set it apart from other Linux distributions. Those features include:

- **Cutting-edge Linux technology** — In Fedora 9, major features include the KDE 4 Desktop, Firefox 3, OpenOffice.org 2.4, new Ext4 file system support, and the latest Linux kernel.

- **Software packaging** — Red Hat, Inc. created the RPM Package Management (RPM) method of packaging Linux. RPMs allow less technically savvy users to easily install, search, manage, and verify Linux software. With RPM tools, you can install from CD, hard disk, over your LAN, or over the Internet. It's easy to track which packages are installed or to look at the contents of a package. Because RPM is available to the Linux community it has become one of the de facto standards for packaging Linux software.

  Tools such as yum and PackageKit, which are built to take advantage of RPM technology, have been added to Fedora to extend your ability to install and update packages. Those tools can point to online repositories, so the latest software packages are often only a click away.

> **CROSS-REFERENCE:** Chapter 5 describes how to install RPM packages and use yum repositories.

- **Easy installation** — The Fedora installation software (called *anaconda*) provides easy steps for installing Linux. During installation, anaconda also helps you take the first few steps toward configuring Linux. You can choose which packages to install and how to partition your hard disk. You can even get your desktop GUI ready to go by configuring user accounts, keyboard, mouse and even your network connection. With Fedora 9, you can install directly from a running live CD, or choose from several different install-only media.

> **CROSS-REFERENCE:** Chapter 2 covers Fedora installation.

- **UNIX System V–style run-level scripts** — To have your system services (daemon processes) start up and shut down in an organized way, Fedora and RHEL use the UNIX System V mechanism for starting and stopping services. Shell scripts (that are easy to read and change) are contained in subdirectories of `/etc`. When the run level changes, such as when the system boots up or you change to single-user mode, messages tell you whether each service started correctly or failed to execute properly. Chapter 12 describes how to use runlevel scripts.

- **Desktop environments (GNOME and KDE)** — To make it easier to use Linux, Fedora and RHEL come packaged with the GNOME and KDE desktop environments. GNOME is installed by default and offers some nice features that include drag-and-drop protocols and tools for configuring the desktop look and feel. KDE is another popular desktop manager that includes a wide range of tools tailored for the KDE environment, such as the Konqueror Web browser. You can try out separate Fedora live CDs for GNOME and KDE, and then install software from those CDs directly to your hard disk. (This book includes the KDE live CD.)

- **GUI Administration tools** — There are some helpful configuration tools for setting up some of the trickier tasks in Linux. Several different GUI tools provide a graphical, form-driven interface for configuring networking, users, file systems, security and initialization services. Instead of creating obtuse command lines or having to create tricky configuration files, these graphical tools can set up those files automatically. (Prior to Fedora Core 2, many of these GUI administration tools were launched from commands that began with `redhat-config-*`. Now, those commands have been renamed to start with `system-config-*`.)

> **NOTE:** There are advantages and disadvantages of using a GUI-based program to manipulate text-based configuration files. GUI-based configuration tools can lead you through a setup procedure and error-check the information you enter. However, some features can't be accessed through the GUI, and if something goes wrong, it can be trickier to debug. With Linux, you have the command-line options available as well as the GUI administration tools.

- **Testing** — The exact configuration that you get on the Fedora or RHEL distribution has been thoroughly tested by experts around the world. Because Fedora is now represented by a single huge software repository, the most intensely tested software will be that which is offered in official CD and DVD versions of Fedora.

- **Automatic updates** — The software packages that make up Fedora are constantly being fixed in various ways. To provide a mechanism for the automatic selection, download, and installation of updated software packages, Fedora and RHEL rely primarily on the yum facility.

  With the addition of yum software repositories on the Internet that include Fedora packages, whole sets of RPM software packages can be updated with a single yum update command. The new PackageKit facility provides graphical tools with Fedora to install from multiple software repositories on the Internet (as opposed to local CD or DVD media A desktop applet automatically alerts you when updated packages are available to download and install. See Chapter 5 for descriptions of these tools.

New Features in Fedora 9

When it comes to versions of different software projects that come with Fedora, the major components in Fedora 9 include (with version numbers):

- **Linux kernel**: version 2.6.25
- **GNOME (desktop environment)**: version 2.22
- **KDE (desktop environment)**: version 4.0.3
- **X Window System (X.org graphical windowing system)**: version 11, Release 1.4
- **OpenOffice.org (office suite)**: version 2.4
- **GIMP (image manipulation application)**: version 2.4.5
- **GCC (GNU C language compilation system)**: version 4.3
- **Apache (Web server)**: version 2.2.8
- **Samba (Windows SMB file/printer sharing)**: version 3.2
- **CUPS (print services)**: version 1.3.7
- **Sendmail (mail transport agent)**: version 8.14.2
- **vsFTPd (secure FTP server)**: version 2.0.6
- **INN (Usenet news server)**: version 2.4.3
- **MySQL (database server)**: version 5.0.51
- **BIND (Domain name system server)**: version 9.5.0

> **TIP:** If you want the latest features in Linux when looking at different Linux distributions, compare the version numbers shown above. Version numbers and names that Linux distributors such as Debian, SUSE, and Fedora associate with their releases can be arbitrary. By comparing versions of the kernel, KDE and GNOME desktops, and GNU compiler they are using, you can tell which distribution actually has the latest features.

The following sections describe major new features of Fedora 9 (besides the latest versions of those basic components just named).

K Desktop Environment (KDE) 4

KDE 4 marks a major revision of the popular desktop environment. The new Plasma desktop shell provides a framework for KDE 4 enhancements. With Plasma, you get a new look-and-feel, new ways of finding applications, files and URLs, and new "widget" technology that lets you run the same mini-applications on the desktop or on panels.

The Dolphin File Manager was added to provide a more streamlined tool for managing files and folders for daily use. Desktop configuration features are now available on a new System Settings window. For details on using the new KDE 4 desktop, refer to Chapter 3.

To let you immediately try out KDE 4, we have included the Fedora 9 KDE desktop live CD. You can boot that live CD directly to a KDE 4 desktop system, then, if you choose, you can install that desktop system directly to your hard disk if you choose.

PackageKit Software Management

In Fedora 9, PackageKit became the default GUI package for managing software updates and adding software packages. It is a community-developed software management system that has replaced the Red Hat-developed Package Updater (pup) and Package Manager (pirut) applications.

With PackageKit, an icon in the top panel alerts you when software updates are available. Or you can use the PackageKit Package Manager for GNOME to search for and install additional packages. PackageKit is described in Chapter 5.

Firefox 3 Web browser

This new major release of Firefox Web browser offers improvements in security, ease-of-use, personalization and performance. There is one-click access to a site's security information (via a favicon in the location bar) when a site uses Extended Validation (EV) SSL certificates. With EV SSL certificates, certificate authorities validate that the site you are visiting is the one it claims to be. Password information bars replace the previous password dialog.

For personalization, bookmarks have improved by letting you add tags to them so they can be sorted by topic. You can use smart bookmarks to immediately access bookmarks that were recently tagged or created. In the location bar, auto-completion is improved to display frequent and recently visited locations as you type a URL.

Preupgrade

A new preupgrade feature lets you install and run a preupgrade application that prepares a Fedora 8 system to be upgraded to Fedora 9. This feature lets you do much of the time-consuming package download and dependency checking that takes place during upgrades while you are still using the existing system. Preupgrade is described in Chapter 2.

Ext4 file systems

Support was added so that Fedora can handle the new ext4 file system type. The ext4 file system was designed to provide better performance and scalability than ext3 systems. While there should be no differences in how people use ext4 file systems, a new set of tools for creating, checking and maintaining ext4 file systems is included with Fedora 9.

Encrypted file systems

Using the crykptsetup and LUKS features in Fedora 9, you can now encrypt file systems other than your root (/) or /boot partitions. Encrypted file systems can be particularly important to secure your data on laptop systems.

Identity management with freeIPA

The freeIPA framework for managing identity, policy, and audit features across an enterprise has been added for the first time in Fedora 9. For this first release, only the identity portion has been implemented. The long-term goal of freeIPA is to provide an open source mechanism for centrally maintaining these critical security and monitoring features. Chapter 14 contains a description of freeIPA.

NetworkManager

To simplify the process of setting up connections to wired and wireless networks, NetworkManager is providing continued improvements. In Fedora 9, it is now the default method of connecting to and managing wired and wireless networks interfaces.

Getting custom Fedora spins

Fedora used to be released as a set of CDs or a DVD containing all the Fedora packages that could be installed from those media. The results of new tools first added in Fedora 7 for creating custom software repositories (Pungi) and custom live CDs (livecd-creator) have continued to improve in the form of a growing set of *custom spins*.

A custom spin of Fedora is a CD, DVD, or USB flash drive image that can be run as a live CD and/or Fedora installer. Official Fedora spins include:

- **Fedora DVD** — Contains about a 3.4GB cross-section of desktop, server, and software development software packages that you can install to hard disk. The contents of this disk are similar to what used to be in Fedora Core.
- **Fedora CD Set** — This six-CD set contains everything from the 3.4GB Fedora install DVD. This is for those who don't have a DVD drive on their computer.

- **Fedora Desktop Live CD (GNOME)** — From this single, 700MB live CD you can run a GNOME desktop Fedora 9 system. An install icon on the desktop then lets you install that desktop system to your hard disk.

- **Fedora Desktop Live CD (KDE)** — Fedora is showing KDE some love by offering a KDE desktop live/install CD of Fedora 9. As with the GNOME desktop, you can select the install icon to install the KDE desktop system to your hard disk. (This CD is included with this book.)

- **Everything DVD Set** — An "Everything" 2-DVD set containing the entire Fedora 9 repository (about 11GB) is expected to be produced shortly after Fedora 9 is released. This set is for people who want every installable software package with Fedora 9. (The DVD that comes with this book contains most of the contents of the two Everything DVDs, respun onto a high-capacity DVD-9.)

The KDE desktop CD and Nearly-Everything DVD included with this book are for standard 32-bit PCs (i386). If you need media to install Fedora on PowerPC (PPC) or 64-bit PC (X86_64) computer architectures, you can download ISO images for those media either using either Bittorrent (`http://spins.fedoraproject.org`) or an official Fedora public mirror site (`http://mirrors.fedoraproject.org`). Refer to Chapter 2 for information on using and installing Fedora from these different media.

Unofficial custom spins are also available from the Custom Spins page (`http://fedoraproject.org/wiki/CustomSpins`). So far there are already Fedora Live Developer, Games, Art, Xfce Desktop, and Electronic Lab spins. (The term *spin* means a compilation of software from the Fedora software repository, combined into the form of one or more bootable images (typically to fit on a CD or DVD), that lets you either run live or install that set of software.)

Creating your own spins

The same tools that the Fedora Project uses to build packages and create live CDs and installation CDs are themselves distributed with Fedora. That means that anyone can use those tools to create their own installation package sets, and then turn those package sets into their own repositories. Using those repositories, you could then create your own CD or DVD images to later install or run live.

Pungi (`http://hosted.fedoraproject.org/projects/pungi`) is the project created for Fedora to build the Fedora system itself. The pungi package contains the `pungi` command and related configuration files. You can use the `pungi` command to fashion your own installation trees that result in installable ISO images.

The Fedora Live CD project (`http://fedoraproject.org/wiki/FedoraLiveCD`) has produced tools for building your own live CDs from Fedora software repositories. The primary tool for creating those live CDs is called livecd-creator. Refer to the Live CD HOWTO (`http://fedoraproject.org/wiki/FedoraLiveCD/LiveCDHowTo`) for information on using livecd-creator.

A nice recent addition to livecd-creator for Fedora is that you can create kickstart files (described in Chapter 2) to direct the creation of live CDs. This means that the same format you use to automate installs with anaconda can be used to save the package list and other settings you use to create your live CDs.

Firewall Configuration

The Firewall Configuration window was enhanced to provide several features that previously needed to be added manually to your iptables firewall. In particular, you can identify selected ports to do port forwarding (for example, if you wanted to have a Web server on a private address behind your firewall). You can also indicate which ICMP types you support, such as the commonly used echo request (`ping`) and echo reply (`pong`).

The Culture of Free Software

I would be remiss to not say something about the culture of free software development from which Linux has thrived and will continue to thrive. The copyright for Fedora and Red Hat Enterprise Linux systems is covered primarily under the GNU public license. That license, which most free software falls under, provides the following:

- **Author rights** — The original author retains the rights to his or her software.
- **Free distribution** — People can use the GNU software in their own software, changing and redistributing it as they please. They do, however, have to include the source code with their distribution (or make it easily available).
- **Copyright maintained** — Even if you were to repackage and resell the software, the original GNU agreement must be maintained with the software. This means that all future recipients of the software must have the opportunity to change the source code, just as you did.

It is important to remember that there is no warranty on GNU software. If something goes wrong, the original developer of the software has no obligation to fix the problem. However, the Linux culture has provided resources for that event. Experts on the Internet can help you iron out your problems, or you can access one of the many Linux newsgroups or forums to read how others have dealt with their problems and to post your own questions about how to fix yours. Chances are that someone will know what to do — maybe even going so far as to provide the software or configuration file you need.

If you need reliable support for your Linux system, commercial Linux support is available from a variety of companies. Also, many of the software projects that go into Linux offer their own support features, which let you get help directly from those who are building the code.

> **NOTE:** The GNU project uses the term *free software* to describe the software that is covered by the GNU license. Many Linux proponents tend to use the term *open source software* to describe software. Although source code availability is part of the GNU license, the GNU project claims that software defined as open source is not the same as free software because it can encompass semi-free programs and even some proprietary programs. See `www.opensource.org` for a description of open-source software.

Summary

Linux is a free computer operating system that was created by Linus Torvalds in 1991 and has grown from contributions from software developers all over the world. Fedora and Red Hat Enterprise versions of Red Hat Linux are distributions of Linux that package together the software needed to run Linux and make it easier to install and use.

This book specifically describes Fedora 9, a nearly complete version of which is included on the DVD that comes with this book, as well as Red Hat Enterprise Linux 5. Fedora includes cutting-edge Linux technology that is slated for inclusion in commercial Red Hat Linux systems. Features in Fedora 9 include a new Online Desktop feature, PulseAudio sound server, and an enhanced Firewall Configuration window. You can get different "spins" of Fedora (both live and install CDs) from the Internet or from distributions that come with books such as this one.

Linux is based on a culture of free exchange of software. Linux's roots are based in the UNIX operating system. UNIX provided most of the framework that was used to create Linux. That framework came from the POSIX standard, the System V Interface Definition, and the Berkeley Software Distribution, pieces of which have all found their way into Linux. Now the Linux Standard Base creates the standards to provide consistency among Linux distributions.

Chapter 2

Installing Fedora

In This Chapter

- Quick installation
- Detailed installation instructions
- Special installation procedures
- Special installation topics
- Troubleshooting installation
- Spinning your own Fedora

A simplified installation procedure is one of the best reasons for using a Linux distribution such as Fedora or RHEL. In many cases, for a computer dedicated to using Fedora, you can just pop in the DVD or CD (that come with this book), choose from several preset configurations, and be up and running with Linux in less than an hour.

If you want to share your computer with both Linux and Microsoft Windows, Fedora offers several ways to go about doing that. A Fedora Desktop Live CD is included with this book, and will help prepare your computer before installation. If your computer doesn't have a DVD or CD drive, network and hard disk installs are available. To pre-configure Fedora to install on multiple, similar computers, you can use the kickstart installation.

In the past few releases of Fedora, the project has made some great improvements to the installation process. Most notably, a recent feature in anaconda (the Fedora installer) lets you install software from multiple online repositories during the initial Fedora install.

Although this procedure focuses on installing Fedora on a standard PC (i386 32-bit architecture), the Fedora Project also produces installable versions of Fedora for PowerPC (ppc) and 64-bit PC architecture (x68_64). Because the latest Apple Mac computers are based on Intel architecture, Fedora can be installed on those machines as well (see Chapter 26 for information on installing Fedora on a Mac Mini).

> **NOTE:** This chapter follows the install procedure for Fedora 9, which comes with this book. The procedure is very similar to the Red Hat Enterprise Linux installation process. For details on installing RHEL, refer to the Red Hat Enterprise Linux 5 Installation Guide: `www.redhat.com/docs/manuals/enterprise/RHEL-5-manual/Installation_Guide-en-US`

Understanding Fedora Installation Media

In earlier releases, the Fedora Project packaged its Linux operating system as both 5-CD and 1-DVD installation media. Extra software packages could be downloaded from the Fedora Extras repository and installed from over the Internet. Recently, that arrangement has changed in several major ways:

- **Fedora Repository** — Instead of separate Fedora Core and Extras repositories, there is just a single Fedora repository that includes all software from those two repositories.

- **New Installation Media** — The merged Fedora repository contains too much software to expect the average person to download. Therefore the Fedora Project offers more reasonable-sized installation media that include a single 3.4G installation DVD , a Desktop Live CD, and a KDE Desktop Live CD. Either of the live CDs can also be used to install the Fedora desktop system contained on that CD to hard drive. After the release, look for custom Fedora *spins* that might include full CD and DVD sets, as well as specialized live CDs for games, art, software development, and other special topics (`http://spins.fedoraproject.org/`). A *spin* is just a selected grouping of Fedora software into a live or install CD or DVD image.

- **New Build Tools** — To help people put together the mass of Fedora software into a form that is useful to them, the Fedora Project created several software tool projects. Using Fedora and optionally other software repositories, Pungi can be used to create a new set of installation media, while livecd-creator can build a live CD or live DVD. (See descriptions of these tools at the end of this chapter.)

With this book, we have included the Fedora KDE Desktop Live CD and a "Combined" Fedora Installation DVD. The live CD is the exact KDE Desktop Live CD produced by the Fedora project. The "Combined" DVD includes most of the contents of the Fedora repository, which we put together especially for this book using the Pungi tools just described. (See the "Choosing an Installation Method" section later in this chapter for details about those two media.)

Using the Fedora 9 Live CD

The official Fedora 9 KDE Desktop Live CD that comes with this book is a great way to try out Fedora before you commit to installing it. In addition to answering the obvious question of "does Fedora run on my PC at all?" the CD itself contains useful tools for examining your hardware and preparing your computer for installation.

A live CD is a bootable medium (usually a CD, but other removable media, such as DVDs or USB flash drives can be used the same way) that contains an entire operating system. In most cases, you can boot the live CD without touching the contents of your hard drive.

With Fedora 9 Desktop Live CD, you can boot up to a working KDE desktop that works like most desktop computer systems installed to hard disk. If you don't like the system, then reboot, remove the CD, and your computer will return to the way it was. If you like it, you can click a single button and install the same desktop system to your hard disk.

Here's a quick set of steps to try out the Fedora 9 KDE Desktop Live CD (included with this book):

> **NOTE:** The live CD will not run well on less than 256MB of RAM. Also, if you find that the live CD hangs at some point in the boot process, refer to boot options later in this chapter. With the boot label highlighted on the boot menu, press the Tab key to be able to add boot options to the boot command.

1. Insert the Fedora 9 KDE Desktop Live CD into your CD drive and reboot.

2. From the boot screen, either let the CD timeout and boot or press any key to see other selections. From the boot menu, highlight either Boot or Verify and Boot, then press Enter. (The verify step makes sure the medium isn't corrupted.)

3. When you see the login screen, you can select a language or just let the login prompt timeout. (No password is required.) The KDE desktop starts up.

4. From the KDE desktop, here are a few things you can try from the live CD:

    - **Run applications** — Try any of the applications you choose from menus in the top panel. If you have an Internet connection (Fedora will automatically configure most wired Ethernet cards), you can try Web browsing and other Internet applications. You can even add more applications. Select Applications → Add/Remove Software to select applications to install over the Internet. (Because the live CD is a read-only medium, software you add will disappear when you reboot.)

    - **Check hardware** — Refer to the "Preparing for Installation using the Live CD" section later in this chapter for suggestions on how to check out your computer hardware.

    - **Prepare for dual booting** — If you want to keep an installed Windows system that is already on your computer's hard disk, you can prepare your computer to be able to dual boot both Windows and a new install of Fedora. Refer to the "Setting up to dual-boot Linux and Windows" section later in this chapter for information on resizing your computer's hard disk partitions to make room for Fedora.

If you like the live CD, and your computer is prepared for you to install to it, you can immediately install the contents of the live CD to your computer's hard drive. Select the Install to Hard Drive icon from the desktop, and then follow along the installation procedure in the next sections.

> **NOTE:** If you prefer the GNOME Desktop Environment over KDE, Fedora offers a live CD spin based on the GNOME desktop. You can download that live CD from any Fedora mirror site.

Quick Installation

It can be a little intimidating to see a thick chapter on installation. But the truth is, if you have a little bit of experience with computers and a computer with common hardware, you can probably install Fedora or RHEL pretty easily. The procedure in this section will get you going quickly if you have:

- **Media** — The Fedora installation DVD or live/install CD that come with this book.

- **PC** — A Pentium-class PC (at least 200 MHz for text mode; 400 MHz Pentium II for GUI) with a built-in, bootable DVD or CD drive, at least 64MB of RAM (for text mode) or 192MB of RAM (for GUI mode; although 256MB is the recommended minimum).

- **Disk Space** — If you are installing from the live CD, you need at least 3GB of disk space. Keep in mind that the live CD install only copies the live CD files to your hard disk. You don't get to select individual packages, as you do when installing from the DVD. (The fact that files are compressed on the CD accounts for the need for more hard disk space than the 700MB CD image would indicate.)

  With the DVD, because there are no preset install types in Fedora 9, essentially every installation is a custom installation (although you can go with a default package set). Therefore, depending on which packages you choose to install, the disk space you need can range from about 600MB (for a minimal server with no GUI install) to 10GB (to install all packages). I would recommend from 2GB to 3GB minimum if you are installing a desktop system. (The Fedora Project recommends at least 5 percent of additional free space, plus any disk space you require for user data.)

For this quick procedure, you must either be dedicating your entire hard disk to Linux, have a preconfigured Linux partition, or have sufficient free space on your hard disk outside any existing Windows partition.

> **CAUTION:** If you are not dedicating your whole hard disk to Fedora and you don't understand partitioning, skip to the following "Detailed Installation Instructions" section in this chapter. That section describes choices for having both Linux and Windows on the same computer.

Here's how you get started:

1. Insert the Fedora 9 installation DVD or CD into your computer's drive.

2. Reboot your computer.

3. The next step depends on whether you are using the live CD or DVD that come with this book:

- For the DVD, select to install or upgrade an existing system.

- For the install/live CD, let the boot screen time out. When the CD boots up to a KDE desktop, double-click the Install to Hard Drive icon to begin the installation.

During installation, you are asked questions about your computer hardware and the network connections. After you have completed each answer, click Next. The following list describes the information you will need to enter. (If you need help, all of these topics are explained later in this chapter.)

- **Media Check** — If you are installing from the DVD, you can optionally check the DVD to be sure it is not damaged or corrupted.

- **Language Selection** — Choose the language used during the install (you can add other languages later).

- **Keyboard Configuration** — If you are installing from DVD, choose your keyboard type.

- **Install or Upgrade** — If you are installing from DVD and have an earlier version of Fedora installed, you can choose Upgrade to upgrade your system without losing data files. Otherwise, you can continue with a new installation by selecting Reinstall System. (Upgrades are not supported when you are installing from the live CD.)

- **Network Configuration** — Set up your LAN connection (not dial-up). You can choose to get addresses simply using DHCP, or you can manually enter your computer's IP address, netmask, hostname, default gateway, and DNS servers. You can also indicate whether to activate your network when Linux boots and, if so, you must enable IP support (probably IPv4).

- **Time Zone Selection** — Identify the time zone in which you are located. Uncheck the System Clock uses UTC box if you are booting multiple operating systems from this machine because most operating systems expect the BIOS clock to match local time.

- **Set Root Password** — Add the root user account password.

- **Disk Partitioning Setup** — Choose to remove Linux partitions, all partitions, or no partitions (and use existing free space) to have space to install Fedora. Because repartitioning can result in lost data, I recommend that you refer to descriptions on repartitioning your hard disk later in this chapter.

- **Boot Loader Configuration** — Add the GRUB boot manager to control the boot process. (GRUB is described later in this chapter.) With multiple operating systems on the computer, select which one to boot by default.

- **Choose Software** — If you are installing from DVD, choose from several preset installation classes, such as Office and Productivity (for laptop, home, or desktop use), Software Development (desktop plus software development), or Web Server (file, print, Web, and other server software). I suggest you also select Customize now so that you can see exactly which packages you have selected (and add others if you want to). If you are installing from the live CD, you won't be able to choose the software to install (in this or the next step) because the entire contents of the CD are installed to hard disk.

- **Installation Categories** — If you are installing from DVD, select each category that appears to see which groups of software packages are installed. Then select the Optional packages button to add or subtract packages from each group.

- **About to Install** — Up to this point, you can quit the install process without having written anything to disk. When you select Next, the disk is formatted (as you chose) and selected packages are installed.

> **NOTE:** After answering the questions, the actual installation of packages from the DVD takes between 20 and 60 minutes, depending on the number of packages and the speed of the computer hardware. For the live CD, the installation process is typically much faster because the contents of the CD are simply copied to hard disk. Upgrades can take much longer.

When installation is done, remove the Fedora DVD and click Exit to reboot your computer. If you installed from the live CD, reboot your computer and remove the live CD before it's time for the installed system to boot. Linux should boot by default. After Linux boots for the first time, the Firstboott runs to let you read the license agreement, set system date and time, configure your display, check your hardware, add a user account, configure your sound card, and install additional CDs. On subsequent reboots, you will see a login prompt. You can log in and begin using your Linux system.

If you need more information than this procedure provides, go to the detailed installation instructions just ahead.

Detailed Installation Instructions

This section provides more detail on installation. Besides expanding on the installation procedure, this section also provides information on different installation types and on choosing computer hardware.

If anything goes wrong during installation and you get stuck, go to the "Troubleshooting Installation" section at the end of this chapter. It gives suggestions for solving common installation problems.

> **CAUTION:** If, when installing Windows or Fedora, you find that the other operating system is no longer available on your boot screen, don't panic and don't immediately reinstall. You can usually recover from the problem by booting the live CD that comes with this book, and then using the `grub-install` command to reinsert the proper master boot record. (You can also enter rescue mode by selecting **Rescue installed system** from the Fedora DVD boot screen.) Refer to the "Using the GRUB boot loader" section later in this chapter. If you are uncomfortable working in emergency mode, seek out an expert to help you.

Installing Fedora 9

This chapter details how to install Fedora 9 from the DVD that comes with this book. If you don't have a DVD drive, you can use the Fedora live/install CD that comes with this book to do a basic desktop install. If you are installing Fedora from those media, you can simply follow the instructions in this chapter.

Choosing an installation method

Fedora offers very flexible ways of installing the operating system. This book comes with the following installation media (described in Appendix A):

- **Fedora 9 DVD**— Contains nearly the entire Fedora 9 operating system, including all binary packages that are associated with a software group (most packages that didn't make the CD are miscellaneous packages).

- **Fedora 9 KDE Desktop Live CD** — If you don't have a DVD drive, you can install from the included official Fedora 9 KDE Desktop Live/install CD. The CD lets you run a live version of Fedora 9 that includes the K Desktop Environment (KDE). From the running live CD system, you can launch an install process that copies the entire contents of the live CD to your hard disk.

If your computer has a DVD drive, I recommend installing Fedora from the DVD that comes with this book after testing your computer with the live CD. However, if you don't have a DVD drive, you also have the option of installing a desktop Fedora system from the CD with this book or from any of several different types of media. There are also several special types of installation. The installation types noted here are described fully in the "Special Installation Procedures" section.

Install or upgrade?

First you should determine if you are doing a new install or an upgrade. If you are upgrading an existing Fedora system to the latest version, the installation process will try to leave your data files and configuration files intact as much as possible. You also need to do the upgrade from the DVD because upgrades are not available from the Fedora live CD.

An upgrade installation takes longer than a new install. A new install will simply erase all data on the Linux partitions (or entire hard disk) that you choose.

> **NOTE:** While you can upgrade to Fedora 9 from previous Fedora releases, you cannot upgrade to Fedora 9 from a Red Hat Enterprise Linux or CentOS system. The older the Fedora release you are upgrading from, however, the more likely you are to have problems upgrading.

If you choose to upgrade, you can save yourself some time (and disk space) by removing software packages you don't need. An upgrade will just skip packages that are not installed and not try to upgrade them. Here are a few other tips related to upgrades:

- **Conflicting packages** — If you upgrade a system on which you installed packages from sources outside of the Fedora project that conflict with Fedora packages, those features may no longer work. For example, if you replaced GNOME with Ximian GNOME or used a third-party KDE package set, you can't upgrade those packages to Fedora 9. (It's probably best to remove those packages before upgrading, and then apply them again later if you like.)

- **Third-party packages** — If you have installed packages from third-party repositories that are specific to your current kernel (such as drivers for NVidia video cards or wireless LAN cards) you will need to get new versions of those packages that match your upgraded kernel.

- **Kernel requirements** — To upgrade, you must have at least a Linux 2.0 kernel installed on the system you are upgrading.

- **Configuration files** — With an upgrade, your configuration files that are replaced are saved as `filename.rpmsave` (for example, the hosts file is saved as `hosts.rpmsave`). More often, however, your old configuration files will remain in place, while the system copies new configuration files to `filename.rpmnew`. The locations of those files, as well as other upgrade information, is written to `/root/upgrade.log`. The upgrade installs the new kernel, any changed software packages, and any packages that the installed packages depend on being there. Your data files and configuration information should remain intact.

- **Digital certificates** — If you are using digital certificates on your system, you must relocate them to the `/etc/pki` directory after the upgrade. (See Chapter 14 for information on setting up digital certificates.)

- **Java** — If you used the Java RPM from Sun Microsystems to provide Java support, conflicts with that package provides may cause it to be erased during an upgrade. If that occurs, you can install the Java RPM from jpackage.org or install the Java tarball from Sun Microsystems into your `/opt` directory. You can also consider removing that version of Java from your system and instead using the open source Java IcedTea packages included with Fedora to provide Java support.

A new feature that is available when you are upgrading to Fedora 9 is the preupgrade package. By installing preupgrade on a Fedora 8 system (`yum install preupgrade`), you can prepare your system to upgrade to Fedora 9 by launching a single application to:

- Determine which packages need to be downloaded to upgrade to Fedora 9.

- Download the packages needed to complete the upgrade (while Fedora 8 is still running)

- Download the boot images needed for the upgrade.

The advantage to using preupgrade is that you can continue using your system while you do most of the time-consuming work (such as downloading packages) that needs to be done to complete an upgrade. Also, before you get into running the installer, you will be able to see if there are any package dependencies you should deal with (before committing to the actual upgrade).

With the preupgrade package installed, you can start the GUI version of preupgrade by typing **preupgrade** from a Terminal window as root user. Files needed for the upgrade are copied to the /var/cache/yum/anaconda-upgrade directory. Once preupgrade is complete, you can reboot to a Fedora 9 install DVD and begin the upgrade.

From DVD, network, or hard disk?

When you install Fedora, the distribution doesn't have to come from the installation DVD or CD. After booting the installation DVD, press Tab with the Install selection highlighted. Then type the word **askmethod** at the end of the boot command line displayed and press Enter. You are offered the choice of installing Fedora from the following locations:

- **Local DVD or CDROM** — This is the most common method of installing Fedora and the one you get by simply pressing Enter from the installation boot prompt. All packages needed to complete the installation are on the DVD that comes with this book.
- **HTTP** — Lets you install from a Web page address (http://).
- **FTP** — Lets you install from an FTP site (ftp://).
- **NFS image** — Allows you to install from any shared directory on another computer on your network using the Network File System (NFS) facility.
- **Hard drive** — If you can place a copy of the Fedora distribution on your hard drive, you can install it from there. (Presumably, the distribution is on a hard drive partition to which you are *not* installing.)

If your computer doesn't have a DVD drive, you can use the boot.iso CD image that comes on the DVD with the book (see below) to start a network install (HTTP, FTP, or NFS). Just type **linux askmethod** at the boot prompt, to begin the installation process.

If you don't have a bootable DVD or CD drive, there are other ways to start the Fedora installation. Unlike some earlier Fedora and Red Hat Linux versions, Fedora doesn't support floppy disk boot images (the Linux 2.6 kernel is too large to fit on a floppy disk). Therefore, if you don't have a bootable DVD or CD drive, you need to start the install process from some other medium (such as a USB device, PXE server, or hard drive, as described later in this chapter).

The following specialty installation types also may be of interest to you:

- **Boot CD** — You can create a boot CD from the boot images contained on the Fedora installation DVD that comes with this book. Copy and burn the file boot.iso from the images directory on the DVD. You can use the CD you create from that image to begin the install process if you have a DVD drive that is not bootable or if you have the Fedora 9 software available on any of the media described in the linux askmethod section.

- **USB or other bootable media** — If your computer can be configured to boot from alternate bootable media, such as a USB pen drive, that is larger than a floppy disk, you can copy the `diskboot.img` file to that medium and install from there. That image is contained in the `images` directory on the DVD.

- **Kickstart installation** — Lets you create a set of answers to the questions Fedora asks you during installation. This can be a time-saving method if you are installing Fedora on many computers with similar configurations.

A Fedora Installation Guide is now available from the Fedora Project, if you find you need further information. It may not be up to date, however. You can access the guide here:

```
http://docs.fedoraproject.org/install-guide
```

Choosing computer hardware

This may not really be a choice. You may just have an old PC lying around that you want to try Fedora on. Or you may have a killer workstation with some extra disk space and want to try out Fedora on a separate partition or whole disk. To install the 32-bit PC version of Fedora successfully (that is, the version on the accompanying DVD), the computer must have the following:

- **x86 processor** — Your computer needs an Intel-compatible CPU. With the latest version, Fedora recommends that you at least have a Pentium-class processor to run Fedora. For a text-only installation, a 200 MHz Pentium is the minimum, while a 400 MHz Pentium II is the minimum for a GUI installation.

- **DVD or CD-ROM drive** — You need to be able to boot up the installation process from a DVD, CD-ROM, or other bootable drive. (Other drives can include a USB flash memory drive that you can use with a `diskboot.img` image included on the DVD.) Once you have booted from one of the media just described, you can use the Internet, a LAN connection to install Fedora software packages from a server on the network or figure out a way to copy the contents of the DVD to a local hard disk to install from there.

- **Hard disk** — The minimum amount of space you need varies depending on the installation type and packages you select. If you are an inexperienced user, you want at least 2.3GB of space so you can get the GUI (with some Office and Productivity apps) or 3GB for a Software Development install (if you want to do software development). Although different install types are no longer supported in Fedora, the following items roughly indicate how much disk space you need to install different types of desktop or server systems:

  - **Office and Productivity** — Requires 2.3GB of disk space.
  - **Software Development** — Requires 3.0GB of disk space.
  - **Web Server** — Requires 1.1GB of disk space.

- **Minimal** — Requires at least 620MB of disk space.

- **RAM** — You should have at least 64MB of RAM to install Fedora (text mode only). If you are running in graphical mode, you will want at least 192MB. The recommended minimum RAM (for decent performance) for GUI mode is at least 256MB.

> **NOTE:** With demanding applications such as the Openoffice.org office suite and automatic features for monitoring your desktop being added, Fedora demands more RAM to use it effectively than it used to. A developer at Red Hat recommends at least 512MB of RAM for good performance from a Fedora desktop.

- **Keyboard and monitor** — Although this seems obvious, the truth is that you need only a keyboard and monitor during installation. You can operate Fedora quite well over a LAN using either a shell interface from a network login or an X terminal.

Fedora versions, not included with this book, are available for the AMD64 architecture and PowerPC. The minimum PowerPC hardware supported is a PowerPC G3/POWER4. Supported PowerPC products include the Apple Power Macintosh (1999 or later), IBM 32-bit RS/6000, Genesi Pegasos II, as well as 64-bit G5 and POWER processors from IBM eServer pSeries computers. Check the Fedora Project download site for information on PPC versions of Fedora.

Installing Fedora on a Laptop

Because laptops can contain non-standard equipment, before you begin installing on a laptop you should find out about other people's experiences installing Linux on your model. Do that by visiting the Linux on Laptops site (`www.linux-on-laptops.com`).

Most modern laptops contain bootable CD-ROM drives. If yours doesn't, you probably need to install from a device connected to a USB or PCMCIA slot on your laptop. PCMCIA slots let you connect a variety of devices to your laptop using credit card–sized cards (sometimes called PC Cards). Linux supports hundreds of PCMCIA devices. You can use your laptop's PCMCIA slot to install Fedora from several different types of PCMCIA devices, including:

- A DVD drive
- A CD-ROM drive
- A LAN adapter

See Chapter 10 for further information on using Linux on laptops.

For other hardware, such as Intel Itanium and IBM mainframe, there are versions of Red Hat Enterprise Linux available (which you have to purchase from Red Hat, Inc.). The DVD that comes with this book and the installation procedures presented here, however, are specific to 32-bit PCs. Most of the software described in this book will work the same in any of those hardware environments. (Check out `http://fedoraproject.org/get-fedora` for sites that offer Fedora for different computer hardware architectures.)

> **NOTE:** The list of hardware supported by Red Hat Enterprise Linux is available on the Internet at `http://bugzilla.redhat.com/hwcert`.

Preparing for installation using the live CD

Before you begin installing Fedora 9, there are ways to check your computer hardware and prepare your computer to install Linux. By booting a live CD, you can make sure that:

- The Linux kernel (the heart of the operating system) will boot.
- Device drivers are available for the hardware on your computer.
- Your hard disk has enough free space to install Fedora or RHEL (and if there's not enough, you can use tools on the live CD to resize your hard disk partitions to make space).

You can try out Fedora using the Fedora 9 KDE Desktop Live CD that comes with this book without making any changes to your existing setup. You can identify your hardware drivers and disk partitions. Then, if you need to, you can change your hard disk to prepare it to install Fedora (primarily if you need to retain an existing operating system, such as Windows, to dual boot with Linux).

To use Fedora live, insert the Fedora 9 Live CD that comes with this book, and then reboot your computer. After a ten-second timeout period, the live CD begins booting Fedora.

After taking a few moments to detect your hardware and start up services, Fedora Live should present you with a graphical (KDE) desktop. With the live CD running on the PC where you want to install Fedora, there are a lot of ways you can check the hardware on your computer. You can also take additional steps to configure and debug any hardware problems before you begin installing Fedora. The following procedures describe what you can do with the Fedora KDE Live CD to prepare to install Fedora or RHEL.

Display hardware information

To display information about your computer's hardware from the Fedora live CD open a Terminal window (from the main menu, select Applications → System Tools → Terminal). Then, from the Terminal window, type the following command:

```
$ /sbin/lspci -vv | less
```

Press the spacebar to page through the list of PCI devices on your computer (press q to exit). Note the model names and numbers of any hardware that doesn't seem to be working. Next plug in any USB devices you want to use (USB flash drives, cameras, Webcams, and so on) and type the following:

```
$ /sbin/lsusb
```

If you would like a more graphical way of displaying hardware information, and you have an active Internet connection, you can install the Hardware Browser to your running Fedora live CD. To install Hardware Browser, type the following:

```
# su -
# yum install hwbrowser
```

You can open the Hardware Browser from the main menu (search for the Hardware application) or type **hwbrowser**. From the Hardware Browser, select the following items from the left column to check out your computer:

- **Hard Drives** — Tells you your available disk partitions. Your hard disk partitions will probably appear as /dev/sc?? (for IDE and SCSI disks) where the two question marks are replaced by a letter (*a* for the first, *b* for the second, and so on), then a number (1, 2, 3, and so on).

  The file system type listed for each partition might give you some idea of the contents of that partition. For example, NTFS and VFAT file systems are common for Windows systems, while ext3, ext2, and reiserfs are generally for Linux or similar systems. For each disk, you can see the sector each partition starts and ends on, the size of the partition (in MB) and the type of file system (in the "Setting up to dual-boot Linux and Windows" section later in this chapter, I describe how to get more information about your partitions).

- **Network Devices** — Displays device information, drivers, and device name for any wired or wireless Ethernet cards installed on your computer.

- **Sound Cards** — Tells which sound cards are installed on your computer.

- **System Devices** — Shows information about the PCI devices on your computer. This could tell you a lot of good information about your computer's bus and bridges.

- **Video cards** — Describes the type of video card and chipset connected to your computer.

To check out information about your computer's memory, open the KDE System Monitor by selecting System → System Monitor from the Applications menu. Then select the Sensor Load tab. The following information about your computer's available memory is displayed:

- **Physical Memory** — Shows how much RAM is available on your computer and how much is being used currently.

- **Swap Memory** — If there is a swap partition (which there won't be if you are starting with a Windows-only PC), you will see the amount of space available on that partition, as well as how much is being used. (If you already have a Linux system installed on the machine, you may need to turn on the swap partition manually. For example, if the swap partition were located at /dev/sda2, you could type **swapon /dev/sda2** from a Terminal window as root user to turn on that swap partition.)

Writing down the information about your hardware and memory will help you later if something goes wrong. So, for example, if you try to use Google to search for an answer or ask a question at a forum, you will know exactly what hardware is not working.

Test your hardware

Although most configuration you do will disappear when you reboot your computer after using the live CD, running through some tests and a bit of setup can help you when you configure the same equipment on the installed Fedora or RHEL. Here are a few ways to test useful hardware devices from the Fedora Live CD:

- **Sound card** — To test your sound card, select System → Soundcard Detection to open the Audio Devices window. The window will show you the vendor, model name, and device (module) associated with the sound card. Click the Play button to see if the driver worked.

- **Network/Internet** — To test your network connection, you can simply open a Web browser to see if you have an active connection. If you don't, select System → Network Configuration. From the Network Configuration window that appears, select New. Use the Add new Device Type window to configure your Ethernet, ISDN, modem, token ring, wireless card, or xDSL connection (as described in Chapters 15 and 16).

- **Video card** — To check your video card, open the Display Settings window (select System → Display). Select the Hardware tab to see your video card type and monitor. If you prefer to use the command line to check what video card was detected, type the following from a Terminal window:

```
# grep Chipset /var/log/Xorg.0.log
```

You can try other hardware devices as well by opening whatever applications you need to access the device (a Web browser, a file manager, and so on). Many USB devices (digital cameras, pen drives, and so on) will be detected and often displayed on the desktop. Running the lsmod and modinfo commands can help you determine which devices were loaded for those modules. Here are a few other quick commands for checking out your computer:

- cat /proc/interrupts — Shows what interrupts are in use.
- cat /proc/cpuinfo — Shows CPU information.
- cat /proc/bus/usb/devices — Shows attached and detected USB devices.
- /sbin/lspci — Shows listing of PCI devices found (-vv for more verbose info).
- cat /proc/cmdline — See command line options the system booted with.
- cat /proc/ioports — Shows ioports in use and the devices using them.
- less /var/log/messages — Page through the log of system start-up messages.

For any hardware that is not working properly, write down as much information you can about it (its name, model number, version, driver, and so on). Check Fedora mailing lists or use your favorite search engine to search for that hardware, plus keywords such as Linux or Fedora.

If your computer has an existing Windows operating system installed, you can use the live CD to set up your computer to dual boot Linux and Windows. See the section "Setting up to dual-boot Linux and Windows" later in this chapter for details. Besides describing how to resize your hard disk to fit Linux on it, the section also describes how you can later mount and access Windows (VFAT and NTFS file systems) from Linux.

Beginning the installation

If you feel you have properly prepared to install Fedora, you can begin the installation procedure. Throughout most of the procedure, you can click Back to make changes to earlier screens. However, once you go forward after being warned that packages are about to be written to hard disk, there's no turning back. Most items that you configure can be changed after Fedora is installed.

> **CAUTION:** If your computer contains any data that you want to keep, be sure to back it up now. Even if you have multiple disk partitions, and don't expect to write over the partitions you want, a backup is a good precaution in case something should go wrong.

1. **Insert the DVD or live CD.** This procedure assumes you are booting and installing from either the DVD or CD that come with this book. (If you are not able to boot from any of those media, refer to the "Alternatives for starting installation" section. If you are booting installation from DVD or CD, but installing the software packages from a network or hard disk, refer to the "Installing from Other Media" section.)

   The DVD can be used for any type of install; the CD with this book can only be used to copy the Fedora 9 desktop system running on the CD to hard disk.

2. **Start your computer.** If you see the Fedora boot screen, continue to the next step.

> **TIP:** If you don't see the boot screen, your DVD or CD-ROM drive may not be bootable. Creating a bootable floppy is no longer an option because the 2.6 kernel doesn't fit on a floppy. However, you may have the choice of making your DVD or CD-ROM drive bootable or copying a boot image to a bootable USB device (such as a pen drive). Here's how: Restart the computer. Immediately, you should see a message telling you how to go into setup, such as by pressing the F1, F2, or Del key. Enter setup and look for an option such as "Boot Options" or "Boot from." If the value is "A: First, Then C:" change it to "CD-ROM First, Then C:" or something similar. Save the changes and try to install again.
>
> If installation succeeds, you may want to restore the boot settings. If your DVD or CD drive still won't boot, you may need to use an alternative method to boot Fedora installation (described in "Alternatives for starting installation" later in this chapter).

3. **Start the boot procedure.** At the boot screen do one of the following, depending on whether you are installing from the DVD or CD:

- Fedora 9 **Install DVD** — With "Install or upgrade" highlighted on the boot menu, press Enter to begin the installation.

- Fedora 9 **Desktop Live CD** — Either wait for the boot screen to time out or with Boot highlighted on the boot menu, press Enter to start the live CD. When the CD boots up to a KDE desktop, double-click the Install to Hard Drive icon to begin the installation.

The boot screen is menu-driven. So if you want to change any of the boot options for a menu selection, highlight that selection and press the Tab key. You can then remove or add options before pressing Enter to continue. For example, to install from a different medium (such as over the network), add the askmethod boot option. See the sidebar "Choosing Different Install Modes" for more boot options.

Although many of the steps are the same, the DVD and CD installs are different in a few key ways. In particular, the DVD install lets you select which packages to install. The CD install simply copies what is essentially an installed system from the live CD to your hard disk. So some of the steps that follow won't apply to the live CD install.

4. **Media check.** At this point, you may be asked to check your installation media. If so, press Enter to check that the DVD is in working order. If a disk is damaged, this step saves you the trouble of getting deep into the install before failing. After the DVD is checked, select Skip to continue.

5. **Continue.** When the welcome screen appears, click Next when you're ready to continue.

6. **Choose a language.** When prompted, indicate the language that you would like to use during the installation procedure by moving the arrow keys and selecting Next. (Later, you will be able to add additional languages.) You are asked to choose a keyboard.

7. **Choose a keyboard.** Select the correct keyboard layout (U.S. English, with Generic 101-key PC keyboard by default). Some layouts enable dead keys (on by default). Dead keys let you use characters with special markings (such as circumflexes and umlauts).

8. **Choose a fresh install or upgrade.** Select either "Install Fedora" for a new install or "Upgrade an existing installation" to upgrade an existing version of Fedora.

9. **Configure networking.** At this point, you are asked to configure your networking. This applies only to configuring a local area network. If you will use only dial-up networking, skip this section by clicking Next. If your computer is not yet connected to a LAN, you should skip this section. If your computer has a wired Ethernet card with a connection to a DHCP server, simply click Next to automatically connect to the network and proceed.

Network address information is assigned to your computer in two basic ways: statically (you type it) or dynamically (a DHCP server provides that information from the network at boot time). One Network Device appears for each wired network card you have installed on your computer. The first Ethernet interface is eth0, the second is eth1, and so on. Repeat the setup for each card by selecting each card and clicking Edit.

Choosing Different Install Modes

Although most computers with more than 192M of RAM automatically install Fedora in the default mode (graphical), there may be times when your video card does not support that mode. Also, although the install process will detect most computer hardware, there may be times when your hard disk, Ethernet card, or other critical piece of hardware cannot be detected and you'll need to enter special information at boot time.

The following is a list of different installation options you can use to start the Fedora install process. You would typically try these modes only if the default mode failed (that is, if the screen was garbled or installation failed at some point). For a list of other supported modes, refer to the `/usr/share/doc/anaconda*/command-line.txt` file (if you have a running Fedora system somewhere with the anaconda package installed) or press F1 through F5 keys to see short descriptions of some of these types.

To use these boot options, highlight the first entry on the boot menu and press Tab. When the boot command appears at the bottom of the screen, type the options you want at the end of that line and press Enter to boot the install process.

- **text:** Type **text** to run installation in a text-based mode. Do this if installation doesn't seem to recognize your graphics card. The installation screens aren't as pretty, but they work just as well.

- **ks:** Type **ks** to run a Fedora installation using a kickstart file. A kickstart file provides some or all of the installation options you would otherwise have to select manually. (A section on creating and using kickstart files is contained later in this chapter.)

- **lowres:** Type **lowres** to run installation in 640 x 480 screen resolution for graphics cards that can't support the higher resolution. To choose a particular resolution, use the **resolution** option. For example: **resolution=1024x768.**

- **nofb:** Type **nofb** to turn off frame buffer. (With frame buffer on, the video display is driven from a memory buffer holding a complete data frame.)

- **noprobe:** Typically, the installation process will try to determine what hardware you have on your computer. In `noprobe` mode, installation will not probe to determine your hardware; you will be asked to load any special drivers that might be needed to install it.

- **mediacheck:** Type **mediacheck** to check your DVD before installing. Because media checking is done next in the normal installation process, you should do this only to test the media on a computer you are not installing on. For Fedora Live CDs, select the Verify and Boot option to check the CD before booting.

- **rescue:** The **rescue** mode is not really an installation mode. This mode boots from DVD or CD, mounts your hard disk, and lets you access useful utilities to correct problems preventing your Linux system from operating properly.

- **vnc vncconnect=*hostname* vncpassword=******:** Run the install in VNC mode to step through the installation process from another system (a VNC client represented by *hostname*). See the "Starting a VNC install" section later in this chapter for information on setting up a VNC server to do this type of install.

- **dd:** Type **dd** if you have a driver disk you want to use to install.

- **expert:** Type **expert** if you believe that the installation process is not properly auto-probing your hardware. This mode bypasses probing so you can choose your mouse, video memory, and other values that would otherwise be chosen for you.

- **askmethod:** Type **askmethod** to have the installation process ask where to install from (local DVD/CD, NFS image, FTP, HTTP, or hard disk).

- **nocddma**: Type **nocddma** to turn off DMA. Errors with some CD drives can be overcome by turning off the DMA feature. This is a good option to try if an install CD or DVD you know to be good fails media check. You could also try `ide=nodma` to turn of DMA for all IDE devices.

- **updates:** Type **updates** to install from an update disk.

You can add other options to the `linux` boot command to identify particular hardware that is not being detected properly. For example, to specify the number of cylinders, heads, and sectors for your hard disk (if you believe the boot process is not detecting these values properly), you could pass the information to the kernel as follows: `linux hd=720,32,64`. In this example, the kernel is told that the hard disk has 720 cylinders, 32 heads, and 64 sectors. You can find this information in the documentation that comes with your hard disk (or stamped on the hard disk itself on a sticker near the serial number).

CROSS-REFERENCE: Refer to Chapter 15 for descriptions of IP addresses, netmasks, and other information you need to set up your LAN and to Chapter 16 for information related to domain names.

If you need to manually configure your Ethernet connection, select the interface you want and click Edit. The Edit Interface dialog box is displayed, allowing you to add the following for both IPv4 and IPv6 support:

- **Enable IPv4 support** — This is the most common TCP/IP protocol version in use today. It should be enabled in most cases.

- **Dynamic IP configuration (DHCP)** — For IPv4 support, if your IP address is assigned automatically from a DHCP server, a checkmark should appear here. With

DHCP checked, you don't have to manually set IPv4 addresses on this page. Remove the checkmark to set your own IP address.

- **Enable IPv6 support** — This is the upcoming TCP/IP standard, which features much longer addresses and some built-in security features. You can enable this without conflicting with IPv4 support.

- **Automatic Neighbor Discovery** — This makes it possible for different machines to exchange messages to implement autoconfiguration. Using this feature, computers can find information on routing and other near-by hosts (neighbors).

- **Dynamic IP configuration (DHCPv6)** — For IPv6 support, if your IP address is assigned automatically from a DHCPv6 server, a checkmark should appear here. Remove the checkmark to set your own IPv6 address.

- **IPv4 and IPv6 Manual Configuration** — If you are not using DHCP to get IP addresses for your Fedora system, you can enter an IPv4 or IPv6 address here. In most cases, an IPv4 address is all that you need. If you set your own IP address, this is the four-part, dot-separated number that represents your computer to the network. An example of a private IP address is 192.168.0.1. See Chapter 15 for a more complete description of how IP addresses are formed and how you choose them.

    In the second part of each IP address, you enter the netmask. The netmask is used to determine what part of an IP address represents the network and what part represents a particular host computer. An example of a netmask for a Class C network is 255.255.255.0.

Click OK. Then add the following information on the main screen:

- **Activate on boot** —You should indicate whether you want the network to start at boot time (you probably do if you have a LAN).

- **Set the hostname** — This is the name identifying your computer within your domain. For example, if your computer were named "baskets" in the handsonhistory.com domain, your full hostname may be baskets.handsonhistory.com. You can either set the domain name yourself (manually) or have it assigned automatically, if that information is being assigned by a DHCP server (automatically via DHCP).

- **Gateway** — This is the IP number of the computer that acts as a gateway to networks outside your LAN. This typically represents a host computer or router that routes packets between your LAN and the Internet.

- **Primary DNS** — This is the IP address of the host that translates computer names you request into IP addresses. It is referred to as a Domain Name System (DNS) server. You may also have a Secondary name server in case the first one can't be reached. (Most ISPs will give you two DNS server addresses.)

10. **Choose a time zone.** Select the time zone. Either click a spot on the map or choose from the drop-down box. Before you click your exact location on the map, click on the area of the map that includes your continent or move the slider to zoom in. Then select the

specific city. You can click "System clock uses UTC" to have your computer use Coordinated Universal Time (also known as Greenwich Mean Time). With multiple operating systems installed, you might want to uncheck this box, because some operating systems expect the BIOS to be set to local time.

11. **Set root password.** You must choose a password for your root user at this point. The root password provides complete control of your Fedora system. Without it, and before you add other users, you will have no access to your own system. Enter the Root Password, and then type it again in the Confirm box. (Remember the root user's password and keep it confidential! Don't lose it!) Click Next to continue.

> **TIP:** Use the `passwd` command to change your password later. See Chapter 14 for suggestions on how to choose a good password. See Chapter 11 for information on setting up user accounts.

12. **Choose your partitioning strategy.** You have the following choices related to how your disk is partitioned for a Fedora installation:

> **NOTE:** Instead of installing to a local hard disk, you can identify an ISCSI initiator as the storage device by selecting the Advanced Storage Configuration button and entering the IP address and ISCSI Initiator Name of the SCSI device. Once that is identified, you can use that device for installing Fedora.

- **Remove all partitions on selected drives and create default layout** — This erases the entire contents of the hard disks you select.

- **Remove Linux partitions on selected drives and create default layout** — This erases all Linux partitions, but leaves Windows partitions intact.

- **Use free space on selected drives and create default layout** — This works only if you have enough free space on your hard disk that is not currently assigned to any partition. (You can choose this option if you resized your Windows partition to make space for Linux, as described in the "Setting up to dual-boot Linux and Windows" section later in this chapter.)

- **Create custom layout** — Select this if you want to create your own custom partitioning.

> **NOTE:** If you selected to create a custom layout, refer to the section on partitioning your hard disk later in this chapter for details on using those tools.

If you have multiple hard disks, you can select which of those disks should be used for your Fedora installation. Check the Review and Modify Partitioning Layout check box to see how Linux is choosing to partition your hard disk. Click Next to continue.

13. **Review and modify partitioning layout.** If you chose to review or customize your partitioning, you will see the Disk Setup tool with your current partitioning layout displayed. You can change any of the partitions you choose, provided that you have at least one root (/) partition that can hold the entire installation and one swap partition. A small /boot partition (about 100MB) is also recommended.

> **WARNING:** Partitioning your disk improperly can cause you to lose your data. Refer to the "Partitioning your disks" section later in this chapter for further information on disk partitioning.

The swap partition is often set to twice the size of the amount of RAM on your computer (for example, for 512MB RAM you could use 1024MB of swap). Linux uses swap space when active processes have filled up your system's RAM. At that point, an inactive process is moved to swap space. You get a performance hit when the inactive process is moved to swap and another hit when that process restarts (moves back to RAM). For example, you might notice a delay on a busy system when you reopen a window that has been minimized for a long time.

The reason you need to have enough swap space is that when RAM and swap fill up, no other processes can start until something closes. Bottom line: add RAM to get better performance; add swap space if processes are failing to start. The Fedora Project suggests a minimum of 32MB and maximum of 2GB of swap space.

Click the Next button (review partitions that are being reformatted and select Format if the changes are acceptable) to continue.

14. **Configure boot loader.** All bootable partitions and default boot loader options that are detected are displayed. By default, the install process will use the GRUB boot loader, install the boot loader in the master boot record of the computer, and choose Fedora as your default operating system to boot.

> **NOTE:** If you keep the GRUB boot loader, you have the option of adding a GRUB password. The password protects your system from having potentially dangerous kernel options sent to the kernel by someone without that password. This password can and should be different from the root password you are asked to enter later. The GRUB boot loader is described later in this chapter.

The names shown for each bootable partition will appear on the boot loader screen when the system starts. Change a bootable partition name by clicking it and selecting Edit. To change the location of the boot loader, click "Configure advanced boot loader options" and continue to the next step. If you do not want to install a boot loader (because you don't want to change the current boot loader), click "No boot loader will be installed." (If the defaults are okay, skip the next step.)

15. **Configure advanced boot loader.** If you selected to configure advanced boot loader options, you can now choose where to store the boot loader. Select one of the following:

- **Master Boot Record (MBR)** — This is the preferred place for GRUB. It causes GRUB to control the boot process for all operating systems installed on the hard disk.

- **First Sector of Boot Partition** — If another boot loader is being used on your computer, you can have GRUB installed on your Linux partition (first sector). This lets you have the other boot loader refer to your GRUB boot loader to boot Fedora. If you take this option, you will need to modify your other boot loader to point to your Fedora partition (or you won't be able to boot the Fedora you are installing).

A useful feature if you have multiple, bootable partitions is the Change Drive Order button. Select this button if you want to change the order in which hard drives are used to boot from. If you have a combination of SCSI and IDE drives, this is a way that you could indicate that the master boot record should go on a SCSI drive.

You can choose to add kernel parameters (which may be needed if your computer can't detect certain hardware). If some piece of hardware is improperly detected and preventing your computer from booting, you can add a kernel parameter to disable that hardware (for example, add `nousb`, `noscsi`, `nopcmcia` or `noagp`). You can select to use linear mode (which was once required to boot from a partition on the disk that is above cylinder 1024, but is now rarely needed).

16. **Install Classes.** For a new install, the installer automatically selects a set of basic software to install. In addition to that set, you can choose one or more of the following groups of software, referred to as tasks. For each of these installation tasks, you have the opportunity to install a set of preset packages or customize that set.

    - **Office and Productivity** — Installs software appropriate for a home or office personal computer or laptop computer. This includes the GNOME desktop (no KDE) and various desktop-related tools (word processors, Internet tools, and so on). Server tools, software development tools, and many system administration tools are not installed.

    - **Software Development** — Similar to a Office and Productivity installation but adds tools for system administration and software development. (Server software is not installed.)

    - **Web Server** — Installs the software packages that you would typically need for a Linux Web server (in particular, Apache Web server and print server). It does not include many other server types by default (FTP, DHCP, mail, DNS, FTP, SQL, or news servers). The default server install also include a GUI (GNOME only).

    A recent feature in Fedora lets you select software repositories outside of Fedora, from which you can select packages to install during the initial Fedora installation. Use the check box to be able to install from other software repositories. Select Add additional software repositories to add other repositories (such as Livna.org or ATRpms repositories, described in Chapter 5). Then, select the Customize Now button if you want to further specifically select which packages in the selected tasks are installed:

    - **Customize Now** — Select the Customize Now button after selecting the task (or tasks) you want to install. This lets you see which categories from each task and which packages within those categories are selected to be installed. It also lets you add or remove package selections. Note that packages from multiple repositories can appear in the same category (for example, you would see games from both Fedora and Livna packages appearing in the Games category if the Livna repository were enabled).

Unlike previous versions, this version of Fedora does not offer an Everything install type or a Minimal install type. Select install classes you want, then choose Customize Now to see the packages to be installed (based on install categories and package groups). Unselecting the major categories can get you a pretty good minimal install, if you like to build from a bare-bones install. In the following step, the procedure will continue as though you had chosen Customize Now.

17. **Customize categories.** If you selected Customize Now, you are presented with categories of software on the left side of the screen and package groups on the right side.

    Select a category to see which groups it contains. Select a group and click the Optional packages to see which optional packages are available in that group and which are selected to be installed. Categories include:

    - **Desktop Environments** — The GNOME desktop environment is selected by default. KDE and XFCE are the other available desktop environment. (Desktop environments are described in Chapter 3.)

    - **Applications** — This category includes packages of office applications, games, sound and video players, Internet tools, and other applications. (Many of these applications are described in Chapters 5 through 9.)

    - **Development** — General and specialized software development tools are included in packages in this category.

    - **Servers** — Packages in this category are for Web, mail, FTP, database, and a variety of other network server types.

    - **Base System** — Contains basic system administration tools, many common utilities, and support for basic system features (such as X Window System, Java, and Legacy software support).

    - **Languages** — Packages containing support for multiple languages are contained in this category.

    After you have chosen the packages you want to install, select Next to continue. The installer will take some time to check for dependencies among the packages you selected.

18. **About to Install.** A screen tells you that you are about to begin writing to hard disk. You can still back out now, and your hard disk will not have changed. Click Next to proceed. (To quit without changes, eject the DVD or CD and restart the computer.) Now the file systems are created and the packages are installed. This typically takes from 20 to 60 minutes to complete, although it can take much longer on older computers.

    For live CD install, the live CD image is simply copied to your hard disk.

19. **Finish installing.** When you see the Congratulations screen, you are done. Eject the DVD or CD and click Reboot.

Your computer will restart. If you installed GRUB, you will see a graphical boot screen that gives you several seconds press a key to view and/or change the bootable partitions. After that, your Fedora installation should boot.

The first time your system boots after installation, Fedora Firstboot runs to do some initial configuration of your system. The next section explains how Fedora Firstboot works.

Running Fedora Firstboot

The first time you boot Fedora, after it is installed, Fedora Firstboot runs to configure some initial settings for your computer.

> **NOTE:** Firstboot runs automatically only if you have configured Fedora to boot to a graphical login prompt. To start it from a text login, log in as root and type the following from a Terminal window:
> ```
> # rm /etc/sysconfig/firstboot
> # /usr/sbin/firstboot
> ```

The first screen you see is the Welcome screen. Click Forward to step through each procedure as follows:

- **License Agreement** — Read and agree to the Fedora License Agreement to be able to continue.

- **Create User** — For your daily use of Fedora, you should have your own user account. You should typically log in with this user name (of your choosing) and use only the root user to perform administrative tasks. In the first of the four text boxes on the screen, type a user name (something such as `jparker` or `alanb`). Next, type your full name (such as John W. Parker or Alan Bourne). Then type your password in the Password text box and again in the Confirm Password text box. Click Forward.

  If some form of network authentication is used, such as LDAP, Kerberos, or SMB authentication, you can click the Use Network Login button. See the "Enabling Authentication" sidebar for information on choosing different authentication types.

- **Hardware Profile** — The Smolt hardware profiler runs to gather and display all kinds of inforrmation about your hardware. Select Sent Profile if you agree to have this information sent to the Fedora Project. Click Forward.

Firstboot is complete. Click Finish to continue. You may need to reboot. See Chapter 3 for a description of how to log in to Fedora and start learning how to use Linux.

When Fedora starts up the next time, it will boot up normally to a login prompt. A graphical boot screen is displayed (instead of a scrolling list of services starting up).

Enabling Authentication

In most situations, you will enable shadow passwords and MD5 passwords (as selected by default) to authenticate users who log in to your computer from local `passwd` and `shadow` password files. To change that behavior, you can select the Use Network Login button during the Create User setup during Firstboot.

The shadow password file prevents access to encrypted passwords. MD5 is an algorithm used to encrypt passwords in Linux and other UNIX systems. It replaces an algorithm called crypt, which was used with early UNIX systems. When you enable MD5 passwords, your users can have longer passwords that are harder to break than those encrypted with crypt.

If you are on a network that supports one of several different forms of network-wide authentication, you may choose one of the following features (on the Authentication tab):

- **Enable Kerberos Support.** Tick this check box to cnable network authentication services available through Kerberos. After enabling Kerberos, you can add information about a Kerberos Realm (a group of Kerberos servers and clients), KDC (a computer that issues Kerberos tickets), and Admin server (a server running the Kerberos kadmind daemon).

- **Enable LDAP Support** — If your organization gathers information about users, you can tick this check box to search for authentication information in an LDAP server. You can enter the LDAP Server name and optionally an LDAP distinguished name to look up the user information your system needs.

- **Enable Smart Card Support** — Tick this check box to allow users to log in using a certificate and key associated with a smart card.

- **Enable SMB Support** — Tick this check box to configure your computer to use Samba for file and print sharing with Windows systems. If you enable SMB authentication, you can enter the name of the SMB server for your LAN and indicate the Workgroup you want your computer to belong to.

- **Enable Winbind Support** — Tick this check box to configure your computer to authenticate users from information retrieved from NTDOM or ADS servers.

Besides those services just mentioned, you can also select from various ways of gathering distributed user information, if any of these methods are supported on your Network.

- **Configure Hesiod** — If your organization uses Hesiod for holding user and group information in DNS, you can add the LHS (domain prefix) and RHS (Hesiod default domain) to use for doing Hesiod queries.

- **Configure NIS** — Select this button and type the NIS Domain name and NIS server location if your network is configured to use the Network Information System (NIS). Instead of selecting an NIS Server, you can click the check box to broadcast to find the server on your network.

Going forward after installation

If your Fedora system installed successfully, you are ready to start using it. Before you head off in your chosen direction, however, there are a few things that I strongly recommend that you do:

- **Get updates** — As bugs and security vulnerabilities are discovered in Fedora or RHEL, updates to your software packages are made available. Look for a desktop applet to alert you that updates are available. Select that icon to see available updates, then select to download and install them when you are ready. As an alternative, you can run yum update from a Terminal window (as root user) to get available updates downloaded and installed on your computer. (See Chapter 5 for further information on getting software updates.)

- **Check your security** — There is a security checklist in Chapter 14. It steps you through different levels of security that are built into your Linux system. I suggest you go through that checklist. Sometimes a feature won't work because of the way permissions, firewalls, SELinux, and other security facilities are set on your system.

- **Learn the desktop and the shell** — Go through Chapter 3 to learn your way around the GNOME and KDE desktops that are available with Fedora and RHEL. After that, learn about the shell in Chapter 4. If something goes wrong with your system, the help you will get from forums and mailing lists will almost always include commands to run from the shell.

- **Check non-working hardware** — If a printer, network card, or other hardware component isn't working immediately, try tools for configuring those items under the System → Administration menu (described throughout this book). If that doesn't work, there are a few standard places to look for information. Review the Fedora Release Notes. From the Release Notes page, look for a link to Help and Support. Visit the Bugzilla page (https://bugzilla.redhat.com) and search for the name or model number of hardware that is giving you trouble.

After you have examined these topics, you can go anywhere else in the book that interests and excites you.

The rest of this chapter is devoted to special topics relating to installing Fedora and RHEL. If you're happy with the way your Fedora system installed, you can skip to the next chapter.

Special Installation Procedures

If you don't want to, or can't, use the procedure to install Fedora from DVD or CD, the procedures in the following sections give you alternatives. The first subsection describes alternate ways of booting the installation, such as PXE or USB flash drives (if your computer doesn't have a bootable DVD or CD drive).

After the install procedure boots, use the "Installing from other media" section that follows to learn how to install Fedora from media other than DVD or CD-ROM (using FTP, HTTP, NFS, or hard disk installs). If you want to have the installation screens appear on another computer as you install, refer to the "Starting a VNC install" section. The subsection following that describes how to do kickstart installations.

Alternatives for starting installation

Your computer may not have a DVD or CD drive or may have one that is unbootable, so you need to find an alternative way to boot the install process. Although booting installation from 1.44MB floppy disks is no longer supported (the 2.6 kernel won't fit on one), you have a few other alternatives:

- Boot installation from hard disk
- Boot from a USB flash drive or other USB device
- Do a PXE install

Procedures for starting installation in those ways are described in the following sections.

Booting installation from hard disk

Booting the install process is similar to booting a regular Linux system. To start an install from your hard disk all you really need to do is:

- Put the files needed to boot installation on your hard disk.
- Configure your boot loader to tell your computer's master boot record about those installation files.

This procedure presumes that there is already a Fedora or Red Hat Enterprise Linux system running on the computer (so you are doing an upgrade or a fresh install of Fedora). It also presumes that you can find a way to get those files on to the hard disk (I'll describe how to do that from a DVD or CD that can be mounted even if it can't be booted).

> **NOTE:** See the section later in this chapter on setting up install servers because presumably you need the contents of the Fedora installation DVD accessible from somewhere other than the DVD itself.

1. Insert the Fedora DVD into the DVD drive while Fedora or Red Hat Enterprise Linux is running.

   If the DVD isn't automatically mounted, as root user type the following to mount it:

   ```
   # mount /media/disk
   ```

   Note that the mount point for the DVD may be in a different location. Another option if the DVD doesn't mount is to create a mount point and mount the DVD there. For example, you could type `mkdir /mnt/dvd ; mount /dev/dvd /mnt/dvd`.

2. Copy the `vmlinuz` and `initrd` files from the installation DVD to your boot directory:

   ```
   # cd /media/disk/isolinux
   # cp initrd.img /boot/initrd-boot.img
   # cp vmlinuz /boot/vmlinuz-boot
   ```

> **NOTE:** If you are not able to mount a DVD or CD on the machine, you could copy the files from another machine on the network using `scp`. Or you could download those files to your `/boot` directory from a Fedora FTP site that contains the Fedora distribution.

3. Change your local `/boot/grub/grub.conf` file to include an entry for the `vmlinux` and `initrd` files you just added to your boot directory. For example:

```
title Fedora 9 installation
        root (hd0,0)
        kernel /vmlinuz-boot
        initrd /initrd-boot.img
```

This example assumes that your `/boot` partition exists on the first partition of your first IDE hard drive (`hd0,0` which is `/dev/sda1`). You can type **df** to see where your `/boot` partition is located.

4. Reboot your computer.

5. When the boot countdown message appears, press any key to display the GRUB boot screen. From there, press the down arrow key to move to the entry titled "Fedora 9 installation" and press Enter. From here you should be able to start installation normally.

Booting installation from a USB device

Most newer computer motherboards can boot from USB devices, allowing you to copy boot disk images to something like a USB flash drive to start the installation. To add the software needed to boot a flash drive or other USB device to start the Fedora install process, you can do the following:

1. Insert the Fedora DVD into the drive while Fedora or RHEL is running. The DVD should be automatically mounted in the `/media` directory.

2. If the DVD isn't automatically mounted, as root user type the following to mount it:

```
# mount /media/disk
```

If you don't know the mount point directory for your DVD drive, check the `/etc/fstab` file to see if it's listed there. If it's not listed, create your own mount point.

3. Insert the pen drive or other USB storage device into a USB port. The device should be automatically mounted under the `/media` directory under a name such as `usbdisk`.

4. Write the `diskboot.img` image from the DVD to the bootable USB drive. (This image needs only about 8MB of disk space.) For example, if the device of the USB flash drive were `/dev/sdb1`, you would type:

```
# dd if=/media/disk/images/diskboot.img of=/dev/sdb1
```

5. To start the installation process from the USB drive you just copied the image to, remove the USB drive and insert it into the computer where you want to install Fedora. Then reboot that computer. It should boot to the Fedora installation boot screen.

6. If the installation boot screen doesn't appear, your computer may not be set to boot USB devices. Go into setup mode when the computer first boots and try to change the boot order in the computer BIOS so that USB devices are booted first.

7. If the installation boot screen does appear, you will use the `linux askmethod` way of installing. Refer to the "Installing from other media" section later in this chapter for information on how to proceed.

Booting installation using PXE

Another method to begin Fedora installation is to use Pre-eXecution Environment (PXE). With PXE, the installation process begins by setting the BIOS of your computer to look on the network for a PXE server to boot from.

For information on how to do a PXE install, refer to `/usr/share/doc/syslinux-*/pxelinux.doc` (provided that the syslinux package is installed). For the PXE install server, you can use the kernel and initrd images from the `images/pxeboot` directory on the Fedora DVD. You need to be able to set up a DHCP server and Tftp server to complete this procedure. Then you can get the Fedora installation files from any of the media types described in the next section.

Installing from other media

Once the installation process has booted (from DVD, as described in the previous section), Fedora will let you get the actual packages that are to be installed from a Web server (HTTP), an FTP server, a shared NFS directory, or local hard disk.

> **NOTE:** To use HTTP, FTP, or NFS installations, your computer must be connected via an Ethernet connection to a network that can reach the computer containing the Fedora distribution. You cannot use a direct dial-up connection. For a local hard disk install, the distribution must have been copied to a local disk (or separate disk partition) that is not being used for installation. See the section "Setting up an HTTP, FTP, or NFS install server" for details on copying the distribution and making it available.

Beginning installation

You can use the DVD that comes with this book (or an alternative method described in the previous section) to start a network or hard disk install.

> **NOTE:** For earlier Red Hat and Fedora distributions, you could use a floppy disk to boot the install process. Because the 2.6 kernel is too large to fit on a floppy disk, however, this method of starting installation is not supported for Fedora Core 2 or later versions.

1. **Insert the Fedora installation DVD into the drive.**

2. **Reboot the computer.** You should see the Fedora boot screen.

3. **Start askmethod.** Press Tab with the first entry on the boot screen highlighted and add the following to the end of the boot prompt:

```
askmethod
```

You are prompted to select a language.

4. **Select the language.** You are prompted to choose a keyboard type.

5. **Select your keyboard type.** You are prompted to select an installation method.

6. **Choose the installation method.** Select any of the following installation methods: Local CDROM, NFS image, FTP, HTTP, or Hard drive.

7. **Configure the network card.** For any of the network installs, you are asked to select your Ethernet card from the list shown. (This may be detected automatically.) If your card is not on the list, you need to obtain a driver disk that contains the driver needed by your network card.

> **NOTE:** The Fedora project does not currently offer a driver disk, so you need to obtain the appropriate driver on your own.

8. **Configure TCP/IP.** For any of the network install types (NFS, FTP, and HTTP), you are prompted to configure TCP/IP for your computer. (See the section on configuring networking earlier in this chapter for information on how to add to these fields.)

9. **Identify the location of the Fedora distribution.** You must identify the NFS server name, FTP site name, or Web site name that contains the Fedora directory that holds the distribution. Or, if you are installing from hard disk, you must identify the partition containing the distribution and the directory that actually contains the Fedora directory.

> **NOTE:** For an FTP install, if you are not downloading from a public FTP site that allows anonymous login, you must select the "Use non-anonymous FTP" check box when you identify the server and directory. You will need a user name and password that has access to the shared directory.

10. **Continue with installation.** If the distribution is found in the location you indicated, continue the installation as described in the previous section.

The next section describes how to set up your own server for installing Fedora.

Setting up an HTTP, FTP, or NFS install server

If you have a LAN connection from your computer to a computer that has at least 2.5GB of disk space and offers NFS, FTP, or Web services, you can install Fedora from that server. Likewise, you can install from a spare disk partition by using a hard disk install. The following procedures let you set up a Linux install server by copying all files from the DVD or by copying images of the DVD.

Configuring an install server using files

To do an FTP or HTTP install, you must copy the files from the installation DVD to a directory that you make available to the network. For example, you could do the following:

```
# mkdir /tmp/rh
# mount /media/disk              With DVD inserted
# cp -r /media/disk/* /tmp/rh/
# umount /media/disk; eject /media/disk
```

In this example, all files were copied. Setting up an NFS install server or hard disk install requires copying the DVD image to the shared NFS directory.

Configuring an install server using disk images

Instead of copying all files from the installation DVD, you can copy the entire DVD image to your hard disk for NFS or hard disk installs. To install the DVD, do the following:

```
# mkdir /tmp/rh
# dd if=/dev/cdrom of=/tmp/rh/disk1.iso   With DVD inserted
# umount /media/disk ; eject /media/disk
```

NFS server

Add an entry to the /etc/exports file to share the distribution directory you created. Remember that for NFS installs, this directory must contain the DVD ISO image. The following entry makes the directory available in read-only form to any computer:

```
/tmp/rh    *(ro)
```

Next, restart NFS by typing the following as root user:

```
# /etc/init.d/nfs restart
```

To set the NFS service to be on permanently (it is off by default), type the following as root:

```
# chkconfig nfs on
```

Web server

If your computer is configured as a Web server, you need to simply make the distribution directory available. For example, with just the ISO image (or images) in the current directory, you could type the following:

```
# mkdir /var/www/html/rh/
# cp *.iso /var/www/html/rh
```

Then simply start the Web server as you would normally (service httpd start). If your computer were named pine.handsonhistory.com, you would identify the install server as pine.handsonhistory.com and the directory as rh.

FTP server

If your computer is configured as an FTP server, you need to make the distribution directory available in much the same way you did with the Web server. For example, after creating the distribution directory as described, type the following:

```
# ln -s /tmp/rh /var/ftp/pub/rh
```

If your computer were named pine.handsonhistory.com, you would identify the install server as pine.handsonhistory.com and the directory as pub/rh.

Hard disk install

With the ISO images of the DVD copied to a disk partition that is not being used for your Fedora install, you can use the hard disk install. If the ISO images exist in the /tmp/rh directory of the first partition of your IDE hard disk, you could identify the device as /dev/sda1 and the directory holding the images as /tmp/rh.

Starting a VNC install

The VNC Fedora installation type doesn't exactly fit into the other installation categories, but I'm adding it here because you might find it useful. With a VNC install, you can boot up the installation process on the machine you want to install Fedora to, and then step through the installation screens on another computer (running a VNC server). This can be convenient if you want to sit at your own desk while you install Fedora on a computer down the hall. Here's what to do:

1. Go the computer from which you want to view the install process (in our example, the one with IP address 10.0.0.1) and start a VNC client process by typing the following from a Terminal window:

    ```
    # vncviewer -listen
    ```

    If vncviewer is not found, install the vnc package (yum install vnc).

2. From the computer you want to install Fedora to insert the installation DVD and reboot the computer. The Fedora installation boot screen should appear.

3. Start the VNC install procedure by identifying the computer screen you want to watch the install from. You should also enter a password (at least six characters). For example, to have the install screens appear on the computer at IP address 10.0.0.1 with a password of myF9pass, press Tab with the Install menu highlighted. Then add the following to the end of the vmlinuz line that appears:

    ```
    vnc vncconnect=10.0.0.1 vncpassword=myF9pass
    ```

4. Answer the first few questions as you would for a normal Fedora install from DVD: Media check, Choose a Language, and Keyboard Type. Next you're asked if you want to configure TCP/IP.

5. Choose either dynamic IP configuration (if you have a BOOTP or DHCP server configured on your network) or enter your own IP address, Netmask, Default gateway, and Primary nameserver for the local computer. Select OK to continue. If the network connection starts up successfully, you will see messages such as the following:

```
Starting VNC...
The VNC server is now running
Attempting to connect to vnc client on host 10.0.0.1...
Connected!
Starting graphical installation...
```

6. Return to the desktop where you are going to view the install procedure. A VNC window should appear on the desktop containing the Fedora Welcome screen. Proceed with installation as you would normally.

> **NOTE:** If you are not able to connect to the vncviewer, make sure that port 5500 is open and accepting connections on your desktop system. Check the descriptions of iptables in Chapter 14 for further information on opening ports in your firewall.

Performing a kickstart installation

If you are installing Fedora or RHEL on multiple computers, you can save yourself some trouble by preconfiguring the answers to questions asked during installation. The method of automating the installation process is referred to as a *kickstart* installation. A kickstart file can not only be used to drive a regular Fedora installation, but can also be used to create Fedora live CDs.

> **CAUTION:** Based on the information you provide in your `ks.cfg` file, kickstart will silently go through and install Fedora without intervention. If this file is not correct, you could easily remove your master boot record and erase everything on your hard disk. Check the `ks.cfg` file carefully and test it on a noncritical computer before trying it on a computer holding critical data.

The general steps of performing a kickstart installation are as follows:

1. **Create a kickstart file.** The kickstart file, named `ks.cfg`, contains the responses to questions that are fed to the installation process.

2. **Install kickstart file.** You have to place the `ks.cfg` on a floppy disk or CD, on a local hard disk, or in an accessible location on the network.

3. **Start kickstart installation.** When you boot the installation procedure, you need to identify the location of the `ks.cfg` file.

In the example in this chapter you create your kickstart file directly with a text editor. If you prefer, you can use the Kickstart Configurator (system-config-kickstart command, from the package of the same name), which is a graphical tool for creating kickstart files.

Creating the kickstart file

A good way to begin creating your kickstart file is from a sample ks.cfg file. When you install Fedora or RHEL, the installation process places a file called anaconda-ks.cfg into the /root directory. You can use this file as the basis for the ks.cfg file that you will use for your kickstart installs.

The particular /root/anaconda-ks.cfg file you get is based on the information you entered during a regular installation (CD, NFS, and so on). Presumably, if you are installing Fedora on other computers for the same organization, multiple computers may have a lot of the same hardware and configuration information. That makes this a great file for you to start creating your ks.cfg file from.

> **NOTE:** For further details about how to use kickstart, refer to the Red Hat Linux Configuration Guide. You can get this guide from any Red Hat mirror site. To use a more graphical tool for configuring kickstart, run the system-config-kickstart command (after installing the package of the same name).

To start, log in as the root user. Then make a copy of the anaconda-ks.cfg file to work on.

```
# cp anaconda-ks.cfg ks.cfg
```

Use any text editor to edit the ks.cfg file. Remember that required items should be in order and that any time you omit an item, the user will be prompted for an answer. Entries from a ks.cfg file that was created from a regular DVD installation of Fedora are used as a model for the descriptions below. You should start with your own anaconda-ks.cfg file, and as a result, your file will start out somewhat differently. Commented lines begin with a pound sign (#).

The first line in the ks.cfg file should indicate whether the installation is an upgrade or an install. The install option runs a new installation. You can use the upgrade keyword instead to upgrade an existing system. (For an upgrade, the only requirements are a language, an install method, an install device, a keyboard, and a boot loader.)

```
install
```

The method of installation is indicated on the next line. Possible locations for the installation media include: NFS (nfs --server=*servername* --dir=*installdir*), FTP (url --url ftp://*user:passwd@server/dir*), HTTP (url --url http://*server/dir*), or hard drive (harddrive --dir=/*dir* --partition=/dev/*partition*). For the default DVD or CD install, you will see:

```
cdrom
```

The required `lang` command sets the language (and to be more specific, the country as well) in which Fedora is installed. The value is U.S. English (`en_US.UTF-8`) by default:

```
lang en_US.UTF-8
```

You can install multiple languages to be supported in Fedora. Here is an example of the default being set to U.S. English:

```
langsupport --default en_US.UTF-8 en_US.UTF-8
```

The required `keyboard` command identifies a United States (`us`) keyboard by default. More than 70 other keyboard types are supported. (Run `system-config-keyboard` to see a list of available keyboard types.)

```
keyboard us
```

The optional `xconfig` command can be used to configure your monitor and video card. If you use the `skipx` command instead (as shown in the following code sample), no X configuration is done. (After the system is installed, run `system-config-desktop` to set up your X configuration.) When you use the `xconfig` command, you can identify the type of X server to use based on your video card (`--card`) and monitor specs (`--hysync` and `--vsync`). A handful of other options enable you to set the color depth in bits (`--depth`), the screen resolution (`--resolution`), whether the default desktop is GNOME or KDE (`--defaultdesktop`), whether the login screen is graphical (`--startxonboot`), and the amount of RAM on your video card (`--videoram`). (All the information after `xconfig` should actually appear on one line.)

```
skipx
```

or

```
xconfig --card="NVIDIA GeForce FX (generic)" --videoram=131072
    --hsync=31.5-37.9 --vsync=50-70 --resolution=800x600
    --depth=16 --startxonboot --defaultdesktop gnome
```

The optional `network` command lets you configure your Fedora or RHEL system's interface to your network. The example tells your computer to get its IP address and related network information from a DHCP server (`--bootproto dhcp`). If you want to assign a particular IP address, use the `--bootproto static` option. Then change the IP address (`--ip`), netmask (`--netmask`), IP address of the gateway (`--gateway`), and IP address of the DNS server (`--nameserver`) to suit your system. You can also add a hostname (`--hostname`).

> **NOTE:** Although the `network` values appear to be on three lines, all values must be on the same line.

```
network --device eth0 --bootproto dhcp
```
or

```
network --device=eth0 --bootproto static --ip=192.168.0.1
    --netmask 255.255.255.0 --gateway 192.168.0.1
    --nameserver 192.168.0.254 --hostname duck.example.com
```

58   Part I: Getting Started in Fedora and RHEL

The rootpw command sets the password to whatever word follows (in the following example, paSSword). It is a security risk to leave this password hanging around, so you should change this password (with the passwd command) after Linux is installed. You also have the option of adding an encrypted password instead (--iscrypted g.UJ.RQeOV3Bg –enablemd5).

```
rootpw paSSword
```
or
```
rootpw --iscrypted g.UJ.RQeOV3Bg --enablemd5
```

The firewall command lets you set the default firewall used by your Fedora or RHEL system. The default value is enabled (if the firewall is turned on). You can also set firewall to disabled (no firewall). (These values are described in the installation procedure earlier in this chapter.) As you can see in the example, you can optionally indicate that there be no restrictions from host computers on a particular interface (--trust eth0). You can also allow an individual service (--ssh) or a particular port:protocol pair (--port 1234:udp).

```
firewall --enabled --trust=eth0 --ssh --port=1234:udp
```

The required authconfig command sets the type of authentication used to protect your user passwords. The --enableshadow option enables the /etc/shadow file to store your passwords. The --enablemd5 option enables up to 256 character passwords. (You would typically use both.)

```
authconfig --enableshadow --enablemd5
```

The selinux command indicates whether or not Security Enhanced Linux is enabled. The following line shows it as enabled and enforcing:

```
selinux --enforcing
```

The timezone command sets the time zone for your Linux system. The default, shown here, is United States, New York (America/New_York). The –utc option indicates that the computer's hardware clock is set to UTC time. If you don't set a time zone, US/Eastern is used. Run the timeconfig command to see other valid time zones.

```
timezone --utc America/New_York
```

The bootloader command sets the location of the boot loader (GRUB, by default). For example, --location=mbr adds GRUB to the master boot record. (Use --location= none to not add GRUB.) The driveorder= option describes which hard disk to look on first for the master boot record. You can also add kernel options to be read at boot time using the append option (--append hdd=ide-scsi) or an optional password for GRUB (--password=GRUBpassword).

```
bootloader --location=mbr --driveorder=sda --append="rghb quiet"
password=GRUBpassword
```

Partitioning is required for a new install, optional for an upgrade. The code that follows is from the sample `ks.cfg` file. The `clearpart --linux` value removes existing Linux partitions (or use `--all` to clear all partitions) on the first hard drive (`--drives=sda`). The `part /boot`, `/` and `swap`, sets the file system type (`--fstype`) and partition name (`onpart`) for each partition assignment. You can also set sizes of the partitions (`--size`) to however many megabytes you want. You can also create logical volume group (`volgroup`) and individual logical volume (`logvol`) entries for your partitioning.

```
# The following is the partition information you requested
# Note that any partitions you deleted are not expressed
# here so unless you clear all partitions first, this is
# not guaranteed to work
#clearpart --linux --drives=sda
#part /boot --fstype ext3 --size=100 --ondisk=sda
#part / --fstype ext3 --size=700 --grow --ondisk=sda
#part swap --size=128 --grow --maxsize=256 --ondisk=sda
```

To indicate which packages to install, begin a section with the `%packages` command. (A few examples follow.) Designate whole installation groups, individual groups, or individual packages. On the `%packages` line, you can indicate whether or not to resolve dependencies by installing those packages needed by the ones you selected (`--resolvedeps`). After `%packages`, start an entry with an @ sign for a group of packages, and add each individual package by placing its name on a line by itself. Here is an example:

> **TIP:** You can find a listing of package groups and individual packages on the Fedora installation DVD. Find the `comps` file in the `Fedora/base` directory. However, if you start with the `anaconda-ks.cfg` file that resulted from installing Fedora or RHEL, you might already have a set of packages that you want to install.

```
%packages --resolvdeps
@base
@editors
@games
@graphical-internet
@kde-desktop
@office
@sound-and-video
        .
        .
        .
```

> **NOTE:** The `%packages` command is not supported for upgrades. To install everything, you can remove the package names shown. Then, after the `%packages` line, you can add an @ everything line.

The `%post` command starts the post-installation section. After it, you can add any shell commands you want to run after installation is completed. A useful thing to do is to add useradd commands for users you want to add during installation. You can also use the usermod command to add the user's password. (See Chapter 22 for information on creating an encrypted password.)

```
%post
/usr/sbin/useradd jake
chfn -f 'John W. Jones' jake
/usr/sbin/usermod -p '$1kQUMYbFOh79wECxnTuaH.' Jake
```

At this point you should have a working ks.cfg file.

Installing the kickstart file

Once the ks.cfg file is created, you need to put it somewhere accessible to the computer doing the installation. Typically, you will place the file on a floppy disk. However, you can also put the file on a computer that is reachable on the network or on a hard disk.

To copy the file to a floppy disk, create a DOS floppy and copy the file as follows:

```
# mcopy ks.cfg a:
```

When you do the Fedora kickstart installation, have this floppy disk with you. As an alternative, you can copy the ks.cfg file to a hard disk partition, Web server, or NFS share.

Being able to place the ks.cfg file on a computer on the network requires a bit more configuration. The network must have a DHCP or a BOOTP server configured that is set up to provide network information to the new install computer. The NFS server containing the ks.cfg file must export the file so that it is accessible to the computer installing Linux. To use a ks.cfg file from the local hard disk, you can place the file on any partition that is a Windows (VFAT) or Linux (ext3) partition.

Booting a kickstart installation

If the kickstart file (ks.cfg) has been created and installed in an accessible location, you can start the kickstart installation. Here is an example of how you can do a kickstart installation using the Fedora DVD and a floppy containing a ks.cfg file:

1. Insert the Fedora or RHEL DVD and restart the computer.

2. When you see the boot screen, insert the floppy containing the ks.cfg file, highlight the first boot entry and press the Tab key. When the boot command line appears, modify it to add the following text:

```
ks=floppy
```

You should see messages about formatting the file system and reading the package list. The packages should install without any intervention. Next you should see a post-install message. Finally, you should see the Complete message.

3. Remove the floppy; then press the Spacebar to restart your computer (the DVD should eject automatically).

> **TIP:** You can install using kickstart over NFS (`ks:nfs:server:path/ks.cfg`), from Web server (`ks=http://server/path/ks.cfg`), or from your hard drive (`ks=hd:device/ks.cfg`).

Special Installation Topics

Some things that you run into during installation merit whole discussions by themselves. Rather than bog down the procedures with details that not everyone needs, I have included instructions in this section to address issues such as setting up a dual-boot Linux and Windows system, disk partitioning, and boot loaders.

Setting up to dual-boot Linux and Windows

It is possible to set up your computer so that you can have two (or more) complete operating systems installed on it. When you power up your computer, you can choose which operating system you want to boot. This setup is referred to as a *dual-boot* computer.

If a Microsoft Windows operating system was installed when you got your PC, it's likely that the entire hard disk is devoted to Windows. Fedora installation procedures retain existing Windows partitions by default, but they don't let you take space from existing disk partitions without destroying them. If you want to be able to run Linux on that machine, you need to do one of the following:

- **Erase the disk**. If you never wanted Windows in the first place (or if Windows is badly broken or infected), you may decide to completely erase it from your hard disk. In this case, you won't have a dual-boot system, but you can jump right to the Fedora or RHEL install procedure and start installing (tell the install process to just erase the whole disk).

- **Add a second disk.** This lets you maintain your Windows installation on the computer without having to do the potentially dangerous resizing of your Windows partitions. (Refer to Chapter 10 for information on adding a second disk, then go right to the Fedora installation section.)

- **Resize your Windows partition(s)**. Many people choose this route for dual-booting Windows and Linux. If done sucessfully, you don't have to add hardware and you can keep your whole Windows system.

The rest of this section is devoted to a discussion and procedure for resizing your Windows partitions to create a dual-boot computer with Windows and Linux.

Resizing your Windows partitions

By resizing your Windows partitions you can free up disk space that can be used for your Fedora or RHEL installation. Because there is some danger in resizing your disk partitions and changing how your computer boots, however, you should carefully read the Caution that follows.

> **CAUTION:** Setting up a dual-boot system is discouraged by Red Hat and by people who write Linux books (like me) because if something goes wrong you can lose all your data or make your computer unbootable (usually temporarily). New users often won't have a backup and will simply erase their hard disk if the computer won't boot after a procedure like the following. Then they complain a lot. So, I'm officially recommending against setting up a dual-boot system, and then telling you how to do it.
>
> Red Hat, Inc. encourages you to use VFAT file systems for your Windows partitions if you plan to dual boot your computer with Linux. In Fedora 9, Fedora offers support for the NTFS file system type. So you can now use tools from within Fedora to resize your Windows NTFS partitions.
>
> If, after resizing your Windows partitions and installing Fedora or RHEL, your computer becomes unbootable, refer to the "Troubleshooting Installation" section later in this chapter for advice on what to do.

Before you begin resizing your Windows system, boot Windows and do the following:

- **Back up your data!** Of course, you should always have a current backup of your important data. However, now is a particularly good time to do a back up, just in case one of those disk catastrophes I warned you about actually happens.

- **Defragment your disk**. Before you resize your hard disk, you should use a defragmenting utility in Windows to have all files stored contiguously on the disk. That way, when you reassign free space to Linux partitions, you have a continuous area of the disk to work with. To defragment a disk in Windows XP, click Start → All Programs → Accessories → System Tools → Disk Defragmenter. Then select Defragment from the Disk Defragmenter window. Defragmenting can take a while, depending on your processor speed and disk size.

While you have the Disk Defragmenter window displayed, note a few things about your hard disk that you will need to know later:

- **File System** — The file system type will most likely be NTFS, although it may also be VFAT. If you have the option to install Windows from scratch, selecting VFAT as the file system type will work much better for Linux. Support for writing to NTFS has been considered unreliable from Linux, although reading from NTFS seems to work well. VFAT file systems, however, will work well for both Linux and Windows.

- **Free Space** — If your entire hard disk consists of a single Windows partition, you can resize your existing partition to use some of the free space to assign to Linux partitions. Note the amount of free space you have here and compare it to the amounts you will need to install Linux (described earlier).

Despite the fact that I have successfully resized several NTFS partitions using the GParted utility, I still recommend caution (and a good backup of your data) before proceeding. If you feel more comfortable using commercial products to resize your partitions, I have listed a few of those below. I have not tested the products so I name them here only because I have heard good reports of success from others:

- **Norton Partition Magic** — I've heard good reports from people using Partition Magic (www.powerquest.com/partitionmagic) to resize NTFS partitions. Partition Magic also helps you create new partitions and manage them. It supports Windows XP Professional/Home, Windows 95b-98SE, Windows Me, Windows 2000 Professional, and NT 4.0 workstation (SP6a). The cost is currently $69.95.

- **Acronis OS Selector** — This is another well-regarded product for managing, creating, and resizing partitions, which is now included in the Acronis Disk Director Suite. It supports a variety of file system types, including FAT12, FAT16, FAT32, NTFS, and Linux partition types (ext2, ext3 and Linux ReiserFS). It also supports the same Windows platforms that Partition Magic does. The cost is currently $49.99 from www.acronis.com.

> **NOTE:** Earlier releases of Fedora included a FIPS utility for resizing FAT and VFAT file systems. FIPS is no longer included with Fedora or RHEL, so no description of FIPS is included here. A description of FIPS from an earlier edition of this book is included at the Wiley Web site: www.wiley.com/go/fedora9bible.

Microsoft Windows Vista now comes with tools for resizing your disk partitions. From the Start menu, right-click on Computer and select Manage. In the left pane that appears, select Storage and click Disk Management. Then right-click on the volume you want to resize and select either Extend Volume or Shrink Volume to change its size.

The open source tool I describe here for resizing your disk is called GParted. It can be used to resize partitions that contain a variety of file system types.

f your Windows system is backed up and your disk defragmented, you can begin the process of resizing your NTFS or VFAT disk partition with GParted using the Fedora 9 Desktop Live CD included with this book. Here's how to resize your NTFS partitions using that CD:

1. Insert the Fedora 9 Desktop Live CD and reboot your computer.

2. At the boot prompt, with the first entry highlighted, press Enter .

3. When the live CD boots to a KDE desktop, to begin resizing your hard disk you need to install the gparted package. Assuming you have an Internet connection, type the following from a Terminal window:

```
$ su -
# yum install gparted
```

4. From the KDE menu, search for the GParted application and select it. The GParted graphical partitioning tool opens, displaying your current disk partitions.

5. Select the disk (probably /dev/sda) and partition (probably NTFS or VFAT for a Windows partition) you want to resize. The Resize/Move button should become available.

6. Select the Resize/Move button to open a Resize/Move pop-up windows.

7. Grab the slider bar from the right and move it to select how much you want to resize your partition. The New Size box shows the new size of your partition. The Free Space Following MiB box shows how much free space you will have after you are done. In my example, on a small disk I resized /dev/sda1 to about 15GB, leaving me about 5GB of free space that I can use later to install Fedora (normally, you would want more for Fedora, if space is available). Figure 2-1 shows the GParted window resizing about a 20GB partition to about 15GB.

8. Click Resize/Move to begin resizing your partition. When it is done, you will see the resized partition and a new entry showing the free space.

> **CAUTION:** The resize is committed in the next step. You can quit now without making any changes if you are nervous. In any case, make sure that the partition you are resizing is not mounted. (In this example, I'd type `umount /dev/sda1` as root user from a shell before running the next step.

9. If the new partition sizes look alright, click Apply to commit the changes.

10. At this point, you can close the GParted window and begin the regular installation procedure for Fedora or RHEL, using the disk space that you just freed up.

Figure 2-1: Use GParted to resize your Windows NTFS partitions.

After you have installed Fedora or RHEL, there are a few other useful things you might want to do so you can use files from your Windows partitions in Linux.

> **NOTE:** By default, Fedora and RHEL are configured to hide the GRUB boot screen that lets you select which operating system to boot. You will have to press any key, as the Fedora boot screen counts down 5 seconds, to see the GRUB boot screen. You might consider editing the `grub.conf` file, as described later in this chapter. Personally, I removed the `hiddenmenu` line and increased the timeout from 5 to 10 seconds.

Using Windows partitions from Linux

With some space available on your disk, when you go to install Linux, consider adding a small FAT16 or FAT32 partition (maybe 2GB) on your disk. Every x86 operating system (Linux, Windows 95, NT, 2000, XP, Vista and DOS) supports those types. With that added, you will be able to freely exchange files between your Linux and Windows system on the FAT16 partition.

With FAT partitions, however, keep in mind that there are limitations. FAT is limited to between 2GB and 4GB file sizes. Also, FAT16 doesn't support long file names. Total partition size for FAT file systems is 32GB.

After you have installed Linux in the space freed up by the previous procedure, you should be able to choose between Linux and Windows when the Fedora or RHEL boot screen appears during boot time. Press any key to go to the GRUB boot screen. Then move the arrow key to choose to boot Linux or Windows.

The first time you boot Windows, you might be asked to check your disk (because your Windows partition will be a different size than expected). After that, there should be no change in how you use your Windows system. Your disk space will just be smaller.

Now, when you boot up Linux, if you have a lot of documents, digital images, music, or other content on your Windows partition, you probably want to be able to use that content from Linux. To do that, you need to:

- Determine which partition is your Windows partition.
- If you didn't do so during installation, add support for the file system type of your Windows partition to Linux. Since VFAT is already built in, that means adding NTFS support if that is the file system type.
- Mount the Windows partition on your Linux file system.

The following procedure describes how to do those things.

1. **Check partitions.** To determine which partition contains your Windows file system, use the `fdisk` command as follows:

```
# fdisk -l
Disk /dev/sda: 60.0 GB, 60011642880 bytes
16 heads, 63 sectors/track, 116280 cylinders
Units = cylinders of 1008 * 512 = 516096 bytes
```

```
   Device Boot    Start       End      Blocks    Id    System
/dev/sda1    *        1      41725   21029053+    7    HPFS/NTFS
/dev/sda2        106741     116280    4808160    12    Compaq diagnostics
/dev/sda3         41725      41932     104422+   83    Linux
/dev/sda4         41932     106734   32660145     5    Extended
/dev/sda5         41932     106718   32652081    8e    Linux LVM
```

In this example, the Windows partition is on device /dev/sda1 and is an NTFS file system. (The other common type of Windows file system is VFAT.)

2. **Get NTFS support.** If you have a VFAT file system, you can skip this step. If you have an NTFS file system, and NTFS support is not already installed, you can install the necessary drivers and tools to be able to mount and use your NTFS file system in Linux by running the following yum command as root user from a Terminal window:

```
# yum install ntfsprogs ntfs-3g
```

Assuming you have an active connection to the Internet, this will install the NTFS support you need to access your NTFS partitions from Linux.

3. **Mount Windows file system.** You can access your Windows file system from Linux using the mount command. Assuming your Windows partition is an NTFS file system on /dev/sda1 (as in the example above), you could type the following to create the Windows mount point and mount the file system there:

```
# mkdir /mnt/win
# chmod 755 /mnt/win
# mount -oro -t ntfs /dev/sda1 /mnt/win
# chmod 755 /mnt/win
# ls /mnt/win
```

The -oro option to mount will mount the file system read-only. Read/write support is not considered to be stable (so if you remove the -oro option to mount read/write, you do so at your own risk). Replace the ntfs with vfat if your Windows partition is a VFAT file system. The ls command is just to find out if you can see the contents of your Windows partition.

You can have the mount occur permanently by adding an entry to the /etc/fstab file. Here's an example of the line you could add to /etc/fstab to have the partition mounted every time the system reboots:

```
/dev/sda1    /mnt/win    ntfs    ro    0 0
```

At this point, you can use the files from your Windows partition as you would any other files on your system. You can open a folder or change directories to the /mnt/win directory to see the contents. Then use any applications you choose to open your documents (OpenOffice.org), music (Rhythmbox), images (Gimp), or any other content type you want to use from your Windows partition in Linux.

> **NOTE:** If your Linux system uses an ext2 or ext3 file system (as Fedora typically does), you can do the reverse of what was just described as well: access your Linux partition from Windows. For information on how to do this, see the Ext2 Installable File System for Windows (`www.fs-driver.org`).

Partitioning your disks

The hard disk (or disks) on your computer provides the permanent storage area for your data files, applications programs, and the operating system (such as Fedora or RHEL). Partitioning is the act of dividing a disk into logical areas that can be worked with separately. There are several reasons you may want to do partitioning:

- **Multiple operating systems** — If you install Fedora or RHEL on a PC that already has a Windows operating system, you may want to keep both operating systems on the computer. To run efficiently, they must exist on completely separate partitions. When your computer boots, you can choose which system to run. Note that you are limited in the number of partitions you can have (with IDE drives you can have 63 partitions; with SCSI devices, you are limited to 15 partitions per device).

- **Multiple partitions within an operating system** — To protect from having their entire operating system run out of disk space, people often assign separate partitions to different areas of the Linux file system. For example, if /home and /var were assigned to separate partitions, then a gluttonous user who fills up the /home partition wouldn't prevent logging daemons from continuing to write to log files in the /var/log directory.

  Multiple partitions also make it easier to do certain kinds of backups (such as an image backup). For example, an image backup of /home would be much faster (and probably more useful) than an image backup of the root file system (/).

- **Different file system types** — Different kinds of file systems have different structures. File systems of different types must be on their own partitions. In Fedora and RHEL, you need at least one file system type for / (typically ext3) and one for your swap area. File systems on CD-ROM use the iso9660 file system type.

> **TIP:** When you create partitions for Fedora or RHEL, you will often assign the file system type as Linux native (using the ext3 type). Reasons to use other types include needing a file system that allows particularly long filenames or many inodes (each file consumes an inode).
>
> For example, if you set up a news server, it can use many inodes to store news articles. Another reason for using a different file system type is to copy an image backup tape from another operating system to your local disk (such as one from an OS/2 or Minix operating system).

If you have used only Windows operating systems before, you probably had your whole hard disk assigned to C: and never thought about partitions. With Fedora and RHEL, you can select to have Linux erase the whole disk, take it over, and partition it or have Linux keep separate partitions for Windows 9x/2000/NT/XP/Vista and Linux. The Fedora and RHEL install processes also give you the opportunity to view and change the default partitioning for the different installation types.

During installation, Fedora and RHEL enable you to partition your hard disk using the Disk Setup utility (a graphical partitioning tool). The following sections describe how to use Disk Setup (during installation) or fdisk (when Fedora or RHEL is up and running or by switching virtual terminals while the install is running). See the section "Tips for creating partitions" for some ideas for creating disk partitions.

Partitioning with Disk Setup during installation

During installation, you are given the opportunity to change how your hard disk is partitioned. Fedora recommends using the Disk Setup. The Disk Setup screen is divided into two sections. The top shows general information about each hard disk. The bottom shows details of each partition. Figure 2-2 shows an example of the Disk Setup window.

For each of the hard disk partitions, you can see:

- **Device** — The device name is the name representing the hard disk partition in the /dev directory. Each disk partition device begins with two letters: sd for IDE disks or SCSI disks, ed for ESDI disks, or xd for XT disks. After that is a single letter representing the number of the disk (disk 1 is a, disk 2 is b, disk 3 is c, and so on). The partition number for that disk (1, 2, 3, and so on) follows that.

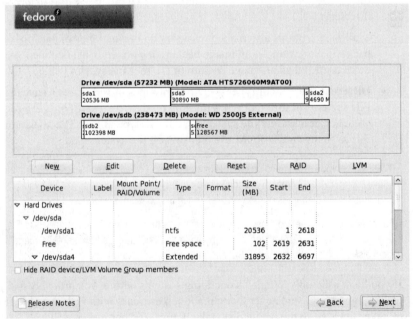

Figure 2-2: Partition your disk during installation from the Disk Setup window.

- **Mount Point/Raid/Volume** — The directory where the partition is connected into the Linux file system (if it is). You must assign the root partition (/) to a native Linux partition before you can proceed. If you are using RAID or LVM, the name of the RAID device or LVM volume appears here.

- **Type** — The type of file system that is installed on the disk partition. In most cases, the file system will be Linux (ext3), Win VFAT (vfat), or Linux swap. However, you can also use the previous Linux file system (ext2), physical volume (LVM), or software RAID. In fact, LVM is used by default for your root file system when you install Fedora or RHEL. This will allow you to add more disk space later to that partition, if needed, without having to create a new partition.

- **Format** — Indicates whether (checkmark) or not (no checkmark) the installation process should format the hard disk partition. Partitions marked with a check are erased! So, on a multiboot system, be sure your Windows partitions, as well as other partitions containing data are not checked!

- **Size (MB)** — The amount of disk space allocated for the partition. If you selected to let the partition grow to fill the existing space, this number may be much larger than the requested amount.

- **Start/End** — Represents the partition's starting and ending cylinders on the hard disk.

In the top section, you can see each of the hard disks that is connected to your computer. The drive name is shown first. That's followed by the model name of the disk. The total amount of disk space, the amount used, and the amount free are shown in megabytes.

Reasons for partitioning

There are different opinions about how to divide up a hard disk. Here are some issues:

- **Do you want to install another operating system?** If you want Windows on your computer along with Linux, you will need at least one Windows (Win95 FAT16, VFAT, or NTFS type), one Linux (Linux ext3), and one Linux swap partition.

- **Is it a multiuser system?** If you are using the system yourself, you probably don't need many partitions. One reason for partitioning an operating system is to keep the entire system from running out of disk space at once. That also serves to put boundaries on what an individual can use up in his or her home directory (although disk quotas are good for that as well).

- **Do you have multiple hard disks?** You need at least one partition per hard disk. If your system has two hard disks, you may assign one to / and one to /home (if you have lots of users) or /var (if the computer is a server sharing lots of data).

Deleting, adding, and editing partitions

Before you can add a partition, there needs to be some free space available on your hard disk. If all space on your hard disk is currently assigned to one partition (as it often is in DOS or

Windows), you must delete or resize that partition before you can claim space on another partition. The section "Resizing your Windows partitions" earlier in this chapter discusses how to take disk space from an existing Windows partition to use later for Linux partitions, without losing information in your existing single-partition system.

> **CAUTION:** Make sure that any data that you want to keep is backed up before you delete the partition. When you delete a partition, all its data is gone.

Disk Setup is less flexible, but more intuitive, than the `fdisk` utility. Disk Setup lets you delete, add, and edit partitions.

> **TIP:** If you create multiple partitions, make sure that there is enough room in the right places to complete the installation. For example, most of the Linux software is installed in the `/usr` directory (and subdirectories), whereas most user data are eventually added to the `/tmp`, `/home` or `/var` directories. It's a good idea to have separate partitions for every directory structure users can write to. Likewise, NFS shares also are often put on separate partitions.

To delete a partition in Disk Setup, do the following:

1. Select a partition from the list of Current Disk Partitions on the main Disk Setup window (click it or use the arrow keys).

2. To delete the partition, click Delete.

3. When asked to confirm the deletion, click Delete.

4. If you made a mistake, click Reset to return to the partitioning as it was when you started Disk Setup.

To add a partition in Disk Setup, follow these steps from the main Disk Setup window:

1. Select New. A window appears, enabling you to create a new partition.

2. Type the name of the Mount Point (the directory where this partition will connect to the Linux file system). You need at least a root (/) partition and a swap partition.

3. Select the type of file system to be used on the partition. You can select from Linux native (ext2 or preferably ext3), software RAID, Linux swap (swap), physical volume (LVM), or Windows FAT (vfat).

> **TIP:** To create a different file system type than those shown, leave the space you want to use free for now. After installation is complete, use `fdisk` to create a partition of the type you want.

4. Type the number of megabytes to be used for the partition (in the Size field). If you want this partition to grow to fill the rest of the hard disk, you can put any number in this field (1 will do fine).

5. If you have more than one hard disk, select the disk on which you want to put the partition from the Allowable Drives box.

6. Type the size of the partition (in megabytes) into the Size (MB) box.

7. Select one of the following Additional Size Options:

   - **Fixed size** — Click here to use only the number of megabytes you entered into the Size text box when you create the partition.

   - **Fill all space up to (MB)** — If you want to use all remaining space up to a certain number of megabytes, click here and fill in the number. (You may want to do this if you are creating a VFAT partition up to the 2048MB limit that Disk Setup can create.)

   - **Fill to maximum allowable size** — If you want this partition to grow to fill the rest of the disk, click here.

8. Optionally select Force to Be a Primary Partition if you want to be sure to be able to boot the partition or Check for Bad Blocks if you want to have the partition checked for errors.

9. Select OK if everything is correct. (The changes don't take effect until several steps later when you are asked to begin installing the packages.)

To edit a partition in Disk Setup from the main Disk Setup window, follow these steps:

1. Click the partition you want to edit.

2. Click the Edit button. A window appears, ready to let you edit the partition definition.

3. Change any of the attributes (as described in the add partition procedure). For a new install, you may need to add the mount point (/) for your primary Linux partition.

4. Select OK. (The changes don't take effect until several steps later, when you are asked to begin installing the packages.)

NOTE: If you want to create a RAID device, you need to first create at least two RAID partitions. Then click the RAID button to make the two partitions into a RAID device. For more information on RAID, refer to Chapter 10 or the Red Hat Linux Customization guide. The latter is available here: `www.redhat.com/docs/manuals/linux/RHL-9-Manual/custom-guide/`. To create an LVM volume group, you must create at least one partition of type "physical volume (LVM)."

Partitioning with fdisk

The fdisk utility does the same job as Disk Setup, but it's no longer offered as an option during Fedora or RHEL installations. (If you are old school, however, you could press Ctrl+Alt+F2 during the installation process and run fdisk from the shell to partition your disk.)

The following procedures are performed from the command line as root user.

> **CAUTION:** Remember that any partition commands can easily erase your disk or make it inaccessible. Back up critical data before using any tool to change partitions! Then be very careful about the changes you do make. Keeping an emergency boot disk handy is a good idea, too.

The `fdisk` command is one that is available on many different operating systems (although it looks and behaves differently on each). In Linux, `fdisk` is a menu-based command. To use `fdisk` to list all your partitions, type the following (as root user):

```
# fdisk -l

Disk /dev/sda: 40.0 GB, 40020664320 bytes
255 heads, 63 sectors/track, 4865 cylinders
Units = cylinders of 16065 * 512 = 8225280 bytes

   Device Boot      Start         End      Blocks   Id  System
/dev/sda1    *          1          13      104391   83  Linux
/dev/sda2              14        4833    38716650   83  Linux
/dev/sda3            4834        4865      257040   82  Linux swap
```

To see how each partition is being used on your current system, type the following:

```
# df -h
Filesystem            Size  Used Avail Use% Mounted on
/dev/sda2              37G   5.4G   30G  16% /
/dev/sda1             99M   8.6M   86M  10% /boot
none                  61M      0   61M   0% /dev/shm
```

From the output of `df`, you can see that the root of your Linux system (/) is on the `/dev/sda2` partition and that the `/dev/sda1` partition is used for `/boot`.

> **CAUTION:** Before using `fdisk` to change your partitions, I strongly recommend running the `df -h` command to see how your partitions are currently being defined. This will help reduce the risk of changing or deleting the wrong partition.

To use `fdisk` to change your partitions, begin (as root user) by typing:

```
# fdisk device
```

where *device* is replaced by the name of the device you want to work with. For example, here are some of your choices:

- `/dev/sda` — For the first IDE or SCSI hard disk; sdb, sdc, and so on for other SCSI disks. (For Fedora 9, IDE hard drives no longer appear as hda, hdb, and so on.)
- `/dev/md0` — For a RAID device.

After you have started `fdisk`, type **m** to see the options. Here is what you can do with `fdisk`:

- **Delete a partition** — Type **d** and you are asked to enter a partition number on the current hard disk. Type the partition number and press Enter. For example, /dev/sda2 would be partition number 2. (The deletion won't take effect until you write the change. Until then, it's not too late to back out.)

- **Create a partition** — If you have free space, you can add a new partition. Type **n** and you are asked to enter l for a logical partition (5 or over) or p for a primary partition (1–4). Enter a partition number from the available range. Then choose the first cylinder number from those available. (The output from fdisk -l shown earlier will show you cylinders being used under the Start and End columns.)

  Next, enter the cylinder number the partition will end with (or type the specific number of megabytes or kilobytes you want: for example, +50M or +1024K). You just created an ext3 Linux partition. Again, this change isn't permanent until you write the changes.

- **Change the partition type** — Press t to choose the type of file system. Enter the partition number of the partition number you want to change. Type the number representing the file system type you want to use in hexadecimal code. (Type **L** at this point to see a list of file system types and codes.) For a Linux file system, use the number 83; use 82 for a Linux swap partition. For a Windows FAT32 file system, you can use the letter b.

- **Display the partition table** — Throughout this process, feel free to type **p** to display (print on the screen) the partition table as it now stands.

- **Saving and quitting** — If you don't like a change you make to your partitions, press **q** to exit without saving. Nothing will have changed on your partition table.

  Before you write your changes, display the partition table again and make sure that it is what you want it to be. To write your changes to the partition table, press **w**. You are warned about how dangerous it is to change partitions and asked to confirm the change.

An alternative to the fdisk command is sfdisk. The sfdisk command is command line-oriented. Type the full command line to list or change partitions. (See the sfdisk man page for details.)

Tips for creating partitions

Changing your disk partitions to handle multiple operating systems can be very tricky. Part of the reason is that each different operating system has its own ideas about how partitioning information should be handled, as well as different tools for doing it. Here are some tips to help you get it right.

- If you are creating a dual-boot system that includes Windows, try to install the Windows operating system first. Otherwise, the Windows installation may make the Linux partitions inaccessible.

- The fdisk man page recommends that you use partitioning tools that come with an operating system to create partitions for that operating system. For example, the DOS `fdisk` knows how to create partitions that DOS will like, and the Fedora or RHEL `fdisk` will happily make your Linux partitions. Once your hard disk is set up for dual boot, however, you should probably not go back to Windows-only partitioning tools. Use Linux `fdisk` or a product made for multiboot systems (such as Partition Magic).

- You can have up to 63 partitions on an IDE hard disk. A SCSI hard disk can have up to 15 partitions. You probably won't need nearly that many partitions.

If you are using Fedora or RHEL as a desktop system, you probably don't need a lot of different partitions within your Linux system. There are, however, some very good reasons for having multiple partitions for Linux systems that are shared by a lot of users or are public Web servers or file servers. Multiple partitions within Fedora or RHEL offer these advantages:

- **Protection from attacks** — Denial-of-service attacks sometimes take action that tries to fill up your hard disk. If public areas, such as /var, are on separate partitions, a successful attack can fill up a partition without shutting down the whole computer. Because /var is the default location for Web and FTP servers, and therefore might hold a lot of data, often entire hard disks are assigned to the /var file system alone.

- **Protection from corrupted file systems** — If you have only one file system (/), corruption of that file system can cause the whole Fedora or RHEL system to be damaged. Corruption of a smaller partition can be easier to correct and can often allow the computer to stay in service while the corruption is fixed.

Here are some directories that you may want to consider making into separate file system partitions:

- **/boot** — Sometimes the BIOS in older PCs can access only the first 1024 cylinders of your hard disk. To make sure that the information in your /boot directory is accessible to the BIOS, create a separate disk partition (of only about 100MB) for /boot and make sure that it exists below cylinder 1024. Then, the rest of your Linux system can exist outside of that 1024-cylinder boundary if you like. Even with several boot images, there is rarely a reason for /boot to be larger than 100MB. For newer hard disks, you can sometimes avoid this problem by selecting the Linear Mode check box during installation. Then the boot partition can be anywhere on the disk.

- **/usr** — This directory structure contains most of the applications and utilities available to Fedora or RHEL users. Having /usr on a separate partition lets you mount that file system as read-only after the operating system has been installed. This prevents attackers from replacing or removing important system applications with their own versions that may cause security problems. A separate /usr partition is also useful if you have diskless workstations on your local network. Using NFS, you can share /usr over the network with those workstations.

- **/var** — Your FTP (/var/ftp) and Web-server (/var/www) directories are, by default, stored under /var. Having a separate /var partition can prevent an attack on those facilities from corrupting or filling up your entire hard disk.

- **/home** — Because your user account directories are located in this directory, having a separate /home account can prevent an indiscriminate user from filling up the entire hard disk. (Disk quotas represent another way of controlling disk use. See Chapter 10.) Also, some people have a separate /home partition so they can reinstall the operating system, erasing the root (/) partition, and simply remounting the /home partition.

- **/tmp** — Protecting /tmp from the rest of the hard disk by placing it on a separate partition can ensure that applications that need to write to temporary files in /tmp are able to complete their processing, even if the rest of the disk fills up.

Although people who use Fedora or RHEL casually rarely see a need for lots of partitions, those who maintain and have to recover large systems are thankful when the system they need to fix has several partitions. Multiple partitions can localize deliberate damage (such as denial-of-service attacks), problems from errant users, and accidental file system corruption.

Using the GRUB boot loader

A boot loader lets you choose when and how to boot the bootable operating systems installed on your computer's hard disks. GRUB is the only boot loader offered for you to configure during Fedora installation. (The LILO boot loader included with earlier versions of Fedora is no longer included as of Fedora Core 5.) The following sections describe the GRUB boot loader.

With multiple operating systems installed and several partitions set up, how does your computer know which operating system to start? To select and manage which partition is booted and how it is booted, you need a boot loader. The boot loader that is installed by default with Fedora is called the GRand Unified Boot loader (GRUB).

GRUB is a GNU software package (www.gnu.org/software/grub) that replaced LILO as the only boot loader available in Fedora. GRUB offers the following features:

- Support for multiple executable formats.

- Support for multiboot operating systems (such as Fedora, FreeBSD, NetBSD, OpenBSD, and other Linux systems).

- Support for non-multiboot operating systems (such as Windows 95, Windows 98, Windows NT, Windows ME, Windows XP, Windows Vista and OS/2) via a chain-loading function. Chain-loading is the act of loading another boot loader (presumably one that is specific to the proprietary operating system) from GRUB to start the selected operating system.

- Support for multiple file system types.

- Support for automatic decompression of boot images.

- Support for downloading boot images from a network.

For more on how GRUB works, type **man grub** or **info grub**. The info command contains more details about GRUB. Or, see the GRUB Wiki: http://grub.enbug.org.

When you install Fedora or RHEL, information needed to boot your computer (with one or more operating systems) is automatically set up and ready to go. Simply restart your computer. When you see the boot message, press the Enter key (quickly before it times out) and the GRUB boot screen appears (it says GRUB at the top and lists bootable partitions below it). Then you can do one of the following:

- **Default** — If you do nothing, the default operating system will boot automatically after a few seconds.
- **Select an operating system** — Use the up and down arrow keys to select any of the operating systems shown on the screen. Then press Enter to boot that operating system.
- **Edit the boot process** — If you want to change any of the options used during the boot process, use the arrow keys to select the operating system you want and type **e** to select it. Follow the next procedure to change your boot options temporarily.

If you want to change your boot options so that they take effect every time you boot your computer, see the section on permanently changing boot options. Changing those options involves editing the /boot/grub/grub.conf file.

Temporarily changing boot options

From the GRUB boot screen, you can select to change or add boot options for the current boot session. First, quickly before GRUB times out and boots the default system, press any key. From the GRUB selection screen that appears, select the operating system you want (using the arrow keys) and type **e** (as described earlier). You will see a graphical screen that contains information like that shown in Figure 2-3.

There are three lines in the example of the GRUB editing screen that identify the boot process for the operating system you chose. The first line (beginning with root) shows that the entry for the GRUB boot loader is on the first partition of the first hard disk (hd0, 0). GRUB represents the hard disk as hd, regardless of whether it is a SCSI, IDE, or other type of disk. You just count the drive number and partition number, starting from zero.

The second line of the example (beginning with kernel) identifies the boot image (/boot/vmlinuz-2.6.25.1-31.fc9) and several options. The rhgb option produces the Red Hat graphical boot screen, while the quiet option prevents details of the boot process from being shown. The options identify the partition as initially being loaded ro (read-only) and the location of the root file system on a partition with the label LABEL=/1. The third line (starting with initrd) identifies the location of the initial RAM disk, which contains the minimum files and directories needed during the boot process.

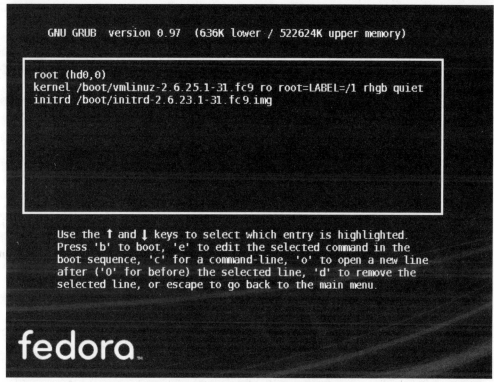

```
          GNU GRUB   version 0.97   (636K lower / 522624K upper memory)

   root (hd0,0)
   kernel /boot/vmlinuz-2.6.25.1-31.fc9 ro root=LABEL=/1 rhgb quiet
   initrd /boot/initrd-2.6.23.1-31.fc9.img
```

      Use the ↑ and ↓ keys to select which entry is highlighted.
      Press 'b' to boot, 'e' to edit the selected command in the
      boot sequence, 'c' for a command-line, 'o' to open a new line
      after ('O' for before) the selected line, 'd' to remove the
      selected line, or escape to go back to the main menu.

      fedora™

Figure 2-3: Edit the boot entry from your Fedora system from the GRUB menu.

If you are going to change any of the lines related to the boot process, you would probably change only the second line to add or remove boot options. Here is how you do that:

1. Position the cursor on the `kernel` line and type **e**.

2. Either add or remove options after the name of the boot image. You can use a minimal set of bash shell command-line editing features to edit the line. You can even use command completion (type part of a filename and press Tab to complete it). Here are a few options you may want to add or delete:

    - **Boot to a shell** — If you forgot your root password or if your boot process hangs, you can boot directly to a shell by adding `init=/bin/sh` to the boot line. (The file system is mounted read-only, so you can copy files out. You need to remount the file system with read/write permission to be able to change files.)

    - **Turn off a service** — If your boot process is hanging on a particular service, you can often turn off that service from the boot prompt. For example, you could add the options `noacpi` (to turn off ACPI power management), `nopcmcia` (to turn off PCMCIA card slot support), or `nodma` (to turn of DMA, if you are getting disk errors). Add `selinux=0` to temporarily turn off SELinux. Sometimes turning off a service at the boot prompt allows you to fix the problem after the system is up and running.

- **Select a run level** — If you want to boot to a particular run level, you can add the word *linux,* followed by the number of the run level you want. For example, to have Fedora boot to run level 3 (multiuser plus networking mode), add linux 3 to the end of the boot line. You can also boot to single-user mode (1), multi-user mode (2), or X GUI mode (5). Level 3 is a good choice if your GUI is temporarily broken.

3. Press Enter to return to the editing screen.

4. Type **b** to boot the computer with the new options. The next time you boot your computer, the new options will not be saved. To add options so they are saved permanently, see the next section.

Permanently changing boot options

You can change the options that take effect each time you boot your computer by changing the GRUB configuration file. In Fedora, GRUB configuration centers around the /boot/grub/grub.conf file.

The /boot/grub/grub.conf file is created when you install Fedora. Here is an example of a grub.conf file:

```
# grub.conf generated by anaconda
#
# Note that you do not have to rerun grub after making
# changes to this file
# NOTICE: You have a /boot partition.  This means that
#         all kernel and initrd paths are relative to /boot/, eg.
#         root (hd0,0)
#         kernel /vmlinuz-version ro root=/dev/sda7
#         initrd /initrd-version.img
#boot=/dev/sda
default=0
timeout=5
splashimage=(hd0,0)/boot/grub/splash.xpm.gz
hiddenmenu
title Fedora (2.6.25.1-31.fc9)
     root (hd0,0)
     kernel /vmlinuz-2.6.25.1-31.fc9 ro root=LABEL=/1 rhgb quiet
     initrd /initrd-2.6.25.1-31.fc9.img
title Windows XP
     rootnoverify (hd1,0)
     chainloader +1
```

The default=0 line indicates that the first partition in this list (in this case Fedora) will be the one that is booted by default. The line timeout=5 causes GRUB to pause for 5 seconds before booting the default partition. (Because of the `hiddenmenu` option, you won't even see the GRUB boot screen if you don't press Enter before 5 seconds.)

> **NOTE:** GRUB indicates disk partitions using the following notation: (`hd0, 0`). The first number represents the disk, and the second is the partition on that disk. So, (`hd0, 1`) is the second partition (1) on the first disk (0). That would equate to `/dev/sda2` in Linux.

The `splashimage` line looks in the second partition on the first disk (`hd0, 0`) for the boot partition (in this case `/dev/sda1`, which is the `/boot` partition). GRUB loads `splash.xpm.gz` as the image on the splash screen (`/boot/grub/splash.xpm.gz`). The splash screen appears as the background of the boot screen.

> **NOTE:** You can replace the splash screen with any image you like, provided that it meets certain specifications. Using GIMP or other image editor, save the image to 640x480 pixels, 14 colors, and xpm format. Next, use gzip to compress the file. Then copy that file to the `/boot/grub` directory. The last step is to edit the `grub.conf` file to have the splashimage value point to the new file.

The two bootable partitions in this example are `Fedora` and `Windows XP`. The title lines for each of those partitions are followed by the name that appears on the boot screen to represent each partition.

For the Fedora system, the `root` line indicates the location of the boot partition as the second partition on the first disk. So, to find the bootable `kernel` and the `initrd` initial RAM disk boot image that is loaded, GRUB looks in the root of `hd0, 0` (which is represented by `/dev/sda1` and is eventually mounted as `/boot`). Other options on the `kernel` line set the partition as read-only initially (`ro`) and set the root file system to LABEL=/1.

For the Windows XP partition, the `rootnoverify` line indicates that GRUB should not try to mount the partition. In this case, Windows XP is on the first partition of the second hard disk (`hd1, 0`) or `/dev/sdb1`. Instead of mounting the partition and passing options to the new operating system, the `chainloader +1` indicates to hand control of the booting of the operating system to another boot loader. The `+1` indicates that the first sector of the partition is used as the boot loader.

> **NOTE:** Microsoft operating systems require that you use the `chainloader` to boot them from GRUB.

If you make any changes to the `/boot/grub/grub.conf` file, you *do not* need to load those changes. Those changes are automatically picked up by GRUB when you reboot your computer. If you are accustomed to using the LILO boot loader, this may confuse you at first, as LILO requires you to rerun the `lilo` command for the changes to take effect.

Adding a new GRUB boot image

You may have different boot images for kernels that include different features. These days, as you get updated kernels for Fedora or RHEL, you simply load an RPM containing the new kernel and that new kernel is added to the `grub.conf` file as the default kernel to be booted. At boot time, you can choose which kernel you want to run.

> **NOTE:** To prevent you from having dozens of entries on your boot screen and lots of kernels hanging around, when you install new kernels on your Fedora system, all but the two most recent kernels are removed. Likewise, instead of getting lots of boot entries as you add new kernels, only the two most recent kernel entries are maintained in your `grub.conf` file.

If you build your own kernel, however, or get one to use from another source, you need to modify the `grub.conf` file yourself to tell Fedora or RHEL to boot that kernel. Here is the procedure for modifying the `grub.conf` file:

1. Copy the new image from the directory in which it was created (such as `/usr/src/kernels/linux-2.6.25-1/arch/i386/boot`) to the `/boot` directory. Name the file something that reflects its contents, such as `bz-2.6.25-1`. For example:

```
# cp /usr/src/linux-2.6.25-1/arch/i386/boot/bzImage /boot/bz-2.6.25-1
```

2. Add several lines to the `/boot/grub/grub.conf` file so that the image can be started at boot time if it is selected. For example:

```
title Fedora (My own IPV6 build)
    root (hd0,1)
    kernel /bz-2.6.20-5 ro root=/dev/sda2
    initrd /initrd-2.6.20-5.img
```

3. Reboot your computer.

4. Press Enter at the boot prompt. When the GRUB boot screen appears, move your cursor to the title representing the new kernel and press Enter.

The advantage to this approach, as opposed to copying the new boot image over the old one, is that if the kernel fails to boot, you can always go back and restart the old kernel. When you feel confident that the new kernel is working properly, you can use it to replace the old kernel or perhaps just make the new kernel the default boot definition.

Troubleshooting Installation

The description of troubleshooting your Fedora or RHEL installation is split into three different areas. The first is what to try if you fail to install Fedora or RHEL. Next, there's what to do if it installs, but fails to boot up. The final area describes how to go forward if Fedora or RHEL is basically working, but selected features or hardware components aren't working.

Insert your Fedora or RHEL boot media and reboot your computer. If your computer bypasses the DVD or CD completely and boots right from hard disk, you may need to change the BIOS (as described earlier in this chapter). If the DVD or CD drive keeps blinking, but doesn't install, you may either have a bad DVD or CD or you might have an older drive that can't use DMA (in the latter case, try adding `nodma` to the boot command line). If it hangs at some point during the install, there are many boot options to try, in case the install is hanging on a bad or non-recognized hardware item (see descriptions of boot options earlier in the chapter).

If you were able to boot Fedora or RHEL, you can see how the installation went by checking different aspects of your system. There are three log files to look at once the system comes up:

- **/root/upgrade.log** — When upgrading packages, output from each installed package is sent to this file. You can see what packages were installed and if any failed.

- **/var/log/dmesg** — This file contains the messages that are sent to the console terminal as the system boots up, including messages relating to the kernel being started and hardware being recognized. If a piece of hardware isn't working, you can check here to make sure that the kernel found the hardware and configured it properly.

- **/var/log/boot.log** — This file contains information about each service that is started up at boot time. You can see if each service started successfully. If a service fails to start properly, there may be clues in this file that will help you learn what went wrong.

If something was set wrong (such as your mouse) or just isn't working quite right (such as your video display), you can always go back after Fedora is running and correct the problem. Here is a list of utilities you can use to reconfigure different features that were set during installation:

- **Changing or adding a mouse** — `mouse-test`
- **Changing a keyboard language** — `system-config-keyboard`
- **Adding or deleting software packages** — `yum`, `PackageKit`, `system-config-packages` or `rpm`
- **Partitioning** — `fdisk`
- **Boot loader** — `/boot/grub/grub.conf`
- **Networking (Ethernet & TCP/IP)** — `system-config-network`
- **Time zone** — `timeconfig` or `firstboot`
- **User accounts** — `useradd` or `system-config-users`
- **Sound** — `system-config-soundcard`
- **X Window System** — `system-config-display`

Here are a few other random tips that can help you during installation:

- If installation fails because the installation procedure is unable to detect your video card, try restarting installation in text mode. After Fedora is installed and running, use the `system-config-display` command to configure your video card and monitor. (For some cards, such as those from NVIDIA, you need to get and install special drivers from the manufacturer's Web site or `rpm.livna.org`.)

> **CAUTION:** Some video card drivers from NVIDIA and ATI will overwrite important Xorg driver files. If you later change to a different video card, features of the new card (such as DRI) might fail. The solution is to entirely remove the NVIDIA or ATI drivers and reinstall your xorg and mesa packages.

- If installation completes successfully, but your screen is garbled when you reboot, you should try to get Fedora or RHEL to boot to a text-login prompt. To do this, add the number 3 to the end of the kernel boot line in GRUB. Linux will start with the GUI temporarily disabled. Run `system-config-display` to try to fix the problem. (See Chapter 3 for other advice related to fixing your GUI.)

- If your mouse is not detected during installation, you can use arrow keys and the Tab key to make selections. Then use `mouse-test` to track down the problem.

- If installation improperly probes your hardware or turns on a feature that causes problems with your hardware, you might be able to solve the problem by disabling the offending feature at the install boot prompt. Try adding one or more of the following after the word `linux` at the installation boot prompt: `ide=nodma` (if your system hangs while downloading the image), `apm=off` or `acpi=off` (if you experience random failures during install), or `nousb`, `nopcmcia`, or `nofirewire` (if you suspect that install is hanging on devices of those types).

- If you are still having problems installing Fedora, try searching FedoraForum.org to see if they have an answer. Sign up for an account and you can ask a question yourself. Probably the best resource for troubleshooting your installation problems for RHEL systems is the Red Hat Support site (`www.redhat.com/apps/support`). Links from that page can take you to documentation, updates and errata, and information about support programs. If you are having problems with a particular piece of hardware, try searching the Solutions Database, using the name of the hardware in the search box. If you are having problems with particular hardware, chances are someone else did, too.

Spinning Your Own Fedora Install or Live Media

All software included in Fedora can be redistributed. Because of that fact, you can not only use the software as you please, but you can also repackage and redistribute it if you care to. Not only is the Fedora Project committed to protecting your rights to redistribute Fedora, but it has gone so far as to give you the tools to build your own brand new Fedora-based distribution to suit your needs.

Fedora has created several tools that let you build your own install or live media images. Using these tools, you can pick the packages you want from the Fedora repository, add new repositories, and combine the content into ISO images that can be burned to CDs, DVDs, USB flash drives or other media. In short, you can make your own custom Linux distribution.

The two major tools that Fedora produces, which the project itself currently uses to produce its own install and live CDs, are Pungi and livecd-creator:

- **Pungi for building install media** — Pungi is a distribution composition tool (http://hosted.fedoraproject.org/projects/pungi) you can use to "spin" your own Linux distribution from Fedora software packages and, optionally, your own packages. You give Pungi the location of one or more software repositories (containing Fedora RPMs) and it will gather that software, along with the anaconda installer, and make ISO images that you can use to install that set of software. Because Pungi uses tools associated with the anaconda installer, you can use anaconda features, including kickstart files to list packages and other items you gather for your custom ISO images.

- **Livecd-creator for building live media** — The livecd-creator tool can be used to make your own Fedora-based live CDs from packages in one or more software repositories (http://fedoraproject.org/wiki/FedoraLiveCD/LiveCDHowTo). Besides gathering up packages, like Pungi livecd-creator can use kickstart files and the anaconda installer to make and recreate the live ISO images that suit you.

While the practice of using Pungi and livecd-creator to create your own Linux derivative is beyond the scope of this book, as you gain experience with Fedora, you might find lots of interesting ways to use these tools. For example, I used Pungi to create the single 8GB DVD that comes with this book, which includes as many packages as I could fit on it. People have used livecd-creator to make a games live DVD, a free digital artwork CD, and a software developer tools DVD. If you develop your own software, you can build live or install CDs that showcase your software in various ways.

Summary

Installing Linux has become as easy as installing any modern operating system. Precompiled binary software and preselected packaging and partitions make most Fedora and RHEL installations a simple proposition. Improved installation and GUI configuration windows have made it easier for computer users who are not programmers to enter the Linux arena.

Besides providing some step-by-step installation procedures, this chapter discussed some of the trickier aspects of Fedora and RHEL installation. In particular, this chapter covered specialty installation procedures (such as dual booting with Windows), ways of partitioning your hard disk, and how to change the boot procedure. The chapter even gives pointers to using tools such as Pungi and livecd-creator to create your own Fedora install and live CD media.

Chapter 3

Getting Started with the Desktop

In This Chapter

- Logging in to Linux
- Getting started with the desktop
- Choosing KDE, GNOME or Xfce desktops
- Using the GNOME desktop environment
- Configuring an Online Desktop
- Switching desktop environments
- Using the KDE desktop environment
- Enabling 3D desktop effects with AIGLX
- Using the Xfce desktop environment
- Getting your desktop to work

The desktop is the most personal feature of your computer. The way that icons, menus, panels, and backgrounds are arranged and displayed should make it both easy and pleasant to do your work. With Fedora and RHEL, you have an incredible amount of control over how your desktop behaves and how your desktop is arranged.

From the initial login screen to the desktop background and screensaver, the latest version of Fedora is sporting distinctive looks for GNOME, KDE, and Xfce desktops. GNOME designs feature the new Waves artwork and Nodoka desktop theme. The new KDE 4 desktop included with Fedora 9 offers a classy new Plasma desktop look and feel. For machines with less horsepower, the Xfce desktop can be an excellent choice.

With each desktop environment, you can get a full set of desktop applications, features for launching applications, and tools for configuring preferences.

The basic desktop is provided by the X.Org X server. The X server provides the framework on which GNOME, KDE, and other desktop applications and window managers rely. If you have used the XFree86 X server in other Linux distributions, special features of the X.org server described later in this chapter might interest you. (See Chapter 1 for a description of the X Window System.)

This chapter takes you on a tour of your desktop — going through the process of logging in, trying out some features, and customizing how your desktop looks and behaves. Sections on KDE, GNOME, and Xfce desktops contain reference information on how to set preferences, run applications, configure panels, and work with the file managers. The last section describes how to use the Display Settings window to configure your video card and monitor, if they were not properly detected.

Newer desktop features described in this chapter include the GNOME Online Desktop and AIGLX desktop effects. Using Online Desktop, you can organize and easily connect to your friends and accounts with Internet services such as Flickr, Amazon, Netflix, Facebook, Mugshot, and many others. With AIGLX, you can get interesting desktop effects, such as windows that wobble when you move them or changing workspaces on a revolving cube.

Logging in to Fedora or RHEL

Because Linux was created as a multiuser computer system, you start by logging in (even if you are the only person using the computer). Logging in accomplishes three functions:

- It identifies you as a particular user.
- It starts up your own shell and desktop (icons, panels, backgrounds, and so on) configurations.
- It gives you appropriate permissions to change files and run programs.

After the computer has been turned on and the operating system has started, you see either a graphical login screen (default) or a text-based login prompt. The text-based prompt should look something like this:

```
Fedora release 9
Kernel 2.6.25 on an i686

localhost login:
```

The graphical login is typically your entry into the graphical user interface (GUI). Figure 3-1 is an example of the login screen you see when you boot the Fedora operating system that comes with this book.

> **NOTE:** If you see a text-based login prompt instead of the graphical login screen, and you want to use the GUI, type your user name and password. Then when you see a command prompt, type **startx** to start up your desktop.

For the current Fedora release, the login screen has been enabled for Face Browsing. This means that user accounts you add will appear on the login screen, so you can click one to log in as that user. Users also can add an image (96x96 pixels by default) to represent themselves in the About Me window (select System → Preferences → Personal → About Me to add your own image).

Figure 3-1: A graphical login screen greets Fedora desktop users.

Notice the several menu buttons on the login screen. If you don't see the one you want, simply select Other and type your user name and password as prompted. Or you can use these buttons as follows:

- **Suspend** — Click Suspend to suspend the current session.
- **Restart** — Click Restart to reboot the computer.
- **Shut Down** — Click Shut Down to shut down the operating system and turn off the computer.

After you select a user, you are prompted for a password (or user name, if you selected Other). You then have the following additional selections:

- **Language** — Click Language to select a language other than the last language you selected when Fedora was installed. (You may need additional software packages to use different languages.)
- **Session** — Click Session and you are asked to choose which desktop environment (GNOME, KDE, Online Desktop, or Xfce) to start when you log in, assuming you have more than one desktop environment installed.

To log in, type your user name and, when prompted, your password. Or you can click on a Face Browser user listing. You can log in as either a regular user or as the root user:

- **A regular user** — As someone just using the Linux system, you probably have your own unique user name and password. Often, that name is associated with your real name (such as johnb, susanp, or djones). If you are still not sure why you need a user login, see the sidebar "Why Do I Need a User Login?" You probably have at least one user account available that was added the first time you booted Fedora.

- **The root user** — Every Linux system has a *root* user assigned when Linux is installed. The root user (literally type the user name **root**) can run programs, use files, and change the computer setup in any way. Because the root user has special powers, and can therefore do special damage, you usually log in as a regular user (which allows access only to that user's files and those that are open to everyone).

CROSS-REFERENCE: See Chapter 10 for a description of the root user and Chapter 11 for information on how to set up and use other user accounts. Refer to Chapter 14 for suggestions on how to choose a good password. For information on instances where the root user doesn't have complete control over the system, refer to the descriptions of SELinux (Security-Enhanced Linux) in Chapter 10.

If your desktop did not start, refer to the "Troubleshooting Your Desktop" section at the end of this chapter. Otherwise, continue on to the next section.

Why Do I Need a User Login?

If you are working on a PC, and you are the only one using your Linux computer, you may wonder why you need a user account and password. Unlike Windows, Linux (as its predecessor UNIX) was designed from the ground up to be a multiuser system. Here are several good reasons why you should use separate user accounts:

- Even as the only person using Linux, you want a user name other than root for running applications and working with files so you don't change critical system files by mistake during everyday computer use.

- If several people are using a Linux system, separate user accounts let you protect your files from being accessed or changed by others.

- Networking is probably the best reason for using a Linux system. If you are on a network, a unique user name is useful in many ways. Your user name can be associated with resources on other computers: file systems, application programs, and mailboxes to name a few. Sometimes a root user is not allowed to share resources on remote Linux systems.

- Over time, you will probably change personal configuration information associated with your account. For example, you may add aliases, create your own utility programs, or set properties for the applications you use. By gathering this information in one place, it's easy to move your account or add a new account to another computer in the future.

- Keeping all your data files and settings under a home login directory (such as /home/chris) makes it easier to back up the data and restore it later if needed.

Getting Familiar with the Desktop

The term *desktop* refers to the presentation of windows, menus, panels, icons, and other graphical elements on your computer screen. Originally, computer systems such as Linux operated purely in text mode — no mouse, no colors, just commands typed on the screen. Desktops provide a more intuitive way of using your computer.

As with most things in Linux, the desktop is built from a set of interchangeable building blocks. The building blocks of your desktop, to use a car analogy, are:

- The X Window System (which is like the frame of the car)
- The GNOME, KDE, or Xfce desktop environment (which is like a blueprint of how the working parts fit together)
- The Metacity window manager (which provides the steering wheel, seat upholstery, and fuzzy dice on the mirror)
- The Fedora desktop theme (the paint job and the pin stripe)

Once Linux is installed (see Chapter 2) and you have logged in (see the previous section), you should see either the GNOME or KDE desktop. At this point, I'll take you on a tour of the desktop and step you through some initial setup to get your desktop going.

Figure 3-2 shows an example of the Fedora default desktop (GNOME).

Because GNOME is the default desktop for Fedora and Red Hat Enterprise Linux when you install from the official DVD or live CD, I'll start by walking you around the GNOME desktop (with a few references to KDE applications, which can also be run from GNOME). The tour steps you through trying out your home folder, changing some preferences, and configuring your panel.

Touring your desktop

If you are unfamiliar with the GNOME desktop that comes with Fedora or RHEL, I suggest you take this quick tour to familiarize yourself with the desktop features. If you are using the KDE desktop, refer to the KDE section later in this chapter for tips on using KDE.

Step 1: Checking out your home folder

Double-click the *user*'s Home icon on the desktop (it should say something like "bill's Home" or "julie's Home," depending on your user name). The window that appears shows your file manager window (Nautilus in GNOME or Dolphin in KDE) as it displays the contents of your home folder.

Notice that your home folder contains several folders that were added by GNOME: Desktop (containing the items you see on your desktop), Documents, Download, Music, Pictures, Public, Templates, and Videos.

Figure 3-2: After login, Fedora starts you off with a GNOME desktop by default.

The location of the home folder (also referred to as a *home directory*) on your computer is usually /home/*user*, where *user* is replaced by your user name. Here are some things to try out with your home folder (assuming the GNOME Nautilus window is your file manager):

1. **Folders** — Create folders and subfolders to store your work (click File → Create Folder, and then type the name of the new folder; something like Images, Memos, or Projects).

2. **Open Location** — To open another folder on your computer, click File → Open Location and type a directory name. For our tour, open a folder that has several different file types in it (for example, /usr/share/doc/bash-3.2/ contains some text, PostScript and HTML files).

> **NOTE:** To move down to a subfolder of the current folder, simply double-click that folder. To move up to a parent folder, click the current folder name in the bottom-left corner of the window frame. From the menu that opens, you can select to go to any higher level folder from there.

3. **Open With** — Click any object in a folder with the right mouse button, and then select Open With. You should be able to see several programs you can use to open the object.

For example, you can choose to open a Web page (`.html` file) with Firefox, Konqueror, or Text Editor (depending on what is installed, you may see different options).

4. **Side Pane** — Right-click any folder in the Nautilus file manager window, and then select Browse Folder to open the new folder with a Side Pane displayed. From the drop-down box at the top of the Side Pane, choose *Information* to show information about the selected folder or file. Next choose *History* to see files and folders previously viewed. Choose *Tree* to see a hierarchical representation of your file system. Select *Places* to see folders from removable media and your home folder. Using the button above the side pane, you can choose to have your location box be text-based or represented by buttons.

5. **Backgrounds** — Click Edit → Backgrounds and Emblems. Drag and drop patterns or colors you like into the pane on your folder window. (I personally like camouflage.) Click Emblems, and then drag and drop an emblem on a file or folder. Use the emblem to remind yourself of something about the object (such as the fact that it's a personal document or of an urgent nature).

6. **Organize your work** — As you create documents, add music, or download images from your camera, organize them into your home folder or any subfolders. Your home folder is not accessible to any other user on the computer except the root user, so you can safely store your work there. With the files you create, you can:

   - **Move** — Drag and drop to move a file to another folder icon or folder window.
   - **Delete** — Drag and drop a file to the Trash icon to delete it.
   - **Rename** — Right-click the file, select Rename, and then type the new name.

As with any window, with the Folder window you can:

   - **Minimize/Unminimize** — Click the Minimize button (first button, upper-right corner of the title bar) to minimize the window to the window pane. Click the minimized window in the desktop panel to return it to your desktop.

   - **Maximize** — Click the Maximize button (second button, upper-right corner of the title bar) to have the window go full screen. (Maximize is now the default action for double-clicking in the title bar. If you prefer the old window shade default, see the Tip below.)

> **TIP:** The window shade feature, where a double-click in the title bar rolls up the window instead of maximizing or restoring it, is not on by default. To turn on that feature from the Desktop menu, click System → Preferences → Look and Feel → Windows. From the pop-up window that appears, change Maximize to Roll Up (under Double-click Title Bar to Perform This Action).

   - **Close** — Click the X button (upper-right corner of the title bar) to close the window.

Step 2: Change some preferences

More than 20 different preference categories are available from the GNOME desktop. Select the System menu, and then choose Preferences. From submenus on the Preferences menu, there are a few preferences you might want to modify when you start out (see the GNOME and KDE preferences sections later in this chapter for further details):

- **Change background** — Select Look and Feel → Appearance, and then select the Background tab. The Appearance Preferences window appears, as shown in Figure 3-3. To change the background image, select one of the Desktop Wallpaper images shown. To add your own image, click the Add button (to choose a file from your disk) or drag and drop an image onto the Location box. Select a Style, such as Centered, Fill Screen, Tiled, Zoom, or Scaled. To use just a color, select the blank wallpaper in the upper-left corner of the Wallpaper box and choose a color under the Colors selector. You can choose a solid color or a vertical or horizontal gradient.

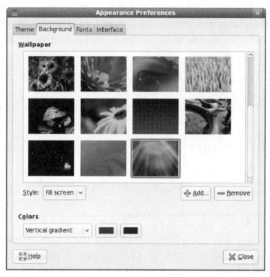

Figure 3-3: Select a color or picture for your desktop background.

The default background for Fedora 9 is actually an animated background. The background consists of a series of images and a specially formatted XML file that indicates when and how the images are changed. See `/usr/share/backgrounds/waves/waves.xml`. Read the comments in that XML file to see how the background images change to reflect different times of day.

- **Choose browsers and other apps** — Select Personal → Preferred Applications. When you open a Web page, mail composer, or shell from the desktop, this preferences window lets you choose which Web browser, mail reader, media player or Terminal window to open by default. Firefox is the default Web browser, but you can choose Epiphany or Konqueror (the KDE browser) to run on your GUI. If you want a text-based Web browser, select W3M or Links. To use a different Web browser, select Custom and type the command line for the browser you want to use into the Command box.

Available Mail Readers include Evolution (the default), KMail, Thunderbird, and Mutt. On the System tab, GNOME Terminal is assigned as the default when you need a shell prompt (you can change that to use KDE Konsole or a standard xterm Terminal). To add a different default terminal, select Custom Terminal and enter the command that starts the Terminal you want. You can also choose default multimedia players and accessibility applications.

> **TIP:** The `konsole` command starts the Konsole (KDE) terminal window. Programmers who use many terminal windows at once often prefer Konsole over `gnome-terminal` (finding it to be more efficient and feature-rich).

- **Add a screensaver** — Select Look and Feel → Screensaver. Try out a few screensavers (the default screensaver is floating Fedora logos). Click different screensavers to see them and click Preview to try them out. (If you see only a few screensaver options, install the rss-glx-gnome-screensaver package to install a lot more screensavers.)

> **TIP:** Click the Lock Screen When Screensaver is Active check box and set the number of minutes after which the screen screensaver comes on and locks. This is a good option for an office environment, where you want your screen locked if you wander away for a few minutes. If you logged into a virtual terminal (for example, you pressed Ctrl+Alt+F2, then logged in, then returned to the desktop with Ctrl+Alt+F7), be sure to log off the virtual terminal as well before leaving your desk.

- **Change the theme** — Select Look and Feel → Appearance and select the Theme tab. You can change the entire theme (colors, icons, borders, and so on) for your desktop. The default theme is called Nodoka. Try any of the others to find one that suits you. Click Customize to mix and match attributes from different themes. Figure 3-4 shows the window for selecting a theme.

Step 3: Configure your panels

Most people manage their desktops from panels that appear at the top and bottom of the screen. These panels provide an intuitive way to:

- Launch applications
- Change workspaces
- Add useful information (clocks, news tickers, CD players, and so on)

Step through the following procedure to learn about the desktop (GNOME) panels:

1. **Applications menu** — Click Applications in the top panel. Most useful GUI applications and system tools that come with Fedora and RHEL are available from the menus and submenus of this Applications menu.

   - **Start an application** — Click Accessories, Education, Games, Graphics, Internet, Office, or Sound & Video menu items, and then select any application to run.

- **Try system tools** — Select System Tools from the Applications menu. The submenu that appears contain some tools for managing certain applications. You can also select Add/Remove Software to open the PackageKit utility to add, delete, or search for software packages.

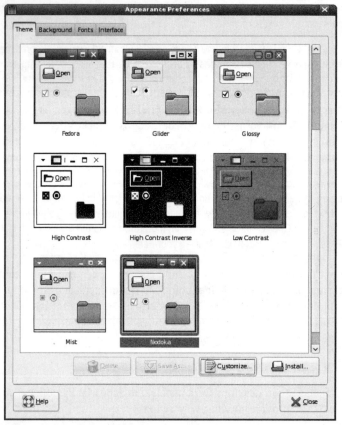

Figure 3-4: Change the default Fedora theme.

2. **System menu** — Click System in the top panel. Here are several actions you can do from that menu:

   - **Change your settings** — Click the Preferences menu item to change preferences or the Administration menu item to change system-wide settings.

   - **Do administrative tasks** — Click Administration to select from a menu of administrative tasks, to do such things as configure your network, firewall, printers, sound cards, or system services. You need the root password to do most of these tasks.

   - **Log out or shutdown** — Click the Log Out menu item to log out from your current desktop session. Click Shut Down to shutdown, restart, or hibernate (for laptop computers) your computer.

3. **Places menu** — Click Places in the top panel. From the menu that appears, you can open your Home Folder, along with special folders to hold your Documents, Music, Pictures, Videos, and Downloads in a Nautlius file manager window. You can also select Connect to Server, to connect to network servers using SSH (remote login), FTP (file transfer), Windows share (file and printer sharing), and WebDAV (HTTP file sharing). Select Search to search your computer for selected files.

4. **Select desktop applications** — Fedora includes icons for popular desktop applications right on the panel. Figure 3-5 shows default icons to launch a Web browser (Firefox), an e-mail reader (Evolution Email), plus several icons I added to open a word processor (OpenOffice.org Writer), a presentation creator (OpenOffice.org Impress), and spreadsheet application (OpenOffice.org Calc), respectively.

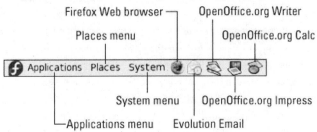

Figure 3-5: Launch popular desktop applications with one click.

> **NOTE:** OpenOffice.org applications are no longer installed by default in Fedora. On the Fedora live CDs, they were left off primarily for space considerations.If you use your Linux system as a desktop, you will probably find it useful to install OpenOffice.org Writer, Impress, and Calc and add them to your panel.

5. **Use workspaces** — Click different panels in the Workspace Switcher (bottom panel, right side). Open an application, and then click another workspace panel. Workspaces are a great way to have multiple windows and still keep your desktop uncluttered. Notice that there are tiny representations of each window you open on the workspace panel it is in. Drag and drop the tiny windows among the Workspace Switcher boxes to move applications to different workspaces, without leaving your workspace.

6. **Add cool stuff to your panel** — Right-click an empty place in a panel so that a panel menu appears. It should say Add to Panel at the top. Because real estate is limited on your panel, I recommend adding a drawer, to which you can add some little applications that run in the panel and icons that launch other applications. To begin, click Add to Panel, and then from the window that appears, select Drawer. A Drawer icon appears on your panel (you can drag it where you want it to go). Click to open the drawer, and then right-click the open drawer and click Add to Drawer. Here are a few things I suggest adding to a drawer on your panel:

- **Terminal** — From the drawer menu, click Add to Drawer → Application Launcher, and then click Forward. Next, select the down arrow next to System Tools, choose Terminal and click Add. Now, when I ask you to type something into a Terminal window, you can launch one from the terminal icon that appears in this drawer.

> **NOTE:** Throughout this book, I give examples that require you to use a Terminal window. Neither the new KDE nor GNOME desktops have a Terminal window launcher on the panel or desktop. I strongly suggest that you add a Terminal window to your desktop or panel in order to launch it easily. The alternative is to select Applications → System Tools → Terminal to open a Terminal window.

- **Weather report** — From the drawer menu, click Add to Drawer → Weather Report. Right-click the temperature icon that appears and choose Preferences. Click the Location tab and select your country, state, and city from the list. Now, whenever you double-click the temperature icon in your drawer, you can see weather conditions and a forecast for your city.

- **Popular folder or Web site** — Folders or Web sites that you visit often should be easily accessible. Click Add to Drawer → Custom Application Launcher and select Add. From the Create Launcher window, select Link (as the Type) and type a URL or Application, and then type **nautilus *folder*** (where *folder* is replaced by the name of the folder you want to open). Click Icon and choose an icon to represent the item. For example, when I write a book, I have a folder containing chapter files. To add a launcher for that file, I select Application from Launcher Properties (`nautilus /home/chris/ToysII`). Then I assign an icon (an image of the book cover) to the launcher. Figure 3-6 shows an example of a drawer, with the launchers I just described added to it.

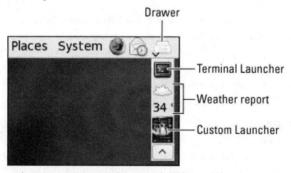

Figure 3-6: A drawer is a great way to contain personal utilities and launchers.

You can do much more with the desktop and the panel. To learn more about configuring your desktop, check out the specific descriptions of the GNOME and KDE desktops later in this chapter.

Tips for configuring your desktop

Now that you have experimented with a few items on the desktop, you should configure certain features to get Fedora and RHEL really working well for you. Most of the tips I describe here will help you get Fedora and RHEL working well on the network.

> **NOTE:** Some of the tips described here should be carried out by the system administrator. They apply to you if you are the system administrator for your organization, or if you are configuring your own home or office network.

- **Getting Updates** — If updates to any of the packages installed on your system are available, an icon and message box will appear in the upper-right corner of your panel. You can select to see the available updates, and then download and install them if you like. Or simply select System → Administration → Update System to use the Update System window to get software package updates.

> **CROSS-REFERENCE:** Refer to Chapter 5 for more information on using the yum utility and PackageKit features to get updates.

- **Set up your network** — You may have configured your network interfaces (dial-up or LAN) during installation. If not, refer to Chapter 15 for setting up a LAN and Chapter 16 for setting up an Internet connection.
- **Configure e-mail** — You must identify information about your e-mail account in order to use e-mail. Click the Evolution Email icon in the panel to start the process of configuring e-mail. Refer to Chapter 9 for information on setting up and using e-mail.
- **Configure the Web browser** — Open the Firefox Web Browser from the panel. Although it should work fine at browsing the Internet once you have a network connection set up, there are a few things you should do to tune your browser. For example, you should choose a home page (click Edit → Preferences, and then type a home page location to use the current page or a bookmarked page). If you have bookmarks from another computer, you can export those bookmarks, copy the file to this computer, and import those bookmarks here (click Bookmarks → Organize Bookmarks, and then select Import and Backup → Import from the Bookmark Manager window).

> **NOTE:** If you are coming from a Windows environment, you may find that some Web content doesn't work by default in Firefox. Refer to Chapter 9 for suggestions on ways to enhance Firefox to change the appearance of some Web pages and improve the ability to play certain multimedia content.

The sections that follow provide more details on using the GNOME and KDE desktops.

Using the GNOME Desktop

GNOME (pronounced *guh-nome*) provides the desktop environment that you get by default when you install Fedora or RHEL. This desktop environment provides the software that is between your X Window System framework and the look-and-feel provided by the window manager. GNOME is a stable and reliable desktop environment, with a few cool features in it.

The GNOME 2.22 desktop comes with the most recent version of Fedora. If you have used an earlier version of GNOME, here are some additions you will find as you use existing GNOME features:

- **Webcam photos and videos** — Using the new Cheese application (install the cheese package and select Applications →Accessories → Cheese) you can take individual photos or videos from your webcam. See Chapter 8 for a description of Cheese.

- **Improved Nautilus file manager**— Nautilus file manager provides new protocols and features for accessing local and remote file system. Use the `cdda://cdrom` protocol to view track information from an audio CD or `gphoto2://` to access connected digital cameras. New information bars are displayed to let you select applications to handle the content displayed in the file manager (such as a music player or image viewer).

- **Multiple time locations** — Using the GNOME Clock applet you can select multiple locations around the world so that when you open your calendar you see the local time and weather for those locations.

- **Google calendars** — You can add Google calendars to your Evolution calendars.

- **Keyboard Preferences simplified** — Settings from keyboard layout and accessibility windows have been merged into a single Keyboard Preferences dialog.

- **Accessibility improvements** — Several accessibility improvements make it easier for people with disabilities to use GNOME. The Orca screenreader includes improved accessibility with Firefox and Web applications. There's support for level 2 contracted braille.

To use your GNOME desktop, you should become familiar with the following components:

- **Metacity (window manager)** — The default window manager for GNOME in Fedora and RHEL is Metacity. The window manager provides such things as themes, window borders, and window controls. If you enable 3D acceleration, you will automatically be switched to the Compiz window manager (if your hardware can support AIGLX).

- **Nautilus (file manager/graphical shell)** — When you open a folder (for example, by double-clicking the Home icon on your desktop), the Nautilus window opens and displays the contents of the selected folder. Nautilus can also display other types of content, such as shared folders from Windows computers on the network (using SMB).

- **GNOME panels (application/task launcher)** — These panels, which line the top and bottom of your screen, are designed to make it convenient for you to launch the applications you use, manage running applications, and work with multiple virtual desktops. By default, the top panel contains menu buttons (Applications, Places, and System), desktop application launchers (Firefox and Evolution Email), Tomboy sticky notes, NetworkManager applet, a clock, and a volume control icon. Other applets you could add include Mugshot, battery monitors, and various launchers.

Using the Fast User Switch applet, you can switch between different desktop users without shutting down the current desktop. The bottom panel has a "hide desktop" icon, a tray of active applications, a workspace switcher (for managing four virtual desktops) and a trash can icon (to drop files for deletion or view deleted files).

- **Desktop area**— The windows and icons you use are arranged on the desktop area. The desktop area supports such things as drag-and-drop actions between applications, a desktop menu (right-click to see it), and icons for launching applications.

Besides the components just described, GNOME includes a set of Preferences windows (select System → Preferences) that let you configure different aspects of your desktop. You can change backgrounds, colors, fonts, keyboard shortcuts, and other features relating to the look and behavior of the desktop. Figure 3-7 shows how the GNOME desktop environment appears the first time you log in, with a few windows added to the screen.

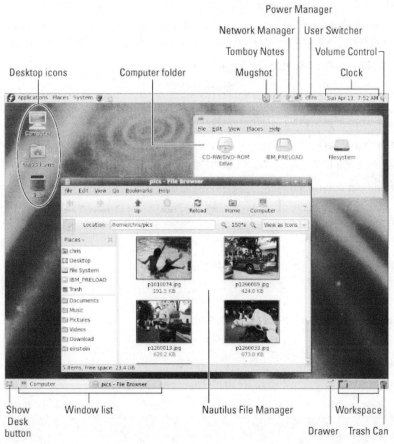

Figure 3-7: In the GNOME desktop environment, you can manage applications from the panels.

The following sections provide details on using the GNOME desktop.

Using the Metacity window manager

The Metacity window manager seems to have been chosen as the default window manager for GNOME because of its simplicity. The creator of Metacity refers to it as a "boring window manager for the adult in you" — then goes on to compare other window managers to colorful, sugary cereal while Metacity is characterized as Cheerios.

There really isn't much you can do with Metacity (except get your work done efficiently). Assigning new themes to Metacity and changing colors and window decorations is done through the GNOME preferences (and is described later). A few Metacity themes exist, but expect the number to grow. Signs that Metacity is willing to inch toward more sparkle for the desktop is its support for GLX extensions that allow 3D screen effects (see the section "Running 3D Accelerated Desktop Effects" later in this chapter).

Basic Metacity functions that might interest you are keyboard shortcuts and the workspace switcher. Table 3-1 shows keyboard shortcuts to get around the Metacity window manager.

Table 3-1: Metacity Keyboard Shortcuts

Actions	Keystrokes
Window focus cycle forward, with pop-up icons	Alt+Tab
cycle backward, with pop-up icons	Alt+Shift+Tab
cycle forward, without pop-up icons	Alt+Esc
cycle backward, without pop-up icons	Alt+Shift+Esc
Panel focus cycle forward among panels	Alt+Ctrl+Tab
cycle backward among panels	Alt+Ctrl+Shift+Tab
Workspace focus move to workspace to the right	Ctrl+Alt+right arrow
move to workspace to the left	Ctrl+Alt+left arrow
move to upper workspace	Ctrl+Alt+up arrow
move to lower workspace	Ctrl+Alt+down arrow
Minimize/unminimize all windows	Ctrl+Alt+D
Show window menu	Alt+Spacebar
Close menu	Esc

Another Metacity feature that may interest you is the workspace switcher. Four virtual workspaces appear in the workspace switcher on the GNOME panel. Here are some things to do with the Workspace Switcher:

- **Choose current workspace** — Four virtual workspaces appear in the Workspace Switcher. Click any of the four virtual workspaces to make it your current workspace.

- **Move windows to other workspaces** — Click any window, each represented by a tiny rectangle in the Workspace Switcher, to drag and drop it to another workspace. Likewise, you can drag an application from the Window List to move that application to another workspace.

- **Add more workspaces** — Right-click the workspace switcher, and select Preferences. You can add workspaces (up to 32).

- **Name workspaces** — Right-click the workspace switcher and select Preferences. Click in the Workspaces pane to change names of workspaces to any names you choose.

You can view and change information about Metacity controls and settings using the gconf-editor window (as root, type **yum install gconf-editor**, then **gconf-editor** as a regular user from a Terminal window). As the window says, it is not the recommended way of changing preferences. So, when possible, you should change the desktop through GNOME preferences. However, gconf-editor is a good way to see descriptions of each Metacity feature.

From the gconf-editor window, select apps → metacity. Then choose from general, global_keybindings, keybindings_commands, window_keybindings, and workspace_names. Click each key to see its value, along with short and long descriptions of the key. (Type **yum install gconf-editor** if it's not yet installed on your system.)

Using the GNOME panels

Fedora includes panels on the top and bottom of the GNOME desktop. From those panels you can start applications (from buttons or menus), see what programs are active, manage network interfaces, monitor power issues, adjust your audio volume, and switch workspaces. There are also many ways to change the top or bottom panel — by adding applications or monitors, or by changing the placement or behavior of the panel, for example.

Click any open space on either panel to see the Panel menu. The Panel menu appears, as shown in Figure 3-8.

Figure 3-8: Right-click any open spot on the GNOME Panel to see the Panel menu.

From the GNOME Panel menu, you can perform a variety of functions, including:

- **Use the Applications menu** — Displayed on the Applications menu are most of the applications and system tools you will use from the desktop.
- **Add to panel** — You can add an applet, menu, launcher, drawer, or button.
- **Delete This panel** — You can delete the current panel.
- **Properties** — Change position, size, and background of the panel.
- **New panel** — You can add panels to your desktop in different styles and locations.

You can also work with items on a panel; for example, you can:

- **Move items** — To move items on a panel, simply drag-and-drop them to a new position.
- **Set Preferences or Properties** — Right-click on an icon on the panel and select Preferences or Properties, depending on which is available. From the pop-up that appears, you can usually set properties of what is launched when the application is selected.

The following sections describe some things you can do with the GNOME panel.

Use the Applications and System menus

Click Applications on the panel and you see categories of applications, programming tools, and system tools that you can select. Click the application you want to launch.

To add a menu or launch item to the panel, right-click the Applications menu and select Edit Menus. The left column shows available menus and the center column shows items on those menus. Here are some ways you can change those menus:

- **Add/Remove Applications** — Click check boxes next to application items to add (check) or remove those items from the Applications menus.
- **Move Applications** — Select an application, and then click Move up or Move down to change its position on a menu.
- **New Menu** — Select New Menu to add a submenu to an existing menu.
- **New Separator** — Select the New Separator button to add a separator between menu entries.
- **New Item** — Select New Item to add an application launcher.

If you are adding a new application, after you select New Item, a Create Launcher pop-up window appears. Here is what you need to add to that window:

- **Type** — Select either Application or Application in Terminal. Select Application for any X-based application and select Application in Terminal if the application is a command that expects to run in a shell.

- **Name** — A name to appear on the menu.
- **Command** — The command that is executed when you select the menu item. You can browse for it.
- **Comment** — A comment for when you hover over the menu item with your mouse.
- **Icon** — Select the No Icon button to display a list of icons from the `/usr/share/pixmaps` directory that you can use on the menu. Select Browse to find an icon from a different directory.

After you click OK, the new item will immediately appear on the menu (no need to restart anything).

Adding an applet

There are dozens of small GNOME applications called *applets* that you can run directly on the GNOME panel. These applets can show information you may want to see on an ongoing basis or may just provide some amusement. To see what applets are available and to add applets that you want to your panel, perform the following steps:

1. Right-click an open space in the panel so that the panel menu appears.

2. Select Add to Panel. An Add to Panel window appears.

3. Select from among several dozen applets, including: a clock, dictionary lookup, stock ticker, weather report, lock screen, log out, run application, take screen shot, fortune-telling fish, eyes that follow your mouse, e-mail Inbox monitor, modem lights monitor and many others. The applet appears on the panel, ready for you to use.

Figure 3-9 shows, from left to right, geyes, system monitor, weather report, network monitor, and wanda the fish.

Figure 3-9: Applets let you monitor activities, play CDs, watch your mail, or check the weather.

After an applet is installed, right-click it to see what options are available. For example, select Preferences for the stock ticker, and you can add or delete stocks whose prices you want to monitor. If you don't like the applet's location, right-click it, click Move, slide the mouse until the applet is where you want it (even to another panel), and click to set its location.

A lot of interesting applets have been added recently that you can try out. Here are some examples of available applets and the packages you need to install to have them available:

- **Deskbar (deskbar-applet)** — A versatile search interface that lets you type words to search for programs and files on your local system, as well as launch a browser or e-mail when you type a URL or e-mail address. From the Deskbar Preferences, you can add many other neat search types as well, such as Fedora Bugzilla entries and dictionary terms.

- **CPU Temperature (gai-temp)** — Watch the temperature of your CPU or hard disk from your panel in Fahrenheit or Celsius. Colors change from green to orange to red if temperature rises above normal limits.

- **Moon data (glunarclock)** — Monitor the phases of the moon on your panel from this applet. Double-click the applet to see more data on moon coordinates, moonrise, and moonset.

- **Network traffic (gnome-applet-netspeed)** — Display the amount of traffic traveling across your network interfaces (both incoming and outgoing).

Keep in mind that applets can be a drain on system resources. If you no longer want an applet to appear on the panel, right-click it, and then click Remove From Panel. The icon representing the applet will disappear. If you find that you have run out of room on your panel, you can add a new panel to another part of the screen, as described in the next section.

Adding another panel

You can have several panels on your GNOME desktop. You can add panels that run along the sides of the screen to go with the ones that already go along the top and bottom. To add a panel, do the following:

1. Right-click an open space in the panel so that the Panel menu appears.

2. Select New Panel. A new panel appears at the right side of the screen.

3. Right-click an open space in the new panel and select Properties.

4. From the Panel Properties, select where you want the panel from the Orientation box (Top, Bottom, Left or Right).

After you've added a panel, you can add applets or application launchers to it as you did to the default panel. To remove a panel, right-click it and select Delete This Panel.

Adding an application launcher

Icons on your panel represent a Web browser and several office productivity applications. You can add your own icons to launch applications from the panel as well. To add a new application launcher to the panel, do the following:

1. Right-click in an open space on the panel.

2. Select Add to Panel → Application Launcher → Forward from the menu. All application categories from your Applications menu appear.

3. Select the arrow next to the category of application you want, select the application, and select Add. (As an alternative, you can simply drag and drop the applet item on to the panel.) An icon representing the application appears.

To launch the application you just added, single-click it.

If the application you want to launch is not on your Applications menu, you can build one yourself as follows:

1. Right-click in an open space on the panel.

2. Select Add to Panel → Custom Application Launcher → Add. The Create Launcher window appears.

3. Provide the following information for the application that you want to add:

    - **Type** — Select Application (to launch an application) or Application in Terminal (to launch and application within a Terminal window). Another selection is Link, to open a Web address in a browser.

    - **Name** — A name to identify the application (this appears in the tool tip when your mouse is over the icon).

    - **Command** — The command line that is run when the application is launched. You should use the full path name, plus any required options.

    - **Comment** — A comment describing the application. As with Name, this information appears when you later move your mouse over the launcher.

4. Click the Icon box (it might say No Icon). Select one of the icons shown and click OK. Alternatively, you can browse the file system to choose an icon.

> **NOTE:** Icons available to represent your application are contained in the `/usr/share/pixmaps` directory. These icons are either in png or xpm formats. If there isn't an icon in the directory you want to use, create your own and assign it to the application.

5. Click OK.

The application should now appear in the panel. Click it to start the application.

Adding a drawer

By adding a drawer to your GNOME panel, you can add several applets and launchers and have them take up only one slot on your panel. You can use the drawer to show the applets and launchers as though they were being pulled out of a drawer icon on the panel.

To add a drawer to your panel, right-click the panel and then select Add to Panel → Drawer. The drawer should appear on the panel. The drawer behaves just like a panel. Right-click the drawer area, and add applets or launchers to it as you would to a panel. Click the drawer icon to retract the drawer.

Figure 3-10 shows a portion of a side panel that includes an open drawer. This example includes an icon for launching a Terminal window, a custom folder icon, a volume monitor, and a weather applet.

Figure 3-10: Add launchers or applets to a drawer on your GNOME panel.

Changing panel properties

Properties you can change that relate to a panel are limited to the orientation, size, hiding policy, and background. To open the Panel properties window that applies to a specific panel, right-click on an open space on the panel, and then choose Properties. The Panel Properties window that appears includes the following values:

- **Orientation** — You can move the panel to different locations on the screen by clicking on a new position.

- **Size** — You can select the size of your panel by choosing its height in pixels (24 pixels by default).

- **Expand** — Click this check box to have the panel expand to fill the entire side or unselect the check box to make the panel only as wide as the applets it contains.

- **Autohide** — You can select whether or not a panel is automatically hidden (appearing only when the mouse pointer is in the area).

- **Show hide buttons** — You can choose whether or not the Hide/Unhide buttons (with pixmap arrows on them) appear on the edges of the panel.

- **Arrows on hide buttons** — If you select Show hide buttons you can select to either have arrows on those buttons or not.

- **Background** — From the Background tab, you can assign a color to the background of the panel, assign a background image, assign a Style (using a slider to go from Transparent to Opaque) or just leave it as None (which causes the panel to get its background from the current system theme). Click the Background Image radio button if you want to select an Image for the background, and then select an image, such as a tile from /usr/share/backgrounds/tiles or other directory.

> **TIP:** I usually turn on the AutoHide feature and turn off the Hide buttons. Using AutoHide gives you more space to work with on your desktop. When you move your mouse to the edge where the panel is, it pops up — so you don't need Hide buttons.

Using the Nautilus file manager

At one time, file managers did little more than let you run applications, create data files, and open folders. These days, file managers are expected to also offer different browsing choices, preview file content, select different applications to use on data files, and access files on other computers. The Nautilus file manager, which is the default GNOME file manager, is an example of just such a file manager.

When you open the Nautilus file manager window (from a GNOME menu or by opening the Home icon or other folder on your desktop), you see the name of the location you are viewing (such as the folder name) and what that location contains (files, folders, and applications). Figure 3-11 is an example of the file manager window displaying the home directory of a user named mike (/home/mike).

The default Nautilus window has been greatly simplified in recent releases to show fewer controls and provide more space for file and directory icons. Double-click a folder to open that folder in a new window. Select your folder name in the lower-left corner of the window to see the file system hierarchy above the current folder (as shown in Figure 3-11). Whatever size, location, and other setting you had for the folder the last time you opened it, GNOME will remember and return it to that state the next time you open it.

To see more controls, as Nautilus showed by default in previous versions, right-click a folder and select Browse Folder to open it. Or select Applications → System Tools → File Browser to open Nautilus in Browser mode directly.

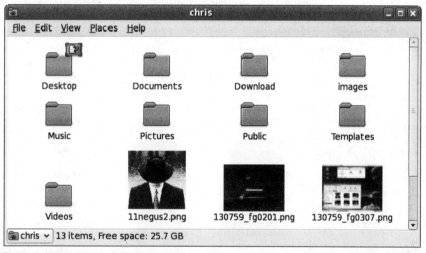

Figure 3-11: Move around the file system, open directories, launch applications, and open Samba folders.

Icons on the toolbar of the Nautilus window let you move forward and back among the directories and Web sites you visit. To move up the directory structure, click the up arrow. To refresh the view of the folder or Web page, click the Reload button. The Home button takes you to your home page and the Computer button lets you see the same type of information you would see from a My Computer icon on a Windows system (CD drive, floppy drive, hard disk file systems, and network folders).

Icons in Nautilus often indicate the type of data that a particular file contains. The contents or file extension of each file can determine which application is used to work with the file. Or, you can right-click an icon to open the file it represents with a particular application or viewer.

Some of the more interesting features of Nautilus are described here:

- **Sidebar** — From the Browse Folder view described previously, click on View → Side Pane to have a sidebar appear in the left column of the screen. From the sidebar, you can click tabs that represent different types of information you can select. The Tree tab shows a tree view of the directory structure, so you can easily traverse your directories.

  The Notes tab lets you add notes that become associated with the current Directory or Web page. The History tab displays a history of directories and Web sites you have visited, allowing you to click those items to return to the sites they represent. Right-click in the sidebar to choose which of the sidebar tabs are displayed.

- **Windows file and printer sharing** — If your computer is connected to a LAN on which Windows computers are sharing files and printers, you can view those resources from Nautilus. Click File → Open Location from a Nautilus window, and then type **smb:** to see available workgroups. Click a workgroup to see computers from that workgroup that are sharing files and printers. Figure 3-12 shows an example of Nautilus displaying an icon representing a folder on a Windows computer called einstein (smb://einstein).

Figure 3-12: Display shared Windows file and printer servers (SMB) in Nautilus.

- **MIME types and file types** — To handle different types of content that may be encountered in the Nautilus window, you can set applications to respond based on MIME type and file type. With a folder being displayed, right-click a file for which you want to assign an application. Click Open With Other Application. If no application has been assigned for the file type, click Associate Application to be able to select an application. From the Add File Types window, you can add an application based on the file extension and MIME type representing the file.

CROSS-REFERENCE: For more information on MIME types, see the description of MIME types in the "Changing GNOME preferences" section later in this chapter.

- **Drag and drop** — You can drag and drop files and folders within the Nautilus window, between the Nautilus and the desktop, or between multiple Nautilus windows. Many GNOME-compliant applications also support the GNOME drag-and-drop feature. So, for example, you could drag an image file from Nautilus and drop it on a gThumb image viewer to work with that image.

If you need more information on the Nautilus file manager, visit the GNOME Web site (`www.gnome.org/nautilus`).

Changing GNOME preferences

There are many ways to change the behavior, look, and feel of your GNOME desktop. Most GNOME preferences can be modified from windows you can launch from the System menu (click Preferences to see features to change).

Unlike earlier versions of GNOME for Fedora and Red Hat Linux, boundaries between preferences relating to the window manager (Metacity), file manager (Nautilus), and the GNOME desktop itself have been blurred. Preferences for all of these features are available from the Preferences menu.

The following items highlight some of the preferences you might want to change:

- **Accessibility** — If you have difficulty operating a mouse or keyboard, the Keyboard Preferences window lets you adapt mouse and keyboard settings to make those devices more accessible. From the Preferences menu select Personal → Assistive Technologies. Then select Keyboard Accessibility. Figure 3-13 shows the Accessibility tab on the Keyboard Preferences window.

- **Desktop Background** — Choose System → Preferences → Look and Feel → Appearance. From the Background tab you can choose a solid color or an image to use as wallpaper. If you choose to use a solid color (by selecting the blank wallpaper in the upper left corner of the Wallpaper box), click the Color box, choose a color from the palette, and select OK.

  To use wallpaper for your background, open a folder containing the image you want to use. Then drag the image into the Wallpaper pane on the Background tab. You can choose from a variety of images in the `/usr/share/nautilus/patterns` and `/usr/share/backgrounds/tiles` directories. Then, choose to have the image as wallpaper that is tiled (repeated pattern), centered, scaled (in proportion), or stretched (using any proportion to fill the screen).

- **Screensaver** — You can choose from dozens of screensavers from the Screensaver window. Select Random Screensaver to have your screensaver chosen randomly from those you mark with a check, or select one that you like from the list to use all the time. Next, choose how long your screen must be idle before the screensaver starts (default is 10 minutes). (If you only see a few screensavers, you might want to install the xscreensaver-extras and xscreensaver-gl-extras packages.)

Figure 3-13: Set keyboard responses from the Keyboard Preferences window.

NOTE: The gnome-screensaver replaced xscreensaver as the default screensaver application as of Fedora 5. While gnome-screensaver seems more stable, xscreensaver includes more flexibility in configuring your screensavers. To use xscreensaver, disable gnome-screensaver, install xscreensaver-base package, and type **xscreensaver-demo** (to configure your screensaver).

- **Theme** — You can choose to have an entire theme of elements be used on your desktop. A desktop theme affects not only the background, but also the way that many buttons and menu selections appear. There are only a few themes available for the window manager (Metacity) in the Fedora and RHEL distributions. You can get a bunch of other Metacity themes from themes.freshmeat.net (click Metacity).

  Choose System → Preferences → Look and Feel → Appearance, and then select the Theme tab. From there you can select from a handful of themes, or click Customize to modify the current theme. The screen appearance changes immediately as you click the new theme. If you download a new theme, click Install to browse to the theme in your file system and select to install it.

Managing removable media (CDs, DVD, and cameras)

The GNOME Volume Manager is a GNOME feature for managing some removable media for your Fedora or RHEL system. Using the Removable Drives and Media Preferences window, you can define how digital video cameras, webcams, PDAs, printers, scanners and other input devices are handled when they are hot-plugged to USB ports.

> **NOTE:** If you are looking for ways to change what happens when you insert CD and DVDs or connect removable storage devices, those preferences have moved. Instead of being on the Removable Drives and Media Preferences window, they are now on the File Management Preferences window associated with the Nautilus File Manager. From a Nautilus File Browser window, select Edit → Preferences and choose the Media tab. You can then change which applications are launched when you insert audio CDs, DVD videos, Blu-Ray discs, blank CDs, and other media.

To open the GNOME Volume Manager from the System menu, select Preferences → Hardware → Removable Drives and Media. The Removable Drives and Media Preferences window appears, as shown in Figure 3-14.

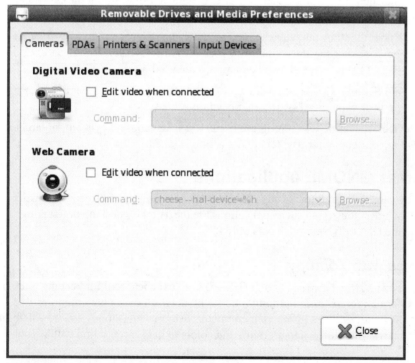

Figure 3-14: Choose which removable drives and media are mounted and played.

As noted, this window can be used to configure a variety of devices. Basically, the window can help you define what happens when you connect one of these devices to your Fedora system. Here is a list of settings that are available from the Removable Drives and Media Preferences window:

- **Digital Video Camera** — Use this selection to add a video editing command to launch when a digital video camera is connected. (None come with Fedora, but digital video editors such as kino are available from `rpm.livna.org`.)

- **Web Camera** — Use this selection to launch an application to use your webcam when that device is plugged in. By default, no application is enabled, although by selecting the check box you can have the cheese window opened to take pictures and videos with your webcam.

- **Portable Music Players** — You can select your own application to launch when a portable music player is connected to your computer (nothing is configured by default). If it is an MP3 player, refer to Chapter 8 for information on getting MP3 support.

- **Digital Camera** — When a digital camera is connected to a USB port on your computer, the camera's storage device is mounted automatically and the gThumb image viewer is launched. You can use that viewer to download images from the camera and manipulate those images. (The gThumb application is described in Chapter 8.)

- **PDAs** — Under the PDA tab, you can select to have the contents of your Palm or PocketPC device synced to the contents on your computer. By default, the `gpilotd-control-applet` and `multisync` commands are used, respectively.

- **Printers and Scanners** — Define which program to run if a USB printer or scanner is connected to your computer. By default, no action is taken.

- **Input Devices** — Define which program to run if a USB mouse, keyboard, or tablet is connected to your computer. By default, no action is taken.

Trying other GNOME applications

The GNOME project stores and tracks bugs for a variety of open source projects that work well with GNOME desktops. Two such applications are the Tomboy desktop note-taking application and the GNOME Network Tools utility.

Taking notes with Tomboy

Tomboy (`www.beatniksoftware.com/tomboy`) is an excellent tool for keeping track of lots of bits of information. Instead of putting little sticky notes all over your computer, Tomboy lets you put sticky notes inside your computer. Features in Tomboy enable you to link notes together, search your notes, and use fonts and colors to help information within your notes stand out.

Add the Tomboy Notes applet to your desktop panel as you would any GNOME applet (select Tomboy Notes from the Add to Panel window). Then click on the sticky notepad icon and select Create New Note to open a small window that's ready for you to start typing your note.

After you have created a stick note with Tomboy, double-click on the title bar to be able to add a title, font, font color, and note color. You can add links to new notes (select some text and click the Link button). You can go back and search for text in existing notes (click the Search button). You can even see a table of contents of your notes (select the Tomboy applet icon, and then select Table of Contents).

Recent new features in Tomboy allow you to add links to items outside of your notes, such as URLs and files. Those items are automatically detected and highlighted as you type them.

If Tomboy is not available on your system, type **yum install tomboy** to install it.

Checking Your Network from GNOME

The GNOME Network Tools window (recently added to GNOME) brings together several tools you would normally run from the command line to monitor network resources from a graphical window on your GNOME desktop. To open the Network Tools window, select Applications → System Tools → Network Tools. Eight tabs on that window let you perform different operations on your network.

> **NOTE:** If the GNOME Network Tools window is not available, you can install it (as root user) by typing **yum install gnome-nettool** from a Terminal window.

The Devices tab displays information about each of your network interfaces. It makes it easy to find the names and addresses associated with each of your network interfaces (IP addresses, broadcast, netmask) as well as information on data transmissions and collisions.

On other tabs, you can run graphical version of the `ping` command (to see if another computer can be reached on your network), `netstat` command (to see information about routes and network services), and `traceroute` command (to watch the network hops from your site to a remote host). You can do a portscan with nmap (to check for open ports on a network interface), DNS lookup (to get information about a domain name system server), finger (to see who's logged into a local or remote host computer), and whois (to get information about domain name registration).

Switching to another user

If you want to log in as another desktop user without closing your current desktop session, you can use the Fast User Switch feature of GNOME. Look for the User Switcher applet in your top panel (by default, it should show your user name on the applet) or add the applet yourself (it's identified as User Switcher from the Add to Panel window).

To use Fast User Switch, click the User Switcher applet to see a list of user names on your system. To log in as one of those users, click on the name and log in (when the login screen appears). A desktop for the new user appears, while the previous desktop keeps running on a different virtual terminal.

After you have logged in and started a desktop for another user, you can use the same User Switcher applet to switch between the multiple user desktops. A check box appears next to the names of users that have desktops launched on the different virtual terminals accessible from your display.

Figure 3-15 shows an example of the User Switcher icon with several active user logins.

Figure 3-15: Switch quickly among user desktops from the User Switcher.

Exiting GNOME

When you are done with your work, you can either log out from your current session or shut down your computer completely. If you have multiple user sessions open, you should log out of each of those first (to make sure you don't lose any unsaved work.)

To exit from GNOME, do the following:

1. Click the System button from the panel.
2. Select Log Out from the menu. A pop-up window appears, asking if you want to Log out.
3. Select OK from the pop-up menu. This will log you out and return you to either the graphical login screen or to your shell login prompt.
4. Select OK to finish exiting from GNOME.

If you are unable to get to the Log out button (if, for example, your Panel crashed), there are two other exit methods. Try one of these two ways, depending on how you started the desktop:

-   If you started the desktop by typing **startx** from your login shell, press Ctrl+Alt+Backspace to kill X and return to your login shell. Or you could type Ctrl+Alt+F1 to return to where you first ran **startx**, and then press Ctrl+C to kill the desktop.
-   If you started the desktop from a graphical login screen (and Ctrl+Alt+Backspace doesn't work), first open a Terminal window (right-click the desktop and then select New Terminal). In the Terminal window, type **ps x | more** to see a list of running processes. Look for a command named gnome-session and determine its number under the PID column. Then type **kill -9 *PID***, where *PID* is replaced by the PID number. You should see the graphical login screen.

Although these are not the most graceful ways to exit the desktop, they work. You should be able to log in again and restart the desktop.

Setting Up an Online Desktop

As more and more services are moving off your desktop and on to the Internet, what features does the next generation of desktop systems need to be relevant? If the developers of the GNOME Online Desktop are right, the desktop will serve primarily as a tool for interconnecting your online services, applications, and friends.

The GNOME Online Desktop (`http://live.gnome.org/OnlineDesktop`) was added as an experimental feature to Fedora 8 and improved for Fedora 9. The centerpiece of the project is an experimental sidebar called Big Board (`http://live.gnome.org/BigBoard`). From Big Board, you consolidate icons and menus to connect to your online photo services (like Flickr), retail accounts (such as Amazon), movie rentals (such as Netflix), and others. It also, however, keeps track of the files and applications you use locally.

You can use Mugshot (`www.mugshot.org`) to tie together connections to your online friends and activities. Mugshot lets you create the connections to your online accounts in a way that allows them to be used either from the Mugshot site or from your Online Desktop sidebar.

To get started with Online Desktop in Fedora, simply select the user you want to log in as and choose Sessions ➔ Online Desktop Demo from the login screen. Then type your password. After that, you can set up online accounts with the Mugshot and GNOME projects. Then begin configuring the services you want on your Online Desktop. (If Online Desktop isn't installed yet, type `yum install online-desktop*` to install it.)

A GNOME desktop configured with the Online Desktop feature appears. The following steps take you through the setup of your Online Desktop:

1. **Register with GNOME.org** — Select Enable Online Desktop from the sidebar. A Web browser will open, taking you to the GNOME.org site where you can create a GNOME Online account.

2. **Sign-up at GNOME.org** — Follow the instructions for creating an account, and log in to that account once you have a user name and password. This account is used to store information about the applications you use, to incorporate into Online Desktop.

3. **Create GNOME.org Account** — Begin adding information to your account. This information includes your name, picture, e-mail account, IM account, and GNOME online services.

4. **Sign-up at Mugshot.org** — Use your Web browser to visit the Mugshot.org site and create your own Mugshot account. This account stores information about your online services, as well as information about other people and groups with online accounts you can connect to. All that information can be added to your Online Desktop.

5. **Add Personal Information** — Open the link to your account information and add your name, a short "About Me" description, and a picture to represent yourself.

6. **Configure Online Accounts** — Set up connections to your personal online services accounts. Figure 3-16 shows an example of the Mugshot screen for adding your online service accounts. Click the heart icon to configure a feature you love, or click the X to announce why it's a feature you hate. Here are some of the features you can add:

Figure 3-16: Configure online accounts in Mugshot to display on your Online Desktop

- **Amazon** — Create links to your Amazon profile, reviews, and wishlist.
- **Del.icio.us** — Save and organize a collection of favorite Web sites.
- **Digg** — Connect to your account on Digg.com to view and vote on popular stories.
- **Facebook** — Get to your Facebook social network site.
- **Flickr** — Visit your online digital image collection at Flickr.com.
- **Lots of Others!** — Besides those just mentioned, Mugshot lets you create connections to your accounts with Google, MySpace, Netflix, Picasa, Rhapsody, YouTube and others.

7. **Add People**— From your Mugshot account, select Active People to get to a link where you can invite friends. Once you invite a friend and the friend accepts, the person is added to the People section of your sidebar.

8. **Add Groups** — From your Mugshot account, select Active Groups to see available Mugshot groups. Select Join Group to add it to a list of groups that you follow.

When you've completed these configuration steps, your Online Desktop should be ready to use. Figure 3-17 shows an example of an Online Desktop and related Mugshot information.

Figure 3-17: Get to your online services and friends using Online Desktop configured with Mugshot

After logging in to Mugshot, you'll see the following information, starting from the top of the Big Board sidebar in Figure 3-17:

- **User Information** — The user name and face image appears in the top box of the My Desktop sidebar. Select that box to logout of the desktop, visit the Mugshot account page, view system preferences, or minimize the sidebar.

- **Tiny Icons** — The tiny icons below the User Information represent the online services you have configured for your Mugshot account. Beginning with the top-left icon in this example, the icons represent Digg, Picasa, Amazon, Netflix, Del.icio.us, my home URL, Reddit, Twitter, and Flickr.

- **Search Box** — Type a term into the search box (flash memory appears in this example) and press Enter. A pop-up lets you select to search for that term at Amazon.com, Answers.com, Creative Commons, eBay, Google, or Yahoo.

- **Files** — See the files that you have opened recently under the Files box. Select More to search or browse for local files.

- **Applications** — Your most-used applications appear in the Applications box, ready for you to start at any time. Select More to search for an application or see statistics about the types of applications you use most.

- **People** —The people you added to your Mugshot account appear, with their names and icons, in the People box. Click on a photo or name to go to that person's Mugshot page.

- **Calendar** — Connect to your online Google calendar from this box.

- **Mugshot Home** — In the example, a Web browser is open to my Mugshot home page. From the Mugshot home page, you can access the same services that are loaded on your Online Desktop, as well as configure all the features that are picked up by your Online Desktop.

- **Mugshot Stacker** — Click the Mugshot icon in the panel to see the Mugshot stacker. That stacker shows information about your activities, as well as activities of others you have added to your People list. In this example, you can see that I joined a group, left another group, and added a movie to my Netflix queue.

Because Online Desktop is still under development, expect to have many more features and services available by the time you read this text. In particular, work is being done to integrate online applications, so you will be able to work with Web applications to use your documents, spreadsheets, and other important information.

Switching Desktop Environments

If you decide you want to try a different desktop environment, the Desktop Switcher provides a graphical means of changing your desktop environments between KDE, GNOME, Xfce and several different window managers (including TWM). To open the Desktop Switcher, select System → Preferences → Desktop Switching Tool.

From the Desktop Switcher, select the desktop environment (GNOME, KDE, or XFce) or window manager (TWM) you want to use next. You can have that change apply to the current display (just the next time you restart X only) or make the change permanent. Click OK. Then log out. The next time you log in, the new environment or window manager will take effect.

> **NOTE:** To use the Desktop Switcher window, you must have the switchdesk-gui package installed. Otherwise, you can use the `switchdesk` command, followed by the name of the Desktop you want to switch to, from a Terminal window to change your Desktop.

If you just want to change your desktop environment temporarily, you can select Session from the login screen and choose the desktop you want. You can choose it just for the current session or to have it be your default desktop.

Using the KDE Desktop

The KDE desktop was developed to provide an interface to Linux and other UNIX systems that could compete with Mac OS or Microsoft Windows operating systems for ease of use. Integrated within KDE are tools for managing files, windows, multiple desktops, and applications. If you can work a mouse, you can learn to navigate the KDE desktop. Fedora 9 includes version 4 of KDE.

> **NOTE:** KDE is not installed by default for Fedora. Therefore, to use the procedures in this section, you might have to install KDE. During installation, you could use a Custom install type to install KDE. Otherwise, see Chapter 5 for information on how to use PackageKit or yum to add KDE. You can also try the KDE 4 Desktop Live CD that comes with this book, and even install that live CD to your hard disk.

The lack of an integrated, standardized desktop environment in the past has held back Linux and other UNIX systems from acceptance on the desktop. While individual applications could run well, you rarely could drag and drop files or other items between applications. Likewise, you couldn't open a file and expect the machine to launch the correct application to deal with it or save your windows from one login session to the next. KDE provides a platform for developers to create programs that easily share information and detect how to deal with different data types.

The following section describes how to get started with KDE. This includes using the KDE Setup wizard, maneuvering around the desktop, managing files, windows, virtual desktops, and adding application launchers.

New Features in KDE 4

KDE 4 marks some major innovations for the KDE desktop. New libraries were added to support multimedia applications and improve handling of removable devices. There are new applications for viewing documents (such as Okular) and managing files (such as Dolphin). The most important new feature, however, is the Plasma desktop shell.

The Plasma desktop shell gives the KDE 4 desktop a whole new look and feel. It features improved ways of finding and presenting information, such as KRunner and KickOff. The new Plasma Panel can incorporate lots of new applets, as well as clocks, pagers, and other useful applications.

Elements in the Plasma desktop shell are referred to as *plasmoids*. What makes plasmoids different from components on many of today's desktop systems is that they can be combined in various ways to interact with each other and can be placed in different locations. For example, if a particular widget (such as a clock or a news ticker) is important to you, instead of having it represented by a tiny icon on the panel, you can put a big version of the applet on your desktop.

Descriptions of these and other KDE 4 features are included in the following section.

Starting with KDE

You can select the KDE desktop from the login screen (provided that KDE is installed). Select your login name and choose Session → KDE. Then type your password, as prompted. A KDE desktop should appear, similar to the one shown in Figure 3-18.

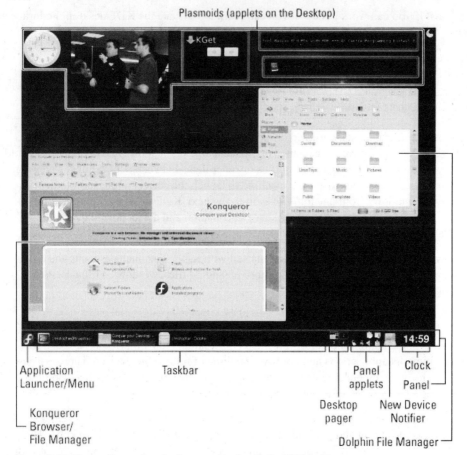

Plasmoids (applets on the Desktop)

Application
Launcher/Menu

Taskbar

Panel
applets

Clock

Panel

Konqueror
— Browser/
File Manager

Desktop
pager

New Device
Notifier

Dolphin File Manager

Figure 3-18: Manage files and applications graphically with the KDE desktop.

KDE desktop basics

Here are some descriptions of what you will find on the KDE 4 Plasma desktop for Fedora 9, as illustrated in Figure 3-18:

- **Plasmoids** — Applets that can be added to the desktop as well as the panel are referred to as *plasmoids* in KDE 4 . Here you can see the clock, picture frame, KGet downloader, news ticker, and dictionary search all added to the desktop. You can drag plasmoids around, group them together, and arrange them as you like on your desktop.

- **Konqueror** — The default Web browser and file manager for KDE.

- **Dolphin**— A new file manager for KDE.

- **Panel** — The panel provides some quick tools for launching applications and managing the desktop. You can adapt the panel to your needs by resizing it, adding tools, and changing its location. By default, you start with an application launcher, taskbar, desktop pager, some mini applets, new device modifier, and a clock.

- **Application Launcher/Menu** — This panel button is represented by a Fedora logo. The button opens the new Kickoff Application menu, which helps you search for applications installed on your system and launch them. Choose between Favorites (applications you use often), Applications (application menus), Computer (places and storage devices), or Recently Used applications. Right-click the button and select Switch to Classic Menu Style to return to a classic view of application categories and menus.

- **Taskbar** — This button shows the tasks that are currently running on the desktop. The button for the window that is currently active appears pressed in. Click a task to toggle between opening and minimizing the window.

- **Desktop Pager** — This box on the panel consists of your virtual desktops, which contain small views of each desktop. There are four virtual desktops available to you, by default. These are labeled 1, 2, 3, and 4. You begin your KDE session on virtual desktop 1. If there are windows on the desktop, small icons representing them may cover the desktop number. You can change to any of the four desktops by clicking it.

- **Mini applets** — Some applications, such as media players, clipboards, and battery power managers, will keep running after you have closed the related window. Some of those applications maintain a tiny applet in the panel. Often clicking on these applets restores the windows they represent. This is convenient for music players if you don't want to take up desktop space while you play music, but you want to be able to open the player quickly to change songs.

- **Clock** — The current time is shown on the far right-hand side of the panel. Click it to see a calendar for the current month. Click the arrow keys on the calendar to move forward and back to other months.

Getting around the desktop

Navigating the desktop is done with your mouse and keyboard. You can use a two-button or three-button mouse. Using the keyboard to navigate requires some Alt and Ctrl key sequences.

Using the mouse

The responses from the desktop to your mouse depend on which button you press and where the mouse pointer is located. Table 3-2 shows the results of clicking each mouse button with the mouse pointer placed in different locations.

The mouse actions in the table are all single-click actions. Use single-click with the left mouse button to open an icon on the desktop. On a window title bar, double-clicking results in a window-shade action, where the window scrolls up and down into the title bar.

Table 3-2: Mouse Actions

Pointer Position	Mouse Button	Results
Window title bar or frame (current window active)	Left	Raise current window.
Window title bar or frame (current window active)	Middle	Lower current window.
Window title bar or frame (current window active)	Right	Open operations menu.
Window title bar or frame (current window not active)	Left	Activate current window and raise it to the top.
Window title bar or frame (current window not active)	Middle	Activate current window and lower it.
Window title bar or frame (current window not active)	Right	Open operations menu without changing position.
Inner window (current window not active)	Left	Activate current window, raise it to the top, and pass the click to the window.
Inner window (current window not active)	Middle	Activate current window and pass the click to the window.
Inner window (current window not active)	Right	Activate current window and pass the click to the window.
Any part of a window	Middle (plus hold Alt key)	Toggle between raising and lowering the window.
Any part of a window	Right (plus hold Alt key)	Resize the window.
On the desktop area	Left (hold and drag)	Select a group of icons.
On the desktop area	Right	Open system pop-up menu.

Using keystrokes

If you don't happen to have a mouse or you just like to keep your hands on the keyboard, there are several keystroke sequences you can use to navigate the desktop. Here are some examples:

- **Step through windows** (Alt+Tab) — To step through each of the windows that are running on the current desktop, hold down the Alt key and press the Tab key until you see the one you want. Then release the Alt key to select it.

- **Open Run Command box** (Alt+F2) — To open a KRunner box on the desktop that lets you type in a command and run it, hold the Alt key and press F2. Next, type the command in the box and KRunner presents you with matching commands as you type. Either click the command you want or press Enter after typing the whole command you want to run. You can also type a URL into this box to view a Web page.

- **Close the current window** (Alt+F4) — To close the current window, press Alt+F4.

- **Close another window** (Ctrl+Alt+Esc) — To close an open window on the desktop, press Ctrl+Alt+Esc. When a skull and cross bones appears as the pointer, move the pointer over the window you want to close and click the left mouse button. (This is a good technique for killing a window that has no borders or menu.)

- **Switch virtual desktops** (Ctrl+F1, F2, F3, or F4 key) — To step through virtual desktops, press and hold the Ctrl key and press F1, F2, F3, or F4 to go directly to desktop one, two, three, or four, respectively. You could do this for up to eight desktops, if you have that many configured.

- **Open window operation menu** (Alt+F3) — To open the operations menu for the active window, press Alt+F3. When the menu appears, move the arrow keys to select an action (Move, Size, Minimize, Maximize, and so on), and then press Enter to select it.

Managing files with Dolphin and Konqueror File Managers

With KDE 4, the KDE desktop offers two file managers: the new Dolphin File Manager and the existing Konqueror File Manager/Browser. Dolphin is a streamlined file manager that is now used by default when you open a folder in KDE. Konqueror can handle a wide range of content from local files and folders to remote Web content.

> **NOTE:** For further information on Dolphin, refer to the Dolphin File Manager home page (`http://enzosworld.gmxhome.de`).

The Konqueror File Manager/Web browser helps elevate the KDE environment from just another X window manager to an integrated desktop that can compete with GUIs from Apple Computing or Microsoft. The features in Konqueror rival those that are offered by those user-friendly desktop systems. Figure 3-19 shows an example of the Konqueror File Manager window.

Some of Konqueror's greatest strengths over earlier file managers are the following:

- **Network desktop** — If your computer is connected to the Internet or a LAN, features built into Konqueror let you create links to files (using FTP) and Web pages (using HTTP) on the network and open them within the Konqueror window. Those links can appear as file icons in a Konqueror window or on the desktop. When a link is opened (single-click), the contents of the FTP site or Web page appears right in the Konqueror window. Given proper folder permission, you could drag and drop files to your FTP server in this way.

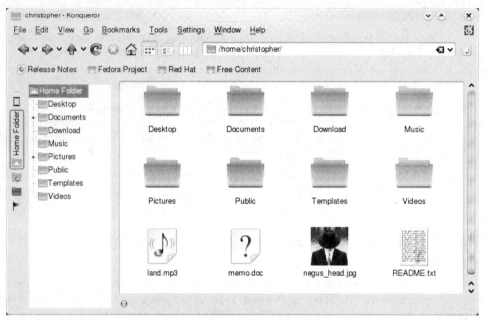

Figure 3-19: Konqueror provides a network-ready tool for managing files.

- **Web browser interface** — The Konqueror interface works like Firefox, Internet Explorer, or another Web browser in the way you select files, directories, and Web content. You can open Web content by typing Web-style addresses in a Location box.

TIP: Web pages that contain Java content will run by default in Konqueror. To double-check that Java support is turned on, choose Settings → Configure Konqueror. From the Settings window, click Java & JavaScript and select the Java tab. To enable Java, click the Enable Java Globally box and click Apply. Try a game from Java.com to see if Java is working. If you need a later version of Java Runtime Environment (JRE), you can download it from `www.java.com/en/download`. After downloading the new JRE, change Path to Java Executable to `/usr/java/jre1.5.0_02/bin/java` to get it to work.

- **File types and MIME types** — If you want a particular type of file to always be launched by a particular application, you can configure that file yourself. KDE already has dozens of MIME types defined that can automatically detect particular file and data types and start the right application. There are MIME types defined for audio, image, text, video, and a variety of other content types.

Of course, you can also perform many standard file manager functions with Konqueror. For manipulating files, you can use features such as Select, Move, Cut, Paste, and Delete. You can search directories for files, create new items (files, folders, and links, to name a few), view histories of the files and Web sites you have opened, and create bookmarks.

Working with files

Because most of the ways of working with files in both Konqueror and Dolphin are quite intuitive (by intention), I'll just give a quick rundown of how to do basic file manipulation:

- **Open a file** — Click a file. The file will open right in the Konqueror or Dolphin window, if possible, or in the default application set for the file type. You can also open a directory (to make it the current directory), application (to start the application), or link (to open the target of a link) in this way.

- **Choose an application** —Right-click to open a menu. When you right-click a data file, select the Open With menu. The menu that appears shows which applications are set up to open the file.

- **Delete a file** — Right-click and select Move to Trash. You are asked if you really want to delete the file. Click Trash to move the item to the Trash folder. (If you are brave, you can use Shift+Delete to permanently delete a selected file. Just keep in mind that you won't be able to restore it from the Trash if you change your mind.)

- **Copy a file** — Right-click and select Copy. This copies the file to your clipboard. After that, you can paste it to another folder. Click the Klipper (clipboard) icon in the panel to see a list of copied files. (See the Move a file bullet item for a drag-and-drop method of copying.)

- **Paste a file** — Right-click (an open area of a folder) and select Paste. A copy of the file you copied previously is pasted in the current folder.

- **Move a file** — With the original folder and target folder both open on the desktop, press and hold the left mouse button on the file you want to move, drag the file to an open area of the new folder, and release the mouse button. From the menu that appears, click Move Here. (You could also copy or create a link to the file using this menu.)

- **Link a file** — Drag and drop a file from one folder to another. When the menu appears, click Link Here. (A linked file lets you access a file from a new location without having to make a copy of the original file. When you open the link, a pointer to the original file causes it to open.)

There are also several features for viewing information about the files and folders in your Konqueror and Dolphin windows. With the addition of Dolphin to KDE 4, some file manager features that were once available in Konqueror have been moved to the more streamlined Dolphin file manager. The following items include file management features supported by those two applications:

- **View quick file information** — Right-click a file in a Konqueror or Dolphin window and select Properties. A pop-up window appears with information about the item, including its filename, file size, modification times and file type.

- **View hidden files** — In Konqueror or Dolphin, select View → Show Hidden Files. This allows you to see files that begin with a dot (.). Dot files tend to be used for configuration and don't generally need to be viewed in your daily work.

- **Change icon size** — In Dolphin, select View → Zoom In to make the file and folder icons bigger (or Zoom Out to make them smaller).

- **Change icon view** — In Konqueror or Dolphin, select View → View Mode, and then select to view the folder contents as icons, details, or columns.

To act on a group of files at the same time, there are a couple of actions you can take. To select a group of files, click in an open area of the folder and drag the pointer across the files you want to select. All files within the box will be highlighted. In Dolphin, you can also select Edit → Select All to select all files and folders in a folder. When files are highlighted, you can move, copy, or delete the files as described earlier.

Searching for files with Dolphin and kfind

If you are looking for a particular file or folder, the Find feature that was previously part of Konqueror can now be launched from Dolphin. To open a Find Files/Folders window to search for a file from a Dolphin file manager, choose Tools → Find File and the window will appear. You could also start the Find/Folders window by typing **kfind** from a Terminal window. Figure 3-20 shows the Find files/Folders window.

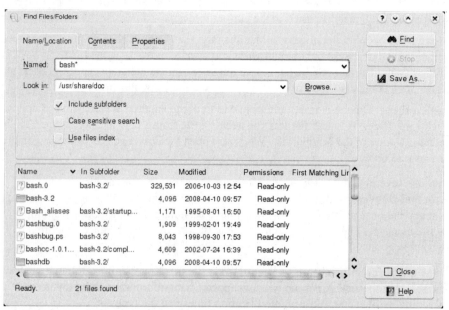

Figure 3-20: Search for files and folders from the Find Files/Folders window.

Simply type the name of the file you want to search for (in the Named text box) and the folder, including all subfolders, you want to search in (in the Look in text box). Then click the Find button. Use metacharacters, if you like, with your search. For example, search for `*.rpm` to find all files that end in `.rpm` or `z*.doc` to find all files that begin with z and end with `.doc`. You can also select to have the search be case sensitive or click the Help button to get more information on searching.

To further limit your search, you can click the Properties tab, and then enter a date range (between), a number of months before today (during the previous x months), or the number of days before today (during the previous x days). Select the Contents tab to choose to limit the search to files of a particular type (of Type), files that include text that you enter (Containing Text), or that are of a certain size (Size is) in kilobytes.

Creating new files and folders

You can create a variety of file types when using the Dolphin window. Choose File → Create New, and select Folder (to create a new folder) or one of the following types under the File submenu:

- **HTML File** — Opens a dialog box that lets you type the name of an HTML file to create.

- **Link to Application** — Opens a window that lets you type the name of an application. Click the Permissions tab to set file permissions (Exec must be on if you want to run the file as an application). Click the Execute tab and type the name of the program to run (in the field: Execute on click) and a title to appear in the title bar of the application (in the field: Window Title). If it is a text-based command, select the Run in terminal check box. Click the check box to Run as a different user and add the user name. Click the Application tab to assign the application to handle files of particular MIME types. Click OK.

- **Link to Location (URL)** — Selecting this menu item opens a dialog box that lets you create a link to a Web address. Type a name to represent the address and and type the name of the URL (Web address) for the site. (Be sure to add the `http://`, `ftp://`, or other prefix.)

- **Text File** — Opens a dialog box that lets you create a document in text format and place it in the Konqueror window. Type the name of the text document to create and click OK.

Under the Link to Device submenu, you can make the following selections:

- **CD-ROM Device** — Opens a dialog box that lets you type a new CD-ROM device name. Click the Device tab and type the device name (`/media/cdrecorder`), the mount point (such as `/media/cdrecorder`), and the file system type (you can use iso9660 for the standard CD-ROM file system, ext2 for Linux, or msdos for DOS). When the icon appears, you can open it to mount the CD-ROM and display its contents.

- **CDWRITER Device** — From the window that opens, enter the device name of your CD writer.

- **DVD-ROM Device** — Opens a dialog box that lets you type a new DVD-ROM device name. Click the Device tab and type the device name (/dev/cdrom), the mount point (such as /media/cdrecorder), and the file system type (you can use iso9660 for the standard CD-ROM file system, ext2 for Linux, or msdos for DOS). When the icon appears, you can open it to mount the DVD-ROM and display its contents.

- **Camera Device** — In the dialog box that opens, identify the device name for the camera devices that provides access to your digital camera.

- **Floppy Device** — Opens a dialog box to type a new floppy name. Click the Device tab and type the device name (/dev/fd0), the mount point (such as /media/floppy), and the file system type (you can use auto to autodetect the contents, ext2 for Linux, or msdos for DOS). When the icon appears, open it to mount the floppy and display its contents.

- **Hard Disc Device** — Opens a dialog box that lets you type the name of a new hard disk or hard-disk partition. Click the Device tab and type the device (such as /dev/sda1), the mount point (such as /mnt/win), and the file system type (you can use auto to autodetect the contents, ext2 or ext3 for Linux, or vfat for a Windows file system). When the icon appears, you can open it to mount the file system and display its contents.

Creating MIME types and applications is described later in this chapter.

Using the Konqueror browser features

Because Konqueror performs like a Web browser as well as a file manager, it includes several other browser features. For example, you can keep a bookmark list of Web sites you have visited, using the bookmarks feature. Any bookmarks that you add to your bookmarks list show up in the drop-down menu that appears when you click Bookmarks. Select from that list to return to a site. There are several ways to add and change your bookmarks list:

- **Add Bookmark** — To add the address of the page that is currently being displayed to your bookmark list, choose Bookmarks → Add Bookmark. The bookmark is silently added. The next time you click Bookmarks, you will see the bookmark you just added on the Bookmarks menu. In addition to Web addresses, you can also bookmark any file or folder.

- **Edit Bookmarks** — Select Bookmarks → Edit Bookmarks to open a tree view of your bookmarks. From the Bookmark Editor window that appears, you can change the URLs, the icon, or other features of the bookmark. There is also a nice feature that lets you check the status of the bookmark (that is, whether the address is still valid).

- **Bookmark Tabs as Folder** — You can add a new folder of bookmarks to your Konqueror bookmarks list. To create a bookmarks folder, choose Bookmarks → Bookmark Tabs as Folder. Then type a name for the new Bookmarks folder and click

OK. The new bookmark folder appears on your bookmarks menu. You can add the current location to that folder by clicking on the folder name and selecting Add Bookmark.

- **New Bookmark Folder** — You can create a new bookmark folder by choosing Bookmarks → New Bookmark Folder. When a pop-up appears, type a new folder name and select OK.

Configuring Konqueror and Dolphin options

You can change many of the visual attributes of the Konqueror window. You can select which menu bars and toolbars appear. You can have any of the following bars appear on the Konqueror window: Menu bar, Toolbar, Extra Toolbar, Location Toolbar, Bookmark Toolbar. Select Settings and then click the menu item for the bar you want to have appear (or not appear). The bar appears when the checkmark is shown next to it.

You can modify a variety of options for Konqueror by choosing Settings → Configure Konqueror. The Konqueror Settings window appears, offering the following options:

- **Behavior (File)** — Changes file manager behavior.

- **Appearance** — Changes file manager fonts and colors.

- **Previews & Meta-Data** — An icon in a Konqueror folder can be made to ressemble the contents of the file it represents. For example, if the file is a JPEG image, the icon representing the file could be a small version of that image. Using the Previews features, you can limit the size of the file used (1MB is the default) because many massive files could take too long to refresh on the screen. You can also select to have any thumbnail embedded in a file to be used as the icon or have the size of the icon reflect the shape of the image used.

- **File Associations** — Describes which programs to launch for each file type.

- **Web Behavior**— Click the Behavior (Browser) button to open a window to configure the Web browser features of Konqueror. By enabling Form Completion, Konqueror can save form data you type and, at a later time, fill that information into other forms. If your computer has limited resources, you can speed up page display by clearing the Automatically load images check box or by disabling animations.

- **Java and JavaScript** — Use this selection to enable or disable Java and JavaScript content contained in Web pages in your Konqueror window.

- **AdBlock Filters** — Click here to create a list of URLs that are filtered as you browse the Web. Filtering is based on frame and image names. Filtered URLs can be either thrown away or replaced with an image. You can also import and export lists of filters here.

- **Fonts** — Choose which fonts to use, by default, for various fonts needed on Web pages (standard font, fixed font, serif font, sans serif font, cursive font, and fantasy font). The serif fonts are typically used in body text, while sans serif fonts are often used in headlines. You can also set the Minimum and Medium font sizes.

- **Web Shortcuts** — Click the Web Shortcuts button to see a list of keyword shortcuts you can use to go to different Internet sites. For example, follow the word "ask" with a search string to search the Ask Jeeves (www.ask.com) Web site.

- **History Sidebar** — Click here to modify the behavior of the list of sites you have visited (the history). By default, the most recent 500 URLs are stored, and after 90 days, a URL is dropped from the list. You will also find a button to clear your history. (To view your history list in Konqueror, open the left side panel, and then click the tiny scroll icon.)

- **Cookies** — Click the Cookies button to select whether or not cookies are enabled in Konqueror. By default, you are asked to confirm that it is okay each time a Web site tries to create or modify a cookie. You can change that to either accept or reject all cookies. You can also set policies for acceptance or rejection of cookies based on host and domain names.

- **Cache** — Click the Cache button to indicate how much space on your hard disk can be used to store the sites you have visited (based on the value in the Disk Cache Size field).

- **Proxy** — Click the Proxy button if you are accessing the Internet through a proxy server. You need to enter the address and port number of the computer providing HTTP or FTP proxy services or both.

- **Stylesheets** —Click the Stylesheets button to select whether to use the default stylesheet, a user-defined stylesheet, or a custom stylesheet. The stylesheet sets the font family, font sizes, and colors that are applied to Web pages. (This won't change particular font requests made by the Web page.) If you select a custom stylesheet, click the Customize tab to customize your own fonts and colors.

- **Crypto** — Click the Crypto button to display a list of secure certificates that can be accepted by the Konqueror browser. By default, Secure Socket Layer (SSL) version 2 and 3 certificates are accepted, as is TLS support (if supported by the server). You can also select to be notified when you are entering or leaving a secure Web site.

- **Browser Identification** — Click the Browser Identification button to set how Konqueror identifies itself when it accesses a Web site. By default, Konqueror tells the Web site that it is the Mozilla Web browser. You can select Konqueror to appear as different Web browsers to specific sites. You must sometimes do this when a site denies you access because you do not have a specific type of browser (even though Konqueror may be fully capable of displaying the content).

- **Plugins** — Click the Plugins button to see a list of directories that Konqueror will search to find plug-ins. Konqueror can also scan your computer to find plug-ins that are installed for other browsers in other locations.

- **Performance** — Select the Performance button to see configuration settings that can be used to improve Konqueror performance. You can preload an instance after KDE startup or minimize memory usage.

In Dolphin, you can change file manager settings by selecting Settings → Configure Dolphin. The Dolphin Preferences window (shown in Figure 3-21) opens. From this window you can set how items in a folder are displayed by default, as well as a variety of other folder start-up settings.

Figure 3-21: Change file manager settings from the Dolphin Preferences window.

Managing windows

If you have a lot of windows open at the same time, tricks for organizing and managing the windows on your desktop are very helpful. KDE helps you out by maintaining window lists you can work with and shortcuts for keeping the windows in order.

Using the taskbar

When you open a window, a button representing the window appears in the taskbar at the bottom of the screen. Here is how you can manage windows from the taskbar:

- **Toggle windows** — You can left-click any running task in the taskbar to toggle between opening the window and minimizing it.

- **Move windows** — You can move a window from the current desktop to any other virtual desktop. Right-click any task in the taskbar, select To Desktop, and then select any desktop number. The window moves to that desktop.

- **Position windows** — You can indicate to have the selected window be above or below other windows or displayed in full screen. Right-click the running task in the taskbar and select Advanced. Then choose Keep Above Others, Keep Below Others, or Fullscreen.

All the windows that are running, regardless of which virtual desktop you are on, appear in the taskbar. If there are multiple windows of the same type shown as a single task, you can right-click that task; then select All to Desktop to move all related windows to the desktop you pick.

To set other preferences related to the panel taskbar, right-click the handle on the left side of the taskbar and choose Configure Taskbar. The Configure window that appears lets you choose settings for how the taskbar appears and how mouse actions affect it.

Moving windows

The easiest way to move a window from one location to another is to place the pointer on the window's title bar; while holding down the mouse button, move the mouse so the window goes to a new location, and release the mouse button to drop the window. Another way to do it is to click the window menu button (top-left corner of the title bar), click Move, move the mouse to relocate the window, and then click again to place it.

> **TIP:** If somehow the window gets stuck in a location where the title bar is off the screen, there is a way you can move it back to where you want it. Hold down the Alt key and press the left mouse button in the inner window. Then move the window where you want it and release. An alternative is to right-click anywhere on the window frame and select Move to move the window.

Resizing windows

To resize a window, place the pointer over a corner or side of the window border, and, while holding down the mouse button, move it until it is the size you want. Grabbing a corner lets you resize vertically and horizontally at the same time. Grabbing the side lets you resize in only one direction.

You can also resize a window from the window menu button. Click the window menu button (top left corner of the title bar) and select Size. Move the mouse until the window is resized and click to leave it there.

Pinning windows on top or bottom

You can set a window to always stay on top of all other windows or always stay under them. Keeping a window on top can be useful for a small window that you want to always refer to (such as a clock or a small TV viewing window). To pin a window on top of the desktop, click in the window title bar. From the menu that appears, select Advanced → Keep Above Others. Likewise, to keep the window on the bottom, select Advanced → Keep Below Others.

Using virtual desktops

To give you more space to run applications than will fit on your physical screen, KDE gives you access to several virtual desktops at the same time. Using the 1, 2, 3, and 4 buttons on the Panel, you can easily move between the different desktops. Just click the one you want.

If you want to move an application from one desktop to another, you can do so from the window menu. Click the window menu button for the window you want to move, click To Desktop, and then select Desktop 1, 2, 3, or 4. The window will disappear from the current desktop and move to the one you selected.

Configuring the desktop

If you want to change the look, feel, or behavior of your KDE desktop, the best place to start is the System Settings window. The System Settings window lets you configure dozens of attributes associated with colors, fonts, and screensavers used by KDE. There are also selections from that window that let you do basic computer administration, such as changing date/time settings and modifying your display. To open the System Settings window, select the Fedora menu and choose System Settings. The System Settings window appears, as shown in Figure 3-22.

Click any item you want to configure, or type into the Search box to find a selection that matches what you type.

There are several ways you can change the look-and-feel of your desktop display from the System Settings window. Under the Look & Feel topic, you can select to change the appearance, desktop, notifications, or window behavior.

Here are a few of the individual desktop features you may want to change:

- **Change the screensaver** — Under the Look & Feel heading, select Desktop → Screen Saver. From the window that appears, there are only a few screensavers available by default. However, by installing the kdeartwork-extras package, you can get a lot more screensavers to choose from. Under the Start Automatically box, select how many minutes of inactivity before the screensaver turns on. You can also click Require Password to require that a password be entered before you can access your display after the screensaver has come on.

- **Change fonts** — You can assign different fonts to different places in which fonts appear on the desktop. Under the Look & Feel heading, select Appearance → Fonts. Select one of the categories of fonts (General, Fixed width, Small, Toolbar, Menu, Window title, Taskbar, and Desktop fonts). Then click the Choose box to select a font from the Select Font list box that you want to assign to that category. If the font is available, you will see an example of the text in the Sample text box.

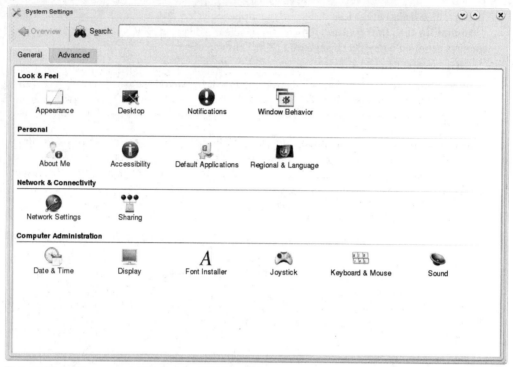

Figure 3-22: Configure your desktop from the KDE Control Center.

- **Change the colors** — Under the Look & Feel heading in the System Settings window, select Appearance → Colors. The window that appears lets you change the color of selected items on the desktop. Select a whole color scheme from the Color Scheme list box. Or select an item from the Colors tab to change a particular item. Items you can change include text, backgrounds, links, buttons, and title bars.

Adding widgets

You want to be able to quickly access the applications that you use most often. One of the best ways to make that possible is to add widgets to the panel or the desktop that can either run continuously (such as a clock or news ticker) or launch the applications you need with a single click. Procedures for adding widgets to the panel and desktop are described in the following sections.

Adding widgets to the panel

You can add any KDE widgets to the KDE panel quite easily. Here's how:

1. Right-click an place on the panel.

2. Select the widget you want to add.

3. Click Add Widget

An icon representing the widget should immediately appear on the panel. (If the panel seems a bit crowded, you might want to remove some widgets you don't use or add a widget directly to the desktop.) At this point, you can change any properties associated with the widget by right-clicking the widget in the panel and then selecting to change its settings

If you decide later that you no longer want this widget to be available on the panel, right-click it and click Remove.

Adding widgets to the desktop

To add an widget to the desktop, you can use the desktop menu. Here's how:

1. Right-click an open area of the desktop.
2. Select Add Widgets from the menu.
3. Select the widget you want from the list that appears.
4. Select Add Widget.

If you decide later that you no longer want this widget to be available on the desktop, hover the mouse over it and click the red X to delete it.

Running 3D Accelerated Desktop Effects

The goal of the Accelerated Indirect GL X project (AIGLX) is to add 3D effects to everyday desktop systems. It does this by implementing OpenGL (`http://opengl.org`) accelerated effects using the Mesa (`www.mesa3d.org`) open-source OpenGL implementation. To learn more about the AIGLX project, refer to this Web site:

`http://fedoraproject.org/wiki/RenderingProject/aiglx`

Currently, AIGLX supports a limited set of video cards and implements only a few 3D effects. However, if you have one of those cards, AIGLX features in the current version of Fedora can give you some insights into the eye candy that is to come in later Fedora and RHEL distributions.

To use AIGLX, you must have one of the following supported video cards.

- **ATI video cards** — The ATI Radeon 7000 through X850 video cards are supported. Generations r100 through r400 are included.
- **Intel video cards** — The Intel i810 and i830 through i945 Intel video cards are supported.
- **3DFX video cards** — 3DFX Voodoo3 through Voodoo5 video cards should work, but have not been tested yet. (3DFX was bought out by NVIDIA a few years ago.)

Because direct rendering infrastructure (DRI) is required for AIGLX, cards that don't support that feature cannot be used. Support for NVidia cards is under development. Although not yet officially supported, the nouveau Xorg driver is an experimental 3D open source driver for NVidia cards that comes with Fedora. Cards that are known to *not* work with AIGLX include ATI Rage 128 and Mach 64, Matrox G200 through G550, and 3DFX Voodoo 1 and 2.

If you have a supported video card, the next trick in getting AIGLX to work in Fedora is to have the right software packages installed. If you have installed the GNOME desktop, you should already have all the packages you need. Those packages include compiz (for the compiz window manager), glx-utils, gtk2-engines, mesa-libGL, mesa-libGLU, and xorg-x11-drv-ati or xorg-x11-drv-i810 (depending on which driver your video card needs).

If your video card was properly detected and configured, you may be able to simply turn on the Desktop Effects feature to see the effects that have been implemented so far. To turn on Desktop Effects from the GNOME desktop, select System → Preferences → Look and Feel → Desktop Effects. When the Desktop Effects pop-up window appears, select Enable Desktop Effects. Enabling this does the following: From the KDE desktop, open the System Settings window, then select Desktop → Desktop Effects. Then choose Enable Desktop Effects.

- Stops the current window manager (metacity, by default) and starts the Compiz window manager.

- Enables the Windows Wobble When Moved effect. With this effect on, when you grab the title bar of the window to move it, the window will wobble as it moves. Menus and other items that open on the desktop also wobble.

- Enables the Workspaces on a Cube effect. Drag a window from the desktop to the right or the left and the desktop will rotate like a cube, with each of your desktop workspaces appearing as a side of that cube. Drop the window on the workspace where you want it to go. You can also click on the Workspace Switcher applet in the bottom panel to rotate the cube to display different workspaces.

Figure 3-23 shows an example of desktop workspaces rotating on a cube.

The following are some interesting effects you can get with your 3D AIGLX desktop:

- **Spin cube** — Hold Ctrl+Alt keys and press right and left arrow keys. The desktop cube spins to each successive workspace (forward or back).

- **Slowly rotate cube** — Hold the Ctrl+Alt keys, press and hold the left mouse button, and move the mouse around on the screen. The cube will move slowly with the mouse among the workspaces.

- **Tab through windows** — Hold the Alt key and press the Tab key. You will see reduced versions of all your windows in a strip in the middle of your screen, with the current window highlighted in the middle. Still holding the Alt key, press Tab or Shift+Tab to move forward or backwards through the windows. Release the keys when the one you want is highlighted.

Figure 3-23: With AIGLX enabled for the Compiz window manager, windows wobble as you move them around on the desktop and workspaces spin on a cube.

- **Scale and separate windows** — If your desktop is cluttered, hold Ctrl+Alt and press the up arrow key. Windows will shrink down and separate on the desktop. Still holding Ctrl+Alt, use your arrow keys to highlight the window you want and release the keys to have that window come to the surface.

- **Scale and separate workspaces** — Hold Ctrl+Alt and press the down arrow key to see reduced images of the workspace shown on a strip. Still holding Ctrl+Alt, use right and left arrow keys to move among the different workspaces. Release the keys when the workspace you want is highlighted.

- **Send current window to next workspace** — Hold Ctrl+Shift+Alt keys together and press the left and right arrow keys. The current window will move to the next workspace to the left or right, respectively.

- **Slide windows around** — Press and hold the left mouse button, and then press the left, right, up, or down arrow keys to slide the current window around on the screen.

If you get tired of wobbling windows and spinning cubes, turning off the AIGLX 3D effects and returning Metacity as the window manager can be done quite simply. Just select System

→ Preferences → Look and Feel → Desktop Effects again and toggle off the Enable Desktop Effects button to turn off the feature.

If you have a supported video card, but find that you are not able to turn on the Desktop Effects, check that your X server started properly. In particular, make sure that your `/etc/X11/xorg.conf` file is properly configured. Make sure that dri and glx are loaded in the Module section. Also, add an extensions section that appears as follows:

```
Section "extensions"
 Option "Composite"
EndSection
```

Another option is to add the following line to the `/etc/X11/xorg.conf` file in the Device section:

```
Option XAANoOffscreenPixmaps"
```

The `XAANoOffscreenPixmaps` option will improve performance.

Check your `/var/log/Xorg.log.0` file to make sure that DRI and AIGLX features were started correctly. The messages in that file can help you debug other problems as well.

Using the Xfce Desktop Environment

The Xfce desktop environment provides a lightweight interface for using your Fedora or RHEL system. Because it is designed to conserve system resources and load applications quickly, Xfce is usually the best choice if you are using Fedora or RHEL on a less powerful computer (for example, if you have less than 512MB of RAM).

To meet its goals of running fast and efficiently, Xfce offers its own applications for doing many desktop operations. Here are some examples:

- **Thunar File Manager** — A fast and efficient way of managing your files and folders.
- **Xfce Application Finder** — A useful tool for finding every desktop-ready application on the system. (From the Xfce menu, select Accessories → Appfinder.)
- **Xfce Settings Manager** — Provides tools for changing desktop, display, file manager, keyboard, mouse, sound and various other desktop settings. (From the Xfce menu, select Settings → Settings Manager.)
- **Mousepad** — A simple and efficient text editor.
- **Panel Items** — Dozens of items are available to add to the Xfce panel to monitor battery life, manage clipboards, display time, search dictionaries, watch system performance, and do many other tasks.

Figure 3-24 shows an example of the Xfce desktop with a Thunar File Manager, Xfce Settings Manager, and Mousepad text editor running.

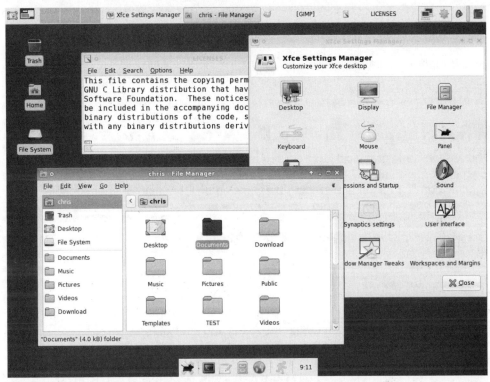

Figure 3-24: Xfce offers a lightweight desktop environment, with applications designed to launch and run quickly.

To use Xfce, you need to install the Xfce desktop packages (`yum install xfce*`). To launch an Xfce desktop, you can either select Xfce from the Sessions box on the login screen or use the switchdesk feature (described earlier in this chapter) to make Xfce your default desktop.

Troubleshooting Your Desktop

If your desktop is not functioning properly (or at all) it may be that your video card was not configured properly. This section helps you get your video card configured properly and your desktop up and running smoothly.

GUI doesn't work at start-up

If Fedora or RHEL has been successfully installed (along with the desired desktop environment) but the GUI wasn't set to start at boot time, you may see only a simple text-based login prompt when you start Fedora or RHEL. This login prompt may look something like this:

```
Fedora release 9
Kernel 2.6.25 on an i686
YourComputer login:
```

Log in as the root user. As noted earlier, you can check if you have a GUI that is at least working well enough for you to correct it. Type the following command:

```
# startx
```

What Happens During Desktop Startup?

The X server and graphical login screen is started by the `prefdm` script. By default, the login screen is displayed by the GNOME display manager (`gdm` command), which handles both logging in and starting the desktop environment for your console monitor, as well as graphical logins from other computers and X terminals.

The `prefdm` script is launched only if the run level in the `/etc/inittab` file is set to `5`, as follows:

```
id:5:initdefault:
```

If the `initdefault` state is `3`, the system boots to a text-based login prompt. See Chapter 12 for information on Linux run states and start-up processes.

Some processes started during every X session are launched from scripts in the `/etc/X11/xinit/xinitrc.d` directory. Check those scripts to see if any of the settings they include might be causing problems. (You can also use those scripts to launch applications of your own each time X starts.)

If you are unable to get the video card and monitor configured properly, or if you don't need a GUI, you can configure the computer to start up in text mode. To do this using any shell text editor (such as the `vi` command described in Chapter 4), change the `initdefault` line in the `/etc/inittab` file from `id:5:initdefault:` to `id:3:initdefault`.

If you prefer to have Fedora or RHEL boot to a GUI, change the 3 to a 5.

If the desktop works fine when you type **startx**, you might want to change to a graphical login, so the GUI starts automatically every time. See the "What Happens During Desktop Startup" sidebar for information on booting to a GUI. If X crashes, see `/var/log/Xorg.0.log` for clues about what went wrong.

If your GUI is so distorted you can't even see to correct it, switch to a virtual terminal to correct the problem. For example, hold the Ctrl and Alt keys, and press F2. You will see a plain text login prompt. Log in as root user and type **init 3** to make the garbled GUI login screen go away. As an alternative, press Ctrl+Alt+Backspace to close the X session. Then you can try tuning your video card as described in the following section.

> **TIP:** Switching virtual terminals is a great way to get out of a GUI that is broken or stuck and run the commands you need to fix a problem. You can use any function key from F1 through F8 with Ctrl+Alt to switch terminals. The GUI itself is probably on the F7 virtual terminal. Linux experts use virtual terminals during Fedora or RHEL installation to debug a problem or during startup to view text startup messages.

Tuning your video card and monitor

If your GUI is starting up but needs some tuning (to get better resolution, more colors, or to fix flickering), you can use the Display Settings window to fix your desktop. For the current Fedora and RHEL versions, the Display Settings window was enhanced so that you can use it from a command line with no GUI running. The next sections describe how to run the Display Settings window, and then how to review the resulting `xorg.conf` file to understand your settings.

Running the Display Settings window

The Fedora Project replaced the `Xconfigurator` tool with a new Display Settings window (`system-config-display` command). This window lets you set the most basic functions relating to your display, monitor, and video card. The Display Settings window is easy-to-use and no longer requires a running X desktop to use it.

To open the Display Settings window from the Desktop menu, click System →Administration → Display. To open that window from a text prompt (even with no GUI running), type **system-config-display** (as root).

From the Settings tab of the Display Settings window, you can try different resolutions (screen width and height in pixels) and color depth (from 256 colors to millions of color). Click the Hardware tab to try to configure your monitor and video card. Click the Dual head tab if you have a video card that supports two monitors that you can use side-by-side with Fedora or RHEL. Click OK to save your changes.

Here are a few tips for using the Display Settings window:

- If you know your monitor type, but it is not being detected, click the Hardware tab and then click Configure. You can select the monitor from a list of monitors (by manufacturer) or, if it's not on the list, enter information about the monitor's horizontal and vertical sync rates from the manufacturer's instructions. If you don't see you monitor on the list, check the Web to find this information for your monitor (for example, try `www.monitorworld.com/monitors_home.html`).

- If you don't know the vertical and horizontal sync rates, you can choose a generic monitor from the list. You could simply choose a generic CRT or Generic LCD at a resolution you would expect the monitor to support. Common resolutions for older monitors include 1280x1024, 1024x768, and 800x600.

Changes made in the Display Settings window result in the creation of a new /etc/X11/xorg.conf file. The next section describes what the xorg.conf file contains.

> **TIP:** If the Display Settings window fails to create a working xorg.conf file, you can try another approach. With no GUI on as root user, type the following commands from a shell:
>
> ```
> # Xorg -configure
>
> # X -xf86config /root/xorg.conf.new
> ```
>
> The first line creates xorg.conf.new in the /root directory. The second tries to start your GUI with that new config file. You should see the mouse cursor (an X) and a blank screen. If the GUI works, press Ctrl+Alt+Backspace to exit, and then copy /root/xorg.conf.new to /etc/X11/xorg.conf. You may need to run system-config-mouse to get the mouse working properly after this.

Understanding the xorg.conf file

Beginning with Fedora Core 2, the XFree86 X server was replaced by the X server from X.Org. Although that change should be invisible to most users, if you like to change X settings directly, you need to know that the main X configuration file is now /etc/X11/xorg.conf and not /etc/X11/XF86Config.

The xorg.conf file (located in the /etc/X11 directory) contains definitions used by the X server to use your video card, keyboard, mouse, and monitor. In general, novice users should not edit this file directly. For some video cards, however, manual configuration may be required to get the card working properly.

The following is a description of the basic information contained in the xorg.conf file:

- **ServerLayout section** — Binds input and output devices for your X session. Lets you set server definitions for different X servers (if necessary).
- **Module section** — Describes which X server modules should be loaded.
- **Files section** — Sets the locations of the RGB (color), modules, and fonts databases.
- **InputDevice sections** — Separate sections identify keyboard and mouse input devices.
- **Monitor section** — Sets the type of monitor, along with its horizontal sync rate, vertical refresh rate, and settings needed to operate at different resolutions.
- **Device section** — Identifies your video card and, optionally, video RAM and clock information for the chipset.
- **Screen section** — Binds the graphics board and monitor information to be referenced later by the ServerLayout section.
- **Keyboard section** — Sets keyboard settings, including the layout of the keyboard and the way certain key sequences are mapped to the keyboard.

- **Pointer section** — Selects the pointer you are using (typically a mouse linked to /dev/mouse). Also sets speed and button emulation, when appropriate.

- **DRI** — Provides information for Direct Rendering Infrastructure (used for accelerated 3D graphics).

Configuring video cards for gaming

Some games and video players require special features to work properly (or at all, in some cases). For games that require 3D hardware acceleration, including some that run under TransGaming's WineX, TransGaming recommends using NVIDIA GeForce Graphics cards.

Because only basic NVIDIA video card drivers are included in Fedora (NVIDIA's own drivers are not open source), you need to get NVIDIA drivers yourself to use those cards for gaming. You can get Linux NVIDIA drivers from www.nvidia.com/object/linux.html or you can install them from the rpm.livna.org Fedora repository.

> **CAUTION:** Some components of the video drivers from NVIDIA can conflict with those that come with Fedora or RHEL. See the section on choosing a video card for gaming in Chapter 7 for further information on getting and using NVIDIA drivers in Fedora.Games that don't require 3D hardware acceleration should work fine with most video cards that are supported by the X.Org X server drivers.

> **TIP:** To use hardware DRI acceleration on Voodoo 3 cards, you must have your display set to use 16bpp resolution. On Voodoo 5 cards, only 16bpp and 24bpp resolutions are supported. Voodoo chipsets and other 3DFX technology is now owned by NVIDIA.

Getting more information

If you tried configuring X and you still have a server that crashes or has a garbled display, your video card may either be unsupported or may require special configuration. Here are several locations you can check for further information:

- **X.Org** (www.x.org) — The latest information about the X servers that come with Fedora and RHEL is available from the X.Org Web site. X.Org is the freeware version of X recently used by many major Linux distributions to replace the XFree86 X server.

- **X documentation** — README files that are specific to different types of video cards are delivered with the X.Org X server. Visit the X doc directory (/usr/X11R6/lib/X11/doc) for a README file specific to the type of video card (or more specifically, the video chipset) you are using. A lot of good information can also be found on the xorg.conf man page (type **man** xorg.conf).

Summary

The X Window System provides the basis for most graphical user interfaces available for Fedora, RHEL, and other Linux systems today. Although X provides the framework for running and sharing applications, the GNOME, KDE, and Xfce desktop environments, along with a window manager and theme, provide the look-and-feel of your desktop.

Using various configuration files and commands, you can change nearly every aspect of your graphical environment. Backgrounds can be assigned a single color or can be filled with single or tiled graphic images. Menus can be changed or enhanced. Multiple virtual workspaces can be used and managed.

A new Online Desktop feature of GNOME represents early attempts to join online services, applications, and people on a networked desktop. Fedora's entry into the 3D hardware acceleration arena is represented by the AIGLX project. By making a few simple selections, as described in this chapter, you can have desktops that rotate on a cube and windows that wobble and fade. Look for more 3D features in the future.

After reading this chapter, you should feel comfortable working with the GNOME and KDE desktops. The next chapter should help you work from the traditional command line interface, referred to as the *shell*.

## Chapter 4

Using Linux Commands

In This Chapter

- Understanding the shell
- Using the shell
- Working with the Linux file system
- Using the vi text editor in Linux

This chapter presents a view of Linux from the shell. The *shell* is a command-line interpreter that lets you access some of the most critical Linux tools. The shell is powerful, complex, and almost completely unintuitive.

Although at first it isn't obvious how to use the shell, with the right help you can quickly learn many of the most important shell features. In Fedora and RHEL, bash is the shell command interpreter used by default (and therefore, the one used for most of the examples in this chapter). Other shells, such as csh, ksh, sh and others, are also available in Fedora and RHEL and are therefore also noted in this chapter.

This chapter is your guide to working with the Linux system commands, processes, and file system from the shell. It describes the shell environment and helps you tailor it to your needs. It also describes how to use and move around the file system.

The Shell Interface

Throughout this book, there are procedures that require you to use a shell to run commands. How you first get to a shell depends on whether your computer is configured to have a graphical user interface (GUI) or not. A desktop system, by its nature, starts with a GUI. Server systems often are run entirely from the command line. Here are ways of reaching a shell, depending on whether you have a desktop GUI running or not:

- **No desktop** — If your Linux system has no GUI (or one that isn't working at the moment), you log in from a text-based prompt and immediately begin working from the shell.

- **With desktop** — With the GNOME desktop running, you can open a Terminal window (select Applications → System Tools → Terminal) to start a shell. You can begin typing commands into the Terminal window.

If you are using a shell interface, the first thing you see is the shell prompt. The default prompt for a normal user is simply a dollar sign:

```
$
```

The default prompt for the root user is a pound sign (also called a hash mark):

```
#
```

If you use a shell other than the default bash shell in Fedora, in some cases you may see a percent sign (%) as the user prompt instead of the pound sign. For most Linux systems, the $ or # prompts are preceded by your user name, system name, and current directory name. So, for example, a login prompt for the user named jake on a computer named pine with /tmp as the current directory would appear as:

```
[jake@pine tmp]$
```

You can change the prompt to display any characters you like. You could use as your prompt the current directory, the date, the local computer name, or any string of characters. When you see a tilde (~) character as the current directory (instead of tmp as shown in the preceding code), it indicates that your home directory is the current directory. (To configure your prompt, see the section "Setting your prompt" later in this chapter.)

Although a tremendous number of features are available with the shell, it's easy to begin by just typing a few commands. Try some of the commands shown in the remainder of this section to become familiar with your current shell environment.

In the examples that follow, the $ or # symbols indicate a prompt. The prompt is followed by the command that you type and then by Enter or Return (depending on your keyboard). The lines that follow show the output that results from the command.

Checking your login session

When you log in to a Linux system, Linux views you as having a particular identity. That identity includes your user name, group name, user ID, and group ID. Linux also keeps track of your login session: it knows when you logged in, how long you have been idle, and where you logged in from.

To find out information about your identity, use the id command as follows:

```
$ id
uid=501(chris) gid=105(sales) groups=105(sales),4(adm),7(lp)
    context=user_u:system_r:unconfined_t
```

This shows that the user name is chris, which is represented by the numeric user ID (uid) 501. Here, the primary group for chris is called sales, which has a group ID (gid) of 105. Chris also belongs to other groups called adm (gid 4) and lp (gid 7). These names and numbers represent the permissions that chris has to access computer resources. (Permissions are described later in this chapter in the section on working with files.)

If your computer has SELinux enabled, the id command also shows context information. In this example, you see context=user_u:system_r:unconfined_t on id output. See Chapter 10 for information on SELinux.

You can see information about your current login session by using the who command. In the following example, the -m option tells the who command to print information about the current user, -u says to add information about idle time and the process ID, and -H asks that a header be printed:

```
$ who -umH
NAME          LINE          TIME                 IDLE      PID     COMMENT
chris         tty1          Jun 13 20:57           .        2013
```

The output from this who command shows that the user name is chris. Here, chris is logged in on tty1 (which is the monitor connected to the computer), and his login session began at 20:57 on June 13. The IDLE time shows how long the shell has been open without any command being typed (the dot indicates that it is currently active). COMMENT would show the name of the remote computer the user had logged in from, if that user had logged in from another computer on the network, or the name of the local X display if you were using a Terminal window (such as :0.0).

Checking directories and permissions

Associated with each shell is a location in the Linux file system known as the *current* or *working directory*. As previously mentioned, each user has a directory that is identified as the user's home directory. When you first log in to Linux, you begin with your home directory as the current directory.

When you request to open or save a file, your shell uses the current directory as the point of reference. Simply give a filename when you save a file, and it will be placed in the current directory. Alternatively, you can identify a file by its relation to the current directory (relative path). Or you can ignore the current directory and identify a file by the full directory hierarchy that locates it (absolute path). The structure and use of the file system is described in detail later in this chapter.

To find out what your current directory is, type the pwd command:

```
$ pwd
/usr/bin
```

In this example, the current or working directory is /usr/bin. To find out the name of your home directory, type the echo command, followed by the $HOME variable:

```
$ echo $HOME
/home/chris
```

In the preceding example, the home directory is /home/chris. To get back to your home directory, you can simply type the change directory (cd) command. Although cd, followed by a directory name, changes the current directory to the directory that you choose, simply typing cd (with no directory name) takes you to your home directory:

```
$ cd
```

You can also use the tilde (~) character to indicate the home directory. So cd ~ would have the same result as just cd. This is useful when changing to long paths in your home directory (such as ~/local/files, instead of /home/chris/local/files).

At this point, list the contents of your home directory, using the ls command. Either you can type the full path to your home directory to list its contents, or you can use the ls command without a directory name to list the contents of the current directory. Using the -a option to ls enables you to view the hidden files (dot files) as well as all other files. With the -l option, you can see a long, detailed list of information on each file. (You can put multiple single-letter options together after a single dash, for example, -la.)

```
$ ls -la /home/chris
total 158
drwxrwxrwx    2    chris    sales     1024   May 12 13:55 .
drwxr-xr-x    3    root     root      1024   May 10 01:49 ..
-rw-------    1    chris    sales     2204   May 18 21:30 .bash_history
-rw-r--r--    1    chris    sales       24   May 10 01:50 .bash_logout
-rw-r--r--    1    chris    sales      230   May 10 01:50 .bash_profile
-rw-r--r--    1    chris    sales      124   May 10 01:50 .bashrc
drw-r--r--    1    chris    sales     4096   May 10 01:50 .kde
-rw-rw-r--    1    chris    sales   149872   May 11 22:49 letter
```

Displaying a long list (-l option) of the contents of your home directory shows you more about file sizes and directories. Directories such as the current directory (.) and the directory above the current directory (..) are noted as directories by the letter d at the beginning of each entry. In this case, dot (.) represents /home/chris and two dots (..), which is also referred to as the parent directory, represent /home. The /home directory is owned by root. All other files are owned by the user chris (who belongs to the sales group).

The file or directory names shown on the right are mostly dot (.) files that are used to store GUI properties (.kde directory) or shell properties (.bash files). The only non-dot file shown in this example is the one named letter. At the beginning of each line is the permissions set for each file. (Permissions and configuring shell property files are described later in this chapter.) Other information in the listing includes the size of each file in bytes (column 4) and the date and time each file was most recently modified (column 5).

> **NOTE:** A symbolic link is a file that points to another file, effectively allowing you to have multiple filenames representing a single physical file. Permissions for a symbolic link appears as lrwxrwxrwx, but are not interpreted as full read/write/execute permissions. If you try to open a symbolic link, the permissions on the file that link points to (the original file) determine whether or not you can access the file.

Checking system activity

In addition to being a multiuser operating system, Linux is also a multitasking system. *Multitasking* means that many programs can be running at the same time. An instance of a running program is referred to as a *process*. Linux provides tools for listing running processes, monitoring system usage, and stopping (or killing) processes when necessary.

The most common utility for checking running processes is the ps command. With ps, you can see which programs are running, the resources they are using, and who is running them. The following is an example of the ps command:

```
$ ps au
USER    PID %CPU %MEM  VSZ    RSS    TTY     STAT START  TIME COMMAND
root    2146 0.0  0.8 1908   1100   tty0    Ss+  14:50  0:00 login -- jake
jake    2147 0.0  0.7 1836   1020   tty0    Ss+  14:50  0:00 -bash
jake    2310 0.0  0.7 2592    912    tty0   R+   18:22  0:00 ps au
```

In this example, the a option asks to show processes of all users who are associated with your current terminal, and the u option asks that user names be shown, as well as other information such as the time the process started and memory and CPU usage. The concept of terminal comes from the old days, when people worked exclusively from character terminals, so a terminal typically represented a single person at a single screen. Now you can have many "terminals" on one screen by opening multiple Terminal windows.

On this shell session, there isn't much happening. The first process shows that the user named jake logged in to the login process (which is controlled by the root user). The next process shows that jake is using a bash shell and has just run the ps au command. The terminal device ttyp0 is being used for the login session. The STAT column represents the state of the process, with R indicating a currently running process and S representing a sleeping process. (A *sleeping* process is one that is still active, but is waiting for some event to complete before continuing. It may be waiting for someone to type something at a shell or for a process to send information it requested.) A small s indicates a session leader and + indicates the foreground process group.

The USER column shows the name of the user who started the process. Each process is represented by a unique ID number, referred to as a process ID (PID). (You can use the PID if you ever need to kill a runaway process.) The %CPU and %MEM columns show the percentage of the processor and random access memory, respectively, that the process is consuming. VSZ (virtual set size) shows the size of the image process (in kilobytes), and RSS (resident set size) shows the size of the program in memory. START shows the time the process began running, and TIME shows the cumulative system time used.

Many processes running on a computer are not associated with a terminal. A normal Linux system has many processes running in the background. Background system processes perform such tasks as logging system activity or listening for data coming in from the network. They are often started when Linux boots up and run continuously until it shuts down. To see and thereby monitor all the processes running on your Linux system, type:

```
$ ps au | less
```

I added the pipe (|) and the less command to ps au to allow you to page through the many processes that will appear on your screen. A pipe lets you direct the output of one command to be the input of the next command. Use the spacebar to page through, and type **q** to end the list. You can also use the arrow keys to move one line at a time through the output.

Exiting the shell

To exit the shell when you are done, type **exit** or press Ctrl+D.

I just showed a few commands designed to familiarize you quickly with your Linux system. Hundreds of other commands that you can try are contained in directories such as /bin and /usr/bin. There are also administrative commands in /sbin or /usr/sbin directories. Many of these commands are described in the remainder of this chapter.

Understanding the Shell

Before icons and windows took over computer screens, you typed commands to interact with most computers. On UNIX systems, from which Linux was derived, the program used to interpret and manage commands was referred to as the *shell*.

The shell provides a way to run programs, work with the file system, compile computer code, and manage the computer. Although the shell is less intuitive than common GUIs, most Linux experts consider the shell to be much more powerful than GUIs. Because shells have been around for so long, many advanced features have been built into them. Many old-school Linux administrators and programmers primarily use a GUI as a way to open lots of shells.

The Linux shell illustrated in this chapter is called the *bash* shell, which stands for Bourne Again SHell. The name is derived from the fact that bash is compatible with the first UNIX shell: the Bourne shell (represented by the sh command). Other popular shells include the C shell (*csh*), which is popular among BSD UNIX users, and the Korn shell (*ksh*), which is popular among UNIX System V users. Linux also has a *tcsh* shell (a C shell look-alike) and an *ash* shell (another Bourne shell look-alike).

> **NOTE**: While you can invoke the Bourne shell with /bin/sh, the command actually runs the bash shell in sh compatibility mode. Running /bin/sh produces a shell that behaves more like sh than bash, but you will probably be able to use bash scripting concepts that the real Bourne shell wouldn't recognize. The sh shell still exists primarily for compatibility with scripts that were written specifically for that shell.

Although most Linux users have a preference for one shell or another, when you know how to use one shell, you can quickly learn any of the others by occasionally referring to the shell's man page (for example, type **man bash**). The bash shell is roughly compatible with the sh shell.

Using the Shell in Linux

When you type a command in a shell, you can also include other characters that change or add to how the command works. In addition to the command itself, these are some of the other items that you can type on a shell command line:

- **Options** — Most commands have one or more options you can add to change their behavior. Options typically consist of a single letter, preceded by a dash. You can also often combine several options after a single dash. For example, the command ls -la lists the contents of the current directory. The -l asks for a detailed (long) list of information, and the -a asks that files beginning with a dot (.) also be listed. When a single option consists of a word, it is usually preceded by a double dash (--). For example, to use the help option on many commands, you would enter --help on the command line. Here's an example of help information for the ls command (Output is piped to the less command to page through it; type **q** to quit):

```
$ ls --help | less
Usage: ls [OPTION]... [FILE]...
List information about the FILEs (the current directory by default).
Sort entries alphabetically if none of the -cftuSUX nor --sort.

Mandatory arguments to long options are mandatory for short options too
  -a, --all               do not hide entries starting with .
  -A, --almost-all        do not list implied . and ..
    .
    .
    .
```

- **Arguments** — Many commands also accept arguments after any options are entered. An argument is an extra piece of information, such as a filename, that can be used by the command. For example, cat /etc/passwd displays the contents of the /etc/passwd file on your screen. In this case, /etc/passwd is the argument.

- **Environment variables** — The shell itself stores information that may be useful to the user's shell session in what are called *environment variables*. Examples of environment variables include $SHELL (which identifies the shell you are using), $PS1 (which defines your shell prompt), and $MAIL (which identifies the location of your mailbox).

> **TIP:** You can check your environment variables at any time. Type **declare** to list the current environment variables. Or you can type echo $*VALUE*, where *VALUE* is replaced by the name of a particular environment variable you want to list.

- **Metacharacters** — These are characters that have special meaning to the shell. Metacharacters can be used to direct the output of a command to a file (>), pipe the output to another command (|), or run a command in the background (&), to name a few. Metacharacters are discussed later in this chapter.

To save you some typing, there are shell features that store commands you want to reuse, recall previous commands, and edit commands. You can create aliases that allow you to type a short command to run a longer one. The shell stores previously entered commands in a history list, which you can display and from which you can recall commands. This is discussed further in the remainder of this section.

Unless you specifically change to another shell, the bash shell is the one you use with Fedora or RHEL. The bash shell contains most of the powerful features available in other shells. Although the description in this chapter steps you through many bash shell features, you can learn more about the bash shell by typing man bash. For other ways to learn about using the shell, refer to the sidebar "Getting Help with Using the Shell."

Locating commands

If you know the directory that contains the command you want to run, one way to run it is to type the full path to that command. For example, you run the date command from the /bin directory by typing:

```
$ /bin/date
```

Of course, this can be inconvenient, especially if the command resides in a directory with a long name. The better way is to have commands stored in well-known directories, and then add those directories to your shell's PATH environment variable. The path consists of a list of directories that are checked sequentially for the commands you enter. To see your current path, type the following:

```
$ echo $PATH
/usr/kerberos/bin:/usr/local/bin:/bin:/usr/bin:/usr/X11R6/bin:/home/chris/bin
```

The results show the default path for a regular Linux user. Directories in the path list are separated by colons. Most user commands that come with Linux are stored in the /bin, /usr/bin, or /usr/local/bin directories. Although most graphical commands (that are used with GUIs) are contained in /usr/bin, there are some special X commands that are in /usr/bin/X11 and /usr/X11R6/bin directories. The last directory shown is the bin directory in the user's home directory. (In Fedora and RHEL systems, the /usr/kerberos/bin directory precedes other directories so that if you are doing network authentication with Kerberos, the Kerberos versions of many network clients are used instead of the regular Linux versions.)

TIP: If you want to add your own commands or shell scripts, place them in the `bin` directory in your home directory (such as `/home/chris/bin` for the user named chris). This directory is automatically added to your path (although you must type `mkdir $HOME/bin` to create the directory). As long as you add the command to your bin with execute permission (described in the "Understanding file permissions" section), you can immediately begin using the command by simply typing the command name at your shell prompt.

Getting Help with Using the Shell

When you first start using the shell, it can be intimidating. All you see is a prompt. How do you know which commands are available, which options they use, or how to use more advanced features? Fortunately, lots of help is available. Here are some places you can look to supplement what you learn in this chapter:

- Check the PATH — Type `echo $PATH`. You see a list of the directories containing commands that are immediately accessible to you. Listing the contents of those directories (with the `ls` command) displays most standard Linux commands.

- Use the `help` command — Some commands are built into the shell, so they do not appear in a directory. The `help` command lists those commands and shows options available with each of them. (Type `help | less` to page through the list.) For help with a particular built-in command, type `help command`, replacing *command* with the name that interests you. The `help` command works with the bash shell only.

- Use `--help` with the command — Many commands include a `--help` option that you can use to get information about how the command is used. For example, type `date --help | less`. The output shows not only options, but also time formats you can use with the date command.

- Use the `man` command — To learn more about a particular command, type `man command`. (Replace *command* with the command name you want.) The command name `man` is short for manual. A description of the command and its options appears on the screen.

- Use the `info` command — Command descriptions that aren't available on man pages are often availble for the info facility. Type `info command` to see a text-based interface for stepping through information on the command.

If you are the root user, directories containing administrative commands are in your path. These directories include `/sbin` and `/usr/sbin`.

The path directory order is important. Directories are checked from left to right. So, in this example, if there is a command called `foo` located in both the `/bin` and `/usr/bin` directories, the one in `/bin` is executed. To have the other `foo` command run, you either type the full path to the command or change your PATH variable. (Changing your PATH and adding directories to it are described later in this chapter.)

Not all the commands that you run are located in directories in your PATH. Some commands are built into the shell. Other commands can be overridden by creating aliases that define any commands and options that you want the command to run. There are also ways of defining a function that consists of a stored series of commands. Here is the order in which the shell checks for the commands you type:

1. **Aliases** — Names set by the `alias` command that represent a particular command and a set of options. (Type **alias** to see what aliases are set.) Often, aliases allow you to define a short name for a long, complicated command. Some users use aliases to map a command name from another operating system to the similar utility in Linux.

2. **Shell reserved word** — Words that are reserved by the shell for special use. Many of these are words that you would use in programming-type functions, such as `do`, `while`, `case`, and `else`.

3. **Function** — A set of commands that are executed together within the current shell.

4. **Built-in command** — A command that is built into the shell.

5. **File system command** — This is a command that is stored in and executed from the computer's file system. (These are the commands that are indicated by the value of the PATH variable.)

To find out where a particular command is taken from, you can use the `type` command. (If you are using a shell other than `bash`, use the `which` command instead.) For example, to find out where the bash shell command is located, type the following:

```
$ type bash
bash is /bin/bash
```

Try these few words with the `type` command to see other locations of commands: `which`, `case`, and `return`. If a command resides in several locations, you can add the `-a` option to have all the known locations of the command printed.

> **TIP:** Sometimes you run a command and receive an error message that the command was not found or that permission to run the command was denied. In the first case, check that you spelled the command correctly and that it is located in your PATH. In the second case, the command may be in the PATH, but may not be executable. Adding execute permissions to a command is described later in this chapter.

Rerunning commands

It's annoying, after typing a long or complex command line, to learn that you mistyped something. Fortunately, some shell features let you recall previous command lines, edit those lines, or complete a partially typed command line.

The *shell history* is a list of the commands that you have entered before. Using the `history` command, you can view your previous commands. Then, using various shell features, you can recall individual command lines from that list and change them however you please.

The rest of this section describes how to do command-line editing, how to complete parts of command lines, and how to recall and work with the history list.

Command-line editing

If you type something wrong on a command line, the bash shell ensures that you don't have to delete the entire line and start over. Likewise, you can recall a previous command line and change the elements to make a new command.

By default, the bash shell uses command-line editing that is based on the `emacs` text editor. So, if you are familiar with `emacs`, you probably already know most of the keystrokes described here.

> **TIP:** If you prefer the `vi` command for editing shell command lines, you can easily make that happen. Add the line
>
> ```
> set -o vi
> ```
>
> to the `.bashrc` file in your home directory. The next time you open a shell, you can use `vi` commands (as described in the tutorial later in this chapter) to edit your command lines.

To do the editing, you can use a combination of control keys, meta keys, and arrow keys. For example, Ctrl+f means to hold the Control key and type f. Alt+f means to hold the Alt key and type f. (Instead of the Alt key, your keyboard may use a meta key or the Esc key instead. On a Windows keyboard, you can sometimes use the Windows key.)

To try out a bit of command-line editing, type the following command:

```
$ ls /usr/bin | sort -f | less
```

This command lists the contents of the /usr/bin directory, sorts the contents in alphabetical order (regardless of upper- and lowercase), and pipes the output to `less` (so you can page through the results). Now, suppose you want to change /usr/bin to /bin. You can use the following steps to change the command:

1. Press Ctrl+a. This moves the cursor to the beginning of the command line.

2. Press Ctrl+f or the right arrow (→) key. Repeat this command a few times to position the cursor under the first slash (/).

3. Press Ctrl+d. Type this command four times to delete /usr.

4. Press Enter. This executes the command line.

As you edit a command line, at any point you can type regular characters to add those characters to the command line. The characters appear at the location of your cursor. You can use right (→) and left (←) arrows to move the cursor from one end to the other on the command line. You can also press the up (↑) and down (↓) arrow keys to step through previous commands in the history list to select a command line for editing. (See the section "Command-line recall" for details on how to recall commands from the history list.)

There are many keystrokes you can use to edit your command lines. Table 4-1 lists the keystrokes that you can use to move around the command line.

Table 4-1: Keystrokes for Navigating Command Lines

Keystroke	Full Name	Meaning
Ctrl+f	Character forward	Go forward one character.
Ctrl+b	Character backward	Go backward one character.
Alt+f	Word forward	Go forward one word.
Alt+b	Word backward	Go backward one word.
Ctrl+a (Home key)	Beginning of line	Go to the beginning of the current line.
Ctrl+e (End key)	End of line	Go to the end of the line.
Ctrl+l	Clear screen	Clear screen and leave line at the top of the screen.

Table 4-2 lists the keystrokes for editing command lines.

Table 4-2: Keystrokes for Editing Command Lines

Keystroke	Full Name	Meaning
Ctrl+d	Delete current	Delete the current character.
Backspace or Rubout	Delete previous	Delete the previous character.
Ctrl+t	Transpose character	Switch positions of current and previous characters.
Alt+t	Transpose words	Switch positions of current and previous characters.
Alt+u	Uppercase word	Change the current word to uppercase.
Alt+l	Lowercase word	Change the current word to lowercase.
Alt+c	Capitalize word	Change the current word to an initial capital.
Ctrl+v	Insert special character	Add a special character. For example, to add a Tab character, press Ctrl+v+Tab.

Table 4-3 lists the keystrokes for cutting and pasting text on a command line.

Table 4-3: Keystrokes for Cutting and Pasting Text in Command Lines

Keystroke	Description
Ctrl+k	Cut text to the end of the line.
Ctrl+u	Cut text to the beginning of the line.
Ctrl+w	Cut the word located behind the cursor.
Alt+d	Cut the word following the cursor.
Ctrl+y	Paste most recently cut text.
Alt+y	Rotate back to previously cut text and paste it.
Ctrl+c	Delete the entire line.

Command-line completion

To save you a few keystrokes, the bash shell offers several different ways of completing partially typed values. To attempt to complete a value, type the first few characters, and then press Tab. Here are some of the values you can type partially:

- **Environment variable** — If the text begins with a dollar sign ($), the shell completes the text with an environment variable from the current shell.

- **User name** — If the text begins with a tilde (~), the shell completes the text with a user name. (This is actually just a case of file or directory expansion. For example, ~chr might expand to ~chris/, which would identify the home directory /home/chris.)

- **Command, alias, or function** — If the text begins with regular characters, the shell tries to complete the text with a command, alias, or function name.

- **Filenames** — After a command has been typed, anything beginning with a / or regular characters is completed as a path to a directory or filename. This is one of the most common forms of command-line completion because it can help you traverse directory paths with long names or complete long filenames.

- **Hostname** — If the text begins with an at (@) sign, the shell completes the text with a hostname taken from the /etc/hosts file.

> **TIP:** To add hostnames from an additional file, you can set the HOSTFILE variable to the name of that file. The file must be in the same format as /etc/hosts.

Here are a few examples of command completion. (When you see <Tab>, it means to press the Tab key on your keyboard.) Type the following:

```
$ echo $OS<Tab>
$ cd ~ro<Tab>
$ fing<Tab>
$ cat /etc/fed<Tab>
$ mail root@loc<Tab>
```

The first example causes $OS to expand to the $OSTYPE variable. In the next example, ~ro expands to the root user's home directory (~root/). Next, fing expands to the finger command. After that, /etc/fed expands to /etc/fedora-release, so you can see your current release of Fedora. Finally, the address of root@loc expands to computer name localhost.

Of course, there will be times when there are several possible completions for the string of characters you have entered. In that case, you can check the possible ways text can be expanded by pressing Tab twice at the point where you want to do completion. The following code shows the result you would get if you checked for possible completions on $P.

```
$ echo $P<Tab><Tab>
$PATH $PPID $PS1 $PS2 $PS4 $PWD
$ echo $P
```

In this case, there are six possible variables that begin with $P. After possibilities are displayed, the original command line returns, ready for you to complete it as you choose.

If text you are trying to complete is not preceded by a $, ~, or @, you can still try to complete the text with a variable, user name, or hostname. Press the following to complete your text:

- **Alt+~** — Complete the text before this point as a user name.
- **Alt+$** — Complete the text before this point as a variable.
- **Alt+@** — Complete the text before this point as a hostname.
- **Ctrl+x+~** — List possible user name text completions.
- **Ctrl+x+$** — List possible environment variable completions.
- **Ctrl+x+@** — List possible hostname completions.
- **Ctrl+x+!** — List possible command name completions.

> **NOTE:** You may find that only the Alt key on the left side of your keyboard works with the preceding examples. Also, remember that characters such as the tilde (~) and dollar sign ($) require the Shift key, as well as the Alt or Ctrl keys.

Command-line recall

After you type a command line, that entire command line is saved in your shell's history list. The list is stored in a history file, from which any command can be recalled to run again. After it is recalled, you can modify the command line, as described earlier.

To view your history list, use the `history` command. Type the command without options or followed by a number to list that many of the most recent commands. For example:

```
$ history 8
 382 date
 383 ls /usr/bin | sort -a | more
 384 man sort
 385 cd /usr/local/bin
 386 man more
 387 useradd -m /home/chris -u 101 chris
 388 passwd chris
 389 history 8
```

A number precedes each command line in the list, using an exclamation point (!). Keep in mind that with an exclamation point, the command is run blind, without giving you a chance to confirm. There are several ways to run a command immediately from this list, including the following:

- **Run Command Number (!*n*)** — Replace the *n* with the number of the command line, and the command line indicated is run. For example, to repeat the `date` command shown as command number 382 from the previous history listing, you could type the following:

```
$ !382
date
Thu May 13 21:30:06 PDT 2008
```

- **Run Previous Command (!!)** — Runs the previous command line. To run that same `date` command again immediately, type the following:

```
$ !!
date
Thu May 13 21:30:39 PDT 2008
```

- **Run Command Containing String (!?*string*?)** — Runs the most recent command that contains a particular *string* of characters. For example, you could run the `date` command again by just searching for part of that command line as follows:

```
$ !?dat?
date
Thu May 15 21:32:41 PDT 2008
```

Instead of just running a `history` command line immediately, you can recall a particular line and edit it. You can use these keys to do that:

- **Step (Arrow Keys)** — Press the up (↑) and down (↓) arrow keys to step through each command line in your history list to arrive at the one you want. (Ctrl+p and Ctrl+n do the same functions, respectively.)

- **Reverse Incremental Search (Ctrl+r)** — After you press these keys, you are asked to enter a search string to do a reverse search. As you type the string, a matching command line appears that you can run or edit.

- **Reverse Search (Alt+p)** — After you press these keys, you are asked to enter a string to do a reverse search. Type a string and press Enter to see the most recent command line that includes that string.

- **Forward Search (Alt+n)** — After you press these keys, you are asked to enter a string to do a forward search. Type a string, and press Enter to see the most recent command line that includes that string.

- **Beginning of History List (Alt+<)** — Brings you to the first entry of the history list.

- **End of History List (Alt+>)** — Brings you to the last entry of the history list.

Another way to work with your history list is to use the `fc` command. Type **fc** followed by a history line number, and that command line is opened in a text editor. Make the changes that you want. When you exit the editor, the command runs. You can also give a range of line numbers (for example, `fc 100 105`). All the commands open in your text editor, and then run one after the other when you exit the editor.

The history list is stored in the `.bash_history` file in your home directory. Up to 1000 history commands are stored for you by default.

Connecting and expanding commands

A truly powerful feature of the shell is the capability to redirect the input and output of commands to and from other commands and files. To allow commands to be strung together, the shell uses metacharacters. As noted earlier, a metacharacter is a typed character that has special meaning to the shell for connecting commands or requesting expansion.

Piping commands

The pipe (`|`) metacharacter connects the output from one command to the input of another command. This lets you have one command work on some data, and then have the next command deal with the results. Here is an example of a command line that includes pipes:

```
$ cat /etc/password | sort | cut -f1,5 -d: | less
```

This command lists the contents of the `/etc/password` file and pipes the output to the `sort` command. The `sort` command takes the user names that begin each line of the `/etc/password` file, sorts them alphabetically, and pipes the output to the `cut` command. The `cut` command takes fields 1 and 5, with the fields delimited by a colon (`:`), then pipes the output to the `less` command. The `less` command displays the output one page at a time, so that you can go through the output a line or a page at a time (press q to quit at the end of the output).

Pipes are an excellent illustration of how UNIX, the predecessor of Linux, was created as an operating system made up of building blocks. A standard practice in UNIX was to connect utilities in different ways to get different jobs done. For example, before the days of graphical word processors, users created plain-text files that included macros to indicate formatting. To see how the document really appeared, they used a command such as the following:

```
$ gunzip < /usr/share/man/man1/grep.1.gz | nroff -c -man | less
```

In this example, the contents of the `grep` man page (`grep.1.gz`) are directed as input to the `gunzip` command to be unzipped. The output from `gunzip` is piped to the `nroff` command to format the man page using the manual macro (`-man`). The output is piped to the `less` command to display the output. Because the file being displayed is in plain text, you could have substituted any number of options to work with the text before displaying it. You could sort the contents, change or delete some of the content, or bring in text from other documents. The key is that, instead of all those features being in one program, you get results from piping and redirecting input and output between multiple commands.

Sequential commands

Sometimes you may want a sequence of commands to run, with one command completing before the next command begins. You can do this by typing several commands on the same command line and separating them with semicolons (`;`):

```
$ date ; troff -me verylargedocument | lpr ; date
```

In this example, I was formatting a huge document and wanted to know how long it would take. The first command (`date`) showed the date and time before the formatting started. The `troff` command formatted the document and then piped the output to the printer. When the formatting was done, the date and time was printed again (so I knew when the `troff` command completed).

Background commands

Some commands can take a while to complete. Sometimes you may not want to tie up your shell waiting for a command to finish. In those cases, you can have the commands run in the background by using the ampersand (`&`).

Text formatting commands (such as `nroff` and `troff`, described earlier) are examples of commands that are often run in the background to format a large document. You also might want to create your own shell scripts that run in the background to check continuously for certain events to occur, such as the hard disk filling up or particular users logging in.

Here is an example of a command being run in the background:

```
$ troff -me verylargedocument | lpr &
```

There are other ways to manage background and foreground processes (described in the "Managing background and foreground processes" section).

Expanding commands

With command substitution, you can have the output of a command interpreted by the shell instead of by the command itself. In this way, you can have the standard output of a command become an argument for another command. The two forms of command substitution are $(command) or `command`. (The first case is the preferred method.)

The command in this case can include options, metacharacters, and arguments. Here is an example of using command substitution:

```
$ vi $(find /home | grep xyzzy)
```

In this command line, the command substitution is done before the vi command is run. First, the find command starts at the /home directory and prints out all files and directories below that point in the file system. This output is piped to the grep command, which filters out all files except for those that include the string xyzzy. Finally, the vi command opens all filenames for editing (one at a time) that include xyzzy.

This particular example might be useful if you knew that you wanted to edit a file for which you knew the name but not the location. As long as the string was uncommon, you could find and open every instance of a filename existing beneath a point you choose in the file system.

Expanding arithmetic expressions

There may be times when you want to pass arithmetic results to a command. There are two forms you can use to expand an arithmetic expression and pass it to the shell: $[expression] or $((expression)). Here is an example:

```
$ echo "I am $[2008 - 1957] years old."
I am 51 years old.
```

In this example, the shell interprets the arithmetic expression first (2008 - 1957), and then passes that information to the echo command. The echo command displays the text, with the results of the arithmetic (51) inserted.

Expanding variables

Environment variables that store information within the shell can be expanded using the dollar sign ($) metacharacter. When you expand an environment variable on a command line, the value of the variable is printed instead of the variable name itself, as follows:

```
$ ls -l $BASH
-rwxr-xr-x 1 root   root   625516 Dec 5 11:13 /bin/bash
```

Using $BASH as an argument to ls -l causes a long listing of the bash command to be printed. For more information on shell environment variables, see the following section.

Using shell environment variables

Every active shell stores pieces of information that it needs to use in what are called *environment variables.* An environment variable can store things such as locations of configuration files, mailboxes, and path directories. They can also store values for your shell prompts, the size of your history list, and type of operating system.

To see the environment variables currently assigned to your shell, type the **declare** command. (It will probably fill more than one screen, so type **declare | more.**) You can refer to the value of any of those variables by preceding it with a dollar sign ($) and placing it anywhere on a command line. For example:

```
$ echo $USER
chris
```

This command prints the value of the USER variable, which holds your user name (chris). Substitute any other variable name for USER to print its value instead.

Common shell environment variables

When you start a shell (by logging in or opening a Terminal window), a lot of environment variables are already set. Here are some variables that are either set when you use a bash shell or that can be set by you to use with different features:

- BASH— Contains the full path name of the bash command. This is usually /bin/bash.

- BASH_VERSION — A number of the current version of the bash command.

- EUID — This is the effective user ID number of the current user. It is assigned when the shell starts, based on the user's entry in the /etc/passwd file.

- FCEDIT — If set, this variable indicates the text editor used by the fc command to edit history commands. If this variable isn't set, the vi command is used.

- HISTFILE — The location of your history file. It is typically located at $HOME/.bash_history.

- HISTFILESIZE — The number of history entries that can be stored. After this number is reached, the oldest commands are discarded. The default value is 1000.

- HISTCMD — This returns the number of the current command in the history list.

- HOME — This is your home directory. It is your current working directory each time you log in or type the cd command with any options.

- HOSTTYPE — A value that describes the computer architecture on which the Linux system is running. For Intel-compatible PCs, the value is i386, i486, i586, i686, or something like i386-linux. For AMD 64-bit and Intel EM64T machines, the value is x86_64. There is also ppc and ppc64, for Apple computers (PowerPC 32-bit and 64-bit).

- MAIL — This is the location of your mailbox file. The file is typically your user name in the `/var/spool/mail` directory.

- OLDPWD — The directory that was the working directory before you changed to the current working directory.

- OSTYPE — A name identifying the current operating system. For Fedora and RHEL, the OSTYPE value is either linux or linux-gnu, depending on the type of shell you are using. (Bash can run on other operating systems as well.)

- PATH — The colon-separated list of directories used to find commands that you type. The default value for regular users is:

```
/usr/kerberos/bin:/usr/local/bin:/usr/bin:/bin: /home/chris/bin
```

For the root user, the value also includes `/sbin`, `/usr/sbin`, and `/usr/local/sbin`.

- PPID — The process ID of the command that started the current shell (for example, its parent process).

- PROMPT_COMMAND — Can be set to a command name that is run each time before your shell prompt is displayed. Setting PROMPT_COMMAND=date lists the current date and time before the prompt appears.

- PS1 — Sets the value of your shell prompt. There are many items that you can read into your prompt (date, time, user name, hostname, and so on). Sometimes a command requires additional prompts, which you can set with the variables PS2, PS3, and so on. (Setting your prompt is described later in this chapter.)

- PWD — This is the directory that is assigned as your current directory. This value changes each time you change directories using the `cd` command.

- RANDOM — Accessing this variable causes a random number to be generated. The number is between 0 and 32767.

- SECONDS — The number of seconds since the time the shell was started.

- SHLVL — The number of shell levels associated with the current shell session. When you log in to the shell, the SHLVL is 1. Each time you start a new bash command (by, for example, using su to become a new user, or by simply typing bash), this number is incremented.

- TMOUT — Can be set to a number representing the number of seconds the shell can be idle without receiving input. After the number of seconds is reached, the shell exits. This is a security feature that makes it less likely for unattended shells to be accessed by unauthorized people. (This must be set in the login shell for it to actually cause the shell to log out the user. You can use it in any terminal session to close the current shell after a set number of seconds, for example TMOUT=30)

- UID — The user ID number assigned to your user name. The user ID number is stored in the `/etc/password` file.

Setting your own environment variables

Environment variables can provide a handy way of storing bits of information that you use often from the shell. You can create any variables that you want (avoiding those that are already in use) so that you can read in the values of those variables as you use the shell. (The `bash` man page lists variables already in use.)

To set an environment variable temporarily, you can simply type a variable name and assign it to a value. Here is an example:

```
$ AB=/usr/dog/contagious/ringbearer/grind/ ; export AB
```

This example causes a long directory path to be assigned to the `AB` variable. The `export AB` command says to export the value to the shell so that it can be propagated to other shells you may open. With `AB` set, you can go to the directory by typing the following:

```
$ cd $AB
```

> **TIP:** You may have noticed that environment variables shown here are in all caps. Although case does matter with these variables, setting them as uppercase is a convention, not a necessity. You could just as easily set a variable to `xyz` as to `XYZ` (variables are case sensitive so they are not the same, but either will work if you use case consistently).

The problem with setting environment variables in this way is that as soon as you exit the shell in which you set the variable, the setting is lost. To set variables more permanently, you should add variable settings to a bash configuration file, as described later in this section.

If you want to have other text right up against the output from an environment variable, you can surround the variable in braces. This protects the variable name from being misunderstood. For example, if you want to add a command name to the `AB` variable shown earlier, you can type the following:

```
$ echo ${AB}adventure
/usr/dog/contagious/ringbearer/grind/adventure
```

Remember that you must export the variable so that it can be picked up by other shell commands. You must add the export line to a shell configuration file for it to take effect the next time you log in. The `export` command is fairly flexible. Instead of running the `export` command after you set the variable, you can do it all in one step, as follows:

```
$ export XYZ=/home/xyz/bin
```

You can override the value of any environment variable. This can be temporary by simply typing the new value. Or you can add the new export line to your $HOME/`.bashrc` file. One useful variable to update is `PATH`. Here is an example:

```
$ export PATH=$PATH:/home/xyz/bin
```

In this example, I added the /home/xyz/bin directory to the `PATH`, a useful technique if you want to run a bunch of commands from a directory that is not normally in your `PATH`, without typing the full or relative path each time. Remember that the order of the PATH is important. If /home/xyz/bin/ls preceded $PATH and the /home/xyz/bin/ls command existed, typing **ls** would use that command instead of /bin/ls.

If you decide that you no longer want a variable to be set, you can use the unset command to erase its value. For example, you could type unset XYZ, which would cause XYZ to have no value set. (Remember to remove the export from the $HOME/.bashrc file — if you added it there — or it will return the next time you open a shell.)

Managing background and foreground processes

If you are using Linux over a network or from a *dumb* terminal (a monitor that allows only text input with no GUI support), your shell may be all that you have. You may be used to a windowing environment where you have a lot of programs active at the same time so that you can switch among them as needed. This shell thing can seem pretty limited.

> **NOTE:** One way to overcome the limitations of a single shell is to use the screen command. Screen allows you to have multiple shells open at the same time, as well as disconnect and reconnect to different shell sessions without completely closing them. Install the screen package to use the screen command. Type **man screen** to read about the screen command.

Although the bash shell doesn't include a GUI for running many programs, it does let you move active programs between the background and foreground. In this way, you can have a lot of stuff running, while selectively choosing the one you want to deal with at the moment.

There are several ways to place an active program in the background. One mentioned earlier is to add an ampersand (&) to the end of a command line. Another way is to use the at command to run commands in a way in which they are not connected to the shell. (See Chapter 12 for more information about the at command.)

To stop a running command and put it in the background, press Ctrl+z. After the command is stopped, you can either bring it to the foreground to run (the fg command) or start it running in the background (the bg command).

Starting background processes

If you have programs that you want to run while you continue to work in the shell, you can place the programs in the background. To place a program in the background at the time you run the program, type an ampersand (&) at the end of the command line. For example:

```
$ find /usr > /tmp/allusrfiles &
```

This command finds all files on your Linux system (starting from /usr), prints those filenames, and puts those names in the file /tmp/allusrfiles. The ampersand (&) runs that command line in the background. To check which commands you have running in the background, use the jobs command, as follows:

```
$ jobs
[1]   Stopped (tty output)   vi /tmp/myfile
[2]   Running              find /usr -print > /tmp/allusrfiles &
[3]   Running              nroff -man /usr/man2/* >/tmp/man2 &
[4]- Running              nroff -man /usr/man3/* >/tmp/man3 &
[5]+ Stopped              nroff -man /usr/man4/* >/tmp/man4
```

The first job shows a text-editing command (vi) that I placed in the background and stopped by pressing Ctrl+z while I was editing. Job 2 shows the find command I just ran. Jobs three and four show nroff commands currently running in the background. Job five had been running in the shell (foreground) until I decided too many processes were running and pressed Ctrl+z to stop job 5 until a few processes had completed.

The plus sign (+) next to number 5 shows that it was most recently placed in the background. The minus sign (-) next to number 4 shows that it was placed in the background just before the most recent background job. Because job 1 requires terminal input, it cannot run in the background. As a result, it is Stopped (preventing terminal output or input) until it is brought to the foreground again.

> **TIP:** To see the process ID for the background job, add a -l option to the jobs command. If you type ps, you can use the process ID to figure out which command is for a particular background job.

Moving commands to the foreground and background

Continuing with the example, you can bring any of the commands on the jobs list to the foreground. For example, to edit myfile again, type:

```
$ fg %1
```

As a result, the vi command opens again, with all text as it was when you stopped the vi job.

> **CAUTION:** Before you put a text processor, word processor, or similar program in the background, make sure you save your file. It's easy to forget you have a program in the background and you will lose your data if you log out or the computer reboots later on.

To refer to a background job (to cancel or bring it to the foreground), use a percent sign (%) followed by the job number. You can also use the following to refer to a background job:

- % — A percent sign alone refers to the most recent command put into the background (indicated by the plus sign). This action brings the command to the foreground.
- %string — Refers to a job where the command begins with a particular string of characters. The string must be unambiguous. (In other words, typing %vi when there are two vi commands in the background results in an error message.)
- %?string — Refers to a job where the command line contains a string at any point. The string must be unambiguous or the match will fail.
- %-- — Refers to the previous job stopped before the one most recently stopped.

If a command is stopped, you can start it running again in the background using the `bg` command. For example, take job number 5 from the jobs list in the previous example:

```
[5]+  Stopped            nroff -man man4/* >/tmp/man4
```

Type the following:

```
$ bg %5
```

After that, the job runs in the background. Its jobs entry appears as follows:

```
[5]   Running            nroff -man man4/* >/tmp/man4 &
```

If you would like to run a job in the background, and have it continue to run after you close the shell from which you ran it, you can run that command by preceding it with the `nohup` command. For example, to update your locate data base (which store all files on your system so you can find them easily with the locate command) so it will keep running after you exit the shell, type the following command:

```
# nohup updatedb &
```

Configuring your shell

You can tune your shell to help you work more efficiently. Your prompt can provide pertinent information each time you press Enter. You can set aliases to save your keystrokes and permanently set environment variables to suit your needs. To make each change occur when you start a shell, you can add this information to your shell configuration files.

Several configuration files support how your shell behaves. Some of the files are executed for every user and every shell. Others are specific to the user who creates the configuration file. Here are the files that are of interest to anyone using the bash shell in Linux:

- `/etc/profile`— This file sets up user environment information for every user. It is executed when you first log in. This file provides values for your path, as well as setting environment variables for such things as the location of your mailbox and the size of your history files. Finally, `/etc/profile` gathers shell settings from configuration files in the `/etc/profile.d` directory.

- `/etc/bashrc` — This file is executed for every user who runs the bash shell, each time a bash shell is opened. It sets the default prompt and may add one or more aliases. Values in this file can be overridden by information in each user's `~/.bashrc` file.

- `~/.bash_profile` — This file is used by each user to enter information that is specific to his own use of the shell. It is executed only once, when the user logs in. By default, it sets a few environment variables and executes the user's `.bashrc` file.

- `~/.bashrc` — This file contains the information that is specific to your bash shells. It is read when you log in and also each time you open a new bash shell. This is the best location to add environment variables and aliases so that your shell picks them up.

- ~/.bash_logout — This file executes each time you log out (exit the last bash shell). By default, it simply clears your screen.

To change the /etc/profile or /etc/bashrc files, you must be the root user. Users can change the information in the $HOME/.bash_profile, $HOME/.bashrc, and $HOME/.bash_logout files in their own home directories.

The following sections provide ideas about items to add to your shell configuration files. In most cases, you add these values to the .bashrc file in your home directory. However, if you administer a system, you may want to set some of these values as defaults for all of your Linux system's users.

Setting your prompt

Your prompt consists of a set of characters that appear each time the shell is ready to accept a command. The PS1 environment variable sets what the prompt contains. If your shell requires additional input, it uses the values of PS2, PS3, and PS4.

When your Fedora or RHEL system is installed, your prompt is set to include the following information: your user name, your hostname, and the base name of your current working directory. That information is surrounded by brackets and followed by a dollar sign (for regular users) or a pound sign (for the root user). Here's an example of that prompt:

```
[chris@myhost bin]$
```

If you change directories, the bin name would change to the name of the new directory. Likewise, if you were to log in as a different user or to a different host, that information would change.

You can use several special characters (indicated by adding a backslash to a variety of letters) to include different information in your prompt. These can include your terminal number, the date, and the time, as well as other pieces of information. Here are some examples:

- \! — Shows the current command history number. This includes all previous commands stored for your user name.
- \# — Shows the command number of the current command. This includes only the commands for the active shell.
- \$ — Shows the user prompt ($) or root prompt (#), depending on which user you are.
- \W — Shows only the current working directory base name. For example, if the current working directory was /var/spool/mail, this value would simply appear as mail.
- \[— Precedes a sequence of nonprinting characters. This could be used to add a terminal control sequence into the prompt for such things as changing colors, adding blink effects, or making characters bold. (Your terminal determines the exact sequences available.)
- \] — Follows a sequence of nonprinting characters.

- \\ — Shows a backslash.
- \d — Displays the day, month, and number of the date. For example: Sat Jan 23.
- \h — Shows the hostname of the computer running the shell.
- \n — Causes a newline to occur.
- \nnn — Shows the character that relates to the octal number replacing *nnn*.
- \s — Displays the current shell name. For the bash shell, the value would be bash.
- \t — Prints the current time in hours, minutes, and seconds (for example, 10:14:39).
- \u — Prints your current user name.
- \w — Displays the full path to the current working directory.

> **TIP:** If you are setting your prompt temporarily by typing at the shell, you should put the value of PS1 in quotes. For example, you could type export PS1="[\t \w]\$ " to see a prompt that looks like this: [20:26:32 /var/spool]$.

To make a change to your prompt permanent, add the value of PS1 to your .bashrc file in your home directory (assuming that you are using the bash shell). There may already be a PS1 value in that file that you can modify. Refer to the Bash Prompt HOWTO (www.tldp.org/HOWTO/Bash-Prompt-HOWTO) for information on changing colors, commands, and other features for your bash shell prompt.

Adding environment variables

You may consider adding a few environment variables to your .bashrc file. These can help make working with the shell more efficient and effective:

- TMOUT— This sets how long the shell can be inactive before bash automatically exits. The value is the number of seconds for which the shell has not received input. This can be a nice security feature, in case you leave your desk while you are still logged in to Linux. To avoid getting logged off while you are working, you may want to set the value to something like TMOUT=1800 (to allow 30 minutes of idle time).
- PATH — As described earlier, the PATH variable sets the directories that are searched for commands you use. If you often use directories of commands that are not in your PATH, you can permanently add them. To do this, add a PATH variable to your .bashrc file. For example, to add a directory called /getstuff/bin, add the following:

```
PATH=$PATH:/getstuff/bin ; export PATH
```

This example first reads all the current path directories into the new PATH ($PATH), adds the /getstuff/bin directory, and then exports the new PATH.

> **CAUTION:** Some people add the current directory to their PATH by adding a directory identified simply as a dot (.), as follows:

```
PATH=.:$PATH ; export PATH
```

This lets you always run commands in your current directory (which people may be used to if they have used DOS). However, the security risk with this procedure is that you could be in a directory that contains a command that you don't intend to run from that directory. For example, a malicious person could put an `ls` command in a directory that, instead of listing the content of your directory, does something devious.

- *WHATEVER* — You can create your own environment variables to provide shortcuts in your work. Choose any name that is not being used and assign a useful value to it. For example, if you do a lot of work with files in the `/work/time/files/info/memos` directory, you could set the following variable:

```
M=/work/time/files/info/memos ; export M
```

You can make that your current directory by typing cd $M. You can run a program called hotdog from that directory by typing $M/hotdog. You can edit a file called bun from there by typing vi $M/bun.

Adding aliases

Setting aliases can save you even more typing than setting environment variables. With aliases, you can have a string of characters execute an entire command line. You can add and list aliases with the `alias` command. Here are some examples:

```
alias p='pwd ; ls -CF'
alias rm='rm -i'
```

In the first example, the letter p is assigned to run the command pwd, and then to run ls -CF to print the current working directory and list its contents in column form. The second runs the rm command with the -i option each time you simply type **rm**. (This is an alias that is often set automatically for the root user, so that instead of just removing files, you are prompted for each individual file removal. This prevents you from removing all the files in a directory by mistakenly typing something such as rm *.)

While you are in the shell, you can check which aliases are set by typing the `alias` command. If you want to remove an alias, you can type **unalias**. (Remember that if the `alias` is set in a configuration file, it will be set again when you open another shell.)

Working with the Linux File System

The Linux file system is the structure in which all the information on your computer is stored. Files are organized within a hierarchy of directories. Each directory can contain files, as well as other directories.

If you were to map out the files and directories in Linux, it would look like an upside-down tree. At the top is the root directory, which is represented by a single slash (/). Below that is a set of common directories in the Linux system, such as bin, dev, home, lib, and tmp, to name a few. Each of those directories, as well as directories added to the root, can contain subdirectories.

Figure 4-1 illustrates how the Linux file system is organized as a hierarchy. To illustrate how directories are connected, Figure 4-1 shows a /home directory that contains subdirectories for three users: chris, mary, and tom. Within the chris directory are subdirectories: briefs, memos, and personal. To refer to a file called inventory in the chris/memos directory, you could type the full path of /home/chris/memos/inventory. If your current directory were /home/chris/memos, you could refer to the file as simply inventory.

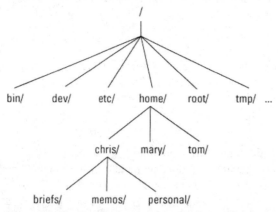

Figure 4-1: The Linux file system is organized as a hierarchy of directories.

The following Linux directories may be of interest to you:

- /bin— Contains common Linux user commands, such as ls, sort, date, and chmod.

- /boot— Has the bootable Linux kernel and boot loader configuration files (GRUB).

- /dev — Contains files representing access points to devices on your systems. These include terminal devices (tty*), floppy disks (fd*), hard disks (hd* or sc*), RAM (ram*), and CD-ROM (cd*). (Applications normally access these devices directly through the device files, but end users rarely access them directly.)

- /etc — Contains administrative configuration files.

- /home — Contains directories assigned to each user with a login account.

- /media — Provides a location for mounting devices, such as remote file systems and removable media (with directory names of cdrom, floppy, and so on). In Fedora and RHEL, many removable media are mounted automatically in this directory when the media is inserted (CD or DVD) or connected (USB pen drives or cameras).

- /proc — Provides a mechanism for the kernel to send information to processes.

- /root — Represents the root user's home directory.

- /sbin — Contains administrative commands and daemon processes.

- `/sys` — A `/proc`-like file system, added with the Linux 2.6 kernel and intended to contain files for getting hardware status and reflecting the system's device tree as it is seen by the kernel. It pulls many of its functions from `/proc`.

- `/tmp` — Contains temporary files used by applications.

- `/usr` — Contains user documentation, games, graphical files (X11), libraries (lib), and a variety of other user and administrative commands and files.

- `/var` — Contains directories of data used by various applications. In particular, this is where you would place files that you share as an FTP server (`/var/ftp`) or a Web server (`/var/www`). It also contains all system log files (`/var/log`). In time, FTP, HTTP, and similar services will move to the `/srv` directory to adhere to the Linux Standards Base (`www.freestandards.org/spec`).

The file systems in the DOS or Microsoft Windows operating systems differ from the Linux file structure. See the sidebar on the Linux file system versus Windows-based file systems.

Linux File Systems Versus Windows-Based File Systems

Although similar in many ways, the Linux file system has some striking differences from file systems used in MS-DOS and Windows operating systems. Here are a few:

- In MS-DOS and Microsoft Windows file systems, drive letters represent different storage devices (for example, A: is a floppy drive and C: is a hard disk). In Linux, all storage devices are fit into the file system hierarchy. So, the fact that all of `/usr` may be on a separate hard disk or that `/mnt/rem1` is a file system from another computer is invisible to the user.

- Slashes, rather than backslashes, are used to separate directory names in Linux. So, `C:\home\chris` in an MS system is `/home/chris` in a Linux system.

- Filenames almost always have suffixes in DOS (such as `.txt` for text files or `.doc` for word-processing files). Although at times you can use that convention in Linux, three-character suffixes have no required meaning in Linux. They can be useful for identifying a file type.

- Every file and directory in a Linux system has permissions and ownership associated with it. Security varies among Microsoft systems. Because DOS and MS Windows began as single-user systems, file ownership was not built into those systems when they were designed. Later releases added features such as file and folder attributes to address this problem.

Creating files and directories

As a Fedora or RHEL user, most of the files you save and work with will probably be in your home directory. Here are commands you use to create and use files and directories:

- cd— Change to another directory
- pwd — Print the name of the current working directory
- mkdir — Create a directory
- chmod — Change the permission on a file or directory
- ls — List the contents of a directory

The following procedure steps you through creating directories within your home directory, moving among your directories, and setting appropriate file permissions:

1. Go to your home directory. To do this, simply type **cd**. (For other ways of referring to your home directory, see the "Identifying Directories" sidebar.)

2. To make sure that you got to your home directory, type **pwd**. When I do this, I get the following response (yours will reflect your home directory):

```
$ pwd
/home/chris
```

3. Create a new directory called test in your home directory, as follows:

```
$ mkdir test
```

4. Check the permissions of the directory by typing:

```
$ ls -ld test
drwxr-xr-x  2 chris  sales   1024  Jan 24 12:17 test
```

Notice that this listing says that test is a directory (d), the owner is chris, the group is sales, and the file was most recently modified on Jan 24 at 12:17 p.m. Suppose that you want to prevent everyone else who uses this computer from using or viewing the files in this directory. The permissions for the directory are rwxr-xr-x. I explain what these permissions mean later in this section.

> **NOTE:** When you add a new user in Fedora or RHEL, by default, the user is assigned to a group of the same name. For example, in the preceding text, the user chris would be assigned to the group chris. This approach to assigning groups is referred to as the *user private group* scheme. For more information on user private groups, refer to Chapter 11.

1. For now, type the following:

```
$ chmod 700 test
```

This step changes the permissions of the directory to give you complete access and everyone else no access at all. (The new permissions should read like rwx------.) (See the "Understanding file permissions" section later in this chapter for more information on permissions.)

2. Make the `test` directory your current directory as follows:

    ```
    $ cd test
    ```

Identifying Directories

When you need to identify your home directory on a shell command line, you can use the following:

- $HOME — This environment variable stores your home directory name.
- ~ — The tilde (~) represents your home directory on the command line.

You can also use the tilde to identify someone else's home directory. For example, ~chris would be expanded to the chris home directory (probably /home/chris).

Other special ways of identifying directories in the shell include the following:

- . — A single dot (.) refers to the current directory.
- .. — Two dots (..) refers to a directory directly above the current directory.
- $PWD — This environment variable refers to the current working directory.
- $OLDPWD — This environment variable refers to the previous working directory before you changed to the current one.

Using metacharacters and operators

To make more efficient use of your shell, the bash shell lets you use certain special characters, referred to as metacharacters and operators. Metacharacters can help you match one or more files without typing each filename completely. Operators let you direct information from one command or file to another command or file.

Using file-matching metacharacters

To save you some keystrokes and to be able to refer easily to a group of files, the bash shell lets you use metacharacters. Anytime you need to refer to a file or directory, such as to list it, open it, or remove it, you can use metacharacters to match the files you want. Here are some useful metacharacters for matching filenames:

- * — This matches any number of characters.
- ? — This matches any one character.
- [...] — This matches any one of the characters between the brackets, which can include a dash-separated range of letters or numbers.

To try out some of these file-matching metacharacters, go to an empty directory (such as the test directory described in the previous section) and create some files. Here's an example of how to create some empty files (although the `touch` command is more commonly used to set assign the current date and time to an existing file than to create new ones):

```
$ touch apple banana grape grapefruit watermelon
```

The next few commands show you how to use shell metacharacters to match filenames so they can be used as arguments to the `ls` command. Using the metacharacters shown in the code that follows, you can match the filenames you just created with the `touch` command. Type the following commands and see if you get the same responses:

```
$ ls a*
apple
$ ls g*
grape
grapefruit
$ ls g*t
grapefruit
$ ls *e*
apple grape grapefruit watermelon
$ ls *n*
banana watermelon
```

The first example matches any file that begins with an `a` (`apple`). The next example matches any files that begin with `g` (`grape`, `grapefruit`). Next, files beginning with `g` and ending in `t` are matched (`grapefruit`). Next, any file that contains an `e` in the name is matched (`apple`, `grape`, `grapefruit`, `watermelon`). Finally, any file that contains an `n` is matched (`banana`, `watermelon`).

Here are a few examples of pattern matching with the question mark (`?`):

```
$ ls ????e
apple grape
$ ls g???e*
grape grapefruit
```

The first example matches any five-character file that ends in `e` (`apple`, `grape`). The second matches any file that begins with `g` and has `e` as its fifth character (`grape`, `grapefruit`).

Here are a few examples of using brackets to do pattern matching:

```
$ ls [abw]*
apple banana watermelon
$ ls [agw]*[ne]
apple grape watermelon
```

In the first example, any file beginning with a, b, or w is matched. In the second, any file that begins with a, g, or w and also ends with either n or e is matched. You can also include ranges within brackets. For example:

```
$ ls [a-g]*
apple banana grape grapefruit
```

Here, any filenames beginning with a letter from a through g is matched.

Using file-redirection metacharacters

Commands receive data from standard input and send it to standard output. Standard input is normally user input from the keyboard, and standard output is normally displayed on the screen. Using pipes (described earlier), you can direct standard output from one command to the standard input of another. With files, you can use less than (<) and greater than (>) signs to direct data to and from files. Here are the file redirection characters:

- < — Direct the contents of a file as input to the command (because many commands take a file name as an option, the < key is not usually needed).
- > — Direct the output of a command to a file, overwriting any existing file.
- >> — Direct the output of a command to a file, adding the output to the end of the existing file.

Here are some examples of command lines where information is directed to and from files:

```
$ mail root < ~/.bashrc
$ man chmod | col -b > /tmp/chmod
$ echo "Finished project on $(date)" >> ~/projects
```

In the first example, the contents of the .bashrc file in the home directory are sent in a mail message to the computer's root user. The second command line formats the chmod man page (using the man command), removes extra back spaces (col -b), and sends the output to the file /tmp/chmod (erasing the previous /tmp/chmod file, if it exists). The final command results in the following text being added to the user's project file:

```
Finished project on Wed Jun 25 13:46:49 PST 2008
```

You could also pipe the output of the previous command to another command. For example, the following command line would send the line just shown in a mail message to the user boss@example.com:

```
$ echo "Finished project on $(date)"|mail -s 'Done' boss@example.com
```

Understanding file permissions

After you've worked with Linux for a while, you are almost sure to get a Permission denied message. Permissions associated with files and directories in Linux were designed to keep users from accessing other users' private files and to protect important system files.

The nine bits assigned to each file for permissions define the access that you and others have to your file. Permission bits appear as rwxrwxrwx. The first three bits apply to the owner's permission, the next three apply to the group assigned to the file, and the last three apply to all others. The r stands for read, the w stands for write, and the x stands for execute permissions. If a dash appears instead of the letter, it means that permission is turned off for that associated read, write, or execute.

You can see the permission for any file or directory by typing the `ls -ld` command. The named file or directory appears as those shown in the following example:

```
$ ls -ld ch3 test
-rw-rw-r--  1 chris   sales     4983   Jan 18 22:13 ch3
drwxr-xr-x  2 chris   sales     1024   Jan 24 13:47 test
```

The first line shows a file (ch3) that has read and write permission for the owner and the group. All other users have read permission, which means they can view the file but cannot change its contents (although a user may be allowed to remove the file, since the ability to remove a file is based on directory permissions). The second line shows a directory (indicated by the letter d before the permission bits). The owner has read, write, and execute permission, while the group and other users have only read and execute permissions. As a result, only the owner can add, change, or delete files in that directory. Any other user, however, can only read the contents, change to that directory, and list the contents of the directory. (Note that by using the -d option, the `test` directory entry is listed without listing its contents.)

If you own a file, you can change the permission on it as you please. You can do this with the `chmod` command. For each of the three sets of permission on a file (read, write, and execute), r is assigned to the number 4, w to 2, and x to 1. So to make permissions wide open for yourself as owner, you would set the first number to 7 (4 plus 2 plus 1). The same would be true for group and other permission. Any combination of permissions can result from 0 (no permission) through 7 (full permission).

Here are some examples of how to change permission on a file and what the resulting permission would be:

```
chmod 777 files  →  rwxrwxrwx
chmod 755 files  →  rwxr-xr-x
chmod 644 files  →  rw-r--r-
chmod 000 files  →  ---------
```

You can also turn file permissions on and off using plus (+) and minus (-) signs, respectively. This can be done for the owner user (u), owner group (g), others (o), and all users (a). For example, each time starting with a file that has all permissions open (rwxrwxrwx), here are some chmod examples with resulting permissions after using a minus sign:

```
chmod a-w files   →  r-xr-xr-x
chmod o-x files   →  rwsrwsrw-
chmod go-rwx files  →  rwx------
```

Likewise, here are some examples, starting with all permissions closed (---------) where the plus sign is used with chmod to turn permissions on:

```
chmod u+rw files  →  rw-------
chmod a+x files   →  --x--x--x
chmod ug+rx files →  r-xr-x---
```

When you try to create a file, by default it is given the permission `rw-r--r--`. A directory is given the permission `rwxr-xr-x`. These default values are determined by the value of umask. Type **umask** to see what your umask value is. For example:

```
$ umask
022
```

The umask value represents the permissions that are not given on a new file. It masks the permissions value of 666 for a file and 777 for a directory. The umask value of 022 results in permission for a directory of 755 (`rwxr-xr-x`). That same umask results in a file permission of 644 (`rw-r--r--`). (Execute permissions are off by default for regular files.)

TIP: Here's a great tip for changing the permission for lots of files at once. Using the `-R` options of chmod, you can change the permission for all of the files and directories within a directory structure at once. For example, if you want to open permissions completely to all files and directories in the `/tmp/test` directory, you can type the following:

```
$ chmod -R 777 /tmp/test
```

This command line runs chmod recursively (`-R`) for the `/tmp/test` directory, as well as any files or directories that exist below that point in the file system (for example, `/tmp/test/hat`, `/tmp/test/hat/caps`, and so on). All would be set to 777 (full read/write/execute permissions).

CAUTION: The `-R` option of chmod works best if you are opening permissions completely or adding execute permission (as well as the appropriate read/write permission). The reason is that if you turn off execute permission recursively, you close off your ability to change to any directory in that structure. For example, `chmod -R 644 /tmp/test` turns off execute permission for the `/tmp/test` directory, and then fails to change any files or directories below that point.

Moving, copying, and deleting files

Commands for moving, copying, and deleting files are fairly straightforward. To change the location of a file, use the mv command. To copy a file from one location to another, use the cp command. To remove a file, use the rm command. Here are some examples:

```
$ mv abc def
$ mv abc ~
$ cp abc def
$ cp abc ~
$ rm abc
$ rm *
```

Of the two move (mv) commands, the first moves the file abc to the file def in the same directory (essentially renaming it), whereas the second moves the file abc to your home directory (~). The first copy command (cp) copies abc to the file def, whereas the second copies abc to your home directory (~). The first remove command (rm) deletes the abc file; the second removes all the files in the current directory (except those that start with a dot).

> **CAUTION:** Be sure to use the * and other wildcard characters wisely, because you might match (and therefore remove) files you don't intend to match.

> **NOTE:** For the root user, the mv, cp, and rm commands are aliased to each be run with the -i option. This causes a prompt to appear asking you to confirm each move, copy, and removal, one file at a time. This is done to prevent the root user from messing up a large group of files by mistake. To temporarily get around an alias, type the full path to the command (for example, /bin/rm -rf /tmp/junk/*).

Using the vi Text Editor

It's almost impossible to use Linux for any period of time and not need to use a text editor. If you are using a GUI, you can run gedit, which is fairly intuitive for editing text. Most Linux shell users will use either the vi or emacs commands to edit text files. The advantage of vi or emacs over a graphical editor is that you can use it from any shell, a character terminal, or a character-based connection over a network (using telnet or ssh, for example). No GUI is required.

This section provides a brief tutorial of the vi text editor. The tutorial was done using the vi or vim (Vi Improved) editors provided with the vim-minimal and vim-advanced packages in Fedora.

Any time in this book that I suggest you manually edit a configuration file, you can use vi to do that editing (from any shell). (If vi doesn't suit you, see the sidebar "Exploring Other Text Editors" for other options.)

The vi editor is difficult to learn at first. But when you know it, you will be able to edit and move around quickly and efficiently within files. Your fingers never have to leave the keyboard to pick up a mouse or press a function key.

Starting with vi

Most often, you start vi to open a particular file. For example, to open a file called /tmp/test, type the following command:

```
$ vi /tmp/test
```

If this is a new file, you should see something similar to the following:

```
~
~
~
~
~
"/tmp/test" [New File]
```

The box at the top represents where your cursor is. The bottom line keeps you informed about what is going on with your editing (here you just opened a new file). In between, there are tildes (~) as filler because there is no text in the file yet. Now here's the intimidating part: there are no hints, menus, or icons to tell you what to do. On top of that, you can't just start typing. If you do, the computer is likely to beep at you. And some people complain that Linux isn't friendly.

Exploring Other Text Editors

Dozens of text editors are available to use with Linux. Here are a few contained in Fedora and RHEL that you can try out if you find vi to be too taxing:

- **emacs** — Most experienced Linux and UNIX users traditionally have used vi or emacs as their text editor. Many extensions are available with emacs to handle editing of many different file types.

- **gedit** — The GNOME text editor that runs in the GUI.

- **joe** — The joe editor is similar to many PC text editors. Use control and arrow keys to move around. Press Ctrl+C to exit with no save or Ctrl+X to save and exit.

- **kate** — A nice-looking editor that comes in the kdebase package. It has lots of bells and whistles, such as highlighting for different types of programming languages and controls for managing word wrap.

- **kedit** — A GUI-based text editor that comes with the KDE desktop.

- **nedit** — A good tool for editing source code.

If you use ssh to log in to other Linux computers on your network, you can use any editor to edit files. A GUI-based editor will pop up on your screen. When no GUI is available, you will need a text editor that runs in the shell, such as vi, jed, or joe.

The first things you need to know are the different operating modes. The vi editor operates in either command mode or input mode. When you start vi, you are in command mode. Before you can add or change text in the file, you have to type a command to tell vi what you want to do. A command consists of one or two letters and an optional number. To get into input mode, you need to type an input command. To start out, type either of the following input commands:

- **a** — Add. After you type a, you can input text that starts to the right of the cursor.

- **i** — Insert. After you type i, you can input text that starts to the left of the cursor.

Type a few words and press Enter. Repeat that a few times until you have a few lines of text. When you are done typing, press Esc. You are now back in command mode. Now that you have a file with some text in it, try moving around in your text with the following keys or letters.

> **TIP:** Remember the Esc key! It always places you back into command mode.

- **Arrow keys** — Use the arrow keys to move up, down, left, or right in the file one character at a time. To move left and right you can also use Backspace and the Spacebar, respectively. If you prefer to keep your fingers on the keyboard, use h (left), l (right), j (down), or k (up) to move the cursor.
- **w** — Moves the cursor to the beginning of the next word.
- **b** — Moves the cursor to the beginning of the previous word.
- **0** (zero) or **^** — Moves the cursor to the beginning of the current line.
- **$** — Moves the cursor to the end of the current line.
- **H** — Moves the cursor to the upper-left corner of the screen (first line on the screen).
- **M** — Moves the cursor to the first character of the middle line on the screen.
- **L** — Moves the cursor to the lower-left corner of the screen (last line on the screen).

Now that you know how to input text and move around, the only other editing you need to know is how to delete text. Here are a few `vi` commands for deleting text:

- **x** — Deletes the character under the cursor.
- **X** — Deletes the character directly before the cursor.
- **dw** — Deletes from the current character to the end of the current word.
- **d$** — Deletes from the current character to the end of the current line.
- **d0** — Deletes from the previous character to the beginning of the current line.

If you feel pretty good about creating text and moving around the file, you may want to wrap things up. Use the following keystrokes for saving and quitting the file:

- **ZZ** — Save the current changes to the file and exit from vi.
- **:w** — Save the current file but continue editing.
- **:wq** — Same as ZZ.
- **:q** — Quit the current file. This works only if you don't have any unsaved changes.
- **:q!** — Quit the current file and *don't* save the changes you just made to the file.

> **TIP:** If you've really trashed the file by mistake, the `:q!` command is the best way to exit and abandon your changes. The file reverts to the most recently changed version. So, if you just did a `:w`, you are stuck with the changes up to that point. If you just want to undo a few bad edits, press u to back out of changes.

You have learned a few `vi` editing commands. I describe more commands in the following sections. However, before I do, here are a few tips to smooth out your first trials with `vi`:

- **Esc** — Remember that Esc gets you back to command mode. (I've watched people press every key on the keyboard trying to get out of a file.) Esc followed by ZZ gets you out of input mode, saves the file, and exits.

- **u** — Press u to undo the previous change you made. Continue to press u to undo the change before that, and the one before that. (With the traditional vi editor, u undoes a single command and r returns what you just undid.)

- **Ctrl+r** — If you decide you didn't want to undo the previous edit, use Ctrl+r for Redo. Essentially, this command undoes your undo.

- **Caps Lock** — Beware of hitting Caps Lock by mistake. Everything you type in `vi` has a different meaning when the letters are capitalized. You don't get a warning that you are typing capitals — things just start acting weirdly.

- **:! *command*** — You can run a shell command while you are in `vi` using `:!` followed by a command name. For example, type **:!date** to see the current date and time, type **:!pwd** to see what your current directory is, or type **:!jobs** to see if you have any jobs running in the background. When the command completes, press Enter and you are back to editing the file. You could even do that with a shell (`:!bash`) to run a few commands from the shell, then type **exit** to return to `vi`. (I recommend doing a save before escaping to the shell, just in case you forget to go back to `vi`.)

- **-- INSERT --** — When you are in input mode, the word INSERT appears at the bottom of the screen. Other messages also appear at the line at the bottom of the screen.

- **Ctrl+g** — If you forget what you are editing, pressing these keys displays the name of the file that you are editing and the current line that you are on. It also displays the total number of lines in the file, the percentage of how far you are through the file, and the column number the cursor is on. This just helps you get your bearings after you've stopped for a cup of coffee at 3 a.m.

Moving around the file

Besides the few movement commands described earlier, there are other ways of moving around a `vi` file. To try these out, open a large file that you can't do much damage to. (Try copying `/var/log/messages` to `/tmp` and opening it in `vi`.) Here are some movement commands you can use:

- **Ctrl+f** — Page ahead, one page at a time.
- **Ctrl+b** — Page back, one page at a time.
- **Ctrl+d** — Page ahead a half page at a time.
- **Ctrl+u** — Page back a half page at a time.
- **G** — Go to the last line of the file.

- **gg** or **1G** — Go to the first line of the file. (Use any number with a G or gg to go to that line in the file.)

Searching for text

To search for the next occurrence of text in the file, use either the slash (/) or the question mark (?) character. Within the search, you can also use metacharacters. Here are some examples:

- `/hello`— Searches forward for the word `hello`.
- `?goodbye` — Searches backward for the word `goodbye`.
- `/The.*foot` — Searches forward for a line that has the word `The` in it and also, after that at some point, the word `foot`.
- `?[pP]rint` — Searches backward for either `print` or `Print`. Remember that case matters in Linux, so using brackets can search for words that could have different capitalization.

The `vi` editor was originally based on the `ex` editor. That editor did not let you work in full-screen mode. However, it did enable you to run commands that let you find and change text on one or more lines at a time. When you type a colon and the cursor goes to the bottom of the screen, you are essentially in `ex` mode. Here is an example of some of those `ex` commands for searching for and changing text. (I chose the words `Local` and `Remote` to search for, but you can use any appropriate words.)

- `:g/Local`— Searches for the word `Local` and prints every occurrence of that line from the file. (If there is more than a screenful, the output is piped to the `more` command.)
- `:s/Local/Remote` — Substitutes `Remote` for the word `Local` on the current line.
- `:g/Local/s//Remote` — Substitutes the first occurrence of the word `Local` on every line of the file with the word `Remote`.
- `:g/Local/s//Remote/g` — Substitutes every occurrence of the word `Local` with the word `Remote` in the entire file.
- `:g/Local/s//Remote/gp` — Substitutes every occurrence of the word `Local` with the word `Remote` in the entire file, then prints each line so that you can see the changes (piping it through `more` if output fills more than one page). Another way to globally search and replace without printing every line that changes is to type `:%s/Local/Remote/g`

Using numbers with commands

You can precede most `vi` commands with numbers to have the command repeated that number of times. This is a handy way to deal with several lines, words, or characters at a time. Here are some examples:

- `3dw` — Deletes the next three words.
- `5cl` — Changes the next five letters (that is, removes the letters and enters input mode).
- `12j` — Moves down 12 lines.

Putting a number in front of most commands just repeats those commands. At this point, you should be fairly proficient at using the `vi` command. If you would like further instruction, I suggest you try the VIM Tutor by running the `vimtutor` command.

> **NOTE**: When you invoke `vi` on Fedora or RHEL, you're actually invoking the `vim` text editor, which runs in `vi` compatibility mode. Those who do a lot of programming might prefer `vim`, because it shows different levels of code in different colors. `vim` has other useful features, such as the ability to open a document with the cursor at the same place where it was when you last exited that file.

Summary

Working from a shell command-line interpreter within Linux may not be as simple as using a GUI, but it offers many powerful and flexible features. This chapter describes how to log in to Fedora or RHEL and use shell commands. Features for running commands include recalling commands from a history list, completing commands, and joining commands.

This chapter describes how shell environment variables can be used to store and recall important pieces of information. It also teaches you to modify shell configuration files to tailor the shell to suit your needs. Finally, this chapter describes how to use the Linux file system to create files and directories, use permissions, and work with files (moving, copying, and removing them), and how to edit text files from the shell using the `vi` command.

Part II
Using Fedora and RHEL

Chapter 5

Accessing and Running Applications

In This Chapter

- Getting and installing software packages
- Getting Fedora and RHEL software updates
- Managing RPM packages
- Running desktop applications
- Using emulators to run applications from other operating systems
- Running DOS applications
- Running Windows applications with WINE
- Running applications in virtual environments (KVM and Xen)

Fedora and RHEL come with thousands of software applications, covering every major category of desktop, server, and programming software. By accessing some third-party, Fedora-specific software repositories on the Internet, you have access to many more software packages. Often, getting a new software package downloaded and installed is as simple as running a single yum command.

Some of the same tools you use to get and install software packages in Fedora and RHEL (such as yum and rpm commands) can also be used to manage your installed software and get updates or security patches when they become available. Options in those tools let you query which packages you installed, as well as list and verify the contents of those packages. Likewise, GUI tools such as PackageKit can be used to automatically grab and install new and updated packages as they become available.

Once an application is installed, launching it can be as easy as it is in any friendly desktop system: by clicking a few menus on the desktop. There are also some neat ways to launch applications from another computer so that you can work with them (securely) from your own desktop.

In those cases where you must have a specific application that isn't available for Linux (such as Microsoft Office or a particular media player), there are several emulators and compatibility software facilities to let you run software made for Windows, DOS, or other operating systems. You can also build and install your own software packages for Fedora or RHEL, starting with software available as source RPMs or as tarballs.

This chapter covers these tools and procedures for getting, installing, and managing software applications in Fedora and RHEL.

Getting and Installing Software Packages

Applications that are packaged specifically to run on Fedora and RHEL systems are usually stored in RPM format. Except for a few components used to start the system, most of the Fedora and RHEL operating systems themselves are in RPM format. When you look for software to install in Fedora or RHEL, you should start in the following locations:

- **Install DVD** — Any package you didn't install during the initial installation process can be installed later from the DVD that comes with this book (aside from a few game-related packages that were left off due to the DVD size limitations). To do that, you can use the rpm command. After initial installation, however, provided you have an Internet connection, using online repositories to add packages using the yum utility or the PackageKit window is often the better method. That's because those tools can not only get and install the packages you request, but they will also find and get updated versions of the packages (if available), as well as any dependent packages required to install the packages you want.

- **Fedora repository** — Prior to Fedora 7, Fedora software was contained in one of two areas: Fedora Core and Fedora Extras. Fedora Core was the basic Fedora Linux operating system (maintained primarily by Red Hat Inc. employees) and Fedora Extras consisted of packages contributed by the Fedora community. Now, all the software from those two initiatives are combined into a single, massive Fedora repository.

  In Fedora today, your yum facility is automatically configured to use the online Fedora repository. Because there are multiple instances of the repository, yum points to mirror lists from the Fedora project (http://mirrors.fedoraproject.org) to choose a Fedora repository that is near to you.

- **Third-party Fedora repositories** — Because of licensing issues and patent questions, some software that is popular to use with Fedora is not included in Fedora itself. For example, commercial DVD movie and MP3 music players are not included in Fedora. There are third-party Fedora repositories, however, that make that software available. In particular, rpmforge.net, rpm.livna.org, dag.wieers.com, freshrpms.net, dribble.org.uk, and ATRPMs.net are popular third-party repositories. You can download packages directly from these sites or (preferably) set up yum so you can download and install packages more easily.

> **CAUTION:** Getting software from any sites that are not sanctioned by the Fedora Project presents potential problems. While the Fedora Project works hard to make sure that package dependencies across all official packages are handled consistently, you don't get the same guarantees with all other repositories. While some repositories make commitments to build their packages on the official Fedora repository, to maintain consistent dependencies across packages, others don't. In the latest Fedora release, several of these repositories (Dribble, Freshrpms, and Livna) are in the process of joining together to form the RPM Fusion Project (http://rpmfusion.org), to help eliminate inconsistencies among those popular repositories.

- **Extra Packages for Enterprise Linux (EPEL)** — Because Red Hat Enterprise Linux is designed to be a stable distro derived from Fedora packages, some Fedora packages are not included with RHEL. To provide many of these extra packages to RHEL users (as well as RHEL derivatives such as CentOS), the Fedora project sponsored the EPEL software repository. If you are using RHEL 4.x or 5.x systems, add the appropriate epel-release package to your system, then use the EPEL repository as you would any other yum software repository (as described later in this chapter). For more on EPEL, refer to the EPEL FAQ (http://fedoraproject.org/wiki/EPEL/FAQ).

- **Software project sites** — Often individual software projects will offer their own set of RPM packages for their own projects. This is particularly useful for projects under continuous development (such as the WINE project). If the project doesn't offer RPMs, they will typically offer code in what is called a *tarball*. The tarball may include binary code or, more often, source code you can build for your environment. (I describe how to install from source code tarballs later in this chapter.)

If you know what software package you want and it is available from more than one location, you should choose one from an official Fedora repository. Besides that, a repository outside of Fedora that's committed to being compatible with the main Fedora repository is your next best choice, since that will help take care of any dependency problems.

Most Fedora repositories are light on descriptions of the packages they offer. The following list summarizes some other Web sites that you can browse to find detailed information about software that runs in Linux. Then you can search Fedora repositories (described later in this chapter) for Fedora- or RHEL-specific versions of those packages.

- **Freshmeat** (www.freshmeat.net) — This site maintains a massive index of Linux software. You can do keyword searches for software projects or browse for software by category.

- **SourceForge** (www.sourceforge.net) — This site hosts thousands of open source software projects. You can download software and documentation from those projects through the SourceForge site.

- **Rpmfind** (www.rpmfind.net) — Provides a way of searching for open source software that is packaged in the RPM Package Management (RPM) format across a variety of repositories. You can do a keyword search from this Web site.

- **Google (**www.google.com**)** — Since we're just looking for help in finding software projects, Google (or other general-purpose search engine) can be used to find information about a the project we are interested in.

Often, you can't just download a single software package to get the software in that package to work. Many packages depend on other packages. For example, software packages for playing audio and video typically rely on other software packages for decoding different kinds of content. To handle software dependency issues (along with the fact that it includes many other valuable features), Fedora has based its packaging tools on the yum facility.

Downloading and installing applications with yum

The Yellow Dog Updater, Modified (yum) software package lets you install and update selected software packages in RPM format from software repositories on the Web. Once you know the software package that you want, yum is probably the best way to download and install that package. There are also features in yum for listing and managing RPMs after they are installed.

Yum is the foundation for software updates in Fedora and RHEL 5. Besides the yum command, the PackageKit windows and even the Fedora installer itself (anaconda) now use yum as the underlying mechanism for getting and updating software in Fedora.

The yum package is included on the Fedora DVD that comes with this book. To use yum to install RPM software packages, follow these basic steps:

1. **Determine the software package you want.** Yum is delivered with the current Fedora repository already configured. Use yum or PackageKit search tools (described later) to find packages you want. Or add more repositories for yum to search to your /etc/yum.conf file or /etc/yum.repos.d directory (also described later). (Many software repositories offer RPM packages that automatically configure entries in the yum.repos.d directory to point to those repositories.)

2. **Configure yum.** You have the option to configure the /etc/yum.conf file to set options that relate to how you use your yum repositories, as described in the next section. Then add any repositories, outside of Fedora , that you want to get packages from. Several popular Fedora software repositories offer RPMs that install the information yum needs to access those repositories.

3. **Run yum.** The yum command can be used to download and install any package from the yum repository, including any packages the one you want depends on.

CAUTION: In Fedora and RHEL, Red Hat, Inc. has gone to great lengths to ensure that software it provides is of good quality and unimpaired by legitimate patent claims. When you download packages that are not official packages for RHEL or Fedora, you are on your own to check the quality and legality of that software.

Besides downloading and installing new software packages, yum can also be used to check for available updates and list various kinds of information about available packages.

Configuring yum (/etc/yum.conf)

The /etc/yum.conf file already comes preconfigured to include options that affect how you download and use RPM packages with yum. All necessary, basic repository listings are contained in files in the /etc/yum.repos.d directory. Here is what the yum.conf file contains:

```
[main]
cachedir=/var/cache/yum
keepcache=0
debuglevel=2
logfile=/var/log/yum.log
exactarch=1
obsoletes=1
gpgcheck=1
plugins=1
metadata_expire=1800
installonly_limit=2

# PUT REPOS HERE OR IN separate file.repo files
# in /etc/yum.repos.d
```

The cachedir (/var/cache/yum) is where the RPM files are downloaded to by yum when you ask to install or upgrade packages. The keepcache=0 option causes all downloaded packages and headers to be erased after they are installed. If you select to save the RPM files (which some people do if they want to share packages with multiple machines, without multiple downloads), you need to set keepcache=1 and make sure the directory has enough disk space to handle it. During a testing cycle, I ended up with about 1GB of RPMs in my /var/cache/yum file system (of course, they can just be deleted after they are installed).

Messages related to yum processing are sent to /var/log/yum.log by default, using a debug level of 2 (0 to 10 is legal, with 2 producing minimal success or failure messages). The exactarch set to 1 indicates that you must match the name and release architecture exactly for a package.

The obsoletes option lets yum determine obsolete packages during updates. The gpgcheck indicates whether or not a check of the package's GPG key is done (1 indicates the check is done). With plugins turned on (set to 1), available extensions to yum are enabled. The value of metadata_expire determines when the metadata you have from a repository expires. The default of 1800 seconds causes metadata to expire 30 minutes after it is received.

Some packages can be installed but never updated. These packages include kernel, kernel-smp, kernel-bigmem and others, as set by the default installonlypkgs value in yum. Because kernel packages are stored separately, you can keep multiple kernel packages installed on your system. By default, the `installonly_limit` value of 2 in `/etc/yum.conf` keeps the latest two `installonlypkgs` on your system, but will delete older packages of the same name as new kernel packages are added.

Here are some tips relating to setting up `yum.conf`:

- **Getting metadata** — The metadata that describes the contents of a yum repository is downloaded to your computer when you run the `yum` command. If you run the command again after the metadata expires (30 minutes by default, as described earlier), you will have to wait again while the metadata downloads before yum proceeds.

    If yum is configured to access several repositories, it can take a long time to repeatedly download the metadata. To get around this problem, you can extend the `metadata_expire` value or run `yum` with a `-C` on the command line (to use the existing metadata). The downside is that if the repository data has changed, you might not be getting the latest packages.

- **Excluding repositories** — Excluding repositories on the `yum` command line is another way to save time by preventing unneeded metadata from being downloaded. For example, if you know the package you want is in Fedora, you can disable the livna repository by adding `--disablerepo=livna` to the `yum` command line.

- **Plugins** — Fedora comes with the `plugins` feature enabled in the `yum.conf` file. This causes plugins in the `/usr/lib/yum-plugins` directory to be enabled. When you start out, you may have no plugins or only the refresh-updatesd plugin. This plugin tells yum to notify the yum-updatesd daemon to refresh yum metadata. For information on other available plugins, refer to theYumPlugins Wiki (`http://wiki.linux.duke.edu/YumPlugins`).

For more information about the `yum.conf` file, type **man yum.conf** from a shell.

Adding yum repositories (/etc/yum.repos.d/)

When you use the `yum` command to request to install a software package, it checks repositories listed in the `/etc/yum.conf` file and in files in the `/etc/yum.repos.d` directory. By default, you begin with repository listings from the following:

- **Fedora (fedora.repo)** — These are all the same packages that are on the DVD that comes with this book (plus a few more we couldn't fit on the DVD). You can install any of those packages, or updates to them, from the repositories using `yum`. There are thousands of software packages in this repository.

- **Fedora Updates (fedora-updates.repo)** — As updates become available from Fedora, you can automatically access those updates from mirror sites listed in fedora-updates.repo.

The following is a list of other repositories you might consider adding to your own `/etc/yum.repos.d/` files. Several of these repositories have made it easy for you by offering an RPM that adds the gpgkey and `yum.repos.d` file needed to access their repositories.

Keep in mind that these repositories change over time, as new ones are added, some are neglected and others are consolidated. The locations of repository directories and GPG keys can change without notice. In fact, the RPM Fusion Project (`http://rpmfusion.org`) is gearing up to merge the Dribble, Freshrpms and Livna repositories.

> **NOTE:** I recommend only adding repositories you need. Adding unnecessary respositories can slow down the performance of yum.

- **Livna.org** (`http://rpm.livna.org`) — Begun as an extension of the `Fedora.us` site, `rpm.livna.org` contains RPM software packages that are outside of the Fedora Project. This is a good place to get audio and video players (such as xine, mplayer, ffmpeg, ogle, and so on) that may not meet the licensing requirements adhered to by Red Hat, Inc. By installing the livna-release RPM, yum is configured to access the rpm.livna.org repository. Look for the Fedora 9 livna-release RPM at the following URL:

  `http://rpm.livna.org/fedora/9/i386/`

- **Dag** (`http://dag.wieers.com/packages`) — This site contains more than 45,000 RPMs from more than 2400 different projects. Currently, the repository has not been updated for the latest Fedora release and there is no RPM to automatically set up access that repository from yum. You can, however, look for Dag packages from the merged RPMForge.net site.

- **FreshRPMs** (`www.freshrpms.net`) — Another site with a good selection of high-quality RPMs is FreshRPMs.net. This site has a good selection of audio and video players that are outside of the mainstream Fedora repositories. By installing the freshrpms-release RPM, yum is configured to access the FreshRPMs repository. Look for the Fedora 9 freshrpms-release RPM at the following URL:

  `http://ayo.freshrpms.net/fedora/linux/9/i386/RPMS.freshrpms/`

- **Dribble** (`http://dribble.org.uk`) — RPM packages focused on fun software are contained in the Dribble repository. Many of the packages are for games and console game emulators. Look for a dribble-release package, which you can use to automatically enable the Dribble repository for your Fedora system, at this URL:

  `http://dribble.org/uk/listrpms1.html`

- **ATRPMs** (`http://atrpms.net/dist/f9`) — This site has RPMs containing many drivers for video cards, wireless cards, and other hardware not included with Fedora. If you want to try out a personal video recorder, this site also has RPMs for the MythTV project. By installing the atrpms-package-config RPM, yum is configured to access the ATRPMs.net repository. Look for the Fedora 9 atrpms-package-config RPM at the following URL:

```
http://atrpms.net/dist/f9
```

- **RPMforge.net** (`http://rpmforge.net`) — This site represented a merge of three separate repositories that offered Fedora RPM packages: `dag.wieers.com`, `www.freshrpms.net`, and `dries.ulyssis.org`. This repository is transitioning to the RPMrepo project (`www.rpmrepo.org`). During the transition, RPMforge offers packages for RHEL and CentOS (`https://rpmrepo.org/RPMforge/Using`).

Running yum to download and install RPMs

With the repositories identified, downloading and installing an RPM you want is as simple as running `yum` with the `install` option to request the RPM. With an active connection to the Internet, open a Terminal window as root user.

The first thing yum does is download metadata and headers for all packages you might want from each repository. Then, after presenting you with the list of dependencies it thinks you need, it asks if you want to install the necessary packages. Here is an example of using the `yum` command to download the `madwifi` media player:

```
# yum install madwifi
Setting up Install Process
Parsing package install arguments
fedora       100% |============| 2.1 kB     00:00
atrpms       100% |============| 951  B     00:00
Reading repository metadata in from local files
primary.xml.gz  100%|=========| 2.5 MB     00:04
    .
    .
    .

Transaction Summary
================================================
Install     4  Package(s)
Update      0  Package(s)
Remove      1  Package(s)
Total download size: 17M
Is this ok [y/N]: y
Downloading Packages
    .
    .
    .
```

As you can see from this example, `yum` checked two different software repositories, Fedora and atrpms packages, for the current Fedora release. After listing the dependencies, yum asks if it is OK to install them. Type **y** and the package and all its dependencies are installed.

Some packages, including the madwifi package shown in the previous example, need to install a version that matches the kernel that you are running. For that reason, installing such a package might also bring an updated kernel package with it.

Using yum to install packages locally

If you want to install RPM packages with yum that are available from your local system (by inserting the Fedora DVD or copying an RPM to a local directory), you can use the localinstall option to yum. For example, if you were to insert the Fedora DVD that comes with this book (and it was mounted on /media/disk), you could type the following to install the gftp package:

```
# yum localinstall /media/disk/Fedora/Packages/gftp-*
yum localinstall /media/disk/Fedora/Packages/gftp-2.0.18-7.fc9.rpm
    .
    .
    .

Resolving Dependencies
--> Running transaction check
---> Package gftp.i386 1:2.0.18-7.fc9 set to be updated
Dependencies Resolved
================================================================
 Package Arch  Version       Repository       Size
================================================================
Installing:
 gftp    i386  1:2.0.18-7.fc9 /media/disk/Fedora/Packages/gftp-2.0.18-7.fc9.rpm  946 k

Transaction Summary
================================================================
Install       1 Package(s)
Update        0 Package(s)
Remove        0 Package(s)

Total download size: 946 k
Is this ok [y/N]: y
```

A good reason for using yum localinstall instead of the rpm command to install RPM packages is that yum will check whether the package you are installing is dependent on any other packages being installed. If yum finds that it needs other packages, it will search any yum repositories you have configured (at least the main Fedora repository) to download and install what you need.

In this example, yum found that gftp didn't require any additional packages be installed. So, typing **y** at the prompt caused only the one package to be installed.

Using yum for listing packages

Besides downloading and installing new RPM packages, yum can also be used to list available packages as well as those that are already installed. The following examples illustrate some uses of yum.

If you want to see a list of all packages that are available for download from the repositories you have configured, type the following:

```
# yum list | less
```

Adding the `less` command to the end lets you scroll through the list of software (it could be long, depending on which repositories you point to). If you try to install a package and it fails with a message like `package xyzpackage needs xyzfile (not provided)`, you can check for packages that include the missing file using the `provides` option as follows:

```
# yum provides missingfile
```

With the `provides` option, yum will search your repositories for whatever file you enter (instead of `missingfile`) and return the name of any packages it finds that include that file.

To search software descriptions in repositories for a particular string, use the `search` option. For example, the following command searches for `arcade` in any package description (this search will find some games):

```
# yum search arcade
```

Because yum packages are not automatically deleted after being installed, you might want to go through on occasion and clean them out. To clear out packages from subdirectories of the `/var/cache/yum` directory, type the following:

```
# yum clean packages
```

If you would like to check to see RPMs that were installed from repositories outside of the main Fedora repository, you can do so using the `list extras` option. Here is an example:

```
# yum list extras
Setting up repositories
Reading repository metadata in from local files
Extra Packages
AdobeReader_enu.i386
flash-plugin.i386   9.0.48.0-release installed
```

The list shown includes Acrobat Reader (which I got from the Adobe Web site), which does a nice job displaying PDF files. The other package is for running the Flash plug-in with the Firefox Web browser. Note that this list includes all packages from repositories configured for your system that are outside of Fedora. (For example, it would list packages installed from Livna and ATRPMs, if those repositories were configured.)

Using yum-utils package

There are several utilities in the yum-utils package for working with yum repositories and managing software packages. To get these utilities, type the following `yum` command:

```
# yum install yum-utils
```

These utilities provide different ways of cleaning up repositories, getting packages without installing them, and doing different query types. Here are some examples:

- **package-cleanup** — Check your local RPM database for dependency problems and packages that are not needed. Options include `--problems` (to check dependency problems in the RPM database), `--orphans` (to list packages that are not currently available in any of your repositories), and `--oldkernels` (to remove old kernel and kernel-devel packages). You can add `--keepdevel` when running `--oldkernels`, to keep the associated kernel-devel packages.

- **repoclosure** — Check remote yum repositories for dependency problems. By default, this checks repositories configured for your machine. To check a specific repository, use the `-r repoid` option (get the repoid from the first line of the `/etc/yum.repos.d` file for the repository). Other options include `-c file` (to use a different configuration *file* containing repositories) or `-a arch` (to indicate which base architecture to check for the repository). Note that this command consumes a lot of memory and can take a long time to run.

- **yumdownloader** — Download a package from a repository to a selected directory. This tool also downloads all dependent packages along with the requested package by adding the `--resolve` option. You can specify a download directory (`--destdir directory`) or just list the URL where the package would be downloaded from (`--urls`) without actually downloading. Use `--source` to download source packages as well.

- **repoquery** — Query yum repositories for information about packages and groups. This command is similar to using `rpmquery` to query your local RPM database. You can list descriptions of a package (`-i`), list package dependencies (`--requires`), and show name, version and release information (`-nvr`). Type `repoquery --help` for other options.

Getting Fedora and RHEL software updates

With new exploits being discovered daily, any computer connected to the Internet should get regular software updates to patch any potential holes and fix broken code. Yum offers several ways of getting updates for Fedora. For Fedora, the GUI utilities for getting updates is called PackageKit.

Getting alerted to available updates

The first time you log in to Fedora and display the desktop, you will probably see an orange star icon in the upper-right, alerting you that updates are available. That icon represents the PackageKit Update Applet. Any time updates are available, that icon will appear.

Click the button on the applet, and then select Show Updates. The PackageKit Update System window will open, listing the number of available updates You can select Review Updates to view and optionally select only particular packages to update. Click the Apply Updates button and all selected updates will be downloaded to your computer and installed. Figure 5-1 shows an example of the PackageKit Update System window:

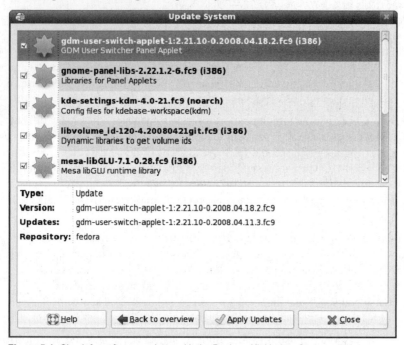

Figure 5-1: Check for software updates with the PackageKit Update System window.

Getting manual updates with yum

At any time you can check whether updates are available for RPM packages installed on your Fedora or RHEL system. Before doing updates with yum, however, you should always update yum itself first:

```
# yum update yum
```

Next, you can check for updates. Then you can choose to either update selected packages or all available packages. Here is how:

```
# yum check-update
```

The check-update option causes yum to check the software repositories for available updated versions of RPM packages you have installed. If you see a package you want to update, you can use the update option. For example, to update the nmap-frontend package, type the following:

```
# yum update nmap-frontend
```

To update all packages that have updates available, type the following:

```
# yum update
```

This command could take a while to complete, depending on how long it has been since the last time you installed updates and on how many total packages are installed on your computer. If, instead of trying to remember to do updates, you want them to happen automatically, the following section describes how to do that.

Managing RPM Packages

Both graphical and command-line tools are available for managing your Fedora or RHEL systems. The PackageKit Add/Remove Software window lets you display categories of software packages installed on and available for your system. The rpm command offers an extensive range of features for installing, uninstalling, listing, and verifying your RPM packages.

Using the PackageKit Add/Remove window

Unless you installed every package that comes with Fedora, as you go through this book you will probably find that you want to add some Fedora software packages after the initial installation. To do that, you can use the yum command (as already described). You can also use rpm, a general-purpose command for installing any software packages in RPM format, described in the following section. However, the application with the most user-friendly interface is the PackageKit Add/Remove Software window, which provides a graphical interface for installing packages.

The PackageKit Add/Remove Software window replaces the Package Manager window in Fedora this release. This window provides a lot of flexibility to search, browse, list, and install software packages from yum repositories To open the Add/Remove Software window in Fedora, select System → Administration → Add/Remove Software from the menu on the top panel.

With the Add/Remove Software window displayed, you can find both available and installed packages as follows:

- Select a category from the left column to see all packages from that category in the right column.
- Enter all or part of a package name the the search box and select find, to have all packages that include that term appear in the right column.

Packages appear with open box icons if they are installed or closed box icons if they are not. Select a package to see information about the contents of that package. With a package selected, you can choose to either install or remove it (depending on its current state).

> **NOTE:** Note that not all packages in a repository will necessarily show up in the groups shown on the left window pane. So, if you believe a package you want is in an enabled repository, but you can't browse for it, use the Find box to search for it by name.

The Add/Remove Software window appears as shown in Figure 5-2. In this example, after searching for xfce and displaying all packages with that term in the right column, I selected one of the packages. In the bottom right window I can then see a description of the package, a complete list of files it contains, and any packages this package depends on or depend on it.

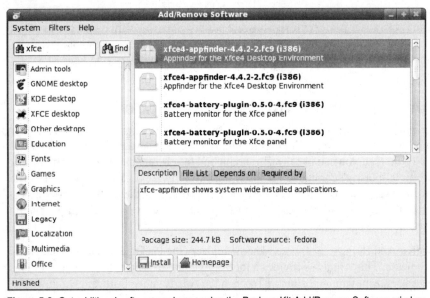

Figure 5-2: Get additional software packages using the PackageKit Add/Remove Software window.

Using the rpm command

The command used to work with RPM package files is rpm. To manage RPM packages, the rpm command has options that let you list all the packages that are installed, upgrade existing packages to newer versions, and query packages for information (such as the files or documentation included with the package). There is also a verify option to check that all files that make up the package are present and unchanged.

The rpm command has the following modes of operation:

- install (-i)
- upgrade (-U)
- freshen (-F)
- query (-q)

- verify (-V)
- signature check (--checksig)
- uninstall (-e)
- rebuild database (--rebuilddb)
- fix permissions (--setperms)
- set owners/groups (--setugids)
- show RC (--showrc)

With these options, you can install RPM packages and verify that their contents are properly installed, correcting any problems that occur. You can also do special things, such as rebuild the RPM database and modify ownership. You must be logged in as the root user to add or remove packages. You may, however, list installed packages, query packages for information, or verify a package's contents without root permission.

The following sections describe how to use rpm to install and work with your RPM applications.

NOTE: While the rpm command is good for installing a single RPM from a local directory, once your system is installed the yum command is often a better choice for installing software. Some advantages to using yum are that, for the package you request, it will search your configured repositories, grab the latest available version, and automatically find dependent packages.

Even if you have an RPM package in a local directory or on a DVD, if the package is dependent on other packages, installing with yum localinstall will try to grab the needed packages from online repositories (while the rpm command would just fail). See the "Using yum to install packages locally" section earlier in this chapter.

Verifying rpm package integrity

When you add repositories to your yum facility, in the cases of rpm.livna.com, ATRPMs, and others that offer a release RPM (such as livna-release), yum is automatically configured to use a valid GPG/DSA key and point to a valid online repository. When you ask to install a package from one of those repositories using yum, the GPG/DSA key is used to validate each package before it is installed. On the other hand, if you are simply installing a local RPM package, you need to do some manual work to verify its contents.

To check all digests and signatures included in an RPM (to make sure it is original and not corrupted), you can use the --checksig option to RPM. For example, say I have a copy of the dvgrab RPM (which is part of Fedora) in my local directory and I wanted to check it. I could run the following command:

```
# rpm --checksig dvgrab-3.1-2.fc9.rpm
dvgrab-3.1-2.fc9.i386.rpm: (sha1) dsa sha1 md5 gpg OK
```

The preceding output shows that the GPG/DSA key was found and used to check that the package's digital signatures (dsa, sha1, and md5) were correct. If, however, you got a package for which you didn't have the GPG/DSA key installed, you would need to get and import that key before you could verify the package.

If you trust the Internet site where you are getting the RPM you want to install, look for an indication that the site has signed its packages. Then download the GPG public key and import it. That will allow you to check the validity of the packages from that site. For example, I decided I wanted to use the KDE-redhat (http://apt.kde-redhat.org) project to replace all my KDE packages from Fedora. I downloaded the digikam package and tried to verify it as follows:

```
# rpm --checksig digikam-doc-0.9.3-1.fc9.rpm
digikam-doc-0.9.3-1.fc9.rpm: (SHA1) DSA sha1 md5 (GPG) NOT OK (MISSING
KEYS: GPG#ff6382fa)
```

Because the GPG public key was not installed, the contents couldn't be verified as correct. So, I went to the KDE-redhat project site and downloaded the GPG public key to the current directory. Then I imported the key as follows:

```
# rpm --import gpg-pubkey-ff6382fa-3e1ab2ca
```

With the GPG public key imported, the second check of the RPM showed that it was clean:

```
# rpm --checksig digikam-doc-0.9.3-1.fc9. rpm
digikam-doc-0.9.3-1.fc9.rpm: (sha1) dsa sha1 md5 gpg OK
```

Most of the GPG public keys you need for the basic repositories used with Fedora are included in the fedora-release package. GPG public keys from other repositories should be stored with those keys in the /etc/pki/rpm-gpg directory.

Remember, however, that it is best to get packages automatically from known repositories with yum (or related tools). Besides checking the signatures of packages, yum will also make sure all dependencies are cleared up.

Installing with rpm

To install an RPM archive file that is not yet installed on your system with the rpm command, most people generally use the same options they would if they were upgrading (the -U option). Here's an example of a command line you could use to install a new RPM package:

```
# rpm -U [options] package
```

Package is the name of the RPM archive file. This package may be in the current directory, on a DVD or CD (for example, /media/disk/Packages/x.rpm), or on an accessible FTP site (for example, ftp://ftp.example.com/pub/whatever.i386.rpm).

> **CAUTION:** Interrupting `rpm` during a package installation can leave stale lock files and possibly corrupt the database. As a result, subsequent `rpm` commands may hang. If this happens, you can probably correct the problem by removing old database locks. If that doesn't work, you can also try checking whether the database is corrupt and, if so, rebuilding the RPM database. Rebuilding the database can take a long time, so only do it if the other options don't clear up the problem. Here's how to remove lock files, check the database, and rebuild the database (as root user):
>
> ```
> # rm -f /var/lib/rpm/__db*
> # rpm --rebuilddb
> ```

Along with the `-U` option, you can use the following options to get feedback during a new installation:

- **-v** — Prints debugging information during installation. This is a good way to see everything that happens during the install process. (This output can be long, so you may want to pipe it to the `less` command.) You can get more information by adding multiple `-v` options (for example, `-vv`).

- **-h** — Prints 50 hash marks (#) as the package unpacks. The intent is to see the progress of the unpacking process (so you can tell if the program is still working or stalled).

- **-percent** — Prints the percentage of the total package that has been installed throughout the install process.

Before installing a package, `rpm` checks to make sure that it is not overwriting newer files or installing a package that has dependencies on other packages that are not installed. The following install options can be used to override conditions that may otherwise cause the installation to fail:

- **--force** — Forces the contents of the current package to be installed, even if the current package is older than the one already installed, contains files placed there by other packages, or is already installed. (This is the same as using the `oldpackage`, `replacefiles`, and `replacepkgs` options.) Although it is dangerous to do so, people often use this option to override any issue that might cause the package install to fail (such as an older RPM).

- **--oldpackage** — Forces the package to be installed, even if the current package is older than the one already installed.

- **--replacefiles** — Forces files in this package to be installed, even if the files were placed there by other packages.

- **--replacepkgs** — Forces packages in this archive to be installed, even if they are already installed on the system.

- **--nodeps** — Skips package dependency checks and installs the package, even if packages it depends on are not installed. This option should be used with extreme caution! By not resolving dependencies properly, you can end up with broken software.

- **--ignorearch** — Forces package to be installed, even if the binaries in the package don't match the architecture of your host computer.

- **--excludedocs** — Excludes any man pages, texinfo documents, or other files marked as documentation.

- **--ignoreos** — Forces package to be installed, even if the binaries in the package don't match the architecture of your operating system.

The following is a simple `rpm` command line used to install an RPM package:

```
# rpm -U AdobeReader_enu-7.0.9-1.i386.rpm
```

I like to see some feedback when I install something (by default, `rpm` is suspiciously quiet when it succeeds). Here is what the command looks like when I add the `-vv` option to get more verbose feedback, along with some of the output:

```
# rpm -Uvv AdobeReader_enu-7.0.9-1.i386.rpm
D: ============== AdobeReader_enu-7.0.9-1.i386.rpm
D: Expected size:    43915056 = lead(96)+sigs(180)+pad(4)+data(43914776)
D:   Actual size:    43915056
D: AdobeReader_enu-7.0.9-1.i386.rpm: Header SHA1 digest: OK
(0d5e873fa8a74542544c1c405f970c8b8983e0e5)
D: opening  db environment /var/lib/rpm/Packages joinenv
D: opening  db index       /var/lib/rpm/Packages rdonly mode=0x0
D: locked   db index       /var/lib/rpm/Packages
D: opening  db index       /var/lib/rpm/Providename rdonly mode=0x0
D: added binary package [0]
D: found 0 source and 1 binary packages
D: ========== +++ AdobeReader_enu-7.0.9-1 i386/linux 0x1
       .
       .
       .
```

From this output, you can see that `rpm` finds one binary package in this archive, verifies the checksum, opens the RPM database, installs the packages, and closes the database when done. Another way to verify that the install is actually working is to add the `-h` option, as follows:

```
# rpm -Uvh AdobeReader_enu-7.0.9-1.i386.rpm
Preparing...      ##############################
AdobeReader_enu   ##############################
```

With the `-h` option, `rpm` chugs out 50 hash marks (#) until the package is done installing. As you can see, when everything goes well, installing with `rpm` is quite simple. Some problems can occur, however. Here are a couple of them:

- **Package dependencies errors** — If the package you are installing requires an additional package for it to work properly, you will see an error noting the missing package. You should get and install that package before trying your package again. (You can override the failure with install options described above, but I don't recommend that because your package may not work without the dependent package.)

- **Nonroot user errors** — If rpm -U is run by someone who is not the root user, the command will fail. The output will indicate that the /var/lib/rpm database could not be opened. Log in as root user and try again.

Upgrading packages with rpm

The upgrade option (-U) with rpm can, as you might expect, also be used to upgrade existing packages. The format is the same as described above:

```
# rpm -U [options] package
```

> **TIP:** Although there is a separate install option (-i), I recommend using the -U option whether you are doing a new install or an upgrade. With -U, the package installs in either case. So rpm -U always works (with one exception), while rpm -i fails if the package is already installed.
>
> The exception is when you are installing kernel packages. Use -i when installing a new kernel or your old (and presumably, working) kernel will be removed and you could be stuck with an unbootable system!

One issue when upgrading is installing an older version of a package. For example, if you install a new version of some software and it doesn't work as well, you will want to go back to the old version. To do this, you can use the --oldpackage option as follows:

```
# rpm -U --oldpackage AnotherLevel-0.7.4-1.noarch.rpm
```

If a later package of this name already exists, it is removed and the older version is installed.

Freshening packages with rpm

An option that is similar to the upgrade (-U) option is the freshen (-F) option. The main difference between the two is what happens if the RPM you are updating or freshening is not already installed on your Fedora system. The -U can do either a fresh install or an upgrade. The -F will only do an upgrade (so if the package is not already installed, rpm -F will do nothing).

A great use for freshen is when you have a directory full of updated RPM files that you want to install on your system. But, you only want to update those packages that are already installed. In other words, there may be a lot of RPMs in the directory you don't want. Freshen lets you just update the packages you already have.

Let's say that you downloaded a directory of RPMs and you want to selectively freshen the ones you have installed. With the directory of RPMs as your current directory, you could type:

```
# rpm -Fhv *.rpm
```

Packages already installed are updated with the new RPMs. All other RPMs are skipped.

> **CAUTION:** Again, note that you should not do freshens or upgrade on kernel packages because it might cause your only working kernel to be removed when you add the new one.

Removing packages with rpm

If you no longer want to use a package (or you just want to recover some disk space), use the -e option to remove a package. In its simplest form, you use rpm with the -e option as follows:

```
# rpm -e package
```

If there are no dependencies on this package, it is silently removed. Before you remove a package, however, you may want to do a quick check for dependencies. The -q option is used for a variety of query options. (Checking for dependencies isn't necessary because rpm checks for dependencies before it removes a package. You may want to do this for your own information, however.) To check for dependencies, do the following:

```
# rpm -q --whatrequires package
```

If you decide to remove the package, I recommend using the -vv option with rpm -e. This lets you see the actual files that are being removed. I also suggest that you either direct the output to a file or pipe it to the less command because the output often runs off the screen. For example:

```
# rpm -evv jpilot | less
```

This example removes the jpilot package and shows you the files that are being removed one page at a time. (Press the Spacebar to page through the output.)

Other options that you can run with rpm -e can be used to override conditions that would prevent the package from being removed or to prevent some processing (such as not running preuninstall and postuninstall scripts). Three of those options are as follows:

- **--nodeps** — Uninstall the package without checking for dependencies
- **--noscripts** — Uninstall the package without running any preuninstall or postuninstall scripts
- **--notriggers** — Uninstall the package without executing scripts that are triggered by removing the package

If you feel nervous about boldly removing a package, you can always run the uninstall in test mode (--test) before you do the real uninstall. Test mode shows you everything that would happen in the uninstall without actually uninstalling. (Add the --vv option to see the details.) Here's an example:

```
# rpm -evv --test jpilot | less
D: opening  db environment /var/lib/rpm/Packages joinenv
D: opening  db index       /var/lib/rpm/Packages rdonly mode=0x0
```

```
D:  locked    db index       /var/lib/rpm/Packages
D:  opening   db index       /var/lib/rpm/Name rdonly mode=0x0
D:  opening   db index       /var/lib/rpm/Pubkeys rdonly mode=0x0
            .
            .
            .
D:  closed    db index       /var/lib/rpm/Name
D:  closed    db index       /var/lib/rpm/Packages
D:  closed    db environment /var/lib/rpm/Packages
```

If the results look fine, you can run the command again, without the `--test` option, to have the package removed.

Querying packages with rpm

You can use the query options (`-q`) of `rpm` to get information about RPM packages. This can be simply listing the packages that are installed or printing detailed information about a package. Here is the basic format of an `rpm` query command (at least one option is required):

```
# rpm -q [options]
```

The following list shows some useful options you can use with an `rpm` query:

- **-qa** — Lists all installed packages.
- **-qf** *file* — Lists the package that owns *file*. (The file must include the full path name or `rpm` assumes the current directory.)
- **-qi** *package* — Lists lots of information about a package.
- **-qR** *package* — Lists components (such as libraries and commands) that *package* depends on.
- **-ql** *package* — Lists all the files contained in *package*.
- **-qd** *package* — Lists all documentation files that come in *package*.
- **-qc** *package* — Lists all configuration files that come in *package*.
- **-qp** *[option] package* — Query packages that are not yet installed. Using this option, along with other query options, allows you to query packages you have that are not yet installed.

To list all the packages installed on your computer, use the `-a` query option. Because this is a long list, you should either pipe the output to `less` or, possibly, use `grep` to find the package you want. The following command line displays a list of all installed RPM packages, and then shows only those names that include the string of characters `xfree`. (The `-i` option to `grep` says to ignore case.)

```
# rpm -qa |grep -i xorg
```

If you are interested in details about a particular package, you can use the `rpm -i` query option. In the following example, information about the `dosfstools` package (for working with DOS file systems in Linux) is displayed:

```
# rpm -qi dosfstools
Name         : dosfstools             Relocations: (not relocatable)
Version      : 2.11                       Vendor: Fedora Project
Release      : 9.fc9             Build Date: Wed 20 Feb 2008 12:32:35 AM CST
Install Date: Wed 26 Mar 2008 11:29:13 PM CDT Build Host: hammer2.fedora.redhat.com
Group        : Applications/System       Source RPM: dosfstools-2.11-9.fc9.src.rpm
Size         : 122533                     License: GPL
Signature    : DSA/SHA1, Tue 04 Mar 2008 09:51:09 AM CST, Key ID da84cbd430c9ecf8
Packager     : Fedora Project
URL          : ftp://ftp.uni-erlangen.de/pub/Linux/LOCAL/dosfstools
Summary      : Utilities for making and checking MS-DOS FAT filesystems on Linux
Description  :
The dosfstools package includes the mkdosfs and dosfsck utilities,
which respectively make and check MS-DOS FAT filesystems on hard
drives or on floppies.
```

To find out about a package's contents, you can use the `-l` (list) option with your query. The following example shows the complete path names of files contained in the `dosfstools` package:

```
# rpm -ql dosfstools | less
/sbin/dosfsck
/sbin/fsck.msdos
/sbin/fsck.vfat
/sbin/mkdosfs
/sbin/mkfs.msdos
/sbin/mkfs.vfat
/usr/share/man/man8/dosfsck.8.gz
  .
  .
  .
```

Would you like to know how to use the components in a package? Using the `-d` option with a query will display the documentation (`man` pages, README files, HOWTOs, and so on) that is included with the package. If you are having trouble getting your X Window System running properly, you can use the following command line to find documents that may help:

```
# rpm -qd xorg-x11 | less
/usr/X11R6/man/man1/Xmark.1x.gz
/usr/X11R6/man/man1/Xorg.1x.gz
/usr/X11R6/man/man1/Xserver.1x.gz
/usr/X11R6/man/man1/appres.1x.gz
/usr/X11R6/man/man1/atobm.1x.gz
/usr/X11R6/man/man1/bitmap.1x.gz
/usr/X11R6/man/man1/bmtoa.1x.gz
```

.
.
.

Many packages have configuration files associated with them. To see what configuration files are associated with a particular package, use the -c option with a query. For example, this is what you would type to find configuration files that are used with the ppp package:

```
# rpm -qc ppp
/etc/logrotate.d/ppp
/etc/pam.d/ppp
/etc/ppp/chap-secrets
/etc/ppp/options
/etc/ppp/pap-secrets
```

If you ever want to know which package a particular command or configuration file came from, you can use the -qf option. In the following example, the -qf option displays the fact that the chgrp command comes from the fileutils package:

```
# rpm -qf /bin/chgrp
coreutils-6.10-11.fc9.i386
```

Before you install a package, you can do the same queries on it that you would do on an installed package. This can be a great tool for finding information from a package while it is in your current directory, or even in a software repository. Here is an example of using the -qp option with -i to see the description of a package in a software repository:

```
# rpm -qp -i \
http://ayo.freshrpms.net/fedora/linux/7/i386/freshrpms/RPMS/a52dec-0.7.4-8.fc7.i386.rpm
Name        : a52dec               Relocations: (not relocatable)
Version     : 0.7.4                      Vendor: Freshrpms.net
Release     : 8.fc7                  Build Date: Wed 30 May 2007 01:02:28 PM CDT
Install Date: (not installed)        Build Host: python3.freshrpms.net
Group       : Applications/Multimedia  Source RPM: a52dec-0.7.4-8.fc7.src.rpm
Size        : 106856                    License: GPL
Signature   : DSA/SHA1, Wed 30 May 2007 01:02:58 PM CDT, Key ID 692ac459e42d547b
Packager    : Matthias Saou <matthias@rpmforge.net>
URL         : http://liba52.sourceforge.net/
Summary     : Library for decoding ATSC A/52 (aka AC-3) audio streams
Description :
liba52 is a free library for decoding ATSC A/52 streams. It is released
under the terms of the GPL license. The A/52 standard is used in a
variety of applications, including digital television and DVD. It is
also known as AC-3.
```

In the previous example, the long command line shown on three lines should actually be typed on one line. If you are concerned about the content or legality of downloading a package, this example is a way to read the description of a package before you even download it.

In the following example, the command lists the files contained in a package that is in the current directory:

```
# rpm -qp -l AdobeReader_enu-7.0.9-1.i386.rpm
```

Again, this is an excellent way to find out what is in a package before you install it.

Verifying installed packages with rpm

If something in a software package isn't working properly, or if you suspect that your system has been tampered with, the verify (-V) option of rpm can help you verify installed software against its original software package. Information about each installed package is stored on your computer in the RPM database. By using the verify option, you can check whether any changes were made to the components in the package.

> **NOTE:** The verify option uses the uppercase letter (-V), while the verbose option uses the lowercase (-v).

Various file size and permissions tests are done during a verify operation. If everything is fine, there is no output. Any components that have changed from when they were installed will be printed along with information indicating how they were changed. Here's an example:

```
# rpm -V ppp
S.5....T. c /etc/ppp/chap-secrets
S.5....T. c /etc/ppp/options
S.5....T. c /etc/ppp/pap-secrets
```

This output shows that the ppp package (used to dial up a TCP/IP network such as the Internet) has had three files changed since it was installed. The notation at the beginning shows that the file size (S), the MD5 sum (5), and the modification time (T) have all changed. The letter c shows that these are all configuration files. By reviewing these files to see that the changes were only those that I made to get PPP working, I can verify that the software is okay.

The indicators that you may see when you verify the contents of a configuration file are:

- **5 (MD5 Sum)** — An MD5 checksum indicates a change to the file contents.
- **S (File size)** — The number of characters in the file has changed.
- **L (Symlink)** — The file has become a symbolic link to another file.
- **T (Mtime)** — The modification time of the file has changed.
- **D (Device)** — The file has become a device special file.
- **U (User)** — The user name that owns the file has changed.
- **G (Group)** — The group assigned to the file has changed.
- **M (Mode)** — If the ownership or permission of the file changed.

> **TIP:** A utility is available to browse the contents of RPM files from Microsoft Windows. With the
> `rpmbrowser.exe` utility, you can list and extract files from an RPM distribution. This utility is available
> from `winsite.com` (search for `rpmbrowser` from `www.winsite.com/search`).

Using Software in Different Formats

There may not be RPMs available for every piece of software you want to install on your
Fedora or RHEL system. Likewise, you may find that an RPM isn't configured exactly the
way you would want it, so that you would be better served by building your own RPM from an
RPM source code package. The following sections describe various forms in which you may
encounter open source software and different ways of building and installing that software for
you to use.

Understanding software package names and formats

Whenever possible, you want to install the applications you use with Fedora from software
packages in RPM format (files with a `.rpm` extension). However, if an RPM isn't available,
the software that you want may come in other package formats.

Say you just downloaded a file from the Internet that contains lots of names, numbers, dots,
gzs, and tars. What does all that stuff mean? Well, when you break it down, it's really not that
complicated.

Most of the names of archive files containing Linux applications follow the GNU-style
package-naming conventions. The following example illustrates the package-naming format:

```
mycoolapp-4.2.3-1.i386.rpm
mycoolapp-4.2.3.tar.gz
mycoolapp-4.2.3.src.tar.gz
mycoolapp-4.2.3.bin.SPARC.tar.gz
mycoolapp-4.2.3.bin.ELF.static.tar.gz
```

These examples represent several different packages of the same software application. The
name of this package is `mycoolapp`. Following the package name is a set of numbers that
represent the version of the package. In this case, it is version 4.2.3 (the major version number
is 4, followed by minor version number and patch level 2.3). After the version number is a dot,
followed by some optional parts, which are followed by indications of how the file is archived
and compressed.

The first line shows a package that is in the RPM Package Management (`.rpm`) format. The
`.i386` before the `.rpm` indicates that the package contains binaries that are built to run Intel
i386 architecture computers (in other words, PCs). The `-1` indicates the build level (the same
package may have been rebuilt multiple times to make minor changes). See the sidebar "Using
Binary RPMs versus Building from Source" for the pros and cons of using prebuilt RPM
binary packages as opposed to compiling the program yourself.

Using Binary RPMs versus Building from Source

Binaries created in RPM format are easily installed, managed, and uninstalled using tools such as rpm and yum. This is the recommended installation method for Fedora and RHEL novices. Sometimes, however, building an application from source code may be preferable. Here are some arguments on both sides:

- RPM — Installing applications from a binary RPM archive is easy. After the application is installed, there are both shell commands and GUIs for managing, verifying, updating, and removing the RPM package. You don't need to know anything about Makefiles or compilers. When you install a binary RPM package, RPM tools even check to make sure that other packages that the package depends on are installed. Because Red Hat has released RPM under the GPL, other Linux distributions also use it to distribute their software. Thus, most Linux applications are, or will be, available in RPM format.

- Source code — Not all source-code packages are made into RPM binaries. If you use RPM, you may find yourself with software that is several versions old, when you could simply download the latest source code and run a few tar and make commands. Also, by modifying source code, you can tailor the package to better suit your needs.

Refer to Appendix A for information on getting source code for Fedora RPM binary packages that are included on the DVD that comes with this book. You can modify that source code yourself and rebuild the RPM binaries. The rebuilt binaries can be tuned to your hardware and include the features you want with the package. For more information on RPMs, refer to the *Red Hat RPM Guide* by Eric Foster-Johnson (Red Hat Press/Wiley, 2003).

In the next two lines of the previous example, each file contains the source code for the package. The files that make up the package were archived using the tar command (.tar) and compressed using the gzip command (.gz). You use these two commands (or just the tar command with the -z option) to expand and uncompress the packages when you are ready to install the applications.

Between the version number and the .tar.gz extension there can be optional tags, separated by dots, which provide specific information about the contents of the package. In particular, if the package is a binary version, this information provides details about where the binaries will run. In the third line, the optional .src tag was added because the developer wanted to differentiate between the source and binary versions of this package. In the fourth line, the .bin.SPARC detail indicates that it is a binary package, ready to run on a SPARC workstation. The final line indicates that it is a binary package, consisting of statically linked ELF format executables.

Instead of using gzip, many software packagers today use the bzip2 utility to compress their software archives. In that case, files names shown in the examples above might instead end with .bz2 or .tar.bz2 extensions.

Here is a breakdown of the parts of a package name:

- **name** — This is generally an all-lowercase string of characters that identifies the application.
- **dash (-)**
- **version** — This is shown as major to minor version number from left to right.
- **dot (.)**
- **src or bin** — This is optional, with src usually implied if no indication is given.
- **dot (.)**
- **type of binary** — This is optional and can include several different tags to describe the content of the binary archive. For example, i386 indicates binaries intended for Intel architectures (Pentium CPU) and SPARC indicates binaries for a Sparc CPU.
- **dot (.)**
- **archive type** — Often tar is used (.tar).
- **compression type** — Often gzip is used (.gz).

Using different archive and document formats

Many of the software packages that are not associated with a specific distribution (such as Fedora or Debian) use the tar/gzip method for archiving and compressing files. However, you may notice files with different suffixes at software project sites.

Table 5-1 describes the different file formats that you will encounter as you look for software at a Linux FTP site. Table 5-2 lists some of the common document formats that are used in distributing information in Linux.

Table 5-1: Linux Archive File Formats

Format	Extension	Description
gzip file	.gz or .z	File was compressed using the GNU gzip utility. It can be uncompressed using the gzip or gunzip utilities (they are both the same).
tar file	.tar	File was archived using the tar command. tar is used to gather multiple files into a single archive file. You can expand the archive into separate files using tar with different options.

Format	Extension	Description
tar and gzip file	`.tgz`	A common practice for naming files that are `tar` archives that were compressed with `gzip` is to use the `.tgz` extension.
bzip2	`.bz2`	File was compressed with the `bzip2` program.
Tar/compressed	`.taz` or `.tz`	File was archived with `tar` and compressed with the UNIX `compress` command.
Linux Software Map	`.lsm`	File contains text that describes the content of an archive.
Debian Binary Package	`.deb`	File is a binary package used with the Debian Linux distribution. (See descriptions of how to convert Debian to Red Hat formats later in this chapter.)
RPM Package Management	`.rpm`	File is a binary package used with Fedora. Format also available to other Linux distributions.

Table 5-2: Linux Document Formats

Format	Extension	Description
Hypertext Markup Language	`.html` or `.htm`	File is in hypertext format for reading by a Web browser program (such as Mozilla).
PostScript	`.ps`	File is in PostScript format for outputting on a PostScript printer.
SGML	`.sgml`	File is in SGML, a standard document format. SGML is often used to produce documents that can later be output to a variety of formats.
DVI	`.dvi`	File is in DVI, the output format of the LaTeX text-processing tools. Convert these files to PostScript or Hewlett-Packard's PCL using the `dvips` and `dvilj` commands.
Plain text		Files in Fedora without a suffix are sometimes plain-text files (in ASCII format). (A note of caution: A lot of the commands in Linux, such as those in `/usr/bin` and `/usr/sbin`, have no extension either. If you have a file with no extension, it's best to use the `file` command on it before proceeding with any operation. In fact, using `file` on a previously untested file can prevent problems. A `.txt` file full of binary code could be used to exploit a text editor and do malicious things to the system.)

If you are not sure what format a file is in, use the `file` command as follows:

```
$ file filename
```

This command tells you if it is a GNU `tar` file, RPM, `gzip`, or other file format. (This is a good technique if a file was renamed and lost its extension.)

If you would like to convert a software package from one of the formats described above, you can try the alien utility (`http://freshmeat.net/projects/alien`). Although alien is not considered stable enough to use with important system packages, it can be a good tool for trying out some simple software packages on your Fedora system.

Building and installing from source code

If no binary version of the package that you want is available, or if you just want to tailor a package to your needs, you can always install the package from source code. To begin, you can get the source code (SRPM) version of any binary packages in Fedora from the Fedora software repository (see Appendix A for details). You can modify the source code and rebuild it to suit your needs.

Software packages that are not available in RPM format are typically available in the form of a tarball (a bunch of files grouped together into a single file formatted by the `tar` utility) that has been compressed (typically by the `gzip` utility). Although the exact instructions for installing an application from a source code archive vary, many packages that are in the `.bz2`, `.tar.bz2`, `.tgz`, `.gz` and `.tar` formats follow the same basic procedure.

> **TIP:** Before you install from source code, you will need to install a variety of software development packages. If you have the disk space, I recommend that you install all software development packages that are recommended during Fedora installation.

The following is a minimal list of C-programming software development tools:

- **gcc** — Contains the `gcc` (GNU C compiler) compiler.
- **make** — Contains the `make` command for making the binaries from Makefiles.
- **glibc** — Contains important shared libraries, the C library, and the standard math library.
- **glibc-devel** — Contains standard header files needed to create executables.
- **binutils** — Contains utilities needed to compile programs (such as the assembler and linker).
- **kernel-devel** — Contains the Linux kernel source code and is needed to rebuild the kernel.
- **rpm-build** — Contains the rpmbuild utility for building the RPM binary package from source code.
- **libc** — Contains libraries needed for programs that were based on `libc` 5, so older applications can run on `glibc` (`libc` 6) systems.

Installing software in SRPM format

To install a source package from the Fedora source directory, do the following:

1. Refer to Appendix A for information on obtaining Fedora source code.

2. Download the package you want to the current directory.

3. Install the source code package using the following command:

   ```
   # rpm -iv packagename*.src.rpm
   ```

   (Replace *packagename* with the name of the package you are installing.) The source is installed in the Fedora source tree (/usr/src/redhat/SOURCES). Spec files are copied to /usr/src/redhat/SPECS.

4. Change to the SPECS directory as follows:

   ```
   # cd /usr/src/redhat/SPECS
   ```

5. Unpack the source code as follows:

   ```
   # rpmbuild -bp packagename*.spec
   ```

6. The package's source code is installed to the /usr/src/redhat/BUILD/*package* directory, where *package* is the name of the software package.

7. You can now make changes to the files in the package's BUILD directory. Read the README, Makefile, and other documentation files for details on how to build the individual package.

The --rebuild option to rpmbuild can be used to rebuild the rpm without installing it first. The resulting binary will be in /usr/src/redhat/RPMS/*arch*, where *arch* is replaced by i386 or other architecture for which you are building the RPM.

Installing software in tar.gz or tar.bz2 formats

Here are some generic instructions that you can use to install many Linux software packages that are in the gzip or tar format:

1. Get the source code package from the Internet or from a CD distribution and copy it into an empty directory (preferably using a name that identifies the package).

2. To check the contents of your tar archive before extracting it to your hard drive, you could use the following command:

   ```
   # tar tvf package.tar.gz
   ```

3. Assuming the file is compressed using gzip, uncompress the file using the following command:

   ```
   # gunzip package.tar.gz
   ```

The result is that the package is uncompressed and the `.gz` is removed from the package name (for example, *package*`.tar`). (If your package ends in `bz2`, use the `bzip2` command instead of `gunzip` shown above.)

4. From the resulting `tar` archive, run the `tar` command as follows:

```
# tar xvf package.tar
```

This command extracts the files from the archive and copies them to a subdirectory of the current directory. (Using `tar xvfz` *package*`.tar.gz` you can do steps 2 and 3 in one step. For a compressed `bzip2` file, run `tar xvfj` *package*`.tar.bz2` instead.)

5. Change directories to the new subdirectory created in Step 3, as follows:

```
# cd package
```

6. Look for a file called `INSTALL` or `README`. One of these files should give you instructions on how to proceed with the installation. In general, the `make` command is used to install the package. Here are a few things to look for in the current directory:

If there is a `Make.in` file, try running:

```
# ./configure -prefix=/usr/local
# make all
```

If there is an `Imake` file, try running:

```
# xmkmf -a
# make all
```

If there is a `Makefile`, try running:

```
# make all
```

After the program is built and installed, you might have to do additional configuration. You should consult the `man` pages or the HOWTOs that come with the software for information on how to proceed.

> **TIP:** With some tar.gz files that include an RPM spec file, you could run the `rpm -ta` `file.tar.gz` and the `rpm` command will build an RPM from that tarball.

To try out this procedure, I downloaded the whichman package, which includes utilities that let you find manual pages by entering keywords. The file I downloaded, `whichman-2.2.tar.gz`, was placed in a directory that I created called `/usr/src/which`. I then ran the `gunzip` and `tar` commands, using `whichman-2.2.tar.gz` and `whichman-2.2.tar` as arguments, respectively.

I changed to the new directory, `cd /usr/sw/which/whichman-2.2`. I then listed its contents. The README file contained information about the contents of the package and how to install it. As the README file suggested, I typed **make**, and then **make install**. The commands `whichman`, `ftwhich`, and `ftff` were installed in `/usr/bin`. (At this point, you can check the `man` page for each component to see what it does.)

The last thing I found in the README file was that a bit of configuration needed to be done. I added a `MANPATH` variable to my `$HOME/.bashrc` to identify the location of `man` pages on my computer to be searched by the `whichman` utility. The line I added looked like this:

```
export
MANPATH=/usr/share/man:/usr/man/man1:/usr/X11R6/man:/usr/share/doc/samba-
2.2.3a/docs
```

In case you are wondering, `whichman`, `ftwhich`, and `ftff` are commands that you can use to search for `man` pages. They can be used to find several locations of a `man` page, `man` pages that are close to the name you enter, or `man` pages that are located beneath a point in the directory structure, respectively.

Using Fedora or RHEL to Run Applications

Although operating systems are nice (and necessary), people use desktop computers to run application programs. There has been a common belief that although Fedora or RHEL can work well as a server, they are not ready to challenge Microsoft's dominance of the desktop arena. There are several reasons why, I believe, Fedora and RHEL can replace Microsoft Windows on the desktop, if you are committed to doing it:

- Every category of desktop application now has an open source offering that will run in Linux. So, for example, although Adobe Photoshop doesn't run natively in Linux, you can use The GIMP or other applications to work with digital images in Linux.

- Your Windows applications that you absolutely must have can usually be run without problems using Windows emulators or compatibilty programs, such as QEMU and WINE. Particular efforts have been made to get Windows games (Transgaming.com) and office productivity applications (Codeweavers.com) running in Linux.

- With viruses and worms running rampant in Microsoft systems, many people now believe that Linux systems offer a more secure alternative, particularly if the desktop system is being used primarily for Web browsing and e-mail. With Linux, corporations that deploy hundreds or even thousands of desktop systems can exercise a great deal of control over the security and features in their employees' systems.

  In the long run, as Linux systems become more profitable targets for viruses and malware, learning good practices in choosing software, using file ownership/permission, and monitoring system resources will become more important. However, such tools (including virus scanners like klamav and clamscan) are already available for any Linux system that chooses to include them. (For more information refer to `www.clamav.net` and `http://klamav.sourceforge.net`.)

- A huge development community is working on open source applications to meet the needs of the Linux community. If you feel more secure having a company backing up your mission-critical applications, some strong commercial software offerings are available for Red Hat systems (see www.redhat.com/apps/isv_catalog).

The bottom line is that it will take some effort for most people to discard their Microsoft Windows operating systems completely. However, if you are committed to making Fedora your sole application platform, there are several ways to ease that transition. Emulation programs let you run many programs that were created for other operating systems. Conversion programs can help you convert graphics and word processing data files from other formats to those supported by Linux applications.

> **CROSS-REFERENCE:** See Chapter 6 for information on importing and exporting word processing and graphics files.

If you are running Linux on a PC, chances are that you already paid for a Microsoft Windows 95, 98, ME, XP, NT, 2000, or Vista operating system. You can either run Linux on a different PC than you use for Windows or have Windows and Linux on separate partitions of your hard disk on the same PC. The latter requires that you reboot each time you want to switch operating systems. (See Chapter 2 for information on setting up a Linux/Windows dual-boot system.) Recently, a third choice has been added, where you can run a virtual Windows system on your Linux desktop (see the descriptions of Xen and KVM later in this chapter).

The following section describes applications that run in Fedora that you can use to replace the Windows applications you are used to.

Finding common desktop applications in Linux

If you are going to use Linux as a desktop computer system, you have to be able to write documents, work with graphics, and crunch numbers. You probably also have other favorite applications, like a music player, Web browser, and e-mail reader.

> **NOTE:** Using WINE technology, the people at Codeweavers, Inc. offer a CrossOver Office product that lets you install and run Microsoft Office in Linux. See the "Running Windows Applications with WINE" section later in this chapter.

To give you a snapshot of what desktop applications are available, Table 5-3 contains a list of popular Windows applications, equivalent Linux applications, and where you can find the Linux applications. Although many of these applications have not reached the level of sophistication of their Windows counterparts, they can be cost-effective alternatives.

Table 5-3: Windows-Equivalent Linux Applications

Windows Applications	Linux Applications	Where to Get Linux Applications	Cost
Microsoft Office (office productivity suite)	OpenOffice.org (`openoffice.org`)	Included on Fedora DVD	Free
	Koffice	Included on Fedora DVD	Free
	StarOffice	`www.sun.com/staroffice`	$69.95
Microsoft Word (word processor)	OpenOffice.org Writer	Included on Fedora DVD	Free
	AbiWord	Included on Fedora DVD	Free
	kword	Included on Fedora DVD	Free
Microsoft Excel (spreadsheet)	OpenOffice.org Calc	Included on Fedora DVD	Free
	gnumeric	Included on Fedora DVD	Free
	kspread	Included on Fedora DVD	Free
Microsoft PowerPoint (presentation)	OpenOffice.org Impress	Included on Fedora DVD	Free
	kpresenter	Included on Fedora DVD	Free
Microsoft Internet Explorer (Web browser)	firefox	Included on Fedora DVD	Free
	seamonkey	Included on Fedora DVD	Free
	epiphany	Included on Fedora DVD	Free
	konqueror	Included on Fedora DVD	Free
	opera	`www.opera.com`	Free
Microsoft Outlook (e-mail reader)	evolution	Included on Fedora DVD	Free
	kmail	Included on Fedora DVD	Free
	thunderbird	Included on Fedora DVD	Free
	Seamonkey Mail	Included on Fedora DVD	Free
Adobe Photoshop (image editor)	The Gimp (gimp)	Included on Fedora DVD	Free
Microsoft Expression or Front Page (HTML editor)	quanta	Included on Fedora DVD	Free
Quicken or Microsoft Money (personal finance)	gnucash	Included on Fedora DVD	Free
AutoCAD (computer-aided design)	LinuxCad	`www.linuxcad.com`	$89

The following sections describe how to find and work with application programs that are included or available specifically for Linux.

Investigating your desktop

More and more high-quality desktop applications are being packaged with or made available for Fedora and RHEL, many as part of the GNOME or KDE desktop environments. In other words, to start finding some excellent office applications, games, multimedia players, and communications tools, you don't have to look any further than the Applications menu button on your desktop panel.

So before you start hunting around the Internet for the software you need, see if you can use something already installed with Fedora or RHEL. The chapters that follow this one describe how to use publishing tools, play games, work with multimedia, and communicate over the Internet — all with programs that are either on the DVD that comes with this book or are easily attainable.

Using your Fedora or RHEL desktop to run applications is relatively easy. If you have used Microsoft Windows operating systems, you already know the most basic ways of running an application from a graphical desktop. X, however, provides a much more flexible environment for running native Linux applications.

> **CROSS-REFERENCE:** See Chapter 3 for information on setting up an X desktop.

Starting applications from a menu

To run applications on your own desktop, most X window managers provide a menu, similar to the Microsoft Start menu, to display and select X applications. Applications are usually organized in categories. From the GNOME or KDE desktops in Fedora, open the Applications menu, select the category, and then select the application to run. Figure 5-3 shows an example of the Applications menu and the Accessories submenu in GNOME.

Starting applications from a Run Application window

Not all installed applications appear on the menus provided with your window manager. For running other applications, some window managers provide a window, similar to the Run Application window, that lets you type in the name of the program you want to run.

To access the Run Application window:

1. Right-click the panel and select Add to Panel.
2. Select Run Application and click Add. The Run Application icon should appear on the panel.
3. Click the Run Application button. The Run Application window appears.
4. Click Show List of Known Applications, click the program you want, and then click Run.

If the application you want isn't on the list, you can either type the command you want to run (along with any options) and click Run, or you can click Run with File to browse through directories to select a program to run. If you are running a program that needs to run in a Terminal window, such as the vi command, click the Run in Terminal button before running the command. Figure 5-4 is an example of the Run Application window.

Figure 5-3: Starting X applications from the Applications menu.

Figure 5-4: Select a program to run from the list in the Run Application window.

Starting applications from a Terminal window

I often prefer to run an X application, at least for the first time, from a Terminal window. There are several reasons why I prefer a Terminal window to selecting an application from a menu or Run Application window:

- If there is a problem with the application, you see the error messages. Applications started from a menu or Run Application usually just fail silently.

- Applications from menus run with set options. If you want to change those options, you have to change the configuration file that set up the menu and make the changes there.

- If you want to try out a few different options with an application, a Terminal window is an easy way to start it, stop it, and change its options.

When you have found an application and figured out the options that you like, you can add it to a menu or a panel (if your window manager supports those features). In that way, you can run a program exactly as you want, instead of the way it is given to you on a menu.

Here is a procedure to run X applications from a Terminal window:

1. Open a Terminal window from your desktop (look for a Terminal icon on your Panel or a Terminal selection on a menu.)

2. Type

```
$ echo $DISPLAY
```

   The result should be something similar to the following:

```
:0.0
```

   This indicates that the Terminal window will, by default, direct any X application you run from this window to display 0.0 on your local system. (If you don't see a value when you type that command, type **export DISPLAY=:0.0** to set the display value.)

3. With the xmms package installed, type the following command:

```
$ xmms &
```

   The xmms program should appear on your desktop, ready to work with. You should note the following:

   - The xmms command runs in the background of the Terminal window (&). This means that you can continue to use the Terminal window while xmms is running.

   - I encountered no errors running xmms on this occasion. With other applications, however, text sometimes appeared in the Terminal window after the command was run. The text may say that the command can't find certain information or that certain fonts or colors cannot be displayed. That information would have been lost if the command were run from a menu.

4. If you want to know what options are available, type:

```
$ xmms --help
```

5. Try it with a few options. For example, if you want to begin by playing a file and you have a Ogg Vorbis audio file named `file.ogg`, you could type:

```
$ xmms file.ogg
```

6. When you are ready to close the xmms window, you can either do so from the xmms box window (right-click on the xmms window and select Exit) or you can kill the process in the Terminal window. Type **jobs** to see the job number of the process. If it was job number 2, for example, you would type **kill %2** to kill the xmms program. If instead you want to continue running xmms in the background, press Ctrl+Z (to put it in the background) and bg (to continue running it in the background).

You should try running a few other X commands. A couple of old X commands you might try are xeyes or xcalc.

Running remote X applications

X lets you start an application from anywhere on the network and have it show up on your X display. Instead of being limited by the size of your hard disk and the power of your CPU and RAM, you can draw on resources from any computer that gives you access to those resources.

Think about the possibilities. You can work with applications launched from any other computer that can run an X application — from a small PC to a supercomputer. Given the proper permission, you can work with files, printers, backup devices, removable drives, other users, and any other resources on the remote computer as though you were on that computer.

With this power, however, comes responsibility. You need to protect the access to your display, especially in networks where the other machines and users are not known or trusted. For example, you wouldn't want to allow anyone to display a login screen on your display, encouraging you to inadvertently give some cracker your login and password.

Traditionally, to run remote X applications, you basically only need to know how to identify remote X displays and how to use whatever security measures are put in place to protect your network resources. Using ssh to launch X applications is even simpler and more secure than the traditional method. Those issues are described in the following sections.

Traditional method to run remote X applications

If there is an X application installed on another computer on your network and you want to use it from your desktop, follow these steps:

- Open permissions to your X server so that the remote application can use your display.
- Identify your X server display to the application when it starts up.

When you run an X client on your local system, your local display is often identified as `:0`, which represents the first display on the local system. To identify that display to a remote system, however, you must add your computer's host name. For example, if your computer were named *whatever*, your display name would be:

```
whatever:0
```

> **TIP:** In most cases, the host name is the TCP/IP name. For the computers on your local network, the name may be in your `/etc/hosts` file, or it may be determined using the Domain Name System (DNS) service. You could also use a full domain name, such as `hatbox.handsonhistory.com`. X does support other types of transport, although transports other than TCP/IP aren't used much anymore.

You will probably use the display name in this form most of the time you run a remote X application. In certain cases, however, the information may be different. If your computer had multiple X displays (keyboard, mouse, and monitor), you may have numbers other than `:0` (`:1`, `:2`, and so on). It is also possible for one keyboard and mouse to be controlling more than one monitor, in which case you could add a screen number to the address, like this:

```
whatever:0.1
```

This address identifies the second screen (`.1`) on the first display (`:0`). The first screen is identified as `.0` (which is the default because most displays only have one screen). Unless you have multiple physical screens, however, you can skip the screen identifier.

There are two ways to identify your display name to a remote X application:

- **DISPLAY shell variable** — The `DISPLAY` shell variable can be set to the system name and number identifying your display. After this is done, the output from any X application run from that shell will appear on the display indicated. For example, to set the `DISPLAY` variable to the first display on `whatever`, type one of the following:

  ```
  export DISPLAY=whatever:0
  ```

  or

  ```
  setenv DISPLAY whatever:0
  ```

- The first example shows how you would set the `DISPLAY` variable on a `bash` or `ksh` shell. The second example works for a `csh` shell.

- **-display option** — Another way to identify a remote display is to add the `-display` option to the command line when you run the X application. This overrides the `DISPLAY` variable. For example, to open an `xterm` window on a remote system so that it appears on the first display on `whatever`, type the following:

  ```
  xterm -display whatever:0
  ```

With this information, you should be able to run an X application from any computer that you can access from your local computer. The following sections describe how you may use this information to start a remote X application.

Launching a remote X application

Suppose you want to run an application from a computer named `remote1` on your local area network (in your same domain). Your local computer is `local1`, and the remote computer is `remote1`. The following steps show how to run an X application from `remote1` from your X display on `local1`.

> **CAUTION:** This procedure assumes that no special security procedures are implemented. It is the default situation and is designed for sharing applications among trusted computers (usually single-user workstations) on a local network. This method is inherently insecure and requires that you trust all users on computers to which you allow access. If you require a more secure method, refer to the section "Using SSH to run remote X applications" later in this chapter.

1. Open a Terminal window on the local computer.

2. Allow access for the remote computer (for example, `remote1`) to the local X display by typing the following from the Terminal window:

    ```
    $ xhost +remote1
    remote1 being added to access control list
    ```

3. Log in to the remote computer using any remote login command. For example:

    ```
    $ telnet -l user remote1
    Password:
    ```

    Replace `user` with the name of the user login that you have on the remote computer. You will be prompted for a password.

> **NOTE:** By default, the `telnet` service is not enabled in Fedora or RHEL. The server's administrator (in this example, `remote1`) must consider security consequences of enabling remote login services.

4. Type the password for the remote user login. (You are now logged in as the remote user in the Terminal window.)

5. Set the `DISPLAY` variable on the remote computer to your local computer. For example, if your computer were named pine in the local domain, the command could appear as:

    ```
    $ export DISPLAY=pine:0
    ```

    (If you are using a `csh` shell on the remote system, you may need to type **setenv DISPLAY pine:0**.)

6. At this point, any X application you run from the remote system from this shell will appear on the local display. For example, to run a remote Terminal window so that it appears locally, type:

    ```
    $ xterm
    ```

    The Terminal window appears on the local display.

You need to remember some things about the remote application that appears on your display:

- If you only use the login to run remote applications, you can add the line exporting the DISPLAY variable to a user configuration file on the remote system (such as .bashrc, if you use the bash shell). After that, any application that you run will be directed to your local display.

- Even though the application looks as though it is running locally, all the work is being done on the remote system. For example, if you ran a word processing program remotely, it would use the remote CPU and when you save a file, it is saved to the remote file system.

> **CAUTION:** Don't forget when a remote shell or file editor is open on your desktop. Sometimes people forget that a window is remote and will edit some important configuration file on the remote system by mistake (such as the /etc/fstab file). You could damage the remote system with this type of mistake.

Using SSH to run remote X applications

Not only does the ssh command provide a secure mechanism for logging in to a remote system, it also provides a way of securely running remote X applications. With X11 forwarding turned on, any X application you run from the remote location during your ssh session will appear on your local desktop.

After you log in to the remote computer using ssh, you can use that secure channel to forward X applications back to your local display. Here is an example:

1. Type the following ssh command to log in to a remote computer (the -X option enables X11 forwarding):

```
$ ssh -X jake@remote1
jake@remote1's password: *******
```

2. Check that the display variable is set to forward any X applications you run through this ssh session to your local display:

```
$ echo $DISPLAY
localhost:10.0
```

3. After you are logged in, type any X command and the window associated with that command appears on your local display. For example, to start the gedit command, type:

```
$ gedit &
```

For this to work, you don't need to open your local display (using xhost). The reason this works is because the SSH daemon (sshd) on the remote system sets up a secure channel to your computer for X applications. So as not to interfere with any real display numbers, the SSH daemon (by default) uses the display name of localhost:10.0.

This X forwarding feature is on by default in the latest version of Fedora (see the
`X11Forwarding yes` value set in the `/etc/ssh/sshd_config` file). It is off in other
systems, however, so you may need to change the `X11Forwarding` value on those systems.

Running Microsoft Windows, DOS, and Macintosh Applications

Linux is ready to run most applications that were created specifically for Linux, the X Window
System, and many UNIX systems. Many other applications that were originally created for
other operating systems have also been ported to Linux. However, there are still lots of
applications created for other operating systems for which there are no Linux versions.

Linux can run some applications that are intended for other operating systems using *emulator*
programs. An emulator, as the name implies, tries to act like something it is not. In the case of
an operating system, an emulator tries to present an environment that looks to the application
like the intended operating system.

> **NOTE:** The most popular of these emulators, called WINE, is not really an emulator at all. WINE is a
> mechanism that implements Windows application-programming interfaces; rather than emulating Microsoft
> Windows, it provides the interfaces that a Windows application would expect. In fact, some people claim
> that WINE stands for "WINE Is Not an Emulator."

In the following sections, I discuss emulators that enable you to run applications that are
intended for the following operating systems:

- DOS
- Microsoft Windows 3.1
- Microsoft Windows 95
- Microsoft Windows 98
- Microsoft Windows 2000
- Microsoft Window ME
- Microsoft Windows NT
- Microsoft Windows XP
- Microsoft Windows Vista
- Macintosh (Mac OS)

As for Mac OS X applications, because that operating system is based on a UNIX-like
operating system called Darwin, many open source applications written for Mac OS X will
have versions available that run in Linux. If you find an application that you like in Mac OS X
and want to run in Linux, check the `Sourceforge.net` site to see if the project that created

the Mac OS X application offers a Linux version of it as well (or at least the source code to try to build the application yourself).

> **NOTE:** In theory, any application that is Win32-compatible should be able to run using software such as WINE (described later). Whether or not a Microsoft Windows application will run in an emulator in Linux must really be checked on a case-by-case basis.

Available emulation programs include:

- DOSBox, for running many classic DOS applications that won't run on new computers. (Install it from Fedora by typing `yum install dosbox` as root.)

- DOSEMU, also for running classic DOS applications. (Refer to the DOSEMU site at `http://dosemu.sourceforge.net` for information. Select the Stable Releases link to find RPM binaries of DOSEMU that run in Fedora.)

- WINE, which lets you run Windows 3.1, Windows 95, Windows 98, Windows 2000, Windows NT, and Windows XP binaries. Windows NT and XP programs are not as well supported. However, because many Windows applications are written to work in earlier Windows systems (why limit their market just to use a couple of XP-specific calls?), they will run just fine in WINE as well. Check the documentation for the Windows application. If it only requires Windows 95 or Windows 98, it will often run in WINE.

- ARDI Executor, which enables you to run applications that are intended for the Macintosh operating system (MAC OS).

In general, the older and less complex the program, the better chance it has to run in an emulator. Character-based applications generally run better than graphics-based applications. Also, programs tend to run slower in emulation, due sometimes to additional debugging code put into the emulators. However, because WINE "is not an emulator," any application that doesn't make system calls should run as fast in WINE as it does natively in Windows.

Yet another approach to running applications from other operating system on Linux is to use virtualization products. One popular virtual machine product is VMWare player (`www.vmware.com/products/player`). However, included in Fedora itself is Xen virtualization software. Another approach to virtualization, called KVM, was added to Fedora in Fedora 7. (Both Xen and KVM are described later in this chapter.)

Running DOS applications

Because Linux was originally developed on PCs, a variety of tools were developed to help developers and users bridge the gap between Linux and DOS systems. A set of Linux utilities called `mtools` enables you to work with DOS files and directories within Linux. A DOS emulator called `DOSbox` lets you run DOS applications within a DOS environment that is actually running in Linux (much the way a DOS window runs within a Microsoft Windows operating system). DOSEMU is another DOS emulator that is available outside of the Fedora repository.

Using mtools

mtools are mostly DOS commands that have the letter *m* in front of them and that run in Linux (though there are a few exceptions that are named differently). Using these commands, you can easily work with DOS files and file systems. Table 5-4 lists mtools that are available with Linux (if you have the mtools package installed).

Table 5-4: mtools Available with Linux

Command	Function
mattrib	The DOS attrib command, which is used to change an MS-DOS file attribute flag.
mbadblocks	The DOS badblocks command, which tests a floppy disk and marks any bad blocks contained on the floppy in its FAT.
mcd	The DOS cd command, which is used to change the working directory to another DOS directory. (The default directory is A:\) that is used by other mtools.
mcheck	The DOS check command, which is used to verify a file.
mcopy	The DOS copy command, which is used to copy files from one location to another.
mdel	The DOS del command, which is used to delete files.
mdeltree	The DOS deltree command, which deletes an MS-DOS directory along with the files and subdirectories it contains.
mdir	The DOS dir command, which lists a directory's contents.
mdu	The Linux du command, which is used to show the amount of disk space used by a DOS directory.
mformat	The DOS format command, which is used to format a DOS floppy disk.
minfo	This command is used to print information about a DOS device, such as a floppy disk.
mkmanifest	This command is used to create a shell script that restores Linux filenames that were truncated by DOS commands.
mlabel	The DOS label command, which is used to make a DOS volume label.
mmd	The DOS md command, which is used to create a DOS directory.
mmount	This command is used to mount a DOS disk in Linux.
mmove	The DOS move command, which is used to move a file to another directory and/or rename it.

Command	Function
mrd	The DOS rd command, which is used to remove a DOS directory.
mren	The DOS ren command, which is used to rename a DOS file.
mshowfat	This command is used to show the FAT entry for a file in a DOS file system.
mtoolstest	This command is used to test the mtools configuration files.
mtype	The DOS type command, which is used to display the contents of a DOS text file.
mzip	This command is used to perform operations with Zip disks, including eject, write protect, and query.

I used to use mtools to copy files between my Linux system and a Windows system that was not on my network. I would use mcopy, which let me copy files using drive letters instead of device names. In other words, to copy the file vi.exe from floppy drive A: to the current directory in Linux, I would type:

```
# mcopy a:\vi.exe .
```

CAUTION: By default, the floppy-disk drive can be read from or written to only by the root user and the floppy group. To make the floppy drive accessible to everyone (assuming it is floppy drive A:), type the following as root user: **chmod 666 /dev/fd0**.

Using DOSBox

To run your classic DOS applications, Fedora includes the dosbox package. To install dosbox, type the following as root user:

```
# yum install dosbox
```

With DOSBox installed, just type **dosbox** to open a DOSBox window on your desktop. From that window, you have an environment when you can run many classic DOS applications. Assuming you have some DOS applications you want to run already stored on your Fedora system, you can make those applications available by mounting the directory containing them. For example, to mount the /home/chris directory to drive C in DOSBox, type the following:

```
Z:\> mount c /home/chris
```

At this point, you can use standard DOS commands to access and run applications from the directory you just mounted. For example, type **dir c:** to see the contents of the directory you just mounted. Type **c:** to go to that directory. Then just run the DOS applications stored in that directory by typing its name.

To mount a CD-ROM, you need to indicate the file system type when you mount it. For example:

```
Z:\> mount d /media/disk -t cdrom
```

For information on using special keys and features in dosbox, refer to the dosbox README file (`/usr/share/doc/dosbox-*/README`).

Running Microsoft Windows applications in Linux

There are several promising approaches you can take to get your Windows applications to work during a running Linux session. Here are a few of them:

- **WINE** — The WINE project (`www.winehq.org`) has been making great strides in getting applications that were created for Microsoft Windows to run in Linux and other operating systems. WINE is not really an emulator because it doesn't emulate the entire Windows operating system. Instead, because it implements Win32 application programming interfaces (APIs) and Windows 3.x interfaces, the WINE project is more of a "Windows compatibility layer." WINE doesn't require that Windows be installed. It can, however, take advantage of Windows .dll files if you have some to add.

- **Win4Lin** — Win4Lin (`www.win4lin.com`) is a commercial product for running a Windows system in Linux. You can try the software free for 14 days. Installation consists of three steps: Installing Win4Lin (available in RPM format), installing the guest operating system (Windows 98, 2000, or ME; XP is still experimental), and setting up a guest session. Then you run a full Windows system from a Linux desktop, installing and running any Windows applications you choose.

- **QEMU** — QEMU (`www.qemu.org`) is an open source project that acts as a processor emulator. It can either emulate a full system or work in user mode emulation (where it can be used to test processes compiled for different CPUs). In full system emulation, QEMU can run a variety of operating systems, including Windows 3.11, 95, 98SE, ME, 2000, and possibly XP.

  To try applications intended for other operating systems, QEMU can also run several Linux (Fedora, KNOPPIX, Mandrake, Morphix, Debian, and others) and other UNIX-like systems (NetBSD, Solaris, and others). QEMU can take advantage of virtualization features, using KVM, that have recently been added to the Linux kernel (described later in this chapter).

The rest of this section describes how to get and use WINE to run Windows applications in Linux. To get WINE for your Fedora system, you can go to the following places:

- **WINE in Fedora** —As of Fedora 7, WINE became part of the main Fedora software repository. The wine and wine-core packages are needed to use WINE. Additional WINE support comes in the following packages: wine-capi (ISDN support), wine-cms (color management), wine-esd (ESD sound support), wine-jack (JACK sound support), wine-ldap (LDAP support), wine-nas (NAS sound support), wine-tools (useful Windows utilities), and wine-twain (scanner support). Add wine-docs for further documentation or wine-devel, for WINE development components.

- **Cedega** — A commercial version of WINE called Cedega (formerly called WineX) is available from TransGaming, Inc. (`www.transgaming.com`). TransGaming focuses on running Windows games in Linux, using WINE as its base. See Chapter 7 for descriptions of Cedega.

- **CodeWeavers** — If you need Microsoft Office or Web browser plug-ins, CodeWeavers (`www.codeweavers.com`) offers CrossOver Linux. Although CrossOver Linux costs some money, it offers friendly interfaces for installing and managing the Windows software. A 30-day free trial is available.

While it's true that you can run many Windows applications using WINE, some fiddling is still required to get many Windows applications to work. If you are considering moving your desktop systems from Windows to Linux, the current state of WINE provides an opportunity to see if some Windows applications you need might run in Linux.

Besides developing software, the WINE project maintains a database of applications that run under WINE (`http://appdb.winehq.org`). More than 1000 applications are listed, although many of them are only partially operational. The point is, however, that the list of applications is growing, and special attention is being paid to getting important Windows 2000 and XP applications running.

Although not an open source product, Win4Lin is another good way to run Windows applications, along with a Linux system on the same running computer. With the open source QEMU project you can simultaneously run Microsoft Windows and Linux operating systems on the same PC. (See `http://qemu.org/ossupport.html` for a complete list of supported operating systems.)

In general, Windows applications are less likely to break in QEMU than they are in WINE (since you actually run the whole Windows operating system), but performance may not be as good (since you run an operating system within an operating system). The next section describes how to set up Linux to run Microsoft Windows applications using WINE.

Running Windows Applications in WINE

For WINE to let you run Microsoft Windows applications, it needs to have an environment set up that looks like a Microsoft Windows system. The following section takes you through the steps of installing and configuring the wine RPM available from Fedora. You can install wine over the Internet by typing the following:

```
# yum install wine wine-tools wine-core wine-docs
```

Although you only need the wine and wine-core packages, wine-tools offers some nice graphical tools for working with your WINE environment and wine-docs offers some useful documents in the /usr/share/doc/wine-docs* directory for developing software and using WINE. The yum command line shown above will also pull in other wine packages from the Fedora repository (such as those that include additional support for sound, scanners, and other features mentioned earlier).

The location of the basic Microsoft Windows operating-system directories for WINE is the $HOME/.wine/drive_c directory for each user, which looks like the C: drive to wine. The $HOME/.wine directory is created automatically in your home directory the first you run Wine Configuration (select Applications → Other → Wine → Wine Configuration) or type the winecfg command:

```
$ winecfg
```

This opens the Wine configuration window, where you can do most of your activities to add applications, configure the operating system, and integrate with the desktop. Figure 5-5 shows an example of the Wine configuration window.

Figure 5-5: Set up your Windows applications in Linux from the Wine configuration window.

Assigning drive letters

Before you begin installing Windows applications in WINE, you should become familiar with your WINE environment. Drive letters are assigned in the $HOME/.wine/dosdevices directory. Select the Drives tab on the Wine configuration window to see which drive letters are assigned. At least drive C: and drive Z: should be set.

To configure additional drive letters, you can select Add (to add an individual drive) or select Autodetect (to have WINE assign all your partitions to drive letters) in the Windows configuration window.

Within the $HOME/.wine/drive_c directory (that is, your C: drive), you should see some things that are familiar to you if you are coming from an older Windows environment: Program Files and windows directories.

> **NOTE:** For details on configuring WINE, see the Wine User Guide. That guide (wineusr-guide.pdf) is stored in the /usr/share/doc/wine-docs* directory when you install the wine-docs RPM.

Installing applications in WINE

For Windows applications that are included on CD or DVD, you can try installing them by simply running the setup program on that medium with the wine command. So, with a CD containing the application you want to install inserted and mounted, you would run a command like the following:

```
# wine d:\Setup.exe
```

Launching applications

Depending on how the application's installer set up the application, there are a couple of ways in which you might launch your Windows application in WINE, as follows:

- **Control Panel** — If the application set up an applet for the Windows control panel, you can open a Windows control panel, and then select the applet to launch the application from there. To start a Windows control panel, type the following:

    ```
    $ wine control
    ```

- **WINE File System Browser** — If you installed the wine-tools package, you can launch the winefile command to see the Wine File window. This window displays a tree structure of the file system, as it relates to the drives you have configured for WINE. Select the drive letter containing the application you want to launch, browse to the application, and double-click it to start.

Just as you launched the application's installer, as described earlier, you can also launch a Windows application installed on your file system from the command line. Again, you can use drive letters to indicate the location of the application you want to launch. However, to have the path to the application interpreted properly, you should typically surround it with quotes:

```
$ wine "C:\program files\appdir\app.exe"
```

As a Windows file path you use backslashes (\) instead of slashes (/) to separate subdirectories. Instead of using double quotes, you can add an extra backslash before each space or backslash.

Once you have a working `wine` command line to run your Windows application, you can add that command to a launcher on your Fedora desktop. See Chapter 3 for information on adding application launchers to your panel, menus, or desktop area.

Tuning and configuring WINE

Because the Windows applications you run with WINE expect to find Windows resources on a Linux system, those resources either have to be provided by WINE or need to be mapped into the existing Linux system. For example, an application may require a specific dll file that WINE doesn't include. Or, you may need to map your COM or LPT ports where WINE expects to find them.

Here are some tips to help you tune your WINE configuration:

- **Windows version** — Different versions of Windows provide different environments for applications to run in. WINE emulates Windows XP by default, but allows you to have WINE run as nearly a dozen different Windows versions for each application. From the Wine configuration window, select the Applications tab and choose the Add application button. Choose the Windows application you want from your file system then choose the Windows version you want it to run under.

- **Changing registry entries** — When you need to change Windows registry entries, WINE provides three files you can work with: `system.reg`, `user.reg`, and `userdef.reg`. All of these files are in the user's `$HOME/.wine` directory. You can use the `wineprefixcreate` utility to update your registry.

- **Configuring ports** — As with Windows drive letters, you can add links to serial and a parallel ports to your `$HOME/.wine/dosdevices` directory. For example, to add entries for your first parallel port (LPT1) and serial port (COM1), you could run the following commands from your `$HOME/.wine/dosdevices` directory:

```
$ ln -s /dev/lp0 lpt1
$ ln -s /dev/ttyS0 com1
```

- **Adding DLLs** — WINE provides many of the basic libraries (DLL files) needed for a functioning Windows system. However, some DLLs that may be required for your application may not be included, or some that are included may not work properly for your application. Using the Windows configuration window (Libraries tab), you can replace DLLs provided by WINE or add other DLLs you have from applications you install.

- **Graphics settings** — You can change settings associated with your graphics display from the Graphics tab on the Windows configuration window. In particular, you can change how closely your Windows applications will can be managed on your Linux desktop.

- **Adding fonts** — To add fonts to your WINE installation, copy TrueType fonts (.ttf files) to the `C:\windows\fonts` directory.

For further information on configuring WINE to run your Windows applications in Linux, refer to the Wine User Guide (`www.winehq.org/docs/en/wineusr-guide.html`).

Finding more Windows applications for WINE

For information on Windows applications that have been tested to run in WINE, refer to the Wine Application Database (`http://appdb.winehq.org`). CodeWeavers also keeps its own database of applications that have been tested to run under WINE. Refer to the CodeWeavers Compatibility Center (`www.codeweavers.com/compatibility`) for information on running Windows applications. From there, you can view CodeWeavers' own application database of more than 3300 Windows applications.

Another Web site for information about WINE applications is Frank's Corner (`www.frankscorner.org`). The site is loaded with good tips for getting graphics, Internet, multimedia, office, games, and other applications running in WINE.

Running Macintosh applications with ARDI Executor

Besides enabling you to run many popular older Macintosh applications on the PC, the commercial product ARDI Executor (`www.ardi.com`) from ARDI, Inc. lets you work with Mac-formatted floppies and a variety of Mac drives. Find more about ARDI Executor from `www.ardi.com/executor.php`.

ARDI also maintains a listing of compatible Mac software in its Compatibility Database. There are literally hundreds of Mac applications listed. Each application is color coded (green, yellow, orange, red, or black) to indicate how well the software runs under ARDI. Green and yellow are fully usable and largely usable, respectively. Orange is mostly unusable. Red means the application won't run at all, and black means it won't run because it requires features that aren't implemented in ARDI. At a glance, about two-thirds of the applications listed were either green or yellow.

> **CROSS REFERENCE:** With Mac OS X being based on a Linux-like operating system, more and more cross-platform applications will be available for Linux and the Mac. Interoperating Mac OS X with Linux systems is discussed in more detail in Chapter 26.

Running Applications in Virtual Environments

Virtualization has become a hot topic in Linux in recent years. Instead of being able to have just one operating system running on a computer at a time, virtualization allows multiple guest operating systems to run on a host system. When acting as the host operating system, Fedora offers two major approaches to virtualization: Xen and KVM.

There are many advantages to running multiple virtualized operating systems on one computer. For example, you can configure one virtual machine to contain only a Web server. By compartmentalizing your Web server in this way, you can have it tuned to run efficiently and to protect software running on the same computer from outside intruders. By running different operating systems separately, you can use the same hardware to run applications that weren't made for the same operating system.

The following sections introduce you to Xen and KVM virtualization software in Fedora.

Running applications virtually with Xen

Xen (www.xensource.com) is virtualization software that is included in Fedora. Using Xen, you can run multiple operating system instances within a running Fedora system. These operating systems, referred to as virtual machines, can not only run applications built specifically for those operating systems. They can also appear to the network as though they are running on completely different machines.

To demonstrate Xen features, the procedures in this section describe how to set up a virtual machine of Fedora that will run on an installed host Fedora system. Currently, to run other operating systems on Xen in Fedora, you need to supply an OS image, rather than build one from scratch as shown in the procedure below.

If you run into road blocks with Xen, there are places to get help. To ask questions about Xen, see the Fedora-Xen mailing list (www.redhat.com/mailman/listinfo/fedora-xen). Try the Xen Tools page (http://fedoraproject.org/wiki/Tools/Xen) for links to further information on Xen in Fedora.

You can find more information about how Xen works and what it is from the Xen Source Wiki (http://wiki.xensource.com/xenwiki). In particular, select the Xen FAQ link (for information on what Xen is) or the HowTos link (for links to the user manual and specialty HowTos).

Before installing Xen

Xen requires a lot of resources to run. Each operating system instance (referred to as a guest operating system) will need almost the full amount of resources it would need to run separately. Therefore, before you begin, make sure your system has at least the following available:

- **RAM** — In general, your compuer should have at least 256MB of RAM available for each guest you want to have, plus the amount of RAM required for the type of Fedora install you selected.

- **Hard Disk** — On top of what you need to install Fedora, you need the entire amount of disk space required by each operating system guest you installed. Of course, these amounts can vary greatly, with minimal server installs starting at around 600MB and average desktop installs typically starting at 2GB or 3GB.

- **Paravirtualization (PAE) support** — Your computer's CPU must support the PAE extension. Many laptops will not have PAE support. To see if your computer has PAE support, type the following:

```
# cat /proc/cpuinfo | grep pae
flags : fpu vme de pse tsc msr pae mce cx8 apic
mtrr pge mca cmov pat pse36 mmx fxsr syscall
mmxext 3dnowext 3dnow up
```

In this example, PAE is supported. If it were not supported, nothing would be returned.

- **Fully-virtualized guest support** — In order to run fully virtualized guests, you need Intel VT or AMD-V support, depending on your processor. Check your cpuinfo again (as shown above) but this time `grep` for `vmx` or `svm` (on Intel or AMD processors, respectively). Again, if you see output, the program is supported.

- **GRUB boot loader** — A final requirement of the computer you are using is that GRUB be your boot loader. When you install Xen, it will automatically add itself to your GRUB boot loader as a secondary choice of operating system kernels that you can select to boot.

Installing Xen

To run Xen in Fedora, you need to install and boot from a specially configured Xen kernel. Xen kernel packages are not installed by default with Fedora, so you have to either select them at install time or add them later. Here's how to install the Xen packages you need:

- **At install time or from PackageKit**— Select Base System → Xen, so a check mark appears in front of it. Select Optional Packages to see other packages that are useful, though not required (gnome-applet-vm and virt-manager are selected by default).

- **Using yum** — As root, type the following from Terminal window:

```
# yum install kernel-xen xen virt-manager gnome-applet-vm vnc kernel-xen-
devel
```

Because Xen automatically adds an entry to your GRUB boot loader and installs it when you reboot, you should be ready to restart Fedora with the Xen kernel running. So the next step is to reboot your computer.

Rebooting to Xen

When you reboot your computer, the GRUB boot loader takes over. When you see the first GRUB screen, press any key (quickly) to display available boot options. You should see options that appear similar to the following:

```
Fedora (2.6.25-0.fc9.i686.xen)
Fedora (2.6.25-0.fc9)
```

Press arrow keys to highlight the Xen boot label and press Enter. Fedora will boot Fedora using the Xen kernel. If it doesn't work, you can reboot using the generic Fedora kernel. Then you can try such things as updating your Xen packages or fixing the boot loader configuration (check the `/boot/grub/grub.conf` file).

Installing a guest operating system

With Fedora up and running with the Xen kernel, the next step is to install a guest operating system to run in Xen on your Fedora system. You do this using the `virt-manager` utility. (If you prefer to create a Xen guest with a command-line utility, try `xenguest-install`.)

For demonstration purposes, the procedure below shows how to install a Fedora 7 instance as a virtual guest operating system on Fedora 9. Before you start, you need a network connection and the location of an online Fedora 7 software repository. That location can be a local DVD that is shared via an NFS connection. This procedure gives you an idea of how the feature works, before you try installing other operating systems.

1. **Start libvirtd service** — If it's not already running, start the libvirtd service:

   ```
   # service libvirtd start
   ```

2. **Start xenguest-install** — As root user from a Terminal window, type the following:

   ```
   # /usr/sbin/virt-manager
   ```

3. **Select Xen host** — Select Local Xen host and click File → Open Connection.

4. **Create new guest** — Right-click on local host and click New. When the Create a new virtual system pop-up appears, click Forward. You are asked to name your virtual system.

5. **Virtual machine name** — Type a name to represent this virtual machine and click Forward. Keep the name simple (one word, fairly short, and no special characters) because the name is used to represent the virtual machine in file names and on menus. You are asked the location of the media.

6. **Virtualization method** — Select Paravirtualization (for faster, lightweight virtualization) or Fully Virtualized (slower, but supports more operating systems) and click Forward.

7. **Installation Media** — Type the location of an online software repository (you can also enter a kickstart file, if you have one). To use your Fedora DVD instead of an online repository, you export it as an NFS share (see the following Note). Here's an example of a

software repository for Fedora 7 so you can create a Fedora 7 system to run on your Fedora 9 system:

```
http://download.fedora.redhat.com/pub/fedora/linux/releases/7/Fedora/i38
6/os
```

> **NOTE:** Here's how to use your Fedora DVD as a Xen guest repository. Install the nfs-utils package. Insert the DVD. Assuming it is mounted as `/media/disk`, add the line:
>
> **/media/disk *(ro)**
>
> to the `/etc/exports` file. Start nfs (**`/etc/init.d/nfs start`**). When you are prompted for a software repository, enter this address: **`nfs:localhost:/media/disk`**. If localhost doesn't work, try using your computer's IP address.

8. **Storage location** — Choose to either use a file on an existing file system or the device name of a disk partition to store the installed system. For example, you could name the disk image /home/chris/xenimageA as the file to use. I created a new disk partition as I was doing this procedure. Just make sure that the location you use has enough disk space to hold the operating system you are about to install. You are asked to allocate memory.

9. **Host network** — Choose how would like your new virtual system to connect to the host network. In most cases, select Virtual network. However, you can also select a shared physical device (such as an Ethernet bridge or MAC address).

10. **Allocate Memory** — Type a number representing the maximum number of megabytes of RAM you want to dedicate to this virtual machine and the amount you want to start with and click Forward. At least 256 megabytes of RAM are recommended. If you have more available, you should use more since it will improve performance. You can also select to use multiple virtual CPUs (1 is the default).

11. **Finish** — When all the information has been entered, a summary of the information you entered appears as shown in Figure 5-6. Click Finish. The new virtual machine should appear on the Virtual Machine Manager window. Select it and click Open.

12. **Start installation** — A virtual machine console should appear, ready to install your guest Fedora 7 installation.

13. **Install Guest** — Because you are installing a Fedora 7 guest on a Fedora 9 system, you can basically follow along the installation instructions in Chapter 2 of this book. For disk partitioning, you can instruct the installer to use the entire partition or you can create multiple partitions.

After Fedora is installed as a guest, you can open that virtual machine as you need it from the Virtual Machine Manager window. If you selected Ethernet bridging, and there is a DHCP server on your network, your virtual machine can be assigned its own IP address. So you can use tools in Fedora to access the Internet and update and get new software as needed.

To manage your virtual machines from the command line you can use the xm command. To see which virtual machines are currently available, type the following:

```
# xm list
Name                      ID   Mem   VCPUs    State    Time
Domain-0                   0   453       1    r-----   1675.5
Fedora                         264       1             243.9
```

If you want to save a snapshot of your virtual machine, use the xm command to save it to a file. For example, to save a virtual machine named Fedora to /tmp/virt-save, you could type the following:

```
# xm save Fedora /tmp/virt-save
```

Later, to restore the virtual machine, you could type:

```
# xm restore /tmp/virt-save
```

For details on working with Xen virtual machines in Fedora, refer to the Fedora Xen Quickstart (http://fedoraproject.org/wiki/Docs/Fedora7VirtQuickStart).

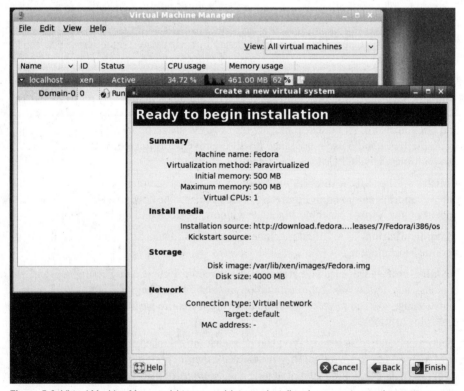

Figure 5-6: Virtual Machine Manager (virt-manager) lets you install and run guest operating systems.

Running applications virtually with KVM and QEMU

As with Xen, Kernel-based Virtual Machine (KVM) virtualization requires a computer that has either an Intel VT or AMD-V processor. KVM, however, is implemented using a loadable kernel module (kvm.ko) that works with the standard kernel, instead of using a special Xen kernel. QEMU (www.qemu.org) is used to ultimately run the guest operating systems.

Within each virtual machine running under KVM is private, virtualized hardware that provides you with access to local hard disks, network interface cards, and other hardware resources. Some of the requirements for beginning with KVM virtualization are the same as they are for Xen:

- You need at least about 256MB of RAM for each guest.

- For hard disk space, you probably need between 2GB and 3GB at least for each guest system (judging from an average-size Fedora desktop install).

- You need to have the GRUB bootloader installed.

- You need an Intel VT or AMD-V processor (see the "Before Installing Xen" section for information on how to check for pae support).

Next, you want to install many of the same packages you installed for Xen. From the Add/Install Software window you can simply search for and install all appropriate xen packages. In particular, add the kvm and qemu packages to those needed by Xen (such as virt-manager).

Before proceeding, make sure that you booted to the regular kernel and not the Xen kernel (if the xen-kernel package is installed, both a regular and xen kernel should be available for you to boot from). Then run the following procedure to install a new guest operating system that will run using KVM and QEMU:

1. **Start libvirtd service** — If it's not already running, start the libvirtd service:

   ```
   # service libvirtd start
   ```

2. **Start KVM guest -install** — As root user from a Terminal window, type the following:

   ```
   # /usr/sbin/virt-manager
   ```

   The Virtual Machine Manager window appears.

3. **Create new guest** — Right-click localhost (qemu) and click New. When the Create a new virtual system pop-up appears, click Forward. You are asked to name your virtual system.

4. **Virtual machine name** — Type a name to represent this virtual machine and click Forward. Keep the name simple (one word, fairly short, and no special characters) because the name is used to represent the virtual machine in file names and on menus. You are asked the virtualization method.

5. **Virtualization method** — Choose Fully Virtualized. You can also choose to create a guest that uses a different CPU architecture (i686, X86_64, ppc, sparc, mips, or mipsel). You are asked to identify the location of the installation media.

6. **Installation media** — Type the location of an ISO image (you can browse for it) or the CD or DVD drive that has your installation media (such as a Fedora Install DVD) inserted. Also identify the type (generic, Linux, UNIX, Windows, or other) and variant (Fedora, Windows Vista, Sun Solaris, for example) of the operating system you are installing. You are asked to assign storage space.

7. **Assign storage space** — You can either identify a disk partition or create a virtual disk by identifying a file name and size. In either case, the storage area must be large enough to hold your installed guest operating system. You are asked to set up a network connection.

8. **Host network** — Identify either a virtual network or shared physical network device to provide network connectivity for your guest operating system. Next allocate memory and CPU.

9. **Allocate memory** — From the total memory shown on the screen, choose the amount of VM memory to use and the maximum amount to use. At least 256MB is recommended. Also, choose the number of virtual CPUs to start with (typically not more than the logical CPUs on the host system). You are asked to review your install information.

10. **Start installation** — If all the information is correct, click Finish to begin the install process.

At this point, you run through the installation process as you normally would for the operating system you selected. Once installation is complete, you can start and shutdown the new virtual environment from the Virtual Machine Manager.

Summary

Between applications written directly for Linux and other UNIX systems, those that have been ported to Linux, and those that can run in emulation, thousands of applications are available to be used with Fedora and RHEL systems. With the merging of Fedora Core and Fedora Extras and other online software repositories, the number of high-quality software packages available to run on Fedora and RHEL systems has grown exponentially.

To simplify the process of installing and managing your Linux applications, Red Hat developed the RPM Package Management (RPM) format. Using tools developed for RPM, such as the rpm command, you can easily install, remove, and perform queries on Linux RPM packages. Tools for finding, downloading, and installing RPM packages include the yum utility and PackageKit window.

Of the types of applications that can run in Linux, those created for the X Window System provide the greatest level of compatibility and flexibility when used in Linux. However, using emulation software, it is possible to run applications intended for DOS, Microsoft Windows

95/98/2000/NT/XP/Vista, and Macintosh operating systems. In the long run, virtualization software such as Xen and KVM will allow multiple operating systems to run as guests on Fedora. That, in turn, will provide a means for running a variety of applications within those systems on Fedora.

Chapter 6

Publishing with Fedora and RHEL

In This Chapter

- Using OpenOffice.org
- Using commercial word processors
- Creating documents with Groff and LaTeX
- Creating DocBook documents
- Printing documents with Linux
- Displaying documents with Ghostscript and Acrobat
- Working with graphics
- Using scanners driven by SANE

To survive as a desktop system, an operating system must be able to perform at least one task well: produce documents. It's no accident that, after Windows, Microsoft Word (which is bundled into Microsoft Office) is the foundation of Microsoft's success on the desktop. Fedora and RHEL include tools for producing documents, manipulating images, scanning, and printing. Almost everything you would expect a publishing system to do, you can do with Fedora and RHEL.

OpenOffice.org is a powerful open-source office suite available as part of the Fedora and RHEL distributions. Based on the Sun Microsystems StarOffice productivity suite, OpenOffice.org includes a word processor, spreadsheet, presentation manager, and other personal productivity tools. In many cases, OpenOffice.org can act as a drop-in replacement for Microsoft Office, in both its features and its ability to support files in Word, Excel, PowerPoint and other Microsoft formats.

The first document and graphics tools for Linux were mostly built on older, text-based tools. Recently, more sophisticated tools for writing, formatting pages, and integrating graphics have been added. Despite their age, many of the older publishing tools (such as Groff and LaTeX) are still used by people in the technical community.

In this chapter, I describe both text-based and GUI-based document preparation software for Fedora and RHEL. I also describe tools for printing and displaying documents, as well as software for working with images.

Using OpenOffice.org

Some have called OpenOffice.org a significant threat to Microsoft's dominance of the desktop market. If a need to work with documents in Microsoft Word format has kept you from using Linux as your desktop computer, OpenOffice.org is a big step toward removing that obstacle.

> **NOTE:** If you are willing to pay a few dollars, CrossOver Office from Codeweavers.com lets you install and run different versions of Microsoft Office (97, 2000, XP, and 2003) from your Linux desktop. See Chapter 5 for further information or check out `www.codeweavers.com/products/cxoffice`.

Fedora and RHEL include the entire OpenOffice.org suite of desktop applications. The latest OpenOffice.org version (2.4) is included with this release of Fedora. Based on the StarOffice source code, OpenOffice.org consists of the following office-productivity applications:

- **OpenOffice.org Writer** — A word processing application that can work with documents in file formats from Microsoft Word, StarOffice, and several others. Writer also has a full set of features for using templates, working with fonts, navigating your documents, including images and effects, and generating tables of contents.

- **OpenOffice.org Calc** — A spreadsheet application that lets you incorporate data from Microsoft Excel, StarOffice, Dbase, and several other spreadsheet formats. Some nice features in Calc enable you to create charts, set up database ranges (to easily sort data in an area of a spreadsheet), and use the data pilot tool to arrange data in different points of view.

- **OpenOffice.org Draw** — A drawing application that enables you to create, edit, and align objects; incorporate textures; include textures and colors; and work with layers of objects. It lets you incorporate images, vector graphics, AutoCAD, and a variety of other file formats into your drawings. Then, you can save your drawing in the OpenOffice.org Drawing or StarOffice Draw formats.

- **OpenOffice.org Math** — A calculation program that lets you create mathematical formulas.

- **OpenOffice.org Impress** — A presentation application that includes a variety of slide effects. Using Impress, you can create and save presentations in the Microsoft PowerPoint, Draw, and Impress formats.

- **OpenOffice.org Base** — A low-end database, similar to Microsoft's Access database. Base can also act as a front-end to other databases.

Unlike other applications that were created to work with Microsoft document and data formats, OpenOffice.org (although not perfect) does a very good job of opening and saving files from many different versions of Microsoft Word (.doc) and Excel (.xls) formats with fewer problems. Very basic styles and formatting that open in OpenOffice.org often don't look noticeably different from the way they appear in Microsoft Office. In fact, some older Word documents will actually work better in OpenOffice.org Writer than they do in the latest Microsoft Office suites.

> **NOTE:** The Open Office XML (OOXML) format, a 6,000-page tome, represent's Microsoft's recent efforts to claim to support standard document formats. This format is the default document type in Word 2007. Some people in the open source community, however, claim that OOXML is so specific in requiring support for Microsoft product features, without providing any guidance in how those Microsoft proprietary features can be implemented, that it is unusable as a standard. In other words, don't think that because Microsoft is claiming to support standards that you will ever be able to fully use Microsoft document formats on other platforms.

To open OpenOffice.org Writer, Impress, Calc and other office applications, click Office from the Applications menu. Then select the OpenOffice.org application you want to open. Figure 6-1 shows an example of OpenOffice.org Writer with a document file that was originally created in Microsoft Word.

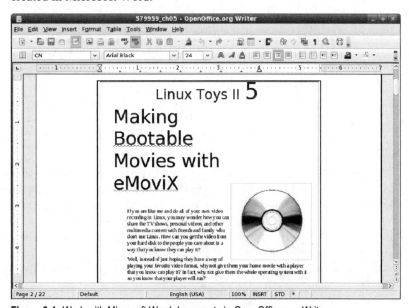

Figure 6-1: Work with Microsoft Word documents in OpenOffice.org Writer.

The controls in OpenOffice.org are similar to the ones you would find in Word prior to Word 2007. So if you were comfortable with those controls, you should find it easy to transition to OpenOffice.org Writer. In fact, you might find it easier than using Microsoft Word 2007, since many people have found the transition to Word 2007 difficult.

Toolbars in OpenOffice.org Writer include boxes for identifying filenames, and changing styles, font types, and font sizes. Buttons enable you to save and print the file, change the text alignment, and cut, copy, and paste text. In other words, Writer includes almost everything you expect in an advanced word processor. In addition, Writer includes a handy PDF button to output a file directly to the PDF format. This is very useful for exchanging documents or placing data on the Internet.

If you are just starting out with OpenOffice.org Writer, here are a few features you can try out:

- **Wizards** — Use a wizard to start a letter, fax, agenda, presentation, Web page, Document Converter, or Euro Converter. Select File → Wizards and then choose one of the document types just mentioned. The Document Converter Wizard lets you convert a directory of Microsoft or StarOffice documents to OpenDocument format. The Euro Converter lets you convert files containing different European currencies to Euros.

- **Document styles and formatting** — Create the format of your documents using character, paragraph, frame, page, and numbering styles (select Format → Styles and Formatting). From the Styles and Formatting window, choose the type of style you want to change, right-click in the Styles box, and choose New to create your own style.

- **Checking Documents** — Try different features for checking and correcting your documents. Writer includes features such as spell checking (Tools → Spellcheck) and autocorrection (Tools → AutoCorrect). You can display the content as a Web page or in print layout and view font and character markup (View → Nonprinting Characters).

- **Drawing and images** — Use drawing tools (View → Toolbars → Drawing) to create drawings, flow charts, callouts, or symbols in your documents. Insert background colors or graphics on your pages (Format → Page, select Background tab, and choose color or graphic). To insert a graphic, select Insert → Picture, and insert the image from a file or from your scanner.

- **Outputting PDF or other formats** — Writer provides a toolbar button that will output your current document to PDF format. PDF is a good format for sharing documents that you want others to read or print, but don't necessarily want to necessarily give them the original source file. You can also save Writer documents to other useful formats, including HTML (to publish your document to the Web) or Rich Text Format (to be able to share the document with different word processors).

> **NOTE**: Find out more about OpenOffice.org at `www.OpenOffice.org`.

Other Word Processors

With the merge of Fedora Core and Fedora Extras that occurred with Fedora 7, there are now many different word processors available from the Fedora software repository. So, popular light-weight word processors such as AbiWord and KOffice (which is part of the KDE desktop), can now be easily installed with a single `yum` command from the Fedora repository. As for commercial offerings, there is StarOffice from Sun Microsystems.

- **StarOffice** — The StarOffice productivity suite (`www.sun.com/staroffice`) contains applications for word processing, spreadsheets, presentation graphics, e-mail, news, charting, and graphics. It was created to run on Linux systems, but it runs in other environments as well. It can import and export a variety of Microsoft file formats. StarOffice is owned by Sun Microsystems, which sells it as a commercial product.

- **AbiWord** — The AbiWord word processor (`abiword` command) is produced by the AbiSource project (`www.abisource.com`). In addition to working with files in its own AbiWord format (`.abw` and `.zabw`), AbiWord can import files in Microsoft Word and several other formats.

- **KOffice** — The KOffice package contains a set of office productivity applications designed for the KDE desktop. It includes a word processor (KWord), spreadsheet (KSpread), a presentation creator (KPresenter), and a diagram drawing program (KChart). These applications can be run separately or within a KOffice Workspace. (The koffice package is on the DVD that comes with this book. You learn more about it from the KOffice Web site at `www.koffice.org`.)

- **TextMaker** — TextMaker is another popular commercial word processing package for Linux (`www.softmaker.com/english/tml_en.htm`). This word processor requires much less memory than OpenOffice.org Writer, but still contains many powerful features. With TextMaker, interchanging documents between different operating systems is easy because there are also versions of TextMaker for Windows, Pocket PCs, Handhelp PCs, FreeBSD, and Zaurus.

Using StarOffice

The StarOffice suite from Sun Microsystems, Inc. is a product that runs on Linux, UNIX, and Windows operating systems. Like OpenOffice.org, StarOffice contains many features that make it compatible with Microsoft Office applications. In particular, it includes the capability to import Microsoft Word and Excel files.

StarOffice is probably the most complete integrated office suite for Linux. If you are working in a cross-platform environment, however, you can also get StarOffice for Sun Solaris and Microsoft Windows operating systems. StarOffice includes:

- **StarOffice Writer** — This is the StarOffice word processing application. It can import documents from a variety of formats, with special emphasis on Word documents.

- **StarOffice Calc** — This is the spreadsheet program that comes with StarOffice. You can import spreadsheets from Microsoft Excel and other popular programs.

- **StarOffice Impress** — This module enables you to create presentations.

- **StarOffice Draw** — This is a vector-oriented drawing program. It includes the capability to create 3D objects and to use texturing.

- **StarOffice Base** — You can manage your data with StarBase, a friendly front end for databases. It can access a variety of database interfaces.

There are also other tools in StarOffice that enable you to create business graphics, edit raster images, and edit mathematical formulas (StarOffice Math).

You can download StarOffice 8 for Linux or purchase a boxed set from the StarOffice Web site at `www.sun.com/software/star/staroffice/`. Although StarOffice was once available free for download, the current price to download the software for home users is $69.95.

> **NOTE**: OpenOffice.org is an open-source project sponsored by Sun Microsystems. Sun takes the OpenOffice.org source code and uses it (along with other modules) to create StarOffice. This is very similar to Mozilla, an open-source Web browser, and Netscape, a commercial product built from the Mozilla sources. Of course, the Fedora Project and Red Hat Enterprise Linux have a similar symbiotic relationship.

AbiWord

The AbiWord word processor is a very nice, free word processor from the AbiSource project (`www.abisource.com`). If you are creating documents from scratch, AbiWord includes many of the basic functions you need to create good-quality documents.

With AbiWord, you can select what type of document the file contains. You can select to save the file in the following formats:

- AbiWord, AbiWord Template, and GZipped AbiWord (`.abw`, `.awt`, `.zabw`)
- HTML/XHTML (`.html`)
- KWord (`.kwd`)
- Multipart HTML (`.mht`)
- Rich Text Format (`.rtf`)
- Microsoft Word (`.doc`)
- OpenDocument format, or ODF, an emerging standard for office documents.
- PalmDoc (`.pdb`)
- Portable Document Format (`.pdf`)
- UNIX nroff/man format (`.nroff`)
- UTF8 (`.utf8`)
- Word Perfect (`.wp`) (requires an added plug-in)
- Text (`.txt`)

AbiWord doesn't yet import all of these file types cleanly. Although the recent version of AbiWord supports Word styles, sometimes tables, graphics, and other features don't translate perfectly. If you want to work with a Word document in AbiWord, open it as AbiWord, correct any font problems, and save the document in AbiWord format. AbiWord has vastly improved in the past few releases, but you can still have problems if you need to exchange files with others who are using Word. (To keep files in the Word format, OpenOffice.org and StarOffice work much better, but not perfectly.)

If you have slow hardware, AbiWord offers better performance than OpenOffice.org Writer. If you are working in a cross-platform environment, you can get versions of AbiWord that run in Windows, Mac OS X, QNX, and most UNIX derivatives (Linux, BSD, Solaris, and so on).

Recently added features, such as styles and bullets, continue to make AbiWord a more useful word processing tool. It's not competitive with comparable commercial products, but its developers continue to improve it.

Using KOffice

There is a KDE office suite of applications that go with the KDE desktop. The KOffice package has the basic applications you would expect in an integrated office suite: a word processor (KWord), spreadsheet (KSpread), a presentation creator (KPresenter), and a diagram drawing program (KChart).

Use the command `yum install koffice-suite` to install the KOffice suite. When you use KOffice, you can select from the different office applications from the left column. Open multiple documents in any of the applications. Then click Documents in the left column to choose which one to display at the moment.

Figure 6-2 shows KWord displaying a Word document.

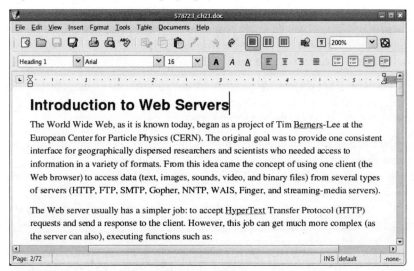

Figure 6-2: You can work with Word documents in KWord.

You can work with a variety of document, spreadsheet, and image types; not many commercial document types are supported yet. So you may need to import documents using other tools before you can read them into KWord. The KSpread program can open several different spreadsheet styles, however, such as Microsoft Excel and GNUmeric spreadsheets. Kivio is a useful flowcharting tool.

Using Traditional Linux Publishing Tools

With old-school text processors (such as Groff and TeX), you can ignore document appearance while writing. Plain-text macros instruct post-processors how to lay out a document for printing after writing is done. With word processors (such as OpenOffice.org Word and StarOffice Writer), you mark up text and see the basic layout of the document as you write.

Some attributes of the traditional Linux publishing tools make them particularly well suited for certain types of document publishing. Groff and LaTeX (which is based on TeX) come with Fedora and RHEL and have been popular among technical people. Reasons for that include:

- You can manipulate files in plain text. Using tools such as `sed` and `grep`, you can scan and change one document or hundreds with a single command or script.

- Scientific notation is supported. With `geqn`, you can create complex equations. LaTeX and TeX are suited for technical notation. Some math publications require LaTeX.

- Editing can be faster because traditional Linux documents are created with a text editor. You usually get better performance out of a text editor than a word processor.

Simple page layouts work well with Linux documentation tools. For example, a technical book with a few flow charts and images can be easily produced and maintained using Groff or TeX documentation tools. Letters and memos are also easy to do with these tools. And, of course, Linux man pages are created with text-based tools.

Also, Linux likes PostScript. Most Linux document-processing software includes print drivers for PostScript. There are many tools for converting PostScript to other formats. Also, some documents on the Web are distributed in PostScript (`.ps`).

The drawback to the traditional Linux document tools is that they are not intuitive. Rarely will a beginner try to use these tools, unless they have a need to support legacy UNIX or Linux documents (such as manual pages or old UNIX guides). Although there are some easier front ends to LaTeX (see the description of LyX later on), if you are creating documents in a text editor, you need to learn what macros to type into your documents and which formatting and print commands to use.

> **NOTE:** For many years, the UNIX system documentation distributed by AT&T was created in troff/nroff formats, which predate Groff. The documents used separate macro packages for man pages and guide material. Using a source code control system (SCCS), thousands of pages of documentation could be ported to different UNIX systems. Today, Fedora and RHEL include the same tools to work with man pages.

Creating Documents in Groff or LaTeX

You can create documents for either of Linux's Groff (troff/nroff) or LaTeX (TeX) styles of publishing using any text editor. Fedora and RHEL come with several text editors, or you can download others from the Internet. See the sidebar "Choosing a Text Editor" for more information.

The process of creating documents in Groff or LaTeX consists of the following general steps:

1. Create a document with any text editor. The document will contain text and markup.

2. Format the document using a formatting command that matches the style of the document that you created (for example, with `groff` or `latex`). During this step, you may need to indicate that the document contains special content, such as equations (`eqn` command), tables (`tbl` command), or line drawings (`pic` command).

3. Send the document to an output device. The device may be a printer or display program.

If you are used to a word processor with a GUI, you may find these publishing tools difficult. In general, Groff is useful to create man pages for Linux. LaTeX is useful if you need to produce mathematical documents, perhaps for publication in a technical journal.

Text processing with Groff

The `nroff` and `troff` text formatting commands were the first interfaces available for producing typeset quality documents with the UNIX system. They aren't editors; rather, they are commands that you send your text through, with the result being formatted pages:

- **nroff** — Produces formatted plain text and includes the ability to do pagination, indents, and text justification, as well as other features.

- **troff** — Produces typeset text, including everything `nroff` can do, plus the ability to produce different fonts and spacing. The `troff` command also supports kerning.

The `groff` command is the front end for producing `nroff`/`troff` documentation. Because Linux man pages are formatted and output in Groff, most of the examples here help you create and print man pages with Groff.

People rarely use primitive `nroff`/`troff` markup. Instead, there are common macro packages that simplify the creation of `nroff`/`troff`-formatted documents:

- **man** — The man macros are used to create Linux man pages. You can format a man page using the `-man` option to the `groff` command.

- **mm** — The mm macros (memorandum macros) were created to produce memos, letters, and technical white papers. This macro package includes macros for creating a table of contents, lists of figures, references, and other features that are helpful for producing technical documents. You can format an mm document using the `-mm groff` option.

- **me** — The me macros were popular for producing memos and technical papers on Berkeley UNIX systems. Format an me document using the -me groff option.

Choosing a Text Editor

Hardcore UNIX or Linux users tend to edit files with either the vi or emacs text editor. These editors have been around a long time and are hard to learn, but efficient to use. (Your fingers never leave the keyboard.) The emacs editor has some GUI support, although it will run fine in a Terminal window. There are also GUI versions of vi such as GVim (gvim command is in the vim-X11 package), while emacs itself supports menus and mouse features in a GUI.

Some of the other, simpler text editors that can run on your graphical desktop are:

- **gedit** (gedit command) — This text editor, which comes with Fedora and RHEL, is the lightweight text editor for GNOME. It has simple edit functions (cut, copy, paste, and select all) and settings let you set indentations and word wrap. Special functions, such as a spell checker and a diff feature are included. You can start gedit by typing **gedit** from a Terminal window. Go to gedit.sourceforge.net for more information.

- **nedit** (nedit **command**) — While being quite simple to use, nedit offers many nice extras accessible from its menu bar. As you edit, you can run shell commands to sort, count, or spell the contents of your text documents. (You may need to install the tcsh package for those features to work.)

- **Advanced Editor** (kwrite command) — This text editor includes a menu bar to create, open, or save files. It also has simple edit functions (cut, copy, paste, undo, and help). Other edit features let you set indents, find and replace text, and select all text. This tool comes with the KDE desktop.

- **Text Editor** (kedit command) — Another simple text editor. Features let you open files from your file system or from a URL. It also includes a convenient toolbar and a spell checker. It comes with the KDE desktop.

- **joe** (joe command) — joe is a text-mode editor that is much simpler than either vi or emacs. joe also has the ability to mimic other text editors, such as vi, emacs, pico, and even the late, lamented WordStar. In addition to standard features such as search and replace, arrow key movements for the cursor, and so on, joe also offers macros, code editing features, and the ability to move or format large chunks of text easily.

Groff macro packages are stored in /usr/share/groff/*/tmac. The man macros are called from the an.tmac file, mm macros are from m.tmac, and me macros are from e.tmac. The naming convention for each macro package is *xxx*.tmac, where *xxx* is replaced by one or more letters representing the macro package. In each case, you can understand the name of the macro package by adding an m to the beginning of the file suffix.

> **TIP:** Instead of noting a specific macro package, you can use -mandoc to choose a macro package.

When you run the groff formatting command, you can indicate on the command line which macro packages you are using. You can also indicate that the document should be run through any of the following commands that preprocess text for special formats:

- **eqn** — This preprocessor formats macros that produce equations in groff.
- **pic** — This preprocessor formats macros that create simple line drawings in groff.
- **tbl** — This preprocessor formats macros that produce tables within groff.

The formatted Groff document is output for a particular device type. The device can be a printer, a window, or (for plain text) your shell. Here are output forms supported by Groff:

- **ps** — Produces PostScript output for a PostScript printer or a PostScript previewer.
- **lj4** — Produces output for an HP LaserJet4 printer or other PCL5-compatible printer.
- **ascii** — Produces plain-text output that can be viewed from a Terminal window.
- **dvi** — Produces output in TeX dvi, to output to a variety of devices described later.
- **X75** — Produces output for an X11 75 dots/inch previewer.
- **X100** — Produces output for an X11 100 dots/inch previewer.
- **latin1** — Produces typewriter-like output using the ISO Latin-1 character set.

Formatting and printing documents with Groff

You can try formatting and printing an existing Groff document using any man pages on your Fedora or RHEL system (such as those in /usr/share/man/*). (Those man pages are compressed, so you can copy them to a temporary directory and unzip them to try out Groff.)

These commands copy the chown man page to the /tmp directory and unzips it. Then, groff formats the chown man page in plain text so you can page through it on your screen.

```
$ cp /usr/share/man/man1/chown.1.gz /tmp
$ gunzip /tmp/chown.1.gz
$ groff -Tascii -man /tmp/chown.1 | less
```

In the previous example, the chown man page (chown.1.gz) is copied to the /tmp directory, is unzipped (using gunzip), and is output in plain text (-Tascii) using the man macros (-man). The output is piped to less, to page through it on your screen. Instead of piping to less (| less), you can direct the output to a file (> /tmp/chown.txt).

To format a man page for typesetting, you can specify PostScript or HP LaserJet output. You should either direct the output to a file or to a printer. Here are a couple of examples:

```
$ groff -Tps -man /tmp/chown.1 > /tmp/chown.ps
```

```
$ groff -Tlj4 -man -l /tmp/chown.1
```

The first example creates PostScript output (-Tps) and directs it to a file called
/tmp/chown.ps. That file can be read by a PostScript previewer (such as Ghostscript) or
sent to a printer (lpr /tmp/chown.ps). The next example creates HP LaserJet output
(-Tlj4) and directs it to the default printer (-l option).

> **TIP:** Using man2html, you can convert man pages to HTML format for display in a browser. For
> example: zcat /usr/share/man/man1/chown.1.gz| man2html |
> /tmp/chown.htm.

Creating a man page with Groff

Before HOW-TOs and info files, man pages were the foundation for information about UNIX
(and UNIX-like) systems. Each command, file format, device, or other component either had
its own man page or was grouped on a man page with similar components. Creating your own
man page requires that you learn a few macros (in particular, man macros). Figure 6-3 shows
the source for a fictitious man page for a command called waycool.

```
.\"
.\" waycool.1 - the *roff document processor source for the waycool command
.\"
.TH waycool 1 "May 12, 2002" GNU "Linux Programmer's Manual"
.SH NAME
waycool \- my cool command
.SH SYNTAX
\fBwaycool\fR [ \fB-abcv\fR ] [ \fI file ... \fR ]
.SH VERSION
This man page documents the GNU waycool version X.XX
.SH DESCRIPTION
\fBwaycool\fR is a way cool command.
.SP
This version of \fBwaycool\fR is better than the last one.
.SH OPTIONS
.IP -a
Run all options with it.
.IP -b
Run some options.
.IP -c
affect symbolic links instead of any referenced file
(available only on systems that can change the
ownership of a symlink)
.IP -v
Print the version number with the command.
.SH COMMENTS
If you don't like the command, don't tell me. It will just hurt my feelings.
.SH ENVIRONMENT VARIABLES
These environment variables are used by \fBwaycool\fR:
.IP "DISPLAY"
This sets the X Display variable.
.IP "WAYCOOL"
This contains the location of the waycool database.
.SH FILES
/usr/local/waycool - Directory containing waycool stuff.
.SH AUTHOR
Chris Craft <chris@handsonhistory.com>
.SH "REPORTING BUGS"
Report bugs to <bug-fileutils@gnu.org>.
.SH COPYRIGHT
Copyright \(co 2001 Free Software Foundation, Inc.
.br
This is free software; see the source for copying conditions.  There is NO
warranty; not even for MERCHANTABILITY or FITNESS FOR A PARTICULAR PURPOSE.
.SH ACKNOWLEDGEMENTS
I'd like to thank all my friends.
```

Figure 6-3: Simple markup is required to create man pages.

> **TIP:** Most man pages are stored in subdirectories of `/usr/share/man`. Before you create a man page, refer to similar man pages to see the markup and the headings they include. In man1 are commands; man2 has system calls; man3 has library functions; man4 has special device files (`/dev/*`); man5 has file formats; man6 has games; man7 has miscellaneous components; and man8 has administrative commands.

A few other kinds of macros are used in the man page. The .IP macros format indented paragraphs for things such as options. The man page also contains some lower-level font requests; for example, \fB says to change the current font to bold, \fI changes the font to italic, and \fR changes it back to regular font. (This markup is better than asking for a particular font type because it just changes to bold, italic, or regular for the current font.) Figure 6-4 shows what the `waycool` man page looks like after it is formatted with `groff`:

```
$ groff -man -Tps -l waycool.1
```

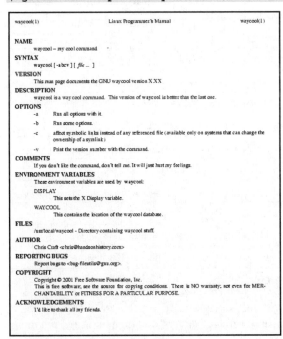

Figure 6-4: Man page formatting adds headers and lays out the page of text.

Table 6-1 lists the macros that you can use on your man pages. These macros are described on the man(7) manual page (type **man 7 man** to view that page).

Table 6-1: man Macros

Macro	Description
.B	Bold.
.BI	Bold, then italics (alternating).

Macro	Description
.BR	Bold, then Roman (alternating).
.DT	Set default tabs.
.HP	Begin a hanging indent.
.I	Italics.
.IB	Italics, then bold (alternating).
.IP	Begin hanging tag. For options. Long tags use .TP.
.IR	Italics, then Roman (alternating).
.LP	Begin paragraph.
.PD	Set distance between paragraphs.
.PP	Begin paragraph.
.RB	Roman, then bold (alternating).
.RE	End relative indent (after .RS).
.RI	Roman, then italics (alternating).
.RS	Begin relative indent (use .RE to end indent).
.SB	Small text, then bold (alternating).
.SM	Small text. Used to show words in all caps.
.SH	Section head.
.SS	Subheading within a .SH heading.
.TH	Title heading. Used once at the beginning of the man page.
.TP	Begin a hanging tag. Begins text on next line, not same line as tag.

Creating a letter, memo, or white paper with Groff

Memorandum macros (which are used with the -mm option of Groff) were once popular among UNIX users for producing technical documents, letters, and memos. Although more modern word processors with a variety of WYSIWYG templates have made mm outdated, in a pinch mm can still be a quick way to create a typeset-style document in a text environment.

To format and print (to a PostScript printer) a document with mm macros, use the following:

```
$ groff -mm -Tps -l letter.mm
```

The following is a simple example of how to use mm macros to produce a letter:

```
.WA "Christopher T. Craft"
999 Anyway Way
Anytown, UT 84111 USA
```

```
.WE
.IA
John W. Doe
111 Notown Blvd.
Notown, UT 84111
.IE
.LO RN "Our telephone conversation"
.LO SA "Dear Mr. Doe:"
.LT
In reference to our telephone conversation on the 4th, I am calling to
confirm our upcoming appointment on the 18th. I look forward to
discussing the merger. I believe we have a win-win situation here.
.FC "Yours Truly,"
.SG
```

The output of the letter, if you use the `groff` command line mentioned in the paragraph preceding the code example, is shown in Figure 6-5.

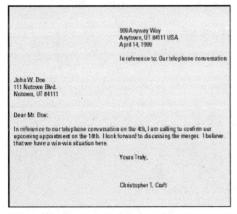

Figure 6-5: Create a simple letter using mm macros.

The mm macros were often used to produce technical memos. The following is an example of a sign-off sheet that might go at the front of a larger technical memo.

```
.TL
Merger Technical Specifications
.AF "ABC Corporation"
.AU "Christopher Craft"
.AT "President"
.AS
This memo details the specifications for the planned merger.
.AE
.MT "Merger Description and Marching Orders"
As a result of our talks with XYZ corporation, we plan to go
forward with the merger. This document contains the following:
.BL
```

```
.LI
Schedule and time tables.
.LI
Financial statements.
.LI
Asset allocations.
.LE
.SP
Please add any corrections you have, then sign the approval line
indicated at the bottom of this sheet.
.FC
.SG
.AV "John W. Doe, XYZ Corporation President"
.AV "Sylvia Q. Public, XYZ Corporation CFO"
.NS
Everyone in the corporation.
.NE
```

Figure 6-6 shows the output of this memo.

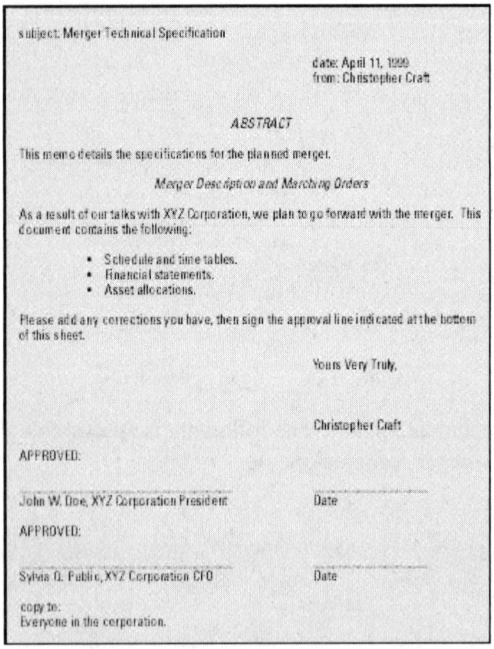

Figure 6-6: Add headings and approval lines automatically to memos.

NOTE: For a complete listing of mm macros, see the `groff_mm` man page. More than 100 mm macros exist. Also, dozens of defined strings let you set and recall information (such as figure names, tables, table of contents information, and text) that is automatically printed with different headings.

Adding equations, tables, and pictures

To interpret special macros for equations, tables, and line drawings, you can run separate commands (eqn, tbl, and pic) on the file before you run the groff command. Alternatively, you can add options to the groff command line to have the file preprocessed automatically by any of the commands (-e for eqn, -t for tbl, and -p for pic).

Here are some examples of EQN, TBL, and PIC markup included in a Groff document. The first example shows an equation that can be processed by eqn for a Groff document:

```
.EQ
a ~ mark = ~ 30
.EN
.sp
.EQ
a sup 2 ~ + ~ b sup 2~lineup = ~ 1000
.EN
.sp
.EQ
x sup 3 ~ + ~ y sup 3 ~ + ~ z sup 3~lineup = ~ 1400
.EN
```

If this appeared in a memo called memoeqn.mm, the memo would be preprocessed by eqn and then sent to the printer using the following command:

```
$ groff -Tps -l -mm -e memoeqn.mm
```

All data between the .EQ and .EN macros are interpreted as equations. The resulting output from the equation would appear as shown in Figure 6-7.

$$a = 30$$
$$a^2 + b^2 = 1000$$
$$x^3 + y^3 + z^3 = 1400$$

Figure 6-7: Produce equations in documents with the use of the eqn command's .EQ and .EN macros.

To create a table in a Groff document, use the .TS and .TE macros of the tbl preprocessor. The following is an example of the markup used to produce a simple table.

```
.TS
center, box, tab(:);
c s s
c | c | c
l | l | l.
Mergers and Acquisitions Team
_

Employee:Title:Location
_
```

```
Jones, James:Marketing Manager:New York Office
Smith, Charles:Sales Manager:Los Angeles Office
Taylor, Sarah:R&D Manager:New York Office
Walters, Mark:Information Systems Manager:Salt Lake City Office
Zur, Mike:Distribution Manager:Portland Office
.TE
```

After the .TS macro starts the table, the next line indicates that the table should be centered on the page (center) and surrounded by a line box and that a colon will be used to separate the data into cells [tab(:)]. The next line shows that the heading should be centered in the box (c) and should span across the next two cells (s s). The line after that indicates that the heading of each cell should be centered (c | c | c) and that the data cells that follow should be left justified (l | l | l).

> **CAUTION:** There must be a period at the end of the table definition line. In this case, it is after the l | l | l. line. If the period is not there, tbl will try to interpret the text as part of the table definition. In this case, tbl will fail and stop processing the table, so the table will not print.

The rest of the information in the table is the data. Note that the tab separators are colon characters (:). When the table is done, you end it with a .TE macro. If the table were in a memo called memotbl.mm, tbl could preprocess the memo and then send it to the printer using the following command:

```
$ groff -Tps -l -mm -t memotbl.mm
```

Data between .TS and .TE macros are interpreted as tables (see Figure 6-8).

Employee	Title	Location
Jones, James	Marketing Manager	Jones, James
Smith, Charles	Sales Manager	Smith, Charles
Taylor, Sarah	R&D Manager	Taylor, Sarah
Walters, Mark	Information Systems Manager	Walters, Mark
Zur, Mike	Distribution Manager	Zur, Mike

Figure 6-8: Set how text is justified and put in columns with the use of the tbl command's .TS and .TE macros.

The PIC macros (.PS and .PE) enable you to create simple diagrams and flow charts to use in Groff. PIC is really qualified to create only simple boxes, circles, ellipses, lines, arcs, splines, and some text. The following is some PIC code that could be in a Groff document:

```
.PS
box invis "Start" "Here"; arrow
box "Step 1"; arrow
circle "Step 2"; arrow
ellipse "Step 3"; arrow
box "Step 4"; arrow
box invis "End"
```

```
.PE
```

After the `.PS`, the first line indicates an invisible box (`invis`) that contains the words Start Here, followed by an arrow. That arrow connects to the next box containing the words Step 1. The next elements (connected by arrows) are a circle (Step 2), an ellipse (Step 3), another box (Step 4), and another invisible box (End). The `.PE` indicates the end of the pic drawing.

If these lines appeared in a document called `memopic.mm`, you could preprocess the PIC code and print the file using the following command:

```
$ groff -Tps -l -mm -p memopic.mm
```

Figure 6-9 shows an example of this drawing.

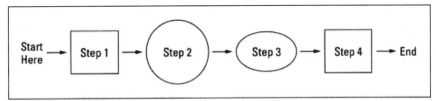

Figure 6-9: Create simple flow diagrams with the pic command's .PS and .PE macros.

Text processing with TeX/LaTeX

TeX (pronounced *tech*) is a collection of commands used primarily to produce scientific and mathematical typeset documents. The most common way to use TeX is by calling a macro package. The most popular macro package for Tex is LaTeX, which takes a higher-level approach to formatting TeX documents. TeX and LaTeX tools are contained in the tetex-latex package.

> **NOTE:** The tetex-* packages needed to use the TeX examples shown in this chapter are found on the DVD that accompanies this book.

TeX interprets the LaTeX macros from the latex format file (`latex.fmt`). By default, the `latex.fmt` and `plain.fmt` format files are the only ones that are built automatically when the TeX package is installed. Other macro files that you can use with TeX include:

- **amstex** — Mathematical publications, including the American Mathematical Society use this as their official typesetting system.
- **eplain** — Includes macros for indexing and table of contents.
- **texinfo** — Macros used by the Free Software Foundation to produce software manuals. Text output from these macros can be used with the Linux `info` command.

You can create a TeX/LaTeX file using any text editor. After the text and macros are created, you can run the `tex` command (or one of several other related utilities) to format the file. The input file is in the form `filename.tex`. The output is generally three different files:

- **filename.dvi** — This is the device-independent output file that can be translated for use by several different types of output devices (such as PostScript).
- **filename.log** — This is a log file that contains diagnostic messages.
- **filename.aux** — This is an auxiliary file used by LaTeX.

The .dvi file produced can be formatted for a particular device. For example, you could use the dvips command to output the resulting .dvi file to your PostScript printer (dvips filename.dvi). Or you could use the xdvi command to preview the .dvi file in X.

Creating and formatting a LaTeX document

Because LaTeX is the most common way of using TeX, this section describes how to create and format a LaTeX document. A LaTeX macro (often referred to as a command) appears in a document in one of the two following forms:

- *\string{option}[required]* — First there is a backslash (\), which is followed by a string of characters. (Replace string with the name of the command.) Optional arguments are contained in braces ({ }), and required arguments are in brackets ([ ])
- *\?{option}[required]* — First there is a backslash (\), which is followed by a single character that is not a letter. (Replace ? with the command character.) Optional arguments are contained in braces ({ }), and required arguments are in brackets ([ ]).

Each command defines some action to be taken. The action can control page layout, the font used, spacing, paragraph layout, or a variety of other actions on the document. The minimum amount of formatting that a LaTeX document can contain is the following:

```
\documentclass{name}
\begin{document}
   TEXT GOES HERE!
\end{document}
```

You should replace {name} with the name of the class of document you are creating. Valid document classes include article, book, letter, report, and slides. The text for the file, along with your formatting commands, goes between the begin and end document commands.

The best way to get started with LaTeX is to use the LyX editor. LyX provides a GUI for creating LaTeX documents. It also contains a variety of templates you can use instead of just creating a document from scratch. Figure 6-10 shows an example of the LyX editor.

NOTE: The LyX editor is available from the Fedora repository; you can install it by typing **yum install lyx**.

If you want to edit LaTeX in a regular text editor, you need to be familiar with the LaTeX commands. For a complete listing of the LaTeX commands, type **info latex** and then go to the section "Commands within a LaTeX document."

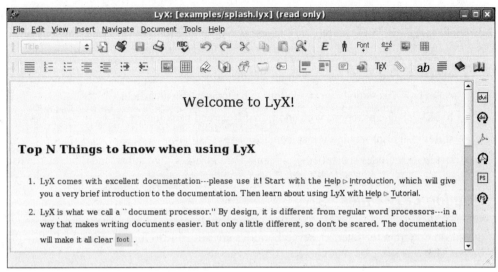

Figure 6-10: Create LaTeX documents graphically with the LyX editor.

Using the LyX LaTeX Editor

Start the LyX LaTeX editor with the `lyx` command. LyX comes with a lot of supporting documentation. Click Help to select a Tutorial, User's Guide, or other information.

To start your first document, I recommend that you select one of the templates provided with LyX. Templates are located in `/usr/share/lyx/templates`. To open a template, click File → New from Template. A list of available templates appears. You can use them to create letters, slides, and articles, for example.

Besides offering standard editing functions, such as cut, copy, and paste, you can perform a variety of markup functions from the Layout menu. As for mathematical functions, the Math menu enables you to insert fractions, square root, exponent, sum, and integral functions into your document. When you are done, you can:

- Print the file to a PostScript printer or output a PostScript (`.ps`) file. (Select File → Print, select the printing method, and then click OK.)
- Export the file to LaTeX, DVI, PostScript, or ASCII Text. (Select File → Export and choose from the list of file formats. LyX simply exports the files to your home directory, without letting you choose where to save them.)

LyX calls itself a WYSIWYM editor — What You See Is What You Mean. As a result, what you see on the screen as you edit is not exactly what the printed document will look like. For example, no extra white space will appear between lines by pressing Enter multiple times.

Because LyX supports style files, it enables you to create documents that meet several different standards. For example, LyX supports typesetting for the American Mathematics Society (AMS) journals using the article text class. Other text classes supported include:

- **article** — One-sided paper with no chapters.
- **report** — Two-sided report, tending to be longer than an article.
- **book** — Same as report, with additional front and back matter.
- **slides** — For producing transparencies.
- **letter** — Includes special environments for addresses, signatures, and other elements.

Printing LaTeX files

Whether you create your own LaTeX file, export one from the LyX LaTeX editor, or download one from the Internet, several utilities are available to format, print, or display the output. Here are some of your choices:

- To format a LaTeX file (`filename.tex`), run the following command:

```
$ latex filename.tex
```

- To print a DVI file (`filename.dvi`), send it to your default PostScript printer, and type the following:

```
$ dvips filename.dvi
```

- To display a DVI file in an X window, type the following (after installing the tetex-xdvi package):

```
$ xdvi filename.dvi
```

If you prefer to output your LaTeX files to PDF format, you can try the `dvipdf` command.

Converting documents

Documents can come to you in many different formats. Search just some of the Linux FTP sites on the Internet and you will find files in PostScript, DVI, man, PDF, HTML, and TeX. There are also a variety of graphics formats. Fedora and RHEL come with lots of utilities to convert documents and graphics from one format to another. The following is a list of document and graphics conversion utilities:

- **dos2unix** — Converts a DOS text file to a UNIX (Linux) text file. A reason you might want to use this command is that DOS text files include double-character carriage returns, whereas Linux (UNIX) text files have a single-character linefeed.
- **fax2ps** — Converts TIFF facsimile image files to a compressed PostScript format. The PostScript output is optimized to send to a printer on a low-speed line. This format is

less efficient for images with a lot of black or continuous tones. (In those cases, tiff2ps might be more effective.)

- **fax2tiff** — Converts fax data (Group 3 or Group 4) to a TIFF format. The output is either low-resolution or medium-resolution TIFF format.
- **gif2tiff** — Converts a GIF (87) file to a TIFF format.
- **man2html** — Converts a man page to an HTML format.
- **pal2rgb** — Converts a TIFF image (palette color) to a full-color RGB image.
- **pdf2dsc** — Converts a PDF file to a PostScript document DSC file. The PostScript file conforms to Adobe Document Structuring Conventions (DSC). The output enables PostScript readers (such as Ghostview) to read the PDF file a page at a time.
- **pdf2ps** — Converts a PDF file to a PostScript file (level 2).
- **pfb2pfa** — Converts Type 1 PostScript font (binary MS-DOS) to ASCII-readable.
- **pk2bm** — Converts a TeX pkfont font file to a bitmap (ASCII file).
- **ppm2tiff** — Converts a PPM image file to a TIFF format.
- **ps2ascii** — Converts PostScript or PDF files to ASCII text.
- **ps2epsi** — Converts a PostScript file to Encapsulated PostScript (EPSI). Some word processing and graphic programs can read EPSI. Output is often low quality.
- **ps2pdf** — Converts a PostScript file to Portable Document Format (PDF).
- **ps2pk** — Converts a Type 1 PostScript font to a TeX pkfont.
- **ras2tiff** — Converts a Sun raster file to a TIFF format.
- **tiff2bw** — Converts an RGB or Palette color TIFF image to a grayscale TIFF image.
- **tiff2ps** — Converts a TIFF image to PostScript.
- **unix2dos** — Converts a UNIX (Linux) text file to a DOS text file.

Besides these tools, many graphical applications, such as The GIMP, enable you to save images into several different formats (BMP, JPEG, PNG, TIFF, and so on), using the Save As feature.

Creating DocBook documents

Documentation projects often need to produce documents that are output in a variety of formats. For example, the same text that describes how to use a software program may need to be output as a printed manual, an HTML page, and a PostScript file. The standards that have been embraced most recently by the Linux community for creating what are referred to as *structured documents* are SGML, XML, and DocBook.

Understanding SGML and XML

Standard Generalized Markup Language (SGML) was created to provide a standard way of marking text so that it could be output later in a variety of formats. Because SGML markup is done with text tags, you can create SGML documents using any plain-text editor. Documents consist of the text of your document and tags that identify each type of information in the text.

Unlike markup languages such as Groff and HTML, SGML markup is not intended to enforce a particular look when you are creating the document. So, for example, instead of marking a piece of text as being bold or italic, you would identify it as an address, paragraph, or a name. Later, a style sheet would be applied to the document to take the tagged text and assign a look and presentation.

Because SGML consists of many tags, to simplify producing documents based on SGML, other projects have cropped up to better focus the ways in which SGML is used. In particular, the Extensible Markup Language (XML) was created to offer a manageable subset of SGML that would be specifically tailored to work well with Web-based publishing.

So far in describing SGML and XML, I have referred only to the frameworks that are used to produce structured documents. Specific documentation projects need to create and, to some extent, enforce specific markup definitions for the type of documents they need to produce. These definitions are referred to as Data Type Definitions (DTDs). For documentation of Linux itself and other open source projects, DocBook has become the DTD of choice.

Understanding DocBook

DocBook is a DTD that is well suited for producing computer software documents in a variety of formats. It was originally created by the OASIS Consortium (`www.oasis-open.org/docbook`) and is now supported by many different commercial and open-source tools.

> **CROSS REFERENCE:** You can find official documentation for DocBook at `www.docbook.org`.

DocBook's focus is on marking content, instead of indicating a particular look (that is, font type, size, position, and so on.). It includes markup that lets you automate the process of creating indices, figure lists, and tables of contents, to name a few. Tools in Fedora and RHEL enable you to output DocBook documents into HTML, PDF, DVI, PostScript, RTF, and other formats.

DocBook is important to the Linux community because many open-source projects are using DocBook to produce documentation. For example, the following is a list of organizations, and related Web sites, that use DocBook to create the documents that describe their software:

- Linux Documentation Project (`www.tldp.org/LDP/LDP-Author-Guide`)
- GNOME Documentation (`developer.gnome.org/projects/gdp/handbook/gdp-handbook`)

- KDE Documentation Project (www.kde.org/documentation)
- FreeBSD Documentation Project (www.freebsd.org/docproj)

If you want to contribute to any of the preceding documentation projects, refer to the Web sites for each organization. In all cases, they publish writers' guides or style guides that describe the DocBook tags that they support for their writing efforts.

Creating DocBook documents

You can create the documents in any text editor, using tags that are similar in appearance to HTML tags (with beginning and end tags appearing between less-than and greater-than signs). There are also word processing programs that allow you to create DocBook markup. You can export documents from OpenOffice.org Writer to DocBook format, for example.

The following procedure contains an example of a simple DocBook document produced with a plain-text editor and output into HTML using tools that come with Fedora and RHEL. (You need to have the set of docbooks packages on the DVD installed to do the following procedure.)

1. Create a directory in your home directory to work in and go to that directory. For example, you could type the following from a Terminal window:

```
$ mkdir $HOME/doctest
$ cd $HOME/doctest
```

2. Open a text editor to hold your DocBook document. For example, you could type:

```
$ gedit cardoc.sgml
```

(A text editor such as jedit, which you can get at www.jedit.org, can also be useful for dealing with the long tag names used in DocBook.)

3. Enter the tags and text that you want to appear in your document. Most DocBook documents are either <book> type (large, multichapter documents) or <article> type (single chapter documents). To try out a DocBook document, type the following:

```
<xml version="1.0">
<article>
  <title>Choosing a new car</title>
  <artheader>
    <abstract>
      In this article, you will learn how to price,
      negotiate for, and purchase an automobile.
    </abstract>
  </artheader>
  <section>
    <title>Getting Started</title>
    <para>
```

```
        The first thing you will learn is how to figure out
        what you can afford.
      </para>
    </section>
    <section>
      <title>The Next Step</title>
      <para>
      After you know what you can afford, you can begin your
      search.
      </para>
    </section>
</article>
```

You should notice a few things about this document. The entire document is wrapped in article tags (`<article>` `</article>`). The article title is in title tags (`<title>` `</title>`). The section tags (`<section>` `</section>`) indicate sections of text that have a title and paragraph each. These sections can later be treated separately in the TOC.

4. Save the file and exit from the text editor.

5. Next, you can try translating the document you just created into several different formats. For example, to create HTML output you can type the following:

```
$ db2html cardoc.sgml
```

The result is a new directory called `cardoc`. The result from `db2html` in the `cardoc` directory was: stylesheet-images directory, `t2.html` file, and `x12.html` file.

6. To view the HTML file just created, I typed the following:

```
$ firefox $HOME/doctest/cardoc/t2.html
```

Figure 6-11 shows an example of the output created from the `db2html` command. The screen on the left shows the first page. Click the Next link at the top of the page. The second page that you see is shown on the right. During conversion to HTML, the `db2html` command adds Next/Previous buttons to each page. It also puts the title of each section in a Table of Contents on page one and in the browser's title bar.

From this point, you can continue to add content and different types of tags. If you are writing documents for a particular project (such as the Linux projects mentioned earlier), you should get information on the particular tags and other style issues they require.

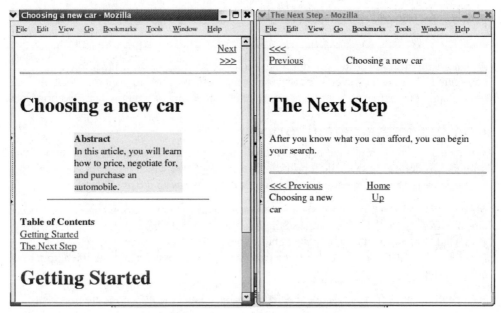

Figure 6-11: The DocBook file is output in HTML with the db2html command.

Converting DocBook documents

The previous example shows how to create a simple DocBook document and convert it to HTML output. The following Fedora and RHEL utilities convert DocBook to other formats:

- **docbook2dvi** — Converts a DocBook file to Device Independent file format.
- **docbook2html** — Converts a DocBook file to HTML format.
- **docbook2man** — Converts a DocBook file to man page format.
- **docbook2pdf** — Converts a DocBook file to Portable Document Format (PDF).
- **docbook2rtf** — Converts a DocBook file to Rich Text Format (RTF).
- **docbook2tex** — Converts a DocBook file to TeX format.
- **docbook2texi** — Converts a DocBook file to GNU TeXinfo format.
- **docbook2txt** — Converts a DocBook file to a bare text format.

Printing Documents with Fedora and RHEL

Printing in Red Hat Linux is provided by the Common UNIX Printing System (CUPS) service. The LPRng service, which is no longer included with Fedora or RHEL, still can be obtained from www.lprng.com/downloads.html. Both services, however, let you print using the same basic set of printing commands described in this section.

> **CROSS-REFERENCE:** For information on configuring local and remote printers for Fedora and RHEL, see Chapter 17.

As a non-administrative user, you don't have a lot of control over how the printers are configured. You can, however, check which printers are available to print to, check the status of print queues (documents waiting to print), and remove any of your own queued print jobs.

Printing to the default printer

When your system administrator (or you) configured printers for your computer, one of those printers was defined as the default printer. If you are not sure which printer is your default, type **system-config-printer** and look for the printer with the check by it.

Most graphical word processors, such as StarOffice and OpenOffice.org, enable you to choose a printer from those available. Some of the less sophisticated Linux utilities that run from the command line, however, use only the default printer. For example, dvips (to print a PostScript file) and groff -1 (to print a troff/nroff file) automatically send the output to the default printer.

As a regular user, you can override the default printer using the PRINTER environment variable. For example, if the default printer on your computer is lp0 and you want to print regularly to lp1, change your default printer by setting the PRINTER variable as follows:

```
$ export PRINTER=lp1
```

To have this take effect all the time, you could add this line to one of your shell configuration files (such as $HOME/.bashrc, if you use the bash shell).

Printing from the shell

The lpr command is used to print files from the shell. You can use lpr to print whether the LPRng or CUPS print service is being used. If you have a file already formatted, use lpr to print it. For example, if you have a PostScript output file (file.ps) and you want to print it to your PostScript printer, use the following command line:

```
$ lpr file.ps
```

If you want to specify a particular printer (other than the default), add the -P*printer* option. For example, to print to the lp0 printer, you could type the following:

```
$ lpr -Plp0 file.ps
```

If you want to print more than one copy of a document, use the -#*num* option, where *num* is replaced by the number of copies you want. For example, to print five copies of a file, use:

```
$ lpr -#5 file.ps
```

The lpr command can also accept standard output for printing. For example, you can print the output of a groff command by piping that output to lpr as follows:

```
$ groff -Tps -man /tmp/chown.1 | lpr -Plp0
```

> **TIP:** The enscript command (in the enscript package) is another useful tool for printing plain-text files. It converts the files to PostScript and sends them to a printer or to a specified file.

Checking the print queues

To check the status of print jobs that have been queued, you can use the lpq command. By itself, lpq prints a listing of jobs that are in the queue for the default printer. For example:

```
$ lpq
hp is ready and printing
Rank       Owner      Job  Files         Total Size
active     root       3    hosts         1024 bytes
1st        root       7    (stdin)       625 bytes
2nd        root       8    memo1.ps      12273 bytes
3rd        chuck      9    bikes.ps      10880 bytes
```

The output from lpq shows the printer status and the files waiting to be printed. Rank lists the order in which they are in the queue. Owner is the user who queued the job. Job shows the job number. The Files column shows the name of the file or standard input (if the file was piped or directed to lpr). Total Size shows how large each file is in bytes.

You can add options to lpq to print different kinds of information. By adding -Pprinter, you can see the queue for any available printer. You can also add the job number (to see the status of a particular print job) or a user name (to see all queued jobs for a user).

Removing print jobs

If you have ever printed a large document by mistake, you understand the value of being able to remove a print job from the queue. Likewise, if a printer is going to be down for a while and everyone has already printed their jobs to another printer, it's sometimes nice to be able to clear all the print jobs when the printer comes back online.

Remove print jobs in Fedora or RHEL using lprm. For example, to remove all jobs for the user named bill (assuming you are either bill or the root user), type the following:

```
$ lprm -U bill
```

The root user can remove all print jobs from the queue (although you can expect to have some unhappy users if you do this often). To do this you add a dash (-) to the lprm command line as follows:

```
$ lprm -
```

You can also remove queued print jobs for a particular printer (-Pprinter) or for a particular job number by just adding the job number to the lprm command line.

Checking printer status

Sometimes nothing comes out of a printer and you have no idea why. The lpc command is a printer status command that might give you a clue as to what is going on with your printer. The lpc command is intended for administrators, so it may not be in your default PATH. To start the lpc command, type the following:

```
# /usr/sbin/lpc
lpc> status
hp:
            printer is on device 'lpd' speed -1
            queuing is enabled
            printing is enabled
            no entries
            daemon present
lpc>
```

When the command returns the lpc> prompt, type the word **status**. This example shows the status of printer hp. Here, queuing and printing are enabled. The printer shows no problems, no print jobs are waiting. To quit the lpc command, type **exit** at the lpc> prompt.

Displaying PDF Files with Adobe Acrobat Reader

Non-WYSIWYG publishing can be very paper-intensive if you send a Groff or LaTeX document to the printer each time you want to make a change to the document's content or formatting. To save paper and time spent running around, you can use some print preview programs to display a document on the screen as it will appear on the printed page. The following sections describe the Adobe Acrobat reader for displaying Portable Document Format (PDF) files.

The Portable Document Format (PDF) provides a way of storing documents as they would appear in print. With Adobe Acrobat Reader, you can view PDF files in a very friendly way. Adobe Acrobat makes it easy to move around within a PDF file. A PDF file may include hyperlinks, a table of contents, graphics, and a variety of type fonts.

A recent version of the Adobe Acrobat Reader (version 8) is available in RPM format from Adobe.com. This version can use many PDF features that aren't available in other PDF readers, including some new compression features in version 1.4. (While you are at it, you can install the Acrobat Plug-in RPM, to use the same reader to play PDF content when you browse the Web.)

After you install Adobe Acrobat Reader, type the following command to start the program:

```
$ acroread
```

Select File → Open, and then select the name of a PDF file you want to display. Figure 6-12 shows an example of a PDF file viewed in Adobe Acrobat Reader.

Acrobat Reader has a lot of nice features. For example, you can display a list of bookmarks alongside the document and click on a bookmark to take you to a particular page. You can also display thumbnails of the pages to quickly scroll through and select a page.

Figure 6-12: Display PDF files in the Adobe Acrobat Reader.

Using the menu bar or buttons, you can page through the PDF document, zoom in and out, go to the beginning or end of the document, and display different views of the document (as well as display bookmarks and page thumbnails). To print a copy, select File → Print.

Working with Graphics

Tools for creating and manipulating graphics are becoming both more plentiful and more powerful in Linux. Leading the list is The GNU Image Manipulation Program (The GIMP, or sometime simply GIMP). GIMP lets you compose and author images as well as retouch photographs. Other tools that come with Fedora and RHEL for creating graphics include `ksnapshot` (a program for taking screen captures).

CROSS-REFERENCE: See Chapter 8 for descriptions of other multimedia applications, such as the gphoto window for working with images from digital cameras.

Manipulating images with GIMP

The GIMP is a free software program that comes with Fedora and RHEL for manipulating photographs and graphical images. To create images with GIMP, you can either import a drawing, photograph, or 3D image, or you can create one from scratch. You can start GIMP from the Applications menu by clicking Graphics → The GIMP or by typing `gimp&` from a Terminal window.

Figure 6-13 shows an example of The GIMP.

Figure 6-13: GIMP is a powerful tool for graphic manipulation.

GIMP 2.4 represents one of the most significant new releases of GIMP for some time. Many of the new features aim at improving the tools needed by professional designers. All new selection tools let designers select rectangular areas with rounded corners. A slider was added to let you more specifically select brush sizes. New grid and alignment features make it easier to align layers, paths or guides. Digital photo editing has improved with built-in red-eye removal, full-screen editing, and new cropping and printing tools.

In many ways, GIMP is similar to Adobe Photoshop. Some people feel that GIMP's scripting features are comparable to, or even better than, Actions in Adobe Photoshop. One capability in which GIMP has been behind Photoshop has been in the area of color management. With the latest features of GIMP, however, you can calibrate screens and work with color profiles from your cameras and scanners (`http://gimp.org/release-notes/gimp-2.4-cm.html`).

One of the easiest ways to become familiar with GIMP is to crop, or trim, an image file already on your computer. To crop a file, follow these steps:

1. Start GIMP and open an image file.

2. Right-click on the image. From the contextual menu that appears, select Tools → Transform Tools → Crop. The crop cursor appears (a cross and knife icon).

3. Position the crop cursor at the upper-left corner of the area of the image that you want to crop. Click and drag the cursor to the lower-right corner of the area to be cropped. A selection rectangle will appear around the selected area as you do so.

4. Release the mouse button. Four selection squares appear in the corners of the border around the selected area. Click and drag the handles to resize the border.

5. When the border is in the right place, press the Enter key. The image will be cropped to the border.

> **TIP**: If you make a mistake, select Edit → Undo from the GIMP menu or press the Ctrl+Z key combination.

Taking screen captures

If you want to show examples of the work you do on Fedora or RHEL, you can use the Screen Capture program to capture screen images. (The `ksnapshot` command is part of the kdegraphics package contained on the media that comes with this book.)

> **NOTE:** If you don't have ksnapshot installed, you can also use `gnome-screenshot` or The GIMP to capture screenshots of your desktop.

To open Screen Capture, from the Applications menu click Graphics → Ksnapshot (or type `ksnapshot`). Figure 6-14 shows an example of the Screen Capture program.

When Screen Capture first opens, it takes a snapshot of the full desktop. Buttons on the window offer the following options:

- **New Snapshot** — Select the capture mode (Full Screen, Window under cursor, or Region). Click here to take a new snapshot of the selected content.

- **Save As** — Save the snapshot to a file in X bitmap, Windows icon, PNG, portable pixmap, JPEG, X pixmap, Encapsulated PostScript, or Windows BMP formats.

- **Copy to Clipboard** — Copy the image to the clipboard, so it can be pasted into a document, image editor, or other application.

- **Print** — Have the snapshot sent to your printer.

You can select a capture mode other than the default Full Screen. For example you can choose to capture the window under the cursor, a particular region of the desktop (hold down the mouse and drag a box open), or a section of a window (the element of the window set to be captured will highlight). You can also delay the snapshot for a set number of seconds.

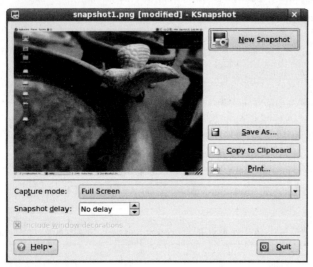

Figure 6-14: Grab a picture of your desktop or selected window with Screen Capture.

Using Scanners Driven by SANE

Software for using a scanner with Linux is being driven by an effort called Scanner Access Now Easy (SANE). This effort hopes to standardize how device drivers for equipment such as scanners, digital still cameras, and digital video cameras are created, as well as help simplify the interfaces for applications that use those devices.

SANE is now included with the Fedora and RHEL distributions. The sane-backends, sane-frontends, xsane, and xsane-gimp packages are all on the DVD that comes with this book. You can get the latest SANE driver packages from www.sane-project.org.

Someone wanting to use Linux as a publishing platform is generally interested in two issues about scanners: which scanners are supported and which applications are available to use the scanners. In the past, more SCSI scanners have been supported than parallel scanners. However, have given way to the more convenient USB scanners.

Because of the ongoing development effort, new scanners are being supported all the time. You can find a current list of supported scanners at www.sane-project.org/sane-supported-devices.html. As for applications, these are currently available with Fedora and RHEL:

- **xsane** — This is an X-based graphical front end for SANE scanners; `xsane` can work as a GIMP plug-in or as a separate application. (From the Applications menu, select Graphics → Scanning.) It supports 8-bit output in JPG, TIFF, PNG, PostScript, and PNM formats. There is experimental 16-bit support for PNM (ASCII), PNG, and raw formats.

- **scanimage** — This is a command-line interface for obtaining scanned images. It supports the same formats as `xscanimage`. The command acquires the scanned image, and then directs the data to standard output (so you can send it to a file or pipe it to another program).

In addition to these applications, the OpenOffice.org suite supports SANE.

Because of the architecture of SANE scanner drivers, it is possible to separate scanner drivers from scanner applications. This makes it possible to share scanners across a network.

Summary

In recent times, modern GUI-based publishing tools have augmented the text-based publishing tools that have always been available Linux systems. Powerful open-source publishing tools such as OpenOffice.org are becoming competitive with commercial office suites. Traditional publishing tools such as Groff (which implements traditional troff/nroff text processing) and LaTeX (a TeX macro interface that is particularly suited for scientific and mathematical publishing) are still available with Fedora.

Tools for working with graphics are gaining ground on professional image manipulation programs. Using The GIMP, you can modify your images in a variety of ways.

Chapter 7

Gaming in Fedora and RHEL

In This Chapter

- Gaming in Linux
- Playing open source games in Fedora
- Finding commercial Linux games
- Running Windows games in Linux

As Linux has grown in popularity, the availability of Linux-based entertainment options has increased. From simple parlor games to fast-paced OpenGL first-person shooters (FPS), there have been great strides recently in Linux gaming opportunities. In fact, the advance of processor-devouring 3D games has helped drive improvements in computer technology in general.

Availability of gaming software that you can use directly in Linux is a mixed bag. Many free and open source board games, card games, and clones of old popular game console games are either packaged with Fedora or available from other sources. Some older commercial games have been either released as open source (such as Doom) or become freely distributable (though only as binaries or with licensing restrictions on how they can be used).

Some experts predict that gaming will be the software category that brings Linux into homes. The unfortunate truth is that many of the current "hot" titles still need to be coaxed onto Linux with some kind of Win32 emulation (such as Cedega). But even this is getting easier and more dependable. While the number of popular game applications is fairly limited at the moment, like everything else in Linux, more games are becoming available each day.

One area where gaming-related software has grown in Linux is in tools for producing high-quality 3D animations. For example, Blender (www.blender.org) is an open source project for doing animations, 3D models, post-production, and rendering that is being used today to produce commercial games and movie animations. Blender's features are beginning to rival those of commercial 3D animation software such as 3D Studio Max (www.autodesk.com/3dsmax), Maya (www.autodesk.com/maya) and SoftImage SXI (www.softimage.com).

> **NOTE:** You can participate in a community of Blender artists and game developers at the BlenderArtists.org site. The site offers many useful forums on blender, including several active forums on the Blender Game Engine.

This chapter examines the current state of gaming in Linux, including the basics on getting your gaming environment going, and hardware considerations for gaming. It also describes the free games (mostly fairly simple X Window games) that come with Fedora and RHEL or that can be found elsewhere on the Web. For running games that were created for other platforms, this chapter describes game emulators such as Cedega.

This chapter also discusses some popular commercial games that have demo versions available for Linux. If you like the demos, you can purchase these games, some of which run natively in Linux.

Basic Linux Gaming Information

There are more than 200 software packages in the Games group in the Fedora software repository. So if you are just looking for a few diverting games or old commercial games that are now publicly available, you can start by looking within that repository. However, if you are interested in learning more about new commercial games that run in Linux, or finding out about the general state of Linux gaming, there are several sites on the Web you should check out.

Where to get information on Linux gaming

To find news on the latest games available for Linux, as well as links to download sites, go to some of the several Web sites available. Here are a few to get you started:

- **TransGaming Technologies** (www.transgaming.com) — This company's mission is to bring games from other platforms (Windows) to Linux. TransGaming is the provider of Cedega, formerly known as WineX, a powerful tool that allows you to play hundreds of PC games on your Linux system.

- **The Linux Game Tome** (http://happypenguin.org) — This site features a database of descriptions and reviews of tons of games that run on Linux. You can do keyword searches for games listed at this site. The site also includes links to where you can get the different games, as well as links to other gaming sites.

- **Linuxgames.com** (http://linuxgames.com) — This site can give you some very good insight into the state of Linux gaming. There are links to HOW-TOs and Frequently Asked Questions (FAQs), as well as forums for discussing Linux games. There are also links to Web sites that have information on particular games.

- **Wikipedia** (http://en.wikipedia.org) — In the past few years, Wikipedia has become a wonderful resource for information on both commercial and open source games available for Linux. From Wikipedia, there is a list of open source games (http://en.wikipedia.org/wiki/List_of_open_source_games) and a general Linux games page (http://en.wikipedia.org/wiki/Linux_games).

- **id Software** (www.idsoftware.com) — Linux versions of Doom 3, the Quake series and Return to Castle Wolfenstein are available from id Software.

- **Garage Games** (www.garagegames.com) — Garage Games is a site that publishes games from independent game makers. Many of the games sold at the Garage Games store (www.garagegames.com/pg) have ports of games specifically for Linux.

- **Linuxgamepublishing.com** (www.linuxgamepublishing.com) — A relatively new entrant into the Linux gaming world, linuxgamepublishing.com aims to be a one-stop shopping portal for native Linux games, as well as for ports of games from other platforms. At the time of writing, they offered 28 games. Note that to purchase games from this site, you must create a user account.

- **Loki Entertainment Software** (www.lokigames.com) — Loki provided ports of best-selling games to Linux, but went out of business in 2001. Its products included Linux versions of Unreal Tournament, Civilization: Call to Power, Myth II: Soulblighter, SimCity 3000, Railroad Tycoon II, and Quake III Arena. While the company itself is no longer in business, the Loki Demo Launcher is still available to see demo versions of these games, and some boxed sets are available for very little money.

- **Tux Games** (www.tuxgames.com) — If you are ready to purchase a game, the Tux Games Web site is dedicated to the sale of Linux games. Besides offering Linux gaming news and products, the site lists its top-selling games and includes notices of games that are soon to be released.

- **Linux Gamers' FAQ** (http://icculus.org/lgfaq) — This FAQ contains a wealth of information about free and commercial Linux games. It lists gaming companies that have ported their games to Linux, tells where to get Linux games, and answers queries related to common Linux gaming problems. For a list of Linux games without additional information, see http://icculus.org/lgfaq/gamelist.php.

Choosing a video card for gaming

Because high-end games place extraordinary demands on your video hardware, choosing a good video card and configuring it properly is one of the keys to ensuring a good gaming experience. For advanced gaming you will need to go beyond what an old 64-bit card can do for you.

Support for video cards in Fedora comes primarily from the X.org project. For details on exactly which features and cards are supported for the current release of Fedora or RHEL, refer to the X.Org Wiki (http://wiki.x.org). Select the link to documentation for the version of X.Org software included in your version of Fedora or RHEL (for example, http://wiki.x.org/wiki/ReleasesX11R7.3).

One video card feature that can greatly improve your gaming experience is Direct Rendering Infrastructure (DRI). Whether you are running the games using Cedega or natively in Linux, a card that supports DRI allows your video display to do hardware acceleration. You can find a more complete list of video cards that support DRI from the DRI project site (http://dri.sourceforge.net/).

Here are some suggestions of video cards you can use with Fedora and RHEL for gaming that either supply proprietary Linux drivers or include DRI support:

- **NVIDIA** — NVIDIA cards are by far the most popular video cards used for gaming in Linux. Open source drivers (nv) are available for NVIDIA cards. However, most Linux users get NVIDIA drivers that are produced by NVIDIA. Although these are not open source drivers, you can download binary NVIDIA drivers from the NVIDIA Web site (www.nvidia.com) or from the rpm.livna.org site. (To install the drivers directly from the NVIDIA site, you must have the kernel-devel and xorg-sdk packages installed.)

> **NOTE:** Because binary-only drivers are not part of the Linux kernel, if you update your kernel at some point, you will need to update your NVIDIA driver as well. The rpm.livna.org site offers a nice service by packaging NVIDIA and ATI video card drivers as RPMs to match new Fedora kernel updates. Refer to this site for further information: http://rpm.livna.org/rlowiki/LivnaSwitcher. Because the drivers direct from NVIDIA have been known to overwrite shared XOrg files in Fedora, sometimes breaking your ability to use other video cards with the system, using the RPMs from livna.org is, in most cases, the best way to install NVIDIA drivers to Fedora.
>
> A new, experimental open source driver called nouveau aims at providing 3D effects for NVIDIA cards. The driver requires DRM support in the kernel and Mesa support for 3D effects. Currently, only 2D rendering is working with the nouveau driver delivered with Fedora. Eventually you should be able to use features such as the AIGLX-enabled Compiz window manager and OpenGL screensavers with the nouveau driver.

- **AMD's ATI Technologies** — In 2006, Advanced Micro Devices (AMD) purchased graphics chip maker ATI Technologies. ATI chipsets that support DRI include the Mach64 (Rage Pro), Radeon 7X00 (R100), Radeon 2 / 8500 (R200), and Rage 128 (Standard, Pro, Mobility). Cards based on these chip sets include All-in-Wonder 128, Rage Fury, Rage Magnum, Xpert 99, Xpert 128, and Xpert 2000. DRI support for Radeon chipsets up to 9200 has recently been added. Proprietary, binary-only drivers for ATI cards are available directly from the AMD site at http://ati.amd.com/support/driver.html or packaged as RPMs from the rpm.livna.org site.

A recent announcement from AMD regarding its ATI graphics chip drivers promises strong support for Linux in the future. AMD has expanded features in its Catalyst software to support ATI Radeon HD 2000 series graphics processors. Features slated for the near future are expected to produce significant performance improvements in popular Linux games (including Doom 3 and Quake 4) as well as adding support for accelerated indirect GLX (AIGLX) for 3D accelerated effects.

- **3dfx** — If you can find a used unit on eBay, there are several 3dfx cards that support 3D. In particular, the Voodoo (3, 4, and 5) and Banshee chip sets have drivers that support DRI. Voodoo 5 cards support 16 and 24 bpp. Scan Line Interleaving (SLI), where two or more 3D processors work in parallel (to result in higher frame rates), is not supported for 3dfx cards.

- **Intel** — Supported video chipsets from Intel include the i810 (e, e2, and -dc100), i815, and i815e. Intel has recently released some of the drivers for these and other graphics chip sets to the open source community. You can find out more about these drivers from the Linux Graphics Drivers from Intel site (`www.intellinuxgraphics.org`).

- **Matrox** — The Matrox chipsets (`www.matrox.com`) that have drivers that support DRI include the G200, G400, and G450. Cards that use these chips include the Millennium G450, Millennium G400, Millennium G200, and Mystique G200.

To find out whether DRI is working on your current video card, you can use the `glxinfo` command (available from the glx-utils package). Type the following:

```
$ glxinfo | grep rendering
direct rendering: Yes
```

This example shows that direct rendering is supported. If it were not supported, the output would say `No` instead of `Yes`. Even if DRI is not supported, you may experience the best game play with a high-end card from NVIDIA, in particular, and ATI to a lesser extent. While DRI support can be important, many games support OpenGL rendering, a feature supported by both NVIDIA and ATI video cards. Both companies have specific driver requirements, so make sure you research the cards, driver requirements, and any game-specific issue before you plop down big money on a top-tier 3D video card.

Running Open Source Linux Games

A lot of diverting open source games come with Fedora and RHEL and run in X. Both the GNOME and KDE environments available with Fedora include a set of games that are installed by default with those desktops. Beyond that, many more games can be installed from the Fedora repository.

Much of the recent increase in Fedora games has come from the Fedora Games SIG (Special Interest Group). You can check out that SIG's activities for information on other games of interest that have not made it into Fedora at `http://fedoraproject.org/wiki/SIGs/Games`. In fact, if you know of a popular game that runs in Linux that is not available currently in Fedora, chances are there have been discussions among the Fedora Games SIG of the pros and cons of including it.

Discussions on the fedora-games-list mailing list provide insights into why some games are difficult to package for Fedora and why some games can't get into Fedora because they don't meet the licensing requirements. Discussion relating to whether or not to include Doom first-person-shooter game in Fedora, for example, was an interesting example of how licensing issues are addressed. Although the Doom engine is freely distributable, there are clauses in the Doom license that prevent people from modifying, disassembling, or reverse engineering the software. For that reason, the Fedora project decided to include the prboom open source Doom clone and the freedoom doom data files.

An on-going activity of the Fedora Gaming SIG is a Fedora gaming LiveCD/LiveDVD. Check out the games slated for that live media on the Games LiveCD/LiveDVD page (http://fedoraproject.org/wiki/SIGs/Games/GamesLive).

GNOME games

The GNOME games consist of some old card games and a bunch of games that look suspiciously like games you would find on Windows systems. If you are afraid of losing your favorite desktop diversion (such as Solitaire, FreeCell, or Minesweeper) when you leave Windows, have no fear. You can find clones of many of them under GNOME games.

Table 7-1 lists the games that are part of the gnome-games software package. After that package is installed, the games are available by selecting Games from the Applications menu. If you installed the kdegames package, many KDE games (shown in Table 7-2) are also available on this menu.

Table 7-1: GNOME Games

Game	Description
AisleRiot (solitaire)	Lets you select from among 28 different solitaire card games.
Blackjack	The popular card game where you try to get to 21.
Five or More	Form lines to remove colored balls from the board.
Four-In-A-Row	Drop balls to beat the game at making four in a row.
FreeCell Solitaire	A popular solitaire card game.
Iagno	Flip black and white chips to maneuver past the opponent.
Klotski	Move pieces around to allow one piece to escape.
Mahjongg	Classic Asian tile game.
Mines	Minesweeper clone. Click safe spaces and avoid the bombs.
Nibbles	Steer a worm around the screen while avoiding walls.
Robots	Later version of Gnobots, which includes movable junk heaps, where you try to get robots to destroy themselves before they get you.
Same GNOME	Eliminate clusters of balls for high score.
Sudoku	Popular Japanese logic puzzle game.
Tali	Yahtzee clone. Roll dice to fill in categories.
Tetravex	Puzzle game where numbers on adjacent pieces must match.

KDE games

If you install KDE, there are a bunch of games in the kdegames package. If you did not install the KDE desktop, you can install the kdegames package separately from the DVD that accompanies this book or using yum over the Internet (yum install kdegames). To see the KDE games (along with some GNOME games) on the Applications menu, select Games and then choose the game you want. The games from the kdegames package are listed by category in Table 7-2.

Table 7-2: Games for the KDE Desktop

Game	Description
Arcade Games	
KAsteroids	Destroy asteroids in the classic arcade game.
KBounce	Add walls to block in bouncing balls.
KFoul Eggs	Squish eggs in this Tetris-like game.
Klickety	Click color groups to erase blocks in this adaptation of Clickomania.
Kolf	Play a round of virtual golf.
KSirtet	Tetris clone. Try to fill in lines of blocks as they drop down.
KSmileTris	Tetris with smiley faces.
KSnakeRace	Race your snake around a maze.
KSpaceDuel	Fire at another spaceship as you spin around a planet.
Boardgames	
Atlantik	Play this Monopoly-like game against others on the network.
KBackgammon	Online version of backgammon.
KBlackBox	Find hidden balls by shooting rays.
Kenolaba	Move game pieces to push opponents' pieces off the board.
KMahjongg	Classic oriental tile game.
KReversi	Flip game pieces to outmaneuver the opponent.
Shisen-Sho	Tile game similar to Mahjongg. Very addictive.
Kwin4	Drop colored pieces to get four pieces in a row.
Cardgames	
KPoker	Video poker clone. Play five-card draw, choosing which cards to hold and which to throw.
Lieutenant Skat	Play the card game Skat.

Game	Description
Patience	Choose from nine different solitaire card games.
Tactics and Strategy	
KAtomic	Move pieces to create different chemical compounds.
KGoldrunner	Strategy puzzle game.
KJumping Cube	Click squares to increase numbers and take over adjacent squares.
KMines	Minesweeper clone. Click safe spaces and avoid the bombs.
Kolor Lines	Move marbles to form five-in-a-row and score points.
Konquest	Expand your interstellar empire in this multiplayer game.
Potato Guy	Build your own potatohead face.
SameGame	Erase game pieces to score points.

The games on the KDE menu range from diverting to quite challenging. If you are used to playing games in Windows, KMines and Patience will seem like old favorites. KAsteroids and KPoker are good for the mindless game category.

Adding more games from Fedora repository

As Fedora continued its role as a proving ground for the Red Hat Enterprise Linux products, some just-for-fun software packages were pushed out of what was called Fedora Core. Luckily, many of them were pushed into Fedora Extras. With the merging of Fedora Extras and Core, all those games are now back in the main Fedora repository.

Because the Fedora Games SIG is an on-going initiative, you can check the Fedora Project Web site to see if more games than are shown in Table 7-3 are available in Fedora by opening the PackageKit window and selecting Games.

You can install each game from the Fedora DVD included with this book. Most, but not all, of the games available in the Fedora repository are included on the DVD. To check games packages that might have been added later, type `yum groupinfo games`. To install a later version of a game from the Fedora repository, as root user type the following, replacing *game* with the name of one of the games listed in Table 7-3:

```
# yum install game
```

Table 7-3 contains a sample from the growing list of games available from the Fedora repository. There are now over 200 games packages in Fedora. Except where noted, all games in Table 7-3 can be launched from the Games list on the Applications menu.

Table 7-3: Games in Fedora

Game	Description
Abe (abe)	Scrolling, platform-jumping, ancient pyramid exploring game.
Beneath a Steel Sky (beneath-a-steel-sky)	A popular commercial science fiction adventure game from the early 1990s, set in a repressive, futuristic city.
BSD Games (bsd-games)	Text-based card games and adventure games dating back to early UNIX systems of the 1970s. (Run from the shell.)
BZFlag (bzflag)	3D multi-player tank battle game.
Celestia (celestia)	OpenGL real-time visual space simulation. (Available under the Other menu.)
CGoban (cgoban)	X board for playing go.
Crystal Stacker (crystal-stacker)	As crystals fall, match three or more of the same color.
Cannon Smash (csmash)	3D tabletennis game.
Enigma (enigma)	Clone of the ATARI game Oxyd.
Extreme Tuxracer (extremetuxracer)	3D racing game featuring Tux.
Flight Gear (FlightGear)	Flight simulator software.
FooBilliard (foobillard)	OpenGL billiard game.
Fortune (fortune-mod)	A program which will display a fortune. (Available by typing the `fortune` command.)
Freeciv (freeciv)	The Freeciv multi-player strategy game.
Freedoom (freedoom)	Data files for Doom game engines (use with prboom package, which provides an open source port of the doom engine).
Freedroid (freedroid)	Clone of the C64 game Paradroid.
Freedroid RPG (freedroidrpg)	Freedroid theme for role playing game with Tux as hero.
GL-117 (gl-117)	Action flight simulator.
Gnofract 4D (gnofract4d)	Gnofract 4D is a Gnome-based program to draw fractals. (Available under the Graphics menu.)
Chess (gnuchess)	The GNU chess program. Used with the xboard package to provide a graphical chess game.
gnogo (gnugo)	Text based go program. (Available by typing the `gnogo` command.)
Grhino (grhino)	GNOME-based reversi game.
Lacewing (lacewing)	Asteroid game sporting different types of ships.

Game	Description
Lincity (lincity-ng)	Build simulated cities.
LMarbles (lmarbles)	Atomix clone where you create figures out of marbles.
LucidLife (lucidlife)	A Conway's life simulator.
NetHack (nethack)	Single-player rogue-like game where you explore dungeons.
Neverball (neverball)	Roll a ball through an obstacle course.
Maelstrom (Maelstrom)	A space combat game.
Nexuiz (nexuiz)	Deathmatch-oriented first person shooter (multiplayer).
Powermanga (powermanga)	Arcade 2D shoot-them-up game.
Qascade (qascade)	Classic puzzle game.
Quake 3 Arena Engine (quake3)	Quake 3 Arena engine, used to play various first person shooter games based on this engine.
Quake 3 Demo (quake3-demo)	Quake 3 Arena tournament game demo installer (will download demo data files).
Raidem (raidem)	Top-down, 2D shooting game.
Rogue (rogue)	Graphical version of classic adventure game.
Scorched Earth (scorched3d)	Game based loosely on the classic DOS game Scorched Earth.
Sirius (sirius)	Othello for Gnome.
Sopwith (sopwith)	SDL port of the sopwith game. (Available by typing the `sopwith` command.)
Starfighter (starfighter)	Project: Starfighter, a space arcade game. (Available by typing the `/usr/games/starfighter` command.)
SuperTux (supertux)	Jump'n run like game similar to Mario Bros.
TORCS (torcs)	The Open Racing Car Simulator.
The Ur-Quan Masters (uqm)	The Ur-Quan Masters, a port of the classic game Star Control II.
Vega Strike (vegastrike)	Spaceflight simulator (3D OpenGL).
Virus Killer (viruskiller)	Frantic shooting game where viruses invade your computer.
Battle for Wesnoth (wesnoth)	Turn-based strategy game with a fantasy theme.
Worminator (worminator)	Multi-level shoot-em up game.
Chess (xboard)	An X Window System graphical chessboard.
X Pilot (xpilot-ng)	Multi-player space arcade game. (The xpilot-ng-server is also available.)

Game	Description
xplanet (xplanet)	Render a planetary image into an X window. (Available by typing the `xplanet` command.)
Zasx (zasx)	Asteroid-style game that includes power-ups.

The following sections describe three of the more interesting games that come with Fedora. First is the xboard game and some related chess programs. Next is a description of Freeciv, and finally a description of PlanetPenguin Racer.

Chess games

Chess was one of the first games played on computer systems. While the game hasn't changed over the years, the way it's played on computers has. The chess programs that are available in Fedora let you play against the computer (in text or graphical modes), have the computer play against itself, or replay stored chess games. You can even play chess against other users on the Internet using Internet Chess Servers (ICS).

The xboard program is an X-based chess game that provides a graphical interface for gnuchess. GNU Chess (represented by the xboard and gnuchess packages) describes itself as a communal chess program. It has had many contributors, and it seeks to advance a "more open and friendly environment of sharing" among the chess community. With xboard, you can move graphical pieces with your mouse.

To play against the computer, type **xboard** from a Terminal window. Then start by just moving a piece with your mouse. While in the xboard window, select Mode → Two Machines to have the computer play itself. Select File → Load Game to load a game in Portable Game Notation (PGN). Figure 7-1 shows the xboard window with a Two Machines game in progress.

You can use xboard to play online against others by connecting an xboard session to an Internet Chess Server (ICS). To start xboard as an interface to an ICS, type the following command line:

```
$ xboard -ics -icshost name
```

In this example, *name* should be replaced with the name of the ICS host (see the list of hosts below). In ICS mode, you can just watch games, play against other users, or replay games that have finished. The ICS host acts as a gathering place for enthusiasts who want to play chess against others on the Internet, watch games, participate in tournaments, or just meet chess people. Here is an example of starting an ICS session at chess.net from a Terminal window:

```
$ xboard -ics -icshost chess.net
```

When you first visit, type **guest** and press Enter. If there are not too many guests already online, you are logged into the chess server as a guest. (You can add a real account later by typing **/register**.) The xboard window opens on your screen. Keep an eye on the Terminal window where you started the session. Someone will probably challenge you to a game within a few moments. For example, if a challenge ends with Type '/accept 102' to accept the sought challenge, you type:

```
chess%   /accept 102
```

You can begin playing. To learn more about how to play, visit http://chess.net/help. Select the Beginners Manual to start. Other chess servers you can try include the Internet Chess Club (ICC) at chessclub.com or Free Internet Chess Server at freechess.org.

Figure 7-1: In the xboard window, you can either play against the computer or replay saved games.

For a list of other chess servers, refer to the U.S. Chess Federation Internet servers list (www.uschess.org/org/sources.html#Servers). If you have trouble reaching a chess server because you are behind a firewall, refer to the Xboard FAQ (/usr/share/doc/xboard-*/FAQ.html) for tips.

Freeciv

Freeciv is a free clone of the popular Civilization game series from Atari. With Freeciv, you create a civilization that challenges competing civilizations for world dominance.

The version of Freeciv that is included in Fedora contains both client software (to play the game) and server software (to connect players together). You can connect to your server and try the game yourself or (with a network connection) play against up to 14 other players on the Internet.

> **NOTE:** A commercial port of Civilization for Linux (Civilization: Call to Power) was created a few years ago by Loki Games. That game is described later in this chapter.

You can start Freeciv from the Applications menu (as a non-root user) by clicking Games →
Freeciv. If Freeciv doesn't start, try starting it from a Terminal window by typing

```
$ civclient &
```

Figure 7-2 shows the window that appears when you start Freeciv.

Figure 7-2: Play Freeciv to build civilizations and compete against others.

> **NOTE:** If Freeciv won't start, it may be that you are logged in as root. You must be logged in as a regular user to run the `civclient` command.

Starting Freeciv

You can play a few games by yourself, if you like, to get to know the game before you play against others on the network. You can select Connect to Network Game to start playing against others on the Internet or you can begin playing locally. The following procedure describes how to start your first practice Freeciv game.

1. Start Freeciv from the Applications menu (Games → Freeciv, or type **civclient&**).The Freeciv windows appear, as shown in Figure 7-2.

2. Select Start New Game. (Besides starting the client, this action also starts `civserver`, which allows others to connect to your game, if you like.) You are asked to choose the number of players, skill level, and other game options.

3. Select 2 to play against the computer or more if you want others to join in, and then click Start. A What Nation Will You Be? window appears on the client, as shown in Figure 7-3.

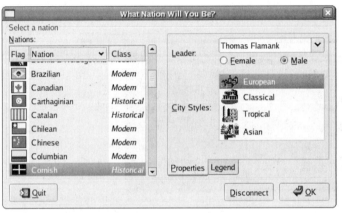

Figure 7-3: Choose a nation to begin Freeciv.

4. Choose a nation, the name of a leader, your gender, and the style of the city, and then click OK. At this point, you are ready to begin playing Freeciv.

Beginning with Freeciv

Check out the Freeciv window. Here are things you should know before you start the game. (You can find more help at the Freeciv site: `www.freeciv.org`.)

- Click the Help button for topical information on many different subjects that will be useful to you as you play.

- The world (by default) is 80×50 squares, with 11×8 squares visible at a time.

- The active square contains an icon of the active unit (flashing alternatively with the square's terrain).

- Some squares contain special resources. Press and hold the middle mouse button for information on what special resources a square contains. (With a two-button mouse, hold the Ctrl key and click the right mouse button.) Try this a few times to get a feel for the land around you. This action also identifies any units on the terrain, as well as statistics for the unit.

- To see the world outside of your 11 × 8 viewing area, click the scroll bars outside of the map. At first the world outside will be black. As units are added, areas closer to those units will be visible. (Press the letter **c** to return to the active part of your map.)

- An overview map is in the upper-left corner of the Freeciv window. As the world becomes more civilized, this provides a good way to get an overview of what is going on. Right-click a spot on the overview map to have your viewport centered there.

- The menu bar contains buttons you can use to play the game. The Game menu lets you change settings and options, view player data, view messages, and clear your log. The Kingdom menu lets you change tax rates, find cities, and start revolutions. The View menu lets you place a grid on the map or center the view. The Orders menu is where you choose the items you build and the actions you take. The Reports menu lets you display reports related to cities, military, trade, and science, as well as other special reports.

- A summary of the economy of your civilization appears under the overview map. Information includes number of people, current year, money in the treasury, and percent of money distributed to tax, luxury, and science.

- Ten icons below the overview information represent how money is divided between luxuries (an entertainer), research (a researcher), and taxes (a tax collector). Essentially, these icons represent how much of your resources are placed into improving each of those attributes of your community.

- When you have made all your moves for a turn, click Turn Done. Next to that, a lightbulb indicates the progress of your research (increasing at each turn). A sun icon starts clear, but becomes brighter from pollution to warn of possible global warming. A government symbol indicates that you begin with a despotic government. The last icon tells you how much time is left in a turn.

The Unit box shows information about your current unit. You begin with two Settlers units and one Explorer unit.

Building your civilization

Start building your civilization. Here are things to try, as suggested by the Freeciv manual:

- To change the distribution of money, choose Government → Tax Rates. Move the slider bars to redistribute the percentage of assets assigned to luxury, research, and taxes. Try increasing research and reducing taxes to start off.

- Change the current unit to be a settler as follows: click the stack of units on the map and click one of the Settlers from the menu that appears.

- Begin building a city by clicking on Orders → Build City. When prompted, type a name for the city and click OK. The window that appears shows information about the city. It starts with one happy citizen, represented by a single icon (more citizens will appear as the game progresses).

- The Food, Prod, and Trade lines reflect the raw productivity statistics for the city. The first number shows how much is being produced, the second (in parens) shows the surplus above what is needed to support the units. The Gold, Luxury, and Science lines indicate the city's trade output. Granary numbers show how much food is stored and the size of the food store. The pollution level begins at zero.

- The Units at this point are not yet supported by a city (so nothing appears under Supported Units). When Units require support, they will be assigned to cities, and they will draw on city resources. Units present appear under that heading.

- The map area shown consists of 21 squares that make up the city. The number 1 indicates the size of the city. The number 211 reflects the production of food, manufacturing production, and trade, respectively. The number 210 shows where the city's citizen is working and the results of the work.

- The Phalanx line shows that the city can build a Phalanx and that it will take 20 production points to produce. Click Change to view other units the city could produce, select one you want to build, and click Change. Below that is a list of your current buildings (of which you have only a Palace to start out).

- Close the city window by clicking Close.

Exploring your world

To begin exploring, move the Settler.

1. Using the numeric keypad, press the 9 key three times to begin exploring. You can move the explorer up to three times per turn. You begin to see more of the world.

2. When the next unit (the Settler) begins blinking, move it one square in another direction. Click Turn Done. Information for the city will be updated.

3. Click the City to see the city window. Notice that information about the city has been updated. In particular, you should see food storage increase. Close the city window.

4. Continue exploring and build a road. With the explorer flashing, use the numeric keypad to move it another three sections. When the Settler begins blinking, press **r** to build a road. A small R appears on the square to remind you that the Settler is busy building a road. Click Turn Done.

Using more controls and actions

Now that you have some understanding of the controls and actions, the game can begin taking a lot of different directions. Here are a few things that might happen next and things you can do:

- After you take a turn, the computer gets a chance to play as well. As it plays, its actions are reported to you. You can make decisions on what to do about those actions. Choose Game → Message Options. The Message options window appears, containing a listing of different kinds of messages that can come from the server and how they will be presented to you.

- As you explore, you will run into other explorers and eventually other civilizations. Continue exploring by selecting different directions on your numeric keypad.

- Continue to move the Settler one square at a time, after it has finished creating the road. (The Settler will blink again when it is available.) Click Turn Done.

- At this point, you should see a message that your city has finished building Warriors. When buildings and units are complete, you should usually check out what has happened. Click the message associated with the city, and then click Popup City. The city window appears, showing you that it has additional population. The food storage may appear empty, but the new citizens are working to increase the food and trade. You may see an additional warrior unit.

- A science advisory may also appear at this point to let you choose your city's research goals. Click Change and select Writing as your new research goal. You can then select a different long-term goal as well. Click Close when you are done.

- If your new Warrior is now blinking, press the **s** key to assign sentry mode to the Warrior.

You should be familiar with some of the actions of Freeciv at this point. To learn some basic strategies for playing the game, choose Help → Help Playing.

Extreme Tuxracer

With Extreme Tuxracer (`yum install extremetuxracer`), you guide Tux the penguin (the Linux mascot) down a snow-covered hill as fast as you can. Extreme Tuxracer (`etracer` command or Games → Extreme Tuxracer) is an open source (GPL) version of TuxRacer, which was once freeware, but was later made into a commercial game by Sunspire Studios.

To advance in Extreme Tuxracer, you need to complete courses in the allotted time while overcoming whatever obstacle is presented (gathering herring or negotiating flags). You move up to try different courses and achieve higher-level cups. Figure 7-4 shows a screenshot of Extreme Tuxracer.

Figure 7-4: Race Tux the penguin down a mountain.

Commercial Linux Games

When Loki Software, Inc., closed its doors a few years ago, the landscape of commercial gaming in Linux changed. Loki produced Linux ports of popular games, including Myth II and Civilization: Call to Power, to name a few, and many hoped it would help Linux become the premier gaming platform. Today, commercial games that run natively are led by several popular games from id Software (described in the next section).

Although Loki Software, Inc. is gone, certain Loki Games are still available for purchase on the Web. Although they sell for a fraction of their original price, you are on your own if they don't work because Loki Software is no longer there to support them. The Loki Games Demo is still around, if you want to get a feel for a particular Loki game before it disappears completely (I describe how to find demo and packaged Loki Games later in this chapter).

In the wake of Loki's demise, TransGaming Technologies has been working on an approach to bringing popular games to Linux that relies on a version of WINE called Cedega (formerly WineX). In most cases, instead of having different ports of popular games (as Loki did), Transgaming enables users to run existing Windows games in Linux by adapting Cedega to each game that needs a tweak here and there.

While the state of Linux gaming has improved somewhat since earlier editions of this book, Linux is still emerging as a gaming platform. Linux has some of the technology needed to support advanced games, but the technology and developer support have not yet really come together.

Most serious gamers still maintain a Windows partition to support their gaming habits. According to top game developers, there are significant hurdles — both technological and economic — that hinder development of games for Linux. In particular, the relatively small size of the Linux gaming market means that incentives to overcome the technical issues are not particularly strong. However, these limitations are not overwhelming. As you'll see later in this chapter, even the hardcore game nut can successfully use Linux.

Getting Started with commercial games in Linux

How you get started with Linux gaming depends on how serious you are about it. If all you want to do is play a few games to pass the time, I've already described plenty of diverting X Window games that come with Linux. If you want to play more powerful commercial games, you can choose from:

- **Games for Microsoft Windows (Cedega 6.0)** — Many of the most popular commercial games created to run on Microsoft operating systems will run in Linux using Cedega. To get RPM versions of Cedega, you must sign up for a Cedega subscription at www.transgaming.com. To see if your favorite Windows game will run in Linux and Cedega, refer to the TransGaming.Org Games Database at http://games.cedega.com/gamesdb.

- **Games for Linux (id Software and others)** — Certain popular games have Linux versions available. Most notably, id Software offers its DOOM and Return to Castle Wolfenstein in Linux versions. Other popular games that run natively in Linux include Unreal Tournament 2004 and 2005 from Atari (www.unrealtournament.com). Commercial games that run in Linux without WINE, Cedega, or some sort of Windows emulation typically come in a boxed version for Windows with some sort of Linux installer included.

Playing commercial Linux games

To get your commercial games running in Linux, you should start from a site such as the Linux Game Tome (www.tuxgames.com) or Linux Gamers' FAQ (http://icculus.org/lgfaq), which both provide information on commercial games that run in Linux and help in getting them to run. In most cases, you need to:

- Purchase a legal copy of the game.
- Go to a Web site that describes how to install, get patches for, and work around any issues related to playing the game in Linux.

Here are examples of a few commercial games that run well in Linux:

- **Duke 3D Atomic Edition for Linux (3D Realms)** — Duke Nukem returns to earth to face aliens and clean up Los Angeles in this third chapter in the Duke Nukem series. Visit 3D Realms for official information about Duke 3D Atomic Edition (www.3drealms.com/duke3d). Visit http://icculus.org/duke3d for tips on getting it running.

- **Unreal Tournament 2003 (Epic Games)** — Multiplayer death match set in the future, where warriors face each other with awesome weapons and stuff. Includes a Linux installer. Go to Epic Games (www.epicgames.com) or the Unreal Tournament site (www.unrealtournament.com) for the official information. Visit the Icculus.org site for tips on installing in Linux (www.icculus.org/lgfaq#ut2k3_install).

- **Unreal Tournament 2004 (Epic Games)** — Adds new maps, characters, vehicles, weapons, and modes of play to the 2003 edition.

The following sections describe Linux games from id Software, information about running Windows games using Cedega in Linux, and games produced by Loki Games (before it went out of business) still available from other sources today.

id Software Games

Among the most popular games running natively in Linux are Quake III Arena, and Return to Castle Wolfenstein from id Software, Inc. You can purchase Linux versions of these games or download demos of each game before you buy.

> **NOTE:** If you have trouble getting any id Software games running in Linux, refer to the Linux FAQs available from id Software at: http://zerowing.idsoftware.com/linux.

Quake III Arena

Quake III Arena is a first-person shooter-type game where you can choose from lots of weapons (lightning guns, shotguns, grenade launchers, and so on) and pass through scenes with highly detailed 3D surfaces. You can play alone or against your friends. There are multiplayer death-match and capture-the-flag competitions. Standalone play allows you to advance through a tournament structure of skilled AI opponents. This version of the game lets you select a difficulty level, from fairly easy to downright impossible.

If you have a commercial copy of Quake III Arena, you can install the open source Quake 3 Arena engine (http://ioquake3.org) and use it with that product. Copy the pak0.pk3 file and q3key from your Quake III Arena CD to the /usr/share/quake3/baseq3 directory. Launch Quake III Arena by selecting Applications → Games → Quake 3 Arena.

Quake III Arena demo is available from the Fedora repository (yum install quake3-demo). Besides what you get with the quake3 package, data files are needed to play the game. Although those data files can be freely downloaded from the Internet, they cannot be distributed with Fedora. Therefore, when you launch Quake III Arena demo, you are asked if you want to download the demo data files before proceeding. Click Accept, and then agree to the licensing agreement and you can start to play. Figure 7-5 shows a screenshot from Quake III Arena.

Figure 7-5: Quake III Arena is a popular first-person shooter game that runs in Linux.

With the open source Quake III Arena engine installed, you can run other first-person shooter games that use that engine as well. For example, install the Urban Terror package (`yum install urbanterror`) and you can launch the Urban Terror downloader to download the data files needed to play that game (the Urban Terror data file is 700MB compressed and requires 1.4GB of disk space.) Also, the OpenArena game (`yum install openarena`) open source Quake III Arena-type game can be downloaded directly from the Fedora repository.

Return to Castle Wolfenstein

Mixing World War II action with creatures conjured up by Nazi scientists, you battle with the Allies to destroy the Third Reich. Return to Castle Wolfenstein is based on the Quake III Arena engine. The game offers single-player mode as well as team-based multiplayer mode.

If you purchase Return to Castle Wolfenstein for Linux, you actually get the Windows version with an extra Linux installer. If you already have the Windows version, you can download the Linux installer and follow some instructions to get it going. I downloaded the installer `wolf-linux-1.41b.x86.run` from `ftp.idsoftware.com/idstuff/wolf/linux`. The `INSTALL` file (in `/usr/local/games/wolfenstein`) describes what files you need to copy from the Windows CD. You can buy the Linux installer from `www.tuxgames.com`.

To get a demo of Return to Castle Wolfenstein, go to `www.idsoftware.com/games/wolfenstein/rtcw/index.php?game_section=overview`. Both a single-player and a multiplayer demo are available.

> **NOTE:** You need an NVIDIA card to run Return to Castle Wolfenstein.

Figure 7-6 is a screenshot from Return to Castle Wolfenstein running in Linux.

Figure 7-6: Return to Castle Wolfenstein combines strange creatures and WWII battles.

Gaming with Cedega

TransGaming Technologies (`www.transgaming.com`) brings to Linux some of the most popular games that currently run on the Windows platforms. Working with WINE developers, TransGaming is developing Cedega, which enables you to run many different games on Linux that were originally developed for Windows. Although TransGaming is producing a few games that are packaged separately and tuned for Linux, in most cases it sells you a subscription service to Cedega instead of the games. That subscription service lets you stay up-to-date on the continuing development of Cedega so you can run more and more Windows games.

> **NOTE:** You may need to obtain a vanilla kernel from `kernel.org` and boot that on your system before running games with Cedega.

To get Windows games to run in Linux, Cedega needs to develop Microsoft DirectX features that are required by many of today's games. There are also issues relating to CD keys and hooks into the Windows operating system that must be overcome (such as requiring Microsoft Active Desktop). In fact, a Cedega subscription has value, in part, because it lets you vote on which games you'd like to see TransGaming work on next.

A full list of games supported by TransGaming, as well as indications of how popular they are and how well they work, is available from the TransGaming.org site (`http://games.cedega.com/gamesdb`). Browse games by category or alphabetically. Games that are officially supported by Transgaming are marked by an asterisk. On each game description page is a link to a related Wiki Node, when one exists, that gives you details about how well the game works under Cedega and tips for getting it to work better.

TransGaming added several new features to the Cedega GUI (formerly called Point2Play). The Cedega GUI provides a graphical window for installing, configuring, and testing Cedega on your computer. It also lets you install and organize your games so you can launch them graphically. Figure 7-7 shows an example of the Cedega GUI window in Linux.

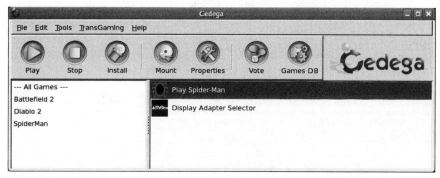

Figure 7-7: Use the Cedega GUI window to check computer hardware for Cedega gaming.

Features in the new Cedega GUI window include a new look-and-feel and tools for individually configuring how each game runs under Cedega. (If a game won't run from the GUI, try launching it from a Terminal window.)

You can download a free 14-day trial of Cedega that is fully functional for that limited time. To get the full benefits of Cedega, you need to subscribe to TransGaming. For details on how to become a "TransGamer," click the Subscribe Here link on the TransGaming home page (www.transgaming.com). Benefits currently include:

- Downloads of the latest version of Cedega
- Access to Cedega support forums
- Ability to vote on which games you want TransGaming to support next
- Subscription to the Cedega newsletter

Cedega used to be known as WineX. The source code for WineX may become available in the near future if you want to build your own WineX/Cedega package. To check availability, try the SourceForge.net project site for WineX (sourceforge.net/projects/winex).

Loki Software game demos

To encourage people to get to know its games, Loki offered a demo program that lets you choose from among more than a dozen Loki games to download and try. Loki also offered boxed sets of its commercial games for purchase. Although Loki Software, Inc. is no longer in business, you can still find some of its games for sale. For example, a recent search for Loki at

Amazon.com turned up 16 different Loki games (including the ones described here), with many selling for $9.99.

> **WARNING:** If you try to download any of the demos described in the next sections, make sure you have plenty of disk space available and a fast connection. It is common for one of these demos to require several hundred megabytes of disk space.

The Loki Demo Launcher for downloading demos is still available from the Demo Launcher page (`www.lokigames.com/products/demos.php3`). From that page, there are links to FTP sites from which you can download the Demo Launcher. The file that you want to save is `loki_demos-full-1.0e-x86.run`. Save it to a directory (such as `/tmp/loki`) and do the following:

1. Change to the directory where you downloaded the demo. For example:

   ```
   # cd /tmp/loki
   ```

> **NOTE:** You may not need to be root user to install these games. However, the default paths where the Demo Launcher tries to write by default are only accessible to the root user.

2. As root user, run the following command (the program may have a different name if it has been updated):

   ```
   # sh loki_demos-full-1.0e.x86.run
   ```

   If you have not used the Demo Launcher before, you are asked to identify the paths used to place the Install Tool.

3. If the default locations shown are okay with you, press Enter (or add a different path if you need to assign a location with more disk space). You will then be asked to identify other locations for Uninstall and Demo files.

   When all locations are defined, the Loki Update Tool window appears.

4. Select the Demos you want to install (hover your cursor over each demo line to see how much disk space each requires) and select Continue. A download window appears.

5. Choose a mirror site from which to download the demo. Each selected demo or upgrade is downloaded.

6. When the download is completed, select Finished. The window will close.

7. Back at the command prompt, press Enter to begin playing the game.

8. Select to start the game, and you're ready to go.

The following sections describe a few games that may still be available. Again, these games may not be available for long.

Civilization: Call to Power

You can build online civilizations with Civilization: Call to Power (CCP). As with earlier versions and public spin-offs (such as the Freeciv described earlier in this chapter), Civilization: Call to Power for Linux lets you explore the world, build cities, and manage your empire. This latest version offers multiplayer network competition and extensions that let you extend cities into outer space and under the sea.

If you like Freeciv, you will love CCP. Engaging game play is improved with enhanced graphics, sound, and animation. English, French, German, Italian, and Spanish versions are available.

The CCP demo comes with an excellent tutorial to get you started. If you have never played a civilization game before, the tutorial is a great way to start. Figure 7-8 shows an example of a scene from the Civilization: Call to Power for Linux demo.

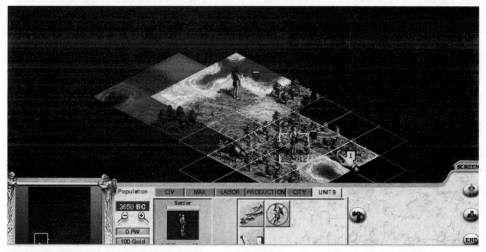

Figure 7-8: Civilization: Call to Power features excellent graphics and network play.

Myth II: Soulblighter

If you like knights and dwarves and storming castles, Myth II: Soulblighter for Linux might be for you. In Myth II, you are given a mission and some troops with various skills. From there, you need strategy and the desire to shed lots of virtual blood to meet your goal.

Myth II was created by Bungie Software (www.bungie.net) and ported to Linux by Loki Entertainment Software (www.lokigames.com). This version of the popular Myth game includes improved graphics and new scenarios.

A demo version is available that runs well in Fedora and RHEL. You can get it via the Demo Launcher described earlier. As usual, you will need a computer that is at least a Pentium 133 MHz, with 32MB RAM, 80MB swap space, and 100MB of free disk space. You need network hardware for multiuser network play (network card or dialup) and a sound card if you want audio. A screenshot of Myth II is shown in Figure 7-9.

Figure 7-9: Use warriors, archers, and dwarves to battle in Myth II.

Heretic II

Based on the Quake Engine, Heretic II sets you on a path to rid the world of a deadly, magical plague. As the main character, Corvus, you explore dungeons, swamps, and cities to uncover and stop the plague. The graphics are rich and the game play is quite engaging.

You will experience some crashing problems with Heretic II out-of-the-box. Be sure to check for the update to Heretic II at `updates.lokigames.com`, which should fix most of the problems.

Neverwinter Nights

BioWare (`www.bioware.com`) dipped its foot into Linux gaming waters with a Linux client for its wildly popular Neverwinter Nights game. Neverwinter Nights is a classic role-playing game in the swords-and-sorcery mold. You can develop your character and go adventuring, or play online with others via a LAN or over the Internet. You can even build your own worlds and host adventures as the Dungeon Master. Neverwinter Nights is licensed by Wizards of the Coast to use Dungeons & Dragons rules and material.

In order to use the Neverwinter Nights Linux client, you must purchase the game itself from BioWare. You must also have access to certain files from a Windows installation of the game. If you or a friend have the Windows version already, you can grab the files from that version. Otherwise, you'll find them online in a number of locations. See the installation instructions at `http://nwn.bioware.com` for links.

Summary

With the addition of hot titles such as Doom 3, Far Cry and EverQuest 2 to the list of playable titles, Linux continues to grow as a gaming platform. You can spend plenty of late nights gaming on Linux. Old UNIX games that have made their way to Linux include a variety of X Window–based games. There are card games, strategy games, and some action games for those less inclined to spend 36 hours playing Doom 3.

On the commercial front, Civilization: Call to Power for Linux and Myth II are available to use on your Fedora or RHEL system. Unfortunately these will probably disappear because Loki Software (which ported those applications to Linux) went out of business. Fortunately, the future of high-end Linux gaming seems to be in the hands of TransGaming Technologies, which has created Cedega from previous WINE technology to allow Windows games to run in Linux. It is also in the hands of cutting-edge developers (id Software) and hardware manufacturers (NVIDIA and AMD) who are expanding driver and application support for Linux.

## Chapter 8

Music, Video, and Images in Linux

In This Chapter

- Listening to music
- Using Webcams and TV cards
- Playing video
- Working with digital cameras and images

Nearly every kind of audio and video format available today can be played, displayed, encoded, decoded, and managed in Linux. With the development of the Theora video codec, there are now patent-free, royalty-free formats available for every major type of multimedia content. If you are starting from scratch, today you can legally create, manipulate, and share your own multimedia content from Linux using all free applications and codecs.

This chapter covers many different tools that come with Fedora and RHEL for playing or displaying digital music, video, and images. It also takes a swipe at explaining some of the legal issues surrounding software for playing commercial movie DVDs, MP3 music, and various audio/video formats in Linux.

Video content that is readily available on the Internet for playing movie clips, commercial films, and other content can be viewed using several different players in or available for Fedora and RHEL. Also, you can view live television and video using TV cards and Webcams.

Because CD-ROM is the physical medium of choice for recorded music, this chapter describes how to set up and use CD burners to create your own music CDs. After your CD burner is set up to record music, you can use the same CD burner to back up your data or to create software CDs. (The same tools can be used to burn DVDs as well.)

Understanding Multimedia and Legal Issues in Linux

You can't play DVD movies or MP3 music with software delivered with Fedora or RHEL because software needed to do so isn't included in those distributions. That's because there are patent claims associated with the formats used to store, encode, and decode that content that would prevent open source software that worked with that content from being freely distributed.

Commercial Linux vendors, including Red Hat, have decided not to add software codecs (which encode and decode multimedia formats), even if they were written from scratch and covered under the GPL, that are encumbered by contentious software patents. After Thomson and Fraunhofer Gesellschaft (which control the MP3 patent) began requesting licensing fees in 2002 of $.075 for MP3 decoders (per system), Red Hat Linux dropped MP3 support. (See `www.mp3licensing.com/royalty` for details.)

Just to clarify, I am not talking about copyright here. Nobody can rightly claim that it is okay to copy someone else's commercial code and release it as free software. It would clearly violate copyright laws. What we are talking about are patents.

The idea of a patent is to allow someone to control the rights regarding who can make, sell, offer to sell, use, or import an invention that the patent applicant dreamed up. As it relates to multimedia software in particular, the encoding and decoding of audio and video content for many commercially released music and video formats are covered by patents. So, even if open source developers write every piece of code from scratch to encode and decode content, it may not be legal to distribute it without paying a royalty to the patent owner.

Major efforts are underway (especially in Europe) to oppose software patents. Refer to the Foundation for a Free Information Infrastructure Web site (`http://ffii.org`) for further information. The contention is that so many ideas related to software are being patented that it could severely cripple the ability to innovate (especially for open source developers or small software companies without huge legal teams).

Patents have been granted in Europe for common items that might appear on a Web page, such as selling things over a network, using an electronic shopping cart, and using rebate codes (see `http://webshop.ffii.org`). Although there are now laws in Europe that are aimed at preventing any further software patents, some software patents are still being granted and existing patents are still being used to discourage innovation.

Despite efforts against software patents, however, the fact remains that Fedora and Red Hat Enterprise Linux distributions do not include some of the software that you would want to use to play your digital media. That doesn't mean, however, that there is nothing you can do to legally play the commercial audio and video content you want to play in Linux. In the latest version of Fedora, some features have been added to make sure that there are legal ways to get the codecs you need.

Extending Freedom to Codecs

Fedora may not be able to give you the audio decoders you need to play every kind of media you want, but it gives you the freedom (and the tools) to go out and get those decoders yourself. To give Fedora users a legal way to play their MP3 audio content, the Fedora Project has added Codeina. Formerly called Codec Buddy, Codeina connects you to services that let you download free (as in no cost) support for MP3 audio content. It also points you to a site where you can purchase codecs for other non-free audio and video content, such as MPEG4 video, Windows Media, and others.

A company called Fluendo (www.fluendo.com), which is responsible for the GStreamer multimedia framework used in Fedora, produced Codeina to hook into the Fluendo's Web site for delivering a range of popular codecs. Fluendo purchased an unlimited MP3 license that allows you to download the Fluendo MP3 Audio Decoder for free, to play your MP3 audio files. You can pay a small fee to get audio/video codecs such as Dolby AC3 Audio Decoder, Windows Media MMS Network Stream Reader, MPEG2 Video Decoder, or MPEG4 Part 2 Video Decoder. If Codeina is not already installed on your system, you can install it by typing:

```
# yum install codeina
```

You can start Codeina to see what codec packages are available from Fluendo to use with your Fedora system in several ways. One way is to just run the codeina command as follows:

```
$ /usr/bin/codeina
```

The other way to start Codeina is to try to play content (such as an MP3 audio file) with a GStreamer application (such as Totem or even Firefox) for which a codec available from Fluendo is needed. Instead of playing the content, a Codeina Codec Installer window pops up with the codec you need selected. You can select View → All Available to see all codecs available from Fluendo that you can use to play multimedia on your Fedora system. Figure 8-1 shows an example of the Codec Installer window:

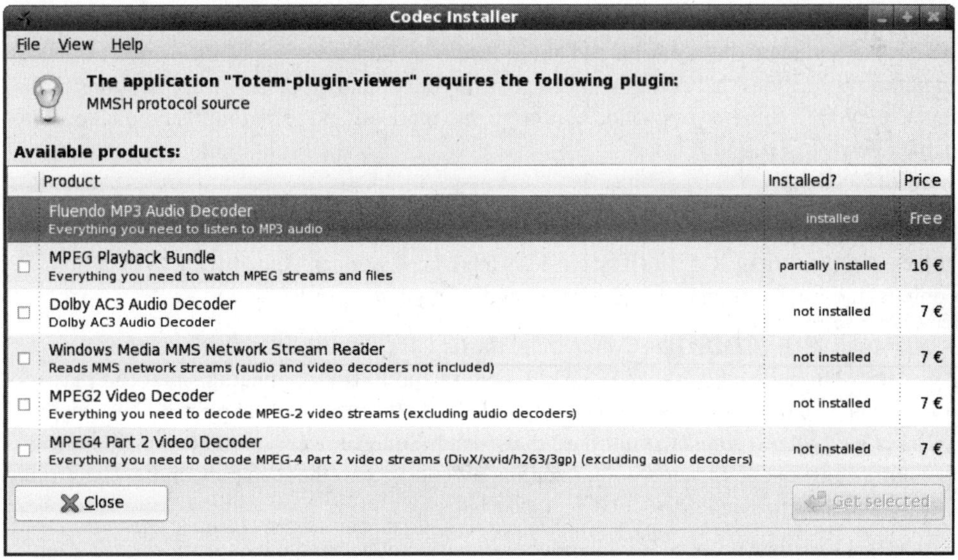

Figure 8-1: Get a free to get a legal MP3 audio decoder or pay fees for other decoders from Fluendo.

Read the licensing agreement that appears before you accept the download. Unlike software that comes with Fedora, you cannot freely redistribute the codecs you get from Fluendo.

Listening to Music in Linux

Good-quality sound hardware is considered a necessity for today's desktop and laptop computer systems. Whether playing songs downloaded from the Internet, sound tracks to digital movies, or audio from a TV card, any user-friendly operating system has to support a healthy list of sound hardware and audio applications.

Most popular sound devices for the PC, whether on separate cards or built into your computer's motherboard, will be automatically detected when a Fedora or RHEL system boots up. Appropriate modules will be loaded, so you can immediately begin using your sound card.

Beginning with Fedora 8, PulseAudio (`www.pulseaudio.org`) became the default sound system used with Fedora, taking over that spot from Advanced Linux Sound Architecture (ALSA). PulseAudio basically provides the interfaces between audio applications and your sound card. A major improvement over other audio systems is that it allows you to control volume levels separately for different applications. Also, by incorporating plug-ins, PulseAudio lets you use audio applications that were designed for ALSA.

To control playback volumes and audio input and output devices, the pulseaudio package includes the PulseAudio Volume Control window. The alsa-utils RPM package contains the commands and configuration files you can use to tune your sound card and adjust audio levels. Other friendly graphical tools have been added by the GNOME and KDE projects for managing sound.

After your sound card is working and audio levels are adjusted, you can use any of the dozens of audio applications that come with Linux with your sound card. Those applications include music players, video players, video conferencing applications, games, and audio recorders, to name a few.

As for audio content, the following list describes the types of audio content you might want to play, which players can be used for each type of content, and whether or not the software comes with Fedora or RHEL. (If not, I describe where you can get software to play that content and issues associated with getting and using that software.)

- **Music CDs (CDDA)** — Commercial music CDs are nearly all stored in the Compact Disc Digital Audio system (CDDA). Fedora and RHEL applications that can play music CDs include CD Player (gnome-cd) and KsCD (kscd). Rhythmbox can play music CDs, as well import songs to your hard disk (using Sound Juicer) so you can manage your music from one location. Other applications in Fedora that can play audio files from CDs include xmms and grip.

- **Ogg Vorbis Audio** — If you are compressing and storing music from scratch, Ogg Vorbis is probably the best choice if you want to avoid completely any royalty issues.

The libvorbis codec is included with Fedora and RHEL and makes it possible to play audio encoded in Ogg Vorbis format in a variety of Linux music players, including xmms, Rhythmbox, ogg123, and many others. The vorbis-tools package also includes utilities for encoding (oggenc) and decoding (oggdec) Ogg Vorbis content to or from WAV and raw music formats. The Xiph.org Foundation develops both Ogg Vorbis audio formats and Theora video formats.

- **MP3 Audio** — MPEG Audio Layer 3 (MP3) has become the standard format for storing audio files that are transmitted over computer networks (such as the Internet). Because of licensing issues associated with distributing MP3 players, Red Hat does not include codecs needed to encode or decode MP3 audio files in any of its distributions. However, Fedora does give you the opportunity to download free, legal MP3 decoders from Fluendo (as described earlier in this chapter).

  Another way to get MP3 support, which may not be legal where you are, is to install the xmms-mp3 package, which contains software needed by Linux audio players to play MP3 audio files with the xmms music player. You need the lame package to create compressed audio files from WAV, AIFF, or raw audio files that play on MP3 players. Many use the mpg321 command-line MP3 player, which is available in the mpg321 package. (All of these packages are available from the Livna.org RPM repository. See Chapter 5 on installing software from the Livna.org repository.)

- **FLAC Audio** — FLAC is an open source lossless audio format. *Lossless* means that it compresses the audio as much as possible without losing sound quality. In comparing the same song compressed in Ogg Vorbis and FLAC (using default settings), FLAC files were on average about six times the size of the Ogg Vorbis files.

  Many of the same applications that can play Ogg Vorbis files can play FLAC files as well. Rhythmbox, ogg123, and xmms can all play FLAC files. You can encode FLAC audio using Sound Juicer or the `flac` command, among others.

- **Other Audio Formats** — While the audio formats mentioned previously are the most common ones used for music files today, there are other audio formats you may want to play from Linux. Refer to the description of the sox utility for several audio formats that are supported by that utility. Use the `play` command (which comes with the sox package) or `aplay` (which is in the alsa-utils package) to play content stored in any of those supported formats.

Audio formats that are sometimes included with video files are described in the section on video players later in this chapter. For an official description of which contentious multimedia encoding software (and other software) Fedora doesn't include, refer to the Fedora Project Forbidden Items page (`http://fedoraproject.org/wiki/ForbiddenItems`).

Configuring a sound card

Configuring a sound card in Linux consists primarily of having the right modules load (which usually happens automatically at boot time) and then using the sound utilities you choose (such as the PulseAudio Volume Control, alsamixer or aumix) to adjust the settings for the sound card. Today's sound cards often have more than the old Mic-In, Line-In, Speaker-out, and Joystick ports. So when you go to adjust your audio levels, there are more items you need to learn about.

Sound card features

Sound cards can pack an amazing number of features these days. Most PCs these days come with built-in sound support. Here are some of the features you should look for if you want to purchase a sound card separately:

- **Sound recording and playback quality** — When you record and play back audio, quality and file size are determined, in part, by word length (the number of bits that are used to hold a numerical value) and sample rates. Typical word lengths include 8-bit (less popular), 16-bit, or 24-bit digital sizes. To convert the sound, the board samples the sound in waves from 8 kHz to 96 kHz, or 8,000 to 96,000 times per second. (Of course, the higher the sampling, the better the sound and larger the output.)

- **Full-duplex support** — This allows for recording and playback to occur at the same time. This is particularly useful for bidirectional Internet communication or simultaneous recording and playback.

- **PCI or USB interface** — Most people purchase a PCI sound card to put in the case of their desktop system, when sound ports on the computer's motherboard are not sufficient. However, if you are using a PC (such as a Shuttle) with limited slots or a laptop, there are USB sound cards that are supported in Linux.

Several different ports on the board enable you to connect input/output devices. These ports can include some or all of the following:

- **Line-In (blue)** — Connects an external CD player, cassette deck, synthesizer, MiniDisc, or other device for recording or playback. If you have a television card, you might also patch that card's line out to your sound card's line in.

- **Microphone (red)** — Connects a microphone for audio recording or communications.

- **Headphone/Line-Out/Speaker Out (green)** — Connects speakers, headphones, or a stereo amplifier. (On sound cards I've tested, this is marked as Headphone in mixer utilities.)

- **Joystick/MIDI (15-pin connector)** — Connects a joystick for gaming or MIDI devices. (Some sound cards no longer have these ports because they are now available from most motherboards.)

- **Digital out (orange)** — A digital out connector can be used to connect a digital audio tape (DAT) device or CD recordable (CD-R) device.

- **Rear out (black)** — Can be used to deliver audio output to powered speakers or an external amplifier.

- **Internal CD Audio** — This internal port connects the sound card to your computer's internal CD-ROM drive (this port isn't exposed when the board is installed).

For some sound applications, you need to identify the device files used to communicate with the sound card and other sound hardware. The devices that the audio programs use to access audio hardware in Fedora and RHEL include:

- **/dev/audio, /dev/audio1** — Devices that are compatible with Sun workstation audio implementations (audio files with the `.au` extension).
- **/dev/cdrom** — Device representing your first CD-ROM drive. (Additional CD-ROM drives are located at `/dev/cdrom1`, `/dev/cdrom2`, and so on.)
- **/dev/dsp, /dev/dsp1** — Digital sampling devices, which many audio applications identify to access your sound card.
- **/dev/mixer, /dev/mixer1** — Sound-mixing devices.
- **/dev/sequencer** — Device that provides a low-level interface to MIDI, FM, and GUS.
- **/dev/midi00** — Device that provides raw access to midi ports.

TIP: Nodes in the `/dev` directory, such as `/dev/audio`, aren't just regular files. They represent access points to the physical devices (hard disks, COM ports, and so on) that are connected to your system, or to pseudo-devices (such as Terminal windows). For example, to find out the device of your current Terminal window, type `tty`. Then send some data to that device. For example, if your device name is `/dev/pts/0`, type:

```
$ echo "Hello There" > /dev/pts/0
```

The words `Hello There` appear in that Terminal window. You can try sending messages among several Terminal windows. If a user who is logged on to the computer has terminal permissions open, you can send messages to him or her in this way, too. (I knew people who would send a dictionary file to an unsuspecting user's terminal. Although it wasn't destructive, it was annoying if you were trying to get work done.)

To get information from the ALSA service about your sound cards, list the contents of the following files (for example, `cat /proc/asound/devices`):

- **/proc/asound/devices** — Contains available capture, playback, and other devices associated with your sound system.
- **/proc/asound/cards** — Contains the names, model numbers, and IRQs of your sound cards.

For general information about sound in Linux, see the Sound-HOWTO (for tips about sound cards and general sound issues) and the Sound-Playing-HOWTO (for tips on software for playing different types of audio files). You can also refer to the Linux Audio Users Guide (`http://lau.linuxaudio.org`).

NOTE: You can find Linux HOWTOs at `www.tldp.org`.

Detecting your sound card driver

During the first start-up after you install Fedora, the Firstboot setup agent tries to detect and configure your sound card. If that process was successful, and your sound card is working, you can skip this procedure. If your sound card wasn't detected or you simply don't hear any sound, try running the Audio Configuration utility.

> **TIP:** Audio may be muted when you first install Fedora or RHEL. If you are not able to hear the test of your sound card, use Volume Control or alsamixer (as described later in this chapter) to unmute and adjust the volume on your audio input.

To open the Audio Configuration window, from the System menu, click Administration → Soundcard Detection (this runs the `system-config-soundcard` command). If your sound card was detected, the Audio configuration window should appear, as shown in Figure 8-2. Click the play button to the left of the slider and you should hear a test sound. You can move the slider to the right to make sure volume is set high enough to hear it.

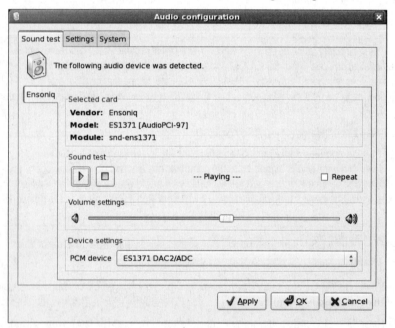

Figure 8-2: The Audio configuration (system-config-soundcard) window detects your sound card.

The Audio Configuration window contains three tabs of settings you might want to adjust:

- **Sound test** — In addition to letting you test your sound card, this tab shows information about each sound card you have installed. If your sound card isn't working, use the Vendor, Model, and Module information when you ask for help. You can also change the PCM device from this tab, for example, to try different outputs from the card.

- **Settings** — If you have multiple sound cards, you can select which card to use by default (Default Audio Card) and the Default PCM Device for that card (identifying where sound is output). From the Settings tab, you can also select Disable Specific Card Configuration, to allow plug-ins to override default settings. Likewise, you can change the order in which audio cards are used on your system.

- **System** — You can view information about the ALSA sound system (driver versions, library packages, and utility packages) from this tab. You can also reload sound drivers or generate a report related to your sound system. The report is copied to `/root/sysconfig.log` and contains output from commands such as `lspci` and `lsmod`, as well as contents of your `/etc/asound.conf` file and output from the `aplay-1` command.

At this point, you can try playing an audio file. Insert a CD and open one of the CD players described in the following section. If you don't hear any sound, but the utility seems to have detected your sound card, refer to the next section and try adjusting your audio levels. If that doesn't work, try some of the debugging procedures suggested in the ALSA Wiki FAQ (`http://alsa.opensrc.org/faq`).

> **TIP:** If there is a data CD in your CD drive, you may not be able to simply eject it to play your music CD. To eject a data CD, close any windows that may have an open file from the CD, and then unmount the CD in your drive (if one is mounted) by typing **umount /media/cdrecorder** as root user from a Terminal window (the mount point name may be something other than `cdrecorder`). Then you can eject the old CD and place an audio CD in the drive. If the CD appears as an icon on the desktop, you can right-click the CD icon and select Eject to eject the disc.

Adjusting sound levels

Every audio output (Playback) and input (Capture) device associated with your sound cards can be adjusted or muted using one of several different tools that come with Fedora and RHEL. To control volume on multiple audio applications, you can use the PulseAudio Volume Control window.

The PulseAudio Volume Control window displays volume slider bars for each active audio application on the system (typically associated with right and left channels). Besides controlling volume, you can also select the default input and output devices, or associate each audio application with particular input and output devices. From the Applications menu, select Sound & Video → PulseAudio Volume Control to see that window.

Figure 8-3 shows an example of the PulseAudio Volume Control window with two active audio applications. The totem-plug-in-viewer is playing an MP3 file from the Firefox browser and the Totem Movie Player is playing a video, in this example. A lock button lets you lock or unlock the two channels for each application. Then you can use the slider to adjust volume levels together or separately. A mute button lets you mute or unmute sound for each application.

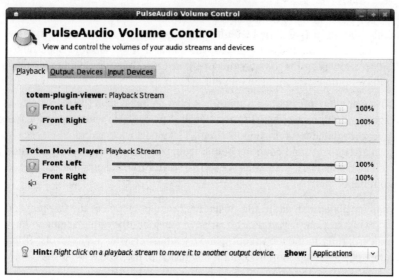

Figure 8-3: The PulseAudio Volume Control window provides simple, intuitive controls for setting audio levels.

On the Output Devices and Input Devices tabs, you can see the available audio devices on your computer. If you have multiple devices, you can click on the device you want to make the default for both input and output. You can also associate your audio applications with specific audio devices.

With GNOME installed, an alternative is to adjust audio levels from the GNOME Volume Control applet on the top panel. Figure 8-4 shows an example of GNOME Volume Control.

Because the example in Figure 8-4 shows a default Fedora system, where PulseAudio is the primary sound system, `alsamixer` doesn't control the sound cards directly. It only acts as a master volume controller for PulseAudio. If you don't happen to have GNOME utilities, such as the Volume Applet, installed, you can use the utilities that come with the alsa-utils package in Fedora and RHEL. In particular, that package contains the alsamixer utility, which lets you adjust or mute the various sound tracks. It also lets you select the device from which you can record or otherwise capture audio input.

The alsamixer utility is an ncurses application, which means that it is viewed graphically from a shell. It can be used to manage sound levels for more than one sound card on a computer, each with multiple devices representing it. Type **alsamixer** from a Terminal window to start it in playback mode (to adjust audio output) or **alsamixer -V capture** (to select an audio capture device and adjust audio capture level).

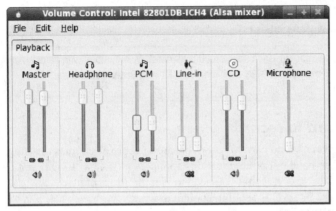

Figure 8-4: Adjust audio levels from the screen-orient command-line alsamixer utility.

Here are some ways to adjust your audio tracks with alsamixer:

- Use the right and left arrow keys to move among the different sound tracks.
- Use the up and down arrow keys to adjust the levels of the current tracks.
- Press m to mute or unmute the current track (playback mode only).
- Press the spacebar to make the current track the capture device, for devices such as microphone or line-in that are appropriate for capturing audio. Then adjust the Capture bar to set the level at which audio is captured. (Note that this feature works in capture mode only: `alsamixer -v capture`.)

Tracks that are muted appear with an MM at the bottom of the slider. When unmuted, 00 appears instead. If more tracks are available than can appear on the screen, the right arrow key enables you to scroll to the right to display additional track bars.

If two channels are available on a track, you can adjust them individually. With the track selected, use the q, w, and e keys to adjust the left, both, and right channels up, respectively. Use z, x, and c to adjust those same channels down, respectively. When you are done using alsamixer, press the Esc key to exit.

Here are a few general rules for adjusting your audio channels:

- To avoid unwanted noise on playback or record, mute any tracks you are not using.
- An icon representing your GNOME Volume Control utility should appear on your desktop panel. The single slider associated with that icon may be set to adjust your master volume or headphone port output. Right-click that icon and select Preferences to change to a different port.
- To test that your audio channels are working, use the `speaker-test` command. For example, `speaker-test -c4` will send a tone to each of four speakers in turn (front

left, front right, rear left, and rear right) to check that each is working. Note that the tone output may surprise you with its loudness.

> **TIP:** If you have more than one sound card, each sound card is identified by a number, with zero identifying the first sound card. For example, to start `alsamixer` for your second sound card, type $ **alsamixer -c 1**.

Setting your sound card to record

I added this section on setting your sound card to record because people often miss this step. You may run the `arecord` command or communications application (such as Ekiga) and wonder why nothing records. The reason is that you need to identify the capture device to use before you record and make sure its level is set high enough to work.

The easiest way to set the channel to use for audio capture is to use the GNOME Volume Control window described earlier. Click File → Change Device and choose the Capture device that controls your computer microphone (or other input device). Then make sure that all audio devices are muted except the one you want to record from. Available devices might include microphone, line-in, and CD. A red *X* through a microphone icon beneath each capture device indicates that it is muted.

Move the slider for your capture device up to an appropriate level. Then connect your microphone or input device (to line in) and start the application you want to record from. With that in place, a quick way to test if you can record is with the `arecord` command. For example:

```
$ arecord -d30 -f cd -t wav /tmp/testing.wav
$ aplay /tmp/testing.wav
```

The example just shown records a CD-quality WAV file for 30 seconds from your default input device (such as your microphone). The output is stored in the `/tmp/testing.wav` file. You can use the `aplay` command to play back the recording.

> **TIP:** Audacity is a nice application for recording and working with recorded sound in Fedora. You can install the audacity package from the Fedora repository (type **yum install audacity**).

Choosing audio players

There are audio players in Fedora and RHEL for playing music and sound files in a variety of formats. Without adding any software, you can play commercial music CDs and Ogg Vorbis audio (which you can rip and encode yourself). MP3 support can be added to some of these players, while MP3 players outside of Red Hat distributions are also available.

- **KsCD Player (kscd)** — The KsCD player comes with the KDE desktop. To use KsCD, the kdemultimedia package must be installed. From the Applications menu (KDE desktop), select Sound & Video → KsCD (or type **kscd** from a Terminal window). This player lets you get title, track, and artist information from the CD database, and lets you submit information you type in yourself to a CD database (if your CD isn't found there).

- **Rhythmbox (rhythmbox)** — Import and manage your music collection with Rhythmbox music management and playback software for GNOME. Rhythmbox uses GStreamer and Sound Juicer to extract music from a CD, and then compresses that music using Ogg Vorbis, FLAC, or a low-quality WAV (for speech) audio format. Besides allowing you to create playlists of your music library, Rhythmbox also has features for playing Internet radio stations. Open Rhythmbox from the Applications menu by selecting Sound & Video → Music Player.

- **XMMS (xmms)** — The X Multimedia System (XMMS) audio player provides a simple, graphical player for playing Ogg Vorbis, WAV, FLAC, and other audio formats. XMMS has a fairly simple Windows winamp-like look and feel, which you can adjust using a few dozen skins. (The xmms package is available in the Fedora repository. To add CD playing support to xmms, install the xmms-cdread package as well.)

- **ogg123**, **mpg321**, **aplay**, or **play** — If you don't have access to the desktop, you can use the text-based `ogg123`, `mpg321`, or `play` commands. The `ogg123` command comes with the vorbis-tools package, `aplay` is part of the alsa-utils package, and `play` comes with the sox package in Fedora and RHEL. The `mpg321` command comes in the mpg321 package, which is available from the Livna.org RPMs site. (The `mpg321` command is covered under the GPL. There is an `mpg123` project, which is no longer maintained and is not fully covered under the GPL.)

The default CD audio player is Rhythmbox for the current release. One advantage of Rhythmbox, and other GStreamer audio applications, is that it will work with the free and legal MP3 codec you can download with the Codeina application.

> **NOTE:** If you try some of these CD players and your CD-ROM drive is not working, see the sidebar "Troubleshooting Your CD-ROM" for further information.

Automatically playing CDs

When you put an audio CD into your CD-ROM drive, a media player (Rhythmbox) automatically pops up on your desktop and begins playing the CD. If you are using the GNOME desktop, you can use the application launcher to handle music CDs (as well as other removable media) from a Nautilus folder window.

If you don't want to have CDs automatically start playing or if you want to use a different CD player by default, you can change that behavior from the File Management Preferences window in Nautilus. Open any folder in Nautilus and select Edit → Preferences and choose the Media tab. Then from the Media tab, select the box next to CD Audio and select to either ask what to do or do nothing when an audio CD is encountered.

Troubleshooting Your CD-ROM

If you are unable to play CDs on your CD-ROM drive, here are a few things you can check to correct the problem:

- Verify that your sound card is installed and working properly (see "Configuring a sound card" earlier in this chapter).

- Verify that the CD-ROM drive was detected when you booted Linux. If your CD-ROM drive is an IDE drive, type **dmesg | grep -i cd**. You should see messages about your CD-ROM that look like this: `ata2.00: ATAPI: HL-DT-STCD-RW/DVD DRIVE GCC-4242N, 0201, max UDMA/33`.

- If you see no indication of a CD-ROM drive, verify that the power supply and cables to the CD-ROM are connected. To make sure that the hardware is working, you can also boot to DOS and try to access the CD.

- Try inserting a software CD-ROM. If you are running the GNOME or KDE desktop, a desktop icon should appear indicating that the CD is mounted by itself. If no such icon appears, go to a Terminal window and type **mount /media/cdrecorder**. Then list the contents using the `ls /media/cdrecorder` command. This tells you if the CD-ROM is accessible.

- Check that your CD-ROM drive is not blacklisted because of buggy firmware or other issues. See `www.tldp.org/HOWTO/Hardware-HOWTO/cdrom.html`.

- If you get the CD-ROM working, but it fails with the message `CDROM device: Permission denied` when you try to play music as a nonroot user, the problem may be that the device related to that medium is not readable by anyone but root. Type **mount |grep media** to see what device name represents the drive. Then (as the root user), if, for example, the CD device were `/dev/scd0`, type **chmod 644 /dev/scd0** to enable all users to read your CD-ROM and to enable the root user to write to it. One warning: If others use your computer, they will be able to read any CD you place in this drive.

Playing and managing music with Rhythmbox

Rhythmbox is a tool for gathering, managing, and playing your music collection from one application. It lets you import music (from a CD, URL, or folder), and then select and sort your music by album, artist, title, or other variables from the Rhythmbox window. Rhythmbox also lets you play Internet radio stations.

The first time you run Rhythmbox, consider setting some Rhythmbox Preferences by selecting Edit → Preferences. On the Music tab, you can tell Rhythmbox the folder in which to store your music files, as shown in Figure 8-5. (Remember this folder name. You will need it later when you configure Sound Juicer to rip CDs.)

> **TIP:** The location you choose for your music collection could require lots of disk space. Some people will add a hard disk or at least have a large, dedicated disk partition for storing their music and other multimedia content. Having this separate disk area can be useful later for doing backups. Also, if you later want to reinstall your operating system, you will be able to do so without harming your music collection.

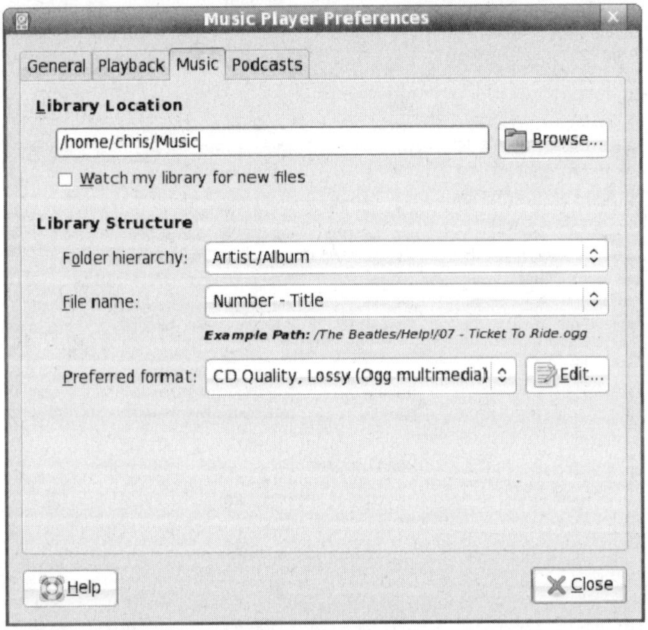

Figure 8-5: Define where you store your music with Rhythmbox.

After you set your Music folder and other preferences, close the Preferences menu and begin using the main music player (see Figure 8-6).

> **NOTE:** To get MP3 support for Rhythmbox, you can use the Codeina feature described earlier in this chapter.

Here are a few ways to use Rhythmbox:

- **Scan Removable Media** — Extract tracks from an audio CD by selecting Music →
  Scan Removable Media. If an audio CD is found, Sound Juicer launches to rip and
  compress the music from your CD (see the section "Extracting music CDs with Sound
  Juicer" for more on ripping audio CDs).

- **Create playlist** — To create a playlist, select Music → Playlist. If you have a really
  large music collection, select New Automatic Playlist. A pop-up window lets you choose
  search criteria to find songs, artists, title, or other criteria to load into your playlist. You
  can also create a new, empty playlist (New Playlist) or load a stored playlist from a file.
  Once a playlist is created, you can add songs to the list by importing (as described

previously) or dragging and dropping from a Nautilus window. Right-click on a song to copy, cut, or delete it.

Figure 8-6: View your music library and play selected songs or albums with Rhythmbox.

- **Check statistics** — Rhythmbox stores the number of times a song has been played, when it was last played, and how you rate it (one to five stars). Select Edit → Preferences to select to have columns of that information appear on your Rhythmbox window.

- **Play music tracks** — With your music available, play that music by double-clicking an album (to play the whole album), artist (to play the artist's first album you have), or track (to start with that track). Buttons at the top of Rhythmbox let you play/pause or go forward or backward a track. Select Shuffle or Repeat boxes on the bottom of Rhythmbox to randomly play the songs in the album or play the same album repeatedly. Use the slider to move ahead or back in a song and select the speaker icon to adjust volume.

- **Play Internet radio** — Rhythmbox can also play Internet radio stations. The easiest way to do this is to find a streaming radio station (you want to look for Shoutcast PLS files, usually with a `.pls` extension). Save the PLS file, right-click the file in the Nautilus file browser, and then select Open with Music Player. Nautilus comes configured to launch Rhythmbox for playing audio. The sites www.di.fm and www.shoutcast.com list a number of free Internet radio channels.

If you are looking for new music, selections under Stores on the Rhythmbox window let you connect to Magnatune and Jamendo online music services. Select either of those services to see lists of music you can try out for free. You can also search those services for music that interests you.

Magnatune makes money by licensing the music of the artists it represents for use in movies, Web sites, commercials, or other media. You can also purchase a whole album or physical music CD through those services. Jamendo provides the music of its artists for free, to help promote the music to a world-wide audience. In either case, those services provide a way for you to explore different kinds of music.

Playing music with XMMS Audio Player

The XMMS (X Multimedia System) Audio Player provides a graphical interface for playing music files in MP3, Ogg Vorbis, WAV, and other audio formats. XMMS has some nice extras, too, which include an equalizer, a Playlist Editor, and the ability to add more audio plug-ins. If the player looks familiar to you, that's because it is styled after the Windows winamp program.

> **NOTE:** Because XMMS is not a GStreamer application, the MP3 support you can get from Fluendo doesn't work with XMMS. You can get MP3 support by installing the lame package from the Livna.org repository or the xmms-mp3 package from Guru Labs (http://gurulabs.com/downloads.html).

The xmms package is available from the Fedora repository (type **yum install xmms** to install the xmms package). To use XMMS to play CDs, you must also add the xmms-cdread package (also in the Fedora repository). With an Internet connection, this command will get both packages for you: yum install xmms xmms-cdread.

Start the XMMS Audio Player from the Applications menu by selecting Sound & Video → Audio Player or by typing the xmms command from a Terminal window. Figure 8-7 consists of the XMMS Audio Player with the associated equalizer (above) and the Playlist Editor (to the right).

> **NOTE:** Although the default theme is one that matches the Fedora Blue Curve theme, you can download different themes from www.xmms.org/skins.php. Copy the skin's zip file to the /usr/share/doc/xmms/Skins directory. Then change the look of the player by right-clicking on XMMS and selecting Options → Skin Browser. The theme shown in Figure 8-7 is called UltrafinaSE.

Figure 8-7: Play Ogg Vorbis and other audio files from the XMMS playlist.

As noted earlier, you can play several audio file formats. Supported audio file formats include the following:

- MP3 (with added xmms-mp3 package)
- Ogg Vorbis
- FLAC (with added xmms-flac package)
- WAV
- AU
- CD Audio
- CIN Movies

You can get many more audio plug-ins from the Fedora repository or directly from xmms.org. The XMMS Audio Player can be used in the following way to play music files:

1. Obtain music files by either:
   - Ripping songs from a CD or copying them from the Web so that they are in an accessible directory.
   - Inserting a music CD in your CD-ROM drive. (xmms expects the CD to be accessible from /dev/cdrom.)

2. From the Applications menu, select Sound & Video → Audio Player. The X Multimedia System player appears.

3. Click the Eject button. The Load files window appears.

4. If you have inserted a CD, the content of that CD appears in the Files pane. (If it doesn't, change to `/dev/cdrom`, `/media/cdrom` or `/media/cdrecorder`, as appropriate.) Select the files you want to add to your Playlist and click the Add Selected Files or the Add All Files in Directory button to add all songs from the current directory. To add audio files from your file system, browse your files and directories and click the same buttons to add the audio files you want. Select Close.

5. Click the Play List button (the tiny button marked PL) on the console. A Playlist Editor window appears.

6. Double-click the music file and it starts to play.

7. With a file selected and playing, here are a few actions you can take:

    *   **Control play** — Buttons for controlling play are what you would expect to see on a physical CD player. From left to right, the buttons let you go to a previous track, play, pause, stop, go to the next track, or eject the CD. The Eject button opens a window, allowing you to load the next file.

    *   **Adjust sound** — Use the left slider bar to adjust the volume. Use the right slider bar to change the right-to-left balance.

    *   **Display time** — Click in the elapsed time area to toggle between elapsed time and time remaining.

    *   **View file information** — Click the button in the upper-left corner of the screen to see the XMMS menu. Then select View File Info. You can often find out a lot of information about the file: title, artist, album, comments, and genre. For an Ogg file, you can see specific information about the file itself, such as the format, bit rate, sample rate, frames, file size, and more. You can change or add to the tag information and click Save to keep it.

8. When you are done playing music, click the Stop button to stop the current song. Then click the X in the upper-right corner of the display to close the window.

Special features of the XMMS Audio Player let you adjust high and low frequencies using a graphic equalizer and gather and play songs using a Playlist Editor. Click the button marked EQ next to the balance bar on the player to open the Equalizer. Click the button marked PL next to that to open the Playlist Editor.

Using the Equalizer

The Equalizer lets you use slider bars to set different levels to different frequencies played. Bars on the left adjust lower frequencies, and those on the right adjust higher frequencies. Click the EQ button to open the Equalizer. Here are tasks you can perform with the Equalizer:

*   If you like the settings you have for a particular song, you can save them as a Preset. Set each frequency as you like it and click the Preset button. Then choose Save → Preset. Type a name for the preset and click OK.

- To reload a preset you created earlier, click the Preset button and select Load → Preset. Select the preset you want and click OK to change the settings.

The small window in the center/top of the Equalizer shows the sound wave formed by your settings. You can adjust the Preamp bar on the left to boost different levels in the set range.

Using the Playlist Editor

The Playlist Editor lets you put together a list of audio files that you want to play. You can add and delete files from this list, save them to a file, and use them again later. Click the PL button in the XMMS window to open the Playlist Editor.

The Playlist Editor allows you to:

- **Add files to the playlist** — Click the Add button. The Load Files window appears. Select the directory containing your audio files (it's useful to keep them all in one place) from the left column. Then either select a file from the right column and click Add selected files or click Add all files in the directory. Click OK. The selected file or files appear in the playlist. You can also drag music files from the nautilus file manager onto the playlist window to add the files to the playlist.

- **Select files to play** — To select from the files in the playlist, use the previous track and next track buttons in the main XMMS window. The selected file is highlighted. Click the Play button to play that file. Alternatively, you can double-click on any file in the playlist to start it playing.

- **Delete files from the playlist** — To remove files from the playlist, select the file or files you want to remove (next/previous track buttons), right-click the playlist window, and click Remove → Selected. The selected files are removed.

- **Sort files on the playlist** — To sort the playlist in different ways, click and hold the Misc button and move the mouse to select Sort List. Then you can select Sort List to sort by Title, Filename, Path and Filename, or Date. You can also randomize or reverse the list.

- **Save the playlist** — To save the current playlist, hold the mouse button down on the List button and then select Save. Browse to the directory you want, and then type the name you want to assign to the playlist and click OK.

- **Load the playlist** — To reload a saved playlist, click the List button. Select a previously saved playlist from the directory in which you saved it and click OK.

There is also a tiny set of buttons on the bottom of the Playlist Editor screen. These are the same buttons as those on the main screen used for selecting different tracks or playing, pausing, stopping, or ejecting the current track.

Using ogg123, mpg321, and play command-line players

Command-line music players are convenient if you happen to be working from a shell (no GUI) or if you want to play audio files from a shell script. Here are a few command-line players that might interest you:

- **ogg123** — The `ogg123` command is a good way to play Ogg Vorbis or FLAC audio files from the command line. From the command line, you can play a file (`abc.ogg`), a playlist containing multiple music files (`--list=/tmp/myownlist`), or an HTTP or FTP location (`http://example.com/song.ogg`). The following is an example of the `ogg123` command playing an Ogg Vorbis file from the current directory:

```
$ ogg123 01-Rhapsody_in_Blue.ogg
Audio Device:   Advanced Linux Sound Architecture (ALSA) output
Playing: 01-Rhapsody_in_Blue.ogg
Ogg Vorbis stream: 2 channel, 44100 Hz
Title: Rhapsody in Blue
Artist: George Gershwin
Track number: 1
Tracktotal: 8
Album: Rhapsody in Blue
Genre: Instrumental
Time: 00:20.36 [15:29.65] of 15:50.01 (181.6 kbps) Output Buffer  96.9%
```

  To stop ogg123 from playing a single song, press Ctrl+C. Do two Ctrl+C keystrokes to quit ogg123 when multiple tracks are queued up.

- **play** — The `play` command can be used to play any of the wide range of audio formats supported by sox. The syntax is simply `play file.xx`. To see what file formats can be played by the `play` command, type **sox -h** to see a list. The `play` command is useful if you are looking in directories of sound effects, voice content, or other audio files that aren't your typical mainstream multimedia audio types. (You need the sox package installed, which comes with Fedora and RHEL, to be able to use `play`.)

- **mpg321** — This is similar to the `ogg123` command, but it's used (as you might guess) to play MP3 audio files. Like ogg123, you can play a file (`abc.mp3`), a playlist containing multiple music files (`--list /tmp/myownlist`), or an HTTP or FTP location (`http://example.com/song.mp3`). Unlike ogg123, mpg321 doesn't come with Fedora or RHEL. You can get the mpg321 package from the Livna.org site.

Using MIDI audio players

MIDI stands for Musical Instrument Digital Interface. MIDI files are created from synthesizers and other electronic music devices. MIDI files tend to be smaller than other kinds of audio files because, instead of storing the complete sounds, they contain the notes played. The MIDI player reproduces the notes to sound like a huge variety of MIDI instruments.

There are lots of sites on the Internet for downloading MIDI files. Try the Ifni MIDI Music site (www.ifnimidi.com), which contains songs by the Beatles, Led Zeppelin, Nirvana, and others organized by album. Most of the MIDI music is pretty simple, but you can have some fun playing with it.

Fedora and RHEL come with the kmid MIDI player. Kmid is not installed by default (find it in the kdemultimedia package on the DVD). Kmid provides a GUI interface for midi music, including the ability to display karaoke lyrics in real time. There is also the timidity MIDI player (from the timidity++ package on the DVD), which lets you run MIDI audio from a Terminal window.

> **NOTE:** Use the timidity MIDI player if your sound card doesn't include MIDI support (install the timidity++ package). It can convert MIDI input into WAV files that can play on any sound card. To start timidity, type **timidity** *file.mid* at the command-line prompt.

To start kmid, type **kmid &** from a Terminal window.

Converting audio files with SoX

If you have a sound file in one format, but you want it to be in another format, Linux offers some conversion tools you can use to convert the file. The sox utility can translate to and from any of the audio formats listed in Table 8-1.

Table 8-1: Sound Formats Supported by the sox Utility

File Extension or Pseudonym	Description	File Extension or Pseudonym	Description
.8svx	8SVX Amiga musical instrument description format.	.aiff	Apple IIc/IIgs and SGI AIFF files. May require a separate archiver to work with these files.
.au, .snd	Sun Microsystems AU audio files. This is a popular format.	.avr	Audio Visual Research format, used on the Mac.
.cdr	CD-R files used to master compact discs.	.cvs	Continuously variable slope delta modulation, which is used for voice mail and other speech compression.
.dat	Text data files, which contain a text representation of sound data.	.gsm	Lossy Speech Compression (GSM 06.10), used to shrink audio data in voice mail and similar applications.

File Extension or Pseudonym	Description	File Extension or Pseudonym	Description
`.hcom`	Macintosh HCOM files.	`.maud`	Amiga format used to produce sound that is 8-bit linear, 16-bit linear, A-law, and u-law in mono or stereo.
`.ogg`	Ogg Vorbis compressed audio, which is best used for compressing music and streaming audio.	`.ossdsp`	Pseudo file, used to open the OSS /dev/dsp file and configure it to use the data type passed to sox. Used to either play or record.
`.prc`	Psion record.app format, newer than the WVE format.	`.sf`	IRCAM sound files, used by CSound package and MixView sample editor.
`.sph`	Speech audio SPHERE (Speech Header Resources) format from NIST (National Institute of Standards and Technology).	`.smp`	SampleVision files from Turtle Beach, used to communicate with different MIDI samplers.
`.sunau`	Pseudo file, used to open a `/dev/audio` file and set it to use the data type being passed to sox.	`.txw`	Yamaha TX-16W from a Yamaha sampling keyboard.
`.vms`	Used to compress speech audio for voice mail and similar applications.	`.voc`	Sound Blaster VOC file.
`.wav`	Microsoft WAV RIFF files. This is the native Microsoft Windows sound format.	`.wve`	8-bit, A-law, 8 kHz sound files used with Psion Palmtop computers.
`.raw`	Raw files (contain no header information, so sample rate, size, and style must be given).	`.ub, .sb, .uw, .sw, .ul, .al, .lu, .la, .sl`	Raw files with set characteristics. ub is unsigned byte; sb is signed byte; uw is unsigned word; sw is signed word; and ul is ulaw.

TIP: Type **sox -h** to see the supported audio types. This also shows supported options and effects.

If you are not sure about the format of an audio file, you can add the `.auto` extension to the filename. This triggers sox to guess what kind of audio format is contained in the file. The

.auto extension can be used only for the input file. If sox can figure out the content of the input file, it translates the contents to the sound type for the output file you request.

In its most basic form, you can convert one file format (such as a WAV file) to another format (such as an AU file) as follows:

```
$ sox file1.wav file1.au
```

To see what sox is doing, use the -V option. For example:

```
$ sox -V file1.wav file1.voc

sox: Reading Wave file: Microsoft PCM format, 2 channel, 44100 samp/sec
sox: 176400 byte/sec, 4 block align, 16 bits/samp, 50266944 data bytes
sox: Input file: using sample rate 11025
        size bytes, style unsigned, 1 channel
sox: Input file1.wav: comment "file1.wav"

sox: Output file1.voc: using sample rate 44100
        size shorts, encoding signed (2's complement), 2 channels
sox: Output file: comment "file1.wav"
```

You can apply sound effects during the sox conversion process. The following example shows how to change the sample rate (using the -r option) from 10,000 kHz to 5,000 kHz:

```
$ sox -r 10000 file1.wav -r 5000 file1.voc
```

To reduce the noise, you can send the file through a low-pass filter. Here's an example:

```
$ sox file1.voc file2.voc lowp 2200
```

For more information on SoX and to get the latest download, go to the SoX — Sound eXchange— home page (http://sox.sourceforge.net).

Extracting and encoding music

Storing your music collection on your computer's hard disk makes it easy to manage and play your music. Using ripping software, you can copy music tracks from a music CD to your hard disk. As part of the same process (or as a separate step), you can encode each track into another form. That encoding is usually done to reduce the size of the audio files.

Tools that come with Fedora and RHEL for extracting audio tracks from CDs and copying them to your hard disk include the Sound Juicer window and the cdparanoia command. Encoders that come with Fedora and RHEL that are typically used for encoding music include oggenc and flac. Although encoding is often done as part of the extraction process (for example, in Sound Juicer), I give an example of how to use oggenc to encode WAV files to Ogg Vorbis format on the command line.

Extracting music CDs with Sound Juicer

Sound Juicer is an intuitive graphical tool for extracting music tracks from commercial music CDs. It can read the tracks of a music CD; get CD album, artist, and track information about the CD (provided you have an Internet connection); and save the tracks to your hard disk. During that process, you can also have Sound Juicer encode the tracks in Ogg Vorbis, FLAC, or Voice-quality WAV format.

> **NOTE:** You can use the Codeina feature, described earlier in this chapter, to get support for MP3 playback. There is a fee for purchasing MP3 decoding software.

To start Sound Juicer, select Applications → Sound & Video → Sound Juicer CD Extractor. (Or you can launch it by typing **sound-juicer** or by selecting Music → Import Audio CD from Rhythmbox.) Figure 8-8 shows an example of the Sound Juicer window.

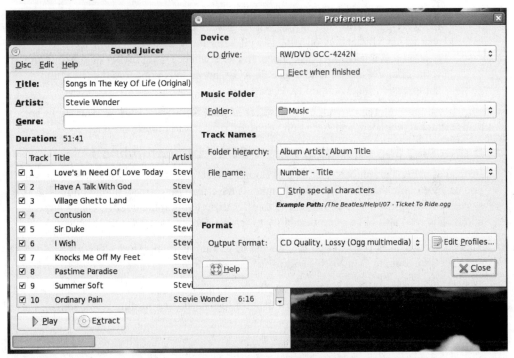

Figure 8-8: Extract songs from music CDs and encode them using Sound Juicer.

Here's how to use Sound Juicer to extract songs from an audio CD and encode them to any supported encoding type:

1. After starting Sound Juicer, insert an audio CD into your computer's CD drive and select Re-read on the Sound Juicer window. (If another audio player starts up, you can close it.)

2. Select Edit → Preferences. The Preferences window appears, as shown in Figure 8-8.

3. Set the following Preferences:

    - **CD Drive** — If you have multiple CD drives, choose the one you want to extract from.

    - **Music Folder** — Choose the folder the music tracks will be written to. Make sure that the disk partition containing the folder has enough space for you to store your music collection. As I noted earlier, a separate partition is a good idea for a large collection.

    - **Track Names** — Here's where you identify the names that will be used to store your music. The Folder hierarchy is set to the artist's name, followed by the Album title. So multiple albums by the same artist will be in the same folder. The tracks themselves, indicated by the File name box, are stored by track number and song title, separated by a dash. You can choose different ways of indicating the files and folder names used to store your music.

    - **Output** — This sets the type of encoding that is done to each track. Your choices are FLAC, Ogg Vorbis, and WAV. With a gstreamer-plugins-mp3 package installed, you should have the choice of MP3 as well. I normally use Ogg Vorbis because the quality is good and it takes less disk space. In cases where I want higher quality output (with some compression), I tend to use FLAC. Choose WAV to store the file without compression (highest quality, largest size).

4. Close the Preferences window and select Extract from Sound Juicer. The tracks are extracted, encoded, and stored on your hard disk to the folder you selected.

Extracting and encoding music CDs from commands

Instead of using a graphical tool (such as Sound Juicer) to extract and encode your music CDs, you can use commands instead. The commands described here are available on most Linux systems, while those systems might tend to offer different graphical tools. Using these commands, you also have more flexibility in setting options to use for your encoding.

This procedure takes you through the process of extracting tracks from CD (cdparanoia) and encoding them to Ogg Vorbis (oggenc).

1. Create a directory to hold the audio files, and change to that directory. Make sure the directory can hold up to 660MB of data (or less if you are burning fewer songs). For example:

    ```
    # mkdir /tmp/cd
    # cd /tmp/cd
    ```

2. Insert the music CD into your CD-ROM drive. (If a CD player opens on the desktop, close it.)

3. Extract the music tracks you want by using the cdparanoia command. For example:

    ```
    # cdparanoia -B
    ```

This example reads all of the music tracks from the CD-ROM drive (the location of your CD drive may be different). The -B option says to output each track to a separate file. By default, the cdparanoia command outputs the files to the WAV audio format.

Instead of extracting all songs, you can choose a single track or a range of tracks to extract. For example, to extract tracks 3 through 5, add the "3+5" option. To extract just track 9, add "9".

Watch the "output smiles" on the progress bar as the tracks are extracted. Normal operation (low/no jitter) is represented by a smily face :-) while errors cause faces that are progressively more worried: :-| :-/ :-P and so on.

4. To encode your WAV files to Ogg Vorbis, you can use the oggenc command. In its most basic form, you can use oggenc with one or more WAV or AIFF files following it. For example:

```
$ oggenc *.wav
```

This command would result in Ogg Vorbis files created from all files ending with .wav in the current directory. An Ogg file is produced for each WAV file, with oggenc substituting .ogg for .wav as the file suffix for the compressed file.

Instead of using oggenc to convert the WAV files to Ogg Vorbis, you can use the flac command to convert the WAV files to FLAC format (*.flac). To give you an idea of the space consumed by each format, I started with a WAV file of 27MB. When I encoded it with FLAC, it went to 11MB, whereas encoding the WAV file to Ogg Vorbis ended in 1.5MB.

> **TIP:** Another tool for ripping and compressing a music CD is grip. Grip allows you to select oggenc or other tools to do the file compression. You can get grip from Fedora repository (type yum install grip). Refer to the Web site associated with this book (www.wiley.com/go/fedora9bible) for information on using grip.

Creating your own music CDs

Fedora and RHEL contain tools for burning CDs and DVDs from either the command line or graphical window. CD and DVD burners are great for backing up your data and system files. The following sections describe how to use CD/DVD burning software specifically to create audio CDs.

Creating audio CDs with cdrecord

You can use the cdrecord command to create either data or music CDs. You can create a data CD by setting up a separate file system and copying the whole image of that file system to CD. Creating an audio CD consists of selecting the audio tracks you want to copy and copying them all at once to the CD.

> **NOTE:** Instead of the cdrecord package, Fedora now uses the wodim package (`www.cdrkit.org`) to implement the `cdrecord` command. Fedora and other Linux distributions switched to the CDR Kit project because cdrecord licensing was changed to the Sun CDDL license, which is believed to be incompatible with the GPL. Now, `cdrecord` is a link to the `wodim` command, although it supports the same options that `cdrecord` supported before the switch to `wodim`.

This section focuses on using `cdrecord` to create audio CDs. The `cdrecord` command can use audio files in `.au`, `.wav`, or `.cdr` format, automatically translating them when necessary. If you have audio files in other formats, you can convert them to one of the supported formats by using the `sox` command (described previously in this chapter).

> **CROSS-REFERENCE:** See Chapter 13 for information on how to use `cdrecord` to create data CDs.

Start by extracting music tracks from your audio CD (using a tool such as cdparanoia, described earlier in this chapter). After you have created a directory of tracks (in WAV format) from your CD, you can copy those files to your CD writer as follows:

```
# cdrecord -v dev=/dev/cdrom -audio *.wav
```

The options to `cdrecord` tell the command to create an audio CD (`-audio`) on the writable CD device located at `/dev/cdrom`. The `cdrecord` command writes all files from the current directory that end in `.wav`. The `-v` option causes verbose output.

If you want to change the order of the tracks, you can type the track names in the order you want them written (instead of using `*.wav`). If you don't indicate a recording speed, cdrecord will try to choose an appropriate one. If you get errors while you are recording, sometimes reducing the recording speed can help. For example, try `speed=2` or `speed=4` on the `cdrecord` command line.

After you have created the music CD, indicate the contents of the CD on the label side of the CD. The CD should now be ready to play on any standard music CD player.

Creating audio and data CDs with K3b

For anyone who has struggled to get the options just right with `cdrecord`, the K3b CD/DVD Burning Facility is a wonderful tool. Modeled after popular CD recording tools you can find in Windows environments, K3b provides a very intuitive way to master and burn your own CDs and DVDs.

Among the best uses of K3b are copying audio CDs and burning ISO images (perhaps containing a Linux distribution you want to try out) that you download from the Internet. To start K3b, select Sound & Video → K3b from the Applications menu. Figure 8-9 shows an example of the K3b window.

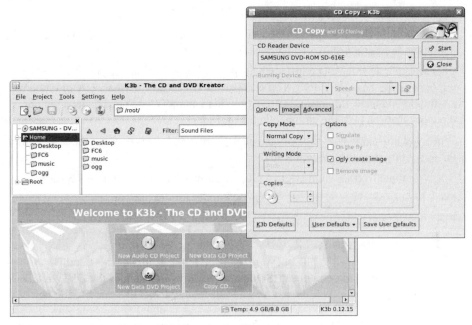

Figure 8-9: Master and burn CDs and DVDs using the K3b window.

Creating a new audio CD

If you have a bunch of audio tracks you want to put together for your own CD, here's how to do that from the K3b window:

1. Select the New Audio CD project icon from the main K3b window.

2. Open a folder window and go to the folder that contains the music track files you want to burn to CD.

3. Drag-and-drop the music tracks you want to the Current Projects pane on the bottom of the K3b screen.

4. Right-click on any track to see properties of that track. You can change or add to the information there. To change the order, you can drag tracks to different locations within the pane.

5. Select the Burn button in the upper-right corner of the K3b Current Projects screen.

6. From the Audio Project window that appears, select options for doing the burn and click the Burn button to burn the CD. As an alternative, you can select Only Create Image, to create an ISO image of all the files that you can burn to CD at a later time.

Copying a CD

If there is an audio or data CD you want to copy, you can do so from the K3b window as follows:

1. Insert the CD you want to copy into your CD drive.

2. Select Tools → CD → Copy CD from the K3b window. The CD Copy window appears (as shown in Figure 8-9).

3. Choose options for the CD copy, such as the CD reader and burner devices (they can be the same if you have only one). You can also choose to do a normal copy or clone copy. Assuming you have only one CD drive (and it's a burner), you need to set a temporary directory that can hold the entire contents of the CD.

4. When you are happy with the options, click Start. K3b begins copying the source disk to the temporary directory you indicated.

5. When prompted, remove the original CD and insert a blank CD into the CD drive.

6. Click Start to continue. K3b will tell you when the copy is complete.

7. Eject the CD and mark it appropriately.

Burning an ISO image to CD

Before your songs are copied to CD, they are gathered together into a single archive, referred to as an ISO image. You can download ISO images of software (such as the DVD or CD images used to install Fedora). Although an ISO image only looks like one big file before you burn it, after it is burned to a CD it appears as a filesystem containing multiple files. To burn any of the images just described to a CD using K3b, do the following:

1. Download or otherwise copy an ISO image to a directory on your hard disk. A CD image will be up to about 700MB, while a DVD image can be over 4GB.

2. From the K3b window, select Tools → CD → Burn CD Image. A Burn CD Image window appears.

3. Next to the Image to Burn box, select the folder icon to browse your file system to find the ISO image. After you select the image, it is loaded into the Burn CD Image window, which will display information about the image, including its MD5sum.

4. Check the MD5sum and compare it with the MD5sum provided with the ISO image when you downloaded it. (There is likely a file ending with md5 in the directory from which you downloaded the image.)

5. If the MD5sums match, continue by checking out the settings on the Burn CD Image window. I've had generally good luck using the default settings. However, I find that if I get a bad burn, often changing the speed from Auto to a slower speed that is auto-detected will result in a good burn.

6. Click Start to begin burning the image to CD. When the writing is done, K3b tells you whether it thought the burn process was successful.

The descriptions for burning CDs apply to DVDs as well (provided you have a DVD burner). Remember that you are going to need a lot more temporary space on your hard disk to work with DVDs than you would to work with CDs.

Creating CD labels with cdlabelgen

The `cdlabelgen` command can be used to create tray cards and front cards to fit in CD jewel cases. You gather information about the CD and `cdlabelgen` produces a PostScript output file that you can send to the printer. The cdlabelgen package also comes with graphics (in `/usr/share/cdlabelgen`) that you can incorporate into your labels. Install the package by typing **yum install cdlabelgen**.

Here is an example of a `cdlabelgen` command line that you can use to generate a CD label file in PostScript format. (Type it all on one line or use backslashes, as shown here, to put it on multiple lines.)

```
cdlabelgen -c "Grunge is Gone" -s "Yep HipHop" \
-i "If You Feed Me%Sockin Years%City Road%Platinum and Copper%Fly Fly \
Fly%Best Man Spins%What A Headache%Stayin Put Feelin%Dreams Do Go \
Blue%Us%Mildest Schemes" -o yep.ps
```

In this example, the title of the CD is indicated by `-c "Grunge is Gone"` and the artist by the `-s "Yep HipHop"` option. The tracks are entered after the `-i` option, with each line separated by a `%` sign. The output file is sent to the file `yep.ps` with the `-o` option. To view and print the results, you can use the `evince` command as follows:

```
$ evince yep.ps
```

The results of this example are shown in Figure 8-10.

You will probably want to edit the command and re-run `evince` a few times to get the CD label correct. When you are ready to print the label (assuming you have a printer configured for your computer), click Print All to print the label.

Viewing TV and Webcams

Getting TV cards, Webcams, and other video devices to play in Linux is still a bit of an adventure. Most manufacturers of TV cards and Webcams are not losing sleep to produce Linux drivers. As a result, most of the drivers that bring video to your Linux desktop have been reverse-engineered (that is, they were created by software engineers who watched what the video device sent and received, rather than seeing the actual code that runs the device).

The first, and probably biggest, trick is to get a TV card or Webcam that is supported in Linux. Once you are getting video output from that device (typically available from `/dev/video0`), you can try out a couple of applications to begin using it. This section describes the TVtime application for watching television and the Ekiga program for video conferencing.

Watching TV with TVtime

The TVtime program (`tvtime` command) enables you to display video output, in particular television channels, on your desktop. You can change the channels, adjust volume, and fine-tune your picture. In addition, TVtime sports a slick onscreen display and support for a widescreen display.

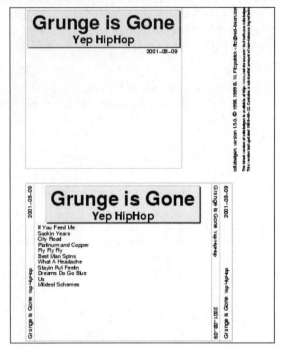

Figure 8-10: Generate CD jewel case labels with cdlabelgen and print them with evince.

TVtime will display, by default, any device producing video on the /dev/video0 device. Therefore, you can use TVtime to view Webcams as well as receive television channels. The following sections describe how to choose a TV capture card and use TVtime to watch television on your desktop.

> **NOTE:** TVtime will not display output from some low-quality Webcams. To use your Webcam, consider obtaining the xawtv package, which is available by typing **yum install xawtv**. A description of xawtv is available from the Web site that accompanies this book at www.wiley.com/ go/fedora9bible.

Getting a supported TV card

Video4Linux is the video interface included with Fedora and RHEL. It supports a variety of TV capture cards and cameras.

To see a list of supported TV cards that you can use with TVtime, refer to the CARDLIST and Cards files. To view these files, you need to have the kernel-doc package installed. You'll find the CARDLIST.tuner file in the following location on your Linux system:

```
/usr/share/doc/kernel-doc*/Documentation/video4linux/
```

The CARDLIST.bttv file applies to the Video4Linux bttv driver, which lists many TV capture cards by card number, name, and sometimes by chip set. Also, the CARDLIST.tuner lists tuner types that might be associated with different TV cards.

Video4Linux is designed to auto-detect your TV capture card and load the proper modules to activate it. So, physically install the TV-card hardware (with the appropriate connection to your TV reception), boot Fedora or RHEL, and run the tvtime command as described in the next section. You should be able to see video displayed on your TVtime window.

If your card appears not to be working, here are a few things you can try:

- To see if your TV card was properly seated in its slot and detected by Linux, type the following:

```
$ /sbin/lspci | less
```

  This will show you a list of all valid PCI cards on your computer. If nothing shows up for the card that says something like "Multimedia video controller," you probably have a hardware problem. My Hauppauge WinTV Go card appears as:

```
Multimedia video controller: Brooktree Corporation Bt878 Video Capture
```

- It is possible that the card is there, but the right card type is not being detected. Improper detection is most likely the issue if you have a card for which there are several revisions, with each requiring a different driver. If you think your card is not being properly detected, find your card in the CARDLIST files. Then add the appropriate line to the /etc/modprobe.conf file. For example, to add a Prolink PV-BT878P, revision 9B card, add the following line to /etc/modprobe.conf:

```
options   bttv   card=72
```

You can also add other options listed in the Insmod-options file for the bttv driver. If you are still having problems getting your card to work, a mailing list is available on which you can ask questions about Video4Linux issues:

```
http://listman.redhat.com/mailman/listinfo/video4linux-list
```

One possible reason that you don't see any video when you try to run TVtime or other video applications is that some other person or video application already has the video driver open. Only one application can use the video driver at a time in Fedora or RHEL. Another quirk of Video4Linux is that the first person to open the device on your system becomes the owner. So you might need to open the permissions of the device file (such as /dev/video0) to allow people other than the first person to use it to access the video4linux driver (for example, chmod 666 /dev/video0).

Starting TVtime

To start up the TVtime viewer, simply select the TVtime Television Viewer choice from the Sound & Video menu. Or, type the following from a Terminal window on your desktop:

```
$ tvtime &
```

A video screen should appear in a window on the desktop. Click the left mouse button on the window to see the current channel number, current time, and current video source (Television, Composite1, and so on). Click the right mouse button to see the onscreen Setup menu.

If your card seems to have been detected and the needed modules were properly loaded, but you don't see any video, try using the keyboard arrow keys to step forward until you find a valid channel. If that doesn't work, try going through the following adjustments (most important, the video source and television standard), to get TVtime working properly:

- **Configure input** — This choice allows you to change the video source, choose the television standard (which defaults to NTSC for the USA), and change the resolution of the input. To change the video source to Composite1, S-Video, Television, or other input source, right-click the TVtime window, select Input configuration → Change video Source. To change Television standard, select Television standard and choose NTSC (U.S.), PAL (Europe), or other available settings.
- **Set up the picture** — Adjust the brightness, contrast, color, and hue. Right-click the TVtime window, select Picture settings, and then choose Brightness, Contrast, Saturation, or Hue to adjust those attributes.
- **Adjust the video processing** — You can control the attempted frame rate, configure the deinterlacer, or add an input filter. Right-click the TVtime window, select Video processing, and then choose Attempted framerate (to slow the frame rate) or a Deinterlacer option (to change other processing features). You can also try Input filters to do some fun things like invert color, flip the video as though in a mirror image, or put the video in black and white (using Chroma killer).

If you view television often from your computer, consider adding an icon to your panel (right-click the panel and select Add to Panel → Application Launcher → Sound & Video → TVtime). With TVtime running, you can put it on top by right-clicking the title bar and selecting On Top.

Selecting channels in TVtime

With video input working and the picture adjusted to your liking, you should set up your channels. Right-click the TVtime window, select Channel management → Scan channels for signal. TVtime will scan for all available channels and note which ones have active signals. Once channels have been scanned, you can use your mouse wheel to change among the active channels. If TVtime missed an active channel, use your keyboard arrow keys to go to the missed channel and select Channel management → Current channel active in list.

> **TIP:** The xmltv project provides a means of identifying and downloading TV listings for your area. TVtime includes support for xmltv listing files, allowing you to display current television shows and station names while you go through TVtime channels. It can be tricky getting xmltv going. If you are interested, I suggest you start at the XMLTV project site (`http://membled.com/work/apps/xmltv`).

Video conferencing and VOIP with Ekiga

The Ekiga application (formerly called GnomeMeeting) enables you to communicate with other people over a network through video, audio, and typed messages. Because Ekiga supports the H323 protocol, you can use it to communicate with people using other video-conferencing clients, such as Microsoft NetMeeting, Cu-SeeMe, and Intel VideoPhone. Besides video conferencing, Ekiga also supports VOIP and IP telephony, to make telephone calls over the Internet.

To be able to send video, you need a Webcam that is supported in Linux. Although not all Webcams are supported in Linux, you still have a few dozen models to choose from. The following sections show you how to set up your Webcam and use Ekiga for video conferencing.

Getting a supported Webcam

As with support for TV capture cards, Webcam support is provided through the Video4Linux interface. Some of the supported cameras have a parallel-port interface, although most Webcams currently supported in Linux require a USB port.

Finding a Webcam to work in Linux is a bit of an adventure. Few (if any) Webcams come with Linux drivers or specs to allow open source developers to create those drivers. Webcam drivers that have been created often have limited features and sometimes break with new kernel releases. Also, Webcam vendors sometimes switch the chip sets they are using without changing the Webcam's name. And there are times when the same Webcam is marketed under different names.

So, instead of just telling you what Webcam to buy, I'll tell you what Webcams are supported by drivers that come with Fedora and RHEL. I suggest you use this information as a starting point. Combine that information with information from some sites where you can do further research and you should have what you need to make the best Webcam choice.

- **IBM C-it USB Webcams** (`ibmcam` driver) — Webcams that work with this driver have been sold under the names Xirlink C-It, IBM PC Camera, Veo Stingray, and Envision 123 Digital Camera. Before purchasing one of these Webcams, refer to the Web site for this driver (`www.linux-usb.org/ibmcam`) for further information on supported cameras, tips for getting different models to work properly, and insights on how these cameras work.

- **Konica Webcams** (`konicawc` driver) — This driver should work with the Intel YC76 or any USB Webcams that have the following vendor or product codes: 0x04c8 or

0x0720. This includes the Intel Create and Share Camera Pack. Information about the driver is available from www.si.org/konica.

- **OmniVision Webcams** (ov511 driver) — Webcams supported by this driver include USB Webcams based on OmniVision camera chips (www.ovt.com/products/app2_table.asp?id=4). Webcams include Creative WebCam 3, MediaForte MV300, AVERmedia Webcam, and D-Link DSB-C300.

- **Philips USB Webcams** (pwc driver) — This driver supports a variety of Philips USB Webcams, including PCA645, PCA646, PCVC675, PCVC680, PCVC690, PCVC730, PCVC740, and Askey VC010. These include a several inexpensive Logitech Webcams, including the QuickCam Pro 3000.

- **EndPoints Webcams** (se401 driver) — Supports Webcams that contain the EndPoints SE401 chip sets. These include the Kensington VideoCam PC cameras (67014, 67015, 67016, and 67017) and the Aox se401 camera (se401).

- **SONiX PC Cameras** (sn9c102 driver) — USB cameras based on the SONiX PC camera controllers are supported by this driver. These include the Sweex 100K, X-Eye, and Chicony Twinklecam Webcam. The sn9c10x driver is maintained by Linux Projects (www.linux-projects.org).

- **STMicroelectronics Webcams** (stv680 driver) — Webcams containing the USB version of STV0680B chips from STMicroelectronics (www.st.com) are supported by this driver. Cameras include the Aiptec Pencam and Nisis Quickpix 2 (Vendor/product ID 0553/0202). For information on the driver, refer to the Linux STV0680 USP Support page (http://stv0680-usb.sourceforge.net).

- **Ultracam Webcams** (ultracam driver) — Supports Webcams such as the IBM UltraPort Camera II. See the ultracam driver page (www.gutwin.org/cam/source) for information about the driver.

- **Vicam Webcams** (vicam driver) — The 3Com HomeConnect USB Webcam is supported by this driver. Refer to the driver's project page for further information (http://homeconnectusb.sourceforge.net).

- **Winbond Webcams** (w9968cf driver) — Supports the W9668cf JPEG USB dual mode camera chip from Winbond Electronics. Webcams that use that chip include the ADG-5000 Aroma Digi Pen, Ezonics EZ-802 EZMega Cam, and the Pretec DigiPen-480. Refer to the Linux Projects site (www.linux-projects.org) for further information.

Check out the following Web sites for a more complete list of Webcams that are and are not supported in Linux. Keep in mind, however, that not all of the drivers for these Webcams will work in the latest kernels in Fedora or RHEL.

- Kamerstöd i Linux (www.cs.umu.se/~c00ahs/exjobb/linuxcams.html)
- Linux USB Device Drivers (www.linux-usb.org/devices.html)

The Logitech QuickCam Pro 300 Webcam that I used for examples in this chapter works well with the pwc driver that comes with Fedora. To check that it was working, I ran the lsmod command to see that the pwc driver was loaded and associated with the videodev module:

```
# lsmod
pwc                      43392     0
compat_ioctl32            5569     1 pwc
videodev                  5120     1 pwc
```

To see information about the pwc module (which is specific to this Webcam), I typed the following modinfo command:

```
# modinfo -p pwc
size:Initial image size. One of sqcif, qsif, qcif, sif, cif, vga
fps:Initial frames per second. Varies with model, useful range 5-30
fbufs:Number of internal frame buffers to reserve
mbufs:Number of external (mmap()ed) image buffers
trace:For debugging purposes
power_save:Turn power save feature in camera on or off
compression:Preferred compression quality. Range 0 (uncompressed) to 3
    (high compression)
leds:LED on,off time in milliseconds
dev_hint:Device node hints
```

Running Ekiga

To start Ekiga, select Applications → Internet → IP Telephone, VOIP and Video Conferencing. To start Ekiga from a Terminal window, type **ekiga &.** If it is not installed, you can install the ekiga package from the DVD that comes with this book. The first time you run Ekiga, the Ekiga Configuration Assistant starts. The assistant lets you enter the following information:

- **Personal Data** — Your first name, last name, e-mail address, comment, and location. You can also select whether or not you want to be listed in the Ekiga ILS directory.

- **Connection Type** — Indicate the speed of your Internet connection (56K modem, ISDN, DSL/Cable, T1/LAN, or Custom).

- **Audio Manager** — Typically you would choose ALSA as your audio manager.

- **Video Manager and Devices** — Typically you would choose Video4Linux as the video manager and your Webcam as the input device.

> **NOTE:** If you want to reconfigure Ekiga later, run the following command to clean out the old settings: ekiga-config-tool --clean. Make sure all instances of Ekiga are stopped before running that configuration tool. Run ekiga again to re-enter your settings.

Figure 8-11 shows the Ekiga window with the history log to the right.

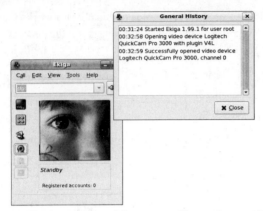

Figure 8-11: Connect to ILS servers to video-conference with Ekiga.

In the Ekiga window that opens, you can click the rolodex icon to open an address book. From the address book, select Ekiga White Pages. By typing a name into the search filter, you can search for people who might be connected to Ekiga server by first name, last name, e-mail address, or location. Select a person from the list that appears and, if he or she accepts your call, you can begin video-conferencing.

By selecting View → Control Panel, you can select to have tabs appear beneath the video window to adjust your audio levels and video appearance. The History tab shows a log of your activities.

Taking Webcam videos and snapshots with Cheese

Fedora has a new application as part of the GNOME desktop for taking snapshots and videos from your Webcam. With a supported Webcam (described earlier), you can use the new Cheese application (www.gnome.org/projects/cheese) to capture images from your Webcam with a few simple mouse clicks.

To install Cheese, type the following from a Terminal as root user:

```
# yum install cheese
```

Then, with your Webcam connected, either select Applications → Accessories → Cheese from the GNOME menu or type cheese from a Terminal window to launch Cheese. Figure 8-12 shows an example of the Cheese window.

As your Webcam output is displayed live in the top of the Cheese window, you can use the Photo or Video buttons to select what you want to capture. The middle button toggles to let you either Take a Photo or Start Recording. For photos, you have a three-second pause to get ready for the shot. For videos, recording starts and you need to click Stop Recording when you have captured all you want.

Figure 8-12: Take pictures or videos from your Webcam with Cheese.

Before grabbing an image or video, you can select Effects to change the images to produce effects such as Black-and-White, Hulk (everything turns green), or some weird Warp or Verdigo effects. Select No Effect to turn off the special effects.

Each photo or video you grab is represented by a thumbnail on the bottom of the window. Right-click on the image you want and you can select to open it, save it, move it to trash, send it via email, or export it to the F-Spot application. You can also select Set As Account Photo to have the image set as the image that appears on the login screen, User Switcher applet, or screensaver window for your user account.

Playing Video

Video recording (encoding) and playback (decoding) remain among the most contentious areas of potential litigation in open source software. On one hand you have patent holders of complex video formats that might ask for royalties for open source codecs (even when the software was written from scratch). On the other, you have the movie industry that has taken aim at those publishing what they had hoped were secret encryption techniques (DeCSS), to prevent the open source decoding of commercial movies. The problem is that the same technique that allows you to play movies in Linux also can be used to copy and share them.

> **NOTE:** Codec stands for COder/Decoder or COmpressor/DECompressor, depending on whom you ask. In either case, codecs are what make it possible to process and encode audio and video on computers.

As with audio recording, if you are starting from scratch, there is an open source codec called Theora (www.theora.org) that you can use without paying any royalties, as of this writing. Provided you own the content you are recording, you can freely distribute that content as well and allow others to play it back.

When it comes to including video codecs (other than the free Theora), Red Hat, Inc. has taken the cautious approach. While Fedora and RHEL now include video players such as Totem (described later in this chapter), they do not include players (such as the MPlayer and Xine media players) that often are packaged with contentious codecs. If you want to play commercial movies, popular video clips, or other video content in a Red Hat Linux system, you have to get those codecs elsewhere.

This section describes some of the issues surrounding playing and creating video in Linux. It also describes video players that come with Fedora and RHEL, as well as those you can obtain to play a wide variety of video content.

Examining laws affecting video and Linux

I need to start out by reminding everyone that I am not a lawyer, so you need to take responsibility yourself regarding any software you put on your computers. However, there are several themes that have arisen in regard to playing video content with open source software in Linux:

- **Licensing fees for patented codecs may be required.** While many video codecs are covered by patents, some patent holders don't charge for personal use. However, you should check current policies of companies who own patents on codecs you plan to use, as the terms of use are constantly changing. For example, this statement that was once posted on the DivX Web site is no longer there: "Personal use of DivX video software is free. Commercial use is not and requires that you obtain a commercial use license from DivXNetworks." (Refer to the DivX Web site www.divx.com for information on DivX licensing).

  Because MPEG-2 and MPEG-4 video formats are covered by a variety of patents, groups of patent holders have joined together to charge licensing fees for related encoders and decoders. These efforts are not sponsored by standards organizations that spearheaded the creation of those formats and may not cover every patent holder related to the software you are paying for. See the MPEG Industry Forum for details on MPEG patent issues (www.m4if.org/patents).

  Remember that there are now ways to purchase codecs for many popular audio/video formats for use with Linux. See the section "Extending Freedom to Codecs" for information on purchasing codecs from Fluendo.

- **Unauthorized copying of copyright-protected material is never legal.** Even legal video codecs do not make it legal to copy commercial movies and other protected content and distribute them to others. There are questions as to whether or not, for example, it is legal to make a personal backup copy of a DVD movie (a commonly accepted legal practice with computer software). But any redistribution of movie, music, or other media content is not legal without the owner's permission.

Because patenting eliminates trade secret protection for the subject matter disclosed in the patent (or published patent application), many people have raised the question of why someone can't freely distribute libdvdcss (based on DeCSS decryption) to play DVD movies. Without copyright or patent coverage on CSS, it should not be illegal to distribute libdvdcss and there's nobody to pay a license fee to for using it. In regards to libdvdcss, another issue arose in the United States: the Digital Millennium Copyright Act (DMCA). DMCA might make DeCSS illegal because the technology is used to break an encryption scheme to circumvent copyrighted material.

As for the software patent issues, those are being fought on several fronts besides those relating to multimedia content. As noted earlier, the contention held by many open source proponents is that software should be copyrighted and not patented (see the section "Understanding Multimedia and Legal Issues in Linux" earlier in this chapter.)

With all that said, the next parts of this chapter go on to describe which players are available to play a wide range of video content in Linux. It is up to you to work out the maze of which codecs are free for you to use and in what ways.

Understanding video content types

Before launching into the video players themselves, I want to try to clear up a bit of confusion relating to video file formats and codecs:

- **Video file formats** — A video file format essentially describes the structure of a video file for combining audio and video content. That structure can also define such things as subtitles and how audio and video are synchronized. However, a variety of video and audio codecs may have been used to encode that content. So, just because you can play a video file that is marked as MPEG (`.mpg`), Audio Video Interleaved (`.avi`), QuickTime (`.mov`), RealMedia (`.rm`), Windows media (`.wvm`), Advanced Streaming Format (`.asf`), or other file format, it doesn't mean that you can play all video files marked as such.

- **Video and audio codecs** — Codecs are used to encode and decode video and audio content. A video encoded entirely with free software might use Theora to encode the video and Ogg Vorbis to encode the audio. Popular video codecs include MPEG-4, DivX, Xvid, RealVideo, and MJPEG.

Not all video codecs and file formats are suitable for streaming video. For example, AVI and MPEG-2 are not streamable. However, RealMedia, MPEG-4, and ASF format can be streamed. Check the descriptions of video players in the following sections for information on which players can support which codecs.

If you have a video file on your hard disk and you'd like to know what type of content it contains, you can use the `file` command. Here's an example of the `file` command for checking the contents of a movie trailer:

```
$ file movie.avi
movie.avi: RIFF (little-endian) data, AVI, 640 x 272, 23.98 fps, video:
DivX 3, audio: MPEG-1 Layer 3 (stereo, 44100 Hz)
```

This example shows that the file contains DivX 3 video and MPEG-1 Layer 3 audio. The size of the video is 640 x 272 pixels. Video was captured at 23.98 frames per second. This can lead you to the type of video player you need to play the content. Given that the right codecs are installed, MPlayer, Xine, VLC, or several other players would be able to play this content.

Watching video with Xine

At the base of the Xine video player (`http://xinehq.de`) is the xine-lib core engine. While Xine has its own xlib-based user interface, you can choose different video player front-ends to use with the core engine instead (including Totem, Kaffeine, and aaxine). You can also use Xine as a Mozilla plug-in, to have videos play in a browser window.

The xine player is an excellent application for playing a variety of video and audio formats. You can get Xine from `http://xinehq.de` (which takes some work to get going) or by downloading RPMs from `rpm.livna.org/fedora`. (See Chapter 5 for information on using Livna.org and other software repositories for getting Fedora and RHEL software. If yum is configured to point to one of those repositories, you should be able to install Xine by typing **yum install xine**).

> **NOTE:** The Xine project offers the following disclaimer before you download or use its software: *Some parts of Xine (especially audio/video codecs) may be subject to patent royalties in some countries. If you provide pre-compiled binaries or intend to build derivative works based on the Xine source please consider this issue. The Xine project is not warranting or indemnifying you in any way for patent royalties. You are solely responsible for your own actions.*

You can start the Xine player by typing **xine&** from a Terminal window. Figure 8-13 shows an example of the Xine video player window and controls.

The Xine Setup window (shown to the right) lets you choose various settings for the video player, such as a different user interface, if one is available. Below the Xine window is the Xine controller, which has buttons that work like many physical DVD players. Right-click the main window to see a menu of options. Select Settings → Video to display another controller (shown at the bottom of Figure 8-13) that lets you adjust hue, saturation, brightness, and contrast.

Xine supports a bunch of video and audio file formats and codecs. However, not all of these codecs are distributed with Xine:

- MPEG (1, 2, and 4)
- QuickTime (see "Xine tips" if this content won't play)
- RealMedia (see "Xine tips" if this content won't play)
- WMV (see "Xine tips" if this content won't play)
- Motion JPEG
- MPEG audio (MP3)
- AC3 and Dolby Digital audio
- DTS audio
- Ogg Vorbis audio

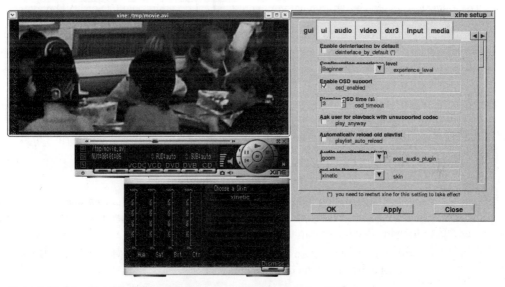

Figure 8-13: Play video CDs, MP3s, QuickTime, and other video formats with Xine.

Using the Xine controller, you can select to play content directly from a DVD, DVB, VCD, VCDO, or CD disk. If you are playing an audio CD (or any audio file), you can choose different visualizations (right-click, and then choose Audio → Visualization and select goom, oscope, fftscope, or fftgraph) to appear in the Xine windows as music plays.

Xine can understand different file formats that represent streaming audio and video. These include .mpg (MPEG program streams), .ts (MPEG transport streams), .mpv (raw MPEG audio/video streams), .avi (MS AVI format), and .asf (Advanced Streaming format). While Xine can play video CDs and DVDs containing other content, it can't play encrypted

DVDs or video-on-CD hybrid format without adding other software (because of the legal issues mentioned earlier related to decrypting DVDs).

Using Xine

With Xine started, right-click in the Xine window to see the controls. The quickest way to play video is to click one of the following buttons, and then press the Play button (right arrow or Play, depending on the skin you are using):

- VCD (looks for a video CD)
- DVD (looks for a DVD in `/dev/dvd`)
- CDA (looks a music CD in `/dev/cdaudio`)

Next, you can use the Pause/Resume, Stop, Play, Fast motion, Slow motion, or Eject buttons to work with video. You can also use the Previous and Next buttons to step to different tracks. The controls are very similar to what you would expect on a physical CD or DVD player.

To select individual files, or to put together your own list of content to play, you can use the Playlist feature.

Creating playlists with Xine

Click the Playlist button on the left side of the xine control window. A Playlist Editor appears, showing the files on your current playlist. You can add and delete content from this list, and then save the list to call on later. Here's how you use the Xine Playlist Editor:

- **CDA, DVD, or VCD** — Click any of the buttons that represent a particular CD or DVD. All content from that CD or DVD is added to the playlist.
- **Add** — Click the Add button to see the MRL Browser window. From that window, click File to choose a file from your Linux file system to add to the list. Click Select to add that file to the Playlist Editor.
- **Move up/Move down** — Use the Move up selected MRL and Move down selected MRL buttons to move up and down the playlist.
- **Delete** — Click the Delete Selected MRL button to remove the current selection.
- **Delete all** — Click the Delete All Entries button to clear the whole playlist.
- **Save** — Click the Save button to save the playlist to your home directory (`$HOME/.xine/playlist.tox` or give it another name).
- **Load** — To read in the playlist you saved, click the Load button.

The Xine content is identified as media resource locators (MRLs). Each MRL is identified as a file, DVD, or VCD. Files are in the regular file path (`/path/file`) or preceded by `file:/`, `fifo:/`, or `stdin:/`. DVDs and VCD are preceded by `dvd` and `vcd`, respectively (for example, `vcd://01`).

To play your playlist, click the Play button (arrow key) on the Playlist Editor.

Xine tips

Getting video and audio to work properly can sometimes be a tricky business. Here are a few quick tips to using Xine:

- **Xine won't start.** To work best, Xine needs an X driver that supports xvid. If there is no xvid support for your video card in X, Xine will shut down immediately when it tries to open the default Xv driver. If this happens to you, try starting the `xine` command with the X11 video driver (which is slower, but should work) as follows:

```
$ xine -V XShm
```

- **Don't run as root.** Run `xine` as a regular user, instead of as root. Once Xine is installed, you should be able to run it from the Applications menu on your panel by selecting Sound & Video → Xine Media Player. There have been recently discovered vulnerabilities of some open source media players related to streaming media. Although that problem was fixed, it again highlighted the fact that running applications as a regular user, whenever possible, is a good idea.

- **Run `xine-check`.** To get an idea of how happy Xine is running on your system, run the `xine-check` command (as the user who will be using Xine). It will tell you if there are problems running Xine on your current operating system, kernel, and processor, among other things.

- **Xine playback is choppy.** If playback of files from your hard disk is choppy, there are a couple of settings you can check: 32-bit IO and DMA. (If these two features are supported by your hard disk, they will generally improve hard disk performance.)

> **CAUTION:** Improper disk settings can result in destroyed data on your hard disk. Do this procedure at your own risk. This procedure is only for IDE hard drives (not SCSI)! Also, be sure to have a current backup and no activity on your hard disk if you change DMA or IO settings as described here.

First, test the speed of hard disk reads. To test the first IDE drive (in Fedora 7, it may appear as /dev/sda instead of /dev/hda), type:

```
# hdparm -t /dev/sda
Timing buffered disk reads: 64 MB in 19.31 seconds = 3.31 MB/sec
```

To see your current DMA and IO settings, as root user type:

```
# hdparm -c -d /dev/sda
/dev/sda:
 I/O support = 0 (default 16-bit)
 using_dma   = 0 (off)
```

This shows that both 32-bit IO and DMA are off. To turn them on, type:

```
# hdparm -c 1 -d 1 /dev/sda
/dev/sda:
```

```
I/O support = 1 (32-bit)
using_dma   = 1 (on)
```

With both settings on, test the disk again:

```
# hdparm -t /dev/sda
Timing buffered disk reads: 64 MB in 2.2 seconds = 28.83 MB/sec
```

As you can see from this example, buffered disk reads of 64MB went from 19.31 seconds to 2.2 seconds after changing the parameters described. Playback should be much better now.

- **Xine won't play particular media.** Messages such as no input plug-in mean that either the file format you are trying to play is not supported or it requires an additional plug-in (as is the case with playing DVDs). If the message is maybe xyx is a broken file, the file may be a proprietary version of an otherwise supported format. For example, I had a QuickTime video fail that required an SVQ3 codec (which is currently not supported under Linux), although other QuickTime files will play fine.

  If a particular multimedia format is not supported, but you have Windows dlls available that support it, you can add those dll files to the /usr/lib/win32 directory. Some of these codec ddls are available from http://www.mplayerhq.hu/design7/dload.html#binary_codecs in a package called essential. Choose a mirror site from the table under the Binary Codec Packages heading.

> **NOTE:** The CrossOver Plugin (described in Chapter 9) can be used to play a variety of content, including the version of QuickTime just mentioned.

Using Totem movie player

The Totem movie player (www.gnome.org/projects/totem) comes with the GNOME desktop environment. In Fedora and RHEL, Totem can play video in Theora format with Ogg Vorbis audio. Totem is based on GStreamer (http://gstreamer.freedesktop.org) so it can be used with other video software from that project. In particular, free and fee-based codecs that you can purchase from www.fluendo.com for playing a variety of commercial audio/video formats will work with Totem.

Totem also supports a xine backend that allows it to play a wide range of video content (in other words, anything xine supports). To play commercial DVD movies, however, you need to replace the version of Totem that comes with Fedora with the totem-xine package available from Livna.org. From that same repository, you can add the libdvdcss, libdvdnav, and xine-lib-extras-nonfree packages (provided the software is legal where you live).

Besides common controls you would expect with a movie player (play, pause, skip forward, skip backwards, and so on), Totem lets you create playlists, take a snapshot of the current frame, and adjust the volume. You can change preferences, which let you add proprietary plug-ins, select your DVD device, and balance color. Figure 8-14 shows an example of the Totem window.

Figure 8-14: Totem plays Theora video, plus any codecs supported by Xine and GStreamer.

Using a Digital Camera

With the GNOME Volume Manager features in Fedora and RHEL, getting images from a digital camera can be as easy in Linux as it is in any desktop operating system. With most digital cameras that can be connected to a USB port on your computer, simply plugging the camera into a USB port (with the camera set to send and receive) causes the GNOME Volume Manager to:

- Immediately prompt you to ask if you want to download images from your camera.
- Run the gThumb image viewer and browser program to look at, manipulate, and download the contents of your digital camera.

Although GNOME Volume Manager will open your camera's contents in an image viewer, you can treat the storage area in your camera much as you would the storage area on a hard disk or a pen drive. I describe how to use your camera to store other data as well.

Displaying images in gThumb

The GNOME Volume Manager mounts the contents of your USB camera, treating the memory of your camera as it would any file storage device. When I tried it with an Olympus digital camera, my images were available from the `/media/usbdisk/dcim/100olymp` directory. Figure 8-15 shows an example of the gthumb-import window displaying the images from a digital camera.

Converting Video to Theora

There are not a lot of tools yet for creating Theora video. To get a video to try out, I shot a video with my Sony Handycam, which stores video in 30-minute, 1.4GB mini DVDs. I downloaded a tool, recommended from the Theora.org site, called ffmpeg2theora (`www.v2v.cc/~j/ffmpeg2theora`). My video camera stored my home movie as a VOB file, which I copied to my hard disk and converted to Theora/Ogg Vorbis as follows:

```
$ ffmpeg2theora VTS_01_1.VOB
Input #0, mpeg, from 'VTS_01_1.VOB':
  Duration: 00:00:00.6, start: 0.197311, bitrate: -2147483 kb/s
  Stream #0.0: Video: mpeg2video, 704x480, 29.97 fps, 9300 kb/s
  Stream #0.1: Audio: ac3, 48000 Hz, stereo, 256 kb/s
  Resize: 704x480 => 320x240
  Resample: 48000Hz => 44100Hz
      .
      .
      .
```

The original file was stored in mpeg-2 video (720 x 480 pixels) and ac3 audio (48,000 Hz). The `ffmpeg2theora` command resized the video to 704 x 480 pixels and resampled the audio to 44,100 Hz. The result was a second file (same filename with an .ogg extension added) that was 82MB, compared to the original 1.1GB.

With your camera connected and the gThumb window open, here are some things you can do with the images on your camera:

- **Download images** — Click a single image or select Edit → Select All to highlight all images from your digital camera. Then select File → Import Photos. From the Import Photos window you can select the destination where you want the images to be downloaded. As an alternative, you can download selected images to a folder on the GNOME desktop.

- **View Slideshow** — Select View → Slide Show. A full-screen slideshow appears on your display, with the images changing every few seconds. The toolbar that appears at the top lets you display information about the photo name, date, and size (click Image Info), go forward and back through the images, and zoom in or out.

- **Manipulate images** — Double-click an image to open it, and select the Image menu. That menu offers a set of tools for enhancing, resizing, cropping, or otherwise transforming the image. You can also adjust the color balance, hue/saturation, and brightness contrast.

- **Assign categories** — With an image selected, click the Categories button. The Categories pop-up window lets you assign the image to a category to help you organize your photos. Assign available categories (such as birthday, family, holidays, or games) or click New and add your own categories.

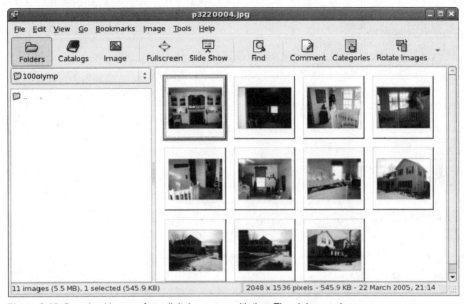

Figure 8-15: Download images from digital cameras with the gThumb image viewer.

Once images are downloaded to your computer's hard disk, you can continue to work with them using gThumb or use any of a number of tools available for manipulating digital images (GIMP, KView, and Kuickshow, to name a few).

> **NOTE:** If you have a camera that saves images to a floppy disk, just insert that disk into your disk drive and the contents of the disk should open automatically on your desktop. In addition, if your camera saves images to SD or CF cards, you can purchase a USB card reader and view these files from Linux.

Check the gPhoto2 Web site (`www.gphoto.org/proj/libgphoto2/support.php`) for information on supported cameras as well as other topics related to gPhoto.

Using your camera as a storage device

As I noted with my example of an Olympus camera with a USB connector, the GNOME Volume Manager is capable of detecting that camera once it is connected, and mounting its contents as a storage device. With the contents of a digital camera mounted, you can use your camera as a USB mass storage device by:

- Opening the mounted directory in a folder window and using any file manager features to work with the images.

- Changing to the mounted directory from the shell and using commands to copy, move, rename, or delete digital images.

Of course, with your camera mounted as a file system, you are not limited to using it only for digital images. You can use it to store any kind of files you like, essentially using the camera as a storage device. The following list is a partial summary of digital cameras that can be used as a USB storage device:

- **Casio** — Supported models: QV-2400UX, QV-2x00, QV-3x00, QV-4000, and QV-8000
- **Fuji** — FinePix 1300, 1400Zoom, 2300Zoom, 2400Zoom, 2800Zoom, 4200Z, 4500, 4700 Zoom, 4900 Zoom, 6800 Zoom, A101, A201, and S1 Pro
- **HP** — PhotoSmart 315, 318xi, 618, and C912
- **Konica** — KD200Z, KD400Z, and Revio KD300Z
- **Kyocera** — Finecam s3
- **Leica** — Digilux 4.3
- **Minolta** — Dimage 5, Dimage 7, and Dimage X
- **Nikon** — CoolPix 2500, 885, 5000, 775, and 995
- **Olympus** — Brio Zoom D-15, C-100, C-200Z, C-2040, C-220Z, C-2Z, C-3020Z, C-3040Z, C-4040Zoom, C-700, C-700UZ, C-860L, D-510, D-520Z, E-10, and E-20
- **Pentax** — EI2000, Optio 330, and Optio 430
- **Sony** — DSC-F505, DSC-F505V, DSC-F707, DSC-P1, DSC-P20, DSC-P5, DSC-P71, DSC-S30, DSC-S70, DSC-S75, DSC-S85, MVC-CD300, and MVC-FD92
- **Vivitar** — Vivicam 3550
- **Yashica** — Finecam s3

Summary

This chapter takes you through the steps of setting up and using audio, video, and digital cameras in Fedora and RHEL. It covers topics such as troubleshooting your sound card and explains how to find software to play music through that card. Many popular music players included with Fedora and RHEL, such as KsCD and Rhythmbox are described.

With nearly every type of audio and video format available today in Linux, the biggest trick is figuring out which software is legal to use freely and which isn't. Because Red Hat tends to be conservative when it comes to patent claims to multimedia, you might need to dig up the audio and video codecs you need on your own. I tried to cover some of the legal issues surrounding multimedia software patents, so you can try to make informed decisions.

Live video from TV cards and Webcams is covered in the sections on TVtime, Cheese, and Ekiga. I cover the xine and Totem players for playing a variety of video formats, followed by the GNOME Volume Manager for downloading images from a digital camera. If your computer has a CD burner, use the descriptions in this chapter to create your own music CDs and CD labels. You can also burn complete CD or DVD ISO images using the K3b window.

Chapter 9

Using the Internet
and the Web

In This Chapter

- Understanding Internet tools
- Browsing the Web
- Communicating via e-mail
- Participating in newsgroups
- Using Pidgin Instant Messaging
- Using BitTorrent cooperative software distribution
- Using remote login, copy, and execution commands

With your Fedora system connected to the Internet, you can take advantage of dozens of tools for browsing the Web, downloading files, getting e-mail, and communicating live with your friends. In most cases, you have several choices of GUI and command-line applications for using Internet services from your Linux desktop or shell.

This chapter describes some of the most popular tools available with Fedora for working with the Internet. These descriptions cover Web browsers, e-mail readers, instant messaging clients, and commands for login and remote execution. With the consolidation of Fedora Core and Fedora Extras software repositories that took place with Fedora 7, many specialty applications (such as BitTorrent file sharing) are now available to Fedora users from the single, common Fedora repository.

Overview of Internet Applications and Commands

When it comes to features and ease-of-use issues, applications that come with Fedora for accessing the Internet can rival those of any operating system. For every major type of Internet client application, there are at least three or four graphical and command-line tools to choose from.

While Linux has offered high-quality servers for Web, mail, FTP, and other Internet services for years, current versions of these desktop Internet applications have become both solid and rich in content. If Web browsing and e-mail are your primary needs in a desktop system, Fedora and RHEL are ready today to let you leave your Windows desktop systems behind.

Figure 9-1 illustrates some of the most valuable Linux applications for using the Internet.

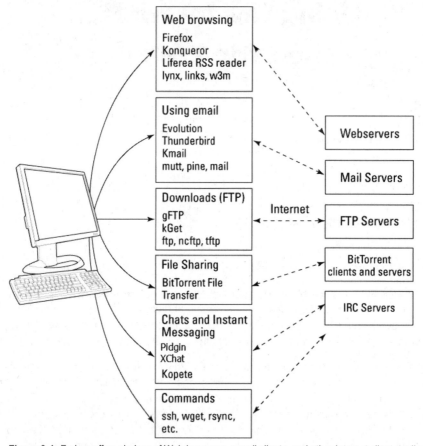

Figure 9-1: Fedora offers choices of Web browsers, e-mail clients, and other Internet client applications.

If you are using Fedora or RHEL as a desktop system, the browsers and e-mail clients make requests to servers available on your LAN or the Internet. Software for configuring a computer as a Web, mail, FTP, or other server type is also included with Fedora and RHEL systems. Someone starting out with Linux, however, can use applications for using the Internet as they would from any Windows or other desktop system.

The following Internet applications available in Fedora are covered in this chapter:

- **Web browsers** — Most Web browsers available for Linux today follow from the legacy of Netscape Navigator. The open source Mozilla project, which was originally spawned from Netscape source code, is responsible for the award-winning Firefox Web browser. Another browser that comes with Fedora is the Konqueror browser/file manager. (The Mozilla suite was renamed SeaMonkey and is available with Fedora in the seamonkey package.)

  Relatively new ways for gathering content from the Web include RSS news feed readers, such as the liferea RSS/RDF feed reader. There are also several browsers, such as lynx and w3m, that can run from the command line (with no graphical interface required).

- **E-mail clients** — The Evolution e-mail client has evolved into a full-fledged groupware suite, combining an e-mail reader with features for managing contacts, calendars, and tasks, as well as connecting to Microsoft Exchange servers. Thunderbird is an up-and-coming e-mail client from the Mozilla project (SeaMonkey mail is also available from the same organization). For those who prefer old-school e-mail readers, mutt, pine, and mail commands let you read mail from the command line, often with limited abilities to handle attachments, HTML, or other modern e-mail features.

- **FTP clients** — If you use the FTP protocol to download files from FTP servers, or to upload Web pages to your server, graphical tools for doing those tasks include the gFTP and kGet applications. There are also many shell commands available for accessing FTP servers to look for files, download files, or upload files. Those commands include `ftp`, `ncftp`, and `tftp`.

- **BitTorrent clients/servers** — BitTorrent is the popular open source software project for sharing files among many computers at the same time. With BitTorrent, as you download a file you can simultaneously safely upload that same file to others. BitTorrent is particularly useful for publishing CD or DVD images containing large software distributions (such as Fedora) the minute they becomes available, without overstressing the original servers releasing the software.

- **Instant messaging and chats** — Typing live messages to friends, family, and associates has become a popular activity in recent years. Pidgin is an instant messaging client that lets you connect to AIM, IRC, MSN, Google, and ICQ servers. XChat is a popular Internet Relay Chat (IRC) client (a popular protocol among Linux enthusiasts for online chats). Kopete is an instant messaging client that integrates with a KDE desktop.

- **Remote commands (login, file copy, and so on)** — As you spend more time working with Linux, you will find that it is often quicker and more convenient to run commands than it is to run graphical applications. Some very powerful command-line tools exist in Linux for doing such things as remote login and remote execution (`ssh`) and remote file copy (`wget`, `scp`, and `rsync`).

> **NOTE:** Besides the applications mentioned here, many more Internet-enabled applications are described in other parts of the book. For example, music players and video players described in Chapter 8 can grab audio and video files or streaming media from the Internet. Likewise, software installation tools such as yum are made to get software from software repositories on the Internet.

Because the Internet client applications featured in Fedora and RHEL are designed to be intuitive, if you are accustomed to using the Internet from Windows or Macintosh the transition to Linux shouldn't be that difficult. While I describe many of the basic features that come in these Internet applications, there are a few tricks you should learn to get the most out of them:

- **Tuning your browser** — While Firefox has made great strides in supporting different kinds of Web content, getting some multimedia, image, and document formats to play in Firefox can require some extra steps. In most cases, this is because software for playing many popular multimedia formats cannot be freely distributed, so you have to add them later. I describe some plug-ins and other software that you will want to add to Firefox (or another Web browser) to get it to play many popular types of content that it can't handle by default.

- **Managing e-mail** — With e-mail volume increasing every day, tools for managing your e-mail are becoming more important. In the e-mail section, I explain how to use filter rules to sort your e-mail and how to identify junk mail. I also discuss ways to manage and use mailing lists effectively.

- **Useful command options** — Besides identifying some useful commands for remote login, file copying, and command execution, I identify options that are particularly helpful to use with them.

To get started with Internet applications in Linux, you need to set up a connection to the Internet from your Linux system (as described in Chapters 15 and 16). Most graphical Internet applications in Fedora and RHEL are available from menus on the GNOME or KDE desktops. Click Applications → Internet to see a list of Internet applications you can choose from. Icons to launch the Firefox browser and Evolution e-mail client are directly on the panel on the top of the display.

Browsing the Web

The most important client Internet program these days is the Web browser. In Fedora and RHEL, you have several choices of Web browsers, including the following:

- **Firefox** — The Firefox browser is touted as the flagship Web browser from the Mozilla project and is aimed squarely at the dominance of Microsoft Internet Explorer in the browser space. Firefox offers easy-to-use features for dealing cleverly with issues that have wreaked havoc with other Internet browsers, such as viruses, spyware, and pop-ups. Firefox is the featured Web browser in Fedora and RHEL.

- **Epiphany** — The Epiphany browser is the official Web browser of the GNOME project. It is powered by the Mozilla Layout Engine (sometimes referred to as Gecko). While Epiphany doesn't have all the features you find in Firefox, it is designed to be fast and efficient.

- **Konqueror** — Although Konqueror is the file manager for the KDE desktop, it can also display Web content. Using Konqueror, you can easily go back and forth between Web sites and local files and folders. A testament to the quality of Konqeror is that the Mac OS X Safari browser uses the WebKit rendering engine, which is based on the Konqueror KHTML and kjs engines.

If you are working from a shell, there are several command-line utilities that allow you to browse the Web without a graphical interface. These include the `links`, `w3m`, and `lynx` commands.

Understanding Web browsing

Although the Internet has been around since the 1960s, the Web is a relatively new technology (ushered in by the creation of the first Web browser in 1990). The Web places an additional framework over Internet addresses that were once limited to hostnames and domain names. Before the Web, finding resources on the Internet was difficult. However, the Web now provides several features that make it much easier to access these resources:

- **Uniform Resource Locators (URLs)** — URLs identify the location of resources on the Web. Besides identifying the domain and host on which a resource resides, they can also identify the type of content and the specific location of the content.

- **Hypertext Markup Language (HTML) Web pages** — When people talk about a Web page, they are generally referring to information that is presented in HTML format. HTML changed the Internet from a purely plain-text–based resource to one that can present graphics and font changes. An HTML page can also contain hypertext links. Links are the threads that join together the Web, enabling someone viewing a Web page to be immediately transported to another Web page (or other content) by simply selecting a linked text string or image on the page.

The primary tool for displaying HTML Web pages is the Web browser. Firefox is the featured Web browser in Fedora and RHEL systems. It can display HTML (Web pages), as well as other types of Web content. Now even file managers, made for displaying local files and folders, have been extended to be able to display Web content (see the description of Konqueror file manager in Chapter 3).

This section contains general information about the Web and some specific hints for using several different browsers (in particular, Firefox) to browse the Web from your Fedora or RHEL system.

Uniform Resource Locators

To visit a site on the Internet, you either type a URL into the location box on your browser or click a link (either on a Web page or from a menu or button on the browser). Although URLs are commonplace these days — you can find them on everything from business cards to cereal boxes — you may not know how URLs are constructed. The URL form is as follows:

```
protocol://host-domain/path
```

The protocol identifies the kind of content that you are requesting. By far, the most common protocol you come across is Hypertext Transfer Protocol (HTTP). HTTP is the protocol used to request Web pages. In addition to HTTP, however, there are other protocols that might appear at the beginning of a Web address. Instead of showing you a Web page, these other types of protocols may display different kinds of information in your browser, or open a completely different application for working with the content.

Table 9-1 lists some of the protocols that can appear in a Web URL. (Some of these are no longer supported in modern browsers, as noted in the table.)

Table 9-1: Protocols in Web URLs

Protocol Name	Description
http	Hypertext Transfer Protocol. Used to identify HTML Web pages and related content. The secure version is Hypertext Transfer Protocol over Secure Socket Layer (https).
file	Identifies a file on a specific host. Most often used to display a file from your local computer.
ftp	File Transfer Protocol. Identifies a location where there are file archives from which you might want to download files.
gopher	Gopher Protocol. Provides databases of text-based documents that are distributed across the Internet. (Gopher is nearly obsolete.)
mailto	Electronic Mail Address. Identifies an e-mail address, such as mailto:joe@example.com. (Usually opens a mail composer.)
news	USENET newsgroup. Identifies a newsgroup, such as news://news.example.com/comp.os.linux.networking. If you type a similar address into Seamonkey, a window appears with the newsgroup displayed from the news server you identified. (In Firefox, news is not a registered protocol by default.)
nntp	USENET news using nntp protocol.
telnet	Log in to a remote computer and begin an interactive session. An example of a telnet address is telnet://localhost. (Replace localhost with any host or IP address that allows you to log in.)
wais	Wide Area Information Server protocol. A WAIS address might look like the following: wais://handsonhistory.com/waisdb. (As with gopher, WAIS databases are nearly obsolete.)

The first part of a URL is the protocol. You don't always have to type the protocol. Most browsers are good at guessing the content you are looking for (mostly they guess HTTP). If the address you type starts with www, the browser assumes HTTP; if it starts with ftp, it assumes FTP.

The second part of a URL takes you to the computer that is hosting the Web content. By convention, Web servers begin with www (or sometimes home). However, if you type the correct protocol (usually http), you will be directed to the right service at the host computer. The next piece of this name is just the host.domain style of Internet address that is always used with the Internet (such as redhat.com, linuxtoys.net, or whitehouse.gov). An optional port number can be tacked on to the host.domain name. For example, to request the port used for HTTP services (port 80) from the host called www.linuxtoys.net, you can type http://www.linuxtoys.net:80.

> **TIP:** You can identify a specific port number to request the service attached to the port on the computer you request. A port number is a lot like a telephone extension in a big company. A main telephone number (such as the host.domain name) gets you to a company switchboard. The telephone extension (like the port number) connects you to the right person (like the service associated with a port).

The third part of a URL identifies the location of the content on the host computer. Sections in a Web page can be identified with a pound sign (#) and an identifier following the Web page location. For example, the craft section of the bsched.htm page at handsonhistory.com would appear as:

```
http://www.handsonhistory.com/bsched.htm#craft
```

The filename extension (such as .htm or .html) further identifies the content type.

Web pages

If you look at the HTML source code that produces Web pages, you see that it consists of a combination of information and markup tags, all of which are in plain-text format. The idea is to have Web pages be very portable and flexible. You can create a Web page with vi, emacs, gedit, or any text editor on any computing platform. Alternatively, simplified front-end programs can be used to provide WYSIWYG (What You See Is What You Get) interfaces that let you see what you are creating as you go.

HTML tags are set apart by right and left angle brackets. Tags come in pairs, with a beginning tag, the information, and then an ending tag. The beginning tag contains the tag name, while an ending tag contains a forward slash (/) and the tag name. Here is a minimal HTML page:

```
<html>
<head>
<title>Greetings from Wisconsin</title>
</head>
<body>
Here we are in beautiful Madison.
```

```
</body>
</html>
```

You can see that the document begins and ends with HTML tags (`<html>` and `</html>`). The beginning part of the Web page is contained within the `head` tags. The body of the page is contained within the `body` tags. The title of the page is set apart by `title` tags.

Between the beginning and ending `body` tags, you can add all kinds of stuff. You can have different types of bulleted or numbered lists. You can have headings, images, and text. More complex pages can include forms, dynamic HTML (which changes the content as you move or select items), or special data. Figure 9-2 shows an example of a Web page as it appears in Firefox.

Figure 9-2: Many Web pages contain text, images, headings, and links.

Some of the HTML code that was used to create the Web page shown in Figure 9-2 is shown here. The title of the Web page appears between two `title` tags:

```
<title>Swan Bay Folk Art Center - American Crafts
in Port Republic, NJ</title>
```

The following code is used to create a link that opens a new mail message window:

```
<A HREF="mailto:webmaster@handsonhistory.com">Contact Us</A>;
```

The text `Contact Us` is a link to an e-mail address. When someone clicks that link, a new message window appears, allowing that person to send e-mail to that address.

```
<A HREF="bsched.htm">
New Basket Class! </A>
```

The words `New Basket Class!` point to a link to another HTML page. If someone were to click on those words, the `bsched.htm` page would appear.

Browsing the Web with Firefox

Firefox Web browser t offers real competition to Microsoft Internet Explorer. Firefox is lightweight (so it performs fast), includes many ease-of-use features, and was built with security as a high priority. If you haven't switched to Fedora yet, you can get Firefox for Windows, Mac OS X, and other Linux systems. With the Fedora CD and DVD that come with this book, you can try Firefox out right now.

Firefox version 3 is offered for the first time in Fedora 9. This version features great improvements in performance, as well as new security, ease-of-use, and personalization features.

> **NOTE:** When this book went to press, it was not clear if the final Firefox 3 or the Firefox 3 release candidate would be included with Fedora 9. However, the expectation is that within a few weeks of the Fedora 9 release, a firefox package update (with `yum` or PackageKit) would download and install the final Firefox 3.

Figure 9-3 shows an example of the Firefox Web browser:

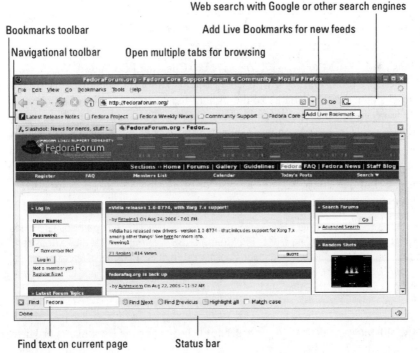

Figure 9-3: Firefox makes it easy to search, do tabbed browsing, and get plugins in a secure way.

Because Firefox is the default browser for the current Fedora and RHEL, if you have done an install that includes the desktop, Firefox should already be installed. (If it's not, you need to install the firefox package from the Fedora DVD.) To start Firefox from your Fedora desktop, either select the globe icon from your panel or select Internet → Firefox Web Browser from the Applications menu. Firefox makes some of its best features available right in its main window (as shown in Figure 9-3). Here are some examples:

- **Tabbed browsing** — Instead of opening multiple windows to have several Web pages available at a time, Firefox includes a very efficient tabbed browsing feature. Select File → New Tab (or by pressing Ctrl+T). Then type the URL for the new Web page you want. Figure 9-3 shows the Firefox window with two open browsing tabs. Tab options set from the Preferences window (Edit → Preferences → Tabs) can be set to automatically force new links to be opened in a new tab or open links from other applications in a new tab. This can help preserve screen real estate by containing multiple Web pages in one window.

    To close a tab, open a new tab, bookmark one or a group of tabs, or reload one or all tabs, right-click one of the tabs at the top of the pane. A drop-down menu enables you to choose the function you want. One of the easiest ways to open a link in a tab is to right-click over a link on an HTML page. Select the Open Link in New Tab choice.

- **Live Bookmarks** — For Web sites that have RSS news and blog headlines available, a small RSS logo icon appears in the location box of the Firefox screen (see Figure 9-3). Using that icon, you can bookmark the advertised RSS feed so that live headlines from that site can be displayed from your Bookmarks menu.

    Try a site such as `http://fedoraforum.org`. Click the RSS button. When prompted, choose to Subscribe Now to Live Bookmarks for the site. Select Bookmarks, and then select the new bookmark. To the right of the bookmark, a list of articles available today from the site appears. You can click to go straight to an article that looks interesting to you. Or, you can choose Open in Tabs to open all the articles in separate tabs.

    There are many sites that include RSS support these days. Try `packers.com`, `cnn.com`, `slashdot.org`, `abcnews.com`, or `cbssportsline.com` for other examples of sites that offer RSS news feeds.

> **NOTE:** If you visit a Web site that you know is an RSS site, but the headlines you want appear in XML code, it means the page is not identifying itself to Firefox as an RSS site. You can add a Live Bookmark for the site anyway by selecting Bookmarks → Manage Bookmarks. From the Bookmarks Manager screen, select File → New Live Bookmark. When prompted, enter a name for the live bookmark, and then type (or cut and paste) the location of the RSS page into the Feed Location box and click OK. That new live bookmark, and today's articles from that site, will appear on your Bookmarks list.

- **Using the sidebar** — Select View → Sidebar to choose to have Bookmarks or History appear as a sidebar in the Firefox window. Add your own bookmarks, return to pages from your history list, or use the Search box to search for content from those lists. Type Ctrl+B and Ctrl+H to toggle on and off Bookmarks and History sidebars, respectively.

- **Web searches** — A box for doing keyword searches from Google is built right into the Firefox navigation toolbar. A drop-down menu lets you choose to search Yahoo!, Answers.com, Creative Commons, Amazon.com, or eBay. Or select "Manage Search Engines" from the drop-down list to go to the Firefox Search Engines page, where you can choose from more than 20 different search engines.

- **Finding text** — Click Edit → Find in This Page to open a toolbar at the bottom of the window for searching the current page for a text string. This allows you to search the page for text without having a little pop-up window get in your way. After typing the text string, click Find Next or Find Previous to search for the string. You can also click Highlight to highlight all instances of the string on the page.

- **Resizing text on Web page** — There is a nice keyboard shortcut that lets you quickly resize the text on most Web pages in Firefox. Hold the Ctrl key and press the plus (+) or minus (-) keys. The text on the Web page (in most cases) gets larger or smaller, respectively. That page with the insanely small type font is suddenly readable. (Remember to hold the Shift key to type a + character.)

- **Checking history** — Select History → Show in Sidebar to have the History sidebar appear on the Firefox screen. From that sidebar, you can do keyword searches for sites you have visited, display the site names you have visited in various ways (by date, site name, most visited, and last visited), and browse through and select to revisit a site.

Some of the best features in Firefox are not as near the surface. In particular, Firefox was designed for safe computing, so Firefox is very careful about what it will and will not allow by default. Here are some important features of Firefox that can contribute to safe and fun Web browsing:

- **Blocking pop-ups** — In Firefox, pop-up windows are blocked by default. To see or change how pop-ups are handled from Firefox, select Edit → Preferences and select Content. The Block Pop-ups Windows option is either selected (to block pop-ups) or unselected (to allow them). If pop-ups are blocked, you can select Exceptions to add selected sites from which you will allow pop-ups.

- **Advanced Security Features** — With Firefox, you have a lot of control over what content can be played and what software can be downloaded to your computer. You can view or change many security features from the Preferences window (select Edit → Preferences). The Content tab lets you choose to enable Java or JavaScript, load images, or block pop-up windows. The Privacy tab lets you manage cookies, passwords, history, and cache information.

If you have been using Firefox for a while, but are new to Firefox 3, there are many new features you may find interesting. Inside Firefox 3 is the new Gecko 1.9 Web rendering platform, with thousands of features to improve performance, rendering and stability. You should notice improvements in color management and fonts.

One improvement that connects you to several new features in Firefox 3 is the location box. Figure 9-4 shows two location box examples that illustrate new ways of dealing with the Web sites you request:

Figure 9-4: Verify sites and work with bookmarks from the location box.

In Figure 9-4, the upper example shows what happens when you click on the icon on the left side of the location box when visiting a secured site. You can see that Equifax verifies the authenticity of the site and that communications are encrypted. By selecting the star on the right side, you can work with bookmark information for a page and modify that information. Other icons that might appear in the Location box include a variety of security warnings, such as warnings for possible forged or dangerous content.

Go to the Mozilla Firefox site (www.mozilla.org/products/firefox) for more information on Firefox. For help transitioning from Internet Explorer to Firefox, see the Firefox site at www.mozilla.org/products/firefox/switch.html.

Setting up Firefox

There are many things you can do to configure Firefox to run like a champ. The following sections describe some ways to customize your browsing experience in Firefox.

Setting Navigator preferences

You can set your Firefox preferences in the Preferences window. To open Firefox Preferences, click Edit → Preferences. The Preferences window appears, as shown in Figure 9-5.

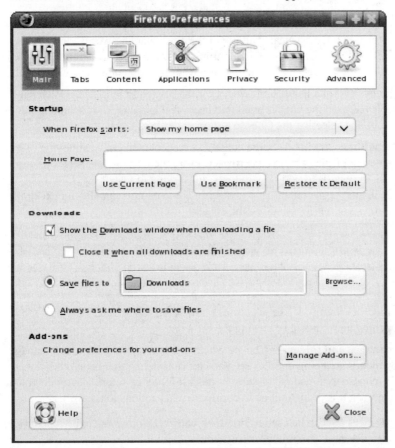

Figure 9-5: Change settings for navigating the Web from the Firefox Preferences window.

The following list shows some preferences that you might want to change from the Firefox Preferences window:

- **Choosing a home page** — To choose a home page from the Main tab, you can simply type a URL in the Location box. It can be a local file (file://) or a Web page (http://). You can also have multiple home pages, with each appearing on a separate tab when Firefox starts, by separating URLs with a pipe (for example, linuxtoys.net|redhat.com).

  To fill in your home page locations, you can also select buttons. Use Current Pages adds the current pages on all tabs of your browser as your home pages. The Use Bookmarks button lets you choose home pages from you bookmarks list. Selecting Use Blank Page sets your home page to `about:blank`.

- **Saving browsing information** — Select the Privacy tab to choose how information about your Web browsing is saved. On the Privacy tab, you can choose how to save data related to your browsing history, data you enter into forms, passwords, downloaded files, and cookies. You can select to clear your history, forms data, passwords, download history, cookies, and cached Web pages. Clearing this information is a good idea if you are using Firefox on someone else's machine and want to keep your browsing private.

- **Setting languages** — Set a list of preferences for the particular language a Web page should be displayed in, if the page is available in several languages, by selecting the Content category and selecting the Choose button under Languages.

- **Blocking or enabling content** — Some content you encounter can be annoying or even dangerous to play or display from your browser. From the Content tab, select what to allow and block in regards to pop-up windows, sites trying to install extensions or themes, image display, ava content, and javascript content. You can also set exceptions to the general rules you set for handling the content just mentioned.

> **NOTE:** The latest Firefox release helps you block forged Web sites by displaying a Suspected Web Forgery pop-up message when it encounters a page that has been reported as forged. You can choose to not display the page or ignore the warning. If you suspect a forged page that doesn't display that message, select Help → Report Web Forgery to try to add the page to the Google Web Forgery list.

- **Defining tabbed browsing** — Use selections on the Tabs tab to determine how tabs are used when opening new content or closing the browser.

- **Download manager and folder** — Choose whether or not to see a download manager when file downloads are being done. Also, you can choose to either be asked where to place each file chosen to download or select a default folder to automatically download your files. Select View & Edit Actions to configure what actions to take.

The Advanced Preferences tab can be used to fine-tune your Web browsing experience. Here are some Advanced Preferences that might interest you:

- **General settings** — Some settings on the General tab in the Advanced section let you change accessibility settings, browsing features (such as auto resizing of windows and scrolling) and system defaults.

- **Choosing connection settings** — If you have direct access to the Internet, you don't need to change any proxy settings. However, if you need to access the Internet via a proxy server, you can identify the location of that server (or servers) by selecting Network → Connection Settings from the Advanced tab. To access the Web via proxy servers, you must explicitly identify the proxy server to use for each type of content you request (HTTP, SSL, FTP, Gopher, and SOCKS).

- **Get browser updates** — From the Update tab, Firefox can be set to automatically check for updates available for the search engine or installed extensions and themes. Select Show Update History to see a history of updates you have installed for Firefox.

- **Choose security settings** — From the Encryption tab of the Advanced section, choose which protocols (SSL and TLS) are acceptable for Firefox to use for secure browsing. There is also a Certificates section that lets you manage certificates to verify the authenticity of secure sites or authenticate yourself to remote sites. (See the "Securing Firefox" section for further information on securing Web browsing with Firefox.)

Extending Firefox

Firefox can handle most standard Web content (HTML, JPEG, text files) without any trouble. As with any browser, however, some content requires additions of plug-ins or helper applications to be able to play or display that content. Firefox also allows you to add extensions that let you enhance the features available in Firefox.

Using plug-ins

From Firefox, you can see what plug-ins are installed to Firefox by typing **about:plugins** in the location bar. As Firefox is delivered in Fedora and RHEL systems, you will have at least a NPAPI plug-ins wrapper installed by default. The NPAPI plug-in allows you to use some plug-ins that were not built for Linux.

To find plug-ins that will work for Firefox in Linux systems, try the Mozilla Plugins page (http://plugindoc.mozdev.org/linux.html). Here are a few plug-ins that you might want to add to Firefox:

- **Adobe Acrobat Plug-in** (www.adobe.com/support/downloads) — Displays files in the Adobe Systems PDF (Portable Document Format) format. (Without this plug-in installed, Firefox will use the evince command to display PDF files in a separate window.)

- **DjVu Plug-in** (djvu.sourceforge.net) — Displays images in DjVu image compression technology. This plug-in is from AT&T.

- **Adobe Flash Player** (www.adobe.com/products/flashplayer) — With the explosion of YouTube and other sites carrying Flash video content, the Adobe Flash Player has become indispensible on desktop systems. By default, Fedora now includes the open source swfdec-mozilla package to play Flash content.

  However, if you have problems playing Flash with swfdec-mozilla (as some have), you can uninstall that package and get an official (non-open source) Flash player directly from Adobe. Follow the links from the Adobe Flash Player site to find the Linux plug-in you need. I recommend the Yum version, which will install the plug-in and make automatic updates of the flash player as they are available.

- **MPlayer Plug-in** (`http://mplayerplug-in.sourceforge.net`) — This plug-in implements the popular mplayer video player to play embedded video content in the browser window. An RPM package of this plug-in (mplayerplug-in) is available from `http://rpm.livna.org`. See Chapter 5 for more on using `rpm.livna.org`.

- **Java Runtime Environment** (`java-1.7.0-icedtea`) — To be able to play Java and JavaScript content from your Web browser, you need a plug-in that provides the functionality you get with the Java Runtime Environment Web plug-in from Sun Microsystems (`http://java.com/en/download/index.jsp`). Instead of using proprietary code from Sun, however, Fedora Project has added a completely free equivalent version by combining software from the OpenJDK project and IcedTea project (`http://fedoraproject.org/wiki/Features/IcedTea`).

  To make sure the plug-in is working, restart Firefox and type `about:plugins` in the location box. You'll see a list of Java content handled by the GCJ Web Browser Plugin. You can also try different Web sites that contain Java content to try out your Java plug-in. For example, you can visit the Java.com test page:

```
http://java.com/en/download/help/testvm.xml
```

  If you are unable to see the Java content, open the PackageKit Update Applet and look for an updated nspluginwrapper package. Installing that updated package and restarting your Firefox browser should be allow you to see the Java content.

  To make sure the plug-in is working, restart Firefox and type `about:plugins` in the location box. You'll see a list of Java content handled by the GCJ Web Browser Plugin.

> **NOTE:** If you are concerned about the experimental nature of IcedTea at the moment, there are other ways of getting a Java Runtime Environment browser plug-in working in Fedora. There are RPMs of that software available from the `dag.wieers.com` Fedora repository. Others have had luck getting the software from `www.jpackage.org`. In the past, I have gotten the package directly from sun.com to work, but have found it more difficult to get working in the latest Fedora release. Because getting Java Runtime Environment software working in Linux is a moving target, so you may want to build your own RPM (see `www.fedorafaq.org/#java`).

- **CrossOver Plugin** (`www.codeweavers.com`) — Linux plug-ins are not yet available for some of the more interesting and popular plug-ins. QuickTime 5 movies, Shockwave Director multimedia content, and various Microsoft movie, file, and data formats simply will not play natively in Firefox. Using software built on WINE for Linux on x86-based processors, CodeWeavers created the CrossOver Plugin. Although no longer offered as a separate product (you must buy the entire Crossover Office product for US$39.95), the CrossOver Plugin lets you play some content that you could not otherwise use in Linux. (Download a demo from `www.codeweavers.com/site/products/download_trial`.)

  After you install the CrossOver Plugin, you see a nice Plugin Setup window that enables you to selectively install plug-ins for QuickTime, Windows Media Player, Shockwave,

Flash, iTunes, and Lotus Notes, as well as Microsoft Word, Excel, and PowerPoint viewers. (Support for later versions of these content formats may be available by the time you read this.) You can also install other multimedia plug-ins, as well as a variety of fonts to use with those plug-ins.

For some plug-ins, you will be prompted for where you want to put the plug-in. You can either install them so they are available to all users on the system or only to the current user. To add a plug-in for the current user only, place it in the `~/.mozilla/plugins` directory. To have the plug-in available for all users who run Firefox on the system, put the plug-in in the `/usr/lib/firefox-*/plugins` directory.

> **NOTE:** When Firefox doesn't have a plug-in assigned to handle a particular data type, a pop-up window asks if you want to use the default application from your desktop environment to handle the data. For GNOME, the `/usr/share/applications/defaults.list` file defines system-wide default applications. For your own desktop, you can change the defaults used to open a particular file type as follows: Open the Nautilus file manager; right-click on any file of the type you want to change; select Properties; select the Open With tab; and choose the application you want to use for that file type from the list. If the application you want to add is not on the list, click Add to add it to the list.

While plug-ins are available for playing select types of content, add-ons can be used to add features to the browser itself.

Getting Add-ons

To extend Firefox to handle content beyond what is delivered with Fedora or RHEL, start from the Mozilla.org Firefox product page (`http://www.mozilla.com/en-US/firefox/`). From there, follow links to Firefox Add-ons. Here are some of the most popular add-ons to Firefox that are available from Mozilla.org:

> **NOTE:** Some Firefox add-ons have been known to cause performance problems with Firefox, primarily from using excessive amounts of memory. If you are having poor performance with Firefox, close all Firefox windows, then restart Firefox in safe mode from a Terminal window by typing the following:
>
> `firefox -safe-mode`
>
> Refer to `http://kb.mozillazine.org/Safe_Mode` for further information on using safe mode to debug firefox problems.

- **Downloading tool (FlashGot)** — If you like to download groups of files from your Web browser, FlashGot can be a very useful tool. With FlashGot installed, you can select to download an individual file, files identified by highlighting links on a Web page, or all files linked from the current Web page. There is also a Build Gallery feature that lets you identify a range of filenames to download at once. When FlashGot is installed, you can access it from Firefox by selecting Tools → FlashGot, and then choosing a feature from the menu. In Fedora, FlashGot passes requests to kGet to complete the download. You can get other download tools to use instead of kGet, such as wget.

- **Selectively block ads (Adblock)** — Using Adblock, you can selectively prevent ads from being displayed on the Web pages you visit. With Adblock installed, an Adblock button appears on the lower-right corner of Firefox. Click that button to see a window containing items on the current page you want to block. Right-click on an image and select Adblock Image to choose to block that image. Use an asterisk to block all content from a particular site (for example, `www.example.com/*`). Open the Adblock preferences window from Firefox (Tools → Adblock → Preferences) to see, edit, or remove blocked sites. With Firefox 1.5 or later, you should use Adblock Plus instead of Adblock.

- **Access FTP servers (FireFTP)** — Contains a useful client application that runs in Firefox for accessing with FTP servers. There is also a FireFTP button add-on for accessing FireFTP from the toolbar.

- **Block Flash animations (Flashblock)** — Prevent Flash animations from playing in your Firefox browser window. Can be particularly useful for dial-up users who don't want to take a performance hit when a visited site tries to play unrequested Flash content.

- **Improve tab browsing (Tabbrowser Preferences)** — Although Firefox already gives you some nice features for using tabs to keep multiple Web pages open in the same Firefox window, Tabbrowser Preferences takes those features a step further. Select Edit → Preferences → Tabbed Browsing. The Tabbed Browsing selections let you refine how tabs work in Firefox. You can set what motion selects tabs (such as mouse-over as opposed to clicking), put tabs on the bottom instead of the top, or choose whether or not to load the home page in a new tab.

- **Watch your weather (ForecastFox)** — With ForecastFox, the latest weather for any region you select can be just a click away in Firefox. After you install ForecastFox and restart Firefox, a pop-up window enables you to configure ForecastFox options. Select at least Find Code, to choose the area in which you want to keep up on weather. Save your options and a weather icon appears in the lower-right corner of Firefox. Move your mouse over that icon to see a quick view of the current weather. Double-click the icon to have a more detailed weather report displayed from `www.weather.com`.

After you have installed an add-on, you need to restart Firefox for it to take effect. In some cases, a change to an add-on's option will also require you to restart Firefox.

If you want to uninstall an add-on, change an add-on's options, or get more add-ons, select Tools → Add-ons from Firefox. The window that appears shows you a list of installed add-ons and lets you change them. Select Browse All Add-ons to go directly to the Mozilla Firefox Add-ons page.

> **NOTE:** On the Firefox Add-ons page, look for the Firefox Extensions RSS feed (an orange-striped icon in the Location box). You can use that RSS feed to be notified when new Firefox Add-ons become available. As new versions of Add-ons become available, you should install them since they might fix security issues.

Changing Firefox themes

There are several themes available for Firefox for changing the look and feel of your Firefox window. From the Mozilla update site (`https://addons.mozilla.org`), select Themes. When you download a theme for Firefox, it knows that it is a Firefox theme and, on the download window, it gives you the option to install the theme by clicking on the Use Theme button.

To change a theme later or get more Themes, select Tools → Add-ons → Themes. After you have installed a new theme and selected it as your current theme, you need to restart Firefox for the new theme to take effect. From the dialog window, you can click on the "Get More Themes" link to download other themes. The link takes you to the Mozilla update site.

Securing Firefox

Security has been one of the strongest reasons for people switching to Firefox. By prohibiting the most unsafe types of content from playing in Firefox, and by warning you of potentially dangerous or annoying content before displaying it, Firefox has become the Web browser of choice for many security-conscious people. Here are some ways that Firefox helps make your Web browsing more secure:

- **ActiveX** — Because of major security flaws found in ActiveX, Firefox will simply not play ActiveX content. If you absolutely must be able to play ActiveX content, a plug-in is in development to provide controlled support for ActiveX. Follow the progress of this project at the Mozilla ActiveX Project home page (`www.iol.ie/~locka/ mozilla/mozilla.htm`). I don't recommend doing this, but it's up to you.

- **Pop-ups** — Pop-up windows are disabled by default in Firefox. You can set preferences to enable all pop-ups or to enable only pop-ups from selected sites.

- **Privacy preferences** — From the Privacy window in Firefox (select Edit → Preferences, and then click the Privacy button), you can clear different categories of stored private information from your browser in a single click. This is a particularly good feature if you have just used a computer that is not yours to browse the Web. You can select to individually clear your History, information saved in forms you might have filled in, any passwords saved by the browser, history of what you have downloaded, cookies, and cached files. If you want all private data cleared, click the Settings button, choose the categories you want cleared, and select OK. You could also select Clear private data when closing Firefox to have all data cleared when you exit Firefox.

- **Certificates** — In Firefox, you can install and manage certificates that can be used for validating a Web site and safely performing encryption of communications to that site. Using the Preferences window (select Edit → Preferences, and then click the Security button), you can manage certificates under the Encryption Tab. Select View Certificates to display a window that lets you import new certificates or view certificates that are already installed. Firefox will check that certificates you encounter are valid (and warn you if they are not). See Chapter 14 for more information on using certificates.

Along with all the excellent security features built into Firefox, it's important that you incorporate good security practices in your Web browsing. Download and install software only from sites that are secure and known to you to be safe. For any online transactions, make sure you are communicating with a secure site (look for the `https` protocol in the location box and closed lock icon in the lower-right corner of the screen). Be careful about being redirected to another Web site when doing a financial transaction. An IP address in the site's address or misspellings on a screen where you enter credit card information are warning signs that you have been directed to an untrustworthy site.

Because new exploits are being discovered all the time, it's important that you keep your Web browser up to date. That means that, at least, you need to get updates of Firefox from the Fedora project as they become available (see Chapter 5 for information on using yum and PackageKit to get the latest software). To keep up on the latest security news and information about Firefox and other Mozilla products, refer to the Mozilla Security Center (`www.mozilla.org/security`).

Tips for using Firefox

There are so many nice features in Firefox, it's hard to cover all of them. Just to point you toward a few more fun and useful features, here are some extra tips about Firefox you might enjoy:

- **Add smart keywords** — Many Web sites include their own search boxes to allow you to look for information on their sites. With Firefox, you can assign a smart keyword to any search box on the Web, and then use that keyword from the location bar in the Firefox browser to search that site.

  For example, go to the Linux Documentation Project site (`http://tldp.org`). Right-click in the Search/Resources search box. Select Add a Keyword for this Search from the menu that appears. Add a name (Linux Documentation) and a keyword (tldp) and select Add to add the keyword to your Bookmarks.

  After you have added the keyword, you can use it by simply entering the keyword and one or more search terms to the Firefox location box (on the navigation toolbar). For example, I entered `tldp Lego Mindstorms` and came up with a list of HOW-TOs for using Lego Mindstorms in Linux.

- **Check config** — Firefox has hundreds of configuration preferences available to set as you please. You can see those options by typing **about:config** into the location box. For true/false options, you can simply click the preference name to toggle it between the two values. For other preferences, click the preference to enter a value into a pop-up box. While many of these values can be changed through the Preferences menu (Edit → Preferences), some technical people prefer to look at settings in a list like the one shown on the about:config page. The `about:buildconfig` page lists the options used to build Firefox.

- **Multiple home pages** — Instead of just having one home page, you can have a whole set of home pages. When you start Firefox, a separate tab will open in the Firefox window for each address you identify in your home page list. To do this, create multiple tabs (File → New Tab) and enter the address for each page you want in your list of home pages. Then select Edit → Preferences → Main and click the Use Current Pages button. The next time you open Firefox, it will start with the selected tabs open to the home pages you chose. (Clicking the Home icon will open new tabs for all the home pages.)

There are many more things you can do with Firefox than I have covered in this chapter. If you have questions about Firefox features or you just want to dig up some more cool stuff about Firefox, I recommend checking out the MozillaZine forum for Firefox support (`http://forums.mozillazine.org/viewforum.php?f=38`). There is a sticky link there to Miscellaneous Firefox Tips and a good FAQ post.

Using text-based Web browsers

If you become a Linux administrator or power user, over time you will inevitably find yourself working on a computer from a remote login or where there is no desktop GUI available. At some point while you are in that state, you will probably want to check an HTML file or a Web page. To solve the problem, Fedora and RHEL include several text-based Web browsers.

With text-based Web browsers, any HTML file available from the Web, your local file system, or a computer where you're remotely logged in can be accessed from your shell. There's no need to fire up your GUI or read pages of HTML markup if you just want to take a peek at the contents of a Web page. Besides letting you call up Web pages, move around with those pages, and follow links to other pages, some of these text-based browsers even display graphics right in a Terminal window!

Which text-based browser you use is a matter of which you are more comfortable with. Browsers that are available include:

- **links** — With links (elinks package), you can open a file or a URL, and then traverse links from the pages you open. Use search forward (`/string`) and back (`?string`) features to find text strings in pages. Use up and down arrows to go forward and back among links. Then press Enter to go to the current link. Use the right and left arrow keys to go forward and back among pages you have visited. Press Esc to see a menu bar of features to select from.

  While links doesn't allow you to display images inline, if you select an image it will be displayed on your desktop in gThumb image viewer (by default). You also have the option of saving the image to your local hard disk.

- **lynx** — The lynx browser has a good set of help files that come with it (press the ? key). Step through pages using the Spacebar. Although lynx can display pages containing frames, it cannot display them in the intended positioning. Use the arrow keys to display the selected link (right arrow), go back to the previous document (left arrow), select the previous link (up arrow), and select the next link (down arrow).

As with links, lynx lets you display a selected image. However, lynx uses ImageMagick instead of gThumb to display the image you choose.

- **w3m** — The w3m text-based Web browser can display HTML pages containing text, links, frames, and tables. It even tries to display images (that feature has improved a lot in recent releases). There are both English and Japanese help files available (press H with w3m running). You can also use w3m to page through an HTML document in plain text (for example, cat index.html | w3m -T text/html). Use the Page Up and Page Down keys to page through a document. Press Enter on a link to go to that link. Press the B key to go back to the previous link. Search forward and back for text using / and ? keys, respectively.

> **NOTE**: You must install the elinks package to get links, the lynx package to get lynx, and the w3m package to get w3m. All of them are included with Fedora.

The w3m command seems the most sophisticated of these browsers. It features a nice default font selection, seems to handle frames neatly, and its use of colors also makes it easy to use. The links browser lets you use the mouse to cut and paste text.

You can start any of these text-based Web browsers by giving it a filename, or if you have an active connection to the network, a Web address. For example, to read the w3m documentation (which is in HTML format) with a w3m browser, you can type the following from a Terminal window or other shell interface:

```
$ w3m /usr/share/doc/w3m-0*/doc/MANUAL.html
```

An HTML version of the W3M Manual is displayed, or you can give w3m a URL to a Web page, such as the following:

```
$ w3m www.handsonhistory.com
```

After a page is open, you can begin viewing the page and moving around to links included in the page. Start by using the arrow keys to move around and select links. Use the Page Up and Page Down keys to page through text.

Communicating with E-mail

Running a close second to Web browsers is the e-mail reader (referred to in network standards terms as a Mail User Agent, or MUA). Evolution is the recommended e-mail client for Fedora and RHEL. However, Mozilla Thunderbird is the new kid on the block of e-mail clients.

Other e-mail options include the Sylpheed mail client and the KDE KMail program. There's also a groupware application that comes with KDE called Kontact that includes an e-mail client. Mail programs that have been around in Linux and other UNIX systems since the time when most mail was plain text include mutt, pine, and mail. In other words, there is no shortage of choices for e-mail clients in Linux.

Here are some pros and cons for different e-mail clients that are available for Fedora and RHEL:

- **Evolution** — This is a full-featured e-mail client that also includes ways of managing your contacts, calendars, and tasks. Because it is so easy to use and rich in features, it provides one of the best ways to transition from Windows e-mail clients (such as Outlook). There are also features in Evolution for connecting to Microsoft Exchange and Novell GroupWise servers. The complaint I hear most often about Evolution is that it demands a lot of resources. So, with slow-processor and low-RAM systems, you would probably find other e-mail clients less frustrating to use over time.

- **Thunderbird** — As with Firefox in the browser arena, Thunderbird is the flagship mail client from the Mozilla project. It was designed from the ground up to be secure, fast, and loaded with important features. It also has versions available on Windows and Mac OS X, so you can use the same mail client on different platforms. Not much on the downside here: Because it is fairly new, they are still shaking out some of the bugs in Thunderbird. Also it doesn't include a lot of the groupware features you get in Evolution. (However, you can check out the new calendar feature, just added to the Thunderbird section of this chapter.)

- **KMail** — People who become frustrated with Evolution performance seem to often switch to KMail. Because KMail is a KDE desktop project, it integrates particularly well with the KDE desktop environment. However, many people insist that KMail runs well in GNOME, too. The look-and-feel is similar to Evolution (folders in the left column and message headers and message to the right). As with Evolution, KMail can easily integrate with clamav (antivirus software) and spamassassin (e-mail spam-checker software).

- **Sylpheed** — The Sylpheed mail client is good for low-end computers, where you still want to use a graphical mail client. Sylpheed is used on bootable business card Linux systems, such as Damn Small Linux. You can install Sylpheed simply by typing `yum install sylpheed`.

- **Text-based mail** — Many techical people who often work from the command line prefer to use a text-based mail reader as well. That way, they can do remote shell login or just not even fire up a GUI to read their mail. The mutt e-mail client will run in a shell, handle some more modern features well (such as attachments), and beat out any graphical e-mail client for performance by a wide margin. The downside is that the learning curve is bigger than you will have with point-and-click interfaces.

After covering some e-mail basics, this section leads you through the steps that allow you to use e-mail with Evolution and Thunderbird. If you are interested in text-based, command-driven mail tools, some of which have been around UNIX systems for many years, you will also find descriptions of many of those commands in this section.

E-mail basics

E-mail is one of the oldest uses of computer networks — predating the Web by more than 20 years. In fact, e-mail was one of the first applications used to transport information on the Internet, when the Internet consisted of only a few computers.

Today, there are millions of users around the world who have e-mail addresses. Although there are several different styles of e-mail addressing, by far the most popular e-mail address format is the domain style address (used with the Internet and other TCP/IP networks). The e-mail address consists of a user name and domain name, separated by an @ sign. For example:

```
webmaster@handsonhistory.com
```

As someone using e-mail, you need an e-mail client (such as Evolution) that enables you to get your e-mail, manage your e-mail messages, and send messages. Although mail messages were originally only plain text, and still are in most cases today, there are some newer features that let you enhance the kinds of content that you can send and receive, such as:

- **Attachments** — You can attach files to your mail messages. Attachments can contain data that you couldn't ordinarily keep in a mail message, such as a binary program, a word processing file, or an image. The recipient of the mail attachment can either save the file to a local hard disk or open it in a program designed to read the attachment.

- **HTML** — The same stuff used to create Web pages can be included in mail messages you create with certain mail clients (including Evolution). This enables you to change fonts and colors, add backgrounds, insert images, or add HTML features.

> **CAUTION:** To people who use text-based mail clients, HTML content can't be interpreted (it shows up as a bunch of markers that overwhelm the text). In general, don't use HTML in messages that are being distributed to a large group of people (such as in a newsgroup). Also, e-mail was never intended to transport large attachments. For larger files, try copying to an FTP site instead of sending e-mail attachments.

Depending on the e-mail client you are using, e-mail management features let you direct incoming e-mail into different folders and sort messages by date, sender, or other attributes. E-mail sending features let you reply to messages, forward messages, and draw names from an address book or directory server.

> **CROSS-REFERENCE:** If you don't have an e-mail account, you can set up your own e-mail server using Fedora. For information on setting up a mail server, see Chapter 19.

If you want to change your default e-mail application in GNOME from Evolution, select System → Preferences → Personal → Preferred Applications. When the Preferred Applications window appears, select the Mail Reader tab and choose the mail reader you want from the Select drop-down box. (You can also change your default Web browser and Terminal window from the Preferred Applications window.) In KDE, from the main KDE menu, select

System Setting → Default Applications → Email Client. Then use either the default KMail client or select "Use a different email client" select the button to select from a list of known applications you can choose as your email client.

Using Evolution e-mail

Evolution is the preferred application for sending and managing e-mail on default GNOME desktops for Fedora and RHEL. Fedora developers gave it a prime spot on the desktop, just to the right of the System menu and Web browser icon. After you launch Evolution for the first time and run the Startup Assistant, the Evolution window appears, showing the different types of operations you can perform.

Figure 9-6 shows an example of the Evolution window.

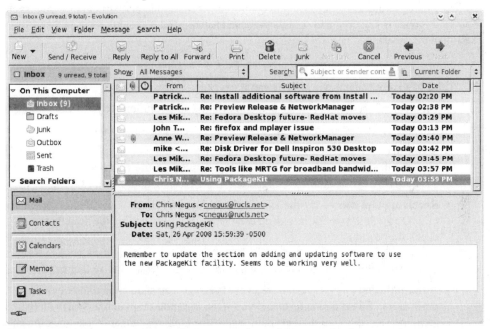

Figure 9-6: Evolution can be used to manage your e-mail, appointments, and tasks.

Evolution is a groupware application, combining several types of applications that help groups of people communicate and work together. The features of Evolution include:

- **Mail** — Includes a complete set of features for getting, reading, managing, composing, and sending e-mail on one or more e-mail accounts.

- **Calendars** — Create and manage appointments on your personal calendar. You can e-mail appointment information to others and do keyword searches of your calendar.

- **Contacts** — Create contact information for friends and associates, such as names, addresses, and telephone numbers. A Categories feature helps you remember who gets birthday and anniversary gifts.

- **Tasks** — Organize ongoing tasks into folders.

- **Exchange** — Connect to an exchange server. If your organization gets its mail from an Exchange server, the Evolution Connector software (included with this version of Evolution) lets you configure this e-mail client to access that server.

In the next section, I focus on the Preferences and e-mail features of Evolution.

Setting Evolution preferences

To really make Evolution your own, you can set preferences that are particular to you, such as how your e-mail is gathered and sorted. You can change Mail Accounts settings by performing the following steps:

1. From the Evolution main window, select Edit → Preferences.
2. Click Mail Accounts in the left column.
3. Select the mail account to change and click Edit. The Evolution Account Editor appears.
4. Here are a few items you may want to change for your e-mail account:

    - **Signature** — Have a signature appear on every e-mail message you send. Either click the Default signature box and select Autogenerated (to use name and e-mail address as a signature) or click Add New Signature to create a signature in a text editor.

    - **Receiving Options** — By default, Evolution doesn't check your mail server for your messages unless you ask it to. You can change that by clicking the Automatically check for new mail every... box on the Receiving Options tab, to have Evolution check your mail server for your mail every 10 minutes. Once downloaded, each message is erased from the server. Select Leave messages on server to change that behavior.

    - **Automatic copy** — You can have every message you send copied to one or more other users. This is a nice feature if you write important e-mail that you want to archive to a different e-mail account. Select the Defaults tab, and then click the check box next to Always Cc or Always Bcc. Next, type the correct e-mail address.

    - **Security** — To help validate that you are who you say you are and keep your e-mail private, Evolution lets you use PGP/GPG (Pretty Good Privacy/GNU Privacy Guard) encryption keys. Click the Security tab, and then enter your PGP/GPG Key ID. Choose settings for signing and encryption as appropriate.

5. Click OK to apply the changes.

Receiving, composing, and sending e-mail

Evolution offers a full set of features for sending, receiving, and managing your e-mail. The folder bar in the left part of the Evolution window makes it easy to create and use multiple mail folders.

Here are some tips for sending, reading, and receiving mail:

- **Read e-mail** — Click Inbox in the Folder column. Your messages appear to the right.

- **Delete e-mail** —After you have read a message, select it and press the Delete key. Click View → Hide Deleted Messages to toggle whether or not you see deleted messages. Click Actions → Expunge to permanently remove all messages marked for deletion in the current folder.

- **Send and receive** — Click the Send/Receive button to send any e-mail queued to be sent and receive any e-mail waiting for you at your mail server.

- **Compose e-mail** — Click New → Mail Message (or click the New button in the toolbar). A Compose a Message window appears. Type the e-mail address, a message for the subject line, and the body of the message. Click Send when you are finished. Buttons on the Compose window let you add attachments, cut and paste text, choose a format (HTML or plain text), and sign the message (if you have set up appropriate keys).

- **Create folders** — If you like to keep old messages, you may want to save them outside your Inbox (so it won't get too crowded). Right-click on the Inbox, and then select New Folder. Type a folder name and click OK (to store it as a subfolder to your Inbox).

- **Sort messages** — With new folders created, you can easily sort messages from your Inbox to another folder. The easiest way is to simply drag and drop each message (or a set of selected messages) from the message pane to the new folder.

- **Search messages** — With your Inbox or other mail folder selected, type a keyword in the search box over your e-mail message pane and select whether to search your message subject lines, sender, recipient, or message body. Click Find Now to search for the keyword. After viewing the messages, click Clear to have the other messages reappear.

- **Filter messages** — You can take action on an e-mail message before it even lands in your Inbox. Click Tools → Filters. A Filters window appears that lets you add filters to deal with incoming or outgoing messages. Click Add to create criteria and set actions.

  For example, you could have all messages from a particular sender, subject, date, status, or size sorted to a selected folder. Or you could have messages matching your criteria deleted, assigned a color, or respond by playing a sound clip.

> **CROSS-REFERENCE:** Refer to Chapter 19 for information on using Spamassassin, along with Evolution filters, to sort out spam from your real e-mail messages. Evolution also includes built-in junk e-mail filtering, using Bayesian statistical analysis.

Besides the features mentioned in the previous sections, Evolution supports many common features, such as printing, saving, and viewing e-mail messages in various ways. The help system that comes with Evolution (click the Help button) includes a good manual, FAQ, and service for reporting bugs.

Thunderbird mail client

As a companion to its Firefox Web browser, the Mozilla project created the Thunderbird e-mail client. If you installed Thunderbird (thunderbird package) from the Fedora media that comes with this book, you can launch it from your Applications menu by selecting Internet → Thunderbird Email.

The first time you run Thunderbird, an import wizard opens, allowing you to import preferences, account settings, address books, and other data from other e-mail clients. Have information about your e-mail account (user name, incoming and outgoing servers, and so on) ready so you can enter it before Thunderbird starts up. Figure 9-7 shows an example of the Thunderbird window.

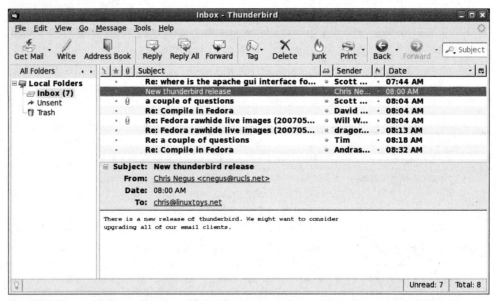

Figure 9-7: Thunderbird is an efficient e-mail client that includes advanced junkmail and message filtering.

In many ways, the layout and selections in the Thunderbird client are similar to those in Evolution. In general, however, Thunderbird seems to offer better performance than Evolution. Here are some features of Thunderbird that may interest you:

- **Display threads** — Click a small callout icon (such as a cartoon speech bubble) in the Thunderbird message pane. Then, instead of simply sorting your messages by date, subject, or sender, messages are sorted by threads (so all messages created in response to a message are sorted together).

- **Junk Mail Controls** — Select Tools → Junk Mail Controls to configure how Thunderbird deals with messages that appear to be junk mail. From the Junk Mail Controls window, select to Delete or Move to the Junk folder any messages you mark as junk mail. To manage your junk mail, click in the junk mail column (a circle with a line through it) next to a message that comes into your mailbox that is junk mail. By marking messages as junk mail, you can train Thunderbird's adaptive junk mail filter to learn when a message is junk mail and mark new messages that come in as such. Select Tools → Run Junk Mail Controls on Folder to apply junk mail filtering to the current folder.

- **HTML messages** — You have the option to create HTML markup in the mail messages you compose. When you write a mail message, from the Compose window you can choose what type of text to use, change font sizes, add bullets or numbers, set text justification, and add emoticons, to name a few features. (Note that in many news groups and mailing lists you should not use HTML markup because some people like to use text-only mail clients to access those groups.)

After using the Thunderbird e-mail client, the biggest improvement over other graphical e-mail clients I have used is performance. Sorting and searching messages is much faster than I've experienced on other clients. Switching to different mail folders and opening messages also seems to work much faster.

Text-based mail programs

If you don't mind text-based interfaces, or if you are a UNIX person who likes to sort, grep, troff, col, and cat your e-mail, there are still plenty of UNIX-like mail tools around. The mail command itself provides an easy-to-use interface for plain-text messages sent to other users on your UNIX system or on your LAN. There are text-based mail applications, such as the mutt command, that let you handle mail attachments.

Many text-based mail programs have been around for a long time, so they are full of features and have been well debugged. Because they are not used much anymore, however, don't expect them to have the latest spiffy features. As a group, text-based mail clients are not very intuitive. The following sections describe some text-based mail clients.

> **TIP:** Most of these programs use the value of your $MAIL environment variable as your local mailbox. Usually, that location is /var/spool/mail/*user*, where *user* is your user name. To set your $MAIL so that it points to your Mozilla mailbox (so you can use a text-based mail program or graphical mail client), add the following line to one of your startup files:
>
> export MAIL=$HOME/.mozilla/default/*/Mail/*hostname*/Inbox
>
> If you usually use Mozilla for mail, set this variable temporarily to try out some of these mail programs.

Mail readers and managers

The mail readers described in the following sections are text-based and use the entire screen. Although some features are different, menu bars show available options right on the screen.

Mutt mail reader

> **NOTE:** To use the mutt mail reader you must have the mutt software package installed from the DVD that come with this book or over the network using `yum`.

The `mutt` command is a text-based, full-screen mail user agent for reading and sending e-mail. The interface is quick and efficient. Type **mutt** to start the mail program. Click the up and down arrow keys to select from your listed messages. Press Enter to see a mail message and type **i** to return to the Main menu.

The menu bar indicates how to mark messages for deletion or undelete them, save messages to a directory, or reply to a message. Type **m** to compose a new message and it opens your default editor (for me, vi) to create the message. Type **y** to send the message. If you want to read mail without having your fingers leave your keyboard, mutt is a nice choice. (It even handles attachments!)

Pine mail reader

> **NOTE:** The pine package is not distributed with Fedora or RHEL, but you can get pine from the Pine project site: `www.washington.edu/pine/getpine/linux.html`. RPM packages for older versions of Fedora or RHEL are available from
> `http://rpmforge.net/user/packages/pine`.

The pine mail reader is another full-screen mail reader, but it offers many more features than does mutt. With pine, you can manage multiple mail folders. You can also manage newsgroup messages, as well as mail messages. As text-based applications go, pine is quite easy to use. It was developed by a group at the University of Washington for use by students on campus, but has become widely used in UNIX and Linux environments.

Start this mail program by typing **pine**. The following menu is displayed, from which you can select items by typing the associated letter or using up and down arrows and pressing Enter:

```
?   HELP               - Get help using Pine
C   COMPOSE MESSAGE    - Compose and send a message
I   MESSAGE INDEX      - View messages in current folder
L   FOLDER LIST        - Select a folder to view
A   ADDRESS BOOK       - Update address book
S   SETUP              - Configure Pine Options
Q   QUIT               - Leave the Pine program
```

To read your e-mail, select either I or L. Commands are listed along the bottom of the screen and change to suit the content you are viewing. Left (←) and right (→) arrow keys let you step backward and forward among the pine screens.

Mail reader

The mail command was the first mail reader for UNIX. It is text-based, but not screen-oriented. Type **mail** and you will see the messages in your mailbox. Because mail is not screen-oriented, you just get a prompt after message headings are displayed — you are expected to know what to do next. (You can use the Enter key to step through messages.) Type **?** to see which commands are available.

While in mail, type **h** to see mail headings again. Simply type a message number to see the message. Type **d#** (replacing # with a message number) to delete a message. To create a new message, type **m**. To respond to a message, type **r#** (replacing # with the message number). Type **man mail** to learn more about the mail command.

Participating in Newsgroups

Usenet news is another feature that has been around almost as long as the Internet. Using a newsreader, and even many regular mail readers, you can select from literally thousands of topics and participate in discussions on those topics. To participate, you simply read the messages people have posted to the group, respond to those that you have something to say about, and send your own messages to start a discussion yourself.

To get started, you basically need a newsreader and access to a news server computer. The Thunderbird e-mail client includes support for accessing Usenet accounts. A popular newsreader that comes with RHEL is called Pan.

> **TIP:** If you have never used a newsgroup before, check out the news.announce.newusers newsgroup. This newsgroup exists to answer questions from new users.

The Pan newsreader is a graphical application for reading, managing, and interacting with newsgroups. It is particularly adept at displaying attached pictures and downloading binaries. The interface is very intuitive and easy to use. A big benefit of using Pan instead of Thunderbird for accessing newsgroups is that Thunderbird combines and decodes split yenc posts.

> **NOTE:** You can get the pan package by typing **yum install pan**.

Although Pan was originally designed for the GNOME desktop, GNOME libraries are no longer required to run Pan. For that reason, Pan will now work on KDE, Window Maker, or other desktop environments without any special software.

To open the Pan newsreader, type **pan** from the shell. The first time you start Pan, the Pan wizard runs to let you set up the newsreader. Have your e-mail address and your news server's name ready. When the wizard is done, you can download the list of newsgroups available from your news server.

Instant Messaging with Pidgin

Pidgin is the predominant instant messaging client in Linux. Originally based on the America Online (AOL) Open IM architecture (www.aim.com), the project recently changed its name to Pidgin from GAIM. Pidgin now supports a wide variety of instant messaging protocols, including the following:

- **Oscar** — Because Oscar is the official AIM protocol created by AOL, it is the most popular one used for Pidgin. To work in Pidgin, Oscar had to be reverse engineered because it is a proprietary protocol of AOL. So, not all features that you might find in AOL's own instant messenger are supported. Messaging is done over TCP-based networks (typically, the Internet), with all messages going through AOL servers, except in the case of direct connections (which are difficult to get working properly).

- **MSN Messenger** — This protocol was based originally on the MSN Messenger Service 1.0 protocol (www.hypothetic.org/docs/msn/ietf_draft.txt). That protocol has been "enhanced" so significantly by Microsoft since it was first published that the version included with Pidgin had to be reverse engineered. To find out more about MSN Messenger (from Pidgin or otherwise), see the MSN Messenger Protocol Resources/Links page (www.hypothetic.org/docs/msn/resources/links.php).

- **ICQ** — Pidgin uses the open source icqlib library to implement the ICQ protocol. Because of recent changes to the ICQ protocol, it is usually recommended to use Oscar to connect to the ICQ network, rather than icqlib.

- **IRC** — The Internet Relay Chat protocol is based on the Internet standard RFC 1459. Although there are differences in implementation of that standard on different IRC servers, this TCP-based protocol should work fine on most IRC servers.

- **Yahoo! Messenger** — This allows you to communicate to others using Yahoo! Messenger servers.

There are other messaging protocols supported by Pidgin as well. These include Jabber (which is used by GoogleTalk and available from www.jabber.org), Napster (instant messaging and buddy lists, but not music downloads), Groupwise Messenger (Novell's instant messaging), Sametime (Lotus messaging from meanwhile.sourceforge.net), TOC (rarely used AOL AIM service for unofficial clients), and Zephyr (IM system from MIT). Pidgin not only supports multiple protocols, but also allows you to communicate over multiple protocols at the same time. There are also available Jabber servers you can get to run your own

Jabber instant messaging server, such as Ejabberd (`http://ejabberd.jabber.ru`). (Type `yum install ejabberd` to install that package.)

To start Pidgin from the Applications menu, choose Internet → Instant Messenger. Figure 9-8 contains an example of the Pidgin Buddy List and other windows.

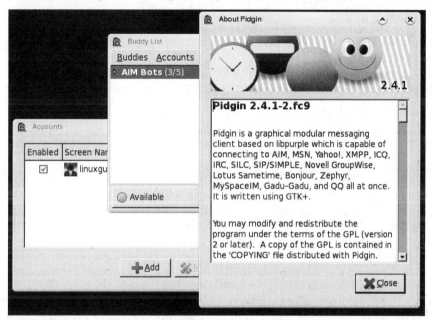

Figure 9-8: Access your AOL or other Instant Messaging account using Pidgin.

If you have never used instant messaging before, you can sign up for free accounts from AOL (`https://my.screenname.aol.com/`) or MSN (`http://messenger.msn.com`). Click Accounts from the initial Pidgin window and add your account. Select your account from the Account list, enter the password, and select Sign on.

Once you are signed on, for example, to AOL, from the Buddy List that appears select the IM button to connect to another IM user who is online. Or select Chat to enter the name of a chat room you want to enter. You can add buddies to your list as appropriate.

A small icon shaped like a yellow man appears in the system tray on your desktop when Pidgin is running. Click that icon to have your buddy list appear and disappear. Right-click that icon and a menu lets you choose to send a new message, join a chat, or work with Pidgin account and preference settings.

Sharing Files with BitTorrent

BitTorrent is a tool for distributing software content to a large number of clients over a network. What makes BitTorrent so unique is that, as you download a file to your computer, someone else can be downloading the same file from your computer. In that way, the server originally offering the file doesn't get hammered and a potentially unlimited number of people can get the file quickly.

BitTorrent is an excellent tool for the free and open source software community. For example, when a new release of Fedora comes out (now including more than 13GB of software), using BitTorrent means you don't have to wait for days for traffic on the Fedora mirror servers to cool down. Likewise, someone who wants to share home videos with the world can do so without having an industrial-size server and bandwidth. Of course, there are also those who are concerned that BitTorrent makes it easy to share files people shouldn't share, such as commercial movies, music, and software.

Both a text-based and graphical (bittorrent-gui) BitTorrent client are available from the Fedora repository. You can get both clients by typing the following as root user from a Terminal window:

```
# yum install bittorrent-gui
```

To use BitTorrent, visit a Web site that offers software downloads and look for a link to a torrent file representing the software, video, or other type of file you want to download. Download the torrent file to your computer. Next open the BitTorrent Window (select Applications → Internet → BitTorrent File Transfer). Open the torrent file (look for a file with a .torrent extension) you downloaded by selecting File → Open torrent file.

The slider on the BitTorrent window lets you control how much bandwidth you will allow for others to upload the files from you that you are downloading. The more you supply, the faster you will be allowed to download the file. You can continue to make the file available to others after you are finished downloading.

To create your own torrent file for a file or directory of files you want to share, select File → Make new torrent. While you can always publish your own torrent on a public server, your firewall may limit your ability to publish your own torrent to the Internet. For more information on BitTorrent, refer to the BitTorrent Introduction at `http://www.bittorrent.org/introduction.html`.

Using Remote Login, Copy, and Execution

This section describes some features for allowing users to use resources across a network. They are the `telnet`, `ssh`, `ftp`, and `wget` commands.

> **CROSS-REFERENCE:** Only the ssh service is turned on by default in Fedora because the other remote login, execution, and copy commands described here do not provide encrypted communications by default, and so they can represent significant security risks. For information on how to turn on the services described in this chapter on a Fedora or RHEL server, refer to Chapter 14 and Appendix B.

Two of the commands described in this section that are generally available are remote login and file transfer programs: `telnet` and `ftp`, respectively. Other commands for accessing FTP servers are `ncftp` and `gFTP`. The `ssh` command is typically used as a secure remote login command, although it can be used for remote execution as well.

Two newer commands for copying files over the network are `wget` and `rsync`. Both of these tools can be used for efficiently downloading files that you can identify on the network.

Using telnet for remote login

Telnet is a service provided by many different types of computer systems to enable remote users to log in to their machines over TCP/IP networks. The `telnet` command is the client program that you use to do the remote login. The most common way to use telnet is with a hostname. The following is a typical telnet session:

```
$ telnet maple
Trying 10.0.0.11 ...
Connected to maple.linuxtoys.net 10.0.0.11
Escape character is '^]'.
Fedora release 9
Kernel 2.6.25-0.234.fc9 on an i686
login: mike
Password: ********
Last login: Mon Jun 16 13:15:57 from pine
[mike@maple mike]$
```

This example shows what happens when the `telnet` command is used to log in from a computer named pine to a computer named maple by typing `telnet maple`. My computer tries to connect to the telnet port on maple (IP address `10.0.0.11`). Because maple is also a Fedora system, once the connection is established, I see the standard `login:` prompt. I type the user name (mike) and the password when prompted. When the login and password are accepted, I see the shell prompt for the user named mike.

The telnet service is disabled by default on Fedora and RHEL systems (as are most network services). So, to be able to log in to your computer using telnet, refer to Appendix B for information on how to turn on the telnet service.

Here are a few useful options you can use with telnet:

- **-a** — Automatic login. With this option, your computer attempts to log in to the remote computer using your local user name. So, if you are logged in to your computer as `mike`, when you use `telnet` to log in to a remote computer, the remote computer assumes that you want to log in as mike. It simply prompts you for mike's password.

- **-l** *user* — User name. This option is similar to the `-a` option, except that instead of using your current user name, you can ask to log in using any user name you choose.

- **-r** — Rlogin-style interface. This option lets you use tilde (~) options. For example, to disconnect while in rlogin mode, type **~.** (tilde+dot), or to suspend the telnet session, type **~^z** (tilde+carat+z). Only use ~ . if your remote shell is hung (exit is a better way to quit normally). If you use ~^z to suspend your telnet session temporarily, you are returned to your local system shell. To get back to the suspended session, type **fg** to put telnet back in the foreground.

Another way to use `telnet` is in command mode. Instead of using a hostname, simply type the word **telnet**. You will see a `telnet` prompt as follows:

```
$ telnet
telnet>
```

At this point, there are several commands available to you. You are not yet connected to a remote host. To open a login session to a remote computer from the telnet prompt (for example, to a computer named `maple`), type:

```
telnet> open maple
```

After you do connect to a remote computer, you can return to the telnet session at any time by typing **Ctrl+]**. Here are other options you can use during your telnet session:

- **?** — Print help information.
- **!** — Escape to the shell. (Type **exit** to leave the subshell and return to telnet.)
- **close** — If you have an open connection, type **close** to close it.
- **display** — Shows the operating parameters that are in effect.
- **logout** — Logs you off any remote connection in this session and closes it.
- **mode** — Tries to enter line mode or character mode. (Type **mode ?** to see other options that go with the mode option.)
- **quit** — Close telnet and exit.
- **z** — Suspend the current telnet session. (Type **fg** to return to the suspended telnet session.)

Copying files with FTP

As with telnet, FTP is a protocol that is available on many different operating systems. Archives of files on the Internet are stored on what are called FTP servers. To connect to those servers from Fedora, you can either type the URL of that server into a Web browser or you can use the `ftp` command or graphical FTP windows such as gFTP. Of the other FTP client programs available for Fedora and RHEL, my favorite is the `ncftp` command (although it is no longer included in the distributions).

Using the ftp command

The `ftp` command is available on Fedora, as well as every other Linux and UNIX system, for copying files to and from FTP servers. As with telnet, FTP has a command mode or you (more typically) can use it to connect directly to a remote computer. For example:

```
$ ftp maple
Connected to maple.
220 (vsFTPd 2.0.6)
Name (maple:mike): jake
331 Please specify the password.
Password: ********
230 Login successful.
Remote system type is UNIX.
Using binary mode to transfer files.
ftp>
```

In this example, `ftp` connects to a computer called maple (`ftp maple`). When I was prompted for a name, it assumed that I was going to use my current login name on maple (`maple:mike`). I could have pressed Enter to use the name mike, but instead I logged in as jake and typed the password when prompted. The password was accepted and, after some information was printed, I was given an `ftp>` prompt.

Because FTP is used for public servers, you can often log in using the word `anonymous` as your user name. By entering a valid e-mail address as your password, you can enter the anonymous FTP site and download files that the server makes available to the public. Sometimes the username and password "ftp" is also reserved for anonymous logins.

Unlike telnet, instead of being in a regular UNIX shell after I logged in with FTP, I was placed in FTP command mode. Command mode with FTP includes a whole lot of commands for moving around the remote file system and for copying files (which is its main job).

> **NOTE:** If you are behind a firewall and having trouble connecting to FTP servers, learn about active and passive FTP. Refer to the following: `http://slacksite.com/other/ftp.html`.

FTP directory commands

To get your bearings and move around the remote file system, you could use some of the following commands from the `ftp>` prompt. The commands are used to work with both the remote and local directories associated with the FTP connection.

- **passive** — Turn passive data transfer mode on and off. Passive mode may be required from behind firewalls that don't allow incoming connections.
- **pwd** — Shows the name of the current directory on the remote system.
- **ls** — Lists the contents of the current remote directory using the UNIX `ls` command. You can use any valid `ls` options with this command, provided that they are supported by the particular FTP server you are connected to.

- **dir** — Same as ls.
- **cd** — Use the cd command to move to the named directory on the remote system.
- **cdup** — Moves up one directory in the file system.
- **lcd** — Use the lcd command to move to the named directory on the local system.

If you want to make changes to any of the remote files or directories, use the following commands:

- **mkdir** — Creates a directory on the remote system.
- **rename** — Renames a file or directory on the remote system.
- **rmdir** — Removes a remote directory.
- **delete** — Removes a remote file.
- **mdelete** — Removes multiple remote files.

Depending on how the FTP server is configured, you may or may not be able to execute some of the file and directory commands shown. In general, if you log in as the anonymous user, you will not be able to modify any files or directories. You will only be able to download files. If you have a real login account, you will typically have the same read and write permission you have when you enter the computer using a standard login prompt.

FTP file copying commands

Before you copy files between the remote and local systems, consider the type of transfer you want to do. The two types of transfer modes are:

- **binary** — For transferring binary files (such as data files and executable commands). This is also referred to as an image transfer.
- **ascii** — For transferring plain-text files.

The Linux ftp command seems to set the default to binary when you start FTP. Binary seems to work well for either binary or text files. However, binary transfers may not work when transferring ASCII files from non-UNIX systems. If you transfer an executable file in ASCII mode, the file may not work when you try to run it on your local system.

But, if you transfer a compressed file, such as a Zip or Gzip archive, an image file, or a word-processor document, you must use binary transfers or the files will get corrupted. To avoid this problem, type in the binary command prior to transferring files. Not using binary mode is a common error.

Most file copying is done with the get and put commands. Likewise, you can use the mget and mput commands to transfer multiple files at once. Some FTP servers will even allow you to use matching characters (for example, mget abc* to get all files beginning with the letters abc). Here are descriptions of those commands:

- **get** *file* — Copies a file from the current directory on the remote file system and copies it to the current directory on the local file system. You can use a full path along with the filename. Here are some examples:

```
ftp> get route
ftp> get /tmp/sting
```

  The first example takes the file `route` from the current remote directory and copies it to the current local directory. The second example copies the file `/tmp/sting` from the remote system to the file `tmp/sting` relative to the current directory on the local system. So if your current directory were `/home/jake`, `ftp` would try to copy the file to `/home/jake/tmp/sting`.

- **put** *file* — Copies a file from the current local directory to the current remote directory. The usage of this command is essentially the same as the `get` command, except that files are copied from the local to the remote system.

> **NOTE:** Anonymous FTP sites (described later) usually let you copy files *from* them, but not *to* them. If they do allow you to put files on their servers, it will usually be in a restricted area.

- **mget** *file* ... — This command lets you download multiple files at once. You can specify multiple files either individually or by using metacharacters (such as the asterisk). If you run the `prompt` command (see below), FTP prompts you for each file to make sure you want to copy it.

- **mput** *file* ... — This command lets you put multiple files on the remote computer. Like `mget`, `mput` can prompt you before transferring each file.

Another useful ftp command is the `prompt` command. After `prompt` is run, `mget` and `mput` commands will offer a prompt to ask if you want to download each file in the list you requested as it is ready to download.

FTP exiting commands

While a connection is open to a remote computer from an FTP client in Fedora, you can use several commands to either temporarily or permanently exit from that connection. Here are some useful commands:

- **!** — This command temporarily exits you to the local shell. After you have done what you need to do, type **exit** to return to your FTP session. You can also use this command to run other local commands. For example, you can type **!pwd** to see what the current directory is on the local system, **!uname -a** to remind yourself of your local system name, or **!ls -l** to see the contents of your current directory.

- **close** — Closes the current connection.

- **bye** — Closes the connection and exits the `ftp` command. You can also use **quit** in place of **bye**.

Using the ncftp command

By virtue of being an FTP client program, the `ncftp` command supports all the standard commands you would expect to find in an FTP client (`get`, `put`, `ls`, `cd`, and so on). However, `ncftp` has added features that make it more efficient and friendlier than some other FTP clients.

> **NOTE:** You can install the ncftp package by typing **yum install ncftp**.

With `ncftp`, you can connect to an FTP server in the same way you did with `ftp`. One convenient difference is that if you enter no user name, `ncftp` assumes you want to use the anonymous user name and just logs you in. Here is an example:

```
$ ncftp ftp.mozilla.org
NcFTP 3.2.1 (July 29, 2007) by Mike Gleason
(http://www.NcFTP.com/contact/).
Connecting to ftp.mozilla.org...
(vsFTPd 2.0.5).
Logging in...
Login successful.
Logged in to ftp.mozilla.org.
ncftp / >
```

To log in as a user name other than anonymous, add a `-u user` option, where *user* is replaced by the name you want to log in as. Enter the password as prompted to continue.

Using ncftp

After you are logged in with the ncftp session running, there are a few nice features you can use that aren't available with other FTP clients. Here are some examples:

- **bookmark** — If you are visiting a site that you want to return to, type the bookmark command and type a name to identify that site. The next time you start an `ncftp` session, type the bookmark name as an option. Not only are you logged into the FTP site you bookmarked; you are taken to the directory where you set the bookmark.

- **lls, lcd, lmkdir, lpwd** — There is a set of commands that enables you to move around the local file system. Just place a letter `l` in front of standard shell commands such as `ls`, `cd`, `mkdir`, `pwd`, `rm`, and `rmdir` and you can move around and work with your local file system while you are in `ncftp`.

- **rhelp** — Use `rhelp` to see commands that are recognized by the remote FTP server. To see commands that are specific to the FTP server, type **help** while you are in an ncftp session.

- **Auto-resume** — If you were disconnected in the middle of a large download, you will appreciate this new feature. After a connection is broken during a download, reconnect to the FTP site and begin downloading the file again in the same local directory. The `ncftp` command resumes downloading where it left off.

Using ncftp for background transfers

If you are moving around to different parts of the FTP site, or jumping between different sites, you might not want to wait around for a file transfer to complete before you can go somewhere else. The ncftp command has an excellent feature for placing transfer commands in a spool file and then running them in the background immediately or later.

To select a file for background transfer, use the bgget command. Here is an example:

```
ncftp /pub > bgget wireless.doc
•Spooled: get wireless.doc
ncftp /pub > jobs
---Scheduled-For-----Host------------Command--------------------
2008-06-01  18:38 maple           GET wireless.doc
ncftp /pub > bgstart
Background process started.
Watch the "/home/br/.ncftp/spool/log" file to see how it is progressing
```

In this example, the bgget command spools the wireless.doc file from the remote current directory (/pub) and sets it to be copied to the local current directory. Typing the jobs command shows that the job (GET wireless.doc), from the host named maple, is scheduled to run immediately (6:38 p.m., June 1, 2008). By running the bgstart command this process, and any other spooled jobs, are run immediately.

Instead of starting the background transfers immediately you can do them later. For background jobs spooled for transfer, the transfer begins when you quit ncftp, leave your current FTP site, or go to another FTP site. In this way, the program that does the transfer (ncftpbatch) can take over your current login session to do the transfer.

If you wanted to wait even longer to do the transfers, you can pass an option to the bgget command to have it start the transfer at a particular time. Here is an example:

```
ncftp /pub > bgget -@ 2008100410000 wireless.doc
```

With this command, the transfer is set to run at 1 a.m. on October 4, 2008 to transfer the file called wireless.doc. Again, you can check the .ncftp/spool/log file in your home directory to see if the transfer has completed.

Using the gFTP window

If you prefer a more graphical interface for accessing FTP servers, you can use the gFTP window. Install gFTP by typing **yum install gftp**). You can open a gFTP window by typing **gftp**. Figure 9-9 shows an example of the gFTP window.

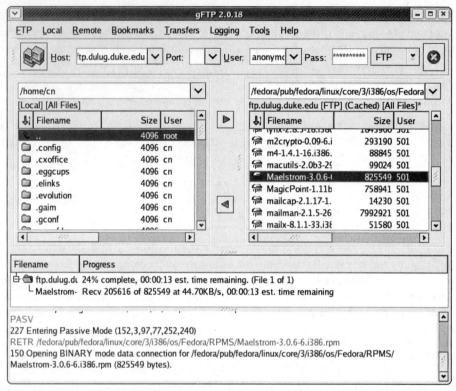

Figure 9-9: View local and remote files simultaneously from the gFTP window.

Unlike the `ftp` command, the gFTP window lets you simultaneously see the contents of the current remote and local directories. To transfer a file from one side to the other, simply double-click it or drag and drop it to the other pane. (Normally, you will just be copying files from FTP sites, unless a site provides you with permission to write to it.)

Follow this procedure to connect to an FTP site:

1. Type the name of the FTP server to which you want to connect (for example, `ftp.dulug.duke.edu`) into the Host box.

2. Type the port number on the FTP server (you can leave this blank to use the default port number 21).

3. Type the user name used to log in to the FTP server. Use the default `anonymous` if you don't have a specific user name and the server is publicly accessible.

4. Type the password for the user name you entered. The convention with anonymous FTP servers is to use your e-mail address as the password.

5. Click the icon displaying two little monitors to connect to the FTP site.

6. If you entered the information correctly, the bottom pane on the window should show that the transfer was complete and the right pane should show the contents of the current directory of the FTP site. Here are some actions you can take once you are connected:

    *   **Move around** — Double-click a directory to move to that directory or double-click on the two dots (. .) to move up a level. You can do this on both the remote and local directories.

    *   **Drag and drop files** — You can drag and drop files from the FTP site on to the left pane (representing your current local directory).

    *   **Save this site** — If you want to return to this site later, choose Bookmarks → Add Bookmark. A pop-up window lets you name this site for the bookmarks list. After you do, you can select that entry from the list at a later date to connect to that site. The gFTP window will have stored not only the host name, but also the port, user name, and password. So you are just one click away from connecting. This is one of the best features of graphical FTP programs such as gFTP.

A nice feature of gFTP is that it stores log information. Choose Logging → View Log. A window appears showing you the conversations that have taken place between your computer and each FTP site. You can look at these messages to see what is wrong if you are unable to connect to a site or to remember where you have been and what you have done on an FTP site.

> **NOTE:** The Bookmarks list comes with several entries under the Red Hat Sites menu that let you connect directly to FTP sites that have software packaged as RPMs. While those sites were useful at one time, it's usually better these days to use `yum` or PackageKit to get software packages. Many of the sites in this Bookmarks list contain out-of-date RPMs and won't automatically take care of dependency issues.

Getting files with wget

If you already know where a file is on the network, there are more efficient ways of downloading that file than opening an FTP session, moving around the FTP server, and running the `get` command. The `wget` command is a simple, efficient tool for doing non-interactive downloads of files over the Internet.

> **NOTE:** Another great command for copying files over the network is the `rsync` command. I often use `rsync` to do backups over the network. See Chapter 13 for descriptions on using `rsync` to do backups.

If there is a file you want to download from an FTP site or Web server (HTTP), and you know exactly where the file is, `wget` is a good way to download. The `wget` command is very useful if you want to copy a whole site, recursively, from one computer to another (for example, containing user home directories). When downloading from FTP sites, `wget` can let you just download as the `anonymous` user or add your own user name and password to the command line.

Downloading a single file

Here is an example of using wget to get a file from a Web server:

```
$ wget http://dag.wieers.com/packages/pan/pan-0.14.2.91-2.1.fc3.rf.i386.rpm
--09:34:11--  http://dag.wieers.com/packages/pan/pan-0.14.2.91-2.1.fc3.rf.i386.rpm
          => `pan-0.14.2.91-2.1.fc3.rf.i386.rpm'
Resolving dag.wieers.com... 212.204.244.42
Connecting to dag.wieers.com[212.204.244.42]:80... connected.
HTTP request sent, awaiting response... 302 Found
Location: http://apt.sw.be/packages/pan/pan-0.14.2.91-2.1.fc3.rf.i386.rpm [following]
--09:34:17--  http://apt.sw.be/packages/pan/pan-0.14.2.91-2.1.fc3.rf.i386.rpm
          => `pan-0.14.2.91-2.1.fc3.rf.i386.rpm'
Resolving apt.sw.be... 193.1.219.82
Connecting to apt.sw.be[193.1.219.82]:80... connected.
HTTP request sent, awaiting response... 200 OK
Length: 1,224,357 [application/x-redhat-package-manager]

100%[====================================================================
====================================>] 1,224,357     53.23K/s    ETA 00:00

09:34:41 (52.08 KB/s) - `pan-0.14.2.91-2.1.fc3.rf.i386.rpm' saved
[1,224,357/1,224,357]
```

By the first part of the URL (http://), wget knows you are copying a file from an HTTP server to the current directory (.) on the local host. After resolving the address (dag.wieers.com), wget connects to the site and transfers the file. As the file downloads, wget shows the progress of the download, and then exits.

Downloading a file with user name and password

If you are doing an FTP file copy and need to log in as a user other than anonymous, you can add that information to the command line or to a .netrc file in your home directory (type **man netrc** to see the format of that file). Here is an example of adding the password to the command line:

```
$ wget ftp://joe:my67chevy@ftp.handsonhistory.com/memo1.doc
```

> **CAUTION:** Adding a password to a command line leaves the password exposed to onlookers. This practice is generally discouraged, except in cases where no one can see your monitor or your history files or view your command line by running the ps command. You can add passwords to your ~/.wgetrc file, to keep your password from being seen.

In the previous example, the user logs in as joe with the password my67chevy. The wget then copies the file memo1.doc from the current directory on the host computer named ftp.handsonhistory.com. That current directory is most likely /home/joe.

Downloading a whole Web site

Using `wget`, you can download a large number of files from Web servers as well. The `wget` command downloads files using the http protocol, if file addresses begin with `http://`. Downloading a single file, you would use the same form as you would for an FTP file (for example: `wget http://host/file.`). The best `wget` option for HTTP downloads is `-r` (recursive).

A recursive download lets you choose a point at a Web site and download all content below that point. Here is an example of a recursive download used to download the contents of the `www.example.com` Web site.

```
$ wget -r http://www.example.com
```

In this example, the HTML pages, images, and other content on the `www.example.com` Web site are copied below the current directory in a new directory named `www.example.com`. This is useful if you want to gather the contents of a Web site but don't have login access to that site. Because content is taken by following links, if there is content in a directory at the Web site that isn't in a link, it won't be downloaded.

Downloading an entire Web site can result in a massive amount of data being downloaded. If you want only part of a Web site, start from a point lower in the site's structure. Or, as an alternative, you can limit the number levels the `wget` will go down the site structure. Using the `-l` option (l as in level), the following example gets two levels of HTML content:

```
$ wget -r -l 2 http://www.example.com
```

To mirror a site, you can use the `-m` option instead of `-r`. Using `wget -m http://site` is like asking to download an infinite number of levels recursively (`-r -l inf`), keep current time stamps (`-N`), and keep FTP directory listings (`-nr`). Note that `wget` will honor a Web site's `robots.txt` file, which might restrict the ability of `wget` to recursively access multiple levels of links from a Web site.

Continuing a download

In the old days, if you were downloading a particularly large file (such as an ISO image of a CD or DVD), if the download stopped for some reason (a disconnected network or errant reboot), you needed to start all over. With `wget`, you can choose to restart a download and have it continue right where it left off. This has been a lifesaver for me on many occasions.

Let's say that you were downloading a 4GB DVD ISO image named `mydvd.iso` from the site `ftp://ftp.example.com` and you killed the `wget` process by mistake after about 3GB of download. Make sure that your current directory is the one that contains the partially downloaded ISO. Then run the same `wget` command you did originally, adding the `-c` (continue) option as follows:

```
$ wget -c ftp://ftp.example.com/mydvd.iso
```

If you had not used the -c option, in this case, a new download would have started using the file name mydvd.iso.1 to download to.

> **NOTE:** Another command that you might be interested in, similar to wget, is the curl command. Like wget, curl can download files using the ftp or http protocols. Curl can also do multiple file transfers on the same connection.

Using ssh for remote login/remote execution

Although the telnet and rlogin login commands and rsh remote execution command have been around much longer, the ssh command is the preferred tool for remote logins and executions. The reason is that ssh provides encrypted communication so you can use it securely over insecure, public networks between hosts that don't know each other.

In the following example, ssh is being used to log in to a computer named maple. Because no user is specified, ssh tries to log in as the current user (which is the root user in this case).

```
# ssh maple
root@maple's password:
```

If you wanted to log in as a different user, you could use the -l option. For example, to log in to the computer named maple as the user named jake, you could type the following:

```
# ssh jake@maple
jake@maple's password:
```

The ssh command can also be used to execute a command on the remote computer. For example, if you wanted to monitor the messages file on a remote computer for a minute, you could type the following command:

```
# ssh root@maple "tail -f /var/log/messages"
root@maple's password:
```

After you typed the password in the preceding case, the last several lines of the /var/log/messages file on the remote computer would be displayed. As messages were received, they would continue to be displayed until you decided to exit (press Ctrl+C to exit the tail command).

> **NOTE:** To learn how to use public keys for passwordless login to ssh, refer to Chapter 14. Find out more about the ssh command from the SSH Web site (www.openssh.org).

Using scp for remote file copy

The scp command is a simple yet secure way of copying files among Linux systems. It uses the underlying ssh facility, so if ssh is enabled, so is scp. Here is an example of using scp to copy a file from one computer to another:

```
# scp myfile toys.linuxtoys.net:/home/chris
root@toys.linuxtoys.net's password: ******
```

In this example, the file `myfile` is copied to the computer named `toys.linuxtoys.net` in the `/home/chris` directory. If you don't provide a user name, `scp` assumes you are using the current user name. Unlike some tools that provide remote login, `scp` and `ssh` do allow you to login as root user over the network, by default. (Many people turn off this feature for security reasons.)

To use `scp` with a different user name, you can append the user name with an @ character. For example, `chris@toys.linuxtoys.net:/home/chris` would attempt to log in as the user named chris to do the file copy.

The first time you connect to a remote computer using `scp` or `ssh`, those commands try to establish the authenticity of the remote host. If it cannot establish the host's authenticity, it will display the RSA key fingerprint and ask you if you want to continue. If you type `yes`, `scp` will not question the authenticity of that computer again for subsequent `scp` commands.

However, if the RSA key fingerprint should change in the future for the remote computer (which will happen if, for example, the operating system is reinstalled on that computer), `scp` will refuse to let you connect to that remote computer. To override that refusal, you need to edit your `$HOME/.ssh/known_hosts` file and delete the entry for the remote computer. You can then verify the authenticity of the remote computer and continue to use `scp`.

The `sftp` command, which also communicates using secure ssh protocols, is a command for copying files from an FTP server. It is considered a more secure way of getting files from an FTP server that has an sshd server running. The `sftp` command can be disabled on the server by commenting out the `sftp` line in the `sshd_config` directory.

Using the "r" commands: rlogin, rcp, and rsh

The `rlogin`, `rcp`, and `rsh` commands all use the same underlying security mechanism to enable remote login, remote file copy, and remote execution, respectively, among computers. These commands are included with Fedora to be compatible with legacy UNIX systems. Because "r" commands are inherently insecure, however, most people use `ssh` and `scp` commands to provide the same functionality in a more secure way.

> **CROSS REFERENCE:** For a description of these "r" commands, refer to the *Fedora 9 and Red Hat Enterprise Linux Bible* Web site at Wiley Publishing: `www.wiley.com/go/fedora9bible`.

Summary

Most use of the World Wide Web centers on the Web browser. Firefox is fast becoming the most popular Web browser to use with Fedora, RHEL, and most other Linux systems, and is accessible from a button on your desktop. Epiphany, Konqueror, and various text-based Web browsers are also available with Fedora and RHEL. The original Mozilla Browser Suite is no longer packaged with Fedora.

Evolution, which can also be used for managing your e-mail, is now the preferred mail reader for Fedora and RHEL. Thunderbird is the latest e-mail application from the Mozilla Project. There are also many text-based mail readers, such as mutt, pine, and mail.

Command-line tools for downloading files include `wget`, `ftp`, and many others. A popular download tool, which offers both command-line and graphical interfaces, is BitTorrent. With BitTorrent, you not only download files, but you can simultaneously upload the files you get to others.

Legacy remote login and file copy commands (`rlogin`, `rcp`, and `rsh`) are still available in Fedora. However, improved programs for remote login and file copy, such as `ssh`, `scp`, and `sftp` are more often used today.

Part III
Administering Fedora and RHEL

Chapter 10

Understanding System Administration

In This Chapter

- Using the root login
- Administrative commands, configuration files, and log files
- Graphical administration tools
- Working with the file system
- Working with hardware devices
- Monitoring system performance
- Managing battery power on laptops
- Using Security Enhanced Linux

Fedora and Red Hat Enterprise Linux, like other Linux and UNIX systems, were intended for use by more than one person at a time. Multiuser features allow many people to have accounts in Linux, with their data kept secure from others. Multitasking allows many people to use the computer at the same time. Sophisticated networking protocols and applications make it possible for a Linux system to extend its capabilities to network users and computers around the world. The person assigned to manage all of this stuff is referred to as the *system administrator.*

Even if you are the only person using a Linux system, system administration is still set up to be separate from other computer use. To do most administrative tasks, you need to be logged in as the root user (also referred to as the super user) or gain temporary root privilege. Other users cannot change, or in some cases, even see some of the configuration information for a Linux system. In particular, security features such as passwords are protected from general view.

This chapter describes the general principles of Fedora and RHEL system administration. In particular, this chapter covers some of the basic tools you need to administer your Linux system. It also helps you learn how to work with file systems and monitor the setup and performance of your Linux system.

Security Enhanced Linux (SELinux) adds another dimension to administering a Fedora or RHEL system. Instead of giving the root user full control of the entire Linux system, access to data, programs, devices, and processes can be assigned to different roles. Because Fedora is delivered with only a limited set of SELinux features turned on (targeted policy), the root user maintains most of its traditional role (whether SELinux is off or on). SELinux is described at the end of this chapter.

Using the root user account

The traditional role of the root user in Linux systems is to have complete control of the operation of your Fedora system. That user can open any file or run any program. The root user also installs software packages and adds accounts for other people who use the system.

During the Fedora or RHEL installation process, you are required to add a password for the root user. You need to remember and protect this password. You will need it to log in as root or to obtain root permission while you are logged in as some other user.

The home directory for the root user is /root. The home directory and other information associated with the root user account is assigned in the /etc/passwd file. Here is what the root entry looks like in the /etc/passwd file:

```
root:x:0:0:root:/root:/bin/bash
```

This shows that for the user named root, the x indicates that the password is stored in /etc/shadow, the user ID is set to 0 (root user), and the group ID is set to 0 (root group). The home directory is /root and the shell for that user is /bin/bash. You can change the home directory or the shell used by changing the values in this file.

> **CROSS-REFERENCE:** It's best to make changes to /etc/passwd with the User Manager window or usermod command. See the section on setting up users in Chapter 11 for more information about the /etc/passwd file.

Among the defaults that are set for the root user are aliases for certain commands that could have dangerous consequences. Aliases for the rm, cp, and mv commands allow those commands to be run with the -i option. This prevents massive numbers of files from being removed, copied, or moved by mistake. The -i option causes each deletion, copy, or move to prompt you before removing or overwriting any files from those commands.

Becoming Super User (The su Command)

Though one way to become the super user is to log in as root, sometimes that is not convenient. For example, you may be logged into a regular user account and just want to make a quick administrative change to your system without having to log out and log back in. Or you may need to log in over the network to make a change to a Linux system but find that the system doesn't allow root users in from over the network (a common practice).

The answer is that you can use the su command. From any Terminal window or shell, you can simply type:

```
$ su
Password: ******
#
```

When you are prompted, type in the root user's password. The prompt for the regular user ($) will be changed to the super user prompt (#). At this point, you have full permission to run any command and use any file on the system. However, one thing that the su command doesn't do when used this way is read in the root user's environment. As a result, you may type a command that you know is available and get the message "command not found." To fix this problem, you can use the su command with the dash (-) option instead, as follows:

```
$ su -
Password: ******
#
```

You still need to type the password, but after you do that, everything that normally happens at login for the root user will happen after the su command is completed. Your current directory will be root's home directory (probably /root), and things like the root user's PATH variable will be used. If you became the root user by just typing su, rather than su -, you would not have changed directories or the environment of the current login session.

> **TIP:** When you become super user during someone else's session, a common mistake is to leave files or directories in the user's directories that are owned by root. If you do this, be sure to use the chown or chmod command to make the files and directories you modify open to the user that you want to own them. Otherwise, you will probably get a phone call in a short time, asking you to come back and fix it.

You can also use the su command to become another user than root. For example, to have the permissions of a user named chum, you could type the following:

```
$ su - chum
```

Even if you were root user before you typed this command, you would only have the permission to open files and run programs that are available to chum. As root user, however, after you type the su command to become another user, you don't need a password to continue. If you type that command as a regular user, you must type the new user's password.

When you are finished using super user permissions, return to the previous shell by exiting the current shell. Do this by pressing Ctrl+D or by typing **exit**.

> **CAUTION:** If you are the administrator for a computer that is accessible to multiple users, don't leave a root shell open on someone else's screen (unless you want to let that person do anything they like to the computer)!

Besides opening a shell session using su (to run a bunch of commands as root), you can instead just apply root permission to a single command or window. This approach is considered more secure than leaving a shell open with root permission if you are just doing one administrative task. For example:

- **GUI admin tools** — When you run GUI administration tools as a regular user, you are usually prompted for the root password (as described the section "Using graphical administration tools" later in this chapter). If a GUI administration tool fails and doesn't prompt you for a password, refer to the sidebar "Becoming Super User in X."

- **sudo command** — You can configure a user in /etc/sudoers to be allowed to run administrative commands. After that is done, that user can run the sudo command, followed by a single administrative command, to run that command as root would. When that single command completes, the root permission to run that command ends as well. (See the description of the sudo command later in this chapter.)

Learning about Administrative GUI Tools, Commands, Configuration Files, and Log Files

Fedora and Red Hat Enterprise Linux systems have advanced enough in recent releases that you can now do most system administration from your desktop GUI, bypassing the shell altogether. Whether you administer Linux from the GUI or from a shell, however, underlying your activities are many administrative commands, configuration files, and log files.

Understanding where GUI administrative tools, commands, and files are located and how they are used will help you effectively maintain your Linux system. Although most administrative features are intended for the root user, other administrative users (described later in this section) have limited administrative capabilities.

Using graphical administration tools

The trend over the past few versions of Fedora and Red Hat Enterprise Linux has been to steer clear of the massive administrative interfaces (such as linuxconf and Webmin) and instead to offer graphical windows that perform individual administrative tasks. Instead of sharing one monolithic interface, they share common menus. Individual graphical windows for configuring a network, adding users, or setting up printers can be launched from those menus.

To administer your Fedora or RHEL system through the GNOME or KDE desktops, Red Hat, Inc. has provided a common set of administrative tools that are accessible from menu buttons on the panel. Selections for starting most graphical administration windows are available from the following menus:

- **Administration** — Select System → Administration from the GNOME desktop panel (or Administration from the KDE menu) to select tools for configuring your system.

These include tools for adding users, setting date and time, configuring your network, setting up printers, and getting sound cards and printers to work.

Becoming Super User in X

There may be times when your desktop (and underlying X Window System) is running on Linux as a non-root user and you want to run a graphical administration program. In most cases, the GUI administration program will simply prompt you for the root password to continue. However, if the program fails, saying that you don't have permission to run the command, here is what you can do:

First, open a Terminal window on the X desktop.

Then, open permission to the X window display to everyone on the local computer (this is just a temporary measure) by typing:

```
$ xhost +localhost
```

Type the following and enter the root password when prompted, to become super user:

```
$ su -
Password: ******
#
```

Next, type the following to see the current display value:

```
# echo $DISPLAY
```

If the value is something like :0 or :0.0, any X command you run from that shell will appear on the console terminal for the computer. If you are at the console and that's what you see, then you can skip the next step. If you see no value (which is quite possible) or the wrong value, you must set the DISPLAY variable.

Type the following (assuming you are using a bash or sh shell):

```
# export DISPLAY=:0
```

At this point, you can run any administrative X command (such as neat or system-config-packages) and have it appear on your X desktop. If you are running an administrative command from a remote computer and you want it to appear on your local desktop, you can set the DISPLAY to host:0, where host is replaced by the name of your computer.

When you are done, be sure to exit the application you are running. Then restore the security of your X desktop by typing the following:

```
$ xhost -
```

- **System Tools** — Select Applications → System Tools from the GNOME desktop panel (or System from the KDE menu) to select tools to monitor and work with your system. These include tools for updating software, monitoring the system, and checking network activity.

Because these administrative tasks require root permission, if you are logged in as a regular user you must enter the root password before the GUI application's window opens. For example, if you launch the Display Settings window (System → Administration → Display) from the desktop panel as a regular user, you see the pop-up window shown in Figure 10-1.

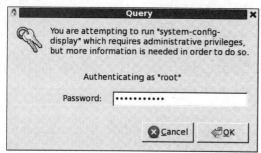

Figure 10-1: Enter the root password to open system administration windows from a regular user's GUI.

After you have entered the root password, most of the system configuration tools will open without requiring you to retype the password during this login session. Look for a yellow "badge" icon in the lower right corner of the panel, indicating that you have root authorization. Click the badge to open a pop-up window that lets you remove authorization. Otherwise, authorization goes away after five minutes.

NOTE: As you configure different features on your Fedora or Red Hat Enterprise Linux system, you are asked to launch different individual graphical windows. In general, if you have a choice of tools for configuring a server or adding a feature, I recommend that you use the tool provided with your distribution. That's because the Red Hat GUI tools more often integrate closely with the way Fedora and RHEL systems store and manage their configuration information.

The following list describes administrative tools you can start from the Administration menu (System → Administration). The name of the package that must be installed to get the feature is shown in parentheses:

- **Server Settings** — This submenu accesses the following server configuration windows:
  - **Domain Name System (system-config-bind)** — Create and configure zones if your computer is acting as a DNS server.
  - **FTP (system-config-vsftpd)** — Configure the vsftpd FTP server.
  - **HTTP (system-config-httpd)** — Configure your computer as an Apache Web server.

- **NFS (system-config-nfs)** — Set up directories from your system to be shared with other computers on your network using the NFS service.

- **Services (system-config-services)** — Display and change which services are running on your Fedora or RHEL system at different run levels.

- **Authentication (authconfig-gtk)** — Change how users are authenticated on your system. Usually, Shadow Passwords and MD5 Passwords are selected. However, if your network supports LDAP, Kerberos, SMB, NIS, or Hesiod authentication, you can select to use any of those authentication types.

- **Boot Loader (system-config-boot)** — Configure the default boot entry and timeout value (in seconds) for your GRUB boot loader.

- **Date & Time (system-config-date)** — Set the date and time or choose to have an NTP server keep system time in sync. Figure 10-2 shows the Date/Time Properties window.

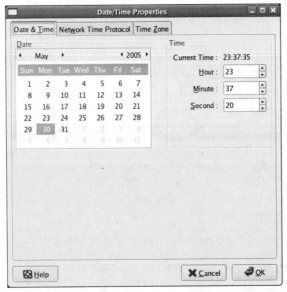

Figure 10-2: Choose an NTP server or set date and time in the Date/Time Properties window.

- **Display (system-config-display)** — Change the settings for your X desktop, including color depth and resolution for your display. You can also choose settings for your video card and monitor.

- **Firewall (system-config-firewall)** — Configure your firewall to allow or deny services to computers from the network.

- **Hardware (hwbrowser)** — View information about your hard drives, network devices, sound cards, and other hardware. (Install the hwbrowser package to see this item.)

- **Keyboard (system-config-keyboard)** — Choose the type of keyboard you are using, based on language.

- **Language (system-config-language)** — Select the default language used for the system.

- **Logical Volume Management (system-config-lvm)** — Display and manage logical volumes and related disk partitions.

- **Network (system-config-network)** — Manage your current network interfaces, as well as add interfaces.

- **Printing (system-config-printer)** — Configure local and network printers.

- **Root Password (system-config-rootpassword)** — Change the root password.

- **Samba (system-config-samba)** — Configure Windows (SMB) file sharing. (To configure other Samba features, you can use the SWAT window. SWAT is described in Chapter 18.)

- **Soundcard Detection (system-config-soundcard)** — Tries to detect and configure your sound card.

- **System Log (gnome-system-log)** — Displays messages (by date) for log files stored in the /var/log directory.

- **Users & Groups (system-config-users)** — Lets you add, display, and change user and group accounts for your Fedora or RHEL system (see Figure 10-3).

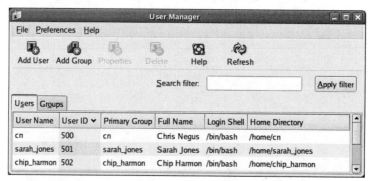

Figure 10-3: Change user and group accounts with the User Manager window.

The following tools associated with system administration can be started from the System Tools menu (Applications → System Tools):

- **Configuration Editor (gconf-editor)** — Change settings associated with your GNOME desktop system.

- **Disk Usage Analyzer (gnome-utils)** — Displays and analyzes data on the use of your computer's hard disks.

- **Kickstart (system-config-kickstart)** — Create a Kickstart configuration file that can be used to install multiple Fedora or RHEL systems without user intervention.

- **System Monitor (frysk-gnome)** — Shows information about running processes and resource usage.

Procedures for using the various system graphical administrative tools are discussed throughout the book.

Administrative commands

Many commands are intended only for root. When you log in as root, your $PATH variable is set to include some directories that contain commands for the root user. These include the following directories:

- **/sbin** — This contains commands for modifying your disk partitions (such as fdisk), changing boot procedures (grub), and changing system states (init).
- **/usr/sbin** — This contains commands for managing user accounts (such as useradd) and checking network traffic (wireshark). Commands that run as daemon processes are also contained in this directory. (Look for commands that end in "d" such as sshd, pppd, and crond.)

Some administrative commands are contained in regular user directories (such as /bin and /usr/bin). This is especially true of commands that have some options available to everyone. An example is the /bin/mount command, which anyone can use to list mounted file systems, but only root can use to mount file systems.

To find commands that are intended primarily for the system administrator, check out the section 8 manual pages (usually in /usr/share/man/man8). They contain descriptions and options for most Linux administrative commands. For example, to see the man page for the fdisk command (/usr/share/man/man8/fdisk.8.gz), type:

```
$ man fdisk
```

Some third-party applications will add administrative commands to directories that are not in your PATH. For example, an application may put commands in /usr/local/bin (this is the most common location), /opt/bin, or /usr/local/sbin. Although /usr/local/bin and /usr/local/sbin are already in each user's and root's path (respectively), you may need to add /opt/bin or other directories to your PATH.

Administrative configuration files

Configuration files are another mainstay of Linux administration. Almost everything you set up for your particular computer — user accounts, network addresses, or GUI preferences — is stored in plain-text files. This has some advantages and some disadvantages.

The advantage of plain-text files is that it is easy to read and change them. Any text editor will do. On the downside, however, is that as you edit configuration files, no error checking is going on. You have to run the program that reads these files (such as a network daemon or the

X desktop) to find out if you set up the files correctly. A comma or a quote in the wrong place can sometimes cause a whole interface to fail.

Throughout this book, I describe the configuration files you need to set up the different features that make up Fedora and RHEL systems. In terms of a general perspective on configuration files, however, there are several locations in a Fedora or RHEL file system where configuration files are stored. Here are some of the major locations:

- $HOME — All users store information in their home directories that directs how their login accounts behave. Most configuration files in $HOME begin with a dot (.), so they don't appear as a user's directory when you use a standard ls command (you need to type ls -a to see them). There are dot files that define how each user's shell behaves, the desktop look and feel, and options used with your text editor. There are even files (such as .ssh/* and .rhosts) that can configure network permissions for each user.

- /etc — This directory contains most of the basic Linux system-configuration files. The following /etc configuration files are of interest:

  - adjtime — Holds to data to adjust the hardware clock (see the hwclock man page).

  - aliases — Can contain distribution lists used by the Linux mail service.

  - bashrc — Sets system-wide defaults for bash shell users. (By default, it sets the shell prompt to include current user name, hostname, current directory, and other values.)

  - cdrecord.conf — Contains defaults used for recording CDs.

  - crontab — Sets cron environment and times for running automated tasks.

  - csh.cshrc (or cshrc) — Sets system-wide defaults for csh (C shell) users.

  - dovecot —Contains information needed to support the dovecot IMAPv4/POP3 mail service.

  - esd.conf — Sets options used by the Enlightenment Sound Daemon to mix multiple audio streams into a single audio output.

  - exports — Contains a list of local directories that are available to be shared by remote computers using the Network File System (NFS).

  - fedora-release — Contains a string identifying the current Fedora release. For RHEL releases, the file is named redhat-release.

  - fstab — Identifies the devices for common storage media (hard disk, floppy, CD-ROM, and so on) and locations where they are mounted in the Linux system. This is used by the mount command to choose which file systems to mount.

  - group — Identifies group names and group IDs (GIDs) that are defined on the systems. Group permissions in Linux are defined by the second of three sets of rwx (read, write, execute) bits associated with each file and directory.

  - gshadow — Contains shadow passwords for groups.

- `host.conf` — Sets the locations in which domain names (for example, redhat.com) are searched for on TCP/IP networks (such as the Internet). By default, the local hosts file is searched, then any nameserver entries in `resolv.conf`.

- `hosts` — Contains IP addresses and hostnames that you can reach from your computer. (Usually this file is used just to store names of computers on your LAN or small private network.)

- `hosts.allow` — Lists host computers that are allowed to use certain TCP/IP services from the local computer.

- `hosts.deny` — Lists host computers that are *not* allowed to use certain TCP/IP services from the local computer (doesn't exist by default).

- `inittab` — Contains information that defines which programs start and stop when Linux boots, shuts down, or goes into different states (runlevels) in between. This is the most basic configuration file for starting Linux.

- `issue` — Contains the lines that are displayed when a terminal is ready to let you log in to your Fedora or RHEL system from a local terminal, or the console in text mode.

- `issue.net` — Contains login lines that are displayed to users who try to log in to the Linux system from a computer on the network using the telnet service.

- `mail.rc` — Sets system-wide parameters associated with using mail.

- `man.config` — Used by the `man` command to determine the default path to the location of `man` pages.

- `modprobe.conf` — Contains aliases and options related to loadable kernel modules used by your computer.

- `mtab` — Contains a list of file systems that are currently mounted.

- `mtools.conf` — Contains settings used by DOS tools in Linux.

- `named.conf` — Contains DNS settings if you are running your own DNS server.

- `ntp.conf` — Includes information needed to run the Network Time Protocol (NTP).

- `passwd` — Stores account information for all valid users for the system. Also includes other information, such as the home directory and default shell.

- `printcap` — Contains definitions for the printers configured for your computer.

- `profile` — Sets system-wide environment and start-up programs for all users. This file is read when the user logs in.

- `protocols` — Sets protocol numbers and names for a variety of Internet services.

- `redhat-release` — Contains a string identifying the current Red Hat release. This file exists on Red Hat Linux and Red Hat Enterprise Linux systems. On Fedora systems, this file exists as a link to the `fedora-release` file, so that applications that look for release information in the `redhat-release` file won't fail.

- `resolv.conf` — Identifies the locations of DNS name server computers that are used by TCP/IP to translate Internet host.domain names into IP addresses.

- `rpc` — Defines remote procedure call names and numbers.

- `services` — Defines TCP/IP services and their port assignments.

- `shadow` — Contains encrypted passwords for users who are defined in the `passwd` file. (This is viewed as a more secure way to store passwords than the original encrypted password in the `passwd` file. The `passwd` file needs to be publicly readable, whereas the `shadow` file can be unreadable by all but the root user.)

- `shells` — Lists the shell command-line interpreters (`bash`, `sh`, `csh`, and so on) that are available on the system, as well as their locations.

- `sudoers` — Sets commands that can be run by users, who may not otherwise have permission to run the command, using the `sudo` command. In particular, this file is used to provide selected users with root permission.

- `syslog.conf` — Defines what logging messages are gathered by the `syslogd` daemon and what files they are stored in. (Typically, log messages are stored in files contained in the `/var/log` directory.)

- `termcap` — Lists definitions for character terminals, so that character-based applications know what features are supported by a given terminal. Graphical terminals and applications have made this file obsolete to most people. (Termcap was the BSD UNIX way of storing terminal information; UNIX System V used definitions in `/usr/share/terminfo` files.)

- `/etc/X11` — Contains subdirectories that each contain system-wide configuration files used by X and different X window managers available for Linux. The `xorg.conf` file (which makes your computer and monitor usable with X) and configuration directories containing files used by `xdm` and `xinit` to start X are in here.

  Directories relating to window managers contain files that include the default values that a user will get if that user starts one of these window managers on your system. Window managers that may have system-wide configuration files in these directories include Motif (`mwm`) and Twm (`twm`). The `fs` directory contains a file for configuring font server settings.

> **NOTE:** Some files and directories in `/etc/X11` are linked to locations in the `/usr/X11R6` directory.

- `/etc/alternatives` — Contains links that the alternatives facility uses to enable a system administrator to exchange one service with another in a way that is invisible to users. (Currently, only mail and printing use the alternatives service.)

- `/etc/amanda` — Contains files and directories that allow the amanda facility to do network backups of other Linux and UNIX systems.

- /etc/cron* — Directories in this set contain files that define how the crond utility runs applications on a daily (cron.daily), hourly (cron.hourly), monthly (cron.monthly), or weekly (cron.weekly) schedule.

- /etc/cups — Contains files that are used to configure the CUPS printing service.

- /etc/default — Contains files that set default values for various utilities. For example, the file for the useradd command defines the default group number, home directory, password expiration date, shell, and skeleton directory (/etc/skel) that are used when creating a new user account.

- /etc/httpd — Contains a variety of files used to configure the behavior of your Apache Web server (specifically, the httpd daemon process).

- /etc/init.d — Contains the permanent copies of run-level scripts. These scripts are linked to files in the /etc/rc?.d directories to have each service associated with a script started or stopped for the particular run level. The ? is replaced by the run-level number (0 through 6).

- /etc/mail — Contains files used to configure your sendmail mail service.

- /etc/pcmcia — Contains configuration files that allow you to have a variety of PCMCIA cards configured for your computer. (PCMCIA slots are those openings on your laptop that allow you to have credit card–sized cards attached to your computer. You can attach such devices as modems and external CD-ROMs.)

- /etc/postfix — Contains configuration files for the postfix mail transport agent.

- /etc/ppp — Contains several configuration files used to set up Point-to-Point protocol (so that you can have your computer dial out to the Internet).

- /etc/rc?.d — There is a separate rc?.d directory for each valid system state: rc0.d (shutdown state), rc1.d (single-user state), rc2.d (multiuser state), rc3.d (multiuser plus networking state), rc4.d (user-defined state), rc5.d (multiuser, networking, plus GUI login state), and rc6.d (reboot state).

- /etc/security — Contains files that set a variety of default security conditions for your computer. These files are part of the pam (pluggable authentication modules) package.

- /etc/skel — Any files contained in this directory are automatically copied to a user's home directory when that user is added to the system. By default, most of these files are dot (.) files, such as .kde (a directory for setting KDE desktop defaults) and .bashrc (for setting default values used with the bash shell).

- /etc/squid — Contains configuration files for the Squid proxy caching server.

- /etc/sysconfig — Contains important system configuration files that are created and maintained by various system services (including iptables, samba, and most networking services).

- /etc/uucp — Contains configuration files used with Taylor UUCP (a nonstandard version of the uucp facility that is used to create modem, direct line, and other serial connections with other computers).

- /etc/vsftpd — Contains configuration files used to set up the vsftpd FTP server.

- /etc/xinetd.d — Contains a set of files, each of which defines a network service that the xinetd daemon listens for on a particular port. When the xinetd daemon process receives a request for a service, it uses the information in these files to determine which daemon processes to start to handle the request.

Administrative log files

One of the things that Linux does well is keep track of itself. This is a good thing, when you consider how much can go wrong with a complex operating system. Sometimes you are trying to get a new facility to work and it fails without giving you the foggiest reason why. Other times you want to monitor your system to see if people are trying to access your computer illegally. In any of those cases, you can use log files to help track down the problem.

The main utilities for logging error and debugging messages for Linux are the syslogd and klogd daemons. General system logging is done by syslogd. Logging that is specific to kernel activity is done by klogd. Logging is done according to information in the /etc/syslog.conf file. Messages are typically directed to log files that are usually in the /var/log directory.

As root user, you can view log files with a text editor (such as gedit or vi) or watch messages as they enter log file using the tail command (tail -f /var/log/messages).

Using other administrative logins

You don't hear much about other administrative logins (besides root) being used with Linux. It was a fairly common practice in UNIX systems to have several different administrative logins that allowed administrative tasks to be split among several users.

In any case, these administrative logins are available with Linux, so you may want to look into using them. At the very least, because individual software packages such as bind, squid, and amanda set up permissions for their log files and configuration files based on their administrative logins, maintaining those permissions can impede someone who hacks into one of those services from gaining control of the whole computer.

> **TIP:** Because most Fedora and RHEL administrative features are expected to be administered by the root user, e-mail for other administrative accounts is routed to the root user. If you want other administrative users to receive their own e-mail, delete the aliases for those users from the /etc/aliases file.

Understanding administrative logins

Here are some of the administrative logins that are configured automatically for Linux systems. By tradition, these logins are assigned UID numbers under 100. Here are examples:

> **TIP:** Most administrative logins have no passwords by default. They also typically have `/sbin/nologin` assigned as their shell, so if you try to log in as one of these users, you see a `This account is currently not available` message. That's why you can't use an administrative login separately until you assign it a password and shell (such as `/bin/bash`).

- **lp** — This user can control some printing features. Having a separate lp administrator allows someone other than the super user to do such things as move or remove lp logs and print spool files. The home directory for lp is `/var/spool/lpd`.

- **mail** — This user can work with administrative e-mail features. The mail group has group permissions to use mail files in `/var/spool/mail` (which is also the mail user's home directory).

- **uucp** — This user owns various `uucp` commands (once used as the primary method for dial-up serial communications). It is the owner of log files in `/var/log/uucp`, spool files in `/var/spool`, administrative commands (such as uuchk, uucico, uuconv, and uuxqt) in `/usr/sbin`, and user commands (uucp, cu, uuname, uustat, and uux) in `/usr/bin`. The home directory for uucp is `/var/spool/uucp`.

- **bin** — This user owns many commands in `/bin` in traditional UNIX systems. This is not the case in Fedora and RHEL because root tends to own most executable files. The home directory of bin is `/bin`.

- **news** — This user could do administration of Internet news services, depending on how you set permission for `/var/spool/news` and other news-related resources. The home directory for news is `/etc/news`.

Using sudo for assigning administrative privilege

One way to give full or limited root privileges to any non-root user is to set up the `sudo` facility. That simply entails adding the user to `/etc/sudoers` and defining what privilege you want that user to have. Then the user can run any command he or she is privileged to use by preceding that command with the `sudo` command.

The following is an example of how to use the `sudo` facility to cause any users that are added to the `wheel` group to have full root privileges:

1. As the root user, edit the `/etc/sudoers` file by running the `visudo` command:

```
# /usr/sbin/visudo
```

   By default, the file is opened in `vi`, unless your `EDITOR` variable happens to be set to some other editor acceptable to `visudo` (for example, `export EDITOR=gedit`). The reason for using `visudo` is that the command will lock the `/etc/sudoers` file and do some basic sanity-checking of the file to ensure it was edited correctly.

> **NOTE:** If you are stuck here, refer to the vi tutorial ("Using the vi Text Editor") in Chapter 4 for information.

2. Uncomment the following line to allow users in the group named `wheel` to have full root privileges on the computer:

```
%wheel       ALL=(ALL)        ALL
```

The previous line causes the user to be prompted for a password to be allowed to use administrative commands. To allow users in the `wheel` group to have that privilege without using a password, uncomment the following line instead:

```
%wheel       ALL=(ALL)        NOPASSWD: ALL
```

3. Save the changes to the `/etc/sudoers` file.

4. Still as root user, open the `/etc/group` file in any text editor and add the users you want to have root privilege to the `wheel` line. For example, if you were to add the users `mary` and `jake` to the `wheel` group, the line would appear as follows:

```
wheel:x:10:root,mary,jake
```

At this point, the users `mary` and `jake` can run the `sudo` command to run commands, or parts of commands, that are normally restricted to the root user. The following is an example of a session by the user `jake` after he has been assigned `sudo` privileges:

```
[jake]$ sudo umount /mnt/win

We trust you have received the usual lecture from the local System
Administrator. It usually boils down to these two things:

        #1) Respect the privacy of others.
        #2) Think before you type.

Password: ********
[jake]$ mount /mnt/win
mount: only root can mount /dev/sda1 on /mnt/win
[jake]$ sudo mount /mnt/win
[jake]$
```

In the preceding session, the user `jake` runs the `sudo` command so he can unmount the `/mnt/win` file system (using the `umount` command). He is given a warning and asked to provide his password (this is `jake`'s password, *not* the root password).

Notice that even after `jake` has given the password, he must still use the `sudo` command to run the command as root (the first mount fails, but the second succeeds). Notice that he was not prompted for a password for the second `sudo`. That's because after entering his password successfully he can enter as many `sudo` commands as he wants for the next five minutes without having to enter it again. (You can change the timeout value from five minutes to however long you want by setting the `passwd_timeout` value in the `/etc/sudoers` file.)

The preceding example grants a simple all-or-nothing administrative privilege to everyone you put in the `wheel` group. However, the `/etc/sudoers` file gives you an incredible amount of flexibility in permitting individual users and groups to use individual applications or groups of applications. I recommend you refer to the `sudoers` and `sudo` man pages for information about how to tune your `sudo` facility.

Administering Your Linux System

Your Linux system administrator duties don't end after you have installed Fedora or RHEL. Your ongoing job as a Linux system administrator includes the following tasks:

- **Configuring hardware** — Often when you add hardware to your Fedora or RHEL computer, that hardware will be automatically detected and configured by tools such as kudzu. In those cases where the hardware was not properly set up, you can use commands such as `lsmod`, `modprobe`, `insmod`, and `rmmod` to configure the right modules to get the hardware working.

- **Managing file systems and disk space** — You must keep track of the disk space being consumed, especially if your Fedora or RHEL system is shared by multiple users. At some point, you may need to add a hard disk or track down what is eating up your disk space (you can use commands like `find`, `du`, and `df` to do this).

- **Monitoring system performance** — You may have a run-away process on your system or you may just be experiencing slow performance. Tools that come with Fedora and RHEL can help you determine how much of your CPU and memory are being consumed.

The aforementioned administrative tasks are described in the rest of this chapter. Other chapters cover other administrative topics, such as managing user accounts (Chapter 11), automating system tasks (Chapter 12), system backups and restores (Chapter 13), and securing your system (Chapter 14). Tasks related to network and server administration are covered in Chapters 15 through 26. Ways of getting updates to your Linux software (using the Add/Remove Software window and `yum` command) are described in Chapter 5.

Configuring Hardware

For many hardware items that you attach to your computer, Linux will simply detect them and configure them. During system boot time, the kernel will probe and identify your IDE drives, SCSI drives, PCI cards, and other hardware. After Linux desktop is running, USB devices that you plug in (such as pen drives or digital cameras) will be detected and any file systems they contain will be automatically mounted.

The following section describes how to add and reconfigure hardware in Linux. This includes sections on checking your hardware, using kudzu (for detecting and configuring hardware) and commands for working with loadable modules when hardware isn't being detected and configured properly.

Checking your hardware

Sometime the fact that Fedora or RHEL can't properly detect and configure your hardware may make it impossible for you to install Linux. In those cases, I suggest you try to determine what hardware you have before you install. See Chapter 2 for information on checking your hardware before installing Fedora or RHEL (you can try the bootable Fedora live CD that comes with this book to test your hardware).

Reconfiguring hardware with kudzu

When you add or remove hardware from your computer and reboot Linux, a window appears during the boot process advising that hardware has either been added or removed and asking if you want to reconfigure it. The program that detects and reconfigures your hardware is called kudzu.

The kudzu program is a hardware autodetection and configuration tool that runs automatically at boot time. If you like, you can also start kudzu while Linux is running. In either case, here is what kudzu does:

1. It checks the hardware connected to your computer.

2. It compares the hardware it finds to the database of hardware information stored in the `/etc/sysconfig/hwconf` file.

3. It prompts you to change your system configuration, based on new or removed hardware that was detected.

The following is a list of hardware that kudzu can detect (according to the kudzu README file), followed by a description of what kudzu does to configure the device. Other devices may be detected as well (such as USB devices).

- **Network devices** — Adds an Ethernet interface alias (eth0, eth1, and so on) if necessary and either migrates the old device configuration or creates a new one.

- **SCSI** — Adds an alias for `scsi_hostadapter`.

- **Sound card** — Runs the `sndconfig` command to configure and test the sound card.

- **Mouse** —Runs the `mouseconfig` command to configure and test the mouse.

- **Modem** — Links the new modem device to `/dev/modem`.

- **CD-ROM** — Links the CD-ROM device to `/dev/cdrom`.

- **Scanner** — Links the new scanner device to `/dev/scanner`.

- **Keyboard** — Runs the `kbdconfig` command to reconfigure the keyboard. Also, if you are using a serial console, it makes sure `/etc/inittab` and `/etc/securetty` are configured to be used by a serial console.

The following is a list of actions kudzu takes when a device is removed:

- **Network** — Removes the alias for the Ethernet interface (eth0, eth1, and so on).
- **SCSI** — Removes the alias for the SCSI host adapter (scsi_hostadapter).
- **Modem** — Removes the link to `/dev/modem`.
- **CD-ROM** — Removes the link to `/dev/cdrom`.
- **Scanner** — Removes the link to `/dev/scanner`.

To run kudzu, either reboot (during the reboot, kudzu is run automatically) or simply run the `kudzu` command (as root user from a shell). For any hardware that has been added or removed since the last time kudzu was run, you are asked if you want to configure it, not configure it, or do nothing.

> **NOTE:** Removable devices, such as digital cameras, USB flash drives, and Webcams, are detected and configured on-the-fly using the hald daemon. The hald daemon relies on the Udev device management facility to dynamically create devices and mount points (if needed) when those types of devices are connected. See Chapter 8 for descriptions of how CDs and digital cameras are detected.

Configuring modules

In a perfect world, after installing and booting Linux, all of your hardware should be detected and available for access. While Fedora and Red Hat Enterprise Linux systems are rapidly moving closer to that world, there are times when you must take special steps to get your computer hardware working.

Fedora and RHEL systems come with tools for configuring the drivers that stand between the programs you run (such as CD players and Web browsers) and the hardware they use (such as CD-ROM drives and network cards). The intention is to have only the most critical drivers your system needs built into the kernel; these are called *resident drivers*. Other drivers that are added dynamically as needed are referred to as *loadable modules*. The trend is to keep the basic kernel as lean as possible, so that each running system has only a few resident drivers and it can dynamically add what it needs.

Listing loaded modules

To see which modules are currently loaded into the running kernel on your computer, you can use the `lsmod` command. Here's an example:

```
# lsmod
Module                  Size  Used by
```

```
snd_seq_oss              38912  0
snd_seq_midi_event        9344  1 snd_seq_oss
snd_seq                  67728  4 snd_seq_oss,snd_seq_midi_event
snd_seq_device            8328  2 snd_seq_oss,snd_seq
.
.
.
autofs                   16512  0
ne2k_pci                  9056  0
8390                     13568  1 ne2k_pci
ohci1394                 41860  0
ieee1394                284464  1 ohci1394
floppy                   65712  0
sg                       36120  0
scsi_mod                124600  1 sg
parport_pc               39724  0
parport                  47336  1 parport_pc
ext3                    128424  2
jbd                      86040  1 ext3
```

This output shows a variety of modules that have been loaded on a Linux system. The modules loaded on this system include several to support the ALSA sound system, including some that provide OSS compatibility (snd_seq_oss).

To find information about any of the loaded modules, you can use the `modinfo` command. For example, you could type the following:

```
# modinfo snd-seq-oss
filename:      /lib/modules/2.6.25-8.fc9.i686/kernel/sound/core/seq/oss/snd-seq-oss.ko
alias:         sound-service-?-1
alias:         sound-service-?-8
license:       GPL
description:   OSS-compatible sequencer module
author:        Takashi Iwai <tiwai@suse.de>
srcversion:    0C66CC71AF1E69F8CC186A6
depends:       snd,snd-seq,snd-seq-midi-event,snd-seq-device
vermagic:      2.6.25-8.FC9.I686 SMP mod_unload 686 4KSTACKS
parm:          maxqlen:maximum queue length (int)
parm:          seq_oss_debug:debug option (int)
```

This output tells you the location of the module (filename), the author, and description, among other information. The output describes snd-seq-oss as an OSS-compatible sequencer module. You can use the -d option to list just the description, the -a option to see the author of the module or -n to see the object file representing the module. The author information often has the e-mail address of the driver's creator, so you can contact the author if you have problems or questions about it.

Loading modules

You can load any module that has been compiled and installed (to the `/lib/modules` directory) into your running kernel using the `modprobe` command. The most common reasons for loading a module are that you want to use a feature temporarily (such as loading a module to support a special file system on a floppy you want to access) or to identify a module that will be used by a particular piece of hardware that could not be autodetected.

Here is an example of the `modprobe` command being used to load the parport module. The parport module provides the core functions to share parallel ports with multiple devices.

```
# modprobe parport
```

After parport is loaded you can load the parport_pc module to define the PC-style ports available through the interface. The parport_pc module lets you optionally define the addresses and IRQ numbers associated with each device sharing the parallel port. For example:

```
# modprobe parport_pc io=0x3bc irq=auto
```

In the previous example, a device is identified as having an address of 0x3bc. The IRQ for the device is autodetected.

The `modprobe` command loads modules temporarily. At the next system reboot, the modules you enter disappear. To permanently add the module to your system, add the `modprobe` command line to one of the start-up scripts that are run a boot time.

> **NOTE:** An alternative to using `modprobe` is the `insmod` command. The advantage of using `modprobe`, however, is that `insmod` will only load the module you request, while `modprobe` will try to load other modules that the one you requested is dependent on.

Removing modules

You can remove a module from a running kernel using the `rmmod` command. For example, to remove the module parport_pc from the current kernel, type the following:

```
# rmmod parport_pc
```

If the module is not currently busy, the parport_pc module is removed from the running kernel. (Instead of `rmmod`, you can use `modprobe -r` to remove the module, plus related modules.)

> **NOTE:** There are times when a piece of hardware is improperly detected and a module is loaded that is either the wrong module or is simply a broken module. In that case, you can consider adding the name of the offending driver to the `/etc/modprobe.d/blacklist` file, to prevent that module from being loaded. After that, you can consider loading the proper module manually or by adding a `modprobe` command to load the module you want from a system startup file.

Managing File Systems and Disk Space

File systems in Linux are organized in a hierarchy, beginning from root (/) and continuing downward in a structure of directories and subdirectories. As an administrator of a Fedora or RHEL system, it is your duty to make sure that all the disk drives that represent your file system are available to the users of the computer. It is also your job to make sure there is enough disk space in the right places in the file system for users to store what they need.

File systems are organized differently in Linux than they are in Microsoft Windows operating systems. Instead of drive letters (for example, A:, B:, C:) for each local disk, network file system, CD-ROM, or other type of storage medium, everything fits neatly into the directory structure. For hard drive partitions, it is up to an administrator to create a mount point in the file system and then connect the disk to that point in the file system. For removable media (such as CD, DVD, USB flash drives, or digital cameras), mount points are automatically created and connected (in the /media directory) when those items are connected or loaded.

> **CROSS-REFERENCE:** Chapter 2 provides instructions for using Disk Setup (formerly Disk Druid) to configure disk partitions. Chapter 4 describes how the Linux file system is organized.

The organization of your file system begins when you install Linux. Part of the installation process is to divide your hard disk (or disks) into partitions. Those partitions can then be assigned to:

- A part of the Linux file system,
- Swap space for Linux, or
- Other file system types (perhaps containing other bootable operating systems)

For our purposes, I want to focus on partitions that are used for the Linux file system. To see what partitions are currently set up on your hard disk, use the fdisk command as follows:

```
# fdisk -l
Disk /dev/sda:  40.0 GB, 40020664320
255 heads, 63 sectors/track, 4825 cylinders
Units = cylinders of 16065 * 512 bytes = 8225280 bytes

   Device Boot      Start         End      Blocks   Id  System
/dev/sda1   *           1          13         104    b  Win95 FAT32
/dev/sda2              84          89       48195   83  Linux
/dev/sda3              90         522     3478072+  83  Linux
/dev/sda4             523         554      257040    5  W95 Ext'd (LBA)
/dev/sda5             523         554      257008+  82  Linux swap / Solaris
```

This output shows the disk partitioning for a computer able to run both Linux and Microsoft Windows. You can see that the Linux partition on /dev/sda3 has most of the space available for data. There is a Windows partition (/dev/sda1) and a Linux swap partition

(/dev/sda5). There is also a small /boot partition (46MB) on /dev/sda2. In this case, the root partition for Linux has 3.3GB of disk space and resides on /dev/sda3.

Next, to see what partitions are actually being used for your Linux system, you can use the mount command (with no options). The mount command can show you which of the available disk partitions are actually mounted and where they are mounted.

```
# mount
/dev/sda3 on / type ext3 (rw)
/dev/sda2 on /boot type ext3 (rw)
/dev/sda1 on /mnt/win type vfat (rw)
none on /proc type proc (rw)
none on /sys type sysfs (rw)
none on /dev/pts type devpts (rw,gid=5,mode=620)
none on /dev/shm type tmpfs (rw)
none on /proc/sys/fs/binfmt_misc type binfmt_misc (rw)
/dev/scd0 on /media/cdrecorder_ type iso9660
(ro,nosuid,nodev,uhelper=hal)
```

> **NOTE:** You may notice that /proc, /sys, /dev/pts, /proc/sys/fs/binfmt_misc, /dev/shm, and other entries not relating to a partition are shown as file systems. This is because they represent different file system types (proc and devpts, and so on). The word none, however, indicates that they are not associated with a separate physical partition.

The mounted Linux partitions in this case are /dev/sda2, which provides space for the /boot directory (which contains data for booting Linux), and /dev/sda3, which provides space for the rest of the Linux file system beginning from the root directory (/). This particular system also contains a Windows partition that was mounted in the /mnt/win directory.

Beginning with Fedora Core 3 and RHEL 4, mount points for removable media (CDs, DVDs, USB pen drives, and so on) moved from /mnt to the /media directory. In this example, an IDE combination CDRW/DVD-ROM drive was mounted on /media/cdrecorder. With most GUI interfaces, the CD or DVD is typically mounted automatically when you insert it. In this example, the uhelper (unprivileged unmount request helper) is assigned to the hald daemon user hal so that the hald facility can unmount the CD as an otherwise non-privileged user.

> **NOTE:** See a description of the GNOME Volume Manager in Chapter 3 for information about how removable media are handled in the current Fedora and RHEL releases.

After the word type, you can see the type of file system contained on the device. (See the description of different file system types in the next section of this chapter.) Particularly on larger Linux systems, you may have multiple partitions for several reasons:

- **Multiple hard disks** — You may have several hard disks available to your users. In that case you would have to mount each disk (and possibly several partitions from each disk) in different locations in your file system.

- **Protecting different parts of the file system** — If you have many users on a system, and the users consume all of the file system space, the entire system can fail. For example, there may be no place for temporary files to be copied (so the programs writing to temporary files may fail), and incoming mail may fail to be written to mail boxes. With multiple mounted partitions, if one partition runs out, others can continue to work.

- **Backups** — There are some fast ways to back up data from your computer that involve copying the entire image of a disk or partition. If you want to restore that partition later, you can simply copy it back (bit by bit) to a hard disk. With smaller partitions, this approach can be done fairly efficiently.

- **Protecting from disk failure** — If one disk (or part of one disk) fails, by having multiple partitions mounted on your file system, you may be able to continue working and just fix the one disk that fails.

When a disk partition is mounted on the file system, all directories and subdirectories below that mount point are then stored on that partition. So, for example, if you were to mount one partition on / and one on /usr, everything below the /usr mount point would be stored on the second partition while everything else would be stored on the first partition. If you then mounted another partition on /usr/local, everything below that mount point would be on the third partition, while everything else below /usr would be on the second partition.

> **TIP:** What if a remote file system is unmounted from your computer, and you go to save a file in that mount point directory? What happens is that you will write the file to that directory and it will be stored on your local hard disk. When the remote file system is remounted, however, the file you saved will seem to disappear. To get the file back, you will have to unmount the remote file system (causing the file to reappear), move the file to another location, remount the file system, and copy the file back there.

Mount points that are often mentioned as being candidates for separate partitions include /, /boot, /home, /usr, and /var. The root file system (/) is the catchall for directories that aren't in other mount points. The root file system's mount point (/) is the only one that is required. The /boot directory holds the images needed to boot the operating system. The /home file systems is where all the user accounts are typically stored. Applications and documentation are stored in /usr. Below the /var mount point is where log files, temporary files, server files (Web, FTP, and so on), and lock files are stored (that is, items that need disk space for your computer's applications to keep running).

> **CROSS-REFERENCE:** See Chapter 2 for further information on partitioning techniques.

The fact that multiple partitions are mounted on your file system is invisible to people using your Linux system. The only times they will care will be if a partition runs out of space or if they need to save or use information from a particular device (such as a floppy disk or remote file system). Of course, any user can check this by typing the `mount` command.

Mounting file systems

Most of your hard disk partitions are mounted automatically for you. When you installed Fedora or RHEL, you were asked to create partitions and indicate the mount points for those partitions. When you boot Fedora or RHEL, all Linux partitions residing on hard disk should typically be mounted. For that reason, this section focuses mostly on how to mount other types of devices so that they become part of your Linux file system.

Besides being able to mount other types of devices, you can also use `mount` to mount other kinds of file systems on your Linux system. This means that you can store files from other operating systems or use file systems that are appropriate for certain kinds of activities (such as writing large block sizes). The most common use of this feature for the average Linux user, however, is to allow that user to obtain and work with files from floppy disks or CD-ROMs.

Supported file systems

To see file system types that are currently available to be used on your system, type **cat /proc/filesystems**. The following file system types are supported in Linux, although they may not be in use at the moment or they may not be built into your current kernel (so they may need to be loaded as modules):

- **adfs** — This is the acorn disc file system, which is the standard file system used on RiscOS operating systems.
- **befs** — This is the file system used by the BeOS operating system.
- **cifs** — The Common Internet File System (CIFS) is the virtual file system used to access servers that comply with the SNIA CIFS specification. CIFS is an attempt to refine and standardize the SMB protocol used by Samba and Windows file sharing.
- **ext3** — The ext file systems are the most common file systems used with Linux. The ext3 file system was new for Red Hat Linux 7.2 and is currently the default file system type in many Linux systems (including Fedora and RHEL). The root file system (/) is typically ext3 (although you can use other file systems as well). The ext3 file system is also referred to as the Third Extended file system. The ext3 file system includes journaling features that improve a file system's ability to recover from crashes, as compared to ext2 file systems.
- **ext2** — The default file system type for versions of Red Hat Linux previous to 7.2. Features are the same as ext3, except that ext2 doesn't include journaling features.
- **ext** — This is the first version of the ext file system. It is not used very often anymore and I recommend you don't use it.
- **iso9660** — This file system evolved from the High Sierra file system (which was the original standard used on CD-ROM). Extensions to the High Sierra standard (called

Rock Ridge extensions), allow iso9660 file systems to support long filenames and UNIX-style information (such as file permissions, ownership, and links). This file system type is used when you mount a CD-ROM.

- **kafs** — This is the AFS client file system. It is used in distributed computing environments to share files with Linux, Windows, and Macintosh clients.

- **minix** — This is the Minix file system type, used originally with the Minix version of UNIX. It only supports filenames of up to 30 characters.

- **msdos**— This is an MS-DOS file system. You can use this type to mount floppy disks that come from Microsoft operating systems.

- **vfat** — This is the Microsoft extended FAT (VFAT) file system.

- **umsdos** — This is an MS-DOS file system with extensions to allow features that are similar to UNIX (including long filenames).

- **proc** — This is not a real file system, but rather a file-system interface to the Linux kernel. You probably won't do anything special to set up a proc file system. However, the /proc mount point should be a proc file system. Many utilities rely on /proc to gain access to Linux kernel information.

- **swap** — This is used for swap partitions. Swap areas are used to hold data temporarily when RAM is currently used up. Data is swapped to the swap area, then returned to RAM when it is needed again.

- **nfs** — This is the Network File System (NFS) type of file system. File systems mounted from another computer on your network use this type of file system.

> **CROSS-REFERENCE:** Information on using NFS to export and share file systems over a network is contained in Chapter 18.

- **hpfs** — This file system is used to do read-only mounts of an OS/2 HPFS file system.

- **ncpfs** — This relates to Novell NetWare file systems. NetWare file systems can be mounted over a network.

- **ntfs** — NTFS support was added to the Fedora repository with Fedora 7. Many people who set up dual-boot computers want to be able to access the Windows (ntfs) drives. To add NTFS file system support to Fedora, you need to install the ntfs-3g package.

- **affs** — This file system is used with Amiga computers.

- **reiserfs** — This is a journaling file system that used to be the default file system for some other Linux distributions (including SUSE, Slackware, and Linspire). Reiserfs is not considered to be well-supported in Red Hat systems. (You must add reiser to the boot prompt when you install Fedora to enable reiserfs partitions. Also, SELinux doesn't support reiserfs file systems.)

- **ufs** — This file system is popular on Sun Microsystems operating systems (that is, Solaris and SunOS).

- **xenix** — This was added to be compatible with Xenix file systems (one of the first PC versions of UNIX). The system is obsolete and will probably be removed eventually.

- **xfs** — This is a journaling file system that is useful in high-performance environments. It includes full 64-bit addressing. An xfs file system can scale up to systems that include multiple terabytes of data that transfer data at multiple gigabytes per second.

- **jfs** — This file system is based on the JFS file system IBM used for OS/2 Warp. It became an open source project in 2000. JFS is most suited for enterprise systems. Like XFS, JFS is tuned for large file systems and high-performance environments.

- **xiafs** — This file system supports long filenames and larger inodes than file systems such as minux.

- **squashfs** — This is a compressed file system, where files are uncompressed on the fly as they are requested. It is often used with live CDs, including all official Fedora Live CDs.

- **fuse** — Fuse behaves like a user-space remote file system. A local user can use ssh tools to mount a remote file system locally, without the remote file system being made available, purely on the basis of the permissions of the user you login as. A very cool way to mount a remote file system without administrative intervention on the remote side.

Two new file system types have been added for Fedora 9: ext4 file systems. and encrypted file systems. Although both are still considered experimental, tools are available in Fedora 9 to create and use these new file system types.

The ext4 file system is the latest version of the ext file system (with ext3 being the current standard). An ext4 file system can be mounted as an ext3 file system. However, if you want to use new ext4 features (called extents), mount it as an ext4 device (`mount -t ext4dev`). See the Ext4 FAQ for information on creating and working with ext4 file systems:

```
http://ext4.wiki.kernel.org/index.php/Frequently_Asked_Questions
```

Encrypted file systems can be used to protect your data if your computer should become lost or stolen. In particular, this feature was created with laptops in mind. Someone stealing your laptop would not be able to mount or access data on an encrypted file system without your password. The `cryptsetup` command from the cryptsetup-luks package is used to create cryptographic volumes. Any file system, other than root (`/`), can be encrypted in Fedora 9. To learn more, refer to the Encrypted Filesystems Feature page:

```
http://fedoraproject.org/wiki/Releases/FeatureEncryptedFilesystems
```

Using the fstab file to define mountable file systems

The hard disks on your local computer and the remote file systems you use every day are probably set up to mount automatically when you boot Linux. The definitions for which of these file systems are mounted are contained in the `/etc/fstab` file. Here's an example of an `/etc/fstab` file:

```
/dev/VolGroup00/LogVol00  /                  ext3    defaults        1 1
LABEL=/boot               /boot              ext3    defaults        1 2
/dev/devpts               /dev/pts           devpts  gid=5,mode=620  0 0
/dev/shm                  /dev/shm           tmpfs   defaults        0 0
/dev/proc                 /proc              proc    defaults        0 0
/dev/sys                  /sys               sysfs   defaults        0 0
/dev/VolGroup00/LogVol01  swap               swap    defaults        0 0
/dev/sda1                 /mnt/win           vfat    noauto              0
0
```

All file systems listed in this file are mounted at boot time, except for those set to `noauto` in the fourth field. In this example, the root (`/`) and swap hard disk partitions are configured as logical volume management (LVM) volumes. This means that they may consist of multiple hard disk partitions. You can use the `pvdisplay` command to see what physical volumes make up each logical volume. An advantage of LVM volumes is that, if you run out of space in a logical volume, you can simply attach a new physical volume (such as a disk partition) to extend its size. You don't have to resize or create a new partition.

The `/proc`, `/sys`, `/dev/shm`, and `/dev/pts` file systems are not associated with particular devices. The floppy disk and CD-ROM drive entries are no longer included in the `/etc/fstab` file by default. That's because those media types are now handled by the hald daemon and mounted automatically when they are inserted. The actual mount points will change based on the CD or DVD's volume name (implanted on that medium itself).

I also added one additional line for `/dev/sda1`, which allows me to mount the Windows (vfat in this case, but ntfs support can be added) partition on my computer so I don't have to always boot Windows to get at the files on my Windows partition.

> **NOTE:** To access the Windows partition described previously, I must first create the mount point (by typing `mkdir /mnt/win`). I can then mount it when I choose by typing (as root) `mount /mnt/win`.

You find the following in each field of the `fstab` file:

- **Field 1** — The name of the device representing the file system. The word `none` is often placed in this field for file systems (such as `/proc` and `/dev/pts`) that are not associated with special devices. Notice that this field can now include the `LABEL` or `UUID` options. Using `UUID`, you can indicate a universally unique identifier (UUID). `LABEL` indicates a volume label instead of a device name. The advantage to the `LABEL` approach is that, since the partition is identified by volume name, you can move a volume to a different device name and not have to change the `fstab` file.

- **Field 2** — The mount point in the file system. The file system contains all data from the mount point down the directory tree structure, unless another file system is mounted at some point beneath it.

- **Field 3** — The file system type. Valid file system types are described in the "Supported file systems" section earlier in this chapter.

- **Field 4** — Options to the `mount` command. In the preceding example, the `noauto` option prevents the indicated file system from being mounted at boot time. Also, `ro` says to mount the file system read-only (which is reasonable for a CD-ROM drive). Commas must separate options. See the `mount` command manual page (under the `-o` option) for information on other supported options.

> **TIP:** Normally, only the root user is allowed to mount a file system using the `mount` command. However, to allow any user to mount a file system (such as a file system on a floppy disk), you could add the `user` or `owner` option to Field 4 of `/etc/fstab`.

- **Field 5** — The number in this field indicates whether or not the indicated file system needs to be dumped. A number 1 assumes that the file system needs to be dumped. A number 0 assumes that the file system doesn't need to be dumped.

- **Field 6** — The number in this field indicates whether or not the indicated file system needs to be checked with `fsck`. A zero indicates that the file system should not be checked. A number 1 assumes that the file system needs to be checked first (this is used for the root file system). A number 2 assumes that the file system can be checked at any point after the root file system is checked.

If you want to add an additional local disk or an additional partition, you can create an entry for the disk or partition in the `/etc/fstab` file. To get instructions on how to add entries for an NFS file system, see Chapter 18.

Using the mount command to mount file systems

Your Fedora or Red Hat Enterprise Linux system automatically runs `mount -a` (mount all file systems) each time you boot. For that reason, you would typically only use the `mount` command for special situations. In particular, the average user or administrator uses `mount` in two ways:

- To display the disks, partitions, and remote file systems that are currently mounted.

- To temporarily mount a file system.

Any user can type the `mount` command (with no options) to see what file systems are currently mounted on the local Linux system. The following is an example of the `mount` command. It shows a single hard disk partition (`/dev/sda1`) containing the root (`/`) file system, and proc and devpts file system types mounted on `/proc` and `/dev`, respectively. The last entry shows a floppy disk, formatted with a standard Linux file system (ext3) mounted on the `/media/floppy` directory.

```
$ mount
/dev/mapper/VolGroup00-LogVol00 on / type ext3 (rw)
/dev/proc on /proc type proc (rw)
/dev/sys on /sys type sysfs (rw)
/dev/devpts on /dev/pts type devpts(rw,gid=5,mode=620)
```

```
/dev/sda3 on /boot type ext3 (rw)
/dev/shm on /dev/shm type tmpfs (rw)
/dev/fd0 on /media/floppy type ext3 (rw)
```

The most common devices to mount by hand are your floppy disk and your CD-ROM. However, by default now in Fedora and other Linux systems, CD-ROMs and floppy disks are mounted for you automatically when you insert them. (In some cases, the autorun program may also run automatically. For example, autorun may start a CD music player or software package installer to handle the data on the medium.)

Mounting removable media

If you want to mount a file system manually, the /etc/fstab file helps make it simple to mount a file system from any disk partition, floppy disk, or a CD-ROM. Although Fedora no longer automatically adds entries for CDs and floppy disks to the /etc/fstab file, you could add entries manually, if you wanted to mount those media in different locations. Here are examples of entries you could add to your /etc/fstab file:

```
/dev/cdrom  /mnt/cdrom  auto noauto,user,exec,ro 0 0
/dev/fd0  /mnt/floppy auto noauto,owner       0 0
```

The /mnt directory is the location traditionally used to mount removable or temporary file systems in Linux. If you are adding mount points manually, it's best to use a location such as /mnt, instead of the newer /media directory, so you don't conflict with any file systems the Hal service (hald daemon) mounts automatically in the /media directory.

With entries added such as those just shown, you can use the mount command with a single option to indicate what you want to mount, and information is taken from the /etc/fstab file to fill in the other options. The following are cases where you could mount a CD or floppy disk file system using a single option (based on the /etc/fstab file shown above):

- **CD-ROM** — If you are mounting a CD-ROM that is in the standard ISO 9960 format (as most software CD-ROMs are), you can mount that CD-ROM by placing it in your CD-ROM drive and typing the following:

```
# mount /mnt/cdrom
```

By default, your CD-ROM is mounted on a point in the /media directory. The command just shown, however, mounts the /dev/cdrom device on the /mnt/cdrom directory.

- **Floppy Disk** — If you are mounting a floppy disk that is in the standard Linux file system format (ext3), based on the /etc/fstab file entry shown above, you can mount that floppy disk by inserting it in your floppy drive and typing the following:

```
# mount /mnt/floppy
```

The file system type (ext3), device (/dev/fd0), and mount options are filled in from the /etc/fstab file. You should be able to change to the floppy disk directory (cd /mnt/floppy) and list the contents of the floppy's top directory (ls).

> **NOTE:** In both of the two previous cases, you could give the device name (/dev/cdrom or /dev/fd0, respectively) instead of the mount point directory to get the same results.

Of course, it is possible that you may get floppy disks you want to use that are in all formats. Someone may give you a floppy containing files from a Microsoft operating system (in MS-DOS format). Or you may get a file from another UNIX system. In those cases, you can fill in your own options, instead of relying on options from the /etc/fstab file. In some cases, Linux autodetects that the floppy disk contains an MS-DOS (or Windows vfat) file system and mount it properly without additional arguments. However, if it doesn't, here is an example of how to mount a floppy containing MS-DOS files:

```
# mount -t msdos /dev/fd0 /mnt/floppy
```

This shows the basic format of the mount command you would use to mount a floppy disk. You could change msdos to any other supported file system type (described earlier in this chapter) to mount a floppy of that type. Instead of using floppy drive A: (/dev/fd0), you could use drive B: (/dev/fd1) or any other accessible drive. Instead of mounting on /mnt/floppy, you could create any other directory and mount the floppy there.

Here are some other useful options you could add along with the mount command:

- -t auto — If you aren't sure exactly what type of file system is contained on the floppy disk (or other medium you are mounting), use the -t auto option to indicate the file system type. The mount command will query the disk to try to guess what type of data it contains.
- -r — If you don't want to make changes to the mounted file system (or can't because it is a read-only medium), use this option when you mount it. This will mount it read-only.
- -w — This mounts the file system with read/write permission.

Mounting CD or DVD images

Another valuable way to use the mount command has to do with ISO disk images. If you download a CD, DVD, or floppy disk image from the Internet and you want to see what it contains, you can do so without burning it to CD or floppy. With the image on your hard disk, create a mount point and use the -o loop option to mount it locally. Here's an example of what to type (as root user):

```
# mkdir /mnt/mycdimage
# mount -o loop whatever-i386-disc1.iso /mnt/mycdimage
```

In this example, the disk image file (whatever-i386-disc1.iso) residing in the current directory is mounted on the /mnt/mycdimage directory I just created. I can now cd to that directory, view the contents of it, and copy or use any of its contents. This is useful for downloaded CD images that you want to install software from without having to burn the image to CD. When you are done, just type umount /mnt/mycdimage to unmount it.

Other options to mount are available only for a specific file system type. See the mount manual page for those and other useful options.

Using the umount command to unmount a file system

When you are done using a temporary file system, or you want to unmount a permanent file system temporarily, you can use the umount command. This command detaches the file system from its mount point in your Linux file system. To use umount, you can give it either a directory name or a device name. For example:

```
# umount /mnt/floppy
```

This unmounts the device (probably /dev/fd0) from the mount point /mnt/floppy. You could also have done this using the form:

```
# umount /dev/fd0
```

In general, it's better to use the directory name because the umount command will fail if the device is mounted in more than one location.

If you get a message that the "device is busy," the umount request has failed. The reason is that either a process has a file open on the device or that you have a shell open with a directory on the device as a current directory. Stop the processes or change to a directory outside of the device you are trying to unmount for the umount request to succeed.

An alternative for unmounting a busy device is the -l option. With umount -l (a lazy unmount), the unmount happens as soon as the device is no longer busy. To unmount a remote NFS file system that is no longer available (for example, the server went down), you can use the umount -f option to forcibly unmount the NFS file system.

Using the mkfs command to create a file system

It is possible to create a file system, for any supported file system type, on a disk or partition that you choose. This is done with the mkfs command. While this is most useful for creating file systems on hard disk partitions, you can create file systems on floppy disks or re-writable CDs as well.

Here is an example of using mkfs to create a file system on a floppy disk:

```
# mkfs -t ext3 /dev/fd0
mke2fs 1.39, (29-May-2006)
Filesystem label=
OS type: Linux
Block size=1024 (log=0)
Fragment size=1024 (log=0)
```

```
184 inodes, 1440 blocks
72 blocks (5.00%) reserved for the super user
First data block=1
1 block group
8192 blocks per group, 8192 fragments per group
184 inodes per group

Writing inode tables: done

Filesystem too small for a journal
Writing superblocks and filesystem accounting information: done

The filesystem will be automatically checked every 23 mounts or
180 days, whichever comes first. Use tune2fs -c or -i to override.
```

You can see the statistics that are output with the formatting done by the mkfs command. The number of inodes and blocks created are output. Likewise, the number of blocks per group and fragments per group are also output. You could now mount this file system (mount /mnt/floppy), change to it as your current directory (cd /mnt/floppy), and create files on it as you please.

Adding a hard disk

Adding a new hard disk to your computer so that it can be used by Linux requires a combination of steps described in previous sections. The general steps are as follows:

1. Install the hard disk hardware.
2. Identify the partitions on the new hard disk.
3. Create the file systems on the new hard disk.
4. Mount the file systems.

The easiest way to add a hard disk to Linux is to have the entire hard disk devoted to a single Linux partition. You can have multiple partitions of different sizes, however, and assign them each to different types of file systems and different mount points, if you like. The following procedure describes how to add a hard disk containing a single Linux partition. Along the way, however, it also notes which steps you need to repeat to have multiple file systems with multiple mount points.

> **NOTE:** This procedure assumes that Fedora or RHEL is already installed and working on the computer. If this is not the case, follow the instructions for adding a hard disk on your current operating system. Later, when you install Fedora or RHEL, you can identify this disk when asked to partition your hard disk(s).

1. Install the hard disk into your computer. Follow the manufacturer's instructions for physically installing and connecting the new hard disk. If, presumably, this is a second

hard disk, you may need to change jumpers on the hard disk unit itself to have it operate as a slave hard disk. You may also need to change the BIOS settings.

2. Boot your computer to Linux.

3. Determine the device name for the hard disk. As root user from a shell, type:

```
# dmesg | less
```

From the output, look for an indication that the new hard disk was found. For example, if it is a second hard disk, you should see sdb: in the output. Be sure you identify the right disk or you will erase all the data from disks you probably want to keep!

> **NOTE:.** Note that prior to Fedora 7, IDE hard drives began with /dev/hd and SCSI drives began with /dev/sd. Now, both IDE and SCSI drives begin with /dev/sd, as in /dev/sda and /dev/sdb.

4. Use the fdisk command to create partitions on the new disk. For example, if you are formatting the second hard disk (sdb), you could type the following:

```
# fdisk /dev/sdb1
```

5. If the disk had existing partitions on it, you can change or delete those partitions now. Or, you can simply reformat the whole disk to blow everything away. Use p to view all partitions and d to delete a partition.

6. To create a new partition, type the following:

```
n
```

You are asked to choose an extended or primary partition.

7. To choose a primary partition, type the following:

```
p
```

You are asked the partition number.

8. If you are creating the first partition (or for only one partition), type the number 1:

```
1
```

You are asked to enter the first cylinder number (with 1 being the default).

9. To begin at the second cylinder, type the number 2 as follows:

```
2
```

You are asked to enter the last cylinder.

10. If you are using the entire hard disk, use the last cylinder number shown. Otherwise, choose the ending cylinder number or indicate how many megabytes the partition should have.

11. To create more partitions on the hard disk, repeat Steps 6 through 10 for each partition.

12. Type **w** to write changes to the hard disk. At this point, you should be back at the shell.

13. To make a file system on the new disk partition, use the `mkfs` command. By default, this command creates an ext2 file system, which is useable by Linux. To create an ext3 file system on the first partition of the second hard disk, type the following:

```
# mkfs -t ext3 /dev/sdb1
```

If you created multiple partitions, repeat this step for each partition (such as `/dev/sdb2`, `/dev/sdb3`, and so on).

> **TIP:** If you don't use `-t ext3` as shown above, an ext2 file system is created by default. Use other commands, or options to this command, to create other file system types. For example, use `mkfs.vfat` to create a VFAT file system, `mkfs.msdos` for DOS, or `mkfs.reiserfs` for Reiser file system type. The `tune2fs` command, described later in this section, can be used to change an ext2 file system to an ext3 file system.

14. Once the file system is created, you can have the partition permanently mounted by editing the `/etc/fstab` and adding the new partition. Here is an example of a line you might add to that file:

```
/dev/sdb1            /abc            ext3        defaults       1 1
```

In this example, the partition (`/dev/sdb1`) is mounted on the `/abc` directory as an ext3 file system. The `defaults` keyword causes the partition to be mounted at boot time. The numbers `1 1` cause the disk to be checked for errors. Add one line like the one shown above for each partition you created.

15. Create the mount point. For example, to mount the partition on `/abc` (as shown in the previous step), type the following:

```
# mkdir /abc
```

Create your other mount points if you created multiple partitions. The next time you boot Linux, the partition will be automatically mounted on the `/abc` directory, as will any other partitions you added.

After you have created the file systems on your partitions, a nice tool for adjusting those file systems is the `tune2fs` command. Using `tune2fs`, you can change volume labels, how often the file system is checked, and error behavior. You can also use `tune2fs` to change an ext2 file system to an ext3 file system so the file system can use journaling. For example:

```
# tune2fs -j /dev/sdb1
tune2fs 1.39 (29-May-2006)
Creating journal inode: done
This filesystem will be automatically checked every 38 mounts or
180 days, whichever comes first. Use tune2fs -c or -i to override.
```

By adding the -j option to tune2fs, you can change either the journal size or attach the file system to an external journal block device. After you have used tune2fs to change your file system type, you probably need to correct your /etc/fstab file to include changing the file system type from ext2 to ext3.

Using RAID disks

RAID (Redundant Arrays of Independent Disks) is spreads the data used on a computer across multiple disks, while appearing to the operating system as if it is dealing with a single disk partition. Using the different RAID specifications, you can achieve the following advantages:

- **Improved disk performance** — RAID0 uses a feature called *striping*, where data is striped across multiple RAID partitions. Striping can improve disk performance by spreading the hits on a computer's file system across multiple partitions, which are presumably on multiple hard disks. However, striping does not provide redundancy.

- **Mirroring** — RAID1 uses partitions from multiple hard disks as mirrors. That way, if one of the partitions becomes corrupted or the hard disk goes down, the data exists on a partition from another disk because it has continuously maintained an exact mirror image of the original partition.

- **Parity** — Although striping can improve performance, it can increase the chance of data loss, since any hard-disk crash in the array can potentially cause the entire RAID device to fail. Using a feature called *parity*, information about the layout of the striped data is kept so that data can be reconstructed if one of the disks in the array crashes. RAID3, 4, and 5 implement different levels of parity.

During installation of Fedora or RHEL, you can use the Disk Setup window to create RAID0, RAID1, and RAID5 disk arrays. The following procedures describe how to set up RAID disks during installation.

Before you begin creating RAID partitions when you install Fedora or RHEL, you will probably want to start with a computer that has two or more hard disks. The reason is that, if you don't have multiple hard disks, you won't get the performance gains that come from spreading the hits on your computer among multiple disks. Likewise, mirroring will be ineffective if all RAID partitions are on the same disk because the failure of a single hard disk would still potentially cause the mirrored partitions to fail as well.

For example, you might begin with 30GB of free disk space on your first hard disk (/dev/sda) and 30GB of free disk space on your second hard disk (/dev/sdb). During the Fedora or RHEL installation procedure, select to partition your disk with Disk Setup. Then follow this procedure:

1. From the Disk Setup window, click the RAID button. A RAID Options window appears.

2. Select Create a Software RAID Partition, and click OK. The Add Partition window appears.

3. With Software RAID selected as the File System Type, choose the drive you want to create the partition on and choose the size (in megabytes). Then click OK.

4. Repeat Steps 2 and 3 (presumably creating software RAID partitions on different hard disks until you have created all the RAID partitions you want to use).

5. Click the RAID button again. Select Create a RAID Device [default=/dev/md0] and click OK. The Make RAID Device window appears, as shown in Figure 10-4.

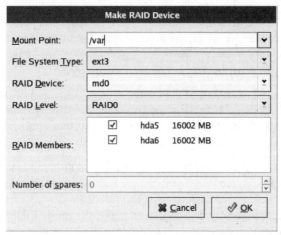

Figure 10-4: Join multiple RAID partitions to form a single RAID device.

6. You need to select the following information about your RAID device and click OK:

    - **Mount Point** — The point in the file system associated with the RAID device. You might be creating the RAID device for a part of the file system for which you expect there to be a lot of hits on the hard disk (such as the /var partition).

    - **File System Type** — For a regular Linux partition, choose ext3. You can also select LVM, swap, or VFAT as the file system type.

    - **RAID Device** — The first RAID device is typically md0 (for /dev/md0).

    - **RAID Level** — Allowable RAID levels are RAID0, RAID1, and RAID5. RAID0 is for striping (essentially dividing the RAID device into stripes across RAID partitions you have selected). RAID1 is for mirroring so that the data is duplicated across all RAID partitions. RAID5 is for parity, so there is always one backup disk if a disk goes bad. You need at least three RAID partitions to use RAID5.

    - **RAID Members** — From the RAID partitions you created, select which ones are going to be members of the RAID device you are creating.

    - **Number of spares** — Select how many spares are available to the RAID device.

The new RAID Device should appear on the Disk Setup window. Click Next to continue with installation.

Once installation is complete, you can check your RAID devices by using a variety of tools that come with Fedora or RHEL. Commands for working with RAID partitions come in the raidtools package. Using raidtools commands, you can list and reconfigure your RAID partitions.

Checking system space

Running out of disk space on your computer is not a happy situation. Using tools that come with Fedora or RHEL, you can keep track of how much disk space has been used on your computer, and you can keep an eye on users who consume a lot of disk space.

Checking Disk Space with Disk Usage Analyzer

The Disk Usage Analyzer, which is part of the gnome-utils package, provides an easy way to see how much and where space is being consumed on your hard disk. To start Disk Usage Analyzer from the GNOME desktop, select Applications → System Tools → Disk Usage Analyzer.

At first, Disk Usage Analyzer displays only the size of the hard disk and amount of space that has been consumed on that disk. However, you can see how much disk space is consumed by files in a particular folder (and its subfolders) by selecting the Folder button and browsing for the folder that interests you. Figure 10-5 shows an example of a music folder containing several subfolders of music. You can sort each subfolder alphabetically or by disk space consumed.

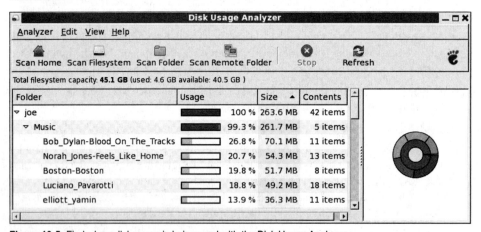

Figure 10-5: Find where disk space is being used with the Disk Usage Analyzer.

Displaying system space with df

You can display the space available in your file systems using the df command. To see the amount of space available on all of the mounted file systems on your Linux computer, type **df** with no options:

```
$ df
Filesystem   1k-blocks      Used   Available  Use%   Mounted on
/dev/sda3    30645460    2958356    26130408   11%   /
/dev/sda2       46668       8340       35919   19%   /boot
/dev/fd0         1412         13        1327    1%   /mnt/floppy
```

The output here shows the space available on the hard disk partition mounted on the root partition (/dev/sda1), /boot partition (/dev/sda2), and the floppy disk mounted on the /mnt/floppy directory (/dev/fd0). Disk space is shown in 1K blocks. To produce output in a more human-readable form, use the -h option as follows:

```
$ df -h
Filesystem         Size  Used  Avail  Use%  Mounted on
/dev/sda3           29G  2.9G    24G   11%  /
/dev/sda2           46M  8.2M    25M   19%  /boot
/dev/fd0           1.4M   13k   1.2M    1%  /mnt/floppy
```

With the df -h option, output appears in a friendlier megabyte or gigabyte listing. Other options with df let you:

- Print only file systems of a particular type (-t type)
- Exclude file systems of a particular type (-x type)
- Include file systems that have no space, such as /proc and /dev/pts (-a)
- List only available and used inodes (-i)
- Display disk space in certain block sizes (--block-size=#)

Checking disk usage with du

To find out how much space is being consumed by a particular directory (and its subdirectories), you can use the du command. With no options, du lists all directories below the current directory, along with the space consumed by each directory. At the end, du produces total disk space used within that directory structure.

The du command is a good way to check how much space is being used by a particular user (du /home/user1) or in a particular file system partition (du /var). By default, disk space is displayed in 1K block sizes. To make the output more friendly (in kilobytes, megabytes, and gigabytes), use the -h option as follows:

```
$ du -h /home/jake
114k    /home/jake/httpd/stuff
234k    /home/jake/httpd
137k    /home/jake/uucp/data
701k    /home/jake/uucp
1.0M    /home/jake
```

The output shows the disk space used in each directory under the home directory of the user named jake (/home/jake). Disk space consumed is shown in kilobytes (k) and megabytes

(M). The total space consumed by /home/jake is shown on the last line. To avoid listing all the subdirectories and see a total for all files and directories below a certain directory, add the -s option as follows:

```
$ du -sh /home/jake
1.0M    /home/jake
```

Finding disk consumption with find

The find command is a great way to find file consumption of your hard disk using a variety of criteria. You can get a good idea of where disk space can be recovered by finding files that are over a certain size or were created by a particular person.

> **NOTE:** You must be root user to run this command effectively, unless you are just checking your personal files.

In the following example, the find command searches the root file system (/) for any files owned by the user named jake (-user jake) and prints the filenames. The output of the find command is then listed with a long listing in size order (ls -ldS). Finally, that output is sent to the file /tmp/jake. When you read the file /tmp/jake, you will find all of the files that are owned by the user jake, listed in size order. Here is the command line:

```
# find / -xdev -user jake -print | xargs ls -ldS > /tmp/jake
```

> **TIP:** The -xdev option prevents file systems other than the selected file system from being searched. This is a good way to cut out a lot of junk that may be output from the /proc file system. It could also keep large remotely mounted file systems from being searched.

The next example is similar to the previous one, except that instead of looking for a user's files, this command line looks for files that are larger than 1000 kilobytes (-size +1000k):

```
# find / -xdev -size +1000k -print | xargs ls -ldS > /tmp/size
```

You can save yourself a lot of disk space by just removing some of the largest files that are no longer needed. Open the /tmp/size file in this example and large files are sorted by size.

Monitoring System Performance

If your Linux system is being used as a multiuser computer, sharing the processing power of that computer can be a major issue. Likewise, any time you can stop a runaway process or reduce the overhead of an unnecessary program running, your Linux server can do a better job serving files, Web pages, or e-mail to the people that rely on it.

Utilities are included with Linux that can help you monitor the performance of your Linux system. The kinds of features you want to monitor in Linux include CPU usage, memory usage (RAM and swap space), and overall load on the system. The following sections describe tools for monitoring Linux.

Watch computer usage with System Monitor

If you like visual representations of your system use, the System Monitor provides a great way to see how much your system is being used. To open the System Monitor from the Applications menu on the GNOME panel, select System Tools → System Monitor. Figure 10-6 shows the System Monitor window with the Resources tab selected.

On the Resource Monitor window, lines scroll from right to left, indicating the percentage of your CPU being used as it rises and falls. You can also see how much of your total memory (RAM) is being used at the moment (and over time), as well as the amount of swap space being used. The bar at the bottom of the window shows the amount of data being sent and received over your computers network interfaces.

Click the Processes tab to see a listing of processes that are running for the current user. Click the columns in that tab to sort processes by name, memory use, percentage of CPU being consumed by the process, and process ID. There are also columns showing the security context of the process (if SELinux is enabled) and the arguments associated with the process.

Click the File Systems tab to see the storage devices (hard disk partitions, CD, USB flash drive, or other) that are currently mounted on your computer. Click columns to sort the devices by device name, directory name, file system type, total disk space, free disk space, or used disk space.

The example in Figure 10-6 shows a computer that is running with over 700MB of RAM. Although there is a fair amount of activity on the System Monitor in this example, there is still User memory available. However, if on your system User memory is running near the maximum, it would indicate the likely occurrence of performance problems as RAM fills up and data has to be moved to swap space. The CPU used is only about 15 percent, which indicates that the CPU is currently keeping up with the demand.

Monitoring CPU usage with top

Start the `top` utility in a Terminal window, and it displays the top CPU consuming processes on your computer. Every five seconds, `top` will determine which processes are consuming the most CPU time and display them in descending order on your screen.

By adding the `-S` option to `top`, you can have the display show you the cumulative CPU time that the process, as well as any child processes that may already have exited, has spent. If you want to change how often the screen is updated, you can add the `-d secs` option, where secs is replaced by the number of seconds between updates.

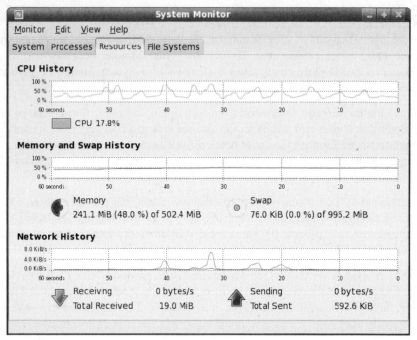

Figure 10-6: System Monitor graphically displays your system's CPU and memory usage.

By default, processes are sorted by CPU usage. You can sort processes numerically by PID (press N), by age (press A), by resident memory usage (press M), by time (press T), or back to CPU usage (press P). The following output shows an example of top running, with information sorted by memory use. The system shown is running a GNOME desktop, with OpenOffice.org Writer, Firefox Web browser and several other applications active. Notice that the amount of memory free is very low. To get good performance out of a Fedora desktop system, 256MB may not be enough once you start running a lot of big applications.

```
top - 16:11:41 up 10:27,  2 users,  load average: 1.60, 0.51, 0.18
Tasks: 107 total,  2 running, 103 sleeping,  0 stopped,  2 zombie
Cpu(s): 16.6%us,  6.5%sy,  0.0%ni,  0.0%id, 76.9%wa,  0.0%hi,  0.0%si,  0.0%st
Mem:    252424k total,  249224k used,  3200k free,  2360k buffers
Swap:  1020088k total,  14240k used, 1005848k free,  86820k cached

 PID USER     PR  NI  VIRT  RES  SHR S %CPU %MEM   TIME+  COMMAND
4242 chris     18   0  183m  37m  25m R 19.9 15.0  0:05.86 swriter.bin
4217 chris     15   0  137m  31m  17m S  0.0 12.9  0:07.27 firefox-bin
4244 chris     15   0 39148  18m 7684 S  0.0  7.6  0:04.94 beagled-helper
4138 chris     15   0  101m  14m 9.8m S  0.0  5.9  0:06.87 baobab
```

Monitoring power usage on laptop computers

To effectively use a laptop computer, you need to be able to monitor and manage the laptop's power usage. Using tools provided in Fedora or RHEL, you can configure your laptop to:

- Monitor the battery level.
- Notify you when the battery is low.
- Notify you when the battery is fully charged.
- Show when the laptop is plugged in.
- Suspend the current session.

Fedora and RHEL offer two facilities that do power management: APM and ACPI.

- **Advanced Power Management (APM)** — APM can be used to monitor the battery of your notebook and notify user-level programs to tell you when your battery is low. It can also be used to place your laptop into suspend mode.

- **Advanced Configuration and Power Interface (ACPI)** — Besides monitoring power features on your laptop, ACPI can also do thermal control, motherboard configuration, and change power states.

Many older laptops do not include support for ACPI in the BIOS, so you must use APM to monitor and manage your batteries. For some newer laptops, ACPI may be required. In general, ACPI offers a more complete feature set for power management, but APM has more user-level support today.

To check whether ACPI or APM are supported on your Linux system, you can use the dmesg command after a reboot. For example, type:

```
# dmesg | less
```

Page through the output looking for lines beginning with text strings ACPI or apm. On a computer where APM wasn't working, I saw the message "apm: overridden by ACPI." When ACPI wasn't working, I saw the message "ACPI: System description tables not found."

The following procedure was performed on a laptop that used ACPI to manage power events. It describes how to use the GNOME Power Manager applet on the desktop to monitor your battery.

> **NOTE:** If it seems that either ACPI or APM are interfering with the proper operation of your laptop, you can turn off either service when you boot your computer. Add either acpi=off or apm=off to the end of the kernel line (from the GRUB boot screen or the /boot/grub/grub.conf file) to turn off ACPI or APM, respectively.

Using the Power Manager applet

If you are using the GNOME desktop, the GNOME Power Manager applet should automatically appear on your panel to keep track of the power levels of your battery (if a battery is present). The following procedure steps you through adding the monitor to your panel (if it is not already there) and configuring it to behave as you like.

1. Move the mouse pointer over the battery icon in the top panel. A tooltip should tell you whether or not your laptop is currently running on AC power and your battery's current charge level. Figure 10-7 shows an example of battery information for a laptop that is on AC power and that is in the process of recharging the battery.

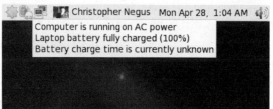

Figure 10-7: View battery status from the Power Management applet in the GNOME panel.

2. Right-click the battery icon and select Preferences. The Power Management Preferences window appears.

3. Change any of the following values related to your battery monitor:

   - **On AC Power** — From the On AC Power tab, you can select how many minutes of idle time should elapse before putting the computer or display to sleep. You can also set what hapens when the laptop lid is closed (Blank Screen Suspend, Hibernate, or do nothing). As for the Display, you can set how long to wait before putting the display to sleep (40 minutes is the default) or whether or not you want to dim the display when it is idle.

   - **On Battery Power** — The same options described for running on AC power are available for when your laptop is running on battery power. You can set what happens to the CPU and display after set amounts of idle time.

   - **General** — From the General tab, you can set the type of notification that occurs when the laptop's power button is pressed or when the suspend button is pressed. You can also set when the battery icon is displayed (when a battery is present, when it is low, or when it is charging or discharging).

Using apm to enter suspend mode

If the apm service is running, the apm command lets you view information about your computer's power management and put the computer in suspend mode (if it is supported on your laptop). Here are some examples of using the apm command:

```
# apm -m
```

Using the -m option, the apm command displays the number of minutes of battery life remaining (if that information is available). It may also give you information about the status of how the battery is charging and whether or not the laptop is currently plugged in.

```
# apm -s
```

The -s option of apm causes the laptop to enter suspend mode. You can start up the laptop again, in most cases, by pressing a key on the keyboard.

Using acpi_listen to monitor ACPI events

If ACPI is running on your system, you can monitor ACPI events using the acpi_listen command. As root user, type the following from a Terminal window:

```
# acpi_listen
ac_adapter AC 00000080 00000000
processor CPU 00000080 00000000
processor CPU 00000081 00000000
battery BAT0 00000080 00000001
ac_adapter AC 00000080 00000001
processor CPU 00000080 00000000
processor CPU 00000081 00000000
battery BAT0 00000080 00000001
button/lid LID 00000080 00000001
button/lid LID 00000080 00000002
```

The message above appeared when the AC power was disconnected, the power was reconnected, the laptop's lid was closed and the lid was again opened.

Choosing Software Alternatives

Because several software packages are available for every major service available in Linux (such as mail, printing, Java environments, and so on), there will be times when people using the system will prefer one service over another. Software packages that have been designed to work with the alternatives system can be configured in Fedora or RHEL to let an administrator choose which of the alternatives to a particular service he or she wants to use by default.

Selecting Java alternatives

If you are developing Java applications, an addition to the alternatives feature lets you switch between using a proprietary Java virtual machine (JVM) to using the GNU compiler for Java (gcj). Type the following to see which implmentation of java is currently in use on your system:

```
# alternatives --display java
```

Selecting mail and printing alternatives

Beginning with Red Hat Linux 7.3, which was the first version to offer the alternatives feature, two major services were configured to use alternatives: mail transport and printing services. The alternatives facility let system administrators choose the following, related to mail transport and printing:

- **Mail Transport Agent (MTA)** — If the sendmail, exim and postfix mail transport agents are installed, as an administrator you can choose which of those services is the default for sending and receiving e-mail.

- **Printing** — If both LPRng and CUPS printing services are installed, you can choose which service is the default for printing documents.

As an administrator, you still need to configure each alternative service to work. Descriptions for configuring sendmail and postfix mail-transport agents are contained in Chapter 19. Information on setting up the CUPS printing service is in Chapter 17. (LPRng is no longer delivered with Fedora or RHEL, although it is still available from sites such as rpmfind.net. Likewise, the feature for switching the printing service described below is not included with Fedora or RHEL, but can still be found in earlier Red Hat Linux systems.)

In terms of setting up the alternatives side of mail services, much of the work of creating links so that the services can be chosen has already been done. Links relating to the default services are set up in the /etc/alternatives directory. Definitions that identify the alternative components of sendmail, exim, and postfix mail servers are contained in the /var/lib/alternatives directory.

Because much of the configuration has been done in advance, the first step in switching between the different mail services installed on your computer is only a couple of clicks away. To switch the default mail services on your computer, do the following:

1. To switch mail service, type **system-switch-mail**. The switcher window appears.

2. Click on the service you want to switch to — Sendmail, Exim, or Postfix for mail, depending on which are installed. (If the one you want is already selected, you can just cancel.)

   If the switch is successful, a pop-up window tells you to restart the new service.

3. Click OK to complete the switch and close the pop-up window.

The next time your computer boots, your new mail service takes over that service. All the links are in place and the start-up scripts are changed. However, your system is still running the old service. The start-up scripts for those services are in the /etc/init.d directory. They are as follows:

- **exim** — for the Exim mail service
- **sendmail** — for the Sendmail mail service

- `postfix` — for the Postfix mail service

To stop the old service so that the new one can take over, type the following (replacing *service* with the name of the service you want to stop):

```
# /etc/init.d/service stop
```

To start the new service, type the following (replacing *service* with the name of the service you want to start):

```
# /etc/init.d/service start
```

Providing that the new service was configured properly, it should now be available to the users of your computer.

Using mail alternatives

The mail-transport services that the alternatives facility allows you to change rely on many of the same command names. For example, both Postfix and Sendmail have a `newalias` command and `mailq` commands for updating aliases and checking the mail queue, respectively.

So, to the user, a change in the local mail service should (in theory) be nearly invisible. Users can send mail as they always did and the fact that a different mail transport is being used should make no difference.

Using Security Enhanced Linux

Security Enhanced Linux (SELinux) is a security model that offers the potential to compartmentalize and secure every component of a Linux system (processes, files, directories, users, devices, and so on). Instead of the all-or-nothing, either-you-have-root-privilege-or-you-don't approach to security in traditional Linux and UNIX systems, SELinux allows much finer granularity in how permissions to run and alter components on the computer are handed out. With SELinux, you can drastically limit the damage caused by a person who cracks one part of a Linux system.

When you first install Fedora or RHEL, you have the opportunity to enable or disable SELinux. If enabled, the targeted policy is used by default. Targeted policies focus on services with vulnerable daemon processes, as well as the resources the services can access.

Targeted policies limit the impact that an attack on the following services can have on your server as a whole: Apache (Web server), Samba (Windows file and print sharing), FTP (file transfer protocol), NFS (network file system), and others. The targeted set of policies is practical today and provides further boundaries around what are already quite secure features. In most cases, you can use this policy set without modification.

This chapter sets out to give you an understanding of what SELinux is. It describes how to turn on SELinux in Fedora or RHEL. Then it provides an overview of how Fedora's targeted policy is set up for you and describes how you can modify the targeted SELinux policies to personalize your SELinux policy settings.

Understanding Security Enhanced Linux

With traditional UNIX and Linux systems, when a user got root access to your computer, he owned the machine. The root user (or whoever took over as root user) could override ownership, read/write/execute permissions, and processor scheduling priorities. Likewise, an attack on a Web server (httpd daemon) could allow an attacker full privileges of the apache user account, instead of limiting the attack to a single set of virtual host resources.

Organizations such as the United States National Security Agency (NSA) recognized the need to have operating systems in secure environments be able to separate information in terms of confidentiality and data integrity. The standard security model made Linux and UNIX systems unacceptable for highly secure environments, where the risk of one exploit taking down the whole operating system was unacceptable. The mechanism that NSA recommended to implement highly secure systems is referred to as *Mandatory Access Control* (MAC).

The SELinux project aims at providing MAC functionality into the Linux kernel. By implementing rules for what all operating system components can and can't do, an application that has security flaws or has been taken over for malicious intent can be contained. In other words, gaining control of one component of a system doesn't allow a cracker to take over the entire computer.

Despite the fact that SELinux is complex, many of the bugs have been worked out of it in recent releases and the default settings are quite easy to work with. I would recommend enabling SELinux on a server you are testing, to prepare to one day enable SELinux to protect your Internet servers.

Types and roles in SELinux

The mechanisms for implementing security rules in SELinux are referred to as *policies*. Any system that implements SELinux selects a particular policy (strict, targeted, and so on) that results in a consistent set of rules that meet the level of security required on the system.

Using policy configuration files, SELinux implements two different security models: *Type Enforcement* (TE) and *Role-Based Access Control* (RBAC).

- **Type Enforcement** — Under the TE model, every object in the operating system is bound to a security attribute called a *type*. Every process is bound to a security attribute called a *domain*. This approach allows for very tight control of every object in the operating system. Every user is allowed to access objects in the operating system based on the domain in which he or she is allowed to operate.

- **Role-Based Access Control** — Using the RBAC model, SELinux lets each user operate in a specific role. The roles are arranged in a hierarchy, with specific permissions associated with each role provided by type enforcement.

In traditional Linux, a user is assigned a specific user ID (UID) and group ID (GID), which affords that user certain access to system resources. For instance, it gives the user certain rights to read, write, or execute files and directories based on whether that user owns the file or directory or is part of a group assigned to that file or directory.

In SELinux, a data file, directory, or application can have many more attributes associated with it. Those attributes might actually give more permissions to access the component than were available in traditional Linux security. At the same time, having access to the component wouldn't necessarily give that user control of that component in a way that could be exploited beyond what the security policies allow the user to do.

Users in SELinux

The model that SELinux uses to define the rights that users have on an SELinux-enabled system can co-exist with the existing Linux user model, rather than replace it. With SELinux enabled, Linux users still have their accounts defined through definitions in the `/etc/passwd` file. A user who is also assigned a role in SELinux is referred to as a *Defined User*.

Special user identities in SELinux include the `system_u` (which is the user identity assigned to system processes) and `user_u` (which is the assignment used to indicate if general users, in particular those without specific user identities, are allowed to use the feature in question). There is also a `root` identity, which is retained to allow compatibility with existing file contexts. This allows existing files to remain valid if they have `root` as their user identity.

Policies in SELinux

As noted earlier, with Fedora and RHEL you have the choice of either turning off SELinux or turning it on. The values set in the `/etc/selinux/config` file determine which type of policy is on (only the targeted policy is available by default, however a strict policy is also available) and whether or not SELinux is:

- **enforcing** — The current SELinux policy is turned on and its policies are enforced.
- **permissive** — The current SELinux policy is on, but not enforced (so you only see warning messages describing how the policy would be enforced).
- **disabled** — SELinux is off, so only standard Linux permissions are enforced (as they always were on systems not including SELinux).

Fedora and RHEL contain a compiled policy file for the targeted policy they deliver. For example, in the current version of Fedora

`/etc/selinux/targeted/policy/policy.23` is the compiled policy set used when that policy is active.

Tools in SELinux

Tools available with SELinux let you work with and change policy settings in SELinux. Many of these tools come in the selinux-policy, selinux-policycoreutils and setroubleshoot-server packages in the current release of Fedora. Tools include the following:

- **SELinux Troubleshooter** — The SELinux Troubleshooter will start an icon in the desktop panel when SELinux detects something that violates SELinux policy. Click that icon to display the setroubleshoot browser window to see descriptions and potential fixes for the problem. You can also start setroubleshoot browser directly by selecting Applications → System Tools → SELinux Troubleshooter.

- **SELinux Policy Generation Tool** — Graphical tool for generating your own SELinux policy framework. Application developers or systems administrators can use this tool to confine users or applications to only access those resources they need.

- **SELinux Administration window** — Open the SELinux Administration window (select System → Administration → SELinux Management) to change the status of SELinux (enabled, disabled, or enforcing) or change the default policy type (targeted by default). You can also modify SELinux settings for users, files and directories, policy modules, and network ports.

- **SELinux commands** — A set of command-line tools can be used to modify SELinux policies. These commands include `chcon` (to label files and directories) and `setsebool` (to turn on and off SELinux attributes). To get information on how specific daemon processes are being handled in SELinux, refer to various SELinux policy man pages (ftpd_selinux, httpd_selinux, kerberos_selinux, named_selinux, nfs_selinux, nis_selinux, rsync_selinux, and ypbind_selinux).

Using SELinux in Fedora and RHEL

If you use the targeted SELinux policy (which is delivered and on by default), you can still administer Linux as you always have. The following procedure describes the software packages you need to use SELinux and starts you off working with the default targeted policy. If you need additional information, refer to the following:

- **Red Hat Enterprise Linux 4 SELinux Guide** — Describes how to use, administer, and troubleshoot SELinux in Red Hat Enterprise Linux 4. While some of the specific policy settings are different for the most recent Fedora, this is an excellent guide for understanding how SELinux works in RHEL and Fedora systems. You can find this document here at `http://www.redhat.com/docs/manuals/enterprise/RHEL-4-Manual/selinux-guide/`.

- **SELinux Documentation** — Most of documents that come in the selinux-doc package are standards-type documents from the National Security Agency (NSA). Look in the `/usr/share/doc/selinux-doc*` directory of your Fedora or RHEL system for these files, using your Web browser or PDF file viewer.

Getting SELinux

Support for SELinux is built into the Linux 2.6 kernel. In fact, SELinux is on by default in the latest release of Fedora. If you prefer to have SELinux off, after you boot the desktop, you can open the SELinux Administration window (select System → Administration → SELinux Management) and set the Enforcing Current selection to Permissive. Permissive causes SELinux to check and note where SELinux would fail, but doesn't actually fail.

With SELinux enabled, might also want the following software packages installed:

- **checkpolicy** — Contains the SELinux policy compiler named `checkpolicy`. Use this package to build or check policies for SELinux. Using `checkpolicy`, you create binary policy files from policy configurations and parameters in a `policy.conf` file. (Type **man checkpolicy** to read about `checkpolicy`.)

- **libselinux** — Contains the application programming interface for SELinux applications. It includes components used by application programs to check SELinux status.

- **policycoreutils** — Contains basic utilities needed to operate an SELinux system. Commands include `fixfiles` (to check and possibly correct security attributes on file systems), `restorecon` (to set security attributes for selected files), `audit2allow` (to translate messages from `/var/log/messages` to rules that SELinux can use), `newrole` (to open a shell in a new role), `load_policy` (to load a policy file), `run_init` (to run an init script using the correct context), `sestatus` (to check whether SELinux is currently enabled), and `setfiles` (to set the security contexts of files).

- **selinux-doc** — Contains a lot of SELinux documentation that is stored in the /usr/share/SELinux directory.

- **selinux-policy-mls** — Contains the multi-level security translation table for SELinux.

- **selinux-policy-targeted** — Contains the sample policy file used to incorporate the targeted SELinux policy into a running Linux system, as well as contexts files and the `booleans` file needed to make run-time changes to SELinux.

- **setools** — Contains tools for managing parts of a running policy that define what access users have to different components of the Linux system.

Checking whether SELinux is on

After Fedora or RHEL is installed, you can check the `/etc/selinux/config` file (which is linked to `/etc/sysconfig/selinux`) to see if SELinux is enabled and, if so, which policies are in effect. That file sets two critical variables for a Fedora system configured to use SELinux:

- **SELinux State** — The `SELINUX` variable sets the state of SELinux. If you enable SELinux during Fedora installation this starts out as `SELINUX=enforcing` (which causes security policies for SELinux to be enforced). If SELinux is disabled during installation, `SELINUX=disabled` is set instead. A third choice is to set `SELINUX=permissive`, which prints warnings based on the policies you have set, instead of enforcing them.

- **SELinux Policy Type** — The `SELINUXTYPE` variable indicates the type of policy to use. `SELINUX=targeted` protects only selected network daemons (as set in files located in the `/etc/selinux/targeted` directory).

For most practical purposes, if you use SELinux you will want to enable the SELinux-targeted policy (which is the default). While not locking down all Fedora components under SELinux, the targeted policy does lock down those daemon processes that are most critical to protect from attacks. Standard Linux security protects everything else in the operating system.

You can override your default settings to place SELinux into permissive mode from the Linux boot prompt by adding the following to the end of the kernel line from the GRUB screen when you boot Fedora:

```
setenforce 0
```

With SELinux in permissive mode (`setenforce 0`), you can still log in and use the system, with any potentially devastating permission failures simply resulting in error messages. If SELinux is in permissive mode, you can likewise return SELinux to enforcing mode from the boot prompt by typing `setenforce 1`. You can change the SELinux state permanently, using the SELinux Administration window.

Checking SELinux status

There are many tools for checking the status of SELinux on your Fedora system. To check whether or not SELinux is enabled, type the following:

```
# sestatus -v | less
SELinux status:        disabled
```

The output shows that SELinux is not enforced on the current system. If SELinux were set to permissive, the output would look more like the following:

```
SELinux status:                 enabled
SELinuxfs mount:                /selinux
Current mode:                   enforcing
Mode from config file:          enforcing
Policy version:                 22
Policy from config file:        targeted
```

```
Process contexts:
Current context:              user_u:system_r:unconfined_t:SystemLow-SystemHigh
Init context:                 system_u:system_r:init_t
/sbin/mingetty                system_u:system_r:getty_t
/usr/sbin/sshd                system_u:system_r:unconfined_t:SystemLow-SystemHigh

File contexts:
Controlling term:             user_u:object_r:devpts_t
/etc/passwd                   system_u:object_r:etc_t
/etc/shadow                   system_u:object_r:shadow_t
/bin/bash                     system_u:object_r:shell_exec_t
/bin/login                    system_u:object_r:login_exec_t
/bin/sh                       system_u:object_r:bin_t ->
system_u:object_r:shell_exec_t
/sbin/agetty                  system_u:object_r:getty_exec_t
/sbin/init                    system_u:object_r:init_exec_t
/sbin/mingetty                system_u:object_r:getty_exec_t
/usr/sbin/sshd                system_u:object_r:sshd_exec_t
/lib/libc.so.6                system_u:object_r:lib_t -> system_u:object_r:lib_t
/lib/ld-linux.so.2            system_u:object_r:lib_t ->
system_u:object_r:ld_so_t
```

Press the Spacebar to page through the output. Besides showing that SELinux is enabled and running in permissive mode, this output shows the process contexts and file contexts that are set.

To see and change basic SELinux settings from a graphical interface, you can open the SELinux Administration window. From the GNOME Desktop, select System → Administration → SELinux Management. From that window, you can set whether SELinux is Disabled, Enforcing, or Permissive. You can also set the SELinux policy to use (targeted is the default).

Changing the policy type or turning the SELinux service from off to on requires that you also relabel the entire file system. Changing policy should never be done lightly. If you do decide to change policy through the SELinux Administration window, that change also requires that the file system be relabeled. By changing the policy through this window, the file system will be relabeled automatically the next time you reboot your computer (or you can select the check box to prevent relabeling the file system on the next reboot).

> **NOTE:** Relabeling the file system can be a long and time-consuming activity. Again, remember that changing policies is a major change to your operating system. The more nodes there are in your file system, the longer it will take to relabel your file system the next time you boot your computer.

You can check the security context in which you are operating using the id command with the -Z option. The following example shows that your current context is the root user, your role is the system_r role, and the type is unconfined_t.

```
# id -Z
unconfined_u:unconfined_r:unconfined_t:s0-s0:c0.c1023
```

SELinux is capable of turning out a lot of error messages. By default, those messages are directed to the `/var/log/messages` file. Because the file contains messages from many different services, you can use the seAudit window (type `seaudit` from a Terminal window) to view messages strictly related to SELinux.

Learning More about SELinux

To dig deeper into SELinux, there are a variety of technical reports, FAQs, and component documents available. Here are a few places you can try:

- **SELinux FAQs (`fedora.redhat.com/docs/selinux-faq`)** — This site provides information specific to the SELinux implementation in Fedora.
- **SELinux Documentation (`www.nsa.gov/selinux/info/docs.cfm`)** — This site provides links to published papers, technical reports, and presentations related to SELinux.

Summary

Although you may be using Fedora or RHEL as a single-user system, many of the tasks you must perform to keep your computer running are defined as administrator tasks. A special user account called the root user is needed to do many of the things necessary to keep a Linux system working as you would like it to. If you are administering a Linux system that is used by lots of people, the task of administration becomes even larger. You must be able to add and support users, maintain the file systems, and ensure that system performance serves your users well.

To help the administrator, Fedora and RHEL come with a variety of command-line utilities and graphical windows for configuring and maintaining your system. The kudzu program can be used to probe and reconfigure Linux when you add or remove hardware. Commands such as `mkfs` and `mount` let you create and mount file systems, respectively. Tools like System Monitor and top let you monitor system performance.

SELinux adds a new layer of security on top of existing Linux security methods. As a systems administrator, you can choose whether or not to turn on SELinux. You can also choose which of your system services are protected by SELinux.

Chapter 11

Setting Up and Supporting Users

In This Chapter

- Creating user accounts
- Setting user defaults
- Creating portable desktops
- Providing support to users
- Deleting user accounts
- Checking disk quotas
- Sending mail to all users

One of the more fundamental and important tasks of administering a Linux system is setting up and supporting user accounts. Computers, after all, are tools to be used by people. Apocalyptic science fiction plots aside, computers have no purpose without users.

When you install Fedora or RHEL, you are required to create the root (administrator) user account. The first time you boot Fedora or RHEL, you are asked to create a regular user account, using any name you choose. Several other administrative user accounts that you will probably never use directly are set up automatically (such as apache, rpm, and lp).

> **CROSS-REFERENCE:** For a description of the root user account and how to use it, see Chapter 10.

This chapter discusses the basics of setting up user accounts and offers tips on easing the burden of supporting a large number of Linux users.

Creating User Accounts

Every person who uses your Fedora or RHEL system should have a separate user account. Having a user account provides each person with an area in which to securely store files. A user account also defines which files and directories a user is permitted to create, modify, or delete throughout the computer's file system.

Some user accounts are already there when you install your Linux system. Administrative users (originally UID 0-100, although now UIDs up to 499 are used) are created to maintain separate control of system files and services from a regular user. Of the administrative user accounts, you will probably only use root (when some system administration is required).

Regular user accounts are created using any names you choose, starting (by default) with a user ID (UID) of 500. Regular users you add to your Fedora or RHEL system typically fall into one of two categories:

- **Desktop users** — A desktop user is one that you expect to use your computer via a graphical interface (typically GNOME or KDE). Create this kind of user account for yourself and anyone else you want to log in directly to your computer (or from a thin client over the network). Most of this section describes how to add this type of user.

- **Server users** — If you are configuring Fedora or RHEL as a server (Web, mail, FTP, and so on), you may want to add accounts for users who have limited access to your system. You may want those users to be able to add content to a Web server or access a mail server, but have only a shell login account (or possibly no login account). See the section "Adding user accounts to servers" later in this chapter for information on adding these types of accounts.

> **CROSS-REFERENCE**: If you have multiple users, you'll also need to be concerned about backup and recovery issues for those users. See Chapter 13 for more information.

You can add user accounts to your Fedora or RHEL system in several ways. This chapter describes how to use the useradd command to add user accounts to Fedora or RHEL from the command line, and how to use the User Manager window to add users from the desktop.

Adding users with useradd

The most straightforward method for creating a new user from the shell is with the useradd command. After opening a Terminal window with root permission, you simply invoke the useradd command at the command prompt, with details of the new account as parameters.

The only required parameter to useradd is the login name of the user, but you will probably want to include some additional information. Each item of account information is preceded by a single letter option code with a dash in front of it. Table 11-1 lists the options that are available with the useradd command.

Table 11-1: useradd Command Options

Option	Description
-c "*comment*"	Provide a description of the new user account. Usually just the person's full name. Replace *comment* with the name of the user account. If the comment contains multiple words, use quote marks.
-d *home_dir*	Set the home directory to use for the account. The default is to name it the same as the login name and to place it beneath /home. Replace *home_dir* with the directory name to use.
-D	Rather than create a new account, save the supplied information as the new default settings for any new accounts that are created.
-e *expire_date*	Assign the expiration date for the account in MM/DD/YYYY or MM-DD-YYYY format. Replace *expire_date* with the expiration date to use. This is best used with temporary employees whom you know only need the account for a limited time.
-f *inactivity*	Set the number of days after a password expires until the account is permanently disabled. Setting this to 0 disables the account immediately after the password has expired. Setting it to -1 disables the option, which is the default behavior. Replace *inactivity* with the number to use.
-g *group*	Set the primary group (as listed in the /etc/group file) that the new user will be in. Replace *group* with the group name to use. The default is to assign the user name as the group name.
-G *grouplist*	Add the new user to the supplied comma-separated list of groups.
-k *skel_dir*	Set the skeleton directory containing initial configuration files and login scripts that should be copied to a new user's home directory. This parameter can only be used in conjunction with the -m option. Replace *skel_dir* with the directory name to use.
-m	Automatically create the user's home directory and copy the files in the skeleton directory (/etc/skel) to it.
-M	Do not create the new user's home directory, even if the default behavior is set to create it.
-n	Turn off the default behavior of creating a new group that matches the name and user ID of the new user.
-o	Use with -u *uid* to create a user account that has the same UID as another user name. (This effectively lets you have two different users with authority over the same set of files and directories.)

Option	Description
-p *passwd*	Enter a password for the account you are adding. This must be an encrypted password. Instead of adding an encrypted password here, you can simply use the passwd *user* command later to add a password for *user*. The user should be asked to immediately change the password you set.
-r	Allows you to create a new account with a user ID in the range reserved for system accounts.
-s *shell*	Specify the command shell to use for this account. Replace *shell* with the command shell.
-u *user_id*	Specify the user ID number for the account. The default behavior is to automatically assign the next available number. Replace *user_id* with the ID number.

As an example, create an account for a new user named Joe Smith with a login name of joe. First, log in as root, and then type the following command:

```
# useradd -c "Joe Smith" joe
```

> **TIP:** When you choose a user name, don't begin with a number (for example, 06jsmith). Also, it is best to use all lowercase letters, no control characters or spaces, and a maximum of eight characters. The useradd command allows up to 32 characters, but some applications can't deal with user names that long. Tools such as ps display UIDs instead of names if names are too long. Having users named Jsmith and jsmith can cause confusion with programs (such as sendmail) that don't distinguish case. Also, some very old applications may not be able to handle user names with more than eight characters.

Next, set Joe's initial password using the passwd command. The password command prompts you to type the password twice. (Asterisks are shown here to represent the password you type. Nothing is actually displayed when you type the password.)

```
# passwd joe
Changing password for user joe.
New password: *******
Retype new password: *******
```

> **CROSS-REFERENCE:** Refer to Chapter 14 for tips on picking good passwords.

In creating the account for Joe, the useradd command performs several actions:

- Reads the /etc/login.defs file to get default values to use when creating accounts.
- Checks command-line parameters to find out which default values to override.
- Creates a new user entry in the /etc/passwd and /etc/shadow files based on the default values and command-line parameters.
- Creates any new group entries in the /etc/group file.

- Creates a home directory based on the user's name and places it in the /home directory.

- Copies any files located within the /etc/skel directory to the new home directory. This usually includes login and application startup scripts.

The preceding example uses only one of the available useradd options. Most account settings are assigned using default values. Here's an example that uses a few more options:

```
# useradd -m -g users -G wheel,sales -s /bin/tcsh -c "Mary Smith" mary
```

In this case, the useradd command is told to create a home directory for the user mary (-m), make users the primary group she belongs to (-g), add her to the groups wheel and sales (-G), and assign tcsh as her primary command shell (-s). Note that the wheel and sales groups must already exist for this example to work. This results in a line similar to the following being added to the /etc/passwd file:

```
mary:x:502:100:Mary Smith:/home/mary:/bin/tcsh
```

In the /etc/passwd file, each line represents a single user account record. Each field is separated from the next by a colon (:) character. The field's position in the sequence determines what it is. As you can see, the login name is first. The password field contains an x because Fedora is using a shadow password file in which to store encrypted password data. The user ID selected by the useradd command was 502. The primary group ID is 100, which corresponds to the users group in the /etc/group file. The comment field was correctly set to Mary Smith, the home directory was automatically assigned as /home/mary, and the command shell was assigned as /bin/tcsh, exactly as specified with the useradd options.

By leaving out many of the options (as I did in the first useradd example), defaults are assigned in most cases. For example, by not using -g users or -G wheel,sales, a group named mary would have been created and assigned to the new user. Likewise, excluding -s /bin/tcsh causes /bin/bash to be assigned as the default shell.

The /etc/group file holds information about the different groups on your Fedora or RHEL system and the users who belong to them. Groups are useful for allowing multiple people to share access to the same files while denying access to others. If you peek at the /etc/group file, you should find something similar to this:

```
bin:x:1:root,bin,daemon
daemon:x:2:root,bin,daemon
sys:x:3:root,bin,adm
adm:x:4:root,adm,daemon
tty:x:5:
disk:x:6:root
lp:x:7:daemon,lp
mem:x:8:
kmem:x:9:
wheel:x:10:root,joe,mary
    .
    .
```

```
nobody:x:99:
users:x:100:
chris:x:500
sheree:x:501
sales:x:601:bob,jane,joe,mary
```

Each line in the group file contains the name of a group, the group ID number associated with it, and a list of users in that group. By default, each user is added to his or her own group, beginning with GID 500. Note that `mary` was added to the `wheel` and `sales` groups instead of having her own group.

It is actually rather significant that `mary` was added to the `wheel` group. By doing this, you grant her the ability to use the `sudo` command to run commands as the root user, provided that the wheel line is uncommented from the `/etc/sudoers` file (as described in Chapter 10), which it is not by default.

In this example, we used the `-g` option to assign `mary` to the `users` group. If you leave off the `-g` parameter, the default behavior is for `useradd` to create a new group with the same name and ID number as the user, which is assigned as the new user's primary group. For example, look at the following `useradd` command:

```
# useradd -m -G wheel,sales -s /bin/tcsh -c "Mary Smith" mary
```

It would result in a `/etc/passwd` line like this:

```
mary:x:502:502:Mary Smith:/home/mary:/bin/tcsh
```

It would also result in a new group line like this:

```
mary:x:502:
```

Note that the user ID and group ID fields now have the same number. If you set up all of your users this way, you will have a unique group for every user on the system, which allows for increased flexibility in the sharing of files among your users.

Adding users with User Manager

If you prefer a graphical window for adding, changing, and deleting user accounts, you can use the User Manager window. To open the window from the GNOME desktop, click System → Administration → Users and Groups (or type `system-config-users` from a Terminal window as root user). Figure 11-1 shows an example of that window.

When you open the User Manager window, you see a list of all regular users who are currently added to your computer. Administrative users (UID 1 through 499) are not displayed. For each user, you can see the user name, UID, primary group, full name, login shell, and home directory. Click any of those headings to sort the users by that information.

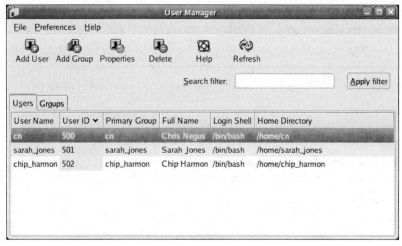

Figure 11-1: Manage users from the User Manager window.

To add a new user from the User Manager window, do the following:

1. Click the Add User icon to open the Create New User window (see Figure 11-2).

Figure 11-2: The Create New User window

2. Type the requested information in the following fields:

    *   **User Name** — A single word to describe the user. Typically, the user name is eight characters, all lowercase, containing the user's real first name, last name, or (more often) a combination of the two (such as jwjones).

- **Full Name** — The user's full name (usually first name, middle initial, and last name). This name is typically just used for display, so using upper- and lowercase is fine.

- **Password** — The user's initial password. (Ask the user to change this password the first time he or she logs in to the new account, using the `passwd` command.)

- **Confirm Password** — Type the password again, to make sure you entered it correctly.

- **Login Shell** — The default shell (for entering typed commands) that the user sees when first logging in to Fedora or RHEL from a character display.

- **Create home directory** — By default, this box is selected and the user's home directory (as indicated by the Home Directory field) is created automatically.

- **Home Directory** — By default, the user is given a home directory of the user's name in the `/home` directory. (For example, the user `sheree` would be assigned `/home/sheree` as her home directory.) Change this field if you want to assign the user to a different home directory.

- **Create a private group for the user** — Check this box if you want a group by the same name as the user, created for this user. The name is added to the `/etc/group` file. This feature is referred to as user private groups (UPGs).

- **Specify user ID manually** — Typically, you would not check this box, so that the UID for the new user would be assigned automatically. New UIDs for regular users start at 500. However, if you want to assign a particular UID for a user (for example, if you want to match the UID with the user's UID from another computer on your network), select this box and type the number you want to use in the UID box.

- **Specify group ID manually** — As with the user ID, you would typically just have the group ID automatically assigned. However, you can assign a different GID to have the user assigned to a particular group.

3. Click OK when you are done. The new user is added to the `/etc/passwd` and `/etc/group` files. The user account is now available for that user to log in.

TIP: Using user private groups (UPGs) can be a benefit for sharing a directory of files among several users. Here's an example:

```
# useradd -m projectx
# mkdir /usr/local/x
# chown root.projectx /usr/local/x
# chmod 2775 /usr/local/x
# ls -ld /usr/local/x
drwxrwsr-x 2 root projectx 4096 Aug 18 01:54 /usr/local/x
# gpasswd -a nextuser projectx
```

In this example, you create a user named `projectx` (with a group named `projectx`). Create a `/usr/local/x` directory and have it owned by root user and `projectx` group. Set the setgid bit to be on for the group (2), open full read/write/execute permissions for user and group (77), and open read and execute permissions for everyone else (5). Add each user to the group that you want to be able to write to the projectx directory (replace *nextuser* with the user you want to add). After that, regardless of a user's primary group, any file created in the `/usr/local/x` directory by a user can be read or modified by anyone in the `projectx` group.

Setting User Defaults

The `useradd` command and User Manager window both determine the default values for new accounts by reading the `/etc/login.defs` file. You can modify those defaults by either editing that file manually with a standard text editor or by running the `useradd` command with the `-D` option. If you choose to edit the file manually, here is what you face:

```
# *REQUIRED*
# Directory where mailboxes reside, _or_ name of file, relative to the
# home directory. If you _do_ define both, MAIL_DIR takes precedence.
# QMAIL_DIR is for Qmail
#
#QMAIL_DIR Maildir
MAIL_DIR    /var/spool/mail
#MAIL_FILE .mail


# Password aging controls:
#
# PASS_MAX_DAYS Maximum number of days a password may be used.
# PASS_MIN_DAYS Minimum number of days allowed between password changes.
# PASS_MIN_LEN  Minimum acceptable password length.
# PASS_WARN_AGE Number of days warning given before a password
# expires.
#
PASS_MAX_DAYS      99999
PASS_MIN_DAYS      0
PASS_MIN_LEN       5
PASS_WARN_AGE      7


#
# Min/max values for automatic uid selection in useradd
#
UID_MIN                 500
UID_MAX                 60000


#
# Min/max values for automatic gid selection in groupadd
#
```

```
GID_MIN                      500
GID_MAX                    60000

#
# If defined, this command is run when removing a user.
# It should remove any at/cron/print jobs etc. owned by
# the user to be removed (passed as the first argument).
#
#USERDEL_CMD /usr/sbin/userdel_local


#
# If useradd should create home directories for users by default.
# On RH systems, we do. This option is ORed with the -m flag on
# useradd command line.
#
CREATE_HOME yes
# The permission mask is initialized to this value. If not
# specified, the permission mask will be initialized to 022.
UMASK             077

# This enables userdel to remove groups if no members exist.
#
USERGROUPS_ENAB yes

# Use MD5 or DES to encrypt password? RedHat use MD5default.
MD5_CRYPT_ENAB yes
ENCRYPT_METHOD SHA512
```

Blank lines and comments beginning with a pound sign (#) are ignored. All other lines contain keyword/value pairs. For example, the keyword MAIL_DIR is followed by some white space and the value /var/spool/mail. This tells useradd that the initial user e-mail mailbox is created in that directory. Following that are lines that enable you to customize the valid range of automatically assigned user ID numbers or group ID numbers. A comment section that explains that keyword's purpose precedes each keyword. Altering a default value is as simple as editing the value associated with that keyword and then saving the login.defs file.

If you want to view the defaults, type the useradd command with the -D option as follows:

```
# useradd -D
GROUP=100
HOME=/home
INACTIVE=-1
EXPIRE=
SHELL=/bin/bash
SKEL=/etc/skel
CREAT_MAIL_SPOOL=yes
```

You can also use the -D option to change defaults. When run with this flag, useradd refrains from actually creating a new user account; instead, it saves any additionally supplied options as the new default values in `/etc/login.defs`. Not all `useradd` options can be used in conjunction with the `-D` option. You can use only the five options listed in Table 11-2.

Table 11-2: useradd Options for Changing User Defaults

Options	Description
`-b` *default_home*	Set the default directory in which user home directories will be created. Replace *default_home* with the directory name to use. Usually this is `/home`.
`-e` *default_expire_date*	Set the default expiration date on which the user account is disabled. The *default_expire_date* value should be replaced with a date in the form MM/DD/YYYY — for example, 10/15/2008.
`-f` *default_inactive*	Set the number of days after a password has expired before the account is disabled. Replace *default_inactive* with a number representing the number of days.
`-g` *default_group*	Set the default group that new users will be placed in. In Fedora, `useradd` creates a new group with the same name and ID number as the user, so this value is ignored. To set a different group primary group for a user, you must set it explicitly with the `-g` option on the command line.
`-s` *default_shell*	Set the default shell for new users. Typically this is `/bin/bash`. Replace *default_shell* with the full path to the shell that you want as the default for new users.

To set any of the defaults, give the `-D` option first; then add any of the defaults you want to set. For example, to set the default home directory location to `/home/everyone` and the default shell to `/bin/tcsh`, type the following:

```
# useradd -D -b /home/everyone -s /bin/tcsh
```

Besides setting up user defaults, an administrator can create default files that are copied to each user's home directory for use. These files can include login scripts and shell configuration files (such as `.bashrc`). The following sections describe some of these files.

Supplying initial login scripts

Many Linux applications, including the command shell itself, read a configuration file at startup. It is traditional practice that these configuration files are stored in the users' home directories. In this way, each user can customize the behavior of the command shell and other applications without affecting that behavior for other users. In this way, global defaults can be assigned from `/etc/profile`, and then those settings can be enhanced by a user's personal files.

The `bash` command shell, for example, looks for a file called `.bashrc` in the current user's home directory whenever it starts up. Similarly, the `tcsh` command shell looks for a file called .tcshrc in the user's home directory. You may see a repeating theme here. Startup scripts and configuration files for various applications usually begin with a dot (.) character and end in the letters rc (which stands for *run commands*). You can supply initial default versions of these and other configuration files by placing them in the /etc/skel directory. When you run the useradd command, these scripts and configuration files are copied to the new user's home directory.

Supplying initial .bashrc and .bash_profile files

By supplying your users with initial .bashrc and .bash_profile files, you give them a starting point from which they can further customize their shell environment. Moreover, you can be sure that files are created with the appropriate access permissions so as not to compromise system security without the user's knowledge.

The .bash_profile script is run each time the user starts a new bash shell and, in turn, runs the .bashrc script. So, security is a concern. The .bash_profile file sets the original PATH used by the user, so it is a good place to add directories containing binaries you want the user to be able to run at your location. You can also add other startup programs you want to run automatically for every user. Here's an example of the .bash_profile file.

```
# .bash_profile

# Get the aliases and functions
if [ -f ~/.bashrc ]; then
        . ~/.bashrc
fi

# User specific environment and startup programs

PATH=$PATH:$HOME/bin
export PATH
```

The .bashrc file is a good place to supply useful command aliases and additions to the command search path. Here's an example of a .bashrc file:

```
# .bashrc


# Source global definitions
if [ -f /etc/bashrc ]; then
        . /etc/bashrc
fi
# User specific aliases and functions
alias rm='rm -i'
alias cp='cp -i'
alias mv='mv -i'
```

This sample .bashrc executes /etc/bashrc (if it exists) to read any further global bash values. Next, the file creates aliases for the rm, cp, and mv commands that result in a -i option always being used (unless overridden with the -f option). This protects against the accidental deletion of files.

Supplying an initial .tcshrc file

The following example .tcshrc file does basically the same thing as the preceding .bashrc example. However, this file (which is for the root user) has the additional task of setting the appearance of the command prompt:

```
# .tcshrc

# User specific aliases and functions

alias rm 'rm -i'
alias cp 'cp -i'
alias mv 'mv -i'

setenv PATH "$PATH:/usr/bin:/usr/local/bin"

set prompt='[%n@%m %c]# '
```

Instead of using the export command to set environment variables, the tcsh shell uses the setenv command. In the example, setenv is used to set the PATH variable. The shell prompt is set to include your user name (%n), your computer name (%m), and the name of the current directory (%c). So, if you were to use the tcsh shell as the root user on a computer named maple with /tmp as your current directory, your prompt would appear as follows:

```
[root@maple /tmp]#
```

The .tcshrc file can also be named .cshrc. The tcsh shell is really an extended version of the csh shell (in fact, you can invoke it by the csh name). When a tcsh shell is started, it first looks for a .tcshrc file in the current user's home directory. If it can't find a file by that name, it looks for the other name, .cshrc. Thus, either name is appropriate.

Configuring system-wide shell options

Allowing individually customizable shell startup files for each user is a very flexible and useful practice. But sometimes you need more centralized control than that. You may have an environment variable or other shell setting that you want set for every user, without exception. If you add that setting to each individual shell, the user has the ability to edit that file and remove it. Furthermore, if that setting must be changed in the future, you must change it in every single user's shell startup file.

Fortunately, there is a better way. There are default startup files that apply to all users of the computer that each command shell reads before reading the user-specific files. In the case of the bash command shell, it reads the /etc/bashrc file before doing anything else.

Similarly, the tcsh shell reads the /etc/csh.cshrc file before processing the .cshrc or .tcshrc file found in the user's home directory. Here is a partial listing of the contents of the /etc/csh.cshrc file that ships with Fedora and RHEL:

```
# /etc/cshrc
#
# csh configuration for all shell invocations.

# by default, we want this to get set.
# Even for non-interactive, non-login shells.
 [ `id -gn` = `id -un` -a `id -u` -gt 99 ]
if $status then
    umask 022
else
    umask 002
endif

if ($?prompt) then
  if ($?tcsh) then
    set prompt='[%n@%m %c]$ '
  else
    set prompt=\[`id -nu`@`hostname -s`\]\$\
  endif
endif
```

The /etc/cshrc and /etc/bashrc files set a variety of shell environment options. If you want to modify or add to the shell environment supplied to every single user on the system, the /etc/bashrc or /etc/cshrc file is the place to do it.

Setting system profiles

Some of the most basic information assigned to each user is added from the /etc/profile file. So, if you want to change any of the following information, you can start from /etc/profile. The contents of the /etc/profile file is sourced into each user's shell only to the initial login shell. Here are some values contained in /etc/profile:

- **PATH** — Assigns the default PATH for the root user and for all other users. You might change this value to add paths to local directories containing applications all users need.

- **ulimit -S -c 0** — The -c 0 option to ulimit prevents core files (typically created when a process crashes) from being created. The -S makes this a "soft" option, so the user has the ability to turn on the core file feature if they choose to.

- **Environment variables** — Shell environment variables that are needed for standard operation are assigned in this file. These include USER (set by the id −un command), LOGNAME (same as USER), MAIL (set to /var/spool/mail/$USER), HOSTNAME (set to the output of the command /bin/hostname), and HISTSIZE (which sets shell command history to 1000 items).

- **INPUTRC** — Sets keyboard mappings for particular situations, based on the contents of the /etc/inputrc file. In particular, the inputrc file makes sure that the Linux console and various Terminal windows (xterm and rxvt) all behave sanely.

The last thing that the /etc/profile file does is look at the contents of the /etc/profile.d directory and source in the files that it finds. Each file contains settings that define environment variables or aliases that affect how users can use the shell. For example, the lang.sh and lang.csh files identify the locations of foreign language files. The vim files create aliases that cause vim to be used when vi is typed. The which-2.sh file defines a set of options used by the which command. You can modify the profile.d files or add your own to have environment variables and aliases set for all of your users.

Adding user accounts to servers

When you set up a server, you often want to allow people to either upload files to it or download files or messages from it. However, you may not want to allow those people access to the entire server. You can begin limiting access to those users when you first create their user accounts.

To prevent a remote user from logging in and accessing a shell (via ssh, telnet, or another login service), you can set the default shell for a user to nologin. For example:

```
# useradd -s /sbin/nologin jerryb
```

With the shell set to nologin, this user would not be able to log in to the server to open a shell. However, the user could still use this account to log in to an FTP service on the server (if the service is available and the user has a password). By default, the user's home directory in this example when he logged in via FTP would be /home/jerryb. (See Chapter 20 for ways in which you can restrict this user to access only his home directory in a chroot environment.)

Another approach to FTP-only access to a server is to use /usr/lib/sftp-server as a user's login shell. While this allows users access to the entire file system that is available to the user account, it restricts them to access the server via secured FTP only.

A common practice with Web hosting is to allow a user to place content on the server, often in that user's /home/*username*/public_html directory, using FTP (but no shell login). However, the administrator could choose to assign the location for the Web content to be any directory, including the system-wide Web server directory. The following command assigns the user named webuser to use /var/www/html as his home directory (you should also change ownership of the files to belong to webuser for this to work):

```
# useradd -s /sbin/nologin -d /var/www/html webuser
```

If you were adding a user for mail service access only, you might choose to prevent any access to FTP as well. One way to do that is to point the user's home directory to /dev/null. For example:

```
# useradd -s /sbin/nologin -d /dev/null jerryb
```

Once you have set up a limited user account, you can further define what your server's users can and cannot access, using features associated with the particular service.

Creating Portable Desktops

Linux is an operating system that was born on the Internet, so it is not surprising that it has strong networking capabilities. This makes Linux an excellent server, but it also allows Linux to be an excellent desktop workstation, especially in a highly networked environment. Fedora and RHEL let you easily set up your users with a portable desktop that follows them from computer to computer. With other leading desktop operating systems, it is not nearly as easy.

Typically, a Linux user's home directory is located within the /home directory. As an alternative, within the home directory you can create a directory named after the system's host name. Within that directory, create the users' home directories. Thus, on a Linux system named dexter, the user mary would have a home directory of /home/dexter/mary instead of /home/mary. There is a very good reason for doing this.

If you are logged into the Linux system ratbert and would like to access your home directory on dexter as if it were stored locally, the best approach is to use Network File System (NFS) to mount dexter's /home directory on the /home on ratbert. This results in having the same contents of your home directory available to you no matter which machine you log in to.

> **CROSS-REFERENCE:** You can read more about NFS in Chapter 18.

To mount dexter's /home directory as described, you would add a line similar to the following in ratbert's /etc/fstab file:

```
dexter:/home /home nfs defaults 0 0
```

You would also add an entry such as the following in dexter's /etc/exports directory:

```
/home ratbert
```

Now, when ratbert boots up, it automatically mounts dexter's home partition over the network. This enables you to treat the remote files and directories on dexter's /home as if they are locally stored on ratbert. Unfortunately, this has the side effect of "covering up" ratbert's actual /home directory.

This is where the extra directory level based on the system name comes to the rescue. With all of dexter's home directories located in /home/dexter and all of ratbert's home directories located in /home/ratbert, you can remove the danger of one system covering up the home directories of another. In fact, let's take this example one step further: Imagine a scenario in which the systems dexter, ratbert, and daffy all have portable desktops that are shared with the other systems. The `/etc/fstab` and `/etc/exports` files for each system should have the following lines added to them as indicated.

The `/etc/exports` and `/etc/fstab` files for `dexter` are as follows:

/etc/exports file

```
/home/dexter ratbert,daffy
```

/etc/fstab file

```
ratbert:/home/ratbert /home/ratbert nfs defaults 0 0
daffy:/home/daffy     /home/daffy   nfs defaults 0 0
```

The `/etc/exports` and `/etc/fstab` files for `ratbert` are:

/etc/exports

```
/home/ratbert dexter,daffy
```

/etc/fstab

```
dexter:/home/dexter /home/dexter nfs defaults 0 0
daffy:/home/daffy   /home/daffy   nfs defaults 0 0
```

The `/etc/exports` and `/etc/fstab` files for `daffy` are:

/etc/exports

```
/home/daffy ratbert,dexter
```

/etc/fstab

```
ratbert:/home/ratbert /home/ratbert  nfs defaults 0 0
dexter:/home/dexter   /home/dexter   nfs defaults 0 0
```

As you can see, each system uses NFS to mount the home directories from the other two systems. A user can travel from server to server and see exactly the same desktop on each system.

Providing Support to Users

Creating new user accounts is just one small administrative task among many. No single chapter can adequately discuss all the tasks that are involved in the ongoing support of users. But I share with you a few hints and procedures to ease that burden.

Creating a technical support mailbox

E-mail is a wonderful communication tool, especially for the overworked system administrator. People usually put more thought and effort into their e-mail messages than into the voice messages that they leave. A text message can be edited for clarity before being sent, and important details can be cut and pasted from other sources. This makes e-mail an excellent method for Linux users to communicate with their system administrators.

In an office with only a few users, you can probably get away with using your personal mailbox to send and receive support e-mails. In a larger office, however, you should create a separate mailbox reserved only for technical support issues. This has several advantages over the use of your personal mailbox:

- Support messages will not be confused with personal, nonsupport-related messages.
- Multiple people can check the mailbox and share administrative responsibility without needing to read each other's personal e-mail.
- Support e-mail is easily redirected to another person's mailbox when you go on vacation. Your personal e-mail continues to go to your personal mailbox.

One easy solution is to simply create a support e-mail alias that redirects messages to an actual mailbox or list of mailboxes. For example, suppose you want to create a support alias that redistributes e-mail to the user accounts for support staff members Joe, Mary, and Bob. You would log in as root, edit the /etc/aliases file, and add lines similar to the following:

```
# Technical support mailing list
support: joe, mary, bob
```

After saving the file, you need to run the `newaliases` command to recompile the /etc/aliases file into a database format. Now your users can send e-mail to the support e-mail address, and the message is automatically routed to everyone on the list. When a member of the list responds to that message, he or she should use the Reply To All option so that the other support staff members also see the message. Otherwise, multiple people may attempt to solve the same problem, resulting in wasteful duplication of effort.

You may also choose to create a support user account. The technical support staff would log in to this account to check messages and send replies. In this manner, all replies are stamped with the support login name and not the personal e-mail address of a staff member.

Resetting a user's password

One common (if not *the* most common) problem that your users will encounter is the inability to log in because:

- They have the Caps Lock key on.
- They have forgotten the password.
- The password has expired.

If the Caps Lock key is not on, then you probably need to reset the user's password. You can't look up the password because Linux stores hashed forms of passwords. Instead, use the `passwd` command to assign a new password to the user's account. Give the user the new password (preferably in person), but then set the password to expire soon so that he or she must choose one (let's hope one that is more easily remembered).

If you must reset a user's password, do so with the passwd command. While logged in as root, type **passwd** followed by the login name you are resetting. You are prompted to enter the password twice. For example, to change the password for mary, type:

```
# passwd mary
```

After resetting the password, set it to expire so that the user is forced to change it the next time she logs in. You can use the chage command to set an expiration period for the password and to trick the system into thinking that the password is long overdue to be changed.

```
# chage -M 30 -d 0 mary
```

The -M 30 option tells the system to expire Mary's password every 30 days. The -d 0 option tricks the system into thinking that her password has not been changed since January 1, 1970. (Keep in mind that using chage activates password aging for any account on which it is used. Adding a -1 to the chage command line disables password aging.)

CROSS-REFERENCE: Administrators who support multiple users might want to consider some newer technologies that make life easier, such as centralized e-mail address books using LDAP. See Chapter 22 for more information.

Modifying Accounts

Occasionally, a user needs more done to an account than just a resetting of the password. You may need to change the groups that a user is in, the drive that a home directory resides on, or a person's name changes with new marital status. The following sections explain how to modify user accounts using one of two methods: usermod or the User Manager window.

Modifying user accounts with usermod

The usermod command is similar to the useradd command and even shares some of the same options. However, instead of adding new accounts, it enables you to change various details of existing accounts. When invoking the usermod command, you must provide account details to change followed by the login name of the account. Table 11-3 lists the available options for the usermod command.

Table 11-3: usermod Options for Changing Existing Accounts

Options	Description
-c "comment"	Change the description field of the account. Non-root users can use the chfn command for to change this field for themselves. Replace comment with a name or other description of the user account. Because the comment can contain multiple words, the quotes are necessary.

Options	Description
-d *home_dir*	Change the home directory of the account to the specified new location. If the -m option is included, copy the contents of the home directory as well. Replace *home_dir* with the full path to the new directory.
-e *expire_date*	Assign a new expiration date for the account, replacing *expire_date* with a date in the MM/DD/YYYY format.
-f *inactivity*	Set the number of days after a password expires until the account is permanently disabled. Setting *inactivity* to 0 disables the account immediately after the password has expired. Setting it to -1 disables the option, which is the default behavior.
-g *group*	Change the primary group (as listed in the /etc/group file) that the user is in. Replace *group* with the name of the new group.
-G *grouplist*	Set the list of groups that user belongs to. Replace *grouplist* with a list of groups.
-l *login_name*	Change the login name of the account to the name supplied after the -l option. Replace *login_name* with the new name. This does not automatically change the name of the home directory; use the -d and -m options for that.
-m	This option is used only in conjunction with the -d option. It causes the contents of the user's home directory to be copied to the new directory.
-o	This option is used only in conjunction with the -u option. It removes the restriction that user IDs must be unique.
-s *shell*	Specify a new command shell to use with this account. Replace *shell* with the full path to the new shell.
-u *user_id*	Change the user ID number for the account. Replace *user_id* with the new user ID number. Unless the -o option is used, the ID number must not be in use by another account.

Assume that a new employee named Jenny Barnes will be taking over Mary's job. We want to convert the mary account to a new name (-l jenny), new comment (-c "Jenny Barnes"), and home directory (-d /home/jenny). You can do that with the following command:

```
# usermod -l jenny -c "Jenny Barnes" -m -d /home/jenny mary
```

Furthermore, if after converting the account you learn that Jenny prefers the tcsh shell, you can make that change with the -s option (-s /bin/tcsh):

```
# usermod -s /bin/tcsh jenny
```

Instead, you can use the chsh command to change the shell. The following is an example:

```
$ chsh -s /bin/tcsh jenny
```

The chsh command is handy because it enables a regular user to change his or her own shell setting to any shell listed in the /etc/shells file. (The root user can change his own shell to any command he chooses.) Simply leave the user name parameter off when invoking the command, and chsh assumes the currently logged-in user as the account to change.

Users can also change their own user information using the chfn command. This information is stored in the /etc/passwd file and displayed when you type the finger command (for example, finger jenny). In this example, the full name, office name, office phone, home phone, and work phone are set by the user jenny:

```
$ chfn -f "J Smith" -o "A-111" -p 555-1212 -h 555-2323 jenny
```

Users can also add information about themselves into the .plan, .project, .forward, and .pgpkey files in their home directory. That information will then be picked up by the finger command.

Modifying user accounts with User Manager

To use the desktop to change an existing account, you can use the User Manager. Here's how to add a new user from the User Manager window:

1. Select System → Administration → Users and Groups (or type system-config-users from a Terminal window as root user). The main User Manager window appears.

2. Select the user name of the account you want to modify, and then click the Properties button to open the User Properties window (see Figure 11-3).

3. There are four tabs of information you can modify for the user you selected:

    • **User Data** — This tab contains the user information you created when you first added the user account.

    • **Account Info** — Select the Enable Account Expiration check box, and then type a date if you want the account to become inaccessible after a particular date. Select the Local Password is Locked check box if you want to prevent access to the account but not delete it. (The latter is a good technique when an employee is leaving the company or if you want to lock out a customer whose account is temporarily disabled. The information isn't removed; it just isn't accessible.)

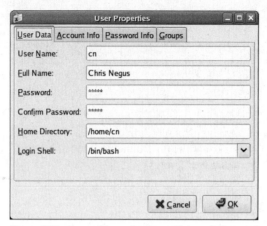

Figure 11-3: Choose Properties to modify an existing user account.

- **Password Info** — Select Enable Password Expiration if you want to control expiration of the user's password. By default, passwords don't expire. Here are your options: "Days before change allowed" (forces the user to keep the password for at least a set number of days before it can be changed); "Days before change required" (allows the user to keep the same password for at least the set number of days); "Days warning before change" (sets how many days before the password expiration day that the user is warned to change the password); "Days before account inactive" (sets the number of days after which the account is deactivated).

- **Groups** — Select from the list of available groups to add the user to one or more of those groups.

4. Click OK to apply the changes to the user account.

Deleting User Accounts

Occasionally, it is necessary to remove a user account from your Linux system. This can be done with either the `userdel` command or the User Manager window.

Deleting user accounts with userdel

The `userdel` command takes a single argument, which is the login name of the account to delete. If you supply the optional `-r` option, it also deletes the user's home directory and all the files in it. To delete the user account with login name `mary`, you would type this:

```
# userdel mary
```

To wipe out her home directory along with her account, type this:

```
# userdel -r mary
```

Files owned by the deleted user but not located in the user's home directory will not be deleted. The system administrator must search for and delete those files manually. The `find` command comes in very handy for this type of task. I won't describe all the capabilities of the `find` command (that would take a very fat chapter of its own). I do, however, provide a few simple examples of how to use `find` to locate files belonging to a particular user, even when those files are scattered throughout a file system. You can even use the `find` command to delete or change the ownership of files as they are located. Table 11-4 has a few examples of the `find` command in action.

Table 11-4: Using find to Locate and Change User Files

Find Command	Description
`find / -user mary`	Search the entire file hierarchy (start at /) for all files and directories owned by `mary` and print the filenames to the screen.
`find /home -user mary -exec rm -i {} \;`	Search for all files and subdirectories under `/home` owned by `mary`. Run the `rm` command interactively to delete each file.
`find / -user mary -exec chown jenny {} \;`	Search for all files and subdirectories under `/home` that are owned by user `mary` and run the `chown` command to change each file so that it is owned by `jenny` instead.
`find / -uid 500 -exec chown jenny {} \;`	This command is basically the same as the previous example, but it uses the user ID number instead of the user name to identify the matching files. This is useful if you have deleted a user before converting her files.

There are a few common things about each invocation of the `find` command. The first parameter is always the directory to start the recursive search in. After that come the file attributes to match. You can use the `-exec` parameter to run a command against each matching file or directory. The `{}` characters designate where the matching filename should be filled in when `find` runs the `-exec` option. The `\;` at the end simply tells Linux where the command ends. These are only a few of `find`'s capabilities. I encourage you to read the online man page to learn more about `find`. (Type **man find** to view the page.)

Deleting user accounts with User Manager

To delete a user from the User Manager window, simply click the line representing the user account, and then click the Delete button.

- The information about the user is removed from the /etc/passwd file; thus, the user can no longer log in.
- The home directory and all files owned by the user will still exist. However, a listing of files previously owned by that user (ls -l) will show only the former user's UID, but no name, as the owner.

See the description in the previous section for information about how to find and remove files previously owned by the user.

Checking Disk Quotas

Limited disk space can be another source of user support calls. Fedora and RHEL offer the quotas software package for limiting and displaying the amount of disk space that a user can consume. You can also use the du command to see how much disk space has been used in a particular directory (and related subdirectories). To automate the process of checking for disk space, you can create your own script. The following sections describe these ways of dealing with potential disk space problems.

Using quota to check disk usage

A careless or greedy user can gobble up all the space on your hard disk and, possibly, bring your computer to a halt. By using disk quotas, you can limit the amount of disk resources a user or group can use up.

The quota package contains a set of tools that lets you limit the amount of disk space (based on disk blocks) and files (based on inodes) that a user can consume. Using quotas, you can limit the amount of usage (on a per-user and -group basis) for each file system on your computer. The general steps for setting disk quotas are:

1. Edit the /etc/fstab file.
2. Create quota files.
3. Create and start a quota startup script.
4. Create quota rules.
5. Check quotas.

You set quotas on file systems listed in your /etc/fstab file. For computers that are shared by many users, there might be a separate /home or /var partition where users are expected to put all their data. That kind of partition boundary can prevent an entire disk from being consumed by one user. Quotas on the /home or /var partition can make sure that the space within those partitions is shared fairly among your computer's users.

> **NOTE:** When you begin setting user disk quotas, keep track of the total amount of disk space that can be consumed by the users you assign. Although quotas can limit how much each user can consume, it doesn't prevent your system from running out of disk space when the total amount of disk space allocated exceeds the total amount available.

The procedure that spans the next few sections assumes that you have a separate /home partition on your computer for which you want to create quotas. You could use any partition, not just the /home partition shown in the procedure. For example, if you have only one partition mounted at the root of the files system (/), you could set quotas for your entire file system by replacing /home with / in the following example.

Editing the /etc/fstab file

You need to add quota support to the file system. To do that, edit the /etc/fstab file and add the usrquota option to field number four of the partition for which you want to set quotas. Here is an example of a line from /etc/fstab:

```
/dev/sda2  /home  ext3   defaults,usrquota,grpquota     1 2
```

Here, the /home file system is used to allow disk quotas for all users' home directories under the /home directory.

Before the usrquota option can take effect, the file system must be remounted. This happens automatically when you reboot, which you will have to do if you are setting quotas for the root (/) file system. Otherwise, you might be able to use the umount and mount commands to cause the usrquota option to take effect or run mount with the remount option.

Creating quota files

You need to have aquota.user and/or aquota.group files in the root directory of the partition on which you want to establish disk quotas. To add quotas based on individual users, you need an aquota.user file, while aquota.group is needed to set quotas based on groups. One way to create these files is with the quotacheck command. Here's an example of the quotacheck command to create an initial aquota.user file:

```
# quotacheck -c /home
```

A /home/aquota.user file is created from the previous command. (To create an initial aquota.group file, type **touch /home/aquota.group**.) Next, you must create the disk usage table for the partition. Here's an example of how to do that:

```
# quotacheck -vug /home
```

The quotacheck command in this example looks at the file system partition mounted on /home and builds a table of disk usage. The -v option produces verbose output from the command, the -u option causes user quotas to be examined, and the -g option causes group quotas to be examined.

Creating a quota startup script

If the quota package doesn't include a startup script (and it doesn't with the current Fedora or RHEL distributions), you can create your own. You want this script to check quotas (quotacheck command), start the quota service (quotaon command), and turn off the service (quotaoff command).

Open a new file called /etc/init.d/quota as root user, using any text editor. Here is an example of the content you can add to that file:

```
#!/bin/bash

# init file for quota
#
# description: Checks disk quotas
#
# processname: quota
# chkconfig: - 90 90
# source function library
. /etc/rc.d/init.d/functions

case "$1" in
  start)
    echo -n "Checking quotas: "
        daemon /sbin/quotacheck -avug
    echo
    echo -n "Starting quotas: "
        daemon /sbin/quotaon -avug
    echo
    ;;
  stop)
    echo -n "Shutting down quotas: "
    daemon /sbin/quotaoff -a
    echo
    ;;
  restart)
        $0 stop
        $0 start
        ;;
  *)
    echo "Usage: quota {start|stop|restart}"
    exit 1
esac

exit 0
```

The quota script, when started, first runs the quotacheck command to check all file systems for which quota checking is on. Then it turns on quota checking with the quotaon command. The line # chkconfig: - 90 90 identifies the names assigned to the startup script

(`S90quota` or `K90quota`) when it is added to the individual run-level directories. When you run `chkconfig --add quota` in the next step, those scripts are automatically put in the correct run-level directories.

Turn on the quota startup script

If you created a quota file, as described in the previous step, you need to make it executable and set it to start automatically when you start Fedora or RHEL. To do those things, type the following as root user:

```
# chmod 755 /etc/init.d/quota
# chkconfig --add quota
# chkconfig quota on
```

At this point, links are created so that your quota script starts when Fedora or RHEL boots.

Creating quota rules

You can use the `edquota` command to create quota rules for a particular user or group. (Valid users and groups are listed in the `/etc/passwd` and `/etc/group` files, respectively). Here is an example of an `edquota` command to set quotas for a user named `jake`.

NOTE: The `edquota` command uses the `vi` text editor to edit your quota files. To use a different editor, change the value of the `EDITOR` or `VISUAL` environment variable before running `edquota`. For example, to use the `emacs` editor, type the following before running `edquota`:

```
#   export EDITOR=emacs
```

```
# edquota -u jake
Disk quotas for user jake (uid 501)
  Filesystem         blocks    soft    hard    inodes    soft   hard
   /dev/sda2             596       0       0         1       0      0
~
~
~
"/tmp//EdP.aBY1zYC" 3L, 215C
```

This example shows that user quotas can be set for the user `jake` on the `/dev/sda2` partition (which is `/home` in my example). Currently, `jake` has used 596 blocks (a block equals 1K on this `ext3` file system). One file was created by `jake` (represented by 1 inode). To change the disk usage limits, you can edit the zeros (unlimited use) under the soft and hard heading for blocks and inodes.

Soft limits set limits that you don't want a user or group to exceed. Hard limits set the boundaries that you will not let a user or group exceed. After a set grace period that a soft limit is exceeded (which is seven days, by default), the soft limit becomes a hard limit. (Type **edquota -t** to check and change the grace periods that you have set.)

Here is an example of how the line in the previous `edquota` example could be changed:

```
/dev/sda2                    596    512000  716800    1    800  1000
```

In this example, the soft limit on the number of blocks that the user jake could consume on the /dev/sda2 device (/home) is 512000 blocks (or 500MB); the hard limit is 716800 blocks (or 700MB). Soft and hard limits on inodes are 800 and 1000, respectively. If either of the soft limits are exceeded by the user jake, he has seven days to get back under the limit, or he will be blocked from using any more disk space or inodes.

Further attempts to write to a partition after the hard limit has been exceeded results in a failure to write to the disk. When this happens, the user who tries to create the file that exceeds his limit will see a message like the following:

```
ide0(3,2): write failed, user block limit reached.
cp: writing 'abc.doc': Disk quota exceeded
```

Exceeding disk quota can also prevent that user from logging in again because logging in from some graphical user interfaces requires being able to write to a user's home directory.

Instead of assigning quotas to users, you can assign quotas to any group listed in the /etc/group file. Instead of the -u option to edquota, use the -g options followed by a group name.

Updating quota settings

After you have changed quota settings for a user, you should rerun the quotacheck command. You should also run the quotacheck command periodically, to keep the quota records up to date. One way to do that is to run the quotacheck command weekly using a cron entry. (See Chapter 12 for more information on the cron facility.)

Checking quotas

To report on how much disk space and how many inodes each user on your computer (for which you have set quotas) has consumed, use the repquota command. Here's an example of the repquota command for reading quota data relating to all partitions that are using quotas:

```
# repquota -a
*** Report for user quotas on device /dev/sda2
Block grace time: 7days: Inode grace time: 7days
                        Block limits                File limits
User          used    soft    hard  grace    used  soft  hard   grace
root    --  1973984      0       0           2506    0     0
jake    --     1296    700    1700  6days        3    0     0
```

In this example, jake has exceeded his soft limit of 700 blocks. He currently has six days left in his grace period to remove enough files so that the soft limit does not become the hard limit.

Using du to check disk use

You can discover the most voracious consumers of disk space using the du command. Invoke du with the -s option and give it a list of directories; it reports the total disk space used by all the files in each directory. Add an -h option to display disk space used in numbers, followed by kilobytes (k), megabytes (M), or gigabytes (G). The -c option adds a total of all requested directories at the end. The following checks disk usage for several home directories:

```
# du -hcs /home/tom /home/bill /home/tina /home/sally
```

This should result in a list of all of your users' home directories preceded by the number of kilobytes (K), megabytes (M), or gigabytes (G) that each directory structure uses. It looks something like this:

```
1G
339M     /home/tom
81M      /home/bill
31M      /home/tina
44K      /home/sally
1.45G    total
```

Removing temp files automatically

Some potential disk-consumption problems are set up to take care of themselves. For example, directories for storing temporary files used by applications (such as /tmp and /var/tmp) can consume lots of disk space over time. To deal with the problem, Fedora and RHEL include the tmpwatch facility. The tmpwatch command runs from the cron file /etc/cron.daily/tmpwatch to delete unused temporary files. Here's what that file contains:

```
flags=-umc
/usr/sbin/tmpwatch "$flags" -x /tmp/.X11-unix -x /tmp/.XIM-unix \
    -x /tmp/.font-unix -x /tmp/.ICE-unix \
    -x /tmp/.Test-unix 10d /tmp
/usr/sbin/tmpwatch "$flags" 30d /var/tmp
/usr/sbin/tmpwatch 720 /var/tmp
for d in /var/{cache/man,catman}/{cat?,X11R6/cat?,local/cat?}; do
    if [ -d "$d" ]; then
   /usr/sbin/tmpwatch "$flags" -f 30d $d
    fi
done
```

Each day, this tmpwatch script runs to delete temporary files that haven't been used for some time. The flags (-umc) indicate that time access is based on the file's access time (u), modification time (m), and inode change time (c). It starts by identifying files that are not to be deleted (tmpwatch -x). Files such as those in the /tmp/.X11-unix directory represent sockets for active X servers and would make an active GUI inaccessible if they were deleted. All other files from the /tmp and /var/tmp directories are removed after 10 and 30 days of not being accessed, respectively. Temporary man page files stored in /var/cache subdirectories are also checked and deleted after 30 days of disuse.

Sending Mail to All Users

Occasionally, you need to send messages to all users on your system. Warning users of planned downtime for hardware upgrades is a good example. Sending e-mail to each user individually is extremely time consuming and wasteful; this is precisely the kind of task that e-mail aliases and mailing lists were invented for. Keeping a mailing list of all the users on your system can be problematic, however. If you are not diligent about keeping the mailing list current, it becomes increasingly inaccurate as you add and delete users. Also, if your system has many users, the mere size of the alias list can become unwieldy.

The following script, called mailfile, provides a simple method of working around these problems. It grabs the login names from the /etc/passwd file and sends e-mail to all users.

> **NOTE:** Because regular user accounts begin with UID 500 in Fedora and RHEL systems, the script excludes all UIDs under 500 (which are typically administrative accounts). It also skips UID 65534, which is the anonymous NFS user account.

```
#!/bin/bash
# mailfile: This script mails the named file to all regular
#           users of the system.  It skips all administrative
#           accounts (accounts under UID 500) as well as the
#           anonymous NFS user (UID 65534).
#
# USAGE: mailfile "Subject goes here" filename.txt

# Check for a subject
#
# Get the subject of the message
    subject=$1

# Check for a filename
    filename=$2

# Loop through all login names, skipping accounts under 500
# as well as the anonymous NFS account (65534)

for x in $(cut -d ":" -f 1,3 /etc/passwd)
do
    USER=$(echo $x | cut -d ":" -f1)
    ID=$(echo $x | cut -d ":" -f2)

    if [[ $ID -gt 499 && $ID -lt 65534 ]]; then

    # Mail the file
    echo Mailing to $USER
```

```
        mail -s "$subject" $USER < $filename

        # Sleep for a few seconds so we don't overload the mailer
        # On fast systems or systems with few accounts, you can
        # probably take this delay out.
        sleep 2
fi
done
```

The script accepts two parameters. The first is the subject of the e-mail message, which is enclosed in quotes. The second is the name of the file containing the text message to send. Thus, to send an e-mail message to all users warning them about an upcoming server hardware upgrade, I may do something similar to the following:

```
mailfile "System upgrade at 5:00pm" upgrade.txt
```

The file `upgrade.txt` contains the text of the message to be sent to each user. The really useful thing about this approach is that I can save this text file and easily modify and resend it the next time I upgrade the system.

> **TIP:** If your users log in to your system using text-based logins instead of graphical logins, you can add messages to the `/etc/motd` file to have them reach your users. Any text in that file will be displayed on each user's screen after the user logs in and before the first shell prompt appears.

Summary

It is not uncommon for a Linux system to be used as a single-task server with no actual users. It sits quietly in a server room, serving Web pages or handling domain name service, never crashing, and rarely needing attention. This is not always the case, however. You may have to support users on your Linux system, and that can be the most challenging part of your system administration duties.

Fedora and RHEL provide a variety of tools that help you with your user administrative chores. The `useradd`, `usermod`, and `userdel` commands enable easy command-line manipulation of user account data. Furthermore, you can lighten your load even more by creating a support mailbox and building shell scripts to automate repetitive tasks. Fedora and RHEL build on top of the rich history of UNIX and provide an ideal platform to support the diverse needs of your users.

Chapter 12

Automating System Tasks

In This Chapter

- Understanding shell scripts
- System initialization
- System startup and shutdown
- Scheduling system tasks

You'd never get any work done if you typed every command that needs to be run on your Fedora or RHEL system when it starts. Likewise, you could work more efficiently if you grouped together sets of commands that you run all the time. Shell scripts can handle these tasks.

A *shell script* is a group of commands, functions, variables, or just about anything else you can use from a shell. These items are typed into a plain-text file. That file can then be run as a command. Fedora and RHEL use system initialization shell scripts during system startup to run commands needed to get things going. You can create your own shell scripts to automate the tasks you need to do regularly.

This chapter provides a rudimentary overview of the inner workings of shell scripts and how they can be used. You learn how shell scripts are responsible for the messages that scroll by on the system console during booting and how simple scripts can be harnessed to a scheduling facility (such as `cron` or `at`) to simplify administrative tasks.

You also learn to fine-tune your machine to start at the most appropriate run level and to run only services you need. With that understanding, you'll be able to personalize your computer and cut down on the amount of time you spend repetitively typing the same commands.

Understanding Shell Scripts

Have you ever had a task that you needed to do over and over that took a lot of typing on the command line? Do you ever think to yourself, "Wow, I wish there was just one command I could type to do all this of this"? Maybe a shell script is what you're after.

Shell scripts are the equivalent of batch files in MS-DOS, and can contain long lists of commands, complex flow control, arithmetic evaluations, user-defined variables, user-defined functions, and sophisticated condition testing. Shell scripts are capable of handling everything from simple one-line commands to something as complex as starting up your Fedora or RHEL system.

In fact, as you will read in this chapter, Fedora and RHEL do just that. They use shell scripts (`/etc/rc.d/rc.sysinit` and `/etc/rc`) to check and mount all your file systems, set up your consoles, configure your network, launch all your system services, and eventually provide you with your login screen. While there are nearly a dozen different shells available in Fedora and RHEL, the default shell is called `bash`, the Bourne-Again SHell.

Executing and debugging shell scripts

One of the primary advantages of shell scripts is that they can be opened in any text editor to see what they do. A big disadvantage is that large or complex shell scripts often execute more slowly than compiled programs. There are two basic ways to execute a shell script:

- The filename is used as an argument to the shell (as in `bash` *myscript*). In this method, the file does not need to be executable; it just contains a list of shell commands. The shell specified on the command line is used to interpret the commands in the script file. This is most common for quick, simple tasks.

- The shell script may also have the name of the interpreter placed in the first line of the script preceeded by `#!` (as in `#!/bin/bash`), and have its execute bit set (using `chmod +x`). You can then run your script just like any other program in your path simply by typing the name of the script on the command line.

> **CROSS-REFERENCE:** See Chapter 4 for more details on `chmod` and read/write/execute permissions.

When scripts are executed in either manner, options to the program may be specified on the command line. Anything following the name of the script is referred to as a *command-line argument*.

As with writing any software, there is no substitute to clear and thoughtful design and lots of comments. The pound sign (#) prefaces comments and can take up an entire line or exist on the same line after script code. It's best to implement more complex shell scripts in stages, making sure the logic is sound at each step before continuing. Here are a few good, concise tips to make sure things are working as expected during testing:

- Place an `echo` statement at the beginning of lines within the body of a loop. That way, rather than executing the code, you can see what will be executed without making any permanent changes.

- To achieve the same goal, you could place dummy `echo` statements throughout the code. If these lines get printed, you know the correct logic branch is being taken.

- You could use `set -x` near the beginning of the script to display each command that is executed or launch your scripts using `bash -x myscript`.

- Because useful scripts have a tendency to grow over time, keeping your code readable as you go along is extremely important. Do what you can to keep the logic of your code clean and easy to follow.

Understanding shell variables

Often within a shell script, you want to reuse certain items of information. During the course of processing the shell script, the name or number representing this information may change. To store information used by a shell script in such a way that it can be easily reused, you can set variables. Variable names within shell scripts are case-sensitive and can be defined in the following manner:

```
NAME=value
```

The first part of a variable is the variable name, and the second part is the value set for that name. Be sure that the `NAME` and `value` touch the equal sign, without any spaces. Variables can be assigned from constants, such as text or numbers. This is useful for initializing values or saving lots of typing for long constants. Here are examples where variables are set to a string of characters (`CITY`) and a numeric value (`PI`):

```
CITY="Springfield"
PI=3.14159265
```

Variables can contain the output of a command or command sequence. You can accomplish this by preceding the command with a dollar sign and open parenthesis, and following it with a closing parenthesis. For example, `MYDATE=$(date)` assigns the output from the `date` command to the `MYDATE` variable. Enclosing the command in backticks (`` ` ``) can have the same effect.

> **NOTE:** Keep in mind that characters such as dollar sign ($), backtick (`), asterisk (*), exclamation point (!), and others have special meaning to the shell, as you will see as you proceed through this chapter. To use those characters in an option to a command, and not have the shell use its special meaning, you need to precede that character with a backslash (\) or surround it in quotes. One place you will encounter this is in files created by Windows users that might include spaces, exclamation points, or other characters. In Linux, to properly interpret a file named **my big! file!**, you either need to surround it in double quotes or type: **my\ big\! file\!**

These are great ways to get information that can change from computer to computer or from day to day. The following example sets the output of the `uname -n` command to the `MACHINE` variable. Then I use parentheses to set `NUM_FILES` to the number of files in the current directory by piping (`|`) the output of the `ls` command to the word count command (`wc -l`).

```
MACHINE=`uname -n`
NUM_FILES=$(/bin/ls | wc -l)
```

Variables can also contain the value of other variables. This is useful when you have to preserve a value that will change so you can use it later in the script. Here BALANCE is set to the value of the CurBalance variable.

```
BALANCE="$CurBalance"
```

> **NOTE:** When assigning variables, use only the variable name (for example, BALANCE). When referenced, meaning you want the *value* of the variable, precede it with a dollar sign (as in $CurBalance). The result of the latter is that you get the value of the string, and not the string itself.

Special shell variables

There are special variables that the shell assigns for you. The most commonly used variables are called the *positional parameters* or *command line arguments* and are referenced as $0, $1, $2, $3 . . . $n. $0 is special and is assigned the name used to invoke your script; the others are assigned the values of the parameters passed on the command line. For instance, if the shell script named myscript were called as:

```
myscript foo bar
```

the positional parameter $0 would be myscript, $1 would be foo, and $2 would be bar.

Another variable, $#, tells you how many parameters your script was given. In our example, $# would be 2. Another particularly useful special shell variable is $?, which receives the exit status of the last command executed. Typically, a value of zero means everything is okay, and anything other than zero indicates an error of some kind. For a complete list of special shell variables, refer to the bash man page.

Parameter expansion in bash

As mentioned earlier, if you want the value of a variable, you precede it with a $ (for example, $CITY). This is really just shorthand for the notation ${CITY}; curly braces are used when the value of the parameter needs to be placed next to other text without a space. Bash has special rules that allow you to expand the value of a variable in different ways. Going into all the rules is probably a little overkill for a quick introduction to shell scripts, but Table 12-1 presents some common constructs that you're likely to see in bash scripts you find on your Fedora or RHEL box.

Table 12-1: Examples of bash Parameter Expansion

Construction	Meaning
${var:-value}	If variable is unset or empty, expand this to *value*
${var#pattern}	Chop the shortest match for *pattern* from the front of *var*'s value
${var##pattern}	Chop the longest match for *pattern* from the front of *var*'s value
${var%pattern}	Chop the shortest match for *pattern* from the end of *var*'s value
${var%%pattern}	Chop the longest match for *pattern* from the end of *var*'s value

Try typing the following commands from a shell to test how parameter expansion works:

```
$ THIS="Example"
$ THIS=${THIS:-"Not Set"}
$ THAT=${THAT:-"Not Set"}
$ echo $THIS
Example
$ echo $THAT
Not Set
```

In the examples here, the THIS variable is initially set to the word Example. In the next two lines, the THIS and THAT variables are set to their current values or to Not Set, if they are not currently set. Notice that because I just set THIS to the string Example, when I echo the value of THIS it appears as Example. However, since THAT was not set, it appears as Not Set.

> **NOTE:** For the rest of this section, I show how variables and commands may appear in a shell script. To try out any of those examples, however, you can simply type them into a shell as shown in the previous example.

In the following example, MYFILENAME is set to /home/digby/myfile.txt. Next, the FILE variable is set to myfile.txt and DIR is set to /home/digby. In the NAME variable, the file name is cut down to simply myfile, then in the EXTENSION variable the file extension is set to txt. (To try these out, you can type them at a shell prompt as in the previous example, then echo the value of each variable to see how it is set.)

```
MYFILENAME="/home/digby/myfile.txt"
FILE=${MYFILENAME##*/}          #FILE becomes "myfile.txt"
DIR=${MYFILENAME%/*}            #DIR becomes "/home/digby"
NAME=${FILE%.*}                 #NAME becomes "myfile"
EXTENSION=${FILE#*.}            #EXTENSION becomes "txt"
```

Performing arithmetic in shell scripts

Bash uses *untyped* variables, meaning it normally treats variables as strings or text, but can change them on the fly if you want it to. Unless you tell it otherwise with declare, your variables are just a bunch of letters to bash. But when you start trying to do arithmetic with them, bash will convert them to integers if it can. This makes it possible to do some fairly complex arithmetic in bash.

Integer arithmetic can be performed using the built-in let command or through the external expr or bc commands. After setting the variable BIGNUM value to 1024, the three commands that follow would all store the value 64 in the RESULT variable. The last command gets a random number between 0 and 10 and echoes the results back to you.

```
BIGNUM=1024
let RESULT=$BIGNUM/16
RESULT=`expr $BIGNUM / 16`
RESULT=`echo "$BIGNUM / 16" | bc -l`
let foo=$RANDOM%10; echo $foo
```

> **NOTE:** While most elements of shell scripts are relatively freeform (where whitespace, such as spaces or tabs, is insignificant), both let and expr are particular about spacing. The let command insists on no spaces between each operand and the mathematical operator, whereas the syntax of the expr command requires whitespace between each operand and its operator. In contrast to those, bc isn't picky about spaces, but can be trickier to use because it does floating-point arithmetic.

To see a complete list of the kinds of arithmetic you can perform using the let command, type **help let** at the bash prompt.

Using programming constructs in shell scripts

One of the features that make shell scripts so powerful is that their implementation of looping and conditional execution constructs is similar to those found in more complex scripting and programming languages. You can use several different types of loops, depending on your needs.

The "if...then" statements

The most commonly used programming construct is conditional execution, or the if statement. It is used to perform actions only under certain conditions. There are several variations, depending on whether you're testing one thing, or want to do one thing if a condition is true, but another thing if a condition is false, or if you want to test several things one after the other.

The first if...then example tests if VARIABLE is set to the number 1. If it is, then the echo command is used to say that it is set to 1. The fi then indicates that the if statement is complete and processing can continue.

```
VARIABLE=1
if [ $VARIABLE -eq 1 ] ; then
echo "The variable is 1"
fi
```

Instead of using −eq, you can use the equals sign (=), as shown in the following example. The = works best for comparing string values, while -eq is often better for comparing numbers. Using the else statement, different words can be echoed if the criterion of the if statement isn't met ($STRING = "Friday"). Keep in mind that it's good practice to put strings in double quotes.

```
STRING="Friday"
if [ $STRING = "Friday" ] ; then
echo "WhooHoo.  Friday."
else
echo "Will Friday ever get here?"
fi
```

You can also reverse tests with an exclamation mark (!). In the following example, if STRING is not Monday, then "At least it's not Monday" is echoed.

```
STRING="FRIDAY"
if ["$STRING" != "Monday" ] ; then
    echo "At least it's not Monday"
fi
```

In the following example, elif (which stands for "else if") is used to test for an additional condition (is filename a file or a directory).

```
filename="$HOME"

if [ -f "$filename" ] ; then
    echo "$filename is a regular file"
elif [ -d "$filename" ] ; then
    echo "$filename is a directory"
else
    echo "I have no idea what $filename is"
fi
```

As you can see from the preceding examples, the condition you are testing is placed between square brackets [ ]. When a test expression is evaluated, it will return either a value of 0, meaning that it is true, or a 1, meaning that it is false. Notice that the echo lines are indented. This is optional and done only to make the script more readable.

Table 12-2 lists the conditions that are testable and is quite a handy reference. (If you're in a hurry, you can type **help test** on the command line to get the same information.)

Table 12-2: Operators for Test Expressions

Operator	What Is Being Tested?
-a *file*	Does the file exist? (same as −e)
-b *file*	Is the file a special block device?
-c *file*	Is the file character special (for example, a character device)? Used to identify serial lines and terminal devices.
-d *file*	Is the file a directory?
-e *file*	Does the file exist? (same as -a)
-f *file*	Does the file exist, and is it a regular file (for example, not a directory, socket, pipe, link, or device file)?
-g *file*	Does the file have the set-group-id bit set?
-h *file*	Is the file a symbolic link? (same as −L)
-k *file*	Does the file have the sticky bit set?
-L *file*	Is the file a symbolic link?
-n *string*	Is the length of the string greater than 0 bytes?
-O *file*	Do you own the file?
-p *file*	Is the file a named pipe?
-r *file*	Is the file readable by you?
-s *file*	Does the file exist, and is it larger than 0 bytes?
-S *file*	Does the file exist, and is it a socket?
-t *fd*	Is the file descriptor connected to a terminal?
-u *file*	Does the file have the set-user-id bit set?
-w *file*	Is the file writable by you?
-x *file*	Is the file executable by you?
-z *string*	Is the length of the string 0 (zero) bytes?
expr1 -a *expr2*	Are both the first expression and the second expression true?
expr1 -o *expr2*	Is either of the two expressions true?
file1 -nt *file2*	Is the first file newer than the second file (using the modification timestamp)?
file1 -ot *file2*	Is the first file older than the second file (using the modification timestamp)?
file1 -ef *file2*	Are the two files associated by a link (a hard link or a symbolic link)?

Operator	What Is Being Tested?
`var1 = var2`	Is the first variable equal to the second variable?
`var1 -eq var2`	Is the first variable equal to the second variable?
`var1 -ge var2`	Is the first variable greater than or equal to the second variable?
`var1 -gt var2`	Is the first variable greater than the second variable?
`var1 -le var2`	Is the first variable less than or equal to the second variable?
`var1 -lt var2`	Is the first variable less than the second variable?
`var1 != var2`	Is the first variable not equal to the second variable?
`var1 -ne var2`	Is the first variable not equal to the second variable?

There is also a special shorthand method of performing tests that can be useful for simple *one-command* actions. In the following example, the two pipes (||) indicate that if the directory being tested for doesn't exist (-d dirname), then make the directory (mkdir $dirname).

```
# [ test] || {action}
# Perform simple single command {action} if test is false
dirname="/tmp/testdir"
[ -d "$dirname" ] || mkdir "$dirname"
```

Instead of pipes, you can use two ampersands to test if something is true. In the following example, a command is being tested to see if it includes at least three command-line arguments.

```
# [ test ] && {action}
# Perform simple single command {action} if test is true
[ $# -ge 3 ] && echo "There are at least 3 command line arguments."
```

The case command

Another frequently used construct is the case command. Similar to a switch statement in programming languages, this can take the place of several nested if statements. A general form of the case statement is as follows:

```
case "VAR" in
   Result1)
      { body };;
   Result2)
      { body };;
   *)
      { body } ;;
esac
```

One use for the case command might be to help with your backups. The following case statement tests for the first three letters of the current day (case `date +%a` in). Then, depending on the day, a particular backup directory (BACKUP) and tape drive (TAPE) is set.

```
# Our VAR doesn't have to be a variable,
# it can be the output of a command as well
# Perform action based on day of week
case `date +%a` in
   "Mon")
         BACKUP=/home/myproject/data0
         TAPE=/dev/rft0
# Note the use of the double semi-colon to end each option
         ;;
# Note the use of the "|" to mean "or"
   "Tue" | "Thu")
         BACKUP=/home/myproject/data1
         TAPE=/dev/rft1
         ;;
   "Wed" | "Fri")
         BACKUP=/home/myproject/data2
         TAPE=/dev/rft2
         ;;
# Don't do backups on the weekend.
   *)
         BACKUP="none"
         TAPE=/dev/null
         ;;
esac
```

The asterisk (*) is used as a catchall, similar to the default keyword in the C programming language. In this example, if none of the other entries are matched on the way down the loop, the asterisk is matched, and the value of BACKUP becomes none. Note the use of esac, or case spelled backwards, to end the case statement.

The "for...do" loop

Loops are used to perform actions over and over again until a condition is met or until all data has been processed. One of the most commonly used loops is the for...do loop. It iterates through a list of values, executing the body of the loop for each element in the list. The syntax and a few examples are presented here:

```
for VAR in LIST
do
     { body }
done
```

The for loop assigns the values in LIST to VAR one at a time. Then for each value, the body in braces between do and done is executed. VAR can be any variable name, and LIST can be composed of pretty much any list of values or anything that generates a list.

```
for NUMBER in 0 1 2 3 4 5 6 7 8 9
do
   echo The number is $NUMBER
done
```

```
for FILE in `/bin/ls`
do
   echo $FILE
done
```

You can also write it this way, which is somewhat cleaner.

```
for NAME in John Paul Ringo George ; do
   echo $NAME is my favorite Beatle
done
```

Each element in the LIST is separated from the next by whitespace. This can cause trouble if you're not careful because some commands, such as ls -l, output multiple fields per line, each separated by whitespace. The string done ends the for statement.

If you're a die-hard C programmer, bash allows you to use C syntax to control your loops:

```
LIMIT=10
# Double parentheses, and no $ on LIMIT even though it's a variable!
for ((a=1; a <= LIMIT ; a++)) ; do
  echo  "$a"
done
```

The "while...do" and "until...do" loops

Two other possible looping constructs are the while...do loop and the until...do loop. The structure of each is presented here:

```
while condition      until condition
do                   do
   { body }             { body }
done                 done
```

The while statement executes while the condition is true. The until statement executes until the condition is true, in other words, while the condition is false.

Here is an example of a while loop that will output the number 0123456789:

```
N=0
while [ $N -lt 10 ] ; do
   echo -n $N
   let N=$N+1
done
```

Another way to output the number 0123456789 is to use an until loop as follows:

```
N=0
until [ $N -eq 10 ] ; do
   echo -n $N
   let N=$N+1
done
```

Some useful external programs

Bash is great and has lots of built-in commands, but it usually needs some help to do anything really useful. Some of the most common useful programs you'll see used are `grep`, `cut`, `tr`, `awk`, and `sed`. As with all the best UNIX tools, most of these programs are designed to work with standard input and standard output, so you can easily use them with pipes and shell scripts.

The general regular expression parser (grep)

The name *general regular expression parser* sounds intimidating, but `grep` is just a way to find patterns in files or text. Think of it as a useful search tool. Getting really good with regular expressions is quite a challenge, but many useful things can be accomplished with just the simplest forms.

For example, you can display a list of all regular user accounts by using `grep` to search for all lines that contain the text `/home` in the `/etc/passwd` file as follows:

```
grep /home /etc/passwd
```

Or you could find all environment variables that begin with `HO` using the following command:

```
env | grep ^HO
```

To find a list of options to use with the `grep` command, type **man grep**.

Remove sections of lines of text (cut)

The `cut` command can extract specific fields from a line of text or from files. It is very useful for parsing system configuration files into easy-to-digest chunks. You can specify the field separator you want to use and the fields you want, or you can break up a line based on bytes.

The following example lists all home directories of users on your system. Using an earlier example of the `grep` command, this line pipes a list of regular users from the `/etc/passwd` file, then displays the sixth field (`-f6`) as delimited by a colon (`-d':'`). The hyphen at the end tells `cut` to read from standard input (from the pipe).

```
grep /home /etc/passwd | cut -f6 -d':' -
```

Translate or delete characters (tr)

The `tr` command is a character-based translator that can be used to replace one character or set of characters with another or to remove a character from a line of text.

The following example translates all uppercase letters to lowercase letters and displays the words "mixed upper and lower case" as a result:

```
FOO="Mixed UPpEr aNd LoWeR cAsE"
echo $FOO | tr [A-Z] [a-z]
```

In the next example, the `tr` command is used on a list of filenames to rename any files in that list so that any tabs or spaces (as indicated by the `:[blank:]` option) contained in a filename are translated into underscores. Try running the following code in a test directory:

```
for file in * ; do
   d=`echo $file | tr [:blank:] [_]`
   ["$file" = "-d" ] || mv -i "$file" "$d"
done
```

The Stream Editor (sed)

The `sed` command is a simple scriptable editor, and as such can perform only simple edits, such as removing lines that have text matching a certain pattern, replacing one pattern of characters with another, and other simple edits. To get a better idea of how `sed` scripts work, there's no substitute for the online documentation, but here are some examples of common uses.

You can use the `sed` command to essentially do what I did earlier with the `grep` example: search the `/etc/passwd` file for the word `home`. Here the `sed` command searches the entire `/etc/passwd` file, searches for the word `home`, and prints any line containing the word `home`.

```
sed -n '/home/p' /etc/passwd
```

In this example, `sed` searches the file `somefile.txt` and replaces every instance of the string `Mac` with `Linux`. Notice that the letter `g` is needed at the end of the substitution command to cause every occurrence of Mac on each line to be changed to Linux. (Otherwise, only the first instance of Mac on each line is changed.) The output is then sent to the `fixed_file.txt` file.

```
sed 's/Mac/Linux/g' somefile.txt > fixed_file.txt
```

You can get the same result using a pipe:

```
cat somefile.txt | sed 's/Mac/Linux/g' > fixed_file.txt
```

By searching for a pattern and replacing it with a null pattern, you delete the original pattern. This example searches the contents of the `somefile.txt` file and replaces extra blank spaces at the end of each line (s/ *$) with nothing (//). Results go to the `fixed_file.txt` file.

```
cat somefile.txt | sed 's/ *$//' > fixed_file.txt
```

Trying some simple shell scripts

Sometimes the simplest of scripts can be the most useful. If you type the same sequence of commands repetitively, it makes sense to store those commands (once!) in a file. Here are a couple of simple, but useful, shell scripts.

A simple telephone list

This idea has been handed down from generation to generation of old UNIX hacks. It's really quite simple, but it employs several of the concepts just introduced.

```
#!/bin/bash
# (@)/ph
# A very simple telephone list
# Type "ph new name number" to add to the list, or
# just type "ph name" to get a phone number

PHONELIST=~/.phonelist.txt

# If no command line parameters ($#), there
# is a problem, so ask what they're talking about.
if [ $# -lt 1 ] ; then
   echo "Whose phone number did you want? "
   exit 1
fi

# Did you want to add a new phone number?
if [ $1 = "new" ] ; then
   shift
   echo $* >> $PHONELIST
   echo $* added to database
   exit 0
fi

# Nope. But does the file have anything in it yet?
# This might be our first time using it, after all.
if [ ! -s $PHONELIST ] ; then
   echo "No names in the phone list yet! "
   exit 1
else
   grep -i -q "$*" $PHONELIST    # Quietly search the file
   if [ $? -ne 0 ] ; then        # Did we find anything?
      echo "Sorry, that name was not found in the phone list"
      exit 1
   else
      grep -i "$*" $PHONELIST
   fi
fi
exit 0
```

So, if you created the file ph in your current directory, you could type the following from the shell to try out your ph script:

```
$ chmod 755 ph
$ ./ph new "Mary Jones" 608-555-1212
Mary Jones 608-555-1212 added to database
```

```
$ ./ph Mary
Mary Jones 608-555-1212
```

The chmod command makes the ph script executable. The ./ph command runs the ph command from the current directory with the new option. This adds Mary Jones as the name and 608-555-1212 as the phone number to the database ($HOME/.phone.txt). The next ph command searches the database for the name Mary and displays the phone entry for Mary. If the script works, add it to a directory in your PATH (such as $HOME/bin).

A simple backup script

Because nothing works forever and mistakes happen, backups are just a fact of life when dealing with computer data. This simple script backs up all the data in the home directories of all the users on your Fedora or RHEL system.

```
#!/bin/bash
# (@)/my_backup
# A very simple backup script
#

# Change the TAPE device to match your system.
# Check /var/log/messages to determine your tape device.
# You may also need to add scsi-tape support to your kernel.
TAPE=/dev/rft0

# Rewind the tape device $TAPE
mt $TAPE rew
# Get a list of home directories
HOMES=`grep /home /etc/passwd | cut -f6 -d': '`
# Backup the data in those directories
tar cvf $TAPE $HOMES
# Rewind and eject the tape.
mt $TAPE rewoffl
```

> **CROSS-REFERENCE:** See Chapter 13 for details on backing up and restoring files and getting the mt command (part of the ftape-tools packages that must be installed separately).

System Initialization

When you turn on your computer, a lot happens even before Fedora or RHEL starts up. Here are the basic steps that occur each time you boot up your computer to run Fedora or RHEL:

1. **Boot hardware** — Based on information in the computer's read-only memory (referred to as the BIOS), your computer checks and starts up the hardware. Some of that information tells the computer which devices (floppy disk, CD, hard disk, and so on) to check to find the bootable operating system.

2. **Start boot loader** — After checking that no bootable operating system is ready to boot in your floppy, CD, or DVD drive, typically, the BIOS checks the master boot record on the primary hard disk to see what to load next. With Fedora or RHEL installed, the GRUB boot loader is started, allowing you to choose to boot Fedora, RHEL, or another installed operating system.

3. **Boot the kernel** — Assuming that you selected to boot Fedora or RHEL, the Linux kernel is loaded. That kernel mounts the basic file systems and transfers control to the init process. The rest of this section describes what happens after the kernel hands off control of system startup to the init process.

Starting init

In the boot process, the transfer from the kernel phase (the loading of the kernel, probing for devices, and loading drivers) to `init` is indicated by the following lines:

```
Welcome to Fedora
Press "I" to enter interactive startup.
```

The init program, part of the sysvinit RPM package, is now in control. The output from `ps` always lists `init` (known as "the father of all processes") as PID (process identifier) 1. Its actions are directed by the `/etc/inittab` file, which is reproduced next.

The inittab file

The following example shows the contents of the `/etc/inittab` file as it is delivered with Fedora and RHEL:

```
#
# inittab      This file describes how the INIT process should set up
#              the system in a certain run level.
      .
      .
      .
id:5:initdefault:

# System initialization.
si::sysinit:/etc/rc.d/rc.sysinit

l0:0:wait:/etc/rc.d/rc 0
l1:1:wait:/etc/rc.d/rc 1
l2:2:wait:/etc/rc.d/rc 2
l3:3:wait:/etc/rc.d/rc 3
l4:4:wait:/etc/rc.d/rc 4
l5:5:wait:/etc/rc.d/rc 5
l6:6:wait:/etc/rc.d/rc 6

# Trap CTRL-ALT-DELETE
ca::ctrlaltdel:/sbin/shutdown -t3 -r now
```

```
# When our UPS tells us power has failed, assume we have a few minutes
# of power left. Schedule a shutdown for 2 minutes from now.
# This does, of course, assume you have powerd installed and your
# UPS connected and working correctly.
pf::powerfail:/sbin/shutdown -f -h +2 "Power Failure; System Shutting Down"

# If power was restored before the shutdown kicked in, cancel it.
pr:12345:powerokwait:/sbin/shutdown -c "Power Restored; Shutdown Cancelled"

# Run gettys in standard runlevels
1:2345:respawn:/sbin/mingetty tty1
2:2345:respawn:/sbin/mingetty tty2
3:2345:respawn:/sbin/mingetty tty3
4:2345:respawn:/sbin/mingetty tty4
5:2345:respawn:/sbin/mingetty tty5
6:2345:respawn:/sbin/mingetty tty6

# Run xdm in runlevel 5
x:5:once:/etc/X11/prefdm -nodaemon
```

The plain-text `inittab` file consists of several colon-separated fields in the format:

```
id:runlevels:action:command
```

The `id` field is a unique identifier, one to four alphanumeric characters in length, that represents a particular action to take during system startup. The `runlevels` field contains a list of run levels in which the command will be run. Common run levels are 0, 1, 2, 3, 4, 5, and 6 (s and S represent single-user mode, which is equivalent to 1). Run levels 7, 8, and 9 can also be used as the special run levels associated with the on-demand action (a, b, and c, which are equivalent to A, B, and C). The next field represents the type of action to be taken by `init` (valid actions and the results of those actions are listed in Table 12-3), and the last field is the actual command that is to be executed.

Table 12-3: Valid init Actions

Action	How the Command Is Run
once	The command is executed once when entering the specified run level.
wait	The same as once, but init waits for the command to finish before continuing with other inittab entries.
respawn	The process is monitored, and a new instance is started if the original process terminates.
powerfail	The command is executed on receiving a SIGPWR signal from software associated with a UPS unit. This assumes a few minutes of power are left so, by default, the system can shut down the system in two minutes.

Action	How the Command Is Run
powerwait	The same as `powerfail`, but `init` waits for the command to finish.
powerokwait	The command is executed on receiving a `SIGPWR` signal if the `/etc/powerstatus` file contains the word OK. This is generally accomplished by the UPS software and indicates that a normal power level has been restored.
powerfailnow	The local system may be able to detect that an external UPS is running out of power and is about to fail almost immediately.
ondemand	The command is executed when `init` is manually instructed to enter one of the special run levels a, b, or c (equivalent to A, B, and C, respectively). No change in run level actually takes place. The program is restarted if the original process terminates.
sysinit	The command is executed during the system boot phase; the `runlevels` field is ignored.
boot	The command is executed during the system boot phase, after all `sysinit` entries have been processed; the `runlevels` field is ignored.
bootwait	The same as `boot`, but `init` waits for the command to finish before continuing with other `inittab` entries; the `runlevels` field is also ignored.
initdefault	The run level to enter after completing the `boot` and `sysinit` actions.
off	Nothing happens (perhaps useful for testing and debugging).
ctrlaltdel	Traps the Ctrl+Alt+Del key sequence and is typically used to gracefully shut down the system.
kbrequest	Used to trap special key sequences, as interpreted by the keyboard handler.

Because the `inittab` file is a configuration file, not a sequential shell script, the order of lines is not significant. Lines beginning with a hash (#) character are comments and are not processed.

The first non-commented line in the preceding sample `inittab` file sets the default run level to 5. A default of 5 (which is the common run level for desktop systems) means that, following the completion of all commands associated with the `sysinit`, `boot`, and `bootwait` actions, run level 5 is entered (booting to a text-based login). The other common `initdefault` level is run level 3 (often used for servers that boot up in text mode and often have no GUI). Table 12-4 describes each of the run levels and helps you choose the run level that is best suited as the default in your environment.

Table 12-4: Possible Run Levels

Run Level	What Happens in This Run Level
0	All processes are terminated and the machine comes to an orderly halt. As the `inittab` comments point out, this is not a good choice for `initdefault` because as soon as the kernel, modules, and drivers are loaded, the machine halts.
1, s, S	This is single-user mode, frequently used for system maintenance and instances where it may be preferable to have few processes running and no services activated. In single-user mode, the network is nonexistent, the X server is not running, and it is possible that some file systems are not mounted.
2	Multiuser mode. Multiple user logins are allowed, all configured file systems are mounted, and all processes except X, the `at` daemon, the `xinetd` daemon, and NIS/NFS are started. If your machine doesn't have (or perhaps doesn't need) a permanent network connection, this is a good choice for `initdefault`.
3	Multiuser mode with network services. Run level 3 is the typical value for `initdefault` on a Fedora or RHEL server.
4	Run level 4 is available as a user-defined run level. It is nearly identical to runlevel 3 in a default Fedora or RHEL configuration.
5	Multiuser mode with network services and X. This run level starts the X server and presents a graphical login window, visually resembling any of the more expensive UNIX-based workstations. This is a common `initdefault` value for a Fedora or RHEL workstation or desktop system.
6	All processes are terminated and the machine is gracefully rebooted. Again, the comments in the `inittab` file mention that this is not a good choice for `initdefault`, perhaps even worse than run level 0. The effect is a possibly infinite cycle of booting, followed by rebooting.
7, 8, 9	Generally unused and undefined, these run levels have the potential to meet any needs not covered by the default options.
a, b, c, A, B, C	Used in conjunction with the `ondemand` action. These don't really specify a run level but can launch a program or daemon "on demand" if so instructed.

NOTE: If there is no `initdefault` specified in the `inittab` file, the boot sequence will be interrupted and you will be prompted to specify a default run level into which the machine will boot.

The next line in the `inittab` file instructs `init` to execute the `/etc/rc.d/rc.sysinit` script before entering the default run level. This script performs many initialization routines such as choosing a `keymap` file, checking and mounting `root` and `proc` file systems, setting the clock and hostname, configuring swap space, cleaning up `temp` files, and loading modules.

The seven following lines control the commands executed within each major run level. In each, the `/etc/rc.d/rc` script is called, using the desired run level as an argument. In turn, it descends into the appropriate directory tree (for example, the `/etc/rc3.d` directory is entered for run level 3).

The `ctrlaltdel` action in the `inittab` file tells `init` to perform exactly what PC users would expect if the Ctrl, Alt, and Delete keys were pressed simultaneously. The system reboots itself in an orderly fashion (a switch to run level 6) after a three-second delay.

The next two lines (with their comments) deal with graceful shutdowns if you have an uninterruptible power supply (UPS) and software installed. The first line initiates a halt (a switch to run level 0) two minutes after receiving a signal from the UPS indicating a power failure. The second line cancels the shutdown in the event that power is restored.

The six `getty` lines start up virtual consoles to allow logins. These processes are always running in any of the multiuser run levels. When someone connected to a virtual console logs out, that `getty` process dies, and then `respawn` action tells `init` to start a new `getty` process. You can switch between virtual consoles by pressing Ctrl+Alt+F1, Ctrl+Alt+F2, and so on.

The last line indicates that as long as the system is in run level 5, the "preferred display manager" (xdm, gnome, KDE, and so on) will be running. This presents a graphical login prompt rather than the usual text-based login, and eliminates the need to run `startx` to start the GUI.

System Startup and Shutdown

During system startup, a series of scripts are run to start the services that you need. These include scripts to start network interfaces, mount directories, and monitor your system. Most of these scripts are run from subdirectories of `/etc/rc.d`. The program that starts most of these services up when you boot and stops them when you shut down is the `/etc/rc.d/rc` script. The following sections describe run-level scripts and what you can do with them.

Starting run-level scripts

As previously mentioned, the `/etc/rc.d/rc` script is integral to the concept of run levels. Any change of run level causes the script to be executed, with the new run level as an argument. Here's a quick run-down of what the `/etc/rc.d/rc` script does:

- **Checks that run-level scripts are correct** — The `rc` script checks to find each run-level script that exists and excludes those that represent backup scripts left by `rpm` updates.

- **Determines current and previous run levels** — Determines the current and previous run levels to know which run-level scripts to stop (previous level) and start (current level).

- **Decides whether to enter interactive startup** — If the `confirm` option is passed to the boot loader at boot time, all server processes must be confirmed at the system console before starting.

- **Kills and starts run-level scripts** — Stops run-level scripts from the previous level, then starts run-level scripts from the current level.

In Fedora and RHEL, most of the services that are provided to users and computers on the network are started from run-level scripts.

Understanding run-level scripts

A software package that has a service to start at boot time (or when the system changes run levels) can add a script to the `/etc/init.d` directory. That script can then be linked to an appropriate run-level directory and run with either the `start` or `stop` option (to start or stop the service).

Table 12-5 lists many of the typical run-level scripts that are found in `/etc/init.d` and explains their function. Depending on the Fedora or RHEL software packages you installed on your system, you may have dozens more run-level scripts than you see here. (Later, I describe how these files are linked into particular run-level directories.)

Each script representing a service that you want to start or stop is linked to a file in each of the run-level directories. For each run level, a script beginning with K stops the service, whereas a script beginning with S starts the service.

The two digits following the K or S in the filename provide a mechanism to select the priority in which the programs are run. For example, `S12syslog` is run before `S90crond`. However, the file `S110my_daemon` is run before `S85gpm`, even though you can readily see that 85 is less than 110. This is because the ASCII collating sequence orders the files, which simply means that one positional character is compared to another. Therefore, a script beginning with the characters `S110` is executed between `S10network` and `S15netfs` in run level 3.

All of the programs within the `/etc/rcX.d` directories (where *X* is replaced by a run-level number) are symbolic links, usually to a file in `/etc/init.d`. The `/etc/rcX.d` directories include the following:

- `/etc/rc0.d`: Run level 0 directory
- `/etc/rc1.d`: Run level 1 directory
- `/etc/rc2.d`: Run level 2 directory
- `/etc/rc3.d`: Run level 3 directory
- `/etc/rc4.d`: Run level 4 directory
- `/etc/rc5.d`: Run level 5 directory
- `/etc/rc6.d`: Run level 6 directory

In this manner, `/etc/rc0.d/K05atd`, `/etc/rc1.d/K05atd`, `/etc/rc2.d/K05atd`, `/etc/rc3.d/S95atd`, `/etc/rc4.d/S95atd`, `/etc/rc5.d/S95atd`, and `/etc/rc6.d/K05atd` are all symbolic links to `/etc/init.d/atd`. Using this simple, consistent mechanism, you can customize which programs are started at boot time.

Table 12-5: Run-Level Scripts Contained in /etc/init.d

Run-Level Scripts	What Does It Do?
acpid	Controls the Advanced Configuration and Power Interface daemon, which monitors events in the kernel and reports them to user level.
anacron	Runs cron jobs that were not run at their intended times due to the system being down.
apmd	Controls the Advanced Power Management daemon, which monitors battery status, and which can safely suspend or shut down all or part of a machine that supports it.
atd	Starts or stops the at daemon to receive, queue, and run jobs submitted via the at or batch commands. (The anacron run-level script runs at and batch jobs that were not run because the computer was down.)
autofs	Starts and stops the automount daemon, for automatically mounting file systems (so, for example, a CD can be automatically mounted when it is inserted).
bluetooth	Starts services such as authentication, discovery, and human interface devices for communicating with Bluetooth devices.
ConsoleKit	Maintains a list of user sessions.
crond	Starts or stops the cron daemon to periodically run routine commands.
cups	Controls the printer daemon (cupsd) that handles spooling printing requests.
dhcpd	Starts or stops the dhcpd daemon, which automatically assigns IP addresses to computers on a LAN.
dovecot	Starts the dovecot IMAP server, which allows e-mail clients to request and view their mail messages from the mail server.
firstboot	Checks to see if firstboot needs to be run and, if so, runs it. This is typically done after Fedora or RHEL is first installed.
gpm	Controls the gpm daemon, which allows the mouse to interact with console- and text-based applications.
haldaemon	Starts hald daemon to discover and set up hardware. Used to mount removable media, manage power, or auto-play multimedia.

Run-Level Scripts	What Does It Do?
halt	Terminates all processes, writes out accounting records, removes swap space, unmounts all file systems, and either shuts down or reboots the machine (depending on how the command was called).
hplip	Starts the HP Linux Imaging and Printing (HPLIP) service for running HP multi-function peripherals.
httpd	Starts the httpd daemon, which allows your computer to act as an HTTP server (that is, to serve Web pages).
iptables	Starts the iptables firewall daemon, which manages any iptables-style firewall rules set up for your computer.
keytable	Loads the predefined keyboard map.
killall	Shuts down any subsystems that may still be running prior to a shutdown or reboot.
kudzu	Detects and configures new hardware at boot time.
ldap	Starts the Lightweight Directory Access Protocol daemon (sldap), which listens for LDAP requests from the network.
mysqld	Runs the MySQL database daemon (mysqld) to listen for request to MySQL databases.
named	Starts and stops the BIND DNS server daemon (named) to listen for and resolve domain name system requests.
netfs	Mounts or unmounts network (NFS, SMB, and NCP) file systems.
network	Starts or stops all configured network interfaces and initializes the TCP/IP and IPX protocols.
NetworkManager	Switches automatically to the best available network connections.
nfs	Starts or stops the NFS-related daemons (rpc.nfsd, rpc.mountd, rpc.statd, and rcp.rquotad) and exports shared file systems.
ntpd	Runs the Network Time Protocol daemon (ntpd), which synchronizes system time with Internet standard time servers.
portmap	Starts or stops the portmap daemon, which manages programs and protocols that utilize the Remote Procedure Call (RPC) mechanism.
routed	Starts or stops the routed daemon, which controls dynamic-routing table updates via the Router Information Protocol (RIP).
rwhod	Starts or stops the rwhod daemon, which enables others on the network to obtain a list of all currently logged-in users.
sendmail	Controls the sendmail daemon, which handles incoming and outgoing SMTP (Simple Mail Transport Protocol) mail messages.
single	Terminates running processes and enters run level 1 (single-user mode).

Run-Level Scripts	What Does It Do?
smb	Starts or stops the smbd and nmbd daemons for allowing access to Samba file and print services.
snmpd	Starts or stops the snmpd (Simple Network Management Protocol) daemon, which enables others to view machine-configuration information.
spamassassin	Starts and stops the spamd daemon to automate the process of checking e-mail messages for spam.
squid	Starts or stops the squid services, which enables proxy service to clients on your network.
sshd	Runs the secure shell daemon (sshd), which listens for requests from ssh clients for remote login or remote execution requests.
syslog	Starts or stops the klogd and syslogd daemons that handle logging events from the kernel and other processes, respectively.
vsftpd	Runs the Very Secure FTP server (vsftpd) to provide FTP sessions to remote clients for downloading and uploading files.
xfs	Starts or stops xfs, the X Window font server daemon.
xinetd	Sets the machine's hostname, establishes network routes, and controls xinetd, the network services daemon that listens for incoming TCP/IP connections to the machine.
yum	Enables you to run automatic nightly updates of your software using the yum facility.
xfs	Regenerates font lists and starts and stops the X font server.

Understanding what startup scripts do

Despite all the complicated rc*X*s, Ss, and Ks, the form of each startup script is really quite simple. Because they are in plain text, you can just open one with a text editor to take a look at what it does. For the most part, a run-level script can be run with a start option, a stop option, and possibly a restart option. For example, the following lines are part of the contents of the smb script that defines what happens when the script is run with different options to start or stop the Samba file and print service:

```
#!/bin/sh
#
# chkconfig: - 91 35
# description: Starts and stops the Samba smbd daemon \
#              used to provide SMB network services.
        .
        .
        .
start() {
```

```
        KIND="SMB"
        echo -n $"Starting $KIND services: "
        daemon smbd $SMBDOPTIONS
        RETVAL=$?
        echo

        [ $RETVAL -eq 0 -a $RETVAL2 -eq 0 ] && touch /var/lock/subsys/smb || \
            RETVAL=1
        return $RETVAL
}

stop() {
        KIND="SMB"
        echo -n $"Shutting down $KIND services: "
        killproc smbd
        RETVAL=$?
        echo
        [ $RETVAL -eq 0 -a $RETVAL2 -eq 0 ] && rm -f /var/lock/subsys/smb
        return $RETVAL
}

restart() {
        stop
        start
}
```

To illustrate the essence of what this script does, I skipped some of the beginning and end of the script (where it checked if the network was up and running and set some values). Here are the actions smb takes when it is run with start or stop:

- **start** — This part of the script starts the smbd server when the script is run with the start option.
- **stop** — When run with the stop option, the /etc/init.d/smb script stops the smbd server.

The restart option runs the script with a stop option followed by a start option. If you want to start the smb service yourself, type the following command (as root user):

```
# service smb start
Starting SMB services:                    [ OK ]
```

To stop the service, type the following command:

```
# service smb stop
Shutting down SMB services:               [ OK ]
```

The `smb` run-level script is different from other run-level scripts in that it supports several other options than `start` and `stop`. For example, this script has options (not shown in the example) that allow you to reload the `smb.conf` configuration file (`reload`) and check the status of the service (`status`).

Changing run-level script behavior

Modifying the startup behavior of any such script merely involves opening the file in a text editor.

For example, the `atd` daemon queues jobs submitted from the `at` and `batch` commands. Jobs submitted via `batch` are executed only if the system load is not above a particular value, which can be set with a command-line option to the `atd` command.

The default *limiting load factor* value of 0.8 is based on the assumption that a single-processor machine with less than 80 percent CPU utilization could handle the additional load of the batch job. However, if you were to add another CPU to your machine, 0.8 would only represent 40 percent of the computer's processing power. So you could safely raise that limit without impacting overall system performance.

You can change the limiting load factor from 0.8 to 1.6 to accommodate the increased processing capacity. To do this, simply modify the following line (in the `start` section) of the `/etc/init.d/atd` script:

```
daemon /usr/sbin/atd
```

Replace it with this line, using the `-l` argument to specify the new minimum system load value:

```
daemon /usr/sbin/atd -l 1.6
```

After saving the file and exiting the editor, you can reboot the machine or just run any of the following three commands to begin using the new batch threshold value:

```
# service atd reload
# service atd restart
# service atd stop ; service atd start
```

> **NOTE:** Always make a copy of a run-level script before you change it. Also, keep track of changes you make to run-level scripts before you upgrade the packages they come from. You need to make those changes again after the upgrade.

If you are uncomfortable editing startup scripts and you simply want to add options to the daemon process run by the script, there may be a way of entering these changes without editing the startup script directly. Check the `/etc/sysconfig` directory and see if there is a file by the same name as the script you want to modify. If there is, that file probably provides values that you can set to pass options to the startup script. Sysconfig files exist for `apmd`, `arpwatch`, `dhcpd`, `kudzu`, `ntpd`, `samba`, `squid`, and others.

Reorganizing or removing run-level scripts

There are several ways to deal with removing programs from the system startup directories, adding them to particular run levels, or changing when they are executed. From a Terminal window, you can use the `chkconfig` command. From a GUI, use the Service Configuration window.

> **CAUTION:** You should never remove the run-level file from the `/etc/init.d` directory. Because no scripts are run from the `/etc/init.d` directory automatically, it is okay to keep them there. Scripts in `/etc/init.d` are only accessed as links from the `/etc/rcX.d` directories. Keep scripts in the `init.d` directory so you can add them later by re-linking them to the appropriate run-level directory.

To reorganize or remove run-level scripts from the GUI, use the Service Configuration window. Either select System → Administration → Services or log in as root user and type the following command in a Terminal window:

```
# system-config-services &
```

Figure 12-1 shows an example of the Service Configuration window.

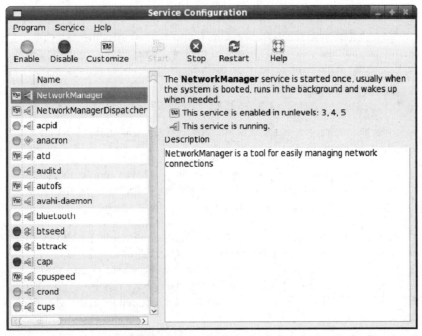

Figure 12-1: Reorganize, add, and remove run-level scripts from the Service Configuration window.

The Service Configuration window enables you to reconfigure services for run levels 2, 3, 4, and 5. Icons next to each service indicate whether the service is currently enabled (green) or disabled (red) for the current run level and whether or not the service is currently running. Select a service to see a description of that service. Here is what you can do from this window:

- **Enable** — With a service selected, click the Enable button to enable the service to start when you start your computer (run levels 2, 3, 4, and 5).

- **Disable** — With a service selected, click Disable to not have the service not start when you boot your computer (or otherwise enter run levels 2, 3, 4, or 5).

- **Customize** — With a service selected, click Customize and select the run levels at which you want the service to start.

- **Start** — Click a service on the list. Select Start to request the service to immediately start.

Some administrators prefer text-based commands for managing run-level scripts and for managing other system services that start automatically. The chkconfig command can be used to list whether services that run-level scripts start, as well as services the xinetd daemon starts, are on or off. To see a list of all system services, with indications that they are on or off, type the following:

```
# chkconfig --list | less
```

You can then page through the list to see those services. If you want to view the status of an individual service, you can add the service at the end of the list option. For example, to see whether the nfs service starts in each run level, type the following:

```
# chkconfig --list nfs
nfs        0:off   1:off   2:off   3:on   4:on   5:on   6:off
```

This example shows that the nfs service is set to be on for run levels 3, 4, and 5, but that it is set to off for run levels 0, 1, 2, and 6.

Another tool that can be run from the shell to change which services start and do not start at various levels is the ntsysv command. Type the following as root user from the shell:

```
# ntsysv
```

A screen appears with a list of available services. Use the up and down arrow keys to locate the service you want. With the cursor on a service, press the Spacebar to toggle the service on or off. Press the Tab key to highlight the OK button, and press the Spacebar to save the change and exit. The ntsysv tool only changes services for the current run level. You can run ntsysv with the --level # option, where # is replaced by the run level for which you want to change services.

Adding run-level scripts

Suppose you want to create and configure your own run-level script. For example, after installing the binaries for the fictitious my_daemon program, it needs to be configured to start up in run levels 3, 4, and 5, and terminated in any other run level. You can add the script to the /etc/init.d directory, then use the chkconfig command to configure it.

To use chkconfig, ensure that the following lines are included in the /etc/init.d/my_daemon script:

```
# chkconfig: 345 82 28
# description: Does something pretty cool - you really \
#    have to see it to believe it!
# processname: my_daemon
```

> **NOTE**: The line chkconfig: 345 82 28 sets the script to start in run levels 3, 4, and 5. It sets start scripts to be set to 82 for those run levels. It sets stop scripts to be set to 28 in all other levels.

With those lines in place, simply run the following command:

```
# chkconfig --add my_daemon
```

Appropriate links are created automatically. This can be verified with the following command:

```
# chkconfig --list my_daemon
```

The resulting output should look like this:

```
my_daemon 0:off 1:off 2:off 3:on 4:on 5:on 6:off
```

The script names that are created by chkconfig to make this all work are:

```
/etc/rc0.d/K28my_daemon
/etc/rc1.d/K28my_daemon
/etc/rc2.d/K28my_daemon
/etc/rc3.d/S82my_daemon
/etc/rc4.d/S82my_daemon
/etc/rc5.d/S82my_daemon
/etc/rc6.d/K28my_daemon
```

Managing xinetd services

There are a bunch of services, particularly network services, which are not handled by separate run-level scripts. Instead, a single run-level script called xinetd (formerly inetd) is run to handle incoming requests for these services. For that reason, xinetd is sometimes referred to as the *super-server*. The xinetd run-level script (along with the xinetd daemon that it runs) offers the following advantages:

- **Fewer daemon processes** — Instead of one (or more) daemon processes running on your computer to monitor incoming requests for each service, the xinetd daemon can listen for requests for many different services. As a result, when you type ps -ax to see what processes are running, dozens of fewer daemon processes will be running than there would be if each service had its own daemon.

- **Access control and logging** — By using xinetd to oversee the management of services, consistent methods of access control (such as PAM) and consistent logging methods (such as the /var/log/messages file) can be used across all of the services.

When a request comes into your computer for a service that xinetd is monitoring, xinetd uses the /etc/xinetd.conf file to read configuration files contained in the /etc/xinetd.d directory. Then, based on the contents of the xinetd.d file for the requested service, a server program is launched to handle the service request (provided that the service is not disabled).

Each server process is one of two types: single-thread or multithread. A single-thread server handles only the current request, whereas a multithread server handles all incoming requests for the service as long as there is still a client holding the process open. Then the multithread server closes and xinetd begins monitoring that service again.

The following are a few examples of services that are monitored by xinetd. The daemon process that is started up to handle each service is also listed.

- **eklogin** (/usr/kerberos/sbin/klogind) — Kerberos-related login daemon
- **finger** (/usr/sbin/in.fingerd) — Handles incoming finger requests for information from remote users about local users
- **gssftp** (/usr/kerberos/sbin/ftpd) — Kerberos-related daemon for handling file transfer requests (FTP)
- **ntalk** (/usr/sbin/in.ntalkd) — Daemon for handling requests to set up chats between a remote user and a local one (using the talk command)
- **rlogin** (/usr/sbin/in.rlogind) — Daemon for responding to remote login requests (from a remote rlogin command)
- **rsh** (/usr/sbin/in.rshd) — Handles requests from a remote client to run a command on the local computer

Other services that can be launched by requests that come to xinetd include services for remote telnet requests, Samba configuration requests (swat), and Amanda network backups. A short description of each service is included in its /etc/xinetd.d file. Many of the services handled by xinetd are legacy services, including rlogin, rsh, and finger, that are considered insecure by today's security standards because they use clear-text passwords.

Manipulating run levels

Aside from the run level chosen at boot time (usually 3 or 5) and the shutdown or reboot levels (0 and 6, respectively), you can change the run level at any time while you're logged in (as root user). The telinit command (really just a symbolic link to init) enables you to specify a desired run level, causing the termination of all system processes that shouldn't exist in that run level, and starting all processes that should be running.

> **NOTE:** The `telinit` command is also used to instruct `init` to reload its configuration file, `/etc/inittab`. This is accomplished with either the `telinit` q or the `telinit` Q commands.

For example, if you encountered a problem with your hard disk on startup, you may be placed in single-user mode (run level 1) to perform system maintenance. After the machine is stable, you can execute the command as follows:

```
# telinit 5
```

The `init` command handles terminating and starting all processes necessary to present you with a graphical login window.

Determining the current run level

You can determine the machine's current run level with the aptly named `runlevel` command. Using the previous example of booting into single-user mode and then manually changing the run level, the output of the `runlevel` command would be:

```
# runlevel
S 5
```

This means that the previous run level was S (for single-user mode) and the current run level is 5. If the machine had booted properly, the previous run level would be listed as N to indicate that there really wasn't a previous run level.

Changing to a shutdown run level

Shutting down the machine is simply a change in run level. With that in mind, other ways to change the run level include the `reboot`, `halt`, `poweroff`, and `shutdown` commands. The `reboot` command, which is a symbolic link to the `halt` command, executes a `shutdown -r now`, terminating all processes and rebooting the machine. The `halt` command executes `shutdown -h now`, terminating all processes and leaving the machine in an idle state (but still powered on).

Similarly, the `poweroff` command, which is also a link to the `halt` command, executes a change to run level 0, but if the machine's BIOS supports Advanced Power Management (APM), it will switch off the power to the machine.

> **NOTE:** A time must be given to the `shutdown` command, either specified as +m (representing the number of minutes to delay before beginning shutdown) or as hh:mm (an absolute time value, where hh is the hour and mm is the minute that you would like the shutdown to begin). Alternatively, now is commonly used to initiate the shutdown immediately.

Scheduling System Tasks

Frequently, you need to run a process unattended or at off-hours. The at facility is designed to run such jobs at specific times. Jobs you submit are spooled in the directory /var/spool/at, awaiting execution by the at daemon atd. The jobs are executed using the current directory and environment that was active when the job was submitted. Any output or error messages that haven't been redirected elsewhere are e-mailed to the user who submitted the job.

The following sections describe how to use the at, batch, and cron facilities to schedule tasks to run at specific times. These descriptions also include ways of viewing which tasks are scheduled and deleting scheduled tasks that you don't want to run anymore.

Using at.allow and at.deny

There are two access control files designed to limit which users can use the at facility. The file /etc/at.allow contains a list of users who are granted access, and the file /etc/at.deny contains a similar list of those who may not submit at jobs. If neither file exists, only the superuser is granted access to at. If a blank /etc/at.deny file exists (as in the default configuration), all users are allowed to utilize the at facility to run their own at jobs. If you use either at.allow or at.deny, you aren't required to use both.

Specifying when jobs are run

There are many different ways to specify the time at which an at job should run (most of which look like spoken commands). Table 12-6 has a few examples. These are not complete commands — they only provide an example of how to specify the time that a job should run.

Table 12-6: Samples for Specifying Times in an at Job

Command Line	When the Command Is Run
at now	The job is run immediately.
at now + 2 minutes	The job will start two minutes from the current time.
at now + 1 hour	The job will start one hour from the current time.
at now + 5 days	The job will start five days from the current time.
at now + 4 weeks	The job will start four weeks from the current time.
at now next minute	The job will start in exactly 60 seconds.
at now next hour	The job will start in exactly 60 minutes.
at now next day	The job will start at the same time tomorrow.
at now next month	The job will start on the same day and at the same time next month.
at now next year	The job will start on the same date and at the same time next year.

Command Line	When the Command Is Run
`at now next fri`	The job will start at the same time next Friday.
`at teatime`	The job will run at 4 p.m. They keywords noon and midnight can also be used.
`at 16:00 today`	The job will run at 4 p.m. today.
`at 16:00 tomorrow`	The job will run at 4 p.m. tomorrow.
`at 2:45pm`	The job will run at 2:45 p.m. on the current day.
`at 14:45`	The job will run at 2:45 p.m. on the current day.
`at 5:00 Apr 14 2008`	The job will begin at 5 a.m. on April14, 2008.
`at 5:00 4/14/08`	The job will begin at 5 a.m. on April 14, 2008.

Submitting scheduled jobs

The `at` facility offers a lot of flexibility in how you can submit scheduled jobs. There are three ways to submit a job to the `at` facility:

- **Piped in from standard input** — For example, the following command will attempt to build the Perl distribution from source in the early morning hours while the machine is likely to be less busy:

```
echo "cd /tmp/perl; make ; ls -al" | at 2am tomorrow
```

An ancillary benefit to this procedure is that a full log of the compilation process will be e-mailed to the user who submitted the job.

- **Read as standard input** — If no command is specified, `at` will prompt you to enter commands at the special `at>` prompt, as shown in the following example. You must indicate the end of the commands by pressing Ctrl+D, which signals an End of Transmission (<EOT>) to `at`.

```
$ at 23:40
at> cd /tmp/perl
at> make
at> ls -al
at> <Ctrl-d>
```

- **Read from a file** — When the `-f` command-line option is followed by a valid filename, the contents of that file are used as the commands to be executed, as in the following example:

```
$ at -f /root/bin/runme now + 5 hours
```

This runs the commands stored in `/root/bin/runme` in five hours. The file can either be a simple list of commands or a shell script to be run in its own subshell (that is, the file begins with `#!/bin/bash` or the name of another shell).

Viewing scheduled jobs

You can use the `atq` command (effectively the same as `at -1`) to view a list of your pending jobs in the `at` queue, showing each job's sequence number, the date and time the job is scheduled to run, and the queue in which the job is being run.

The two most common queue names are `a` (which represents the `at` queue) and `b` (which represents the `batch` queue). All other letters (upper- and lowercase) can be used to specify queues with lower priority levels. If the `atq` command lists a queue name as `=`, it indicates that the job is currently running. Here is an example of output from the `atq` command:

```
# atq
2       2008-09-02 00:51 a
3       2008-09-02 00:52 a
4       2008-09-05 23:52 a
```

Here you can see that there are three `at` jobs pending (job numbers 2, 3, and 4, all indicated as a). After the job number, the output shows the date and hour each job is scheduled to run.

Deleting scheduled jobs

If you decide that you'd like to cancel a particular job, you can use the `atrm` command (equivalent to `at -d`) with the job number (or more than one) as reported by the `atq` command. For example, using the following output from `atq`:

```
# atq
18      2008-09-01 03:00 a
19      2008-09-29 05:27 a
20      2008-09-30 05:27 a
21      2008-09-14 00:01 a
22      2008-09-01 03:00 a
```

you can remove the jobs scheduled to run at 5:27 a.m. on September 29 and September 30 from the queue with the following command:

```
# atrm 19 20
```

Using the batch command

If system resources are at a premium on your machine, or if the job you submit can run at a priority lower than normal, the `batch` command (equivalent to `at -q b`) may be useful. It is controlled by the same `atd` daemon, and it allows job submissions in the same format as `at` submissions (although the time specification is optional).

However, to prevent your job from usurping already scarce processing time, the job will run only if the system load average is below a particular value. The default value is 0.8, but specifying a command-line option to `atd` can modify this. This was used as an example in the earlier section describing startup and shutdown. Here is an example of the `batch` command:

```
$ batch
at> du -h /home > /tmp/duhome
at> <Ctrl+d>
```

In this example, after I type the `batch` command, the `at` facility is invoked to enable me to enter the command(s) I want to run. Typing the `du -h /home > /tmp/duhome` command line has the disk usages for everything in the `/home` directory structure output to the `/tmp/duhome` file. On the next line, pressing Ctrl+D ends the batch job. As soon as the load average is low enough, the command is run. (Run the `top` command to view the current load average.)

Using the cron facility

Another way to run commands unattended is via the `cron` facility. Part of the vixie-cron rpm package, `cron` addresses the need to run commands periodically or routinely (at least, more often than you'd care to manually enter them) and allows lots of flexibility in automating the execution of the command.

As with the `at` facility, any output or error messages that haven't been redirected elsewhere are e-mailed to the user who submitted the job. Unlike using `at`, however, cron jobs are intended to run more than once and at a regular interval (even if that interval is only once per month or once per year).

Also like the `at` facility, `cron` includes two access control files designed to limit which users can use it. The file `/etc/cron.allow` contains a list of users who are granted access, and the file `/etc/cron.deny` contains a similar list of those who may not submit `cron` jobs. If neither file exists (or if `cron.deny` is empty), all users are granted access to `cron`.

There are four places where a job can be submitted for execution by the `cron` daemon `crond`:

- **The `/var/spool/cron/`*`username`* file** — This method, where each individual user (indicated by *username*) controls his or her own separate file, is the method used on UNIX System V systems.
- **The `/etc/crontab` file** — This is referred to as the *system crontab file*, and was the original crontab file from BSD UNIX and its derivatives. Only root has permission to modify this file.
- **The `/etc/cron.d` directory** — Files placed in this directory have the same format as the `/etc/crontab` file. Only root is permitted to create or modify files in this directory.

- **The `/etc/cron.hourly`, `/etc/cron.daily`, `/etc/cron.weekly`, and `/etc/cron.monthly` directories** — Each file in these directories is a shell script that runs at the times specified in the `/etc/crontab` file (by default, at one minute after the hour every hour; at 4:02 a.m. every day; Sunday at 4:22 a.m.; and 4:42 a.m. on the first day of the month, respectively). Only root is allowed to create or modify files in these directories.

The standard format of an entry in the `/var/spool/cron/username` file consists of five fields specifying when the command should run: minute, hour, day of the month, month, and day of the week. The sixth field is the actual command to be run.

The files in the `/etc/cron.d` directory and the `/etc/crontab` file use the same first five fields to determine when the command should run. However, the sixth field represents the name of the user submitting the job (because it cannot be inferred by the name of the file as in a `/var/spool/cron/username` directory), and the seventh field is the command to be run. Table 12-7 lists the valid values for each field common to both types of files.

Table 12-7: Valid /etc/crontab Field Values

Field Number	Field	Acceptable Values
1	minute	Any integer between 0 and 59
2	hour	Any integer between 0 and 23
3	day of the month	Any integer between 0 and 31
4	month	Any integer between 0 and 12, or an abbreviation for the name of the month (Jan, Feb, Mar, Apr, May, Jun, Jul, Aug, Sep, Oct, Nov, Dec)
5	day of the week	Any integer between 0 and 7 (where both 0 and 7 can represent Sunday, 1 is Monday, 2 is Tuesday, and so on), or abbreviation for the day (Sun, Mon, Tue, Wed, Thu, Fri, Sat)

The latest version of cron (vixie-cron and crontabs packages) includes the ability to indicate that a cron job be run at boot time. Refer to the crontab man page (type **man 5 crontab**) for information on using the reboot option to have a command run once at startup time.

An asterisk (*) in any field indicates all possible values for that field. For example, an asterisk in the second column is equivalent to 0,1,2 . . . 22,23, and an asterisk in the fourth column means Jan,Feb,Mar . . . Nov,Dec. In addition, lists of values, ranges of values, and increments can be used. For example, to specify the days Monday, Wednesday, and Friday, the fifth field could be represented as the list Mon,Wed,Fri. To represent the normal working hours in a day, the range 9–17 could be specified in the second field. Another option is to use an increment, as in specifying 0–31/3 in the third field to represent every third day of the month, or */5 in the first field to denote every five minutes.

Lines beginning with a # character in any of the crontab-format files are comments, which can be very helpful in explaining what task each command is designed to perform. It is also possible to specify environment variables (in Bourne shell syntax, for example, NAME="value") within the crontab file. Any variable can be specified to fine-tune the environment in which the job runs, but one that may be particularly useful is MAILTO. The following line sends the results of the cron job to a user other than the one who submitted the job:

```
MAILTO=otheruser
```

If the following line appears in a crontab file, all output and error messages that haven't already been redirected will be discarded:

```
MAILTO=
```

Modifying scheduled tasks with crontab

The files in /var/spool/cron should not be edited directly. They should only be accessed via the crontab command. To list the current contents of your own personal crontab file, type the following command:

```
$ crontab -l
```

All crontab entries can be removed with the following command:

```
$ crontab -r
```

Even if your personal crontab file doesn't exist, you can use the following command to begin editing it:

```
$ crontab -e
```

The file automatically opens in the text editor that is defined in your EDITOR or VISUAL environment variables, with vi as the default. When you're done, simply exit the editor. Provided there were no syntax errors, your crontab file will be installed. For example, if your user name is jsmith, you have just created the file /var/spool/cron/jsmith. If you add a line (with a descriptive comment, of course) to remove any old core files from your source code directories, that file may look similar to this:

```
# Find and remove core files from /home/jsmith/src
5 1 * * Sun,Wed find /home/jsmith/src -name core.[0-9]* -exec rm {} \; > /dev/null 2>&1
```

Because core files in Fedora and RHEL consist of the word core, followed by a dot (.) and process ID, this example will match all files beginning with core. and followed by a number. The root user can access any user's individual crontab file by using the -u username option to the crontab command.

Understanding cron files

Separate `cron` directories are set up to contain `cron` jobs that run hourly, daily, weekly, and monthly. These `cron` jobs are all set up to run from the `/etc/crontab` file. The default `/etc/crontab` file looks like this:

```
SHELL=/bin/bash
PATH=/sbin:/bin:/usr/sbin:/usr/bin
MAILTO=root
HOME=/

# run-parts
01 * * * * root run-parts /etc/cron.hourly
02 4 * * * root run-parts /etc/cron.daily
22 4 * * 0 root run-parts /etc/cron.weekly
42 4 1 * * root run-parts /etc/cron.monthly
```

The first four lines initialize the run-time environment for all subsequent jobs (the subshell in which jobs run, the executable program search path, the recipient of output and error messages, and that user's home directory). The next five lines execute (as the user root) the `run-parts` program that controls programs that you may want to run periodically.

`run-parts` is a shell script that takes a directory as a command-line argument. It then sequentially runs every program within that directory (shell scripts are most common, but binary executables and links are also evaluated). The default configuration executes programs in `/etc/cron.hourly` at one minute after every hour of every day; `/etc/cron.daily` at 4:02 a.m. every day; `/etc/cron.weekly` at 4:22 a.m. on Sundays; and `/etc/cron.monthly` at 4:42 a.m. on the first day of each month.

Here are examples of files that are installed in `cron` directories for different software packages:

- **`/etc/cron.daily/logrotate.cron`** — Automates rotating, compressing, and manipulating system logfiles.

- **`/etc/cron.daily/makewhatis.cron`** — Updates the `whatis` database (contains descriptions of man pages), which is used by the `man -k`, `apropos`, and `whatis` commands to find man pages related to a particular word.

- **`/etc/cron.daily/slocate.cron`** — Updates the `/var/lib/slocate/slocate.db` database (using the `updatedb` command), which contains a searchable list of files on the machine.

- **`/etc/cron.daily/tmpwatch`** — Removes files from `/tmp`, `/var/tmp`, and `/var/catman` that haven't been accessed in ten days.

The `makewhatis.cron` script installed in `/etc/cron.weekly` is similar to the one in `/etc/cron.daily`, but it completely rebuilds the `whatis` database, rather than just updating the existing database.

Finally, in the `/etc/cron.d` directory are files that have the same format as `/etc/crontab` files.

> **NOTE:** If you are not comfortable working with `cron` from the command line, there is a KCron Task Scheduler window that comes in the kdeadmin package for managing cron tasks. To launch KCron, type **kcron** from a Terminal window.

Summary

Shell scripts are an integral part of a Fedora or RHEL system for configuring, booting, administering, and customizing Fedora or RHEL. They are used to eliminate typing repetitive commands. They are frequently executed from the scheduling facilities within Fedora or RHEL, allowing much flexibility in determining when and how often a process should run. They also control the startup of most daemons and server processes at boot time.

The `init` daemon and its configuration file, `/etc/inittab`, also factor heavily in the initial startup of your Fedora or RHEL system. They implement the concept of run levels that is carried out by the shell scripts in `/etc/rc.d/init.d`, and they provide a means by which the machine can be shut down or rebooted in an orderly manner.

To have shell scripts configured to run on an ongoing basis, you can use the `cron` facility. Cron jobs can be added by editing `cron` files directly or by running commands such as `at` and `batch` to enter the commands to be run.

Chapter 13

Backing Up and Restoring Files

In This Chapter

- Doing a simple backup
- Selecting a backup strategy
- Selecting a backup medium
- Backing up to a hard drive
- Backing up files with dump
- Automating backup with cron
- Restoring backed-up files
- Backing up over the network with Amanda
- Performing network backups with multiple computers
- Using the pax archiving utility

If you've ever suffered a hard drive crash, you know just how aggravating it can be. You can lose irreplaceable data. You likely spend countless hours reinstalling your operating system and applications. It is not a fun experience. It need happen only once for you to learn the importance of making regular backups of your critical data.

Today, larger and faster backup media can simplify the process of backing up your data. Fedora and RHEL support many different types of media — such as writable CD (CD-R and CD-RW), DVD (DVD-R, DVD+R, DVD+RW, and DVD-RW), and magnetic tape — for creating backups. Using tools such as cron, you can configure backups to run unattended at scheduled times.

This chapter describes how to create a backup strategy and how to select media for backing up data on your Fedora or RHEL system. It tells you how to do automated backups and backups over a network. It also describes how to restore individual files, or entire file systems, using tools such as the restore command.

Making a Simple Backup Archive

Improvements in the GNOME desktop for handling removable media (CDs, DVDs, USB flash drives and so on) can help you to do a quick backup of your personal data. With the GNOME desktop running on your Fedora system, use the following procedure to back up all the data in your home directory:

1. Insert a blank CD or DVD into your computer's drive. An icon appears on the desktop, indicating that a blank disc is ready to be used.

2. Double-click the Blank Disc icon to see the CD/DVD Creator window.

3. Open the folder icon representing your home directory (such as Joe's Home) on the desktop and browse to the /home folder.

4. Drag-and-drop your home directory from the /home folder on to the CD/DVD Creator window.

5. Add other files and folders you want to back up to the CD/DVD Creator window in the same way.

6. When all the files and folders you want to back up are copied to the CD/DVD Creator window, click Write to Disc and the Write to Disc pop-up window appears.

7. Type a disc name for the backup medium and optionally choose the write speed. (The disc name will be used as the name of the mount point if you later open the CD/DVD on the GNOME desktop). Figure 13-1 shows the Write to Disc pop-up and the CD/DVD Creator window (with the home folder of the user joe dragged into that folder).

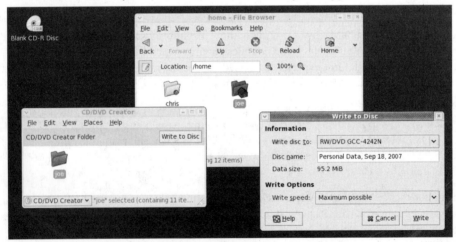

Figure 13-1: Drag-and-drop files and folders on the CD/DVD Creator window for a simple backup. Click Write to have the files and folders written to the disc.

This procedure results in a standard ISO9660 image (with Rock Ridge extensions) being burned to the CD or DVD. That disc can be read from Linux, Windows, or other systems that support that ISO standard. While the procedure is a quick way to save your critical files, you should consider using other backup tools described in this chapter for more flexible and powerful backup methods.

Doing a Simple Backup with rsync

Cheap hard disk space, fast networks, and some really neat new tools have given Linux users some nice backup alternatives to the old reliable removable media (such as tapes and CDs). To back up your personal data or the data from a small office computer, the examples in this section provide fairly simple ways of creating usable backups of your data.

To do this procedure, you need to have hard disk space on a computer that is at least slightly larger than the hard disk you are backing up. That hard disk space could be on:

- **A different partition** — By backing up to a separate disk partition, you are protected in case the partition you are backing up becomes corrupted. However, you are not protected if your hard disk goes bad.

- **A different hard disk** — Backing up to a separate hard disk can protect from a corrupted disk, but won't help you if your computer is hit by lightning, a flood, or other acts of God.

- **A different computer** — By backing up over the network, you can back up to another computer that is as far away from the source of your data as makes you feel comfortable. You can back up to the computer down the hall or one across the country.

To do the actual backup, you use the `rsync` command. The `rsync` command is like a remote copy command (similar to `rcp`) on steroids. In essence, `rsync` lets you copy files from one location to another. However, it also has some nice extra features that enable you to do the following:

- **Transfer differences only** — If you transfer a file that was transferred during an earlier backup, `rsync` uses a checksum-search algorithm to determine the differences between the old file and the new one. Then it sends only the data needed to account for the differences between the two files.

- **Transfer data securely** — `rsync` combines with `ssh` (or another remote shell) to encrypt the data, so it can travel securely across a network.

- **Maintain ownership** — The transferred files can keep their same permissions, ownership, timestamps, and group designations. (Because ownership is based on numeric UID and GID, matching user and group accounts must be set up between machines for the files to appear to be owned by the same users and groups after the files are copied.)

The following sections show examples of the `rsync` command at work.

Backing up files locally

The first example shows a simple backup of a user's personal files. Here I'm copying the `/home/chris` directory (including all its files and subdirectories) to another directory on the local computer. That directory (`/mnt/backup/homes`) could be on a separate partition (see Chapter 2 for creating separate partitions), hard disk (see Chapter 10 to add a hard disk), or a remote NFS file system (see Chapter 18 to mount an NFS file system):

```
# rsync -av /home/chris /mnt/backup/homes/
```

> **NOTE:** Notice that there's no trailing slash after `/home/chris` (so it's not `/home/chris/`). Without that trailing slash, rsync will copy files from that directory to a target directory named `chris` (`/mnt/backup/homes/chris`). With a trailing slash, all files from `/home/chris/` are copied directly to the `homes` directory (`/mnt/backup/homes/`).

In this example, the entire contents of the `/home/chris` directory structure are added to the `/mnt/backup/homes/chris` directory. All files, subdirectories, links, devices, and other file types are copied. By using the archive option (`-a`), all ownership, permissions, and creation times are maintained on the copied files. Using the `-a` option saves you from having to enter the following options individually: `-r` (recursive), `-l` (copy symbolic links), `-p` (preserve permissions), `-t` (preserve times), `-g` (preserve group), `-o` (preserve owner) and `-D` (preserve devices and special files). The verbose option (`-v`) results in more messages being displayed as rsync progresses.

If `/mnt/backup/homes` is on a separate disk, you now have your entire `/home/chris` directory copied in two places on the same machine. If the `/mnt/backup/homes` directory is an NFS shared directory (with write permission on), the files are now backed up to another machine.

Because the example is a backup of my personal files that don't change too often, after a few days of changes to the files, I might want to run the exact same command again:

```
# rsync -av /home/chris /mnt/backup/homes/
```

This time any new files are copied to the target directory and the changes to any files I modified are applied to the original backup files. Any files I deleted from my home directory will still be in the target directory (`rsync` doesn't remove deleted files unless you specifically tell it to). The result is, again, a complete copy of the `/home/chris` directory at the moment the `rsync` command is run, plus any files that have been deleted from any `/home/chris` directories.

> **NOTE:** If you want files that were deleted from the sending directory to be likewise deleted from the target directory, you can add the `--delete` option to `rsync`.

Backing up files remotely

While the previous example was a quick, informal backup method, with more critical data, you want to make sure that the data are being backed up to another computer and that the backup is done at regular intervals. This can be accomplished by using `rsync` in concert with `ssh` and `cron`.

Having `ssh` as the transport mechanism ensures that data will be encrypted when it is transferred. Also, because the SSH service (`sshd`) is enabled by default on many Fedora and Red Hat Enterprise Linux systems, you need only a user name and password to the remote system to do the backup. (As long as you can use `ssh` to connect to the remote machine, port number 873 is open in your firewall, and `rsync` is installed remotely, you can use the `rsync` command to transfer files there.) Here's an example:

```
# rsync -azv -e ssh /home/chris duck:/mnt/backup/homes/
root@duck's password: *******
building file list ... done
```

In this example, I identify the remote computer (named duck in this case) by putting it before the remote directory name, separated with a colon. I use some different options as well. To the archive (`-a`) and verbose (`-v`) options, I add the `-z` option to compress the data (making it more efficient to transfer). I also use the `-e ssh` option to have `rsync` use an `ssh` remote shell to transfer data. The password prompt you see is the `ssh` login prompt. The `-a` option is important if you want to be able to restore files exactly as they were copied, because it recursively copies a whole directory structure as it preserves ownership, date/time stamps, and permissions.

You can repeat this command each time you want to back up your files. However, the more efficient way to do this is to set up this command to run as a cron job so that the backups happen automatically at set intervals.

To have `rsync` run automatically, you can't have it prompt you for a password. To have the `rsync` command run without prompting for a password, follow this procedure:

1. Set up SSH to do no-password logins for the user who is going to perform the backup (see the section "Using ssh, scp, and sftp without passwords" in Chapter 14 for information on how to do this).

2. Decide how often you want the backup to run. For example, if you want to run the `rsync` command once each day, as root user you could create a file called `/etc/cron.daily/mybackup`.

3. Set permissions to be executable:

```
# chmod 755 /etc/cron.daily/mybackup
```

4. Add the command line to the `mybackup` file that you want to use:

```
rsync -azv -e ssh /home/chris chris@duck:/mnt/backup/homes/
```

Notice that I added the user name chris as the login user name on the remote computer (duck). For you, this will be the name of the person for which you set up a no-password login in Step 1.

At this point, a backup will be done once each day to the machine specified.

> **NOTE:** With the simple backup command just shown, you can build on more complex features. In particular, you might want to think about building in a snapshot feature. Snapshots allow you to go back to a particular date and time to restore a backed-up file. Mike Rubel has an excellent procedure for doing `rsync` snapshots at `www.mikerubel.org/computers/rsync_snapshots` entitled "Easy Automated Snapshot-Style Backups with Linux and Rsync."
>
> Another useful feature is the `--bwlimit=` option, which can prevent `rsync` commands from consuming too much of the available network bandwidth. For example, `--bwlimit=100` would limit the maximum transfer rate to 100 kilobytes per second.

Choosing Backup Tools

While the `rsync` command is one of the best choices for doing backups, it is by no means the only tool available. Many Linux systems administrators use a variety of commands for doing backups, often writing scripts to combine commands to work together. They might group together files in a single archive using `tar` or `cpio`, compress files to backup using `bzip2` or `gzip`, or write whole directory structures of files using `mkisofs`.

Descriptions of backup tools in this chapter focus on those that are particularly designed for backups. The `dump` and `restore` commands are traditional UNIX commands for backing up and restoring files. The `mkisofs` and `cdrecord` commands can combine to gather a file system into an ISO image and copy that image to CD or DVD. As for networked backup features, the Amanda facility is described later in this chapter. The pax facility provides a means of creating cpio and tar archives.

If the tools for backing up files described in this chapter are not exactly what you are looking for, there are many open source backup facilities that you can add to your Fedora or RHEL system. Here are a few examples:

- **Bacula** (`www.bacula.org`) — Bacula is a tool for managing network backups. It includes features to make it easy to recover files that have been lost or damaged. Support for backup media includes tape, CD, and hard disk media.

- **Mondo Rescue** (`www.mondorescue.org`) — Mondo supports backups from LVM, RAID, ext2, ext3, JFS, XFS, ReiserFS, and VFAT file systems. Backups can be done to CD-R, CD-RW, NFS, or hard disk.

- **BackupPC** (`http://backuppc.sourceforge.net`) — BackupPC is useful for backing up both Linux and Windows systems over a network. Using BackupPC, you can extract backups using Samba, `tar` (over `ssh`, `rsh`, or `nfs`) or `rsync`.

Selecting a Backup Strategy

While it is tempting to do the quick-and-easy backup, backing up important data requires more planning and forethought. There are several approaches you can take to backing up your data. You need to ask yourself a few questions to decide which approach is best for you. Some things that you should consider are:

- In the event of a crash, how much downtime can I tolerate?
- Will I need to recover older versions of my files or is the most recent revision sufficient?
- Do I need to back up files for just one computer or for many computers on a network?

Your answers to these questions will help you decide how often to do full backups and how often to do incremental backups. If the data is particularly critical, you may even decide that you need to have your data duplicated constantly, using a technique called *disk mirroring*. The following sections describe different backup methods.

Full backup

A full backup is one that stores every file on a particular disk or partition. If that disk should ever crash, you can rebuild your system by restoring the entire backup to a new disk. Whatever backup strategy you decide on, some sort of full backup should be part of it. You may perform full backups every night or perhaps only once every week; it depends on how often you add or modify files on your system, as well as the capacity of your backup equipment.

Incremental backup

An incremental backup is one that contains only those files that have been added or modified since the last time a more complete backup was performed. You may choose to do incremental backups to conserve your backup media.

Incremental backups also take less time to complete, because they only back up data that has changed since the most recent backup (full or incremental). Incremental and other partial backup types can be important when systems are in high use during the workweek and running a full backup would degrade system performance. Full backups can be reserved for the weekend when the system is not in use.

Disk mirroring

Full and incremental backups can take time to restore, and sometimes you just can't afford that downtime. By duplicating your operating system and data on an additional hard drive, you can greatly increase the speed with which you can recover from a server crash.

With disk mirroring, it is usually common for the system to continuously update the duplicate drive with the most current information. In fact, with a type of mirroring called RAID1 (described in Chapter 10), the duplicate drive is written to at the same time as the original, and if the main drive fails, the duplicate can immediately take over. This is called *fault-tolerant* behavior, which is a must if you are running a mission-critical server of some kind.

You can tailor different RAID levels to use features other than mirroring. Other RAID levels use striping and can be tuned for performance, data redundancy, and cost. Software RAID is supported in the Linux kernel and several hardware vendors have RAID controller cards for SATA, IDE, and SCSI disk configurations that work well in Linux. Vendors include LSI Logic (www.lsilogic.com), Promise (www.promise.com), and 3Ware (www.3ware.com). See http://tldp.org/HOWTO/Software-RAID-HOWTO.html for further information on RAID in Linux.

Network backup

All of the preceding backup strategies can be performed over a network. This is good because you can share a single backup device with many computers on a network. This is much cheaper and more convenient than installing a tape drive or other backup device in every system on your network. If you have many computers, however, your backup device will require a lot of capacity. In such a case, you might want to consider a mechanical tape loader, DVD-RW drive, or CD or DVD jukebox (which is capable of recording multiple CDs or DVDs without operator intervention).

It is even possible to do a form of disk mirroring over the network. For example, a Web server may store a duplicate copy of its data on another server. If the first server crashes, a simple TCP/IP hostname change can redirect the Web traffic to the second server. When the original server is rebuilt, it can recover all of its data from the backup server and be back in business.

Selecting a Backup Medium

Armed with a backup strategy in mind, it's time to select a backup medium. Several types of backup hardware and media are available for use with Fedora and RHEL. Each type has its advantages and disadvantages.

The type of medium to choose depends largely on the amount of data you need to archive, how long you will store backups, how often you expect to recover data from your backups, and how much you can afford to spend. Table 13-1 compares the most common backup media.

The following sections describe how to use magnetic tape, writable DVDs, and writable CDs as backup media. Using additional hard drives as backup media is described later in this chapter.

Table 13-1: Comparison of Common Backup Media

Backup Medium	Advantages	Disadvantages
Magnetic tape	High capacity, low cost for archiving massive amounts of data.	Sequential access medium, so recovery of individual files can be slow.
Writable CDs	Random access medium, so recovery of individual files is easier. Backups can be restored from any CD-ROM drive.	Limited storage space (up to 700MB per CD).
Writable DVDs	Random access medium (such as CDs). Large capacity (4.7GB, although the actual capacity you can achieve might be less). DVDR-9 and DVD-9 DVDs can store up to 8.5GB of data.	DVD-RW drives and DVD-R disks are relatively expensive (although they are coming down in price). As more manufacturers add DVD writers to their PCs, DVD will eventually replace CDs as the most common removable media drives.
Additional hard drive	Allows faster and more frequent backups. Fast recovery from crashes. No media to load. Data can be located and recovered more quickly. You can configure the second disk to be a virtual clone of the first disk, so that you can boot off of the second disk if the first disk crashes.	Data cannot be stored offsite; thus there is a risk of data loss if the entire server is destroyed. This method is not well suited to keeping historical archives of the many revisions of your files. The hard drive will eventually fill up. By using removable hard drives, you can overcome this limitation by removing the backup drive when it is full and moving it to a secure location.

Magnetic tape

Magnetic tape was for years the most common medium used for backing up large amounts of computer data. Tapes provide a low-cost, convenient way to archive your files. Today's high-capacity tape drives can back up many gigabytes of data on an amazingly small tape, allowing vast amounts of information to be safely stored. Tapes are also easy to transport offsite so that data will be secure in case of fires, hurricanes, or other disasters.

The primary disadvantage of magnetic tape is that it is a sequential access medium. This means that tapes are read or written from beginning to end, and searching for a particular file can be time-consuming. For this reason, tape is a good choice for backing up and restoring entire file systems, but not the ideal choice to recover individual files on a regular basis.

Fedora and RHEL can use a wide variety of tape drives. Most SCSI tape drives will work without loading special modules. Even many IDE tape drives are now supported natively, without requiring the drive to operate in a "SCSI emulation" mode. Some drives, however, require installation of additional software.

Using ftape tools for magnetic tape

If your tape drive is attached to an IDE floppy controller cable, you will need to use the ftape driver to access it. Fortunately, the ftape loadable module is bundled with the Linux 2.6 kernel. When your Linux system boots, it should autodetect the tape drive and load the ftape driver. To verify that your system loaded the tape driver, type the following command shortly after you boot your computer:

```
dmesg | grep ftape
```

This searches the most recent kernel messages for lines containing the word ftape. If the ftape module was loaded, you should see something like this:

```
ftape v4.04d 25/11/97
[000] ftape-init.c (ftape_init) - installing QIC-117 floppy tape
hardware drive... .
[001] ftape-init.c (ftape_init) - ftape_init @ 0xd08b0060.
[002] ftape-buffer.c (add_one_buffer) - buffer nr #1 @ c1503914, dma
area @ c02c0000.
[003] ftape-buffer.c (add_one_buffer) - buffer nr #2 @ c1503c44, dma
area @ c0298000.
[004] ftape-buffer.c (add_one_buffer) - buffer nr #3 @ c50abaac, dma
area @ c0328000.
[005] ftape-calibr.c (time_inb) - inb() duration: 1109 nsec.
[006] ftape-calibr.c (ftape_calibrate) - TC for `ftape_udelay()' = 310
nsec (at 20479 counts).
[007] ftape-calibr.c (ftape_calibrate) - TC for `fdc_wait()' = 2208 nsec
(at 2559 counts).
```

If the module was not loaded, then you should check whether your kernel is compiled with support for the ftape module and your particular tape drive. It should be available and ready to include as a loadable module.

In most cases, an ftape device can be accessed just like a SCSI device. The primary difference is that an ftape device file contains the letters qft (for QIK Floppy Tape) where a SCSI tape contains st. For example, the device file for the first SCSI tape on your system will probably be /dev/st0; the device file for the first floppy tape will likely be /dev/qft0.

All of the standard tape- and archiving-related programs should work fine with both types of hardware. Nevertheless, there are a few extra programs that you might find useful when working with a floppy tape drive. These programs can be found in the mt-st package in Fedora. The mt command is used to control magnetic tape operation. The stinit command can initialize SCSI magnetic tape drives.

Testing the magnetic tape drive

With the mt-st package installed, you should now be ready to test your tape drive. Insert a blank tape into the tape drive and type the following commands:

```
$ mt -f /dev/qft0 status
$ mt -f /dev/qft0 rewind
```

The first command will present a status of the tape drive. After the second command, you should hear the tape spin as the system rewinds the tape. This will be a very short process if the tape is already rewound. The mt command provided with mt-st package is used to scan, rewind, and eject magnetic tapes in a tape drive.

Writable CD drives

Another backup medium that is gaining popularity is the writable CD drive. Writable CD drives have several advantages over tape, the primary one being that CDs are a random access medium. This means that the CD drive can quickly locate a particular file on the CD without sequentially scanning through the entire disc. This is useful when you need to keep a revision history of frequently changing data files (such as source code for a software project or drafts of legal documents).

Although people used to believe that CDs had a very long life span, that belief has recently come into question. CDs are probably still a good choice if the backup will be needed for two years or less. For longer time periods, a tape backup will generally last longer than a writable CD. If your backups are intended for short-term storage, you should probably consider a rewritable or CD-RW CD drive. A rewritable CD (unlike plain writable CDs) can be reformatted and used to store new backups.

The biggest drawback is that a CD can store, at most, about 700MB of data. In contrast, DVDs can store 4.7GB of data (or about 8.5GB for dual-layer CDs) and many tape drives can store multiple gigabytes of data. For example, DAT DDS-3 tapes can hold up to 24GB of compressed data, while 8mm AIT-2 tapes can hold up to 100GB of compressed data.

Getting cdrecord for writable CDs

To write CDs with Fedora or RHEL you can use the cdrecord package, which is installed by default with Fedora and RHEL. This package contains components such as the cdrecord, devdump, isodump, isoinfo, isovfy, and readcd commands.

Writing to CDs

Because the data written to a CD-R or CD+R disc becomes permanent once it is written, you need to format the CD and copy files to it all in one step. If you formatted it first, you would end up with an empty file system on a CD that can no longer be written to.

> **NOTE:** Using a command called growisofs (described later in this chapter), you can write to a CD in such a way that the session is not closed. Later, you can add more data, in multiple sessions, before you finally close the CD. The cdrecord command itself also now supports a -multi option, which can keep the session open for further writing. Not all CD drives will support multi-session writing (which reqires that the hardware support CD-ROM XA mode 2 form 1).

The first step is to create an image of the CD file system as a file on your computer. You do this with the mkisofs command. The second step is to burn the image to CD or DVD using a tool such as the cdrecord command.

> **NOTE:** In recent releases of Fedora, the cdrecord command has been replaced by a command called wodim from the CDR Kit project (http://cdrkit.org). Fedora and other Linux distributions switched to the CDR Kit project because cdrecord licensing was changed to the Sun CDDL license, which is believed to be incompatible with the GPL. Because wodim is backward compatible with cdrecord and that command is linked to cdrecord, you can still use the cdrecord command as you always have.

As an example, imagine that you want to back up the home directory for user mary. You would invoke the mkisofs command and pass it the name of the file system image file to create, followed by the directory to base it on:

```
$ mkisofs -R -o /var/tmp/mary.iso /home/mary
```

This creates an ISO9660 file system image in a file named mary.iso located in the /var/tmp directory. The -R option causes Linux-specific file ownership and long filenames to be used. If your /var partition does not have enough room for the image, choose a different location.

> **TIP:** By default, mkisofs preserves the ownership and access rights of files and directories when it creates the file system image. This is appropriate when you are making a backup, but not when you are creating a software distribution CD. In such a case, add the -r option instead of -R as the first parameter to mkisofs. It will then store all files as publicly readable and, where appropriate, executable.

If you have an ATAPI CD drive, you no longer need a SCSI ID for that drive to be able to record to it. You could enter the device name instead of the SCSI ID (such as dev=/dev/cdrom). However, if you have a SCSI CD drive, before you can write the image file to a CD, you must first discover the SCSI bus number, device ID number, and Logical Unit Number (LUN) of the CD drive. You can find out which SCSI device ID the CD drive is using. Invoke the cdrecord command with the single parameter -scanbus:

```
# cdrecord -scanbus
```

You should see a response similar to the following:

```
scsibus0:
        0,0,0     0) 'IDE-CD ' 'R/RW 4x4x24  ' '1.04' Removable CD-ROM
        0,0,1     1) *
        0,0,2     2) *
        0,0,3     3) *
        0,0,4     4) *
        0,0,5     5) *
        0,0,6     6) *
        0,0,7     7) *
```

This tells you that the CD drive is using SCSI ID zero. The Logical Unit Number in this case should always be zero, so you now have all three numbers. You supply them to `cdrecord` as part of the `dev` parameter.

The SCSI bus number is listed first; it is followed by the ID number, and then by the LUN. The entire command should look similar to this:

```
# cdrecord -v speed=2 dev=0,0,0 -data /var/tmp/mary.iso
```

For an ATAPI CD drive, with the CD drive as `/dev/cdrom`, your command line might appear as follows instead:

```
# cdrecord -v speed=2 dev=/dev/cdrom -data /var/tmp/mary.iso
```

Several additional parameters are included in the command. The `-v` parameter tells `cdrecord` to supply verbose output to the screen. The `speed` parameter tells `cdrecord` what speed to record at (in this case X2). (You might choose to leave off `speed=2` and let `cdrecord` autodetect the record speed of your CD burner.) The `-data` parameter tells `cdrecord` to burn WAV or AU files as data, instead of audio tracks. (Without that option, those file types are burned as audio tracks while all other files are burned as data.)

Before running `cdrecord` live, you might consider adding the `-dummy` option, which runs through the CD burn process without actually turning on the laser. You can add the `-eject` parameter to eject the CD when it is done. As it works, `cdrecord` should display status messages that look similar to the following:

```
cdrecord: No write mode specified.
cdrecord: Asuming -tao mode.
cdrecord: Future versions of cdrecord may have drive dependent defaults.
cdrecord: Continuing in 5 seconds...
Cdrecord-Clone 2.01-dvd (i686-pc-linux-gnu) Copyright (C) 1995-2004 Jörg
Schilling
TOC Type: 1 = CD-ROM
scsidev: '/dev/cdrom'
devname: '/dev/cdrom'
scsibus: -2 target: -2 lun: -2
Warning: Open by 'devname' is unintentional and not supported.
Linux sg driver version: 3.5.27
Using libscg version 'schily-0.8'.
SCSI buffer size: 64512
atapi: 1
Device type    : Removable CD-ROM
Version        : 0
Response Format: 1
Vendor_info    : 'IDE-CD  '
Identifikation : 'R/RW 4x4x24      '
Revision       : '1.04'
Device seems to be: Generic mmc CD-RW.
Using generic SCSI-3/mmc   CD-R/CD-RW driver (mmc_cdr).
```

```
Driver flags    : MMC SWABAUDIO
Supported modes: TAO PACKET RAW/R16
Drive buf size : 1572864 = 1536 KB
FIFO size       : 4194304 = 4096 KB
Track 01: data      0 MB
Total size:         0 MB (00:04.02) = 302 sectors
Lout start:         1 MB (00:06/02) = 302 sectors
Current Secsize: 2048
ATIP info from disk:
  Indicated writing power: 5
  Is not unrestricted
  Is not erasable
  Disk sub type: Medium Type B, low Beta category (B-) (4)
  ATIP start of lead in:  -12369 (97:17/06)
  ATIP start of lead out: 359849 (79:59/74)
Disk type:    Short strategy type (Phthalocyanine or similar)
Manuf. index: 69
Manufacturer: Moser Baer India Limited
Manufacturer is guessed because of the orange forum embargo.
The orange forum likes to get money for recent information.
The information for this media may not be correct.
Blocks total: 359849 Blocks current: 359849 Blocks remaining: 359547
Starting to write CD/DVD at speed 4 in real TAO mode for single session.
Last chance to quit, starting real write     0 seconds. Operation starts.
Waiting for reader process to fill input buffer ... input buffer ready.
trackno=0
Performing OPC...
Starting new track at sector: 0
Track 01:  322 of  322 MB written (fifo 100%)  [buf  99%]   2.0x.
Track 01: Total bytes read/written: 338395136/338395136 (165232
sectors).
Writing  time: 1110.710s
Average write speed   2.0x.
Fixating...
Fixating time:  126.108s
cdrecord: fifo had 5331 puts and 5331 gets.
cdrecord: fifo was 0 times empty and 5262 times full, min fill was 96%.
```

After cdrecord finishes writing the CD and your shell prompt returns, delete the file system image file /var/tmp/mary.iso. Label the CD appropriately and store it in a safe place.

If you need any files that were copied to the CD, just return the CD to the CD drive. If it doesn't automatically open a window displaying the contents of the CD, type **mount /media/cdrecorder**. Open /media/cdrecorder in a folder window and copy the files you want.

Note that the mount point name for the CD drive may be something other than /media/cdrecorder. The way that the udev facility works in the latest version of Fedora is to use generic names such as cdrecorder, disk, or cdrom for CDs or DVDs that include no volume id. However, if a volume ID was added to the CD header when the CD was created, that name will be used as the mount point. For example, a game CD with a volume ID of GAMEDISK would be mounted as /media/GAMEDISK.

> **CROSS-REFERENCE:** See Chapter 8 for more information on cdrecord. You can also learn more about installing and troubleshooting writable CD drives from the CD-Writing-HOWTO. If you are using a desktop Fedora or RHEL system, you might want to use a graphical CD writer instead. Chapter 8 also describes the K3B graphical tool for copying and burning CDs and DVDs.

Writable DVD drives

In previous versions of Fedora and RHEL, the dvdrecord command was used to write DVDs. Now, cdrecord can be used to write both CDs and DVDs. Using a writable DVD drive and the cdrecord command, you can back up your data to DVD-R, DVD-RW, DVD+R, and DVD+RW disks.

The first trick with recording to DVDs in Linux is to make sure that you have a drive that supports DVD writing. You can check by removing any disks in the CD/DVD drive and typing the following:

```
$ cdrecord -prcap -dev=/dev/cdrom | less
Cdrecord-Clone 2.01-dvd (i686-pc-linux-gnu)
    .
    .
    .
Device type    : Removable CD-ROM
Version        : 0
Response Format: 2
Capabilities   :
Vendor_info    : 'PIONEER '
Identifikation : 'DVD-RW   DVR-105 '
Revision       : '1.30'
Device seems to be: Generic mmc2 DVD-R/DVD-RW.

Drive capabilities, per MMC-3 page 2A:

  Does read CD-R media
  Does write CD-R media
  Does read CD-RW media
  Does write CD-RW media
  Does read DVD-ROM media
  Does read DVD-R media
  Does write DVD-R media
  Does not read DVD-RAM media
  Does not write DVD-RAM media
  Does support test writing
    .
    .
```

In the preceding output, you can see that this drive supports reading and writing of both CDs and DVDs. Use the Spacebar to page through the output (and q to quit). Near the end of the output, you should see read and write speeds supported by the drive. Note that those are maximum *possible* speeds, so the actual maximum write speeds will depend on the CD or DVD media you are using.

The procedure for writing to DVDs is almost identical to backing up data onto a CD disk, with the following exceptions:

- Each backup disk can hold a lot more data (4.7GB for single-layer and 8.5GB for dual-layer DVD, as compared to 700MB for CDs).

- Both the DVD writer and medium are more expensive than the CD counterparts, although the cost of DVD writers has come down drastically in the past few years.

> **NOTE:** When manufacturers say 4.7GB, they are talking about 1000MB per GB, not 1024MB. Therefore, you can really only store up to about 4.3GB of data on a DVD (or, more precicely, 4,294,967,296 bytes).

There are also a few other issues you should be aware of that relate to using DVD media to record from Linux:

- While most new writable DVD drives today support both DVD-R and DVD+R formats, some older drives may not support DVD+R.

- DVD+RW media that have not been formatted must be formatted before you can write to it. However, you can use cdrecord on an unformatted DVD+RW because it will automatically detect and format an unformatted disk. To force a format, you can use the -format option to cdrecord. There is also a dvd+rw-format that you can use to format a DVD drive (just run dvd+rw-format with your DVD device as the option).

- You don't need to reformat DVD-RW media more than once. Multiple reformats can make the DVD-RW media unusable.

Follow the procedure in the "Writable CD drives" section to create a file system image file (using mkisofs) and determine the location of your DVD-R driver. Then use the cdrecord command to actually burn the DVD. Here is an example of a cdrecord command line that burns a file system image called bigimage.iso:

```
# cdrecord -v speed=2 dev=/dev/cdrom -data bigimage.iso
```

Writing CD or DVDs with growisofs

Instead of doing separate mkisofs and cdrecord commands, as just shown, you can use the growisofs command to combine the function of those two commands. The growisofs command is particularly useful for mastering of large ISO images (such as those for double-layer DVD recording). That's because instead of copying the ISO image you create to a file (as mkisofs does), growisofs sends the ISO image directly to the CD or DVD to be burned.

The growisofs command is also nice for backups because it has simple options for doing multisession DVDs. For example, if you want to back up your /home/chris directory today, then back up your /var/www directory later, you start the first backup as follows:

```
$ growisofs -Z /dev/cdrom -R -J /home/chris
```

The -Z indicates that this is an initial session being written to the CD or DVD. The device of the CD/DVD drive is /dev/cdrom. The -R and -J options allow longer Linux filenames on ISO9660 images (so the disk can be read by other operating systems, yet still retain Linux extensions). The last option (in this case, /home/chris) is whatever directories or files you want to copy to DVD.

When you are ready to write more to the CD or DVD, use the -M options instead, to indicate that you are adding on to an existing CD or DVD. Here is an example:

```
$ growisofs -M /dev/cdrom -R -J /var/www
```

Here, the -M indicates to add a new session to the existing session on the CD or DVD. The content of the /var/www directory (and its subdirectories) is written to the media. You can mount the media between sessions. Just be sure to unmount it before you try to write to it again (using the umount command).

Backing Up to a Hard Drive

As noted in the simple backup procedure in the beginning of this chapter, removable media such as tapes, DVDs, and CDs are not the only choice for backing up your data. You may find it useful to install a second hard drive in your system and use that drive for backups. This has several advantages over other backup media:

- Data can be backed up quickly and throughout the day; thus, backed-up data will be more current in the event of a crash.

- There's no medium to load. Data can be located and recovered more quickly.

- You can configure the second disk to be a virtual clone of the first one. If the first disk crashes, you can simply boot off of the second disk rather than installing new hardware. With disk mirroring software, this process can even be automated. The downside to this approach is that a mirrored drive that is online all the time is more prone to error than would be the case when copying files to removable media, and then removing the media to a safe location.

- With new, cost-effective removable hard drives (including those connected via USB and FireWire), you have the convenience of removable media with what was once usually thought of as non-removable media.

There are some disadvantages to backing up to a hard drive. For example, the hard drive backup method is not well suited to keeping historical archives of the many revisions of your

There are some disadvantages to backing up to a hard drive. For example, the hard drive backup method is not well suited to keeping historical archives of the many revisions of your files because the hard drive will eventually fill up. This problem can be reduced substantially, however, by using `rsync` snapshots, which store changes that are applied to modified files.

The simplest form of second-hard-drive backup is to simply copy important files to the other drive using the `cp` or `tar` command. The most sophisticated method is to provide fault-tolerant disk mirroring using RAID software.

A method in-between RAID and a simple `cp` command is to add an `rsync` command to a cron file so that backups are done automatically as often as you please. For example, you can add a script that does your rsync backup to `/etc/cron.hourly`, `/etc/cron.daily`, `/etc/cron.weekly`, or `/etc/cron.monthly`, to have your backup run automatically each hour, day, week or month, respectively. Keep in mind that you would have to catch any problems within the set time frame (an hour, a day, and so on) before the bad data overwrites the backup. (I describe how to use the cron facility to do backups with `dump` later in this chapter.)

Backing Up Files with dump

The `dump` command was historically one of the most commonly used tools for performing backups on UNIX systems. This command traces its history back to the early days of UNIX and thus is a standard part of nearly every version of UNIX. Likewise, the dump package is included in Fedora and Red Hat Enterprise Linux. If it was not installed by default when you first set up your Linux system, you can install it from the `dump` RPM file located on the Fedora installation DVD.

> **NOTE:** The `dump` and `restore` commands, while widely used for many years, are not considered to be particularly reliable or robust backup and restore tools these days. Also, they can be used only on ext2 and ext3 file system types and it is safest to use `dump` and `restore` on unmounted file systems. Descriptions of those tools are included here to support those with legacy backup media and automated scripts that still use those commands.

The dump package actually consists of several commands. You can read online man pages for more information about them. Table 13-2 provides a short description of the programs.

Table 13-2: Programs in the dump Package

Command	Description
dump	Creates backup archives of whole disk partitions or selected directories.
restore	Can be used to restore an entire archive or individual files from an

Command	Description
	archive to the hard drive.
rmt	A program used by the dump and restore commands to copy files across the network. You should never need to use this command directly.

Creating a backup with dump

When making a file system backup using the dump command, you must supply parameters specifying the dump level, the backup media, and the file system to back up. You can also supply optional parameters to specify the size of the backup media, the method for requesting the next tape, and the recording of file system dump times and status.

The first parameter to dump is always a list of single-letter option codes. This is followed by a space-separated list of any arguments needed by those options. The arguments appear in the same order as the options that require them. The final parameter is always the file system or directory being backed up.

```
# dump options arguments filesystem
```

Table 13-3 lists the various one-letter option codes for the dump command.

Table 13-3: Options to dump

Dump Options	Description
0-9	The dump level. Selecting a dump level of 0 backs up all files (a full dump). A higher number backs up only those files modified since the last dump of an equal or lower number (in essence, an incremental dump). The default dump level is 9.
-B records	The number of dump records per volume. Basically, the amount of data you can fit on a tape. This option takes a numeric argument.
-b kbperdump	The number of kilobytes per dump record. Useful in combination with the -B option. This option takes a numeric argument.
-h level	Files can be marked with a nodump attribute. This option specifies the dump level at or above which the nodump attribute is honored. This option takes a numeric argument of 1-9.
-f file	The name of the file or device to write the dump to. This can even be a file or device on a remote machine.
-d density	Sets the tape density. The default is 1600 bits per inch. This option takes a numeric argument.
-n	When a dump needs attention (such as to change a tape), dump will send a message to all of the users in the operator group. This option takes no arguments.

Dump Options	Description
-s *feet*	Specifies the length in feet of the dump tape. This calculation is dependent on tape density (option d) and the dump record (options B and b). This option takes a numeric argument.
-u	Record this backup in the /etc/dumpdates file. It is a good idea to use this option, especially if you create incremental backups.
-t *date*	Specify a date and time on which to base incremental backups. Any files modified or added after that time will be backed up. This option causes dump to ignore the /etc/dumpdates file. It takes a single argument, a date in the format specified by the ctime man page.
-W	This option causes dump to list the file systems that need to be backed up. It does this by looking at the /etc/dumpdates file and the /etc/fstab file.
-w	This works like the W option but lists the individual files that should be backed up.

Thus, a typical dump command may look similar to the following:

```
# dump 0uBf 500000 /dev/qft0 /dev/sda6
```

This command results in dump performing a level zero (full) backup of the /dev/sda6 file system, storing the backup on the tape drive /dev/qft0, and recording the results in /etc/dumpdates. The B option is used to increase the expected tape block count to 500000; otherwise, dump would prompt for a new tape far earlier than required. The dump command prints status messages to the screen, letting you know how far along the backup has progressed and estimating how much time it will take to complete. The output looks similar to this:

```
DUMP: Date of this level 0 dump: Sat Aug 23 23:33:37 2003
DUMP: Dumping /dev/sda6 (/home) to /dev/qft0
DUMP: Exclude ext3 journal inode 8
DUMP: Label: /home
DUMP: mapping (Pass I) [regular files]
DUMP: mapping (Pass II) [directories]
DUMP: estimated 93303 tape blocks on 0.19 tape(s).
DUMP: Volume 1 started with block 1 at: Sat Aug 23 23:33:47
DUMP: dumping (Pass III) [directories]
DUMP: dumping (Pass IV) [regular files]
DUMP: Closing /dev/qft0
DUMP: Volume 1 completed at: Sat Aug 23 23:35:35 2003
DUMP: Volume 1 94360 tape blocks (92.15MB)
DUMP: Volume 1 took 0:01:48
DUMP: Volume 1 transfer rate: 873 kB/s
DUMP: 94360 tape blocks (92.15MB) on 1 volume(s)
DUMP: finished in 108 seconds, throughput 873 kBytes/sec
DUMP: Date of this level 0 dump: Sat Aug 23  23:33:37 2003
DUMP: Date this dump completed: Sat Aug 23  23:35:35 2003
DUMP: Average transfer rate: 873 kB/s
```

```
DUMP: DUMP IS DONE
```

Understanding dump levels

The dump command can back up all files on a file system, or it can selectively back up only those files that have changed recently. The dump level parameter is used to specify this behavior. A dump level of 0 results in a full backup of all files on the file system. Specifying a higher number (1-9) backs up only those files that have been changed or added since the most recent dump of the same or lower dump level. I recommend you use dump levels to implement a full and incremental backup schedule similar to the one shown in Table 13-4.

Table 13-4: Recommended dump Schedule

Day of Week	Dump Level
Sunday	Level 0 (full dump). Eject the tape when done.
Monday	Level 9 (incremental dump).
Tuesday	Level 8 (incremental dump).
Wednesday	Level 7 (incremental dump).
Thursday	Level 6 (incremental dump).
Friday	Level 5 (incremental dump).
Saturday	Level 4 (incremental dump).

Note that after the full backup on Sunday, a level 9 incremental dump is done the next day, and a successively lower dump level is done each day after that. This results in all the files that have changed since Sunday being backed up on every single incremental backup. Each incremental backup is thus larger than the previous one; the backup contains all of the files from the previous incremental backup plus any files that have changed since then. This may seem wasteful of storage space on the backup tape, but it will save a lot of time and effort should there be a need to restore the file system. (This is referred to as a differential backup.)

For example, imagine that your hard drive crashed on Friday. After replacing the hard drive, you can restore the entire file system in two steps: Restore the full backup from the prior Sunday, and then the most recent incremental backup from Thursday. You can do this because Thursday's backup contains all of the files from Monday, Tuesday, and Wednesday's tape as well as the files that changed after that. If the dump levels had progressed in positive order (level 1 for Monday, level 2 for Tuesday, and so on), *all* of the incremental backups would have to be restored in order to restore the file system to its most current state.

Automating Backups with cron

You can automate most of your backups with shell scripts and the cron daemon. Use the su command to become root, and then cd to the /usr/local/bin directory. Use any text editor to create a shell script called backups.sh that looks similar to the following:

```
#!/bin/sh
#
# backups.sh - A simple backup script, by Thad Phetteplace
#
# This script takes one parameter, the dump level.
# If the dump level is not provided, it is
# automatically set to zero. For level zero (full)
# dumps, rewind and eject the tape when done.
#

if [ $1 ]; then
        level=$1
else
        #
        # No dump level was provided, so set it
        # to zero
        #
        level="0"
fi

/sbin/dump $level'uf' /dev/nrft0 /
/sbin/dump $level'uf' /dev/nrft0 /home
/sbin/dump $level'uf' /dev/nrft0 /var
/sbin/dump $level'uf' /dev/nrft0 /usr


#
# If we are doing a full dump, rewind and eject
# the tape when done.
#
if [ $level = "0" ]; then
        /bin/mt -f /dev/nrft0 rewind
        /bin/mt -f /dev/nrft0 offline
fi
```

You might have to change the partitions being backed up to match your setup, but this script should otherwise work quite well for you. After saving and exiting the editor, change the permissions on the file so that it is executable and readable only by root:

```
# chmod 700 backups.sh
```

You can now back up your entire system by running the backups.sh script when logged in as root. The script accepts the dump level as its only parameter. If you leave the parameter off, it will automatically assume a level zero dump. Thus, the following two commands are equivalent:

```
# backups.sh
# backups.sh 0
```

You may need to customize this script for your situation. For example, I am using the tape device /dev/nrft0. You might be using a different tape device. Whatever device you use, you should probably use the version of its device name that begins with the letter *n*. That tells the system that after it finishes copying data to the tape, it should *not* rewind the tape. For example, I used /dev/nrft0 instead of /dev/rst0 in the preceding script. If I had used /dev/rst0, each successive incremental backup would have overwritten the previous one.

Other things that you may change in this script include the partitions being backed up and the dump level at which the tape is ejected. It is common practice to eject the tape after the last incremental backup just before performing a full backup.

The most useful thing about this script is that you can easily configure your system to run it automatically. Simply add a few lines to the root crontab file, and the cron daemon will invoke the script on the days and times specified. While logged in as root, enter the crontab command with the -e option:

```
# crontab -e
```

This opens the root crontab file in an editor. Add the following lines at the end of the file:

```
0 22 * * 0 /usr/local/bin/backup.sh 0
0 22 * * 1 /usr/local/bin/backup.sh 9
0 22 * * 2 /usr/local/bin/backup.sh 8
0 22 * * 3 /usr/local/bin/backup.sh 7
0 22 * * 4 /usr/local/bin/backup.sh 6
0 22 * * 5 /usr/local/bin/backup.sh 5
0 22 * * 6 /usr/local/bin/backup.sh 4
```

Save and exit the file. The cron daemon will now run the backup script at 10:00 p.m. (22:00 in military time) every day of the week. This example implements the dump schedule outlined earlier. A full dump is performed on Sunday, and the tape is ejected when it is done. A new tape should be loaded on Monday, and then incremental backups will be written to that same tape for the rest of the week. The next full dump will be written to the end of that tape, unless someone is around on Sunday to eject and replace the tape before 10:00 p.m. Keep in mind that the person set to receive e-mail for the root user will be the one to be notified of the actions of this, or any, root-owned cron script.

Restoring Backed-Up Files

The restore command is used to retrieve files from a backup tape or other medium that was created by dump. You can use restore to recover an entire file system or to interactively select individual files. It recovers files from the specified media and copies them into the current directory (the one you ran the recover command in), re-creating subdirectories as needed. Much as with the dump command, the first parameter passed to the restore command is a list of single-character option codes, as shown in Table 13-5.

Table 13-5: Restore Command Options

Restore Options	Description
-r	Restore the entire dump archive.
-C	Compare the contents of the dump file with the files on the disk. This is used to check the success of a restore.
-R	Start the restore from a particular tape of a multitape backup. This is useful for restarting an interrupted restore.
-X *filelist*	Extract only specific files or directories from the archive. This option takes one argument, a list of files or directories to extract.
-T *file*	List the contents of the dump archive. If a file or directory is given as an argument, list only the occurrence of that file, directory, or anything within the directory.
-i	Restore files in interactive mode.
-b *blocksize*	Specify the block size of the dump in kilobytes. This option takes a numeric argument.
-D *filesystem*	Specify the name of the file system to be compared when using the -C option. The file system name is passed as an argument.
-F *script*	Specify the name of the dump archive to restore from. This option takes an alphanumeric argument.
-h	If this option is specified, restore re-creates directories marked for extraction but will not extract their contents.
-m	Files are extracted by inode number instead of name. This is generally not very useful.
-N	Instead of extracting files, print their names.
-s *file#*	Specify the dump file to start with on a multiple file tape. This takes a numeric argument.
-T *directory*	Tells restore where to write any temporary files. This is useful if you booted from a floppy disk (which has no space for temporary files).
-v	Run in verbose mode. This causes restore to print information about each file as it restores it.
-y	The restore command will always continue when it encounters a bad block, rather than asking you if you want to continue.

Restoring an entire file system

Let's return to our earlier example of the Friday disk crash. You installed a shiny new hard drive and your backup tapes are in hand. It is time to restore the files. For the purposes of this example, I assume that the crashed drive contained only the /home partition and that the

Linux operating system is still intact. If the crashed drive had contained the Linux operating system, you would first have to reinstall Linux before restoring the backup.

Before any files can be recovered to your new hard drive, an empty file system must be created on it. You use the mkfs command to do this. The mkfs command can accept a variety of parameters, but usually you need to supply only the name of the device to create the file system on. Thus, to prepare the new hard drive, type:

```
# mkfs -t ext3 /dev/sda6
```

Alternatively, because your /home drive is listed in the /etc/fstab file, you can simply specify the /home mount point and mkfs will figure out the correct device. Thus, the preceding command could be replaced with this:

```
# mkfs /home
```

> **CAUTION:** You should, of course, exercise extreme caution when using the mkfs command. If you specify the wrong device name, you could unintentionally wipe out all data on an existing file system.

After creating a file system on your new disk, mount the partition to a temporary mount point.

```
# mkdir /mnt/test
# mount /dev/sda6 /mnt/test
```

This connects the new file system to the /mnt/test directory. Now change into the directory (cd /mnt/test) and use the restore command to recover the entire file system off of your backup tape. Of course, it is assumed that you have loaded the tape into the tape drive.

```
# cd /mnt/test
# restore rf /dev/nrft0
```

When the restore is finished, you can unmount the partition and remount it to the appropriate mount point. If you have restored the file system to a different physical partition than it was originally on, be sure to modify the /etc/fstab file appropriately so that the correct partition is mounted next time the system is rebooted.

Recovering individual files

The restore command can also be used to recover individual files and directories. By using restore in interactive mode, you can type a series of restore commands to selectively restore files. To run restore in interactive mode, use the i parameter instead of r:

```
# restore if /dev/nrst0
```

The restore command will then read the file index from the backup tape and present you with a restore prompt. At this prompt, you can type the commands that enable you to select which directories and files to recover. You can navigate the directory structure of the backup index much the same way that you navigate an actual file system using a shell prompt. The interactive restore command even has its own version of the familiar cd and ls commands, as shown in Table 13-6.

Table 13-6: Interactive restore Commands

Command	Description
add	Add a file or directory to the list of files to be extracted. If a directory is marked for extraction, all of the directories and files within it will also be extracted.
cd	Change the current directory being viewed within the dump archive. Works much like the cd command used at a shell prompt.
delete	Delete a file or directory from the list of files to be extracted. Deleting a directory from the list results in all of the files and directories within it also being deleted from the list of files to be extracted.
extract	Extract all of the marked files and directories from the archive and write them back to the file system.
help	List the available commands.
ls	List the contents of the current directory. If a directory name is provided as an argument, list the contents of that directory. Files or directories marked for extraction have a * character in front of them.
pwd	Print the full pathname of the current directory of the dump archive.
quit	Exit the interactive restore program.
setmodes	Do not restore the files; instead, set the modes of already existing files on the target disk to match the modes recorded in the dump file. This is useful for recovering from a restore that was prematurely aborted.
verbose	Toggles verbose output versus quiet output during the restore process. Verbose output mode will echo information to the screen for every file that is restored.

As an example, pretend that the user joe has accidentally deleted his Mail subdirectory from his home directory. Joe happens to be your boss, so it is urgent that you recover his files. Here is how you can go about it.

Load the appropriate tape into the tape drive and log in as root. Use the cd command to go to the top of the /home partition, and then run the restore program in interactive mode:

```
# cd /home
# restore if /dev/nrft0
```

Verify that you have the backup tape for the /home partition by entering the ls command. You should see something like the following list of directories, representing users who have home directories in /home:

```
restore > ls
```

```
.:
bob/         jane/         joe/         lost+found/ mary/         thad/
```

Yes, this is the home partition. Now change the current directory to Joe's home directory using the cd command. Type **ls** again to view the contents of his home directory.

```
restore > cd joe
restore > ls
./joe:
.mozilla/            Desktop/            report.html
.tcshrc              Mail/               letter.txt
.xinitrc             News/               www/
```

Now mark the Mail directory for extraction using the add command:

```
restore > add Mail
```

If you use the ls command again, you see that the Mail directory is preceded with an asterisk (*) character, which means it has been marked for extraction.

```
restore > ls
./joe:
.mozilla/            Desktop/            report.html
.tcshrc              *Mail/              letter.txt
.xinitrc             News/               www/
```

Now use the extract command to begin the extraction process. restore will prompt you for the number of the tape to start with. This is a single tape backup, so just enter the number 1. When it prompts you to set owner/mode for '.'?, answer yes by typing y and pressing Enter. restore will then restore the file permissions (if necessary) of the directory it is restoring to. This isn't critical when extracting individual files like this, but you should always answer yes to this prompt when doing a full restore. Anyway, your screen should now contain the following:

```
restore > extract
You have not read any tapes yet.
Unless you know which volume your file(s) are on you
should start with the last volume and work toward the first.
Specify next volume #: 1
set owner/mode for '.'? [yn] y
restore >
```

At this point, the files have been recovered and you can exit the restore program by issuing the quit command. That's all there is to it. You now know the basics of using the dump and restore commands.

Configuring Amanda for Network Backups

Using Amanda (the Advanced Maryland Automatic Network Disk Archiver), you can use a single large-capacity tape drive on a server to back up files from multiple computers over a network. The Amanda packages (amanda, amanda-client, and amanda-server) include a variety of commands. The online man page for Amanda describes the commands as shown in Table 13-7.

Table 13-7: Backup Commands Used with Amanda

Command	Description
amdump	Do automatic Amanda backups. This command is normally run by cron on a computer called the tape server host and requests backups of file systems located on backup clients. amdump backs up all disks in the disklist file to tape or, if there is a problem, to a special holding disk. After all backups are done, amdump sends mail reporting failures and successes.
amflush	Flush backups from the holding disk to tape. amflush is used after amdump has reported it could not write backups to tape. When this happens, backups stay in the holding disk. After the tape problem is corrected, run amflush to write backups from the holding disk to the tape.
amcleanup	Clean up after an interrupted amdump. This command is needed only if amdump was unable to complete for some reason, usually because the tape server host crashed while amdump was running.
amrecover	Provide an interactive interface to browse the Amanda index files and select which tapes to recover files from. amrecover can also run amrestore and the system restore program (such as tar) sometimes.
amrestore	Read an Amanda tape, searching for requested backups. amrestore is suitable for everything from interactive restores of single files to a full restore of all partitions on a failed disk.
amlabel	Write an Amanda format label onto a tape. All Amanda tapes must be labeled with amlabel. amdump and amflush will not write to an unlabeled tape.
amcheck	Verify the correct tape is in the tape drive and that all file systems on all backup client systems are ready to be backed up. Can optionally be run by cron before amdump, so someone will get mail warning that backups will fail unless corrective action is taken.
amadmin	Take care of administrative tasks, such as finding out which tapes are needed to restore a file system, forcing hosts to do full backups of selected disks, and looking at schedule balance information.
amtape	Take care of tape changer control operations, such as loading particular tapes, ejecting tapes, and scanning the tape rack.
amverify	Check Amanda backup tapes for errors (GNU tar format backups only).
amrmtape	Delete a tape from the tape list and from the Amanda database.
amstatus	Give the status of a running amdump.

The `amdump` command is the one that you will use the most, but before you can get started, you need to configure a few things on both the backup server (the system with the tape drive) and the backup clients (the systems being backed up). On amanda clients, you need to install the amanda package. On the amanda server, you need to install the amanda-server package as well.

Creating Amanda directories

You need to create some directories to hold the Amanda configuration files and to provide a location to write Amanda log files. The configuration files go in the `/etc/amanda` directory, and the log files go in `/var/lib/amanda`. In both cases, you should log in as the amanda user and create subdirectories within those directories, one subdirectory for each backup schedule that you intend to run and an index file, as shown in the following example.

> **NOTE:** For security reasons, you should do all amanda administration as the amanda user. To do this, the root user can create a password for amanda by typing `passwd amanda` and entering the new password. A better alternative, however, might be to lock the amanda user account, and then simply type `su - amanda` (as in the following example) to do amanda tasks as root user without an extra password. The rest of this procedure assumes that you are logged in as the amanda user.

```
# su - amanda
$ mkdir -p /var/lib/amanda/normal/index
$ mkdir -p /etc/amanda/normal
```

For the purpose of this example, I have created only a `normal` backup configuration that backs up the data drives on several machines. You may also decide to create an upgrade backup configuration that backs up the operating system partitions. You could then run that backup before you perform any operating system upgrades.

You also need to specify a holding disk that Amanda can use to spool backups temporarily before it writes them to disk. This directory should have a lot of free space. I have a large `/home` partition on my server, so I created an Amanda directory there to use as a holding disk:

```
# mkdir /home/amanda
# chmod 700 /home/amanda
# chown amanda /home/amanda
# chgrp disk /home/amanda
```

Creating the amanda.conf file

Next, as the amanda user, you must create two configuration files for Amanda and store them in the `/etc/amanda/normal` directory: `amanda.conf` and `disklist`. You can start by copying samples of these files from the `/etc/amanda/DailySet1` directory as follows:

```
$ cd /etc/amanda/DailySet1
$ cp amanda.conf disklist /etc/amanda/normal
```

The amanda.conf file sets a variety of general configuration values, and the disklist file
defines which machines and partitions to back up. The amanda.conf file can be rather
complicated but, fortunately, most of its values can be left at their default values. Here is a
simplified amanda.conf file with some comments embedded in it to help explain things:

```
#
# amanda.conf - sample Amanda configuration file. This started life as
#               the actual config file in use at CS.UMD.EDU.

org "GLACI"          # your organization name for reports
mailto "amanda"      # space separated list of operators at your site
dumpuser "amanda"    # the user to run dumps under

# Specify tape device and/or tape changer. If you don't have a tape
# changer, and you don't want to use more than one tape per run of
# amdump, just comment out the definition of tpchanger.

runtapes 1                # number of tapes to be used in a single
                          # run of amdump
tapedev "/dev/nrft0"      # the no-rewind tape device to be used
rawtapedev "/dev/rft0"    # the raw device to be used (ftape only)

tapetype HP-DAT   # what kind of tape it is
          # (see tapetypes below)
labelstr "^normal[0-9][0-9]*$"   # label constraint all
                                 # tapes must match

# Specify holding disks. These are used as a temporary
# staging area for dumps before they are written to tape and
# are recommended for most sites.

holdingdisk hd1 {
    comment "main holding disk"
    directory "/home/amanda"    # where the holding disk is
    use 290 Mb                  # how much space can we use on it
    chunksize -1                # size of chunk
    }

# Note that, although the keyword below is infofile, it is
# only so for historic reasons, since now it is supposed to
# be a directory (unless you have selected some database
# format other than the 'text' default)

infofile "/var/lib/amanda/normal/curinfo"   # database DIRECTORY
logdir   "/var/lib/amanda/normal"       # log directory
indexdir "/var/lib/amanda/normal/index"    # index directory


# tapetypes
```

```
# Define the type of tape you use here, and use it in "tapetype"
# above. Some typical types of tapes are included here. The
# tapetype tells amanda how many MB will fit on the tape, how
# big the filemarks are, and how fast the tape device is.

define tapetype HP-DAT {
    comment "DAT tape drives"
    # data provided by Rob Browning <rlb@cs.utexas.edu>
    length 1930 mbytes
    filemark 111 kbytes
    speed 468 kbytes
}


# dumptypes
#
# These are referred to by the disklist file.

define dumptype global {
    comment "Global definitions"
    # This is quite useful for setting global parameters, so you
    # don't have to type them everywhere.
}

define dumptype always-full {
    global
    comment "Full dump of this filesystem always"
    compress none
    priority high
    dumpcycle 0
}
```

This example `amanda.conf` file was trimmed down from a larger example I copied from the `/etc/amanda/DailySet1` directory. The example `amanda.conf` file provides additional information on the available configuration options. Also, the online man page for Amanda should be helpful (type **man amanda** to read it). You can find more instructions in the `/usr/share/doc/amanda-server*` directory. Generally, you have to do the following:

- Modify the org name for reports.
- Change the device names set for tapedev and rawtapedev to match your tape device.
- Select a tape type entry that is appropriate for your tape drive.
- Change the name of the directory specified in the holding disk section to match the directory you created earlier.

Creating a disklist file

You also must create a `disklist` file in the `/etc/amanda/normal` directory. This simply contains a list of the systems and disk partitions to back up. The qualifier `always-full` is included on each entry to tell Amanda what type of backup to perform. It means to use full, rather than incremental, backups.

```
# sample Amanda2 disklist file
#
# File format is:
#
#       hostname diskdev dumptype [spindle [interface]]
#
# where the dumptypes are defined by you in amanda.conf.

dexter sda5 always-full
dexter sda6 always-full
dexter sda7 always-full
dexter sda8 always-full

daffy sda5 always-full
daffy sda6 always-full
daffy sda7 always-full
daffy sdb1 always-full
daffy sdb2 always-full
```

This example file backs up two systems, dexter and daffy. The order of the systems and the partitions is selected so that the most important data is backed up first. This way, if a tape drive becomes full, you have still managed to back up the most important data.

Adding Amanda network services

Amanda is designed to perform backups over a network. The following amanda services are defined in the /etc/services file:

```
amanda          10080/udp
amanda          10080/tcp
amandaidx       10082/tcp
amidxtape       10083/tcp
```

On the amanda server

To offer these services to the network in Fedora or RHEL, you need to configure the xinetd daemon to listen for those services. You do this by enabling the amandaidx and amidxtape services by typing the following (as root user):

```
# chkconfig amidxtape on
# chkconfig amandaidx on
```

This enables Amanda to accept requests from the client system and to start the backup process without any user intervention. You need to tell the xinetd daemon to reload the /etc/xinetd.d files before this change takes effect. You can do this by typing the following as root user:

```
# /etc/init.d/xinetd reload
```

On each amanda client

Next you need to configure the `.amandahosts` file in the `/var/lib/amanda` directory on each computer (client) that the amanda server will back up from. This file should contain the fully qualified host and domain name of any backup servers that will connect to this client. When you begin, only your localhost is defined in this file as your backup server. To add another computer as a backup server, type the following (replacing *amandahost* with the name of the backup server, while you are logged in as the `amanda` user):

```
$ echo amandahost >> /var/lib/amanda/.amandahosts
```

You also need to make sure that the amanda client daemon is configured to run on the client. You do this by enabling the `amanda` service by typing the following (as root user):

```
# chkconfig amanda on
```

This enables the amanda client to communicate with the amanda server. You need to tell the `xinetd` daemon to reload the `/etc/xinetd.d` files before this change takes place. Do this by typing the following as root user:

```
# /etc/init.d/xinetd reload
```

Performing an Amanda backup

Now that everything is configured, you are ready to perform an Amanda backup. Before running the actual backup, you should run `amcheck` to check your drive and configuration. While logged in as root, type the following commands:

```
# /usr/sbin/amcheck DailySet1
# /usr/sbin/amdump normal
```

This runs the `amdump` command and tells it to read the configuration files it finds in the `/etc/amanda/normal` directory created earlier. It then works its way down the list of systems and partitions in the `disklist` file, backing up each partition in the order it occurs. The results of the `amdump` are written to the `/var/lib/amanda/normal` directory. Read the files you find there to check on the results of the backup. (See the previous section on how to create a `disklist` file to understand the process that `amdump` goes through.)

You can, of course, automate this process with `cron`. To create an `amdump` schedule similar to the regular dump schedule discussed in an earlier section, do the following. While logged in as root, enter the `crontab` command with the `-e` option:

```
# crontab -e
```

This opens the root `crontab` file in an editor. Add the following lines to the end of the file:

```
0 22 * * 0 /usr/sbin/amdump normal
0 22 * * 1 /usr/sbin/amdump incremental
0 22 * * 2 /usr/sbin/amdump incremental
0 22 * * 3 /usr/sbin/amdump incremental
0 22 * * 4 /usr/sbin/amdump incremental
```

```
0 22 * * 5 /usr/sbin/amdump incremental
0 22 * * 6 /usr/sbin/amdump incremental
```

Save and exit the file. The `cron` daemon will now run `amdump` at 10:00 p.m. (22:00 in military time) every day of the week. This example assumes that a second incremental configuration has been created. You can do this by creating a subdirectory named `incremental` under `/etc/amanda` and populating it with appropriately modified `amanda.conf` and `disklist` files. You must also create a subdirectory named `incremental` under `/var/lib/amanda` so that `amanda` has somewhere to write the log files for this configuration.

It may be a bit of work to get it all in place, but when you do, Amanda can make your network backups much easier to manage. It may be overkill for a small office, but in a large enterprise network situation, it enables Fedora or RHEL to act as a powerful backup server.

Using the pax Archiving Tool

Over the years, a variety of UNIX operating systems have arisen, resulting in a variety of similar but incompatible file archiving formats. Even tools that go by the same name may use slightly different storage formats on different systems. This can lead to big problems when trying to archive and retrieve data in a multiplatform environment. Fortunately, there is a solution.

The pax program is a POSIX standard utility that can read and write a wide variety of archive formats. An RPM package for pax is included with Fedora and RHEL. If it is not already installed, type the following as root user to get the latest version of pax (provided you have an Internet connection):

```
# yum install pax
```

If you don't have an Internet connection, mount the CD/DVD containing your Fedora or RHEL distribution, change to the RPMS directory, and then use the `rpm` command to install pax.

```
# rpm -Uhv pax-*
```

Remember that you need to be logged in as root when installing software with the `rpm` command.

The `pax` command takes a variety of command-line options. The last parameter is usually the file or directory to archive. You may use wildcard characters such as * or ? to specify multiple files or directories. The options you will use most often include the `-r` and `-w` parameters for specifying when you are reading or writing an archive. These are usually used in conjunction with the `-f` parameter, which is used to specify the name of the archive file.

By using `pax` parameters in different combinations, it is possible to extract an archive, create an archive, list the contents of an archive, or even copy an entire directory hierarchy from one location to another. Table 13-8 shows a few examples of the `pax` command in action.

Table 13-8: Examples of pax Use

The pax Command	Description
pax -f *myfiles*	List the contents of the archive named myfiles.
pax -r -f *myfiles*	Extract the contents of the archive named myfiles.
pax -w -f *myfiles* /etc	Create an archive named myfiles containing everything within the /etc directory.
pax -w -f *myfiles* *.txt	Archive all of the files in the current directory that have a .txt file extension.
pax -r -w */olddir* */newdir*	Copy the entire contents of the directory /oldir into a new directory called /newdir.
pax -w -B 1440000 -f /dev/fd0 *	Archive the contents of the current directory onto multiple floppy disks.
pax -w -x cpio -f *myfiles* *	Archive the contents of the current directory into an archive file named myfiles using the cpio format.
pax -r -U mary -f *backups*	Extract all of the files owned by user mary from the archive named backups.

Note that by leaving off both the -r and -w options, you cause pax to simply list the contents of the archive. If you specify both the -r and -w options, then you should leave off the -f option and supply source and destination directories instead. This will cause the source directory to be completely cloned in the specified destination directory.

You can use additional parameters to further modify the pax command's behavior. For example, you can use the -x option in conjunction with the -w option to specify the specific archive type to create, or you can use the -B option to specify the number of bytes to write to each volume of a multivolume archive.

Table 13-9 describes the many optional parameters to the pax command.

Table 13-9: Options to pax

Options to pax	Description
-r	Read files from an archive.
-w	Write files to an archive.
-a	Append files to a previously created archive.
-b *blocksize*	Specify the archive's data block size. It must be a multiple of 512.
-c *pattern*	Match all files except those that match the specified pattern.

Options to pax	Description
-d	Match filename wildcards against file or directory names only, not the complete path.
-f archive	Specify the name of the archive.
-i	Interactively rename files when archiving.
-k	Do not overwrite existing files.
-l	Link files with hard links when in copy mode (-r -w).
-n pattern	Match only the first file that matches the supplied pattern.
-o options	Extra options specific to the archiving format used.
-p string	Specify the file characteristics to retain when archiving or copying. Read the pax man page for more information on this option.
-s replstr	Modify the archived filenames using the supplied regular expression.
-t	Preserve the access times of archived files.
-u	Do not overwrite files with older versions.
-v	Provide verbose output when running.
-x format	Specify the format of the archive. Valid formats include cpio, bcpio, sv4cpio, sv4crc, tar, and ustar. The default is to use ustar when creating an archive. The pax command will automatically determine the correct file type when reading an archive.
-z	Indicates that gzip should be used to compress and decompress the archive.
-B bytes	Specify the number of bytes per archive volume. Use this option to create multivolume archives on removable media.
-D	Do not overwrite existing files with files that have an older inode modification time.
-E limit	Limit the number of times pax will retry on encountering a read or write error.
-G group	Select files based on a group name or GID. To select by GID, place a # sign in front of the group number.
-H	Follow only command-line symbolic links while performing a physical file system traversal.
-L	Follow all symbolic links when traversing a directory hierarchy.
-P	Do not follow symbolic links. This is the default.
-T time	Select files based on their modification time. Read the pax man page for complete discussion of this parameter's syntax.

Options to pax	Description
-U *user*	Select files based on the owner's user name, or by UID with a # sign in front of it.
-X	Do not traverse into directories that reside on a different device.
-Y	This option is the same as the -D option, except that the inode change time is checked using the pathname created after all the filename modifications have completed.
-Z	This option is the same as the -u option, except that the modification time is checked using the pathname created after all the filename modifications have completed.

As you can see, pax is a very flexible and powerful archiving tool. It can be particularly helpful in migrating data from older legacy systems to your new Linux system. When you are faced with the task of recovering archived data from an antiquated or even nonfunctioning UNIX system, the multiple file format support of pax can be a literal lifesaver.

Summary

I hope that you never experience a major hard drive crash, but if you do, the effort of making backups will repay itself many times over. A variety of low-cost backup hardware is available to use with your Fedora or RHEL system. The traditional tape drive is an excellent choice for backing up large amounts of data or data that you need to keep for years. However, simply copying your /home directories to another medium offers some level of protection for your data.

For convenience, a writable DVD or CD drive is a good choice. As for the tools you choose to do your backups, the dump and restore commands are old favorites, dating back to the early UNIX days (although they are considered somewhat unreliable these days). The Amanda backup facility is excellent for network backups. If you are dealing with backups in several different formats, the pax command might be helpful.

Chapter 14

Computer Security Issues

In This Chapter

- Linux security checklist

- Using password protection

- Protecting Linux with iptables firewalls

- Service access control with TCP wrappers

- Checking log files

- Using secure shell package

- Understanding attack techniques

- Securing servers with SELinux

- Protecting servers with encryption and certificates

With the growth of the Internet, computer and network security has become more important than ever. Assaults on your Fedora or Red Hat Enterprise Linux system can come in many forms, such as denial-of-service attacks, break-in attempts, or hijacking your machine as a spam relay, to name a few.

In many cases, good practices for setting and protecting passwords, monitoring log files, and creating good firewalls will keep out many would-be intruders. Keeping up with critical security software updates will help patch vulnerabilities as they become known. The addition of SELinux adds another layer of protection on your Linux system. Sometimes, more proactive approaches are needed to respond to break-ins. This chapter will familiarize you, as a Linux administrator, with the dangers that exist and the tools necessary to protect your system.

Linux Security Checklist

While Linux offers all the tools you need to secure your computer, if you are careless, someone can (and probably will) harm your system or try to steal your data. The following checklist covers a range of security measures to protect your Linux desktop or server.

- **Add users and passwords** — Creating separate user accounts (each with a good password) is your first line of defense in keeping your data secure. Users are protected from each other, as well as from an outsider who takes over one user account. Setting up group accounts can extend the concept of ownership to multiple users. See Chapter 11 for more on setting up user accounts and "Using Password Protection" later in this chapter.

- **Read, write, and execute permissions** — Every item in a Linux file system (including files, directories, applications, and devices) can be restricted by read, write, and execute permissions for that item's owner and group, as well as by all others. In this way, for example, you can let other users run a command or open a file, allowing them to change it. See Chapter 4 for information on setting file and directory permissions.

- **Protect root** — In standard Linux systems, the root users (as well as other administrative user accounts such as apache) have special abilities to use and change your Linux system. Protect the root account's password and don't use the root account when you don't need to. An open shell or desktop owned by the root user can be a target for attack. Running `system-config-*` windows as a regular user (and then entering the root password as prompted) and running administrative commands using `sudo` can reduce exposure to attacks on your root account. See Chapter 10 for information on handling the root user account.

- **Use trusted software** — While there are no guarantees with any open source software, you have a better chance of avoiding compromised software by using an established Linux distribution (such as Fedora or RHEL). Software repositories where you get add-on packages or updates should likewise be scrutinized. Using valid GPG public keys (which use signatures and encryption) you can ensure that the software you install comes from a valid vendor. And, of course, always be sure of the source of data files you receive before opening them in a Linux application.

- **Get software updates** — As vulnerabilities and bugs are discovered in software packages, every major Linux distribution (including RHEL and Fedora) offers tools for getting and installing those updates. Be sure to get those updates, especially if you are using Linux as a server. See Chapter 5 for information on using PackageKit and yum to get software updates.

- **Use secure applications** — Even with software that is valid and working, some applications offer better protection from attack or invasion than others. For example, if you want to log in to a computer over the Internet, the secure shell service (ssh) is considered more secure than `rlogin` or `telnet` services. Also, some services that are thought to be insecure if you expose them on the Internet (such as Samba and NFS), can be used more securely over the Internet through virtual private network (VPN) tunnels (such as IPsec or CIPE).

- **Use restrictive firewalls** — A primary job of a firewall is to accept requests for services from a network that you want to allow and turn away requests that you don't (primarily based on port numbers requested). A desktop system should refuse requests that come in on most ports. A server system should allow requests for a controlled set of ports. This chapter describes how to set up a firewall using iptables.

- **Enable only services you need** — To offer services in Linux (such as Web, file, or mail services), a daemon process will listen on a particular port number. Don't enable services you don't need. In fact, you shouldn't even install server software you don't need. See Chapter 12 for information on using system services.

> **NOTE:** A program that runs quietly in the background handling service requests (such as sendmail) is called a *daemon*. Usually, daemons are started automatically when your system boots up, and they keep running until your system is shut down. Daemons may also be started on an as-needed basis by `xinetd`, a special daemon that listens on a large number of port numbers, and then launches the requested process.

- **Limit access to services** — You can restrict access for a service you want to have on to a particular host computer, domain, or network interface. For example, a computer with interfaces to both the Internet and a local area network (LAN) might limit access to a service such as NFS to computers on the LAN, but not offer those same services to the Internet. Services may limit access in their own configuration files or using TCP/IP wrappers (described later in this chapter).

- **Check your system** — Linux has tons of tools available for checking the security of your system. After you install Linux, you can check access to its ports using nmap or watch network traffic using Wireshark (formerly called Ethereal). You can also add popular security tools such as Nessus, to get a more complete view of your system security.

- **Monitor your system** — You can log almost every type of activity on your Linux system. System log files, using the syslogd and klogd facilities, can be configured to track as much or as little of your system activity as you choose. The logwatch facility provides an easy way to have the potential problem messages forwarded to your administrative e-mail account. Linux logging features are described later in this chapter. You can get add-on packages such as tripwire and portsentry, to check your system for tampering and deal with someone scanning your ports, respectively.

- **Use SELinux** — SELinux is an extraordinarily rich (and complex) facility for managing the access of nearly every aspect of a Linux system. It addresses the if-I-get-root-access-I-own-your-box shortcomings of Linux and UNIX systems for highly secure environments. Red Hat systems offer a useful, limited set of SELinux policies that are turned on by default in Fedora. Despite improvements, however, many Linux system administrators still just turn off SELinux because the find it difficult to use. Chapter 10 provides an overview of SELinux, along with explanations of how it is implemented in Fedora and RHEL.

This checklist should give you a good starting point with many aspects of security in Linux. Each of these topics is covered in greater depth throughout this chapter and in other chapters throughout this book that I have just referenced. However, computer security is an ongoing battle, so I recommend you check out the following Web sites to get a deeper, continuing experience with Linux security:

- **CERT (`www.cert.org`)** — The CERT Coordination center follows computer security issues. Check their home page for the latest vulnerability issues. The site has articles on security practices (`www.cert.org/nav/articles_reports.html`). It also has recommendations on what you should do if your computer has been compromised (`www.cert.org/tech_tips/win-UNIX-system_compromise.html`).

- **Red Hat Security Alerts (`www.redhat.com/security`)** — For RHEL security issues (that typically relate to Fedora systems as well), you should check out the resources available from this site. From here you can look for and read about available updates. You can also get information on security training and consulting from Red Hat, Inc.

- **Red Hat Enterprise Linux 4.5 Security Guide** — This guide provides an in-depth look at Linux security, specifically as it relates to Red Hat Enterprise Linux and Fedora. You can access this guide online from the following address:

```
www.redhat.com/docs/manuals/enterprise/RHEL-4-Manual/en-
US/Security_Guide/
```

Using Password Protection

Passwords are the most fundamental security tool of any modern operating system and consequently, the most commonly attacked security feature. It is natural to want to choose a password that is easy to remember, but very often this means choosing a password that is also easy to guess. Crackers know that on any system with more than a few users, at least one person is likely to have an easily guessed password.

By using the "brute force" method of attempting to log in to every account on the system and trying the most common passwords on each of these accounts, a persistent cracker has a good shot of finding a way in. Remember that a cracker will automate this attack, so thousands of login attempts are not out of the question. Obviously, choosing good passwords is the first and most important step to having a secure system.

Here are some things to avoid when choosing a password:

- Do not use any variation of your login name or your full name. Even if you use varied case, append, or prepend numbers or punctuation, or type it backwards, this will still be an easily guessed password.

- Do not use a dictionary word, even if you add numbers or punctuation to it.

- Do not use proper names of any kind.

- Do not use passwords based on a contiguous line of letters or numbers on the keyboard (such as "qwerty", "1q2w3e4r" or "asdfg").

Choosing good passwords

A good way to choose a strong password is to take the first letter from each word of an easily remembered sentence. The password can be made even better by adding numbers, punctuation, and varied case. The sentence you choose should have meaning only to you, and should not be publicly available (choosing a sentence on your personal Web page is a bad idea). Table 14-1 lists examples of strong passwords and the tricks used to remember them.

Table 14-1: Ideas for Good Passwords

Password	How to Remember It
Mrci7yo!	My rusty car is 7 years old!
2emBp1ib	2 elephants make BAD pets, 1 is better
ItMc?Gib	Is that MY coat? Give it back

The passwords look like gibberish, but are actually rather easy to remember. As you can see, I can place emphasis on words that stand for capital letters in the password. You set your password using the `passwd` command. Type the `passwd` command within a command shell, and it will enable you to change your password. First, it will prompt you to enter your old password. To protect against someone "shoulder surfing" and learning your password, the password will not be displayed as you type.

As long as you type your old password correctly, the `passwd` command will prompt you for the new password. When you type in your new password, the `passwd` command checks the password against `cracklib` to determine if it is a *good* or *bad* password. Non-root users will be required to try a different password if the one they have chosen is not a good password. The root user is the only user who is permitted to assign *bad* passwords. Once the password has been accepted by `cracklib`, the `passwd` command will ask you to enter the new password a second time to make sure there are no typos (which are hard to detect when you can't see what you are typing). When running as root, it is possible to change a user's password by supplying that user's login name as a parameter to the `passwd` command. Typing this:

```
# passwd joe
```

results in the `passwd` command prompting you for joe's new password. It does not prompt you for his old password in this case. This allows root to reset a user's password when that user has forgotten it (an event that happens all too often).

Using a shadow password file

In early versions of UNIX, all user account and password information was stored in a file that all users could read (although only root could write to it). This was generally not a problem because the password information was encrypted. The password was encrypted using a *trapdoor algorithm*, meaning the non-encoded password could be encoded into a scrambled string of characters, but the string could not be translated back to the non-encoded password.

How does the system check your password in this case? When you log in, the system encodes the password you entered, compares the resulting scrambled string with the scrambled string that is stored in the password file, and grants you access only if the two match. Have you ever asked a system administrator what the password on your account was only to be told that the system administrator doesn't know? If so, this is why: The administrator really doesn't have the password, only the encrypted version. The non-encoded password exists only at the moment you type it.

Breaking encrypted passwords

There is a problem with people being able to see encrypted passwords, however. Although it may be difficult (or even impossible) to reverse the encryption of a trapdoor algorithm, it is very easy to encode a large number of password guesses and compare them to the encoded passwords in the password file. This is, in order of magnitude, more efficient than trying actual login attempts for each user name and password. If a cracker can get a copy of your password file, the cracker has a much better chance of breaking into your system.

Fortunately, Linux and all modern UNIX systems support a shadow password file by default. The shadow file is a special version of the `passwd` file that only root can read. It contains the encrypted password information, so passwords can be left out of the `passwd` file, which any user on the system can read. Linux supports the older, single password file method as well as the newer shadow password file. You should always use the shadow password file (it is used by default).

Checking for the shadow password file

The password file is named `passwd` and can be found in the `/etc` directory. The shadow password file is named `shadow` and is also located in `/etc`. If your `/etc/shadow` file is missing, then it is likely that your Linux system is storing the password information in the `/etc/passwd` file instead. Verify this by displaying the file with the `less` command.

```
# less /etc/passwd
```

Something similar to the following should be displayed:

```
root:DkkS6Uke799fQ:0:0:root:/root:/bin/bash
bin:*:1:1:bin:/bin:
daemon:*:2:2:daemon:/sbin:
      .
      .
      .
mary:KpRUp2ozmY5TA:500:100:Mary Smith:/home/mary:/bin/sh
joe:0sXrzvKnQaksI:501:100:Joe Johnson:/home/joe:/bin/sh
jane:ptNoiueYEjwX.:502:100:Jane Anderson:/home/jane:/bin/sh
bob:Ju2vY7A0X6Kzw:503:100:Bob Renolds:/home/bob:/bin/sh
```

Each line in this listing corresponds to a single user account on the Linux system. Each line is made up of seven fields separated by colon (:) characters. From left to right the fields are the login name, the encrypted password, the user ID, the group ID, the description (usually a person's name), the home directory, and the default shell. Looking at the first line, you see that it is for the root account and has an encrypted password of DkkS6Uke799fQ. You can also see that root has a user ID of zero, a group ID of zero, and a home directory of /root, and root's default shell is /bin/sh.

All of these values are quite normal for a root account, but seeing that encrypted password should set off alarm bells in your head. It confirms that your system is not using the shadow password file. At this point, you should immediately convert your password file so that it uses /etc/shadow to store the password information. You do this by using the pwconv command. Simply log in as root (or use the su command to become root) and enter the pwconv command at a prompt. It will print no messages, but when your shell prompt returns, you should have a /etc/shadow file and your /etc/passwd file should now look like this:

```
root:x:0:0:root:/root:/bin/bash
bin:x:1:1:bin:/bin:
daemon:x:2:2:daemon:/sbin:
   .
   .
   .
mary:x:500:100:Mary Smith:/home/mary:/bin/sh
joe:x:501:100:Joe Johnson:/home/joe:/bin/sh
jane:x:502:100:Jane Anderson:/home/jane:/bin/sh
bob:x:503:100:Bob Renolds:/home/bob:/bin/sh
```

Encrypted password data is replaced with an x. Password data has been moved to /etc/shadow.

To check the type of password authentication your system is using, open the Authentication window (System → Administration → Authentication from the GNOME desktop). This tool lets you choose to use MD5 passwords, LDAP authentication, Kerberos 5, or other authentication methods.

To work with passwords for groups, you can use the grpconv command to convert passwords in /etc/groups to shadowed group passwords in /etc/gshadow. If you change passwd or group passwords and something breaks (you are unable to log in to the accounts), you can use the pwunconv and grpunconv commands, respectively, to reverse password conversion.

So, now you are using the shadow password file and picking good passwords. You have made a great start toward securing your system. You may also have noticed by now that security is not just a one-time job. It is an ongoing process, as much about policies as programs. Keep reading to learn more.

Securing Linux with iptables Firewalls

What is a firewall? In the non-computer world, a firewall is a physical barrier that keeps a fire from spreading. *Computer firewalls* serve a similar purpose, but the "fires" that they attempt to block are attacks from crackers on the Internet. In this context, a firewall, also known as a *packet filter*, is a physical piece of computer hardware that sits between your network and the Internet, regulating and controlling the flow of information.

The most common types of firewalls used today are filtering firewalls. A filtering firewall filters the traffic flowing between your network and the Internet, blocking certain things that may put your network at risk. It can limit access to and from the Internet to specific computers on your network. It can also limit the type of communication, selectively permitting or denying various Internet services.

For Fedora or RHEL to act as a filtering firewall, you can use the iptables features. The iptables feature replaced ipchains as the default Red Hat Linux firewall several releases ago. With Fedora Core 2, ipchains was dropped altogether. This chapter describes the iptables facility and the Firewall Configuration window for starting out with a simple iptables firewall.

Using the Firewall Configuration window

When you first installed your Fedora or RHEL system, you were given the opportunity to create a basic iptables firewall for your system. Using the Firewall Configuration window, you can see those settings and modify them further.

If you are not familiar with firewalls in general, or iptables in particular, it can be a bit daunting to start out. To make your start with iptables easier for new users, Fedora and RHEL systems offer the Firewall Configuration window. Look through the settings on this window, and then refer to other iptables descriptions that follow for more details on each feature.

To open the Firewall Configuration window, from the System menu select Administration → Firewall (or type **system-config-firewall**). Figure 14-1 shows an example of this window.

You can Enable or Disable the firewall using the radio buttons on the Firewall Configuration window. If you are connected to the Internet or other public network, I strongly suggest you enable your firewall. Even if you are on a trusted LAN you should turn the firewall on, but possibly open some services you might not expose to the Internet (such as NFS and Samba). If the firewall is enabled, select from the following topics in the left column to configure your firewall:

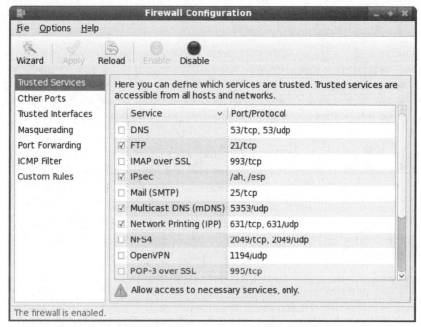

Figure 14-1: Set up a basic firewall using the Firewall Configuration window.

- **Trusted Services** — You can open access to ports associated with your network interfaces to provide the services you want to make available from your system. Some services, such as Samba, require that multiple ports be open.

  Services that are selected (open) by default include IPsec, Multicast DNS, Network Printing (IPP), and SSH (Secure Shell). Other services available from this screen include DNS , FTP, IMAP over SSL, Mail (SMTP), NFS4, OpenVPN, POP-3 over SSL, RADIUS, Samba, secure Web services (HTTPS), and standard Web service (HTTP). Selecting a service opens the common port(s) associated with that service, for the appropriate protocol, in your firewall, but does not configure the service itself.

> **NOTE:** If you need more information about what a particular service is used for, hover your mouse over the service name in this window that interests you for a further description.

- **Other Ports** — You can allow access to any other port numbers by adding them to the Other Ports box. Select Add and then select the protocol type (TCP or UDP) and port number pair you want to allow. About 1000 ports are available to select from. To enable different ports, select the User Defined box and type the port number and select the protocol you want to enable. Click OK when you are done.

- **Trusted Interfaces** — You can identify any of your network interfaces as being trusted. No incoming ports are blocked from requests from a trusted interface. You should never assign an external interface to a public network to be trusted. However, you might have a dedicated network connection or a connection to a small local LAN that you want to be trusted.

- **Masquerading** — By identifying an interface as a Masquerading interface, you can allow other computers on your LAN with private IP addresses to use your computer as a router to the Internet (or other network). This presumes that your Fedora system has another network interface with a route to the Internet. By selecting at least one network interface as providing IP Masquerading, packet forwarding support is automatically turned on. (See descriptions of Masquerading later in this chapter.)

- **Port Forwarding** — You indicate that traffic directed to a specific port on the local interface be redirected to either another local port or to a port on another computer. This is one way to allow a server behind the firewall to provide public Web, SSH, FTP or other service.

- **ICMP** — Allow or disallow Internet Control Message Protocol (ICMP) error messages to be sent between networked computers. For example, a `ping` request is often used to check if a computer on the network is up and running.

- **Custom Rules** — Creating custom rules can be a bit tricker than simply opening access for a port. You can create an iptables rule in a separate file (in iptables-save format as described later in this chapter) and assign that rule to a filter, NAT, or mangle iptables table. Click Add and indicate the address type (ipv4 or ipv6), type of table, and file containing the rule. Click OK to add the rule.

Before clicking Apply to save your settings, consider that doing so will overwrite your existing firewall rules. If you have done any hand editing of the configuration file (`/etc/sysconfig/iptables`), those changes will be overwritten. Make a backup copy of that file before continuing.

Configuring iptables to set up logging, port forwarding, network address translation, and other features can all be done manually, as described in the next sections.

Configuring an iptables firewall

The remaining sections on iptables in this chapter describe a more manual way of working with your iptables firewall in Linux. I also cover how to implement special iptables features that are not available from the Firewall Configuration window (such as port forwarding and NAT).

Turning on iptables

The iptables firewall feature (also referred to as netfilter) is the default firewall software when you install Fedora or RHEL.

This section describes how to turn on iptables and set up firewall rules for several different types of situations. It also tells how to turn on features related to firewalls that allow your iptables firewall to do Network Address Translation (NAT), IP masquerading, port forwarding, and transparent proxies.

> **NOTE:** The Fedora startup scripts will "punch a hole" through your firewall if you use certain services, and will therefore work even if they are not explicitly enabled in your iptables configuration. For example, NTP (which sets your system time from a network time server) and DNS resolution (which lets you contact a DNS server to resolve addresses) both open the ports they need in your firewall.

The following procedure describes how to get iptables going on your Fedora or RHEL system.

1. Set the iptables script to start automatically at boot time:

   ```
   # chkconfig iptables on
   ```

2. Before you can start iptables you must have a working set of rules that has been placed in your /etc/sysconfig/iptables file. To create those rules, refer to the examples in the following sections. (Without the configuration file in place, iptables fails silently.)

> **TIP:** If you are new to iptables, you can start with a workable set of default values by configuring your firewall during Fedora or RHEL installation. I recommend selecting to enable the firewall and enabling only those services you are ready to offer. The resulting /etc/sysconfig/iptables file will let you study how Fedora or RHEL creates its firewalls rules.

3. If you are doing NAT or IP Masquerading, turn on IP packet forwarding. One way to allow this is to change the value of net.ipv4.ip_forward to 1 in the /etc/sysctl.conf file. Open that file as root user with any text editor and change the line to appear as follows:

   ```
   net.ipv4.ip_forward = 1
   ```

4. Restart your network interfaces to have IP packet forwarding take effect.

   ```
   # /etc/init.d/network restart
   ```

5. Once the rules file is in place, start up iptables:

   ```
   # /etc/init.d/iptables start
   ```

6. At this point, iptables is installed as your firewall. You can check to see that the modules used by iptables are loaded by using the lsmod command. Here are some examples:

   ```
   # lsmod |less
   Module                   Size   Used by
   nf_conntrack_ftp        10656   0
   ipt_REJECT               6784   3
   nf_conntrack_ipv4       11396   6
   nf_conntrack            51264   4
       nf_conntrack_ftp,nf_conntrack_ipv4,xt_state
   ```

```
iptable_filter          6528  1
ip_tables              13840  1 iptable_filter
x_tables               15380  7
   xt_tcpudp,ipt_REJECT,xt_state,ip_tables
```

7. If you want to allow passive FTP or IRC connections from computers on your LAN, you may need to load those modules by adding them to the `/etc/modprobe.conf` file. The basic connection tracking module, ip_conntrack, should be loaded by default already. (See the description of passive FTP and IRC after the firewall-example sections.)

If there is an error in your `/etc/sysconfig/iptables` file, you can make a copy of that file, and then try to make a workable configuration by running `system-config-firewall` and setting up a basic firewall. You can then make changes to your firewall to add the features that you need.

TIP: As you add iptables rules, more modules will have to be loaded. Appropriate modules should be loaded automatically when a new rule is entered. Run `lsmod | grep ^ip` again after you have added a few rules to see which modules were added. Note that these modules will not be unloaded if you decide to stop iptables. They will stay loaded until the next reboot or until you remove them (`modprobe -r`).

The following sections contain examples of iptables firewall rules.

Creating iptables firewall rules

One way to configure iptables is to start by adding and deleting rules to your kernel from the command line. Then when you get a set of rules that you like, you save the rules that are currently running on your system. The tools you use to create your firewall rules and then make them permanent are as follows:

- **iptables** — Use this command to append (-A), delete (-D), replace (-R) or insert (-I) a rule. Use the -L option to list all current rules.

- **service iptables save** — Use this command to save the rules from the kernel and install them in the configuration file.

- **/etc/sysconfig/iptables** — This is the configuration file that contains the rules that were saved from the `service iptables save` command.

- **/etc/sysconfig/iptables-config** — You can add settings for managing your iptables rules to the `iptables-config` file. For example, any iptables modules, such as ip_conntrack and others described later in this chapter, can be added to the `IPTABLES_MODULES` line to be loaded automatically. You can also set whether the iptables table in your running kernel is saved to a file when iptables stops.

- **/etc/init.d/iptables** — This is the iptables start-up script that must run automatically each time Fedora reboots. When it starts, it clears all iptables rules and counters and installs the new rules from the /etc/sysconfig/iptables file. You can also use this script with different options from the command line to check the status of iptables (status) or to run iptables-save for you to save the current rules (save).

To get you started with iptables, I'm providing a sample set of iptables rules along with descriptions of how you might change those rules for different situations. Here's how you could load and save any of the sets of rules described in the following example:

1. Stop iptables and clear all existing rules:

```
# /etc/init.d/iptables stop
```

2. Add the rules shown in the following example to a file, using any text editor. Modify the rules to suit your situation and save the file.

3. As root user, run the file as a shell script. For example, if you named the file firescript, you could run it as follows:

```
# sh firescript
```

4. See how the rules were loaded into the kernel:

```
# iptables -L
```

5. If everything looks okay, save the rules that are now in the kernel into the /etc/sysconfig/iptables file:

```
# cp /etc/sysconfig/iptables /etc/sysconfig/iptables-old
# service iptables save
```

From now on, the rules will be read each time you reboot or restart iptables. Save a copy of the script you used to create the rules, in case you ever need it again.

Example 1: Firewall for shared Internet connection (plus servers)

Because firewall configurations can be vastly different depending on what you are trying to achieve, I've illustrated how to configure firewalls based on several different example setups. These setups combine different levels of security requirements.

This example features a home- or small-office LAN with a Fedora system acting as an iptables firewall between the LAN and the Internet. The firewall computer also acts as a Web server, FTP server, and DNS server. Figure 14-2 shows this configuration.

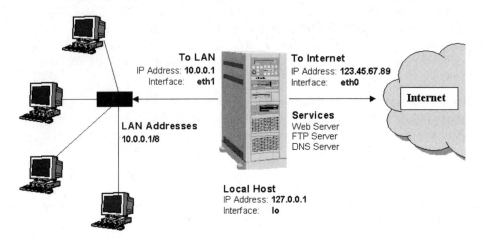

Figure 14-2: Using iptables as a firewall between the Internet and a LAN

If you want to use the sample firewall script that follows, you must change the following information to match your configuration:

Firewall computer — The firewall computer is set up as follows:

- **Local host** — 127.0.0.1 (IP address) and lo (interface). You shouldn't need to change these.

- **Connection to the Internet** — 123.45.67.89 (IP address) and eth0 (interface). Replace them with the static IP address and interface name associated with your connection to the Internet, respectively.

- **Connection to the LAN** — 10.0.0.1 (IP address) and eth1 (interface). Replace 10.0.0.1 and eth1 with the static IP address and interface name associated with your connection to your LAN, respectively.

- **Computers on the LAN** — Each computer on the LAN in the example has an IP address from 10.0.0.2 to 10.0.0.254. Change 10.0.0.255 to a number that matches your LAN's range of addresses.

Here is an example of a script to load firewall rules that could be used for the configuration shown in Figure 14-2:

```
# (1) Policies (default)
iptables -P INPUT DROP
iptables -P OUTPUT DROP
iptables -P FORWARD DROP

# (2) User-defined chain for ACCEPTed TCP packets
iptables -N okay
```

```
iptables -A okay -p TCP --syn -j ACCEPT
iptables -A okay -p TCP -m state --state ESTABLISHED,RELATED -j ACCEPT
iptables -A okay -p TCP -j DROP


# (3) INPUT chain rules

# Rules for incoming packets from LAN
iptables -A INPUT -p ALL -i eth1 -s 10.0.0.0/24 -j ACCEPT
iptables -A INPUT -p ALL -i lo -s 127.0.0.1 -j ACCEPT
iptables -A INPUT -p ALL -i lo -s 10.0.0.1 -j ACCEPT
iptables -A INPUT -p ALL -i lo -s 123.45.67.89 -j ACCEPT
iptables -A INPUT -p ALL -i eth1 -d 10.0.0.255 -j ACCEPT

# Rules for incoming packets from the Internet

# Packets for established connections
iptables -A INPUT -p ALL -d 123.45.67.89 -m state --state \
ESTABLISHED,RELATED -j ACCEPT

# TCP rules
iptables -A INPUT -p TCP -i eth0 --destination-port 21 -j okay
iptables -A INPUT -p TCP -i eth0 --destination-port 22 -j okay
iptables -A INPUT -p TCP -i eth0 --destination-port 80 -j okay
iptables -A INPUT -p TCP -i eth0 --destination-port 113 -j okay

# UDP rules
iptables -A INPUT -p UDP -i eth0 --destination-port 53 -j ACCEPT
iptables -A INPUT -p UDP -i eth0 --destination-port 2074 -j ACCEPT
iptables -A INPUT -p UDP -i eth0 --destination-port 4000 -j ACCEPT

# ICMP rules
iptables -A INPUT -p ICMP -i eth0 --icmp-type 8 -j ACCEPT
iptables -A INPUT -p ICMP -i eth0 --icmp-type 11 -j ACCEPT

# (4) FORWARD chain rules
# Accept the packets we want to forward
iptables -A FORWARD -i eth1 -j ACCEPT
iptables -A FORWARD -m state --state ESTABLISHED,RELATED -j ACCEPT

# (5) OUTPUT chain rules
# Only output packets with local addresses (no spoofing)
iptables -A OUTPUT -p ALL -s 127.0.0.1 -j ACCEPT
iptables -A OUTPUT -p ALL -s 10.0.0.1 -j ACCEPT
iptables -A OUTPUT -p ALL -s 123.45.67.89 -j ACCEPT

# (6) POSTROUTING chain rules
iptables -t nat -A POSTROUTING -o eth0 -j SNAT --to-source 123.45.67.89
```

I divided the commands in the preceding script into six sections. The following text describes each of those sections.

(1) Policies — The `iptables -P` commands set the default policies for INPUT, OUTPUT, and FORWARD chains. By assigning each of those policies to DROP, any packet that isn't matched is discarded. In other words, for a packet to get through, it has to be specifically matched and ACCEPTed by one of the other rules in the script.

(2) User-defined chain — A user-defined chain I call okay is created to do a few more checks on packets requesting certain TCP services that I'm going to allow through (Web, FTP, and DNS services). The `-N okay` option creates the okay chain. The next line says that a SYN packet (`--syn`), which requests a new connection, is fine to let through. The next line allows through packets associated with an ESTABLISHED connection (one that has already had traffic pass through the interface) or a RELATED connection (one that is starting a new connection related to an already established connection). The final line in this set tells iptables to DROP packets that don't meet one of those checks.

(3) INPUT chain rules — The bulk of the packet filtering is done in the INPUT chain. The first set of input rules indicates to iptables when to always accept packets from the Internet and from the LAN. The next three sets determine which requests for specific protocols (TCP, UDP, and ICMP) are accepted:

- **Packets from LAN** — Because you want the users on your LAN and the firewall computer itself to be able to use the Internet, this set of rules lets through packets that are initiated from those computers. The first line tells iptables to accept packets for ALL protocols for which the source is an acceptable address on your LAN (`-s 10.0.0.0/24`, which represents IP numbers `10.0.0.1` through `10.0.0.254`). The next three lines allow packets that come from all valid IP addresses on the firewall computer itself (`-s 127.0.0.1`, `10.0.0.1` and `123.45.67.89`). The last line accepts broadcast packets (`-d 10.0.0.255`) on the LAN.

- **Packets from Internet (already connected)** — This line is split in two (I just used the backslash to join the lines because the page wasn't wide enough to show it as one line). It ACCEPTs packets that are both associated with connections that are already established (`--state ESTABLISHED,RELATED`) and are requested directly to the firewall's IP address (`123.45.67.89`).

- **TCP rules (new connections)** — Here is where you open up the ports for the TCP services you want to provide to anyone from the Internet. In these lines you open ports for FTP service (`--destination-port 21`), secure shell service (22), Web service (80), and IDENTD authentication (113), the last of which might be necessary for protocols such as IRC. Instead of accepting these requests immediately, you jump to the okay chain you defined to further check that the packets were formed properly.

> **CAUTION:** You want to ensure that the services on the ports to which you are allowing access are properly configured before you allow packets to be accepted to them.

- **UDP rules (new connections)** — These lines define the ports where connection packets are accepted from the Internet for UDP services. In this example I chose to accept requests for DNS service (`--destination-port 53`) because the computer is set up as a DNS server. The example also illustrates lines that accept requests for a couple of other optional ports. Port 2074 is needed by some multimedia applications the users on your LAN might want to use, and port 4000 is used by the ICQ protocol (for online chats).

- **ICMP rules** — ICMP messages are really more for reporting conditions of the server than for actually providing services. Packets from the Internet that are accepted for ICMP protocol requests in our example are those for ICMP types 8 and 11. Type 8 service, which allows your computer to accept *echo request messages*, makes it possible for people to ping your computer to see if it is available. Type 11 service relates to packets whose *time to live* (TTL) was exceeded in transit, and for which you are accepting a Time Exceeded message that is being returned to you. (You need to accept type 11 messages to use the `traceroute` command to find broken routes to hosts you want to reach.)

(4) FORWARD chain rules — Because this firewall is also acting as a router, `FORWARD` rules are needed to limit what the firewall will and will not pass between the two networks (Internet and local LAN). The first line forwards everything from the local LAN (`-A FORWARD -i eth1`). The second line forwards anything from the Internet that is associated with an established connection (`--state ESTABLISHED,RELATED`).

(5) OUTPUT chain rules — These rules basically exist to prevent anyone from your local computer from *spoofing* IP addresses (that is, from saying packets are coming from somewhere that they are not). According to these three rules, each packet output from your firewall must have as its source address one of the addresses from the firewall computer's interfaces (`127.0.0.1`, `10.0.0.1`, or `123.45.67.89`).

(6) POSTROUTING chain rules — The `POSTROUTING` chain defines rules for packets that have been accepted, but need additional processing. This is where the actual network-address translation (NAT) work takes place. For the NAT table (`-t nat`), in the `POSTROUTING` chain, all packets that go out to the Internet have their addresses translated to that of the firewall's external interface (`--to-source 123.45.67.89`). In this case I used the Source Network Address Translation (`SNAT`) chain because I have a static IP address (`123.45.67.89`) associated with my Internet connection. If I were using a dynamic IP address (via DHCP), I would use `MASQUERADE` instead of `SNAT`. I would also have to change any references to `-d 123.45.67.89` to `-i eth0`. (Of course, you would be using a different IP address and possibly a different Ethernet interface.)

Example 2: Firewall for shared Internet connection (no servers)

In this scenario, the firewall is protecting a Linux system (firewall) and several systems on the LAN that only are used to connect to the Internet. No servers are behind this firewall, so you want to prevent people from the Internet from requesting services.

You could use the same script shown in Example 1, but not use lines that request TCP services. So you could drop the user-defined chain in section 2 and drop the TCP rules from section 3. You could also remove the ICMP rules, if you don't want your firewall to be visible to ping requests (Type 8) and if you don't care about receiving messages when your packets exceed their time-to-live values (Type 11), such as when a packet runs into a broken router.

Example 3: Firewall for single Linux system with Internet connection

In this example, there is one network interface, connecting your Fedora system to the Internet. You are not sharing that connection with other computers and you are not offering any services from your computer.

In this case, you could cut sections 2, 4, and 6. From section 3, you could cut all rules relating to incoming requests from the LAN and all TCP services. As I mentioned in Example 2, you could also remove the Type 8 ICMP rule to make your firewall invisible to ping requests from the Internet and the Type 11 ICMP rule to not accept messages about failed time-to-live packets.

Understanding iptables

Now that you've seen something about what iptables rules look like and how you can get them going, step back a bit and see how iptables works.

The iptables feature works by having IP packets (that is, network data) that enter or leave the firewall computer, traverse a set of chains that define what is done with the packet. Each rule that you add essentially does both of the following:

- Checks whether a particular criterion is met (such as that a packet requests a particular service or comes from a particular address)

- Takes an action (such as dropping, accepting, or further processing a packet)

Different sets of rules are implemented for different types of tables. For example, tables exist for filtering (`filter`), network address translation (`nat`), and changing packet headers (`mangle`). Depending on the packet's source and destination, it traverses different chains. Most of the rules you create will relate to the `filter` table (which is implied if no other table is given).

The chains associated with the filter table are INPUT, OUTPUT, and FORWARD. You can add user-defined chains as well. You will probably be most interested in adding or removing particular TCP and UDP services using the basic rules shown in the previous example. Assign ACCEPT to packets you want to go through and DROP to those you want to discard. You can also assign REJECT to drop a packet but return a message to the sender, or LOG to neither drop nor accept the message, but to log information about the packet.

A lot of great features are built into iptables. The following descriptions tell you about some cool things you can do with iptables and give you some tips on using it.

Allowing FTP and IRC services through an iptables firewall

With passive FTP, the FTP client sends its IP address and the port number on which it will listen for data to the server. If that client is on a computer that is behind your firewall, for which you are doing NAT, that information must be translated as well or the FTP server will not be able to communicate with the client.

iptables uses connection-tracking modules to track connections. Using this feature, it can look inside the data area of each FTP packet (that is, not in the IP packet header), to get the information it needs to do NAT (remember that computers from the Internet can't talk directly to your private IP addresses). To do FTP connection tracking (to allow passive FTP connections to the clients on your LAN), you need to have the following modules loaded:

- `nf_ip_conntrack`
- `nf_ip_conntrack_ftp`
- `nf_ip_nat_ftp`

The same is true for chats and DCC sends, used to establish and monitor direct connections to IRC chat sessions. Addresses and port numbers are stored within the IRC protocol packets, so those packets must be translated, too. To allow clients on your LAN to use IRC services, you need to load the following modules:

- `nf_ip_conntrack_irc`
- `nf_ip_nat_irc`

The default port for IRC connections is 6667. If you don't want to use the default you can add different port numbers when you load the connection-tracking modules:

```
modprobe nf_ip_conntrack_irc ports=6668,6669
```

Using iptables to do SNAT or IP Masquerading

As noted in the iptables example, you can use Source Network Address Translation (SNAT) or IP Masquerading (MASQUERADE) to allow computers on your LAN with private IP addresses to access the Internet through your iptables firewall. Choose SNAT if you have a static IP address for your Internet connection and MASQUERADE if the IP address is assigned dynamically.

When you create the MASQUERADE or SNAT rule, it is added to the NAT table and the POSTROUTING chain. For MASQUERADE you must provide the name of the interface (such as eth0, ppp0, or slip0) to identify the route to the Internet or other outside network. For SNAT you must also identify the actual IP address of the interface. Here is an example of a MASQUERADE rule:

```
# iptables -t nat -A POSTROUTING -o eth0 -j MASQUERADE
```

Here is an example of a SNAT rule:

```
# iptables -t nat -A POSTROUTING -o eth0 -j SNAT --to-source 12.12.12.12
```

You can add several source addresses if you have multiple addresses that provide a route to the Internet (for example, `--to-source 12.12.12.12.1-12.12.12.12.254`). Although `MASQUERADE` uses some additional overhead, you probably need to use it instead of `SNAT` if you have a dial-up or other Internet connection for which the IP address changes on each connection.

Remember that you need to make sure that IP forwarding is turned on in the kernel. (It is off by default.) To turn it on permanently, edit the `/etc/sysctl.conf` file as described earlier. To turn it on temporarily, you can do the following:

```
# echo 1 > /proc/sys/net/ipv4/ip_forward
```

If you require dynamic IP addressing (in common cases where you don't know the IP address when you first establish the connection to the Internet through a dial-up, DSL, or cable modem connection), turn on that service:

```
# echo 1 > /proc/sys/net/ipv4/ip_dynaddr
```

Using iptables as a transparent proxy

With the `REDIRECT` target you can cause traffic for a specific port on the firewall computer to be directed to a different one. Using this feature you can direct host computers on your local LAN to a proxy service on your firewall computer without those hosts knowing it.

The following is an example of a set of command-line options to the `iptables` command that causes a request for Web service (port 80) to be directed to a proxy service (port 3128):

```
-t nat -A PREROUTING -p tcp --dport 80 -j REDIRECT --to-ports 3128
```

You can use `REDIRECT` targets in `PREROUTING` and `OUTPUT` chains only within a `nat` table. You can also give a range of port numbers to spread the redirection across multiple port numbers.

Using iptables to do port forwarding

What if you have only one static IP address, but you want to use a computer other than your firewall computer to provide Web, FTP, DNS, or some other service? You can use the Destination Network Address Translation (DNAT) feature to direct traffic for a particular port on your firewall to another computer.

For example, if you want all requests for Web service (port 80) that are directed to the firewall computer (`-d 15.15.15.15`) to be directed to another computer on your LAN (such as `10.0.0.25`), you can use the following `iptables` command:

```
# iptables -t nat -A PREROUTING -p tcp -d 15.15.15.15 --dport 80 \
        -j DNAT --to-destination 10.0.0.25
```

(Note that the preceding example should actually appear on one line. The backslash indicates continuation on the next line.)

You can also spread the load for the service you are forwarding by providing a range of IP addresses (for example, `--to-destination 10.0.0.1-10.0.0.25`). Likewise, you can direct the request to a range of ports as well.

Using logging with iptables

Using the `LOG` target you can log information about packets that meet the criteria you choose. In particular you might want to use this feature to log packets that seem like they might be improper in some way. In other words, if you don't want to drop a packet for some reason, you can just log its activity and decide later if something needs to be corrected.

The `LOG` target directs log information to the standard tools used to do logging in Fedora: `dmesg` and `syslogd`. Here's an example of a rule using a `LOG` target:

```
-A FORWARD -p tcp -j LOG --log-level info
```

Instead of `info`, you could use any of the following log levels available with `syslog`: `emerg`, `alert`, `crit`, `err`, `warning`, `notice`, `info`, or `debug`. Using the `--log-prefix` option as follows, you could also add information to the front of all messages produced from this logging action:

```
-A FORWARD -p tcp -j LOG --log-level info --log-prefix "Forward INFO "
```

Enhancing your iptables firewall

You can modify or expand on the iptables examples given in this chapter in many ways. iptables is tremendously flexible.

When you actually create your own iptables firewall, you should refer to the iptables man page (type **man iptables**) for detailed descriptions of options, ways of matching, ways of entering addresses, and other details. I also recommend an excellent iptables Tutorial by Oskar Andreasson (`http://iptables-tutorial.frozentux.net`).

Here are a few tips for using iptables features:

- **Reduce rules** — Try to improve performance by reducing the number of rules. Using subchains can keep a packet from seeing rules that don't apply to it.
- **Deal with fragments** — Use the `-f` option to refer to the second and subsequent packets of a packet that was split into fragments. In general, it is safe to not drop second and third fragments for which you don't have a first packet fragment because they won't be reassembled. If you use NAT, the fragments are assembled before filtering, so you shouldn't have problems with unfiltered fragments being sent through.
- **Opposite** — To make a rule its opposite, use an exclamation mark (!).
- **All interfaces** — To match all interfaces of a type, use a plus sign (+), as in `eth+`.
- **Blocking connections** — Use the `--syn` option to block SYN packets (that is, those packets requesting connections). This option applies only to TCP packets.

- **Limiting** — Use the `--limit` option to restrict the rate of matches that result in log messages. This option allows matches to produce messages only a limited number of times per second (the default is three per hour with bursts of five).

- **Denial of Service (DOS) Attacks** — You can use the `--limit` option to reduce the impact of DOS attacks, but it still won't stop them altogether. As long as the traffic is directed at your server, your network bandwidth is being leeched away, and the machine still utilizes resources to ignore the data.

- **Table types** — The default table type is `filter`. The other types of tables are `nat` (for IP Masquerading) and `mangle` (for altering packets). To use a table other than `filter` you must add a `-t table_type` option, where `table_type` is either `nat` or `mangle`.

Controlling Access to Services with TCP Wrappers

Completely disabling an unused service is fine, but what about the services that you really need? How can you selectively grant and deny access to these services? In previous versions of Red Hat Linux, the TCP wrapper daemon (`tcpd`) was used to facilitate this sort of selective access. In the current version of Fedora, TCP wrapper support has been integrated into `xinetd`. `xinetd` will look at the files `/etc/hosts.allow` and `/etc/hosts.deny` to determine when a particular connection should be granted or refused for services such as rlogin, rsh, telnet, finger, and talk. TCP wrappers are also enabled by default for other services, such as a vsftpd FTP server (with `tcp_wrappers=YES` in your `vsftpd.conf` file).

When a service is requested that relies on TCP wrappers, the `hosts.allow` and `hosts.deny` files are scanned and checked for an entry that matches the IP address of the connecting machine. These checks are made when connection attempts occur:

- If the address is listed in the `hosts.allow` file, the connection is allowed and `hosts.deny` is not checked.

- If the address is in `hosts.deny` (but not the `hosts.allow` file), the connection is denied.

- If the address is in neither file, the connection is allowed.

It is not necessary (or even possible) to list every single address that may connect to your computer. The `hosts.allow` and `hosts.deny` files enable you to specify entire subnets and groups of addresses. You can even use the keyword `ALL` to specify all possible addresses. You can also restrict specific entries in these files so they apply only to specific network services. Look at an example of a typical pair of `hosts.allow` and `hosts.deny` files. Here's the `/etc/hosts.allow` file:

```
#
# hosts.allow    This file describes the names of the hosts which are
#                allowed to use the local INET services, as decided
#                by the '/usr/sbin/tcpd' server.
```

```
#

cups-lpd: 199.170.177.
in.telnetd: 199.170.177., .linuxtoys.net
vsftpd: ALL
```

Here's the /etc/hosts.deny file:

```
#
# hosts.deny    This file describes the names of the hosts which are
#               *not* allowed to use the local INET services, as
#               decided by the '/usr/sbin/tcpd' server.
#

ALL: ALL
```

The preceding example is a rather restrictive configuration. It allows connections to the cups-lpd and telnet services from certain hosts, but then denies all other connections. It also allows connections to the FTP service (vsftp) to all hosts. Let's examine the files in detail.

As usual, lines beginning with a # character are comments and are ignored by xinetd when it parses the file. Each noncomment line consists of a comma-separated list of daemons followed by a colon (:) character and then a comma-separated list of client addresses to check. In this context, a client is any computer that attempts to access a network service on your system.

A client entry can be a numeric IP address (such as 199.170.177.25) or a hostname (such as jukebox.linuxtoys.net), but is more often a wildcard variation that specifies an entire range of addresses. A client entry can take four different forms. The online manual page for the hosts.allow file describes them as follows:

- **A string that begins with a dot (.) character.** A hostname is matched if the last components of its name match the specified pattern. For example, the pattern .tue.nl matches the hostname wzv.win.tue.nl.

- **A string that ends with a dot (.) character.** A host address is matched if its first numeric fields match the given string. For example, the pattern 131.155. matches the address of (almost) every host on the Eindhoven University network (131.155.x.x).

- **A string that begins with an at (@) sign is treated as an NIS netgroup name.** A hostname is matched if it is a host member of the specified netgroup. Netgroup matches are not supported for daemon process names or for client user names.

- **An expression of the form *n.n.n.n/m.m.m.m* is interpreted as a *net/mask* pair.** A host address is matched if *net* is equal to the bitwise *and* of the address and the mask. For example, the net/mask pattern 131.155.72.0/255.255.254.0 matches every address in the range 131.155.72.0 through 131.155.73.255.

The example host.allow contains the first two types of client specification. The entry 199.170.177. will match any IP address that begins with that string, such as

199.170.177.25. The client entry .linuxtoys.net will match hostnames such as jukebox.linuxtoys.net or picframe.linuxtoys.net.

Let's examine what happens when a host named jukebox.linuxtoys.net (with IP address 199.170.179.18) connects to your Fedora system using the Telnet protocol:

1. xinetd receives the connection request.

2. xinetd begins comparing the address and name of jukebox.linuxtoys.net to the rules listed in /etc/hosts.allow. It starts at the top of the file and works its way down the file until finding a match. Both the daemon (the program handling the network service on your Fedora box) and the connecting client's IP address or name must match the information in the hosts.allow file. In this case, the second rule that is encountered matches the request:

    ```
    in.telnetd: 199.170.177., .linuxtoys.net
    ```

3. Jukebox is not in the 199.170.177 subnet, but it is in the linuxtoys.net domain. xinetd stops searching the file as soon as it finds this match.

How about if Jukebox connects to your box using the CUPS-lpd protocol? In this case, it matches none of the rules in hosts.allow; the only line that refers to the lpd daemon does not refer to the 199.170.179 subnet or to the linuxtoys.net domain. xinetd continues on to the hosts.deny file. The entry ALL: ALL matches anything, so tcpd denies the connection.

The ALL wildcard was also used in the hosts.allow file. In this case, we are telling xinetd to permit absolutely any host to connect to the FTP service on the Linux box. This is appropriate for running an anonymous FTP server that anyone on the Internet can access. If you are not running an anonymous FTP site, you probably should not use the ALL flag.

A good rule of thumb is to make your hosts.allow and hosts.deny files as restrictive as possible and then explicitly enable only those services that you really need. Also, grant access only to those systems that really need access. Using the ALL flag to grant universal access to a particular service may be easier than typing in a long list of subnets or domains, but better a few minutes spent on proper security measures than many hours recovering from a break-in.

> **TIP:** You can further restrict access to services using various options within the /etc/xinetd.conf file, even to the point of limiting access to certain services to specific times of the day. Read the manual page for xinetd (by typing **man xinetd** at a command prompt) to learn more about these options.

Checking Log Files

Preparing your system for a cracker attack is only part of the battle. You must also recognize a cracker attack when it is occurring. Understanding the various log files in which Fedora and RHEL record important events is critical to this goal. The log files for your Fedora or RHEL system can be found in the /var/log directory.

Because the system logs are plain text files, you can view the contents of logs directly using any text editor or paging command (such as `less` or `more`). The logwatch facility (which comes with Fedora and RHEL) sends daily highlights from your log files in an e-mail message to the root user. You can also add packages, such as logsentry, to monitor your log files. (A description of logsentry is contained on the Wiley Web site for this book at `www.wiley.com/go/fedora9bible`.)

Understanding the syslogd service

Most of the files in the `/var/log` directory are maintained by the `syslogd` service. The `syslogd` daemon is the System Logging Daemon. It accepts log messages from a variety of other programs and writes them to the appropriate log files. This is better than having every program write directly to its own log file because it allows you to centrally manage how log files are handled. It is possible to configure `syslogd` to record varying levels of detail in the log files. It can be told to ignore all but the most critical message, or it can record every detail.

The `syslogd` daemon can even accept messages from other computers on your network. This is particularly handy because it enables you to centralize the management and reviewing of the log files from many systems on your network. There is also a major security benefit to this practice. If a system on your network is broken into, the cracker cannot delete or modify the log files because those files are stored on a separate computer.

It is important to remember, however, that those log messages are not, by default, encrypted. Anyone tapping into your local network will be able to eavesdrop on those messages as they pass from one machine to another. Also, although the cracker may not be able to change old log messages, he will be able to affect the system such that any new log messages should not be trusted.

It is not uncommon to run a dedicated loghost, a computer that serves no other purpose than to record log messages from other computers on the network. Because this system runs no other services, it is less likely that it will be broken into. This makes it nearly impossible for a cracker to erase his or her tracks. It does not, however, mean that all of the log messages are accurate after a cracker has broken into a machine on your network.

Redirecting logs to a loghost with syslogd

To redirect your computer's log files to another computer's syslogd, you must make some changes to your local syslogd's configuration file. The file that you need to work with is `/etc/syslog.conf`. If you are not already root, become root and then open the `/etc/syslog.conf` file in a text editor (such as `vi`). You should see something similar to this:

```
# Log all kernel messages to the console.
# Logging much else clutters up the screen.
#kern.*                                    /dev/console
```

```
# Log anything (except mail) of level info or higher.
# Don't log private authentication messages!
*.info;mail.none;news.none;authpriv.none;cron.none   /var/log/messages

# The authpriv file has restricted access.
authpriv.*                              /var/log/secure

# Log all the mail messages in one place.
mail.*                                  -/var/log/maillog

# Log cron stuff
cron.*                                  /var/log/cron

# Everybody gets emergency messages
*.emerg                                      *

# Save news errors of level crit and higher in a special file.
uucp,news.crit                          /var/log/spooler

# Save boot messages also to boot.log
local7.*                                /var/log/boot.log

#
# INN
#
news.=crit                              /var/log/news/news.crit
news.=err                               /var/log/news/news.err
news.notice                             /var/log/news/news.notice
```

The lines beginning with a # character are comments. Other lines contain two columns of information, separated by spaces or tabs. The left field is a semicolon-separated list of message types and message priorities. The right field is the log file to which those messages should be written.

> **NOTE:** Notice the dash (-) before the `/var/log/maillog` file. Normally, each log file is synced after every logging. A dash preceding the full path to the log file indicates that the file is not synced after each logging. While this might result in lost information if your machine crashes before the log is written, it can result in better performance on your system if you run verbose logging.

To send the messages to another computer (the loghost) instead of a file, simply replace the log filename with the @ character followed by the name of the loghost. For example, to redirect the output normally sent to the `messages`, `secure`, and `maillog` log files, make these changes to the previous file:

```
# Log anything (except mail) of level info or higher.
# Don't log private authentication messages!
*.info;mail.none;news.none;authpriv.none;cron.none   @loghost
```

```
# The authpriv file has restricted access.
authpriv.*                              @loghost

# Log all the mail messages in one place.
mail.*                                  @loghost
```

The messages will now be sent to the `syslogd` running on the computer named loghost. The name loghost was not an arbitrary choice. It is customary to create such a hostname and make it an alias to the actual system acting as the loghost. That way, if you ever need to switch the loghost duties to a different machine, you need to change only the loghost alias; you do not need to re-edit the `syslog.conf` file on every computer.

Understanding the messages logfile

Because of the many programs and services that record information to the messages log file, it is important that you understand the format of this file. Examining this file often gives you a good early warning of problems developing on your system. Each line in the file is a single message recorded by some program or service. Here is a snippet of an actual messages log file:

```
Feb 25 11:04:32 toys network: Bringing up loopback interface:    succeeded
Feb 25 11:04:35 toys network: Bringing up interface eth0:    succeeded
Feb 25 13:01:14 toys vsftpd(pam_unix)[10565]: authentication failure;
     logname= uid=0 euid=0 tty= ruser= rhost=10.0.0.5  user=chris
Feb 25 14:44:24 toys su(pam_unix)[11439]: session opened for
     user root by chris(uid=500)
```

This is really very simple when you know what to look for. Each message is divided into five main parts. From left to right they are:

- The date and time that the message was logged
- The name of the computer that the message came from
- The program or service name that the message pertains to
- The process number (enclosed in square brackets) of the program sending the message
- The actual text message itself

Let's examine the previous file snippet. In the first two lines, you can see that I restarted the network. The next line shows that I tried to log in as the user named chris to get to the FTP server on this system from a computer at address `10.0.0.5` (I typed the wrong password and authentication failed). The last line shows that I used the `su` command to become root user.

By occasionally reviewing the messages file and the secure file, it is possible to catch a cracking attempt before it is successful. If you see an excessive number of connection attempts for a particular service, especially if they are coming from systems on the Internet, you may be under attack.

Tracking log messages with logwatch

Another way to keep up with the contents of your log files is with the logwatch facility. Logwatch flags messages that might reflect a problem with your system and forwards them each day in an e-mail message to your system's root user. When you install Fedora or RHEL, the logwatch package is installed and configured to watch your log files and report suspicious activities to your system administrator. Based on the logwatch cron file (/etc/cron.daily/0logwatch), the logwatch facility will:

- Run each morning at 4:00 a.m.

- Choose which log files to scan and where to send the e-mail message, based on the configuration file /etc/logwatch/conf/logwatch.conf. (The defaults are listed in /usr/share/logwatch/default.conf.)

- Send an e-mail message to the local computer's root user that reports potentially suspicious activity on your system, based on the contents of your log files.

- Report on administrative activities that could reflect a problem with the system.

The kind of information logwatch reports on includes users and groups that have been deleted, packages installed or uninstalled, and disk space consumed. The daily messages also show login activity through ssh over the network and file transfer activities. Failure messages are flagged and reported for each log file scanned.

Review the /usr/share/logwatch/default.conf/logwatch.conf file to see the options you have for configuring your logwatch service. To change any options, you can add them to the /etc/logwatch/conf/logwatch.conf file. Here are examples of some logwatch settings:

```
LogDir = /var/log
TmpDir = /var/cache/logwatch
MailTo = root
MailFrom = Logwatch
Print = No
Service = "-zz-network"      # Prevents execution of zz-network service, which
                             # prints useful network configuration info.
Service = "-zz-sys"          # Prevents execution of zz-sys service, which
                             # prints useful system configuration info.
Service = "-eximstats"       # Prevents execution of eximstats service, which
                             # is a wrapper for the eximstats program.
Range = yesterday
Detail = Low
Service = All
mailer = "sendmail -t"
```

LogDir sets the log file directory as /var/log (so any log files listed are shown as relative to that directory). The /var/cache/logwatch directory is used to hold temporary files. The daily e-mail report is sent to the root user on the local system (you can change MailTo to any valid e-mail address), with the sender (MailFrom) listed as Logwatch. You can change the Print value to Yes to have the report sent to standard output, instead of being mailed to the MailTo recipient. The Range is set to yesterday, which causes logwatch to search log files for the past day only. You can change the Range to All to search all past files available for a particular log file, as in messages, messages.1, messages.2, and so on. To increase the amount of detail (which is set to Low by default), you can identify Detail as Medium or High (or a number from 0 to 10). The mail application used to send the report is /bin/mail.

Most of the action that takes place by logwatch is based on the value of the Service entry. With Service set to All, all files in the /usr/share/logwatch/conf/services directory are used to produce the logwatch report. Files in this directory are each related to a service that is checked by logwatch and defines the type of information that is gathered for that service. Precede any service name that you want to disable with a dash (-). (By default, zz-network, zz-sys, and eximstats are disabled.)

Using the Secure Shell Package

The Secure Shell package (SSH) provides shell services similar to other remote execution, remote copy, and remote login commands (such as the old UNIX rsh, rcp, and rlogin commands), but encrypts the network traffic. It uses private-key cryptography, so it is ideal for use with Internet-connected computers. The Fedora and RHEL distributions contain the following client and server software packages for SSH: openssh, openssh-clients, and openssh-server packages.

Starting the SSH service

If you have installed the openssh-server software package, the SSH server is automatically configured to start. The SSH daemon is started from the /etc/init.d/sshd start-up script. To make sure the service is set up to start automatically, type the following (as root user):

```
# chkconfig --list sshd
sshd       0:off   1:off   2:on    3:on    4:on    5:on    6:off
```

This shows that the sshd service is set to run in system states 2, 3, 4, and 5 (normal boot-up states) and set to be off in all other states. You can turn on the SSH service, if it is off, for your default run state, by typing the following as root user:

```
# chkconfig sshd on
```

This line turns on the SSH service when you enter run levels 2, 3, 4, or 5. To start the service immediately, type the following:

```
# /etc/init.d/sshd start
```

TIP: If you aren't able to connect to the sshd service from another computer, check that the firewall is open on your server to allow access to tcp port 22. That's the default port on which sshd listens for requests.

Using the ssh, sftp, and scp commands

Three commands you can use with the SSH service are ssh, sftp, and scp. Remote users use the ssh command to log in to your system securely. The scp command lets remote users copy files to and from a system. The sftp command provides a safe way to access FTP sites.

Like the normal remote shell services, secure shell looks in the /etc/hosts.equiv file and in a user's .rhost file to determine whether it should allow a connection. It also looks in the ssh-specific files /etc/shosts.equiv and .shosts. Using the shosts.equiv and the .shosts files is preferable because it avoids granting access to the nonencrypted remote shell services. The /etc/shosts.equiv and .shosts files are functionally equivalent to the traditional hosts.equiv and .rhosts files, so the same instructions and rules apply. (Type man hosts.equiv for further information.)

Now you are ready to test the SSH service. From another computer on which SSH has been installed (or even from the same computer if another is not available), type the ssh command followed by a space and the name of the system you are connecting to. For example, to connect to the system ratbert.glaci.com, type:

```
$ ssh ratbert.glaci.com
```

If this is the first time ever you have logged in to that system using the ssh command, it will ask you to confirm that you really want to connect. Type **yes** and press Enter when it asks this:

```
The authenticity of host 'ratbert.glaci.com (199.170.177.18)' can't be
established.
RSA key fingerprint is xx:xx:xx:xx:xx:xx:xx:xx:xx:xx:xx:xx:xx:xx:xx:xx.
Are you sure you want to continue connecting (yes/no)? yes
```

If you don't specify a user name when you start the ssh connection, the SSH daemon assumes you want to use the user name you are logged in as from the client. If you want to log in as a different user name (such as chris, for example), you could type the following:

```
$ ssh chris@ratbert.glaci.com
```

or

```
$ ssh -l chris ratbert.glaci.com
```

Once you are logged in, a shell prompt appears and you can begin using the remote system as you would from a local shell.

The scp command is similar to the rcp command for copying files to and from Linux systems. Here is an example of using the scp command to copy a file called memo from the home directory of the user named jake to the /tmp directory on a computer called maple:

```
$ scp /home/jake/memo maple:/tmp
jake@maple's password: ********
memo            100%|****************|   153     0:00
```

Enter the password for your user name (if a password is requested). If the password is accepted, the remote system indicates that the file has been copied successfully.

Similarly, the `sftp` command starts an interactive FTP session with an FTP server that supports SSH connections. Many security-conscious people prefer `sftp` to other `ftp` clients because it provides a secure connection between you and the remote host. Here's an example:

```
$ sftp ftp.handsonhistory.com
Connecting to ftp.handsonhistory.com
jake@ftp.handsonhistory.com's password: ********
sftp>
```

At this point you can begin an interactive FTP session. You can use `get` and `put` commands on files as you would using any FTP client, but with the comfort of knowing that you are working on a secure connection.

> **TIP:** The `sftp` command, as with `ssh` and `scp`, requires that the SSH service be running on the server. If you can't connect to an FTP server using `sftp`, the SSH service may not be available.

Using ssh, scp, and sftp without passwords

For machines that you use a great deal, it is often helpful to set them up so that you do not have to use a password to log in. The following procedure shows you how to do that.

These steps will take you through setting up password-less authentication from one machine to another. In this example, the local user is named chester on a computer named host1. The remote user is also chester on a computer named host2.

1. Log in to the local computer (in this example, I log in as chester to host1).

> **NOTE:** Run Step 2 only once as local user on your local workstation. Do not run it again unless you lose your ssh keys. When configuring subsequent remote servers, skip right to Step 4.

2. Type the following to generate the ssh key:

```
$ ssh-keygen -t dsa
Generating public/private dsa key pair.
Enter file in which to save the key
(/home/chester/.ssh/id_dsa): <Enter>
Enter passphrase (empty for no passphrase): <Enter>
Enter same passphrase again: <Enter>
Your identification has been saved in /home/chester/.ssh/id_dsa.
Your public key has been saved in /home/chester/.ssh/id_dsa.pub.
The key fingerprint is:
3b:c0:2f:63:a5:65:70:b7:4b:f0:2a:c4:18:24:47:69 chester@host1
```

3. Accept the default key file location by pressing Enter. Then press Enter again (twice) to assign a blank passphrase. (If you enter a passphrase, you will be prompted for that passphrase and won't be able to log in without it.)

4. You must secure the permissions of your authentication keys by closing permissions to your home directory, .ssh directory, and authentication files as follows:

```
$ chmod go-w $HOME
$ chmod 700 $HOME/.ssh
$ chmod go-rwx $HOME/.ssh/*
```

5. Type the following to copy the key to the remote server (replace `chester` with the remote user name and `host2` with the remote hostname):

```
$ cd ~/.ssh
$ scp id_dsa.pub chester@host2:/tmp
chester@host2's password: *******
```

6. Type the following to add the ssh key to the remote user's authorization keys (the code should be on one line, not wrapped):

```
$ ssh chester@host2 'cat /tmp/id_dsa.pub >>
/home/chester/.ssh/authorized_keys2'
```

> **NOTE:** The previous two steps will ask for passwords. This is okay.

7. In order for the sshd daemon to accept the `authorized_keys2` file you created, your home directories and authentication files must have secure permissions. To secure those files and directories, type the following (note that the double quotes are needed to prevent the * from being interpreted by the local shell):

```
$ ssh chester@host2 chmod go-w $HOME
$ ssh chester@host2 chmod 700 $HOME/.ssh
$ ssh chester@host2 "chmod go-rwx $HOME/.ssh/*"
```

8. Type the following to remove the key from the temporary directory:

```
$ ssh chester@host2 rm /tmp/id_dsa.pub
```

It is important to note that once you have this working, it will work regardless of how many times the IP address changes on your local computer. IP address has nothing to do with this form of authentication.

Securing Linux Servers

Opening up your Fedora or RHEL system as a server on a public network creates a whole new set of challenges when it comes to security. Instead of just turning away nearly all incoming requests, your computer will be expected to respond to requests for supported services (such as Web, FTP, or mail service) by supplying information or possibly running scripts that take in data.

Entire books have been filled with information on how to go about securing your servers. Many businesses that rely on Internet servers assign full-time administrators to watch over the security of their servers. So, think of this section as an overview of some of the kinds of attacks to look out for and some tools available to secure your Fedora or RHEL server.

Understanding attack techniques

Attacks on computing systems take on different forms, depending on the goal and resources of the attacker. Some attackers want to be disruptive, while others want to infiltrate your machines and utilize the resources for their own nefarious purposes. Still others are targeting your data for financial gain or blackmail. Here are three major categories of attacks:

- **Denial of service (DOS)** — The easiest attacks to perpetrate are denial-of-service attacks. The primary purpose of these attacks is to disrupt the activities of a remote site by overloading it with irrelevant data. DOS attacks can be as simple as sending thousands of page requests per second at a Web site. These types of attacks are easy to perpetrate and easy to protect against. Once you have a handle on where the attack is coming from, a simple phone call to the perpetrator's ISP will get the problem solved.

- **Distributed denial of service (DDOS)** — More advanced DOS attacks are called distributed denial-of-service attacks. DDOS attacks are much harder to perpetrate and nearly impossible to stop. In this form of attack, an attacker takes control of hundreds or even thousands of weakly secured Internet connected computers. The attacker then directs them in unison to send a stream of irrelevant data to a single Internet host. The result is that the power of one attacker is magnified thousands of times. Instead of an attack coming from one direction, as is the case in a normal DOS, it comes from thousands of directions at once. The best defense against a DDOS attack is to contact your ISP to see if it can filter traffic at its border routers.

  Many people use the excuse, "I have nothing on my machine anyone would want" to avoid having to consider security. The problem with this argument is that attackers have a lot of reasons to use your machine. The attacker can turn your machine into an agent for later use in a DDOS attack. More than once, authorities have shown up at the door of a dumbfounded computer user asking questions about threats originating from their computer. By ignoring security, the owners have opened themselves up to a great deal of liability.

- **Intrusion attacks** — To remotely use the resources of a target machine, attackers must first look for an opening to exploit. In the absence of inside information such as passwords or encryption keys, they must scan the target machine to see what services are offered. Perhaps one of the services is weakly secured and the attacker can use some known exploit to finagle his or her way in.

  A tool called nmap is generally considered the best way to scan a host for services (note that nmap is a tool that can be used for good and bad). Once the attacker has a list of the available services running on his target, he needs to find a way to trick one of those services into letting him have privileged access to the system. Usually, this is done with a program called an *exploit*.

While DOS attacks are disruptive, intrusion type attacks are the most damaging. The reasons are varied, but the result is always the same. An uninvited guest is now taking up residence on your machine and is using it in a way you have no control over.

Protecting against denial-of-service attacks

As explained earlier, a denial-of-service attack attempts to crash your computer or at least degrade its performance to an unusable level. There are a variety of denial-of-service exploits. Most try to overload some system resource, such as your available disk space or your Internet connection. Some common attacks and defenses are discussed in the following sections.

Mailbombing

Mailbombing is the practice of sending so much e-mail to a particular user or system that the computer's hard drive becomes full. There are several ways to protect yourself from mailbombing. You can use the Procmail e-mail-filtering tool or configure your sendmail daemon.

> **CROSS-REFERENCE:** See Chapter 19 for a more complete description of sendmail.

Blocking mail with Procmail

The Procmail e-mail-filtering tool is installed by default with Fedora and RHEL and is tightly integrated with the sendmail e-mail daemon; thus, it can be used to selectively block or filter out specific types of e-mail. You can learn more about Procmail at the Procmail web site: www.procmail.org.

To enable Procmail for your user account, create a .procmailrc file in your home directory. The file should be mode 0600 (readable by you but nobody else). Type the following, replacing *evilmailer* with the actual e-mail address that is mailbombing you:

```
# Delete mail from evilmailer
:0
* ^From.*evilmailer
/dev/null
```

The Procmail recipe looks for the From line at the start of each e-mail to see if it includes the string evilmailer. If it does, the message is sent to /dev/null (effectively throwing it away).

Blocking mail with sendmail

The Procmail e-mail tool works quite well when only one user is being mailbombed. If, however, the mailbombing affects many users, you should probably configure your sendmail daemon to block all e-mail from the mailbomber. Do this by adding the mailbomber's e-mail address or system name to the access file located in the /etc/mail directory.

Each line of the access file contains an e-mail address, hostname, domain, or IP address followed by a tab and then a keyword specifying what action to take when that entity sends you a message. Valid keywords are OK, RELAY, REJECT, DISCARD, and ERROR. Using the REJECT keyword will cause a sender's e-mail to be bounced back with an error message. The keyword DISCARD will cause the message to be silently dropped without sending an error back. You can even return a custom error message by using the ERROR keyword.

Thus, an example /etc/mail/access file may look similar to this:

```
# Check the /usr/share/doc/sendmail/README.cf file for a description
# of the format of this file. (search for access_db in that file)
# The /usr/share/doc/sendmail/README.cf is part of the sendmail-doc
# package.
#
# by default we allow relaying from localhost...
localhost.localdomain           RELAY
localhost                       RELAY
127.0.0.1                       RELAY
#
# Senders we want to Block
#
evilmailer@yahoo.com    REJECT
stimpy.glaci.com        REJECT
cyberpromo.com          DISCARD
199.170.176.99          ERROR:"550 Die Spammer Scum!"
199.170.177             ERROR:"550 Email Refused"
```

As with most Linux configuration files, lines that begin with a pound (#) sign are comments. Our list of blocked spammers is at the end of this example file. Note that the address to block can be a complete e-mail address, a full hostname, a domain only, an IP address, or a subnet.

To block a particular e-mail address or host from mailbombing you, log in to your system as root, edit the /etc/mail/access file, and add a line to DISCARD mail from the offending sender.

After saving the file and exiting the editor, you must convert the access file into a hash-indexed database called access.db. The database is updated automatically the next time sendmail starts. Or you can convert the database immediately, as follows:

```
# cd /etc/mail
# make
```

Sendmail should now discard e-mail from the addresses you added.

Spam relaying

Another way in which your e-mail services can be abused is by having your system used as a spam relay. *Spam* refers to the unsolicited junk e-mail that has become a common occurrence on the Internet. Spammers often deliver their annoying messages from a normal dial-up Internet account. They need some kind of high-capacity e-mail server to accept and buffer the payload of messages. They deliver the spam to the server all in one huge batch and then log off, letting the server do the work of delivering the messages to the many victims.

Naturally, no self-respecting Internet service provider (ISP) will cooperate with this action, so spammers resort to hijacking servers at another ISP to do the dirty work. Having your mailserver hijacked to act as a spam relay can have a devastating effect on your system and your reputation. Fortunately, open mail relaying is deactivated by default on Fedora and Red Hat Enterprise Linux installations. Open mail relaying is one security issue that you will not have to worry about.

You can allow specific hosts or domains to relay mail through your system by adding those senders to your /etc/mail/access file with keyword RELAY. By default, relaying is allowed only from the local host. Refer to Chapter 19, as well as the sendmail documentation, for more information.

> **TIP:** One package you might consider using to filter out spam on your mail server is spamassassin. Spamassassin examines the text of incoming mail messages and attempts to filter out messages that are determined to be spam. Spamassassin is described in Chapter 19. You should also check out The Spamhaus Project (www.spamhaus.org), which maintains the Spamhaus Block List to help you block verified spam sources and spam operations.

Smurf amplification attack

Smurfing refers to a particular type of denial-of-service attack aimed at flooding your Internet connection. It can be a difficult attack to defend against because it is not easy to trace the attack to the attacker. Here is how smurfing works.

The attack makes use of the ICMP protocol, a service intended for checking the speed and availability of network connections. Using the ping command, you can send a network packet from your computer to another computer on the Internet. The remote computer will recognize the packet as an ICMP request and echo a reply packet to your computer. Your computer can then print a message revealing that the remote system is up and telling you how long it took to reply to the ping.

A smurfing attack uses a malformed ICMP request to bury your computer in network traffic. The attacker does this by bouncing a ping request off an unwitting third party in such a way that the reply is duplicated dozens or even hundreds of times. An organization with a fast Internet connection and a large number of computers is used as the relay. The destination address of the ping is set to an entire subnet instead of a single host. The return address is forged to be your machine's address instead of the actual sender. When the ICMP packet arrives at the unwitting relay's network, every host on that subnet replies to the ping! Furthermore, they reply to your computer instead of to the actual sender. If the relay's network has hundreds of computers, your Internet connection can be quickly flooded.

The best fix is to contact the organization being used as a relay and inform them of the abuse. Usually, they need only to reconfigure their Internet router to stop any future attacks. If the organization is uncooperative, you can minimize the effect of the attack by blocking the ICMP protocol on your router. This will at least keep the traffic off your internal network. If you can convince your ISP to block ICMP packets aimed at your network, it will help even more.

Protecting against distributed DOS attacks

DDOS attacks are much harder to initiate and nearly impossible to stop. A DDOS attack begins with the penetration of hundreds or even thousands of weakly secured machines. These machines can then be directed to attack a single host based on the whims of the attacker.

With the advent of DSL and cable modem, millions of people are enjoying Internet access with virtually no speed restrictions. In their rush to get online, many of those people neglect to implement even the most basic security. Because the vast majority of these people run Microsoft operating systems, they tend to get hit with worms and viruses rather quickly. After the machine has been infiltrated, quite often the worm or virus installs a program on the victim's machine that instructs it to quietly *call home* and announce that it is now ready to do *the master's bidding*.

At the whim of the master, the infected machines can now be used to focus a concentrated stream of garbage data at a selected host. In concert with thousands of other infected machines, a *scriptkiddie* (someone, often a youngster, who doesn't have the knowledge to create worms or viruses, but has the inclination and small bit of skill needed to find and launch them) now has the power to take down nearly any site on the Internet.

Detecting a DDOS is similar to detecting a DOS attack. One or more of the following signs are likely to be present:

- Sustained saturated data link
- No reduction in link saturation during off-peak hours
- Hundreds or even thousands of simultaneous network connections
- Extremely slow system performance

To determine if your data link is saturated, the act of pinging an outside host can tell much of the story. Much higher than usual latency is a dead giveaway. Normal ping latency (that is, the time it takes for a ping response to come back from a remote host) looks like the following:

```
# ping www.example.com
PING www.example.com (192.0.34.166) from 10.0.0.11: 56(84) bytes of data
64 bytes from 192.0.34.166: icmp_seq=1 ttl=49 time=40.1 ms
```

```
64 bytes from 192.0.34.166: icmp_seq=2 ttl=49 time=42.5 ms
64 bytes from 192.0.34.166: icmp_seq=3 ttl=49 time=39.5 ms
64 bytes from 192.0.34.166: icmp_seq=4 ttl=49 time=38.4 ms
64 bytes from 192.0.34.166: icmp_seq=5 ttl=49 time=39.0 ms

--- www.example.com ping statistics ---
5 packets transmitted, 5 received, 0% loss, time 4035ms
rtt min/avg/max/mdev = 38.472/39.971/42.584/1.432 ms
```

In the preceding example, the average time for a ping packet to make the round trip was about 39 thousandths of a second.

A ping to a nearly saturated link will look like the following:

```
# ping www.example.com
PING www.example.com (192.0.34.166): from 10.0.0.11: 56(84)bytes of data
64 bytes from 192.0.34.166: icmp_seq=1 ttl=62 time=1252 ms
64 bytes from 192.0.34.166: icmp_seq=2 ttl=62 time=1218 ms
64 bytes from 192.0.34.166: icmp_seq=3 ttl=62 time=1290 ms
64 bytes from 192.0.34.166: icmp_seq=4 ttl=62 time=1288 ms
64 bytes from 192.0.34.166: icmp_seq=5 ttl=62 time=1241 ms

--- www.example.com ping statistics ---
5 packets transmitted, 5 received, 0% loss, time 5032ms
rtt min/avg/max/mdev = 1218.059/1258.384/1290.861/28.000 ms
```

In this example, a ping packet took, on average, 1.3 seconds to make the round trip. From the first example to the second example, latency increased by a factor of 31! A data link that goes from working normally to slowing down by a factor of 31 is a clear sign that link utilization should be investigated.

For a more accurate measure of data throughput, a tool such as ttcp can be used. To test your connection with ttcp you must have installed the ttcp RPM package on machines inside *and* outside of your network. (The ttcp package comes on the DVD included with this book.) If you are not sure whether the package is installed, simply type **ttcp** at a command prompt. You should see something like the following:

```
# ttcp
Usage: ttcp -t [-options] host [ < in ]
       ttcp -r [-options > out]
Common options:
  -4    Use IPv4
  -6    Use IPv6
  -l ## length of bufs read from or written to network (default 8192)
  -u    use UDP instead of TCP
  -p ## port number to send to or listen at (default 5001)
  -s    -t: source a pattern to network
        -r: sink (discard) all data from network
  -A    align the start of buffers to this modulus (default 16384)
```

```
 -O    start buffers at this offset from the modulus (default 0)
 -v    verbose: print more statistics
 -d    set SO_DEBUG socket option
 -b ## set socket buffer size (if supported)
 -f X  format for rate: k,K = kilo{bit,byte}; m,M = mega; g,G = giga
Options specific to -t:
 -n ## number of source bufs written to network (default 2048)
 -D    don't buffer TCP writes (sets TCP_NODELAY socket option)
 -w ## number of microseconds to wait between each write
Options specific to -r:
 -B    for -s, only output full blocks as specified by -l (for TAR)
 -T    "touch": access each byte as it's read
 -I if Specify the network interface (e.g. eth0) to use
```

The first step is to start up a receiver process on the server machine:

```
# ttcp -rs
ttcp-r: buflen=8192, nbuf=2048, align=16384/0, port=5001  tcp
ttcp-r: socket
```

The −r flag denotes that the server machine will be the receiver. The −s flag, in conjunction with the −r flag, tells ttcp that you want to ignore any received data.

The next step is to have someone outside of your data link, with a network link close to the same speed as yours, set up a ttcp sending process:

```
# ttcp -ts server.example.com
ttcp-t: buflen=8192, nbuf=2048, align=16384/0, port=5001  tcp  ->
server.example.com
ttcp-t: socket
ttcp-t: connect
```

Let the process run for a few minutes and then press Ctrl+C on the transmitting side to stop the testing. The receiving side will then take a moment to calculate and present the results:

```
# ttcp -rs
ttcp-r: buflen=8192, nbuf=2048, align=16384/0, port=5001  tcp
ttcp-r: socket
ttcp-r: accept from 64.223.17.21
ttcp-r: 2102496 bytes in 70.02 real seconds = 29.32 KB/sec +++
ttcp-r: 1226 I/O calls, msec/call = 58.49, calls/sec = 17.51
ttcp-r: 0.0user 0.0sys 1:10real 0% 0i+0d 0maxrss 0+2pf 0+0csw
```

In this example, the average bandwidth between the two hosts was 29.32 kilobytes per second. On a link suffering from a DDOS, this number would be a mere fraction of the actual bandwidth the data link is rated for.

If the data link is indeed saturated, the next step is to determine where the connections are coming from. A very effective way of doing this is with the netstat command, which is included as part of the base Fedora installation. Type the following to see connection information:

```
# netstat -tupn
```

Table 14-3 describes each of the netstat parameters used here.

Table 14-3: netstat Parameters

Parameter	Description
-t, --tcp	Show TCP socket connections.
-u, --udp	Show UDP socket connections.
-p, --program	Show the PID and name of the program to which each socket belongs.
-n, --numeric	Show numerical address instead of trying to determine symbolic host, port, or user names.

The following is an example of what the output might look like:

```
Active Internet connections (w/o servers)
Proto Recv-Q Send-Q Local Address      Foreign Address      State        PID/Program name
tcp        0      0 65.213.7.96:22     13.29.132.19:12545   ESTABLISHED 32376/sshd
tcp        0    224 65.213.7.96:22     13.29.210.13:29250   ESTABLISHED 13858/sshd
tcp        0      0 65.213.7.96:6667   13.29.194.190:33452  ESTABLISHED 1870/ircd
tcp        0      0 65.213.7.96:6667   216.39.144.152:42709 ESTABLISHED 1870/ircd
tcp        0      0 65.213.7.96:42352  67.113.1.99:53       TIME_WAIT   -
tcp        0      0 65.213.7.96:42354  83.152.6.9:113       TIME_WAIT   -
tcp        0      0 65.213.7.96:42351  83.152.6.9:113       TIME_WAIT   -
tcp        0      0 127.0.0.1:42355    127.0.0.1:783        TIME_WAIT   -
tcp        0      0 127.0.0.1:783      127.0.0.1:42353      TIME_WAIT   -
tcp        0      0 65.213.7.96:42348  19.15.11.1:25        TIME_WAIT   -
```

The output is organized into columns defined as follows:

- **Proto** — Protocol used by the socket.
- **Recv-Q** — The number of bytes not yet copied by the user program attached to this socket.
- **Send-Q** — The number of bytes not acknowledged by the host.
- **Local Address** — Address and port number of the local end of the socket.
- **Foreign Address** — Address and port number of the remote end of the socket.
- **State** — Current state of the socket. Table 14-4 provides a list of socket states.
- **PID/Program name** — Process ID and program name of the process that owns the socket.

Table 14-4: Socket States

State	Description
ESTABLISHED	Socket has an established connection.
SYN_SENT	Socket actively trying to establish a connection.
SYN_RECV	Connection request received from the network.
FIN_WAIT1	Socket closed and shutting down.
FIN_WAIT2	Socket is waiting for remote end to shut down.
TIME_WAIT	Socket is waiting after closing to handle packets still in the network.
CLOSED	Socket is not being used.
CLOSE_WAIT	The remote end has shut down, waiting for the socket to close.
LAST_ACK	The remote end has shut down, and the socket is closed, waiting for acknowledgement.
LISTEN	Socket is waiting for an incoming connection.
CLOSING	Both sides of the connection are shut down, but not all of your data has been sent.
UNKNOWN	The state of the socket is unknown.

During a DOS attack, the foreign address is usually the same for each connection. In this case, it is a simple matter of typing the whois command, followed by the foreign IP address, to determine who owns the IP address of the machine causing the attack.

During a DDOS attack, the foreign address will likely be different for each connection. In this case, it is impossible to track down all of the offenders because there will likely be thousands of them. The best way to defend yourself is to contact your ISP and see if it can filter the traffic at its border routers.

Protecting against intrusion attacks

Crackers have a wide variety of tools and techniques to assist them in breaking into your computer. Intrusion attacks focus on exploiting weaknesses in your security, so the crackers can take more control of your system (and potentially do more damage) than they could from the outside.

Fortunately, there are many tools and techniques for combating intrusion attacks. This section discusses the most common break-in methods and the tools available to protect your system. Although the examples shown are specific to Fedora and Red Hat Enterprise Linux systems, the tools and techniques are generally applicable to any other Linux or UNIX-like operating system.

> **CROSS-REFERENCE:** The tripwire package, which is included in the Fedora repository, is a good tool for detecting whether intrusion attacks have taken place. The description of tripwire is not in this edition. However, if you are interested in installing the package on your own, you can find the description of tripwire on the companion Web site of this book at `www.wiley.com/go/fedora9bible`.

Evaluating access to network services

Fedora, Red Hat Enterprise Linux, and its UNIX kin provide many network services, and with them many avenues for cracker attacks. You should know these services and how to limit access to them. Refer to Appendix B for listings and short descriptions of available services.

What do I mean by a network service? Basically, I am referring to a resource or facility that a remote user can request of the server machine, such as a login, file sharing, instant messaging, or other service. Routing e-mail is a network service. So is serving Web pages. Your Linux box has the potential to provide thousands of services. Many of them are listed in the `/etc/services` file. Look at a snippet of that file:

```
# /etc/services:
# service-name   port/protocol   [aliases ...]     [# comment]
chargen          19/tcp               ttytst source
chargen          19/udp               ttytst source
ftp-data         20/tcp
ftp-data         20/udp
# 21 is registered to ftp, but also used by fsp
ftp              21/tcp
ftp              21/udp          fsp fspd
ssh              22/tcp                         # SSH Remote Login Protocol
ssh              22/udp                         # SSH Remote Login Protocol
telnet           23/tcp
telnet           23/udp
# 24 - private mail system
smtp             25/tcp          mail
```

After comment lines, you will notice three columns of information. The left column contains the name of each service. The middle column defines the port number and protocol type used for that service. The rightmost field contains an optional alias or list of aliases for the service.

As an example, examine the last entry in the file snippet. It describes the SMTP (Simple Mail Transfer Protocol) service, which is the service used for delivering e-mail over the Internet. The middle column contains the text 25/tcp, which tells us that the SMTP protocol uses port 25 and uses the Transmission Control Protocol (TCP) as its protocol type.

What exactly is a *port number*? It is a unique number that has been set aside for a particular network service. It allows network connections to be properly routed to the software that handles that service. For example, when an e-mail message is delivered from some other computer to your Linux box, the remote system must first establish a network connection with your system. Your computer receives the connection request, examines it, sees it labeled for port 25, and thus knows that the connection should be handed to the program that handles e-mail (which happens to be sendmail).

I mentioned that SMTP uses the TCP protocol. Some services use UDP, the User Datagram Protocol. All you really need to know about TCP and UDP (for the purpose of this security discussion) is that they provide different ways of packaging the information sent over a network connection. A TCP connection provides error detection and retransmission of lost data. UDP doesn't check to ensure that the data arrived complete and intact; it is meant as a fast way to send non-critical information.

Disabling network services

Although there are hundreds of services (listed in /etc/services) that potentially could be available and subject to attack on your Fedora or Red Hat Enterprise Linux system, in reality only a few dozen services are installed and only a handful of those are on by default. Most network services are started by either the xinetd process or by a start-up script in the /etc/init.d directory.

xinetd is a daemon that listens on a great number of network port numbers. When a connection is made to a particular port number, xinetd automatically starts the appropriate program for that service and hands the connection to it. The xinetd daemon improves on its predecessor, inetd, by offering features that include more flexible access control, more logging settings, and denial-of-service prevention.

The configuration file /etc/xinetd.conf is used to provide default settings for the xinetd server. The directory /etc/xinetd.d contains files telling xinetd what ports to listen on and what programs to start. Each file contains configuration information for a single service, and the file is usually named after the service it configures. For example, to enable the rsync service, edit the rsync file in the /etc/xinetd.d directory and look for a section similar to the following:

```
service rsync
{
    disable = yes
    socket_type      = stream
    wait             = no
    user             = root
    server           = /usr/bin/rsync
    server_args      = --daemon
    log_on_failure   += USERID
}
```

Note that the first line of this example identifies the service as rsync. This exactly matches the service name listed in the /etc/services file, causing the service to listen on port 873 for TCP and UDP protocols. You can see that the service is off by default (disable = yes). To enable the rsync services, change the line to read like this:

```
disable = no
```

> **TIP:** The rsync service is a nice one to turn on if your machine is an FTP server. It allows people to use an rsync client (which includes a checksum-search algorithm) to download files from your server. With that feature, users can restart a disrupted download without having to start from the beginning.

Because most services are disabled by default, your computer is only as insecure as you make it. You can double-check that insecure services, such as rlogin and rsh (which are included in the rsh-server package), are also disabled by making sure that `disabled = yes` is set in the `/etc/xinetd.d/rlogin` and `rsh` files.

> **TIP:** You can make the remote login service active but disable the use of the `/etc/host.equiv` and `.rhosts` files, requiring `rlogin` to always prompt for a password. Rather than disabling the service, locate the server line in the `rsh` file (`server = /usr/sbin/in.rshd`) and add a space followed by `-L` at the end. Of course, that doesn't change the fact that your password and data will still be sent unencrypted over the network.

You now need to send a signal to the `xinetd` process to tell it to reload its configuration file. The quickest way to do that is to reload the xinetd service. As the root user, type the following from a shell:

```
# service xinetd reload
Reloading configuration:          [ OK ]
```

That's it — you have enabled the rsync service. Provided that you have properly configured your mail server (see Chapter 19), clients should now be able to download files from your computer via the rsync protocol.

Securing servers with SELinux

Red Hat, Inc. did a clever thing when it took its first swipe at implementing SELinux in Red Hat systems. Instead of creating only policies to control every aspect of your Linux system, it created a "targeted" policy type that focused on securing those services that are most vulnerable to attacks. Red Hat then set about securing those services in such a way that, if they were compromised, a cracker couldn't compromise the rest of the system as well.

After you have opened a port in your firewall so others can request a service, and then started that service to handle requests, SELinux can be used to set up walls around that service. As a result, its daemon process, configuration files, and data can't access resources they are not specifically allowed to access. The rest of your computer, then, is safer.

As Red Hat continues to work out the kinks in SELinux, there has been a tendency for users to experience SELinux failures and just disable SELinux. If you have tried SELinux in the past and turned it off when you had a problem, consider that SELinux has improved quite a bit in recent versions and it might be time for you to try it again.

If you do encounter a failure related to SELinux, try to find out if SELinux should have caused the failure. In other words, maybe you were doing something that was unsafe and SELinux was right to fail. However, if the failure you encounter turns out to be a bug with SELinux, file a bug report to `http://bugzilla.redhat.com` and help make the service better.

See Chapter 10 for a more in-depth description of SELinux in Fedora and RHEL.

Protecting Web servers with certificates and encryption

Previous sections told you how to lock the doors to your Fedora or RHEL system to deny access to crackers. The best dead bolt lock, however, is useless if you are mugged in your own driveway and have your keys stolen. Likewise, the best computer security can be for naught if you are sending passwords and other critical data unprotected across the Internet.

A savvy cracker can use a tool called a *protocol analyzer* or a *network sniffer* to peek at the data flowing across a network and pick out passwords, credit card data, and other juicy bits of information. The cracker does this by breaking into a poorly protected system on the same network and running software, or by gaining physical access to the same network and plugging in his or her own equipment.

You can combat this sort of theft by using encryption. The two main types of encryption in use today are symmetric cryptography and public-key cryptography.

Symmetric cryptography

Symmetric cryptography, also called *private-key* cryptography, uses a single key to both encrypt and decrypt a message. This method is generally inappropriate for securing data that will be used by a third party, because of the complexity of secure key exchange. Symmetric cryptography is generally useful for encrypting data for one's own purposes.

A classic use of symmetric cryptography is for a personal password vault. Anyone who has been using the Internet for any amount of time has accumulated a quantity of user names and passwords for accessing various sites and resources. A personal password vault lets you store this access information in an encrypted form. The end result is that you have to remember only one password to unlock all of your access information.

Until recently, the United States government was standardized on a symmetric encryption algorithm called DES (Data Encryption Standard) to secure important information. Because there is no direct way to crack DES-encrypted data, to decrypt DES encrypted data without a password you would have to use an unimaginable amount of computing power to try to guess the password. This is also known as the *brute force* method of decryption.

As personal computing power has increased nearly exponentially, the DES algorithm has had to be retired. In its place, after a very long and interesting search, the U.S. government has accepted the Rijndael algorithm as what it calls the AES (Advanced Encryption Standard).

Although the AES algorithm is also subject to brute force attacks, it requires significantly more computing power to crack than the DES algorithm does.

For more information on AES, including a command line implementation of the algorithm, you can visit `http://aescrypt.sourceforge.net/`.

Public-key cryptography

Public-key cryptography does not suffer from key distribution problems, and that is why it is the preferred encryption method for secure Internet communication. This method uses two keys, one to encrypt the message and another to decrypt the message. The key used to encrypt the message is called the public key because it is made available for all to see. The key used to decrypt the message is the private key and is kept hidden. The entire process works like this:

Imagine that you want to send me a secure message using public-key encryption. Here is what we need:

1. I must have a public and private key pair. Depending on the circumstances, I may generate the keys myself (using special software) or obtain the keys from a key authority.

2. You want to send me a message, so you first look up my public key (or more accurately, the software you are using looks it up).

3. You encrypt the message with the public key. At this point, the message can only be decrypted with the private key (the public key cannot be used to decrypt the message).

4. I receive the message and use my private key to decrypt it.

Secure Sockets Layer

A classic implementation of public-key cryptography is with secure sockets layer (SSL) communication. This is the technology that enables you to securely submit your credit card information to an online merchant. The elements of an SSL-encrypted session are as follows:

- SSL-enabled Web browser (Firefox, Mozilla, Internet Explorer, Opera, Konquerer, and so on)
- SSL-enabled Web server (Apache)
- SSL certificate

To initiate an SSL session, a Web browser first makes contact with a Web server on port 443, also known as the HTTPS port (Hypertext Transport Protocol Secure). After a socket connection has been established between the two machines, the following occurs:

1. The server sends its SSL certificate to the browser.

2. The browser verifies the identity of the server through the SSL certificate.

3. The browser generates a symmetric encryption key.

4. The browser uses the SSL certificate to encrypt the symmetric encryption key.

5. The browser sends the encrypted key to the server.

6. The server decrypts the symmetric key with its private key counterpart of the public SSL certificate.

7. The browser and server can now encrypt and decrypt traffic based on a common knowledge of the symmetric key.

Secure data interchange can now occur.

Creating SSL certificates

In order to be able to use SSL certificates for secure HTTP data interchange, you must have an SSL-capable Web server. The Apache Web server (httpd package), which comes with Fedora and RHEL, is SSL-capable. Here are some of the files you will need to create your own SSL certificates for the Apache Web server:

- `/etc/httpd/conf/httpd.conf` — Web server configuration file
- `/etc/pki/tls/certs/Makefile` — Certificate building script
- `/etc/httpd/conf.d/ssl.conf` — Primary Web server SSL configuration file

Now that you're familiar with the basic components, take a look at the tools used to create SSL certificates:

```
# cd /etc/pki/tls/certs
# make
This makefile allows you to create:
  o public/private key pairs
  o SSL certificate signing requests (CSRs)
  o self-signed SSL test certificates

To create a key pair, run "make SOMETHING.key".
To create a CSR, run "make SOMETHING.csr".
To create a test certificate, run "make SOMETHING.crt".
To create a key and a test certificate in one file, run "make
SOMETHING.pem".

To create a key for use with Apache, run "make genkey".
To create a CSR for use with Apache, run "make certreq".
To create a test certificate for use with Apache, run "make testcert".

To create a test certificate with serial number
other than zero, add SERIAL=num

Examples:
  make server.key
  make server.csr
  make server.crt
  make stunnel.pem
```

```
make genkey
make certreq
make testcert
make server.crt SERIAL=1
make stunnel.pem SERIAL=2
make testcert SERIAL=3
```

The make command utilizes the Makefile to create SSL certificates. (The make command is used for a variety of software tasks with C and C++ programming.) Without any arguments the make command simply prints the information listed above. The following defines each argument you can give to make:

- make server.key — Creates generic public/private key pairs.
- make server.csr — Generates a generic SSL certificate service request.
- make server.crt — Generates a generic SSL test certificate.
- make stunnel.pem — Generates a generic SSL test certificate, but puts the private key in the same file as the SSL test certificate.
- make genkey — Same as make server.key except it places the key in the ssl.key directory.
- make certreq — Same as make server.csr except it places the certificate service request in the ssl.csr directory.
- make testcert — Same as make server.crt except it places the test certificate in the ssl.crt directory.
- make server.crt SERIAL=1 — Generate the keys mentioned above using keys serial numbers other than zero.

Using third-party certificate signers

In the real world, I know who you are because I recognize your face, your voice, and your mannerisms. On the Internet, I cannot see these things and must rely on a trusted third party to vouch for your identity. To ensure that a certificate is immutable, it has to be signed by a trusted third party when the certificate is issued and validated every time an end user taking advantage of your secure site loads it. The following is a list of the trusted third-party certificate signers:

- **GlobalSign** — www.globalsign.com/
- **GeoTrust** — www.geotrust.com/
- **VeriSign** — www.verisign.com/
- **RapidSSL.com** — www.rapidssl.com/
- **Thawte** — www.thawte.com/
- **Entrust** — www.entrust.com/
- **ipsCA** — www.ipsca.com/
- **COMODO Group** — www.comodogroup.com/

> **NOTE:** Because of the fluid nature of the certificate business, some of these companies may not be in business when you read this, while others may have come into existence. To get a more current list of certificate authorities, from your Mozilla Firefox browser select Edit → Preferences. From the Preferences window that appears, select Advanced → Encryption → View Certificates. From the Certificate Manager window that appears, refer to the Authorities tab to see Certificate Authorities from which you have received certificates. Consider using well-known certificate authorities for your publicly accessible resources.

Each of these certificate authorities has gotten a chunk of cryptographic code embedded into nearly every Web browser in the world. This chunk of cryptographic code allows a Web browser to determine whether or not an SSL certificate is authentic. Without this validation, it would be trivial for crackers to generate their own certificates and dupe people into thinking they are giving sensitive information to a reputable source.

Certificates that are not validated are called *self-signed certificates*. If you come across a site that has not had its identity authenticated by a trusted third party, your Web browser will display a message similar to the one shown in Figure 14-3.

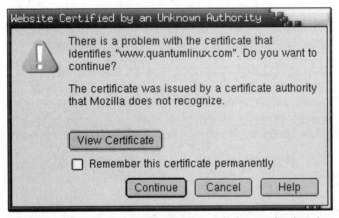

Figure 14-3: A pop-up window alerts you when a site is not authenticated.

This does not necessarily mean that you are encountering anything illegal, immoral, or fattening. Many sites opt to go with *self-signed* certificates, not because they are trying to pull a fast one on you, but because there may not be any reason to validate the true owner of the certificate and they do not want to pay the cost of getting a certificate validated. Some reasons for using a *self-signed* certificate include:

- **The Web site accepts no input** — In this case, you as the end user have nothing to worry about. There is no one trying to steal your information because you aren't giving out any information. Most of the time this is done simply to secure the Web transmission from the server to you. The data in and of itself may not be sensitive, but, being a good netizen, the site has enabled you to secure the transmission to keep third parties from sniffing the traffic.

- **The Web site caters to a small clientele** — If you run a Web site that has a very limited set of customers, such as an Application Service Provider, you can simply inform your users that you have no certificate signer and that they can browse the certificate information and validate it with you over the phone or in person.

- **Testing** — It makes no sense to pay for an SSL certificate if you are just testing a new Web site or Web-based application. Use a *self-signed* certificate until you are ready to go live.

Creating a Certificate Service Request

To create a third-party validated SSL certificate, you must first start with a Certificate Service Request (CSR). To create a CSR, do the following on your Web server:

```
# cd /etc/pki/tls/certs
# make certreq
/usr/bin/openssl


You are about to be asked to enter information that will be incorporated
into your certificate request.
What you are about to enter is what is called
a Distinguished Name or a DN.
There are quite a few fields but you can leave some blank
For some fields there will be a default value,
If you enter '.', the field will be left blank.
-----
Country Name (2 letter code) [GB]:US
State or Province Name (full name) [Berkshire]: Connecticut
Locality Name (eg, city) [Newbury]: Mystic
Organization Name (eg, company) [My Company Ltd]:Acme Marina, Inc.
Organizational Unit Name (eg, section) []:InfoTech
Common Name (eg, your name or your server's hostname)
[]:www.acmemarina.com
Email Address []: webmaster@acmemarina.com
```

To complete the process, you will be asked if you want to add any extra attributes to your certificate. Unless you have a reason to provide more information, you should simply press Enter at each of the following prompts to leave them blank.

```
Please enter the following 'extra' attributes
to be sent with your certificate request
A challenge password []:
An optional company name []:
```

Getting the CSR signed

Once your CSR has been created, you need to send it to a signing authority for validation. The first step in this process is to select a signing authority. Each signing authority has different deals, prices, and products. Check out each of the signing authorities listed in the "Using third-party certificate signers" section earlier in this chapter to determine which works best for you. The following are areas where signing authorities differ:

- Credibility and stability
- Pricing
- Browser recognition
- Warranties
- Support
- Certificate strength

After you have selected your certificate signer, you have to go through some validation steps. Each signer has a different method of validating identity and certificate information. Some require that you fax articles of incorporation, while others require a company officer be made available to talk to a validation operator. At some point in the process you will be asked to copy and paste the contents of the CSR you created into the signer's Web form.

```
# cd /etc/pki/tls/certs
# cat localhost.csr
-----BEGIN CERTIFICATE REQUEST-----
MIIB6jCCAVMCAQAwgakxCzAJBgNVBAYTAlVTMRQwEgYDVQQIEwtDb25uZWN0aWN1
dDEPMA0GA1UEBxMGTXlzdGljMRowGAYDVQQKExFBY21lIE1hcmluYSwgSW5jLjER
MA8GA1UECxMISW5mb1RlY2gxGzAZBgNVBAMTEnd3dy5hY21lbWFyaW5hLmNvbTEn
MCUGCSqGSIb3DQEJARYYd2VibWFzdGVyQGFjbWVtYXJpbmEuY29tMIGfMA0GCSqG
SIb3DQEBAQUAA4GNADCBiQKBgQDcYH4pjMxKMldyXRmcoz8uBVOvwlNZHyRWw8ZG
u2eCbvgi6w4wXuHwaDuxbuDBmw//Y9DMI2MXg4wDq4xmPi35EsO1Ofw4ytZJn1yW
aU6cJVQro46OnXyaqXZOPiRCxUSnGRU+0nsqKGjf7LPpXv29S3QvMIBTYWzCkNnc
gWBwwwIDAQABoAAwDQYJKoZIhvcNAQEEBQADgYEANv6eJOaJZGzopNR5h2YkR9Wg
18oBl3mgoPH60Sccw3pWsoW4qbOWq7on8dS/++QOCZWZI1gefgaSQMInKZ1II7Fs
YIwYBgpoPTMC4bp0ZZtURCyQWrKIDXQBXw7BlU/3A25nvkRY7vgNL9Nq+7681EJ8
W9AJ3PX4vb2+ynttcBI=
-----END CERTIFICATE REQUEST-----
```

You can use your mouse to copy and paste the CSR into the signer's Web form.

After you have completed the information validation, paid for the signing, and answered all of the questions, you have completed most of the process. In 48 to 72 hours you should receive an e-mail with your shiny new SSL certificate in it. The certificate will look similar to the following:

```
-----BEGIN CERTIFICATE-----
MIIEFjCCA3+gAwIBAgIQMI262Zd6njZgN97tJAVFODANBgkqhkiG9w0BAQQFADCB
ujEfMB0GA1UEChMWVmVyaVNpZ24gVHJ1c3QgTmV0d29yazEXMBUGA1UECxMOVmVy
aVNpZ24sIEluYy4xMzAxBgNVBAsTKlZlcmlTaWduIEludGVybmF0aW9uYWwgU2Vy
dmVyIENBIC0gQ2xhc3MgMzFJMEcG10rY2g0Dd3d3LnZlcmlzaWduLmNvbS9DUFMg
SW5jb3JwLmJ5LmJ51FJlZi4gTElBQklMSVRZIExURC4oYyk5NyBWZXJpU2lnbjEeFw0w
MzAxMTUwMDAwMDBaFw0wNDAxMTUyMzU5NTlaMIGuMQswCQYDVQQGEwJVUzETMBEG
A1UECBMKV2FzaG1uZ3RvbHHiThErE371UEBxQLRmVkZXJhbCBXYXkxGzAZBgNVBAoU
EklETSBTZXJ2aWMlcywgSW5jLjEMMAoGA1UECxQDd3d3MTMwMQYDVQQLFCpUZXJt
cyBvZiB1c2UgYXQgd3d3LnZlcmlzawduLmNvbS9ycGGgKGMpMDAxFDASBgNVBAMU
C21kbXNlcnYuY29tMIGfMA0GCSqGSIb3DQEBAQUAA4GNADCBiQKBgQDaHSk+uzOf
7jjDFEnqT8UBa1L3yFILXFjhj3XpMXLGWzLmkDmdJjXsa4x7AhEpr1ubuVNhJVI0
FnLDopsx4pyr4n+P8FyS4M5grbcQzy2YnkM2jyqVF/7yOW2pD130t4eacYYaz4Qg
q9pTxhUzjEG4twvKCAFWfuhEoGu1CMV2qQ1DAQABo4IBJTCCASEwCQYDVR0TBAIw
ADBEBgNVHSAEPTA7MDkGC2CGSAGG+EUBBxcDMCOwKAYIKwYBBQUHAgEWGEWHGh0dHBz
Oi8vd3d3LnZlcmlzaWduLmNvbS9ycGEwCwYDVRRPBAQDAgWgMCgGA1UdJQQhMB8G
CWCGSAGG+EIEM00c0wIYBQUHAwEGCCsGAQUFBwmCMDQGCCsGAQUFBwEBBCgwJjAk
BggrBgEFBQcwAYYYaHR0cDovL29jc2AudmVyaXNpZ24uY29tMEYGA1UdHwQ/MD0w
O6A5oDeGNWh0dHA6Ly9jcmwudmVyaxNpZ24uY29tL0NsYXNzM30ludGVybmF0aW9u
YWxTZXJ2ZXIuY3JsMBkGCmCGSAgG+E+f4Nfc3zYJODA5NzMwMTEyMA0GCSqGSIb3
DQEBBAUAA4GBAJ/PsVttmlDkQai5nLeudLceb1F4isXP17B68wXLkIeRu4Novu13
81LZXnaR+acHeStR01b3rQPjgv2y1mwjkPmC1WjoeYfdxH7+Mbg/6fomnK9auWAT
WF0iFW/+a8OWRYQJLMA2VQOVhX4znjpGcVNY9AQSHm1UiESJy7vtd1iX
-----END CERTIFICATE-----
```

Copy and paste this certificate into an empty file called `server.crt`, which must reside in the `/etc/pki/tls/certs` directory, and restart your Web server:

```
# service httpd restart
```

Assuming your Web site was previously working fine, you can now view it in a secure fashion by placing an "s" after the http in the Web address. So if you previously viewed your Web site at `http://www.acmemarina.com`, you can now view it in a secure fashion by going to `https://www.acmemarina.com`.

Creating self-signed certificates

Generating and running a self-signed SSL certificate is much easier than having a signed certificate. To generate a self-signed SSL certificate, do the following:

1. Remove the key and certificate that currently exist:

```
# rm /etc/pki/tls/certs/localhost.crt
# rm /etc/pki/tls/private/localhost.key
```

2. Create your own server key:

```
# make genkey
```

3. Create the self-signed certificate by typing the following:

```
# make testcert
umask 77 ; \
/usr/bin/openssl req -new -key /etc/httpd/conf/ssl.key/server.key
    -x509 -days 365 -out /etc/httpd/conf/ssl.key/server.crt
    .
    .
    .
```

At this point, it is time to start adding some identifying information to the certificate. Before you can do this, you must unlock the private key you just created. Do so by typing the password you typed earlier. Then follow this sample procedure:

```
You are about to be asked to enter information that will be
  incorporated into your certificate request.
What you are about to enter is what is called
a Distinguished Name or a DN.
There are quite a few fields but you can leave some blank
For some fields there will be a default value,
If you enter '.', the field will be left blank.
-----
Country Name (2 letter code) [GB]:US
State or Province Name (full name) [Berkshire]: Ohio
Locality Name (eg, city) [Newbury]: Cincinnati
Organization Name (eg, company) [My Company Ltd]:Industrial Press, Inc.
Organizational Unit Name (eg, section) []:IT
Common Name (eg, your name or your server's hostname)
[]:www.industrialpressinc.com
Email Address []: webmaster@industrialpressinc.com
```

The preceding generation process places all files in the proper place. All you need to do is restart your Web server and add `https` instead of `http` in front of your URL. Don't forget: you'll get a certificate validation message from your Web browser, which you can safely ignore.

Restarting your Web server

By now you've probably noticed that your Web server requires you to enter your certificate password every time it is started. This is to prevent someone from breaking into your server and stealing your private key. Should this happen, you are safe in the knowledge that the private key is a jumbled mess. The cracker will not be able to make use of it. Without such protection, a cracker could get your private key and easily masquerade as you, appearing to be legitimate in all cases.

If you just cannot stand having to enter a password every time your Web server starts, and are willing to accept the increased risk, you can remove the password encryption on your private key. Simply do the following:

```
# cd /etc/pki/tls/private
# /usr/bin/openssl rsa -in localhost.key -out  localhost.key
```

Exporting Encryption Technology

For many years, the United States government treated encryption technology like munitions. As a result, anyone wanting to export encryption technology had to get an export license from the Commerce Department. This applied not only to encryption software developed within the United States, but also to software obtained from other countries and then re-exported to another country (or even to the same country you got it from). Thus, if you installed encryption technology on your Linux system and then transported it out of the country, you were violating federal law! Furthermore, if you e-mailed encryption software to a friend in another country or let him or her download it from your server, you violated the law.

In January 2000, the U.S. export laws relating to encryption software were relaxed considerably. However, often the U.S. Commerce Department's Bureau of Export Administration requires a review of encryption products before they can be exported. U.S. companies are also still not allowed to export encryption technology to countries classified as supporting terrorism.

Troubleshooting your certificates

The following tips should help if you are having problems with your SSL certificate:

- It's usual to use one SSL certificate per IP address. If you want to add more than one SSL-enabled Web site to your server, you usually bind another IP address to the network interface. Now, however, you can do SSL-enabled name-based virtual hosting, where multiple hosts share the same IP address and port, using the Apache mod_gnutls module. If that interests you, refer to this site:

```
www.g-loaded.eu/2007/08/10/ssl-enabled-name-based-apache-virtual-hosts-with-
mod_gnutls/
```

- Make sure you aren't blocking port 443 on your Web server. All `https` requests come in on port 443. If you are blocking it, you will not be able to get secure pages.

- The certificate lasts for only one year. When that year is up, you have to renew your certificate with your certificate authority. Each certificate authority has a different procedure for doing this; check the authority's Web site for more details.

- Make sure you have the mod_ssl package installed. If it is not installed, you will not be able to serve any SSL-enabled traffic.

Managing Identities with freeIPA

The freeIPA project (www.freeipa.org) aims at providing software to manage security information across an entire Enterprise or other computing environment. The "IPA" part of freeIPA stands for *identity* (identifying and authenticating users and machines), *policy* (settings for access control of applications and machines), and *audit* (methods for collecting and auditing security events, logs, and user activities).

The "identity" area of freeIPA represents the first set of freeIPA features to be implemented. If you want to centralize management of security information, you can try these features in Fedora 9. You can use this first release of freeIPA to configure IPA servers for user identity management and centralized authentication. Then use freeIPA clients to work with that information.

The software features that freeIPA works with in this initial release include:

- Network Time Protocol Daemon
- Fedora Directory Server
- Kerberos Key Distribution
- Apache Web Server
- TurboGears Web Applications

> **CAUTION:** Note that freeIPA modifies the services just mentioned, so it is best to try freeIPA only on test systems. In other words, don't use freeIPA on your production servers.

Setting up the freeIPA Server

Both server and client freeIPA features are available in Fedora 9. However, you need to start with a server system that can essentially be taken over in many respects by freeIPA. To use a server prior to Fedora 9, you need to add the latest patches and upgrades. The server you use should have the following attributes:

- **Fedora 7 or Red Hat Enterprise Linux 5.1 Server (at least)** — If possible, start with a clean Fedora 9 system. You will need the latest patches and upgrades to use freeIPA on the earlier systems just mentioned.

- **Installed freeIPA Software** — To configure a freeIPA server, you need to install the ipa-server and ipa-admintools packages. Support for SELinux and Radius are provided by the ipa-server-selinux, ipa-radius=server, and ipa-radius-admintools packages. You can get all freeIPA packages by simply typing **yum install ipa-*** as root user.

- **Clean Fedora Directory Server**— Another reason for a clean install is that you cannot currently use freeIPA on any system that has existing Directory Server instances. There is no upgrade feature included yet.

- **Fully-qualified Domain Name** — Your freeIPA server must have a fully functional DNS host name (not localhost) that can resolve forward and reverse addresses.

- **Available ports** — Port numbers for HTTP/HTTPS (80, 443, and 8080), LDAP/LDAPS (389 and 636), and Kerberos (88 and 464) associated with the TCP protocol must be available to freeIPA and not assigned to other services. Likewise, port numbers for Kerberos (88 and 464) and NTP (123) must be available to freeIPA for UDP protocol.

The amount of RAM and disk space you need on the server depends on the number of entries the server will hold. For details on configuring a freeIPA server, first refer to the freeIPA concepts page (`www.freeipa.com/page/IpaConcepts`). Next, follow the instructions on the freeIPA Install and Deploy page (`www.freeipa.com/page/InstallAndDeploy`). Because freeIPA is under active development, check back to those pages for the latest information.

Setting up freeIPA Clients

Clients for freeIPA services are available for a wide range of systems. Supported systems include Red Hat Enterprise Linux, Fedora, Solaris, AIX, HP-UX, Mac OS X, and Windows.

To use freeIPA client services from a Fedora 9 or RHEL 5 system, install the ipa-client and ipa-admintools package. For more on setting up freeIPA clients, see the freeIPA Client Configuration Guide (`www.freeipa.com/page/ClientConfigurationGuide`).

Summary

With the rise of the Internet, security has become a critical issue for nearly all computer users. Properly using passwords, securely configuring network services, and monitoring log files are critical ways of keeping your computer secure. Using encryption keys you can help verify the authenticity of those you communicate with, as well as make the data you transmit more secure. By following the recommendations in this chapter, you can begin to learn the techniques and tools that are available for keeping your Fedora and RHEL systems secure.

Part IV
Fedora and RHEL Network and Server Setup

Chapter 15

Setting Up Network Connections and LANs

In This Chapter

- Using NetworkManager for network connections
- Understanding local area networks
- Connecting to a LAN with NetworkManager
- Setting up a wired Ethernet LAN
- Setting up a wireless LAN
- Troubleshooting your LAN

With computers becoming more mobile, and wireless networks more common, setting up network connections is more diverse than in the days when most computers were at fixed locations and addresses. But, whether you are connecting to your own local area network (LAN) or a public wireless network, Fedora and RHEL include tools to set up the kind of network connections you want.

To allow you to interactively manage your network connections, Fedora includes NetworkManager. NetworkManager is described here for choosing and connecting to a wireless LAN, because it includes an easy-to-use desktop applet that detects available wireless LANs and lets you choose the one you want to connect to.

In the home or in a small business, Fedora and RHEL can help you connect to other Linux, Windows, and Macintosh computers so that you can share your computing equipment (files, printers, and devices). Add a connection to the Internet and routing among multiple LANs (described in Chapter 16), and Fedora or RHEL can serve as a focal point for network computing in a larger enterprise. For times when you need more manual configuration for your LAN connections, his chapter describes how to use the Network Configuration window.

Connecting to the Network with NetworkManager

NetworkManager is designed to make your network connections "Just Work." It finds your network interface cards, then connects to the network (when possible) or gives you easy choices to let you choose your network connection. If you change network connections, NetworkManager will likewise try to change attributes of your connection, such as IP addresses, DNS servers, and routes.

Although NetworkManager has been included in the past several releases of Fedora, it is just becoming mature enough that you should consider using it as the facility for managing your network interfaces. In most cases with NetworkManager, connecting to an existing network is simple:

- **Wired Network** — If a wired network interface is available and a DHCP server is found, Fedora will automatically connect you to that interface and use it as your default route.

- **Wireless Network** — If a wireless network interface is available, the NetworkManager applet menu shows all wireless networks that your wireless card can find. You simply choose the network you want and authenticate as needed.

If the NetworkManager service is enabled on your Fedora system, you should see a two-computer-screen icon on the desktop top panel, as shown in Figure 15-1.

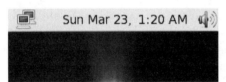

Figure 15-1: The NetworkManager applet icon (upper left) shows NetworkManager is running.

If you see the NetworkManager applet icon, you can immediately start using NetworkManager. If it is not displayed, check that NetworkManager is installed and start the service, as follows:

1. **Check for NetworkManager** — Type the following from a Terminal window to see if NetworkManager packages are installed:

```
$ rpm -qa NetworkManager*
NetworkManager-0.7.0-0.9.1.svn3417.fc9
NetworkManager-vpnc-0.7.0-0.7.7.svn3204.fc9
NetworkManager-glib-0.7.0-0.9.1.svn3417.fc9
NetworkManager-gnome-0.7.0-0.9.1.svn3417.fc9
NetworkManager-openvpn-0.7.0-8.svn3302.fc9
```

2. **Install NetworkManager** — If NetworkManager packages are not installed, type the following as root user from a Terminal window:

```
# yum install NetworkManager*
```

3. **Start NetworkManager** — Type the following commands (as root) to start the NetworkManager service immediately (service) and set it to start on every reboot:

```
# service NetworkManager start
# chkconfig NetworkManager on
```

With NetworkManager installed and running, you can begin using the NetworkManager applet on your GNOME desktop to manage your network interfaces. If you are using a KDE desktop, you need to run the `knetworkmanager` command to have the NetworkManager applet appear in your desktop panel.

With NetworkManager service started, you can manage your network connections from the NetworkManager applet icon. With NetworkManager, you can work with wireless and wired Ethernet connections, as well as select to set up a virtual private network (VPN) from those connections.

Connecting to a wireless network

To see wireless networks detected by your computer, click on the NetworkManager applet icon in the top panel. Provided that Fedora has a working driver for your wireless card, you will see a list of wireless networks that have been detected.

> **NOTE:** Although Fedora has dramatically improved support for wireless LAN cards in recent releases, there are still many wireless cards that are not supported out of the box. If your wireless card is not properly detected, refer to the "Getting wireless drivers" section later in this chapter for descriptions of how to get and load appropriate wireless drivers.

Figure 15-2 shows an example of a NetworkManager applet menu that has found three wireless networks.

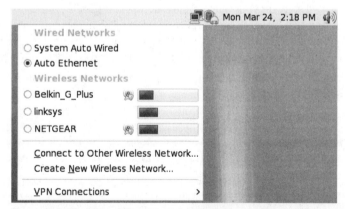

Figure 15-2: The NetworkManager applet icon displays available wireless networks

Assuming the network you want to connect to shows up under the Wireless Networks heading, you can click on that network. Type a password or encryption key and click Connect when you see the Wireless Network Secrets Required window, shown in Figure 15-3.

Figure 15-3: Enter the password to connect to the selected wireless network

If the password is correct, NetworkManager will use your new wireless connection as the default network route from your computer (disconnecting any wired Ethernet connection you may have).

Here are some other ways to work with wireless networks from the NetworkManager applet:

- **Existing Wireless Network** — If your wireless card is working, but the network you want doesn't appear, click the NetworkManager icon and select Connect to Other Wireless Network to select a different wireless network by name.

- **New Wireless Network** — To create your own wireless network, click the NetworkManager icon and select Create New Wireless Network. When prompted, enter the network name and select the type of Wireless Security you want. You can then enter the passphrase that others would use to connect to your new wireless network.

- **Disable Wireless Network** —Right-click the NetworkManager applet icon and uncheck the Enable Wireless box (so the check box disappears).

After you have established a connection, you can check information about that connection by right-clicking the NetworkManager icon and selecting Connection information. You will see the interface name, connection speed, driver name, IP address, and locations of DNS servers (among other information).

Connecting to a wired network

As noted earlier, with your wired network plugged in and a DHCP server on the line, you probably don't have to do anything to start your wired Ethernet network interface. However, if you want instead to configure static IP addressing, I recommend that you use the Network Configuration window, described later in this chapter.

Once a wired network connection is working, however, you can use the NetworkManager applet to enable and disable the interface. To do that, right-click the NetworkManager applet icon and select Enable Networking. That will toggle the network interface on and off.

Setting up a virtual private network connection

NetworkManager applet offers some simple graphical tools for configuring your Fedora system to connect to a virtual private network (VPN). The following procedure describes how to configure NetworkManager to communicate with a remote openvpn server.

Sometimes the people and offices that have to work closely together are not physically close together. For example, you may have:

- Two branch offices that need to constantly share sales databases, or
- An employee who needs to access office computers, printers, and files from home.

Rather than purchase expensive leased lines from a phone company, you want to use an inexpensive network medium, like the Internet, to let the two sides communicate. The problem is that you don't want to open up access to file sharing, print sharing, and other private services to the Internet. You also don't want communication between these sites to be exposed to anyone who is watching Internet traffic. One solution is to set up a virtual private network (VPN).

A VPN provides a way to set up secure communications over an otherwise insecure network. With a VPN connection in place, the two sides of a connection can communicate as safely as they do on the same corporate LAN. To do this, a VPN usually offers the following features:

- **Authentication** — Using passwords or other techniques, two ends of a communication can prove that they are who they say they are before accepting a connection. After the connection is in place, communications can flow in both directions across it.

- **Encryption** — By encrypting all data being sent between the two points on the public network, you can be assured that even if someone could see the packets you send, they couldn't read them. Creating a connection between two public network addresses to use for exchanging encrypted data is known as *tunneling*.

Before you can set up a VPN connection with NetworkManager, the basic service needs to be installed and running. Also, make sure the NetworkManager-openvpn and openvpn packages are installed. The following procedure assumes that NetworkManager is running and you can reach a computer on your network that has an active openvpn service. (See Chapter 16 for information on setting up a VPN server with openvpn.)

Click the NetworkManager applet icon, then select VPN Connections → Configure VPN. A VPN Connections window appears.

1. Select Add to see the Create VPN Connection window and select Forward to continue.

2. For this example, select OpenVPN Client (Cisco VPN client is also available), and click Forward. You are asked to enter VPN connection information.

3. Fill in the following information for your openvpn client connection:

   - **Connection name** — Name the connection anything you like.

   - **Gateway address** — The name or IP address of the openvpn server that is acting as the gateway for your VPN connection.

   - **Connection type** — Select the default X.509 Certificates (if you are using the example server from Chapter 16). You can also select Pre-shared key, Password Authentication, or X.509 with Password Authentication.

   - **CA file** — Identify the location of the root CA certificate you copied from the key server (possibly to /etc/openvpn/keys/ca.crt).

   - **Certificate** — Identify the location of the client certificate you copied from the key server (possibly to /etc/openvpn/keys/client01.crt).

   - **Key** — Identify the location of the client key you copied from the key server (possibly to /etc/openvpn/keys/client01.key).

   Select Forward to continue.

4. If everything looks correct, select Apply to apply your new vpn connection.

5. If the openvpn server is up and running, you can try your new VPN connection. Select the NetworkManager applet. Then choose VPN Connects and select the name of the new VPN connection you just configured.

NetworkManager is still a work in progress, so the automated features may not extend as far as you would like. For example, when you change between wired and wireless interfaces, besides just bringing VPN interfaces up or down, you may also want to unmount and mount shared file systems. Work is underway in this area, but has not yet been included in any formal release.

Understanding Local Area Networks

Connecting the computers in your organization via a LAN can save you a lot of time and money. By putting a small amount of money into networking hardware, even in a small configuration (less than five or six users), can save you from buying multiple printers, backup media, and other hardware. Add a single, shared Internet connection and you no longer need multiple modems and Internet accounts.

With a LAN, you don't have to run down the hall anymore with your file on a disk or USB thumb drive to print it on your friend's printer. Information that had to wait for the mailroom to make the rounds can be sent in an instant to anyone (or everyone) on your LAN.

With a LAN, you begin to open the greatest potential of Linux — its ability to act as a server on a network. Because Fedora and RHEL are more robust and feature-rich than other computing systems (certainly for the price), adding it to your LAN can provide a focal point to workstations that could use Linux as a file server, a mail server, a print server, or a boot server. (Those features are described later in this book.)

Creating and configuring a LAN consists of these steps:

1. **Planning, Getting, and Setting up LAN hardware** — This entails choosing a network topology, purchasing the equipment you need, and installing it (adding cards and connecting wires or using wireless antennas).

2. **Configuring TCP/IP** — To use most of the networking applications and tools that come with Linux, you must have TCP/IP configured. TCP/IP lets you communicate not only with computers on your LAN, but with any computers that you can reach on your LAN, modem, or other network connection (particularly via the Internet).

Planning, getting, and setting up LAN hardware

Even with a simple LAN, you must make some decisions about network topology (that is, how computers are connected). You must also make some decisions about network equipment (network interface cards, wires, switches, and so on).

LAN topologies

Most small office and home LANs connect computers together in one of the following topologies:

- **Star topology** — The star topology is by far the most popular LAN topology. In this arrangement, each computer contains a Network Interface Card (NIC) that connects with a cable to a central network switch or hub. The cabling is typically Category 5 (unshielded twisted pair) wiring with RJ-45 connectors. Other equipment, such as printers and fax machines, can also be connected to the hub in a star topology. Figure 15-4 is an example of a star topology.

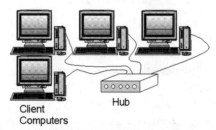

Figure 15-4: In a star topology, machines on the network connect to a central switch or hub.

- **Bus topology** — Instead of using switches or hubs, the bus topology connects computers in a chain from one to the next. The cabling usually used is referred to as coaxial, or

Thin Ethernet cable. A "T" connector attaches to each computer's NIC, then to two adjacent computers in the chain. At the two ends of the chain, the T connectors are terminated. Figure 15-5 illustrates an example of a bus topology.

Bus Topology

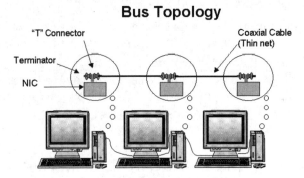

Figure 15-5: A bus topology chains computers together without using a hub.

- **Ring topology** — This is a less popular topology than star and bus topologies. In a ring topology, computers connect to a ring of wires on which tokens are taken and passed by computers that want to send information on the network. This type of topology typically uses IBM's token ring protocols.

You can configure a wireless Ethernet LAN in several different topologies, depending on how you want to use the LAN. With a wireless LAN, each computer broadcasts in the air rather than across wires. Here are some examples of wireless topologies:

- **Wireless peer-to-peer** — In this topology, frames of data are broadcast to all nodes within range, but are consumed only by the computers for which they are intended. This arrangement is useful if you are sharing file and print services among a group of client computers. Figure 15-6 shows an example of a peer-to-peer wireless LAN.

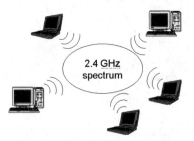

Figure 15-6: Wireless LANs can communicate as peers by broadcasting data.

- **Wireless access point** — A wireless interface can act as an access point for one or more wireless clients. Clients can be configured to communicate directly with the access point, instead of with every client that is within range. This arrangement is useful for point-to-point connections between two buildings, where the access point is acting as a gateway to the Internet or, for example, a campus intranet. It is also the most popular topology for home wireless LANs. Figure 15-7 depicts a point-to-point wireless LAN.

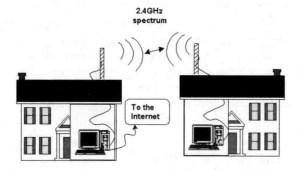

Figure 15-7: Wireless communication can go through an access point.

- **Multiple wireless access points and roaming** — Each wireless network can be configured as a separate cell. Multiple cells can be joined together in what is called a *Managed Wireless LAN*. In this arrangement, each cell's access point acts as a bridge (in fact, its actions are referred to as *bridging*) by passing all data from the cell to other cells without changing any node's MAC address. In other words, the managed wireless LAN masks the fact that there are multiple wireless cells invisible to the clients on those cells. This arrangement allows users to roam among cells as they come in and out of range without losing continuity of communication.

> **NOTE:** Although Linux does not support any wireless LAN cards that can act as a bridging wireless access point, you can have the Linux system act as a client to a bridging access point. Set your card to Managed mode and identify the MAC address for your wireless LAN's access point. For information on the current state of wireless Ethernet bridging, refer to the Bridging page at the OSDL Web site (`http://linux-net.osdl.org/index.php/Bridge`).

For our purposes, we focus on star (wired) and peer-to-peer (wireless) topologies. Common to both of these topologies is the protocol used to send data over those wired and wireless media — the Ethernet protocol.

LAN equipment

The equipment that you need to connect your LAN can include some or all of the following:

> **CROSS-REFERENCE:** For a complete description of wireless hardware, see the "Choosing wireless hardware" section later in this chapter.

- **Network Interface Card (NIC)** — Typically, one of these cards goes into a slot in each computer. For wired Ethernet networks, the cards can transmit data at 10 Mbps or 100

Mbps. Gigabit (1000 Mbps) NICs are also now available, and have recently dropped quite a bit in price. An 802.11b wireless NIC card can operate at speeds of up to 11 Mbps, but is more expensive than a wired NIC card. Recently, 802.11g cards have become much more popular, as well as coming down drastically in price.

- **Cables** — For star topologies, cables are referred to as *twisted-pair*. Category 5e wiring, which contains four twisted-pair sets per wire, is the most common type of wiring used for LANs today. A connector at each end of the cable is an RJ-45 plug, similar to those used on telephone cables. Ethernet interfaces are either 10Base-T (10 Mbps speeds) or 100Base-TX (100 Mbps speeds). These cables plug into the computer's NIC at one end and the hub at the other.

Figure 15-8 shows an example of a twisted-pair cable with an RJ-45 connector used for star topologies.

Figure 15-8: A star topology's twisted-pair cables have RJ-45 connectors (similar to telephone-cable connectors).

- **Hubs** — With the star topology, hubs were once the most popular ways to connect computers. With low-cost network switches becoming more popular, however, hubs are now less often used. Sometimes hubs are also referred to as repeaters because they receive signals from the nodes connected to them and send the signals on to other nodes.

- **Switches** — Switches are now more commonly used than hubs. Switches let you divide a LAN that is getting too large into segments that are more manageable. A switch can reduce network traffic by directing messages intended for a specific computer directly to that computer. This is as opposed to a hub, which broadcasts all data to all nodes. Because switches have come down so much in price, in most cases you should just pay a few extra dollars and get a switch instead of a hub. Besides the common 10/100 Mbps switches, Gigabit switches (1000 Mbps) are now available for economical prices.

One piece of equipment that I won't go into yet is a router. A router is used to direct information from the LAN to other LANs or the Internet.

CROSS-REFERENCE: Machines that carry out routing functions are described in Chapter 16.

LAN equipment setup

With an Ethernet NIC, appropriate cables, and a hub or switch, you are ready to set up your wired Ethernet LAN. Most new computers include built-in Ethernet ports. If your computer doesn't have one, most PCI Ethernet cards you can purchase for only a few dollars can be used with Linux. The steps for setting up an Ethernet LAN are:

1. Power down each computer and physically install the NIC card (following the manufacturer's instructions).

2. Using cables appropriate for your NIC cards and switch, connect each NIC to the network switch.

3. Power up each computer.

4. If Fedora or RHEL is not installed yet, install the software and reboot (as instructed). Chapter 2 tells you how to configure your Ethernet card while installing Linux.

5. If Fedora or RHEL is already installed, refer to the section "Configuring TCP/IP for your LAN" for information on configuring your Ethernet cards.

6. When the system comes up, your Ethernet card and interface (eth0) should be ready to use.

For most wired Ethernet cards, Linux will properly detect the card and load the module needed for that card to start communicating. Wireless cards, however, often require special firmware to be installed on your Fedora system. If your card is not immediately detected and configured, descriptions later in this chapter will help you get the firmware and drivers you need.

If your card is working, you can continue on to configure TCP/IP for that card. If not, refer to the section "Troubleshooting Your LAN" later in this chapter to learn how to check your Ethernet connection.

Configuring TCP/IP for your LAN

When you install Fedora or RHEL, you are given the opportunity to add your TCP/IP host name and IP address, as well as some other information, to your computer or choose to have that information automatically provided using Dynamic Host Configuration Protocol (DHCP). You also can set up a way to reach other computers on your LAN by name. With very small LANs, that can be done by adding computer names and IP addresses to your /etc/hosts file (as described here) or (with more than a few machines) using a DNS server.

> **CROSS-REFERENCE:** DNS is discussed in Chapter 16. Configuring your own DNS server is described in Chapter 25.

If you did not configure your LAN connection during installation of Linux, you can either use NetworkManager (described earlier) to connect to your wired or wireless networks or the Network Configuration window (run the neat command to start it). Using the Network

Configuration window, the IP address and host names can be assigned statically to an Ethernet interface or retrieved dynamically at boot time from a DHCP server.

> **NOTE:** A computer can have more than one IP address because it can have multiple network interfaces. Each network interface must have an IP address (even if the address is assigned temporarily). So, if you have two Ethernet cards (eth0 and eth1), each needs its own IP address. Also, the address `127.0.0.1` represents the local host, so users on the local computer can access services in loopback.

To use the Network Configuration window to define your IP address for your Ethernet interface, follow this procedure:

1. Start the Network Configuration. From the top panel, click System → Administration → Network or, as root user from a Terminal window, type **neat**. (If prompted, type the root password.) The Network Configuration window appears.

2. Click the Devices tab. A listing of your existing network interfaces appears.

3. Double-click the eth0 interface (representing your first Ethernet card). A pop-up window appears, enabling you to configure your eth0 interface. Figure 15-9 shows the Network Configuration window and the pop-up Ethernet Device window configuring eth0.

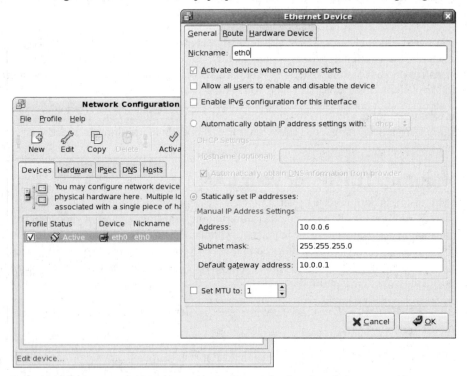

Figure 15-9: Configure your LAN interface using the Network Configuration window.

4. On the Ethernet Devices window that appears, you can enter the following information:

- **Activate device when computer starts:** Check here to have eth0 start at boot time.

- **Allow all users to enable and disable the device:** Check to let non-root users enable and disable the network interface.

- **Enable IPv6 configuration for this interface:** Check here if you are connected to an IPV6 network. (Most networks are still IPV4.)

5. On the same window, you must choose whether to get your IP addresses from another computer at boot time or enter the adresses yourself:

    - **Automatically obtain IP address settings with:** Select this check box if you have a DHCP or BOOTP server on the network from which you can obtain your computer's IP address, netmask, and gateway. DHCP is the most common way to connect to your ISP. You should consider setting up your own DHCP server if you have more than just a few computers on your LAN. (See Chapter 23 for how to set up a DHCP server.) You can, optionally, set your own host name, which can be just a name (such as `jukebox`) or a fully qualified domain name (such as `jukebox.linuxtoys.net`).

    - **Statically set IP addresses:** If there is no DHCP, or other boot server, on your LAN, you can add necessary IP address information statically by selecting this option and adding the following information:

        Address: Type the IP address of this computer into the Address box. This number must be unique on your network. For your private LAN, you can use private IP addresses (see the section, "Understanding IP Addresses" later in this chapter).

        Subnet Mask: Enter the netmask to indicate what part of the IP address represents the network. (Netmask is described later in this chapter.)

        Default Gateway Address: If a computer or router connected to your LAN is providing routing functions to the Internet or other network, type the IP address of the computer into this box. (Chapter 16 describes how to use NAT or IP masquerading and use Fedora or RHEL as a router.)

    - **Set MTU to:** The maximum transfer unit (MTU) sets the number of 8-bit bytes that are available to the Internet Protocol in a link-layer frame. Click the check box and enter a number to change from the default 1500 MTU used by default for Ethernet interfaces in Linux. Lower rates can result in fewer packets being dropped on unreliable networks (some gamers like to lower the rate slightly, so fewer small actions are dropped). Higher rates can improve performance of large data transfers on reliable networks. In most cases, you don't need to modify this.

6. Click OK in the Ethernet Device window to save the configuration and close the window.

7. Click File → Save to save the information you entered.

8. Click Activate in the Network Configuration window to start your connection to the LAN.

Identifying other computers (hosts and DNS)

Each time you use a name to identify a computer, as when browsing the Web or using an e-mail address, the computer name must be translated into an IP address. To resolve names to IP addresses, Fedora and RHEL go through a search order (based on the contents of three files in the /etc directory: resolv.conf, nsswitch.conf, and host.conf). By default, it checks:

- Hostnames you add yourself (which end up in the /etc/hosts file).
- Hosts available via NIS (if an NIS server is configured as described in Chapter 23).
- Hostnames available via DNS.

You can use the Network Configuration window to add:

- **Hostnames and IP addresses.** You might do this to identify hosts on your LAN that are not configured on a DNS server.
- **DNS search path.** By adding domain names to a search path (such as linuxtoys.net), you can browse to a site by its hostname (such as jukebox), and have Linux search the domains you added to the search path to find the host you are looking for (such as jukebox.linuxtoys.net).
- **DNS name servers.** A DNS server can resolve addresses for the domains it serves and contact other DNS servers to get addresses for all other DNS domains.

> **NOTE:** If you are configuring a DNS server, you can use that server to centrally store names and IP addresses for your LAN. This saves you the trouble of updating every computer's /etc/hosts file every time you add or change a computer on your LAN. Refer to Chapter 25 to learn how to set up a DNS server.

To add hostnames, IP addresses, search paths, and DNS servers, do the following:

1. Start the Network Configuration. As root user from a Terminal window, type **neat** or from the Desktop menu, click System Settings → Network. The Network Configuration window appears.
2. Click the Hosts tab. A list of IP addresses, hostnames, and aliases appears.
3. Click New. A pop-up window appears asking you to add the IP address, hostname, and aliases for a host that you can reach on your network. Figure 15-10 shows the Network Configuration window and the pop-up window for adding a host.
4. Type in the IP address number, hostname, and, optionally, the host alias.
5. Click OK.
6. Repeat this process until you have added every computer on your LAN.
7. Click the DNS tab.
8. Type the IP address of the computers that serve as your Primary and Secondary DNS servers. You get these IP addresses from your ISP or, if you created your own DNS server, you can enter that server's IP address.

9. Type the name of the domain (probably the name of your local domain) to be searched for hostnames into the DNS Search Path box.

10. Select File → Save to save the changes.

11. Select File → Quit to exit.

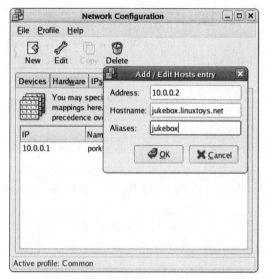

Figure 15-10: Add hosts to /etc/hosts using the Network Configuration window.

Now, when you use programs such as `ftp`, `ssh`, or other TCP/IP utilities, you can use any hostname that is identified on your local computer, exists in your search path domain, or can be resolved from the public Internet DNS servers. (Strictly speaking, you don't have to set up your `/etc/hosts` file. You could use IP addresses as arguments to TCP/IP commands, but names are easier to work with.)

Adding Windows computers to your LAN

It is likely that you have other types of computers on your LAN in addition to those running Linux systems (at least for a few more years). If a DHCP server is available on your LAN (or if you have configured one yourself as described in Chapter 23), Windows and most other computer systems can simply start up and begin using the network. In cases where your network card is not properly detected, or you want to set static IP addresses, you need to do some extra configuration.

If you are using Windows Vista, Vista will detect when you connect a network cable. A Set Network Location window appears, allowing you to choose whether the network is a Home, Work, or Public location. After you choose the connection type, you can take the defaults or select to change or view your network and sharing settings.

For Windows XP or earlier Windows systems, the following are general steps for manually adding your Windows computers to the Ethernet LAN you just created:

1. Power down your computer and install an Ethernet card. (Most PC Ethernet cards will run on Windows.)

2. Connect an Ethernet cable from the card to your switch.

3. Reboot your computer. If your card is detected, Windows will either automatically install a driver or ask you to insert a disk that comes with the card to install the driver.

4. Open the window to configure networking. (Select Start → Settings → Control Panel; then double-click the Network icon. If you have Windows XP, you also need to click Set up or change your Internet connection.). A window to change network properties appears.

5. What you do next depends on the version of Windows you are running:

   For Windows 98:

   - Find the Ethernet card you have just installed in the list and select it.
   - Click Add. The Select Network Component Type pop-up window appears.
   - Double-click Protocol. The Select Network Protocol window appears.
   - Click Microsoft, and then double-click TCP/IP. A new entry should appear in your Network window that looks similar to the following, depending on your card:

   ```
   TCP/IP -> 3Com Etherlink III ISA
   ```

   - Double-click on that new entry. The TCP/IP Properties window should appear, similar to the one in Figure 15-11 for Windows XP.

   For Windows 2000 or XP:

   - Click Switch to classic view.
   - Double-click the Network connections.
   - Double-click Local Area Connection. The Local Area Connection Status window appears.
   - Click Properties. The Local Area Connection Properties window appears.
   - Select Internet Protocol (TCP/IP), and click the Properties button. The Internet Protocol (TCP/IP) Properties window appears as shown in Figure 15-11.
   - Click Use the following IP address to configure your IP address manually.

   NOTE: If you are using a DHCP server to assign IP addresses, click Obtain an IP address automatically instead. See Chapter 23 for information on setting up Linux as a DHCP server.

   - Add the IP address, Subnet mask, and Default Gateway for this computer.
   - Add the IP addresses of up to two DNS servers.

- Click OK. You may need to reboot Windows for the settings to take effect.

At this point, your Windows computer knows to listen on the network (via its Ethernet card) for messages addressed to the IP address you have just entered.

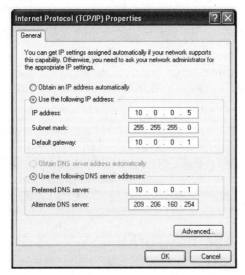

Figure 15-11: Configure TCP/IP on Windows XP for your Ethernet LAN.

Setting Up a Wireless LAN

Sometimes it's not convenient to run wires to all the computers on your network. Pulling Ethernet cables through existing walls can be a pain. Dragging wires into your garden so you can sit in a lounge chair and surf the Internet can ruin the ambiance. With inexpensive, high-speed wireless equipment available today, a wireless LAN is an economical solution.

Although you can use wireless LAN cards with other computer systems, you may want to use Linux systems for one or more nodes in your wireless network. For example, the features in Linux can eliminate the need to buy other types of equipment. Some additional features that make Linux a valuable asset on a wireless LAN include:

- **Internet access** — You don't need a separate router or gateway machine to attach your wireless LAN to the Internet. Having wired and wireless Ethernet LAN cards on a Linux system enables your wireless clients to access the Internet through your Linux system.

- **Firewall** — Owing to some inherent security weaknesses with wireless encryption protocols, you may want to add an extra measure of security to your network by configuring firewalls. With a Linux firewall (iptables) at the boundary between your wireless LAN and your larger network, you still have a measure of protection for your larger network if someone cracks your wireless LAN.

- **Monitoring and logging** — All the tools you use for monitoring and logging activity on your wired networks in Linux are also available for your wireless network.

> **NOTE:** Keep in mind that you don't have to use Fedora or RHEL to provide Internet access, firewalls, and monitoring. There are several Linux firewall distributions that were created specifically for this purpose that can run from live CDs or even floppy disks.

In the past few Fedora releases, support for different wireless cards and tools for connecting to wireless networks have improved tremendously. In most cases, to connect to a wireless network you can just use NetworkManager (as described earlier in this chapter), and you can skip this section altogether. However, in cases where your wireless card isn't properly detected or configured, this section should help you find the drivers you need and do any manual configuration necessary.

This section describes how to use wireless LAN equipment on computers running Fedora or RHEL to create a wireless Ethernet LAN. It focuses on configuring two Linux systems for wireless communication; however, once you configure these nodes, you can add Windows, Linux, or other types of systems to your wireless LAN by installing compatible wireless cards on each system.

Understanding wireless networks

Wireless LANs are most appropriate in environments where wires are impractical. Despite some challenges such as security and interference, a wireless LAN provides these advantages:

- You don't have to run wires in places that are hard to reach. In many cases, a single wireless LAN can extend your network throughout a building or to another building without the need for wires between each node.
- For the price of a wireless card, you can save the expense of wires, network switches (the air is your switch), and wall repairs (to fix the holes from pulling wires through).
- You can freely move computers around within the transmission range that your environment allows (distances being limited by such variables as antenna power, obstacles, and rates of transmission).

Although several different wireless networking standards exist, this chapter focuses on the installation of relatively low-cost, standard IEEE 802.11b and 802.11g wireless-networking equipment. An 802.11b or 802.11g wireless network uses space in the spectrum available to the public (in other words, you use space in the air for which no special license is required). The 802.11 standards are often referred to as the *Wi-Fi,* or *Wireless Fidelity*, standard.

An 802.11 network is characterized by the following:

- It provides transmission rates of up to 11 Mbps (802.11b) or up to 54 Mbps (802.11g). Transmission rates can also be set (or auto-detected) to lower rates for each standard.

- It uses the 2.4 GHz band of the spectrum. Microwave ovens, Bluetooth devices, and some high-end mobile phones also use this band. (Check local regulations if you are setting up an 802.11 network outside the United States.) To reduce congestion, 14 separate channels have been made available within the 2.4 GHz range.

- It allows transmission over distances as short as a desktop away to as long as several miles away (using special antennas). Greater distances can be gained at lower transmission speeds.

- Makes connections between multiple clients or clients and a base station (usually referred to as an *access point*). On the clients, the wireless LAN cards run in Ad hoc mode, while the base station uses infrastructure mode (also called Managed mode).

Other 802.11 standards exist (such as 802.11a, which can operate at higher speeds), but for the most part wireless-equipment manufacturers originally rallied around the 802.11b standard, and now rally around the 802.11g standard (which can communicate at lower speeds with 802.11b equipment as well). Prices of 802.11b and 802.11g equipment are so close these days that in most cases you will want the 802.11g equipment.

> **CROSS-REFERENCE:** To see a complete list of Wi-Fi–certified products, visit the WECA Web site (`www.wirelessethernet.org`, and click Wi-Fi Certified™ Products). Although these products should be able to communicate with one another; they do not all have drivers that are compatible with Linux.

After your wireless network has been configured, you can use the wireless connections as you would a regular wired Ethernet connection. For example, you can configure TCP/IP on top of your wireless network so that it acts as a gateway to your network's Internet connection. If you are using Linux as a wireless network client as well, you can take full advantage of firewall, masquerading, network proxy, or other networking features to protect and make full use of your wireless network.

Choosing wireless hardware

Getting wireless cards working in Fedora and RHEL, without some scrambling around, has been hit-or-miss until recently. In a recent release of Fedora, the Fedora project made the decision to track down and include firmware drivers for as many wireless LAN cards as they could find (provided they could be legally redistributed with Fedora). You can follow the progress of this effort here:

`http://fedoraproject.org/wiki/Releases/FeatureWirelessFirmware`

Some of the results of that effort are the following Fedora software packages that include support for different wireless cards:

- **atmel-firmware** — Contains firmware needed for Amtel at76c50x wireless network chips.

- **ipw2100-firmware** — Contains firmware needed for Intel PRO/Wireless 2100 Network Connection mini PCI adapters in Linux. Read about the Linux driver for these cards at the project's Web site (`http://ipw2100.sourceforge.net/index.php`).

- **ipw2200-firmware** — Contains firmware needed for Intel PRO/Wireless 2915ABG Network Connection and Intel PRO/Wireless 2200BG Network Connection mini PCI adapters in Linux. Read about the Linux driver for these cards at the project's Web site (`http://ipw2200.sourceforge.net/index.php`).

- **iwl3945-firmware** — Contains firmware needed for Intel xc2 xae PRO/Wireless 3945 A/B/G network adaptors. The project page for the Linux drivers used for these cards is located at: `http://intellinuxwireless.org`.

- **iwl4965-firmware** — Contains firmware needed for Intel xc2 xae PRO/Wireless 4965 A/G/N network adaptors.

- **zd1211-firmware** — Contains firmware needed to work with wireless LAN USB sticks based on ZyDAS ZD1211 and ZD1211B chips. Source code and docs on the Linux driver for these wireless cards an be found here: `www.deine-taler.de/zd1211/`.

- **rt61pci-firmware** — Contains firmware needed for Ralink xc2 xae RT2561/RT2661 A/B/G network adaptors.

- **rt73usb-firmware** — Contains firmware needed for Ralink xc2 xae RT2571W/RT267.1 A/B/G network adaptors.

- **bcm43xx-fwcutter** — Contains the `bcm43xxx-fwcutter` command for extracting firmware from drivers created from Broadcom 43xx wireless cards. Because the firmware for these cards cannot be freely distributed, you need to download the driver that comes with the card and extract the firmware to the `/lib/firmware` directory.

If you have a wireless card that is supported by any of these packages, you can try installing the package, rebooting, and starting NetworkManager. If your card is not supported in this way, refer to the next section for information on getting other wireless cards going.

Selecting wireless LAN cards

Wireless LAN card manufacturers have not shown much interest in providing Linux drivers. Most wireless card drivers that are native to Linux were created without the help of those manufacturers. Also, in many cases Linux drivers are not available at all.

Another issue related to purchasing a wireless LAN card is that manufacturers often change their hardware without notice. Wireless cards with the same name and model number may include different wireless chipsets. While this may not be a problem for Windows users (because the vendor will include a Windows driver to match), the card may fail on your Linux machine despite that fact that others using a card of the same name in Linux swear it is working just fine.

So, now that you know that your wireless card may not work once you get it home, let's talk about how to have the best chance of picking a card that will work. Here are some places to begin looking:

- **Native Linux driver** — Some wireless cards have drivers that were created specifically for Linux systems (see the previous section). Cards with those drivers have a good chance of being detected automatically and working after you install the wireless card. A project called Madwifi (`http://madwifi.org`) has additional Linux wireless drivers, created specifically for wireless LAN cards that use chipsets from Atheros (`www.atheros.com`). Select Compatibility List from the Madwifi Wiki (`http://madwifi.org/wiki/Compatibility`) to see supported wireless cards. There are Madwifi RPMs available from the Livna.org repository (See Chapter 2 for information on installing packages from the Livna.org repository).

- **Windows driver** — In cases where no native Linux driver is available, it's sometimes possible to use an open source driver called ndiswrapper along with the Windows driver to use a wireless card in Linux. To see which cards are supported by ndiswrapper, refer to the list of ndiswrapper-supported cards. Go to the NDISwrapper wiki(`http://ndiswrapper.sourceforge.net/joomla/`) and select Documents/Wiki → List of Cards.

Table 15-1 shows a list of network cards that have Linux-specific open source drivers included with Fedora and RHEL.

> **NOTE:** It's possible that even if your wireless card isn't listed in Table 15-1 that it might still work with drivers included with Fedora or RHEL. Some wireless cards that include the same chipset (and therefore work with the same driver) may be referred to by different names. Rather than try to keep track of all the various acquisitions and name changes in the wireless industry, I refer you to the Linux Wireless LAN HOWTO (`www.hpl.hp.com/personal/Jean_Tourrilhes/Linux`). The Drivers section provides more insight into which drivers work with which cards.

Table 15-1: Supported Wireless Network Adapters and Modules

Wireless Network Adapter	Module
350 Series Wireless LAN Adapter (Cisco Systems)	`airo_cs.ko`
ADMtec ADM8211 wireless	`adm8211.ko`
Aironet PC4500 (Cisco Systems)	`airo_cs.ko`
Aironet PC4800 (Cisco Systems)	`airo_cs.ko`
AT&T WaveLAN Adapter	`wavelan_cs.ko`
Atheros 802.11 wireless	`ath5k.ko`
Atmel AT76C50X wireless	`atmel_cs.ko`
Atmel AT76C50X wireless (PCI version)	`atmel_pci.ko`

Wireless Network Adapter	Module
Broadcom 43xx wireless	`bcm43xx.ko`
Cabletron RoamAbout 802.11 DS	`wvlan_cs.ko`
Compaq WL100 11 Mbps Wireless Adapter	`orinoco_cs.ko`
Digital RoamAbout/DS	`wavelan_cs.ko`
ELSA AirLancer MC-11	`wvlan_cs.ko`
Intel PRO/Wireless 2100 Network Connection mini PCI adapters	`ipw2100.ko`
Intel PRO/Wireless 2915ABG and 2200BG Network Connection mini PCI adapters	`ipw2200.ko`
Lucent Technologies WaveLAN Adapter	`wavelan_cs.ko`
Intersil PRISM2 11 Mbps Wireless Adapter	`wvlan_cs.ko`
Lucent Technologies WaveLAN/IEEE Adapter	`orinoco_cs.ko`
MELCO WLI-PCM-L11	`orinoco_cs.ko`
MELCO WLI-PCM-L11G	`orinoco_cs.ko`
NCR WaveLAN Adapter	`wavelan_cs.ko`
Orinoco PC Cards	`orinoco_cs.ko`
PLANEX GeoWave/GW-CF110	`orinoco_cs.ko`
Planet WL3501	`wl3501_cs.ko`
Prism54 PCI wireless	`prism54pci.ko`
Prism54 USB wireless	`prism54usb.ko`
Realtek RTL8187 USB wireless	`rtl8187`
Xircom CreditCard Netwave	`netwave_cs.ko`
ZCOMAX AirRunner/XI-300	`orinoco_cs.ko`
ZyDAS ZD1201 wireless LAN USB sticks	`zd1201.ko`
ZyDAS ZD1211 wireless LAN USB sticks	`zd1211rw.ko`

Selecting antennas

If you are setting up your wireless LAN among several computers in close proximity to each other, you may not need an additional antenna. To deal with obstructions and longer distances, however, you can add indoor or outdoor antennas to your wireless hardware.

In the sections that follow, I illustrate different types of indoor and outdoor antennas that are compatible with those cards.

Using indoor antennas

The antennas that are built into wireless LAN cards often work well enough to enable communication among computers in an open area. Additional indoor antennas are useful if the direct line of sight between the wireless LAN cards is blocked. A computer may be locked in a storage closet or stuck under a desk. A pile of papers might inhibit transmission, or a sheet of metal might stop it dead. A small antenna that draws the transmission away from the card might be the answer to these problems.

While most wireless LAN cards don't require a completely unobstructed line of sight, an obstacle can certainly slow reception. To get around this problem, an antenna such as the Orinoco IEEE range-extender can plug directly into an Orinoco Gold or Silver wireless LAN card. A 1.5-meter extension cable can bring the signal out from behind a closed door or out on top of a desk. When you set up the antenna, it is recommended that it be:

- Placed in a central location
- Mounted vertically
- Located away from obstructions (metal surfaces in particular, and, to a lesser extent, solid objects such as concrete walls or stacks of papers)

Refer to the instructions that come with your antenna for specific guidelines regarding placing and mounting the antenna.

Using outdoor antennas

Choosing and setting up outdoor antennas for your wireless LAN can be more difficult and expensive than setting them up indoors. Once the outdoor antennas are in place, however, you can save money because you won't need multiple Internet access accounts (monthly fees, DSL/cable modems, and so on).

Although a complete description of the use of outside antennas with your wireless LAN is outside the scope of this chapter, here are some tips that will help you choose the best antennas for your wireless LAN.

- **Point-to-point versus multipoint** — If you are creating a point-to-point link between two outdoor locations (for example, to share an Internet connection between two buildings), a directional antenna can help you achieve greater distance and transmission speeds. However, if your antenna is providing multipoint access for several other outdoor antennas or wireless clients (such as students working from laptops on the campus lawn), an omnidirectional antenna may be more appropriate.

- **Clearance** — The clearer the line of sight between each outdoor antenna, the greater the distance and transmission speed you can achieve. Placing antennas at the highest possible points can prevent diminished performance caused by trees, cars, buildings, and other objects. The amount of distance between obstacles and the coverage area of your wireless transmission is referred to as the *clearance factor* (see Figure 15-12).

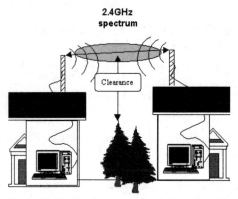

Figure 15-12: The distance of obstructive objects from the wireless signal is called the *clearance*.

- **Distance** — Although the actual distances over which antennas can send and receive data varies greatly based on different factors, you can achieve distances of many miles with outdoor antennas. For example, two Orinoco 24 dBi directional parabolic-grid antennas can theoretically achieve distances of up to 52 miles at an 11 Mbps transmission speed with a 180-meter clearance. Reduce that transmission rate to 1 Mbps and you can achieve distances of up to 149 miles with a 1200-meter clearance. Shorter distances are achieved with less expensive equipment, such as the Orinoco 14 dBi directional antenna which can achieve distances of up to 5.3 miles at 11 Mbps with a 13-meter clearance.

- **Cable factor** — The distances that transmissions travel on the cables between the wireless cards and the antennas can be a factor in choosing the right antenna. The shorter the cables, the greater the distance and speed you will get on your antenna.

The power of an antenna is rated in terms of *gain*. Gain is measured in decibels, based on a *theoretic isotropic radiator* (or *dBi*). Higher gains offer opportunities for reaching greater distances at greater speeds. However, the ability of the antenna to focus that power (directional versus omnidirectional), greatly affects the speeds and distances that can be achieved. If you want to see some interesting home made antennas, search the Web for the word *cantenna*.

Getting wireless drivers

If you are using a wireless card that includes a supported driver in Fedora or RHEL, the system might detect that card and load the proper driver, so that you will be able to configure it as described later in this section. In other cases, you will need to install the associated firmware for the driver that comes with the hardware (usually intended for Windows systems). If the driver you need for your wireless card is not included with Fedora, you may be able to use ndiswrapper and a Windows driver to configure your wireless card. The following procedure contains an example of configuring ndiswrapper with a Linksys 802.11g wireless PCI adapter card.

If you find you need further information about using ndiswrapper, refer to the Fedora Ndiswrapper wiki page (`ndiswrapper.sourceforge.net/joomla/`). Then select Documents/Wiki.

```
http://ndiswrapper.sourceforge.net/mediawiki/index.php/Fedora
```

> **NOTE:** Because there is now a BCM43xx driver available in Fedora, you can use the `bcm43xx-fwcutter` command to extract the firmware from the package to use with that native Linux driver. After that, a reboot should properly detect and load the modules needed for the card. For example, after unzipping the `wpc54g` zip file shown in the procedure below, type the following command with the `bcmwl5.sys` file in the current directory:
>
> **# bcm43xx-fwcutter -w /lib/firmware/ bcmwl5.sys**
>
> If you find that your wireless card is not working using the Fedora drivers, you can use ndiswrapper instead to get your wireless card working. However, because Fedora will try to use the native driver first instead of ndiswrapper, you may need to blacklist the driver that Fedora wants to use.

1. Determine the kind of wireless card you are using. If you have a PCI card, type:

    ```
    # lspci -v | less
    00:0a.0 Network controller: Broadcom Corporation BCM4306 802.11b/g
    Wireless LAN Controller (rev 03)
    Subsystem: Linksys: Unknown device 0014
    Flags: bus master, fast devsel, latency 64, IRQ 5
    Memory at ee000000 (32-bit, non-prefetchable) [size=8K]
    ```

    In this example, the PCI card is a BCM4306 802.11b/g Wireless Controller from Broadcom Corporation. (If your wireless card is a USB device, type the `lsusb` instead.)

2. Check the following list of wireless card drivers known to run under ndiswrapper:
    `http://ndiswrapper.sourceforge.net/mediawiki/index.php/List`.

3. If your card is on the list, download the driver recommended on that page. I used the Linksys WMP54GS Wireless-G PCI Adapter (which was reflected by the chipset BCM4306 802.11g, rev 03 shown in the preceding lspci output). So I downloaded the driver as follows:

    ```
    # mkdir wireless
    # cd wireless/
    # wget ftp://ftp.linksys.com/pub/network/wpc54g_v2_driver_utility_v2.0.zip
    ```

4. After the file is done downloading, unzip the driver file. For the example, I typed:

    ```
    # unzip wpc54g_v2_driver_utility_v2.0.zip
    ```

5. Install the kernel-devel and gcc packages. Then link the kernels directory to the modules directory or your current kernel (replacing `<kernel-version>` with the version of your kernel development package and current kernel, where shown):

```
# yum install kernel-devel gcc
# ln -s /usr/src/kernels/<kernel-version> /lib/modules/<kernel-
version>/build
```

6. Get the ndiswrapper source code by downloading it to your Fedora or RHEL system from the following site: `http://sourceforge.net/projects/ndiswrapper`.

> **NOTE:** There are also ndiswrapper RPM packages available for Fedora at `rpm.livna.org`. If you decide to go that route, instead of installing the source code, make sure that the you find the ndiswrapper package that matches your kernel version. See Chapter 5 for information on enabling the `rpm.livna.org` repository.

7. With the ndiswraper source code package in the current directory, unzip and untar it as follows:

```
# tar xvfz ndiswrapper-*tar.gz
```

8. As root user, change to the ndiswrapper directory and run the `make` command as follows:

```
# cd ndiswrapper*
# make install
```

9. Get the INF file from the unzipped driver package. From our example, the file we needed was `lsbcmnds.inf`. Then run the `ndiswrapper -i` command to install the driver. For example, with the `lsbcmnds.inf` file in the current directory, I ran:

```
# ndiswrapper -i lsbcmnds.inf
```

10. Check that the driver is now available and the hardware is available:

```
# ndiswrapper -l
lsbcmnds        driver present, hardware present
```

11. To load the ndiswrapper module, type the following

```
# modprobe ndiswrapper
```

12. Type the following command to see your wireless lan (wlan) entry:

```
# iwconfig
```

13. Type the following to see your access point:

```
# iwlist wlan0 scan
```

14. Create an alias for your wireless device to wlan0, so that the interface is loaded automatically at boot time:

```
# ndiswrapper -m
```

15. To check that the ndiswrapper module loaded properly, you can check the `/var/log/messages` file. These messages appeared after the module was loaded:

```
Nov  2 20:28:53 toys kernel: ndiswrapper version 1.42 loaded
        (preempt=no,smp=no)
Nov  2 20:28:53 toys kernel: ACPI: PCI interrupt 0000:00:0a.0[A] ->
        GSI 5 (level, low) -> IRQ 5
Nov  2 20:28:53 toys kernel: ndiswrapper: using irq 5
Nov  2 20:28:54 toys udev: creating device node '/dev/ndiswrapper'
Nov  2 20:28:54 toys kernel: wlan0: ndiswrapper ethernet
        device 00:0f:66:6f:b9:0a using driver lsbcmnds
Nov  2 20:28:54 toys kernel: wlan0: encryption modes supported:
        WEP, WPA with TKIP, AES/CCMP
Nov  2 20:28:54 toys kernel: ndiswrapper: driver lsbcmnds
        (The Linksys Group, Inc.,07/17/2003, 3.30.15.0) added
```

From the output, you can see that the ndiswrapper module was loaded, that it found the wireless PCI card, and that the wlan0 interface was assigned to that device using the lsbcmnds driver. With the card properly detected, you can configure TCP/IP to use with that card.

Installing wireless Linux software

For most Fedora or RHEL install types, the software packages you need to create your wireless LAN will already be installed. Drivers and modules needed to support PCMCIA cards and wireless cards should be in your system. Besides the wireless drivers, the following software packages contain tools for configuring and working with your wireless LAN cards in Fedora and RHEL:

- **pcmciautils** — Contains commands and configuration files to support your wireless card if it happens to be a PCMCIA card.

- **wireless-tools** — Contains commands for setting extensions for your wireless LAN interface. Commands include `iwconfig` (for configuring your wireless interface) and `iwlist` (for listing wireless statistics).

After you have established a wireless LAN interface, you can use a variety of Linux software to monitor and control access to that interface. You will need to install the appropriate software packages as well. Here are some examples of other wireless software packages in Fedora that you might find useful:

- **aircrack-ng** — Can be used to audit wireless networks
- **wifi-radar** — Scans for available wireless networks

- **kismet** — Sniffing 802.11 wireless networks
- **wifiroamd** — Lets you search for the best available access point
- **airsnort** — Has tools for checking the strength of your wireless encryption keys

Configuring the wireless LAN

Before you begin testing the distances you can achieve with your wireless Linux LAN, I recommend that you configure wireless cards on two computers within direct sight of each other. After the two computers are communicating, you can change wireless settings to tune the connection and begin experimenting with transmission distances.

The following sections describe the steps you need to take to set up a wireless LAN between two Linux systems. Although only two nodes are described, you can add more computers to your wireless LAN once you know how. This procedure describes how to operate your wireless Linux LAN in two different modes:

- **Ad hoc** — All the computers in your wireless LAN are gathered into a single virtual network made up of only one cell. A single cell means that you cannot roam among different groups of wireless nodes and continue your communication invisibly. To do that requires a managed network.

- **Managed** — As I noted earlier, many wireless cards supported in Linux cannot operate as access points. A Linux wireless card, however, can operate as a node in a managed network. The wireless configuration tools that come with Fedora and RHEL let you identify the access point for Linux to use by indicating the access point's MAC address.

Install your wireless cards per the manufacturer's instructions. Then configure the interface for each card as described in the following procedure.

Configuring the wireless interface

The Network Configuration window (`neat` command) can be used to configure wireless Ethernet card interfaces, as well as regular wired Ethernet cards. The following procedure describes how to configure a wireless Ethernet card using the Network Configuration window.

> **NOTE:** If your wireless card driver does not appear on the list, you may need to configure your wireless card manually, as described later in this chapter. Step through this procedure and if you are not able to activate the wireless card, refer to the description of the `ifcfg-eth1` file.

1. Start the Network Configuration. From the Desktop menu, click System → Administration → Network, or, as root user from a Terminal window, type **neat**. The Network Configuration window appears.

2. Click the New button. The Select Device Type window appears.

3. Click Wireless connection and Forward. The Select Wireless Device window appears.

4. Select your wireless card from the list of cards shown, and click Forward. The Configure Wireless Connection window appears, as shown in Figure 15-13.

5. Add the following information and click Forward:

- **Mode** — Indicates the mode of operation for the wireless LAN card. Because I am setting up a wireless LAN consisting of only one cell (in other words, with no roaming to cells set up in other areas), I could set the mode to Ad hoc. Ad hoc mode allows the card to communicate directly with each of its peers. You can use Managed mode if you have multiple cells, requiring your card to communicate directly to an access point. You can also use Managed mode for a point-to-point network.

- **Network Name (SSID)** — The network name (or Network ID) that identifies cells that are part of the same network. If you have a group of cells (which might include multiple nodes and repeaters among which a client could roam), this name can identify all of those cells as falling under one virtual network. Choose any name you like and then use that name for all computers in your virtual network. (SSID stands for Service Set ID.)

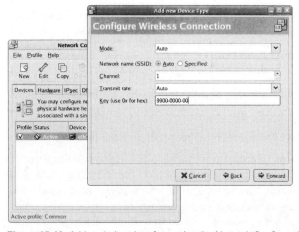

Figure 15-13: Add a wireless interface using the Network Configuration window.

- **Channel** — Choose a channel between 1 and 14. You can begin with channel 1; if you get interference on that channel, try changing to other channels.

- **Transmit Rate** — Choose the rate of transmission from the following rates: 11M, 5.5M, 2M, 1M, or Auto. Choosing Auto allows the interface to automatically ramp down to lower speeds as needed. Lower speeds allow the interface to transmit over greater distances and deal with noisy channels.

- **Key** — You need the same encryption key for all wireless LAN cards that are communicating with each other. It is critical to get this value right. This key is used to encrypt all data transmitted and decrypt all data received on the wireless interface. You can enter the number (up to 40 bits, depending on what is supported by your card) as XXXXXXXXXX or XXXX-XXXX-XX (where each X is a number from 0 to 9 or letter between A and F). For 64-bit encryption, the key must be ten hexadecimal characters; for 128-bit encryption, the key must be 32 hexadecimal characters.

A Configure Network Settings window appears.

6. You can enter the following information:

    - **Automatically obtain IP address settings with:** If you want to get your IP address from a DHCP server, click this box and the rest of the information is obtained automatically. Otherwise, set the IP address statically using the other options.

    - **Hostname:** If you are using DHCP, you can optionally add a hostname to identify this network interface. If none is entered here, the output from the /bin/hostname command is used.

    - **Statically set IP addresses:** Click here to manually set your IP addresses.

    - **Address:** If you selected static IP addresses, type the IP address of this computer into the Address text box. This number must be unique on your wireless network.

    - **Subnet Mask:** Enter the netmask to indicate what part of the IP address represents the network. (Netmask is described later in this chapter.)

    - **Default Gateway Address:** If a computer on your wireless LAN is providing routing to the Internet or other network, type the IP address of the computer here.

7. Click Forward to see a listing of the information you just entered.

8. Click Apply to complete the new wireless network interface.

9. Select File → Save (on the main window) to save the interface.

This procedure creates an interface configuration file in your /etc/sysconfig/network-scripts directory. The name of the configuration file is ifcfg- followed by the interface name (such as eth0, eth1, and so on). So, if your wireless card is providing your only network interface, it might be called ifcfg-eth0.

Using any text editor, open the ifcfg-eth? file (replacing ? with the interface number) as root user. The following is an example of an ifcfg-eth1 file:

```
# Please read /usr/share/doc/initscripts-*/sysconfig.txt
# for the documentation of these parameters.
ONBOOT=no
USERCTL=no
PEERDNS=no
GATEWAY=10.0.0.1
TYPE=Wireless
DEVICE=eth1
HWADDR=00:02:2d:2e:8c:a8
BOOTPROTO=none
NETMASK=255.255.255.0
IPADDR=10.0.1.1
```

```
DOMAIN=
ESSID=
CHANNEL=1
MODE=Ad-Hoc
RATE=11Mb/s
NETWORK=10.0.1.0
BROADCAST=10.0.1.255
```

In this example, the wireless card's hardware (MAC) address is automatically set to
`00:02:2d:2e:8c:a8`. (Your MAC address will be different.) The interface is not yet set to
come up at boot time (`ONBOOT=no`). The interface device is `eth1` (which matches the
interface filename `ifcfg-eth1`), because this particular computer has another Ethernet card
on the `eth0` interface. The interface type is set to `Wireless`.

Other information in the file sets standard TCP/IP address information. The NETMASK is set
to `255.255.255.0` and the IP address for the card is set to `10.0.1.1`. The broadcast
address is `10.0.1.255`.

You can also set many options that are specific to your wireless network in this file. The
following list explains some additional options that you might want to set:

- **NWID** — Identifies the name of this particular computer on the network. The
  computer's hostname (determined from the `uname -n` command) is used by default if
  you don't set it with NWID.

- **FREQ** — You can choose a particular frequency in which to transmit. No value is
  required because selecting a channel implies a certain frequency. If you do enter a
  frequency, the value must be a number followed by a k (kilohertz), M (megahertz), or G
  (gigahertz). The default values for the channels you select range from `2.412G` (channel
  1) to `2.484G` (channel 14), with other channels occurring at increments of .005G. The
  default is `2.422G`.

- **SENS** —You can select the sensitivity level of the access point. SENS can be set to 1
  (low density), 2 (medium density), or 3 (high density). The default is 1. The
  `sensitivity threshold` has an impact on roaming.

CAUTION: The encryption algorithm used with 802.11 networks is the Wired Equivalent Privacy (WEP)
algorithm. Although using the encryption key is more secure than not using it, experts feel that WEP has
some inherent flaws that might allow a drive-by hacker to decrypt your wireless LAN traffic. For that reason,
I strongly recommend using additional techniques to protect your wireless LANs, such as firewalls and
diligent log-checking. See the "Wireless Security" sidebar for further information. (In the future, keep your
eyes open for support for WPA encryption standards, which are expected to be more secure than WEP.)

Besides those options just shown, you can also pass any valid options to the `iwconfig`
command (which actually interprets these values), by adding an IWCONFIG option to the
configuration file. Display the `iwconfig` man page (`man iwconfig`) to see all wireless
options. Also view the `/etc/sysconfig/network-scripts/ifup-wireless` script to
see how the options you just added are processed.

> **NOTE:** On the computer that is acting as a gateway from your wireless network to the Internet, you need to turn on IP packet forwarding. Change the value of `net.ipv4.ip_forward` to 1 in `/etc/sysctl.conf`. Open that file as the root user with a text editor and change the line as follows:
>
> `net.ipv4.ip_forward = 1`

Repeat the configuration procedure for each wireless Fedora and RHEL computer on your LAN. At this point, your wireless network should be ready to go. Restart your network, as described in the following steps, to make sure that it is working.

Activating the wireless interfaces

To immediately activate the wireless interface you just configured, select the Wireless entry on the Network Configuration window and click the Activate button. After a few seconds, the Status should appear as Active.

To have the interface start when you reboot your computer, click the wireless interface from the Network Configuration window and select Edit. From the Wireless Device Configuration window that appears, click the box next to Activate device when computer starts.

If you want to explicitly enter a Network Name (SSID), click the Wireless Settings tab on the Wireless Device Configuration window. From there, select Specified, type the network name (any name you choose to match others on your wireless network), and click OK.

Be sure to save your changes on the Network Configuration window by clicking File → Save.

Checking your wireless connection

Your wireless LAN interface should be operating at this point. If another wireless computer is available on your wireless network, try communicating with it using the `ping` command and its IP address (as described in the section "Can you reach another computer on the LAN?" later in this chapter).

If you are not able to communicate with other wireless nodes or if transmission is slow, you may have more work to do. For example, if you see messages that say "Destination Host Unreachable," instead of the output shown earlier, refer to the section on "Troubleshooting a wireless LAN" for help.

Testing distances

Although you may be thrilled to have a wireless LAN working between two computers, you will probably want these computers to be located some distance from each other to make the LAN useful. Getting your wireless LAN to work at the desired distances can be quite a challenge. See the section "Selecting antennas" earlier in this chapter for suggestions on selecting and using antennas to configure the type of wireless LAN you are interested in.

Wireless Security

The Wireless Ethernet Compatibility Alliance (WECA) has recommended changes in response to security concerns about wireless networks. They did this because, unlike wired networks, which can often be physically protected within a building, wireless networks often extend beyond physical boundaries that can be protected.

The Wireless Equivalent Privacy (WEP) standard adds encryption to the 802.11 wireless standard. WECA refers to WEP as its way of providing "walls" that make wireless Ethernet as secure as wired Ethernet. However, you need to implement WEP, as well as other security methods that would apply to any computer network, in order to make your wireless network secure. Here are WECA's suggestions:

- Change the default WEP encryption key on a regular basis (possibly weekly or even daily). This prevents casual drive-by hackers from reading your encrypted transmissions.
- Use password protection on your drives and folders.
- Change the default Network Name (SSID).
- Use session keys, if available in your product (session keys are not supported in current Linux wireless drivers).
- Use MAC address filtering (supported in a limited way in Linux).
- Don't broadcast from the access point, if possible.
- Use a VPN (Virtual Private Network) system, which can add another layer of encryption beyond that which is available on your wireless network.

For larger organizations requiring greater security, WECA suggests such features as firewalls and user-verification schemes (such as Kerberos). As I mentioned earlier in this chapter, features for protecting from intrusions and restricting services are already built into Fedora and RHEL. Refer to the descriptions of security tools in Chapters 14, 15, and 16 for methods of securing your network, its computers, and their services. In particular, you could consider adding a VPN to further secure all data sent on your wireless LAN.

Wi-Fi Protected Access (WPA) features have recently become available for wireless cards in Linux. Wireless cards for Linux that support WPA include Cisco Aironet 802.11a/b/g, Linksys Dual-Band Wireless A+G, Proxim Gold 11a/b/g Combo card (8480-WD), and Netgear Dual Band WAG511. WPA-Supplicant software for implementing WPA in Linux is available from http://hostap.epitest.fi/wpa_supplicant.

Setting wireless extensions

After the wireless module is loaded, you can change wireless extensions using the `iwconfig` command. The `iwconfig` command is the command that is actually used to set the options added to the `ifcfg` configuration script (for example, for the eth1 interface, the script would be `/etc/sysconfig/network-scripts/eth1`).

Some of the same options that you set when the module was loaded can be reset using the `iwconfig` command. The `iwconfig` command can be useful for testing different settings on an active wireless LAN. The syntax of the `iwconfig` command is as follows:

```
# iwconfig interface parameter value
```

The `interface` is the name of the wireless interface you want to change, such as `eth1` or `wvlan0`. The `parameter` is the name of the option, and the *value* is replaced by its value. For example, to set your network name (ESSID) to Homelan, you could type the following as root user:

```
# iwconfig eth0 essid "Homelan"
```

Table 15-2 contains a list of available options for the `iwconfig` command. Refer back to the "Configuring the wireless interface" section for further details on these options.

Table 15-2: Options for the iwconfig Command

Option	Description
essid *name*	Indicates the network name.
ap *address*	Indicates that the access point is at a particular MAC address. For low-quality connections, the client driver may return to trying to automatically detect the access point. This setting is useful in Managed mode only.
channel *#*	Picks the channel number to operate on.
frag *frag_size*	Sets the fragmentation threshold for splitting up packets before they are transmitted.
freq 2.4??G	Sets the frequency of the channel to communicate on.
key *xxxx-xxxx-xx*	Sets the key used for WEP encryption.
mode *option*	Sets the mode used for communications to Ad-hoc, Managed, Master, Repeater, Secondary, or Auto.
nick *name*	Sets the station name to define this particular computer.
rate *XX*M	Defines the transmission rate to use.
rts *number*	Sets the RTS/CTS threshold for packet transmission.

Option	Description
`retry` *number*	For cards that support MAC retransmissions, you can use this option to determine how many retries are made before the transmission fails. The value can be a number (indicating number of seconds allotted for retries), or a number followed by an `m` (for milliseconds) or `u` (for microseconds). Instead of a number, you can set a number of retries using the limit parameter. For example: `retry limit 100` indicates that the transmission can retry up to 100 times.
`sens number`	Sets the lowest possible sensitivity threshold for which the wireless interface will try to receive a packet. Raising this level can help block out interference from other wireless LANs that might weakly encroach on your transmission area.

The best place to add `iwconfig` options permanently in Fedora or RHEL is the configuration file for your wireless interface in the `/etc/sysconfig/network-scripts` directory.

Options to `iwconfig` are added to the wireless interface file (such as `ifcfg-eth0` or `ifcfg-eth1`) using the `IWCONFIG` parameter. For example, to add an encryption-key value of 1234-1234-12 for your wireless LAN card, you could add the following line to your wireless-interface file:

```
IWCONFIG="key 1234-1234-12"
```

Understanding Internet Protocol Addresses

Whether you are using a wired or a wireless network, each computer you communicate with (including yours) must have a unique address on the network. In TCP/IP, each computer must be assigned an Internet Protocol (IP) address. This section gives you some background in IP addresses.

There are two basic ways to assign a hostname and IP address to a network interface in Linux:

- **Static addresses** — With static IP addresses, each computer has an IP address that doesn't change each time the computer reboots or restarts its network interface. Its IP address can be entered manually because it's not assigned on-the-fly. You can do this at Fedora or RHEL installation time, or later using the Network Configuration window.

- **Dynamic addresses** — With dynamic addresses, a client computer gets its IP address assigned from a server on the network when the client boots. The most popular protocol for providing dynamic addresses is called Dynamic Host Configuration Protocol (DHCP). With this method, a client computer may not have the same IP address each time it boots.

> **TIP:** If you expect to add and remove computers regularly from your LAN or if you have a limited number of IP addresses, you should use DHCP to assign IP addresses. Chapter 23 describes how to set up a DHCP server.

An IP address is a four-part number, with each part represented by a number from 0 to 255 (256 numbers total). Part of that IP address represents the network the computer exists on, while the remainder identifies the specific host on that network. Here's an example of an IP address:

```
192.168.35.121
```

Originally, IP addresses were grouped together and assigned to an organization that needed IP addresses, based on IP address classes. These days, a more efficient method, referred to as Classless Inter-Domain Routing (CIDR), is used to improve routing and waste fewer IP addresses. These two IP address methods are described in the following sections.

IP address classes

Unfortunately, it's not so easy to understand which part of an IP address represents the network and which represents the host without explaining how IP addresses are structured. IP addresses are assigned in the following manner. A network administrator is given a pool of addresses. The administrator can then assign specific host addresses within that pool as new computers are added to the organization's local network. There were originally three basic classes of IP addresses, each representing a different size network.

- **Class A** — Each Class A address has a number between 0 and 127 as its first part. Host numbers within a Class A network are represented by any combination of numbers in the next three parts. A Class A network therefore contains millions of host numbers (approximately 256 x 256 x 256, with a few special numbers being invalid). A valid Class A network number is:

```
24.
```

- **Class B** — A Class B IP address has a number between 128 and 191 in its first part. With a Class B network, however, the second part also represents the network. This enables a Class B network to have more than 64,000 host addresses (256 x 256). A valid Class B network number is:

```
135.84
```

- **Class C** — A Class C IP address begins with a number between 192 and 223 in its first part. With a Class C network, the first three parts of an IP address represent the network, while only the last part represents a specific host. Thus, each Class C network can have 254 numbers (the numbers 0 and 255 can't be assigned to hosts). Here is an example of a Class C network number:

```
194.122.56
```

To tell your computer which part of a network address is the network and which is the host, you must enter a number that masks the network number. That number is referred to as the *netmask*.

Understanding netmasks

Suppose you are assigned the Class B address 135.84, but you are only given the pool of numbers available to the address 135.84.118. How do you tell your network that every address beginning with 135.84.118 represents a host on your network, but that other addresses beginning with 135.84 should be routed to another network? You can do it with a netmask.

The netmask essentially identifies the network number for a network. When you assign the IP address that is associated with your computer's interface to the LAN (eth0), you are asked for a netmask. By default, your computer fills in a number that masks the part of your IP address that represents the class of your network. For example, the default netmasks for Class A, B, and C networks are the following:

- Class A netmask: 255.0.0.0
- Class B netmask: 255.255.0.0
- Class C netmask: 255.255.255.0

Now, if your network was assigned the network number 135.84.118, to tell your computer that 135.84.118 is the network number and not 135.84 (as it normally would be for a Class B address), add a netmask of 255.255.255.0. So you could use host numbers from 1 to 254 (which would go into the fourth part of the number).

To further confuse the issue, you could mask only one or more bits that are part of the IP address. Instead of using the number 255, you could use any other numbers between 0 and 255, including 128, 192, 224, 240, 248, 252, and 254, to mask only part of the numbers in that part of the address.

> **NOTE:** The reason that only the numbers just mentioned are valid netmasks is that each part is represented by eight binary numbers, but all 1s that are included must be to the left. So 240 would be allowed (11110000) but 242 would not (11110010). This limitation is what leads to the creation of CIDR (see the next section).

Classless Inter-Domain Routing

The class method of allocating IP addresses had several major drawbacks. First, few organizations fell neatly into one class or another. For most organizations, a Class C address (up to 256 IP addresses) was too small, and a Class B address (up to 65,534 IP addresses) was too big. The result was a lot of wasted numbers in a world where IP addresses were running short. Second, IP classes resulted in too many routing table entries. As a result, routers were becoming overloaded with information.

The Classless Inter-Domain Routing (CIDR) addressing scheme set out to deal with these problems. The scheme is similar to IP address classes, but offers much more flexibility in assigning how much of the 32-bit IP address is the network identifier. Instead of the first 8, 16, or 32 bits identifying the network, 13 to 27 bits could identify the network. As a result, groups of assigned IP addresses could contain from 32 to about 524,000 host addresses.

To indicate the network identifier, a CIDR IP address is followed by a slash (/) and then a number from 13 to 27. A smaller number indicates a network containing more hosts. Here's an example of an IP address that uses the CIDR notation:

```
128.8.27.18/16
```

In this example, the first 16 bits (128.8) represent the network number, and the remainder (27.18) represents the specific host number. This network number can contain up to 65,536 hosts (the same as a class B address). The following list shows how many hosts can be represented in networks using different numbers to identify the network:

```
/13     524,288 hosts
/14     262,144 hosts
/15     131,072 hosts
/16      65,536 hosts
/17      32,768 hosts
/18      16,382 hosts
/19       8,192 hosts
/20       4,096 hosts
/21       2,048 hosts
/22       1,024 hosts
/23         512 hosts
/24         256 hosts
/25         128 hosts
/26          64 hosts
/27          32 hosts
```

The CIDR addressing scheme also helps reduce the routing overload problem by having a single, high-level route represent many lower-level routes. For example, an ISP could be assigned a single /13 IP network and assign the 500,000-plus addresses to its customers. Routers outside the ISP would only need to know how to reach the ISP for those half-million addresses. The ISP would then be responsible for maintaining routing information for all of the host routes with that network address.

Getting IP addresses

So, what is the impact of assigning IP addresses for the computers on your LAN? Your choice of which IP addresses to use depends on your situation. If you are part of a large organization, you should get addresses from your network administrator. Even if you don't connect to other LANs in your organization at the moment, having unique addresses can make it easier to connect to them in the future.

If you are setting up a network for yourself (with no other networks to consider in your organization), you can use private addresses. However, if you need to connect computers to the Internet as servers, apply for your own domain name (from an Internet domain registrar) and IP addresses (from your ISP).

> **CROSS-REFERENCE:** Refer to Chapter 25 for information about getting the IP addresses and domain names you need to configure a public server on the Internet.

If you don't need to have your LAN accessible from the Internet, choose IP addresses from the set of available general-purpose IP addresses. Using these private IP addresses, you can still access the Internet from your LAN for such things as Web browsing and e-mail by using IP masquerading or Network Address Translation (NAT), as described in Chapter 16. Table 15-3 lists the private IP addresses not used on any public part of the Internet.

Table 15-3: Private IP Addresses

Network Class	Network Numbers	Addresses per Network Number
Class A	10.0.0.0	167,777,216
Class B	172.16.0.0 to 172.31.0.0	65,536
Class C	192.168.0.0 to 192.168.255.255	256

So, for a small private LAN, the following numbers are examples of IP addresses that could be assigned to the host computers on your network. (You could use any of the network numbers, plus host numbers, from the table. These are just examples.)

- 192.168.1.1
- 192.168.1.2
- 192.168.1.3
- 192.168.1.4
- 192.168.1.5

You could continue that numbering up to 192.168.1.254 on this network, and you could use a network mask of 255.255.255.0.

Troubleshooting Your LAN

After your LAN has been set up, your Ethernet cards installed, and hostnames and addresses added, there are several methods you can use to check that everything is up and working. Some troubleshooting techniques are shown in the following sections.

Did Linux find your Ethernet driver at boot time?

Type the following right after you boot your computer to verify whether Linux found your card and installed the Ethernet interface properly:

```
dmesg | grep eth
```

The dmesg command lists all the messages that were output by Linux at boot time. The grep eth command causes only those lines that contain the word *eth* to be printed. The first message shown below appeared on my laptop computer with the NETGEAR card. The second example is from my computer with the EtherExpress Pro/100 card:

```
eth0: NE2000 Compatible: port 0x300, irq3, hw_addr 00:80:C8:8C:8E:49
eth0: OEM i82557/i82558 10/100 Ethernet at 0xccc0, 00:90:27:4E:67:35, IRQ 17.
```

The message in the first example shows that a card was found at IRQ3 with a port address of 0x300 and an Ethernet hardware address of 00:80:C8:8C:8E:49. In the second example, the card is at IRQ 17, the port address is 0xccc0, and the Ethernet address is 00:90:27:4E:67:35.

> **NOTE:** If the eth0 interface is not found, but you know that you have a supported Ethernet card, check that your Ethernet card is properly seated in its slot.

Can you reach another computer on the LAN?

Try communicating with different network interfaces on your LAN. The ping command can be used to send a packet to another computer or local network interface and to ask for a packet in return. You could give ping either a host name (pine) or an IP address (10.0.0.10). The following is a succession of ping commands you can use to test your local network interfaces and connections to other computers (your external and router IP addresses will probably be different):

```
# ping localhost            Local loopback
# ping 10.0.0.10            Local external interface
# ping 10.0.0.1             Local router to Internet
# ping 208.77.188.166       Remote server
# ping example.com          Remote server by name
```

If you are able to ping a remote server by name, you know that both name service and routing are working. If the remote server can be reached, the output will look similar to the following:

```
PING example.com (208.77.188.166): 56(84) bytes of data.
64 bytes from www.example.com (208.77.188.166): icmp_seq=1 ttl=255
time=0.351 ms
64 bytes from www.example.com (208.77.188.166): icmp_seq=2 ttl=255
time=0.445 ms
64 bytes from www.example.com (208.77.188.166): icmp_seq=3 ttl=255
time=0.409 ms
```

```
64 bytes from www.example.com (208.77.188.166): icmp_seq=4 ttl=255
time=0.457 ms
64 bytes from www.example.com (208.77.188.166): icmp_seq=5 ttl=255
time=0.401 ms
64 bytes from www.example.com (208.77.188.166): icmp_seq=6 ttl=255
time=0.405 ms
64 bytes from www.example.com (208.77.188.166): icmp_seq=7 ttl=255
time=0.443 ms
64 bytes from www.example.com (208.77.188.166): icmp_seq=8 ttl=255
time=0.384 ms
64 bytes from www.example.com (208.77.188.166): icmp_seq=9 ttl=255
time=0.365 ms
64 bytes from www.example.com (208.77.188.166): icmp_seq=10 ttl=255
time=0.367 ms

--- example.com ping statistics ---
10 packets transmitted, 10 packets received, 0% packet loss, time 9011ms
rtt min/avg/max/mdev = 0.351/0.402/0.457/0.042 ms, pipe 2
```

A line of output is printed each time a packet is sent and received in return. It shows how much data was sent and how long it took for each package to be received. After you have watched this for a while, press Ctrl+C to stop ping. At that point, you will see statistics on how many packets were transmitted, received, and lost.

If you don't see output that shows packets have been received, it means you are not contacting the other computer. Try to verify that the names and addresses of the computers that you want to reach are in your /etc/hosts file or that your DNS server is accessible. Next, confirm that the names and IP addresses you have for the other computers you are trying to reach are correct (the IP addresses are the most critical).

Is your Ethernet connection up?

Using the ifconfig command, you can determine whether your Ethernet (and other network interfaces) are up and running. Type the following command:

```
# ifconfig
```

The output that appears is similar to the following:

```
eth0 Link encap:Ethernet HWaddr 00:90:27:4E:67:35
     inet addr:10.0.0.10 Bcast:10.0.0.255 Mask:255.255.255.0
     UP BROADCAST RUNNING MULTICAST MTU:1500 Metric:1
     RX packets:156 errors:0 dropped:0 overruns:0 frame:0
     TX packets:104 errors:0 dropped:0 overruns:0 carrier:0
     collisions:0 txqueuelen:100
     RX bytes:20179 (19.7 Kb)    TX bytes:19960 (19.4 Kb)
     Interrupt:11 Base address:0xe000 Memory:ff8ff000-ff8ff038

lo   Link encap:Local Loopback
```

```
inet addr:127.0.0.1 Mask:255.0.0.0
UP LOOPBACK RUNNING MTU:3924 Metric:1
RX packets:56 errors:0 dropped:0 overruns:0 frame:0
TX packets:56 errors:0 dropped:0 overruns:0 carrier:0
collisions:0 txqueuelen:0
RX bytes:3148 (3.0 Kb)  TX bytes:3148 (3.0Kb)
```

In this example, two network interfaces are up on the current computer. The first section shows your Ethernet interface (eth0), and its Ethernet hardware address, IP address (inet addr), broadcast address, and netmask. The next lines provide information on packets that have been sent, along with the number of errors and collisions that have occurred.

> **NOTE:** The lo entry is for loopback. This enables you to run TCP/IP commands on your local system without having a physical network up and running.

If your eth0 interface does not appear, it may still be configured properly, but not running at the moment. Try to start the eth0 interface by typing the following:

`# ifconfig eth0 up`

After this, type **ifconfig** again to see if eth0 is now running. If it is, it may be that eth0 is simply not configured to start automatically at boot time. You can change it so Ethernet starts at boot time (which I recommend), using the Network Configuration window described earlier in this chapter.

> **TIP:** If your network interfaces are not running at all, you can try to start them from the network initialization script. This interface reads parameters and basically runs ifconfig for all network interfaces on your computer. Type the following to restart your network:
>
> `# /etc/init.d/network restart`

Another way to see statistics for your Ethernet driver is to list the contents of the process pseudo file system for network devices. To do that, type the following:

`# cat /proc/net/dev`

The output should look like this:

```
Inter-|  Receive                                            |Transmit
face  |bytes packets errs drop fifo frame compressed multicast|bytes
  lo:  5362   64   0  0  0   0       0        5362    64  0  0  0   0
 sit0:    0    0   0  0  0   0       0           0     0  0  0  0   0
 eth0: 3083   35   0  0  0   0       0        3876    31  0  0  0   0
```

The output is a bit hard to read. (This book isn't wide enough to show it without wrapping around, so the output was truncated at the right.) With this output, you can see Receive and Transmit statistics for each interface. This output also shows you how many Receive and Transmit errors occurred in communication. (Transmit information is cut off in this example.)

For a more detailed look at your network, you can use the Wireshark window. Wireshark is described in the section "Watching LAN traffic with Wireshark" later in this chapter.

> **NOTE:** The `sit0` network interface (which stands for Simple Internet Transition) can be used to encapsulate IPv6 packets into an IPv4 network. This allows IPv6 network communications to be routed across IPv4 networks. You would only use this interface if you have IPv6 networking enabled.

Troubleshooting a wireless LAN

If you set up your two (or more) wireless LAN cards to enable Fedora and RHEL systems to communicate, and they are not communicating, you can troubleshoot the problem in several different ways.

Checking wireless settings

You can use the `iwlist` and `iwconfig` commands to check your wireless settings. The `iwconfig` command provides a quick overview of your wireless settings, while the `iwlist` command shows you information about parameters that you specify.

Use the `iwconfig` command, along with the name of the wireless LAN interface, to see information about that interface. For example, if the wireless interface were `eth1`, you could type the following:

```
# iwconfig eth1
eth0    IEEE 802.11-DS  ESSID:"Homelan"  Nickname:"pine"
        Mode:Ad-Hoc  Frequency:2.412GHz  Cell: 02:02:2D:2D:3B:30
        Bit Rate=11Mb/s  Tx-Power=15 dBm  Sensitivity:1/3
        RTS thr:off  Fragment thr:off
        Encryption key:7365-6375-31
        Power Management:off
        Link Quality:0/92  Signal level:-102 dBm  Noise level:-102 dBm
        Rx invalid nwid:0  invalid crypt:0  invalid misc:0
```

With `iwconfig`, you can see details about the wireless aspects of the Ethernet interface. In this example, the network name (`ESSID`) is `Homelan`, and the station name (`Nickname`) is `pine`. The interface is operating in Ad hoc mode on channel 1 (frequency of 2.412 GHz). Transmission rates are at the maximum speed of 11 Mbps. The encryption key that must be used by every node the card connects with is `7365-6375-31`. Other settings describe the link and signal quality.

The `iwlist` command lets you request specific information about the wireless LAN interface. The syntax is to follow the `iwlist` command with the interface name and the information you are interested in. For example:

```
# iwlist eth1 freq
eth 0     14 channels in total; available frequencies :
          Channel 01 : 2.412 GHz
```

```
Channel 02 : 2.417 GHz
Channel 03 : 2.422 GHz
Channel 04 : 2.427 GHz
Channel 05 : 2.432 GHz
Channel 06 : 2.437 GHz
Channel 07 : 2.442 GHz
Channel 08 : 2.447 GHz
Channel 09 : 2.452 GHz
Channel 10 : 2.457 GHz
Channel 11 : 2.457 GHz
Channel 12 : 2.457 GHz
Channel 13 : 2.457 GHz
Channel 14 : 2.462 GHz
Current Frequency:2.412GHz (Channel 1)
```

The freq parameter displays the available frequencies (and channels) available for communication. Note that all the available frequencies are in the 2.4 GHz range.

```
# iwlist eth0 rate
eth0      6 available bit-rates :
          1Mb/s
          2Mb/s
          5.5Mb/s
          11Mb/s
          58Mb/s
          39.5Mb/s
          Current Bit Rate=54Mb/s
```

The preceding rate parameter displays the transmission rates available for the wireless interface. You can see that 1, 2, 5.5, and 11 Mbps rates are available for the current interface.

```
# iwlist eth0 key
eth0      2 key sizes : 40, 104bits
          4 keys available :
                  [1] 7365-6375-31 (40 bits)
                  [2] off
                  [3] off
                  [4] off
          Current Transmit Key: [1]
```

The key parameter lets you see the encryption keys available with the interface. It also shows the key sizes currently available. Because the card reflected in the preceding example supports 64- and 128-bit encryption, the key sizes available are 40 and 104 bits. (The encryption algorithm automatically generates the last 24 bits of each key.)

If you are troubleshooting your wireless LAN connection, some settings are more likely than others to cause problems. It is important to set the following wireless LAN settings properly — if you don't, they may keep your network from working:

- **Network ID (ESSID)** — You may not be able to communicate among peer computers if the Network ID (ESSID) doesn't match on each of them. Network IDs are case sensitive — for example, Mylan is not the same as MyLAN.

- **Encryption key** — Having encryption keys that don't match is like trying to log in to Linux with the wrong password. Check that all nodes are using the same key. (If nodes were unable to connect, check the encryption key first, because typing long hexidecimal keys can be prone to error.)

- **Mode** — If you are communicating through an access point, your mode should be set to Managed and you must provide the MAC address for that access point. In most single-cell networks, you should set all nodes to Ad hoc. The Ad hoc mode allows all nodes to communicate directly to each other as peers.

- **Channel or frequency** — The channel and frequency options are just two different means of setting the same value. For example, setting the channel to 1 is the same as setting the frequency to 2.412G (GHz). Make sure that the nodes on your network are able to communicate on the samefrequency.

Checking TCP/IP

To ensure that your wireless LAN is communicating with its peers, use the `ping` command (as described earlier in this chapter). If you believe that your cards are working properly, but the `ping` command continues to give you a `Network Unreachable` message, you may have a problem with your TCP/IP configuration. Here are some items you can check from the Network Configuration window:

- **IP address** — Know the correct IP address of the peer you are trying to reach.

- **Hostname** — If you ping the peer computer by name, make sure that your computer can properly resolve that name into the correct IP address, or have the peer's hostname and IP address properly listed in the `/etc/hosts` file locally. The former option will probably require that you have one or more DNS servers identified to resolve the name.

If you can reach another computer on the wireless LAN, but not computers outside of that LAN (such as Internet addresses), check that you have properly identified the location of your gateway. If the gateway address is correct, and you can reach that gateway, it may be that the gateway itself is not configured to allow packet forwarding.

If you found that any of the preceding information needed to be changed and you changed it, you should restart the wireless LAN interface. One way to do that is to restart the PCMCIA interface and the network interfaces as follows:

```
# /etc/init.d/pcmcia restart
# /etc/init.d/network restart
```

Adapting to poor reception

Your wireless LAN might be working fine while your two wireless computers are sitting on the same desk. But if performance degrades when you separate the computers, you may need to identify any potential obstructions. Then you must decide how to get around them. For desktop systems, a small indoor antenna can bring the signal out from under a desk or out of a closet. For adjacent buildings, a roof antenna might be the answer.

In cities or other congested areas, many people and pieces of equipment can be competing for the 2.4 GHz range. You may want to move a microwave oven or high-end remote phone that may be interfering with your wireless LAN. These settings might help adapt to poor reception:

- **Reduce transmission rate** — Instead of using 11 Mbps, you can explicitly ramp down to 5.5, 2, or 1 Mbps. Slower rates can mean more efficient operation in noisy places.

- **Use smaller fragment sizes** — Although there is more total overhead to transmitting packets broken up into smaller fragments, they can often provide better overall performance in noisy environments. Change the `frag` parameter to reduce fragment sizes.

- **Use different frequencies** — By specifically requesting that certain frequencies (or channels) be used for transmission, you can avoid congested channels.

Use debugging tools

Because most wireless LAN cards were created for Windows systems, debugging tools from the manufacturers are available only on those systems. If your computer is a dual-boot system (Windows and Linux), try booting in Windows to test the quality of your wireless network.

In Fedora and RHEL, you can use many of the tools you use for wired Ethernet networks and other TCP/IP network interfaces. Here are a couple of examples:

- **Wireshark** — The Wireshark window (type **wireshark** as the root user from a Terminal window) lets you watch Ethernet frames being sent and received by your wireless LAN interface. For example, the output of Wireshark can tell you whether a failed connection reflects a lack of reception or rejected requests. (Wireshark is described in the next section.)

- **/var/log/messages** — When the wireless LAN interface starts up, messages related to that startup are sent to the `/var/log/messages` file. In some cases, these messages will reflect improper options being set for the wireless LAN module.

Watching LAN traffic with Wireshark

If you really want to understand the coming and going of information on your LAN, you need a tool that analyzes network traffic. Wireshark (formerly called Ethereal) is a graphical tool for capturing and displaying the packets being sent across your network interfaces. Using filters to select particular hosts, protocols, or direction of data, you can monitor activities and track problems on your network.

In addition to reading Ethernet packet data gathered by Wireshark, the Wireshark window can be used to display captured files from LanAlyzer, Sniffer, Microsoft Network Monitor, Snoop, and a variety of other tools. These files can be read from their native formats or after being compressed with gzip (.gz).

Wireshark can track more than 100 packet types (representing different protocols). It can also display specific fields related to each protocol, such as various data sizes, source and destination addresses, port numbers, and other values.

Starting Wireshark

To start Wireshark from the Applications menu, select Internet → Wireshark Network Analyzer. Or type the following (as root user) from a Terminal window:

```
# wireshark &
```

The Wireshark window, shown in Figure 15-14, appears. (If the wireshark command is not found, the package is probably not installed. You can install the wireshark and wireshark-gnome packages from the Internet by typing yum install wireshark wireshark-gnome, or you can use the rpm command to install them from the installation DVD.)

The primary function of Wireshark is to take a snapshot of the packets coming across your network interfaces and display that data in the Wireshark window. You can filter the data based on a variety of filter primitives. When the capture is done, you can step through and sort the data based on the values in different columns. Optionally, you can save the captured data to a file to study the data at a later time.

> **TIP:** If you can't use Wireshark because you don't have a GUI available, you can use the tcpdump command from the shell. It is not as friendly as Wireshark, but it supports the same filtering syntax. Because tcpdump can produce a lot of output, you will probably want to use some form of filtering or direct the output of the command to a file. (Type **man tcpdump** for information on filter options.)

Capturing Ethernet data

With the Wireshark window displayed, you can capture data relating to packet activities on any of your Ethernet network interfaces by doing the following:

1. Click Capture → Interfaces. You will see a list of network interfaces available on your computer.

2. Click Prepare next to the interface you want to capture from (probably eth0 for a wired Internet or wlan0 for a wireless interface). A Wireshark Capture Options window appears.

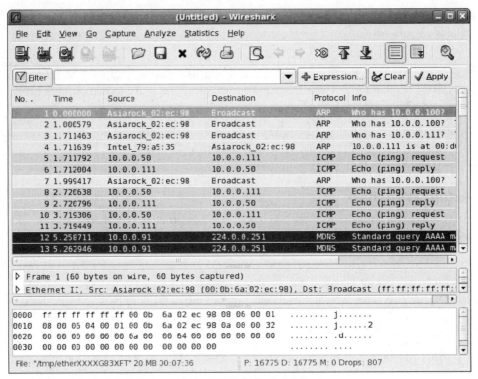

Figure 15-14: Configure your Ethernet card for TCP/IP during installation.

3. Choose options relating to what data is captured:

- **Limit each packet to:** Limits the size of each packet to a maximum number of bytes.

- **Capture packets in promiscuous mode:** Any computer on a LAN can see all packets that traverse the LAN, except those packets intended for switched portions of the LAN. With this on, all packets seen by your network interface are captured. With this mode off, only packets intended specifically for your network interface (including multicast and broadcast packets) are captured. In other words, turn on promiscuous mode to monitor the whole LAN and turn it off to monitor only your interface.

- **Capture Filter:** This optional field lets you enter a filter that can be used to filter capture data. You can type in filters individually or click the Filter button to use a filter you have stored earlier.

> **CROSS-REFERENCE:** Filtering is one of the most powerful features of Wireshark. See the sidebar "Using Wireshark Filters" for further information on how to enter filters into the Filter field.

- **Capture file(s):** Enter the name of a file in which you want to capture the data gathered. If you don't enter a filename, the information will be displayed on the Wireshark window without being saved to a file.

- **Ring buffer (Number of files):** Select this option to have packets captured in a set number of files. To use this feature, you must also specify a filename (such as /tmp/abc) and a file size. Data will be put into files you chose, named from the root filename you have provided. Once the files fill up, Wireshark will go back and write to the first file again and continue filling up the files. When you stop the capture, you are left with the number of capture files you chose, containing the most recent data.

- **Update list of packets in real time:** Select this option to have packet information appear in the Wireshark window as each packet crosses the interface. With this option off, the information is displayed after you stop capturing it.

- **Automatic scrolling in live capture:** If you are updating packets in real time, select this option to have packet information scroll up after the screen fills. With this off, you just see the first screen of packets and have to scroll down manually to see the rest.

- **Hide capture info dialog:** Prevents the Capture Info box from appearing to display the number and types of packets being captured.

- **Stop Capture after . . . :** By default, Wireshark will capture data from the moment you click OK until you click Stop (with this value set to 0). Or, select one of the three Stop Capture fields and type a number to capture only that number of packets; a number to stop capture after a set number of bytes, kilobytes, megabytes, or gigabytes of data; or a number to indicate the number of seconds minutes, hours or days to capture data. When the limit is reached, capture stops and the file is stored in /tmp/etherXXXX???????, where ??????? is replaced by a string of characters.

- **Enable MAC/network/transport name resolution:** With any of these three options on, names are displayed instead of addresses (if possible). For example, for transport names, Source and Destination IP addresses are displayed as hostnames (if they can be resolved from /etc/hosts or DNS). With this option off, IP addresses appear in the Source and Destination columns.

4. Click Capture. Wireshark begins gathering data on packets encountered by the interface.

   The Wireshark Capture window displays information on how many incoming and outgoing packets have crossed the interface since the capture began. The number of packets that are associated with each protocol Wireshark monitors is displayed, along with the percentage of total packets associated with each protocol.

5. Click Stop (or the capture might stop automatically, if it has reached a size or time limit set by you). The snapshot of data you just took will appear on the Wireshark window. Packets are displayed in the order in which they traversed the interface.

6. You can choose to save the data to your hard disk by selecting File → Save As.

At this point, you can start interpreting the data.

Interpreting captured Ethernet data

With the captured data displayed in your Wireshark window, you can get a detailed view of the network traffic that your computer is exposed to. The Wireshark window is divided into three parts. The top part contains a scrollable list of packets. The protocol tree for the current packet appears in the middle part of the display. A hexadecimal dump of the entire contents of the packet appears in the bottom part.

You can sort data in different ways from the top part of the window by clicking the column headings. To see more details relating to different items in the protocol tree for the current packet, you can click the triangle-shaped icon next to the protocol information that interests you.

Using Wireshark Filters

If you are monitoring a busy server or a busy network, Wireshark can gather so much data that it can become almost unusable. If you know what you are looking for, however, you can filter what packets are captured based on values you enter.

Filters in Wireshark are implemented using the pcap library (type **man pcap** to read about it). The filter expressions you can use with Wireshark are described on the `tcpdump` man page. Here are some examples of filters that you could enter into the Filter box when you capture Ethernet data with Wireshark:

```
host 10.0.0.15
```

The `host` primitive lets you capture only packets that are either to or from a particular host computer (by IP address or hostname). By preceding `host` with `src` or `des`, you can indicate that you only want packages sent from a particular source or to a particular destination host.

```
tcp port 80
```

You can enter a protocol name (such as `tcp`, `ether`, `udp`, or `ip`) to limit captured packets to those that are assigned to that protocol. As shown in the previous example, with `tcp` you could also indicate a port number (such as 80, to monitor traffic to and from your Web server).

You can filter for certain special activities on the network, using the `gateway`, `broadcast`, or `multicast` primitives. Entering `gateway host` lets you find packets sent to a gateway host that is neither a Source nor Destination for the packet (which is determined because the Ethernet address doesn't match either of those IP addresses). Enter `ether broadcast` to monitor broadcast packets on your Ethernet network, such as announcements from name servers announcing availability. Likewise, you could filter for multicast packets on ether or ip protocols (`ether multicast`).

The following tips will help you interpret what the data means:

- The Source and Destination columns show where each packet came from and where it went. If the Enable name resolution option is on (which is recommended), the hostname associated with IP packets is displayed. This makes it much easier to see which computer is communicating with you.

- To see all activity associated with a particular location, click the Source or Destination column. Packets will be sorted alphabetically, making it easier for you to scroll through the activity list for the location that interests you.

- If you are trying to debug a particular feature, click the Protocol column to gather activities based on protocol. For example, if you were trying to get Samba to work (for Windows file or printer sharing), sorting by protocol would enable you to see all NetBIOS and NBNS (NetBIOS name server) requests that came to your computer.

- To mark a packet of interest to you, click the middle mouse button. This will highlight the packet, making it easier to find later. (If you have only a two-button mouse, and you indicated during installation that it should emulate a three-button mouse, you can click both mouse buttons together to emulate the middle mouse button.)

The Info column gives you details about the intention of the packet. For example, you can see the type of service that was requested (such as http for Web service or FTP for file transfer). You can see what information is being broadcast and determine when attempts to find particular host computers are failing. If you believe someone is using your network improperly, you can see which sites they are visiting and the services they are requesting.

Another handy option is one that lets you follow the stream of TCP information. Click Tools → Follow TCP Stream. The Contents of TCP stream window that appears lets you see the total output of the HTTP, SMTP, or other protocol being used. Of course, viewing data being transmitted by protocols is useful only if it is in plain text. Although the fact that more and more data and service requests are being encrypted makes it more difficult to debug using Wireshark, it also makes it harder for bad guys on your network to steal your data.

Summary

Linux is at its best when it is connected to a network. Configuring a LAN enables you to share resources with other computers in your home or organization. These resources can include files, printers, CD-ROM drives, and backup media.

This chapter describes how to connect to wired and wireless networks and create a LAN with a Fedora or RHEL system being used on one of the computers on that LAN. It helps you determine the kind of equipment you need to obtain, and the layout (topology) of the network. In particular, the chapter describes how to use NetworkManager for making network connections, and Network Configuration for manually configuring your network interfaces.

If something isn't working with your network interface to the LAN, you can use utilities such as `ifconfig` to check that your Ethernet interface is configured and running properly. You can also check that Linux found and installed the proper driver for your Ethernet card. After an Ethernet interface is working, you can use the Wireshark window to monitor the packets coming and going across the interface between your computer and the network.

If a wired network is not possible or convenient, Linux includes support for wireless LAN cards. A wireless LAN can be an effective means of extending your network to areas that are difficult or expensive to reach with wired connections. Using ndiswrapper, you can also get drivers working for many Windows wireless cards.

Chapter 16

Connecting to the Internet

In This Chapter

- Understanding how the Internet is structured
- Using dial-up connections to the Internet
- Connecting your LAN to the Internet
- Setting up Linux as a router
- Configuring a virtual private network
- Setting up Linux as a proxy server
- Setting up proxy clients

This chapter demonstrates how to connect Fedora or RHEL to any TCP/IP-based network, such as the Internet, a private LAN, or a company WAN. The differences in how you connect have more to do with the network medium you use (that is, telephone lines, LAN router, and so on) than they do with whether you are connecting to the public Internet or a company's private network.

Connections to the Internet described in this chapter include a simple dial-up connection from your own Linux system. The most popular protocol for making dial-up connections to the Internet is Point-to-Point Protocol (PPP). It also builds on the procedures in Chapter 15 for creating your own Local Area Network (LAN) by teaching you how to connect your LAN to the Internet.

This chapter first provides an overview of the structure of the Internet, including descriptions of domains, routing, and proxy services. It then discusses how to connect your Linux system to the Internet using PPP dial-up connections. For those who want to connect a LAN to the Internet, it describes how to use Linux as a router and set it up to do IP masquerading (to protect your private LAN addresses). Finally, it describes how to configure Linux as a proxy server, including how to configure client applications such as Firefox.

Understanding How the Internet Is Structured

In order to operate, the Internet relies on maintaining a unique set of names and numbers. The names are domain names and hostnames, which enable the computers connected to the

Internet to be identified in a hierarchy. The numbers are Internet Protocol (IP) addresses and port numbers, which enable computers to be grouped together into interconnected sets of subnetworks, yet remain uniquely addressable by the Internet.

An Internet service provider (ISP) will give you the information you need to set up a connection to the Internet. You plug that information into the programs used to create that connection, such as scripts to create a PPP connection over telephone lines. See the section "Using Dial-up Connections to the Internet" later in this chapter for descriptions of the information needed from your ISP and the procedures for configuring PPP to connect to the Internet. With a broadband connection (and the default DHCP configuration), you might just be able to plug in your Ethernet card and go.

The following list describes the basic Internet structure in more detail:

- **IP addresses** — These are the numbers that uniquely define each computer known to the Internet. Internet authorities assign pools of IP addresses (along with network masks, or netmasks) so that network administrators can assign addresses to each individual computer that they control. An alternative to assigned addresses is to use a reserved set of private IP addresses, so multiple computers in your home or business can share a single public IP address.

> **CROSS-REFERENCE:** See Chapter 15 for a further description of IP addresses.

- **Port numbers** — Port numbers provide access points to particular services. Port numbers are like channels on a television. While all ports are inherently the same, many ports are associated with a particular service. A server computer will listen on the network for packets that are addressed to its IP address, along with one or more port numbers. For example, a Web server listens to port 80 to respond to requests for HTTP content. A Web browser will know, by default, to make its request for HTTP service (in other words, a Web page) to port 80 on the server.

> **NOTE:** In reality, you can assign any service to any port you choose. In fact, system administrators sometimes assign services to unusual ports for the express purpose of keeping most outsiders from finding them. If you decide to use a non-standard port for a service, you should try to avoid port numbers that are already assigned for common services, since those ports might end up being scanned by an intruder anyway. A client of your service would have to know to request that port specifically. For example, `http://www.example.com:4863` would request content from port `4863` from the host `www.example.com`.

- **Domain names** — On the Internet, computer names are organized in a hierarchy of domain names and host names. If you want to have and maintain your own Internet domain, you need to be assigned one that fits into one of the top-level domains (domains such as .com, .org, .net, .edu, .info, and so on).

- **Hostnames** — If a domain name is assigned to your organization, you are free to create your own hostnames within that domain (sometimes called subdomains). This is a way of associating a name (host name) with an address (IP address). When you use the

Internet, you use a *fully qualified domain name* to identify a host computer. For example, in the domain `handsonhistory.com`, a host computer named `baskets` would have a fully qualified domain name of `baskets.handsonhistory.com`.

Within an organization, you should choose a host-naming scheme that makes sense to you. For example, for `handsonhistory.com`, you could have hostnames dedicated to different crafts (`baskets`, `decoys`, `weaving`, and so on). Some organizations use the names from Norse mythology such as thor, odin, and loki, or beer brands such as summit, jamespage, guinness, and so on.

> **TIP:** For some naming schemes, see
> `http://c2.com/cgi/wiki?NamesGivenToComputers.`

- **Routers**— If you have a LAN or other type of network in your home or organization that you want to connect to the Internet, you can share an Internet connection. You do this by setting up a router. The router connects to both your network and the Internet, providing a route for data to pass between your network and the Internet. This is especially useful if you connect to the Internet over a dial-up or broadband connection, since your Linux box can act as a router and you can share the connection among all your computers.

- **Firewalls and IP masquerading** — To keep your private network somewhat secure, yet still allow some data to pass between it and the Internet, you can set up a firewall. The firewall restricts the kind of data packets or services that can pass through the boundary between the private and public networks. If your network uses private addresses, or if you just want to protect the addresses of computers behind your firewall, you can use techniques such as Network Address Translation (NAT) or IP masquerading.

> **NOTE:** Although you can set up a firewall to filter packets on any computer on your private network, firewalls are typically configured most stringently on the machine that routes packets between the public and private networks. In this way, intruders can be stopped before they get on your private network and security can be relaxed somewhat between your computers behind the firewall.

- **Proxies** — You can bypass some of the configuration required to allow the computers on your LAN to communicate directly with the Internet by configuring a proxy server. A proxy server can store (referred to as *caching*) Internet objects (such as data from Web and FTP servers) so that clients of that proxy server don't have to contact the server originating that data each time it is requested. With a proxy server, a computer on your LAN can also run Internet applications (such as a Web browser) and have them appear to the Internet as if they are actually running on the proxy server.

> **CROSS-REFERENCE:** You can read about firewalls in Chapter 14. IP masquerading and proxy servers are described in the sections "Enable forwarding and masquerading" and "Setting Up Linux as a Proxy Server" later in this chapter.

Internet domains

You can't read a magazine, watch a TV commercial, or open a cereal box these days without coming across a "`something.com`." When a company, organization, or person wants you to connect to them on the Internet, it relies on the uniqueness of its particular domain name. However, within that domain name, the company or organization to which it has been assigned can arrange its content however it chooses.

Internet domains are organized in a structure called the *domain name system* (DNS). At the top of that structure is a set of *top-level domains* (or TLDs). Some of the top-level domains are used commonly in the United States, although they are available for worldwide use. TLDs such as `edu` (for colleges and universities), `gov` (for United States government), and `mil` (for United States military sites) were among the most used TLDs in the early Internet. In more recent years, `com` (for commercial sites) has experienced the most growth.

The `us` domain was added to include U.S. institutions, such as local governments and elementary schools, as well as to individuals within a geographical region of the United States. Recently, new domains such as `info` (for people and business to publish information about themselves) and `biz` (an alternative to `com` for businesses) have been added.

To facilitate the entry of other countries to the Internet, the International Organization for Standardization (ISO) has defined a set of two-letter codes that are assigned to each country; examples include codes such as `tv` for Tuvalu and `de` for Germany (*Deutschland* in German). Within each country are naming authorities responsible for organizing the subdomains. Some subdomains are organized by categories, while others are structured by geographic location. Some locales have offered their domain names for general use, including the `cc` domain (from the Cocos Keeling Islands territory of Australia) and `ws` (representing Western Samoa).

Domain names are hierarchical, which means there can be subdomains beneath second-level domains, as well as host computers. (Second-level domains are the names directly below the TLDs that are assigned to individual people and organizations.) Each subdomain is separated by a dot (`.`), starting with the top-level domain on the right and with the second-level domain and each subsequent subdomain appearing to the left. Here is an example of a fully qualified domain name for a host:

```
baskets.crafts.handsonhistory.com
```

In this example, the top-level domain is `.com`. The second-level domain name assigned to the organization that controls the domain is `handsonhistory`. Within that domain is a subdomain, or third-level domain, called `crafts`. The last name (`baskets`) refers to a particular computer within that third-level domain. From other hosts in the third-level domain, the host can be referred to simply as `baskets`. From the Internet, you would refer to it as `baskets.crafts.handsonhistory.com`.

> **CROSS-REFERENCE:** For more details on how the domain-name system is structured, and for information on how to set up your own DNS server in Linux, see Chapter 25.

TIP: Several RFCs (Request for Comments) define the domain name system. RFC 1034 covers domain name concepts and facilities. RFC 1035 is a technical description of how DNS works. RFC 1480 describes the `us` domain. For a more general description of DNS, there is RFC 1591. You can view RFCs at the RFC Database (`www.rfc-editor.org/rfc.html`).

Hostnames and IP addresses

In the early days of the Internet, every known host computer name and address was collected into a file called `HOSTS.TXT` and distributed throughout the Internet. This quickly became cumbersome because of the size of the list and the constant changes being made to it. The solution was to distribute the responsibility for resolving hostnames into IP addresses to many DNS servers throughout the Internet.

To make the domain names friendly, the names contain no network addresses, routes, or other information needed to deliver messages. Instead, each computer must rely on some method to translate domain names and hostnames into IP addresses. The DNS server is the primary means of resolving the names to addresses. If you request a service from a computer using a fully qualified domain name (including all domains and subdomains), the request will go to a DNS server to resolve that name into an IP address. It will gather that information either directly from the DNS server that owns that information or, which is more likely, from another DNS server along the way that has gathered that information.

If you have a private LAN or other network, you can keep your own list of hostnames and IP addresses. For the computers you work with all the time, it's easier to type `baskets` than `baskets.crafts.handsonhistory.com`. There are a couple of ways (besides DNS) that your computer can resolve the IP address for computers for which you give only the host name:

- **Check the /etc/hosts file.** In your computer's `/etc/hosts` file, you can place the IP addresses and names for the computers on your local network. In this way, your computer doesn't need to query the DNS server to get the address (which may not be there anyway if you are on a private network and don't have your own DNS server). Another use of the `/etc/hosts` file is to override an address that a DNS server is giving you, for example if it is giving you an errant IP address for that host, or if you wanted to point your system to a different mail server.

- **Check specified domains.** You can specify that if the hostname requested doesn't include a fully qualified domain name and the hostname is not in your `/etc/hosts` file, then your computer should check certain specified domain names. You can do this in the `/etc/resolv.conf` file.

On your Linux system, when you make a request to resolve a hostname into an IP address, the contents of the `/etc/resolv.conf` file will most likely determine where your computer searches for that information. That file can specify your local domain, an alternative list of

domains, and the location of one or more DNS servers. Here is an example of an
`/etc/resolv.conf` file:

```
domain crafts.handsonhistory.com
search crafts.handsonhistory.com handsonhistory.com
nameserver 10.0.0.10
nameserver 10.0.0.12
```

In this example, the local domain is `crafts.handsonhistory.com`. If you try to contact a
host by giving only its hostname (with no domain name), your computer can check in both
`crafts.handsonhistory.com` and `handsonhistory.com` domains to find the host. If
you give the fully qualified domain name, it can contact the name servers (first `10.0.0.10`
and then `10.0.0.12`) to resolve the address. (You can specify up to six name servers that
your computer will query in order until the address is resolved. The total search line is limited
to 256 characters, however.)

If your system uses DHCP, where another server on your network assigns your Linux system
an IP address, your `/etc/resolv.conf` file can look more like the following:

```
; generated by /sbin/dhclient-script
search ce1.client2.big_isp.com
nameserver 10.0.0.10
nameserver 10.0.0.12
```

In this example, the `/etc/resolv.conf` file was created by the DHCP client code, based on
information from the DHCP server. Note that `big_isp.com` is an alias for a large
communications company.

> **TIP:** Your resolver knows to check your `/etc/hosts` file first because of the contents of the
> `/etc/host.conf` and `/etc/nsswitch.conf` files. By default, the `nsswitch.conf` file
> has your resolver check local files first, followed by DNS to resolve addresses. The `host.conf` file
> indicates that local files (hosts) be checked first for the address, followed the DNS system (`bind`). You can
> change that behavior by modifying those files. See the `resolv.conf` man page for further information.

Routing

Knowing the IP address of the computer you want to reach is one thing; being able to reach
that IP address is another. Even if you connect your computers on a LAN, to have full
connectivity to the Internet there must be at least one node (that is, a computer or dedicated
device) through which you can route network traffic that is destined for locations outside your
LAN. That is the job of a *router*.

A router is a device that has interfaces connected to at least two networks and is able to route
network traffic between the two networks. In my example of a small business that has a LAN
that it wants to connect to the Internet, the router would have a connection and IP address on
the LAN, as well as a connection and IP address to a network that provides access to the
Internet.

A computer running Linux can act as a router between any two TCP/IP interfaces, for example, if the computer has two LAN cards or if it has a network interface card and a modem (for a dial-up connection to the Internet). Alternatively, you can purchase a dedicated router, such as Cisco ADSL routers, that can exclusively perform routing between your LAN and the Internet or network service provider.

> **TIP:** Unlike regular dial-up modems, xDSL routers or bridges have several different standards that are not all compatible. Before purchasing an xDSL modem, check with your ISP. If your ISP supports xDSL, it can tell you the exact models of xDSL modems you can use to get xDSL service.

Proxies

Instead of having direct access to the Internet (as you do with routing), you can have indirect access via the computers on your LAN by setting up a *proxy server*. With a proxy server, you don't have to configure and secure every computer on the LAN for Internet access. When, for example, a client computer tries to access the Internet from a Web browser, the request goes to the proxy server. The proxy server then makes that request to the Internet. A proxy server can also be used to filter undesirable Web sites from being accessed by users on your local network.

With a proxy server, Internet access is fairly easy to set up and quite secure to use. Linux can be configured as a proxy server using several different projects, including Squid (as described later in this chapter).

Using Dial-Up Connections to the Internet

Although high-speed Internet connections have become widely available, if no high-speed connection is available modems and telephone lines may be your only option. An external modem typically connects to a serial port (COM1, COM2, and so on) or USB port on your computer and then into a telephone wall jack. Then your computer dials a modem at your ISP or business that has a connection to the Internet.

The most common protocol for making dial-up connections to the Internet (or other TCP/IP network) is Point-to-Point Protocol (PPP). This section describes how to use PPP protocol to connect to the Internet.

Getting information

To establish a PPP connection, you need to get some information from the administrator of the network that you are connecting to. This is either your ISP when you sign up for Internet service, or the person in your workplace who walks around carrying cables, two or more cellular phones, and a couple of beepers. (When a network goes down, these people are in demand!) Here is the kind of information you need to set up your PPP connection:

- **Telephone number** — This telephone number gives you access to the modem (or pool of modems) at the ISP. If it is a national ISP, make sure that you get a local or toll-free telephone number (otherwise, you will rack up long distance fees on top of your ISP fees).

- **Account name and password** — This information is used to verify that you have an Internet account with the ISP. This is referred to as an *account name* when you connect to a Linux or other UNIX system. (When connecting to an NT server, the account name may be referred to as a *system name*.)

- **An IP number** — Most ISPs use Dynamic IP numbers, which means that you are assigned an IP number temporarily when you are connected. Your ISP assigns a permanent IP number if it uses static IP addresses. If your computer or all the computers on your LAN need to have a more permanent presence on the network, you may be given one static IP number or a set of static IP addresses to use.

- **DNS Server IP addresses** — Your computer translates Internet hostnames to IP addresses by querying a Domain Name System (DNS) server. Your ISP should give you at least one IP address for a preferred (and possibly alternate) DNS server.

- **PAP or CHAP secrets** — You may need a PAP id or CHAP id and a secret, instead of a login and password when connecting to a Windows NT system at your ISP. These features are used with authentication on Microsoft operating systems, as well as other systems. Linux and other UNIX servers don't typically use this type of authentication, although they support PAP and CHAP on the client side.

Besides providing an Internet connection, your ISP typically also provides services for use with your Internet connection. Although you don't need this information to create your connection, you will need it soon afterward to configure these useful services. Here is some information you should acquire:

- **Mail server** — If your ISP is providing you with an e-mail account, you must know the address of the mail server, the type of mail service (such as Post Office Protocol or POP3), and the authentication password for the mail server in order to get your e-mail.

- **News server** — To enable you to participate in newsgroups, the ISP may provide the name of a news server. If the server requires you to log on, you will also need a password.

After you have gathered this information, you are ready to set up your connection to the Internet. To configure Fedora or RHEL to connect to your ISP, follow the PPP procedure described in the section that follows.

Setting up dial-up PPP

Point-to-Point Protocol (PPP) is used to create Internet Protocol (IP) connections over serial lines. Most often, the serial connection is established over a modem; however, it will also work over serial cables (null modem cables) or digital lines (including ISDN and DSL).

Although one side must dial out while the other side must receive the call to create a PPP connection over a modem, after the connection is established, information can flow in both directions. For the sake of clarity, however, I refer to the computer placing the call as the client and the computer receiving the call as the server.

To simplify the process of configuring PPP (and other network interfaces), Fedora and RHEL let you configure dial-up by using either the Network Configuration Window or another tool, such as kppp:

- **Network Configuration Window** — From the GNOME desktop panel, choose System → Administration → Network. From the Network Configuration window, select New. The Select Device Type window that appears lets you configure and test your dial-up PPP modem connection.

- **KPPP Window** — Select Applications → Internet → KPPP, or from a Terminal window run the kppp command. From the KPPP window you can set up a PPP dial-up connection and launch it. (You must have the kdenetwork package installed to get KPPP.)

Before you begin either of the two dial-up procedures, physically connect your modem to your computer, plug it in, and connect it to your telephone line. If you have an internal modem, you will probably see a telephone port on the back of your computer that you need to connect. If your modem isn't detected, you can reboot your computer or run wvdialconf create (as described later in this chapter) to have it detected.

Creating a dial-up connection with the Network Configuration window

You can use the Network Configuration window to set up dial-up networking. To start it, choose System → Administration → Network from the desktop panel. (Type the root password, if prompted.) Select New and a Select Device Type window appears to help you select the device for your Internet connection (a dial-up modem, in this case), as shown in Figure 16-1.

Follow the procedure below from the first Select Device Type window.

1. From the Select Device Type window that appears, select Modem connection and click Forward. The utility searches for a modem and the Select Modem window appears.

2. Select the following modem properties:
   - **Modem Device** — If the modem is connected to your first serial port (COM1) you can select /dev/ttyS0; for the second serial port (COM2) choose /dev/ttyS1. (By convention, the device is often linked to /dev/modem. Type **ls –l /dev/modem** to see if it is linked to a tty device.)

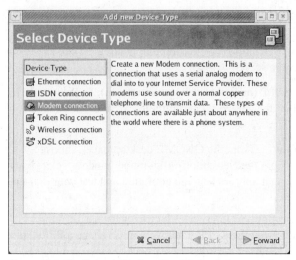

Figure 16-1: The Network Configuration Window helps you set up a PPP Internet connection.

NOTE: If you see the message `no such file or directory` when you list `/dev/modem`, it is possible that dial-up will fail later. If you determine that your modem's serial port is `/dev/ttyS0`, you can create the necessary link by typing the following command (as root user):

 # ln -s /dev/ttyS0 /dev/modem

- **Baud Rate** — This is the rate at which the computer talks to the modem (which is typically considerably faster than the modem can talk over the phone lines). The default is 115200. For dial-up connections, the value of 57600 is probably fine.

- **Flow Control** — Check the modem documentation to see if the modem supports hardware flow control (CRTSCTS). If it doesn't, select software flow control (XON/XOFF).

- **Modem Volume** — This is off by default, because the modem noise can be annoying. However, I usually select medium while I am setting up the modem. Then I turn it off once everything is working. The sound can give you a sense of where things are stopping if you can't get a connection.

- **Use touch tone dialing** — Leave this check box on in most cases. If for some reason your phone system doesn't support touch-tone dialing, you can turn it off.

Click Forward. The Select Provider window appears.

3. Enter the following provider information:

- **Internet Provider** — If you are using Internet service in any of the countries shown in the Internet Provider window, select the plus sign next to that country name. If your Internet provider appears under the National list, select it. Information is automatically filled in for that provider. Otherwise, you need to fill in the rest of the dialog window. Click Forward.

- **Phone Number** — Enter the telephone number of the ISP you want to dial into. (An optional prefix is available in case you need to dial 9 or some other number to get an outside dial tone.)

- **Provider Name** — The name of the Internet service provider. You could use `ppp0` here as the provider name, to identify the interface. (For multiple dial-up accounts, use `ppp1`, `ppp2`, and so on.)

- **Login Name** — The login name assigned to you from the ISP. The ISP may have called the login name a login ID or something similar.

- **Password** — The password associated with the login name.

Click Forward, and the IP Settings window appears.

4. With a dial-up connection, you would typically select Automatically obtain IP address settings. However, if the ISP has assigned a static IP address that you can use, click the Statically set IP addresses check box, and then enter your IP address, Subnet Mask, and Default Gateway Address. Then click Forward to continue.

   The Create Dialup Connection window appears, displaying information you just entered.

5. If all the information looks correct, click Apply (otherwise, click the Back button to change any information). The window closes.

6. The Network Configuration window appears, with a new PPP connection of modem type appearing in the window.

7. Click the new dial-up entry so it is highlighted.

8. Click File → Save to save the new dial-up configuration you just created.

9. Click the ppp device name and click the Activate button. The Internet dialer starts up and dials your ISP. (If you have sound turned on, you should hear your modem dialing out.)

If everything is working properly, you should see your login and password accepted and the PPP connection completed. Try opening a Web browser and see if you can access a Web site on the Internet. If this doesn't work the first time, don't be discouraged. There are many things to check to get your dial-up PPP connection working. If your dial-up connection isn't working yet, skip ahead to the "Checking your PPP connection" section.

Launching your PPP connection

Although your dial-up connection should now be configured (as described in the previous section), it is not set to connect automatically. One way to start the connection is to set it up to launch from the desktop panel. Here's how:

From the GNOME desktop (after installing the gnome-ppp package):

1. Right-click the Panel and then choose Add to Panel → Application Launcher, and select Forward.

2. Select the down arrow next to the Internet menu, select GNOME PPP, and select Add. A GNOME PPP phone icon appears on the panel.

3. Select the new icon from the panel. You are asked if you want to start a connection with your modem.

4. Fill in the user name, password, and phone number, and then select Connect to start the connection.

From the KDE desktop (after installing the kppp package):

1. Right-click the panel and then choose Add Application to Panel → Internet → KPPP.

2. Select the KPPP icon from the panel (type the root password, if prompted). A KPPP window appears.

3. Select the dial-up interface you added (probably ppp0) and click Connect to connect.

From this point forward, icons will appear on your desktop that you can select to connect immediately to your ISP over the dial-up connection you configured.

Launching your PPP connection on demand

Instead of starting a dial-up PPP connection manually each time you want to contact the Internet, you can set your dial-up connection to start automatically when an application (such as a Web browser or e-mail program) tries to use the connection. On-demand dialing is particularly useful if:

- The dial-up connection on your Linux system is acting as the gateway for other computers in your home or office. You don't have to run over to your Linux box to start the connection when another computer needs the dial-up connection.

- You run programs at off hours that require an Internet connection (like remote backups).

- You don't want to be bothered clicking an extra icon when you just want to browse the Web a bit.

The risk of on-demand dialing is that dial-up connections can start up when you don't want them to because the connection starts automatically. (Some people get worried when their computer starts dialing by itself in the middle of the night.)

Here is an example of settings you can add to your dial-up configuration file (probably /etc/sysconfig/network-scripts/ifcfg-??? where ??? is replaced by your provider name) to configure on-demand dialing:

```
ONBOOT=yes
DEMAND=yes
IDLETIMEOUT=600
RETRYTIMEOUT=30
```

The `ONBOOT=yes` starts the pppd daemon (but doesn't immediately begin dialing because `DEMAND` is set to `yes`). Also, because `DEMAND=yes`, a dial-up connection attempt is made any time traffic tries to use your dial-up connection. With `IDLETIMEOUT` set to `600`, the connection is dropped after 600 seconds (10 minutes) with no traffic on the connection. With `RETRYTIMEOUT` set to `30`, a dropped connection is retried after 30 seconds (unless the connection was dropped by an idle timeout, in which case there is no retry). You can change the timeout values as it suits you.

> **NOTE:** Because it can take a bit of time for dial-up connections to be established, operations may fail while dialing occurs. In particular, DNS requests can time out in 30 seconds, which may not be long enough to establish a dial-up connection. If you have three DNS servers configured for each client, you have a 90-second timeout period. As a result, the modem connection may be running before the request fails.

Checking your PPP connection

To debug your PPP connection or simply to better understand how it works, you can run through the steps below. They will help you understand where information is being stored and how tools can be used to track this information.

Checking that your modem was detected

It is possible that your modem is not supported under Linux. If that is the case, your PPP connection might be failing because the modem was not detected at all. To scan your serial ports to see where your modem might be, type the following (as root user):

```
$ wvdialconf /etc/wvdial.conf.new
```

The `wvdialconf` command is really made to build a configuration file (the `/etc/wvdial.conf` file) that is used by the dialer command (`wvdial`). If it succeeds, you can copy the `wvdial.conf.new` file to the `/etc/wvdial.conf`. Its first action, however, is to scan the serial ports on your computer and report where it finds modems. If it tells you that no modem was detected, it's likely that either your modem isn't connected properly or no driver is available to support the modem.

If the modem wasn't detected, you should determine whether or not it is a modem supported in Linux. You can do this by finding out what type of chip set is used in the modem. This is even more important than finding out the manufacturer of the modem because the same manufacturer can use chips from different companies. (This applies primarily to internal, software-based modems, because most external serial modems, internal PCI controller–based modems, and many USB modems are supported in Linux.)

After you have determined the chip set being used, check the Web site `linmodems.org`. This site contains information on so-called Win-modems. Search for the chip set on your modem from this site. It will tell you if there is a driver available for your modem.

A nice tool for determining what type of Win-modem you have and how to get it working is scanModem. If you have access to the Internet from another machine, you can download scanModem from this address:

```
http://linmodems.technion.ac.il/packages/scanModem.gz
```

Because you probably don't have a working Internet connection yet, find a way to copy scanModem.gz to your Linux system (maybe copy it to a floppy disk or burn it to a CD). As root user from a Terminal window, type these commands, with that file in the current directory:

```
# gunzip scanModem.gz
# chmod 755 scanModem
# ./scanModem
```

The result is a Modem directory containing text files describing your modem and what you can do to configure it.

> **NOTE:** If you are a new Linux user with a Win-modem and you are still baffled after referring to the linmodems.org site, you might consider getting a serial or USB modem. To try to get your Win-modem working, you might need to download, compile and load a modem driver. Especially with some older Win-modems, drivers have not been updated to work with the latest kernels. Picking up a cheap serial modem (under $20) from a used computer store can save hours of frustration that may still result in failure.

Checking that your PPP interface is working

One way to check that the PPP interface is working is with the ping command. From the Terminal window, type **ping** along with any Internet address you know. For example:

```
$ ping www.handsonhistory.com
PING handsonhistory.com (198.60.22.8) from 192.168.0.43 : 56(84) bytes
of data.
64 bytes from handsonhistory.com (198.60.22.8): icmp_seq=0 ttl=240
time=120 msec
64 bytes from handsonhistory.com (198.60.22.8): icmp_seq=1 ttl=240
time=116 msec
64 bytes from handsonhistory.com (198.60.22.8): icmp_seq=2 ttl=240
time=120 msec

--- www.handsonhistory.com ping statistics ---
4 packets transmitted, 3 packets received, 25% packet loss
round-trip min/avg/max/mdev = 116.816/119.277/120.807/1.779 ms
```

Press Ctrl+C to end the ping command. The previous lines show the responses from www.handsonhistory.com. It sent back packets from the IP address 198.60.22.8 in response to each one it received. You can see the sequence of packets (icmp_seq) and the time it took for each response (in milliseconds). If you receive packets in return, you will know two things: first, that your connection is working, and second, that your name to address translation (from the DNS addresses in /etc/resolv.conf) is working.

Checking the default route

After starting a dial-up connection, check that the default route is set using route -n, as shown in the following example:

```
# /sbin/route -n
Kernel IP routing table
Destination    Gateway        Genmask          Flags Metric Ref  Use Iface
198.62.1.1     0.0.0.0        255.255.255.255  UH    0      0      0 ppp0
10.0.0.0       0.0.0.0        255.0.0.0        U     0      0      0 eth0
169.254.0.0    0.0.0.0        255.255.0.0      U     0      0      0 eth0
127.0.0.0      0.0.0.0        255.0.0.0        U     0      0      0 lo
0.0.0.0        198.62.1.1     0.0.0.0          UG    0      0      0 ppp0
```

This shows that the gateway was set to the remote PPP server (198.62.1.1), as well as showing the other interfaces running on my computer. There are two ppp0 entries. The first shows the destination as a host (UH). The second shows the destination as a gateway (UG). The address entry 169.254.0.0 indicates that all addresses for subnetwork 169.254 should be directed to the local network. (Microsoft clients that can't get an IP address via DHCP or other means will assign themselves IP addresses in this range.) All addresses that can't be resolved on the local LAN are directed to the gateway address.

Checking that the name servers are set

If you are able to ping a remote computer by IP address, but are not able to resolve any addresses, your DNS servers may not be set correctly. As root user from a Terminal window, open the /etc/resolv.conf file and check that there are lines identifying one or more DNS servers in this file. These should be supplied to you by your ISP (unless you run your own DNS server). Here are some examples (the numbers are fictitious):

```
nameserver 111.11.11.111
nameserver 222.22.22.222
```

Try using the ping command to make sure that the name servers are live.

> **NOTE:** When you connect to your ISP using DHCP, it's possible that during the connection process, new name server information will appear in your /etc/resolv.conf file and old entries will be lost. This can be a problem if you are relying on your own server for providing DNS service and its entry is erased.

Checking the chap-secrets or pap-secrets file

PPP supports two authentication protocols in Fedora and RHEL: Challenge Handshake Authentication Protocol (CHAP) and Password Authentication Protocol (PAP). Here is what each protocol does to authenticate:

- **CHAP** — The server sends the client a challenge packet (which includes the server name). The client sends back a response that includes its name and a value that combines the secret and the challenge. The client name and secret are stored in your `/etc/ppp/chap-secrets` file.

- **PAP** — The client sends its name and a password (clear text) for authentication. The client name and secret are stored in your `/etc/ppp/pap-secrets` file.

By default, PPP will authenticate if the server requests it, unless it has no secrets to share. If it has no secrets, PPP (or, more specifically, the PPP daemon `pppd`) will refuse authentication. It is likely that you will find the user names and passwords you provided when you set up your PPP connection in both of these files (PPP assumes that you may be using CHAP or PAP authentication).

The chap-secrets and pap-secrets formats are the same. Each authentication line can contain the client name, the server name, and the secret. The server name can be represented by an * (to allow this secret to be used to authenticate any server). This is useful if you don't know what the server name will be. Also, remember that case is significant (that is, Myserver is not the same as myserver).

> **TIP:** For more about PAP and CHAP in PPP for Linux, see the pppd man page (type **man pppd**).

In any case, here's an example of what a chap-secrets file may look like:

```
# Secrets for authentication using CHAP
# client           server        secret                    IP addresses
###### redhat-config-network will overwrite this part!!! (begin) ######
"abcusername"       "ppp0"     "MySecretPassword"
```

> **CAUTION:** The pap-secrets and chap-secrets files should not be accessible by anyone but the root user. Anyone gaining this information could use it to access your Internet account. By default, permissions are closed to all but the root user. (To close permission, type **chmod 600 /etc/ppp/*-secrets**.)

Looking at the ifcfg file

The `ifcfg` file for your PPP connection is stored in a file name that includes the provider name you entered (such as `/etc/sysconfig/network-scripts/ifcfg-ATT`). That file contains options that are passed to the pppd daemon for features that are negotiated with the remote PPP server. Most of the problems that can occur with your PPP connection result from getting some of the options wrong (particularly asking for features the server can't or won't provide).

Here is an example of the `ifcfg-???` file (in this case named `ifcfg-ATT`) used to connect to a Windows NT PPP server:

```
DEVICE=ppp0
PROVIDER=ATT
```

```
MODEMPORT=/dev/ttyS0
LINESPEED=115200
PAPNAME=guest
ONBOOT=yes
DEFROUTE=yes
DEMAND=yes
```

The device name is `ppp0`. The `PROVIDER` is the name you assigned to the connection (which is associated with the configuration file, for example `ifcfg-ATT`). `MODEMPORT` is the device name associated with the port the modem is connected to (in this case, `COM1`). `LINESPEED` sets the speed, in bps, between the computer and the modem (not the dial-up speed, which is typically slower). `PAPNAME` is the user name that you log in with, assuming you are using PAP authentication.

`ONBOOT` is set to `yes` to start the `pppd` daemon at boot time (but not dial out yet, since `DEMAND=yes` is set). `DEFROUTE=yes` sets the default route to be this PPP connection. `DEMAND=yes` causes the link to be initiated only when traffic is present.

> **TIP:** If you want to see the exact options set by each of these parameters, look at the contents of the `/etc/sysconfig/network-scripts/ifup-ppp` script. For example, if `DEFROUTE=yes`, then the option defaultroute is sent to the pppd daemon. See the pppd man page for a description of each option (type **man pppd**).

You can add a `PPPOPTIONS` line to set any additional options you want passed to the pppd daemon process. There are some cases where the ISP will require other values that are not included here. Likewise, there are some options that you should not put in this file when connecting to certain types of servers. Here are some suggestions of values that either should not be in this file or should be (in some cases) for some Windows NT servers. For descriptions of these options, see the pppd man page:

- **remotename=*remotename*** — You may need this value for PAP authentication, but it should not be entered for CHAP authentication. (For CHAP, the remote PPP server sends you its name.)

- **require-chap, require-pap, auth, noauth** — It's a nice idea to ask a Windows NT server to authenticate itself (which is what `require-chap` and `require-pap` do for their respective protocols). The `auth` value requires the server to authenticate itself before packets can be sent or received. However, I'm told on good authority that Windows NT will not let you do any of this. Authentication will fail and you will not get a connection. You may need to indicate explicitly that the server is not required to authenticate itself by entering the `noauth` option.

- **default-asyncmap** — PAP can fail to authenticate because of "link transparency problems." If authentication fails and you are sure you have the authentication information correct, try adding this value.

- **ipcp-accept-local, ipcp-accept remote** — Sometimes a server will request your local IP address, even if it wants to assign one itself. The same is true of the remote address. Try adding these lines to the options file:

```
192.168.0.1:192.168.0.2
ipcp-accept-local
ipcp-accept-remote
demand
```

This gives temporary local and remote addresses and tells the remote server that it can replace those values. Instead of using private IP addresses (as shown here), you could use 0.0.0.0 instead.

- **bsdcomp, deflate** — Certain kinds of compression are not supported with Windows NT PPP servers. So, you should not request BSD compression (bsdcomp) or Deflate compression (deflate). In some cases, you may want to prohibit those types of compression: nobsdcomp, nodeflate, and noccp (for no compression control protocol).

As noted earlier, the best place for descriptions of pppd options is the pppd man page. For a sample options file, look in /usr/share/doc/ppp*/sample.

> **NOTE:** Additional scripts for dial-up connections, particularly if you are using the newer IPv6 addresses, are contained in the /etc/ppp directory.

Running debugging

If your modem is working, but you are not getting connected at all, the first thing to do is turn on logging for PPP. This will help you track down the problem. If you are still stumped after looking at the logging output, have an expert review the log file. Make sure that debugging is turned on by setting DEBUG=yes in the ifcfg-??? file.

> **TIP:** If you can get on the Internet from another machine, I recommend posting your failed PPP output to the comp.protocol.ppp newsgroup, where some very smart PPP experts can help answer your questions. Before you post, however, read a few days' worth of messages from the group. Chances are that someone has already run into the same problem and has a solution. Also, post only the parts of the log file that are relevant. You can also ask your local Linux user group for help.

To have debugging directed to a separate log file for PPP, add these lines to the /etc/syslog.conf file:

```
daemon.*        /var/log/pppmsg
local2.*        /var/log/pppmsg
```

After this, restart the syslogd daemon process (as root user) by typing the following:

```
# service syslog restart
```

It's best to try to do this debugging process from the desktop because it helps to have several Terminal windows open (I would suggest at least three). From the first window, start a command that lists the contents of the log file we just defined above (pppmsg) as debug messages come in:

```
# tail -f /var/log/pppmsg
```

In the next window, start the PPP interface. Assuming it is the ppp0 interface, use the following command as root user:

```
# ifup ppp0
```

Here is a partial listing of the output:

```
Jun  6 20:43:51 maple pppd[2077]: pppd 2.4.1 started by root, uid 0
Jun  6 20:43:51 maple ifup-ppp: pppd started for ppp0 on /dev/modem at 115200
Jun  6 20:43:52 maple chat[2079]: abort on (BUSY)
Jun  6 20:43:52 maple chat[2079]: abort on (ERROR)
Jun  6 20:43:52 maple chat[2079]: abort on (NO CARRIER)
Jun  6 20:43:52 maple chat[2079]: abort on (NO DIALTONE)
Jun  6 20:43:52 maple chat[2079]: abort on (Invalid Login)
Jun  6 20:43:52 maple chat[2079]: abort on (Login incorrect)
Jun  6 20:43:52 maple chat[2079]: send (ATZ^M)
Jun  6 20:43:52 maple chat[2079]: expect (OK)
Jun  6 20:43:53 maple chat[2079]: ATZ^M^M
Jun  6 20:43:53 maple chat[2079]: OK
Jun  6 20:43:53 maple chat[2079]:  -- got it
Jun  6 20:43:53 maple chat[2079]: send (ATDT5551212^M)
Jun  6 20:43:53 maple chat[2079]: expect (CONNECT)
Jun  6 20:43:53 maple chat[2079]: ^M
Jun  6 20:44:10 maple chat[2079]: ATDT5551212^M^M
Jun  6 20:44:10 maple chat[2079]: CONNECT
Jun  6 20:44:10 maple chat[2079]:  -- got it
Jun  6 20:44:10 maple chat[2079]: send (\d)
Jun  6 20:44:14 maple pppd[2077]: Serial connection established.
Jun  6 20:44:14 maple pppd[2077]: Using interface ppp0
Jun  6 20:44:14 maple pppd[2077]: Connect: ppp0 <--> /dev/modem
                .
                .
                .
Jun  6 20:44:17 maple pppd[2077]: local  IP address 222.62.137.121
Jun  6 20:44:17 maple pppd[2077]: remote IP address 222.62.1.105
Jun  6 20:44:17 maple pppd[2077]: primary  DNS address 111.222.111.253
Jun  6 20:44:17 maple pppd[2077]: secondary DNS address 111.222.111.254
```

This output shows starting the PPP connection on /dev/modem. After verifying that the modem is working, the chat script sends the telephone number. The connection is made, and the PPP interface is started. After some parameter negotiations, the server assigns IP addresses to both sides of the communication, and the connection is ready to use.

If you do get connected, but none of your applications (Web browser, FTP, and so on) seem to work, check that your PPP interface is noted as the default route (`/sbin/route -n`). If it is, check that you have the DNS servers specified correctly in your `/etc/resolv.conf` file. Use the `ping` command on those DNS servers' IP addresses to make sure you can get through.

Connecting Your LAN to the Internet

The users on your LAN are happy that you made it so that they can share files and printers with each other. With your users already connected on a LAN, the next logical step is to set up a connection to the Internet that everyone can share. The advantages of doing this are as follows:

- **Save on modems** — Instead of each computer having its own modem, you can have one high-speed device (such as a DSL router or cable modem) that routes all traffic to the Internet.

- **Save on telephone lines** — Instead of using a telephone line for each person who wants to get to the Internet, you can use one line to your ISP. (In the case of DSL, the telephone company will even let you use the same telephone line for both analog voice and high-speed digital data.)

- **Central maintenance** — If information related to your Internet connection changes (such as your dial-out number or name server addresses), you can administrate those changes in one location instead of having to change it on every computer.

- **Central security** — You can better control the Internet traffic that comes in to and goes out of your network.

The procedures in this section assume that you have already set up a LAN, as described in Chapter 15. It is also assumed that you have an outgoing connection from your Linux system to the Internet that all traffic between the computers on your LAN and the Internet can pass through. That outgoing connection may be dial-up or may come through another LAN card connected (to a DSL router) or other LAN. This section describes two ways to set up your Linux system so clients on the LAN can access the Internet:

- **As a router** — By configuring Linux as a router, it can route IP packets from clients on the LAN to the Internet through the dial-up connection.

- **As a proxy server** — You can configure Linux as a proxy server. In this way, client computers on your LAN can access the Internet as though the connection were coming from the Linux computer.

Setting Up Linux as a Router

There are several different ways to set up routing from your LAN to the Internet. You can have a dedicated router or you can have a computer already connected to your LAN that will act as a router. This section describes how to use your Linux system as a router.

A computer may have several network interfaces, such as a loopback, an Ethernet LAN, a direct line to another computer, or a dial-up interface. For a client computer to use a router to reach the Internet, it may have a private IP address assigned to it on the LAN. A connection to a routing computer would act as the gateway to all other addresses.

Here's an example of Linux being used as a router between a LAN and the Internet:

- The Linux system has at least two network interfaces: one to the office LAN and one to the Internet. The interface to the Internet may be a dial-up PPP connection or, more likely these days, a higher-speed DSL or cable modem connection.

- Packets on the LAN that are not addressed to a known computer on the LAN are forwarded to the router (that is, the Linux system acting as a router). So, each client identifies that Linux system as the gateway system.

- The Linux router/firewall is set up to receive packets from the local LAN, then forwards those packets to its other interface (possibly a PPP connection to the Internet). If the LAN uses private IP addresses, the firewall is also configured to use IP masquerading or Network Address Translation.

The following sections describe how to set up the Linux router, as well as the client computers from your LAN (Linux and MS Windows clients) that will use this router. Using Linux as a router also provides an excellent opportunity to improve the security of your Internet connection by setting up a firewall to filter traffic and hide the identity of the computers on your LAN (IP masquerading).

Configuring the Linux router

To configure your Linux computer as a router, you need to have a few things in place. Here's what you need to do before you set up routing:

- **Connect to your LAN.** Add a network card and configure the computers on your LAN (as described in Chapter 15).

- **Connect to the Internet.** Set up a dial-up or other type of connection from your Linux computer to your ISP. This is described earlier in this chapter in the section on setting up outgoing PPP connections.

- **Configure your Linux computer as a router.** See the rest of this section.

Selecting IP addresses

The type of IP addresses you are using on your LAN will have an impact on a couple of steps in this procedure. Here are the differences:

- **Private IP addresses** — If the computers on your LAN use private IP addresses (described in Chapter 15), you need to set up Linux as a firewall to do IP masquerading or NAT (as described in Chapter 14). Because those numbers are private, they must be hidden from the Internet when the Linux router forwards their requests. Packets

forwarded with masquerading or NAT look to the outside world as though they came
from the Linux computer forwarding the packets.

- **Valid IP addresses** — If your LAN uses addresses that were officially assigned by your
  ISP or other registration authority, you don't need to do IP masquerading or NAT.
  (Actually, for any machine you want to expose to the world, such as a public server, you
  will want to have a valid, public IP address.)

In most cases where you are not configuring the computers on your LAN as servers, you will
probably want to use private IP addresses.

Enable forwarding and masquerading

With your Linux computer's LAN and Internet interfaces in place, use the following procedure
to set up Linux as a router. After this procedure is completed, any client computer on your
LAN can identify your Linux computer as its gateway so it can use Linux to get to the Internet.

1. Open the `/etc/sysconfig/network` file in a text editor as the root user. Then add
   either a default gateway or default gateway device as described below.

   Your default gateway is where traffic destined for networks outside of your own is sent.
   This is where you would identify your Internet connection. Here is how you choose
   which one to enter:

   - **Default Gateway** — If there is a static IP address you use to reach the Internet, enter
     that IP address here. For example, if your Internet connection goes through a DSL
     modem connected to your NIC card at address `192.168.0.1`, enter that address as
     follows:

   ```
   GATEWAY=192.168.0.1
   ```

   - **Default Gateway Device** — If you reach the Internet using a dynamic address that is
     assigned when you connect to a particular interface, enter that interface here. For
     example, if you had a dial-up interface to the Internet on the first PPP device, you
     would enter `ppp0` as the default gateway device as follows:

   ```
   GATEWAYDEV=ppp0
   ```

   When you are done, the contents of this file should look similar to the following:

   ```
   NETWORKING=yes
   HOSTNAME='maple.handsonhistory.com'
   DOMAINNAME='handsonhistory.com'
   #GATEWAY=
   GATEWAYDEV=ppp0
   ```

   In this case, the computer is configured to route packets over a dial-up connection to the
   Internet (`ppp0`).

2. Turn on IP packet forwarding. One way to do this is to change the value of `net.ipv4.ip_forward` to 1 in the `/etc/sysctl.conf` file. Open that file as root user with any text editor and change the line to appear as follows:

```
net.ipv4.ip_forward = 1
```

> **NOTE:** You can restart your network for this change to take effect (`service network restart`). To have the change take place without a network restart, type **echo 1 > /proc/sys/net/ipv4/ip_forward**.

3. If the computers on your LAN have valid IP addresses, skip ahead to the "Configuring network clients" section. If your computers have private IP addresses, continue with this procedure.

> **CAUTION:** The lines shown below for configuring your iptables firewall to do IP masquerading should be used in addition to your other firewall rules. They do not, in themselves, represent a secure firewall, but merely describe how to add masquerading to your firewall. See Chapter 14 for details about how to configure a more complete firewall and when to use NAT versus IP masquerading.

4. To get IP masquerading going on your Linux router, you need to define which addresses will be masqueraded and forwarded, using iptables.

   The following examples assume that you are masquerading all computers on your private LAN 10.0.0 (that is, 10.0.0.1, 10.0.0.2, and so on) and routing packets from that LAN to the Internet over your dial-up (ppp0) interface.

   Type the following as root user:

```
# iptables -t nat -A POSTROUTING -o ppp0 -j MASQUERADE
# iptables -A FORWARD -s 10.0.0.0/24 -j ACCEPT
# iptables -A FORWARD -d 10.0.0.0/24 -j ACCEPT
# iptables -A FORWARD -s ! 10.0.0.0/24 -j DROP
```

   The previous commands turn on masquerading in the NAT table by appending a POSTROUTING rule (`-A POSTROUTING`) for all outgoing packets on the first dial-up PPP interface (`-o ppp0`). The next two lines accept forwarding for all packets from (`-s`) and to (`-d`) the 10.0.0 network (`10.0.0.0/24`). The last line drops packets that don't come from the 10.0.0 network.

   The previous lines add rules to your running iptables firewall in the Linux kernel. To make the current rules permanent, save them as follows:

```
# service iptables save
```

   This copies all the current rules to the `/etc/sysconfig/iptables` file, from which the rules are read each time you reboot your system. If the new rules don't work, just copy the `iptables.save` file back to the original `iptables` file.

5. At this point, you may want to restart your network as follows:

```
# /etc/init.d/network restart
```

6. Then, to restart your firewall, type the following:

```
# /etc/init.d/iptables restart
```

7. To see if your new rules have gone into effect, type `iptables -L`. To view NAT rules, type `iptables -L -t nat`.

If the route to the Internet from Linux is being provided by a dial-up connection, you probably want to turn on on-demand dialing (as described earlier in this chapter).

Configuring network clients

In this example, there are a variety of Linux and Windows operating system clients on a LAN. One Linux computer has a connection to the Internet and is set up to act as a router between the Internet and the other computers on the LAN (as described previously). To be able to reach computers on the Internet, each client must be able to do the following:

- Resolve the names it requests (for example, `www.redhat.com`) into IP addresses.

- Find a route from the local system to the remote system, using its network interfaces.

Each Linux client computer knows how to find another computer's address based on the contents of the `/etc/host.conf`, `/etc/hosts`, and `/etc/resolv.conf` files. The contents of the `host.conf` file, by default, is the following:

```
order hosts,bind
```

This tells your system to check for any hostnames (hosts) that you request by first checking the contents of the `/etc/hosts` file and then checking with name servers that are identified in the `/etc/resolv.conf` file. In our case, we will put the addresses of the few hosts we know about on our private network (whether on the LAN, direct connection, or other network interface) in the `/etc/hosts` file. Then, the system knows to resolve addresses using a DNS server (`bind`) based on addresses of name servers we add to the `/etc/resolv.conf` file.

Next, each client machine must know how to get to the Internet. Do this by adding a default route (sometimes called a *gateway*) to each client. To permanently add a default route on the client Linux system, do the following:

1. Set the default route to point to the router. This entails setting the GATEWAY or GATEWAYDEV value in the `/etc/sysconfig/network` file as described in the previous procedure. (This time, the address will point to the LAN interface of the router.)

2. Restart your network interfaces by typing the following as root user:

```
# /etc/init.d/network restart
```

3. When the computer comes back up, type the following:

```
# netstat -r
Kernel IP routing table
Destination  Gateway  Genmask        Flags  MSS Window  irtt Iface
10.0.0.0     *        255.255.255.0  U          0 0         0 eth0
```

```
169.254.0.0    0.0.0.0 255.255.0.0      U          0 0          0 eth0
default        10.0.0.1 0.0.0.0         UG         0 0          0 eth0
```

You can see that the default gateway was set to the host at the IP address `10.0.0.1` on the `eth0` Ethernet interface. Assuming that router is ready to route your packets to the Internet, your Linux client is now ready to use that router to find all IP addresses that you request that you do not already know where to find. (The `netstat -r` command provides the same output as the `/sbin/route` command.)

Configuring a Virtual Private Network Connection

There are several ways of going about setting up VPN connections in Linux:

- **Internet Protocol SECurity (IPsec)** — IPsec is a standard developed by the Internet Engineering Task Force (IETF) as the required method of encryption when the IP version 6 becomes the standard Internet protocol (right now IPv4 is the standard in North America and Europe). There are several implementations of IPsec over IPv4 in Linux these days. Linux includes IPsec support by including the Linux 2.6 kernel and offering an administrative interface for configuring it (via the ipsec-tools package).

- **PPP over OpenSSH** — With this method, using software that is already in Linux, you can configure a PPP interface (as you would a regular dial-up connection) to use SSH to encrypt all data that goes across the PPP interface. While this method is not too difficult to configure, it can provide poor performance. To see how to create a PPP over OpenSSH VPN, refer to the VPN PPP-SSH HOW-TO (search `www.tldp.org`).

- **OpenVPN** — With OpenVPN (`http://openvpn.net`), you can use all OpenSSL encryption and authentication features to create a tunnel to remote systems over public networks (such as the Internet). An OpenVPN package for Fedora is available from the Fedora software repository (type `yum install openvpn`).

- **Openswan** — The Openswan project (`www.openswan.org`) produces an implementation of IPsec that was originally based on code from the FreeS/WAN project (`www.freeswan.org`). Openswan is included in the Fedora software repository (to install it, type `yum install openswan`).

- **Crypto IP Encapsulation (CIPE)** — Using this method, IP packets are routed across selected IP interfaces as encrypted UDP packets. CIPE is easy to set up and carries less overhead than PPP over OpenSSH, so you should get better performance. One drawback is that, because it is not a standard VPN, CIPE is not available on all platforms and was dropped from Fedora and RHEL.

Chapter 15 explained the basic idea behind using a VPN and described how to configure NetworkManager to communicate with a remote openvpn server. In this chapter, I provide an overview of the features and tools in IPsec and a detailed description of configuring an OpenVPN server in Fedora.

Understanding IPsec

To provide more secure transmission of TCP/IP data in the new Internet Protocol version 6 (IPv6) standard, developers of that standard created the Internet Protocol Security (IPsec) architecture. With IPsec, encrypted communication is possible right at the IP level and methods for providing access control, data integrity, authentication, and traffic flow confidentiality are standardized as well.

In practical terms, organizations that have computers that need to communicate on public networks in ways are secure and private can create VPNs with IPsec. Unlike other VPN implementations (such as CIPE), which require a manual exchange of keys to work, IPsec offers an automated way of creating security associations between communications endpoints and managing keys.

With slow adoption of IPv6 in the United States and other places, IPsec has been included (backported) into the IPv4 protocol, which is still the most common IP version used on the Internet. That backport was added into the IP protocol included with the Linux 2.6 kernel that comes with Fedora starting with version 2. The Internet standard RFC2401 document describes the IPsec architecture.

Using IPsec protocols

IPsec consists of two primary protocols: Authentication Header (AH) and Encapsulating Security Payload (ESP). Look in the `/etc/protocols` file and you'll see that AH is assigned to protocol number 50 and ESP is assigned to protocol number 51.

To authenticate peer computers and exchange symmetric keys, IPsec uses the Internet Key Exchange (IKE) protocol. At the beginning of communication between two host computers using IPsec, IKE does the following:

- Authenticates that the peer computers are who they say they are
- Negotiates security associations
- Chooses secret symmetric keys (using Diffie-Hellmann key exchange)

The security associations established by IKE are stored in a security association database (SAD). A security association holds information about the communications endpoints (possibly public Internet IP addresses), whether Authentication Header (AH) or Encapsulating Security Payload (ESP) protocols are being used with IPsec, and the secret key/algorithm being used.

IPsec itself has two possible modes of operation: tunnel mode and transport mode.

- **Tunnel mode** — The entire IP datagram is encapsulated into the new IP datagram by IPsec. This protects both the data and the control information from being seen by anyone except the communications endpoint that is allowed to decrypt the communication.

- **Transport mode** — Only the data (the payload intended for the client receiving the data) is encrypted. To do this, IPsec inserts its own header between the Internet Protocol header and the protocol header for the upper layer.

Included in the protocol header of each packet transmitted is information referred to as Hash Message Authentication Codes (HMAC). Including these codes with transmitted data in IPsec offers the following advantages:

- **Data integrity** — By using a hash algorithm to create a hash from a secret key and the data in the IP datagram, the resulting HMAC is added to the IPsec protocol header. The receiver can then check that the HMAC is correct using its own copy of that secret key. Supported authentication algorithms include MD5, SHA1, and SHA2 (256, 384, and 512).
- **Data privacy** — By using symmetric encryption algorithms (such as DES, NULL, AES, 3DES, and Blowfish), datagrams are encrypted so their contents cannot be seen by outsiders.

By recording a sequence of packets during data communications, an intruder can attempt denial-of-service attacks by replaying that sequence of packets. IPsec combats that type of attack by accepting packets that are within a "sliding window" of sequence numbers or higher. Packets using older sequence numbers are dropped.

Using IPsec in Fedora or RHEL

Using IPsec in Fedora or RHEL, you can configure VPNs between Fedora or RHEL and other systems that support IPsec. It is important that hosts at both ends of the IPsec VPN are configured in the same way. In fact, you may have the best results by using the same operating system version and IPsec software. In Fedora and RHEL, you have the choice of using OpenVPN, Openswan, or IPsec-Tools.

By default, the necessary modules to use IPsec are already available in Fedora and RHEL. If you choose to use IPsec, all the tools you need to configure a VPN are contained in the ipsec-tools packages. You set up IPsec in the kernel in much the same way that you set up firewalls with iptables: you run commands that load settings into the kernel, either from command line options (standard input) or from a file containing your preconfigured options.

The commands you use to set up a VPN with IPsec include the following:

- **setkey** — Use this command to load the data about your VPN connections into the kernel. It can add, change, flush, or dump information in the Security Association Database (SAD) and the Security Policy Database (SPD) for your IPsec VPN. Typically, you would create a configuration file in the format described on the `setkey` man page, then run `setkey -f filename` to load that data into the kernel.
- **racoon** — Use this command to create IKE security associations between host computers communicating together over an IPsec VPN. Security data are loaded into

`racoon` from the `/etc/racoon/racoon.conf` file (unless that file is overridden from the `racoon` command line using the `-f` option).

Sample configuration files to use with `setkey` are available from the IPsec-HOWTO (`www.ipsec-howto.org`). A sample `racoon.conf` file is included with the ipsec-tools package (in the `/usr/share/doc/ipsec-tools-*` directory). For an in-depth description of the tools used with IPsec, refer to the Kame Project Web site (`www.kame.net`).

Configuring an OpenVPN Server

Virtual private networks were created to allow computer systems to have secure connections using insecure public networks. Setting up an OpenVPN server at your place of business can provide an inexpensive way for branch offices or telecommuters to securely access your company's private network.

Because VPN technologies, such as OpenVPN, provide encrypted connections between two transport-level network interfaces, any applications communicating between those two systems are secure. This is as opposed to user-space applications, such as SSL, that must implement features from every application they want to offer to users.

For Linux systems, OpenVPN provides a very good choice of software for configuring a VPN server. The following are some of the features of OpenVPN:

- A single port can provide access to up to 128 clients.
- The server can control client setup, doing tasks such as pushing configuration data to clients through the VPN tunnel.
- You can use telnet to access the server.
- OpenVPN includes TUN/TAP virtual network interface drivers at the networking layer, with device names like `/dev/tun`*X* and `/dev/tap`*X*. Applications can use the TUN devices as virtual point-to-point interface to VPN partner (routed mode). TAP devices provide a virtual Ethernet adapter, so daemons listening on TAP can capture Ethernet frames.

The OpenVPN procedure in this chapter describes how to set up an OpenVPN server. This includes:

- Setting up information needed to create certificate authority certificates and keys. In the process you create a root RSA Private Key (`ca.key`) that you need to keep confidential and a root certificate (`ca.crt`) that you share.
- Setting up configuration files and starting the OpenVPN service.

Decisions before configuring OpenVPN

The decisions you need to make before setting up your OpenVPN connection include the following:

- **Do you want a public key infrastructure or static key?** If you have a single VPN client connection to a single server you can use a static key. That way you don't have to maintain a key infrastructure. See the OpenVPN HOWTO for more information:

```
http://openvpn.net/index.php/documentation/howto.html#examples
```

- **Will your VPN do routing or bridging?** Routing, where data are routed from the VPN server to the LAN (instead of just being passed through), is usually a better choice than bridging. Routing is easier to set up and provides more control for specific client features.

The following assumes you decided to set up a public key infrastructure and are using a routing OpenVPN server. For information on using OpenVPN to do bridging, refer to the Ethernet Bridging FAQ (`http://openvpn.net/faq.html#bridge1`).

Create a public key infrastructure

Using certificates and private keys, you can create a safe environment for allowing multiple clients to access your private networks over the Internet. The following procedure is done on a Fedora system that doesn't necessarily have to be the same one that you use for your VPN server. In this example, however, the entire procedure is run on the OpenVPN server.

To begin setting up your public key infrastructure, open a Terminal window as root and do the following:

1. **Copy the sample configuration files**:

```
# cp -r /usr/share/openvpn/easy-rsa/ /etc/openvpn/
# cd /etc/openvpn/easy-rsa/2.0
```

2. **Choose Variables**: Edit the vars file (in this example, the vars file is located in /etc/openvpn/easy-rsa/2.0). Most of the defaults will work, as long as you work from this configuration directory. However, you need at least to set the key values that are placed in your certificate. Replace the examples in quotes with your own values:

```
export KEY_COUNTRY="US"
export KEY_PROVINCE="WI"
export KEY_CITY="Madison"
export KEY_ORG="Reedsburg-LUG"
export KEY_EMAIL="chris@linuxtoys.net"
```

In the vars file, you can also change such values as the default key size (1024) and days to certificate expiration (3650 days).

3. **Set Variables**: Export the variables in the vars file to the current shell so they can be used by the later commands you run:

```
# source ./vars
```

4. **Prepare to create new keys**: If there are any keys in your KEY_DIR (probably named keys/ in the current directory), this command removes them and creates index.txt and serial files in that directory:

```
#./clean-all
```

Next you will create the server certificates and keys.

5. **Build root certificate authority certificate and key**: Run the following script, which in turn will use the pkitool command to create a 1024 bit RSA private key:

```
# ./build-ca
Generating a 1024 bit RSA private key
.......................++++++
....++++++
writing new private key to 'ca.key'
      .
      .
      .

Country Name (2 letter code) [US]:
State or Province Name (full name) [WI]:
Locality Name (eg, city) [Madison]:
Organization Name (eg, company) [Reedsburg-LUG]:
Organizational Unit Name (eg, section) []:
Common Name (eg, your name or your server's hostname) [Reedsburg-LUG CA]:
Email Address [chris@linuxtoys.net]:
```

You should have two new files in the keys directory. The ca.key file holds the private key and the ca.crt key holds the new certificate generated from your KEYS values.

6. **Create parameters for SSL/TLS**: Type the following to build the server-side Diffie-Hellman parameters needed for SSL/TLS connection:

```
# ./build-dh
Generating DH parameters, 1024 bit long safe prime, generator 2
This is going to take a long time
.....+....................+..........+
```

This creates a file named dh1024.pem in the keys directory.

7. **Create server keys and certificates**: Run the the following command to create the keys and certificates needed on the OpenVPN server, replacing server1 with your server's hostname or other common name to identify it:

```
# ./build-key-server server1
Generating a 1024 bit RSA private key
..++++++
.....................++++++
writing new private key to 'server.key'
      .
      .
      .
```

```
A challenge password []: chzypassw77
An optional company name []:
Using configuration from /etc/openvpn/easy-rsa/2.0/openssl.cnf
    .
    .
    .
Sign the certificate? [y/n]:y
1 out of 1 certificate requests certified, commit? [y/n]  y
Write out database with 1 new entries
Data Base Updated
```

The command just run produces the `server.crt`, `server.csr`, and `server.key` files in the `keys` directory. The `server.key` file must be kept secret! Next you need to create client certificates and keys for each client you want to connect to your OpenVPN server.

8. **Create client certificates and keys**: Run the `build-key` (or `build-key-pass`) script for every client that you want to use the OpenVPN server. Here are examples running the `build-key` script for two clients, named `client01` and `client02`:

```
# ./build-key client01
    .
    .
    .
A challenge password []: my67ChvyB
Sign the certificate? [y/n] y
1 out of 1 certificate requests certified, commit? [y/n]  y
# ./build-key client02
    .
    .
    .
```

After you have run `build-key` for every client, you will have a crt (`client01.crt`), csr (`client01.csr`), and key (`client01.key`) file in the keys directory for each client. The next step is to make sure each of those keys is transported to the appropriate computer.

For this example, we will copy the keys to a directory on the Fedora client machine we are calling client01 in the `/etc/openvpn/keys/` directory on that machine. (See the "Create OpenVPN client configuration" section later in this chapter.)

Create OpenVPN server configuration

Before starting the OpenVPN service on the server, you need to create a `server.conf` file in the `/etc/openvpn` directory. You can do this by copying a sample `server.conf` file and editing it. Here is an example of one you can use:

```
# cd /usr/share/doc/openvpn-2.1/sample-config-files
# cp server.conf /etc/openvpn/
```

As root user, open the `server.conf` file in any text editor. This is an example for a multi-client server that is doing routing (not bridging). The locations of key files should match those you created in the key server section earlier. Many of the comments have been left out of this example, though you should read them in the `server.conf` file to guide your configuration.

```
port 1194
proto udp
dev tun

ca /etc/openvpn/easy-rsa/2.0/keys/ca.crt
cert /etc/openvpn/easy-rsa/2.0/keys/server.crt
key /etc/openvpn/easy-rsa/2.0/keys/server.key      # This file should be kept secret
dh /etc/openvpn/easy-rsa/2.0/keys/dh1024.pem

server 10.8.0.0 255.255.255.0

keepalive 10 120
comp-lzo

persist-key
persist-tun

status openvpn-status.log

verb 3
```

In this configuration, the OpenVPN server listens on port 1194, UDP protocol, as a routing VPN server (`dev tun`). You can use a different port number, to make the service more obscure, but the clients must use that port number as well. The private network that OpenVPN clients will be able to reach from this VPN connection is on the subnetwork `10.8.0` (identified by `10.8.0.0 255.255.255.0`). With the configuration file completed, you can start the OpenVPN service on the server by typing the following:

```
# service openvpn start
```

The last step you need to do to make your OpenVPN server ready to accept connections is to open your firewall to accept connections on port 1194 and to allow your system to route packets to your private subnetwork. In this example, we used a private subnetwork with IP addresses of 10.8.0.1 through 10.8.0.254. See the "Firewall" section of Chapter 14 for details.

Create OpenVPN client configuration

To configure an OpenVPN client to connect to the OpenVPN server you just configured, you need to copy the key files to the client, create a client configuration file, and start the service. Here is an example of how you might copy the keys from the server:

```
# cd /etc/openvpn
# mkdir keys
```

```
# scp root@server1:/etc/openvpn/easy-rsa/2.0/keys/ca.crt keys
# scp root@server1:/etc/openvpn/easy-rsa/2.0/keys/client01.crt keys
# scp root@server1:/etc/openvpn/easy-rsa/2.0/keys/client01.key keys
```

Copy a client configuration file to your `/etc/openvpn` directory and edit it as appropriate. For example, type the following:

```
# cd /usr/share/doc/openvpn-2.1/sample-config-files
# cp client.conf /etc/openvpn/
```

Here is an example of an edited `client.conf` file:

```
client

dev tun
proto udp

ns-cert-type server

remote example.com 1194

resolv-retry infinite

nobind

persist-key
persist-tun

ca /etc/openvpn/keys/ca.crt
cert /etc/openvpn/keys/client01.crt
key /etc/openvpn/keys/client01.key

comp-lzo
verb 3
```

To test that your VPN client configuration is working, type the following:

```
# openvpn --config client.conf
```

The output you see from this command will help you debug any problems you have connecting to the OpenVPN server. If you use a GUI interface to start your OpenVPN client, be sure to identify the location of your client configuration file and keys.

Setting Up Linux as a Proxy Server

You have a LAN set up, and your Linux computer has both a connection to the LAN and a connection to the Internet. One way to provide Web-browsing services to the computers on the LAN without setting up routing is to configure Linux as a proxy server.

The Squid proxy caching server software package comes with Fedora and RHEL. In a basic configuration, you can get the software going very quickly. However, the package is full of features that let you adapt it to your needs. You can control which hosts have access to proxy services, how memory is used to cache data, how logging is done, and a variety of other features. Here are the basic proxy services available with Squid:

- **HTTP** — Allowing HTTP proxy services is the primary reason to use Squid. This is what lets client computers access Web pages on the Internet from their browsers (through your Linux computer). In other words, HTTP proxy services will find and return the content to you for addresses that look similar to this: `www.ab.com`.

- **FTP** — This represents File Transfer Protocol (FTP) proxy services. When you enable HTTP for a client, you enable FTP automatically (for example, `ftp://ftp.ab.com`).

- **Gopher** — The gopher protocol proxy service was one of the first mechanisms for organizing and searching for documents on the Internet (it predates the Web by more than a decade). Nobody uses gopher anymore. However, gopher is automatically supported when you enable HTTP for a client.

Besides allowing proxy services, Squid can also be part of an Internet cache hierarchy. Internet caching occurs when Internet content is taken from the original server and copied to a caching server that is closer to you. When you, or someone else in the caching hierarchy, requests that content again, it can be taken from the caching server instead of from the original server.

You don't have to cache Internet content for other computers to participate in caching with Squid. If you know of a parent caching-computer that will allow you access, you can identify that computer in Squid and potentially speed your Web browsing significantly.

Caching services in Squid are provided through your Linux system's ICP port. Besides ICP services, you can also enable Simple Network Management Protocol (SNMP) services. SNMP lets your computer provide statistics and status information about itself to SNMP agents on the network. SNMP is a feature for monitoring and maintaining computer resources on a network.

> **CAUTION:** SNMP poses a potential security risk if it is not configured properly. Use caution when configuring SNMP with Squid.

The squid daemon process (`/usr/sbin/squid`) can be started automatically at system boot time. After it is set up, most of the configuration for Squid is done in the `/etc/squid/squid.conf` file. The `squid.conf` file contains lots of information about how to configure Squid (the file contains more than 4300 lines of comments and examples, although there are only 35 lines of active settings).

For further information about the Squid proxy server, refer to the Squid Web Proxy Cache home page (`www.squid-cache.org`).

Starting the squid daemon

When you install Fedora or RHEL, you have an opportunity to install Squid (squid package). If you are not sure whether or not Squid was installed, type the following:

```
# rpm -q squid
squid-3.0.STABLE2-2.fc9.i386
```

If squid is not installed, you can install it from the DVD that comes with this book or by typing **yum install squid** to install it over the network. Next you can check whether or not squid is configured to run. To do that, type the following:

```
# chkconfig --list squid
squid           0:off   1:off   2:off   3:off   4:off   5:off   6:off
```

If the squid service is off for run levels 3, 4, and 5 (it's off at all run levels by default), you can set it to start automatically at boot time. To set up the squid daemon to start at boot time, type the following:

```
# chkconfig squid on
```

At this point, the squid daemon should start automatically when your system boots. By default, the squid daemon will run with the -D option. The -D option enables Squid to start without having an active Internet connection. If you want to add other options to the squid daemon, you can edit the /etc/sysconfig/squid configuration file. Look for the line that looks similar to the following:

```
SQUID_OPTS="-D"
```

You can add any options, along with the -D option, between the quotes. Most of these options are useful for debugging Squid:

- **-a** *port#* — Substitute for port# a port number that will be used instead of the default port number (3128) for servicing HTTP proxy requests. This is useful for temporarily trying out an alternative port.

- **-f** *squidfile* — Use this option to specify an alternative squid.conf file (other than /etc/squid/squid.conf). Replace *squidfile* with the name of the alternative squid.conf file. This is a good way to try out a new squid.conf file before you replace the old one.

- **-d** *level* — Change the debugging level to a number indicated by *level*. This also causes debugging messages to be sent to stderr.

- **-X** — Use this option to check that the values are set properly in your squid.conf file. It turns on full debugging while the squid.conf file is being interpreted.

You can restart the squid service by typing /etc/init.d/squid restart. While the squid daemon is running, there are several ways you can run the squid command to change how the daemon works, using these options:

- **squid -k reconfigure** — Causes Squid to again read its configuration file.
- **squid -k shutdown** — Causes Squid to exit after waiting briefly for current connections to exit.
- **squid -k interrupt** — Shuts down Squid immediately, without waiting for connections to close.
- **squid -k kill** — Kills Squid immediately, without closing connections or log files. (Use this option only if other methods don't work.)

With the squid daemon ready to run, you need to set up the `squid.conf` configuration file.

Using a simple squid.conf file

You can use the `/etc/squid/squid.conf` file that comes with Squid to get started. Although the file contains lots of comments, the actual settings in that file are quite manageable. The following paragraphs describe the contents of the default `squid.conf` file:

```
http_port 3128
```

The `http_port` tag identifies the port on which Squid listens for HTTP client requests. The normal port to use (which is the default) is 3128. Optionally, you can add a hostname (such as `example.com:3128`) or IP address (such as `10.0.0.1:3128`) to limit allowed incoming requests to those made to a particular host name or IP address.

```
hierarchy_stoplist cgi-bin ?
```

The `hierarchy_stoplist` tag indicates that when a certain string of characters appears in a URL, the content should be obtained from the original server and not from a cache peer. In this example, requests for the string `cgi-bin` and the question mark character (?) are all forwarded to the originating server.

```
acl QUERY urlpath_regex cgi-bin \?
cache deny QUERY
```

The preceding two lines can be used to cause URLs containing certain characters to never be cached. These go along with the previous line by not caching URLs containing the same strings (`cgi-bin` and ?) that are always sought from the original server.

```
acl apache rep_header Server ^Apache
acl all src 0.0.0.0/0.0.0.0
acl manager proto cache_object
acl localhost src 127.0.0.1/255.255.255.255
```

The `acl` tags are used to create access control lists. The first line in the preceding code creates an access control list called apache and assigns any response headers containing `Server` `^Apache` to the apache `acl`. After that, the `all` acl is defined to include all IP addresses. The next `acl` line assigns the manager acl to handle the `cache_object` protocol. The `localhost` source is assigned to the IP address of `127.0.0.1`.

```
access_log /var/log/squid/access.log squid
```

The preceding line identifies the location of the Squid `access.log` file. As the name implies, this file contains messages about requests to access the Squid server.

Squid includes default settings for how long different types of content in cache are still considered to be fresh. The following `refresh_pattern` values are included in the `squid.conf` file:

```
refresh_pattern    ^ftp:      1440    20%    10080
refresh_pattern    ^gopher:   1440     0%     1440
refresh_pattern    .             0    20%     4320
```

In the code just shown, all lines that begin (^) with `ftp` or `gopher` are set to expire in 1440 minutes. The percentage of the object's age during which it is considered to be fresh is shown in the next column (20%, 0%, and 20%). The last column indicates the maximum number of minutes during which the object will be considered fresh. The next several entries define how particular ports are handled and how access is assigned to HTTP and ICP services.

```
acl SSL_ports port 443
acl Safe_ports port 80              # http
acl Safe_ports port 21              # ftp
acl Safe_ports port 443             # https
acl Safe_ports port 70              # gopher
acl Safe_ports port 210             # wais
acl Safe_ports port 1025-65535      # unregistered ports
acl Safe_ports port 280             # http-mgmt
acl Safe_ports port 488             # gss-http
acl Safe_ports port 591             # filemaker
acl Safe_ports port 777             # multiling http
acl CONNECT method CONNECT
http_access allow manager localhost
http_access deny manager
http_access deny !Safe_ports
http_access deny CONNECT !SSL_ports
http_access allow localhost
http_access deny all
http_reply_access allow all
icp_access allow all
```

The following sections describe these settings in more detail, as well as other tags you might want to set in your `squid.conf` file. By default, no clients can use the Squid proxy server, so you at least want to define which computers can access proxy services.

To make sure that this simple Squid configuration is working, follow this procedure:

1. On the Squid server, restart the squid daemon. To do this, type **/etc/init.d/squid restart**. (If Squid isn't running, use start instead of restart.)

2. On the Squid server, start your connection to the Internet (if it is not already up).

3. On a client computer on your network, set up Firefox (or another Web browser) to use the Squid server as a proxy server (described later in this chapter). (In Firefox, select Edit → Preferences → Advanced and click the Network tab, then choose Settings. From the Connection Setting window that pops up, select Manual proxy configuration. Then add the Squid server's computer name and, by default, port 3128 to each protocol. You can also check the Use this proxy server for all protocols option to use the same proxy for all service requests from the browser.

4. On the client computer, try to open any Web page on the Internet with the browser you just configured.

If the Web page doesn't appear, see the "Debugging Squid" section for how to fix the problem.

Modifying the Squid configuration file

If you want to set up a more complex set of access permissions for Squid, you should start with the default `squid.conf` configuration file (described earlier).

To begin, open the `/etc/squid/squid.conf` file (as the root user). You will see a lot of information describing the values that you can set in this file. Most of the tags that you need to configure Squid are used to set up caching and provide host access to your proxy server.

> **TIP:** Don't change the `squid.conf.default` file! If you really mess up your `squid.conf` file, you can start again by making another copy of this file to `squid.conf`. If you want to recall exactly what changes you have made so far, type the following from the `/etc/squid` directory:
>
> `# diff squid.conf squid.conf.default | less`
>
> This will show you the differences between your actual `squid.conf` and the version you started with.

Configuring access control in squid.conf

To protect your computing resources from being used by anyone, Squid requires that you define which host computers have access to your HTTP (Web) services. By default, all hosts are denied access to Squid HTTP services except for the local host. With the `acl` tag, you can create access lists. Then, with the `http_access` tag, you can authorize access to HTTP (Web) services for the access lists you create.

The form of the access control list tag (`acl`) is:

```
acl  name  type  string
acl  name  type  file
```

The name is any name you want to assign to the list. A `string` is a string of text, and `file` is a file of information that applies to the particular `type` of acl. Valid acl types include `dst`, `src`, `dstdomain`, `srcdomain`, `url_path_pattern`, `url_pattern`, `time`, `port`, `proto`, `method`, `browser`, and `user`.

Several access control lists are set up by default. You can use these assigned acl names to assign permissions to HTTP or ICP services. You can also create your own acl names to assign to those services. Here are the default acl names from the /etc/squid/squid.conf file that you can use or change:

```
acl all src 0.0.0.0/0.0.0.0
acl manager proto cache_object
acl localhost src 127.0.0.1/255.255.255.255
acl SSL_ports port 443 563
acl Safe_ports port 80          # http
acl Safe_ports port 21          # ftp
acl Safe_ports port 443 563     # https, snews
acl Safe_ports port 70          # gopher
acl Safe_ports port 210         # wais
acl Safe_ports port 1025-65535  # unregistered ports
acl Safe_ports port 280         # http-mgmt
acl Safe_ports port 488         # gss-http
acl Safe_ports port 591         # filemaker
acl Safe_ports port 777         # multiling http
acl CONNECT method CONNECT
```

When Squid tries to determine which class a particular computer falls in, it goes from top to bottom. In the first line, all host computers (address/netmask are all zeros) are added to the acl group all. In the second line, you create a manager group called manager that has access to your cache_object (the capability to get content from your cache). The group localhost is assigned to your loopback address. Secure socket layer (SSL) ports are assigned to the numbers 443 and 563, whereas Safe_ports are assigned to the numbers shown above. The last line defines a group called CONNECT (which you can use to allow access to SSL ports).

To deny or enable access to HTTP services on the Squid computer, the following definitions are set up:

```
http_access allow manager localhost
http_access deny manager
http_access deny !Safe_ports
http_access deny CONNECT !SSL_ports
http_access allow localhost
http_access deny all
```

These definitions are quite restrictive. The first line allows someone requesting cache objects (manager) from the local host to do so, but the second line denies anyone else making such a request. Access is not denied to ports defined as safe ports. Also, secure socket connections via the proxy are denied on all ports, except for SSL ports (!SSL_ports). HTTP access is permitted only from the local host and is denied to all other hosts.

To allow the client computers on your network access to your HTTP service, you need to create your own http_access entries. You probably want to do something more restrictive than simply saying `http_access allow all`. Here is an example of a more restrictive acl group and how to assign that group to HTTP access:

```
acl ourlan src 10.0.0.1-10.0.0.100
http_access allow ourlan
```

In the previous example, all computers at IP addresses `10.0.0.1` through `10.0.0.100` are assigned to the `ourlan` group. Access is then allowed for `ourlan` with the `http_access` line.

Configuring caching in squid.conf

Caching, as it relates to a proxy server, is the process of storing data on an intermediate system between the Web server that sent the data and the client that received it. The assumption is that later requests for the same data can be serviced more quickly by not having to go all the way back to the original server. Instead, the proxy server can simply send you the content from its copy in cache. Another benefit of caching is that it reduces demands on network resources and on the information servers.

You can arrange caching with other caching proxy servers to form a cache hierarchy. The idea is to have a *parent cache* exist close to an entry to the Internet backbone. When a *child cache* requests an object, if the parent doesn't have it, the parent goes out and gets the object, sends a copy to the child, and keeps a copy itself. That way, if another request for the data comes to the parent, it can probably service that request without making another request to the original server. This hierarchy also supports *sibling caches*, which can, in effect, create a pool of caching servers on the same level.

> **CAUTION:** Caching can consume a lot of your hard disk space if you let it. If you have separate partitions on your system, make sure that you have enough space in `/var` to handle the added load.

Here are some cache-related tags that you should consider setting:

- **cache_peer** — If there is a cache parent whose resources you can use, you can add the parent cache using this tag. You would need to obtain the parent cache's hostname, the type of cache (parent), proxy port (probably 3128), and ICP port (probably 3130) from the administrator of the parent cache. (If you have no parent cache, you don't have to set this value.) Here's an example of a `cache_peer` entry:

  ```
  cache_peer parent.handsonhistory.com parent 3128 3130
  ```

  You can also add options to the end of the line, such as `proxy-only` (so that what you get from the parent isn't stored locally) and `weight=n` (where *n* is replaced by a number above 1 to indicate that the parent should be used above other parents). Add `default` if the parent is used as a last resort (when all other parents don't have the requested data).

- **cache_mem** — Specifies the amount of cache memory (RAM) used to store in-transit objects (ones that are currently being used), hot objects (ones that are used often), and negative-cached objects (recent failed requests). The default is 8MB, although you can raise that value. To set `cache_mem` to 16MB, enter the following:

```
cache_mem   16 MB
```

> **NOTE:** Because Squid will probably use a total of three times the amount of space you give it for all its processing, Squid documentation recommends that you use a `cache_mem` size one-third the size of the space that you actually have available for Squid.

- **cache_dir** — Specifies the directory (or directories if you want to distribute cache across multiple disks or partitions) in which cache swap files are stored. The default is the `/var/spool/squid` directory. You can also specify how much disk space to use for cache in megabytes (100 is the default), the number of first-level directories to create (16 is the default), and the number of second-level directories (256 is the default). Here's an example:

```
cache_dir  ufs /var/spool/squid 100 16 256
```

> **NOTE:** The cache directory must exist. Squid won't create it for you. It will, however, create the first- and second-level directories.

- **cache_mgr** — Add the e-mail address of the user who should receive e-mail if the cache daemon dies. By default, e-mail is sent to root. To explicitly set `cache_mgr` to the root user, use the following:

```
cache_mgr   root
```

- **cache_effective_user** — After the squid daemon process is started as root, subsequent processes are run as `squid` user and group (by default). To change that subsequent user to a different name (for example, to `nobody`) set the `cache_effective_user` as follows:

```
cache_effective_user nobody
```

> **NOTE:** When I changed the `cache_effective_user` name so that a user other than `squid` ran the `squid` daemon, the messages log recorded several failed attempts to initialize the Squid cache before the process exited. When I changed the user name back to `squid`, the process started properly. To use the `cache_effective_user` feature effectively, you must identify which files are not allowing access.

Configuring port numbers in squid.conf

When you configure client computers to use your Squid proxy services, the clients need to know your computer's name (or IP address) and the port numbers associated with the services.

For a client wanting to use your proxy to access the Web, the HTTP port is the needed number. Here are the tags that you use to set port values in Squid for different services, along with their default values:

- **http_port 3128** — The `http_port` is set to 3128 by default. Client workstations need to know this number (or the number you change this value to) to access your proxy server for HTTP services (that is, Web browsing).

- **icp_port 3130** — ICP requests are sent to and from neighboring caches through port 3130 by default.

- **htcp_port 4827** — ICP sends HTCP requests to and from neighboring caches on port 4827 by default.

Debugging Squid

If Squid isn't working properly when you set it up, or if you just want to monitor Squid activities, there are several tools and log files to help you.

Checking the squid.conf file

By running the squid daemon with the `-X` option (described earlier), you can check what is being set from the `squid.conf` file. You can add an `-X` option to the `SQUID_OPTS` line in the `/etc/init.d/squid` file. Then run `/etc/init.d/squid restart`. A whole lot of information is output, which details what is being set from `squid.conf`. If there are syntax errors in the file, they appear here.

Checking Squid log files

Squid log files (in Fedora and RHEL) are stored in the `/var/log/squid` directory by default. The following are the log files created there, descriptions of what they contain, and descriptions of how they might help you debug potential problems:

- **access.log** — Contains entries that describe each time the cache has been hit or missed when a client requests HTTP content. Along with that information is the identity of the host making the request (IP address) and the content they are requesting. Use this information to find out when content is being used from cache and when the remote server must be accessed to obtain the content. Here is what some of the access result codes mean:

  - **TCP_DENIED** — Squid denied access for the request.
  - **TCP_HIT** — Cache contained a valid copy of the object.
  - **TCP_IMS_HIT** — A fresh version of the requested object was still in cache when the client asked if the content had changed.
  - **TCP_IMS_MISS** — An If-Modified-Since request was issued by the client for a stale object.

- **TCP_MEM_HIT** — Memory contained a valid copy of the object.

- **TCP_MISS** — Cache did not contain the object.

- **TCP_NEGATIVE_HIT** — The object was negatively cached, meaning that an error was returned (such as the file not being found) when the object was requested.

- **TCP_REF_FAIL_HIT** — A stale object was returned from cache because of a failed request to validate the object.

- **TCP_REFRESH_HIT** — A stale copy of the object was in cache, but a request to the server returned information that the object had not been modified.

- **TCP_REFRESH_MISS** — A stale cache object was replaced by new, updated content.

- **TCP_SWAPFAIL** — An object could not be accessed from cache, despite the belief that the object should have been there.

- **cache.log** — Contains valuable information about your Squid configuration when the squid daemon starts up. You can see how much memory is available (Max Mem), how much swap space (Max Swap), the location of the cache directory (`/var/spool/squid`), the types of connections being accepted (HTTP, ICP, and SNMP), and the port on which connections are being accepted. You can also see a lot of information about cached objects (such as how many are loaded, expired, or canceled).

- **store.log** — Contains entries that show when content is being swapped out from memory to the cache (`SWAPOUT`), swapped back into memory from cache (`SWAPIN`), or released from cache (`RELEASE`). You can see where the content comes from originally and where it is being placed in the cache. Time is logged in this file in raw UNIX time (in milliseconds).

You might also be interested in another log file: `/var/log/messages`. This file contains entries describing the startup and exit status of the squid daemon.

Using the top command

Run the `top` command to see information about running processes, including the Squid process. If you are concerned about performance hits from too much Squid activity, type **M** from within the top window. The M option displays information about running processes, sorted by the percent of memory each process is using. If you find that Squid is consuming too large a percentage of your system memory, you can reduce the memory usage by resetting the `cache_mem` value in your `squid.conf` file.

Setting Up Proxy Clients

For your Linux proxy server to provide Web-browsing access (HTTP) to the Windows and Linux client computers on your network, each client needs to do a bit of set-up within the Web browser. The beauty of using proxy servers is in what your client computers don't need to know, such as the following:

- Addresses of DNS servers
- Telephone numbers of ISPs
- Chat scripts to connect to the ISP

There are probably other things that clients don't need to know, but you get the idea. After the proxy server has a connection to the Internet and has allowed a client computer on the LAN access to that service, all the client needs to know is the following:

- **Hostname** — The name or IP address of the proxy server. (This assumes that the client can reach the proxy over the company's LAN or other IP-based network.)
- **Port numbers** — The port number of the HTTP service (3128 by default). That same port number can be used for FTP service as well.

How you go about setting up proxy service on the client has more to do with the browser you are using than with the operating system you are using. Follow the procedures outlined in the following sections for setting up Firefox, Microsoft Internet Explorer, Mosaic, or lynx browsers.

Configuring Firefox to use a proxy

Normally, you would set up Firefox to browse the Web directly over a TCP/IP connection to the Internet (over telephone lines or via a router on your LAN). Follow this procedure to change Firefox to access the Web through your proxy server:

1. Open Firefox.
2. Choose Edit → Preferences. The Preferences window appears.
3. Select the Advanced category and select the Network tab.
4. Click the Settings button. The Connection Settings window appears.
5. Click Manual proxy configuration to enable proxy configuration (see Figure 16-2 for an example of the Foxfire Connection Settings page).
6. Type the proxy server's name or IP address in the address boxes for HTTP, FTP, and Gopher services.
7. Type the port number for HTTP services on your proxy server (probably 3128) in the Port boxes for HTTP, FTP, and Gopher services. (You can just fill in the information for the HTTP Proxy and check the Use this proxy server for all protocols option to have those other services filled in automatically.)
8. Click OK.

The next time you request a Web address from Firefox, it will contact the proxy server to try to obtain the content.

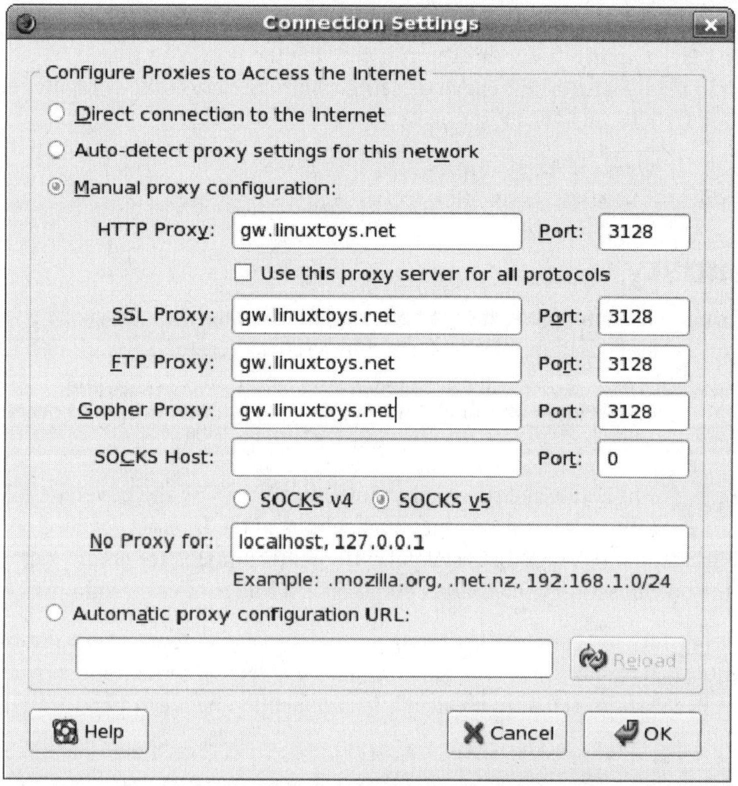

Connection Settings

Configure Proxies to Access the Internet

○ <u>D</u>irect connection to the Internet

○ Auto-detect proxy settings for this net<u>w</u>ork

◉ <u>M</u>anual proxy configuration:

| HTTP Pro<u>x</u>y: | gw.linuxtoys.net | P<u>o</u>rt: | 3128 |

☐ Use this pro<u>x</u>y server for all protocols

<u>S</u>SL Proxy:	gw.linuxtoys.net	Po<u>r</u>t:	3128
<u>F</u>TP Proxy:	gw.linuxtoys.net	Por<u>t</u>:	3128
<u>G</u>opher Proxy:	gw.linuxtoys.net	Port:	3128
SO<u>C</u>KS Host:		Port:	0

○ SOC<u>K</u>S v4 ◉ SOCKS <u>v</u>5

| <u>N</u>o Proxy for: | localhost, 127.0.0.1 |

Example: .mozilla.org, .net.nz, 192.168.1.0/24

○ Autom<u>a</u>tic proxy configuration URL:

| | 🔄 Reload |

🔧 Help   ✖ Cancel   ↩ OK

Figure 16-2: The Preferences window identifies proxy servers and port numbers in Firefox.

Configuring other browsers to use a proxy

There are different methods for indicating a proxy server to other browsers available with Linux. To have a Mosaic or lynx browser use a proxy server to access the Internet, add an environment variable to the shell where the browser will run. Here's how you would set the environment variables for HTTP and FTP proxy services to a proxy computer named maple using a `csh` or `tcsh` shell:

```
setenv http_proxy http://maple:3128/
setenv ftp_proxy http://maple:3128/
```

If you are using a `ksh` or `bash` shell, type the following:

```
export http_proxy=http://maple:3128
export ftp_proxy=http://maple:3128
```

You can add any of these values to your start-up scripts. Or, to make them available on a system-wide basis, you could add them to a system configuration file, such as `/etc/profile` or `/etc/skel/.bash_profile`.

For the elinks and links browsers, you can indicate to use a proxy server in the /etc/elinks.conf file. For example, here are the lines you would add to the /etc/elinks.conf file to have elinks and links use the computer named maple act as a proxy for FTP and HTTP services:

```
protocol.ftp.proxy.host maple:3128
protocol.http.proxy.host maple:3128
```

Summary

Connecting to the Internet opens a whole world of possibilities for your Fedora or RHEL computer. Using Fedora or RHEL as a public Web server, mail server, or FTP server depends on its capability to connect to the Internet. Likewise, if your computers are already connected in a LAN, adding an Internet connection can provide Internet access to everyone on the LAN in one stroke.

Descriptions of how Internet domains are organized built on the coverage of IP addresses in the previous chapter. Creating dial-up connections to the Internet focused on descriptions of PPP. This chapter also discusses several different techniques for connecting your LAN to the Internet. You can set up your Linux computer as a router or as a Squid proxy server.

To use your Internet connection to transport sensitive data to another location in your company's private network, you can configure a VPN. This chapter describes how to use IPsec in Fedora and RHEL to create a VPN connection between two locations.

Chapter 17

Setting Up a Print Server

In This Chapter

- Understanding printing in Linux
- Setting up printers
- Using printing commands
- Managing document printing
- Sharing printers

Sharing printers is a good way to save money and make your printing more efficient. Very few people need to print all the time, but when they do want to print something, they usually need it quickly. Setting up a print server can save money by eliminating the need for a printer at every workstation. Some of those savings can be used to buy printers that can output more pages per minute or have higher-quality output.

You can attach printers to your Fedora or RHEL system to make them available to users of that system or to other computers on the network. You can configure your Fedora or RHEL printer as a remote CUPS printer or Samba printer. With Samba, you are emulating a Windows print server.

This chapter describes configuring and using printers in Fedora or RHEL. It focuses on Common UNIX Printing Service (CUPS), which is the recommended print service for the current versions of Fedora and RHEL. To configure CUPS printers, this chapter focuses on the Printer Configuration window (`system-config-printer` command).

When a local printer is configured, print commands (such as `lpr`) are available for carrying out the actual printing. Commands also exist for querying print queues (`lpq`), manipulating print queues (`lpc`), and removing print jobs (`lprm`). A local printer can also be shared as a print server to users on other computers on your network.

Common UNIX Printing Service

CUPS has become the standard for printing from Linux and other UNIX-like operating systems. Instead of being based on older, text-based line printing technology, CUPS was designed to meet today's needs for standardized printer definitions and sharing on IP-based networks (as most computer networks are today). Here are some features of CUPS:

- **IPP** — At its heart, CUPS is based on the Internet Printing Protocol (www.pwg.org/ipp), a standard that was created to simplify how printers can be shared over IP networks. In the IPP model, printer servers and clients who want to print can exchange information about the model and features of a printer using the HTTP protocol. A server can also broadcast the availability of a printer, so a printing client can easily find a list of locally available printers.

- **Drivers** — CUPS also standardized how printer drivers are created. The idea was to have a common format that could be used by printer manufacturers that could work across all different types of UNIX systems. That way, a manufacturer had to create the driver only once to work for Linux, Mac OS X, and a variety of UNIX derivatives.

- **Printer classes** — Using printer classes, you can create multiple print server entries that point to the same printer or one print server entry that points to multiple printers. In the first case, multiple entries could each allow different options (such as pointing to a particular paper tray or printing with certain character sizes or margins). In the second case, you could have a pool of printers so that printing is distributed. This would decrease the occurrence of congested print jobs, caused by a malfunctioning printer or a printer that is dealing with very large documents.

- **UNIX print commands** — To integrate into Linux and other UNIX environments, CUPS offers versions of standard commands for printing and managing printers that have been traditionally offered with UNIX systems.

The Printer configuration window (system-config-printer command) lets you configure printers in Fedora and RHEL that use the CUPS facility. However, CUPS also offers a Web-based interface for adding and managing printers. Configuration files for CUPS are contained in the /etc/cups directory. In particular, you might be interested in the cupsd.conf file (which identifies permission, authentication, and other information for the printer daemon) and printers.conf (which identifies addresses and options for configured printers).

Setting Up Printers

Most parallel printers and USB printers can be detected and set up using the Printer configuration window. However, the Printer configuration window also lets you configure Fedora or RHEL so that you can use printers that are available on your LAN as a Windows printer (Samba), AppleSocket or HP JetDirect, Internet Printing Protocol (IPP) printer, or UNIX printer (LPD or LRP daemons).

Choosing a Printer

If you are choosing a new printer to use with your Fedora or RHEL system, look for one that is PostScript-compatible. The PostScript language is the preferred format for Linux and UNIX printing and has been for many years. Every major word and image processing application that runs on Fedora, Red Hat Enterprise Linux, and UNIX systems supports PostScript printing.

If you get a PostScript printer and it is not explicitly shown in the list of supported printers, simply select the PostScript filter when you install the printer locally. No special drivers are needed. Your next best choice is to choose a printer that supports PCL (Hewlett Packard's Printer Control Language). In either case, make sure that the PostScript or PCL is implemented in the printer hardware and not in the Windows driver.

When selecting a printer, avoid those that are referred to as *Winprinters*. These printers use nonstandard printing interfaces (those other than PostScript or PCL). Support for these low-end printers is hit-or-miss. For example, some low-end HP DeskJet printers use the pnm2ppa driver to print documents in Printing Performance Architecture (PPA) format. Some Lexmark printers use the pbm217k driver to print. Although drivers are available for many of these Winprinters, many of them are not fully supported.

Ghostscript may also support your printer; if it does, you can use that tool to do your printing. Ghostscript (`www.ghostscript.com`) is a free PostScript and PDF file interpreter program. It can convert that content to output that can be interpreted by a variety of printers. With the ghostscript package installed, type `gs -h` to see a list of available output device formats.

You'll find an excellent list of printers supported in Linux at the Free Standards Group OpenPrinting site (`www.linux-foundation.org/en/OpenPrinting`). I strongly recommend that you visit that site before you purchase a printer to work with Linux. The site offers a Printer Compatibility database, so you can find out if your printer is supported and, if so, what print driver is needed to get your printer working in Linux. For useful information on purchasing a printer that will work in Linux, refer to the Supported Printers section of the Printing HOWTO (`www.tldp.org/HOWTO/Printing-HOWTO/printers.html`).

Using the Printer configuration window

To install a printer from your desktop, use the Printer configuration window (`system-config-printer` command). This tool enables you to add printers, delete printers, and edit printer properties. It also lets you send test pages to those printers to make sure they are working properly.

The key here is that you are configuring printers that are managed by your print daemon (`cupsd` for the CUPS service). After a printer is configured, users on your local system can use it. Following that, you can refer to the "Configuring Print Servers" section to learn how to make the server available to users from other computers on your network.

The printers that you set up can be connected locally to your computer (as on a parallel or USB port) or to another computer on the network (for example, from another UNIX system, Windows system, or NetWare server).

Configuring local printers

Add a local printer (in other words, a printer connected directly to your computer) with the Printer configuration window using the following procedure. (See the "Choosing a Printer" sidebar if you don't yet have a printer.)

> **TIP:** You should connect your printer before starting this procedure. With the printer connected, the Printer configuration window might be able to scan for the printer to determine the printer's location and to test the printer immediately when you have finished adding it.

Adding a local printer

To add a local printer, follow these steps as root user:

1. Make sure that the CUPS service (`cupsd` daemon) is running. Just to make sure, type the following:

```
# service cups restart
```

2. To open the Printer configuration window, either select System → Administration → Printing from the panel or type the following from a Terminal window:

```
# system-config-printer &
```

The Printer configuration window appears. Note that printers detected on the local LAN appear under the Remote Printers heading.

3. Click New Printer. A New Printer window appears, as shown in Figure 17-1.

4. If the printer you want to configure is detected, simply select it and click Forward. If it is not detected, choose the device to which the printer is connected (LPT #1 and Serial Port #1 are the first parallel and serial ports, respectively) and click Forward. (Type **/usr/sbin/lpinfo -v | less** in a shell to see all available ports.)

You are asked to identify the printer's driver.

5. To use an installed driver for your printer, choose Select Printer From Database, and then choose the manufacturer of your printer. As an alternative, you could select Provide PPD File and supply your own PPD file (for example, if you have a printer that is not supported in Linux and you have a driver that was supplied with the printer). PPD stands for PostScript Printer Description. Select Forward to see a list of printer models from which you can choose.

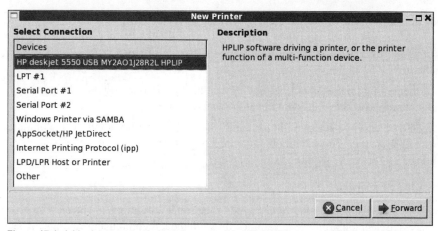

Figure 17-1: Add printers connected locally or remotely with the Printer configuration window.

6. Select the printer model for your printer. If there are multiple drivers available for the model, you can choose which one you want from the Drivers box.

> **TIP:** If your printer doesn't appear on the list but supports PCL (which is HP's Printer Control Language), select from one of several generic PCL drivers. If your printer supports PostScript, you can select PostScript printer from the list. Selecting Raw Print Queue enables you to send documents to the printer that are already formatted for that printer type.

7. With your printer model selected, click the Printer, Driver, or PPD buttons at the bottom of the screen. In many cases, you will see good information from the Linux Printing Database about how your printer is configured and how to tune it further. Click Forward to continue.

8. Add the following information and then click Forward:

    - **Printer Name** — Add the name you want to give to identify the printer. The name must begin with a letter, but after the initial letter, it can contain a combination of letters, numbers, dashes (-), and underscores (_). For example, an HP printer on a computer named maple could be named `hp-maple`.

    - **Description** — Add a few words describing the printer, such as its model name and features (an HP LaserJet 2100M with PCL and PS support).

    - **Location** — Indicate its location (in Room 205 under the coffee pot).

    In this example, my HP Laserjet 2100 and HP Deskjet 5550 printers were detected (as you will see later). One is detected on the computer's parallel port (HP Laserjet 2100) and one is detected on a USB port (hp deskjet 5550).

9. If the information looks correct, click Apply to create the entry for your printer. You are returned to the Printer configuration main window, with the new printer listed under Local Printers.

10. Click the name of the printer you just added, and then click Print Test Page. (Click OK when told the test page has printed.) This test page will tell you interesting information about your printer, such as the resolution and the type of interpreter used (such as PostScript).

    To further configure the printer, using the tabs that appear to the right of the selected printer, continue to the "Editing a Local Printer" section.

Printing should be working at this point for users who are printing from your local computer. (If you want to share this printer with other computers on your network, refer to the "Configuring Print Servers" section of this chapter.)

Editing a local printer

After you have added a local printer, you can edit the printer definitions to change how that printer behaves. Select the printer you want to edit from the left column and settings for that printer appear to the right, as shown in Figure 17-2.

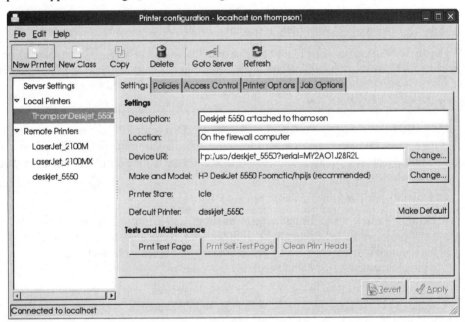

Figure 17-2: Change printer settings, policies, and access from the Printer configuration window.

With the printer you want to configure selected, choose from the following tabs to change its configuration:

- **Settings** — The Description, Location, Device URI, and Make and Model information you created earlier are displayed on this tab. The following bullets describe how to change options in addition to those you added originally:

- **Make Default** — Click this button to make this printer be the default printer.

- **Print Test Page** — Although this isn't technically an option, it lets you send a test page to the printer.

- **Policies** — Click the Policies tab. From this tab, you can set the following items:

  - **State** — Select check boxes to indicate whether the printer will print jobs that are in the queue (Enabled), accept new jobs for printing (Accepting Jobs), or be available to be shared with other computers that can communicate with your compter (Shared). You also must select Server Settings and click the "Share published printers connected to this system" check box before the printer will accept print jobs from other computers.

  - **Policies** — In case of error, the stop-printer selection causes all printing to that printer to stop. You can also select to have the job discarded (abort-job) or retried (retry-job) in the event of an error condition.

  - **Banner** — Add banner pages at the beginning or end of a job. This is good practice for a printer that is shared by many people. The banner page helps you sort who gets which print job. The standard banner page shows the ID of the print job, the title of the file, the user that requested the print job, and any billing information associated with it.

- **Access control** — If your printer is a shared printer, you can select this tab to create a list of users who are either allowed access to the printer (with all others denied) or denied access to the printer (with all others allowed).

- **Printer Options** — Click Printer Options to set defaults for options related to the printer driver. The available options are different for different printers. Many of these options can be overridden when someone prints a document. Here are a few of the options you might have available to set:

  - **Watermark** — There are several Watermark settings that let you add and change watermarks on your printed pages. By default, Watermark and Overlay are off (None). By selecting Watermark (behind the text) or Overlay (over the text), you can set the other Watermark settings to determine how watermarks and overlays are done. Watermarks can go on every page (All) or only the first page (First Only).

    Select Watermark Text to choose what words are used for the watermark or overlay (Draft, Copy, Confidential, Final, and so on). You can then select the font type, size, style, and intensity of the watermark or overlay.

  - **Resolution Enhancement** — You can use the printer's current settings or choose to turn resolution enhancement on or off.

  - **Page Size** — The default is U.S. letter size, but you can also ask the printer to print legal size, envelopes, ISO A4 standard or several other page sizes.

  - **Media Source** — Choose which tray to print from. Select Tray 1 to insert pages manually.

- **Levels of Gray** — Choose to use the printer's current levels of gray or have enhanced or standard gray levels turned on.

- **Resolution** — Select the default printing resolution (such as 300, 600, or 1,200 dots per inch). Higher resolutions result in better quality, but take longer to print.

- **EconoMode** — Either use the printer's current setting or choose a mode where you save toner or one where you have the highest possible quality.

- **Job Options** — Click the Job Options tab to set common default options that will be used for this printer if the application printing the job doesn't already set them. These include Common Options (number of copies, orientiation, scale to fit, and pages per side), Image Options (scaling, saturation, hue, and gamma), and Text Options (characters/inch, lines/inch, and margin settings).

> **NOTE:** For a description of other driver options, refer to the CUPS Software User Manual (`/usr/share/doc/cups-*/sum.html`) under the Standard Printer Options heading.

Click Apply when you are satisfied with the changes you made to the local printer.

Configuring remote printers

To use a printer that is available on your network, you must identify that printer to your Fedora or RHEL system. Supported remote printer connections include Networked CUPS (IPP) printers, Networked UNIX (LPD) printers, Networked Windows (SMB) printers, Networked Novell (NCP) printers, and JetDirect printers. (Of course, both CUPS and UNIX print servers can be run from Linux systems, as well as other UNIX systems.)

In each case, you need a network connection from your Fedora or RHEL system that enables you to reach the servers to which those printers are connected. To use a remote printer, of course, requires that someone set up that printer on the remote server computer. See the section "Configuring Print Servers" later in this chapter for information on how to do that in Fedora and RHEL.

You can use the Printer configuration window to configure each of the remote printer types:

1. From the GNOME desktop, select System → Administration → Printing.

2. Click New Printer. The New Printer window appears.

3. Besides the local ports listed (LPT and Serial ports), you can select one of the following types of network printers:

   - AppleSocket/HP JetDirect — For a JetDirect printer.

   - Internet Printing Protocol (IPP) — For a CUPS or other IPP printer.

   - LPD/LPR Host or Printer — For a UNIX printer.

   - Windows Printer via SAMBA — For a Windows system printer.

4. Continue following the steps in whichever of the following sections is appropriate.

Adding a remote CUPS printer

After choosing to add an Internet Printing Protocol (IPP) CUPS printer from the Select Connection window, you must add the following information to the window that appears:

- **Host** — The host of the computer to which the printer is attached (or otherwise accessible). This can be an IP address or TCP/IP hostname for the computer (the TCP/IP name is typically accessible from your /etc/hosts file or through a DNS name server).

- **Queue** — The printer name on the remote CUPS print server, which might look something like /printers/HP722C. CUPS supports the concept of printer instances, which allows each printer to have several sets of options. So, if the remote CUPS printer is configured this way, you might be able to choose a particular path to a printer, such as hp/300dpi or hp/1200dpi. A slash character separates the print queue name from the printer instance.

I suggest you fill in the host name and select Find Queue, to find the available IPP Printers from that host. After selecting the printer from a list, the Host and Queue information are automatically filled in. Click the Verify button to make sure the printer is accessible. Click Forward and complete the rest of the procedure as you would for a local printer.

Adding a remote UNIX printer

After you have selected to add an LPD/LPR (UNIX) host or printer from the Select Connection window, you must add the following information to the window that appears:

- **Host** — The hostname of the computer to which the printer is attached (or otherwise accessible). This is the IP address or TCP/IP name for the computer (the TCP/IP name is typically accessible from your /etc/hosts file or through a DNS name server). The host computer might be a UNIX or Linux print server running the lpd print daemon. (If you know the hostname, but not the printer name, type the hostname and select the Probe button. Available LPD printers from the host will appear in a list in the Queue field.)

- **Queue** — The printer name on the remote UNIX computer.

Although CUPS is the more popular printing system for Linux and UNIX systems today, some UNIX-like systems still use the Berkeley LPR print spooler system (see RFC1179). Early Red Hat Linux systems included LPRng print spooling software to provide this same interface for managing print servers (lpd daemon). So, to print to a really old Red Hat system at your location, you might need to identify a printer there as a UNIX printer. For older clients, CUPS can also act like an LPD print spooler (see the bullet on enabling LPD-style printing in the "Configuring a shared CUPS printer" section later in this chapter).

Click Forward and complete the configuration as you would for a local printer.

> **TIP:** If the print job is rejected when you send it to test the printer, the print server computer may not have allowed you access to the printer. Ask the remote computer's administrator of the UNIX printer to add your host name to the `/etc/lpd.perms` file. (Type **lpq -P** *printer* to see the status of your print job.)

Adding a Windows (SMB) printer

Enabling your computer to access an SMB printer (the Windows printing service) involves adding an entry for that printer in the Select Connection window.

> **NOTE:** Before you can add an SMB printer queue to Linux, you must first have configured that printer to work on the Windows machine. You must also indicate that the printer can be shared and is accessible to your Linux machine on your LAN.

After you have selected Windows Printer via SAMBA to the Select Connection window (described previously), you can browse for computers on your network that offer SMB services (file or printing service) by clicking the Browse button. When the SMB Browser list appears, you can:

- Select the group (click the arrow next to the group you want).
- Select the server (click the arrow next the server you want).
- Select the printer from the list of available printers shown.

Alternatively, you could identify a server that does not appear on the list of servers. Type a server name and share into the `smb://` box at the top of the page. For example, you could type:

```
smb://MYGROUP/EINSTEIN/hp2100m
```

> **TIP:** To find a remote printer name on most Windows systems, first go to the Printers folder (Start → Settings → Printers), and double-click the printer being shared. From the printer queue window that appears, choose Printer → Properties, and then select the Sharing tab. The Sharing tab indicates whether the printer is shared and, if so, the name under which it is shared.

Next, select the Authentication required box to enter a user name and password, if that is required to access the shared printer:

- **Username** — The user name is the name required by the SMB server system to give you access to the SMB printer. A user name is not necessary if you are authenticating the printer based on share-level, rather than user-level, access control. With share-level access, you can add a password for each shared printer or file system.

- **Password** — The password associated with the SMB user name or the shared resource, depending on the kind of access control being used. Click the Verify button to check that the Username and Password are correct.

> **CAUTION:** When you enter a User and Password for SMB, that information is stored unencrypted in the `/etc/cups/printers.conf` file. Be sure that the file remains readable only by root.

Click Forward and complete the configuration as you would for a local printer.

If everything is set up properly, you should be able to use the standard `lpr` command to print the file to the printer. With this example, you could use the following form for printing:

```
$ cat file1.ps | lpr -P hp2100m
```

> **TIP:** If you are receiving failure messages, make sure that the computer to which you are printing is accessible. For the previous example, you could type **smbclient -L NS1 -U jjones**. Type the password (`my9passswd`, in this case). If you get a positive name query response after you enter a password, you should see a list of shared printers and files from that server. Check the names, and try printing again.

Adding a JetDirect printer

A JetDirect printer (AppSocket/HP JetDirect) is one that is connected directly to your Ethernet network via a JetDirect device. You typically use port 9100 to print to a JetDirect printer, although additional interfaces may use ports 9101, 9102, and so on. To use a JetDirect printer from Fedora or RHEL, enter the following information:

- **Host** — Enter the name of the JetDirect printer.
- **Port number** — Enter the port number (typically 9100) to identify the interface to the JetDirect printer.

Using Web-based CUPS administration

The Printer configuration window effectively hides the underlying CUPS facility. There may be times, however, when you want to work directly with the tools and configuration files that come with CUPS. The following sections describe how to use some special CUPS features.

> **CAUTION:** Plain-text configuration files are at the base of the CUPS printing facility. When different tools, such as the CUPS Web-based interface and Printer Configuration window, manipulate the same config files, those files can become unusable by the other tools. When possible, you should use the `system-config-printer` (Printer configuration window) to work with printers in Fedora and RHEL. You will see warnings to this effect if you start to use the CUPS interface.

Although the preferred way to configure CUPS printing in Fedora or RHEL is with the Printer configuration window, CUPS offers its own Web-based administrative tool.

If CUPS is already running on your computer, you can immediately use CUPS Web-based administration from your Web browser. If CUPS is not running yet, refer to the following section describing the `cupsd` daemon for information on starting it.

CUPS listens on port 631 to provide access to the CUPS Web-based administrative interface. On the local computer, type the following into your Web browser's location box:

```
http://localhost:631/admin
```

A screen similar to the one shown in Figure 17-3 appears.

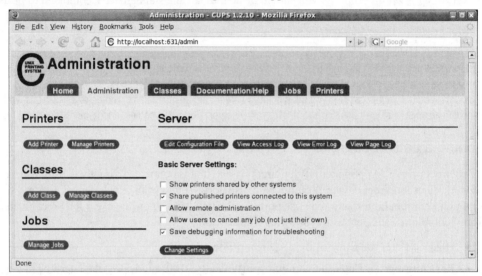

Figure 17-3: CUPS enables Web-based administration via port 631.

By default, Web-based CUPS administration is available only from the localhost. To access Web-based CUPS administration from another computer, you must change the `/admin` section in the `/etc/cups/cupsd.conf` file. As recommended in the text of this file, you should limit access to CUPS administration from the Web. Also keep in mind that passwords are passed as clear text, so someone sniffing your network could see your password. Consider accessing this service through an ssh tunnel if you want to do CUPS administration over an insecure network.

In the following example, I tell CUPS to listen on its LAN interface for outside connections (in this example, the IP address of eth0 is `10.0.0.20`). I changed `BrowseAllow` to `ALL`. I then added `Allow` lines to allow access from a host from IP address `10.0.0.5` for the root of the server (/), `/admin`, and `/admin/conf`, as shown in the following example.

```
Listen 10.0.0.20
BrowseAllow ALL

<Location />
```

```
   Order allow,deny
   Allow @LOCAL
   Allow 10.0.0.5
</Location>

<Location /admin>
  Encryption Required
  Order allow,deny
  Allow localhost
  Allow 10.0.0.5
</Location>

<Location /admin/conf>
  AuthType Basic
  Require user @SYSTEM
  Order allow,deny
  Allow localhost
  Allow 10.0.0.5
</Location>
```

From the computer at address `10.0.0.5`, I typed the same address line shown in Figure 17-3 in my Web browser (substituting the CUPS server's name or IP address for localhost). When prompted, I entered the root user name and password.

Now, with the Admin screen displayed, you can set up a printer as follows:

1. Click the Add Printer button. The Add New Printer screen appears.

2. Type a Name, Location, and Description for the printer and click Continue.

3. Select the device to which the printer is connected. The printer can be connected locally to a Parallel, SCSI, Serial, or USB port directly on the computer. Alternatively, you can select a network connection type for Apple printers (AppSocket/HP JetDirect), Internet Printing Protocol (http or ipp), or Window printer (using SAMBA or SMB).

4. If prompted for further information, you may need to further describe the connection to the printer. For example, you may need to enter the baud rate and parity for a serial port or you might be asked for the network address (Device URI) for an IPP or Samba printer.

5. Select the make of the print driver (if you don't see the manufacturer of your printer listed, choose PostScript for a PostScript printer or HP for a PCL printer). For the make you choose, you will be able to select a specific model. If options are available for that printer, the Set Printer Options screen appears.

6. Depending on the printer driver, there may be a few or a lot of options available for your printer. For example, you may be able to choose page size, manual feed, print quality and other features. After you have chosen the settings you want, select Set Printer Options.

7. If the printer was added successfully, the next page you see should show a link to the description of that printer. Click that link. From the new printer page, you can print a test page or modify the printer configuration.

After you are able to print from CUPS, you can return to the CUPS Web-based administration page and do further work with your printers. Here are a few examples:

- **List print jobs** — Click Manage Jobs to see what print jobs are currently active from any of the printers configured for this server. Click Show Completed Jobs to see information about jobs that are already printed.

- **Create a printer class** — Click Add Class; then identify a name, location and description for a printer class. Then, from the list of printers configured on your server, select which ones will go into this class and click Add Class.

- **View printers** — You can click Manage Printers and view the printers you have configured. For each printer that appears, you can click Stop Printer (to stop the printer from printing, but still accept print jobs for the queue), Reject Jobs (to not accept any further print jobs for the moment), or Print Test Page (to print a page). Those and other actions you can do from the Printers page appears in Figure 17-4.

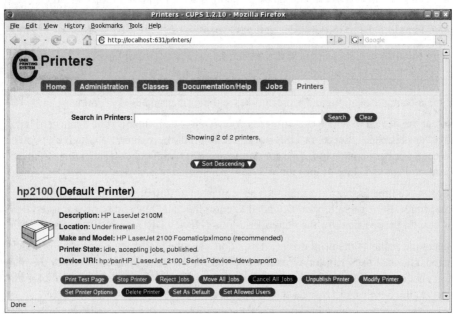

Figure 17-4: Temporarily stop printing or print test pages from the Printers page.

Configuring the CUPS server (cupsd.conf)

The cupsd daemon process listens for requests to your CUPS print server and responds to those requests based on settings in the /etc/cups/cupsd.conf file. The configuration variables in `cupsd.conf` file are in the same form as those of the Apache configuration file (`httpd.conf`). After changing `cupsd.conf`, restart the server for changes to take effect.

The Printer configuration window adds access information to the `cupsd.conf` file. You can step through the `cupsd.conf` file to further tune your CUPS server. Here are a few suggestions:

```
Classification topsecret
```

No classification is set by default. With the classification set to `topsecret`, you can have Top Secret displayed on all pages that go through the print server. Other classifications you can substitute for `topsecret` include: `classified`, `confidential`, `secret`, and `unclassified`.

```
ServerCertificate /etc/cups/ssl/server.crt
ServerKey /etc/cups/ssl/server.key
```

The `ServerCertificate` and `ServerKey` lines (not set by default) can be set up to indicate where the certificate and key are stored, respectively. Activate these two lines if you want to do encrypted connections. Then add your certificate and key to the files noted. Keep in mind that these keys are for the CUPS Web interface and are not used for sending print jobs.

```
Browsing On
BrowseProtocols cups
BrowseOrder Deny,Allow
BrowseAllow from @LOCAL
BrowseAddress 255.255.255.255
Listen *:631
```

Browsing is the feature whereby you broadcast information about your printer on your local network and listen for other print servers' information. Browsing is on by default, but only for the local host (`@LOCAL`). You can allow incoming CUPS browser information for additional selected addresses. Browsing information is broadcast, by default, on address `255.255.255.255`.

To enable Web-based CUPS administration, the `cupsd` daemon listens on port 631 for all network interfaces to your computer based on this entry: `Listen *:631`.

```
BrowseRelay source-address destination-address
```

By turning on `BrowseRelay` (it's off by default), you can allow CUPS browse information to be passed among two or more networks. The *source-address* and *destination-address* can be individual IP addresses or can represent network numbers. This is a good way to allow users on several connected LANs to discover and use printers on other nearby LANs.

You can allow or deny access to different features of the CUPS server. An access definition for a CUPS printer (created from the Printer configuration window) might appear as follows:

```
<Location /printers/ns1-hp1>
Order Deny,Allow
Deny From All
Allow From 127.0.0.1
AuthType None
</Location>
```

Here, printing to the ns1-hp1 printer is allowed only for users on the local host (127.0.0.1). No password is needed (AuthType None). To share this printer with any remote machine that has access to it, you could add Allow From All just before the </Location> line.

If you change any of the settings in the cupsd.conf file, you must reload the CUPS service to have the changes take effect. As root user, type **service cups reload**. (The reload option reads the new configuration without restarting the daemon.)

Configuring CUPS printer options

When a new printer is created from the Printer configuration window, that printer is defined in the /etc/cups/printers.conf file. Here's an example of a printer definition in printers.conf:

```
</DefaultPrinter hp2100>
Info HP LaserJet 2100M
Location HP LaserJet 2100M in hall closet
DeviceURI hp:/par/HP_LaserJet_2100_Series?device=/dev/parport0
State Idle
Accepting Yes
Shared Yes
JobSheets none none
QuotaPeriod 0
PageLimit 0
KLimit 0
OpPolicy default
ErrorPolicy stop-printer
</Printer>
```

This is an example of a local printer that serves as the default printer for the local system. The most interesting information relates to the DeviceURI, which shows us that the printer is connected to parallel port /dev/parport0. The State is Idle (ready to accept printer jobs) and the Accepting value is Yes (the printer is accepting print jobs by default).

The DeviceURI has several ways to identify the device name of a printer, reflecting where the printer is connected. Here are some examples listed in the printers.conf file:

```
DeviceURI parallel:/dev/plp
DeviceURI serial:/dev/ttyd1?baud=38400+size=8+parity=none+flow=soft
DeviceURI scsi:/dev/scsi/sc1d6l0
DeviceURI socket://hostname:port
DeviceURI tftp://hostname/path
DeviceURI ftp://hostname/path
```

```
DeviceURI http://hostname[:port]/path
DeviceURI ipp://hostname/path
DeviceURI smb://hostname/printer
```

The first three examples show the form for local printers (`parallel`, `serial`, and `scsi`). The other examples are for remote hosts. In each case, `hostname` can be the host's name or IP address. Port numbers or paths identify the locations of each printer on the host.

> **TIP:** If you find that you are not able to print because a particular printer driver is not supported in CUPS, you can set up your printer to accept jobs in raw mode. This can work well if you are printing from Windows clients that have the correct print drivers installed on those clients. To allow raw printing in CUPS, uncomment the following line from the `/etc/cups/mime.types` file in Linux:
>
> `application/octet-stream`
>
> And uncomment the following line from the `/etc/cups/mime.convs` file:
>
> `application/octet-stream`
>
> After that, you can print files as raw data to your printers without using the `-oraw` option to print commands. As an alternative, you can just select the Raw Print Queue driver when you first configure printing through the Printer configuration window.

Using Printing Commands

To remain backward compatible with older UNIX and Linux printing facilities, CUPS supports many of the old commands for working with printing. Most command-line printing with CUPS can be performed with the `lpr` command. Word processing applications for Linux, such as StarOffice, OpenOffice.org, and AbiWord, are set up to use this facility for printing.

With the Printer configuration window, you can define the filters needed for each printer so that the text can be formatted properly. Options to the `lpr` command can add filters to process the text properly. Other commands for managing printed documents include `lpq` (for viewing the contents of print queues), `lprm` (for removing print jobs from the queue), and `lpc` (for controlling printers).

> **CROSS-REFERENCE:** Chapter 6 provides examples of how to format and print documents in several different formats, including `troff` and TeX.

Using lpr to print

With the `lpr` command, you can print documents to both local and remote printers. Document files can be either added to the end of the `lpr` command line or directed to the `lpr` command using a pipe (|). Here is an example of a simple `lpr` command:

```
$ lpr doc1.ps
```

When you just specify a document file with lpr, output is directed to the default printer. As an individual user, you can change the default printer by setting the value of the PRINTER variable. Typically, you would add the PRINTER variable to one of your startup files, such as $HOME/.bashrc. Here is a line to add to your .bashrc file to set your default printer to lp3:

```
export PRINTER=lp3
```

For the new PRINTER value to take effect immediately, source the .bashrc file (type source $HOME/.bashrc). To override the default printer, specify a particular printer on the lpr command line. The following example uses the -P option to select a different printer:

```
$ lpr -P canyonps doc1.ps
```

The lpr command has a variety of options that enable lpr to interpret and format several different types of documents. These include -# *num*, where *num* is replaced by the number of copies to print (from 1 to 100) and -l (which causes a document to be sent in raw mode, presuming that the document has already been formatted).

Listing status with lpc

The lpc command in CUPS has limited features. You can use lpc to list the status of your printers. Here is an example:

```
$ lpc status
hp:
        printer is on device 'parallel' speed -1
        queuing is enabled
        printing is disabled
        no entries
        daemon present
deskjet_5550:
        printer is on device 'usb' speed -1
        queuing is enabled
        printing is disabled
        no entries
        daemon present
```

This output shows two active printers. The first (hp) is connected to the parallel port. The second (deskjet_5550) is a USB printer (shown as usb). The hp printer is currently disabled (offline), although the queue is enabled so people can continue to send jobs to the printer.

Removing print jobs with lprm

Users can remove their own print jobs from the queue with the lprm command. Used alone on the command line, lprm removes all of the user's print jobs from the default printer. To remove jobs from a specific printer, use the -P option, as follows:

```
$ lprm -P lp0
```

To remove all print jobs for the current user, type the following:

```
$ lprm -
```

To remove an individual print job from the queue, indicate the job number of that print job on the `lprm` command line. To find the job number, type the `lpq` command. Here's what the output of that command may look like:

```
$ lpq
printer is ready and printing
Rank    Owner               Job Files               Total Size Time
active  root                133 /home/jake/pr1          467
2       root                197 /home/jake/mydoc      23948
```

The output shows two printable jobs waiting in the queue. (In this case, they're not printing because the printer is off.) Under the Job column, you can see the job number associated with each document. To remove the first print job, type the following:

```
# lprm 133
```

Configuring Print Servers

You've configured a printer so that you and the other users on your computer can print to it. Now you want to share that printer with other people in your home, school, or office. Basically, that means configuring that printer as a print server.

The printers that are configured on your Linux system can be shared in different ways with other computers on your network. Not only can your computer act as a Linux print server, it can also look to client computers like an SMB print server. In other words, a Windows client would just see your printer as a printer from another Windows machine.

After a local printer is attached to your Linux system, and your computer is connected to your local network, you can use the procedures in this section to share it with client computers using a Linux (UNIX) or SMB interface.

> **CROSS-REFERENCE:** See Chapter 26 for information on configuring Linux as an AppleTalk server using the netatalk package.

Configuring a shared CUPS printer

After a local printer is added to your Linux computer, making it available to other computers on your network is fairly easy. If a TCP/IP network connection exists among the computers sharing the printer, you can simply grant permission to individual hosts or users from remote hosts to access your computer's printing service. The procedures for setting up local printers are discussed earlier in this chapter.

To share a local printer as a print server with other computers on your network, do the following:

1. From the desktop panel, select System → Administration → Printing. The Printer configuration window appears.

2. Click the name of the printer you want to share. (If the printer is not yet configured, refer to the "Setting Up Printers" section earlier in this chapter.)

3. Select the Shared box on the Settings tab so that a checkmark appears in the box.

4. If you want only selected users to access your printer, select the Access Control tab. Select Deny Printing for Everyone Except These Users, type each user you want to allow to use the printer, and click Add to add each user. Likewise, you could select Allow Printing for Everyone Except These Users and add selected users to be excluded from those allowed to print.

5. Select Server Settings in the right column. From the Basic Server Settings screen that appears, select the Share Published Printers Connecteed to this System check box.

6. Click Apply to make the changes permanent.

At this point, you can configure other computers to use your printer. If you try to print from another computer and it doesn't work, here are a few things to try:

- **Open your firewall** — If you have a restrictive firewall, it may not permit remote users to access your printers. You must allow access to port 513 (UDP and TCP) and possibly port 631 to allow access to printing on your computer. See Chapter 14 for information on configuring your firewall.

- **Enable LPD-style printing** — Certain applications may require an older LPD-style printing service in order to print on your shared printer. To enable LPD-style printing on your CUPS server, you must turn on the cups-lpd service. As root user, type **chkconfig cups-lpd on**. Then restart the xinetd daemon (`service xinetd restart`). To use this service, you may need to install the cups-lpd package (`yum install cups-lpd`).

- **Check names and addresses** — Make sure that you entered your computer's name and print queue properly when you configured it on the other computer. Try using the IP address instead of the hostname (if that worked, it would indicate a DNS name resolution problem). Running a tool such as wireshark can let you watch where the transaction fails.

Access changes to your shared printer are made in the `/etc/cups/cupsd.conf` file.

Configuring a shared Samba printer

Your Linux printers can be configured as shared SMB printers. To share your printer as a Samba (SMB) printer, all you need to do is configure basic Samba server settings as described in Chapter 18. All your printers should be shared on your local network by default. The next section shows what the resulting settings look like and how you might want to change them.

Understanding smb.conf for printing

When you configure Samba, as described in Chapter 18, the `/etc/samba/smb.conf` file is configured to allow all your configured printers to be shared. Here are a few lines you might find in the `[global]` and `[printers]` sections of the `smb.conf` file that relate to printer sharing:

```
[global]
   workgroup = MYGROUP
   serverstring = Samba Server
   security = share
   printcap name = /etc/printcap
   load printers = yes
   printing = cups
   encrypt passwords = yes
   smb passwd file = /etc/samba/smbpasswd
   unix password sync = Yes

[printers]
        comment = All Printers
        path = /var/spool/samba
        guest ok = yes
        browseable = no
        writeable = no
        printable = yes
```

The settings shown resulted from configuring Samba from the Samba Server Configuration (System → Administration → Samba) window. You need to install the system-config-samba package to use the Samba Server Configuration window. In this case, I selected to use encrypted passwords. The lines show that printers from `/etc/printcap` were loaded and that the CUPS service is being used. The `/etc/samba/smbpasswd` file stores the encrypted passwords. Because password sync is on, each user's Samba password is synchronized with the local UNIX password for the user.

The last few lines shown here make up the `[printers]` section, which determines the defaults for how printers are shared in Samba. The final line (`printable = yes`) defines that users can print to all printers.

Summary

Sharing printers is an economical and efficient way to use your organization's printing resources. A centrally located printer can make it easier to maintain a printer, while still allowing everyone to get his or her printing jobs done.

You configure your printer with the Printer configuration window. A variety of filters make it possible to print to different kinds of printers, as well as to printers that are connected to computers on the network.

The default printing service in Fedora and RHEL is the Common UNIX Printing Service (CUPS). Besides being able to set up your computer as a Linux print server, you can also have your computer emulate an SMB (Windows) print server. After your network is configured properly and a local printer is installed, sharing that printer over the network as a UNIX or SMB print server is not very complicated.

Chapter 18

Setting Up a File Server

In This Chapter

- Setting up an NFS file server in Linux
- Setting up a Samba file server in Linux

When groups of people need to work together on projects, they usually need to share documents. Likewise, it can be efficient for groups of people on a computer network to share common applications and directories of information needed to do their jobs. A common way to store files centrally and share them on a network is by setting up a file server.

Fedora and Red Hat Enterprise Linux systems include support for each of the most common file server protocols in use today. The Network File System (NFS) has always been the file-sharing protocol of choice for Linux and other UNIX systems. Networks with many Windows and OS/2 computers tend to use Samba, or SMB/CIFS (Server Message Block/Common Internet File System) protocol. This chapter describes how to set up file servers and clients associated with NFS and Samba, and file servers set up in Linux.

> **CROSS-REFERENCE:** Two other types of file servers are also described in this book: FTP (using vsFTPd) and AppleTalk (using netatalk). To set up public FTP file servers, refer to Chapter 20. Chapter 26 describes how to set up a netatalk server for file sharing with Apple computers.

Goals of Setting Up a File Server

By centralizing data and applications on a *file server*, you can accomplish several goals:

- **Centralized distribution** — You can add documents or applications to one location and make them accessible to any authorized computer or user. In this way, you don't have to be responsible for placing necessary files on every computer.

- **Transparency** — Using protocols such as NFS, clients of your file server (Windows, Linux, or UNIX systems) can connect your file systems to their local file systems as if your file systems existed locally. (In other words, no drive letters on the Linux or UNIX systems. Just change to the remote system's mount point and you are there.)

Setting Up an NFS File Server

Instead of representing storage devices as drive letters (A, B, C, and so on), as they are in Microsoft operating systems, Linux systems connect file systems from multiple hard disks, floppy disks, CD-ROMs, and other local devices invisibly to form a single Linux file system. The Network File System (NFS) facility lets you extend your Linux file system in the same way, to connect file systems on other computers to your local directory structure as well.

> **CROSS-REFERENCE:** See Chapter 10 for a description of how to mount local devices on your Linux file system. The same command (`mount`) is used to mount both local devices and NFS file systems.

Creating an NFS file server is an easy way to share large amounts of data among the users and computers in an organization. An administrator of a Linux system that is configured to share its file systems using NFS has to perform the following tasks to set up NFS:

1. **Set up the network** — If a LAN or other network connection is already connecting the computers on which you want to use NFS (using TCP/IP as the network transport), you already have the network you need.

2. **On the server, choose what to share** — Decide which file systems on your Linux NFS server to make available to other computers. You can choose any point in the file system and make all files and directories below that point accessible to other computers. However, it is most secure to share a directories from the root of a file system partition.

3. **On the server, set up security** — You can use several different security features to suit the level of security with which you are comfortable. Mount-level security lets you restrict the computers that can mount a resource and, for those allowed to mount it, lets you specify whether it can be mounted read/write or read-only. With user-level security, you map users from the client systems to users on the NFS server. In this way, users can rely on standard Linux read/write/execute permissions, file ownership, and group permissions to access and protect files.

4. **On the client, mount the file system** — Each client computer that is allowed access to the server's NFS shared file system can mount it anywhere the client chooses. For example, you may mount a file system from a computer called oak on the `/media/oak` directory in your local file system. After it is mounted, you can view the contents of that directory by typing **ls /media/oak**. Then you can use the `cd` command below the `/media/oak` mount point to see the files and directories it contains.

Figure 18-1 illustrates a Linux file server using NFS to share (export) a file system and a client computer mounting the file system to make it available to its local users.

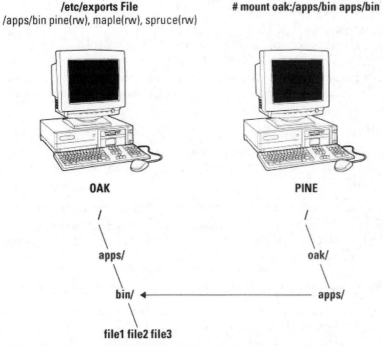

/etc/exports File
/apps/bin pine(rw), maple(rw), spruce(rw)

 # mount oak:/apps/bin apps/bin

OAK

PINE

/

apps/

bin/ ◄─────────────────────── apps/

oak/

/

file1 file2 file3

Figure 18-1: NFS can make selected file systems available to other computers.

In this example, a computer named oak makes its /apps/bin directory available to clients on the network (pine, maple, and spruce) by adding an entry to the /etc/exports file. The client computer (pine) sees that the resource is available, then mounts the resource on its local file system at the mount point /oak/apps. At this point, any files, directories, or subdirectories from /apps/bin on oak are available to users on pine (given proper permissions).

Although it is often used as a file server (or other type of server), Linux is a general-purpose operating system. So, any Fedora or Red Hat Enterprise Linux system can share file systems (export) as a server or use another computer's file systems (mount) as a client. Contrast this with dedicated file servers, such as NetWare, which was created to share files with client computers (such as Windows workstations) and was not intended to act as a client.

Many people use the term *file system* rather loosely. A file system is usually a structure of files and directories that exists on a single device (such as a hard disk partition or CD-ROM). When I talk about the Linux file system, however, I am referring to the entire directory structure (which may include file systems from several disks or NFS resources), beginning from root (/) on a single computer. A shared directory in NFS may represent all or part of a computer's file system, which can be attached (from the shared directory down the directory tree) to another computer's file system.

Sharing NFS file systems

To share an NFS file system from your Linux system, you need to export it from the server system. Exporting is done in Fedora and Red Hat Enterprise Linux by adding entries into the `/etc/exports` file. Each entry identifies the directory in your local file system that you want to share with other computers. The entry identifies the other computers that can share the resource (or opens it to all computers) and includes other options that reflect permissions associated with the directory.

Remember that when you share a directory, you are sharing all files and subdirectories below that directory as well (by default). So, you need to be sure that you want to share everything in that directory structure. (There are still ways to restrict access within that directory structure. Those methods are described later).

Fedora and RHEL provide a graphical tool for configuring NFS called the NFS Server Configuration window (`system-config-nfs` command). The following sections explain how to use the NFS Server Configuration window to share directories with other computers, and then describe the underlying configuration files that are changed to make that happen.

Using the NFS Server Configuration window

The NFS Server Configuration window (`system-config-nfs` command from the package of the same name) allows you to share your NFS directories using a graphical interface. Start this window from the Desktop menu by clicking System→ Administration → Server Settings → NFS. (If it's not there, type **yum install system-config-nfs** to install it.)

To share a directory with the NFS Server Configuration window, do the following:

1. From the NFS Server Configuration window, click File → Add Share. The Add NFS Share window appears, as shown in Figure 18-2.

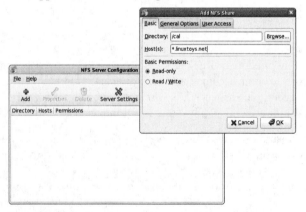

Figure 18-2: Identify a directory to share and access permissions with the NFS Server Configuration window.

2. In the Add NFS Share window Basic tab, enter the following information:

   - **Directory** — Type the name of the directory you want to share. (The directory must exist before you can add it.)

   - **Host(s)** — Enter one or more hostnames to indicate which hosts can access the shared directory. Hostnames, domain names, and IP addresses are allowed here. Separate each name with a space. (See the "Hostnames in /etc/exports" section later in this chapter for valid hostnames.) Add an asterisk (*) to place no restrictions on which hosts can access this directory.

   - **Basic permissions** — Click Read-only or Read/Write to let remote computers mount the shared directory with read access only or read/write access, respectively.

3. Click the General Options tab. This tab lets you add options that define how the shared directory behaves when a remote host connects to it (mounts it):

   - **Allow connections from ports 1024 and higher** — Normally, an NFS client will request the NFS service from a port number under 1024. Select this option if you need to allow a client to connect to you from a higher port number. (This sets the insecure option.) To allow a Mac OS X computer to mount a shared NFS directory, you must have the insecure option set for the shared directory.

   - **Allow insecure file locking** — If checked, NFS will not authenticate any locking requests from remote users of this shared directory. Older NFS clients may not deliver their credentials when they ask for a file lock. (This sets the insecure_locks option.)

   - **Disable subtree checking** — By selecting this option, NFS won't verify that the requested file is actually in the shared directory (only that it's in the correct file system). You can disable subtree checking if an entire file system is being shared. (This sets the no_subtree_check option.)

   - **Sync write operations on request** — This is on by default, which forces a write operation from a remote client to be synced on your local disk when the client requests it. (This sets the sync option.)

   - **Force sync of write operations immediately** — If keeping the shared data immediately up-to-date is critical, select this option to force the immediate synchronization of writes to your hard disk. (This sets the no_wdelay option.)

   - **Hide filesystems beneath** — By default (hide option), if a shared NFS file system has another local file system mounted on it, the second file system will not appear when the client mounts the original file system. If this box is checked, the nohide option is set instead, causing the second mounted file system to be accessible from clients.

   - **Export only if mounted** — If a file system that is set to be shared is a mount point that is currently not mounted, the file system will not be exported if this option is on (represented by the mp option). This can prevent sharing empty directories and having contents stored to the empty directory disappear the next time the resource is mounted.

- **Optional mount point** —You can also identify the mount point directly by checking this box and setting the file system mount point. For example, if you are sharing the /mnt/files/isos directory and you identify /mnt/files as the mount point (mp=/mnt/files), the /mnt/files/isos directory will not be shared if the /mnt/files directory isn't mounted.

- **Set explicit Filesystem ID** — Because not all file systems have UUIDs to identify them, you can identify a further file system you want to share using its file system ID. The result is that the fsid option is set to that value (fsid=???). If you prefer, you can identify a file system as the root of your shared file systems (fsid=0).

4. Click the User Access tab, then select any of the following options:

- **Treat the remote root user as local root** — If this option is on, it enables the remote root user host accessing your shared directory to save and modify files as though he or she were the local root user. Having this on is a security risk, since the remote user can potentially modify critical files. (This sets the no_root_squash option.)

- **Treat all client users as anonymous users** — When this option is on, you can indicate that particular user and group IDs be assigned to every user accessing the shared directory from a remote computer. Enter the user ID and group ID you want assigned to all remote users. (This sets the anonuid and anongid options to the numbers you choose.)

5. Click OK. The new shared directory appears in the NFS Server Configuration window.

At this point, the configuration file (/etc/exports) should have the shared directory entry created in it. To turn on the NFS service and make the shared directory available, type the following from a Terminal window as root user:

1. To immediately turn on NFS, type:

```
# service nfs start
```

2. To permanently turn on the NFS service, type:

```
# chkconfig nfs on
```

3. If you have a firewall configured, you must ensure that UDP ports 111 and 2049 are accepting requests. (See Chapter 14 for information on configuring your firewall.)

The next few sections describe the /etc/exports file you just created. At this point, a client can only use your shared directory if he mounts it on his local file system. Refer to the "Using NFS file systems" section later in this chapter.

Configuring the /etc/exports file

The shared directory information you entered into the NFS Server Configuration window is added to the /etc/exports file. As root user, you can use any text editor to configure the /etc/exports file to modify shared directory entries or add new ones. Here's an example of an /etc/exports file, including some entries that it could include:

```
/cal     *.linuxtoys.net(rw,sync)                  # Company events
/pub     (ro,insecure,all_squash)          # Public dir
/home    maple(rw,squash uids=0-99)  spruce(rw,squash uids=0-99)
```

The following text describes those entries:

- **/cal** — Represents a directory that contains information about events related to the company. It is made accessible to everyone with accounts to any computers in the company's domain (*.linuxtoys.net). Users can write files to the directory as well as read them (indicated by the rw option).

  The sync option, which is the default behavior, is explicitly entered here to indicate that NFS will only reply to new requests after changes have been committed to storage. (The alternative is to enter async, which allows new requests before changes are committed to improve performance, but can result in data corruption.) The comment (# Company events) simply serves to remind you of what the directory contains.

- **/pub** — Represents a public directory. It allows any computer and user to read files from the directory (indicated by the ro option), but not to write files. The insecure option enables any computer, even one that doesn't use a secure NFS port, to access the directory. The all_squash option causes all users (UIDs) and groups (GIDs) to be mapped to the nfsnobody user, giving them minimal permission to files and directories.

- **/home** — This entry enables a set of users to have the same /home directory on different computers. Say, for example, that you are sharing /home from a computer named oak. The computers named maple and spruce could each mount that directory on their own /home directory. If you gave all users the same user name/UIDs on all machines, you could have the same /home/user directory available for each user, regardless of which computer they logged into. The uids=0-99 is used to exclude any administrative login from another computer from changing any files in the shared directory.

Of course, you can share any directories that you choose (these were just examples), including the entire file system (/). There are security implications of sharing the whole file system or sensitive parts of it (such as /etc). Security options that you can add to your /etc/exports file are described throughout the sections that follow.

The format of the /etc/exports file is:

```
Directory    Host(Options)    # Comments
```

Directory is the name of the directory that you want to share. *Host* indicates the host computer that the sharing of this directory is restricted to. *Options* can include a variety of options to define the security measures attached to the shared directory for the host. (You can repeat Host/Option pairs.) *Comments* are any optional comments you want to add (following the # sign).

Hostnames in /etc/exports

You can indicate in the `/etc/exports` file which host computers can have access to your shared directory. Be sure to have a space between each hostname. Here are ways to identify hosts:

- **Individual host** — You can enter one or more TCP/IP hostnames or IP addresses. If the host is in your local domain, you can simply indicate the hostname. Otherwise, you can use the full host.domain format. These are valid ways of indicating individual host computers:

```
maple
maple.handsonhistory.com
10.0.0.11
```

- **IP network** — To allow access to all hosts from a particular network address, indicate a network number and its netmask, separated by a slash (/). These are valid ways of indicating network numbers:

```
10.0.0.0/255.0.0.0
172.16.0.0/255.255.0.0
192.168.18.0/24
192.168.18.0/255.255.255.0
```

- **TCP/IP domain** — Using wildcards, you can include all or some host computers from a particular domain level. Here are some valid uses of the asterisk and question mark wildcards:

```
*.handsonhistory.com
*craft.handsonhistory.com
???.handsonhistory.com
```

The first example matches all hosts in the `handsonhistory.com` domain. The second example matches `woodcraft`, `basketcraft`, or any other hostnames ending in `craft` in the `handsonhistory.com` domain. The final example matches any three-letter hostnames in the domain.

> **NOTE:** You can also separate multiple hostnames with spaces, but if you add options after each hostname, leave no spaces between the hostname and the parentheses. For example:
>
> ```
> *.handsonhistory.com(rw) *.example.net(ro)
> ```

- **NIS groups** — You can allow access to hosts contained in an NIS group. To indicate an NIS group, precede the group name with an at (@) sign (for example, @group).

Access options in /etc/exports

You don't have to just give away your files and directories when you export a directory with NFS. In the options part of each entry in /etc/exports, you can add options that allow or limit access by setting read/write permission. These options, which are passed to NFS, are as follows:

- ro — Only allow the client to mount this exported file system read-only. The default is to mount the file system read/write.

- rw — Explicitly ask that a shared directory be shared with read/write permissions. (If the client chooses, it can still mount the directory read-only.)

User mapping options in /etc/exports

Besides options that define how permissions are handled generally, you can also use options to set the permissions that specific users have to NFS shared file systems.

One method that simplifies this process is to have each user with multiple user accounts have the same user name and UID on each machine. This makes it easier to map users so that they have the same permission on a mounted file system as they do on files stored on their local hard disk. If that method is not convenient, user IDs can be mapped in many other ways. Here are some methods of setting user permissions and the /etc/exports option that you use for each method:

- **root user** — Normally, the client's root user is mapped into the nfsnobody user name (UID 65534). This prevents the root user from a client computer from being able to change all files and directories in the shared file system. If you want the client's root user to have root permission on the server, use the no_root_squash option.

> **TIP:** There may be other administrative users, in addition to root, that you want to squash. I recommend squashing UIDs 0–99 as follows: squash_uids=0-99.

- **nfsnobody user/group** — By using the nfsnobody user name and group name, you essentially create a user/group whose permissions will not allow access to files that belong to any real users on the server (unless those users open permission to everyone). However, files created by the nfsnobody user or group will be available to anyone assigned as the nfsnobody user or group. To set all remote users to the nfsnobody user/group, use the all_squash option.

  The nfsnobody user is assigned to UIDs and GIDs of 65534. This prevents the ID from running into a valid user or group ID. Using anonuid or anongid options, you can change the nfsnobody user or group, respectively. For example, anonuid=175 sets all anonymous users to UID 175 and anongid=300 sets the GID to 300. (Only the number is displayed when you list file permission, however, unless you add entries with names to `/etc/password` and `/etc/group` for the new UIDs and GIDs.)

- **User mapping** — If the same users have login accounts for a set of computers (and they have the same IDs), NFS, by default, will map those IDs. This means that if the user named mike (UID 110) on maple has an account on pine (`mike`, UID 110), he could use his own remotely mounted files from either computer.

  If a client user who is not set up on the server creates a file on the mounted NFS directory, the file is assigned to the remote client's UID and GID. (An `ls -l` on the server would show the UID of the owner.) You can identify a file that contains user mappings using the `map_static` option.

> **TIP:** The `exports` man page describes the `map_static` option, which should let you create a file that contains new ID mappings. These mappings should let you remap client IDs into different IDs on the server.

Exporting the shared file systems

After you have added entries to your `/etc/exports` file, you can actually export the directories listed using the `exportfs` command. If you reboot your computer or restart the NFS service, the `exportfs` command is run automatically to export your directories. However, if you want to export them immediately, you can do so by running `exportfs` from the command line (as root).

> **TIP:** It's a good idea to run the `exportfs` command after you change the exports file. If any errors are in the file, `exportfs` will identify those errors for you. If you are not able to immediately access changed NFS shares from clients, you might need to restart the NFS and portmap services.

Here's an example of the `exportfs` command:

```
# /usr/sbin/exportfs -a -v
exporting maple:/pub
exporting spruce:/pub
exporting maple:/home
exporting spruce:/home
exporting *:/media/win
```

The `-a` option indicates that all directories listed in `/etc/exports` should be exported. The `-v` option says to print verbose output. In this example, the `/pub` and `/home` directories from the local server are immediately available for mounting by those client computers that are named (maple and spruce). The `/media/win` directory is available to all client computers.

Running the `exportfs` command makes your exported NFS directories immediately available. Any changes to your `/etc/export` file will be used again the next time you reboot or otherwise restart the NFS service.

Starting the nfsd daemons

For security purposes, the NFS service is turned off by default on your Fedora or RHEL system. You can use the `chkconfig` command to turn on the NFS service so that your files are exported and the `nfsd` daemons are running when your system boots.

There are two startup scripts you want to turn on for the NFS service to work properly. The `nfs` service exports file systems (from `/etc/exports`) and starts the `nfsd` daemon that listens for service requests. The `nfslock` service starts the `lockd` daemon, which helps allow file locking to prevent multiple simultaneous use of critical files over the network.

> **NOTE:** If you see the message "Cannot register service: RPC: Unable to receive; errno= connection refused," you probably need to start the portmap service on the client machine.

You can use the `chkconfig` command to turn on the nfs service by typing the following commands (as root user):

```
# chkconfig nfs on
```

The next time you start your computer, the NFS service will start automatically and your exported directories will be available. If you want to start the service immediately, without waiting for a reboot, you can type the following:

```
# /etc/init.d/nfs start
```

The NFS service should now be running and ready to share directories with other computers on your network.

Using NFS file systems

After a server exports a directory over the network using NFS, a client computer connects that directory to its own file system using the `mount` command. The `mount` command is the same one used to mount file systems from local hard disks, CDs, and USB flash drives. Only the options to give to `mount` are slightly different.

`Mount` can automatically mount NFS directories that are added to the `/etc/fstab` file, just as it does with local disks. NFS directories can also be added to the `/etc/fstab` file in such a way that they are not automatically mounted. With a `noauto` option, an NFS directory listed in `/etc/fstab` is inactive until the `mount` command is used, after the system is up and running, to mount the file system.

Manually mounting an NFS file system

If you know that the directory from a computer on your network has been exported (that is, made available for mounting), you can mount that directory manually using the `mount` command. This is a good way to make sure that it is available and working before you set it up to mount permanently. Here's an example of mounting the `/home/chris/files` directory from a computer named maple on your local computer:

```
# mkdir /media/maple
# mount maple:/home/chris/files /media/maple
```

The first command (`mkdir`) creates the mount point directory (`/media` is a common place to put temporarily mounted disks and NFS file systems). The `mount` command then identifies the remote computer and shared file system separated by a colon (`maple:/home/chris/files`). Then, the local mount point directory follows (`/media/maple`).

> **NOTE:** If the mount failed, make sure the NFS service is running on the server and that the server's firewall rules don't deny access to the service. From the server, type **ps ax | grep nfsd**. You should see a list of `nfsd` server processes. If you don't, try to start your NFS daemons as described in the previous section. To view your firewall rules, type **iptables -L** (see Chapter 14 for a description of firewalls). By default, the nfsd daemon listens for NFS requests on port number 2049. Your firewall must accept udp requests on ports 2049 (nfs) and 111 (rpc).

To ensure that the mount occurred, type **mount**. This command lists all mounted disks and NFS file systems. Here is an example of the `mount` command and its output:

```
# mount
/dev/sda3 on / type ext3 (rw)
none on /proc type proc (rw)
none on /sys type sysfs (rw)
none on /dev/pts type devpts (rw,gid=5,mode=620)usbdevfs on
/proc/bus/usb type usbdevfs (rw)
/dev/sda1 on /boot type ext3 (rw)
none on /dev/shm type tmpfs (rw)
maple:/home/chris/files on /media/maple type nfs (rw,addr=10.0.0.11)
```

The output from the `mount` command shows your mounted disk partitions, special file systems, and NFS file systems. The first output line shows your hard disk (`/dev/sda3`), mounted on the root file system (`/`), with read/write permission (`rw`), with a file system type of `ext3` (the standard Linux file system type). The small `/boot` file system is also of type `ext3`. The `/proc`, `/sys`, `/dev/shm`, `/dev/pts`, and `usbdevfs` mount points represent special file system types. The just-mounted NFS file system is the `/home/chris/files` directory from maple (`maple:/home/chris/files`). It is mounted on `/media/maple` and its mount type is `nfs`. The file system was mounted read/write (`rw`) and the IP address of maple is `10.0.0.11` (`addr=10.0.0.11`).

I just showed a simple case of using `mount` with NFS. The mount is temporary and is not remounted when you reboot your computer. You can also add options to the `mount` command line for NFS mounts:

- **-a** — Mount all file systems in `/etc/fstab` (except those indicated as `noauto`).

- **-f** — This goes through the motions of (fakes) mounting the file systems on the command line (or in /etc/fstab). Used with the -v option, -f is useful for seeing what mount would do before it actually does it.

- **-F** — When used with -a, you tell mount to fork off a new incarnation of mount for each file system listed to be mounted in the /etc/fstab file. An advantage of using this option, as it relates to NFS shared directories, is that other file systems can be mounted if an NFS file system isn't immediately available. This option should not be used, however, if the order of mounting is important (for example, if you needed to mount /mnt/pcs and then /mnt/pcs/arctic).

- **-r** — Mounts the file system as read-only.

- **-w** — Mounts the file system as read/write. (For this to work, the shared file system must have been exported with read/write permission.)

The next section describes how to make the mount more permanent (using the /etc/fstab file) and how to select various options for NFS mounts.

Automatically mounting an NFS file system

To set up an NFS file system to mount automatically each time you start your Fedora or RHEL system, you need to add an entry for that NFS file system to the /etc/fstab file. The /etc/fstab file contains information about all different kinds of mounted (and available to be mounted) file systems for your Fedora or RHEL system.

The format for adding an NFS file system to your local system is the following:

```
host:directory    mountpoint    nfs    options    0    0
```

The first item (host:directory) identifies the NFS server computer and shared directory. mountpoint is the local mount point on which the NFS directory is mounted, followed by the file system type (nfs). Any options related to the mount appear next in a comma-separated list. (The last two zeros just tell Fedora or RHEL not to dump the contents of the file system and not to run fsck on the file system.)

The following are two examples of NFS entries in /etc/fstab:

```
maple:/home/chris/files /media/maple nfs    rsize=8192,wsize=8192  0 0
oak:/apps    /oak/apps    nfs    noauto,ro            0 0
```

In the first example, the remote directory /home/chris/files from the computer named maple (maple:/home/chris/files) is mounted on the local directory /media/maple (the local directory must already exist). The file system type is nfs, and read (rsize) and write (wsize) buffer sizes are set at 8192 to speed data transfer associated with this connection. In the second example, the remote directory is /apps on the computer named oak. It is set up as an NFS file system (nfs) that can be mounted on the /oak/apps directory locally. This file system is not mounted automatically (noauto), however, and can be mounted only as read-only (ro) using the mount command after the system is already running.

> **TIP:** The default is to mount an NFS file system as read/write. However, the default for exporting a file system is read-only. If you are unable to write to an NFS file system, check that it was exported as read/write from the server.

Mounting noauto file systems

In your /etc/fstab file there can also be devices for other file systems that are not mounted automatically. For example, you might have multiple disk partitions on your hard disk or an NFS shared file system that you might want to mount only occasionally. A noauto file system can be mounted manually. The advantage is that when you type the mount command, you can type less information and have the rest filled in by the contents of the /etc/fstab file. So, for example, you could type:

```
# mount /oak/apps
```

With this command, mount knows to check the /etc/fstab file to get the file system to mount (oak:/apps), the file system type (nfs), and the options to use with the mount (in this case ro for read-only). Instead of typing the local mount point (/oak/apps), you could have typed the remote file system name (oak:/apps) instead, and had other information filled in.

> **TIP:** When naming mount points, including the name of the remote NFS server in that name can help you remember where the files are actually being stored. This may not be possible if you are sharing home directories (/home) or mail directories (/var/spool/mail).

Using mount options

You can add several mount options to the /etc/fstab file (or to a mount command line itself) to impact how the file system is mounted. When you add options to /etc/fstab, they must be separated by commas. The following are some options that are valuable for mounting NFS file systems:

- hard — With this option on, if the NFS server disconnects or goes down while a process is waiting to access it, the process will hang until the server comes back up. This option is helpful if it is critical that the data you are working with not get out of sync with the programs that are accessing it. (This is the default behavior.)

- soft — If the NFS server disconnects or goes down, a process trying to access data from the server will time out after a set period of time when this is on.

- rsize — The number of bytes of data read at a time from an NFS server. The default is 1024. Using a larger number (such as 8192) will get you better performance on a network that is fast (such as a LAN) and is relatively error-free (that is, one that doesn't have a lot of noise or collisions).

- `wsize` — The number of bytes of data written at a time to an NFS server. The default is 1024. Performance issues are the same as with the `rsize` option.

- `timeo=#` — Sets the time after an RPC timeout occurs that a second transmission is made, where # represents a number in tenths of a second. The default value is seven-tenths of a second. Each successive timeout causes the timeout value to be doubled (up to 60 seconds maximum). You should increase this value if you believe that timeouts are occurring because of slow response from the server or a slow network.

- `retrans=#` — Sets the number of minor retransmission timeouts that occur before a major timeout. When a major timeout occurs, the process is either aborted (soft mount) or a `Server Not Responding` message appears on your console.

- `retry=#` — Sets how many minutes to continue to retry failed mount requests, where # is replaced by the number of minutes to retry. The default is 10,000 minutes (which is about one week).

- `bg` — If the first mount attempt times out, try all subsequent mounts in the background. This option is very valuable if you are mounting a slow or sporadically available NFS file system. By placing mount requests in the background, Fedora or RHEL can continue to mount other file systems instead of waiting for the current one to complete.

> **NOTE:** If a nested mount point is missing, a timeout to allow for the needed mount point to be added occurs. For example, if you mount `/usr/trip` and `/usr/trip/extra` as NFS file systems, if `/usr/trip` is not yet mounted when `/usr/trip/extra` tries to mount, `/usr/trip/extra` will time out. Hopefully, `/usr/trip` will come up and `/usr/trip/extra` will mount on the next retry.

- `fg` — If the first mount attempt times out, try subsequent mounts in the foreground. This is the default behavior. Use this option if it is imperative that the mount be successful before continuing (for example, if you were mounting `/usr`).

Any of the options that don't require a value can have `no` prepended to have the opposite effect. For example, `nobg` indicates that the mount should not be done in the background.

Using autofs to mount NFS file systems on demand

Recent improvements to auto-detecting and mounting removable devices have meant that you can simply insert or plug in those devices to have them detected, mounted, and displayed. However, to make the process of detecting and mounting remote NFS file systems more automatic, you still need to use a facility such as autofs.

With the autofs facility configured and turned on, you can cause any NFS shared directories to mount on demand. If you know the hostname and directory being shared by another host computer, you can simply change (`cd`) to the autofs mount directory (`/net` by default) and have the shared resource automatically mount and be accessible to you.

The following steps explain how to turn on the autofs facility:

1. As root user from a Terminal window, open the /etc/auto.master file and look for a
    line that appears as follows:

    ```
    /net    -hosts
    ```

    This causes the /net directory to act as the mount point for the NFS shared directories
    you want to access on the network. (If there is a comment character at the beginning of
    that line, remove it.)

2. Start the autofs service by typing the following as root user:

    ```
    # service autofs start
    ```

3. Set up the autofs service to restart every time you boot your system:

    ```
    # chkconfig autofs on
    ```

Believe it or not, that's all you have to do. Provided that you have a network connection to the
NFS servers from which you want to share directories, you can try to access a shared NFS
directory. For example, if you know that the /usr/local/share directory is being shared
from the computer on your network named shuttle, do the following:

1. Type the following:

    ```
    $ cd /net/shuttle
    ```

    If the computer named shuttle has any shared directories that are available to you, you
    will be able to successfully change to that directory. Another thing to note is that you
    could use an IP address instead of a hostname (for example, cd /net/10.0.0.1).

2. Type the following:

    ```
    $ ls
    usr
    ```

    You should be able to see that the usr directory is part of the path to a shared directory.
    If there are shared directories from other top-level directories, you should see those as
    well (such as /var or /home). Of course, seeing any of those directories is dependent on
    how security is set up on the server.

3. Next, you could try going straight to the shared directory. For example:

    ```
    $ cd /net/shuttle/usr/local/share
    $ ls
    info man music television
    ```

    At this point, the ls should reveal the contents of the /usr/local/share directory on
    the computer named shuttle. What you can do with that content depends on how that
    content was configured for sharing by the server.

Unmounting NFS file systems

After an NFS file system is mounted, unmounting it is simple. You use the `umount` command with either the local mount point or the remote file system name. For example, here are two ways you could unmount `maple:/home/chris/files` from the local directory `/media/maple`:

```
# umount maple:/home/chris/files
# umount /media/maple
```

Either form will work. If `maple:/home/chris/files` is mounted automatically (from a listing in `/etc/fstab`), the directory will be remounted the next time you boot Fedora or RHEL. If it was a temporary mount (or listed as `noauto` in `/etc/fstab`), it will not be remounted at boot time.

> **TIP**: The command is not `unmount`, it is `umount`. This is easy to get wrong.

If you get the message `device is busy` when you try to unmount a file system, it means the unmount fails because the file system is being accessed. Most likely, one of the directories in the NFS file system is the current directory for your shell (or the shell of someone else on your system). The other possibility is that a command is holding a file open in the NFS file system (such as a text editor). Check your Terminal windows and other shells, and `cd` out of the directory if you are in it, or just close the Terminal windows.

If an NFS file system won't unmount, you can force unmount it (`umount -f /media/maple`) or unmount and clean up later (`umount -l /media/maple`). The `-l` option is usually the better choice because a forced unmount can disrupt a file modification that is in progress.

Other cool things to do with NFS

You can share some directories to make it consistent for a user to work from any of several different Linux computers on your network. Some examples of useful directories to share are:

- `/var/spool/mail` — By sharing this directory from your mail server, and mounting it on the same directory on other computers on your network, users can access their mail from any of those other computers. This saves users from having to download messages to their current computers or from having to log in to the server just to get mail. There is only one mailbox for each user, no matter from where it is accessed.

- `/home` — This is a similar concept to sharing mail, except that all users have access to their home directories from any of the NFS clients. Again, you would mount `/home` on the same mount point on each client computer. When the user logs in, that user has access to all the user's start-up files and data files contained in the `/home/user` directory.

> **TIP:** If your users rely on a shared /home directory, you should make sure that the NFS server that exports the directory is fairly reliable. If /home isn't available, the user may not have the start-up files to log in correctly, or any of the data files needed to get work done. One workaround is to have a minimal set of start-up files (.bashrc, .Xdefaults, and so on) available in the user's home directory when the NFS directory is not mounted. Doing so allows the user to log in properly at those times.

- /project — Although you don't have to use this name, a common practice among users on a project is to share a directory structure containing files that people on the project need to share. This way everyone can work on original files and keep copies of the latest versions in one place. (Of course, a better way to manage a project is with CVS or some other version control-type software, but this is a simple work-around.)

- /var/log — An administrator can keep track of log files from several different computers by mounting the /var/log file on the administrator's computer. (Each server may need to export the directory to allow root to be mapped between the computers for this to work.) If there are problems with a computer, the administrator can then easily view the shared log files live.

If you are working exclusively with Fedora, Red Hat Enterprise Linux, and other Linux and UNIX systems, NFS is probably your best choice for sharing file systems. If your network consists primarily of Microsoft Windows computers or a combination of systems, you may want to look into using Samba for file sharing.

Setting Up a Samba File Server

Samba is a software package that comes with Fedora, RHEL, and most other Linux systems. Samba enables you to share file systems and printers on a network with computers that use the Server Message Block (SMB) or Common Internet File System (CIFS) protocols. SMB is the Microsoft protocol that is delivered with Windows operating systems for sharing files and printers. CIFS is an open, cross-platform protocol that is based on SMB. Samba contains free implementations of SMB and CIFS.

Although you can't always count on NFS being installed on Windows clients (unless you install it yourself), SMB is always available (with a bit of setup). If Samba is not currently installed, refer to the "Getting and Installing Samba" section later in this chapter.

On Fedora or RHEL, the Samba software package contains a variety of daemon processes, administrative tools, user tools, and configuration files. To do basic Samba configuration, you can start with the Samba Server Configuration window. This window provides a graphical interface for configuring the server and setting directories to share.

Most of the Samba configuration you do ends up in the /etc/samba/smb.conf file. If you need to access features that are not available through the Samba Server Configuration window, you can edit /etc/samba/smb.conf by hand or use SWAT, a Web-based interface to configure Samba.

Daemon processes consist of smbd (the SMB daemon) and nmbd (the NetBIOS name server). The smbd daemon makes the file sharing and printing services you add to your Linux system available to Windows client computers. The client computers this package supports include:

- Windows 9*x*
- Windows 2000
- Windows Server 2003
- Windows NT
- Windows ME
- Windows XP
- Windows Vista
- Windows for Workgroups
- MS Client 3.0 for DOS
- OS/2
- Dave for Macintosh Computers
- Mac OS X
- Samba for Linux

As for administrative tools for Samba, you have several shell commands at your disposal. You can check your configuration file using the testparm and testprns commands. The smbstatus command tells you which computers are currently connected to your shared resources. Using the nmblookup command, you can query for NetBIOS names (the names used to identify host computers in Samba).

Because SMB is considered a Windows system technology, some of the terms used to describe Samba sound more Windows than Linux. For example, a shared directory or file system is often referred to as a *share*.

Although Samba uses the NetBIOS service to share resources with SMB clients, the underlying network must be configured for TCP/IP. Although other SMB hosts can use TCP/IP, NetBEUI, and IPX/SPX to transport data, Samba for Linux supports only TCP/IP. Messages are carried between host computers with TCP/IP and are then handled by NetBIOS.

Getting and installing Samba

To see if Samba is installed on your Fedora or RHEL system, type the following:

```
# rpm -qa | grep samba
samba-*
system-config-samba
samba-swat-*
samba-common-*
samba-client-*
```

You should see the name of each of the five packages, followed by the version number (I represented version numbers with an asterisk). Although not installed with all installation groups in Fedora and RHEL, the packages that make up Samba are all included on the DVD that comes with this book. To install Samba, insert the DVD. Then run the following (note that the device may have a name other than `cdrecorder` and that you can skip the first step if it mounts automatically):

```
# mount /media/cdrecorder
# cd /media/cdrecorder/Fedora/RPMS
# rpm -Uhv samba*
# cd ; umount /media/cdrecorder
```

If you have an Internet connection, you could try `yum install samba` instead. Before you start trying to configure Samba, read the README file (located in `/usr/share/doc/samba*`). It provides a good overview of the SMB protocol and Samba.

> **NOTE:** With the expanded Fedora software repository, other useful tools for working with Samba are now available. The smb4k package lets you search for available shared SMB/CIFS resources and mount them on your computer. The fuse-smb package lets you find and browse available SMB shares on your network.

Configuring a simple Samba server

The Samba Server Configuration window enables you to do a basic Samba configuration and then identify which directories you want to share. To make this procedure useful, I'm setting up a particular type of shared environment (which you can modify later if you prefer). Here are the characteristics:

- **A single local area network** — Contains multiple Windows and Linux machines.

- **User-level security** — Any user who wants to get to the shared Samba files must have a valid login and password on the Linux Samba server.

- **Encrypted passwords** — Many clients use encrypted passwords with Samba (SMB) by default. I'll describe how to turn on encrypted passwords for clients that don't use encrypted passwords.

- **A guest user account** — The guest user account will be useful later, so you can set up Samba to let users without special accounts use the server's printers via Samba.

The following procedure describes how to configure Samba and create a shared directory in Samba:

1. To open the Samba Server Configuration window, click System → Administration → Samba. The Samba Server Configuration window opens. (You will likely need to enter the root password.)

2. Click Preferences → Server Settings. The Server Settings window appears, as shown in Figure 18-3.

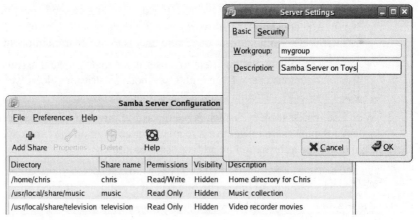

Figure 18-3: Define the workgroup and description for your Samba server.

3. Type the workgroup name (to match that of other computers with which you want to share files) and a short description.

4. Click the Security tab. A window appears like the one shown in Figure 18-4.

Figure 18-4: Fill in Security information for your Samba server.

5. Provide the following information for the fields on the Security tab and click OK:

   • **Authentication Mode** — Select User, Share, Server, ADS (Active Directory Server), or Domain. For this example, I selected User. (See the "Security options" section later in this chapter for details on each of the authentication modes.)

   • **Authentication Server** — This field is only valid if your Samba server is configured to use Server or Domain security. It identifies the server (NetBIOS name) that will be used to authenticate the user name and password the Samba client enters to gain access to this Samba server. With user authentication, passwords are checked on the Samba server (in this example, therefore, this field is blank.)

   • **Kerberos Realm** — If your network uses Kerberos for user authentication, enter the name of your Kerberos realm here.

- **Encrypt Passwords** — Select Yes (to expect clients to send encrypted passwords) or No (to expect clear-text password). See the section on Samba clients later in this chapter to determine how to configure clients to use encrypted passwords.

- **Guest Account** — Set this field to a user name that you want assigned to requests from anonymous users. Even with User mode security set globally, you can assign guest access to particular Samba shares (such as printers).

With User mode security (which is being used in this example), any user who wants to access a Samba share must have a regular user account on the Linux system. (Refer to Chapter 11 for information on adding user accounts.)

6. To add a user as a Samba user (that is, one who can access your Samba server), select Preferences → Samba Users. The Samba Users window appears.

7. Click Add User. The Create New Samba User window appears.

8. Provide information for the following fields in the Create New Samba User window and click OK:

   - **Unix Username** — Click this check box, and then select the Linux user name to which you want to give access to the Samba server.

   - **Windows Username** — This is the user name provided by the user when he or she requests the shared directory. (Often, it is the same as the Unix Username.)

   - **Samba Password** — Type the Samba password, then retype it into the Confirm Samba Password field.

9. Repeat the previous step for each user you want to access the Samba shared directory.

10. Now that you have configured the default values for your Samba server, add a directory to share by clicking File → Add Share. The Create Samba Share window appears.

11. Fill in the following fields shown in the Create Samba Share window:

   - **Directory** — Type the name of the directory you want to share. For example, you might want to share a user's home directory, such as /home/chris.

   - **Description** — Type any description you like of the Shared directory.

   - **Basic Permissions** — Select either Read-only or Read/Write. For Read-only, files can be viewed, but not changed, on the shared directory. For Read/Write, the user is free to add, change, or delete files, provided he or she has Linux file access to the particular file.

12. Click the Access tab, select one of the following choices for access to the share, and then click OK:

   - **Only allow access to specific users** — Click here, and then choose which users will be allowed to access the shared directory. For example, if you are sharing a user's directory (such as /home/chris), you probably want to restrict access to that directory to the directory's owner (for example, chris). Read and write access to particular files and directories are determined by the Linux ownership and group assigned to them.

- **Allow access to everyone** — Choose this option if you want to allow anyone to access this directory. (All users will have privileges assigned to the guest user when accessing the directory.)

After you click OK, Samba is started and the new directory is immediately available. You can close the Samba Server Configuration window.

13. Although Samba should be running at this point, you probably need to set Samba to start automatically every time you reboot Linux. To do that, type the following as root user in a Terminal window:

```
# chkconfig smb on
```

If Samba isn't running yet, type `service smb start` to start it right now. You can repeat the steps for adding a Samba shared directory for every directory you want to make available on your network. At this point, you can do one of the following:

- Go through your Samba server settings in more detail (as described in the "Configuring Samba with SWAT" section) to understand how you might want to further tune your Samba server.

- Try accessing the shared directories you just created from a client computer on your network. To do that, refer to the "Mounting Samba directories in Linux" section later in this chapter.

If you cannot open the shared directory you just configured from a Windows computer or other Linux computer on your LAN, you are probably experiencing one of the following problems:

- The client isn't supplying a valid user name and password.
- The client isn't supplying an encrypted password.

The quick way around these problems is to use only share-level security (which, of course, throws your security right out the window). The other solution is to get passwords up-to-date and make sure that clients are using encrypted passwords (as described in the "Setting up Samba clients" section later in this chapter).

Configuring Samba with SWAT

The Samba Web Administration Tool (SWAT) is a Web-based interface for configuring Samba. While it's not quite as easy to use as the Samba Server Configuration window, it does offer more options for tuning Samba and Help descriptions for each option. Also, because SWAT is Web-based, you can configure your system remotely from any Web browser.

> **CAUTION:** Both SWAT and the Samba Server Configuration window configure Samba by modifying the `/etc/samba/smb.conf` file. Different GUI tools can overwrite each other's settings, sometimes in a way that causes the other tool not to work.
>
> In general, it's best to make a backup copy of your files before switching GUI tools. Eventually, you should choose one tool and stick with it.

Turning on SWAT

Before you can use SWAT, you must have the samba-swat package installed (type **yum install samba-swat**) and start the swat service. To set up SWAT to run from your browser, follow these steps:

1. To turn on the swat service, type the following, as root user, from a Terminal window:

   ```
   # chkconfig swat on
   ```

2. To pick up the change to the swat service, reload data for the running xinetd start-up script as follows:

   ```
   # service xinetd reload
   ```

If xinetd is not already running, use `start` instead of `reload`. When you have finished this procedure, use the SWAT program, described in the next section, to configure Samba.

Starting with SWAT

You can run the SWAT program by typing the following URL in your local browser:

```
http://localhost:901/
```

At this point, the browser will prompt you for a user name and password. Enter the root user name and password. The SWAT window should appear, as shown in Figure 18-5.

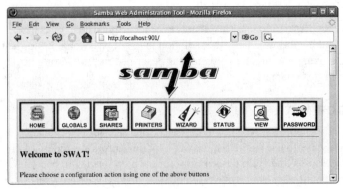

Figure 18-5: Use SWAT from your browser to manage your Samba configuration.

> **TIP:** Instead of running SWAT from your local browser, you can run it from another computer on the network by substituting the server computer's name for `localhost`. (To allow computers besides the local computer to access the swat service, you must change or remove the `only_from = 127.0.0.1` line from the `/etc/xinetd.d/swat` file and reload the xinetd service.) Keep in mind that you are entering clear-text passwords when you connect to the SWAT service, so using this feature outside of the local computer is not particularly secure.

The rest of this section describes how to use SWAT to create your configuration entries (in `/etc/samba/smb.conf`) and to work with that configuration.

> **CAUTION:** Any time you use a GUI to change a plain-text configuration file (as you do with SWAT), you may lose some of the information that you put in by hand. In this case, SWAT deletes comment lines and rearranges other entries. To protect changes you have made manually, make a backup copy of your `/etc/samba/smb.conf` file before you edit it with SWAT.

Creating global Samba settings in SWAT

A group of global settings affects how file and print sharing are generally accomplished on a Samba server. They appear under the `[global]` heading in the `/etc/samba/smb.conf` file. To edit global variables, click the GLOBALS option on the SWAT window.

Nine option types are available: base options, security options, logging options, protocol, printing options, browse options, WINs, eventlog, and winbind options. To view and modify your global Samba server settings, click the GLOBALS option. Then add the following options.

> **NOTE:** Each option shown relates to the exact parameters used in the `/etc/samba/smb.conf` file. You can refer to the `smb.conf` man page (type **man smb.conf**) to get more information on these parameters.

Base options

The following options relate to basic information associated with your Samba server:

- **workgroup** — The name of the workgroup associated with the group of SMB hosts. By default in Fedora and RHEL, the value for this field is `MYGROUP`.

- **realm** — If you are using kerberos authentication, this value indicates the kerberos realm to use. Typically, that is reflected by the hostname of the server providing the service.

- **netbios name** — The name assigned to this Samba server. You can use the same name as your DNS hostname or leave it blank, in which case the DNS hostname is used automatically.

- **netbios alias** —This enables you to set a way of referring to a host computer (an alias) that is different from the host's TCP/IP DNS name.

- **server string** — A string of text identifying the server. This name appears in places such as the printer comment box. By default, it says Samba and the version number.

- **interfaces** — Lets you set up more than one network interface. This enables Samba to browse several different subnetworks. The form of this field can be *IP Address/Subnetwork Mask*. Or, you could identify a network interface (such as eth0 for the first Ethernet card on your computer). For example, a Class C network address may appear as `192.168.24.11/255.255.255.0`.

Security options

Of the security options settings, the first option (`security`) is the most important one to get right. It defines the type of security used to give access to the shared file systems and printers to the client computers. (To see some of the fields described here, you need to click the Advanced view.)

- **security** — Sets how password and user information is transferred to the Samba server from the client computer. As noted earlier, it's important to get this value right. The default value for security (`security=user`) is different than the default value for security (`security=share`) in pre-2.0 versions of Samba. If you are coming from an earlier version of Samba and clients are failing to access your server, this setting is a good place to start. Here are your options:

  - `user` — The most common type of security used to share files and printers to Windows 95/98/2000 and Windows NT clients. It is the default set with Samba in the current release. This setting is appropriate if users are doing a lot of file sharing (as opposed to a Samba server used mostly as a print server). It requires that a user provide a user name/password before using the server.

    The easiest way to get this method working is to give a Linux user account to every client user who will use the Fedora or RHEL Samba server. This provides basically the same file permissions to a user account through Samba as the same user would get if he or she were logged in directly to Linux.

  - `share` — The `share` value for security works best for just print sharing or for providing file access that is more public (guest sharing). A client doesn't need to provide a valid user name and password to access the server. However, the user will typically have a "guest" level of permission to access and change files. See the sidebar describing guest accounts for further information.

  - `server` — The security option that, from the client's point of view, is the same as *user* security, in that the client still has to provide a valid user name/password combination to use the Samba server at all. The difference is on the server side. With `server` security, the user name/password is sent to another SMB server for validation. If this fails, Samba will try to validate the client using *user* security.

  - `domain` — This security option also, from the client's point of view, looks the same as *user* security. This setting is used only if the Samba server has been added to a Windows NT domain (using the `net join` command). When a client tries to connect to the Samba server in this mode, its user name and password are sent to a Windows NT Primary or Backup Domain controller. This is accomplished the same way that a Windows NT server would perform validation. Valid Linux user accounts must still be set up.

- `ads` — This security option causes Samba to act as a domain member in an ADS realm. Kerberos must be installed on the Samba machine to use this option. Samba must also join the ADS realm (see the `net` utility).

- **auth methods** — Sets the authentication method used by the Samba server (`smbd`). Leave the default in most cases. Authentication methods you can choose include anonymous access (`guest`), relay authentication through winbind (`winbind`), pre-winbind NT authentication (`ntdomain`), local lookups based on netbios or domain name (`sam`), or remote DC authentication of trusted users (`trustdomain`).

- **encrypt passwords** — Controls whether encrypted passwords can be negotiated with the client. This is on (`Yes`) by default. For *domain* security, this value must be `Yes`. Later versions of Windows NT (4.0 SP3 or later) and Windows 98 and Windows 2000 expect encrypted passwords to be on. (See the "Setting up Samba clients" section for information on getting clients to use encrypted passwords.)

- **client schannel** —Choose if the client is to require the use of netlogin schannel (`yes`), offer schannel but doesn't enforce it (`auto`) or not even offer schannel (`no`).

- **server schannel** — Choose if the server requires clients to use of netlogin schannel (`yes`), offers schannel but doesn't enforce it (`auto`) or doesn't even offer schannel (`no`). If you set this to `no`, you must apply the Windows XP WinXP_SignOrSeal.reg patch available from the Samba project.

- **passdb backend** — Choose the method of storing the backend database used to store passwords. By default. a TDB-based method is used (`tdbsam`) using a file named `passdb.tdb`. Other options include `smbpasswd` (Samba password storage style) and `ldapsam` (LDAP-based storage style).

- **guest account** — Specifies the user name for the guest account. When a service is specified as Guest OK, the user name entered here will be used to access that service. The account is usually the *nobody* user name.

> **TIP:** Make sure that the guest account is a valid user. (The default of *nobody* should already be set up to work.) With an invalid user as the guest account, the IPC$ connection that lists the shared resources fails.

- **invalid users** — Can contain a list of users that should not be allowed to log in for Samba service. Add an at sign (@) before a name to have it interpreted as an NIS or UNIX (Linux) group name.

- **valid users** — Add a list of user names that should be allowd to log in to the Samba service. If nothing is in this or the invalid users field, any user is allowed to log in.

- **admin users** — Can contain a list of users who have administrative privileges associated with a Samba share.

- **read list** — Can contain a list of users who have only read-only access to a service.

- **write list** — Can contain a list of users who have read/write access to a service.

- **printer admin** —Add users to this list that you want to allow remote administrative privilege to control Samba printers using the MS-RPC service, typically from a NT workstation.

- **hosts allow** — Contains a list of one or more hosts that are allowed to use your computer's Samba services. By default, users from any computer can connect to the Samba server (of course, they still have to provide valid user names and passwords). Usually, you use this option to allow connections from specific computers (such as 10.0.0.1) or computer networks (such as 10.0.0.) that are excluded by the hosts deny option.

- **hosts deny** — Contains a list of one or more hosts from which users are not allowed to use your computer's Samba services. You can make this option fairly restrictive, and then add the specific hosts and networks you want to use the Samba server. By default, no hosts are denied.

- **preload modules** — Contains a list of modules you want to be loaded into the smbd daemon before any clients can connect to the service.

Assigning Guest Accounts

Samba always assigns the permissions level of a valid user on the Linux system to clients who use the server. In the case of share security, the user is assigned a guest account (the *nobody* user account by default).

If the guest account value isn't set, Samba goes through a fairly complex set of rules to determine which user account to use. The result is that it can be hard to assure which user permissions will be assigned in each case. This is why it is recommended to use *user* security if you want to provide more specific user access to your Samba server.

Logging options

The following options help define how logging is done on your Samba server:

- **log file** — Defines the location of the Samba smb log file. By default, Samba log files are contained in `/var/log/samba` (with file names `nmbd.log` and `smbd.log`, and `smb.log`). In this option, the `%m` is replaced by the name of each host that tries to connect to the local Samba server.So, for example, for a client computer named maple, the smb log file would be `/var/log/samba/maple.log`.

- **max log size** — Sets the maximum amount of space, in kilobytes, that the log files can consume. By default, the value is set to 0 (no limit).

Printing options

The cups options field is used to define options that are passed to the cups service. By default, only the raw option is set (which causes printing data to be passed directly to the Samba printer).

Browse options

A browse list is a list of computers that are available on the network to SMB services. Clients use this list to find computers that are not only on their own LAN, but also computers in their workgroups that may be on other reachable networks.

In Samba, browsing is configured by options described below and implemented by the nmbd daemon. If you are using Samba for a workgroup within a single LAN, you probably don't need to concern yourself with the browsing options. If, however, you are using Samba to provide services across several physical subnetworks, you might want to consider configuring Samba as a domain master browser. Here are some points to think about:

- Samba can be configured as a master browser. This allows it to gather lists of computers from local browse masters to form a wide-area server list.

- If Samba is acting as a domain master browser, Samba should use a WINS server to help browse clients resolve the names from this list.

- Samba can be used as a WINS server, although it can also rely on other types of operating systems to provide that service.

- There should be only one domain master browser for each workgroup. Don't use Samba as a domain master for a workgroup with the same name as an NT domain.

If you are working in an environment that has a mix of Samba and Windows NT servers, you should use an NT server as your WINS server. If Samba is your only file server, you should choose a single Samba server (nmbd daemon) to supply the WINS services.

> **NOTE:** A WINS server is basically a name server for NetBIOS names. It provides the same service that a DNS server does with TCP/IP domain names: it can translate names into addresses. A WINS server is particularly useful for allowing computers to communicate with SMB across multiple subnetworks where information is not being broadcast across the subnetworks' boundaries.

To configure the browsing feature in Samba, you must have the workgroup named properly (described earlier in this section). Here are the global options related to SMB browsing.

> **NOTE:** If browsing isn't working, check the nmbd log file (/var/log/samba/log.nmbd). To get more detail, increase the debug information level to 2 or 3 (described earlier in the "Logging options" section) and restart Samba. The log can tell you if your Samba server is the master browser and, if so, which computers are on its list.

- **os level** — Set a value to control whether your Samba server (nmbd daemon) may become the local master browser for your workgroup. Raising this setting increases the

Samba server's chance to control the browser list for the workgroup in the local broadcast area.

If the value is 0, a Windows machine will probably be selected. A value of 65 will probably ensure that the Samba server is chosen over an NT server. The default is 20.

- **preferred master** — Set this to Yes if you want to force selection of a master browser. By setting this to Yes, the Samba server also has a better chance of being selected. (Setting Domain Master to Yes along with this option should ensure that the Samba server will be selected.) This is set to Auto by default, which causes Samba to try to detect the current master browser before taking that responsibility.

- **local master** — Set this to Yes if you want the Samba server to become the local browser master. (This is not a guarantee, but gives it a chance.) Set the value to No if you do not want your Samba server selected as the local master. Local Master is Auto by default.

- **domain master** — Set this to Yes if you want the Samba server (nmbd daemon) to identify itself as the domain master browser for its workgroup. This list will then allow client computers assigned to the workgroup to use SMB-shared files and printers from subnetworks that are outside of their own subnetwork. This is set to No by default.

WINS options

Use the WINS options if you want to have a particular WINS server provide the name-to-address translation of NetBIOS names used by SMB clients. As noted earlier, you probably don't need to use a WINS server if all of the clients and servers in your SMB workgroup are on the same subnetwork. That's because NetBIOS names can be obtained through addresses that are broadcast. It is possible to have your Samba server provide WINS services.

- **wins server** — If there is a WINS server on your network that you want to use to resolve the NetBIOS names for your workgroup, you can enter the IP address of that server here. Again, you will probably want to use a WINS server if your workgroup extends outside of the local subnetwork.

- **wins support** — Set this value to Yes if you want your Samba server to act as a WINS server. (It's No by default.) Again, this is not needed if all the computers in your workgroup are on the same subnetwork. Only one computer on your network should be assigned as the WINS server.

Besides the values described here, you can access dozens more options by clicking the Advanced View button. When you have filled in all the fields you need, click Commit Changes on the screen to have the changes written to the /etc/samba/smb.conf file.

Configuring shared directories with SWAT

To make your Samba share (shared directory) available to others, you can add an entry to the SWAT window. To use SWAT to set up Samba to share directories, do the following:

> **NOTE:** You may see one or more security warnings during the course of this procedure. These messages warn you that someone can potentially view the data you are sending to SWAT. If you are working on your local host or on a private LAN, the risk is minimal.

1. From the main SWAT window, click the SHARES button.

2. Type the name of the directory that you want to share in the Create Share box, then click Create Share.

3. Click Advanced if you would like to change to the Advanced view.

4. There are a few dozen options to choose from. Here are a few that might particularly interest you:

   - **comment** — A few words to describe the shared directory (optional).

   - **path** — The path name of the directory you are sharing.

   - **invalid users** — Enables you to add a list of users who are not allowed to log in to the Samba service. Besides identifying user names directly (from your /etc/passwd file), invalid users can be identified by Linux group or NIS netgroup, by adding a + or & in front of the name, respectively. Preceed the name with @ to have Samba first check your NIS netgroup, and then the Linux group for the name.

   - **valid users** — Add names here to identify which Linux user accounts can access the Samba service. As with invalid users, names can be preceeded with +, &, or @ characters.

   - **admin users** — Lets you identify users who have administrative privilege on a particular share. This is available with `security = share` type of security only.

   - **read list** — Add users to this list if you want to only grant read access to shares (even if a share is available with read-write access). This is available with `security = share` type of security only.

   - **write list** —Add users to this list to grant write access by those users to shares, even if the share is available with read-only access to all others. This is available with `security = share` type of security only.

   - **read only** — If Yes, then files can only be read from this file system, but no remote user can save or modify files on the file system. Select No if you want users to be allowed to save files to this directory over the network.

   - **guest ok** — Select Yes to enable anyone access to this directory without requiring a password.

   - **hosts allow** — Add the names of the computers that will be allowed to access this file system. You can separate hostnames by commas, spaces, or tabs. Here are some valid ways of entering hostnames:

        localhost — Allow access to the local host.

        192.168.74.18 — IP address. Enter an individual IP address.

192.168.74. — Enter a network address to include all hosts on a network. (Be sure to put a dot at the end of the network number or it won't work!)

maple, pine — Enable access to individual hosts by name.

EXCEPT *host* — If you are allowing access to a group of hosts (such as by entering a network address), use EXCEPT to specifically deny access from one host from that group.

- **hosts deny** — Deny access to specific computers by placing their names here. By default, no particular computers are excluded. Enter hostnames in the same forms you used for hosts allow.

- **browseable** — Indicates whether you can view this directory on the list of shared directories. This is on (Yes) by default.

- **available** — Enables you to leave this entry intact, but turns off the service. This is useful if you want to close access to a directory temporarily. This is on (Yes) by default. Select No to turn it off.

5. Select Commit Changes.

At this point, the shared file systems should be available to the Samba client computers (Windows 9*x*, Windows NT, Windows 2000, Windows Vista, Mac OS X, OS/2, Linux, and so on) that have access to your Linux Samba server. Before you try that, however, you can check a few things about your Samba configuration.

Checking your Samba setup with SWAT

From the SWAT window, select the STATUS button.

From this window, you can restart your smbd and nmbd processes. Likewise, you can see lists of active connections, active shares, and open files. (The preferred way to start the smbd and nmbd daemons is to set up the smb service to start automatically. Type **chkconfig smb on** in a Terminal window to set the service to start at boot time.)

Working with Samba files and commands

Although you can set up Samba through the Samba Server Configuration window or SWAT, many administrators prefer to edit the /etc/samba/smb.conf directly. As root user, you can view the contents of this file and make needed changes. If you selected *user* security (as recommended), you will also be interested in the smbusers and smbpasswd file (also in the /etc/samba directory). These files, as well as commands such as testparm and smbstatus, are described in the following sections.

Editing the smb.conf file

Changes you make using the Samba Server Configuration window or SWAT Web interface are reflected in your /etc/samba/smb.conf file. Here's an example of an smb.conf file (with comments removed):

```
[global]
workgroup = ESTREET
server string = Samba Server on Maple
hosts allow = 192.168.0.
printcap name = /etc/printcap
load printers = yes
printing = cups
log file = /var/log/samba/%m.log
max log size = 0
smb passwd file = /etc/samba/smbpasswd
security = user
encrypt passwords = Yes
unix password sync = Yes
passwd program = /usr/bin/passwd %u
passwd chat = *New*password* %n\n *Retype*new*password* %n\n *passwd:
        *all*authentication*tokens*updated*successfully*
pam password change = yes
obey pam restrictions = yes
socket options = TCP_NODELAY SO_RCVBUF=8192 SO_SNDBUF=8192
username map = /etc/samba/smbusers
dns proxy = no

[homes]
comment = Home Directories
browseable = no
writable = yes
valid users = %S
create mode = 0664
directory mode = 0775

[printers]
comment = All Printers
path = /var/spool/samba
browseable = no
guest ok = no
writable = no
printable = yes
```

In the [global] section, the workgroup is set to ESTREET, the server is identified as the Samba Server on Maple, and only computers that are on the local network (192.168.0.) are allowed access to the Samba service. You must change the 'hosts allow =' parameter to match your network.

Definitions for the local printers that will be shared are taken from the `/etc/printcap` file, the printers are loaded (`yes`), and the cups printing service (which is the default print service used by Fedora and RHEL) is used.

Separate log files for each host trying to use the service are created in `/var/log/samba/ %m.log` (with `%m` automatically replaced with each hostname). There is no limit to log file size (0).

In this case, we are using user-level security (`security = user`). This allows a user to log in once and then easily access the printers and the user's home directory on the Linux system. Password encryption is on (`encrypt passwords = yes`) because most Windows systems have password encryption on by default. Passwords are stored in the `/etc/samba/ smbpasswd` file on your Linux system.

The `dns proxy = no` option prevents Linux from looking up system names on the DNS server (used for TCP/IP lookups) when they can't be found among registered NetBIOS names.

The `[homes]` section allows each user to be able to access his or her Linux home directory from a Windows system on the LAN. The user will be able to write to the home directory. However, other users will not be able see or share this directory. The `[printers]` section allows all users to print to any printer that is configured on the local Linux system.

Adding Samba users

Doing user-style Samba security means assigning a Linux user account to each person using the Linux file systems and printers from his or her Windows workstation. (You could assign users to a guest account instead, but in this example, all users have their own accounts.) Then you need to add SMB passwords for each user. For example, here is how you would add a user whose Windows 98 workstation login is `chuckp`:

1. Type the following as root user from a Terminal window to add a Linux user account:

   ```
   # useradd -m chuckp
   ```

2. Add a Linux password for the new user as follows:

   ```
   # passwd chuckp
   Changing password for user chuckp
   New UNIX password: ********
   Retype new UNIX password: ********
   ```

3. Repeat the previous steps to add user accounts for all users from Windows workstations on your LAN that you want to give access to your Linux system to.

4. Type the following command to create the Samba password file (`smbpasswd`):

   ```
   # cat /etc/passwd | /usr/bin/mksmbpasswd.sh > /etc/samba/smbpasswd
   ```

5. Add an SMB password for the user as follows:

```
# smbpasswd chuckp
New SMB password: **********
Retype new SMB password: **********
```

(The `smbpasswd -a user` command can be used to create the `smbpasswd` file at the same time you set a user password.) Repeat this step for each user. Later, each user can log in to Linux and rerun the `passwd` and `smbpasswd` commands to set private passwords.

> **NOTE:** In the most recent version of Samba, options are available in the `smb.conf` file that cause SMB and Linux passwords to be synchronized automatically. See descriptions of the passwd program, passwd chat, and UNIX password sync options in the SWAT section of this chapter.

Starting the Samba service

To start the Samba SMB and NMB daemons, you can run the `/etc/init.d/smb` start-up script by typing the following as the root user:

```
# service smb start
```

This runs the Samba service during the current session. To set up Samba to start automatically when your Linux system starts, type the following:

```
# chkconfig smb on
```

This turns on the Samba service to start automatically in run levels 3, 4, or 5. You can now check SMB clients on the network to see if they can access your Samba server.

Testing your Samba permissions

You can run several commands from a shell to work with Samba. One is the `testparm` command, which you can use to check the access permissions you have set up. It lists global parameters that are set, along with any shared directories or printers.

Checking the status of shared directories

The `smbstatus` command can view who is currently using Samba shared resources offered from your Linux system. The following is an example of the output from `smbstatus`:

```
# smbstatus

Samba version 3.2.0pre2-8.fc9
PID     Username     Group        Machine
-----------------------------------------------------------------
25770   chris        chris        booker      (10.0.0.50)
25833   chris        chris        10.0.0.50   (10.0.0.50)
```

```
Service       pid    machine        Connected at
-----------------------------------------------------
IPC$          25729  booker         Tue Apr 22 12:06:29 2008
mytmp         25770  booker         Tue Apr 22 12:16:03 2008
mytmp         25833  10.0.0.50      Tue Apr 22 12:25:52 2008
IPC$          25730  booker         Tue Apr 22 12:06:29 2008


Locked files:
Pid   Uid DenyMode  Access   R/W  Oplock SharePath    Name    Time
---------------------------------------------------------------------------
25833 501 DENY_NONE 0x12019f RDWR NONE    /home/chris/files/.b.txt.swp Tue Apr 22
12:26:18 2008
```

This output shows that from your Linux Samba server, the `myhome` service (which is a share of the `/home/chris/files` directory) is currently open by the computer named booker. PID 25833 is the process number of the smbd daemon on the Linux server that is handling the service. The file that is open is the `/home/chris/files/.b.swap` file, which happens to be opened by a `vi` command. It has read/write access.

Setting up Samba clients

Once you have configured your Samba server, you can try using the shared directories from a client computer on your network. The following sections describe how to use your Samba server from another Linux system or from various Windows systems.

Using Samba shared directories from Linux

There are several methods of connecting to shared directories from your Samba client. The following sections address these methods.

Using Samba from Nautilus

To connect to a Samba share from Nautilus, use the Open Location box by clicking File →
Open Location. Then type **smb:** into your Nautilus file manager Open Location box.

A list of SMB workgroups on your network appears in the window. You can select a workgroup, choose a server, and then select a resource to use. This should work for shares requiring no password.

The Nautilus interface requires you to either send clear-text passwords or type the user and password into your location box. For example, to get to my home directory (`/home/chris`) through Nautilus, I can type my user name, password, server name, and share name as follows:

```
smb://chris:my72mgb@toys/chris
```

Instead of just typing this information into the Location box, you can use the Connect to Server feature of Nautilus. Select File → Connect to Server. From the Connect to Server window that appears, select the Service Type as Windows Share and type the server name to see all available shares from that window. Optionally, you can request a specific Share, Folder or User Name. Then you can also choose a particular name to use for the connection. You can also drop the password portion (such as `smb://chris@toys/chris`) and be prompted for the password.

Mounting Samba directories in Linux

Linux can view your Samba shared directories as it does any other medium (hard disk, NFS shares, CD-ROM, and so on). Using the `mount` command, you can mount a Samba shared file system so that it is permanently connected to your Linux file system.

The following example of the `mount` command shows how I would mount my home directory (`/home/chris`) from a computer named `toys` on a local directory (`/mnt/toys`). As root user, from a Terminal window, type:

```
# mkdir /mnt/toys
# mount -t cifs -o username=chris,password=a72mg //toys/chris /mnt/toys
```

The file system type for a Samba share is cifs (`-t cifs`). I pass the user name (`chris`) and password (`a72mg`) as options (`-o`). The remote share of my home directory on `toys` is `//toys/chris`. The local mount point is `/mnt/toys`. At this point, you can access the contents of `/home/chris` on `toys` as you would any file or directory locally. You will have the same permission to access and change the contents of that directory (and its subdirectories) as you would if you were the user `chris` using those contents directly from `toys`.

To mount the Samba shared directory permanently, you can add an entry to your `/etc/fstab` file. For the example just described, you could add the following line (as root user):

```
//toys/chris    /mnt/toys    cifs    username=chris,password=a72mg
```

You can add a credentials file and use that to contain your user name and password, instead of exposing that information to the command line. That way, someone running the `ps` command on your system won't be able to see that information. For example, you could create a file named `/etc/samba/creds.smbpub` containing the following two lines:

```
username=chris
password=a72mg
```

You could then change the mount command shown earlier to appear as follows:

```
# mount -t cifs -o credentials=/etc/samba/creds.smbpub //toys/chris
```

Using Samba shared directories from Windows

While using a Windows system, to see the file and print services available from your Linux Samba server (as well as from other computers on the network), open the Network and Sharing Center window in Windows Vista. Selections at the bottom of that window let you see all the files and folders you and others are sharing.

For other Windows systems, open the My Network Places window (for Windows XP) or Network Neighborhood (Windows 98 and older Windows systems). To open the window, select Start → My Network Places from the Windows XP desktop. Figure 18-6 shows an example of the My Network Places window with shares available from the local Windows XP system (named Bluestreak) and the Samba server in Linux (named Waldo).

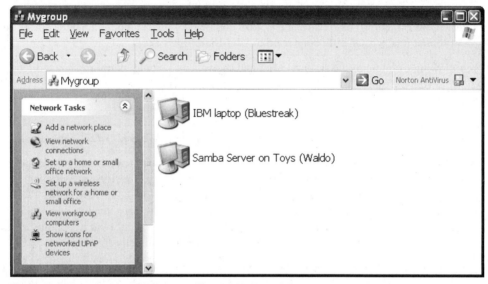

Figure 18-6: View your Linux Samba server from the My Network Places window.

The My Network Places window shows the computers that Windows found on your network. If your server appears on the screen (in my case, the server's name is Waldo), double-click it. Otherwise, you may need to double-click Entire Network, and then open the workgroup that your server is a part of to find your server. The server should show two kinds of resources:

- **Printers and Faxes** — A name and an icon should represent each printer and fax shared from the server. To access a printer or fax, double-click it. Windows will have you set up the printer or fax for your computer. After that, you can use the printer or fax as you would any local printer or fax.

- **Directories** — A name and folder icon should represent shared directories from the server. Open the directory to see the files and folders in that directory.

Double-click a folder to view the contents of that folder. At this point, you may receive a request to enter a password. Type the password and click OK. You should be able to view the contents of the folder, and its subfolders, at this time.

> **TIP:** If you plan to use the directory often, you may want to assign a drive letter to it. Right-click the folder icon, then select Map Network Drive. Select a drive from the list and, if you like, choose Reconnect at logon to have it available when you log on. Then click OK.

If the file server that you are looking for does not appear in your Network Neighborhood, you can try to search for it. Choose Start → Search → Computers or people → Computers. Type the name of the computer to search for, and then select Find Now. If the computer name appears, double-click it. A window should open, displaying the shared directories and printers from the server.

Alternatively, you can also create an lmhosts file to help your Windows computer find your Linux Samba server. Copy the sample C:\windows\lmhosts.sam file to C:\windows\lmhosts. Then edit the file to add the hostnames and IP addresses of the SMB servers on your network.

Troubleshooting your Samba server

A lot can go wrong with a Samba server. If your Samba server isn't working properly, the descriptions in this section should help you pinpoint the problem.

Basic networking in place?

Before computers can share directories and printers from Samba, they must be able to communicate on your LAN. Refer to Chapter 15 for information on setting up a LAN.

In Samba, your Samba server can use the TCP/IP name as the NetBIOS name (used by Window networks for file and printer sharing), or a separate NetBIOS name can be set in the smb.conf file. It is critical, however, that the broadcast address be the same as those for all clients communicating with your Samba server. To see your broadcast address, type the following:

```
$ ifconfig -a
eth0      Link encap:Ethernet  HWadd 00:D1:B3:75:A5:1B
          inet addr:10.0.0.1  Bcast:10.0.0.255  Mask:255.255.255.0
```

The important information is the broadcast address (Bcast:10.0.0.255). This is determined by the netmask (Mask:255.255.255.0). If the broadcast address isn't the same for the Samba server and the clients on the LAN, the clients cannot see that the Samba server has directories or printers to share.

Samba service running?

First, try the smbclient command from your Linux system to check that everything is running and being shared as you expect it to be. The smbclient command is a great tool for getting information about a Samba server and even accessing shared directories from both

Linux and Windows computers. While logged in as root or any user who has access to your Samba server, type the following:

```
$ smbclient -L localhost
Password: **********
Domain=[ESTREET] OS=[Unix] Server=[Samba 3.0.23c-2]

    Sharename       Type        Comment
    ---------       ----        -------
    homes           Disk        Home Directories
    IPC$            IPC         IPC Service (Samba Server)
    ADMIN$          Disk        IPC Service (Samba Server)
    hp-ns1          Printer
Domain=[ESTREET] OS=[Unix] Server=[Samba 3.0.23c-2]

    Server                  Comment
    ---------               -------
    PINE                    Samba Server
    MAPLE                   Windows XP
    NS1                     Samba Server


    Workgroup               Master
    ---------               -------
    ESTREET                 PINE
```

This shows that the Samba server is running on the local computer. Shared directories and printers, as well as servers in the workgroup, appear here. If the Samba server is not running, you will see `Connection refused` messages. You need to start the Samba service as described in the "Starting the Samba service" section earlier in this chapter.

Firewall open?

If the Samba server is running, it should begin broadcasting its availability on your LAN. If you try to access the server from a Windows or Linux client on your LAN, but get a `Connection refused` error, the problem may be that the firewall on your Linux Samba server is denying access to the NetBIOS service. If you have a secure LAN, you can type the following (as root user) to flush your firewall rules temporarily:

```
# iptables -F
```

Then, try to connect to the Samba Server from a Windows or Linux client. If you find that you can connect to the server, turn the firewall back on:

```
# service iptables restart
```

You then need to open access to ports 137, 138, and 139 in your firewall so that the Samba server will be able to accept connections for services. (See Chapter 14 for information on modifying your firewalls.)

User passwords working?

Try accessing a shared Samba directory as a particular user (from the local host or other Linux system on your LAN). You can use the `smbclient` command to do this. Here's an example:

```
# smbclient //localhost/home/chris/files -U chris
added interface ip=10.0.0.1 bcast=10.0.0.255 nmask=255.255.255.0
Password: *******
Domain=[ESTREET] OS=[Unix] Server=[Samba 2.2.7a]
smb: \>
```

In this example, `smbclient` connects to the directory share named `tmp` as the Samba user named `chris`. If the password is accepted, you should see information about the server and a `smb:\>` prompt. If you cannot access the same shared directory from a Windows client, it's quite possible that the client is passing an improper user name and password. Part of the problem may be that the Windows client is not providing encrypted passwords.

For certain Windows clients, using encrypted passwords requires that you change a Windows registry for the machine. One way to change the registry is with the Windows `regedit` command. Registry changes required for different Windows systems are contained within the `/usr/share/doc/samba-*/docs/registry` directory.

> **TIP:** The `smbclient` command, used here to list server information and test passwords, can also be used to browse the shared directory and copy files after you are connected. After you see the `smb:\>` prompt, type **help** to see the available commands. The interface is similar to any ftp client, such as sftp.

Summary

By providing centralized file servers, an organization can efficiently share information and applications with people within the organization, with customers, or with anyone around the world. Several different technologies are available in Fedora and RHEL to enable you to make your Linux computer a file server.

The Network File System (NFS) protocol was one of the first file server technologies available. It is particularly well suited for sharing file systems among Fedora, RHEL, and other UNIX systems. NFS uses standard `mount` and `umount` commands to connect file systems to the directory structures of client computers.

The Samba software package that comes with Fedora and RHEL contains protocols and utilities for sharing files and printers among Windows and OS/2 operating systems. It uses SMB protocols that are included with all Microsoft Windows systems, and therefore provides a convenient method of sharing resources on LANs containing many Windows systems.

Chapter 19

Setting Up a Mail Server

In This Chapter

- Introducing SMTP and sendmail
- Installing and running sendmail
- Configuring sendmail
- Introducing Postfix
- Stopping spam with SpamAssassin
- Getting mail from the server (IMAPv4 and POP3)
- Configuring SquirrelMail
- Administering a mailman mailing list

Today, electronic messaging is part of the communication backbone, the core of information dissemination within companies of all sizes. Everyone uses e-mail, from the mailroom to the laboratories to the CEO's office. And if you're in charge of an organization's mail server, you'll be notified (incessantly) when it stops working.

This chapter explains how to set up a mail server in Fedora to send and receive messages. In particular, it focuses on configuring a sendmail mail server, but also tells how to configure a Postfix mail server (which is also in the Fedora distribution). Once the mail server is configured, Fedora provides your mail server's users with different ways of getting their e-mail from your server, such as downloading it to their mail clients (with IMAPv4 or POP3) or reading it from a Web browser (using SquirrelMail).

Mailing list configuration and administration (using the mailman software package) are also discussed in this chapter, detailing how mailing list management software integrates and interfaces with the mail server.

> **NOTE:** Although the primary aspects of mail server configuration are discussed in this chapter, many configuration aspects are beyond its scope and thus are not addressed. Because security is an important concern when you're connected to the Internet, it is given considerable focus here.

Introducing SMTP and sendmail

Even with multimedia attachments and HTML encoding prevalent in e-mail messages today, the technology behind message transfer hasn't changed significantly since the early 1980s. The framework for the Simple Mail Transfer Protocol (SMTP) was initially described in RFC 821 in 1982. The protocol itself was extended in 1993 (RFC 1425), yielding the Extended Simple Mail Transfer Protocol (ESMTP), which provides more commands and new delivery modes.

The three parts to message transfer are the Mail Transfer Agent (MTA), the Mail Delivery Agent (MDA), and the Mail User Agent (MUA). The MTA, commonly referred to as the mail server (of which sendmail and postfix are examples), actually handles distributing outgoing mail and listening for incoming mail from the Internet. The MDA accepts messages from the MTA and copies the message into a user's mailbox. Fedora uses procmail as the default MDA, as specified in the sendmail configuration file (`sendmail.cf`).

End users, for whom the mail is ultimately intended, use MUAs to get mail from the server and read it from their desktops. Most MUAs support Post Office Protocol (POP3) and Internet Message Access Protocol (IMAPv4) features for getting mail from the server so it can be read and managed from the user's desktop computer.

> **CROSS-REFERENCE:** See Chapter 9 for details on Mail User Agents available with Fedora.

This chapter focuses on the sendmail MTA, the most common mail server on the Internet. Nearly 70 percent of all e-mail messages on the Internet are delivered by sendmail. With the growing Internet population, billions of e-mail messages are sent and received each day. As an alternative to sendmail, this chapter also includes a short description of postfix.

For getting mail from the server, this chapter describes the dovecot software package, which includes POP3 and IMAPv4 server software. As an alternative, for allowing users to read and manage e-mail from a Web browser, this chapter describes how to configure SquirrelMail.

There have been three major releases of sendmail. The original sendmail (sendmail version 5) was written in 1983 by Eric Allman, a student at the University of California at Berkeley. He maintained the code until 1987, when Lennart Lövstrand enhanced the program and developed IDA sendmail. Eric Allman returned to Berkeley in 1991 and embarked on a major code revision, releasing sendmail V8 in 1993, which incorporated the extensions from IDA sendmail. The current version (8.14) is based on this "version 8" code.

Installing and Running sendmail

In Fedora, the sendmail distribution consists of three RPM packages: sendmail, sendmail-cf, and sendmail-doc. Only the first package is truly necessary to send and receive mail on your machine. The second package includes configuration macros and other files that can help you reconfigure your site's sendmail installation if the defaults are insufficient. The third package contains documentation files that help to explain some of the details of the current version.

The sendmail binary packages are included in the Fedora distribution. The sendmail, sendmail-cf, and sendmail-doc packages are on the Fedora DVD that comes with this book. From the Fedora RPMS directory on the DVD, the following command installs the packages:

```
# rpm -Uhv sendmail*
```

Because sendmail is a common target of intruders, it's a good idea to get immediately any updates that are available for sendmail before proceeding. You can do that using the yum command or the PackageKit utility. To update sendmail using yum, type:

```
# yum update sendmail*
```

Starting sendmail

Once installed, the sendmail service is turned on by default. To start sendmail immediately, you can either reboot the machine or just run `service sendmail start` to start the server. The procedure for starting and stopping sendmail is similar to that of any other server process.

Other Mail Servers for Fedora or Red Hat Linux

The open-source version of sendmail is not the only mail server available for Fedora and Red Hat Enterprise Linux systems, but it is definitely the most common. The following list describes other servers and provides URLs for further information:

- **Postfix** — As with sendmail, the Postfix MTA is also included with Fedora. Written by Wietse Venema (of tcp_wrappers fame), this free mail server was designed with security in mind and executes most functions as an unprivileged user in a restricted chroot environment. The server encompasses more than a dozen small programs (each performing a simple, distinct task) and several single-purpose queues. You can find more information and source code at www.postfix.org.

- **Exim** — The Exim MTA is a free mail server (under GPL) that runs on Linux and other UNIX systems. Exim is included in the Fedora distribution. This MTA includes flexible features for checking and routing mail. Find out more about Exim from the Exim Home Page (www.exim.org).

- **Qmail** — Also conceived with security as a high priority, this mail server (written by Daniel J. Bernstein) offers secure and reliable message transfer, mailbox quotas, virtual domains, and antispam features. More information is available from www.qmail.org/top.html.

- **Smail** — Smail offers many of the same features as sendmail but is somewhat easier to configure and requires less memory. Smail is most appropriate for small- to medium-sized mail servers. The Smail project page is available at www.weird.com/~woods/projects/smail.html. The source code can be downloaded from ftp://ftp.planix.com/pub/Smail/.

By default, incoming messages received by sendmail are processed and stored in the `/var/spool/mail` directory. Each file in this directory represents a valid user name on the local machine. The file is created automatically the first time e-mail is sent to the user (or if it's otherwise missing). People with login accounts use this directory and their user account name as their incoming mailboxes (for example, `/var/spool/mail/johnq`).

Outgoing messages go in the `/var/spool/mqueue` directory while waiting to be sent. Filenames in this directory follow a consistent naming scheme. The first two characters indicate what type of data is stored in the file (see Table 19-1). Subsequent characters form a unique random identifier based on the PID of the sendmail process that is handling that message.

Table 19-1: File Prefixes in /var/spool/mqueue

Filename Prefix	Type of Data Stored
df	The data that constitutes the body of an e-mail message.
qf	The queue control file that contains the message headers and other administrative details.
tf	A temporary copy of the qf file, created if delivery errors occur.
xf	Any error messages generated while trying to send the message.

Other programs

Several other executable programs are included in the distribution. These are described in Table 19-2.

Table 19-2: Other Related sendmail Programs

Program	Description
mailq	Displays a summary of the messages awaiting processing in the mail queue (the command is equivalent to `sendmail -bp`).
mailstats	Displays message quantity and byte count statistics.
makemap	Translates text files (`/etc/mail/virtusertable`) to hashed Berkeley databases (`/etc/mail/virtusertable.db`). This command runs each time the sendmail script starts.
newaliases	Translates the plain-text `/etc/aliases` file into the hashed Berkeley database file `/etc/aliases.db` (the command is equivalent to `sendmail -bi`).
praliases	Prints out all aliases defined in `/etc/aliases`.
procmail	Not included with the sendmail package, but is used as an MDA for sendmail. (It is included in Fedora and RHEL in the procmail package.)
purgestat	Clears the directory where host status information is stored. The command is equal to `sendmail -bH`, which is disabled by default.

Program	Description
rmail	Handles incoming mail via UUCP (Unix to Unix Copy).
smrsh	Implements a restricted shell for running programs from sendmail.

Logging performed by sendmail

The amount of logging performed by sendmail is configurable in the `sendmail.mc` file, but the default level provides good coverage of informational notices and error messages. By default, the syslog facility configuration file (`/etc/syslog.conf`) tells syslog to store logging information from sendmail in the `/var/log/maillog` file. A few examples from this file are shown in this section.

An informational message similar to the following is written in the `/var/log/maillog` file each time the daemon starts (which also causes the hashed alias database to be regenerated):

```
May 16 12:52:40 toys sendmail[1758]: alias database /etc/aliases
    rebuilt by root
May 16 12:52:40 toys sendmail[1758]: /etc/aliases: 63 aliases, longest
    10 bytes, 625 bytes total
May 16 12:52:40 toys sendmail[1787]: starting daemon (8.12.8):
    SMTP+queueing@01:00:00
```

Each time a message is sent or received, a log file entry is created:

```
May 16 12:54:34 toys sendmail[1120]: OAA01120: from=root, size=161,
  class=0, pri=3 0161, nrcpts=1,
  msgid=<199907191254.OAA01120@toys.linuxtoys.net>, relay=root@localhost
May 16 12:54:35 toys sendmail[1127]: OAA01120: to=jkpat, ctladdr=root
  (0/0), delay=00:00:01, xdelay=00:00:00, mailer=local, stat=Sent
```

Besides showing normal mail server activities, the logs also show when people attempt to break into your mail server. The `wiz` and `debug` commands were implemented in earlier versions of sendmail and were found to be a huge security problem. You may see log file entries, such as those shown in the following code examples, as people with malicious intent check to make sure that you're not running a vulnerable sendmail daemon. Also, the `expn` and `vrfy` commands (which can be disabled via a configuration option) could give out more information than you'd care to distribute.

```
May 16 13:03:27 toys sendmail[699]: NOQUEUE: "wiz" command from
localhost
    [127.0.0 .1] (127.0.0.1)
May 16 13:03:29 toys sendmail[699]: NOQUEUE: "debug" command from
    localhost [127.0 .0.1] (127.0.0.1)
May 16 13:03:37 toys sendmail[701]: NOQUEUE: localhost [127.0.0.1]:
    expn oracle
May 16 13:03:43 toys sendmail[702]: NOQUEUE: localhost [127.0.0.1]:
    vrfy oracle
```

Configuring sendmail

To configure the sendmail facility, you edit configuration files in /etc/mail and /etc that are then used to by the sendmail start-up script to generate database files. Those database files are, in turn, used by the sendmail daemon to control the behavior of your sendmail server. Once sendmail is configured, you can begin adding user accounts to have mailboxes on your server. The general steps I describe in this section for configuring sendmail are:

1. **Getting a domain name** — You need a unique Internet domain name to assign to your mail server. You can purchase an Internet domain name from one of many different places, and then have DNS mail exchange (MX) records for your domain point to the mail server you are creating.

2. **Configuring basic sendmail settings** — In this step, you edit the /etc/mail/sendmail.mc file. That file defines such things as the locations of other configuration and log files, as well as letting you configure some behavior of the sendmail daemon.

3. **Defining outgoing mail access** — The most critical security issue associated with your mail server is which mail messages it will accept to relay to other mail servers. By editing the /etc/mail/access file, you can indicate the hosts and users from which your server will accept mail for local delivery or relay.

4. **Configuring virtual servers** — By default, sendmail assumes that you are setting up the mail server for the domain of which the server is a member. To have sendmail on a single computer be the mail server for multiple domains (referred to as virtual servers), you need to define each domain name in the /etc/mail/local-host-names file.

5. **Configuring virtual users** — Using the /etc/mail/virtusertable configuration file, you can instruct the sendmail daemon what to do with the mail it receives for the users and domains it's configured to handle. This file gives you a lot of flexibility to take mail addressed to a particular user and direct it to a particular mailbox, forward it to a different mail address, or reject that mail in various ways.

6. **Adding user accounts** — You need to add a user account for every user that has a mailbox on your mail server.

7. **Starting sendmail and generating database files** — Starting the sendmail service causes two major action to happen: it runs the sendmail server daemon and it compiles your configuration files into database files that can be used by sendmail. If the server is already running, you can simply compile the configuration files and have any new settings take effect without restarting the server.

The following subsections provide details on each of these steps.

Getting a domain name

For people to be able to send mail to the users on your mail server, you must have your own domain name. Chapter 25 describes how to get your own domain names and set up a DNS server. The critical issue for your mail server is to make sure that the MX record for your domain on the DNS server points to the address of your mail server.

> **NOTE:** It is possible that your ISP will not allow you to have a private mail server on your residential Internet account. To enforce this, the ISP may block packets from being addressed to port 25. You may need to contact them to open that port before you can set up a mail server on that connection. Because many spamming and otherwise evil (or at least poorly controlled) e-mail servers try to hide behind dynamic IP addresses, many ISPs will neither allow e-mail addresses from dynamic IP addresses nor accept e-mail sent from those servers.

Configuring basic sendmail settings (sendmail.mc)

Much of the configuration of your sendmail server comes from information in your `/etc/mail/sendmail.mc` file. Because this file sets sendmail default values that can be used in most cases, you may not have to do much with `sendmail.mc`. However, I recommend you step through this section so you understand how your mail server is configured.

Changes you make to the `sendmail.mc` file do not immediately take effect. First you must compile the `sendmail.mc` settings to generate the `/etc/mail/sendmail.cf` file. I describe how to do that in the "Starting sendmail and generating database files" section.

The resulting `/etc/mail/sendmail.cf` file contains over 1,800 lines of settings and comments that are used to direct the behavior of your sendmail daemon. The m4 macros you use in the `sendmail.mc` file are different from the resulting settings in the `sendmail.cf` file.

> **NOTE**: The m4 utility can be used to process text files containing macros in IEEE Standard 1003.1-2001 format (Section 12.2, Utility Syntax Guidelines). This compiler is particular about how you use single quotes versus backticks, so be careful editing `sendmail.mc`. For details on the m4 utility, type **info m4**.

To find out which macros to use for a setting you find in the `sendmail.cf` file, refer to the `/usr/share/doc/sendmail*/README.cf` file. If you are interested in details on the contents of your `sendmail.cf` file, I have included an exhaustive description of `sendmail.cf` at the *Fedora 9 and Red Hat Enterprise Linux Bible* Web site (`www.wiley.com/go/fedora9bible`).

> **CAUTION:** Because of the way sendmail is configured in Fedora, you should not directly modify the `sendmail.cf` file. The `sendmail.cf` file is regenerated automatically when sendmail restarts if `sendmail.mc` changes. As a result, any modifications made directly to `sendmail.cf` will be lost.

The following code samples are from the `/etc/mail/sendmail.mc` file that accompanies the Fedora version of sendmail.

> **NOTE:** Lines that begin with dnl (delete to new line) in the sendmail.mc file are comment lines. In most cases, I have left them out in the examples shown. Also, notice that sendmail uses backticks as opening quotes and straight quotes as ending quotes.

```
divert(-1)dnl
include(`/usr/share/sendmail-cf/m4/cf.m4')dnl
VERSIONID(`setup for linux')dnl
OSTYPE(`linux')dnl
```

The first few lines of the sendmail.mc file do some housekeeping. The divert line removes extra output when the configuration file is generated. The include line causes rule sets needed by sendmail to be included. The VERSIONID line identifies the configuration file as being for Linux systems, such as Fedora (although this setting is not checked, so it could be anything you like). The OSTYPE, however, must be set to linux to get the proper location of files needed by sendmail.

```
dnl define(`confSMTP_LOGIN_MSG', `$j Sendmail; $b')dnl
dnl define(`SMART_HOST', `smtp.your.provider')dnl
```

Here are two lines you can consider uncommenting (removing the dnl string). The confSMTP_LOGIN_MSG definition can be used to disguise the mail server you are using (change Sendmail to whatever). As for the second line, by default, the sendmail daemon tries to send your outgoing e-mails directly to the mail server to which they are addressed. If you want all e-mail to be relayed through a particular mail server instead, you can remove the comment (dnl, which stands for "delete to new line") from the beginning of the SMART_HOST line above (leave the one at the end). Then, change smtp.your.provider to the fully qualified domain name of the mail server you want to use. Of course, you need to be sure that the SMART HOST you define will accept relays from your mail server.

```
define(`confDEF_USER_ID', ``8:12'')dnl
```

Instead of running as the root user, the daemon runs as the mail user (UID 8) and mail group (GID 12), based on the confDEF_USER_ID line set previously. This is a good policy, because it prevents someone who might compromise your mail server from gaining root access to your machine.

```
dnl define(`confAUTO_REBUILD')dnl
define(`confTO_CONNECT', `1m')dnl
```

If you remove the initial dnl, the confAUTO_REBUILD line will tell sendmail to rebuild automatically the aliases database, if necessary. The confTO_CONNECT line sets the time sendmail will wait for an initial connection to complete to one minute (1m).

```
define(`confTRY_NULL_MX_LIST', `True')dnl
define(`confDONT_PROBE_INTERFACES', `True')dnl
```

With confTRY_NULL_MX_LIST true, if a receiving server is the best mail exchange (MX) for a host, sendmail will try connecting to that host directly. If confDONT_PROBE_INTERFACES is true, the sendmail daemon will not insert local network interfaces into the list of known equivalent addresses.

```
define(`PROCMAIL_MAILER_PATH', `/usr/bin/procmail')dnl
define(`ALIAS_FILE', `/etc/aliases')dnl
dnl define(`STATUS_FILE', `/var/log/mail/statistics')dnl
```

The next three lines (PROCMAIL_MAILER_PATH, ALIAS_FILE, and STATUS_FILE) set locations for the program that distributes incoming mail (procmail, by default), the mail aliases file, and the mail statistics file, respectively.

```
define(`UUCP_MAILER_MAX', `2000000')dnl
define(`confUSERDB_SPEC', `/etc/mail/userdb.db')dnl
define(`confPRIVACY_FLAGS', `authwarnings,novrfy,noexpn,restrictqrun')dnl
define(`confAUTH_OPTIONS', `A')dnl
```

The UUCP_MAILER_MAX line sets the maximum size (in bytes) for messages received by the UUCP mailer. The confUSERDB_SPEC line sets the location of the user database (where you can override the default mail server for specific users). The confPRIVACY_FLAGS line causes sendmail to insist on certain mail protocols. For example, authwarnings causes X-Authentication-Warning headers to be used and noted in log files. The novrfy and noexpn settings prevent those services from being requested. The restrictqrun option prevents the -q option to sendmail.

```
dnl define(`confAUTH_OPTIONS', `A p')dnl
dnl TRUST_AUTH_MECH(`EXTERNAL DIGEST-MD5 CRAM-MD5 LOGIN PLAIN')dnl
dnl define(`confAUTH_MECHANISMS', `EXTERNAL GSSAPI DIGEST-MD5 CRAM-MD5
    LOGIN PLAIN')dnl

dnl define(`confCACERT_PATH', `/etc/pki/tls/certs')dnl
dnl define(`confCACERT', `/etc/pki/tls/certs/ca-bundle.crt')dnl
dnl define(`confSERVER_CERT', `/etc/pki/tls/certs/sendmail.pem')dnl
dnl define(`confSERVER_KEY', `/etc/pki/tls/certs/sendmail.pem')dnl
dnl define(`confDONT_BLAME_SENDMAIL', `groupreadablekeyfile')dnl
```

Some of the group of lines just shown that begin with dnl (so they are commented out) can be uncommented (remove the initial dnl) to provide certain features. Others are set explicitly. The confAUTH_OPTIONS line can be used to set options used with SMTP authentication. This example (with A and p options) would allow authenticated users with plain text logins to send mail. The TRUST_AUTH_MECH line would cause sendmail to allow authentication mechanisms other than plain passwords (if dnl were removed). The confAUTH_MECHANISMS line can configure the types of authentication mechanisms that can be used (if dnl were removed). The next few lines above set the location of the certificates directory for sendmail to /etc/pki/tls/certs, then identify different files in that directory that hold the certificates and keys needed for authentication. The confDONT_BLAME_SENDMAIL line should be uncommented if the key file needs to be readable by applications other than sendmail. (Typically, you would not want the file to be readable by everyone.)

```
dnl define(`confTO_QUEUEWARN', `4h')dnl
dnl define(`confTO_QUEUERETURN', `5d')dnl
dnl define(`confQUEUE_LA', `12')dnl
dnl define(`confREFUSE_LA', `18')dnl
define(`confTO_IDENT', `0')dnl
```

The commented lines above actually show the default values set for certain timeout conditions. You can remove comments and change these values if you like. The `confTO_QUEUEWARN` option sets how long after delivery of a message has been deferred to send a warning message to the sender. Four hours (`4h`) is the default. The `confTO_QUEUERETURN` option sets how long before an undeliverable message is returned. The `confQUEUE_LA` and `confREFUSE_LA` options set the system load average levels at which mail received is queued or refused, respectively. The `confTO_IDENT` option sets the timeout when waiting for a response to an `IDENT` query to be received (by default it is `0`, which means no timeout).

```
FEATURE(`no_default_msa', `dnl')dnl
FEATURE(`smrsh', `/usr/sbin/smrsh')dnl
FEATURE(`mailertable', `hash -o /etc/mail/mailertable.db')dnl
FEATURE(`virtusertable', `hash -o /etc/mail/virtusertable.db')dnl
FEATURE(redirect)dnl
FEATURE(always_add_domain)dnl
FEATURE(use_cw_file)dnl
FEATURE(use_ct_file)dnl
FEATURE(local_procmail, `', `procmail -t -Y -a $h -d $u')dnl
FEATURE(`access_db', `hash -T<TMPF> -o /etc/mail/access.db')dnl
FEATURE(`blacklist_recipients')dnl
```

The `FEATURE` macro is used to set some special sendmail features. The `no_default_msa` feature tells sendmail not to generate a default MSA daemon (which normally is set to listen on port 587). The `smrsh` feature defines `/usr/sbin/smrsh` as the simple shell used by sendmail to receive commands. The `mailertable` and `virtusertable` options set the locations of the `mailertable` and `virtusertable` databases. The `redirect` option allows you to reject mail for users who have moved and provide new addresses. The `always_add_domain` option causes the local domain name to be added to the hostname on all delivered mail. The `use_cw_file` and `use_ct_file` options tell sendmail to use the file `/etc/mail/local-host-names` for alternative hostnames for this mail server and `/etc/mail/trusted-users` for trusted user names, respectively. (A trusted user can send mail as another user without resulting in a warning message.)

The `local_procmail` option sets the command used to deliver local mail (procmail), as well as options to that command (including the `$h` hostname and `$u` user name). The `access_db` option sets the location of the access database, which identifies which hosts and users are allowed to relay mail through the server. The `blacklist_recipients` option turns on the ability of the server to block incoming mail for selected users, hosts, or addresses. (The `access_db` and `blacklist_recipients` features are useful for blocking spam.)

```
EXPOSED_USER(`root')dnl
DAEMON_OPTIONS(`Port=smtp,Addr=127.0.0.1, Name=MTA')dnl
```

The EXPOSED_USER line allows the root user name to be displayed instead of a masquerade name. As it stands, the DAEMON_OPTIONS line allows only incoming mail created by the local host to be accepted. Be sure to comment this line out if you want to allow incoming mail from the Internet or other network interface (such as the local LAN).

```
FEATURE(`accept_unresolvable_domains')dnl
```

The accept_unresolvable_domains option is on, causing you to accept mail from host computers that don't have resolvable domain names. If you have client computers (such as dial-up computers) that need to use your mail server, leave this option on. Turning it off, however, can help eliminate spam.

```
LOCAL_DOMAIN(`localhost.localdomain')dnl
MAILER(smtp)dnl
MAILER(procmail)dnl
```

The LOCAL_DOMAIN option here causes the name localhost.localdomain to be accepted as a name for your local computer. The last lines in your sendmail.mc file define the mailers to use on your server. The /usr/share/sendmail-cf/mailer directory contains definitions for smtp, procmail, and other mailers. After you have made the changes you want to the sendmail.mc file, you can regenerate the sendmail.cf file as described in the "Starting sendmail and generating database files" section.

Defining outgoing mail access

Every time an e-mail message intended for outgoing mail is received by your sendmail server, the server needs to decide if it will accept or reject relaying of that message. Policies that are too restrictive might prevent legitimate mail from getting out. Policies that are too loose can leave your server open to spammers.

With e-mail abuse the way it is these days, you should run an open relay (where your server simply relays all messages it receives to the requested mail servers). Spammers can use software referred to as spiders to look for open relays. If you leave your mail server open, they will find you quickly and use your machine to relay their spam. The results of a spammer using your machine can include the following:

- **You can end up on blacklists.** Some e-mail blacklist maintainers look for open relays themselves and block them before abuse is even reported. Servers that use those blacklists will block all mail from you, even legitimate e-mail.

- **People will hate you.** Your mail server will be identified as the one sending the spam. As a result, people may retaliate against your server, or at the very least really wish you would stop sending them ads to help them get out of debt or enhance themselves in some way.

- **You face possible fines and jail.** More and more laws are being written to try to stop the spread of spam. You could be found guilty of negligence, or have your machines shut down or confiscated, even if you didn't initiate the spam yourself.

This section describes how to set up the sendmail access file (`/etc/mail/access`) to include a sensible set of rules defining for whom your server will relay mail. Using the `access` file, sendmail can make decisions about whether or not to relay a message based on the sender's host/domain name, IP address, or e-mail address. You can further refine the match by checking for those addresses in Connect, From, or To data associated with the message.

There are then four basic actions you can have the server take on a match:

- **RELAY** — Your mail server could simply send the message on to the mail server requested in the mail message.
- **REJECT** — The message is rejected (not relayed) and the sender is told it was rejected.
- **DISCARD** — The message is silently discarded and the sender is not told.
- **ERROR:** *text you choose* — You can add some informative text here, to give the sender some reason why the relay did not occur.

The `/etc/mail/access` file, by default, relays messages only from users who are directly logged into the mail server (`localhost`). Without being explicitly allowed, users from all other machines are not allowed to relay messages. Here's how the access file is set up by default:

```
localhost.localdomain    RELAY
localhost                RELAY
127.0.0.1                RELAY
```

With these defaults set, only mail sent from the local machine is relayed. So, if the only outgoing mail you send is done while you are logged in directly to the server, you don't need to change this file. The following examples illustrate how you can selectively choose to relay or reject mail received by your sendmail server:

```
Connect:192.168                  RELAY
Connect:linuxtoys.net            RELAY
Connect:spammer-domain.com       REJECT

From:chris@linuxtoys.net         RELAY
To:spidermaker.com               RELAY
To:former-user@linuxtoys.net     ERROR: User no longer works here
```

On the `Connect:192.168` line, the network address (presumably the first part of the IP addresses used on your LAN) is allowed to relay mail. This is a good way to allow everyone sending mail from a machine on the local LAN to have their mail relayed. On the next line (`Connect:linuxtoys.net`), mail coming from any machine in the named domain is allowed to be relayed. The third line represents a domain that you know to be a spam relay, so you reject messages originating from that domain.

The next three lines indicate how to treat mail received for relaying, based on the From and To names associated with the message. As you can see, the first example allows relay of any messages from chris@linuxtoys.net. In the last example, mail being forwarded to a particular person (*former-user*@linuxtoys.net) is rejected and a custom error message (in this case `User no longer works here`) is sent back to the sender.

> **NOTE:** Use some caution when you are creating relay rules based on user e-mail address. Because those values are reported by the users themselves, they are vulnerable to being spoofed.

Once you have adjusted this file to suit you, you must rebuild the access database (`access.db` file) for the changes to take effect. See "Starting sendmail and generating database files" for information on this topic.

Configuring virtual servers

If you have set up a sendmail mail server for one domain, it's quite possible that you will someday want to have multiple domains served from that same computer. To create virtual servers on the same computer, you must add the name of every domain being served to the `/etc/mail/local-host-names` file.

For example, if your sendmail server were handling e-mail accounts for `linuxtoys.net`, `example.com`, and `example.net` domains, the `local-host-names` file would appear as follows:

```
# local-host-names - include all aliases for your machine here.
linuxtoys.net
example.com
example.net
```

Even if you are serving only one domain with your mail server, it is a good idea to identify that domain in this file. When messages come to the server for the domains listed here, sendmail knows to try to deliver the messages locally. Sendmail interprets messages for domains not listed here as needing to be relayed.

> **NOTE:** If you want to off-load the processing of mail for a particular domain that is currently being directed to your sendmail server, you can use the `/etc/mail/mailertable` file. After setting up a DNS MX record to point to your sendmail server for this domain, and listing that domain name in the `mailertable` file, you can identify another computer that sendmail will forward all the traffic to for that domain. For example:
>
> ```
> example.com        smtp:mx1.linuxtoys.net
> ```

This example shows that all messages destined for example.com that are received by your sendmail server are forwarded to the server named `mx1.linuxtoys.net`. The `smtp` indicates that the server supports Simple Mail Transfer Protocol.

Configuring virtual users

Incoming mail to your sendmail server will be directed to your machine with a request to deliver the message to a particular person at a particular domain name. For each domain that the sendmail server supports, you can identify how e-mail to mail recipients of that domain is treated.

With sendmail, you set up virtual user definitions in the `/etc/mail/virtusertable` file. Essentially, you are telling sendmail to redirect messages addressed to particular user names or domain names based on definitions you set up.

Configuring the `virtusertable` file is particularly important if your server is handling mail for multiple domains. That's because, by default, mail for the same user name (regardless of the domain name) will be stored in the same mailbox. For example, if your server handles mail for `example.com` and `linuxtoys.net` domains, mail for `chris@example.com` and `chris@linuxtoys.net`, would all be directed to `/var/spool/mail/chris` mailbox. With the `virtusertable` file, you can change that behavior in a lot of ways.

The `virtusertable` file is empty by default. The following are some examples that illustrate how incoming messages can be directed in different ways based on `virtusertable` definitions.

```
chris@linuxtoys.net        chris
cnegus@linuxtoys.net       chris
francois@linuxtoys.net     francois@spidermaker.com
info@linuxtoys.net         info-list
bogus@linuxtoys.net        error:nouser No such user here
@example.net               example-catchall
@example.com               %1@linuxtoys.net
```

In the first two lines, incoming mail destined for `chris` or `cnegus` at `linuxtoys.net` is directed to the mailbox for the local mail server user named `chris`. In the next line, any e-mail directed to `francois` in the same domain goes to `francois@spidermaker.com`. After that, e-mail sent to the info user name is saved to the local `info-list` mail account.

The line beginning with `bogus@linuxtoys.net` illustrates an error condition. Here, e-mail destined for the user named `bogus` will be rejected with the error message `No such user here` being directed back to the sender. Besides creating custom error messages, you can also use any Enhanced Mail System Status codes that are compliant with RFC 1893.

> **NOTE:** In general, it's not a good idea to tell a potential spammer that a user account doesn't exist. Spammers often query mail servers looking for such information, often addressing e-mail to common names in an attempt to determine what real users exist on the server. As a general rule, try to give as little information as possible to someone phishing for information on your mail server.

The last two lines (beginning with @example.net and @example.com) illustrate how e-mail for all recipients for a given domain can all be directed to the same place. In the first case, all example.net messages go into the mailbox for the user named example-catchall. The last line shows how the users from a particular domain can all be mapped into their same user name (%1) on a selected domain name.

Once you have made changes to this file to suit you, you must rebuild the virtusertable database (virtusertable.db file) for the changes to take effect. See "Starting sendmail and generating database files" for information on this topic.

Adding user accounts

Ultimately, the e-mail received by your mail server is placed in a user's mailbox, where the user can pick it up and read it at his or her leisure. Each of those user names must be added as a real user on your Fedora system. For example, to add the user chris to your Fedora sendmail server, you could type (as root user):

```
# useradd -s /sbin/nologin chris
```

This action creates a user account named chris in the /etc/passwd file, sets the shell to /sbin/nologin, and creates a mail box for that user in /var/spool/mail/chris. The /sbin/nologin shell prevents the user from logging in to a shell (which is a good security practice when you only want a user to have mail or FTP access, for example). Now, sendmail can direct e-mail to that user's mail box.

For that user to be able to access his e-mail later from his POP3 client, he will need a password for his user account. Set the password for that user with the passwd command as follows:

```
# passwd chris
Changing password for user chris
New UNIX password: ********
Retype new UNIX password: ********
passwd: all authentication tokens updated successfully
```

Make sure that the user has this user account name and password so it can be configured into the user's e-mail client.

Starting sendmail and generating database files

None of the configuration that you just did to your sendmail.mc, virtusertable, access, domaintable, and mailertable configuration files take effect until they are regenerated into database (.db) files. There are a few different ways you can go about loading your configuration files into database files:

- **Restarting sendmail** — Each time you reboot your computer or restart the sendmail daemon (`service sendmail restart`), all sendmail configuration files (including `sendmail.mc`) are compiled into database files that are ready to be used by the sendmail server. You can also just rebuild the databases without stopping the sendmail daemon (including the `/etc/aliases.db` file) using the sendmail startup script. To simply rebuild the database type:

```
# /etc/init.d/sendmail reload
```

  This command rebuilds all the database files, including the `/etc/aliases` file. (If the reload doesn't update your `sendmail.cf` file, be sure that the sendmail-cf package is installed: `yum install sendmail-cf`.)

- **Making the configuration files** — Using the `make` command, you can have some or all of the configuration files made into database files, so they become immediately usable by the sendmail daemon. To do that, change to the `/etc/mail` directory, and then type either **make all** or **make** with the target database file you are creating. For example:

```
# cd /etc/mail
# make virtusertable.db
```

  You can replace `virtusertable.db` with `access.db`, `domaintable.db`, `mailertable.db`, or `sendmail.db`. (Note that you use the `.db` target name and not the name of the original configuration file.) As mentioned, you can also use the `make all` command to rebuild all database files.

At this point, your sendmail server should be up and running. You can test your server by sending mail to it and checking log files to see how the server reacted. Make sure that your firewall allows requests on TCP port 25. Then check that your mail server is responding to requests by typing the following:

```
# telnet 127.0.0.1 25
Trying 127.0.0.1...
Connected to localhost.localdomain (127.0.0.1).
Escape character is '^]'.
220 toys.linuxtoys.net ESMTP Sendmail 8.14.1/8.14.1;
    Sun, 15 Jun 2008 03:34:02 -0500
```

You can see that the sendmail daemon is running and responding to port number 25. Try typing **HELO**. (That's literally HELO and not HELLO.) When you are done, type **QUIT** to exit.

NOTE: For more information on troubleshooting your mail server, refer to *Linux Troubleshooting Bible*, from Wiley Publishing.

Redirecting mail

At times, your e-mail users may want to redirect mail to some place other than their own mailboxes on the local server. Each user can redirect his or her mail using the `.forward` file. System-wide, you as the administrator can set aliases to redirect mail in the `/etc/aliases` file.

The .forward file

One way for users to redirect their own mail is through the use of the `.forward` file, which users can place in their own home directories (for example, `/home/jkpat/.forward`). The format of a plain-text `.forward` file is a comma-separated list of mail recipients. Common uses of the `.forward` file include:

- Piping mail to a program to filter the mailbox contents:

  ```
  "| /usr/bin/procmail"
  ```

- Sending mail destined for one user (for example, jkpat) to another (for example, cht09, on a different machine in this case):

  ```
  cht09@other.mybox.com
  ```

- Delivering mail to the local user (jkpat again) *and* sending it to two others (cht09 and brannigan):

  ```
  \jkpat, cht09@other.mybox.com, \brannigan
  ```

> **TIP:** You are not allowed to have a `.forward` file in a directory that can be read by all users. If you leave permissions open on a `.forward` file, sendmail will ignore that file and not forward mail as you want. To allow `.forward` files with open permissions to be used by sendmail, you can remove the `dnl` from the `confDONT_BLAME_SENDMAIL` line in the `sendmail.mc` file.

The aliases file

A more flexible method of handling mail delivery (system-wide rather than being specific to one particular user) involves the `/etc/aliases` file, which is also a plain-text file. The aliases file contains a name followed by a colon, and then a user name, another alias, a list of addresses, a file, or a program to which mail will be delivered. The name to the left of the colon (which can be a valid user name or just an alias) can then be used as an e-mail recipient on the local machine or on a remote machine.

Some aliases are already set by default in `/etc/aliases`. For example, because there are a lot of administrative users defined in Fedora (bin, adm, lp, and so on), instead of having separate mailboxes for each one, messages for all of them are directed to the root user's mailbox as follows:

```
bin:        root
daemon:     root
```

```
adm:           root
lp:            root
```

Using the aliases file for mail-aliasing allows for several extensions to normal mail-handling behavior:

- You can use the aliases file yourself to create mini-mailing lists. Here's an example:

```
info-list:  chris, tweeks, francois@spidermaker.com
```

  In this example, any messages sent to `info-list` are distributed to `chris`, `tweeks`, and `francois@spidermaker.com`. Notice that the user list can be a combination of local users and outside mail addresses.

- One account can receive mail under several different names:

```
patterson: jkpat
```

  This indicates that any mail addressed to `patterson@mybox.com` (just an alias) will arrive in the mailbox of jkpat (an actual user account).

- Mail can be received under a name that isn't a valid (or reasonable) user name:

```
eric.foster-johnson@objectpartners.com: efjohnson
```

  He may not want to type eric.foster-johnson as a user name, but that doesn't mean he can't receive mail as such.

- Messages intended for one user can be redirected to another account (or to several accounts):

```
oldemployee: bradford
consultant: bradford, jackson, patterson
users: :include:/root/mail/lists/users
```

  Here, any message for `oldemployee@mybox.com` would be delivered to the mailbox of user bradford. Also, the users bradford, jackson, and patterson would receive any mail addressed to consultant. The third line indicates that the recipients of the "users" alias are specified in the file `/root/mail/lists/users`.

- Mail can be sent directly to a file on the local machine:

```
acsp-bugs: /dev/null
trouble-ticket: /var/spool/trouble/incoming
```

  In the first line, because the fictional ACSP program is no longer used on the machine, there's no need to track its errors, so the mail is effectively ignored. The second line stores incoming trouble tickets in the `/var/spool/trouble/incoming` file. Remember that if you enable this, anyone anywhere can send you a sufficiently large message to fill up the partition on which that directory resides. This is a security risk and should be carefully evaluated before being implemented.

When you are done adding new aliases, type the following to have those changes take effect:

```
# newaliases
```

> **TIP:** When resolving addresses, sendmail doesn't actually use the /etc/aliases text file. For faster access, the text file is turned into a Berkeley database file, /etc/aliases.db, which resolves aliased addresses. For this reason, the newaliases command (equivalent to sendmail -bi) must be run to rebuild the database file each time the /etc/aliases text file is modified. This happens automatically each time sendmail is restarted.

Introducing Postfix

Postfix is a Mail Transfer Agent that you can use in place of sendmail to handle mail service on your Fedora or Red Hat Enterprise Linux system. There are several reasons that Postfix proponents give for using Postfix instead of sendmail for their mail service:

- Postfix is designed to be easier to administer. Instead of using m4 syntax in the sendmail.mc file, Postfix uses the same types of directives used in the Apache Web server.

- Postfix has multiple layers of security built in, including the ability to run in a chroot jail. It also filters any sender-provided information before exporting that information into the Postfix environment.

Although some of the configuration files and other components are different from those in sendmail, many are meant to replace sendmail components (such as aliases, access, and .forward files, as well as the /var/mail directory structure). To help you make the transition to Postfix from sendmail, Fedora and RHEL have configured the two packages to use the alternatives system. Chapter 10 describes how to use the Mail Transport Agent Switcher to change from one transport to the other.

When you switch to Postfix and start the Postfix daemon, as described in Chapter 10, Postfix takes over as the MTA, replaces sendmail components with Postfix components, and uses some of the same locations for mailboxes and log files. Postfix takes over mail transport based on configuration files set in the /etc/postfix directory. The following is an overview of the default locations used by the Postfix service:

- **Mail configuration** (/etc/postfix/main.cf) — The primary configuration file for Postfix. Identifies the locations of Postfix queues, commands, and aliases, as well as defining the host and domain names that Postfix is serving. If you do not add a fully qualified domain name to this file, Postfix will use your local hostname as the name of the mail service it represents.

- **Mailboxes** (/var/spool/mail) — Directory containing incoming mail files, with each user's mailbox represented by a file of the user's name. (This is the same default spool directory used by sendmail.)

- **Mail queue** (`/var/spool/postfix`) — Location of directories where mail messages are queued for delivery.

- **Mail log** (`/var/log/maillog`) — Location of mail log files.

Although most options you need for Postfix are described in the `/etc/postfix/main.cf` file, you can see many more available options in the `main.cf.default` file in the same directory. Based on the default configuration in the `main.cf` file, here is how Postfix will handle outbound and incoming mail:

- **Outbound mail** — The local hostname is added as the sending host for the mail posted from this computer. You might want to change it to the local domain name (set `myorigin = $mydomain`).

- **Incoming mail** — Only mail destined for the local hostname is kept on the local server by default. Other mail is forwarded. To have all mail for your domain kept on the local server, add $mydomain to the `mydestination` line.

For complete information on configuring Postfix, refer to `www.postfix.org/docs.html`.

Stopping Spam with SpamAssassin

Despite the fact that it is rude and antisocial, there are people who send out thousands of unsolicited e-mail messages (referred to as spam), hoping to get a few responses. Due to the economics of the Internet, spammers can send out literally millions of messages. A very small number of respondents is enough to make a profit for the spammers. Furthermore, modern spam can be dangerous, including messages designed to fool users into entering user names and passwords (called *phishing*) or messages that try to exploit vulnerable systems (particularly Windows systems).

Because Linux systems are often used as mail servers, tools for scanning mail messages for spam and viruses have become quite sophisticated over the years. In this chapter, I describe how to use a tool called SpamAssassin to deal with spam and viruses on your mail server. If this doesn't meet your needs, here are a few links where you can learn about the ClamAV virus scanner and how to use it with different mail software:

- **ClamAV** (`www.clamav.net`) — Command-line virus scanner with database update features. The clamav package is in the Fedora repository (`yum install clamav`).

- **Klamav** (`http://klamav.sourceforge.net/klamavwiki/index.php`) — The KDE version of ClamAV (`yum install klamav`).

- **Third-party ClamAV Apps** (`www.clamav.net/3rdparty.html`) — Find links to third-party software that works with ClamAV.

Using SpamAssassin

With SpamAssassin, you can configure your incoming mail service to tag messages it believes to be spam so you and your users can deal with those messages as you choose.

There are several methods that SpamAssassin uses to identify spam:

- **Checking mail headers** — Examining the headers of your incoming mail to look for well-known tricks used to make the e-mail look valid.

- **Checking mail text** — Looking for text style, content, and disclaimers in message bodies that are commonly used in spam.

- **Checking blacklists** — Checking blacklists to find e-mail sent from sites known before to relay spam. (The `mail-abuse.com` site provides a search tool for checking if a server at a particular IP address has been blacklisted. To use that tool, go to `www.mail-abuse.com/cgi-bin/lookup`.)

- **Checking spam signatures** — Comparing e-mail signatures. Because spam often consists of the exact same message sent thousands of times, taking signatures of spam messages lets SpamAssassin compare your message to a database of known spam messages. SpamAssassin uses Vipul's Razor (see `http://razor.sourceforge.net`).

Although there are many different ways to deal with spam (or rather, e-mail that *might* be spam), most of the experts I have consulted like to configure SpamAssassin to simply tag incoming e-mail messages that appear to be spam. Then they encourage each user of the e-mail server to create his or her own rules for filtering the spam.

> **NOTE:** Although the procedure here describes how to use SpamAssassin from the RPM package that comes with the latest version of Fedora, many people get their version of SpamAssassin directly from the `SpamAssassin.org` Web site. Because anti-spam software is evolving so quickly (to keep ahead of spammers), some people like to make sure they have the very latest software. Instructions for installing spamassassin from source code are available from the SpamAssassin download page: `http://spamassassin.apache.org/downloads.cgi`. Typically you can simply run the `rpmbuild -tb` command on the Mail-Spamassassin tar file to create a new RPM.

Setting up SpamAssassin on your mail server

Here's a quick procedure for enabling SpamAssassin and having your users choose what to do with spam messages that are encountered:

1. Configure your Mail Transport Agent (sendmail or Postfix) to use the `procmail` command as its mailer. For sendmail, it is already configured as the default mailer, based on the following line in the `/etc/mail/sendmail.mc` file:

```
FEATURE(local_procmail,`',`procmail -t -Y -a $h -d $u')dnl
```

2. Make sure that the SpamAssassin `spamd` daemon is running (it should already be on for run levels 2-5), and if it isn't, start it by typing the following (as root user):

```
# chkconfig --list spamassassin
spamassassin  0:off  1: off  2:on  3:on  4:on  5:on  6:off
# chkconfig spamassassin on
```

3. Create an `/etc/procmailrc` file (using any text editor, as root user). This `procmailrc` file example pipes all mail messages received by procmail through `spamc` (which is the client side of the `spamd` daemon turned on in the previous step):

```
:0fw
| /usr/bin/spamc
```

If you like, you can do a lot more in the `procmailrc` file to deal with spam on a system-wide basis. You could, for example, create procmail recipes that take reported spam e-mail messages and sorts them into a system-wide spam folder or deletes them completely. Likewise, each user can create an individual `$HOME/.procmailrc` file to create personal procmail recipes. (Type **man procmailex** for examples of rules in a `procmailrc` file.)

4. Check the `/etc/mail/spamassassin/local.cf` file. This file contains rules that are used system-wide by SpamAssassin, unless they are overridden by a user's individual `$HOME/.spamassassin/user_prefs.cf` file. Here are the contents of the `local.cf` file:

```
required_hits 5
report_safe 0
rewrite_header Subject [SPAM]
```

In SpamAssassin, a scoring system is used to guess at whether a particular message is spam or not. The `required_hits` line shows that a score of 5 is needed to flag the message as spam. You should set that higher for a public mail server (such as 8 or 10). Setting `rewrite_header` to [SPAM] has SpamAssassin add the text [SPAM] to the Subject line of spam it finds. (Type **man Mail::SpamAssassin::Conf** to see other settings you can use in the `local.cf` file.)

Because false-positives sometimes occur, you risk preventing your users from seeing an e-mail they need if you do system-wide filtering. To avoid this problem, the approach shown here lets the user decide what to do with e-mail tagged as spam. Users can even adjust their own threshold for when a message is believed to be spam.

Next, you should have the users of that mail server set up their own user preferences in their home directories. The preferences set in each user's `$HOME/.spamassassin/user_prefs.cf` file help tell SpamAssassin how to behave for that user's e-mail. Here are examples of lines a user might want to have in that file:

```
required_score          3
whitelist_from          jsmith@example.com bjones@example.net
blacklist_from          *.example.org
```

The `required_score` line (which is set to 5 by default, but set to 3 here) sets the score needed to consider the message to be spam. Scores are based on matching or not matching criteria in the tests SpamAssassin performs. (See `http://spamassassin.org/tests.html`.)

The `whitelist_from` and `blacklist_from` lines let you set addresses for people, individual hosts, or entire domains that should not be considered as spam (`whitelist_from`) or should always be considered as spam (`blacklist_from`). For other ways to modify SpamAssassin behavior, type the following command:

```
man Mail::SpamAssassin::Conf
```

At this point, SpamAssassin should be running and identifying spam based on input from you and the people using your e-mail server. Next, each user needs to decide what to do with the messages that are marked as spam, as described in the following section.

> **TIP:** Techniques you can use along with SpamAssassin include services such as SpamCop. SpamCop (`www.spamcop.net`) provides a service that allows you to enter spam messages you receive into a database that helps others block the same spam messages.

Setting e-mail readers to filter spam

Each user can turn on filtering in his or her e-mail reader to decide what to do with each message tagged as spam by SpamAssassin. A common practice is to direct e-mail marked as spam to a separate folder. Because some real mail can occasionally be mistakenly marked as spam, you can check the spam folder every week or two, just to make sure you don't miss anything.

Here's an example of how to add a filter rule from Evolution Email:

1. Create a folder labeled SPAM under your incoming mailbox.

2. Click Edit → Message Filters.

3. From the Filters window, click Add. An Add Rule window appears.

4. Identify a rule name (such as Spam) that adds a criterion that looks for a specific header (X-Spam-Flag) containing specific text (YES). Then under Add Action, select an action (Move to Folder) and identify the folder to contain the spam messages (SPAM).

When you ask to receive mail from your mail server, all messages with the X-Spam-Flag set to `yes` are sorted into your SPAM folder. As an alternative, you can check for the text `[SPAM]` to appear in the subject line as the criterion for sorting the spam messages.

Other mail readers (Sea Monkey mail, pine, Netscape mail, and others) also include features for filtering and sorting e-mail based on criteria you enter.

A fairly new feature in Evolution includes some SpamAssassin features within the Evolution framework. Evolution runs a daemonized version of SpamAssassin using the spamd daemon. The spamd daemons automatically filter your mail to find junk mail. When it finds junk mail, it automatically puts it into the Junk folder in the Evolution window. You can ignore those messages or simply scan through them quickly and delete them.

Getting Mail from the Server (POP3 or IMAPv4)

After you have set up your mail server, you will want to let users access their e-mail from that server. That means either having each user log in to the mail server to read his or her e-mail or, more likely, configuring POP3 or IMAPv4 to let users access their mail from their workstations. Here are descriptions of POP3 and IMAPv4:

- **POP3** — With POP3, users download and manage their e-mail messages on their local workstations. POP3 is simpler and requires fewer server resources.

- IMAPv4 — With IMAPv4, messages stay on the server, although you can manipulate those messages from the mail client. Because the messages stay on the server, an IMAPv4 server requires more disk space and uses more CPU. However, you do have the advantage of logging in to different workstations to read your mail and having the mail and folders you have set up appear the same. With all the e-mail on the server, an administrator needs to back up only one machine to keep permanent records of everyone's e-mail.

Fedora comes with software that is able to provide POP3 and IMAPv4 service. The dovecot package is primarily an IMAPv4 server that also contains a small POP3 server. It supports mail in both maildir (where each mail account can contain multiple folders on the server) and mbox (where all messages are in a single file) formats.

This section describes how to use POP3 to allow the users of your mail server to download their mail messages from your server over the network. POP3 is the simpler of the two protocols for accessing mailboxes over networks.

Accessing mailboxes in Linux

When e-mail messages are received on your sendmail or postfix mail server, they are sorted to separate files, each of which represents a user's mailbox. The default location of mailbox files is the /var/spool/mail directory. So the login account jsmith would have a mailbox:

```
/var/spool/mail/jsmith
```

While logged into the mail server, jsmith could simply type **mail** from a Terminal window to read his e-mail (using the simple, text-based mail command). However, because most people prefer to get their e-mail from the comfort of their own desktop computer, you can set up either Post Office Protocol (POP3) or Internet Message Access Protocol (IMAPv4).

POP3 and IMAPv4 servers listen on the network for requests for a user's e-mail, and then either download the entire contents of the mailbox to the user's mail reader (as with POP3) or let the user manage the messages while the messages stay on the server (as with IMAPv4).

Typically, your mail server will be configured to use either POP3 or IMAPv4 to provide e-mail messages to your users (although it is possible to have both running on the same machine).

The next section explains how to set up an IMAPv4 or POP3 service to allow access to e-mail accounts.

> **TIP:** At times, you may want to check your e-mail on a computer that is not your regular computer, but be able to save messages later. In that case, most mail readers let you choose a setting that copies the e-mail messages without deleting them from your POP3 server. That way, when you get back to your regular computer, you can copy the messages again. IMAPv4 avoids that problem by always keeping the mail messages on the server and letting the user create and work with additional folders on the server.

Configuring IMAPv4 and POP3 with dovecot

When a user is added to Fedora, a mailbox is configured under that user name in the `/var/spool/mail` directory (such as `/var/spool/mail/chris`). The format of that file, by default, is the traditional `mbox` format, with all messages and attachments stored in that one file. By configuring the POP3 service on your mail server, users will be able to download their e-mail messages from e-mail clients on other machines. By configuring IMAPv4, users can work with messages and folders directly on the server.

The following procedure describes how to configure the IMAPv4 or POP3 service in Fedora using dovecot.

1. Review the values set in the `/etc/dovecot.conf` file. For this example, I assume the defaults, so you can try dovecot without changing anything in this file. For the purpose of this example, the POP3 protocol is enabled, plain-text passwords are enabled from the standard `/etc/passwd` file, and PAM is used for anthentication. Read through the comments in the file to see if there are any settings you want to change.

2. Turn on the dovecot service by typing the following (as root user):

   ```
   # chkconfig dovecot on
   ```

   (If dovecot is not installed, install it by typing **yum install dovecot**.)

3. Start the POP3 service immediately by starting up the dovecot service as follows:

   ```
   # /etc/init.d/dovecot start
   ```

4. Open port 110 on your firewall to allow other computers to request POP3 service on your mail server. If you were using POP3 with SSL support, you would open port 995 instead

(or port 993 for IMAPv4 over SSL). An easy way to open a port is through the Security Level and Firewall window (select System →Administration →Security Level and Firewall). Select Other ports and click the Add button to add 110 as the port and TCP and UDP as the protocols.

All users who have user accounts on your mail server are configured, by default, to accept e-mail. For example, if e-mail comes in to the `mail.handsonhistory.com` server for a user named jsmith, the message is copied to the `/var/spool/mail/jsmith` file on the server. Continuing the example, the user named jsmith could set up his mail reader as follows:

- **Mail server:** mail.handsonhistory.com
- **User name:** jsmith
- **Password:** *theuserspassword*
- **Protocol:** POP3

After the mail reader is configured, when jsmith clicks Send & Receive from his mail reader, all e-mail messages in the `/var/spool/mail/jsmith` file are downloaded to his local mail reader. The messages are then erased from the server.

> **NOTE:** Keep in mind that regular POP3 and IMAPv4 service uses plain text protocols to carry user names and passwords across the network. Depending on your network environment, this may pose a security threat.

Getting Mail from Your Browser with SquirrelMail

Once your mail server is up and running, you can configure SquirrelMail to allow the users of your mail server to get their mail from their Web browsers. To use SquirrelMail, you must install the squirrelmail package from the Fedora installation DVD that comes with this book (or type **yum install squirrelmail**). Also, to use SquirrelMail, you need to have configured and started the following components:

- Mail server (sendmail or postfix)
- IMAPv4 server (dovecot)
- Web server (httpd)
- User accounts that will read mail through SquirrelMail

SquirrelMail has a very intuitive, menu-based administrative interface. That interface includes a variety of plug-ins you can add to SquirrelMail, to use features such as spell checking, calendar, password changing, and fetching mail from a POP3 server. You can get more plug-ins from `squirrelmail.org` as well.

To configure SquirrelMail, type the following as root user from a Terminal window:

```
# /usr/share/squirrelmail/config/conf.pl
```

Features you might want to consider tuning include: Organization Preferences (such as the organization's name and logo to put into the SquirrelMail interface), Themes (more than two dozen are available), and Plugins (just check whether any of those that are available to install are interesting).

Also, by default, mail can be accessed only from a browser on the local host, so you will probably want to change Server Settings. For example, change the Domain name to the name of the domain from which you will allow users to access their mail.

For users to get to mail using squirrelmail, they simply need to type the following address into the location box of their Web browser (replacing *server* with `localhost` or the name of the computer, if you are running this outside of the localhost):

```
http://server/webmail
```

Figure 19-1 shows an example of the webmail browser interface with the webmail logo replaced with the logo from my organization (in this case, LinuxToys.net).

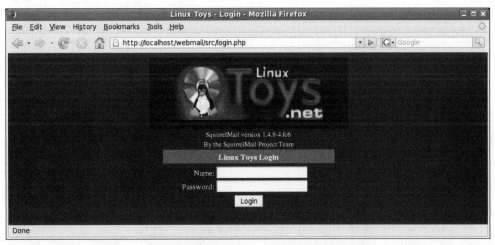

Figure 19-1: Add a logo to SquirrelMail and let users log in from the Web to get mail.

Type your user name and password. Your mailbox should appear, as illustrated in Figure 19-2.

Administering a Mailing List with mailman

Mailman is a popular open source package for managing e-mail discussion lists. Besides offering flexible administrative interfaces for setting up and managing lists, it also has Web-based interfaces that make it easy for people to join lists, access discussion list archives, and tune their own preferences.

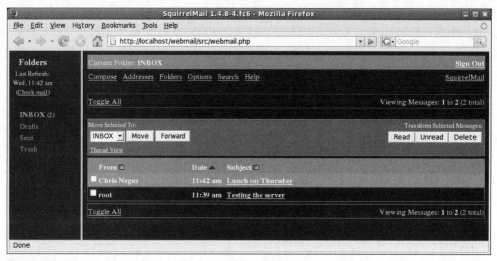

Figure 19-2: Manage your mail from multiple folders in SquirrelMail.

If you need more information about configuring mailman, there are plenty of places to go. Check the mailman Web site at www.gnu.org/software/mailman/mailman.html. Also view README files in /usr/share/doc/mailman-*.

> **NOTE:** If you used mailman previously in an earlier version of Fedora or Red Hat Linux, note that the mailman installation directory has moved from /var/mailman to /usr/lib/mailman. If you made any changes to files in the /var/mailman directory, you need to move those files to the /var/lib/mailman directory after you upgrade the mailman software package.

The following is a brief procedure for configuring a discussion list using mailman:

1. Install the mailman RPM from the Fedora DVD or type **yum install mailman**.

2. Start your Web server (if it isn't already running) as follows:

    ```
    # service httpd start
    # chkconfig httpd on
    ```

3. Create a password for your site as follows:

    ```
    # /usr/lib/mailman/bin/mmsitepass
    New site password: *****
    Again to confirm password: *****
    ```

4. Edit the /usr/lib/mailman/Mailman/mm_cfg.py file and change the DEFAULT_URL_HOST and DEFAULT_EMAIL_HOST values. For example, the hostname of the computer I'm configuring my mailing list on is toys.linuxtoys.net. The default e-mail host is linuxtoys.net. The values would appear as follows:

    ```
    DEFAULT_EMAIL_HOST   = 'toys.linuxtoys.net'
    DEFAULT_URL_HOST DEF = 'linuxtoys.net'
    ```

You can leave these values as `fqdn` to simply use the local computer's fully qualified domain name.

5. Edit the `/etc/httpd/conf.d/mailman.conf` file. To cause queries to mailman to go to the listinfo page, uncomment the `RedirectMatch` line at the bottom of the file and change that line to include your fully qualified domain name. For example, when I did this for the linuxtoys.net mailing list, the line appeared as follows:

```
RedirectMatch ^/mailman[/]*$ http://www.linuxtoys.net/mailman/listinfo
```

6. To create a mailman mailing list, you must first create an unpopulated mailing list called mailman. Along with that list, you must assign the e-mail and initial password for the person responsible for administering the list. To do that, type the following:

```
# /usr/lib/mailman/bin/newlist mailman
Enter the email of the person running the list: chris@linuxtoys.net
Initial mailman password: ********
Hit enter to notify mailman owner...
```

7. Start the mailman service as follows:

```
# service mailman start
# chkconfig mailman on
```

8. Create a new mailing list, using the `newlist` command as follows:

```
# /usr/lib/mailman/bin/newlist
Enter the name of the list: pro
Enter the email of the person running the list: chris@linuxtoys.net
Initial pro password: *****
To finish creating your mailing list, you must edit /etc/aliases (or
equivalent) file by adding the following lines, and running the
`newaliases' program:

## pro mailing list
pro:              "|/usr/lib/mailman/mail/mailman post pro"
pro-admin:        "|/usr/lib/mailman/mail/mailman admin pro"
pro-bounces:      "|/usr/lib/mailman/mail/mailman bounces pro"
pro-confirm:      "|/usr/lib/mailman/mail/mailman confirm pro"
pro-join:         "|/usr/lib/mailman/mail/mailman join pro"
pro-leave:        "|/usr/lib/mailman/mail/mailman leave pro"
pro-owner:        "|/usr/lib/mailman/mail/mailman owner pro"
pro-request:      "|/usr/lib/mailman/mail/mailman request pro"
pro-subscribe:    "|/usr/lib/mailman/mail/mailman subscribe pro"
pro-unsubscribe:  "|/usr/lib/mailman/mail/mailman unsubscribe pro"
```

9. Copy and paste the text just shown (starting from the line `## projectlist mailing list`) into the end of your `/etc/aliases` file.

10. Run the `newaliases` command. At this point you should be able to view the new mailing list from your Web browser. From a Web browser on the local system, type the following name in the address box:

```
http://localhost/mailman/listinfo
```

11. If everything appears to be working, begin adding more mailing lists. In my example, I created a mailing list called projectlist. The name of that project appears on the list shown in Figure 19-3.

12. Select that project name (click on it). The Info page should appear for the project.

13. Scroll to the bottom of that page and click on the project administrative interface link.

14. When prompted, type in the List Administrator Password. Now you can configure the look, feel, and behavior of your mailing list. Important information you will want to consider includes:

   - **Privacy options** — Do you want the list to be public or private (as in, just within your organization)? Who do you want to allow to see your member list?

   - **Send filters** — Who can post messages to the list? Is the list moderated or unmoderated? Might the list just go in one direction, for example, as a way to contact customers?

   - **Membership management** — Can your members see other member information? What are your policies for adding and removing members?

15. When you are finished configuring the options, be sure to submit your changes.

At this point, you can allow users to join the list. Encourage them to explore and set their own user preferences.

If you encounter problems configuring mailman, refer to the `INSTALL.REDHAT` and `README` files in the `/usr/share/doc/mailman-*` directory.

Figure 19-3: Create multiple mailing lists in mailman.

Summary

Fedora includes a full range of tools for configuring and managing mail servers. For Mail Transfer Agents, Fedora includes the sendmail and Postfix software packages. Both are considered to be excellent, professional-quality mail servers.

To allow users to access their mailboxes from the server, Fedora includes the dovecot package. That package implements POP3 and IMAPv4 protocols to allow e-mail to be downloaded or manipulated on the server. You can also configure SquirrelMail to allow users to access their mail through a Web-based interface.

Information is included to help keep your mail service safe from intruders. In particular, filtering software such as SpamAssassin and virus scanner software such as Clamav are critical to keeping your mail service clients safe from harm.

To set up mailing lists in Fedora, you can use the mailman package. In addition to including some very flexible configuration tools, mailman also provides simple Web-based access to mailing list preferences and archives.

Chapter 20

Setting Up an FTP Server

In This Chapter

- Understanding FTP servers
- Using the vsFTPd FTP server
- Getting more information about FTP servers

File Transfer Protocol (FTP) has been the standard method for sharing files over the Internet for many years. Even with the popularity of the Web, which made document database services such as Gopher and WAIS obsolete, FTP servers are still the most common way to make directories of documents and software available to the public over the Internet.

File-sharing applications, such as NFS and Samba, are excellent tools for sharing files and directories over a private network. For organizations that need to share large numbers of files over public networks, however, FTP server software provides more robust tools for sharing files and protecting your computer systems. Also, FTP client software (for accessing FTP servers) is available for any type of computer that can access a network.

This chapter describes how to set up and maintain an FTP server using the Very Secure FTP Server package (vsFTPd).

Configuring your FTP server to allow users to upload files to your server involves more risk than just allowing downloads. Anyone could upload a malicious file, overwrite other files, or depending on the configuration, place a file in an undesired location. To help mitigate this risk, you can set your server up in a chrooted environment to limit access to the filesystem.

Also, keep in mind that authentication information and file transfers are sent in plain text across the network. If this traffic contains sensitive information, you might want to configure encryption. FTPS (also sometimes called FTP/SSL) is FTP over a secure sockets layer connection. Space permits me only to cover a basic installation in this chapter. You can visit `http://chrootssh.sourceforge.net/docs/chrootedsftp.html` for more on setting up sftp in a chrooted environment.

> **NOTE:** In discussing secure file transfer options you may come across both SFTP and FTPS. FTPS is a newer protocol designed by the Internet Engineering Task Force (IETF) and offers more features than traditional FTP, including secure transfers. FTPS is FTP transacted over an encrypted SSL connection, while SFTP is SSH File Transfer Protocol.

Understanding FTP Servers

The first implementations of FTP date back to 1971, predating the Web by almost two decades. FTP was created at a time when most computing was done on large mainframe computers and minicomputers. The predominant platforms using FTP were UNIX systems.

FTP set out to solve the need to publish documents and software so that people could get them easily from other computer systems. On the FTP server, files were organized in a directory structure. Users could connect to the server over the network (originally Darpanet and now the Internet), move up and down the directory structure to find the files that interested them, and download files from (and possibly upload files to) the server.

Originally, one drawback with FTP servers was that when people looked for a file or a document on the Internet, they had to know which FTP server held the file they were looking for. Tools such as Gopher and WAIS helped in searches. With the advent of the Web, however, users can now rely on a variety of search engines and links from Web pages to help identify FTP servers that have the files they want. In fact, since most modern web browsers have integrated multiple protocols to access content, when you download files by clicking a link from a Web page, you may not even be aware that the file is being downloaded from an FTP server.

Attributes of FTP servers

That FTP was implemented on large, multiuser UNIX systems accounts for many of the design decisions that remain a part of FTP today. FTP servers in Linux draw on FTP features that have resulted from years of testing and experience gained from other UNIX versions of FTP. Some attributes of FTP servers follow:

- Because FTP was originally used on multiuser systems, only limited parts of the file system in Fedora and RHEL are devoted to public FTP access. Those who access FTP from a public user account (by default, the `anonymous` user name) are automatically given an FTP directory (often `/var/ftp`) as their root directory. From there, the anonymous user can access only files and directories below that point in the file system.

- Access to the FTP server relies on a login process that uses standard UNIX login names (that is, those user names found in `/etc/passwd`). Although strangers to the system could log in using `anonymous` as a user name, users with their own accounts on the system could log in with their own user names through FTP and most likely have access to a greater part of the file system (in particular, their own private files and directories).

- The `ftp` command and other FTP client programs let you log in and then operate from a command interpreter (similar to a very simple shell). Many of the commands that you use from that command interpreter are familiar UNIX commands. You change directories with `cd`, list files with `ls`, change permissions with `chmod`, and check your location with `pwd` (to name a few). When you find where you want to be, you use the `get` command to download a file or the `put` command to upload one.

As an administrator of an FTP server, it is your responsibility to make sure that you share your files in a way that gives people access to the information you want them to have without compromising the security of your system. This means implementing a strong security policy and relentlessly monitoring the system to prevent abuse.

> **CROSS-REFERENCE:** See Chapter 14 for information on computer security issues.

FTP user types

Several different types of users can log in to and use an FTP server. *Real users* represent the category of users who have login accounts to the Fedora or RHEL system that contains your FTP server (that is, you know them and have given them permission for other uses besides FTP). With vsFTPd (described in the following section), you can configure settings for each real user separately, if you choose.

A *guest user* is similar to a real user account, except that guest user access to the computer's file system is more restricted. The user name `anonymous` is the most common for providing public (guest type) access.

The vsFTPd server also supports the concept of virtual users. The recommended method for creating virtual users for vsFTPd is to configure PAM (pluggable authentication modules) to point to per-user configuration files. Sample files for configuring virtual users are included with the vsftpd package. Refer to the `/usr/share/doc/vsftpd*/EXAMPLE` directory for directories containing virtual user example configuration files.

> **CROSS-REFERENCE:** See Chapter 11 for information on creating user accounts that have restricted access to your server.

Using the Very Secure FTP Server

The Very Secure FTP Server (vsFTPd) is the only general-purpose FTP server software included in Fedora and RHEL distributions. vsFTPd is becoming the FTP server of choice for sites that need to support thousands of concurrent downloads. It was also designed to secure your systems against most common attacks.

> **NOTE:** The Trivial File Transfer Protocol server (tftp-server package), which is distributed with Fedora and RHEL systems, can also be used to provide FTP service. The tftpd daemon is used primarily to provide support for diskless devices, which gather the files they need to boot and run from a TFTP server. TFTP is not intended for general, public FTP service. Because TFTP is considered a security risk to use publicly, it is generally used only on private LANs that are not accessible to public networks. Other FTP server package now available from the Fedora software repository include ProFTPD (`http://proftpd.org`) and Pure-FTPD (`http://pureftpd.org`).

Red Hat, Inc. itself uses vsFTPd on its own FTP servers (`ftp.redhat.com`). Other organizations in the open source software world have also made the switch to vsFTPd, including Debian Linux (`ftp.debian.org`), OpenBSD (`ftp.openbsd.org`) and the GNU Project (`ftp.gnu.org`).

Besides security and scalability, vsFTPd was designed for simplicity. Therefore, fewer options exist for configuring vsFTPd than you find in WU-FTPD, an older FTP server package that is still commonly used, so you are expected to rely on standard Linux file and directory permissions to provide refined access to your server. Getting started with vsFTPd, or using it to replace WU-FTPD, is fairly straightforward.

> **NOTE:** Although vsFTPd is the recommended FTP server software in Fedora and RHEL, the WU-FTPD FTP server software, which was once part of Red Hat Linux, is still available on the Web. However, WU-FTPD is considered by most to be far less secure than vsFTPd and should, therefore, not be used in most cases.

Quick-starting vsFTPd

By enabling the vsFTPd service, you can almost instantly have an FTP service running with the default values (set in the `/etc/vsftpd/vsftpd.conf` file). The following is a quick procedure for getting your vsFTPd server up and running. In case you didn't install vsFTPd when you originally installed Fedora, install it now by typing:

```
# yum install vsftpd
```

Here's how to start and try out the vsFTPd service.

1. To use the vsFTPd server, you must make sure that the vsFTPd software package is installed.

   ```
   # rpm -q vsftpd
   ```

2. Enable the vsFTPd server by typing the following line (as root user):

   ```
   # chkconfig vsftpd on
   ```

3. Start the vsFTPd server as follows:

   ```
   # service vsftpd start
   ```

4. Try to log in to the FTP server as anonymous (using any e-mail address as the password):

```
$ ftp localhost
Connected to yourhost (127.0.0.1)
220 (vsFTPd 2.0.6)
Name (localhost:chris): anonymous
331 Please specify the password.
Password: ******
230 Login successful.
Remote system type is UNIX.
Using binary mode to transfer files.
ftp>
```

If you saw messages similar to the preceding, your vsFTPd server is now up and running. Next, try to access the server from another computer on the network to be sure that it is accessible.

> **NOTE:** If your FTP server is not accessible to the outside world, you may need to ensure that your network is configured properly and that your firewall allows access to port 21 and possibly port 20. The quick way is to run `system-config-firewall` and add FTP as a trusted service. Refer to Appendix B for information on getting your network services working.

The next section explains the `/etc/vsftpd/vsftpd.conf` configuration file.

Configuring vsFTPd

Most of the configuration of vsFTPd is done in the `/etc/vsftpd/vsftpd.conf` file. Although many values are not set explicitly in `vsftpd.conf`, you can override the defaults by setting *option=value* statements in this file. You can set such things as which users have access to your vsFTPd server, how logging is done, and how timeouts are set.

Read the following sections for more information about how vsFTPd is configured by default and how you can further configure your vsFTPd server.

User accounts

Users who can access your vsFTPd server are, by default, the anonymous user and any users with real user accounts on your system. (A *guest* user is simply a real user account that is restricted to its own home directory.) The following lines set these user access features:

```
anonymous_enable=YES
local_enable=YES
```

The `anonymous_enable` line lets users log in anonymously using either the anonymous or `ftp` user name. If you want to disable access by anonymous users, don't just comment out `anonymous_enable`. Anonymous access is on by default, so you must set `anonymous_enable=NO` to disable it.

Any users with local accounts (in `/etc/passwd`) and valid passwords can log into the FTP server with `local_enable` set to `YES`. An exception to this rule is that, by default, all user accounts listed in the `/etc/vsftpd/user_list` file are denied access.

> **NOTE:** Before you start logging into an FTP server with your personal user name and password, keep in mind that FTP login service uses clear text passwords. Because of this fact, a network sniffer is capable of seeing this information. If you want to use an FTP interface to access files on an FTP server using your personal account, consider using the `sftp` command instead of a normal FTP client. If the FTP server includes an SSH server, you can use `sftp` to connnect to that server using encrypted passwords.

Check the `user_list` file to see which users are denied access to the vsFTPd server. Note that root and other administrative logins are excluded. You can add other users to this list or change the location of the list by setting the `userlist_file` parameter to the file you want. To add a user to the `user_list` or use the `userlist_file` parameter to create a new list, you must also have `userlist_enable` set to `YES` (as it is by default). For example:

```
userlist_file=/etc/vsftpd/user_list_local
userlist_enable=YES
```

If you like, you can change the meaning of the `/etc/vsftpd/user_list` file so that only the users in that list are allowed to use the vsFTPd service. Set `userlist_deny=NO` and change the `/etc/vsftpd/user_list` to include only names of users to whom you want to grant access to the server. All other users, including `anonymous` and `ftp`, will be denied access.

Setting FTP access

The vsFTPd server software provides a simple and seemingly secure approach to access permissions. Instead of using settings in the FTP service to selectively prevent downloads and uploads of particular directories (as FTP servers such as WU-FTPD do), you can use standard Linux file and directory permissions to limit access. There are, however, the following general settings in the `/etc/vsftpd/vsftpd.conf` file to let users get files from and put files onto your vsFTPd server.

Downloading files

Any users with valid logins (anonymous or real users, excluding some administrative logins) can download files from the vsFTPd server by default. The ability to download a particular file or a file from a particular directory is governed by the following basic Linux features:

- **File and directory permissions** — Standard file and directory permissions apply as a means of limiting access to particular files, even in accessible file systems. So, if the root user puts a file with 600 permission (read/write to root only) in the `/var/ftp` directory, an anonymous user is not able to download that file.

- **Root directory** — The root directory (chroot) for anonymous users is /var/ftp. The root directory for regular users is the entire computer's root directory (/), although their current directory after connecting to FTP is /home/*user*, where *user* is the user name. So an anonymous user is restricted to downloads from the /var/ftp directory structure, while a regular user potentially has access to the whole file system. Another possibility is to create *guest* accounts by restricting some or all users to their home directories.

You can use the chroot_local_user option to change the root directory for regular users so that they are restricted to their home directory. To restrict all regular users to their home directory when using vsFTPd, add this line to the vsftpd.conf file:

```
chroot_local_user=YES
```

To enable the concept of *guest* users, you can choose to limit only selected users to their home directories. You do this by setting chroot_list_enable to YES, and then adding a list of guest users to a file noted with the chroot_list_file option. The following example lets you add such a list (one user name per line) to the /etc/vsftpd/vsftpd.chroot_list file:

```
chroot_list_enable=YES
chroot_list_file=/etc/vsftpd/vsftpd.chroot_list
```

> **TIP**: To restrict a user to FTP access only, set the user's shell to /sbin/nologin in the /etc/passwd file. Do this by running the system-config-users command or usermod command and changing properties for the user, as described in Chapter 11.

You can add a setting to the vsftpd.conf file to affect how files are downloaded. To enable ASCII downloads, you can enable that feature as follows:

```
ascii_download_enable=YES
```

Without making that change, all downloads are done in binary mode. Although vsFTPd will seem to allow the user to change to ascii mode, ascii mode will not work if this setting is NO. Allowing ASCII file transfers is considered to be a security risk (vulnerable to denial-of-service attacks from an FTP client using the size command to check the size of large files on the server) and should be avoided. With ASCII downloads disabled, it is up to the client side to handle ASCII mangling when required.

Uploading (writing) files from local users

Two values set in the vsftpd.conf file allow the uploading of files during a vsFTPd session. The following defaults allow any users with regular, local user accounts to upload files:

```
write_enable=YES
local_umask=022
```

The write_enable value must be YES if you intend to allow any users the capability to write to the FTP server. The umask=022 value sets the default file permission used when a local user creates a file on the server. (The 022 value causes files created to have 644 permission, allowing the user read and write permission and everyone else only read permission.)

As with downloading, uploading in ascii mode is prohibited by default. Although ascii downloads create a potential security hole for draining resources from your server, ascii uploads are apparently not as dangerous and can be useful for uploading text files. To allow ascii uploads, add the following line:

```
ascii_upload_enable=YES
```

Uploading (writing) files from anonymous users

The ability to upload files is turned off for anonymous FTP users. If you want to turn it on, add the following line to the vsftpd.conf file:

```
anon_upload_enable=YES
```

To use anonymous upload, the global write enable must be activated. You must also make sure that the /var/ftp directory contains one or more directories with write permissions open to anonymous users. For example, you might want to create an incoming directory and open its permissions (chmod 777 /var/ftp/incoming).

Files uploaded by anonymous users will be created with 600 permission by default (read/write permission for the ftp user, not accessible to any other users so that even the user who uploaded the files can't remove them or even see them). To allow 644 permission, for example, you can add the following line:

```
anon_umask=022
```

When you allow the anonymous user to upload files, you can grant limited ability to change the files he or she uploads. By adding the following line, you can allow anonymous users to rename or delete any files owned by anonymous users (provided that the files are in directories for which the users have write permission):

```
anon_other_write_enable=YES
```

If you also want to allow anonymous users to create their own directories, add the following:

```
anon_mkdir_write_enable=YES
```

By default, the ftp user is given ownership of uploaded files from anonymous users. If you want to indicate that anonymous uploads be owned by a different user (of your choice), you can use the chown_uploads and chown_username options. For example, if you have a user account named mynewuser, you can set these options as follows:

```
chown_uploads=YES
chown_username=mynewuser
```

Of course, you can create and use any user name you want. However, for security reasons you should not use the root login or any other administrative login for this purpose.

Adding message files

Although vsFTPd doesn't support the arrangement of README and welcome files that FTP servers such as WU-FTP support, you can add .message files to any accessible directory on your vsFTPd server. Then, if you use the default dirmessage_enable option as follows, the text from the .message file will be displayed when the user enters the directory:

```
dirmessage_enable=YES
```

You will probably at least want to add a .message file to the root directory of the FTP server for anonymous users. By default, that location is /var/ftp/.message. If you want to use files other than .message files, you can set the message_file option. For example, to have text from the .mymessage file displayed when you enter a directory, you can add the following line:

```
message_file=.mymessage
```

A .message file provides an opportunity for you to add information about the contents of your server, copyright information, or instructions on how to use the software. By allowing different message files, you can tailor what you want to say to visitors, depending on where they are located on your file server.

You can also set a one-line message to appear before the login prompt. You can do this by entering the following line, replacing the text with anything you want to say:

```
ftpd_banner=Welcome to My FTP service.
```

As a security measure, you could consider adding a banner that indicates a different operating system than you have running. Any information that can slow down a potential intruder from finding out what software you are running makes it easier for you to keep that intruder out.

Logging vsFTPd activities

Logging is enabled in vsFTPd by default, and the activities of your vsFTPd site are written to the /var/log/xferlog file. The following options enable logging and change the log file to /var/log/vsftpd.log:

```
xferlog_enable=YES
xferlog_file=/var/log/vsftpd.log
```

You can turn off logging if you like by changing YES to NO. (Note, however, that logging enables you to watch for potential break-ins, so turning it off is not recommended.) Or you can change the location of the log file by changing the value of the xferlog_file option. Keep in mind that with a lot of usage, your FTP server can produce a lot of log messages. So, to be useful, you need to monitor the logs fairly often.

If you want to be able to use tools that generate transfer statistics, you can have vsFTPd log data written in the standard xferlog format that is used by WU-FTPD and other FTP servers. To store your transfer data in xferlog format, set the following option:

```
xferlog_std_format=YES
```

Setting timeouts

The following timeouts are set by default in vsFTPd (these values are built in, so you don't have to make any changes to the `/etc/vsftpd/vsftpd.conf` file for them to take effect):

```
accept_timeout=60
connect_timeout=60
idle_session_timeout=600
data_connection_timeout=120
```

The `accept_timeout=60` and `connect_timeout=60` values determine how long the client has to establish a PASV or PORT style connection, respectively, before the connection times out. Both are set to 60 seconds. (Note that these two lines are not automatically included in the configuration file; you can add them by hand if you want to change their values.) The `idle_session_timeout=600` option causes the FTP session to be dropped if the user has been inactive for more than 10 minutes (600 seconds). The `data_connection_timeout` value sets the amount of time, during which no progress occurs, that the server will wait before dropping the connection (the default here is 120 seconds).

Navigating a vsFTPd site

Most shell wildcard characters that a user might expect to use, such as question marks and brackets, are supported by vsFTPd. There is one particularly useful wildcard character you can use with the `ls` command, and one option you can turn on. The asterisk (*) wildcard can be used with the `ls` command. Multiple asterisks in the same line are supported. You can add support for the `-R` option of `ls` so that a user can recursively list the contents of the current directory and all subdirectories. To turn on this feature, which is off by default, you can add the following line to the `vsftpd.conf` file:

```
ls_recurse_enable=YES
```

Setting up vsFTPd behind a firewall

If you are configuring an FTP server behind a firewall, you need to do some special configuration to allow communications to pass through that firewall to those you want to allow access to your server. To deal with the issue, you can use ephemeral port numbers (which provide random, temporary port numbers within a range of numbers as needed). For a description of the issue, refer to the FTP and Your Firewall page at `www.ncftp.com/ncftpd/doc/misc/ftp_and_firewalls.html`.

Getting More Information about FTP Servers

There are plenty of resources for gaining more information about FTP servers. Here are some of your options:

- **FAQ** — To check out the vsFTPd FAQ, go to `/usr/share/doc/vsftpd*/FAQ`.

- **RFCs** — Requests For Comments are the documents that define standard protocols used with the Internet. The main RFC for FTP is RFC959. You can obtain RFCs from a variety of locations on the Internet, including the Internet RFC/FYI/STD/BCP Archives (`www.faqs.org/rfcs`).

- **CERT** — This organization provides useful documents for setting up FTP servers. Anonymous FTP Abuses describes how to respond to and recover from FTP server abuse. It also tells how to deal with software piracy issues. Anonymous FTP Configuration Guidelines provide general guidance in setting up your FTP area, as well as specific challenges of setting up a writable FTP area. Both of those documents are available from the CERT Tech Tips page (`www.cert.org/tech_tips`).

> **TIP:** I strongly recommend reading the FTP documents from CERT. The tips in these documents will help keep your FTP server secure, while enabling you to offer the services that you want to share.

Summary

The FTP service is the primary method of offering archives of document and software files to users over the Internet. The only FTP server package delivered with Fedora and RHEL is the Very Secure FTP (vsFTPd) server. The vsFTPd server relies on standard Linux file and user permissions to provide a simple, yet secure, FTP environment to run in Fedora.

Chapter 21

Setting Up a Web Server

In This Chapter

- Introduction to Web servers
- Quick starting the Apache Web server
- Configuring the Apache Web server
- Starting and stopping the server
- Monitoring server activities

Approximately 50 percent of all Web sites today are powered by the open source Apache Web Server Project (compared to about 31 percent for Microsoft Web servers). In February 2008, Netcraft (www.netcraft.com) reported receiving responses from more than 158 million sites, more than 80,000 of which were running Apache. As registration of Internet domain names continues to grow at an average rate of more than 1 million a month, Apache is getting the lion's share of new Web sites being launched.

The Web has also been a boon to organizations seeking an inexpensive means to publish and distribute information. Using the Fedora distribution that comes with this book or RHEL, you can launch your own Web site using software available from the Apache project. Combine your own domain name, Internet connection, and Fedora or RHEL to create your own presence on the World Wide Web.

This chapter shows you how to install and configure the Apache Web server. Each of the server's configuration files is described and explained in detail. You learn about various options for starting and stopping the server, as well as how to monitor the activity of a Web server. Related security concerns and practices are addressed throughout the chapter in the descriptions and examples, as well as in a special Web server security section ("Protecting Web servers with certificates and encryption") in Chapter 14.

> **NOTE:** The current version of Fedora comes with Apache version 2.2. Apache 2.2 includes support for a new Apache application programming interface, UNIX threading (for multiprocessing), Internet Protocol version 6 (IPv6), and multiple protocols. If you have been using a pre-2.0 version of Apache, you should note that the package names apache and apache-manual have changed to httpd and httpd-manual.

Introduction to Web Servers

The World Wide Web, as it is known today, began as a project of Tim Berners-Lee at the European Center for Particle Physics (CERN). The original goal was to provide one consistent interface for geographically dispersed researchers and scientists who needed access to information in a variety of formats. From this idea came the concept of using one client (the Web browser) to access data (text, images, sounds, video, and binary files) from several types of servers (HTTP, FTP, SMTP, Gopher, NNTP, WAIS, Finger, and streaming-media servers).

The Web server usually has a simpler job: to accept HyperText Transfer Protocol (HTTP) requests and send a response to the client. However, this job can get much more complex (as the server can also), executing functions such as:

- Performing access control based on file permissions, username/password pairs, and host name/IP address restrictions.

- Parsing a document (substituting appropriate values for any conditional fields within the document) before sending it to the client.

- Spawning a Common Gateway Interface (CGI) script or custom Application Programming Interface (API) program to evaluate the contents of a submitted form, presenting a dynamically created document, or accessing a database.

- Logging any successful accesses, failures, and errors.

The Apache Web server

The Apache Web server was originally based on HTTPd, a free server from the National Center for Supercomputing Applications (NCSA). At the time, HTTPd was the first and only Web server on the Internet. Unfortunately, the development of the server wasn't keeping up with the needs of Webmasters, and several security problems had been discovered. Many Webmasters had been independently applying their own features and fixes to the NCSA source code.

In early 1995, a group of these developers pooled their efforts and created a new project from this code base called Apache. Since then, what is now the Apache Software Foundation (www.apache.org) has largely rewritten the code and created a stable, multiplatform Web server daemon. More than two dozen related projects are also sponsored by the Apache Software Foundation. Those projects include mod_perl (to create dynamic Web sites with the Perl language), Jakarta (to provide server-side Java content), DB (to create and maintain commercial-quality database solutions), and spamassassin (to identify and deal with junk e-mail).

The main features of the Apache Web server include:

- The stability and rapid development cycle associated with a large group of cooperative volunteer programmers.

- Full source code, downloadable at no charge.

- Ease of configuration using plain-text files.

- Access control based on client host name/IP address or username/password combinations.

- Support for server-side scripting as well as CGI scripts. This includes the ability to have different users controlling script execution (to limit the vulnerability of a whole Web server if a single script is compromised).

- A custom API that enables external modules (for example, for extended logging capabilities, improved authentication, caching, connection tracking, and so on) to be used by the server daemon.

Apache is not the only Web server for Fedora and RHEL systems, but it is the one most often used with Linux, and is still the most popular server used on the Internet according to Netcraft (`http://news.netcraft.com/archives/web_server_survey.html`). In addition to Apache, Fedora and RHEL come with the lighttpd and thttpd lightweight Web servers.

Other Web servers available for Fedora and RHEL

Some other Web servers that can run on Fedora and other Red Hat Linux distributions are described in the following list, with URLs that provide more detailed information.

- **lighttpd** — The lighttpd Web server (`www.lighttpd.net`) is built for security, speed, compliance and flexibility. It is particularly optimized for high performance environments because it has a low memory footprint and balances cpu-load. Sites such as YouTube, Wikipedia, and meebo have used lighttpd for some specialty Web applications.

- **tclhttpd** — TheTclHttpd Web server (tclhttpd package) is created in the Tool Command Language (TCL). Besides acting as a Web server, TclHttpd can also be used as a TCL application server.

- **thttpd** — The thttpd HTTP server (`http://acme.com/software/thttpd`) was designed to be simple, small, portable, fast, and secure. Its creators call it a tiny, turbo, throttling HTTP server. It implements little more than the minimum needed to be HTTP/1.1 compliant, so it can run much faster than many larger Web servers under extreme loads.

- **XSP** — The XSP Web server (xsp package) can run ASP.NET applications, as well as related services for working with ASP.NET applications.

- **Zope** — In addition to being able to serve Web content, Zope includes features for adding news, membership information, and search capabilities. Originally created by Zope Corporation (`www.zope.org`), Zope is now available as an open source project covered under the GPL. Zope is not included with the current version of Fedora or

RHEL. You can get Zope from the Zope development site
(`zope.sourceforge.net`). Zope is python-based.

- **CERN (W3C) Jigsaw 2.2.6** —The latest HTTP/1.1 reference server, written completely
  in Java and freely available, can be found at `www.w3.org/Jigsaw`. It features
  extensive caching, an improved mechanism for executing external programs (although
  CGI is also supported), and a graphical administration tool.

Quick Starting the Apache Web Server

If Apache wasn't installed during the Fedora installation, you can install it later from the DVD
or CD that comes with this book. You will need the httpd package and optionally the httpd-
manual package (named apache and apache-manual in earlier versions).

Here's a quick way to get your Apache Web server going. From here, you'll want to customize
it to match your needs and your environment (as described in the section that follows).

1. Make sure that Apache is installed by typing the following from a Terminal window:

```
$ rpm -qa | grep httpd
system-config-httpd-1.4.4-1.fc9
httpd-tools-2.2.8-3.i386
httpd-devel-2.2.8-3.i386
httpd-2.2.8-3.i386
httpd-manual-2.2.8-3.i386
```

   The version number you see may be different. You need only the httpd package to get
   started. I recommend httpd-manual because it has excellent information on the whole
   Apache setup. The httpd-devel package includes the `apxs` tool for building and installing
   extension modules. The httpd-tools package includes tools for running benchmarks and
   managing passwords for Apache.

   The system-config-httpd package contains a GUI-based Apache Configuration tool.
   Depending on the type of content you are serving, you might also add packages
   containing modules to run that code within the Apache server (such as mod_perl,
   mod_python, and mod_mono).

2. A valid host name is recommended if it is a public Apache server (for example,
   `abc.handsonhistory.com`). If you don't have a real, fully qualified domain name,
   you can edit the `/etc/httpd/conf/httpd.conf` file and define the `ServerName` as
   your computer's IP address. Open the `httpd.conf` file (as the root user) in any text
   editor, search for the line containing `ServerName www.example.com:80`, and
   uncomment it. It should appear as follows:

```
ServerName www.example.com:80
```

   To make the Web server available to your LAN, you can use your IP address instead of
   `www.example.com` (for example, `ServerName 10.0.0.1`). The `:80` represents the
   port number (which is the default). For a public Web server, get a real DNS hostname.

(Refer to Chapter 25 for information on DNS and making a server public.) No changes are required to this file to make Apache available on the local host.

3. Add an administrative e-mail address where someone can contact you in case an error is encountered with your server. In the `/etc/httpd/conf/httpd.conf` file, the default administrative address appears as follows:

```
ServerAdmin root@localhost
```

Change `root@localhost` to the e-mail address of your Apache administrator.

4. Start the `httpd` server. As root user, type the following:

```
# service httpd start
```

If all goes well, this message should appear: `Starting httpd: [OK]`. Now you're ready to go.

5. To have `httpd` start every time you boot your system, run the command as root user.

```
# chkconfig httpd on
```

6. To make sure that the Web server is working, open Firefox (or another Web browser) and type the following into the location box and press Enter:

```
http://localhost/
```

7. You should see the Test Page for the Apache Web server, as shown in Figure 21-1. To access this page from another computer, you will need to enter your Apache server's host name or IP address.

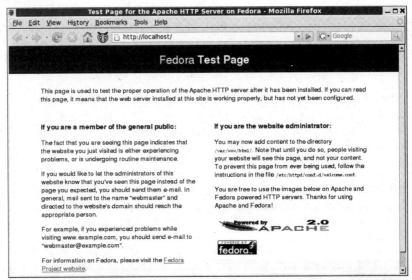

Figure 21-1: Appearance of the Test Page indicates that the Apache installation succeeded.

> **TIP:** It is not necessary to be connected to a network (or even to have a network connection) just to test the server or to view the files on your local Apache machine. Rather than specify the server's real name in the URL, just use "localhost" (that is, `http://localhost/`) from a browser on the same computer. In fact, it's best to fully test the configuration before making the server accessible on an unprotected network.

8. The Test Page is actually an error condition, indicating that you haven't added any content to your Web site yet. To get started, you can add an `index.html` file that contains your own home page content in the `/var/www/html` directory. Then you can continue to add your own content to that directory structure.

Now that your Web server is working (or at least, I hope it is), you should step through the next section. It helps you understand how to set up more complex Web server arrangements and protect your server from misuse. Stepping through that section will also help you troubleshoot your Web server, in case it isn't working.

> **TIP:** If your Web server is accessible from your local host, but not available to others from your LAN or the Internet, you may need to change your firewall rules to allow greater access. Appendix B explains how to make your Web or other server accessible. In particular, you need to open tcp port 80.

Configuring the Apache Server

The primary file for configuring your Apache Web server is `httpd.conf` (located in the `/etc/httpd/conf` directory). A few years ago, the Apache project began recommending not using additional configuration files, such as `srm.conf` and `access.conf`, and simply put everything in `httpd.conf`. In recent releases, however, there has been a trend toward having modules and other components that are used with Apache have their own configuration files (usually located in the `/etc/httpd/conf.d/` directory).

All Apache configuration files are plain-text files and can be edited with your favorite text editor. The `/etc/httpd/conf/httpd.conf` file is reproduced in its entirety in the following section, with explanations inserted after related blocks of options (intended to supplement the comments provided with each file).

Some individual modules, scripts and other services related to Apache, such as perl, php, ssl, webalizer, and mysql, have individual configuration files that may interest you. Those files are contained in the `/etc/httpd/conf.d/` directory. The "Configuring modules and related services (/etc/httpd/conf.d/*.conf)" section later in this chapter discusses modules and related features.

> **CROSS-REFERENCE:** More information on Apache can be obtained on your own Web server, from `http://localhost/manual/` (if the httpd-manual package is installed).

Configuring the Web server (httpd.conf)

The `httpd.conf` file is the primary configuration file for the Apache Web server. It contains options that pertain to the general operation of the server. The default filename (`/etc/httpd/conf/httpd.conf`) can be overridden by the `-f filename` command-line argument to the httpd daemon or the `ServerConfigFile` directive. The following sections list the contents of the `httpd.conf` file and describe how to use the file.

The first section contains comments about the `httpd.conf` file:

```
# This is the main Apache server configuration file. It contains the
# configuration directives that give the server its instructions.
# See <URL:http://httpd.apache.org/docs/2.2/> for detailed information.
# In particular, see
# <URL:http://httpd.apache.org/docs/2.2/mod/directives.html>
# for a discussion of each configuration directive.
#
# Do NOT simply read the instructions in here without understanding
# what they do.  They're here only as hints or reminders.  If you are
# unsure consult the online docs. You have been warned.
#
# The configuration directives are grouped into three basic sections:
#  1. Directives that control the operation of the Apache server
#     process as a whole (the 'global environment').
#  2. Directives that define parameters of the main or default server,
#     which responds to requests that aren't handled by a virtual host.
#     These directives also provide default values for the settings
#     of all virtual hosts.
#  3. Settings for virtual hosts, which allow Web requests to be sent
#     to different IP addresses or hostnames and have them handled by
#     the same Apache server process.
#
# Configuration and logfile names: If the filenames you specify for
# many of the server's control files begin with "/" (or "drive:/" for
# Win32), the server will use that explicit path.  If the filenames do
# *not* begin with "/", the value of ServerRoot is prepended -- so
# "logs/foo.log"with ServerRoot set to "/usr/local/apache" will be
# interpreted by the server as "/usr/local/apache/logs/foo.log".
#
```

This section consists entirely of comments. It basically tells you how information is grouped together in this file and how the httpd daemon accesses this file. By default, log files are in the `/var/log/httpd` directory.

Setting the global environment

In "Section 1: Global Environment" of the `httpd.conf` file, you set directives that affect the general workings of the Apache server. Here is what the different directives are for:

```
### Section 1: Global Environment
#
# The directives in this section affect overall operation of Apache,
# such as the number of concurrent requests it can handle or where it
# can find its configuration files.
#
```

Revealing subcomponents

The ServerTokens directive lets you prevent remote computers from finding out what subcomponents you are running on your Apache server. Comment out this directive if you don't mind exposing this information. To prevent exposure, ServerTokens is set as follows:

```
#
# Don't give away too much information about all the subcomponents
# we are running.  Comment out this line if you don't mind remote sites
# finding out what major optional modules you are running
ServerTokens OS
```

Setting the server root directory

The ServerRoot directive specifies the directory that contains the configuration files, a link to the log file directory, and a link to the module directory. An alternative ServerRoot path name can be specified using the -d command-line argument to httpd.

```
# ServerRoot: The top of the directory tree under which the server's
# configuration, error, and log files are kept.
#
# NOTE! If you intend to place this on an NFS (or other network) mounted
# filesystem then please read the LockFile documentation (available
# at <URL:http://httpd.apache.org/docs/2.2/mod/core.html#lockfile>);
# you will save yourself a lot of trouble.
#
# Do NOT add a slash at the end of the directory path.
#
ServerRoot "/etc/httpd"
```

Storing the server's PID file

The Apache Web server keeps track of the PID for the running server process. You can change the locations of this file using the entry described next:

```
#
# PidFile: The file in which the server should record its process
# identification number when it starts.
#
PidFile run/httpd.pid
```

Apache uses the PidFile to store the process ID of the first (root-owned) master daemon process. This information is used by the /etc/init.d/httpd script when shutting down the server and also by the server-status handler (as described later).

Configuring timeout values

You can set several values that relate to timeout. Some of these values are described in the text following the code:

```
#
# Timeout: The number of seconds before receives and sends time out.
#
Timeout 120

#
# KeepAlive: Whether or not to allow persistent connections (more than
# one request per connection). Set to "Off" to deactivate.
#
KeepAlive Off

#
# MaxKeepAliveRequests: The maximum number of requests to allow
# during a persistent connection. Set to 0 to allow unlimited amount.
# We recommend you leave this number high, for maximum performance.
#
MaxKeepAliveRequests 100

#
# KeepAliveTimeout: Number of seconds to wait for the next request from
# the same client on the same connection.
#
KeepAliveTimeout 15
```

The `Timeout` directive determines the number of seconds that Apache will hold a connection open between the receipt of packets, between the receipt of acknowledgments on sent responses, or while receiving an incoming request. The default of two minutes (120 seconds) can be lowered if you find an excessive number of open, idle connections on your machine.

The `KeepAlive` directive instructs Apache to hold a connection open for a period of time after a request has been handled. This enables subsequent requests from the same client to be processed faster, as a new connection doesn't need to be created for each request.

The `MaxKeepAliveRequests` directive sets a limit on the number of requests that can be handled with one open connection. The default value is certainly reasonable because most connections will hit the `KeepAliveTimeout` before `MaxKeepAliveRequests`.

The `KeepAliveTimeout` directive specifies the number of seconds to hold the connection while awaiting another request. You might want to increase the default (15 seconds). Reasons for having a longer timeout could be to allow all the images on the page to be downloaded on the same connection or to take into account how long it may take a client to peruse your average page and select a link from it. The Web application you are using may also need a longer persistent connection. (Of course, a longer `KeepAliveTimeout` prevents each server from moving on to another client during this time period, so you may find that you need to add more request processes to account for that.)

Setting the number of server processes

To operate efficiently, a Web server has to be able to handle lots of incoming requests for content simultaneously. To be ready for requests for Web content, Apache (as it is set up in Fedora) has multiple server processes (httpd daemons) running and listening to service requests. Those servers can, in turn, direct requests to multiple threads to service the content requests.

With the Multi-Processing Module (MPM) feature (introduced in Apache 2.0), support for threads was added to Apache. On an operating system that supports Native POSIX Thread Libraries (which Fedora and RHEL do), threading allows Apache to improve performance by needing fewer process slots and less memory for the number of servers it needs. Adding threads consumes fewer resources than adding processes.

For a low-volume Web server, you can probably leave the parameters alone that support the MPM feature. You will probably have enough processes to handle your incoming requests, but not so many that they will be a drain on your server. However, if your server needs to serve up lots of content consistently, or needs to respond occasionally to large spikes of requests, you should consider tuning the MPM-related parameters in the httpd.conf file.

Here are a few issues to consider if you want to change any of the MPM-related parameters:

- **RAM is critical** — Every process and thread that is active consumes some amount of memory. If the number of active processes and threads goes beyond the amount of RAM you have, your computer will begin to use swap space and performance will degrade quickly. Make sure this is enough RAM on your system to handle the maximum number of server processes and threads you expect to run on your Apache Web server.

- **Configure for maximum load** — Apache is able to create new server processes and threads as they are needed. You don't need to have the maximum number of processes and threads available at all times. Instead, you can configure the maximum number of servers and threads that Apache can dynamically add as demand on the server requires.

- **Configure for performance** — Performance degrades when Apache has to start a new thread (small amount), start a server process (greater amount), or use swap space (greatest amount). In the perfect world, the exact number of servers you need should be the default number of servers running, with a few spares to handle reasonable spikes. If response is critical, you might opt to have more servers running than you need so that performance isn't hurt when spikes come.

When Apache starts up, it launches a set number of httpd server processes (one parent and multiple child httpd processes) to handle incoming requests for content for the Web server. Parameters for defining how many httpd server processes are available include those that set:

- How many child server processes should be started by the parent httpd server (`StartServers`)

- The minimum number of server processes kept spare (`MinSpareServers`)

- The maximum number of server processes kept spare (`MaxSpareServers`)

- The maximum value `MaxClients` can be over the life of the server (`ServerLimit`)

- The maximum number of server processes allowed to start (`MaxClients`)

- The maximum number of requests a process can serve (`MaxRequestsPerChild`)

Parameters for defining how many threads are available for each httpd server process include those that set:

- The minimum number of spare threads that should always be available, after which more will be created (`MinSpareThreads`)

- The maximum number for spare threads, after which active threads will be deleted to get back to the number of threads per child (`MaxSpareThreads`)

- The number of threads always available to each child process (`ThreadsPerChild`)

The following code example shows how MPM-specific parameters in the `httpd.conf` file are set for the `prefork.c` module (non-threaded module for managing servers processes) and `worker.c` (multithread, multiprocess Web server module).

```
##
## Server-Pool Size Regulation (MPM specific)
##
<IfModule prefork.c>
StartServers        8
MinSpareServers     5
MaxSpareServers     20
ServerLimit         256
MaxClients          256
MaxRequestsPerChild  4000
</IfModule>

<IfModule worker.c>
StartServers         2
MaxClients           150
MinSpareThreads      25
MaxSpareThreads      75
ThreadsPerChild      25
MaxRequestsPerChild  0
</IfModule>
```

Apache starts a master daemon process owned by root that binds to the appropriate port, and then switches to a nonprivileged user. More servers (equivalent to the value of the

StartServers directive in `prefork.c`) will then be started as the same nonprivileged user (the apache user in this case).

Apache attempts to intelligently start and kill servers based on the current load. If the amount of traffic decreases and there are too many idle servers, some will be killed (down to the number of servers noted in `MinSpareServers`). Similarly, if many requests arrive in close proximity and there are too few servers waiting for new connections, more servers will be started (up to the number of servers noted in `MaxClients`).

> **NOTE:** Getting the value of `MaxClients` right is critical because it puts a lid on the total number of simultaneous client connections that can be active at a time. If the number of `MaxClients` servers are in use, no more will be created and subsequent requests to the server will fail until one is freed up.

Using the values specified above, when the daemon is started, the parent and eight child server processes will run, waiting for connections (as defined by `StartServers`). As more requests arrive, Apache will ensure that at least five server processes are ready to answer requests. When requests have been fulfilled and no new connections arrive, Apache will begin killing processes until the number of idle Web server processes is below 20. The value of `StartServers` should always be somewhere between `MinSpareServers` and `MaxSpareServers`.

Apache limits the total number of simultaneous threads with the `MaxClients` directive. The default value is 150, which should be sufficiently high. However, if you find that you frequently have nearly that many threads running, remember that any connection beyond the 150th will be rejected. In such cases, if your hardware is sufficiently powerful (and if your network connection can handle the load), you should increase the value of `MaxClients`.

> **NOTE:** You can see the state of your Apache server processes and get a feel for the server's activity by viewing the server-status page for your server, as described later in this chapter. The `ps -fU apache` command will show you if the Apache server processes (httpd daemon) are currently running.

To minimize the effect of possible memory leaks (and to keep the server pool "fresh"), each server process is limited in the number of requests that it can handle (equal to the value of `MaxRequestsPerChild`). After servicing 4000 requests (the value specified above), the process will be killed. It is even more accurate to say that each process can service 4000 *connections* because all `KeepAlive` requests (occurring prior to encountering a `KeepAliveTimeout`) are calculated as just one request.

In a multiprocessor environment, setting thread values described previously can both limit the number of threads that servers can consume and supply as many threads as you will allow to handle server processing. `MinSpareThreads` and `MaxSpareThreads` control the number of threads available that are not being used. More are added if available threads fall below `MinSpareThreads`. If spare threads go above `MaxSpareThreads`, some are dropped.

Binding to specific addresses

You can bind to specific IP addresses using the `Listen` directive. `Listen` directives can be used to add to the default bindings you already have:

```
# Listen: Allows you to bind Apache to specific IP addresses and/or
# ports, in addition to the default. See also the <VirtualHost>
# directive.
#
# Change this to Listen on specific IP addresses as shown below to
# prevent Apache from glomming onto all bound IP addresses (0.0.0.0)
#Listen 12.34.56.78:80
Listen 80
```

The `Listen` directive is more flexible than the `BindAddress` and `Port` directives. Multiple `Listen` commands can be specified, enabling you to specify several IP address/port number combinations. It can also be used to specify just IP addresses (in which case the `Port` directive is still necessary) or just port numbers.

By default, Apache listens to port 80 (for standard http services) and port 443 (for secure https services) on all interfaces on the local computer (which is where Web browsers expect to find Web content). Listening on only `localhost:80` restricts access only to users on the local machines. A Web server run by a non-privileged user often will bind to port 8080 (only root can bind to ports lower than 1024). If you have multiple network interface cards, you can limit which interfaces Apache will listen on (for example, you can have a Web server only intended for the company LAN which is not exposed to your Internet interface).

Selecting modules in httpd.conf

During the compilation process, individual Apache modules can be selected for dynamic linking. Dynamically linked modules are not loaded into memory with the httpd server process unless `LoadModule` directives explicitly identify those modules to be loaded. The blocks of code that follow select several modules to be loaded into memory by using the `LoadModule` directive with the module name and the path to the module (relative to `ServerRoot`). The following text shows a partial listing of these modules:

```
#
# Dynamic Shared Object (DSO) Support
# Example:
# LoadModule foo_module modules/mod_foo.so
#
LoadModule auth_basic_module modules/mod_auth_basic.so
LoadModule auth_digest_module modules/mod_auth_digest.so
LoadModule authn_file_module modules/mod_authn_file.so
    .
    .
    .
LoadModule file_cache_module modules/mod_file_cache.so
LoadModule mem_cache_module modules/mod_mem_cache.so
LoadModule cgi_module modules/mod_cgi.so
```

Apache modules are included in the list of active modules via the LoadModule directive. The ClearModuleList directive removes all entries from the current list of active modules. Each of the standard modules that come with Apache is described in Table 21-1.

If a particular module contains features that are not necessary, it can easily be commented out of the preceding list. In fact, it is a good security practice to comment out unused modules. Similarly, you might want to add the features or functionality of a third-party module (for example, mod_perl, which integrates the Perl runtime library for faster Perl script execution, or mod_php, which provides a scripting language embedded within HTML documents) by including those modules in the list.

> **NOTE:** Some modules, including core, prefork, http_core, and mod_so, are compiled into the httpd daemon in Fedora and RHEL. To see the list of modules compiled into the daemon, type the httpd -l command.

Table 21-1: Dynamic Shared Object (DSO) Modules

Module	Description
mod_actions	Conditionally executes CGI scripts based on the file's MIME type or the request method.
mod_alias	Allows for redirection and mapping parts of the physical file system into logical entities accessible through the Web server.
mod_asis	Enables files to be transferred without adding any HTTP headers (for example, the Status, Location, and Content-type header fields).
mod_auth_basic	Provides HTTP Basic Authentication. It is used in combination with authentication modules (such as mod_authn_file) and authorization modules (such as mod_authz_user).
mod_auth_digest	Provides MD5 Digest user authentication.
mod_authn_alias	Lets you create extended authentication providers that are assigned to aliases. Later you can reference the aliases through AuthBasicProvider or AuthDigestProvider directives.
mod_authn_anon	Similar to anonymous FTP, this module enables predefined usernames access to authenticated areas by using a valid e-mail address as a password.
mod_authn_dbd	Provides access to SQL tables to authenticate users. It lets you use mod_auth_basic and mod_auth_digest front-ends.
mod_authn_dbm	Provides access control based on username/password pairs. The authentication information is stored in a DBM binary database file, with encrypted passwords.
mod_authn_default	Offers a fallback authentication module, if no other is in use. Any credentials presented by the user are rejected.

Module	Description
mod_authn_file	Provides access control by user look-up in plain text password files. (Similar to mod_authn_dbm, but without encryption.)
mod_authnz_ldap	Lets you use an LDAP directory to store the HTTP Basic authentication database.
mod_authz_dbm	Provides access control to authenticated users based on group name. The authentication information is stored in a DBM binary database file.
mod_authz_default	If modules such as mod_authz_user or mod_authz_groupfile are not configured, the module provides a fallback (simply rejecting authorization requests).
mod_authz_groupfile	Provides access control based on group membership.
mod_authz_host	Provides access control based on client hostname, IP address or other environment variable characteristics.
mod_authz_owner	With a verified username and password, this module allows access to files based on ownership.
mod_authz_user	Allows access to files based on whether an authenticated user is listed in a Required User directive.
mod_autoindex	Implements automatically generated directory indexes.
mod_cache	Allows local or proxied Web content to be cached. Used with the mod_disk_cache or mod_mem_cache modules.
mod_cern_meta	Offers a method of emulating CERN HTTPD meta file semantics.
mod_cgi	Controls the execution of files that are parsed by the "cgi-script" handler or that have a MIME type of x-httpd-cgi. ScriptAlias sets the default directory.
mod_cgid	Similar to mod_cgi with the exception that this module offers a ScriptSock directive to name the socket used with the cgi daemon.
mod_dav	Provides Web-based Distributed Authoring and Versioning (WebDAV) to upload Web content using copy, create, move, and delete resources.
mod_dav_fs	Used to provide file system features to the mod_dav module, used with Web-based Distributed Authoring and Versioning (WebDAV).
mod_dbd	Uses apr_dbd to manage SQL database connections. (The apr_dbd framework offers a common API for different SQL databases.)
mod_deflate	Includes the DEFLATE output filter, to compress data before it is sent to the client.

Module	Description
mod_dir	Sets the list of filenames that may be used if no explicit filename is selected in a URL that references a directory.
mod_disk_cache	Enables a disk-based storage manager to use with mod_proxy.
mod_dumpio	Lets you log all input received by or sent from Apache. Because this can involve a lot of data, it is used mostly for debugging purposes.
mod_env	Controls environment variables passed to CGI scripts.
mod_expires	Implements time limits on cached documents by using the Expires HTTP header.
mod_ext_filter	Before delivering a resonse to the client, pass it through an external filter.
mod_file_cache	Allows caching of frequently requested static files.
mod_filter	Allows you to configure context-sensitive output filtering.
mod_headers	Enables the creation and generation of custom HTTP headers.
mod_ident	Lets you query an RFC 1413–compatible daemon on a remote host to request information on the owner of a connection.
mod_imagemap	Replaces the functions of the imagemap CGI program to process .map files.
mod_include	Implements Server-Side Includes (SSI), which are HTML documents that include conditional statements parsed by the server prior to being sent to a client. This module also has the ability to include files one into another.
mod_info	Provides a detailed summary of the server's configuration, including a list of actively loaded modules and the current settings of every directive defined within each module.
mod_ldap	Used to speed performance of Web sites using LDAP servers.
mod_logio	Can be used to log bytes of data that are sent and received.
mod_log_config	Enables a customized format for information contained within the log files.
mod_log_forensic	Provides the ability to do forensic logging of client requests.
mod_mem_cache	Used with mod_cache to provide memory-based storage.
mod_mime	Alters the handling of documents based on predefined values or the MIME type of the file.
mod_mime_magic	Similar to the UNIX file command, this module attempts to determine the MIME type of a file based on a few bytes of the file's contents.

Module	Description
mod_negotiation	Provides for the conditional display of documents based on the Content-Encoding, Content-Language, Content-Length, and Content-Type HTTP header fields.
mod_proxy	Implements an HTTP 1.1 proxy/gateway server.
mod_proxy_ajp	Uses mod_proxy to provide support for Apache JServ Protocol (version 1.3).
mod_proxy_balancer	Extension to mod_proxy to handle load balancing.
mod_proxy_connect	Extension to mod_proxy to handle CONNECT requests.
mod_proxy_ftp	Extension to mod_proxy to handle FTP requests.
mod_proxy_http	Extension to mod_proxy to handle HTTP requests.
mod_rewrite	Provides a flexible and extensible method for redirecting client requests and mapping incoming URLs to other locations in the file system.
mod_setenvif	Conditionally sets environment variables based on the contents of various HTTP header fields.
mod_speling	Attempts to correct misspellings automatically in requested URLs.
mod_ssl	Implements cryptography using SSL and TLS protocols.
mod_status	Provides a summary of the activities of each individual httpd server process, including CPU and bandwidth usage levels.
mod_suexec	Lets CGI scripts run with permission of a particular user or group.
mod_unique_id	Assigns the UNIQUE_ID environment variable to provide a unique identifier for each request.
mod_userdir	Specifies locations that can contain individual users' HTML documents.
mod_usertrack	Uses cookies to track the progress of users through a Web site.
mod_version	Allows you to use <IFVersion> containers to allow version-dependent configuration.
mod_vhost_alias	Contains support for dynamically configured mass virtual hosting.

More information about each module (and the directives that can be defined within it) can be found on your server at `http://localhost/manual/mod/`.

Including module-specific configuration files

The following lines cause Apache to load configuration files from the
/etc/httpd/conf.d/ directory. This directory contains configuration files associated with
specific modules.

```
#
# Load config files from the config directory "/etc/httpd/conf.d".
#
Include conf.d/*.conf
```

> **CROSS-REFERENCE:** The "Configuring modules and related services (/etc/httpd/conf.d/*.conf)"
> section, later in this chapter, describes some of the configuration files in the conf.d directory that may
> interest you.

Choosing the server's user and group

The httpd daemon doesn't have to run as the root user; the fact that it doesn't run as root by
default makes your system more secure. By setting User and Group entries, you can have the
httpd daemon run using the permissions associated with a different user and group:

```
# If you wish httpd to run as a different user or group, you must run
# httpd as root initially and it will switch.
#
# User/Group: The name (or #number) of the user/group to run httpd as.
#  . On SCO (ODT 3) use "User nouser" and "Group nogroup".
#  . On HPUX you may not be able to use shared memory as nobody, and
#  the suggested workaround is to create a user www and use that user.
#  NOTE that some kernels refuse to setgid(Group) or semctl(IPC_SET)
#  when the value of (unsigned)Group is above 60000;
#  don't use Group #-1 on these systems!
#
User apache
Group apache
```

By default, apache is defined as both the user and group for the server. If you change the User
and Group directives, you should specify a nonprivileged entity. This minimizes the risk of
damage if your site is compromised. The first daemon process that is started runs as root. This
is necessary to bind the server to a low-numbered port and to switch to the user and group
specified by the User and Group directives. All other processes run under the user ID (UID)
and group ID (GID) defined by those directives.

Setting the main server's configuration

The second section of the http.conf file relates to directives handled by your main server
(the one defined by the ServerName directive). In other words, these values are used by the
default server and for all virtual hosts, unless they are explicitly changed for a virtual host. To
change the same directives for particular virtual hosts, add them within virtual host containers.

Setting an e-mail address

You can identify an address where users can send e-mail if there is a problem with your server. This is done with the `ServerAdmin` directive:

```
#
# ServerAdmin: Your address, where problems with the server should be
# e-mailed.  This address appears on some server-generated pages, such
# as error documents. e.g. admin@your-domain.com
#
ServerAdmin you@your.address
```

The `ServerAdmin` directive can be set to any valid e-mail address. The default is `root@localhost`.

Setting the server name

If your server name is anything but your exact registered host or domain name, you should identify your server name here. As the comments point out, the `ServerName` directive can be set to a value other than the actual hostname of your machine. However, this other name should still point to your machine in DNS if the server is to be a public Internet server. Frequently, www is just an alias for the real name of the machine (for example, a machine may respond to `www.linuxtoys.net`, but its real name may be `al.linuxtoys.net`).

```
ServerName jukebox.linuxtoys.net
```

Apache tries to use your hostname as the `ServerName`, if you don't enter a valid server name. It is recommended that you explicitly enter a `ServerName` here.

Setting canonical names

Use the `UseCanonicalName` directive to create a self-referencing URL, as follows:

```
## UseCanonicalName: Determines how Apache constructs self-referencing
# URLs and the SERVER_NAME and SERVER_PORT variables.
# When set "Off", Apache will use the Hostname and Port supplied
# by the client.  When set "On", Apache will use the value of the
# ServerName directive.
#
UseCanonicalName Off
```

The `UseCanonicalName` directive provides a form of naming consistency. When it is set to `On`, Apache uses the `ServerName` and `Port` directives to create a URL that references a file on the same machine (for example, `http://www.linuxtoys.net/docs/`). When `UseCanonicalName` is `Off`, the URL consists of whatever the client specified (for example, the URL could be `http://al.linuxtoys.net/docs/` or `http://al/docs/` if the client is within the same domain).

This can be problematic, particularly when access-control rules require username and password authentication: if the client is authenticated for the host `al.linuxtoys.net` but a link sends him or her to `www.linuxtoys.net` (physically the same machine), the client will

be prompted to enter a username and password again. It is recommended that
UseCanonicalName be set to On. In the preceding situation, the authentication would not
need to be repeated because any reference to the same server would always be interpreted as
www.linuxtoys.net.

Identifying HTTP content directories

There are several directives for determining the location of your server's Web content. The
main location for your Web content is set to /var/www/html by the DocumentRoot
directive. (Note that this location has changed from early versions of Red Hat Linux. The
location was formerly in /home/http.)

```
# DocumentRoot: The directory out of which you will serve your
# documents. By default, all requests are taken from the directory, but
# symbolic links and aliases may be used to point to other locations.
DocumentRoot "/var/www/html"
```

Setting access options and overrides

You can set individual access permissions for each directory in the Web server's directory
structure. The default is fairly restrictive. Here is the default:

```
<Directory />
    Options FollowSymLinks
    AllowOverride None
</Directory>
```

This segment sets up a default block of permissions for the Options and AllowOverride
directives. The <Directory />...</Directory> tags enclose the directives that are to
be applied to the / directory (which is /var/www/html by default, as defined by
DocumentRoot).

The Options FollowSymLinks directive instructs the server that symbolic links within the
directory can be followed to allow content that resides in other locations on the computer.
None of the other special server features will be active in the / directory, or in any directory
below that, without being explicitly specified later. Next, the following access options are
specifically set for the root of your Web server (/var/www/html). (I removed the comments
here for clarity.)

```
<Directory "/var/www/html">
    Options Indexes FollowSymLinks
    AllowOverride None
    Order allow,deny
    Allow from all
</Directory>
```

If you have changed the value of DocumentRoot earlier in this file, you need to change the
/var/www/html to match that value. The Options set for the directory are Indexes and
FollowSymLinks. Those and other special server features are described in Table 21-2. The

`AllowOverride None` directive instructs the server that an `.htaccess` file (or the value of `AccessFileName`) cannot override any of the special access features. You can replace `None` with any of the special access features described in Table 21-3.

Table 21-2: Special Server Features for the Options Directive

Feature	Description
`ExecCGI`	The execution of CGI scripts is permitted.
`FollowSymLinks`	The server will traverse symbolic links.
`Includes`	Server-Side Includes are permitted.
`IncludesNOEXEC`	Server-Side Includes are permitted, except the `#exec` element.
`Indexes`	If none of the files specified in the `DirectoryIndex` directive exists, a directory index will be generated by mod_autoindex.
`MultiViews`	The server allows content negotiation based on preferences from the user's browser, such as preferred language, character set, and media type.
`SymLinksIfOwnerMatch`	The server will traverse symbolic links only if the owner of the target is the same as the owner of the link.
`None`	None of the features above are enabled.
`All`	All the features above are enabled, with the exception of `MultiViews`. This must be explicitly enabled.

Table 21-3: Special Access Features for the AllowOverride Directive

Feature	Description
`AuthConfig`	Enables authentication-related directives (`AuthName`, `AuthType`, `AuthUserFile`, `AuthGroupFile`, `Require`, and so on).
`FileInfo`	Enables MIME-related directives (`AddType`, `AddEncoding`, `AddLanguage`, `LanguagePriority`, and so on).
`Indexes`	Enables directives related to directory indexing (`FancyIndexing`, `DirectoryIndex`, `IndexOptions`, `IndexIgnore`, `HeaderName`, `ReadmeName`, `AddIcon`, `AddDescription`, and so on).
`Limit`	Enables directives controlling host access (`Allow`, `Deny`, and `Order`).
`Options`	Enables the `Options` directive (as described in Table 21-2).
`None`	None of the access features above can be overridden.
`All`	All the access features above can be overridden.

> **NOTE:** Remember that unless you specifically enable a feature described in Tables 21-2 and 21-3, that feature is not enabled for your server (with the exceptions of `Indexes` and `FollowSymLinks`).

Identifying user dirctories

If you have multiple users on your server and you want each to be able to publish their own Web content, it is common practice to identify a directory name that users can create in their own home directories to store that content. When you identify the name that is appended to a user's home directory, that directory is used to respond to requests to the server for the user's name (~*user*). This directory name used to be set to `public_html` by default; however, it is now turned off by default.

To allow access to your users' personal Web pages, add a comment character (#) to the `UserDir disable` line. Then remove the # from the `UserDir public_html` line to make users' personal `public_html` directories accessible through the Web server. After removing extra comment lines, the following text shows what the enabled section looks like:

```
# UserDir: The name of the directory which is appended onto a user's
# home directory if a ~user request is received.

<ifModule mod_userdir.c>
#   UserDir disable
UserDir public_html
</IfModule>
```

Besides uncommenting the `UserDir public_html` line shown in the previous example, you must make both the user's home directory and `public_html` directory executable by everyone in order for the `UserDir` directive to allow access to a particular user's `public_html` directory. For example, the user `cjb` could type the following to make those directories accessible.

```
$ chmod 711 /home/cjb
$ mkdir /home/cjb/public_html
$ chmod 755 /home/cjb/public_html
```

For `UserDir` to work, the `mod_userdir` module must also be loaded (which it is by default).

There are two ways in which the `UserDir` directive can handle an incoming request that includes a username (for example, ~`cjb`). One possible format identifies the physical path name of the individual users' publicly accessible directories. The other can specify a URL to which the request is redirected. A few examples are presented in Table 21-4, using the URL `http://www.mybox.com/~cjb/proj/c004.html` as a sample request.

Table 21-4: UserDir Path Name and URL Examples

UserDir Directive	Referenced Path or URL
UserDir public_html	~cjb/public_html/proj/c004.html
UserDir /public/*/WWW	/public/cjb/WWW/proj/c004.html
UserDir /usr/local/web	/usr/local/web/cjb/proj/c004.html
UserDir http://www.mybox.com/users	http://www.mybox.com/users/cjb/proj/c004.html
UserDir http://www.mybox.com/~*	http://www.mybox.com/~cjb/proj/c004.html
UserDir http://www.mybox.com/*/html	http://www.mybox.com/cjb/html/proj/c004.html

The UserDir directive can also be used to explicitly allow or deny URL-to-path name translation for particular users. For example, it is a good idea to include the following line to avoid publishing data that shouldn't be made public:

```
UserDir disable root
```

Alternatively, use the following lines to disable the translations for all but a few users:

```
UserDir disable
UserDir enable wilhelm cjb jsmith
```

> **NOTE:** You should always be careful about content you publish about yourself on the Internet (names, addresses, personal information,and so on) and also keep in mind that you can be held accountable for the content you publish on your Web server. When you allow others to publish on your Web server, your liability can extend to what those users publish as well. Be sure to have a clear policy about what is acceptable (and legal) to publish on your Web server and give that information to those you allow to use the server.

Setting default index files for directories

The DirectoryIndex directive establishes a list of files that is used when an incoming request specifies a directory rather than a file. For example, a client requests the URL http://www.mybox.com/~jsmith. Because it's a directory, it is automatically translated to http://www.mybox.com/~jsmith/. Now that directory is searched for in any of the files listed in the DirectoryIndex directive. The first match (from the default list of index.html and index.html.var) is used as the default document in that directory. If none of the files exist and the Indexes option (as in the httpd.conf file) is selected, the server will automatically generate an index of the files in the directory.

```
# DirectoryIndex: sets the file that Apache will serve if a directory
# is requested.
#
# The index.html.var file (a type-map) is used to deliver content-
# negotiated documents.  The MultiViews Option can be used for the
# same purpose, but it is much slower.
#
DirectoryIndex index.html index.html.var
```

Sometimes dynamic content (such as index.php or index.cgi) will be added to the
DirectoryIndex to make sure that dynamic content is accessed before static content when
a user simply requests a domain name or directory.

Setting directory-access control

You and your users can add an access file to each directory to control access to that directory.
By default, the AccessFileName directive sets .htaccess as the file containing this
information. The following lines set this filename and prevent the contents of that file from
being viewed by visitors to the Web site. If you change the file to a name other than
.htaccess, be sure to change the line below ("^\.ht") that denies access to that file.

```
#
# AccessFileName: The name of the file to look for in each directory
# for access control information.
#
AccessFileName .htaccess

<Files ~ "^\.ht">
    Order allow,deny
    Deny from all
</Files>
```

You can add the same access directives to a .htaccess file as you do to the httpd.conf
file. In general, it is more efficient to use a <Directory> directive in the httpd.conf file
than it is to create a .htaccess file. With a <Directory> directive, you can specifically
identify the access associated with that directory alone. Because directives you put in
.htaccess apply to all directories below the current directory, any time you add a
.htaccess file to a directory, Apache must search all directories above that point (for
example, /, /var, /var/www. and so on) to include settings from possible .htaccess files
in those directories as well.

Setting MIME-type defaults

The location of the MIME type definitions file is defined by the TypesConfig directive. The
DefaultType directive sets the MIME type:

```
# TypesConfig describes where the mime.types file (or equivalent) is
# to be found.
#
TypesConfig /etc/mime.types

#
# DefaultType is the default MIME type the server will use for a
# document if it cannot otherwise determine one, such as from filename
# extensions. If your server contains mostly text or HTML documents,
# "text/plain" is a good value.  If most of the content is binary, such
# as applications or images, you may want to use "application/octet-
# stream" instead to keep browsers from trying to display binary files
# as though they are text.
#
DefaultType text/plain
```

With the mod_mime_magic module, a server can look for hints to help figure out what type of file is being requested. You must make sure this module is loaded to Apache for it to be used (it is loaded by default). The module can use hints from the /usr/share/magic.mime (off by default) and /etc/httpd/conf/magic (on by default) files to determine the contents of a requested file. Here are the directives that cause that module to be used:

```
<IfModule mod_mime_magic.c>
#   MIMEMagicFile /usr/share/magic.mime
    MIMEMagicFile conf/magic
</IfModule>
```

Setting hostname lookups

With the Apache Web server, you can have the server look up addresses for incoming client requests. Turning on the HostnameLookups entry can do this:

```
# HostnameLookups: Log the names of clients or just their IP addresses
HostnameLookups Off
```

If the HostnameLookups directive is turned on, every incoming connection will generate a DNS lookup to translate the client's IP address into a hostname. If your site receives many requests, the server's response time could be adversely affected. The HostnameLookups should be turned off unless you use a log file analysis program or statistics package that requires fully qualified domain names and cannot perform the lookups on its own. The logresolve program that is installed with the Apache distribution can be scheduled to edit log files by performing host name lookups during off-peak hours.

Configuring HTTP logging

You can set several values related to logging of Apache information. When a relative path name is shown, the directory set by ServerRoot (/etc/httpd/ by default) is appended (for example, /etc/httpd/logs/error_log). As shown in the following example, you can set the location of error logs, the level of log warnings, and some log nicknames:

```
#
# ErrorLog: The location of the error log file.
# If you do not specify an ErrorLog directive within a <VirtualHost>
# container, error messages relating to that virtual host will be
# logged here.  If you *do* define an error logfile for a <VirtualHost>
# container, that host's errors will be logged there and not here.
#
ErrorLog logs/error_log


#
# LogLevel: Control the number of messages logged to the error_log.
# Possible values include: debug, info, notice, warn, error, crit,
# alert, emerg.
#
LogLevel warn


#
# The following directives define some format nicknames for use with
# a CustomLog directive (see below).
#
LogFormat "%h %l %u %t \"%r\" %>s %b \"%{Referer}i\"\"%{User-
    Agent}i\"" combined
LogFormat "%h %l %u %t \"%r\" %>s %b" common
LogFormat "%{Referer}i -> %U" referer
LogFormat "%{User-agent}i" agent


#
# Location and format of the access logfile (Common Logfile Format).
# If you do not define any access logfiles within a <VirtualHost>
# container, they will be logged here.  Contrariwise, if you *do*
# define per-<VirtualHost> access logfiles, transactions will be
# logged therein and *not* in this file.
#
# CustomLog logs/access_log common

# If you would like to have separate agent and referer logfiles,
# uncomment the following directives.

#
#CustomLog logs/referer_log referer
#CustomLog logs/agent_log agent


#
# For a single logfile with access, agent, and referer information
# (Combined Logfile Format), use the following directive:
#
CustomLog logs/access_log combined
```

These lines deal with how server errors, client tracking information, and incoming requests are logged. The `ErrorLog` directive, which can specify an absolute path name or a path name relative to the `ServerRoot` (which is `/etc/httpd` by default), indicates where the server should store error messages. In this case the specified file is `logs/error_log`, which expands to `/etc/httpd/logs/error_log` (which in reality is a symlink to the `error_log` file in the `/var/log/httpd` directory).

The `LogLevel` directive controls the severity and quantity of messages that appear in the error log. Messages can range from the particularly verbose `debug` log level to the particularly silent `emerg` log level. With `debug`, a message is logged anytime the configuration files are read, when an access-control mechanism is used, or if the number of active servers has changed. With `emerg`, only critical system-level failures that create panic conditions for the server are logged.

The level specified by the `LogLevel` directive indicates the least-severe message that will be logged — all messages at that severity and above are recorded. For example, if `LogLevel` is set to `warn`, the error log will contain messages at the `warn`, `error`, `crit`, `alert`, and `emerg` levels. The default value of `warn` is a good choice for normal use (it will log only significant events that may eventually require operator intervention), but `info` and `debug` are perfect for testing a server's configuration or tracking down the exact location of errors.

The four `LogFormat` lines define (for later use) four types of log file formats: combined, common, referer, and agent. You can also add a fifth format called *combinedio*. The tokens available within the `LogFormat` directive are described in Table 21-5. The `LogFormat` definitions can be modified to your own personal preference, and other custom formats can be created as needed.

Table 21-5: Available Tokens within LogFormat

Token	Description
%a	The IP address of the client machine.
%b	The number of bytes sent to the client (excluding header information).
%{VAR}e	The contents of the environment variable VAR.
%f	The filename referenced by the requested URL.
%h	The hostname of the client machine.
%{Header}i	The contents of the specified header line in the HTTP request.
%l	As reported by the identd daemon (if available), the user on the client machine who initiated the request.
%{Note}n	The contents of the message Note from a different module.
%{Header}o	The contents of the specified header line in the HTTP response.

Token	Description
%p	The port number on which the request was received.
%P	The PID of the server process that handled the request.
%r	The actual HTTP request from the client.
%s	The server response code generated by the request.
%t	The current local time and date. The time format can be altered using %{Format}t, where Format is described in the strftime(3) man page.
%T	The number of seconds required to fulfill the client request.
%u	If access-control rules require username and password authentication, this represents the username supplied by the client.
%U	The URL requested by the client.
%v	The hostname and domain name of the server according to the Domain Name System (DNS).
%V	The hostname and domain name of the server handling the request according to the ServerName directive.

The *common* format includes the client host's name or IP address, the username as reported by the ident daemon and the server's authentication method (if applicable), the local time at which the request was made, the actual HTTP request, the server response code, and the number of bytes transferred. This format is a de facto standard among Web servers (and lately even among FTP servers).

For the purpose of connection tracking, the *referer* format stores the URL (from the same site or an external server) that linked to the document just delivered (relative to the ServerRoot). For example, if the page http://www.example.com/corp/about_us.html contained a link to your home page at http://www.mybox.com/linuxguy/bio.html, when a client accessed that link, the referer log on www.mybox.com would look like:

```
http://www.example.com/corp/about_us.html -> /linuxguy/bio.html
```

This information can be used to determine which path each client took to reach your site.

The *agent* format stores the contents of the User-agent: HTTP header for each incoming connection. This field typically indicates the browser name and version, the language, and the operating system or architecture on which the browser was run. On a Pentium II running Fedora, Mozilla will produce the following entry:

```
Mozilla/5.0 (X11; U; Linux i686; en-US; rv:1.6)
```

The *combined* format includes all the information from the other three log file formats into one line. This format is useful for storing all connection-related log entries in one centralized file. The *combinedio* format, which is commented out by default, can be enabled (by removing the # character) to log the actual number of bytes received (%I) and sent (%0), provided the mod_logio module is loaded.

The CustomLog directive assigns one of the defined LogFormat formats to a filename (again, specified as an absolute path name or a path name relative to the ServerRoot). The only uncommented definition assigns combined format to the /etc/httpd/logs/ access_log file. To retain the agent or referer information separately, uncomment the definitions. Also, you could choose to comment out the CustomLog logs/access_log combined line and use the definition for the common format instead.

Adding a signature

Any page that is generated by the Apache server can have a signature line added to the bottom of the page. Examples of server-generated pages include a directory listing, error page, a status page, or an info page. The ServerSignature directive can be set to On, Off, or EMail. Here is how ServerSignature appears by default:

```
# Optionally add a line containing the server version and virtual
# host name to server-generated pages (error documents, FTP directory
# listings, mod_status and mod_info output etc., but not CGI generated
# documents).
# Set to "EMail" to also include a mailto: link to the ServerAdmin.
# Set to one of:  On | Off | EMail
#
ServerSignature On
```

With ServerSignature On, a line similar to the following appears at the bottom of server-generated pages:

```
Apache/2.2.8 (Fedora) Server at toys.linuxtoys.net Port 80
```

With ServerSignature set to EMail, a link to the Web page's administrative e-mail account is added to the signature line (the server name becomes the link). If the directive is set to Off, the line doesn't appear at all. With SSL or webdav enabled, this information will appear in the server signature as well.

Aliasing relocated content

There are various ways to define alias content. These include the Alias and the ScriptAlias directives. Here are alias-related settings in httpd.conf (with comments removed):

```
#
# Aliases: Add here as many aliases as you need (with no limit). The
format is
# Alias fakename realname
```

```
#
Alias /icons/ "/var/www/icons/"

<Directory "/var/www/icons">
    Options Indexes MultiViews FollowSymLinks
    AllowOverride None
    Order allow,deny
    Allow from all
</Directory>

# ScriptAlias: This controls which directories contain server scripts.
ScriptAlias /cgi-bin/ "/var/www/cgi-bin/"

# "/var/www/cgi-bin" should be changed to whatever your ScriptAliased
# CGI directory exists, if you have that configured.
#
<Directory "/var/www/cgi-bin">
    AllowOverride None
    Options None
    Order allow,deny
    Allow from all
</Directory>
```

The `Alias` directive points to a file system location (not necessarily within the DocumentRoot). For example, with the following line in place, requests for documents in /bigjob (`http://www.mybox.com/bigjob/index.html`) would result in the retrieval of /home/newguy/proj/index.html.

```
Alias /bigjob /home/newguy/proj
```

The `icons` alias allows access to the Apache icons used by the Web server for your Web site. The `icons` directory is accessible from the /var/www directory.

The `ScriptAlias` directive performs a related function, but directories that it aliases contain executable code (most likely CGI scripts). The syntax is the same as for the `Alias` directive. Pay special attention whenever you use `ScriptAlias`. Because `ScriptAlias` defines where scripts that can be run from Web content on the server are located, you should make sure that you assign only those directories that contain scripts that are secured and won't open security holes in your system.

Redirecting requests for old content

As content changes on your Web server, some content will become obsolete while other content may move to a different place in the file system or to a different server. Using the `Redirect` directive, you can redirect requests for old content to new locations.

By default, there are no `Redirect` directives set for your Apache server. However, you can uncomment the following example and tailor it to your needs:

```
# Redirect permanent /foo http://www.example.com/bar
```

Redirect can be used to instruct clients that the document they seek has moved elsewhere (to the same server or to an external location) by simply indicating the old and new locations. If the previous Redirect option were in place, a client's attempt to access http://www.mybox.com/foo would redirect to http://www.example.com/bar.

Besides using permanent as the service for Redirect (which results in a redirect status 301), you could instead use temp (a redirect status of 302), seeother (a replaced status of 303), or gone (a permanently removed status of 401). You could also give any status code between 300 and 399 as the service, which represent different error responses. (These numbers are HTTP status codes.)

> **CROSS REFERENCE:** The HTTP status codes are defined as part of the HTTP protocol in RFC 2616. Refer to that document at www.w3.org/Protocols/rfc2616/rfc2616.txt.

Defining indexing

It's possible to have your Apache server show different icons for different types of files. To use this feature, IndexOptions should be set to FancyIndexing, and AddIconByEncoding, AddIconByType, and AddIcon directives should be used:

```
# Directives controlling display of server-generated directory listings.

# FancyIndexing is if you want fancy directory indexing or standard.
# VersionSort is whether files containing version numbers should be
# compared in the natural way, so that `apache-1.3.9.tar' is placed
# before `apache-1.3.12.tar'.
#
IndexOptions FancyIndexing VersionSort NameWidth=* HTMLTable
#
# AddIcon* directives tell the server which icon to show for different
# files or filename extensions.  These are only displayed for
# FancyIndexed directories.
#
AddIconByEncoding (CMP,/icons/compressed.gif) x-compress x-gzip

AddIconByType (TXT,/icons/text.gif) text/*
AddIconByType (IMG,/icons/image2.gif) image/*
AddIconByType (SND,/icons/sound2.gif) audio/*
AddIconByType (VID,/icons/movie.gif) video/*

AddIcon /icons/binary.gif .bin .exe
AddIcon /icons/binhex.gif .hqx
AddIcon /icons/tar.gif .tar
AddIcon /icons/world2.gif .wrl .wrl.gz .vrml .vrm .iv
AddIcon /icons/compressed.gif .Z .z .tgz .gz .zip
AddIcon /icons/a.gif .ps .ai .eps
```

```
AddIcon /icons/layout.gif .html .shtml .htm .pdf
AddIcon /icons/text.gif .txt
AddIcon /icons/c.gif .c
AddIcon /icons/p.gif .pl .py
AddIcon /icons/f.gif .for
AddIcon /icons/dvi.gif .dvi
AddIcon /icons/uuencoded.gif .uu
AddIcon /icons/script.gif .conf .sh .shar .csh .ksh .tcl
AddIcon /icons/tex.gif .tex
AddIcon /icons/bomb.gif core

AddIcon /icons/back.gif ..
AddIcon /icons/hand.right.gif README
AddIcon /icons/folder.gif ^^DIRECTORY^^
AddIcon /icons/blank.gif ^^BLANKICON^^

#
# DefaultIcon: which icon to show for files which do not have an icon
# explicitly set.
#
DefaultIcon /icons/unknown.gif

#
# AddDescription: allows you to place short description after a file in
# server-generated indexes.  These are only displayed for FancyIndexed
# directories.
# Format: AddDescription "description" filename
#
#AddDescription "GZIP compressed document" .gz
#AddDescription "tar archive" .tar
#AddDescription "GZIP compressed tar archive" .tgz

#
# ReadmeName: the name of the README file the server will look for by
# default, and append to directory listings.
#
# HeaderName is the name of a file which should be prepended to
# directory indexes.
#
ReadmeName README.html
HeaderName HEADER.html

#
# IndexIgnore is a set of filenames which directory indexing should
# ignore and not include in the listing.  Shell-style wildcarding is
# permitted.
#
IndexIgnore .??* *~ *# HEADER* README* RCS CVS *,v *,t
```

The previous block of options deals with how server-generated directory indexes are handled. The `IndexOptions FancyIndexing VersionSort NameWidth=*` directive enables an autogenerated directory index to include several bits of information about each file or directory, including an icon representing the file type, the filename, the last modification time for the file, the file's size, and a description of the file. Figure 21-2 shows an example of a directory using default `FancyIndexing` settings.

The `VersionSort` option allows files that include version numbers to be sorted as would be most natural (so, for example, version-2 would come before version-10 with this option on). The `NameWidth=*` option allows filenames of any length to be displayed. You change the asterisk to a number representing the maximum number of characters that can be displayed in the Name column. If `IndexOptions` is not set to `FancyIndexing`, the index lists only the file's name.

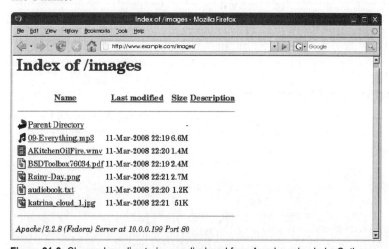

Figure 21-2: Change how directories are displayed from Apache using IndexOptions.

The `AddIconByEncoding` directive is used to configure the output of `FancyIndexing`. It causes a particular icon to be displayed for files matching a particular MIME encoding. In the `AddIconByEncoding` line in the previous example, `compressed.gif` (with an alternative image tag of `CMP` for browsers that don't load images) will be displayed for files with a MIME encoding of x-compress and x-gzip. The `AddIconByType` directive has the same syntax but matches files based on their MIME type.

The `AddIcon` directive performs a similar function, but the icons are displayed based on a pattern in the filename. In the lines above, for example, `bomb.gif` will be displayed for files ending with `core`, and `binary.gif` will be displayed for files ending in `.bin` and `.exe`. The `folder.gif` icon represents a subdirectory.

If there is a conflict between the `AddIcon`, `AddIconByEncoding`, or `AddIconByType` directives, the `AddIcon` directive has precedence. The `DefaultIcon` directive specifies the image to be displayed (unknown.gif, according to the line above) if no previous directive has associated an icon with a particular file.

The HeaderName and ReadmeName directives specify files that will be inserted at the top and bottom of the autogenerated directory index, if they exist. Using the default values, the server first looks for HEADER.html, then HEADER, to include at the top of the "fancy index." At the end of the index, README.html or README (whichever is located first) is inserted.

The IndexIgnore directive specifies files that should not appear in an autogenerated directory index. The line above excludes:

- Any filename starting with a dot and containing at least two additional characters
- Any filename ending with a tilde (~) or what is commonly called a hash mark (#) (typically used by text editors as temporary files or backup files)
- Filenames beginning with HEADER or README (the files displayed at the top and bottom of the directory listing, according to the HeaderName and ReadmeName directives)
- The RCS (Revision Control System) or CVS (Concurrent Versions System) directories

Defining encoding and language

The AddEncoding directive lets you set compression definitions that can be used by browsers to encode data as it arrives. The AddLanguage directive lets you indicate the language of a document, based on its file suffix.

```
#
# AddEncoding: allows you to have certain browsers (Mosaic/X 2.1+)
# uncompress information on fly. Note: Not all browsers support this.
# Despite name similarity, the following Add* directives have nothing
# to do with the FancyIndexing customization directives above.
#
AddEncoding x-compress Z
AddEncoding x-gzip gz tgz


#
# DefaultLanguage and AddLanguage allows you to specify the language of
# a document. You can then use content negotiation to give a browser a
# file in a language it can understand.
         .
         .
         .
# Spanish (es) - Swedish (sv) - Catalan (ca) - Czech(cz)
# Polish (pl) - Brazilian Portuguese (pt-br) - Japanese (ja)
# Russian (ru)
#
AddLanguage da .dk
AddLanguage nl .nl
AddLanguage en .en
```

```
AddLanguage et .ee
AddLanguage fr .fr
      .
      .
      .
# LanguagePriority: allows you to give precedence to some languages
# in case of a tie during content negotiation.
#
# Just list the languages in decreasing order of preference. We have
# more or less alphabetized them. You probably want to change this.
#
LanguagePriority en da nl et fr de el it ja ko no pl pt pt-br ru ltz ca
        es sv tw
```

The `AddEncoding` directive supplements or overrides mappings provided by the `TypesConfig` file (`/etc/mime.types` by default). Knowledge of the MIME type/encoding may allow certain browsers to manipulate files automatically as they are being downloaded or retrieved.

The `AddLanguage` directive performs similar mappings, associating a MIME language definition with a filename extension. The `LanguagePriority` directive determines the precedence if a particular file exists in several languages (and if the client does not specify a preference). Using the preceding definition, if the file `index.html` were requested from a directory that contained the files `index.html.de`, `index.html.en`, `index.html.fr`, and `index.html.it`, the `index.html.en` file would be sent to the client.

Using `LanguagePriority`, you can set which language is used in case a decision on what language to use can't be made during content negotiation. If you are expecting multilanguage use of your Web content, you should check (and probably change) the priority here.

Choosing character sets

The default character set to use and character sets to use for files with particular file extensions are set using the `AddDefaultCharset` and `AddCharset` directives, respectively. Although UTF-8 is the default character set, I recommend specifically UTF-8 as the default character set (as shown in the following code example). Other standard ISO fonts, as well as some nonstandard fonts, are set using `AddCharset` directives.

```
AddDefaultCharset UTF-8
#
AddCharset ISO-8859-1   .iso8859-1   .latin1
AddCharset ISO-8859-2   .iso8859-2   .latin2 .cen
AddCharset ISO-8859-3   .iso8859-3   .latin3
AddCharset ISO-8859-4   .iso8859-4   .latin4
AddCharset ISO-8859-5   .iso8859-5   .latin5 .cyr .iso-ru
AddCharset ISO-8859-6   .iso8859-6   .latin6 .arb
         .
         .
         .
```

You can retrieve an official list of character sets and the file extensions that are assigned to them at `www.iana.org/assignments/character-sets`.

Adding MIME types and handlers

With the `AddType` directive, you can enhance the MIME types assigned for your Apache Web server without editing the `/etc/mime.types` file. With the `AddHandler` directive, you can map selected file extensions to handlers (that result in certain actions being taken):

```
# AddType allows you to add to or override the MIME configuration
# file mime.types for specific file types.

AddType application/x-tar .tgz

#
# For server-parsed imagemap files:
#
AddHandler imap-file map

#
# For type maps (negotiated resources):
# (This is enabled by default to allow the Apache "It Worked" page
#  to be distributed in multiple languages.)
#
AddHandler type-map var
```

Defining actions and headers

Some types of media can be set to execute a script when they are opened. Likewise, certain handler names, when opened, can be set to perform specified scripts. The `Action` directive can be used to configure these scripts:

```
# Action lets you define media types that execute a script whenever
# a matching file is called. This eliminates the need for repeated URL
# pathnames for oft-used CGI file processors.
# Format: Action media/type /cgi-script/location
# Format: Action handler-name /cgi-script/location
```

The `Action` directive maps a CGI script to a handler or a MIME type, whereas the `Script` directive maps a CGI script to a particular HTTP request method (`GET`, `POST`, `PUT`, or `DELETE`). These options allow scripts to be executed whenever a file of the appropriate MIME type is requested, a handler is called, or a request method is invoked.

Customizing error responses

For different error conditions that occur, you can define specific responses. The responses can be in plain text, redirects to pages on the local server, or redirects to external pages:

```
#
# Customizable error responses come in three flavors:
# 1) plain text 2) local redirects 3) external redirects
#
# Some examples:
#ErrorDocument 500 "The server made a boo boo."
#ErrorDocument 404 /missing.html
#ErrorDocument 404 "/cgi-bin/missing_handler.pl"
#ErrorDocument 402 http://www.example.com/subscription_info.html
#
```

As the comments suggest, the `ErrorDocument` directive can customize any server response code, redirecting it to an external page, a local file or CGI script, or to a simple text sentence. Table 21-6 lists the most common server response codes and their meanings.

Table 21-6: HTTP Response Codes

Response Code	Meaning
200 OK	The request was successfully processed.
201 Created	Using the `POST` request method, a new file was successfully stored on the server.
202 Accepted	The request has been received and is currently being processed.
204 No Content	The request was successful, but there is no change in the current page displayed to the client.
301 Moved Permanently	The requested page has been permanently moved, and future references to that page should use the new URL that is displayed.
302 Moved Temporarily	The requested page has been temporarily relocated. Future references should continue to use the same URL, but the current connection is being redirected.
304 Not Modified	A cached version of the page is identical to the requested page.
400 Bad Request	The client's request contains invalid syntax.
401 Unauthorized	The client specified an invalid username/password combination.
402 Payment Required	The client must provide a means to complete a monetary transaction.
403 Forbidden	Access-control mechanisms deny the client's request.
404 Not Found	The requested page does not exist on the server.
500 Internal Server Error	Usually encountered when running a CGI program, this response code indicates that the program or script contains invalid code or was given input that it cannot handle.
501 Not Implemented	The request method (for example, `GET`, `POST`, `PUT`, `DELETE`, `HEAD`) is not understood by the server.

Response Code	Meaning
502 Bad Gateway	With the Web server acting as a proxy server, an error was encountered when trying to fulfill the request to an external host.
503 Service Unavailable	The server is currently processing too many requests.
505 HTTP Version Not Supported	The request version (for example, HTTP/1.0, HTTP/1.1) is not understood by the server.

To make it easier to internationalize error messages and standardize how these messages are presented, the latest version of Apache includes what are referred to as variant pages (ending in a `.var` suffix). These variant pages, which offer variable output based on language, are stored in the `/var/www/error` directory.

```
Alias /error/ "/var/www/error/"

<IfModule mod_negotiation.c>
<IfModule mod_include.c>
    <Directory "/var/www/error">
        AllowOverride None
        Options IncludesNoExec
        AddOutputFilter Includes html
        AddHandler type-map var
        Order allow,deny
        Allow from all
        LanguagePriority en es de fr
        ForceLanguagePriority Prefer Fallback
    </Directory>

    ErrorDocument 400 /error/HTTP_BAD_REQUEST.html.var
    ErrorDocument 401 /error/HTTP_UNAUTHORIZED.html.var
    ErrorDocument 403 /error/HTTP_FORBIDDEN.html.var
    ErrorDocument 404 /error/HTTP_NOT_FOUND.html.var
    ErrorDocument 405 /error/HTTP_METHOD_NOT_ALLOWED.html.var
        .
        .
        .
```

The `ErrorDocument` directive associates a particular error code number with a particular `.var` file that contains multiple possible responses based on language.

Setting responses to browsers

If file extensions are not enough to determine a file's MIME type, you can define hints with the `MimeMagicFile` directive. With the `BrowserMatch` directive, you can set responses to conditions based on particular browser types:

```
#
# The following directives modify normal HTTP response behavior to
```

```
# handle known problems with browser implementations.
#
BrowserMatch "Mozilla/2" nokeepalive
BrowserMatch "MSIE 4\.0b2;" nokeepalive downgrade-1.0 force-response-1.0
BrowserMatch "RealPlayer 4\.0" force-response-1.0
BrowserMatch "Java/1\.0" force-response-1.0
BrowserMatch "JDK/1\.0" force-response-1.0


#
# The following directive disables redirects on non-GET requests for
# a directory that does not include the trailing slash.  This fixes a
# problem with Microsoft WebFolders which does not appropriately handle
# redirects for folders with DAV methods.
# Same deal with Apple's DAV filesystem and Gnome VFS support for DAV.
#
BrowserMatch "Microsoft Data Access Internet Publishing Provider"
    redirect-carefully
BrowserMatch "MS FrontPage" redirect-carefully
BrowserMatch "^WebDrive" redirect-carefully
BrowserMatch "^WebDAVFS/1.[0123]" redirect-carefully
BrowserMatch "^gnome-vfs/1.0" redirect-carefully
BrowserMatch "^XML Spy" redirect-carefully
BrowserMatch "Dreamweaver-WebDAV-SCM1" redirect-carefully
```

The `BrowserMatch` directive enables you to set environment variables based on the contents of the `User-agent:` `header` field. The `force-response-1.0` variable causes a HTTP/1.0 response, indicating that Apache will respond to the browser in basic HTTP 1.0 operations.

> **NOTE:** If you are following the `httpd.conf` file, you notice that we are skipping descriptions of the server-status lines and server-info lines. They are described in the section "Monitoring Server Activities" later in this chapter.

Enabling proxy and caching services

Proxy and caching services are turned off by default. You can turn them on by uncommenting the following directives:

```
#
# Proxy Server directives. Uncomment the following lines to
# enable the proxy server:
#
#<IfModule mod_proxy.c>
#    ProxyRequests On
#
#<Proxy:*>
#    Order deny,allow
#    Deny from all
```

```
#      Allow from .example.com
#</Proxy>

#
# Enable/disable the handling of HTTP/1.1 "Via:" headers.
# ("Full" adds server version; "Block" removes outgoing Via: headers)
# Set to one of: Off | On | Full | Block
#
#ProxyVia On

# To enable a cache of proxied content, uncomment the following lines.
# See http:/httpd.apache.org/docs/2.2/mod/mod_cache.html for more
details.
#
#<IfModule mod_disk_cache.c>
# CacheEnable disk /
# CacheRoot "/var/cache/mod_proxy"
#</IfModule>

#</IfModule>
# End of proxy directives.
```

Apache can function as a proxy server, a caching server, or a combination of the two. If ProxyRequests is set to Off, the server will simply cache files without acting as a proxy. If CacheRoot (which specifies the directory used to contain the cache files) is undefined, no caching will be performed. Both proxy and caching services are Off (commented out) by default.

If you turn on caching, the CacheRoot should exist on a file system with enough free space to accommodate the cache, which is limited by the CacheSize directive. However, you should have 20 to 40 percent more space available in the file system because cache cleanup (to maintain the CacheSize, in kilobytes) occurs only periodically (which you can set using the CacheGcInterval directive).

You can add other directives to this example to enable other caching features. The CacheMaxExpire directive can indicate the maximum number of hours that a document will exist in the cache without checking the original document for modifications. The CacheLastModifiedFactor applies to documents that do not have an expiration time, even though the protocol would support one. To formulate an expiration date, the factor (a floating-point number) is multiplied by the number of hours since the document's last modification. For example, if the document were modified three days ago and the CacheLastModifiedFactor were 0.25, the document would expire from the cache in 18 hours (as long as this value is still below the value of CacheMaxExpire).

The CacheDefaultExpire directive (specifying the number of hours before a document expires) applies to documents received via protocols that do not support expiration times. The

`NoCache` directive contains a space-separated list of IP addresses, hostnames, or keywords in hostnames that should not have documents cached.

Here's how the caching server behaves if you uncomment the previous `Cache` lines:

- The cached files would exist in `/var/cache/mod_proxy`.
- Cache size is limited to 500 Kbytes.

You might want to allow a much larger `CacheSize`, and possibly set a short `CacheGcInterval`, but otherwise the supplied values are reasonable. The `CacheGcInterval` value can be a floating-point number (for example, 1.25 indicates 75 minutes).

Configuring virtual hosting

If you have one Web server computer, but more than one domain that you want to serve with that computer, you can set up Apache to do virtual hosting. With name-based virtual hosting, a single IP address can be the access point for multiple domain names on the same computer. With IP-based virtual hosting, you have a different IP address for each virtual host, which you achieve by having multiple network interfaces to a machine.

With virtual hosting, when a request comes into your Apache server from a Web browser through a particular IP address on your computer, Apache checks the domain name being requested and displays the content associated with that domain name. As an administrator of a Web server that supports virtual hosting, you must make sure that everything that needs to be configured for that virtual server is set up properly (you must define such things as locations for the Web content, log files, administrative contact, and so on).

Virtual hosting is defined with the `VirtualHost` tags. Information related to virtual hosts in the `/etc/httpd/conf/httpd.conf` file is shown in the following code:

```
### Section 3: Virtual Hosts
#
# VirtualHost: If you want to maintain multiple domains/hostnames on
# your machine you can setup VirtualHost containers for them. Most
# configurations use only name-based virtual hosts so the server
# doesn't need to worry about IP addresses. This is indicated by the
# asterisks in the directives below.
#
# Please see the documentation at
# <URL:http://httpd.apache.org/docs/2.2/vhosts/>
# for further details before you try to setup virtual hosts.
#
# You may use the command line option '-S' to verify your virtual host
# configuration.
#
# Use name-based virtual hosting.
#
```

```
#NameVirtualHost *:80
#
# NOTE: NameVirtualHost cannot be used without a port specifier
# (e.g. :80) if mod_ssl is being used, due to the nature of the
# SSL protocol.

#
# VirtualHost example:
# Almost any Apache directive may go into a VirtualHost container.
# The first VirtualHost section is used for requests without a known
# server name.
#
#<VirtualHost *:80>
#     ServerAdmin webmaster@dummy-host.example.com
#     DocumentRoot /www/docs/dummy-host.example.com
#     ServerName dummy-host.example.com
#     ErrorLog logs/dummy-host.example.com-error_log
#     CustomLog logs/dummy-host.example.com-access_log common
#</VirtualHost>
```

The following example lists virtual host directives that would allow you to host the domains
handsonhistory.com and linuxtoys.net on the same computer:

```
NameVirtualHost *:80

<VirtualHost *:80>
     DocumentRoot /var/www/handsonhistory
     ServerName www.handsonhistory.com
     ServerAlias handsonhistory.com
     ServerAdmin webmaster@handsonhistory.com
     ErrorLog logs/handsonhistory.com-error_log
     CustomLog logs/handsonhistory.com-access_log common
</VirtualHost>

<VirtualHost *:80>
     DocumentRoot /var/www/linuxtoys
     ServerName www.linuxtoys.net
     ServerAlias linuxtoys.net
     ServerAdmin webmaster@linuxtoys.net
     ErrorLog logs/linuxtoys.net-error_log
     CustomLog logs/linuxtoys.net-access_log common
</VirtualHost>
```

To experiment with virtual hosts, you can add the new host name to your local /etc/hosts
file and point at your localhost IP address. For example:

```
127.0.0.1        www.linuxtoys.net
```

If you see the content you set up for your virtual host, and not the Fedora error page or default
content you set up, then you probably set up your virtual host properly.

Configuring modules and related services (/etc/httpd/conf.d/*.conf)

Any module that requires special configuration will typically have a configuration file (`.conf` file) in the `/etc/httpd/conf.d/` directory. Here are modular configuration files that might be contained in that directory, along with some ways of using those files and the packages associated with them (use `yum install package` to install each package you want):

- **auth_kerb.conf** — Configure Kerberos authentication over a Web (HTTP) connection. The example in this file suggests using Kerberos authentication over an SSL connection. (Install the mod_auth_kerb package.)

- **auth_mysql.conf** — Configure authentication based on data you add to a MySQL database. Comments in the file describe how to set up the database and then use it to do user or group authentication before allowing a client to access your Web content. (Install the mod_auth_mysql package.)

- **auth_pgsql.conf** — Configure authentication based on data in a PostgreSQL database. (Install the mod_auth_pgsql package.)

- **authz_ldap.conf** — Configure authentication to access an LDAP database to authenticate users. (Install the mod_authz_ldap package.)

- **htdig.conf** — Identify the location of the htdig search content that can be used on your Web site (`/usr/share/htdig` is the default location). To see the htdig search screen from a Web browser, type **http://localhost/htdig**. The htdig system lets you set up tools for indexing and searching your Web site or company intranet. It is optional for your Web server. (Install the htdig-web package.)

- **mailman.conf** — Set up mailman list server software to allow features such as making mailing-list archives available from Apache. (Install the mailman package.)

- **manual.conf** — Defines the location of Apache manuals (`/var/www/manual`) on the server for different languages. Type **http://localhost/manual** in a browser window. (Install the httpd-manual package.)

- **mrtg.conf** — Defines the location of daily mrtg output (`/var/www/mrtg`), which tracks network traffic. Type **http://localhost/mrtg** in a browser window. (Install the mrtg package.)

- **perl.conf** — Identifies and loads the `mod_perl` module so that your Web pages can include Perl code. (Install the mod_perl package.)

- **php.conf** — Identifies and loads the libphp5 module so that your Web pages can include PHP scripting language. There is also a `DirectoryIndex` setting that allows an `index.php` file you add to a directory to be served as a directory index. (Install the php package.)

- **python.conf** — Identifies and loads the `mod_python` module so Web pages can include Apache handlers written in Python. (Install the mod_python package.)

- **squirrelmail.conf** — Identifies the location of the SquirrelMail Web-based mail interface so that it can be incorporated into your Apache Web server. To see the SquirrelMail login screen, type **http://localhost/webmail** into a browser window. (Install the squirrelmail package.)

- **ssl.conf** — Configure SSL support so that Apache knows how to serve pages requested over a secure connection (https). (Install the mod_ssl package.)

- **subversion.conf** — Loads the `mod_dav_svn` and `mod_authz_svn` modules to let you access a Subversion repository from Apache. By uncommenting lines in this file, you can set `/home/svnroot` as the location where you hold authorization files. (Install the mod_dav_svn package.)

- **webalizer.conf** — Lets you identify who can access the webalizer data (statistics about your Web site). (Install the webalizer package.)

- **wordtrans.conf** — Identifies the location of the WordTrans language translation window so that it can be incorporated into your Apache Web server. To see the WordTrans login screen, type **http://localhost/wordtrans** into a browser window. (Install the mod_auth_pgsql package.)

These configuration files are read when the httpd server starts. The information in these files could have been added to `httpd.conf`. However, files are put here so that different packages can add their own configuration settings without having the RPM software package incorporate some automated method of adding their configuration information to the `httpd.conf` file.

Starting and Stopping the Server

The procedure for starting and stopping the Apache Web server is no different from that of many other daemons. You can use the `chkconfig` command to set the httpd service to start at boot time.

> **CROSS-REFERENCE:** See Chapter 12 for detailed information on the inner workings of the shell scripts that control starting and stopping daemons and server processes.

The `/etc/init.d/httpd` shell script accepts any of a handful of command-line arguments. If it is called with the argument `start`, the `httpd` script will run one master daemon process (owned by `root`), which will spawn other daemon processes (equal to the number specified by the `StartServers` directive) owned by the user `apache` (from the `User` and `Group` directives). These processes are responsible for responding to incoming HTTP requests. If called with `stop`, the server will be shut down as all `httpd` processes are terminated.

If given a command-line argument of `restart`, the script will simply execute `stop` and `start` procedures in sequence. Using `reload` as the argument will send the hangup signal (`-HUP`) to the master `httpd` daemon, which causes it to reread its configuration files and restart all the other `httpd` daemon processes. The shell script also supports an argument of `status`, which will report if the daemon is running and, if it is, the PIDs of the running processes. All other command-line arguments result in an error and cause a usage message to be printed.

The actual binary for Apache, `/usr/sbin/httpd`, supports several command-line arguments, although the default values are typically used. The possible command-line arguments are listed in Table 21-7.

Table 21-7: Command-Line Arguments to httpd

Argument	Description
`-c directive`	Read the configuration files and then process the *directive*. This may supersede a definition for the directive within the configuration files.
`-C directive`	Process the *directive* and then read the configuration files. The directive may alter the evaluation of the configuration file, but it may also be superseded by another definition within the configuration file.
`-d directory`	Use *directory* as the `ServerRoot` directive, specifying where the module, configuration, and log file directories are located.
`-D parameter`	Define *parameter* to be used for conditional evaluation within the `IfDefine` directive.
`-f file`	Use *file* as the `ServerConfigFile` directive, rather than the default of `/etc/httpd/conf/httpd.conf`.
`-h`	Display a list of possible command-line arguments.
`-l`	List the modules linked into the executable at compile time.
`-L`	Print a verbose list of directives that can be used in the configuration files, along with a short description and the module that contains each directive.
`-S`	List the configured settings for virtual hosts.

`-t`	Perform a syntax check on the configuration files. The results will either be:
	
	`Syntax OK`
	
	or an error notification; for example:
	
	`Syntax error on line 118 of /etc/httpd/conf/httpd.conf`

`-T`	Same as `-t`, except that there is no check of the `DocumentRoot` value.

`-v`	Print the version information:
	
	`Server version: Apache/2.2.8 (Unix)`
	`Server built:   Feb 25 2008 07:05:32`

Argument	Description

-V	List the version information and any values defined during compilation:
	
	`Server version: Apache/2.2.8 (Unix)`
	`Server built: Feb 25 2008 07:05:32`
	`Server's Module Magic Number: 20051115:11`
	`Architecture:       32-bit`
	`. . . . .`
	`Server compiled with....`
	`-D APACHE_MPM_DIR="server/mpm/prefork"`
	`-D APR_HAS_MMAP`
	`-D APR_HAVE_IPV6 (IPV4-mapped addresses enabled)`
	`            .`
	`            .`
	`            .`
	`-D SERVER_CONFIG_FILE="conf/httpd.conf"`

-X	Only the single master daemon process is started, and no other httpd processes will be spawned. This should be used only for testing purposes directly from the command line.

Monitoring Server Activities

An Apache Web server is a tempting target for someone with a desire to hijack a computer for bad purposes. There are many techniques you can use to secure your server (covered in Chapter 14), which range from SELinux to using certificates to controlling how scripts are run. Described here, however, are techniques for keeping an eye on the performance and security of your Apache Web server. Watching your server carefully can often stop an attack before it gets anywhere.

Apache provides two unique built-in methods to check the performance and status of your Web server. The server-status handler can be configured to show information about server processes. The server-info handler can be configured to display a detailed summary of the Web server's configuration. You can activate these services by adding the following lines to the /etc/httpd/conf/httpd.conf file:

```
<Location /server-status>
    SetHandler server-status
    Order deny,allow
    Deny from all
    Allow from 127.0.0.1
</Location>

<Location /server-info>
    SetHandler server-info
    Order deny,allow
    Deny from all
    Allow from 127.0.0.1
</Location>
```

In this example, all users from the local computer can display the server-info and server-status pages. You can change 127.0.0.1to the name of any domain or host that your Apache server is hosting.

Displaying server information

The Server Information (server-info) page contains the server version information and various general configuration parameters and breaks up the rest of the data by module. Each loaded module is listed, with information about all directives supported by that module, and the current value of any defined directives from that module.

The Server Information is usually quite verbose and contains much more information than can be displayed in Figure 21-3, which shows only the links to each module's section and the general Server Settings section.

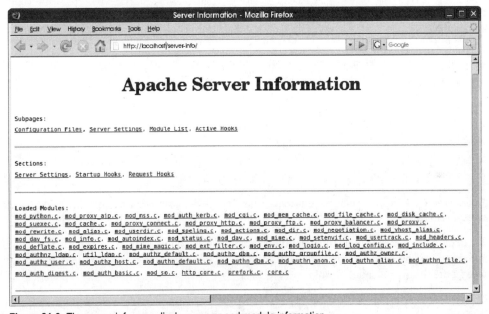

Figure 21-3: The server-info page displays server and module information.

Displaying server status

The contents of the server-status page include version information for the server, the current time, a timestamp of when the server was last started, and the server's uptime. The page also details the status of each server process, choosing from several possible states (waiting for a connection, just starting up, reading a request, sending a reply, waiting to read a request before reaching the number of seconds defined in the `KeepAliveTimeout`, performing a DNS lookup, logging a transaction, or gracefully exiting).

The bottom of the server-status page lists each server by process ID (PID) and indicates its state, using the same possible values. Figure 21-4 shows an example of this page.

The server-status page can also perform automatic updates to provide even closer monitoring of the server. If the URL `http://localhost/server-status?refresh=40` is specified, the server-status page displayed in your browser will be updated every 40 seconds. This enables a browser window to be entirely devoted to continually monitoring the activities of the Web server.

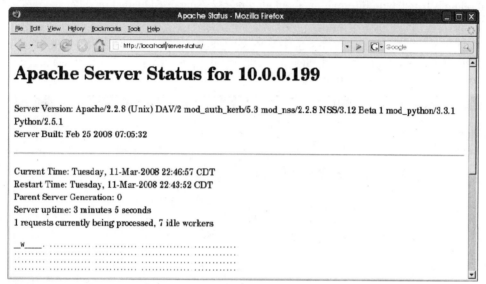

Figure 21-4: The Apache server-status page displays general Apache information and reports on individual server process activities.

By default, only basic status information is generated. If you would like to generate full status information, you need to turn on the `ExtendedStatus` directive by uncommenting the last line in the following code:

```
#
# ExtendedStatus: controls whether Apache will generate "full" status
# information (ExtendedStatus On) or basic information (ExtendedStatus
# Off) when the "server-status" handler is called. The default is Off.
#
#ExtendedStatus On
```

Further security of server-info and server-status

Because both the server-info and server-status pages contain private information that should not be accessible to just anyone on the network, there are a few extra ways you can secure that information. You can restrict that information only to the local host; however, in some environments that may not be practical.

If you must allow other machines or networks access to such detailed configuration information, allow only as many machines as is necessary, and preferably only those machines on your local network. Also, be aware that, in the wrong hands, the information displayed by the server-info and server-status pages can make it much easier for the security of your entire machine to be compromised.

It may also be beneficial to change the URL used to reference both of the aforementioned pages. This is an example of "security through obscurity," which should not be relied on but which can make it just a little more difficult for unauthorized individuals to obtain information about your Web server's configuration (particularly if you cannot restrict such connections to the local network). To accomplish this, simply change the filename in the `Location` directive, as in the following lines:

```
<Location /server.information.page>
```

and:

```
<Location /server.status.page>
```

Logging errors

The error log contains messages generated by the server that describe various error conditions. The `ErrorLog` and `LogLevel` directives in the `httpd.conf` file (as described in the section on configuring the server) can modify the filename and the amount of information that is logged. The default file is `/etc/httpd/logs/error_log` (which is a link to `/var/log/httpd/error_log`). Here are a few sample lines from the error log:

```
[Mon Apr 28 10:29:13 2008] [notice] Apache/2.2.4 (Fedora)
    configured -- resuming normal operations
[Mon Apr 28 10:43:07 2008] [error] [client 127.0.0.1] client denied by
    server configuration: /var/www/html/server-status
[Mon Apr 28 10:06:42 2008] [error] [client 127.0.0.1] File
    does not exist: /var/www/html/newfile.html
[Mon Apr 28 01:12:28 2008 [notice] caught SIGTERM, shutting down
```

The first line indicates that the server has just been started and will be logged regardless of the `LogLevel` directive. The second line indicates an error that was logged to demonstrate a denied request. The third line shows an error, which represents a request for a file that does not exist. The fourth line, also logged regardless of the `LogLevel` directive, indicates that the server is shutting down. The error log should also be monitored periodically because it will contain the error messages from CGI scripts that might need repair.

Logging hits

Every incoming HTTP request generates an entry in the transfer log (by default, `/etc/httpd/logs/access_log`, which is a link to `/var/log/httpd/access_log`). Statistics packages and log file analysis programs typically use this file because manually reading through it can be a rather tedious exercise. (See the information on the logwatch facility in Chapter 14.)

The format of the transfer log can be altered by the `LogFormat` and `CustomLog` directives in the `httpd.conf` file, as described in the "Configuring the Web server (httpd.conf)" section. If you attempted to access `http://localhost/` following the installation procedure (from Figure 21-1), the following lines (in the "common" format) would be written to the `access_log`:

```
127.0.0.1 - - [28/Apr/2008:00:23:33 -0600] "GET / HTTP/1.1" 403 3931 "-""Mozilla/5.0
    (X11; U; Linux i686; rv:1.7.3) Gecko/20041002 Firefox/0.10.1"
127.0.0.1 - - [28/Apr/2008:00:23:34 -0600] "GET /icons/apache_pb2.gif HTTP/1.1" 200
    2414 "http://localhost/" "Mozilla/5.0 (X11; U; Linux i686; rv:1.7.3)
    Gecko/20041002 Firefox/0.10.1"
127.0.0.1 - - [28/Apr/2008:00:23:34 -0600] "GET /icons/powered_by_fedora.png HTTP/1.1"
    200 2243 "http://localhost/" "Mozilla/5.0 (X11; U; Linux i686; rv:1.7.3)
    Gecko/20041002 Firefox/0.10.1"
```

The Apache Test Page actually is an error condition (403), which indicates that the Apache server is running, but that the administrator of the server hasn't added a home page yet. The next two lines show the Apache (`apache_pb2.gif`) and Fedora (`powered_by_fedora.png`) icons that appear on the test page, respectively, for Fedora. (RHEL systems have a Red Hat icon.)

Viewing the server-info and server-status pages (as shown in Figures 21-3 and 21-4, respectively) generated the following entries:

```
127.0.0.1 - - [26/Apr/2008:23:40:41 -0400] "GET /server-info HTTP/1.1"
    200 42632
127.0.0.1 - - [26/Apr/2008:23:41:49 -0400] "GET /server-status
    HTTP/1.1" 200 1504
```

The denied attempt to access the server-status page logged the following line (note the 403 server response code):

```
127.0.0.1 - - [26/Apr/2008:23:43:07 -0400] "GET /server-status
    HTTP/1.1" 403 211
```

Analyzing Web-server traffic

The webalizer package can take Apache log files and produce usage reports for your server. Those reports are created in HTML format so you can display the information graphically. Information is produced in both table and graph form.

To use the `webalizer` command, the webalizer package must be installed (`yum install webalizer`). You can run `webalizer` with no options and have it take the values in the `/etc/webalizer.conf` files to get the information it needs. As an alternative, you can use command-line options to override settings in the `webalizer.conf` file. To use the defaults, simply run the following:

```
# webalizer
```

If all goes well, the command should run for a few moments and exit silently. Based on the information in the `/etc/webalizer.conf` file, the `/var/log/httpd/access_log` log file is read and an `index.html` file is copied to the `/var/www/html/usage/` directory. You can view the output by opening the file in any browser window. For example, you could type the following in the location box:

```
http://localhost/usage
```

The output report shows a 12-month summary of Web server activity. On the bar chart, for each month a green bar represents the number of hits on the Web site, a dark blue bar shows the number of different files hit, and a light blue bar shows the number of pages opened. It also shows data for the number of visits and the number of sites that visited in the right column. The amount of data transferred, in kilobytes, is displayed as well.

Figure 21-5 shows an example of a `webalizer` output file for a Web server that has been running for several months.

Below the chart, a table shows daily and monthly summaries for activity during each month. Users can click the name of a month to see detailed activity.

> **TIP:** Because Webalizer supports both common log format (CLF) and combined log format, it can be used to display information for log files other than those produced for Apache. For example, you could display statistics for your FTP server or Squid server.

Several other software tools are available for analyzing transfer statistics. The accompanying sidebar on statistics packages available for Fedora and Red Hat Enterprise Linux systems describes some of these tools.

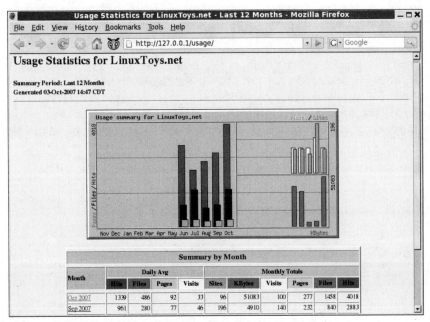

Figure 21-5: Webalizer displays Web data in chart and column formats.

Statistics Packages Available for Fedora and RHEL

Analyzing the transfer log by hand isn't much fun. Several packages have been written to automate this task, including the following two:

- **Analog** — This free log-file analyzer is very fast and easily configurable, and it produces very detailed output (including bar graphs and hypertext links). More information can be found at `www.analog.cx`.

- **AWStats** — The Advanced Web Statistics tool (awstats package) produces graphical statistics representing Web-server access. AWStats can work with log files in the Apache common log format, as well as log files from sendmail, FTP, and other network servers. It can report statistics, such as the number of people who have visited, visits made per person, the domain and country of each visitor, and the number of visits made by robots.

Summary

Web servers are responsible for storing and delivering the vast amount of content available on the World Wide Web to clients all over the world. Although several Web-server software packages are available for Fedora and RHEL systems, the most popular is by far the Apache Web server.

This chapter describes how to install, configure, and run an Apache server in Fedora. The `httpd` daemon process handles requests for Web content (HTTP). Configuration files define what content is made available and how it can be accessed. In particular, the `/etc/httpd/conf/httpd.conf` file is used to configure the server.

The Apache httpd package also includes facilities for logging error and transfer messages. You can look for the `access_log` and `error_log` files in the `/etc/httpd/logs` directory. The `access_log` file contains information on content requests that have been serviced by the server. The `error_log` file lists error conditions that have occurred and times when service has been denied. You can use tools such as Webalizer to simplify the viewing of Apache log data.

Chapter 22

Setting Up an LDAP
Address Book Server

In This Chapter

- Understanding LDAP
- Using OpenLDAP
- Configuring an LDAP server
- Creating an LDAP address book
- Using Thunderbird to access the address book

Sometimes an organization needs a convenient way to gather, store, and distribute information for access by the applications that need it. The Lightweight Directory Access Protocol (LDAP) simplifies the process of creating and using directories of information by network-ready applications.

The intention of LDAP is to simplify the overhead needed to provide directory services described in the X.500 specification. LDAP is a subset of X.500 features. By standardizing the structure of database information, LDAP can get around proprietary storage formats to allow many different applications to share the same data.

> **NOTE:** X.500 is a CCITT specification that has become part of the Open Systems Interconnection (OSI) standards that define a layered framework for interconnecting networks and related services. With the dominance of TCP/IP networks (such as the Internet) in the world, OSI never became the predominent network framework that some expected it to be. Despite that, the seven-layer OSI reference model is often used in classrooms to teach networking theory. Likewise, some of these specifications, such as X.500, have been adopted (and sometimes adapted) where standard, cross-platform features are required.

Fedora and RHEL systems include OpenLDAP software packages to implement LDAP server and client services. To illustrate how to configure and use an LDAP server with OpenLDAP, and make it accessible to user applications, this chapter goes through the process of setting up a shared address book to run on a Fedora or RHEL system. It also describes how to use e-mail clients that can access the LDAP address book.

> **NOTE:** Fedora Directory Server was released in June, 2005 as an alternative open source LDAP server to the OpenLDAP software described in this chapter. Fedora Directory Server (FDS) is now part of the Fedora repository (fedora-ds-base and fedora-das-base-devel packages). To learn more about FDS, see `http://directory.fedoraproject.org`.

Understanding LDAP

LDAP lets people create directories of information that can be shared among client applications over a network. It is particularly geared toward applications that are used to look up information that is fairly stable over and over again (in other words, information that's being looked at more than it's being changed). That's why LDAP is popular for uses such as storing information about people, addresses, and other kinds of data that may require high access with relatively few changes.

Because of LDAP's extraordinarily flexible design, as an LDAP developer or administrator you have a lot of control over:

- How the information in the directories is organized.
- How and by whom information can be accessed.
- The scale, local to global, by which information is distributed. (Information can be replicated to other servers at any scale you choose and synced up automatically.)

Despite its flexibility, however, you don't have to begin designing each directory you create from scratch. LDAP has many predefined structures of information you can rely on to build your LDAP directories. Those data structures are defined in several different standards documents referred to as RFCs (Request for Comments). There are RFCs for almost every aspect of the Internet protocols and related application services. Important RFCs for LDAP definitions include:

- **RFC 2252** — Defines the framework for LDAP.
- **RFC 2256** — Defines the X.500 user schema for LDAPv3.
- **RFCs 1274, 2079, 2247, 2307, 2587, 2589** — Define specifications for including user attributes, Uniform Resource Identifiers, domain names, NIS data, public key infrastructure (PKI), and dynamic directory services in LDAP directories.

The documents on which these RFCs are based include the CCITT X.500 standard and the related ISO IS9594 directory services standards. In particular, X.521 and X.520 define some of the most basic object classes and attribute types.

Keep in mind, however, that these standards provide guidelines. When you put together your own LDAP directory, your OpenLDAP server will have to deal directly with the schemas that implement those standards on the OpenLDAP server.

> **TIP:** Microsoft's Active Directory (AD) is often touted as an "LDAP-based" entity, giving some users high hopes of integrating OpenLDAP and AD. While it is possible to exchange information between AD and OpenLDAP, setting this up requires a lot of patience and skill. Unless you must interoperate with AD, a better path for supporting Windows clients is through the use of OpenLDAP and Samba.

Defining information in schemas

The elements that make up LDAP directories are organized into what are called *schemas*. When you create or use an LDAP directory, the types of information in the schemas you will be working with include the following types of items:

- **Object classes** — An object provides a name under which you would group together a bunch of attributes. So, with an address book, you might include the `inetOrgPerson` object class, under which you could store attributes associated with a person.

- **Attributes** — As its name implies, an attribute holds a piece of information associated with an object class. For example, the `inetOrgPerson` object class could have attributes such as telephone number, e-mail address, and so on.

> **NOTE:** If you are familiar with databases, the LDAP directory terminology might seem a bit different to you. LDAP is more of a directory structure provider than a real database. You can think of attributes as fields and object classes as tables.

Examples of object classes include `country`, `locality`, `organization`, and many others. For each object class, there may be required attributes and a list of optional attributes. You can see the definitions for many standard object classes and attributes in the schema files that come with any LDAP server.

In OpenLDAP, several default schemas are included in the `/etc/openldap/schema` directory. The example e-mail address book I show you how to create in this chapter relies entirely on schemas provided with OpenLDAP. You don't have to create any schema files yourself to do the examples in this chapter. If you need more objects and attributes than are provided by default, you can get schemas from other places or create your own.

> **CROSS-REFERENCE:** For information on schemas included with OpenLDAP, refer to the OpenLDAP Schema Specification page (`www.openldap.org/doc/admin22/schema.html`). That page also describes how you can go about extending those schemas. Check those schemas, as well as the schema definitions in RFCs described earlier, before you create your own object classes or attributes.

As you begin dealing with your LDAP directory, you will access the object classes and attributes as names. To the LDAP server, however, each of those items is represented by a unique string of numbers and dots. Each string is referred to as an Object Identifier (OID). If you are not creating your own object classes or attributes, you don't need to deal with OIDs. To understand what OIDs are and when you might want to get your own OID assignment, refer to the sidebar "Understanding OIDs."

Understanding OIDs

If you look into a schema file (`/etc/openldap/schema/*`), you will see that every LDAP object class and attribute is mapped into a dot-separated number. That number is a hierarchical string that is referred to as an Object Identifier (OID).

Because LDAP is intended to be a global directory (where all entries can be unique), if you want to create a directory that can be accessed globally, you should try to use items that have existing OIDs assigned whenever possible. However, if you find that you need to create object classes or attributes that are not already defined, you can consider getting an Object Identifier (OID) for your organization. The alternative is to make up your own attribute name and OID, in which case you should either never expect that data to be globally accessible or try not to conflict with existing OIDs.

Like a domain name, an OID assignment enables you to create branches under that OID as you need them. If your organization has its own OID assigned, you are guaranteed of having every item you create under that number be globally unique (as long as you maintain those assignments properly yourself).

Private enterprise numbers are examples of useful information that is stored as OIDs. Private enterprise numbers used primarily for companies using SNMP are stored under the OID number 1.3.6.1.4.1. Companies represented under that OID include IBM (1.3.6.1.4.1.2), Cisco Systems (1.3.6.1.4.1.9), and Hewlett Packard (1.3.6.1.4.1.11). For Red Hat Software, the OID is 1.3.6.1.4.1.2312.

If you break down each number into its component parts, you see that they start with the top-level OID 1 (for ISO-assigned OIDs), then 3 (ISO-identified organizations), then 6 (U.S. Department of Defense), then 1 (Internet), then 4 (private), then 1 (enterprise). After that is the number representing each company.

You can see the complete list of enterprise numbers on the Private Enterprise Numbers list at `www.iana.org/assignments/enterprise-numbers`. Search for OID assignments (from the top node) at `www.alvestrand.no/objectid/top.html`. You can request your OID from the Internet Assigned Numbers Authority (`www.iana.org/cgi-bin/mediatypes.pl`).

Structuring your LDAP directories

While standards documents are used to keep the object classes, attributes, and other elements of LDAP directories unique, you are free to put together those elements into your own LDAP directories however you want. The structure you use to create your directories is the LDAP Data Interchange Format (LDIF).

Every piece of information you store in your LDAP directory must fall under a base distinguished name (or *base dn*). Because many organizations these days can be represented by a unique Internet domain name, the domain name is a popular way to identify your LDAP base dn. In fact, for the examples in this chapter, the base distinguished name I use is linuxtoys.net. If you are creating an LDAP directory for an organization that can be represented by a domain name, you can replace linuxtoys.net with your domain name.

If you are creating an LDAP directory structure for a larger organization (in other words, more than just a single address book as I am doing here), you need to think hard about how you want the directory structured. You may want to add country codes (us, de, it, and so on) under your base distinguished name for a multinational company.

Setting Up the OpenLDAP Server

All the software packages you need to set up an OpenLDAP server are included on the DVD that comes with Fedora and RHEL distributions. As an alternative, you can easily install the packages over the Internet using yum. With those packages installed, you can start configuring your OpenLDAP server.

Installing OpenLDAP packages

To configure your OpenLDAP server, you should start by installing all the openldap packages from your Fedora or RHEL distribution. First, check which openldap packages are installed:

```
# rpm -qa "openldap*"
openldap-2.4.8-3
openldap-servers-2.4.8-3
openldap-devel-2.4.8-3
openldap-clients-2.4.8-3
```

You need the openldap-devel package only if you are developing LDAP applications. Otherwise, you can install the openldap, openldap-clients, and openldap-servers packages from the DVD that comes with this book.

Configuring the OpenLDAP server (slapd.conf)

You configure the access and use of your OpenLDAP databases in the configuration file, /etc/openldap/slapd.conf.

> **NOTE:** For a more complete description on features you can use in your slapd.conf file, refer to the slapd.conf man page.

1. **Edit slapd.conf.** Make a backup copy of the /etc/openldap/slapd.conf, and then open the file as root user, using any text editor. The following steps tell you some of the information you might want to change.

2. **Review the schemas.** In the `slapd.conf` file, schemas that are generally useful for creating LDAP directories are included from the `/etc/openldap/schema` directory. Other schemas you might use will often rely on these schemas being included. So, unless you know you don't need them, don't delete any of these schemas:

```
include    /etc/openldap/schema/corba.schema
include    /etc/openldap/schema/core.schema
include    /etc/openldap/schema/cosine.schema
include    /etc/openldap/schema/duaconf.schema
include    /etc/openldap/schema/dyngroup.schema
include    /etc/openldap/schema/inetorgperson.schema
include    /etc/openldap/schema/java.schema
include    /etc/openldap/schema/misc.schema
include    /etc/openldap/schema/nis.schema
include    /etc/openldap/schema/openldap.schema
include    /etc/openldap/schema/ppolicy.schema
include    /etc/openldap/schema/collective.schema
```

Because schemas are plain text files, you can open them with any text editor to read what they do. Several of the schema are of interest to us. The `core.schema` file is required for all LDAP directories. The `cosine.schema` and `inetorgperson.schema` files are particularly useful (and needed for this procedure). The `nis.schema` file is used to provide Network Information System data in an LDAP directory. The `misc.schema` file contains some miscellaneous mail-related schema definitions.

TIP: The LDAP Schema Viewer (`http://ldap.akbkhome.com`) enables you to view object classes, attributes, syntaxes, and matching rules for common schemas for LDAP. Definitions also point to RFCs that more fully define each object class.

---

3. **Add backend database definitions.** In the `slapd.conf` file, you need to define some backend database definitions. Each set of backend definitions applies to a group of databases of the same type.

Here's an example of how the backend database definitions would appear for a computer in the domain named `linuxtoys.net` (of course, you would replace `linuxtoys` and `net` with those of your own domain):

```
####################################################
# ldbm and/or bdb database definitions
####################################################

database           bdb
suffix             "dc=linuxtoys,dc=net"
directory          /var/lib/ldap
rootdn             "cn=Manager,dc=linuxtoys,dc=net"
cachesize 10000
searchstack 8
dbnosync
dirtyread
```

This `database` is of the type `bdb` (Berkeley DB transactional backend), which defines how that data for this directory are stored. The `ldbm` (Lightweight Directory Access Protocol Proxy backend) database is another type you could use. The suffix specifies that queries to this `slapd` server for `linuxtoys.net` are directed to this database. The directory line identifies the `/var/lib/ldap` directory as the location for this LDAP directory.

The `rootdn` line indicates that root access can be granted to change data in databases associated with the `linuxtoys.net` distinguished name (provided the password is supplied with `rootpw`, as described in the next step). I added the last four options to improve performance of the bdb database (type **man slapd-bdb** for details).

4. **Add a password.** In the `slapd.conf` file, you need to enter the password that is required to modify your OpenLDAP backend database. By default, the `rootpw` line defines a clear-text string that is your password. The password will give you full control of the backend database. It will look something like the following:

```
rootpw        mysecret
```

> **NOTE:** If you are going to use a clear-text password, you should make sure that your `slapd.conf` file has read permissions closed to the world (`chmod 640 /etc/openldap/slapd.conf`). See the sidebar "Creating an Encrypted Password" for information on creating an encrypted password to access your OpenLDAP backend database.

5. **Save slapd.conf.** Save your changes to the `slapd.conf` file and close it.

6. **Check slapd.conf.** You can check for syntax errors in your `slapd.conf` file by running the `slaptest` command, as follows:

```
# slaptest -u
config file testing succeeded
```

If something was wrong with the syntax of the file (for example, if you left off a quote or misplaced a comma), the message would say `slaptest: bad configuration file!` instead. Try to correct the problem and check the file again. Later, when the databases are created, you can run `slaptest` again (without the `-u` option) to make sure that `slapd.conf` points to existing, properly configured data bases.

At this point, you can try starting the OpenLDAP service.

Creating an Encrypted Password

To create an encrypted password for the administrator of the OpenLDAP database you can use the `slappasswd` command. You can create the password using Crypt, SSHA, SMD5, MD5, or SSH encryption. Here's an example of creating a password for OpenLDAP using MD5 encryption:

```
# slappasswd -h {md5} > /tmp/myslap
New password: ********
Re-enter new password: ********
# cat /tmp/myslap
{MD5}uBoM+LOQg5GHHJ2Z4NLu9A==
```

Enter a password (twice) to create an encrypted MD5 password. This example directs the encrypted password into the `/tmp/myslap` file; you can read into the `slapd.conf` file later. In this example, I had you `cat` the file so you could see what the encrypted password looks like. Your password will be different. Here's what the `rootpw` line will look like with an encrypted, rather than a clear-text password:

```
rootpw     {MD5}uBoM+LOQg5GHHJ2Z4NLu9A==
```

Starting the OpenLDAP service

You start the OpenLDAP as you do most services in Fedora and RHEL systems, using the `service` and `chkconfig` commands. The service name for OpenLDAP is ldap. To start the service immediately, type the following:

```
# service ldap start
Starting slapd:        [ OK ]
```

To set the ldap service to start each time the system is rebooted, type the following:

```
# chkconfig ldap on
```

By default, the ldap service will have read permissions open to everyone.

Setting Up the Address Book

When I set up the structure of the address book database, I base the distinguished name (dn) for the database on the organization's name (in this example, linuxtoys).

With the suffix set to linuxtoys.net (`suffix "dc=linuxtoys,dc=net"`) in the `slapd.conf` file (yours will be different), the backend database is set up to handle queries to the distinguished name (dn) linuxtoys.net. Next, you can create the structure for the address book for that organization under that distinguished name.

> **NOTE:** The `dc=` stands for Domain Component. When you include a domain name as your distinguished name, the order in which you put the parts of that domain name places the part closest to the DNS root last. In this example, the `dc=linuxtoys` comes before `dc=net`. See RFC 2247 if you are interested in the specification for including domain names in LDAP directories.

You want to create the address book file in a format that can be loaded into the OpenLDAP database. The format you need is referred to as the LDAP Data Interchange Format (LDIF). Information you enter in this format can be used to build the database and load a lot of data into the directory at once from a file.

The following steps explain how to create an LDIF file containing the definitions of your address book for the `linuxtoys.net` LDAP directory (distinguished name), and then load that file into your LDAP server:

1. **Create an ldif file.** As root user, using any text editor, create a file to hold your LDAP directory entry. In my example, I used the file `/etc/openldap/toypeople.ldif`.

> **NOTE:** When you create your ldif file, be sure to leave a blank line before each new distinguished name (`dn:`) line. The blank line tells ldapadd to start a new entry. Without the blank line, LDAP will not think that you are starting a new distinguished name. Also, remove any blank spaces before each line, making sure that all new lines begin on column 1. (A space at the beginning of a line indicates that the new line is actually part of the preceding line.)

2. **Define the organization.** You need to define the directory that you will be loading into the LDAP server. For my example, I added information defining the organization as Linux Toys under the distinguished name linuxtoys.net (`dc=linuxtoys,dc=net`), by adding the following information to my `toypeople.ldif` file.

```
dn:              dc=linuxtoys,dc=net
objectClass:     dcObject
objectClass:     organization
dc:              linuxtoys
o:               Linux Toys
```

3. **Add an organizational role.** I identified the role of administrator of the address book by adding the following lines to the `toypeople.ldif` file.

```
dn:              cn=Manager,dc=linuxtoys,dc=net
objectClass:     organizationalRole
cn:              Manager
description:     LinuxToys Address Book Administrator
```

4. **Add an organizational unit.** Because in this example the address book basically consists of names and addresses of members of the organization, I call the organizational unit (`ou`) members.

```
dn:              ou=members,dc=linuxtoys,dc=net
objectClass:     top
```

```
objectClass:    organizationalUnit
ou:             members
```

> **NOTE:** Although in my example I am creating an address book that is at the top of my directory structure, if you are in a large company chances are that you will want a more complex directory structure. For example, instead of having one address book at the top of your directory structure, you may create additional organizational units for countries, locations, or departments. Then, every single unit might have its own address book. You also might want to support multiple directories under each unit. For example, there may be a separate directory for keeping track of computer equipment or company vehicles.

5. **Add people.** With the directory structure in place, and with a `members` unit under the `linuxtoys.net` distinguished name, I can begin adding people to the directory. I define each person as `organizationalPerson` and `inetOrgPerson` object classes. There are a lot of different attributes I could add to each person's information. However, most of the attributes I've chosen are attributes that will be read by the Thunderbird mail client (which I will show later in this chapter). Here are the two entries:

```
dn:             cn=John Jones,dc=linuxtoys,dc=net
objectClass:    organizationalPerson
objectClass:    inetOrgPerson
cn:             John Jones
mail:           jwjones@linuxtoys.net
givenname:      John
sn:             Jones
uid:            jwjones
o:              Linux Toys
telephoneNumber: 800-555-1212
homePhone:      800-555-1313
mobile:         800-555-1414
pager:          800-555-1515
facsimileTelephoneNumber: 800-555-1414
title:          Account Executive
homePostalAddress: 1515 Broadway$New York NY 99999

dn:             cn=Sheree Glass,dc=linuxtoys,dc=net
objectClass:    organizationalPerson
objectClass:    inetOrgPerson
cn:             Sheree Glass
mail:           sheree@linuxtoys.net
givenname:      Sheree
sn:             Glass
uid:            slglass
o:              Linux Toys
telephoneNumber: 800-555-2893
homePhone:      800-555-4329
mobile:         800-555-8458
pager:          800-555-4955
facsimileTelephoneNumber: 800-555-3838
```

```
title:              Interior Decorator
homePostalAddress: 167 E Street$Salt Lake UT 99999
```

As you can see here, the two people listed in the address book directory (called `members`) are each associated with a common name (cn), John Jones and Sheree Glass, which falls under the linuxtoys.net domain components. You can add as many people as you want to this file by repeating this structure. (Notice that a `$` is used to separate lines in an address.)

> **NOTE:** You may find that you don't need all of the attributes shown here or may want to add others. Refer to the schema files to see a list of attributes that are available with `organizationalPerson`, `inetOrgPerson`, and other object classes you might want to use with your address book.

6. **Save the ldif file.** Save the changes to your ldif file (in my case, the file is called `/etc/openldap/toypeople.ldif`).

7. **Add the information to the LDAP server.** You can use the `ldapadd` command to add the entire contents of the ldif file you created to your LDAP directory. Here is the command I used to add the contents of my ldif file (called `toypeople.ldif`) to my LDAP directory:

```
# ldapadd -xv -D "cn=Manager,dc=linuxtoys,dc=net" -W -f toypeople.ldif
Enter LDAP Password: mysecret
add objectClass:
        dcObject
        organization
add dc:
        linuxtoys
add o:
        Linux Toys
adding new entry "dc=linuxtoys,dc=net"
modify complete

add objectClass:
        organizationalRole
add cn:
        Manager
add description:
        LinuxToys Address Book Administrator
adding new entry "cn=Manager,dc=linuxtoys,dc=net"
modify complete
    .
    .
    .
add cn:
        John Jones
add mail:
        jwjones@linuxtoys.net
```

```
add givenname:
        John
add sn:
        Jones
    .
    .
    .
add cn:
        Sheree Glass
add mail:
        sheree@linuxtoys.net
add givenname:
        Sheree
add sn:
        Glass
    .
    .
    .
```

The password shown here (which will not display as you type it) is the one you added to
your `slapd.conf` file. In the example, I used `mysecret` as the password. The `-x` says
to use simple authentication (no SASL). The `-D` says to use the distinguished name
defined earlier in the slapd.conf file (`cn=Manager,dc=linuxtoys,dc=net`). The `-W`
says to prompt for the password, instead of entering it on the command line. The `-f`
indicates the file to load (in the example presented here, `toypeople.ldif`).

As the `ldapadd` command successfully adds each entry, it lists the objects associated
with each one.

8. **Restart the server.** You can restart the server at this point by typing the following:

```
# /etc/init.d/ldap restart
```

9. **Search the directory.** To make sure that everything was properly inserted into the
directory, you can run the following search command:

```
# ldapsearch -x -W -D 'cn=manager,dc=linuxtoys,dc=net' \
  -b 'dc=linuxtoys,dc=net' '(objectClass=*)'
# extended LDIF
#
# LDAPv3
# base <dc=linuxtoys,dc=net> with scope subtree
# filter: (objectClass=*)
# requesting: ALL
#

# linuxtoys.net
dn: dc=linuxtoys,dc=net
objectClass: top
objectClass: dcObject
```

```
objectClass: organization
dc: linuxtoys
o: Linux Toys

# Manager, linuxtoys.net
dn: cn=Manager,dc=linuxtoys,dc=net
objectClass: organizationalRole
cn: Manager
description: LinuxToys Address Book Administrator

# members, linuxtoys.net
dn: ou=members,dc=linuxtoys,dc=net
objectClass: top
objectClass: organizationalUnit
ou: members

# John Jones, linuxtoys.net
dn: cn=John Jones,ou=members,dc=linuxtoys,dc=net
objectClass: organizationalPerson
objectClass: inetOrgPerson
cn: John Jones
mail: jwjones@linuxtoys.net
givenName: John
sn: Jones
uid: jwjones
o: Linux Toys
   .
   .
   .

# Sheree Glass, linuxtoys.net
dn: cn=Sheree Glass,ou=members,dc=linuxtoys,dc=net
objectClass: top
objectClass: organizationalPerson
objectClass: inetOrgPerson
cn: Sheree Glass
mail: sheree@linuxtoys.net
   .
   .
   .
```

In this example, I asked to use simple authentication (clear-text passwords with the -x option), start at the base (-b) of the linuxtoys.net directory to begin the search, and list all object classes (objectClass=*). If you like, you can pipe the output to less so you can page through it.

10. **Debug your directory.** Don't expect your ldif file to load the first time without any errors. While you debug your address book directory, I recommend that you use a non-production machine and just clear out the database files after each failed attempt to load

your directory. Assuming that you kept your LDAP directory files in `/var/lib/ldap` and that it's okay to erase the whole database while you debug your entries, you can do the following:

> **CAUTION:** You're about to erase the LDAP directory files you created. Don't do this step if you have information in your LDAP directory files that is not in your ldif file. Don't erase your ldif file because you need it to recreate your directory files.

```
# /etc/init.d/ldap stop
# rm /var/lib/ldap/*
# /etc/init.d/ldap restart
# ldapadd -x -D "cn=Manager,dc=linuxtoys,dc=net" -W -f toypeople.ldif
```

Repeat this process until you feel that your ldif file, and all the information it contains, has been properly loaded into your LDAP directory files.

At this point, you can decide if you need to further tune your LDAP directory (as described in the section "More ways to configure LDAP"). After that, I recommend that you check that your LDAP address book directory is working properly by trying to access it from Thunderbird, using its Contacts feature (as described later in this chapter).

More Ways to Configure LDAP

If you plan to scale up your LDAP directory to be used by more than just a small office or home e-mail server, there are some additional configuration options you might want to consider. Here are a few suggestions:

- **Replicate the LDAP directory** — You can make your LDAP directory accessible from multiple LDAP servers and have updates to your directory be disseminated to those servers. See the man page for the slurpd daemon (which handles update replication) and the OpenLDAP Administrator's Guide for information on setting up LDAP directory replication (`/usr/share/doc/openldap-servers*/guide.html`).

- **Add certificates** — Transport Layer Security is built into the OpenLDAP server. For information on defining certificates and ciphers that will be accepted by the slapd daemon, refer to the `slapd.conf` man page.

- **Change log levels** — You can specify the level of debugging that is done by the slapd daemon. By adding the `loglevel <integer>` option to the `slapd.conf` file, you can have slapd do the following types of logging:

    1   Trace function calls

    2   Debug packet handling

    4   Heavy trace debugging

    8   Connection management

```
16        Print out packets sent and received
32        Search filter processing
64        Configuration file processing
128       Access control list processing
256       Stats log connections/operations/results
512       Stats log entries sent
1024      Print communication with shell backends
2048      Entry parsing
```

By default, the loglevel is 256. To log everything, set the loglevel to 4095. To get combinations of loglevel features, simply add the numbers you want together. For example, for trace function calls, heavy trace debugging and connection management, use the number 13 (as in 1 + 4 + 8).

- **Limit searches** — You can limit the number of entries that can be returned by a search (`sizelimit 500`, by default) and the amount of time `slapd` will take to answer a search request in seconds (`timelimit 3600`). Add new values that you want for your LDAP directory to your `slapd.conf` file.

- **Add access control policy** — In the `slapd.conf` file, the default database access is set to allow read access by anyone who can access the database. If you want to change that behavior, you can add access lines to selectively decide who can read and write to your database. For this example, I want to allow everyone to be able to read from the database, but only allow people to change their own information. Refer to the `slapd.conf` man page for further information.

Accessing an LDAP Address Book from Thunderbird

With your LDAP address book configured and running, you should be able to use it to get e-mail addresses from any e-mail client that supports LDAP directories. Assuming your LDAP directory is up and running, the following example shows how to use Thunderbird (which is available with Fedora and RHEL distributions) to search your LDAP directory for e-mail addresses.

1. From Thunderbird, click the Address Book button.

2. From the Address Book window, select File → New → LDAP Directory. From the Thunderbird Directory Server Properties window that appears, enter at least the following information on the General tab:

   - **Name** — The name that identifies the server on your LDAP Servers list.

   - **Hostname** — The name or IP address of computer hosting the LCAP content.

   - **Port** — Enter an IP address for the LDAP server. The port number is 389 by default.

- **Base DN** — Indicates the point in the LDAP directory to begin searching. You can select Find to have Thunderbird check your LDAP server for the Search base. In the example, `dc=linuxtoys,dc=net` is the search base.

Figure 22-1 shows the Directory Server Properties window that was just filled out.

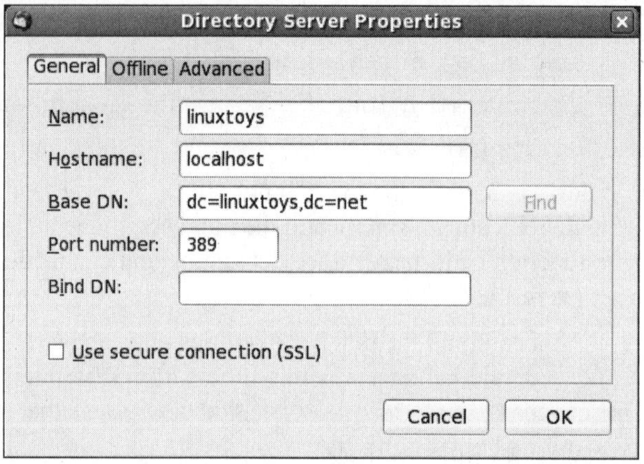

Figure 22-1: Enter information about your LDAP directory server to search for addresses from Thunderbird.

Click OK to save the configuration.

3. If you want to search the directory for an e-mail address, with the name of the LDAP address book selected in the left column, type a search term into the search box on the Thunderbird Address Book window and press Enter. Figure 22-2 shows one of the entries that were added during the example of setting up the LDAP directory. After an entry is found, you can do the following:

- Double-click the entry to see an address book card with as much information as is available for the person displayed.

- Click the highlighted e-mail address for an entry to open a compose window, ready to send an e-mail to the person selected.

If your LDAP directory is not accessible from the Thunderbird client, run the Thunderbird or other LDAP-enabled e-mail application on the LDAP server. If you are able to access the LDAP directory from the local server, it means that for some reason requests are being rejected from the server to outside hosts. Verify that the firewall on the server has port 389 open (which is used by default to access LDAP services). Next, check how access permissions are being set in the `slapd.conf` file.

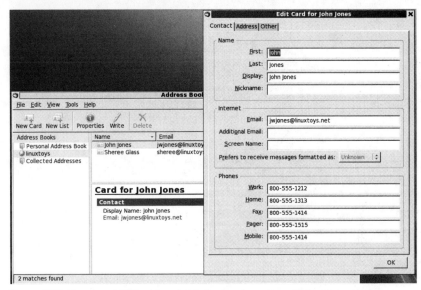

Figure 22-2: Search an LDAP address book directory by name, e-mail address, or other information.

Summary

Lightweight Directory Access Protocol (LDAP) is a popular tool for creating directories of information that need to be accessed by a variety of different network-ready applications. LDAP is based on the CCITT X.500 standard, but provides a more workable subset of those features for creating directories of information that needs to be highly accessible.

In Fedora and RHEL systems, OpenLDAP is included for you to use if you want to offer LDAP services from your computer. To configure an LDAP server, you need to set up the slapd.conf file (to configure the slapd daemon) and create entries that are then loaded into your LDAP directory files. Those entries are typically added to a file in LDIF format and loaded into files in the /var/lib/ldap directory by the ldapadd command.

To check the address book created by the example in this chapter, you can use the Thunderbird e-mail client. Using Thunderbird, or other LDAP-enabled e-mail application, you can search the LDAP directory for names, e-mail addresses and other information contained in that directory.

Chapter 23

Setting Up a DHCP Boot Server

In This Chapter

- Using Dynamic Host Configuration Protocol (DHCP)
- Setting up a DHCP server
- Setting up a DHCP client

If you are tasked with maintaining a network, you are probably interested in automating as much of the routine maintenance as possible. As your network grows this becomes particularly important. When a new computer is added to your network or when a new employee joins your organization, you need to make configuration changes. You'd probably like a painless means of getting the changes pushed out quickly and preferably without having to touch each and every computer on your network. This is where DHCP (Dynamic Host Configuration Protocol) comes in.

The Internet Protocol (IP) has enabled network functionality that could scarcely be imagined when IP was first developed. In order for your network client and servers to take advantage of the numerous IP network services, software, and devices, each of your clients needs an IP address.

For all but the smallest networks, manually assigning and then tracking IP addresses can be a risky proposition. On top of the hassle of tracking who has which address, you could find yourself having to reconfigure every network client you have if you need to make a change in your IP addressing structure to accommodate new users or ISP services. Because DHCP can be used to dynamically assign IP addresses to DHCP clients, all of these pitfalls become irrelevant when DHCP is in use.

This chapter describes how to set up Fedora or RHEL as a DHCP server. It then explains how to verify that the services are working and how to set up client computers to use those services.

Using Dynamic Host Configuration Protocol

Did you ever wonder why you can just plug your computer's Ethernet cable into a LAN jack at work, a hotel, or a DSL router in your home and immediately be up on the Internet? In most cases, it's because that LAN is set up to do DHCP. Linux and Windows systems are set up by default to look for a DHCP server on all Ethernet cards when the systems boot up. If your ISP or support staff has configured DHCP, you can be on the Internet faster than you can open your browser.

Setting up a DHCP server enables you to centrally manage the addresses and other network information for client computers on your private network. With DHCP configured on your network, a client computer can simply indicate that it wants to use DHCP and the DHCP server can provide its IP address, network mask, DNS server, NetBIOS server, router (gateway), and other information needed to get up and running on the network.

With DHCP, you can greatly simplify the initial network configuration that each client computer on your network needs to do. Later, as your network evolves, you can easily update that information, having changes automatically picked up by clients when they restart their network interfaces.

> **NOTE:** Although this chapter focuses on the configuration of DHCP client and server services on your Fedora and RHEL systems, your Fedora or RHEL DHCP client can use the services of other network devices. For example, you might have a Cisco routing swtich, a DSL/Cable device with DHCP services, or even a Windows-based DHCP server. DHCP clients for Fedora and RHEL will not have trouble working with any standards-compliant DHCP server.

To configure the DHCP server described in this chapter, you need to have the dhcp package installed (`yum install dhcp`).

Setting Up a DHCP Server

To configure a DHCP server you need to install the dhcp package. Assuming you have already set up the physical connections between your DHCP server and the client computers on your network (presumably an Ethernet LAN), the minimum tools you need to get the DHCP server working are:

- A firewall that allows requests for DHCP service
- A configured `/etc/dhcpd.conf` file
- A running `dhcpd` server daemon (which can be started at boot time)

After the DHCP server is running, it listens to UDP port 67 for requests from DHCP clients on the LAN. A client simply boots up (with an Ethernet network interface turned on and DHCP identified as its method of getting network addresses). This causes the client to send out a DHCP discovery request to 255.255.255.255 (the global broadcast address). The DHCP server picks up that request and feeds the client the information it needs to get up and running on the network.

> **NOTE:** The `dhcpd.conf` file can serve a wide range of configuration information to DHCP clients. To see the full set of options and parameters you can set in that file, refer to the `dhcp-options` and `dhcpd.conf` man pages (type **man dhcp-options**).

Opening your firewall for DHCP

The firewall on your DHCP server must be configured to allow access to UDP ports 67 and 68. The easiest way to do this is to select System → Administration →Firewall from the GNOME desktop. From the Firewall Configuration window that appears select Other Ports and add UDP ports 67 and 68.

If you prefer to use iptables directly to change your firewall, you can add a new rule to iptables and then save the changes permanently. Type the following as root user:

```
# iptables -I INPUT -i eth0 -p udp --sport 67:68 --dport 67:68 -j ACCEPT
```

In this example, requests are allowed to and from source and destination ports 67 and 68 (`--sport 67:68` and `--dport 67:68`) on the eth0 interface (which is your first Ethernet card). DHCP uses the UDP protocol (`-p udp`). If your DHCP server is also a routing firewall for your network, you want to make sure that you are only offering DHCP services to your LAN and not to the Internet. (You need to figure out if eth0, eth1, or some other card is connected to your LAN.)

If the rule was accepted (type **iptables -L -n** to make sure), you can save your entire firewall configuration so that the new rule is included permanently. (You may need to change an SELinux policy for this to work.) To change your firewall, type the following (as root user):

```
# iptables-save > /etc/sysconfig/iptables
```

This updates your `/etc/sysconfig/iptables` file so that all the current rules (including the one you just added) are included the next time iptables is restarted. To restore those firewall settings without rebooting, use the `iptables-restore` command:

```
# iptables-restore < /etc/sysconfig/iptables
```

Configuring the /etc/dhcpd.conf file

Suppose you have a single pool of IP addresses that you want to distribute to a set of computers that are all on the same subnetwork. In other words, all the computers are connected to one switch or cluster of switches with no routing between the devices. Here is an example of a simple `dhcpd.conf` file:

```
ddns-update-style interim;
ignore client-updates;

subnet 10.0.0.0 netmask 255.255.255.0 {

   option routers            10.0.0.1;
   option domain-name-servers  10.0.0.1;
   option subnet-mask        255.255.255.0;
   option domain-name        "handsonhistory.com";

   range dynamic-bootp 10.0.0.150 10.0.0.225;
```

```
default-lease-time 21600;
max-lease-time 43200;

# Set name server to appear at a fixed address
host ns {
  next-server ns1.handsonhistory.com;
  hardware ethernet 00:D0:B3:79:B5:35;
  fixed-address 10.0.0.1;
  }
}
```

In this example, this DHCP server provides IP addresses for client computers on a small LAN. The first two lines tell the DHCP server not to update DNS records for the local domain based on the IP addresses it assigns.

The DHCP server is serving a single LAN, represented by a 10.0.0.0 network address with a 255.255.255.0 netmask. Other data in this file define what information the DHCP server will hand out to clients on this LAN.

A single server at address 10.0.0.1 is used as the router (or gateway) and DNS server for the LAN. To ensure that this server always gets the fixed address of 10.0.0.1, a host entry is set to the hardware address (00:D0:B3:79:B5:35) for the Ethernet card on the host named ns.

The pool of addresses handed out by this DHCP server is 10.0.0.150 to 10.0.0.225, as set by the range dynamic-bootp line. (Using dynamic-bootp allows bootp and dhcp clients to get addresses.) Along with the IP address that each client is assigned, the client is also given the associated subnet-mask and domain name.

The IP addresses that the DHCP server hands out are leased to each client for a particular time. The default-lease-time (set to 21,600 seconds here, or 6 hours) is the time assigned if the client doesn't request a particular lease period. The max-lease-time (43,200 seconds here, or 12 hours) is the highest amount of time the server will assign, if the client requests it. Clients can renew leases, so they don't have to lose the IP address while they are still using it.

Expanding the dhcpd.conf file

As I noted earlier, this is a very simple example that works well for a single network of client computers. The following are some examples of ways that you can expand your dhcpd.conf file.

- If you have multiple ranges of addresses on the same subnetwork, you can add multiple range options to a subnet declaration. Here is an example:

```
subnet 10.0.0.0 netmask 255.255.255.0 {
   range 10.0.0.10 10.0.0.100;
   range 10.0.0.200 10.0.0.250;
}
```

This example causes the DHCP server to assign IP addresses between the ranges of 10 and 100 and between 200 and 250 on network number 10.0.0.

- You can set fixed addresses for particular host computers, also called *address reservations*. In particular, you would want to do this for your server computers so that their addresses don't change. While you could simply omit the fixed IP addresses from your pool of DHCP assigned addresses, you would lose centralized management of IP configurations. The DHCP reservations allow you to centrally configure all IP address information. One way to do this is based on the Ethernet hardware address of the server's Ethernet card. All information for that computer can be contained in a host definition, such as the following:

```
host pine {
    hardware ethernet 00:04:5A:4F:8E:47;
    fixed-address 10.0.0.254;
}
```

Here, when the DHCP server encounters the Ethernet address, the `fixed-address` `10.0.0.254` is assigned to it. Type **ifconfig -a** on the server computer to see the address of its Ethernet hardware (while the interface is up). Within this host definition, you can add other options as well. For example, you could set the location of different routes (`routers` option).

- Many of the options enable you to define the locations of various server types. These options can be set globally or within particular host or subnet definitions. For example:

```
option netbios-name-servers 10.0.0.252;
option time-servers 10.0.0.253;
```

In these examples, the `netbios-name-servers` option defines the location of the WINS server (if you are doing Windows file and print server sharing using Samba). The `time-servers` option sets the location of a time server on your network.

- The DHCP server can be used to provide the information an X Terminal or diskless workstation could use to boot up on the network. The following is an example of a definition you could use to start such a computer on your network:

```
host maple {
    filename "/dwboot/maple.nb";
    hardware ethernet 00:04:5A:4F:8E:47;
    fixed-address 10.0.0.150;
}
```

In the previous example, the boot file used by the diskless workstation from the DHCP server is located at `/dwboot/maple.nb`. The `hardware ethernet` value identifies the address of the Ethernet card on the client. The client's IP address is set to `10.0.0.150`. All of those lines are contained within a host definition, where the host name is defined as `maple`. (See

Table 23-1 for descriptions of data types and the Thin Clients heading in Table 23-2 for other options that may be useful for configuring thin clients.)

Adding options

There are dozens of options you can use in the `/etc/dhcpd.conf` file to pass information from the DHCP server to DHCP clients. Table 23-1 describes data types you can use for different options. Table 23-2 describes options that are available.

Table 23-1: Data Types

Data Types	Description
ip-address	Enter *ip-address* as either an IP address number (`11.111.111.11`) or a fully qualified domain name (`comp1.handsonhistory.com`). To use a domain name, the name must be resolvable to an IP address number.
int32, int16, int8, uint32, uint16, uint8	Used to represent signed and unsigned 32-, 16-, and 8-bit integers.
"string"	Enter a string of characters, surrounded by double quotes.
Boolean	Enter `true` or `false` when a Boolean value is required.
data-string	Enter a string of characters in quotes (`"client1"`) or a hexadecimal series of octets (00:04:5A:4F:8E:47).

Options contain values that are passed from the DHCP server to clients. Although Table 23-2 lists valid options, the client computer will not be able to use every value you could potentially pass to it. In other words, not all options are appropriate in all cases.

Table 23-2 is divided into the following categories:

- **Names, Addresses, and Time** — These options set values that are used by clients to have their hostnames, domain names, network numbers, and time zones (offset from GMT) defined.
- **Servers and Routers** — These options are used to tell DHCP clients where on the network to find routers and servers. Although more than a dozen server types are listed, most often you will just indicate the address of the router and the DNS servers the client will use.
- **Routing** — These options indicate whether or not the client routes packets.
- **Thin Clients** — These options are useful if DHCP is being used as a boot server for thin clients. A thin client may be an X Terminal or diskless workstation that has processing

power, but no disk (or a very small disk) so it can't store a boot image and a file system itself.

> **NOTE:** The Linux Terminal Server Project (LTSP) contains all the software you need to set up a server and thin clients. You can find a description of LTSP in another of my books: *Linux Toys II* (Wiley Publishing, 2005). The Fedora K12Linux project (`http://fedoraproject.org/wiki/K12Linux`) is an example of an LTSP-based project that provides educational tools to thousands of students in schools.

Table 23-2: DHCP Options

Options	*Descriptions*
Names, Addresses, and Time	
option host-name *string*;	Indicates the name that the client computer can use to identify itself. It can either be a simple hostname (for example, `pine`) or a fully qualified domain name (for example, `pine.handsonhistory.com`). You may use this in a `host` declaration, where a host computer is identified by an Ethernet address.
option domain-name *string*;	Identifies the default domain name the client should use to resolve DNS hostnames.
option *subnet-mask ip-address*;	Associates a subnetwork mask with an IP address. For example, `option 255.255.255.0 10.0.0.1;`
option time-offset *int32*;	Indicates the offset (in seconds) from Coordinated Universal Time (UTC). For example, a UTC offset for U.S. Eastern Standard Time is set as follows: `option time-offset -18000;`
Servers and Routers	
option routers *ip-address* [, *ip-address*...];	Lists, in order of preference, one or more routers connected to the local subnetwork. The client may refer to this value as the gateway.
option domain-name-servers *ip-address* [, *ip-address*...];	Lists one or more Domain Name System (DNS) servers that the client can use to resolve names into IP addresses. List servers in the order in which they should be tried.
option time-servers *ip-address* [, *ip-address*...];	Lists, in order of preference, one or more time servers that can be used by the DHCP client.
option ien116-name-servers *ip-address* [, *ip-address*...];	Lists, in order of preference, one or more IEN 116 name servers that can be used by the client. (IEN 116 name servers predate modern DNS servers and are considered obsolete.)

Options	Descriptions
option log-servers *ip-address* [, *ip-address*...];	Lists one or more MIT-LCS UDP log servers. Lists servers in the order in which they should be tried.
option cookie-servers *ip-address* [, *ip-address*...];	Lists one or more Quote of the Day (cookie) servers (see RFC 865). List servers in the order in which they should be tried.
option lpr-servers *ip-address* [, *ip-address*...];	Lists one or more line printer servers that are available. List servers in the order in which they should be tried.
option impress-servers *ip-address* [, *ip-address*...];	Lists one or more Imagen Impress image servers. List servers in the order in which they should be tried.
option resource-location-servers *ip-address* [, *ip-address*...];	Lists one or more Resource Location servers (RFC 887). List servers in the order in which they should be tried.
option nis-domain *string*;	Indicates the name of the NIS domain, if an NIS server is available to the client.
option nis-servers *ip-address* [, *ip-address*...];	Lists addresses of NIS servers available to the client, in order of preference.
option ntp-servers *ip-address* [, *ip-address*...];	Lists addresses of network time protocol servers, in order of preference.
option netbios-name-servers *ip-address* [, *ip-address*...];	Lists the addresses of WINS servers, used for NetBIOS name resolution (for Windows file and print sharing).
option netbios-dd-server *ip-address* [, *ip-address*...];	Lists the addresses of NetBIOS datagram distribution (NBDD) servers, in preference order.
option netbios-node-type *uint8*;	Contains a number (a single octet) that indicates how NetBIOS names are determined (used with NetBIOS over TCP/IP). Acceptable values include: 1 (broadcast: no WINS), 2 (peer: WINS only), 4 (mixed: broadcast, then WINS), 8 (hybrid: WINS, then broadcast).
option font-servers *ip-address* [, *ip-address*...];	Indicates the location of one or more X Window font servers that can be used by the client, listed in preference order.
option nisplus-domain *string*;	Indicates the NIS domain name for the NIS+ domain.
option nisplus-servers *ip-address* [, *ip-address*...];	Lists addresses of NIS+ servers available to the client, in order of preference.
option smtp-server *ip-address* [, *ip-address*...];	Lists addresses of SMTP servers available to the client, in order of preference.

Options	*Descriptions*
option pop-server *ip-address* [, *ip-address*...];	Lists addresses of POP3 servers available to the client, in order of preference.
option nntp-server *ip-address* [, *ip-address*...];	Lists addresses of NNTP servers available to the client, in order of preference.
option www-server *ip-address* [, *ip-address*...];	Lists addresses of WWW servers available to the client, in order of preference.
option finger-server *ip-address* [, *ip-address*...];	Lists addresses of Finger servers available to the client, in order of preference.
option irc-server *ip-address* [, *ip-address*...];	Lists addresses of IRC servers available to the client, in order of preference.
Routing	
option ip-forwarding *flag*;	Indicates whether the client should allow (1) or not allow (0) IP forwarding. This would be allowed if the client were acting as a router.
option non-local-source-routing *flag*;	Indicates whether or not the client should allow (1) or disallow (0) datagrams with nonlocal source routes to be forwarded.
option static-routes *ip-address ip-address* [, *ip-address ip-address*...];	Specifies static routes that the client should use to reach specific hosts. (List multiple routes to the same location in descending priority order.)
option router-discovery *flag*;	Indicates whether the client should try to discover routers (1) or not (0) using the router discovery mechanism.
option router-solicitation-address *ip-address*;	Indicates an address the client should use to transmit router solicitation requests.
Thin Clients	
option boot-size *uint16*;	Indicates the size of the default boot image (in 512-octet blocks) that the client computer uses to boot.
option merit-dump *string*;	Indicates where the core image should be dumped if the client crashes.
option swap-server *ip-address*;	Indicates where the client computer's swap server is located.
option root-path *string*;	Indicates the location (path name) of the root disk used by the client.
option tftp-server-name *string*;	Indicates the name of the TFTP server that the client should use to transfer the boot image. Used more often with DHCP clients than with BOOTP clients.

Options	Descriptions
option bootfile-name *string*;	Indicates the location of the bootstrap file that is used to boot the client. Used more often with DHCP clients than with BOOTP clients.
option x-display-manager *ip-address* [, *ip-address*...];	Indicates the locations of X Window System Display Manager servers that the client can use, in order of preference.

Starting the DHCP server

After the `/etc/dhcpd.conf` file is configured, you can start the DHCP server immediately. As root user from a Terminal window, type the following:

```
# service dhcpd start
```

Your DHCP server should now be available to distribute information to the computers on your LAN. If there are client computers on your LAN waiting on your DHCP server, their network interfaces should now be active.

If everything is working properly, you can have your DHCP server start automatically each time your computer boots by turning on the dhcpd service as follows:

```
# chkconfig dhcpd on
```

There are a few ways you can verify that your DHCP server is working:

- Check the `/var/log/messages` file. If the DHCP service has trouble starting, you will see messages in this file indicating what the problem is.
- Check the `/var/lib/dhcpd/dhcpd.leases` file. If a client has been assigned addresses successfully from the DHCP server, a lease line should appear in that file. There should be one set of information that looks like the following for each client that has leased an IP address:

```
lease 10.0.0.225 {
        starts 2 2006/05/04 03:48:12;
        ends 2 2006/05/04 15:48:12;
        hardware ethernet 00:50:ba:d8:03:9e;
        client-hostname "pine:;
}
```

- Launch Wireshark (type **yum install wireshark** to install and **wireshark&** to run) and start capturing data (in promiscuous mode). Restart the DHCP server and restart the network interface on the client. You should see a series of DHCP packets that show a sequence like the following: DHCP Discover, DHCP Offer, DHCP Request, and DHCP ACK.

- From the client computer, you should be able to start communicating on the network. If the client is a Linux system, type the **ifconfig -a** command. Your Ethernet interface (probably eth0) should appear, with the IP address set to the address assigned by the DHCP server. If your client is a Windows system, open a command prompt and type **ipconfig /all**. You will see the configuration information for all of your network interfaces.

When the server is running properly, you can continue to add DHCP clients to your network to draw on the pool of addresses you assign.

Setting Up a DHCP Client

Most client computers (Window, Linux, or Mac) are configured by default to boot up using DCHP to connect to the network. However, when that is not the case, you may need to indicate manually that DHCP be used.

Configuring a network client to get addresses from your DHCP server is fairly easy. Different types of operating systems, however, have different ways of using DHCP. Here are examples for setting up Windows and Linux DHCP clients.

Windows (Vista)

1. From Windows Vista, select Start → Control Panel → Network and Internet → Network and Sharing Center → Manage Network Connections.

2. Select Local Area Connection.

3. Select Properties. The Properties window appears.

4. Select Internet Protocol Version 4 and click Properties.

5. On the General tab, make sure the Obtain an IP Address Automatically button is selected.

Windows (95, 98, 2000, or XP)

1. From most older Windows operating systems (Windows 95, 98, and 2000), you open the Network window from the Control Panel (Start → Settings → Control Panel). For Windows XP systems, select Start → Control Panel → Network and Internet Connections → Network Connections, and then select your Local Area Connection and choose Properties.

2. From the Configuration tab (or General tab in Windows XP), click the TCP/IP interface associated with your Ethernet card (something like TCP/IP → 3Com EtherLink III).

3. Click Properties. The Properties window appears.

4. Click the IP Address tab (or General tab in Windows XP) and then select the Obtain an IP Address Automatically check box.

5. Click OK and reboot the computer so the client can use the new IP address.

Fedora/RHEL

1. While you are initially installing Linux, click Configure using DHCP on the Network Configuration screen. Your network client should automatically pick up its IP address from your DHCP server when it starts up.

2. To set up DHCP after installation, open the Network Configuration window (select System → Administration → Network or run the `neat` command).

3. From the Network Configuration window:

    a. Click the Devices tab (on by default).

    b. Click your Ethernet device (probably eth0).

    c. Click Edit.

    d. Click the General tab.

    e. Click "Automatically obtain IP address settings with" and select dhcp.

    f. Click OK.

    g. Click Activate.

4. Then, from a Terminal window, type:

```
# service network restart
```

By default, a Fedora or RHEL client will not accept all information passed to it from the DHCP server. The way that the Fedora or RHEL client handles DHCP server input is based on settings in the `/etc/sysconfig/network-scripts/ifup` script. If the client has DHCP turned on, when the system starts up networking, the `ifup` script runs the `dhclient` command. You can adjust the behavior of `dhclient` by creating the `/etc/dhclient.conf` file. (Type **man dhclient.conf** to find out how you can set your `dhclient.conf` file.)

Summary

DHCP provides a mechanism for centrally administering computers on your network, and can provide information that helps client computers get up and running quickly on the network.

DHCP is used to provide information about your network to Windows, Linux, Mac, or other client computers on your network. IP addresses can be assigned dynamically, meaning they are distributed from a pool of IP addresses. Or specific addresses can be assigned to clients, based on specific Ethernet hardware addresses.

Chapter 24

Setting Up a MySQL Database Server

In This Chapter

- Finding MySQL packages
- Configuring the MySQL server
- Working with MySQL databases
- Displaying MySQL databases
- Making changes to tables and records
- Adding and removing user access
- Checking and fixing databases

MySQL is a popular structured query language (SQL) database server. Like other SQL servers, MySQL provides the means of accessing and managing SQL databases. However, MySQL also provides tools for creating database structures, as well as for adding, modifying, and removing data from those structures. Because MySQL is a relational database, data can be stored and controlled in small, manageable tables. Those tables can be used in combination to create flexible yet complex data structures.

A Swedish company called MySQL AB was responsible for developing MySQL (www.mysql.com). MySQL AB released MySQL as an open-source product several years ago, gaining revenue by offering a variety of MySQL support packages, commercial licenses, and MySQL brand franchise products. In February, 2008, Sun Microsystems Inc. acquired MySQL AB for about $1 billion dollars. (Who says you can't make money with open source software?)

Although all the ramifications of Sun's acquisition of MySQL have not all played out yet, for now MySQL software is still available as open-source software. According to stories on the Web, however, Sun is expected to begin close sourcing parts of the MySQL code base. Some predict that, in time, this could cause a migration to other open source database applications, in particular PostgreSQL (www.postgresql.org).

MySQL has been ported to several different operating systems (primarily UNIX and Linux systems, although there are Windows versions and now even a Mac OS X version as well). As you may have guessed, these include binary versions of MySQL that run on Fedora and RHEL. This chapter contains descriptions of and procedures for the version of MySQL that is contained in the Fedora and RHEL distributions.

The version of MySQL that comes with this release of Fedora is 5.0.51. For many releases, Fedora and RHEL stayed on MySQL 3.23 because of licensing issues that Red Hat felt prevented it from distributing later versions freely. Sun Microsystem's plans to close sourcing parts of MySQL in the future makes the question of redistributing MySQL that much more uncertain.

Finding MySQL Packages

You need at least the mysql and mysql-server packages installed to set up MySQL using the procedures described in this chapter. The following MySQL packages that come with the Fedora and RHEL distributions are what you need to get started:

- **mysql** — This software package contains a lot of MySQL client programs (in /usr/bin), several client shared libraries, the default MySQL configuration file (/etc/my.cnf), a few sample configuration files, files to support different languages, and documentation.

- **mysql-server** — This software package contains the MySQL server daemon (mysqld) and the mysqld startup script (/etc/init.d/mysqld). The package also creates various administrative files and directories needed to set up the MySQL databases.

- **mysql-devel** — This software package contains libraries and header files required for developing MySQL applications.

Other packages available to add functionality to your MySQL databases include php-mysql (contains a shared library to allow PHP applications access to MySQL databases) , mod_auth_mysql (tools to authorize Apache Web server access from data in a MySQL database), and perl-DBD-MySQL (provides a perl interface to MySQL databases). Packages including tools for using MySQL databases include mysql-bench (contains scripts for benchmarking MySQL databases), MySQL-python (contains a Python interface to MySQL), and qt-MySQL (MySQL drivers for QT SQL classes).

If MySQL isn't installed yet, type the following:

```
# yum install mysql mysql-server
```

If MySQL was installed during initial Fedora installation, you should update your MySQL packages (run yum with update instead of install). If no Internet connection is available, you can install the mysql packages using the rpm command or the system-config-packages window (as described in Chapter 5), using the DVD that comes with this book.

Getting More MySQL Packages

While most of this chapter focuses on using and administering a MySQL database from the command line, some graphical tools are available for working with MySQL databases. In particular, the mysql-administrator package contains GUI software for connecting to a MySQL server. To install the mysql-administrator package, type the following as root user:

```
# yum install mysql-administrator
```

If you are familiar with MySQL, you can go ahead and use MySQL Administrator to connect to your MySQL database (assuming it is already running). If MySQL is new to you, I recommend you run through the procedures in this chapter to become familiar with how MySQL works and how to use it from the command line.

To launch the MySQL Administrator window, type **mysql-administrator**. If your MySQL database server is running, as described later in this chapter, enter the server hostname (such as localhost), user name (such as root), and password. The MySQL Administrator window will appear, as shown in Figure 24-1.

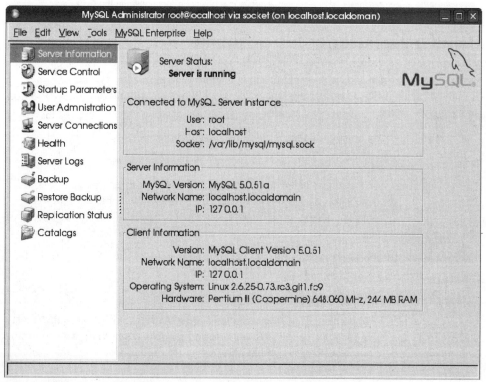

Figure 24-1: Connect to your MySQL database using the MySQL Administrator window.

At this point, you can use the MySQL Administrator window to find information about your MySQL server, backup and restore data, or select Catalogs to display information about each database. You can even select the Health option to all kinds of information about activity and usage of your server machine. (If you want to try another MySQL graphical utility, check out the mysql-query-browser package. That tool is made for designing MySQL tables and running queries.)

Configuring the MySQL Server

Like most server software in Fedora and RHEL, the MySQL server relies on a startup script and a configuration file to provide the service. Server activities are logged to the mysqld.log file in the /var/log directory. There are also mysql user and group accounts for managing MySQL activities. The following sections describe how these components all work together.

> **TIP:** For many of the steps described in this section, the MySQL server daemon must be running. Starting the server is described in detail later in this chapter. For the moment, you can start the server temporarily (as root, type **service mysqld start**). Then add a password, as shown in the next section.

Using mysql user/group accounts

When the MySQL software is installed, it automatically creates a mysql user account and a mysql group account. These user and group accounts are assigned to MySQL files and activities. In this way, someone can manage the MySQL server without needing to have root permission.

The mysql user entry appears in the /etc/password file as follows:

```
mysql:x:27:27:MySQL Server:/var/lib/mysql:/bin/bash
```

The mysql entry just shown indicates that both the UID and GID for the mysql user are 27. The text string identifying this user account is MySQL Server. The home directory is /var/lib/mysql and the default shell is /bin/bash. The home directory identified will contain directories that hold each table of data you define for the MySQL server.

The group entry for mysql is even simpler. The following entry in the /etc/group file indicates that the mysql group has a group ID (GID) of 27.

```
mysql:x:27:
```

If you care to check the ownership of files associated with MySQL, you will see that most of these files have mysql assigned as the user account and group account that own each file. This allows daemon processes that are run by the mysql user to access the database files.

Adding administrative users

To administer MySQL, you need to have at least one administrative account. By default, the root user has full access to your MySQL server database and no password assigned. You can assign a password to the root user using the `mysqladmin` command, once the mysqld server is running. To add the root user as a MySQL administrator, log in as the root user and type the following from a Terminal window (substituting your own password in place of *myownpasswd*):

```
# mysqladmin -u root password myownpasswd
```

After this command is run, the MySQL root user can run any MySQL administrative commands using the password.

MySQL maintains a list of users and passwords that is separate from the list maintained by Fedora. If you don't provide a user name on the command line (as in `-u root` shown above), MySQL assumes you want to use your current Fedora user name to log in to MySQL. However, you will still need to provide the MySQL password (not the Fedora password) for that user to use the MySQL service.

If you want to do MySQL administration, simply add the `-u root` argument to the command line of the MySQL command you are running. The Linux root user account has no connection to the MySQL root user account after the MySQL account is created. You would typically use different passwords for the two accounts.

> **TIP:** To save yourself the trouble of typing in the password each time you run a MySQL client command, you can add a password option under the `[client]` group in one of the option files. The most secure way to do that is to create a `.my.cnf` file in the root user's home directory that can only be accessed by root (`chmod 600 /root/.my.cnf`) and contains the following lines (substituting your password for the last argument shown):
>
>   [client]
>   password=myownpasswd

Setting MySQL options

You can set options that affect how the MySQL applications behave by using options files or command-line arguments. The MySQL server (as well as other administrative tools) reads the following options files when it starts up (if those files exist):

- `/etc/my.cnf` — Contains global options read by `mysqld` (server daemon) and `mysql.server` (script to start the server daemon).
- `-defaults-extra-file` — You can identify a file on the command line that contains options to be used by the server. For example, the following command would cause the file `/home/jim/my.cnf` to be read for options after the global options and before the user-specific options:

      # mysqld --defaults-extra-file=/home/jim/my.cnf

- $HOME/.my.cnf — Contains user-specific options. (The $HOME refers to the user's home directory, such as /home/susyq.)

Table 24-1 shows the MySQL commands that read the options files (in the order shown in the previous bullet list) and use those options in their processing. Options are contained within groups that are identified by single words within brackets. Group names that are read by each command are also shown in the table.

Although you can use any of the options files to set your MySQL options, begin by configuring the /etc/my.cnf file. Later, if you want to override any of the values set in that file, you can do so using the other options files or command-line arguments.

Table 24-1: Option Groups Associated with MySQL Commands

Command	Description	Group names
mysqld (in /usr/libexec)	The MySQL server daemon	[mysqld] [server]
mysqld_safe	Run by the mysqld startup script to start the MySQL server	[mysql] [server] [mysql.server]
mysql	Offers a text-based interface for displaying and working with MySQL databases	[mysql] [client]
mysqladmin	Used to create and maintain MySQL databases	[mysqladmin] [client]
myisamchk	Used to check, fix, and optimize MyISAM databases (.myi suffix)	[myisamchk]
myisampack	Used to compress MyISAM database tables	[myisampack]
mysqldump	Offers a text-based interface for backing up MySQL databases	[mysqldump] [client]
mysqlimport	Loads plain-text data files into MySQL databases	[mysqlimport] [client]
mysqlshow	Shows MySQL databases and tables you select	[mysqlshow] [client]

Creating the my.cnf configuration file

Global options that affect how the MySQL server and related client programs run are defined in the /etc/my.cnf file. The default my.cnf file contains only a few settings needed to get a small MySQL configuration going. The following is an example of the /etc/my.cnf file that comes with MySQL:

```
[mysqld]
datadir=/var/lib/mysql
socket=/var/lib/mysql/mysql.sock

old_passwords=1

[mysql.server]
user=mysql
basedir=/var/lib

[mysql_safe]
err-log=/var/log/mysqld.log
pid-file=/var/run/mysqld/mysqld.pid
```

Most of the settings in the default my.cnf file define the locations of files and directories needed by the mysqld server. Each option is associated with a particular group, with each group identified by a name in square brackets. The previous options are associated with the mysqld daemon ([mysqld]), the MySQL server ([mysql.server]), and the safe_mysqld script that starts the mysqld daemon ([mysql_safe]). (Refer to Table 24-1 for a list of these groups.)

The default datadir value indicates that /var/lib/mysql is the directory that stores the MySQL databases you create. The socket option identifies /var/lib/mysql/mysql.sock as the socket that is used to create the MySQL communications end-point associated with the mysqld server. The basedir option identifies /var/lib as the base directory in which the mysql software is installed. The user option identifies mysql as the user account that has permission to do administration of the MySQL service. Based on the old_passwords=1 value, your MySQL database will use the password format use in previous MySQL 3.x databases.

The err-log and pid-file options tell the safe_mysqld script the locations of the error log (/var/log/mysqld.log) and the file that stores the process ID of the mysqld daemon when it is running (/var/run/mysqld/mysqld.pid). The safe_mysqld script actually starts the mysqld daemon from the mysqld startup script.

> **NOTE:** Each option that follows a group name is assigned to that group. Group assignments end when a new group begins or when the end of a file is reached.

Choosing options

Many values are used by the MySQL server that are not explicitly defined in the my.cnf file. The easiest way to see which options are available for MySQL server and clients is to run each command with the --help option. For example, to view the available mysqld options (as well as other information) type the following from a Terminal window:

```
# /usr/libexec/mysqld --verbose --help | less
```

Then press the Spacebar to step through the information one screen at a time. (An example of this output is shown in the next section.)

You can also use the `man` command to find which options are available. For example, to see which options are available to set for the `mysqld` daemon, type the following:

```
man mysqld
```

It's quite likely that you can try out your MySQL database server without changing any options at all. However, after you set up your MySQL database server in a production environment, you will almost surely want to tune the server to match the way the server is used. For example, if it is a dedicated MySQL server, you will want to allow MySQL to consume more of the system resources than it would by default.

The following list shows a few examples of additional options that you might want to set for MySQL:

- **password** = *yourpwd* — Adding this option to a [client] group in a user's $HOME/.my.cnf file allows the user to run MySQL client commands without having to enter a password each time. (Replace *yourpwd* with the user's password.)

- **port** = **#** — Defines the port number to which the MySQL service listens for MySQL requests. (Replace # with the port number you want to use.) By default, MySQL listens to port number 3306 on TCP and UDP protocols.

- **safe-mode** — Tells the server to skip some optimization steps when the server starts.

- **tmpdir** = *path* — Identifies a directory, other than the default /tmp, for MySQL to use for writing temporary files. (Substitute a full path name for *path*.)

In addition to the options you can set, MySQL clients also have a lot of variables that you can set. Variables set such things as buffer sizes, timeout values, and acceptable packet lengths. These variables are also listed on the `--help` output. To change a variable value, you can use the `--set-variable` option, followed by the variable name and value. For example, to set the `sort_buffer` variable to 10MB, you could add the following option under your [mysqld] group:

```
[mysqld]
set-variable = sort_buffer=10M
```

The following list identifies other variables you could set for your server. In general, raising the values of these variables improves performance, but also consumes more system resources. So you need to be careful raising these values on machines that are not dedicated to MySQL or that have limited memory resources.

> **NOTE:** For variables that require you to enter a size, indicate Megabytes using an M (for example, 10M) or Kilobytes using a K (for example, 256K).

- **key_buffer_size** = *size* — Sets the buffer size that is used for holding index blocks that are used by all threads. This is a key value to raise to improve MySQL performance.

- **max_allowed_packet** = *size* — Limits the maximum size of a single packet. Raise this limit if you require processing of very large columns.

- **myisam_sort_buffer_size** = *size* — Sets the buffer size used for sorting while repairing an index, creating an index, or altering a table.

- **sort_buffer** = *size* — Defines how much buffer size is allocated for each thread that needs to do a sort. Raising this value makes sorting threads go faster.

- **table_cache** = # — Limits the total number of tables that can be open at the same time for all threads. The number of this variable represents the total number of file descriptors that MySQL can have open at the same time.

- **thread_cache_size** = *size* — Sets the number of threads that are kept in cache, awaiting use by MySQL. When a thread is done being used, it is placed back in the cache. If all the threads are used, new threads must be created to service requests.

Checking options

In addition to seeing how options and variables are set in the options files, you can also view how all variables are set on your current system. You can view both the defaults and the current values being used by the MySQL server.

The --help command-line argument lets you see the options and variables as they are set for the server and for each MySQL client. Here is an example of the output showing this information for the mysqld server daemon:

```
# /usr/libexec/mysqld --verbose --help | less
      .
      .
      .

Variables (--variable-name=value)
and boolean options {FALSE|TRUE}    Value (after reading options)
---------------------------------   -----------------------------
help                                TRUE
abort-slave-event-count             0
allow-suspicious-udfs               FALSE
auto-increment-increment            1
automatic-sp-privileges             TRUE
basedir:                            /usr/
      .
      .
      .
tmp_table_size                      33554432
transaction_alloc_block_size        8192
transaction_prealloc_size           4096
updatable_views_with_limit          1
```

```
wait_timeout                         28800

To see what values a running MySQL server isusing, type
'mysqladmin variables' instead of 'mysqld --verbose --help
```

After the server is started, you can see the values that are actually in use by running the mysqladmin command with the variables option. (Pipe the output to the less command so you can page through the information.) Here is an example (if you haven't stored your password, you will be prompted to enter your password before you see any output):

```
# mysqladmin -u root -p variables | less
+---------------------------+------------------------------------------|
| Variable_name             | Value                                    |
+---------------------------+------------------------------------------
| auto_increment_increment  | 1                                        |
| auto_increment_offset     | 1                                        |
| automatic_sp_privileges   | ON                                       |
| back_log                  | 50                                       |
| basedir                   | /usr/                                    |
| bdb_cache_size            | 8388600                                  |
| bdb_log_buffer_size       | 32768                                    |
| bdb_home                  | /var/lib/mysql/                          |
| bdb_max_lock              | 10000                                    |
| bdb_logdir                |                                          |
| bdb_shared_data           | OFF                                      |
| bdb_tmpdir                | /tmp/                                    |
                    .
                    .
                    .
| tmp_table_size            | 33554432                                 |
| tmpdir                    | /tmp/                                    |
| version                   | 5.0.51a                                  |
| wait_timeout              | 28800                                    |
+---------------------------+------------------------------------------+
```

If you decide that the option and variable settings that come with the default MySQL system don't exactly suit you, you don't have to start from scratch. Sample my.cnf files that come with the mysql package let you begin with a set of options and variables that are closer to the ones you need.

Using sample my.cnf files

Sample my.cnf files are available in the /usr/share/doc/mysql-server* directory. To use one of these files, do the following:

1. Keep a copy of the old my.cnf file:

   ```
   # mv /etc/my.cnf /etc/my.cnf.old
   ```

2. Copy the sample `my.cnf` file you want to the `/etc/my.cnf` file. For example, to use the `my-medium.cnf` file, type the following:

```
# cp /usr/share/doc/mysql-server*/my-medium.cnf /etc/my.cnf
```

3. Edit the new `/etc/my.cnf` file (as root user) using any text editor to further tune your MySQL variables and options.

The following bullets describe each of the sample `my.cnf` files.

- **my-small.cnf** — This options file is recommended for computer systems that have less than 64MB of memory and are used only occasionally for MySQL. With this options file, MySQL won't be able to handle a lot of usage but it won't be a drag on the performance of your computer.

  For the mysqld server, buffer sizes are set low — only 64K for the `sort_buffer` and 16K for the `key_buffer`. The `thread_stack` is set to only 64K and `net_buffer_length` is only 2K. The `table_cache` is set to 4.

- **my-medium.cnf** — As with the small options file, the `my-medium.cnf` file is intended for systems where MySQL is not the only important application running. This system also has a small amount of total memory available — between 32MB and 64MB — but more consistent MySQL use is expected.

  The `key_buffer` size is set to 16M in this file, while the `sort_buffer` value is raised to 512K for the mysqld server. The `table_cache` is set to 64 (allowing more simultaneous threads to be active). The `net_buffer_length` is raised to 8K.

- **my-large.cnf** — The `my-large.cnf` sample file is intended for computers that are dedicated primarily to MySQL service. It assumes about 512M of available memory.

  Server buffers allow more active threads and better sorting performance. Half of the system's assumed 512M of memory is assigned to the `key_buffer` variable (256M). The `sort_buffer` size is raised to 1M. The `table_cache` allows more simultaneous users (up to 256 active threads).

- **my-huge.cnf** — As with the `my-large.cnf` file, the `my-huge.cnf` file expects the computer to be used primarily for MySQL. However, the system for which it is intended offers much more total memory (between 1G and 2G of memory).

  Sort buffer size (`sort_buffer`) is raised to 2M while the `key_buffer` is set to consume 384M of memory. The `table_cache` size is doubled to allow up to 512 active threads.

- **my-innodb-heavy-4G.cnf** — This sample configuration file is best suited for computers with 4GB of RAM that are expected to service complex queries without too many connections (using the InnoDB transaction storage engine). Special `innodb` options in this file allow MySQL to take advantage of a large buffer pool size (2G).

Starting the MySQL Server

For Fedora and RHEL, the MySQL server is off by default. To turn it on, however, is fairly simple. The /etc/init.d/mysqld startup script is delivered with the mysql-server package. To start the server, you can run the mysqld startup script to have it start immediately, and then set it to start each time your system boots.

To start the MySQL server immediately, type the following from a Terminal window as root user:

```
# service mysqld start
```

To set the MySQL server to start each time the computer reboots, type the following (as root):

```
# chkconfig mysqld on
```

This sets mysqld to start during most multiuser run states (levels 3, 4, and 5). To check that the service is turned on for those levels, type **chkconfig --list mysqld** from a Terminal window.

Checking That MySQL Server Is Working

You can use the mysqladmin or mysqlshow commands to check that the MySQL server is up and running. Here's an example of how to check information about the MySQL server using the mysqladmin command.

```
# mysqladmin -u root -p version proc
Enter password: ******
mysqladmin  Ver 8.41 Distrib 5.0.51a, for redhat-linux-gnu on i386
Copyright (C) 2000-2006 MySQL AB
This software comes with ABSOLUTELY NO WARRANTY. This is free software,
and you are welcome to modify and redistribute it under the GPL license

Server version         5.0.51a
Protocol version       10
Connection             Localhost via UNIX socket
UNIX socket            /var/lib/mysql/mysql.sock
Uptime:                2 days 10 hours 47 min 35 sec

Threads: 2  Questions: 184  Slow queries: 0  Opens: 11  Flush tables: 1  Open
tables: 0  Queries per second avg: 0.004
+----+------+-----------+----+---------+------+-------+------------------+
| Id | User | Host      | db | Command | Time | State | Info             |
+----+------+-----------+----+---------+------+-------+------------------+
| 2  | root | localhost |    | Query   | 0    |       | show processlist |
+----+------+-----------+----+---------+------+-------+------------------+
```

Each of the two options to mysqladmin shown here provides useful information. The version information shows the mysqladmin version is 8.41 and the number assigned to this distribution of the mysql server is 5.0.51a. The binary package was created for PC versions of Linux/GNU on the i386 processor. The connection to the server is through a UNIX socket (`mysql.sock`) on the local host. The server has been up for 2 days, 10 hours, 47 minutes, and 35 seconds. Statistics show that there is one thread (connection to the server) currently active. There have been 184 requests to the server.

The `proc` option shows that one client is currently connected to the server. That client is logged into MySQL as the root user on the `localhost`. The client that has an Id of 2 (which tells you who the user is, allowing you to use that information, as the server's administrator, if you wanted to disconnect the user) is currently querying the MySQL database.

If the server were not running at the moment, the `mysqladmin` command shown in the previous example would result in a failure message:

```
mysqladmin: connect to server at 'localhost' failed.
```

The recommended remedy is to try to restart the server (by typing `service mysqld restart`).

Working with MySQL Databases

The first time you start the MySQL server (using the startup script described previously), the system creates the initial grant tables for the MySQL database. It does this by running the `mysql_install_db` command.

The `mysql_install_db` command starts you off with two databases: mysql and test. As you create data for these databases, that information is stored in the `/var/lib/mysql/mysql` and `/var/lib/mysql/test` directories, respectively.

Because the MySQL root user doesn't have to be the system's root user (provided you have the MySQL root user's password), you can be logged into Fedora or RHEL as any user you choose. In the following examples, be sure to provide the MySQL root user password when you run the commands shown.

> **NOTE:** If you are using the old ISAM tables instead of MyISAM, support for ISAM tables was removed for MySQL 5.0. You need to convert your tables to MyISAM using a statement such as the following:
>
> `ALTER TABLE` *table* `ENGINE=MYISAM`
>
> where *table* is your table name. Refer to the MySQL Reference Manual (`http://dev.mysql.com/doc/refman/5.0/en/upgrade.html`) for further information on upgrading to MySQL 5.0.

Starting the mysql command

To get started creating databases and tables, you can use the `mysql` command. From any Terminal window, open the `mysql` database on your computer by typing the following:

```
$ mysql -u root -p mysql
Enter password: *********

Welcome to the MySQL monitor. Commands end with ; or \g.
Your MySQL connection id is 39
Server version: 5.0.51a Source distribution
Type 'help;' or '\h' for help. Type '\c' to clear the buffer

mysql>
```

Type in the root user's MySQL password as prompted. (If no password has been set, you can skip the -p option.) The mysql> prompt appears, ready to accept commands for working with the mysql default database on the localhost. If you are connecting to the MySQL server from another host computer, add -h *hostname* to the command line (where *hostname* is the name or IP address of the computer on which the MySQL server is running). Remember that you can also log in as any valid mysql login you created, regardless of which Linux login account you are currently logged in under.

> **NOTE:** It is possible, but not recommended, to enter your password directly to the mysql command line by appending the password to the -p option (for example, -pMyPassword). Although this saves you the step of entering the password separately, it could expose your password to others who have access to your machine.

As the MySQL monitor welcome text notes, be sure to end each command that you type with a semicolon (;) or \g. If you type a command and it appears to be waiting for more input, it's probably because you forgot to put a semicolon at the end.

Before you begin using the mysql interface to create databases, try checking the status of the MySQL server using the status command. The following is an example of output from the status command:

```
mysql> status
--------------
mysql  Ver 14.12 Distrib 5.0.51a, for redhat-linux-gnu (i386) using readline 5.0

Connection id:          26
Current database:       mysql
Current user:           root@localhost
Current pager:          stdout
Using outfile:          ''
Server version:         5.0.51a
Protocol version:       10
Connection:             Localhost via UNIX socket
Server characterset:    latin1
Db      characterset:   latin1
Client characterset:    latin1
Conn.   characterset:   latin1
UNIX socket:            /var/lib/mysql/mysql.sock
```

```
Uptime:                 1 day 2 hours 57 min 19 sec

Threads: 1  Questions: 136  Slow queries: 0  Opens: 12
Flush tables: 1  Open tables: 6 Queries per second avg: 0.001
--------------
```

The status information tells you about the version of the MySQL server (14.12) and the distribution (5.0.51a). The output also reminds you of the current database (mysql) and your user name (root@localhost). You can see how long the server has been up (Uptime). You can also see how many threads are currently active and how many commands have been run to query this server (Questions).

Creating a database with mysql

Within an interactive mysql session, you can create and modify databases and tables. If you are not already connected to a mysql session, type the following command (assuming the mysql user name of root):

```
$ mysql -u root -p
Enter password: *******
mysql>
```

The general steps for creating a MySQL database include creating the database name, identifying the new database as the current database, creating tables, and adding data to the tables. While you are connected to a mysql session, you can run the following procedure to create a sample database.

1. To create a new database name, use the CREATE DATABASE command at the mysql> prompt. For example, to create a database named allusers, type the following:

    ```
    mysql> CREATE DATABASE allusers;
    ```

    This action creates a database called allusers in the /var/lib/mysql directory. (While you don't have to use capitals for the commands just shown, it makes it easier to distinguish the commands from the database entries.)

> **NOTE:** Alternatively, you can create a database from the command line using the mysqladmin command. For example, to create the database named allusers with mysqladmin, you could type the following: **mysqladmin -u root -p create allusers**

2. To see what databases are available for your mysql server, type the following at the mysql> command prompt. The databases shown are named information_schema, allusers, mysql, and test. The information_schema database contains metadata about information in other databases on your server (such as the types of data, columns, or tables used in each). The allusers database is the one created in the previous step. The mysql database contains user access data. The test database is created automatically for creating test mysql databases.

```
mysql> SHOW DATABASES;
+--------------------+
| Database           |
+--------------------+
| information_schema |
| allusers           |
| mysql              |
| test               |
+--------------------+
4 rows in set (0.00 sec)
```

3. To work with the database you just created (`allusers`), you need to make `allusers` your current database. To do that, type the following at the `mysql>` command prompt:

```
mysql> USE allusers;
Database changed
```

4. Creating a table for your database requires some planning and understanding of table syntax. You can type in the following commands and column information to try out creating a table. For more detailed information on creating tables and using different data types, refer to the section "Understanding MySQL Tables" later in this chapter.

   To create a table called `name`, use the following CREATE TABLE command at the `mysql>` prompt:

```
mysql> CREATE TABLE name (
-> firstname      varchar(20)     not null,
-> lastname       varchar(20)     not null,
-> streetaddr     varchar(30)     not null,
-> city           varchar(20)     not null,
-> state          varchar(20)     not null,
-> zipcode        varchar(10)     not null
-> );
Query OK, 0 rows affected (0.00 sec)
```

   You have now created a table called `name` for a database named allusers. It contains columns called `firstname`, `lastname`, `streetaddr`, `city`, `state`, and `zipcode`. Each column allows record lengths of between 10 and 30 characters. Although MySQL supports several different database formats, because none is specified here, the default MyISAM database type is used.

With a database and one table created, you can now add data to the table.

Adding data to a MySQL database table

After the database is created and the structure of a database table is in place, you can begin working with the database. You can add data to your MySQL database by manually entering each record during a `mysql` session or by adding the data into a plain-text file and loading that file into the database.

> **NOTE:** While you are in a mysql session, keep in mind that you can use the up arrow key to retrieve and change previous commands. This is particularly useful if you are manually entering database records that contain similar information.

Manually entering data

To do the procedure in this section, I assume you have an open interactive `mysql` session and that you have created a database and table as described in the previous section. If you are not already connected to a `mysql` session, type the following command (assuming the `mysql` user name of root):

```
$ mysql -u root -p
Enter password: *******
mysql>
```

To add data to an existing MySQL database, the following procedure describes how to view the available tables and load data into those tables manually. The next section describes how to create a plain-text file containing database data and how to load that file into your database.

1. To make the database you want to use your current database (in this case, allusers), type the following command from the `mysql>` prompt:

    ```
    mysql> USE allusers;
    Database changed
    ```

2. To see the tables that are associated with the current database, type the following command from the `mysql>` prompt:

    ```
    mysql> SHOW tables;
    +-------------------+
    | Tables_in_allusers |
    +-------------------+
    | name              |
    +-------------------+
    1 row in set (0.00 sec)
    ```

    You can see that the only table defined so far for the allusers database is the one called `name`.

3. To display the format of the `name` table, type the following command at the `mysql>` prompt:

    ```
    mysql> DESCRIBE name;
    +-----------+-------------+------+-----+---------+-------+
    | Field     | Type        | Null | Key | Default | Extra |
    +-----------+-------------+------+-----+---------+-------+
    | firstname | varchar(20) | NO   |     |         |       |
    | lastname  | varchar(20) | NO   |     |         |       |
    ```

```
| streetaddr| varchar(30)|  NO  |       |        |        |
| city      | varchar(20)|  NO  |       |        |        |
| state     | varchar(20)|  NO  |       |        |        |
| zipcode   | varchar(10)|  NO  |       |        |        |
+-----------+------------+------+-------+--------+--------+
```

4. To add data to the new table, you can use the INSERT INTO command from the mysql> prompt. Here is an example of how to add a person's name and address to the new table:

```
mysql> INSERT INTO name
-> VALUES ('Jerry','Wingnut','167 E Street',
-> 'Roy','UT','84103');
```

In this example, the INSERT INTO command identifies the name table. Then it indicates that values for a record in that table include the name Jerry Wingnut at the address 167 E Street, Roy, UT 84103.

5. To check that the data has been properly entered into the new table, type the following command from the mysql> prompt:

```
mysql> SELECT * FROM name;
+-----------+----------+-------------+-------+-------+---------+
| firstname | lastname | streetaddr  | city  | state | zipcode |
+-----------+----------+-------------+-------+-------+---------+
| Jerry     | Wingnut  | 167 E Street| Roy   | UT    | 84103   |
+-----------+----------+-------------+-------+-------+---------+
```

The resulting output shows the data you just entered, displayed in the columns you defined for the name table. If you like, you can continue adding data in this way.

Typing each data item individually can be tedious. As an alternative, you can add your data to a plain-text file and load it into your MySQL database, as described in the following section.

Loading data from a file

Using the LOAD DATA command during a mysql session, you can load a file containing database records into your MySQL database. Here are a few things you need to know about creating a data file to be loaded into MySQL:

- You can create the file using any Linux text editor.
- Each record, consisting of all the columns in the table, must be on its own line. (A line feed indicates the start of the next record.)
- Separate each column by a Tab character.
- You can leave a column blank for a particular record by placing a \N in that column.
- Any blank lines you leave in the file result in blank lines in the database table.

In this example, the following text is added into a plain-text file. The text is in a format that can be loaded into the name table created earlier in this chapter. To try it out, type the following text into a file. Make sure that you insert a Tab character between each value.

```
Chris    Smith      175 Harrison Street    Gig Harbor   WA   98999
John     Jones      18 Talbot Road NW      Coventry     NJ   54889
Howard   Manty      1515 Broadway          New York     NY   10028
```

When you are done entering the data, save the text to any filename that is accessible to the mysql server daemon (for example, /tmp/name.txt). Remember the filename so that you can use it later. If you are not already connected to a mysql session, type the following command (assuming mysql is the user name root):

```
$ mysql -u root -p
Enter password: *******
mysql>
```

Next, identify the database (allusers in this example) as the current database by typing the following:

```
mysql> USE allusers;
Database changed
```

To actually load the file into the name table in the allusers database, type the following command to load the file (in this case, /tmp/name.txt) from the mysql> prompt.

> **NOTE:** Either enter the full path to the file or have it in the directory where the mysql command starts. In the latter case, you can type the filename without indicating its full path.

```
mysql> LOAD DATA INFILE "/tmp/name.txt" INTO TABLE name;
Query OK, 3 rows affected (0.02 sec)
Records: 3  Deleted: 0  Skipped: 0  Warnings: 0
```

Type the following at the mysql> prompt to make sure that the records have been added correctly:

```
mysql> SELECT * FROM name;
+----------+----------+--------------------+------------+-------+-------+
| firstname| lastname | streetaddr         | city       | state |zipcode|
+----------+----------+--------------------+------------+-------+-------+
| Chris    | Smith    | 175 Harrison Street| Gig Harbor | WA    | 98999 |
| John     | Jones    | 18 Talbot Road NW  | Coventry   | NJ    | 54889 |
| Howard   | Manty    | 1515 Broadway      | New York   | NY    | 10028 |
+----------+----------+--------------------+------------+-------+-------+
```

At this point, you have a database that includes some data that you can begin working with. If something went wrong, refer to the "Updating and deleting MySQL records" section later in this chapter. If you find you need more information that is provided in this chapter, refer to the MySQL documentation at http://dev.mysql.com/doc.

Although MySQL doesn't support all of SQL, it does contain enough features for most users. If you find that MySQL doesn't meet your needs, you can try the PostgreSQL object-relational database management system (which also comes with Fedora and RHEL systems). For further information on PostgreSQL, refer to `www.postgresql.org`. Firebird (`www.firebirdsql.org`) is another open source relational database that might interest you.

Understanding MySQL Tables

You have a lot of flexibility when it comes to setting up MySQL tables. To have your MySQL database operate as efficiently as possible, you want to have the columns be assigned to the most appropriate size and data type to hold the data you need to store.

Use the following tables as a reference to the different data types that can be assigned to your columns. Data types available for use in MySQL fall into these categories: numbers, time and date, and character strings. Here are a few things you need to know as you read these tables:

- The maximum display size for a column is 255 characters. An M data type option sets the number of characters that are displayed and, in most cases, stored for the column.

- There can be up to 30 digits following the decimal point for floating-point or fixed-point data types. A D option to a data type indicates the number of digits allowed for a number following the decimal point. (The value should be no more than two digits less than the value of the display size being used.)

- The UNSIGNED option (shown in brackets) indicates that only positive numbers are allowed in the column. This allows the column to hold larger positive numbers.

- The ZEROFILL option (shown in brackets) indicates that the data in the column will be padded with zeros. For example, the number 25 in a column with a data type of INTEGER(7) ZEROFILL would appear as 0000025. (Any ZEROFILL column automatically becomes UNSIGNED.)

- All values shown in brackets are optional.

- The parentheses shown around the (M) and (D) values are necessary if you enter either of those values. In other words, don't type the brackets, but do type the parentheses.

Table 24-2 shows numeric data types that you can use with MYSQL.

Table 24-2: Numeric Data Types for Columns

Data Type	Description	Space Needed
BIGINT[(M)] [UNSIGNED] [ZEROFILL]	Can contain large integers with the following allowable values: −9223372036854775808 to 9223372036854775807 (signed) 0 to 18446744073709551615 (unsigned)	Uses 8 bytes.
DECIMAL[(M[,D])] [ZEROFILL]	Contains an unpacked fixed-point number (signed only). Each digit is stored as a single character. When you choose the display value (M), decimal points and minus signs are not counted in that value. The value of (M) is 10 by default. Setting D to zero (which is the default) causes only whole numbers to be used.	Uses M+2 bytes if D is greater than 0. Uses M+1 bytes if D is equal to 0.
DOUBLE[(M,D)] [ZEROFILL]	Contains a double-precision, floating-point number of an average size. Values that are allowed include: −1.7976931348623157E+308 to −2.2250738585072014E−308 0 2.2250738585072014E−308 to 1.7976931348623157E+308.	Uses 8 bytes.
DOUBLE PRECISION	Same as DOUBLE.	Same as DOUBLE.
FLOAT(X) [ZEROFILL]	Contains a floating-point number. For a single-precision floating-point number X can be less than or equal to 24. For a double-precision floating-point number, X can be between 25 and 53. The display size and number of decimals are undefined.	Uses 4 bytes if X is less than or equal to 24. Uses 8 bytes if X is greater than or equal to 25 and less than or equal to 53.

Data Type	Description	Space Needed
FLOAT[(M,D)] [ZEROFILL]	Contains a single-precision floating-point number. Values that are allowed include: –3.402823466E+38 to –1.175494351E–38 0 1.175494351E-38 to 3.402823466E+38. If the display value (M) is less than or equal to 24, the number is a single-precision floating-point number.	Uses 4 bytes.
INT[(M)] [UNSIGNED] [ZEROFILL]	Contains an integer of normal size. The range is –2147483648 to 2147483647 if it's signed, and 0 to 4294967295 if unsigned.	Uses 4 bytes.
INTEGER[(M)] [UNSIGNED] [ZEROFILL]	Same as INT.	Same as INT.
MEDIUMINT[(M)] [UNSIGNED] [ZEROFILL]	Contains an integer of medium size. The range is –8388608 to 8388607 if it's signed and 0 to 16777215 if unsigned.	Uses 3 bytes.
NUMERIC(M,D) [ZEROFILL]	Same as DECIMAL.	Same as DECIMAL.
REAL	Same as DOUBLE.	Same as DOUBLE.
SMALLINT[(M)] [UNSIGNED] [ZEROFILL]	Contains an integer of small size. The range is –32768 to 32767 if it's signed and 0 to 65535 if it's unsigned.	Uses 2 bytes.
TINYINT[(M)] [UNSIGNED] [ZEROFILL]	A very small integer, with a signed range of –128 to 127 and a 0 to 255 unsigned range.	Uses 1 byte.

The default format of dates in MySQL is YYYY-MM-DD, which stands for the year, month, and day. Any improperly formatted date or time values will be converted to zeros. Table 24-3 shows time and date data types that you can use with MySQL.

Table 24-3: Time/Date Data Types for Columns

Data Type	Description	Space Needed
DATE	Contains a date between January 1, 1000 (1000-01-01) and December 31, 9999 (9999-12-31).	Uses 3 bytes.
DATETIME	Contains a combination of date and time between zero hour of January 1, 1000 (1000-01-01 00:00:00) and the last second of December 31, 9999 (9999-12-31 23:59:59).	Uses 8 bytes.
TIMESTAMP[(M)]	Contains a timestamp from between zero hour of January 1, 1970 (1970-01-01 00:00:00) and a time in the year 2037. It is stored in the form YYYYMMDDHHMMSS. Using (M), you can reduce the size of the TIMESTAMP displayed to less than the full 14 characters (although the full 4-byte TIMESTAMP is still stored).	Uses 4 bytes.
TIME	Contains a time between −838:59:59 and 838:59:59. The format of the field is in hours, minutes, and seconds (HH:MM:SS).	Uses 3 bytes.
YEAR[(2|4)]	Contains a year, represented by either two or four digits. For a four-digit year, YEAR means 1901–2155 (0000 is also allowed). For a two-digit year, the digits 70-69 can represent 1970-2069.	Uses 1 byte.

Table 24-4 shows string data types that you can use with MYSQL.

Table 24-4: String Data Types for Columns

Data Type	Description	Space Needed
BLOB	Contains a binary large object (BLOB) that varies in size, based on the actual value of the data, rather than on the maximum allowable size. Searches on a BLOB column are case-sensitive.	Uses up to L+2 bytes, where L is less than or equal to 65535.

Data Type	Description	Space Needed
[NATIONAL] CHAR(M) [BINARY]	Contains a character string of fixed length, with spaces padded to the right to meet the length. To display the value, the spaces are deleted. The value of (M) determines the number of characters (from 1 to 255). If the BINARY keyword is used, sorting of values is case-sensitive (it is case-insensitive by default). The NATIONAL keyword indicates that the default character set should be used.	Uses between 1 and 255 bytes, based on the value of (M).
ENUM('val1','val2', . . .)	Contains enumerated strings that are typically chosen from a list of values indicated when you create the column. For example, you set a column definition to ENUM("dog","cat","mouse"). Then, if you set the value of that column to "1" the value displayed would be "dog", "2" would be "cat", and "3" would be mouse. It lets you take a number as input and have a string as output. Up to 65535 values are allowed.	Uses either 1 byte (for up to about 255 values) or 2 bytes, (for up to 65535 values).
LONGBLOB	Contains a binary large object (BLOB) that varies in size, based on the actual value of the data, rather than on the maximum allowable size. LONGBLOB allows larger values than MEDIUMBLOB. Searches on a LONGBLOB column are case-sensitive.	Uses up to L+4 bytes, where L is less than or equal to 4294967295.
LONGTEXT	Same as LONGBLOB, except that searching is done on these columns in case-insensitive style.	Uses up to L+4 bytes, where L is less than or equal to 4294967295.
MEDIUMBLOB	Contains a binary large object (BLOB) that varies in size, based on the actual value of the data, rather than on the maximum allowable size. MEDIUMBLOB allows larger values than BLOB. Searches on a MEDIUMBLOB column are case-sensitive.	Uses up to L+3 bytes, where L is less than or equal to 16777215.
MEDIUMTEXT	Same as MEDIUMBLOB, except that searching is done on these columns in case-insensitive style.	Uses up to L+3 bytes, where L is less than or equal to 16777215.

Data Type	Description	Space Needed
SET('val1','val2',...)	Contains a set of values. A SET column can display zero or more values from the list of values contained in the SET column definition. Up to 64 members are allowed.	Uses 1, 2, 3, 4, or 8 bytes, varying based on how many of the up to 64 set members are used.
TEXT	Same as BLOB, except that searching is done on these columns in case-insensitive style.	Uses up to L+2 bytes, where L is less than or equal to 65535.
TINYBLOB	Contains a binary large object (BLOB) that varies in size, based on the actual value of the data, rather than on the maximum allowable size. TINYBLOB allows smaller values than BLOB. Searches on a TINYBLOB column are case-sensitive.	Uses up to L+1 bytes, where L is less than or equal to 255.
TINYTEXT	Same as TINYBLOB, except that searching is done on these columns in case-insensitive style.	Uses up to L+1 bytes, where L is less than or equal to 255.
[NATIONAL] VARCHAR(M) [BINARY]	Contains a character string of variable length, with no padded spaces added. The value of (M) determines the number of characters (from 1 to 255). If the BINARY keyword is used, sorting of values is case-sensitive (it is case-insensitive by default). The NATIONAL keyword indicates that the default character set should be used.	Uses L+1 bytes, where L is less than or equal to M and M is from 1 to 255 characters.

Displaying MySQL Databases

There are many different ways of sorting and displaying database records during a mysql session. If you are not already connected to a mysql session, type the following command (assuming the mysql user name of root):

```
$ mysql -u root -p
Enter password: *******
mysql>
```

When you are in your mysql session (and have chosen a database), you can display all or selected table records, choose which columns are displayed, or choose how records are sorted.

Displaying all or selected records

Assuming that the current database is allusers (as shown in the previous examples), type the following command to choose (SELECT) all records (*) from the name table and display them in the order in which they were entered into the database.

```
mysql> SELECT * FROM name;
+-----------+---------+--------------------+------------+-------+---------+
| firstname |lastname |streetaddr          | city       | state | zipcode |
+-----------+---------+--------------------+------------+-------+---------+
| Chris     |Smith    |175 Harrison Street | Gig Harbor | WA    | 98999   |
| John      |Jones    |18 Talbot Road NW   | Coventry   | NJ    | 54889   |
| Howard    |Manty    |1515 Broadway       | New York   | NY    | 10028   |
+-----------+---------+--------------------+------------+-------+---------+
```

The following command displays all records from the name table that have the lastname column set to Jones. Instead of using lastname, you could search for a value from any column name used in the table.

```
mysql> SELECT * FROM name WHERE lastname = "Jones";
+-----------+---------+--------------------+------------+-------+---------+
| firstname |lastname |streetaddr          | city       | state | zipcode |
+-----------+---------+--------------------+------------+-------+---------+
| John      |Jones    |18 Talbot Road NW   | Coventry   | NJ    | 54889   |
+-----------+---------+--------------------+------------+-------+---------+
```

Using the OR operator, you can select records that match several different values. In the following command, records that have either Chris or Howard as the firstname are matched and displayed.

```
mysql> SELECT * FROM name WHERE firstname = "Chris" OR firstname = "Howard";
+-----------+----------+--------------------+------------+-------+---------+
| firstname | lastname | streetaddr         | city       | state | zipcode |
+-----------+----------+--------------------+------------+-------+---------+
| Chris     | Smith    | 175 Harrison Street| Gig Harbor | WA    | 98999   |
| Howard    | Manty    | 1515 Broadway      | New York   | NY    | 10028   |
+-----------+----------+--------------------+------------+-------+---------+
```

To match and display a record based on the value of two columns in a record, you can use the AND operator. In the following command, any record that has Chris as the firstname and Smith as the lastname is matched.

```
mysql> SELECT * FROM name WHERE firstname = "Chris" AND lastname = "Smith";
+-----------+----------+--------------------+------------+-------+---------+
| firstname | lastname | streetaddr         | city       | state | zipcode |
+-----------+----------+--------------------+------------+-------+---------+
| Chris     | Smith    | 175 Harrison Street| Gig Harbor | WA    | 98999   |
+-----------+----------+--------------------+------------+-------+---------+
```

Displaying selected columns

You don't need to display every column of data. Instead of using the asterisk (*) shown in the previous examples to match all columns, you can enter a comma-separated list of column name. The following command displays the firstname, lastname, and zipcode records for all of the records in the name table:

```
mysql> SELECT firstname,lastname,zipcode FROM name;
+------------+----------+---------+
| firstname  | lastname | zipcode |
+------------+----------+---------+
| Chris      | Smith    | 98999   |
| John       | Jones    | 54889   |
| Howard     | Manty    | 10028   |
+------------+----------+---------+
```

Likewise, you can sort columns in any order you choose. Type the following command to show the same three columns with the zipcode column displayed first:

```
mysql> SELECT zipcode,firstname,lastname FROM name;
+---------+------------+----------+
| zipcode | firstname  | lastname |
+---------+------------+----------+
| 98999   | Chris      | Smith    |
| 54889   | John       | Jones    |
| 10028   | Howard     | Manty    |
+---------+------------+----------+
```

You can also mix column selection with record selection as shown in the following example:

```
mysql> SELECT firstname,lastname,city FROM name WHERE firstname = "Chris";
+------------+----------+------------+
| firstname  | lastname | city       |
+------------+----------+------------+
| Chris      | Smith    | Gig Harbor |
+------------+----------+------------+
```

Sorting data

You can sort records based on the values in any column you choose. For example, using the ORDER BY operator, you can display the records based on the lastname column:

```
mysql> SELECT * FROM name ORDER BY lastname;
+-----------+----------+------------------+------------+-------+---------+
| firstname |lastname  |streetaddr        | city       | state | zipcode |
+-----------+----------+------------------+------------+-------+---------+
| John      |Jones     |18 Talbot Road NW | Coventry   | NJ    | 54889   |
| Howard    |Manty     |1515 Broadway     | New York   | NY    | 10028   |
| Chris     |Smith     |167 Small Road    | Gig Harbor | WA    | 98999   |
+-----------+----------+------------------+------------+-------+---------+
```

To sort records based on city name, you can use the following command:

```
mysql> SELECT * FROM name ORDER BY city;
+-----------+---------+--------------------+------------+-------+--------+
| firstname |lastname |streetaddr          | city       | state | zipcode|
+-----------+---------+--------------------+------------+-------+--------+
| John      |Jones    |18 Talbot Road NW   | Coventry   | NJ    | 54889  |
| Chris     |Smith    |167 Small Road      | Gig Harbor | WA    | 98999  |
| Howard    |Manty    |1515 Broadway       | New York   | NY    | 10028  |
+-----------+---------+--------------------+------------+-------+--------+
```

You can also add ASC or DESC to indicate the sorting order, because MySQL doesn't otherwise guarantee the order in which data are displayed. Now that you have entered and displayed the database records, you may find that you need to change some of them. The following section describes how to update database records during a mysql session.

Making Changes to Tables and Records

As you begin to use your MySQL database, you will find that you need to make changes to both the structure and content of the database tables. The following section describes how you can alter the structure of your MySQL tables and change the content of MySQL records. If you are not already connected to a mysql session, type the following command (assuming the mysql user name of root):

```
$ mysql -u root -p
Enter password: *******
mysql>
```

To use the examples shown in the following sections, identify the database (allusers in this example) as the current database by typing the following:

```
mysql> USE allusers;
Database changed
```

Altering the structure of MySQL tables

After you have created your database tables, there will inevitably be changes you want to make to them. This section describes how to use the ALTER command during a mysql session for the following tasks: adding a column, deleting a column, renaming a column, and changing the data type for a column.

To add a column to the end of your table that displays the current date, type the following:

```
mysql> ALTER TABLE name ADD curdate TIMESTAMP;
```

The previous line tells mysql to change the table in the current database called name (ALTER TABLE name), add a column named curdate (ADD curdate), and assign the value of that column to display the last edit date (TIMESTAMP data type). If you decide later that you want to remove that column, you can remove it by typing the following:

```
mysql> ALTER TABLE name DROP COLUMN curdate;
```

If you want to change the name of an existing column, you can do so using the CHANGE option to ALTER. Here is an example:

```
mysql> ALTER TABLE name CHANGE city town varchar(20);
```

In the previous example, the name table is chosen (ALTER TABLE name) to change the name of the city column to town (CHANGE city town). The data type of the column must be entered as well (varchar(20)), even if you are not changing it. In fact, if you just want to change the data type of a column, you would use the same syntax as the previous example but simply repeat the column name twice (in this case, zipcode). Here's an example:

```
mysql> ALTER TABLE name CHANGE zipcode zipcode INTEGER;
```

The previous example changes the data type of the zipcode column from its previous type (varchar) to the INTEGER type.

> **NOTE:** If you specify a column when you first create a table (CREATE TABLE command), it will change a column's default value. By running an ALTER TABLE statement, you can respecify the column default value, if you want to return to that value.

Updating and deleting MySQL records

You can select records based on any value you choose and update any values in those records. When you are in your mysql session, you can use UPDATE to change the values in a selected table. Here is an example:

```
mysql> UPDATE name SET streetaddr = "933 3rd Avenue" WHERE firstname = "Chris";
Query OK, 1 row affected (0.00 sec)
Rows matched: 1 Changed: 1 Warnings: 0
```

This example attempts to update the name table (UPDATE name). In this example, each record that has the firstname column set to "Chris" will have the value of the streetaddr column for that record changed to "933 3rd Avenue" instead. Note that the query found one (1) row that matched. That one row matched was also changed, with no error warnings necessary. You can use any combination of values to match records (using WHERE) and change column values (using SET) that you would like. After you have made a change, it is a good idea to display the results to make sure that the change was made as you expected.

To remove an entire row (that is, one record), you can use the DELETE command. For example, if you wanted to delete any row where the value of the firstname column is "Chris", you would type the following:

```
mysql> DELETE FROM name WHERE firstname = "Chris";
Query OK, 1 row affected (0.00 sec)
```

The next time you show the table, there should be no records with the first name Chris.

Adding and Removing User Access

There are several different methods you can use to control user access to your MySQL databases. To begin with, assign a user name and password to every user who accesses your MySQL databases. Then you can use the GRANT and REVOKE commands of mysql to specifically indicate the databases and tables users and host computers can access, as well as the rights they have to those databases and tables.

> **CAUTION:** Database servers are common targets of attacks from crackers. While this chapter gives some direction for granting access to your MySQL server, you need to provide much more stringent protection for the server if you are allowing Internet access. Refer to the General Security Issues section of the MySQL manual (`/usr/share/doc/mysql*/manual.txt`) for further information on securing your MySQL server.

Adding users and granting access

Although you have a user account defined to create databases (the root user, in this example), to make a database useful, you might want to allow access to other users as well. The following procedure describes how to grant privileges for your MySQL database to other users.

> **NOTE:** If you are upgrading your MySQL from a version previous to 3.22, run the `mysql_fix_privilege_tables` script. This script adds new GRANT features to your databases. If you don't run the script, you will be denied access to the databases.

In this example, I am adding a user named bobby who can log in to the MySQL server from the localhost. The password for bobby is i8yer2shuz. (Remember that there does not have to be a Fedora or RHEL user account named bobby. So any user on the localhost with the password for bobby can log in to that MySQL account.)

1. If you are not already connected to a `mysql` session, type the following command (assuming the `mysql` user name of root):

    ```
    $ mysql -u root -p
    Enter password: *******
    mysql>
    ```

2. To create the user named bobby and a password i8yer2shuz, use the GRANT command as follows:

    ```
    mysql> GRANT USAGE ON *.*
        -> TO bobby@localhost IDENTIFIED BY "i8yer2shuz";
    ```

    At this point, someone could log in from the localhost using the name bobby and i8yer2shuz password (`mysql -u bobby -p`). But the user would have no privilege to work with any of the databases. Next you need to grant privileges.

3. To grant bobby privileges to work with the database called allusers, type the following:

```
mysql> GRANT DELETE,INSERT,SELECT,UPDATE ON allusers.*
    -> TO bobby@localhost;
```

In this example, the user named bobby is allowed to log in to the MySQL server on the localhost and access all tables from the allusers database (USE allusers). For that database, bobby can use the DELETE, INSERT, SELECT, and UPDATE commands.

4. To see the privileges that you just granted, select mysql as your current database, and then select the db table as follows:

```
mysql> USE mysql;
Database changed
mysql> SELECT * FROM db WHERE db="allusers";
+----------------+-----------+--------+----------------+---------------+--
----------------+-----------------+
|Host           |Db         |User    |Select_priv |Insert_priv
|Update_priv |Delete_priv
+----------------+-----------+--------+----------------+---------------+--
----------------+-----------------+
|localhost      |allusers   |bobby | Y                      | Y           |
Y                | Y
+----------------+-----------+--------+----------------+---------------+--
----------------+-----------------+
```

The output here shows all users who are specifically granted privileges to the allusers database. Only part of the output is shown here because it is very long. You can make a very wide Terminal window to view the output if you don't like reading wrapped text. Other privileges on the line will be set to N (no access).

Revoking access

You can revoke privileges you grant using the REVOKE command. To revoke all privileges for a user to a particular database, use the following procedure:

1. If you are not already connected to a mysql session, type the following command (assuming the mysql user name of root):

```
$ mysql -u root -p
Enter password: *******
mysql>
```

2. To revoke all privileges of a user named bobby to use a database named allusers on your MySQL server, type the following:

```
mysql> REVOKE ALL PRIVILEGES ON allusers.*
    -> FROM bobby@localhost;
```

At this point, bobby has no privileges to use any of the tables in the allusers databases.

3. To see the privileges that you just granted, select `mysql` as your current database, then select the `db` table as follows:

```
mysql> USE mysql;
Database changed
mysql> SELECT * FROM db WHERE db="allusers";
```

The output should show that the user named bobby is no longer listed as having access to the allusers database. (The results might just say `Empty set`.)

Backing Up Databases

You can use the `mysqldump` command to back up your MySQL databases. The following command backs up all your MySQL databases.

```
# mysqldump -u root -p --opt --all-databases > /root/all-databases
```

In this case, all databases on the local system are copied to the file `all-databases` in the root directory. You can also use `mysqldump` to back up a single database, several databases, or tables within a database. Refer to the `mysqldump` man page for further information.

Checking and Fixing Databases

Over time, databases can become corrupted or store information inefficiently. MySQL comes with commands that you can use to check and repair your databases. The `myisamchk` command is available to check MyISAM database tables.

MyISAM tables are used by default with MySQL. (To use a different table type, you can assign it when you first create your MySQL table.) The tables are stored in the directory `/var/lib/mysql/`*dbname* by default, where *dbname* is replaced by the name of the database you are using. For each table, there are three files in this directory. Each file begins with the table name and ends with one of the following three suffixes:

.frm   Contains the definition (or form) or the table

.MYI   Contains the table's index

.MYD   Contains the table's data

The following procedure describes how to use the `myisamchk` command to check your MyISAM tables.

> **CAUTION:** Do a backup of your database tables before running a repair with `myisamchk`. Although `myisamchk` is unlikely to damage your data, backups are still a good precaution.

1. Stop MySQL temporarily by typing the following from a Terminal window as root user:

```
# /etc/init.d/mysqld stop
```

2. You can check all or some of your database tables at once. The first example shows how to check a table called name in the allusers database.

```
# myisamchk /var/lib/mysql/allusers/name.MYI
Checking MyISAM file: /var/lib/mysql/allusers/name.MYI
Data records:      5    Deleted blocks:      0
- check file-size
- check key delete-chain
- check record delete-chain
- check index reference
- check record links
```

You could also check tables for all your databases at once as follows:

```
# myisamchk /var/lib/mysql/*/*.MYI
```

The preceding example shows a simple, five-record database where no errors were encountered. If instead of the output shown in the previous example, you see output like the following, you may need to repair the database:

```
Checking MyISAM file: name.MYI
Data records:      5    Deleted blocks:      0
- check file-size
myisamchk: warning: Size of datafile is: 89 Should be: 204
- check key delete-chain
- check record delete-chain
- check index reference
- check record links
myisamchk: error: Found wrong record at 0
MyISAM-table 'name.MYI' is corrupted
Fix it using switch "-r" or "-o"
```

3. To fix a corrupted database, you could run the following command:

```
# myisamchk -r /var/lib/mysql/allusers/name.MYI
- recovering (with keycache) MyISAM-table 'name.MYI'
Data records: 5
Found wrong stored record at 0
Data records: 4
```

4. If for some reason the -r option doesn't work, you can try running the myisamchk command with the -o option. This is a slower, older method of repair, but it can handle a few problems that the -r option cannot. Here is an example:

```
# myisamchk -o /var/lib/mysql/allusers/name.MYI
```

If your computer has a lot of memory, you can raise the key buffer size value on the myisamchk command line, which will lessen the time it takes to check the databases. For example, you could use the following command line:

```
myisamchk -r -O --key_buffer_size=64M *.MYI
```

This would set the key buffer size to 64MB.

Summary

MySQL is a structured query language (SQL) database server that runs on Fedora and RHEL, as well as other operating systems. Using a startup script (/etc/init.d/mysqld) and a configuration file (/etc/my.cnf), you can quickly get a MySQL server up and running.

With tools such as the mysqladmin and mysql commands, you can administer the MySQL server and create databases and tables that are as simple or complex as you need. During mysql sessions, you can modify the structure of your database tables or add, update, and delete database records. You have a variety of options for querying data and sorting the output. You also have a lot of control over who can access your database tables and what privileges users have to modify, add to, or delete from the databases you control.

Chapter 25

Making Servers Public with DNS

In This Chapter

- Determining goals for your server
- Connecting a public server
- Configuring a public server
- Setting up a DNS server

In previous chapters you built Web, mail, and FTP servers in Linux. Now you want to expose those servers to the outside world. Options range from handing them to a hosting company and saying, "Take care of it," to managing the servers yourself out of your own home or office.

The following are some cases where you may want to consider some level of self-hosting:

- You're willing to provide the level of support that your organization needs in its servers.
- You just want an inexpensive way to publish some documents on the Web or maintain a public mail server for a few people, and 24/7 support isn't critical.
- You think self-hosting is cool and you want to try it.

The first goal of this chapter is to help you decide how much server support you want to maintain or provide to someone else. The second goal is to suggest how to set up your own public servers, including possibly configuring your own Domain Name System (DNS) server.

The descriptions of setting up your LAN (see Chapter 15) and connecting it to the Internet (see Chapter 16) focus on how to share information locally and let local users share an outgoing Internet connection, respectively. Building on that information, this chapter explains how to set up a DNS server, as well as other issues that relate to securing and maintaining public servers.

> **CAUTION:** After you open your server to Internet traffic, break-in attempts will occur. Most will come from automated scripts, sent from infected computers on the Internet. Because Fedora and RHEL come with good built-in security features, many attacks bounce off harmlessly (after logging messages). Allowing incoming connections, however, creates vulnerabilities that aren't there with an outgoing-only Internet connection. I strongly recommend you use security tools, described in Chapter 14, to protect your servers.

Determining Goals for Your Server

Before you open up that server sitting in your back office to the Internet, stop for a moment and think about your goals. Here are a few questions that you may want to ask yourself:

- How critical is this server for supporting your business?
- How much traffic do you expect on your server?
- Do you need to support the server 24 hours per day, 365 days per year?
- Do you know enough to maintain and secure your server?
- Can you get the connection speed that you require at a reasonable cost for your location?
- Do you need special equipment to keep the server running, such as an uninterruptible power supply?

Maintaining a public server requires some resources. If the server is critical to your business and in high demand, you may not have the time or expertise to support this server yourself. Also, if no high-speed Internet access is available to your location, even a well-configured server may not have the bandwidth to support your clients.

Using a hosting service

Tons of places are ready and willing to host your Web content. The number gets a bit smaller, however, if you need to find a place that can help you maintain your Fedora or RHEL server. In that case, you want to find a company that offers dedicated hosting (that is, gives you control of an entire server) or permits you to co-locate your server on its premises. In either case, you want to make sure that your server:

- Is physically secure.
- Can access enough Internet bandwidth.
- Has someone there if the server goes down.

You can use such a hosting provider in these ways and still use Fedora or Red Hat Enterprise Linux as your server:

- **Co-locate your server at a hosting provider or ISP.** In this arrangement, you can get lots of bandwidth and retain your root privileges so that you can still maintain the server yourself. The downside is that the provider probably isn't expected to fix your server if a hardware failure occurs.
- **Rent a server (at a place such as Rackspace.com)**, where you get the bandwidth and someone to fix the hardware (which that organization often puts together and maintains) if something goes wrong. A place such as Rackspace.com can also assure you that the hardware has been tested to run Linux.

Although this setup probably costs more money, the added support and security may prove well worth it. In either of the preceding cases, where the server resides at the hosting provider, you can also expect that service to include such extras as the use of its DNS service. (In other words, after you register a domain name and sign up with the hosting service, you can probably skip the rest of this chapter.)

Connecting a Public Server

If your organization's Internet service is currently used for outgoing connections, you must consider different security issues if you intend to allow incoming connections. The following are some differences:

- **Outgoing connection** — By providing outgoing Internet access, you need only enable your users to connect to the Internet and gain access to other computers' services. You don't need a domain name, and you don't need your own static IP address. (Chapter 16 describes how to set up a LAN to share an Internet service used primarily for outgoing service.) The focus of your network is on outgoing requests for services.

- **Incoming connection** — If you're setting up a public server, you want people from the Internet to find you and access services that you offer. The focus is on incoming requests for your computer's services, which means that you probably want a public host/domain name for the server and one or more static, public IP addresses for the server.

You have many different ways to connect your Fedora or Red Hat Enterprise Linux server to the Internet and offer its services to the public. In the following sections, I describe what you need to get your server up and running on the Internet.

Choosing an ISP

Although every ISP expects to see outgoing traffic on your Internet connection, not all of them expect incoming traffic (that is, traffic that someone initiates from outside your network). Although your ISP — which may be your local phone company, your cable TV company, or an independent ISP — may expect you to download files from remote servers, it may not expect people to download large files from you.

Assuming that you're going to house the server in your place of work or residence, you need to obtain the following information from a potential ISP:

- Does its Terms of Service agreement enable you to offer services over its connection?
- Does it have static IP addresses that it's willing to assign to you?
- Does it provide connections robust enough to handle the traffic demands on your server?

Checking Terms of Service

Any ISP that handles more than a few users has a document that describes what you can do with the Internet connection that it provides you. That document probably carries a name such as Terms of Service or User Agreement. If you can't find it on the ISP's Web site, you will almost certainly see it after you click a link to sign up for an account.

Typically, an ISP requires you to sign up for a business account if you want to do any kind of business on your Internet service. Here are some excerpts from agreements for several ISPs:

> *". . . you are not permitted to use your Internet connection to sell or advertise goods or services. This is permitted only to those who have purchased a business account or a virtual server."*

> *"Dialup clients are not to use their dialup connection for active or constantly connected Web/FTP/mail or other server services."*

> *"Anyone wanting to promote a business or sell a product must use a business account."*

Internet access is the volume business for most ISPs, and they consider business accounts for those who want to manage their own Web presence as premium services. Although you can technically use a personal account to set up a server (TCP/IP doesn't care what goes across the wire), the ISP's Terms of Service or Acceptable Use Policy may not permit you to do so. Although your DSL connection may easily handle a handful of hits a day on your Web server, offering that service can result in the termination of your account by the ISP. Check into what the ISP considers acceptable use before you use any Internet account to set up a public server.

Getting static IP addresses

Most dialup and DSL Internet-access accounts use dynamic IP addresses, so whenever you connect to your Internet service, the provider assigns the IP address to that connection. After you disconnect, the ISP can reclaim that IP address to assign to someone else. The next time you connect, it is possible that you will get a different IP address.

For a server to have constant, reliable presence on the Internet, it will typically have one or more *static IP addresses*. Most ISPs charge an additional fee for static IP addresses. Each static IP address typically costs between $3 and $20 per month.

> **NOTE:** You can assign a public DNS hostname to a server without a static IP address using Dynamic DNS. Dynamic DNS involves running software on your server that monitors your IP address and notifies the Dynamic DNS provider when that IP address changes.

The number of static IP addresses that you need varies, depending on how you configure your servers. Most likely, you want at least two static IP addresses, one for each of two DNS servers (if you're configuring DNS). In a small organization, those same servers may also offer your Web server, mail server, and other services as well. In general, you want one static IP address for each computer that you make publicly accessible to the Internet.

> **TIP:** You can do some tricks with services such as port forwarding (iptables in Chapter 14) and virtual hosting (Apache Web server in Chapter 21) that enable multiple physical computers to offer services or give the appearance of having multiple computers on a single static IP address. These tricks can reduce the number of IP addresses you need to buy. (To simplify the discussion here, however, I'm describing a case where each public server has its own static, public IP address.)

Choosing a connection speed

Another difficulty with keeping your servers in your own home or business is choosing how fast an Internet connection you need. Although most data centers at ISPs offer more than enough bandwidth for your needs, high-speed Internet connections may not be available to your location — or may prove prohibitively expensive.

Although it's technically possible, using a dialup connection (up to 56 Kbps) to support an Internet server is generally considered unacceptable. Always-on connection services that you may want to consider include the following:

- **Digital Subscriber Line (DSL)** — DSL service is widely available these days. Using only the standard telephone wiring in your home, you can maintain an always-on Internet connection and telephone service on the same wires. Speeds of between 256 Kbps and 7 Mbps are available with DSL service (although the actual speeds that you attain are typically slower than those in the advertisements).

- **Integrated Services Digital Network (ISDN)** — ISDN has been around longer than DSL to offer high-speed network services, and it's comparable to DSL in the speeds that it can offer. However, ISDN is typically more expensive to implement than DSL at comparable speeds.

- **Cable Internet** — Often, cable television providers will offer Internet access as well. Some cable Internet services offer higher download speeds than you can get with DSL, but may limit upload speeds (which may restrict its value for use with a server). For example, a major cable television provider currently offers a basic 3 Mbps download speed, but only 256 Kbps upload speed for its standard service. To use your cable television provider to run your Internet server, find out about the business Internet services it offers.

- **Frame relay** — This service is a packet-switching protocol that runs across wide-area networks. Although it can prove much more expensive than either DSL or ISDN, it can achieve much higher rates of speed. Speeds can range from 56 Kbps to 1.544 Mbps, or even as much as 45 Mbps. Frame relay can operate across a variety of network media. A primary advantage is that it uses virtual circuits that offer a fixed rate of speed, because the circuit between you and the ISP isn't shared with other ISP customers.

If your business can afford it, you might want dedicated T-1 or T-3 lines for your business. A *T-1 connection* can operate at data rates of 1.544 Mbps. A *T-3 line* can support rates of 44.736 Mbps. Check with your local ISPs for available connection types and pricing.

Getting a domain name

Domain names are available from dozens of different domain registrars these days. You can check the availability of domain names from any of these registrar's Web sites, such as GoDaddy (godaddy.com) or Network Solutions (networksolutions.com). You can also use the whois command that comes with Fedora and RHEL.

The *top-level domain* (TLD) in which you register your own domain should reflect the type of business or organization that you represent. Commercial businesses typically use the .com TLD. Newer TLDs, however, such as .biz and .info, are now available for domains that represent a business community or for information about businesses and individuals. Some people choose .ws to represent their Web site, although the .ws TLD is actually owned by the government of Western Samoa, which agreed to license it as a general-purpose Web site domain.

Other common TLDs are .net (originally for network services companies) and .org (originally intended for organizations). Although those domains were intended for special purposes, there are really no restrictions on who can get and use those domain names.

Institutions of higher education in the United States use the .edu TLD. A TLD that has recently become available for public use is the .us TLD, for organizations within the United States (public K-12 schools in the U.S. typically use the .us TLD). Countries outside of the United States each already have their own TLD.

Checking domain name availability

With an active Internet connection, you can use the whois command in Red Hat Linux to check if a domain name is available in the .com, .net, .org, or .edu domains. Following is an example of using whois to check the availability of the domain handsonhistory.com:

```
$ whois handsonhistory.com
[Querying whois.internic.net]
.

       .
       .

Registrant:
Hands-On-History (HANDSONHISTORY-DOM)
   PO Box 943
   Port Angeles, NJ 98221
   US

   Domain Name: HANDSONHISTORY.COM
       .
       .

   Technical Contact:
       Support   domains@XMISSION.COM
       Xmission Domain (XDS)
```

```
        51 East 400 South, Suite #200
        Salt Lake City , UT 84111
        US
        801-539-0852 fax: 999 999 9999

     Record expires on 17-May-2012.
     Record created on 18-May-1998.
     Database last updated on 16-Apr-2008 01:21:40 EST.

     Domain servers in listed order:

     NS.XMISSION.COM                    198.60.22.2
     NS1.XMISSION.COM                   198.60.22.22
```

If the name were available, you'd see the message No match for HANDSONHISTORY.COM. Because the name is already taken, you can see information about the domain name registrar, name servers containing address records for the domain, and a variety of contact information.

Reserving a domain name

At one point, Network Solutions was the only company from which you could get a domain name in the most popular U.S. domains (.com, .net, and .org). Now, there are new TLDs and dozens of domain registrars from which you can select a domain name.

You can have your ISP obtain your domain name for you, or you can go to one of the domain registrars yourself and register online to get your domain name.

> **NOTE:** Because prices and services can vary so widely, I recommend that you shop around for a domain registrar. The Internet Corporation for Assigned Names and Numbers (ICANN) maintains a list of accredited registrars at www.icann.org/registrars/accredited-list.html. The list contains links to registrar sites and a list of the TLDs that they support.

Although each registrar offers different domain and hosting-related services, the following list describes the information that you want to collect before you register your domain (and if you don't have all this information at the moment, don't worry — you can go back and fill in most of it later):

- **Domain name** — If you haven't already chosen a domain name by using the whois command, each registrar offers a search tool at its Web site that enables you to check the availability of any name that interests you.

- **Term of registration** — You must decide how many years of use you want to pay for on the domain name. You can typically pay in one-year increments, with the cost per year usually less the more years for which you reserve the name. Before the domain name expires, you can reregister it.

- **Contact information** — Provide the name, e-mail address, street address, company name, and phone numbers for the person in charge of the domain-name registration (probably you). You fill in separate sets of information for the registrant, technical contact, administrative contact, and billing contact.

> **NOTE:** If you don't fill in the other contact information, the registrar uses the registrant contact information for each of those categories. If someone else is managing your server, you are the registrant and the hosting company provides a technical contact.

- **Hosting options** — If you're providing your own hosting in Fedora or Red Hat Enterprise Linux, you want to decline the Web-hosting service offer that you're given as you register the domain. Along with hosting, the registrar is likely to offer you other hosting options (such as support for ASP pages and FrontPage extensions). It may also offer you e-mail service.

- **Domain Name System servers** — The registrar asks you to supply the primary DNS server and one or more secondary DNS servers. If your ISP is providing your DNS service, you can add that information now. If you're getting set up on DNS later, you can usually "park" the domain at the domain registrar and then come back after you obtain DNS to identify the DNS servers with the registrar.

To pay for the domain name, the service expects you to provide a credit card number. Some registrars accept other forms of payment, although credit cards are the most popular means.

Configuring Your Public Server

With a domain name, a suitable Internet connection, and one or more static IP addresses, you need to prepare your server to share it on the Internet. In addition to choosing the types of services you want to offer, you must be more thoughtful about the security of your servers.

Configuring networking

Whether you're configuring your computer for browsing the Web or offering up a server, procedures for creating network interfaces are very similar. See Chapters 15 and 16 for information on configuring TCP/IP for your computer. Following is a quick review of what you need to do to get a live connection to the Internet that's suitable for your server:

- **Add network interfaces** — Depending on what type of network connection you have, you must configure TCP/IP to work across that connection. Most likely, that connection requires that you configure an Ethernet, PPP, or ISDN interface. If you didn't already configure the connection when you installed Fedora, you can do so at any time by using the Network Configuration window (via the `neat` command).

> **NOTE:** One major difference between configuring a server for connection to the Internet and a computer that you use primarily for Internet access is in how you set your IP address. You quite likely got the IP address for your Internet connection by using DHCP. Now you will probably enter the IP address that you got from your ISP as a static IP address.

- **Add DNS server information** — Although the server IP addresses that you enter for DNS servers are probably ones that your ISP configured, you may want to add your own DNS servers. If so, make sure that your server points to your master and slave DNS servers for IP address resolution. You can also have the other computers on your LAN point to your DNS servers to resolve domain names to IP addresses. (The `/etc/resolv.conf` file is where you identify your DNS servers.) After you add your own DNS server, all your clients should change their `/etc/resolv.conf` files to include the new domain name and DNS server information.

- **Add hostname** — As soon as you have a real domain name, you can name your computer within the structure of that domain name. If you haven't installed Fedora or Red Hat Enterprise Linux, you can enter this hostname during installation. For example, to add a host called `duck` at `handsonhistory.com`, you'd enter `duck.handsonhistory.com` as you install Fedora. Later, you can change the name in the `/etc/sysconfig/network` file.

> **NOTE:** Changing your hostname after you install Fedora or RHEL can sometimes cause problems. Services such as printing and the X server (for your graphical desktop) sometimes fail after you change your hostname. Check to make sure that printing and other network services are still working after you change your hostname. Sometimes restarting the network interface can solve the problem.

After you set up your network interfaces and related information for your server, test the Internet connection by using the `ping` command, as described in Chapter 16. Next, if DNS is already configured for your domain, try to `ping` your server by name to see whether those in the outside world can reach you by name. Make sure that the static IP address that appears in response matches the static IP address that you were assigned.

Configuring servers

Some services are more appropriate for public exposure than others. You probably don't want to offer your print server, for example, to anyone on the Internet. Similarly, file sharing with Samba or NFS isn't appropriate to share those services natively across the public Internet. (To access those services over an Internet connection, however, you could run them over a virtual private network.)

If you're creating your first public server, you may want to consider setting up at least the following basic types of servers:

- **Web server** — This type of server, of course, provides the most common way to publish text, images, and a variety of other content to the Internet. Refer to Chapter 21 for information on configuring an Apache Web server.

- **FTP server** — This type of server provides the most common way of sharing directories of documents, images, application programs, and other content that users can download from your site. See Chapter 20 for information on setting up an FTP server.

- **Mail server** — Presumably, if you have a domain name that you like and a Linux server up and running, you may very well want to get a mail server running too. That way, you can create one or more e-mail addresses that look like `chris@linuxtoys.net`. Because mail servers are high-risk targets for spammers, if this is your first mail server you might consider setting it up for incoming mail only and use your ISP for outgoing mail. See Chapter 19 for information on configuring a mail server.

Of course, you can share any type of server that you choose. Web, FTP, and mail servers, however, are designed for sharing publicly. The basic configuration for these types of servers isn't that difficult. Securing and monitoring these — or any — public servers, however, requires special effort, as the following sections describe.

Managing security

Before you set up your Fedora or RHEL system as a server, you can use it simply to make outgoing connections to the Internet. You can use your firewall (iptables) to close off the ports on your interface to the Internet (making your computer quite secure). Now, however, you need to open some of the ports on that interface to accept incoming requests. With more ports open, you must also become more consistent in monitoring those ports. You can use SELinux to set boundaries around your Internet services.

Opening your firewall

Making your server public doesn't mean leaving your computer wide open. By using firewall rules, you can set your computer to allow outsiders to open connections to certain ports and block requests on other ports. Assuming that you set up your firewall to block incoming connections, here's a list of services (and the associated port numbers) that you may want to consider accepting through your firewall from your external interface to the Internet:

- **Web server** — Port 80
- **Mail server** — Port 25
- **FTP server** — Ports 20 and 21
- **DNS server** — Port 53 (if you're supporting your own DNS)
- **SSH server** — Port 22 (allows secure login service to administer the computer remotely or remote users to add Web content or other server content to the server)

To see which ports are assigned to which services by default, refer to the `/etc/services` file. See `http://www.iana.org/assignments/port-numbers` for a full list of service ports. In most cases, a configuration file for a service indicates the default port number the service listens on. One way of making a service more private is to change the port number that a service listens on. Then the user must know to ask for the service at that particular port. To see which ports are currently exposed on your system, you can use the `nmap` command.

Chapter 14 describes how to change your firewall to accept requests for these services. I start with the iptables example in that chapter when I create the DNS example later in this chapter. You can use that description as a model for setting up a firewall to go with DNS. In the DNS example, you have separate computers for mail, FTP, and Web services. For a low-volume server, however, you can have them all on the same computer.

Enabling SELinux

Security Enhanced Linux (SELinux) is enabled by default in Fedora and RHEL starting with version 4. As it is implemented with targeted policies, most popular server types (including Web, FTP, and DNS) have policies set that restrict what intruders can do if they manage to break into the service. You should look over how policies are set on the Security Level Configuration (`system-config-securitylevel` command) for services you are offering. Refer to Chapter 10 for more information on SELinux.

Checking logs and system files

By making your servers public, you also make them more open to attacks. Although firewalls are a good first line of defense, you still need to watch the activity on those ports that you leave open. A consistent program of monitoring traffic and checking changes to your server, therefore, becomes more critical. The following are a few techniques that you can use to help secure your servers:

- **General security** — Make sure that you protect all your user accounts by using good passwords and the correct file permissions settings.

- **Tripwire** — Use tripwire to take a snapshot of your critical system files so that you can check later whether anyone's altered those files. The tripwire package is included in the latest Fedora repository.

- **File System Saint** — As with Tripwire, File System Saint maintains a database of every file on your system. You can find out more information from the project's SourceForge.net site (`http://sourceforge.net/projects/fss`).

- **Logwatch** — Use Logwatch, which is on by default in Fedora and RHEL, to screen log files and e-mail suspicious messages to you. At the very least, you should change the `MailTo` value in the `/etc/logwatch/conf/logwatch.conf` file to an e-mail address you keep up with (this is where Logwatch will send its screened log messages).

I describe these and other security techniques in Chapter 14.

Keeping up with updates

You can expect to find and correct security issues continuously. You must keep up with software updates that are published to plug security holes. Although some of these updates address theoretical security problems, others are created in response to real break-ins or denial-of-service attacks that are known to exploit weaknesses in the components that come with your operating system.

For Red Hat Enterprise Linux systems, using the Red Hat Network is the best way of getting security updates that are approved for Red Hat Enterprise Linux. For Fedora, you can use the PackageKit or yum to download and install updates from Fedora mirror sites that carry those updates (see Chapter 5 for information on using PackageKit and yum). You should also check CERT and other organizations (which I describe in Chapter 14) for security alerts.

After your server is secure and correctly configured, your last step is to start the server on the Internet with a domain name that points to it. Either ask your service provider to configure DNS for you, or set up your own DNS server, as I describe in the following section.

Setting Up a Domain Name System Server

The *Domain Name System* (*DNS*) is essentially a distributed database that translates hostnames into IP addresses (and IP addresses back to hostnames). That database also contains information related to each domain, such as how the domain is organized into zones, where to route mail for that domain, and whom to contact with questions associated with the domain.

By setting up a DNS server, you become part of a hierarchy of DNS servers that make up the Internet. At the top of this hierarchy is the root server, represented by a dot (.). Below the root server are the Top Level Domains, or TLDs (such as .com, .org, and so on). Domains that individual organizations own and maintain lie below the TLDs, branching in a way that looks like an upside-down tree structure. That's where you come in.

As someone who's setting up a DNS server, you're responsible for managing the hostnames and IP addresses for the computers in the domain (or domains) for which you're responsible. Keeping your DNS information correct means that people can access the services that you want to share, and the Internet as a whole works that much better as a result.

Besides using your DNS server to help people from the Internet find the public servers in your domain, you can also use DNS to provide name and IP address mapping for computers on your private network. The example in the "DNS name server example" section later in this chapter describes how to configure both private and public name and IP address records for a domain.

> **CAUTION:** Setting up a DNS server can be a complex and (these days) potentially dangerous undertaking. A compromised DNS server can cause requests for host addresses to be directed to a cracker's server. The sample DNS server in this section is one created as an example of a DNS server for a home or small office environment. For information on the many different ways to set up a DNS server, go to the BIND 9 Administrator Reference manual at `/usr/share/doc/bind-9*/arm/Bv9ARM.html`.

Understanding DNS

The basic function of a *name server* is to answer queries by providing the information that those queries request. A DNS name server primarily translates domain and hostnames into IP addresses. Each domain is typically represented by at least two DNS servers.

- **Primary (master) name server** — This name server contains the master copy of authoritative information about the domains that it serves. In response to queries for information about its domains, this server provides that information marked as being authoritative. The primary is the ultimate source for data about the domain.

- **Secondary (slave) name server** — This name server gets all information for the domain from the primary name server. As is the case for the primary server, DNS considers the secondary's information about the domain that it serves authoritative, although the domain records can be overwritten from the primary.

NS (which stands for Name Server) records in the parent zone for a domain list the primary and one or more secondary name servers. This *delegation* of servers defines the servers that have authority for the zone.

Because zone records change as you add, remove, or reconfigure the computers in the zone, you assign expiration times for information about your zone. You set the expiration time in the time to live (TTL) field, in the `named.conf` file (which I describe later).

Other specialized types of DNS servers are possible as well. Although these types of servers don't have authority for any zones, they can prove useful for special purposes:

- **Caching name server** — This type of server simply caches the information it receives about the locations of hosts and domains. It holds information that it obtains from other authoritative servers and reuses that information until the information expires (as set by the TTL fields).

- **Forwarding name server** — Creating a server that's not authoritative for a zone but that can forward name server requests to other name servers may prove efficient. This server is essentially a caching name server, but is useful in cases where computers lie behind a firewall and in which only one computer can make DNS queries outside that firewall on behalf of all the internal computers.

Understanding authoritative zones

As an administrator of a DNS server, you need to configure several zones. Each zone represents part of the DNS namespace as you view it from your DNS server. Besides the one or more zones representing your domain, you have a zone that identifies your local host and possibly your local, private LAN.

If you configure a server as authoritative for a zone, that server has the last word on resolving addresses for that zone. In the upcoming "DNS name server example" section, your primary master name server is authoritative for the domain you control (as are the secondary name servers it passes its records to), but not for domains outside your domain.

Remember that the DNS server that you configure is the ultimate authority for your zone. Other zones don't know how you configure your hostnames and IP addresses unless you properly set up your DNS server to distribute that information across the Internet.

The definitive data that you set up for your domain exists in the form of *resource records*. Resource records consist of the data associated with all names below the authoritative point in the tree structure. When the DNS server uses these records to reply to queries, it sets the *authoritative answer* (*AA*) bit in the packet that includes the reply. The AA bit indicates that your name server has the best and most current information available about your domain.

Understanding DNS risks

When you set up a public DNS server, you are essentially responsible for providing reliable name-to-address conversion for the clients that use that server. Because of the potential security risks in maintaining a DNS server, you should not take this responsibility lightly.

Someone breaking in to control the information in a DNS server has the potential to redirect queries to the server for addresses to sites that the intruder chooses. So, for example, if someone is trying to contact a Web server in the domain your DNS server controls, they might be entering their credit card number or other personal information into a Web site that the intruder set up to for the purpose of stealing that information.

There are several different types of attacks directed at DNS servers. DNS cache poisoning is where fraudulent addresses are attached to hostnames that are placed in a DNS server's cache. Pay-per-click frauds will infect DNS servers in such a way that the Web browsers are directed to sites that set off a string of clicks to sites that pay each time you visit them. The person using the browser may never even see any indication that he has contacted those sites.

While Bind servers seem to have a better record of resisting attacks than Microsoft servers, there is still enough risk to warrant educating yourself against such attacks. Here are a few links where you can learn more about DNS attacks:

- **DNS Poisoning** (`http://isc.sans.org/presentations/dnspoisoning.html`) — Contains a good description of DNS poisoning and ways of dealing with it.

- **DNS Amplification** (`www.isotf.org/news/DNS-Amplification-Attacks.pdf`) — Contains a description of DNS amplification attacks, where DDoS attacks are used recursively along a chain of DNS servers.

Refer to the ISC Bind site for security alerts that relate to DNS service with Bind.

Understanding BIND

In Fedora, Red Hat Enterprise Linux, and most other Linux and UNIX systems, you implement DNS services by using the *Berkeley Internet Name Domain* (*BIND*) software. The Internet Software Consortium maintains BIND (at `www.isc.org/sw/bind`). The particular version of BIND that I describe in this chapter is BIND 9.5. To use BIND as described in this section, you need to install these packages: bind, bind-utils, bind-chroot, and bind-libs. There is also a system-config-bind package that contains a graphical means of working with your DNS files.

For the latest Fedora and RHEL distributions, BIND can be configured to run in a changed root (chroot) environment (provided you install the bind-chroot package). This means that instead of having configuration files in `/etc` and `/var/named` as they always have been with BIND, they are located in `/var/named/chroot/etc` and `/var/named/chroot/var/named` instead. This is a security measure to limit the access that an intruder could gain by taking control of the `named` daemon. SELinux also is configured to limit access to the `named` and `nscd` daemons (see the Security Level Configuration window for details).

> **NOTE:** Because `/etc/named.conf` file and files in the `/var/named/` directory are linked to their counterparts in `/var/named/chroot`, you can edit those files in either directory. However, as you add zone files to the `/var/named/chroot/var/named` directory, you will need to create new links to those files in `/var/named` directory to continue to edit them from that location.

The basic components of BIND include the following:

- **DNS server daemon** (`/usr/sbin/named`) — The `named` daemon listens on a port (port number 53 by default) for DNS service requests and then fulfills those requests based on information in the configuration files that you create. Mostly, `named` receives requests to resolve the hostnames in your domain to IP addresses.

> **NOTE:** The `named` daemon actually launches from the `/etc/init.d/named` startup script. You need to set that script to start automatically after your DNS server is ready to go. You can also use the `named` startup script to check the status of the `named` daemon.

- **DNS configuration files** (`named.conf` file and `named` directory) — The `/var/named/chroot/etc/named.conf` file is where you add most of the general configuration information that you need to define the DNS services for your domain. Separate files in the `/var/named/chroot/var/named` directory contain specific zone information. The location of the chrooted DNS configuration files in Fedora and RHEL (`/var/named/chroot`) is set in the `/etc/sysconfig/named` file.

> **NOTE:** If you run BIND in a non-chrooted environment, configuration files are located in `/etc/named.conf` file and the `/var/named` directory. You must uninstall the bind-chroot package to do this.

- **DNS lookup tools** — You can use several tools to check that your DNS server is resolving hostnames properly. These include commands such as `host`, `dig`, and `nslookup` (which are part of the bind-utils software package).

To maintain your DNS server correctly, you can also perform the following configuration tasks with your DNS server:

- **Logging** — You can indicate what you want to log and where log files reside.

- **Remote server options** — You can set options for specific DNS servers to perform such tasks as blocking information from a bad server, setting encryption keys to use with a server, or defining transfer methods.

You don't need to give out DNS information to everyone who requests it. You can restrict access to those who request it based on the following:

- **Access control list (acl)** — This list can contain those hosts, domains, or IP addresses that you want to group together and apply the same level of access to your DNS server. You create acl records to group those addresses, and then indicate what domain information the locations in that acl can or can't access.

- **Listen-on ports** — By default, your name server accepts only name server requests that come to port 53 on your name server. You can add more port numbers if you want your name server to accept name service queries on different ports.

- **Authentication** — To verify the identities of hosts that are requesting services from your DNS server, you can use keys for authentication and authorization. (The `key` and `trusted-keys` statements are used for authentication.)

> **CROSS-REFERENCE:** You should already know what domain names and IP addresses are. Refer to Chapter 15 for IP addresses and Chapter 16 for DNS information, if you need to refresh your memory.

DNS name server example

To get an idea of what you need to set up your DNS server, the following sections step you through an example of a DNS server for a domain called *yourdomain.com*. In the example, you're creating a DNS server for a small office network that includes the following:

- A private, local network that resides behind a firewall
- A server providing DNS service

In this office, other computers on the LAN are using the same Internet connection for outgoing communications, so the firewall on the server does network address translation (NAT) to enable the client computers to use the firewall as a router to the Internet. Figure 25-1 shows the configuration of the example *yourdomain.com* domain.

Figure 25-1 illustrates a small office network that's sharing a single Internet connection. The DNS, Web, mail, and FTP servers all have public IP addresses. (These addresses are fictitious, so please don't try to use them.) Behind the DNS server (which is also operating as a firewall) are four client computers that have private IP addresses. (You can reuse these addresses and other private addresses that I describe in Chapter 15.)

> **NOTE:** Because this is an example of how DNS works, it doesn't deal with all the complexities you might face in setting up the computing infrastructure at your company. For example, you might well want a dedicated firewall protecting your Internet connection, with the DNS server being placed with the other servers behind what is referred to as a *demilitarized zone* that is separated from the company LAN.

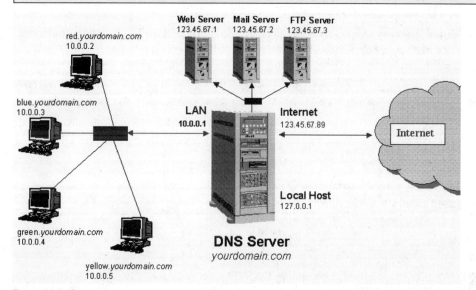

Figure 25-1: The sample *yourdomain.com* DNS server has a combination of public servers and private client computers.

The job of the DNS server, in this configuration, is to map the names of the public servers (www.yourdomain.com, mail.yourdomain.com, ftp.yourdomain.com, and ns1.yourdomain.com) into the static IP addresses that the ISP assigns (123.45.67.1, 123.45.67.2, 123.45.67.3, and 123.45.67.89, for our example). The DNS server also provides DNS service from the private addresses on the LAN, so each computer can reach the others on the LAN without needing to store all computer names in their own /etc/hosts file.

A key feature to this example is that it divides the view of this domain between what the outside world can see and what the computers on the private network can see. Using the view feature of BIND, I create an *outside* view that lets queries from the Internet find only public servers (Web, Mail, and FTP) in the domain. Then I create an *inside* view that lets queries from the local LAN find both the public servers and private computers (red, blue, green and yellow) in the domain.

The sections that follow describe how to set up a DNS server for the example in Figure 25-1.

Quick-starting a DNS server

The DNS server software that comes with the current Fedora and RHEL versions is Berkeley Internet Name Domain (BIND) version 9.5. To configure BIND 9.5, you work with the following components:

- **Configuration file** (`/var/named/chroot/etc/named.conf`) — The main DNS server configuration file.

- **Zone directory** (`/var/named/chroot/var/named`) — The directory containing files that keep information about Internet root DNS servers (`named.ca` file) and information about the zones that you create for your DNS server.

- **Daemon process** (`/usr/sbin/named`) — The daemon process that listens for DNS requests and responds with information that the `named.conf` file presents.

- **Debugging tools** (`named-checkconf`, `named-checkzone`, and `named-compilezone`) — What you use to determine whether you created your DNS configuration correctly.

> **NOTE:** Fedora and RHEL come with a GUI tool for configuring Bind called `system-config-bind`. (Type **yum install system-config-bind** to install it.) If you decide to use that tool, you need to be careful editing the Bind configuration files by hand. It is recommended that if there are changes you want to make to the `named.conf` file that are not supported by the `system-config-bind` window, you should put those changes in the `/etc/named.custom` file instead.

BIND 9.5 also includes tools for creating DNSSEC secured zones. By using these tools, you can create and generate keys to provide authentication and secure address resolution. The example illustrated in these sections doesn't include DNSSEC configuration.

The basic steps in creating a DNS server for your example are as follows:

- Identifying your DNS servers
- Creating DNS Configuration files (`named.conf` file and the `named` directory)
- Starting the named daemon
- Monitoring named activities

In the example configuration, you set up a primary master DNS server and a slave DNS server. The primary server holds the master copy of the authoritative records for the domain. The secondary server is there to share requests for information about the domain, particularly in case the primary goes down. The secondary typically gets its records from the primary server. The secondary is also considered to be authoritative in regards to the DNS records for the domains it controls.

Identifying your DNS servers

If you didn't have your DNS servers set up at the time that you purchased your domain name with a registration authority, you might have just "parked" the domain name there until you configured your DNS servers. Whenever you're ready to set up your DNS servers, return to that registration authority and provide the following information about your DNS servers:

- DNS server IP addresses (the static IP addresses of your DNS servers, probably primary and slave)

- DNS server hostnames (often `ns1.`*`yourdomain.com`*, where you replace *`yourdomain.com`* with your domain name for the primary; the slave hostname is `ns2.`*`yourdomain.com`*)

You should register both the primary and slave DNS servers. After you update this record, that information typically takes a day or two to propagate throughout the Internet. When your DNS servers are registered, you also need to tell the registration authority to use those DNS servers as the authority for addresses in your domain. The registration authority probably offers an online form you can fill out to identify your DNS servers.

Creating DNS configuration files (named.conf and var/named)

In configuring a DNS server, you're actually creating definitions that apply to a particular *zone* in the public DNS tree, as well as several local zones that apply to your computer and local network. To create a useful DNS server for your example small-office environment, you have the following zones:

- **Public DNS server zone** — The DNS server is authoritative for the domain that you're serving. This zone serves the names and IP addresses for your public servers. In the example `named.conf` file shown in the next section, you need to replace the name *yourdomain.com* with the domain that you're creating. These records become accessible to everyone on the Internet.

- **Private DNS server zone** — So each computer on the private network doesn't need to know the IP addresses for other computers on your private network, a zone is added in the example `named.conf` file to let the DNS server resolve these addresses. The names and IP addresses (which are private) are available only to computers on your LAN.

Note that by creating different views of these zones, different information will be returned to queries, depending on where the queries come from. For example, when someone from the Internet requests the address of the DNS server (`ns1.`*`yourdomain.com`*), they will get the address 123.45.67.89. However, when a query for `ns1.`*`yourdomain`*`.com` comes from inside the LAN, the address 10.0.0.1 is returned. Also, any queries from the Internet for addresses of private computers (`red.`*`yourdomain.com`*, `blue.`*`yourdomain.com`*, and so on) are rejected.

Editing named.conf

To begin, you configure the `/var/named/chroot/etc/named.conf` file on the primary master DNS server representing your example *yourdomain*.com domain. This example starts from the `/etc/named.conf` file that comes with the caching-nameserver package in Fedora and RHEL. (Make sure that you install the caching-nameserver and bind packages before you continue and make a backup copy of any configuration files you edit.) Following are a few tips relating to editing the `named.conf` file:

- If a statement contains substatements, make sure that you end the last substatement with a semicolon.

- Comments can appear in the same formats that popular programming languages use. These languages include C (begin with `/*` and end with `*/`), C++ (begin with `//` and go to the end of the physical line), and shell or Perl styles (begin from a `#` and go to the end of the physical line).

- A leading exclamation mark (`!`) negates an element. Putting `!123.45.67.89` in a statement causes the IP address 123.45.67.89 not to match the element. (Just make sure that the negation occurs before a positive match or the positive match takes precedence.)

The edited version of the `/var/named/chroot/etc/named.conf` file is as follows:

```
options {
    directory "/var/named";
    dump-file "/var/named/data/cache_dump.db";
    statistics-file "/var/named/data/named_stats.txt";
};

acl "mylan" {
    127/8; 10.0.0.0/24;
};

controls {
        inet 127.0.0.1 allow { localhost; } keys { rndckey; };
};

view "inside" {
    match-clients { "mylan"; };
    recursion yes;

    zone "." IN {
    type hint;
    file "named.ca";
    };

    zone "0.0.10.in-addr.arpa" IN {
    type master;
    file "yourlan.db";
```

```
    };

    zone "yourdomain.com" {
    type master;
    file "db.yourdomain.com.inside";
    allow-transfer { 10.0.0.2; };
      };
};

view "outside" {
    match-clients { any; };
    recursion no;

    zone "." IN {
    type hint;
    file "named.ca";
    };

    zone "yourdomain.com" {
    type master;
    file "db.yourdomain.com.outside";
    allow-transfer { 123.45.67.2; };
      };
};

include "/etc/rndc.key";
```

The options definition lies at the beginning of the named.conf file and identifies the
/var/named directory as the location where the zone files reside. The acl lines define the
mylan access-control list, which consists of host computers on the 10.0.0.0 local private
network and the localhost (127/8). (See Chapter 15 for information on the form of IP
addresses, CIDR and netmasks.) You use this definition in the 0.0.10.in-addr.arpa zone
to enable only users on the LAN to perform reverse lookups of names of computers on the
LAN.

The DNS server is broken up into two views: inside and outside. The inside view defines
how IP addresses are resolved for requests that come from the private LAN and localhost (as
defined in mylan). By having recursion on (recursion yes), the named daemon will
allow name server queries to any domain (even domains that the local DNS server doesn't
control) from any computer on the LAN. The outside view defines how queries coming
from all other places (presumably, the Internet) are handled. With recursion off (recursion
no), only queries from other name servers for domains controlled by the local DNS server are
honored. Requests for information about other domains will be rejected with a not found
message. (Turning recursion off can help eliminate a common attack, where a cracker causes
your server to seek information from a DNS server controlled by the cracker.)

Each zone entry in the `named.conf` file describes the type of server this computer is for the zone (master in all cases here, except the root zone), the database file (in the `named` directory) that contains records for the zone, and other options relating to the zone records. The `named.ca` file is set up for you by default. It identifies the locations of the Internet root servers.

I made the other zones (`yourlan.db`, `db.yourdomain.com.inside`, `db.yourdomain.com.outside` and `0.0.10.in-addr.arpa`) for this example. For the "inside" view, the `yourlan.db` file lets the computers on your LAN do reverse address lookups (getting the names for IP address queries). The `db.yourdomain.com.inside` file contains names and addresses for all computers in your domain (including those on the local LAN). The DNS slave server for the inside view of this domain is at 10.0.0.2. (Clients in your LAN would use 10.0.0.1 and 10.0.0.2 as DNS servers in `/etc/resolv.conf`.)

For the "outside" view, the `db.yourdomain.com.outside` file contains names and IP addresses for any computers in your domain you want to make public (computers on your private LAN are excluded). The DNS slave server for the outside view of this domain is 123.45.67.2.

Notice that each zone points to a zone file in the `named` directory. Table 25-1 shows which file in the `named` directory each zone points to.

Table 25-1: Zones and Related Zone Files in DNS Example

Zone	Zone File (located in the /var/named/chroot/var/named directory)
. (a single dot representing Internet root servers)	`named.ca`
0.0.10.in-addr.arpa	`yourlan.db`
yourdomain.com (inside view)	`db.yourdomain.com.inside`
yourdomain.com (outside view)	`db.yourdomain.com.outside`

Be very careful editing the `named.conf` file. Forgetting a semicolon is all too easy, and results in the entire file not loading. To ensure that the `named.conf` file doesn't contain any syntax errors, you can run the following command (as root user):

```
# named-checkconf
```

If a syntax error is present, a message identifies the problematic line and informs you what seems to be wrong with it. If the syntax is correct, continue to create the zone files in the `/var/named` directory.

Setting up the zone files (inside)

The /var/named/chroot/var/named directory contains the zone files that the
/var/named/chroot/etc/named.conf file points to. For the example, you need to
create only three zone files from scratch. You can (and should) leave the named.ca file alone.

Most of the real work of the domain name server occurs in the zone files. In the example, the
db.*yourdomain.com*.inside file contains the basic records for the *yourdomain*.com
domain, including all private names and addresses. The following is an example of that file:

```
$TTL      86400
@         IN          SOA         yourdomain.com. hostmaster.yourdomain.com.
(
                                  2008042701  ; Serial
                                  28800       ; Refresh
                                  14400       ; Retry
                                  3600000     ; Expire
                                  86400 )     ; Minimum
; Name servers
          IN    NS          ns1.yourdomain.com.
          IN    NS          ns2.yourdomain.com.

; Mail server for domain
          IN    MX   10     mail.yourdomain.com.

; Public servers
ns1       IN    A           10.0.0.1
ns2       IN    A           10.0.0.2
mail      IN    A           123.45.67.2
www       IN    A           123.45.67.3
ftp       IN    A           123.45.67.4

; Private clients on the LAN
red       IN    A           10.0.0.2
blue      IN    A           10.0.0.3
green     IN    A           10.0.0.4
yellow    IN    A           10.0.0.5

; EOF
```

The zone file for your "inside" *yourdomain*.com contains resource records that include
information about the zone. Your DNS server uses the TTL (time-to-live) record to tell name
servers that store the information that you provide for this domain how long they can keep the
information before they need to throw it out and get fresh information. The first value is the
default for the entire zone, and the time is in seconds. So a value of 86,400 seconds indicates
that a client that is using the information should obtain fresh records about this domain every
24 hours.

The SOA line identifies the start of authority for the domain. The at (@) sign represents the *yourdomain*.com. name — the dot (.) must appear at the end of the domain name. The dot represents the root server of the Internet. If you leave the dot off, your DNS server appends the domain name, so the DNS server will use the name *yourdomain*.com.*yourdomain*.com. The hostmaster.*yourdomain*.com string indicates the e-mail address of the person who is to receive e-mail regarding the domain. (The first dot changes to an @ sign, resulting in hostmaster@*yourdomain*.com). Other information regarding the SOA record is as follows:

- **Serial** — Start with any number here. If the zone records change, increase the serial number to alert other servers that they need to get fresh data about your domain.

> **CAUTION:** If you forget to increase the serial number after changing zone records, other servers that cache this data never pick up your changes. To help remember, use the date in the serial number. The number 2008042701 would be for April 27, 2008. The 01 represents the first change made on that day.

- **Refresh** — Defines how often the slave DNS server for the zone checks for changes. (Here, 28,800 seconds represents 8 hours.)

- **Retry** — If the slave can't reach the master, it tries again after this retry interval. (Here, 14,400 seconds represents 4 hours.)

- **Expire** — If the slave can't contact the master within the expire time (here, 3,600,000 seconds, or 1,000 hours), the slave discards the data.

- **Minimum** — Defines the cache time to live for negative answers. (Here, it's 86,400 seconds, or 24 hours.)

The name server (NS) records define the name servers that represent this zone. In this case, NS records define hosts with the names ns1 and ns2 in *yourdomain*.com. The MX record indicates the location of the mail server for the domain, so that the DNS server can direct e-mail to users in *yourdomain*.com. The rest of the file defines IP addresses for the private clients and public servers that are associated with the domain. Notice that the server at address 10.0.0.2 serves as a client on the LAN and a slave DNS server.

Setting up the zone files (outside)

For the "outside" *yourdomain*.com zone you made a db.*yourdomain*.com.outside file using the same information from the "inside" file, with the following exceptions:

- Removed all references to private clients on the LAN. That way, someone poking around from the Internet can't get information about your private computers.

- Changed the addresses of the primary and slave DNS servers (ns1 and ns2) to 123.45.67.1 and 123.45.67.2, respectively. In that way, only public addresses for name servers are seen by the public. (Of course, you need to use your own public IP addresses instead of the examples 123.45.67.1 and 123.45.67.2.)

Setting up the zone files (reverse lookup)

The other new file in the example is the `yourlan.db` file, which contains the information necessary to perform reverse IP lookups for the computers on your LAN. Here's an example:

```
$TTL      86400
@         IN        SOA       ns1.yourdomain.com hostmaster.yourdomain.com. (
                                        2006042701   ; Serial
                                        28800        ; Refresh
                                        14400        ; Retry
                                        3600000      ; Expire
                                        86400 )      ; Minimum
          IN        NS        ns1.yourdomain.com
1         IN        PTR       yourdomain.com.
2         IN        PTR       red.yourdomain.com.
3         IN        PTR       blue.yourdomain.com.
4         IN        PTR       green.yourdomain.com.
5         IN        PTR       yellow.yourdomain.com.

; EOF
```

The `SOA` record identifies `0.0.10.in-addr.arpa.` as the start of authority for the zone. The `NS` line defines `0.0.10.in-addr.arpa.` as the name server for the zone. Other records are pointers to hostnames that reverse-map on the `10.0.0.` network. The records represent the address for the DNS server (`yourdomain.com`) and each of the clients on the LAN (`red`, `blue`, `green`, and `yellow`).

After you finish creating your own zone files, you can use the `named-checkzone` command to make sure that each zone file is formed correctly. Here is how you'd run the `named-checkzone` command (as root user) to check the two `yourdomain.com` zone files (be sure to type each command on one line, even though each is shown here on two):

```
# named-checkzone yourdomain.com
/var/named/chroot/var/named/db.yourdomain.com.inside
zone yourdomain.com/IN: loaded serial 2008042701
OK
# named-checkzone yourdomain.com
/var/named/chroot/var/named/db.yourdomain.com.outside
zone yourdomain.com/IN: loaded serial 2008042701
OK
```

The output indicates that both files are okay and that `named-checkzone` command is able to load the new serial numbers. In this case, the serial number represents the first serial number (01) on April 27, 2008 (2008042701).

> **NOTE:** Instead of using the `named-checkzone` command, you can use the `named-compilezone`. The difference between the two commands is that `named-compilezone` dumps the zone contents into a file you choose.

Starting the named (DNS) daemon

To start the `named` daemon and see whether it's working, type the following (as root user):

```
# /etc/init.d/named start
```

If the `named` daemon starts successfully, clients of your DNS server should start getting information about your domain. To set the `named` daemon to start each time that the system boots up, type the following:

```
# chkconfig named on
```

Remember that, whenever you make changes to the `named.conf` or any of the zone files, you must increase the serial number for anyone checking your domain records to pick up those changes. After that, you should restart the `named` service too (as root user) as follows:

```
# /etc/init.d/named restart
```

Then you should consider adding the server's own local address to its own `/etc/resolv.conf` file. For example, the `/etc/resolv.conf` file could include the following:

```
search yourdomain.com
nameserver 127.0.0.1
```

If you see the `Starting named` message, your DNS server is probably up and running. If you want to make sure that your server is correctly resolving addresses, the next section, "Checking that DNS is working," describes some tools that you can use to check your DNS name server.

Checking that DNS is working

The best way to verify whether your DNS server is working correctly is to watch it in action. Here are a few commands you can use to check out your DNS server. The first example uses the `host` command to get the IP address for the host computer named `blue` in the local domain:

```
# host blue
blue.yourdomain.com has address 10.0.0.3
```

Instead of using the simple hostname to get the computer's IP address, you can enter an IP address (instead of the name) or a fully qualified hostname. In the following example, the `dig` command is used with a domain name to get information about the addresses for a domain:

```
# dig yourdomain.com
; <<>> DiG 9.5.0b2<<>> yourdomain.com
;; global options:  printcmd
;; Got answer:
;; ->>HEADER<<- opcode: QUERY, status: NOERROR, id: 43728
;; flags: qr aa rd ra; QUERY: 1, ANSWER: 1, AUTHORITY: 2, ADDITIONAL: 0

;; QUESTION SECTION:
```

```
;yourdomain.com.                    IN      A

;; AUTHORITY SECTION:
yourdomain.com.          604800 IN    NS     ns1.yourdomain.com.
yourdomain.com.          604800 IN    NS     ns2.yourdomain.com.

;; Query time: 24 msec
;; SERVER: 10.0.0.1#53(10.0.0.1)
;; WHEN: Mon Jun   9  02:12:32 2008
;; MSG SIZE  rcvd: 129
```

Sections in the output from `dig` include a question section and an authority section. The results show name server assignments and addresses associated with the domain you're querying about. The `nslookup` command is another tool you can use to look up domain information. In the following example, `nslookup` looks up the server that is resolving *ftp.yourdomain.com*:

```
# nslookup -sil ftp.yourdomain.com
Server:         123.45.67.1
Address:        123.45.67.1#53

Name:   ftp.yourdomain.com
Address: 123.45.67.4
```

The output from the `nslookup` command includes the name of the computer fulfilling the request and its IP address, along with the name and address of the computer you're asking for. (The `-sil` option prevents a message that `nslookup` might soon be removed from Fedora and RHEL.) Try `nslookup` with an IP address (such as 10.0.0.1) to make sure reverse lookup works.

To check the status of the named server that is running on your local system, use the same script that starts `named`. Type the following to check the status of your DNS server daemon:

```
# /etc/init.d/named status
number of zones: 5
debug level: 0
xfers running: 0
xfers deferred: 0
soa queries in progress: 0
query logging is OFF
recursive clients: 0/1000
tcp clients: 0/100
server is up and running
```

If you can't reach the computers that your DNS server is serving by name or IP address, you should make sure that each client's address records are correct. You can also try to `ping` each client and server computer using the full hostname or IP address.

Getting More Information about BIND

For details on many other BIND options that I don't describe in this chapter, you can refer to several places, as the following list relates:

- **/usr/share/doc/bind-9*/arm** — Contains HTML and XML versions of the BIND 9 Administrator Reference Manual.

- **Man pages** — Type the `man` command, following it with `named` or `named.conf`. These man pages contain terse descriptions of options and variables that relate to the `named` daemon and `named.conf` file, respectively.

- **Internet Software Consortium** (`www.isc.org/sw/bind`) — The ISC Web site contains information and downloads related to BIND. On this site, find links to BIND mailing lists, security advisories relating to BIND, and BIND history.

Summary

The choice to connect your Fedora or Red Hat Enterprise Linux server to the Internet isn't one to make lightly. If the server is critical to your business and support for the server is too much for you to handle, you should consider handing your server over to a hosting provider.

If you do decide to expose your Fedora or Red Hat Enterprise Linux server to the Internet to offer Web, FTP, mail, or other types of services, you should carefully consider the security implications and prepare for them. By using Linux features that I describe in other parts of this book, you can create firewalls, monitor log files, and track changes to system files to protect your computers.

One way of controlling the public exposure of your servers is to obtain a domain name and configure your own Domain Name System (DNS) server. You can set up your DNS server to resolve hostnames to IP addresses for clients that request the information from the Internet, as well as to the users on your local, private LAN.

Chapter 26

Integrating Fedora
with Apple Macs

In This Chapter

- Inside Mac OS X
- Using Mac OS X network services
- Accessing Samba servers
- Accessing AppleTalk (netatalk) servers
- Configuring an AppleTalk (netatalk) server in Linux
- Installing Fedora on an Intel-based Mac to dual boot

In the old days (like, a couple of years ago), you had to make Linux look like a file and printer server on an AppleTalk network in order to use a Linux server from an Apple Mac. While that is still true with an older Mac (OS 8 or 9), if you have an iMac with OS X, the whole world changes. That's because Mac OS X is a lot like Linux on the inside.

This chapter is for people who have (or want to have) Macs on their desktops and Linux as their servers. It covers a variety of server types that you can set up in Linux, then access from a Mac OS 8, OS 9, or OS X operating system. In particular:

- **For Mac desktop users** — The chapter describes how users can access shared resources from their Linux servers.

- **For system administrators** — The chapter explains how to set up an AppleTalk server in Linux using the netatalk software package. (Chapters 17 through 25 describe how to configure other types of native Linux servers that you can access from your Mac computers.)

The latest Mac computers have moved to Intel-based architectures. So now Apple operating systems are like Linux on the inside and the computer hardware is like the PCs that Windows and a majority of Linux systems run on. Because of this change, you can actually install Fedora on new iMac and Mac Mini computers. Procedures for installing Fedora on a Mac Mini are included at the end of this chapter.

I wrote this chapter in response to several readers of earlier editions of this book who wanted to replace their Windows servers with Linux servers. I hope this chapter will help start them, and you, on the road to taking full advantage of powerful networked Linux features from your easy-to-use Mac desktops.

Looking Inside Mac OS X

Inside Apple computers for the past few years is an operating system referred to as *Mac OS X*. You might also hear Mac OS X referred to as *Jaguar, Panther, Tiger* or *Leopard*. As with Linux, OS X has a free UNIX-like operating system at its core that, in this case, has been turned into a commercial product. That core, instead of being a Linux kernel, was originally based on a BSD-derivative open source project called Darwin.

Although Mac OS X and Linux are very different on the surface, there are many striking similarities. If you open a Terminal (shell) window on your Mac, you'll find that you can use many of the same basic commands that you can use from Linux. In addition, many of the same open source projects are included in both operating systems. These include:

- Samba (Windows file/printer server)
- Apache (Web server)
- CUPS (CommonUNIX Printing Solution)
- Sendmail (mail transport agent)
- BIND (DNS server)

There are also a few differences:

- Fedora is primarily covered under the General Public License, while OS X is based partly on an Open Source license and partly on a proprietary license. In August, 2003, the Apple Public Source License (APSL 2.0) was released (www.opensource.apple.com/apsl) and is now certified as a Free Software License from the Free Software Foundation.

- Fedora uses the Linux kernel; Mac OS X is based on a Mach micro-kernel surrounded by FreeBSD services. (Apple refers to this kernel as XNU and released it as a component of the Darwin open source operating system.)

- Most configuration in Fedora and RHEL is done using system-config windows, which often create text-based configuration files (mostly in the /etc directory) from command-line or GUI applications; Mac OS X stores the configuration file in its own NetInfo database, which is manipulated primarily by GUI tools as well as by the niutil command.

- Fedora requires root permission for many administrative operations; OS X discourages overuse of the root login and encourages user accounts that are granted administrative privileges.

For the examples in this chapter, I originally used an iMac running Mac OS X 10.3.9 (Panther), although the later 10.4 (Tiger) is also available. For this latest edition of the book, I checked the text against Mac OS X version 10.4.8, running on an Intel-based Mac Mini.

Because there were big improvements made after 10.1, I recommend that you upgrade your software if you are using 10.1. To see what version is installed on your Mac, choose About This Mac from the Apple menu on your Mac computer.

Using Network Services from Mac OS X

You can easily connect your Mac OS X computer to your LAN by configuring the Network window. If Fedora or RHEL (or the equipment provided by your ISP) is configured as a DHCP server (see Chapter 23), your Mac OS X client can detect that. Or, you can configure your LAN interfaces manually, as follows:

1. From the Dock bar, click System Preferences and select Network. This opens the Network window, which enables you to configure your network interfaces.

2. If you are connecting to your Linux servers from a LAN, click the Show field and select Built-in Ethernet. The Network window appears, as shown in Figure 26-1.

3. Click the TCP/IP tab. Then select either DHCP or Manually in the Configure Ipv4 field. If you select Manually, you can add the IP address of your computer, its netmask, the location of the router, the location of the DNS servers, and the domains to search. (For a home or small business, you might have a single Linux server serving as your router and DNS server. In this example, 10.0.0.1 is serving both of those functions.)

4. Click the AppleTalk tab. If you have configured your Linux server as an AppleTalk file and printer server (using netatalk), select the Make AppleTalk Active check box to turn on AppleTalk network protocols.

5. Click the Proxies tab. If you need to use a proxy server to access the Internet or other wide area network, use this tab to identify the proxies you are using.

The latest Mac computers have built-in Ethernet jacks that you can use to plug into your network switch or directly into your Internet hardware (such as DSL or cable modem). Plug your iMac into your network hardware and you should be ready to use your Linux servers from Mac OS X.

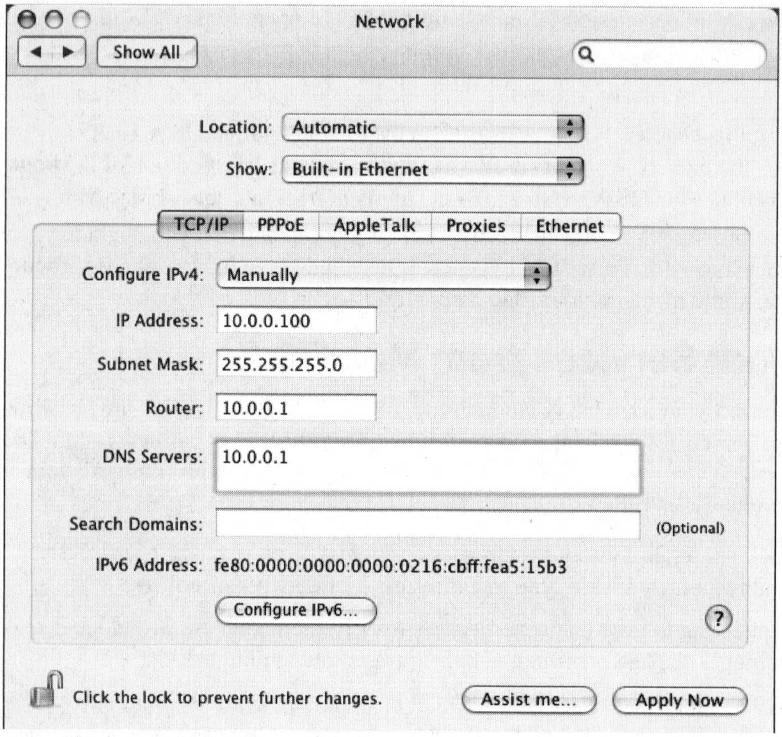

Figure 26-1: Configure your Mac OS X network interface to connect to Linux servers.

Using AppleTalk (netatalk) from Mac OS X

AppleTalk is the traditional set of protocols used by Apple computers to share files and printers over a LAN. Although Mac OS X can support Samba file sharing, AppleTalk is still a familiar way for Mac users to get to networked printers and files.

Fedora and RHEL include a software package called netatalk that you can use to configure Linux as an AppleTalk file and printer server. To a Mac client, the netatalk server looks no different than any other AppleTalk server.

> **CROSS-REFERENCE:** Refer to the "Setting up the netatalk server" section later in this chapter.

To access a shared directory from an AppleTalk server, click Go in the Finder bar at the top of the screen, and then select Connect to Server. The Connect to Server window appears, as shown in Figure 26-2.

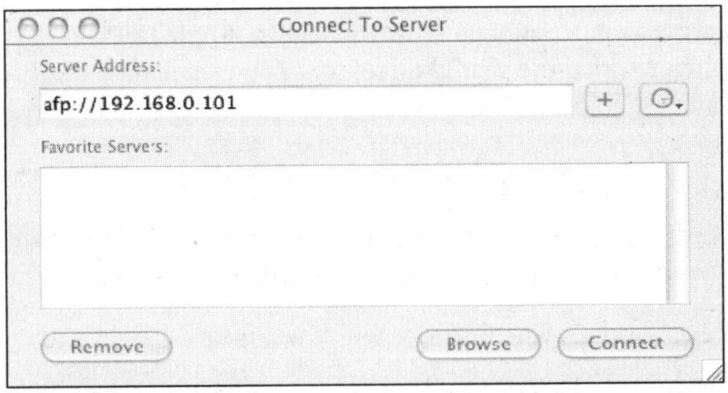

Figure 26-2: In Mac OS X, see Samba and AppleTalk shares from the Connect To Server window.

Enter the address, as shown in Figure 26-2, or click the Browse button to see a list of available servers.

After you click Connect, a pop-up window appears, prompting for a user name and password. Use the Options window to set up your preferences for logging on to the server. You can have the password added to your keychain so you don't have to type it in each time you access the server.

From the Options window, you can also select to send the password in clear text (which is the default) and be warned that you are doing that. The server determines whether you need to enter a clear-text or encrypted password (so if you send the wrong type of password, it will fail). You can also request a secure connection over SSH for your login (which is a good idea to prevent someone from sniffing out your password from the network).

Figure 26-3 shows the Options window for selecting password options as just described.

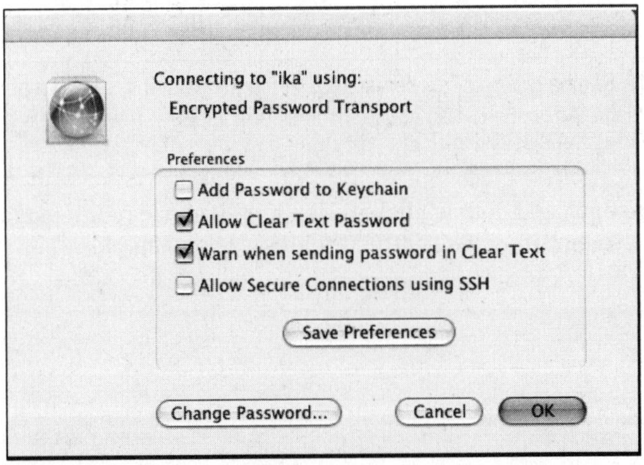

Figure 26-3: Select authentication options when you connect to your AppleTalk (netatalk) server.

After the user name and password are accepted, an icon representing the AppleTalk share appears on your desktop. Double-click to open the shared directory. You can change the contents of that directory in any way that your login allows.

Using AppleTalk from Mac OS 8 or OS 9

Prior to Mac OS X, Mac clients accessed AppleTalk shares from the Chooser window. The procedure for accessing a netatalk (or other AppleTalk) server went something like this:

1. Click the Apple menu and select Chooser. The Chooser window appears.

2. Click AppleShare. The file servers available on the local network appear in the Select a File Server window.

3. Click the file server you want to access and click OK. You are prompted for a user name and password (or just presented with a guest login).

4. Add the requested information and click OK. An icon representing the server appears on the desktop.

At this point, you can open the icon representing the shared directories and begin using the files and subfolders contained within.

Using Mac, Windows, and Linux servers (Samba)

The procedure for accessing Samba servers from your Mac OS X system is similar to the procedure for accessing an AppleTalk server from Mac OS X. As with the AppleTalk procedure, you open the Go menu from the Finder bar and select Connect to Server. From the Connect to Server window, do the following:

1. Click the Browse button, and then click the workgroup name that contains the Samba server that you want.

> **TIP:** If you're not sure if the server is a Samba or AppleTalk server, look at the address at the bottom of the window after you click the server name. A Samba (SMB) address begins with smb://, while an AppleTalk server begins with afp://.

2. Choose the server you want to open and double-click it. You will likely be prompted for your Samba user name and password from the SMB/CIFS Filesystem Authentication window (see Figure 26-4).

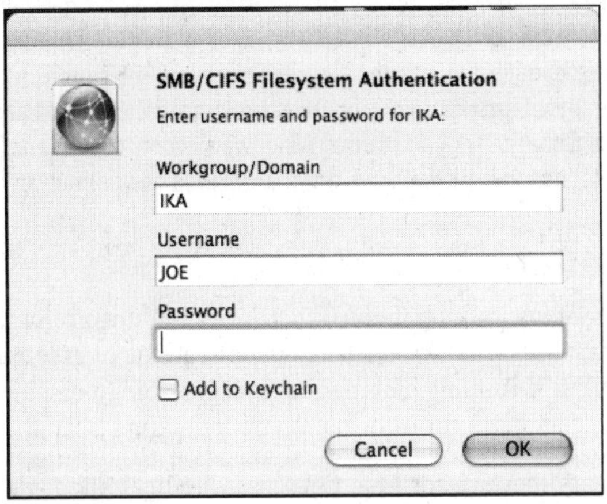

Figure 26-4: After requesting a Samba share, you must authenticate to the server.

3. Type the user name and password. (Optionally, you can click the Add to Keychain box. The keychain lets you store your user name and password, so you don't have to type it again the next time you access this Samba share.) An icon representing the Samba share should appear on your desktop.

If the Samba server doesn't appear on the Connect to Server window, you can type the name or IP address of the server, followed by the share name you want in the address box on the bottom of the window. Here's an example of an address for accessing a Samba share from the Connect to Server window:

```
smb://192.168.0.3/toyprojects
```

In this example, smb tells Mac OS X that it is looking for a Samba share. The Samba server in this example is located at IP address 192.168.0.3 (you could use a NetBIOS name instead of an IP address here). The name of the share is toyprojects. You could also add the workgroup and user name to the command line. Here's an example that asks for a share named toyprojects on a server named toys, in the ESTREET workgroup, as the user named chris:

```
smb://ESTREET:chris@toys/toyprojects
```

Here are a few things you should know about accessing Samba shares from Mac OS X:

- When authenticating your password (see Figure 26-4), Mac OS X sends your password in clear text. Unlike when authenticating an AppleTalk share, there is no way to select to send encrypted passwords from this window.

- The example of setting up Linux Samba shares in Chapter 18 shows how to set up Samba to ask for encrypted passwords (and therefore will fail authentication from Mac OS X). To get around the problem (on a secure network), you can create a share that either accepts clear-text passwords or have the share be available to guest users.

> **NOTE:** To configure Samba to work from a Mac OS X client, edit the `/etc/samba/smb.conf` file (as root user). In a shared directory definition, add the line `guest ok = yes` (to allow guest users access to the share). You can also set `encrypt passwords = no` to accept clear-text passwords. Because `encrypt passwords` is a global setting, and newer Windows systems expect encrypted passwords by default, you may only want to set that value if you have only Mac clients on your network.

Sharing X applications

Most UNIX-like computer systems rely on the *X Window System* (also referred to as *X11* or simply *X*) to display windows over a network. Sharing applications over the network with X requires little more than having X running and making it accessible to displays that are directed to your display (see Chapter 3 for information on launching X applications).

Although the default graphical interface for Mac OS X is a facility called Aqua, there is now an X11 for Mac OS X available for Mac users. The latest version of Mac OS X includes a native X installation. You must choose a Custom install or upgrade when you install Mac OS X to get the X packages on your system. For further information on the state of the X Window System in Mac OS X, go to `www.apple.com/macosx/features/x11`. To download your own copy of X11 for Mac OS X, visit this site:

`www.apple.com/downloads/macosx/apple/macosx_updates/x11formacosx.html`

When I last checked the site just mentioned, they did not have the latest version of X11 available. For my new Mac Mini, I was able to install X11 from the installation disks that came with the computer. Open DVD 1 and select the Optional Installs package. Under applications, select the X11 package.

With X11 installed and running on your Mac OS X, you can run the same X applications you run on Linux systems. However, you also can launch X applications from your Linux system and have them appear on your Mac OS X desktop. From my Mac Mini (Mac OS X 10.4.8), I did the following to start X and display an X application from Fedora on my Mac desktop:

1. Start X11 on the Mac (from the Finder bar, select Go → Applications → Utilities → X11). X11 starts and opens a Terminal window.

2. From the Terminal window on the Mac, use the `xhost` command to tell X11 that it's okay to display an application from your Fedora machine. For example, to open permission to display X clients from the Fedora machine at IP address 10.0.0.100, type the following:

   `$ xhost + 10.0.0.100`

3. Open a Terminal window on the Fedora machine and set your `DISPLAY` variable to the X11 instance on the Mac machine. For example, if you started X11 on a machine located at the address 10.0.0.50, you could identify the first X11 display on that computer by typing the following from the Terminal on your Fedora system:

```
$ export DISPLAY=10.0.0.50:0
```

4. From this same Terminal window on the Fedora system, launch any X application by typing its name. For example, to run a clock program (xclock), type the following:

```
$ xclock
```

The clock application will appear on the desktop of the Mac OS X system. You can run any X11 application you like from that Terminal window in Fedora to have it appear on the Mac's desktop.

Configuring an AppleTalk Server in Linux

If you have a mixture of older Macs (such as a Power Macintosh with Mac OS 8.1) and newer Macs (such as an iMac or Mac Mini with Mac OS X) on the same LAN, an AppleTalk server could be the best way to share files and printers among them. With the netatalk package installed on your Fedora server, netatalk can be configured to act as that AppleTalk server.

Using netatalk, you can allow multiple Mac clients to use the following features from a computer running Fedora:

- **AppleShare file server** — Files and directories you share from your AppleTalk server (via netatalk) are stored with features and permissions that a Mac user would expect.

- **AppleTalk printer server** — Printers configured on your Linux server can be shared as though they were AppleTalk printers.

- **AppleTalk router** — Your Linux system can act as a router between multiple AppleTalk networks.

The netatalk project site is located at `http://netatalk.sourceforge.net`. There, you can find documentation (including an FAQ), as well as links to helpful netatalk Web sites.

To use netatalk in its most basic configuration, all you need to do is:

- Create a LAN connecting your Linux netatalk server and Mac client computers. (You can configure netatalk as a router to connect multiple LANs.)

- Start netatalk as described in the "Starting netatalk" section. This enables any users with user logins to your Linux computer to access their home directories from a Mac (using Linux logins and passwords). You can also add printers and other directories to share.

Before you fire up netatalk, however, I recommend that you check out the following section.

Before you start using netatalk

Know that when you are creating an AppleTalk server on a Linux file system, you are creating a hybrid-type file system. Strange issues can arise because the two types of servers handle ownership, access, and file attributes (such as what applications launch a file) differently.

On the netatalk shared directory structure (referred to as a *volume* or *share*), special directories exist to hold attributes (file type and creator), trash, temporary items, and find content. If you change files or directories on AppleTalk volumes from Linux without taking special precautions, you'll delete a file and leave its attributes around or create a file that has no attributes (so a Mac doesn't know how to launch it). You can't even move a whole directory structure from one Linux partition to another without losing the connection between the files and their attributes.

Here are a few tips to think about before you start using netatalk:

- Use Mac clients to create, move, and copy files on the Mac volume whenever possible. This is the best way to keep your volumes clean and working properly.

- If you must manipulate netatalk files and folders from a Linux shell, use the `apple_mv`, `apple_cp`, and `apple_rm` commands (described later in this chapter).

- You can share the same volumes with both your Mac clients (using netatalk) and Windows clients (using Samba), but this involves certain risks and caveats as well. See the "Sharing files with netatalk and Samba" section later in this chapter for ways to avoid trouble.

- Mac users expect permissions on files and directories to be more open than many Linux administrators are comfortable with. Check the "Securing netatalk volumes" section for information on the best ways to securely provide the necessary access.

- Tools for tracking down network services and troubleshooting problems for AppleTalk networks are different than those used for pure TCP/IP networks. Refer to the "Troubleshooting netatalk" section for information on the tools you can use for tracking down network problems.

Setting up the netatalk server

The following steps provide a high-level overview of how to set up your netatalk server. (The sections that follow contain details on how to do these steps.)

1. **Install netatalk** — The netatalk package is in Fedora, so to install netatalk, you can type **yum install netatalk**.

2. **Start netatalk** — As with most Linux network services, netatalk can be set to start automatically from a start-up script, in this case `/etc/init.d/atalk`. (You can do some limited file sharing with the default configuration, as described in the next section.)

3. **Open firewall** — If you have enabled your firewall, you need to open several ports for netatalk to allow users from other computers to access your system.

4. **Configure general settings** (`/etc/atalk/netatalk.conf` file) — Use the `netatalk.conf` file to add your own general netatalk server settings. The default settings for the general netatalk configuration are:

   - **Clients** — Up to 50 Mac clients can connect to your server at a time.

- **AppleTalk host name** — Your computer's hostname (type **hostname -s** to see it) is used as your computer's AppleTalk server hostname.

- **Authentication** — Netatalk will allow users to connect using a guest login (*nobody* user) with no password, a clear-text password, or an encrypted password (Diffie-Hellman style authentication).

- **Guest user** — A guest user can connect without entering a password and access shared volumes that are open to the world. This guest user is assigned to the Linux *nobody* user name. (By default, no guest shares are set up.)

- **Daemon processes** — Netatalk starts daemon processes to manage your AppleTalk network interface (atalkd daemon), start the AppleTalk print sharing service (papd daemon), and start the AppleTalk filing protocol (afpd daemon) for sharing volumes.

5. **Configure server settings (/etc/atalk/afpd.conf file)** — Configuring afpd.conf lets you set up specific settings for your netatalk server (you can even have multiple, virtual servers configured that each look different to the outside world). The contents of the afpd.conf file affect how the AppleTalk filing protocol daemon (afpd) shares its volumes with Mac clients.

6. **Set up users** — The netatalk server can rely on the Linux users you add to the computer (using clear-text passwords), then limit access to your shared volumes based on those permissions. Or, you can configure netatalk to use encrypted passwords to validate users.

7. **Share volumes (/etc/atalk/AppleVolumes.default file)** — When netatalk starts, each user with a valid Linux login to your computer can, by default, access his or her own home directory as an AppleTalk share from a Mac client. You can (and probably will) have more shared volumes by configuring them in the AppleVolumes.default file.

8. **Securing shared volumes** — Netatalk can take advantage of Linux security features to protect shared volumes. You can secure volumes at the host, user, and file and directory level.

9. **Share printers (/etc/atalk/papd.conf file)** — Netatalk can share any printer you have connected to Linux (or otherwise configured locally) by adding a definition to the papd.conf file. No printers are shared until you add them.

As you work with your shared volumes and printers, you will find that maintenance issues arise from time to time. In particular, you should refer to the following sections: "File- and directory-level security" (for dealing with hidden attribute files and directories), "Sharing files with netatalk and Samba" (to share the same directories from netatalk and Samba), and "Troubleshooting netatalk" (for general troubleshooting tips).

Starting netatalk

Start up netatalk as you would most Linux network services: from a start-up script. The netatalk script is called atalk (/etc/init.d/atalk). To turn it on, type the following as root user:

```
# chkconfig atalk on
```

The previous command causes netatalk to start the next time you reboot. To start it now, type:

```
# service atalk start
```

Here's what happens when you start the AppleTalk service:

- The AppleTalk daemon (`atalkd`) starts from the contents of the `/etc/atalk/atalkd.conf` file.

- The `papd` daemon registers print services using the contents of the `/etc/atalk/papd.conf` file.

- The `afpd` daemon registers volumes from the contents of the `/etc/atalk/AppleVolumes.default` file (using settings from the `AppleVolumes.system` file).

To check that the netatalk service started properly, as root user type the following from any Linux system on the network (the output may take a minute or two to appear):

```
# nbplkup
toys:AFPServer          65280.115:128
toys:netatalk           65280.115:4
toys:Workstation        65280.115:4
```

To check whether your netatalk server is available from a Mac client, go to the Mac client and perform the appropriate procedure:

- **For a pre–Mac OS X client** — Click the Apple Chooser. From the Chooser window, click AppleShare. The netatalk server should appear in the Select a file server pane. Click it and click OK, and then use any valid user login and password from Linux to open that user's home directory.

- **For a Mac OS X client** — From the Finder bar, click Go, then Connect to server. Type the URL of the netatalk shared directory. For example, for the home directory on the computer named `toys` for the user named `chris`, you could type the following:

```
afp://toys/chris
```

You can use an IP address instead of a computer name. By default, your user's home directory (in this case, `/home/chris`) is offered as an AppleTalk volume. When prompted, type the password for that user and select the volume representing the home directory. If you can't find and open the netatalk server from your Mac, see the "Troubleshooting netatalk" section in this chapter for some suggestions.

Open firewall ports

If you enabled iptables service to protect your computer with a firewall, you need to open several ports in that firewall before someone from a remote computer can access your netatalk server. The easiest way to do that is to open the Security Level and Firewall window (System → Administration → Security Level and Firewall).

With the firewall set to Enabled, select Other ports → Add. Then add each port number (for the tcp protocol) needed to open the netatalk server. Port numbers include: 201, 202, 204, 206, and 548. (See the `/etc/services` file for descriptions of those port numbers.) Click OK and the new ports will be opened.

Defining general AppleTalk server settings

Settings in the `/etc/atalk/netatalk.conf` file define information related to the general operation of your netatalk server. Step 2 of "Setting up the netatalk server" describes the default settings in this file. The following code lines illustrate a few things you might want to change (as root user).

```
AFPD_MAX_CLIENTS=100
```

Instead of limiting the number of Mac clients who can simultaneously use your netatalk server to 50, you can use any number you like (I used 100 in the previous example). To change the zone and server name, you could change the following settings:

```
ATALK_ZONE=GSTREET
ATALK_NAME="History 101"
```

This example sets the zone name to `GSTREET` and the server name to `History 101`. To change how authentication is performed, you could use one of the following two `AFPD_UAMLIST` examples:

```
AFPD_UAMLIST="-U uams_guest.so"
AFPD_UAMLIST="-U uams_clrtxt.so"
```

The first example makes netatalk a guest-only server. The second line allows only valid users from the Linux system using clear-text passwords. The following line enables you to change the guest user account:

```
AFPD_GUEST=nobody
```

You could change `nobody` to any valid user account on Linux, and that account will be used as your guest user.

Other settings in the `netatalk.conf` file let you set which daemons run and export MAC and UNIX character sets to use with netatalk.

Defining specific AppleTalk servers settings

Your netatalk server can appear as multiple file servers, each with different attributes. You can set up these "virtual" servers in the `/etc/atalk/afpd.conf` file. Within each file server entry, you name the server, and then assign a variety of options to set how it is accessed. A few examples of how to do this are shown as comments in the `afpd.conf` file itself:

```
"Guest Volume" -uamlist uams_guest.so -loginmesg "Welcome guest!"
"User Volume" -uamlist uams_clrtxt.so -port 12000
```

The "Guest Volume" example causes a "Welcome guest!" message to appear when a user logs into the server. Because it is a guest server (uams_guest.so), no password is required. In the "User Volume" example, clear-text passwords and valid user accounts are needed for the volume. The service is provided on port number 12000. Guest Volume and User Volume appear as the names of the two servers, respectively, in the Mac's chooser window.

If your Linux computer is a router, with one or more network interfaces connected to public networks, you should use the -ipaddr IPaddress option. With that option, you can restrict access to the netatalk server from a particular network interface (probably one that only allows access from your local LAN). There are more than 30 options listed in afpd.conf that you can consider.

Setting up users

As mentioned earlier, the netatalk server (by default) allows users with valid user names and passwords to log in to the server with clear-text (unencrypted) passwords and gain access to (at least) their own home directories. See the "Securing netatalk volumes" section later in this chapter to see how to set up the server to use encrypted passwords.

Sharing netatalk volumes

You use the AppleVolumes.default file to indicate which volumes from the netatalk server are made available to your Mac clients. This file is located in /etc/atalk/AppleVolumes.default.

> **NOTE:** See the "File- and directory-level security" section for detailed information on hidden files and directories, as well as user and group permissions issues related to sharing volumes.

Look at the last line in the AppleVolumes.default file. The single tilde (~) on a line by itself tells the AppleTalk daemon to make all Linux home directories (usually in the /home directory) available as AppleTalk shared directories. When a user logs into the netatalk server, the user's own home directory appears as an available shared directory. A user who chooses to open that directory has the same rights to change, add, and delete files that he has when logged in directly to Linux.

A common practice is to add the text "Home Directory" to the line that contains the single tilde (~) so that it appears as follows:

```
~    "Home Directory"
```

To share additional directories, simply add a full path name to the directory you want to share and the volume name you want to assign to it. For example:

```
/var/toyprojects "Linux Toys"
```

As you can see in this example, /var/toyprojects is shared under the name "Linux Toys." The volume name is limited to 27 characters and cannot contain the ":" character. In this simple case, access permissions to the volume are determined by the user, host, and folder-level security that is set up for the volume (see the "Securing netatalk volumes" section for more information).

You can also add options directly to each listing in the AppleVolumes.default file. On the same line, after the path (/var/toyprojects) and volume name ("Linux Toys") options as shown in the previous example, you can add some options. Here are a few options that might interest you (look inside the AppleVolumes.default file for others):

- **casefold:*option*** — Normally, when a shared volume appears on the Mac client's screen, file and directory names appear in upper- and lowercase as they exist on the Linux system. By replacing *option* in the casefold option with tolower or toupper, you can have lowercase or uppercase apear in both directions, respectively. Or, you could have case translated (xlatelower or xlateupper) to set what the client sees.
- **allow:*users/@groups*** or **deny:*users/@groups*** — You could add specific users or groups to an allow or deny option to have those users or groups allowed or denied access to the shared *volume*. (Separate each with a comma; indicate a group with an @ sign.)
- **password:*pwd*** — Replace *pwd* with a password (up to eight characters) to define a password that is specific to the volume.
- **rolist:*users/@groups*** or **rwlist:*users/@groups*** — Use rolist or rwlist options to allow read-only or read/write access, respectively, to the users or groups you add to the list. (Separate each with a comma; indicate a group with an @ sign.)

By opening these shared volumes and creating files and folders in them, Mac clients automatically create some files and folders that are invisible to the Mac client. These files and folders hold resource fork information and other features that would not normally be in a Linux file system. The "File- and directory-level security" section describes these files and folders.

> **NOTE:** Although most of the files and folders described in the following section are invisible to Mac clients, if you share the same directories using Samba or some Linux file-sharing feature (such as NFS), they will be visible. You can use the veto files feature of Samba to hide these files from Windows users.

Securing netatalk volumes

Some Linux and netatalk features can be used to secure your volumes from unwanted access or misuse. The following sections describe how to protect your netatalk servers at the user, host, and file and directory levels.

User-level security

When you create a shared volume (in `AppleVolumes.default`), you can indicate which users can access that volume. Users can be authenticated using clear-text passwords (to log in to their basic Linux user accounts) or by setting up a special encrypted password file using netatalk.

Users can be assigned to particular volumes when you define those volumes in the `AppleVolumes.default` file as described earlier. Here's an example where the users `mike` and `jojo` and anyone in the group `wheel` are allowed access to a volume:

```
/var/homework "History homework" allow:mike,jojo,@wheel
```

To use the default clear-text passwords, you need only set up user accounts as you normally would in Linux (see Chapter 11). However, to use encrypted passwords for users (on a server configured to use encrypted passwords in the `afpd.conf` file as described earlier), you must create an AppleTalk password file (`/etc/atalk/afppasswd`). As root, type the following:

```
# afppasswd -c
```

This command gathers all regular users (UID 100 and above) and the guest user (*nobody*) and adds them to the `afppasswd` file.

Next, you need to add proper passwords for each of the users just added to the `afppasswd` file that will be allowed access to your netatalk shares. For example:

```
# afppasswd jake
Enter NEW AFP password: *******
Enter NEW AFP password again: *******
```

After you create `afppasswd` initially, you can later add individual users manually to that file (provided they also have valid Linux accounts). Do that using `-a` option to `afppasswd`:

```
# afppasswd -a cindy
Enter NEW AFP password: *********
Enter NEW AFP password again: *********
```

Issues related to choosing a good password (see Chapter 14) are true for setting AppleTalk passwords as well. If the passwords match, the user will be able to log in using the assigned user name and password when he tries to mount the AppleTalk volume from the netatalk server, provided the netatalk service is using encrypted authentication (`uams_dxh.so`).

Host-level security

You can restrict which computers on your network have access to your netatalk services using the `/etc/hosts.allow` and `/etc/hosts.deny` files. These files are described in the "Using TCP wrappers" section of Chapter 14. These are the same files you use to allow or restrict access to other Linux networking services.

The following is an example of an entry in the `hosts.allow` file.

```
ALL: .linuxtoys.com EXCEPT abc.linuxtoys.com
```

This example allows access to netatalk (and all other services) from all computers in the `linuxtoys.com` domain except for the computer named `abc.linuxtoys.com`. See Chapter 14 for details about other ways to indicate services (instead of ALL) and hosts.

File- and directory-level security

Netatalk creates hidden files and directories to handle Mac features that are not in Linux. Understanding those files and directories and working with standard Linux ownership and permissions are the best ways to refine access to the AppleTalk volumes you share.

Understanding hidden Mac files and directories

Netatalk creates special files and directories that you can't see from the Mac Finder. Because these files begin with a dot (.), they are hidden from normal directory listings (`ls`) in Linux as well. The following descriptions should help you understand these files and directories.

> **NOTE:** To see hidden files from a folder window (from the GNOME desktop), click Edit → Preferences. Then from the Views tab, select the "Show hidden and backup files" check box. Type **ls -a** to see them from a Terminal window.

- **.AppleDouble** — Every directory within your shared AppleTalk (netatalk) volume contains a `.AppleDouble` directory. This directory is created automatically as soon as you create a file or directory from a Mac client on the netatalk server. Within this directory are separate files representing attributes of each file in the associated directory. For example, creating a text file in `/var/toyprojects` called `mytext.txt` would create a file called `/var/toyprojects/.AppleDouble/mytext.txt` that contained attributes about that file.

You can create an Icon directory within any `.AppleDouble directory for a shared volume` (`/var/toyprojects/.AppleDouble/Icon` for example), enabling you to add custom icons to the shared volume. Permissions of those directories must be open to writing (for anyone you want to be able to add and change icons), and reading (to anyone you want to all to see icons).

- **.AppleDouble/.Parent** — This directory within each `.AppleDouble` directory contains information about the shared directory.

- **.AppleDesktop** — For each shared volume, this directory is located in the top-level directory. This directory contains information about the applications that created the data stored on the volumes and the icons used to represent that data.

- **Network Trash Folder** — This folder, in the top-level shared directory, holds deleted files from the client. (Note spaces in the directory name, which must be preceded with a backspace to access the folder from the Linux shell.)

- **Temporary Items** — Some applications need this folder (located in the top-level directory) to create temporary files.

Other directories may also appear because applications that work on files in a volume need special directories to get their work done.

Setting file and directory permissions

Permissions on shared netatalk volumes tend to be more wide open than would typically be the case on shared Linux directories in order to match the expectations that Mac users generally have about permissions.

In particular, the set-GID (group) bit is often turned on for directories. By using the set GID feature, any file or directory created in the directory would be owned by the associated group. For example, follow these steps as root user from the shell (creating any directory name you want to share):

```
# mkdir /var/toyprojects
# chown chris /var/toyprojects
# chgrp toygroup /var/toyprojects
# chmod 2775 /var/toyprojects
# ls -ld /var/toyprojects
drwxrwsr-x     2     chris     toygroup     4096   Mar 16 13:32
/var/toyprojects
```

In this example, I prepared a directory to be shared by netatalk called /var/toyprojects. I made the owner of the directory the user chris (use your own user name). I created a group (see Chapter 11 for creating groups) and called it toygroup. Then I set the permission to 2775 on the directory, which means that the group set-GID bit is on (2), the owner (chris) has full read/write/execute permission (7), the group (toygroup) has full read/write/execute permission (7), and other has only read and execute permissions (5).

Turning on the group set-GID bit causes all files and directories created in /var/ toyprojects (and its subdirectories) to be assigned to the toygroup group, regardless of who created it. Because I set group permissions wide open (7), anything created in /var/toyprojects and its subdirectories will be under the complete control of anyone assigned to toygroup. This is a nice technique for sharing files in a group project.

After the top-level directory is created, netatalk will create the files and directories it needs (such as .AppleDouble and Network Trash Folder) as the Mac clients add files and folders. Netatalk should also propagate the correct permissions to those items.

Here are some tips about setting permissions:

- A user must have write permission to the .AppleDesktop directory (and subdirectories) to create an application in a shared directory.

- Make permissions to the Network Trash Folder writable by everyone who has access to the shared volume or their files will always be permanently deleted instead of put in the folder.

- Open permissions to the Temporary Items directory or applications (such as Photoshop) will fail to work with files from the shared volume.

- Turn off write permissions to programs (executable files) to protect them from being exploited.

Setting Appletalk file and folder type and creator

To check type and creator attributes on Mac files, use the `afile` command as follows:

```
# afile file
```

In this form, you can see attributes for files and directories of known types. To see all files (even those without associated attributes stored in the `.AppleDouble` directory), use the `-a` option to `afile`.

Use the `achfile` command to change the type (`-t`) and creator (`-c`) of the Macintosh file. Creator and file type pairs are defined in the `/etc/atalk/AppleVolumes.system` file. You can change these entries to cause different applications to be used for selected file types.

Moving, copying, and deleting netatalk files

When you access files on your netatalk volumes from a Mac client computer, file attributes are maintained or removed properly. Linux commands don't deal with Mac file attributes, however, so you need to run special commands from Linux to move these files and maintain their attributes, instead of the regular Linux commands (`mv`, `cp`, `rm`, and so on).

> **NOTE:** Before you use the `apple_cp` and related commands to add files to your Appletalk volume, open the volume from a Mac client and create a file there. This will cause the appropriate directories and files (`.AppleDouble` and so on) to be created so they are available to add attributes from Linux `apple_*` commands.

The commands for copying, moving, and removing files from a shell in Linux on your netatalk server volumes are `apple_cp`, `apple_mv`, and `apple_rm`. For example:

```
# apple_cp memo1.doc /var/av1/memos/
```

This command copied my `memo1.doc` file from my current directory to the `/var/av2/memos/` directory (presumably on the same netatalk volume). This action also copies the resource forks associated with the file to the `.AppleDouble` directory to the directory you are moving to. Here are examples of move and remove commands:

```
# apple_mv memo1.doc /var/av1/memos/oldmemos/
# apple_rm memo1.doc
```

The `apple_mv` command moves the `memo1.doc` file from the current directory to the `oldmemos` directory (moving attribute information from `.AppleDouble` to the new `.AppleDouble` directory). The `apple_rm` command deletes `memo1.doc` and removes its attribute information.

Sharing files with netatalk and Samba

A common practice if you have both Mac and Windows clients on the same network that need to share the same files is to have both Samba and netatalk configured to share the same volume (that is, set of directories). Before you do that, however, be aware of the following:

- By default, creating files from Mac clients (on netatalk volumes) will make the files you create easiest to work with from the Mac.

- You can hide files from Mac users with the `veto` option in `AppleVolumes.default`.

- The `veto files` option for Samba (in `smb.conf`) can be used to hide Mac files (such as `.AppleDouble` directories) from Samba users.

- If you don't care about Mac attributes, you can set the `noadouble` option in the `AppleVolumes.default` file to create files without them.

- Avoiding certain characters in your file and directory names can make it easier for you to share those items among different types of clients. When possible, avoid characters such as slash (/), backslash (\) and colon (:) when naming files. Also, wildcard characters such as asterisks (*) and pound signs (#) can cause problems.

Here's an example of a veto line you might want to add to your `/etc/samba/smb.conf` file. It prevents Samba users from accessing hidden netatalk-specific directories:

```
veto files = /.AppleDouble/.AppleDesktop/Network Trash
Folder/TheVolume/SettingsFolder
```

The previous `veto files` line, although it appears on two lines, should actually be typed in as one line in the file. Here's a veto line you can add to your `/etc/atalk/atalkd.conf` file to keep netatalk users from accessing directories used by Samba:

```
veto: recycled/desktop.ini/Folder.htt/Folder Settings/
```

Here are a few issues related to `veto` options:

- Get the upper- and lowercase letters right (the option is case-sensitive).

- Type veto names completely. The veto feature doesn't support asterisks (*), brackets ([ ]) and other wildcard characters to match multiple file names.

- If Samba tries to delete a directory that contains only veto files, that deletion will fail unless you set the `delete veto files` parameter to `yes` in the `/etc/samba/smb.conf` file. (The value is set to `no` by default.)

Printer Sharing

You can set up printer sharing using netatalk so that Mac clients using the standard AppleTalk print service (called *Printer Access Protocol*, or *PAP*) can print to your Linux computer. To do that, you must:

- Configure a local Linux printer (see Chapter 17).
- Set up the /etc/atalk/papd.conf file to point to that printer.
- Restart the atalk service (or, more specifically, the papd daemon).

When a Mac client prints to a Linux printer configured in this way, the print job is handed to the standard Linux lpd daemon and put into a spool file for printing, along with Linux print jobs for the printer.

> **NOTE:** Mac OS X computers can print directly to Linux print services (CUPS or LPRng) without requiring netatalk printing. Older Mac OS 9 clients, however, might need to see an AppleTalk printer that you set up in this way with netatalk.

The papd.conf file follows the same basic format as the /etc/printcap file (traditionally used for Linux printing). Here's an example of a printer configured in the papd.conf file:

```
LaserJet2100M:\
            :pr=| /usr/bin/lpr -P hp01:\
            :pd=/etc/atalk/laserjet.ppd:\
            :op=root:\
            :am:uams_guest.so:
```

The printer in this example is named LaserJet2100M. To print the file from the Mac client, it takes the output file and pipes it to the lpr -P hp01 command (hp01 is the name of the local printer). The ppd file is /etc/atalk/laserjet.ppd. The root user is the operator, and guests are allowed to print to the printer (no password is needed).

The printer definition file (ppd) must be installed on both the netatalk server (at the location noted in the papd.conf file) and on the Mac client.

To test that the interface to your AppleTalk printer is working, use the pap command:

```
# pap -p LaserJet2100M /etc/hosts
```

The -p option identifies your netatalk printer. In this example, it prints a copy of your /etc/hosts file. Or, you can just check the status of the printer:

```
# papstatus -p LaserJet2100M
```

Troubleshooting netatalk

Several tools are available that enable you to see the status of your AppleTalk network. The aecho command can test whether a particular AppleTalk host computer is alive. The

nbplkup command can be used to check out the services that are currently available on your
AppleTalk network.

> **NOTE:** In general, AppleTalk should be used on trusted networks. If you are running a firewall on your
> netatalk server, however, you must open access to several ports for netatalk to work. In particular, you may
> need to open ports 548 (AFP over TCP/IP), 201 (AppleTalk routing), 202 (AppleTalk name binding), 204
> (AppleTalk echo), and 206 (AppleTalk zones).

Use the aecho command (similar to the TCP/IP ping command) to check whether an
AppleTalk host computer is alive. The aecho command sends an Apple Echo Protocol (aep)
packet to the host you want to check. Here's an example:

```
# aecho toys
14 bytes from 65280.115: aep_seq=0. time=0, ms
14 bytes from 65280.115: aep_seq=1. time=0, ms

----65280.115 AEP Statistics----
2 packets sent, 2 packets received, 0% packet loss
round-trip (ms)  min/avg/max = 0/0/0
```

If the AppleTalk server is up and running, you can use the nbplkup command to see what
printers and volumes are currently available. For large networks, you can limit the output of
nbplkup by adding a share name or printer name (such as :hpjet), or by entering a host
name (for example, toys). Here's an example:

```
# nbplkup :AFPServer
duck:AFPServer            65280.115:130
User Volume:AFPServer     65280.21:129
Guest Volume:AFPServer    65280.21:130
```

By querying for :AFPServer, nbplkup listed all AppleTalk file servers on the local
network. The first one shown is from the host named duck. The second and third line were
from the same computer (at address 65280.21), but were registered as separate servers.

After restarting your netatalk server, you can check that the daemons all started properly. The
following are lines from the /var/log/messages file.

```
May 14 17:44:23 toys atalkd[2013]: zip_getnetinfo for eth0
May 14 17:44:33 toys atalkd[2013]: zip_getnetinfo for eth0
May 14 17:44:43 toys atalkd[2013]: config for no router
May 14 17:44:44 toys atalkd[2013]: ready 0/0/0
May 14 17:44:44 toys atalk: atalkd startup succeeded
May 14 17:44:57 toys atalk: papd startup succeeded
May 14 17:44:57 toys papd[2070]: restart (1.5.5)
May 14 17:44:57 toys atalk: afpd startup succeeded
May 14 17:45:03 toys afpd[2074]: toys:AFPServer@* started on
65280.96:128 (1.5.5)
```

```
May 14 17:45:03 toys afpd[2074]: ASIP started on 10.0.0.100:548(1)
(1.5.5)
May 14 17:45:03 toys afpd[2074]: uam: uams_clrtxt.so loaded
May 14 17:45:03 toys afpd[2074]: uam: uams_dhx.so loaded
May 14 17:45:03 toys afpd[2074]: uam: "DHCAST128" available
May 14 17:45:03 toys afpd[2074]: uam: "Cleartxt Passwrd" available
```

In the previous example, you can see that the atalk start-up script successfully started up the atalkd, papd, and afpd daemons. The atalkd daemon looks for AppleTalk network information on the first Ethernet interface (eth0). The papd daemon started, but had no printers to register. The afpd daemon started an AppleTalk file server on the server (toys:AFPServer). It then identified the user authentication methods (uams) that are available (both clear-text and encrypted passwords are available here).

Accessing NFS Servers from the Mac

For many years, Network File System (NFS) was the preferred method for sharing files among Linux and other UNIX-like computer systems. Although Mac OS X does support NFS connections from its Connect to Server window, you need to perform a little trick on the Linux server for that server to accept connections from the Mac OS X computer.

The following procedure describes how to use the Connect to Server window from a Mac OS X client to access files and directories from a shared Linux NFS server. You can then use the files and directories (also called folders) that reside on the Linux NFS server as though they existed on your Mac OS X computer.

As I've mentioned, the procedure relies on being able to make a small change to how the Linux NFS server offers the shared directory. If you don't have access to the Linux server, you either need to ask the administrator of the Linux server to make the change or connect your Mac to the Linux NFS server manually. (I describe the manual procedure at the end of this section.)

Connecting to NFS from the Connect to Server window

To create an NFS shared directory in Linux and connect to it from a Mac client, do the following:

1. On the Linux server, export a shared directory using the NFS facility as described in Chapter 18. To be able to use the shared directory from Mac OS X, however, you must be sure to add the insecure option. For example, to share the /var/music directory from the Linux server named jukebox.linuxtoys.net, you can add the following line to the /etc/exports file on that server:

   ```
   /var/music     *(rw,insecure)
   ```

   This example allows the /var/music directory to be shared with all computers (*) and provides read and write permission (rw). The insecure option lets clients that request the exported directory make the request from an insecure port (ports above 1024). This is important because the Mac OS X Connect to Server window makes its request to mount the shared directory from a port above 1024, and fails without the option.

2. On the Linux server, verify that the NFS service is running and re-export the shared directory by typing the following (as root user):

```
# exportfs -a -v
```

3. On the Mac OS X client, select Go in the Finder bar at the top of the screen, and then select Connect to Server. The Connect to Server window appears.

4. On the Mac OS X client, type the address of the share directory into the Address box. For example, to connect to the shared NFS (nfs://) directory called /var/music from the computer named jukebox.linuxtoys.net, you can type the address nfs://jukebox.linuxtoys.net/var/music (see Figure 26-5).

If everything is working properly, an icon representing the server should appear on your Mac OS X desktop. Depending on which version of Mac OS X you are using, a window might just pop open, displaying the contents of the directory or you may need to open that icon to see the contents of the shared directory. You can use the shared files and directories as though they were on your Mac (if permissions on the server permit you to do so). Drop the icon in the trash when you are done.

> **NOTE:** If you are unable to connect to the shared directory, go through the NFS procedures in Chapter 18 more carefully. In particular, make sure that firewall ports are open on the server and that the user and host permissions are set to allow the level of access that you require.

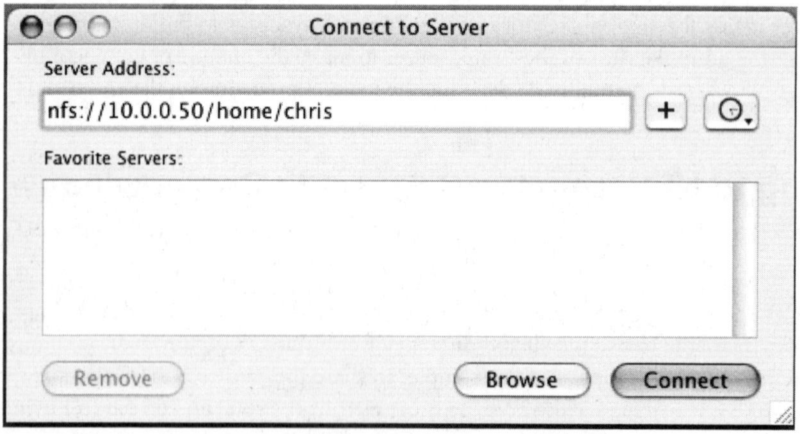

Figure 26-5: Connect to an NFS server from the Connect to Server window.

Connecting to NFS from the command line

You might very well not have any control over how the Linux NFS server is configured. So if the `insecure` option isn't set, you will fail to mount an NFS directory from the Mac's Connect to Server window. A possible workaround is to manually mount the NFS directory from Mac OS X and use a secure port. Here's how:

1. On the Mac OS X computer, gain access to the root user account as follows:

   a. With the Folder icon selected, select Go → Applications. The Applications folder appears.

   b. Open the Utilities folder, then the NetInfo Manager utility.

   c. Click the lock icon on the NetInfo Manager window so that it unlocks.

   d. Select Security → Enable Root User. (If you see a NetInfo error, click OK.)

   e. Type in and verify the new root user password, and then click Verify. (Remember that password!)

   f. Click the open lock icon to close it and prevent further changes.

2. On the Mac OS X computer, click the Terminal icon to open a shell and log in as root:

```
$ su -
Password: *******
```

3. Create a directory that is accessible to the user account of the person who wants to use the shared NFS directory on the Mac. For example, for the user `chris` you might type:

```
# mkdir /Users/chris/music
# chown chris /Users/chris/music
```

4. Mount the NFS shared directory on the directory you just created. For example:

```
# mount -o "-P" jukebox.linuxtoys.net:/var/music /Users/chris/music
```

   The `-P` says to use a privileged port. Replace `jukebox.linuxtoys.net` and `/var/music` with the server's name and the shared directory, respectively. The user can now access `/var/music` from the `/Users/chris/music` directory on the Mac OS X client.

Installing Fedora on an Intel-based Mac

The latest Apple computers feature Intel-based computer architecture. The Fedora Project has enhanced Fedora so that it can be installed (either by itself or dual booting with Mac OS X) on this new Apple hardware. Reasons you might want to install Fedora on one of these "Mactel" computers include:

- **Dual booting** — You might like the Mac OS X desktop (Aqua) and proprietary applications (such as iPhoto or iTunes) for yourself or family members some of the time.

However, you might sometimes want access to server applications, administration tools, development environment, or thousands of free applications you can get with Fedora.

- **Fedora only** — Although you pay a bit of a premium for Apple hardware (though not as much as you used to), you might like the form and features of those cute Apple Mac computers enough to pay a bit extra to have it as your primary desktop Fedora computer.

This section describes how to start with an Intel-based Apple Mac computer (I used a Mac Mini for this example) and configure it to either dual boot with Mac OS X or run Fedora alone.

> **CAUTION:** Installing Fedora on Intel-based hardware is still a technology that is experimental in the Fedora community. Some hardware components still require extra tweaking or won't work at all. I recommend that you don't do this procedure if you can't afford the possibility that your disk may be blown away and have to be reinstalled from scratch.

Before installing Fedora on your Mac

Let's start with a reminder that this procedure is only for Apple Mac computers that are based on Intel architecture. I ran this procedure on a new Mac Mini 1.1 (Intel Core Duo CPU, 512MB RAM). However, the same procedure should work for Intel-based iMac, MacBook, MacBook Pro, or Mac Pro computers.

This procedure is not for Macs with PowerPC architectures. Fedora does support that configuration, but you need to download the ppc installation media from Fedora instead of using the DVD that comes with this book. (Get the media for installing on PowerPCs from `http://fedoraproject.org/wiki/Distribution/Download`.) When you purchase your Mac, the entire hard disk is devoted to Mac OS X. To keep your Mac OS X installation on the computer (so you can boot either Mac OS X or Fedora), you need to reduce the amount of space devoted to Mac OS X. Then you need to use that space to create one or more partitions for installing Fedora.

Although the procedure for resizing and repartitioning your disk is fairly safe, there is some risk that you could corrupt your Mac OS X partition or make the machine (temporarily) unbootable. For that reason, before starting the procedure that follows, please . . .

. . . BACK UP ANY IMPORTANT DATA!

Installing Fedora

Mac OS X Leopard offers software called Boot Camp that can be used to resize Mac hard disks (using the default HFS+ file system type). Until Leopard was released, the beta version of Boot Camp was available as a free download from Apple. The following procedure describes how to update your firmware, resize your disk, and install Fedora.

1. **Check for firmware updates** — Update your Mac OS X system to the latest firmware. Refer to the Mac OS X Firmware Updates page for information on how to do that (`http://docs.info.apple.com/article.html?artnum=303880`). Then go to

Apple Downloads (`www.apple.com/support/downloads`) to get the firmware update, if necessary.

2. **Run Boot Camp** — Start Boot Camp Assistant (it's located in the Utilities folder). Because your interest in Boot Camp is to resize the Mac disk partition, skip the request to burn a Mac CD. Then move the divider to choose how much disk space will be devoted to Mac OS X and how much to Windows XP (you're going to be reusing the Windows area). Select the Partition button when each operating system has the disk space you want. (I chose to create a 10GB Windows partition.)

> **NOTE:** Because Boot Camp is no longer available for Mac OS X versions prior to Leopard, there is no official way to resize your disk to allow multiple boot partitions on your Mac. However, in theory you should be able to use a partitioning tool that supports HFS+ resizing to prepare your disk to install Fedora along side Mac OS X. Refer to Chapter 2 for information on how GParted can be used to resize partitions, such as HFS+ partitions. If you decide to try it, your results come without warranty. (In other words, you're on your own.)

3. **Insert Fedora DVD** — When partitioning is done, instead of inserting a Windows XP Installation CD as requested, insert a Fedora installation CD or DVD and click Restart Mac OS X or Install Windows to reboot the computer. When the computer reboots, you should see the Fedora installer boot screen.

4. **Install Fedora** — Begin a normal Fedora install (as described in Chapter 2), with just a couple of notes:

   - **Partitioning** — Default partitioning by the Fedora installer should work properly (leaving your Mac HFS+ partition alone and creating a Fedora /boot and LVM partition using the rest of the space).

   - **Boot loader** — Again, the installer should do the correct thing and configure the boot loader to be installed on a Fedora partition and not in the master boot record, as would normally be the case. (The boot loader must not be installed in the master boot record of the whole disk or the disk will become unbootable.)

5. **Reboot and Alt key** — When Fedora installation is completed, reboot as instructed. Hold the Alt key as the machine reboots. When you see the Boot Camp menu, select Windows and the computer will boot to Fedora. Just use the default boot entry for Fedora because trying to change GRUB boot labels will probably cause the computer to lock up. (By the way, if you DVD gets stuck in the drive, hold down the mouse button when you reboot and the DVD will eject.)

Remember that installing Fedora on an Intel-based MAC is still considered to be experimental. The less you stray from the defaults (partitioning, boot loaders, and so on), the better chance of getting a workable Fedora system running on your Mac.

If you run into problems, I recommend you refer to the Fedora Project's Fedora On Mactel page (`http://fedoraproject.org/wiki/FedoraOnMactel`). There are also resources available from other Linux projects to get Linux to boot on Intel Mac architecture.

Summary

Because Darwin, a UNIX-like operating system, lies at the heart of the Mac OS X operating system, native Linux and UNIX network servers can be easily connected to these new Macs in a variety of ways. Mac OS X can take advantage of files shared from a Linux server over Samba (Windows file/printer sharing) and NFS (UNIX file/printer sharing).

Instead of just using native Linux server features, you can also configure Linux to act like an AppleTalk file and printer server using the netatalk package. With netatalk, you can set up multiple file servers and protect the volumes (directories) they share with various password and permissions techniques. With Apple's recent move to Intel-based architecture, you can now install Fedora on Intel Mac computers. You can either choose to have Fedora take over the whole computer, or have Fedora set up to dual boot with Mac OS X.

Appendix A

About the Media

If you have a CD-ROM or DVD drive on a standard PC (32-bit i386 architecture), you can install Fedora 9 from the media that come with this book. Those media include:

- **Fedora 9 Install DVD** — Instead of offering the Fedora 9 Prime DVD (3.4GB), we put together most of the software from the massive Fedora 9 software repository on this DVD (over 8GB). This represents the combination of what was called Fedora Core and Fedora Extras in versions of Fedora prior to Fedora 7.

> **NOTE:** The Fedora 9 DVD that comes with this book includes all Fedora packages that are associated with the software groups you see when you install Fedora. There are other Fedora packages available that are not part of any group. To search for or add any of that extra software, use the List or Search features of the PackageKit utility.

- **Fedora 9 KDE Live/Install desktop CD** — This is an official live CD from the Fedora project. It boots to a KDE desktop with a nice variety of applications, regardless of what is installed on your computer's hard disk. You can install the contents of this CD to hard disk by starting the installer icon from the live CD's desktop. Once the software is installed, you can install any other software you need from online repositories.

If you have a drive that supports both DVDs and CDs, use the DVD. It gives you greater options for selecting software and does not require access to online repositories to go beyond a basic desktop system. However, for the average desktop user, the CD set will work well as a starting point for a useable Fedora desktop system.

> **NOTE:** The CD and DVD included with this book are for 32-bit PC architectures. They will not work on other computer architectures. However, you can download ISO images of Fedora live and installation CDs and DVDs for X86 64-bit (x86_64), PowerPC (ppc) or PowerPC 64-bit (ppc64) architectures from the Fedora download page (http://fedoraproject.org/get-fedora.html).

To install Fedora 9 from the DVD or CD follow the instructions provided in Chapter 2 and on the README files on the DVD or CD.

If for some reason you don't have your DVD handy, you can find information on how to download different live and install CDs and DVDs from the Fedora Project Web site at http://fedoraproject.org. If you have a DVD drive on another computer on your

LAN, see Chapter 2 for information on setting up a Fedora install server, so you can install Fedora on your chosen machine over your LAN.

Repositories such as `rpm.livna.org/fedora` can help you find extra, useful software packages that are not in Fedora (or any other Red Hat distribution). Some of these sites act as yum or apt repositories that allow you to download sets of dependent packages (see the descriptions of `yum` and useful third-party Fedora software repositories in Chapter 5).

Fedora Source Code

From time to time, you may want to recompile the Linux kernel or other software package that comes with Fedora. Like the binary software packages, the source code packages are available from the Fedora Project site (`http://fedoraproject.org/get-fedora.html`). To work with Fedora source code packages, here is what you need:

- **kernel-devel** — The kernel-devel package comes with the Fedora binary packages. Included in the package name is the version number of the kernel it contains. The source code for the current kernel is contained in the `/usr/src/kernels` directory, ready to be recompiled, if the kernel-devel package is installed.

- **SRPMS directory** — Source code for each binary package outside of the kernel that is included in Fedora is available from any Fedora repository. Install the source code package for the software that interests you (the name ends in `.src.rpm`) and a copy of that software in subdirectories of the `/usr/src/redhat` directory.

To do the actual compilations, you will need to install at least the gcc package. As with the installation DVDs, if you want to download DVDs containing Fedora source code, you can get them from a Fedora download site. Individual software packages for Fedora source code are available in `SRPMS` directories at the same Fedora mirror sites.

Fedora Rescue CD

In addition to the full Fedora 9 software installation set, the Fedora Project provides a rescue CD. As with the other Fedora CDs and DVDs, you can download this CD image separately from `http://fedoraproject.org`. Look for an image name that includes the current release name and number and ends with `rescuecd.iso`.

The Fedora 9 Rescue CD contains those features needed to rescue your Fedora system if, for example, the system fails to boot because of a corrupted file system or broken master boot record. It's a good idea to make a separate boot CD and store it for an emergency.

The Rescue CD functionality is built into the DVD that comes with this book. To boot that medium into rescue mode, simply press Tab from the first entry on the boot screen and type the word **rescue** at the end of the `boot` command line that appears. Press Enter and the medium will boot into rescue mode.

If you decide to download and burn your own Fedora 9 Rescue CD, you can do the following to use that CD:

1. Insert the Rescue CD into the CD drive.

2. Reboot your computer. You will see the Fedora Rescue CD welcome screen with the `boot:` prompt at the bottom.

3. Press Enter to begin rescue mode. (You could also type **linux** to begin a Fedora install with this CD, or press the F2 function key to see other options.) The rescue CD asks you to choose a language.

4. Choose a language and select OK. You are asked to choose a keyboard type.

5. Choose a keyboard type and select OK. You are asked if you want to start network interfaces.

6. Choose Yes (to start a network interface, if you have a network interface card installed) or No (to continue booting without a network interface).

7. If you said Yes, choose DHCP, or type a static IP address and Netmask for your computer. Also, identify your gateway (the machine that connects you to the Internet or other outside network) and one or more DNS servers you need for address resolution.

8. When you enter the rescue environment, you need to choose whether or not to mount your Linux installation (under the `/mnt/sysimage` directory) by selecting Continue, to mount it as read-only (select Read-Only), or to not mount it (select Skip).

If everything went well, you should receive the message: `Your system is mounted under the /mnt/sysimage directory`. You will see a shell prompt. Now you can:

*   Try to fix any errors in your Linux configuration, beginning at `/mnt/sysimage` to find your normal root (/) directory.

*   Back up or transfer files from your computer to other media or computers, if your system remains unbootable, so you can save any critical files.

When you are done, remove the CD and reboot your computer.

> **NOTE:** As noted earlier, everything you do with the rescue CD you can also do with the Fedora DVD that comes with this book. The rescue CD is just more convenient in some cases because it is smaller to copy (only about 88MB as compared with multiple GB for the Fedora DVD) and quicker to boot up. It will also fit on a medium that is smaller than a full-size CD.

Appendix B

Running Network Services

Because Fedora and RHEL can provide so many different kinds of services (serving Web pages, printers, files, and other resources), it's not always easy to find all the components you need to use those services. Let's say you install all server software packages with Fedora or RHEL. How do you know which servers will start up automatically and which will need special configuration to work? Where do you start to look for configuration files, start-up scripts, and daemon processes? How do you know if your firewall configuration is blocking access to the services?

This appendix provides a quick reference to the network services that come with Fedora and RHEL. It offers an overview of the services described in detail in other chapters. You can use this appendix to help you remember how to get services working or as a guide to help you debug a service that needs fixing.

> **CAUTION:** Any services your computer offers to users who can reach it over a network pose a potential security threat. Refer to Chapter 14 for information on security, as well as the sections in the book that describe configuration of each feature in detail.

Checklist for Running Networking Services

As computer security issues increase with the rising onslaught of computer crackers and viruses, operating systems (such as Fedora or RHEL), in regards to the services they provide, are moving toward more security rather than more ease-of-use. Simply installing server software is no longer enough to get the service up and running.

If a service isn't working, check the following items to hunt down the problem:

1. **Is the software package installed?** Each network service is represented by one or more software packages. Use the command `rpm -qc packagename` to find configuration files, and the command `rpm -qd packagename` to find documentation. If you selected only packages associated with Desktop categories when you first installed Fedora, most network server software may not be installed on your computer at all. Check Table B-1 (at the end of this appendix) to see which package is needed for a particular service to work. (There might be other package dependencies as well, to which you will be alerted

when you try to install the package.) Then use the `rpm` command to install the software from the installation DVD or CD.

2. **Is the start-up script set up to launch the service automatically?** Most network services are launched from start-up scripts that cause daemon processes to listen to the network continuously for requests for the service. See the "Networking Service Daemons" section for information on how to find start-up scripts and have them launch automatically.

3. **Does SELinux permit access to the service?** When SELinux is enabled, it puts an additional layer of security over selected network services. If you get *permission denied* messages when you are sure that the firewall and file/directory permissions are set appropriately, run `system-config-selinux`. On the SELinux tab, check that the appropriate service (Web, FTP, Samba, and so on) is enabled.

4. **Is the configuration file created for the service?** Even if the daemon process is listening for requests for a network service, one or more configuration files associated with the service must probably be set up before requests will be accepted. Table B-1 lists important configuration files for each type of server.

5. **Does the configuration file permit proper access to the service?** Within the configuration file for a service, there might be several levels of permissions that a user must go through to get permission to the service. For example, a configuration file might allow access to the service from a particular host computer, but deny access to a particular user.

6. **Does the firewall permit access to the service?** The first time you boot Fedora after installation, the firstboot procedure enables you to configure a firewall. If you choose the default firewall, most services will not be available outside your local computer. Refer to Chapter 14 for information on how to change your firewall configuration to open ports that provide the different services.

7. **Are there other restrictions to the service being shared?** Some standard Linux security measures might block access to a service that is otherwise open to being shared. For example, you can share a Linux directory using NFS or FTP servers, but local file permissions might block access to the directory or files within the shared directory.

To begin determining where a service failure actually occurs, look to the log files contained in the `/var/log` directory. The `messages` and `dmesg` files contain general messages about processing that occurs when services and hardware are initialized. Many services, such as Sendmail and Apache, have their own log files. Setting debug levels on service daemons is a way to get more details about how a server is working (see the Debugging Services sidebar).

The rest of this appendix provides an overview of the daemon processes, start-up scripts, configuration files, and software packages that are associated with the networking services that come with Fedora and RHEL.

Debugging Services

Nearly every service also has an option for running in different debug levels. By turning on debugging, you can see everything from failure messages to detailed information on everything the service does. Usually, you can either add a debug option to an init script (often passed by options set in `/etc/sysconfig/` files) or run a daemon process manually from the shell with debug options added. For example:

 # /usr/sbin/sshd -ddd -f /etc/ssh/sshd_config -p 52222

This example starts the secure shell daemon (sshd) in maximum debug mode (-ddd). It uses the sshd_config for its configuration and listens for connections on port number 52222. This port is just being used for testing purposes, so not to conflict with any common ports. Watch the debug messages appear in the Terminal window. Next you could have an ssh client from another computer try to connect to this server:

$ ssh -l testuser 192.168.1.246 -p 52222

Assuming here that the server's IP address is 192.168.1.246, this example attempts to connect to the sshd server run earlier on port 52222. It tries to log in as the user named testuser. By watching sshd debug messages, you can check that the client can communicate with the server and that the configuration file is working properly.

Networking Service Daemons

This section provides a quick review of how networking services (as well as other services) are started in Fedora and RHEL. The two main directories containing files that define how services are started are `/etc/xinetd.d` and `/etc/init.d`.

- **/etc/xinetd.d** — Contains configuration files used by the `xinetd` daemon.
- **/etc/init.d** — Contains start-up scripts that are linked from `/etc/rc?.d` directories so they can be started at different run levels.

Each of these methods for handling network services is described in the following sections.

> **NOTE:** Some Fedora and RHEL configuration tools also store configuration information in the `/etc/sysconfig` directory. For example, there are configuration files for `iptables` and `sendmail` in `/etc/sysconfig`. If you search the scripts in the `/etc/init.d` directory for the word `sysconfig`, you will see just how many services look in that directory for configuration information.

The xinetd super-server

The `xinetd` daemon is referred to as the *super-server*. It listens for incoming requests for services based on information in separate files in the `/etc/xinetd.d` directory. When a request for a service is received by the `xinetd` daemon (for a particular network port number), xinetd typically launches a different daemon to handle the request. So instead of having separate daemons running for every network service, only the xinetd daemon needs to run — plus an additional daemon process for each service currently in use.

To see if a particular service handled by xinetd is on or off, go to the /etc/xinetd.d directory and open the file representing that service with a text editor. The disable line sets whether or not the service is currently disabled. The following example is an excerpt from the /etc/xinetd.d/amanda file:

```
service amanda
{
        socket_type      = dgram
        protocol         = udp
        wait             = yes
        user             = amanda
        server           = /usr/lib/amanda/amandad
        server_args      = -auth=bsd amdump
        disable          = yes
}
```

In this example, the amanda configuration file represents a means of retrieving backup index files from amanda clients. By default, the service is turned off. When the service is on, a request to the xinetd server daemon for the amandad service from the network is handed to the amandad daemon. Arguments to that daemon are set on the server_args line.

To enable a service in an /etc/xinetd.d file, edit the file using any text editor as the root user. Turning on the service is as easy as changing the disable option from yes to no and restarting the xinetd daemon. For example, you could change the line in the /etc/xinetd.d/amanda so that it appears as follows:

```
disable      =  no
```

Then you could restart the xinetd daemon (without turning off the daemon itself):

```
# service xinetd restart
```

> **NOTE:** Although not all services support this, the xinetd service lets you use the reload instead of the restart option with the service command just shown. With xinitd already running, a reload can occur faster and with less interruption to system services by not completely shutting down xinetd.

> **CROSS-REFERENCE:** The xinetd super-server is described in Chapter 12.

The init.d start-up scripts

Network services that are not available via the xinetd daemon are typically handled by scripts in the /etc/init.d directory. For a script in the /etc/init.d directory to activate a service, it must be linked to a file in one of the run-level directories (`/etc/rc?.d`) that begins with the letter *S* followed by a two-digit number.

For example, the script for starting the print service daemon (`/etc/init.d/cups`) is linked to the file `S98cups` in the `/etc/rc2.d`, `/etc/rc3.d`, `/etc/rc4.d`, and `/etc/rc5.d` directories. In that way, the print service is started when Fedora or RHEL are running in initialization states 2, 3, 4, or 5.

> **CROSS-REFERENCE:** See Chapter 12 for more details on run levels and start-up scripts.

For the most part, system administrators are not expected to modify these start-up scripts. However, to have a service turned on or off for a particular run level, change the script to a filename that begins with an *S* (start) to one that begins with a *K* (kill). You can easily do this with the `chkconfig` command or the Service Configuration window. To start that window, type **serviceconf** from a Terminal window while you are logged in as the root user.

Start-up scripts typically start one or more daemon processes that represent a particular service. To add options to a particular daemon, you typically don't have to edit the start-up script directly. Instead, look for configuration files in the `/etc/sysconfig` directory. For example, the DNS (`named`), Samba (`smbd` and `nmbd`), and system logging (`syslogd`) services have options files in the `/etc/sysconfig` directory.

Choosing Alternatives

Some services in Fedora and RHEL can be implemented by several different software packages. Although you can, you probably don't want to run multiple mail and print servers on the same computer. At the very least, you should set the software you want to use by default.

In Fedora and RHEL, an *alternatives* feature is packaged into the operating system. Alternatives is an implementation of the Debian GNU/Linux alternatives feature. In essence, alternatives links the software you choose (or leave by default) into the common locations where the service being implemented is launched or made available.

> **CROSS-REFERENCE:** See the "Choosing Software Alternatives" section in Chapter 10 for more information on the alternatives feature.

The first services to be implemented under alternatives in Fedora and RHEL were print and mail server packages. However, when the LPRng print service was dropped from Fedora and RHEL, it left mail as the only service that's supported by the alternatives feature.

Assuming you have multiple mail agents, you can use system-switch-mail to switch among those services. Figure B-1 shows an example of the system-switch-mail window.

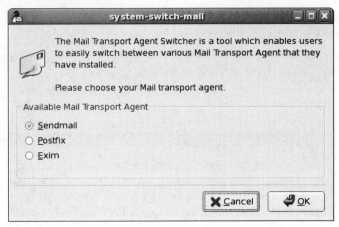

Figure B-1: Change your default mail-transport agent with system-switch-mail.

Referencing Network Services

This section contains the quick reference information related to Fedora and RHEL network services. The table listing these services (Table B-1) contains the following information:

- **Feature** — What type of service is it?
- **Package names** — What software packages must be installed to use the service?
- **Start-up scripts** — Which start-up scripts launch the service?
- **Daemon** — What daemon process is running to provide the service?
- **Configuration files** — What configuration files can you modify to tailor the service to your specific needs?

The descriptions following the table provide additional information about the service, including whether or not the service is started by default and where you can find more information about the service.

> **NOTE:** When the `xinetd` daemon is noted as the start-up script, the daemon process to which the service is handed off is also noted.

The following sections provide some additional information about the services described in Table B-1. (You'll find the table at the end of this appendix.)

Web server

In most cases, you use the Apache project (httpd package) to create a Web server in Fedora or RHEL. If httpd is installed, you must turn on the service, and then start it to use the service (as root user, type **chkconfig httpd on** and then type **service httpd start**). Start-up will fail unless you have a valid name (and IP address) for your Web server. To define a server name, add a `ServerName` entry to the `httpd.conf` file and restart the service.

Users who can access your system from the network will be able to view the contents of the `/var/www/html` directory, by default. Replace the `index.html` file and add your own content. If the `httpd-manual` package is installed, `/var/www/manual` contains the apache manual.

> **CROSS-REFERENCE:** See Chapter 21 for information on configuring an Apache Web server.

File servers

File services in Fedora and RHEL can be provided using FTP servers, Samba (Windows) servers, Network File System (NFS) servers, and NetWare servers. The following sections describe each of these.

FTP servers

The Very Secure FTP daemon (`vsftpd`) package was designed from scratch to be very scalable and fast. It is geared toward FTP sites that require support for lots of simultaneous users. Configure vsftpd by editing the `/etc/vsftpd/vsftpd.conf` and `/etc/vsftpd/user_list` files. The vsftpd package shares the `/var/ftp` directory structure and listens on port 21 for service requests.

To turn on FTP service, type the following (as root user):

```
# service vsftpd start
# chkconfig vsftpd on
```

Another popular FTP server is the Trivial FTP server (tftp). Tftp is often used as a boot server for projects such as the Linux Terminal server project.

> **CROSS-REFERENCE:** See Chapter 20 for information on how to configure the `vsftpd` FTP server.

> **NOTE:** An FTP server with Kerberos 5 support is also included with Fedora and RHEL. The `krb5-workstation` package contains the `ftpd` daemon that includes Kerberos 5 support. The wu-ftp FTP server software is no longer in the Fedora or RHEL distributions.

Samba server

The Samba server software supports the Server Message Block (SMB) and CIFS file- and printer-sharing protocols. SMB and CIFS are most often used to share resources on local networks consisting of computers running Microsoft Windows. You would not typically share SMB/CIFS files and printers over a public network, such as the Internet.

Samba services are off by default in Fedora and RHEL. To have Samba start automatically when you boot your computer, simply type **chkconfig smb on** as the root user. To start the service now, type **service smb start**.

In order for Samba to be useful, edit the Samba configuration file, /etc/samba/smb.conf. An easy way to configure this file is with the Samba Server Configuration window (described in Chapter 18).

> **CROSS-REFERENCE:** For more information about configuring Samba, see Chapters 17 and 18.

Netatalk server

The netatalk server software enables Linux to act as an AppleTalk server for Macintosh computers. To use netatalk, you must install the netatalk package and turn on the service by typing **chkconfig atalk on**. Then start the service by typing **service netatalk start.** Configuration is done from files in the /etc/atalk directory.

> **CROSS-REFERENCE:** See Chapter 26 for information on setting up netatalk.

Login servers

A variety of login servers are available for use with Fedora and RHEL. Both telnet and rlogin services can be used to allow users from other computers to log in to Fedora or RHEL from the network. These days, however, sshd is the preferred login service. For most of these services, you need to remember to allow access to that service from your firewall.

If the telnet-server package is installed, the telnet service is off by default. If telnet is enabled, the xinetd daemon passes all requests for telnet service (by default, port 23) to the in.telnetd daemon to present the telnet login prompt. Once it is on, only users with real logins to the computer can log in to the computer — anonymous users are not supported. Users who log in using telnet are presented with a shell interface for accessing the computer.

Fedora and RHEL also include login daemons that provide Kerberos 5 support. Kerberos 5 provides a higher level of security than is available with other login servers. Kerberos 5–enabled login servers include Klogin (Kerberos 5) and EKlogin (Kerberos 5 with encryption).

The rlogin service has been available for UNIX systems for a long time, though it is generally less secure than the other login services described here. The rlogin service is off by default on your Fedora or RHEL system.

A newer addition to the login servers available with Fedora and RHEL is the OpenSSH server. This service is on by default. To access this service, use applications that come with the openssh-client software package, such as the ssh, sftp, and slogin remote login commands. Many Linux administrators use OpenSSH tools, as opposed to older remote login tools such as rlogin and telnet. OpenSSH is more secure because it encrypts network traffic to protect passwords and data from being sniffed (while `telnet` and `rlogin` send data in clear text).

> **CAUTION:** Not only is the SSH service on by default, but unlike other login services, it will allow root login over the network. If you are uncomfortable with that, you should change the `PermitRootLogin yes` line in the `/etc/ssh/sshd_config` file as follows:
>
>   PermitRootLogin no

E-mail servers

The most common protocols used to download e-mail from a mail server to a client workstation are Post Office Protocol (POP3) and Internet Message Access Protocol (IMAPv4). If you configure Fedora or RHEL as your mail server, you can configure the dovecot package to provide POP and IMAP services.

Dovecot is an IMAP/POP3 mail server that works with both maildir and mbox formats. You use IMAP or POP3 if your users get their mail from their own desktops instead of by running their mail clients on the mail server. By default, all POP or IMAP services are off. Choose the POP or IMAP server you would like to use from those provided in the e-mail reader servers listing in Table B-1.

The default mail-transfer agent that comes with Fedora and RHEL is called sendmail. If sendmail software is installed, the sendmail service is started automatically. However, you must configure various files in the `/etc/mail` directory for the service to work beyond the localhost.

Postfix is an alternative to sendmail, as is the exim mail transport agent. Using the alternatives feature (described earlier in this appendix and in Chapter 10), you can easily make any of those packages your default mail-transfer agent. Configuration files for postfix are located in the `/etc/postfix` directory, while exim configuration files are in the `/etc/exim` directory. Also make sure that you turn sendmail off (`chkconfig sendmail off`) and turn postfix or exim on (`chkconfig postfix on` or `chkconfig exim on`).

> **CROSS-REFERENCE:** Chapter 19 contains details on how to configure sendmail and postfix.

News server

Fedora and RHEL come with the Internet Network News Server (INN) software to let you set up a Fedora or RHEL system as a news server. INN can provide your users access to thousands of Internet newsgroups. It can also be used as a corporate e-mail repository so workgroups can share information about a project.

By default, INN service is off in Fedora and RHEL. To turn it on, type **chkconfig inn on**. Then start it by typing **service inn start.** To make the service usable, you must edit files in the `/etc/news` directory.

> **CAUTION:** Because a news server can potentially consume huge amounts of system resources, you must think carefully about how you configure it. Details about how to configure an INN news server are available from the *Fedora 9 and Red Hat Enterprise Linux Bible* Web site: `www.wiley.com/go/fedora9bible`.

Print servers

The Common UNIX Printing System (CUPS) print server software is included as the default printer software for the current releases of Fedora and RHEL. As an alternative, the LPR New Generation (LPRng) software is still available but is no longer provided with Fedora or RHEL distributions.

> **CROSS-REFERENCE:** Information on setting up printers can be found in Chapter 17.

The Common UNIX Printing System (CUPS) is an alternative to LPRng and other printing interfaces that were built on facilities originally designed for line printers in the 1970s. CUPS is based on the Internet Printing Protocol (RFC 2616). Although it is compatible with other UNIX/Linux print facilities, CUPS is intended to make it easier to support new printers, protocols, and other devices as they become available.

The CUPS server (`cupsd`) is set up to run by default. Configuration files for CUPS are located in the `/etc/cups` directory.

Network administration servers

Some network servers offer services that monitor or configure network configurations. Several of these services, listed in Table B-1, are described in the following sections.

Network Time Protocol server

The Network Time Protocol (NTP) Server synchronizes time among computers on a network.

The Fedora and RHEL firstboot processes lets you turn on the NTP service. To further tune ntp, you must edit the `/etc/ntp.conf` file. The `/etc/ntp.conf` file contains information that identifies the addresses of synchronization sources and modes of operation. The `/etc/ntp/keys` file can be used to turn on authentication.

Portmap server

The portmap server translates Remote Procedure Call (RPC) numbers to TCP/IP and UDP port numbers. Certain network services, such as NFS (`nfs`) and Wall (`rwalld`), only work properly if this server is running. RPC numbers are stored in the `/etc/rpc` file.

SWAT

The Samba Web Administration Tool (SWAT) provides a Web-based interface for configuring Samba file and print services. When properly configured, a Web browser can access the SWAT service (with a root user password). Although this is a well-tested interface, the Samba Server Configuration window is the preferred tool for configuring Samba in Fedora and RHEL.

By default, the SWAT service is off in Fedora and RHEL. To turn the service on, edit the `/etc/xinetd.d/swat` file and change the `disable = yes` entry to `disable = no`. This makes the service available to a Web browser on the local host that asks for port number 901 (for example, `http://localhost:901`). You can remove the line `only_from = 127.0.0.1` to allow a Web browser from any computer that has access to your computer on the network to use SWAT. (Of course, a remote user would also need to know your root password.)

Arpwatch server

The Arpwatch service can be turned on to monitor Ethernet/IP activities on your network. Any potential problems (such as two different computers using the same IP address) are logged to the `syslog` facility (usually to the `/var/log/messages` file).

By default, the Arpwatch service is turned off. To turn it on, type **chkconfig arpwatch on**. To start the service, type **service arpwatch start**. You can check the `/var/log/messages` file to see if the Arpwatch services started successfully and watch for changes on your network.

Simple Network Management Protocol server

The Simple Network Management Protocol (SNMP) server enables your Fedora or RHEL system to listen for SNMP requests from the network. With this server running, other computers using SNMP tools can monitor the activities of your computer (based on configuration files set up on your system).

To use SNMP, you must have the net-snmp package installed. By default, SNMP is turned off. To turn it on, type **chkconfig snmpd on** and **chkconfig snmptrapd on**. SNMP configuration can be quite complex. Start by referring to the `snmpd.conf` man page (type **man snmpd.conf**).

Information servers

By distributing such information as hostnames, user account information, and network addresses, an administrator can more easily manage groups of networked computers. Popular types of servers for managing network information include Network Information System (NIS), Dynamic Host Configuration Protocol (DHCP), and Lightweight Directory Access Protocol (LDAP).

Network Information System servers

Network Information System (NIS) is a software feature developed by Sun Microsystems to manage information needed to configure a group of UNIX (and now Linux) computers on a network. Using NIS, a group of computers can share common passwd, groups, hosts, and other configuration files.

By default, NIS services are off. You can turn on NIS services for your Linux computer as either an NIS client (using shared information) or an NIS server (distributing shared information). NIS client computers need to start the /etc/init.d/ypbind script and identify the NIS servers in the /etc/yp.conf file.

To use Fedora or RHEL as an NIS server, you must gather up the configuration files you want to share, then start the /etc/init.d/ypserv script. The script runs the /usr/sbin/ypserv daemon, which takes care of the distribution of information to the NIS client computers.

Dynamic Host Configuration Protocol server

Instead of going to each computer on your local network and adding all the TCP/IP information they need in order to work (IP address, netmasks, gateways, and so on), you can configure Fedora or RHEL as a Dynamic Host Configuration Protocol (DHCP) server to distribute that information. The client computer simply identifies the IP address of the DHCP server so that when the client starts up its network connection, the DHCP server automatically assigns its network address.

By default, DHCP is turned off. To turn it on, type **chkconfig dhcpd on**. Then start the service by typing **service dhcpd start**. Besides starting the service, you must also configure the /etc/dhcpd.conf file.

> **CROSS-REFERENCE:** Chapter 23 describes how to set up a DHCP server.

Lightweight Directory Access Protocol server

If your organization uses Lightweight Directory Access Protocol (LDAP) databases of information, running the LDAP server that comes with Fedora or RHEL enables you to access those databases. Likewise, the LDAP server enables you to use LDAP-enabled applications, such as Netscape Roaming Access and sendmail 8.

By default, the LDAP service is turned off. To turn it on, type **chkconfig ldap on**. To start the service, type **service ldap start**. In addition to running the start-up script, you must configure files in the /etc/ldap/ directory.

> **CROSS-REFERENCE:** Chapter 22 shows how to set up an e-mail address book using LDAP.

Domain Name System server

A Domain Name System (DNS) server is set up to translate host names to IP addresses on a TCP/IP network. Fedora and RHEL can be configured as a DNS server using the `named` daemon.

By default, the DNS server is not configured to start automatically in Fedora or RHEL. To turn on a DNS server, type **chkconfig named on**. To start the service, type **service named start**. In addition to starting the service, you must configure the `/etc/named.conf` file and configure zone files (in the `/var/named` directory).

Reverse Address Resolution Protocol server

The Reverse Address Resolution Protocol (RARP) daemon responds to requests from RARP clients that must obtain their own IP addresses. Today, RARP is not used very often.

By default, the RARP package (rarpd-ss981107-18) is not installed by default. When it is installed, the service is off. To turn on an RARP server, type **chkconfig rarpd on**. To start the service, type **service rarpd start**. When requests come in for addresses, the `/usr/sbin/rarpd` daemon checks the `/etc/ethers` or NIS+ databases for addresses.

Database services

Database servers provide tools for accessing and managing databases of information. The Postgresql service uses the `postmaster` daemon to handle requests for its services. The MySQL server runs the `mysqld` daemon to handle access to its databases. These daemons are started from start-up scripts in `/etc/init.d`: postgresql and mysqld scripts, respectively.

CROSS-REFERENCE: Chapter 24 describes how to set up a MySQL database server.

User services

Fedora and RHEL can provide end users with a variety of network services. These services let users run remote programs, send messages in real time, and get information on active users.

Remote execution servers

Remote execution servers respond to requests from other computers to run commands on the local computer. This can be a security issue, so be careful in configuring these services. Three remote execution service daemons are available with Fedora and RHEL: Rsh, Rexec, and Kshell.

- The Rsh service (`/usr/sbin/in.rshd`) accepts requests for remote execution requests that were initiated by the `rsh` command (from other Linux or UNIX systems). By default, the service is off. The host or user (or both) must be allowed access before remote execution is permitted. Access is configured in the `/etc/hosts.equiv` file or in the `.rhosts` file in each user's home directory.

- The Rexec service (/usr/sbin/in.rexecd) accepts remote execution requests from the rexec command (from other Linux or UNIX systems). By default, the service is off. To allow remote execution, the user making the request must provide a valid user name and password.

- The Kshell service (/usr/kerberos/sbin/kshd) receives remote execution requests from the rsh command. It uses Kerberos authentication and encryption, making it more secure than the alternative in.rshd daemon. By default, the service is off. However, if you turn it on (by editing the /etc/xinetd.d/kshell file and changing the disable = yes entry to disable = no), it takes precedence over the in.rshd daemon.

The OpenSSH service (using the sshd daemon) described earlier can also be used for remote execution. OpenSSH is a more secure way to do remote execution than the other methods just described. Therefore, in most cases you should bypass these services and use OpenSSH for remote execution.

CROSS-REFERENCE: Login commands for using login services are described in Chapter 16.

Talk server

Use the in.talk or in.ntalk servers to allow users to communicate using the talk command. The talk command enables users to type messages back and forth in real time. The talk daemon handles requests on port 517, and the ntalk daemon handles requests on port 518.

Both services are turned off by default. To turn on either service, edit the /etc/xinetd.d/talk and/or /etc/xinetd.d/ntalk files and change the disable = yes entry to disable = no. Then restart the xinetd daemon: service xinetd restart.

Finger server

The finger (/usr/sbin/in.fingerd) server lets people use the finger command to request information about active users on Linux or UNIX systems locally or over a network. This service is off by default. If the in.fingerd server accepts a request from a finger command, the output to the user who made the request looks something like the following:

```
[maple]
Login: jake                 Name: Jake W. Jones
Directory: /home/jake       Shell: /bin/bash
Last login Mon May 12 13:34 (PDT) on pts/2 from maple
Mail last read Mon May 12 12:10 2008 (PDT)
```

The output shows the user's login name, real name, home directory, and shell. It also shows when the user last logged in and accessed his or her e-mail. Because this service can expose personal or corporate information that you may not want exposed, you typically won't open the finger service to public networks.

Remote user identification

The rusers server (`/usr/sbin/rpc.rusersd`) enables users to query the system from a remote computer to list who is currently logged in to the Fedora or RHEL system. The `rusers` command can be used to query the `rpc.rusersd` server.

By default, the rusers service is off. To start the server, type **chkconfig rusersd on**. To start the service now, type **service rusersd start**. As with the finger services, rusers should rarely be exposed to public networks.

Write-to-All server

The Write-to-All (rwall) server (`/user/sbin/rpc.rwalld`) accepts requests to broadcast a text message to the screens of all users currently logged in to the Fedora, RHEL, or other UNIX system. The request is made with the `rwall` command. By default, the rwall service is off. To start an rwall server, type **chkconfig rwalld on**. To start the service, type **service xinetd start**.

Security services

Fedora and RHEL provide some services to protect your local network from outside attacks. These services include system logging, virtual private network servers, and caching servers. The following sections describe those services.

System logging

Though not specifically a network service, the system-logging facility (`syslogd` package) logs information and error messages from most of the network services (and other services) on your computer. The system-logging daemon (`/sbin/syslogd`) should be running at all times.

The `syslogd` daemon is, by default, started at all multiuser run levels (2, 3, 4, and 5). You can change what messages are logged or have logging messages directed to different files by reconfiguring the `/etc/syslog.conf` file. You can change options used by the `syslogd` daemon by editing the `/etc/sysconfig/syslog` file.

Virtual private network servers

By encrypting data that travels across cpublic networks, a virtual private network (VPN) can provide a secure way for users to access your local network from remote locations. Fedora Core 1 came with the Crypto IP Encapsulation (CIPE) virtual private network software. In current releases of Fedora and RHEL, the openswan package is included to provide IPsec VPN service. Fedora also includes openvpn, which is an SSL VPN service.

CROSS-REFERENCE: See Chapter 16 for more information on IPsec.

Proxy/caching server

The Squid server (/usr/sbin/squid) can be used as both a proxy server and a caching server. A proxy server can allow computers on your local network to communicate with the Internet by passing all requests through the proxy server. A caching server stores Web content that has been accessed by a local user on a computer that is physically closer to the user than the originating computer.

By default, the Squid server is off. To start the Squid server, type **chkconfig squid on**. To install squid, type **yum install squid**.

To start the service, type **service squid start**. You must also set up the /etc/squid/squid.conf file to identify who has access to the server and what services they can access.

CROSS-REFERENCE: Chapter 16 provides details for configuring Squid.

Table B-1: Quick Reference for Network Services

Feature	Package Names	Startup Script(s)	Daemon	Configuration File(s)
Web Server				
Web-Servers (Apache)	httpd httpd-manual httpd-devel	`/etc/init.d/httpd`	`/usr/sbin/httpd`	`/etc/httpd/conf/` `httpd.conf`
File Servers				

FTP Servers (Vs-ftpd)	vsftpd	`/etc/init.d/vsftpd`	`/usr/sbin/vsftpd`	`/etc/vsftpd/`
				`vsftpd.conf`
				`/etc/vsftpd/`
				`user_list`

FTP Server with Kerberos Support (Gss-FTP)	krb5-workstation	`/etc/init.d/xinetd`
		`(/etc/xinetd.d/gssftp)`
			`/usr/sbin/xinetd`
			`(/usr/kerberos/`
			`sbin/ftpd)`
				`/etc/krb5.conf`

Samba Windows File and Printers (SMB)	samba
	samba-common
	samba-client
	samba-swat
	system-config-samba
		`/etc/init.d/smb`
		`/etc/init.d/winbind`
			`/usr/sbin/smbd`
			`/usr/sbin/nmbd`
			`/usr/sbin/`
			`winbindd`
				`/etc/samba/`
				`smb.conf`

UNIX Network File System (NFS)	nfs-utils
	system-config-nfs
		`/etc/init.d/nfs`
		`/etc/init.d/nfslock`
			`/usr/sbin/rpc.nfsd`
			`/usr/sbin/rpc.mountd`
			`/sbin/rpc.statd`
				`/etc/exports`

AppleTalk File and Print Server (Netatalk)	netatalk	`/etc/init.d/atalk`	`/usr/sbin/atalkd`	`/etc/atalk/*`

Table B-1 (continued)

Feature	Package Names	Startup Script(s)	Daemon	Configuration File(s)
Login Servers				
Telnet	telnet-server	/etc/init.d/xinetd (etc/xinetd.d/telnet)	/usr/sbin/xinetd (/usr/sbin/in.telnetd)	/etc/issue.net
Telnet with Kerberos Support (Krb5-telnet)	krb5-workstation	/etc/init.d/xinetd (etc/xinetd.d/krb5-telnet)	/usr/sbin/xinetd (/usr/kerberos/ sbin/telnetd)	/etc/krb5.conf
Open Secure Shell (Openssh)	openssh-server	/etc/initd/sshd	/usr/sbin/sshd	/etc/ssh/*
Remote Login (Rlogin)	rsh-server	/etc/init.d/xinetd (etc/xinetd.d/rlogin)	/usr/sbin/xinetd (/usr/sbin/in.rlogind)	/etc/hosts.equiv $HOME/.rhosts
Remote Login with Kerberos Support (Eklogin)	krb5-workstation	/etc/init.d/xinetd (etc/xinetd.d.eklogin)	/usr/sbin/xinetd (/usr/kerberos/ sbin/klogind)	/etc/krb5.conf $HOME/.k5login $HOME/.klogin
(Klogin)	krb5-workstation	/etc/init.d/xinetd	/usr/sbin/xinetd(/usr/ kerberos/sbin/klogind)	/etc/krb5.conf $HOME/.k5login $HOME/.klogin
E-mail Servers				
Remote Mail Access Servers (IMAP)	dovecot	/etc/init.d/dovecot	/usr/sbin/dovecot	/etc/dovecot
(POP3)	dovecot	/etc/init.d/dovecot	/usr/sbin/dovecot	/etc/dovecot
E-mail Transfer Servers (Sendmail)	sendmail sendmail-cf sendmail-doc	/etc/init.d/sendmail	/usr/sbin/sendmail	/etc/sendmail.cf /etc/mail/*
(Postfix)	postfix	/etc/init.d/postfix	/usr/sbin/postfix	/etc/postfix/*

Table B-1 (continued)

Feature	Package Names	Startup Script(s)	Daemon	Configuration File(s)
News Server				
Internet Network News (INN)	inn	/etc/init.d/innd	/usr/bin/innd	/etc/news/*
Print Server				
Common UNIX Printing System (CUPS)	cups cups-drivers cups-libs cups-drivers-hpijs	/etc/init.d/cups	/usr/sbin/cupsd	/etc/cups/*
Network Administration Servers				
Network Time Protocol Server (NTP)	ntp	/etc/init.d/ntpd	/usr/sbin/ntpd	/etc/ntp.conf /etc/ntp/keys
Network Portmap (RPC to DARPA)	portmap	/etc/init.d/portmap	/sbin/portmap	/etc/rpc
Samba Administration (SWAT)	samba-swat	/etc/init.d/xinetd (/etc/xinetd.d/swat)	/usr/sbin/xinetd (/usr/sbin/swat)	/etc/smb.conf
Network Management (arpwatch)	arpwatch	/etc/init.d/arpwatch	/usr/sbin/arpwatch	/etc/sysconfig/arpwatch
Simple Network Management Protocol (SNMP)	net-snmp	/etc/init.d/snmpd /etc/init.d/snmptrapd	/usr/sbin/snmpd	/etc/snmp/snmpd.conf
Information Servers				
Network Information Server (Ypbind)	ypbind	/etc/init.d/ypbind	/sbin/ypbind	/etc/yp.conf
(Yppasswdd)	ypserv	/etc/init.d/yppasswdd	/usr/sbin/rpc.yppasswd	/etc/passwd /etc/shadow
(Ypserv)	ypserv	/etc/init.d/ypserv	/usr/sbin/ypserv	/etc/ypserv.conf

Table B-1 (continued)

Feature	Package Names	Startup Script(s)	Daemon	Configuration File(s)
Information Servers *(continued)*				
Dynamic Host Configuration Protocol Server (DHCP)	dhcp	`/etc/init.d/dhcpd`	`/usr/sbin/dhcpd`	`/etc/dhcpd.conf`
Lightweight Directory Access Protocol (LDAP)	openldap-servers	`/etc/init.d/ldap`	`/usr/sbin/slapd` `/usr/sbin/slurpd`	`/etc/openldap/slapd.conf`
Domain Name System Server (DNS)	bind bind-utils bind-chroot	`/etc/init.d/named`	`/usr/sbin/named`	`/etc/named.conf` `/var/named/*`
Reverse Address Resolution Protocol Server (RARP)	rarpd	`/etc/init.d/rarpd`	`/usr/sbin/rarpd`	`/etc/ethers`
Database Services				
MySQL Database	mysql mysql-server	`/etc/init.d/mysqld`	`/usr/libexec/mysqld`	`/etc/my.cnf`
Postgresql	postgresql-libs postgresql postgresql-server	`/etc/init.d/postgresql`	`/usr/bin/postmaster`	`/var/lib/pgsql/data`
User Services				
Remote Execution Servers (Rsh)	rsh-server	`/etc/init.d/xinetd` `(/etc/xinetd.d/rsh)`	`/usr/sbin/xinetd` `(/usr/sbin/in.rshd)`	`/etc/hosts.equiv` `$HOME/.rhosts`
(Rexec)	rsh-server	`/etc/init.d/xinetd` `(/etc/xinetd.d/rexec)`	`/usr/sbin/xinetd` `(/usr/sbin/in.rexecd)`	`/etc/passwd`
(Kshell)	krb5-workstation	`/etc/init.d/xinetd` `(/etc/xinetd.d/kshell)`	`/usr/sbin/xinetd` `(/usr/kerberos/sbin/kshd)`	`/etc/krb5.conf`

Table B-1 (continued)

Feature	Package Names	Startup Script(s)	Daemon	Configuration File(s)
User Services *(continued)*				
Talk Server (ntalk)	talk-server	/etc/init.d/xinetd (/etc/xinetd.d/ntalk)	/usr/sbin/xinetd (/usr/sbin/in.ntalkd)	
(talk)	talk-server	/etc/init.d/xinetd (/etc/xinetd.d/talk)	/usr/sbin/xinetd (/usr/sbin/in.talkd)	
Finger Server (Finger)	finger-server	/etc/init.d/xinetd (/etc/xinetd.d/finger)	/usr/sbin/xinetd (/usr/sbin/in.fingerd)	
Identify Users (Rusers)	rusers-server	/etc/init.d/rusersd	/usr/sbin/rpc.rusersd	
Write All Users (Rwall)	rwall-server	/etc/init.d/rwalld	/usr/sbin/rpc.rwalld	
Security Services				
System Logging (syslog)	sysklogd	/etc/init.d/syslog	/sbin/syslogd	/etc/syslog.conf
Caching Server (Squid)	squid	/etc/init.d/squid	/usr/sbin/squid	/etc/squid/squid.conf

Appendix C

Red Hat Enterprise Linux 5 Features

With its Red Hat Enterprise Linux (RHEL) commercial product line, Red Hat, Inc. is clearly positioning itself to go after customers looking to put Linux computing infrastructures in place. So, when you look at the differences between features in Fedora distributions and RHEL products, many features surrounding RHEL products are geared toward managing multiple desktop and server systems within a large organization.

Despite the fact that Red Hat is aimed primarily at customers who want to build large-scale Linux infrastructures, there are ways of starting with RHEL that require a much smaller investment. Later in this appendix, I describe how to get an evaluation copy of RHEL to try out that you can then upgrade to an affordable subscription program.

The current version of Red Hat Enterprise Linux, RHEL 5, was released in March 2007 and is now generally available. Information about RHEL and related products is available from the Red Hat Web site: `www.redhat.com/rhel`.

What's in RHEL 5?

Red Hat, Inc. released RHEL 5 in March, 2007, based on software that was included in Fedora 6. Since RHEL 4, RHEL software product names have changed. Instead of Workstations, Desktops, Enterprise servers, and Application servers, there are two main categories: Servers and Clients.

- **RHEL 5 Servers** — Subsets of RHEL 5 server products include storage, cluster, and virtualization servers. The RHEL 5 Advanced Platform allows unlimited virtualization, GFS filesystem storage support, and improved clustering.

- **RHEL 5 Desktops** — For desktop systems, there are Workstation, Desktop, and virtualization systems.

While there are many new features in RHEL 5 compared to RHEL 4, here are some of the most striking new features:

- **Virtualization** — In RHEL 5, virtualization features are based on XenSource technology. XenSource is owned by Citrix Systems Inc. (http://www.citrixxenserver.com) through a recent acquisition. The concept of virtualization is to allow multiple operating systems to run on a single computer. For RHEL 5, this includes the ability to run multiple instances of RHEL 5 on one machine (in what is called *para-virtualization*) or to run guest operating systems, such as Microsoft Windows. In most cases, special virtualized hardware is needed, such as Intel Virtualization Technology or AMD Virtualization processors.

  Virtualization is seen as a critical feature for enterprise computing, where often a single machine is configured to run only a single application. With virtualization, a large enterprise can have multiple virtualized operating systems each running a single application and sharing the same computer hardware. As demand increases or decreases for a particular service, the entire virtualized O/S can be moved to a different computer or duplicated to handle more load.

  Virtualization also improves efficiency in other ways. For example, virtualization makes it easier to back up snapshots of the operating system, deploy system images in different ways, and enable virtual desktops and thin clients.

- **Security** — Security Enhanced Linux (SELinux) continues to be one of the main features that Red Hat offers to distinguish itself from other Enterprise players. With tools such as the SELinux Troubleshooter and SELinux Management Tool, it has become easier for systems administrators to lock down security on many of the most important services. These include Web service (httpd), name service (bind), network information service (ypbind), and DHCP (dhcpd).

- **Software Package Management** — With RHEL 5, the yum facilities have become the backbone of the software installation and maintenance features. Improvements to anaconda allow RHEL 5 servers to install from multiple yum-enabled software repositories. Graphical tools such as PackageKit make it easy to get updates, search for packages, and add and remove software.

Other features of RHEL 5 desktop and server systems include (but aren't limited to):

- **Linux 2.6 Kernel** — The 2.6 kernel is part of both the latest Fedora and RHEL distributions. Features in the 2.6 kernel that make it particularly valuable in RHEL are its ability to handle more processors, larger memory pools, more devices, larger file systems, and higher-bandwidth networks, than could the previous major kernel release (2.4).

- **GNOME and KDE desktops** — Like Fedora, RHEL 5 offers both GNOME and KDE desktop software, with GNOME installed by default. Aside from menus, logos and backgrounds being different, you can follow most of the descriptions of Fedora desktop features in Chapter 3 to learn about how the RHEL 5 desktops work.

- **Applications** — Hundreds of desktop applications for creating documents, using the Internet, working with graphics, and playing with sound and video are included with RHEL 5.

- **Extras** — To offer RHEL customers the same range of software available to Fedora users, Red Hat created the Extra Packages for Enterprise Linux (EPEL) software repository. This project has been spearheaded by the Fedora project, providing ports of packages from the Fedora repository that are not in RHEL. These packages should work with RHEL, as well as direct RHEL derivatives, such as CentOS.

- **Development tools** — Tools for building and creating applications are available for a wide range of software environments. Besides the common C compilation system tools, a range of tools is available for developing applications specific to the kernel, X Window System, GNOME desktop, KDE desktop, and legacy C and C++ applications.

- **System administration tools** — Red Hat's own graphical system configuration tools are included with a full set of system administration commands and interfaces.

- **Network servers** — The same file, Web, mail, DNS, news, database, and other network servers available with Fedora are included with RHEL distributions.

Nearly every software feature included in the Fedora distribution that comes with this book and is described in these chapters will work as described here for RHEL systems as well. So this book can serve as a guide and learning tool, regardless of whether you are using Fedora or RHEL systems.

While many features overlap between Fedora and RHEL systems, there is a great difference between the two systems when it comes to service and support. For RHEL, Red Hat offers:

- **Hardware certification** — More than 1500 servers have been certified to run Red Hat Enterprise Linux.

- **Training** — Red Hat offers individual courses in system administration and development, with both live instructors and online training. Red Hat also has specialized solutions available to ensure that customer's entire staff is prepared to deploy Red Hat solutions.

- **Technical support** — Using Red Hat Network, you can manage and update your RHEL subscriptions and track your open support tickets. Also part of Red Hat Global Support Services is a complete set of documentation, mailing lists, and other online resources.

- **Certified applications** — Red Hat has certified thousands of independent software vendor (ISV) applications to run on RHEL, with hundreds of new applications being added every month.

Red Hat will help a company migrate to RHEL, and then scale up the company's computing needs as high as they need to go. Red Hat also offers consulting service to help companies put a Linux infrastructure in place.

What's New in RHEL 5.1?

The central theme for new features in RHEL 5.1 is: "Any application, anywhere, anytime." Virtualization is the cornerstone of this initiative. RHEL 5.1 was released in November, 2007.

Using virtualization within Red Hat's Linux Automation initiative, a customer can deploy an application as a separate instance that includes not only the application itself, but also the specific operating system and settings needed to run that application. Each instance can then be deployed to multiple locations and easily moved to different servers to make best use of available computing resources.

Within the RHEL 5.1 framework, virtualized applications can actually be running on Linux or Windows operating systems (Window XP, Windows 2000, Windows Server 2003, and others), so even existing applications can take advantage of Red Hat's framework for deploying and managing applications.

Choosing an RHEL System

Red Hat, Inc. is not geared up for selling and supporting only one or two Linux systems at a time, so the packaging and pricing of Red Hat systems is aimed at orders of multiple systems. With RHEL, you aren't really paying for the software. Instead, you're paying for a subscription, which includes access to all released versions of RHEL, support from Red Hat, and maintenance updates for seven years. The prices in the following list are actually yearly subscription prices.

> **NOTE:** Visit the Red Hat site (`www.redhat.com/rhel`) for the latest subscription rates and terms for Red Hat Enterprise Linux. Make sure that cookies are enabled before your visit the Red Hat site.

Here are the major forms in which RHEL systems are available:

- **RHEL Advanced Platform Server** — Yearly subscriptions for this type of server are available for $1,499 (standard) and $2,499 (premium). This is the recommended configuration for large, multi-system deployments.

- **RHEL Server** — A basic RHEL server subscription is available for $349, a standard subscription is $799, and a premium subscription is $1299 per year. These systems are designed for smaller deployment. The basic subscription includes only Web support, while the standard and premium subscriptions offer phone support. The premium offers 24x7 phone support. Supported architectures include Intel and AMD (x86/x86-64), Intel Itanium2, and IBM Power.

- **RHEL for Mainframe Computing Server** — Red Hat offers both standard and premium subscriptions on IBM z-Series and S/390 processors. You need to contact Red Hat directly for pricing on those subscriptions, although standard subscriptions begin at $15,000 per mainframe. You can run up to 1000 Enterprise Linux AS instances for each subscription.

- **RHEL Desktop** — The Red Hat Desktop systems are designed for general-purpose desktop use. These systems are appropriate, for example, for a university or business that needs to allow students or employees to browse the Web, check e-mail, or run applications. The Basic RHEL Desktop subscription starts at $80 per year. There are Multi-OS Desktop versions that you can purchase for $120/year with a basic subscription. Workstation systems with basic subscriptions start at $179/year. Standard subscriptions on Workstation and Multi-OS desktop systems start at $219/year.

To compare pricing and services of different RHEL desktop subscriptions, refer to the Compare Desktops page at www.redhat.com/rhel/desktop/compare. To compare server subscriptions, refer to www.redhat.com/rhel/server/compare.

To encourage students and teachers to use Red Hat Enterprise Linux, Red Hat offers special pricing (www.redhat.com/solutions/education). Pricing for the Red Hat Enterprise Linux Academic Desktop Edition starts at $30 per subscription. Red Hat Enterprise Linux Academic Server Editions starts at $60 per subscription.

Getting RHEL Evaluation Subscriptions

A free 30-day evaluation subscription is available for any of the RHEL 5 products. You can sign up for that evaluation subscription from the Red Hat Web site (www.redhat.com/rhel/details/eval). You can't, however, just sign up and download the software. By signing up for a free evaluation, you must agree to have Red Hat contact you to assess your interest in Red Hat Enterprise Linux.

Before you can get updates for your demo system, you need to activate the product. Red Hat Network will send you an e-mail, notifying you of where to go to activate a single *entitlement* that comes with the evaluation subscription. When I did this, I was directed to go to the following site:

```
https://www.redhat.com/apps/activate
```

Sign in with the login and password associated with your evaluation subscription.

If you decide you want to continue using your RHEL system after the demo period, you can purchase a single entitlement for your system. That allows you to continue getting updates and provides access to Red Hat online support features (documentation, errata, and so on).

Hardware Compatibility and Commercial Software

While support for hardware can be hit-or-miss with Fedora, Red Hat maintains lists of hardware that has been certified to work with RHEL 5 systems. To find information on certified hardware for RHEL 5, visit the Red Hat Hardware Catalog at the Red Hat Web site (http://hardware.redhat.com).

On the commercial software side, Red Hat maintains a catalog of several hundred certified software vendors whose products will run on RHEL systems. This vendor list includes several partner companies, such as Oracle, IBM, BEA Systems, Veritas Software, and Sybase. You can see lists of Red Hat commercial software vendors in the Red Hat Software Catalog (`https://www.redhat.com/apps/isv_catalog`).

Red Hat also helps companies that want to develop commercial applications to run on RHEL systems. You can get information on support available to application developers from the Developer Support page (`www.redhat.com/developers/subscriptions.html`).

Training and Certification

If you are looking for a career in Linux, Red Hat offers some well-respected programs for becoming a certified expert in Red Hat Linux software. You can learn about available programs from Red Hat's training Web site (`https://www.redhat.com/training`).

If you plan to pursue any of the Red Hat certification programs, don't be surprised if after some theoretical training you are given a misconfigured computer and asked to fix it. Those who get Red Hat certifications are expected to be able to clean up and repair Linux systems in the real world.

Here is a list of available certifications from Red Hat:

- **Red Hat Certified Technician (RHCT)** — An RHCT is the most basic Red Hat certification. It focuses on core skills needed by a Red Hat system administrator. Besides being able to install and configure an RHEL system to come up on a corporate network, you are also expected to understand basic troubleshooting techniques.

- **Red Hat Certified Engineer (RHCE)** — The RHCE program builds on the skills developed in the RHCT program. For an RHCE, however, additional capabilities in security and deploying network services are expected.

- **Red Hat Certified Security Specialist (RHCSS)** — As the name implies, an RHCSS becomes proficient in security-related aspects of managing Red Hat Enterprise Linux systems. Courses with this certification include Enterprise Network Services Security, Enterprise Directory Services and Authentication, and SELinux Policy and Administration.

- **Red Hat Certified Architect (RHCA)** — An RHCA's skills are expected to go beyond those of an RHCT or RHCE. The RHCA program focuses on deploying and managing multiple Linux systems across an enterprise, with special attention given to systems management, storage management, performance tuning, and directory services.

For courses on RHCT, RHCE, RHCSS, and RHCA certifications, visit the Red Hat Certified Engineer Program page (`https://www.redhat.com/training/`). Red Hat offers many courses online for Red Hat Linux training, as well as courses in networking, programming (Java, Object, Web, and general programming), IT management, and e-business.

Documentation and Support

A great many tools are available to help you from the Red Hat Global Support Services site (`https://www.redhat.com/apps/support`). If you have an evaluation subscription, you can use your login ID and password to try out the support services. Access to these resources is reason enough for getting an RHEL subscription once your demo subscription runs out.

Red Hat offers lots of avenues to get help using RHEL products from the support site. Red Hat Enterprise Linux documentation (`www.redhat.com/docs/manuals/enterprise`) includes manuals for installation, system administration, security, SELinux, reference materials, and release notes for different products. You can use keyword searches to find answers to your questions from the Red Hat Knowledgebase.

Managing RHEL Systems

The ability to manage and grow your Linux infrastructure efficiently (and inexpensively) are probably the best reasons for using RHEL systems. Red Hat created the Red Hat Network to allow you to track and update your RHEL systems properly. With different subscription levels come increased levels of support and features for maintaining anywhere from one to thousands of systems.

Using features including global file systems (GFS) and high performance computing (HPC) clustering techniques, Red Hat offers help creating a flexible and efficient Linux software infrastructure. This infrastructure lets you expand your computing capacity incrementally without discarding (or even stopping) the structure you put in place.

Using Red Hat Network

The Red Hat Network (`https://rhn.redhat.com`) offers a service for managing your Linux systems. You can try out Red Hat Network when you sign up for an evaluation subscription. From the Red Hat Network site, you can upgrade your demo system to a paid subscription or sign up for additional entitlements to manage multiple RHEL systems.

Red Hat developed Red Hat Network to help companies implement and manage their Linux infrastructure. There are several different architectures in which Red Hat Network can be configured. These different architectures allow you to choose whether or not your RHEL systems talk directly to Red Hat Network (to manage system entitlements and updates), or to a satellite or proxy server set up on your premises.

The architecture you choose will impact the level of control you can exert over your RHEL systems. Here are the choices:

- **Hosted model** — With a hosted model, each RHEL system communicates directly with Red Hat Network servers for managing the updates it gets. Those updates are based on the appropriate channel for the hardware and software you are using. That information is stored by Red Hat servers, as opposed to being managed locally on your own network.

- **Proxy model** — The proxy model works similarly to the hosted model, but instead of having each system on your premises get updates individually from Red Hat Network, a proxy server is set up on the customer premises, so each set of updates needs to be downloaded to your network only once. Individual systems will then get the updates they need from the local proxy server. Although updates are stored locally, information about channels and entitlements are still managed by Red Hat Network servers.

- **Satellite model** — All Red Hat Network features (system management, updates, and so on) are located on your local network. Updates are downloaded from Red Hat Network to your satellite server, as they are with a proxy server. However, features for managing custom channels and other tasks normally done by RHN can be offloaded to the satellite server. The satellite model is typically used for large enterprises that want to maintain more control and security over their deployment of software. Different levels of support and training are available, although the intent is to have Red Hat act as technical consultant while your own employees manage system and database administration for your network satellite server.

Beyond the basic Update service, there are levels of support you can purchase from Red Hat. The Management and Provisioning support programs are aimed at helping you manage RHEL systems across an entire organization. Here's what you get with those services:

- **Management** — With this subscription level, an organization can set up administrative users to manage groups of systems. An Organization Administrator has the ability to assign those users and the systems to which they have access. To manage their systems, a user can do such things as compare package sets installed on different systems, search groups of systems for information on installed packages or hardware tags, group systems together so they can be managed as a group, and process adding or removing software packages for a batch of systems.

- **Provisioning** — The Provisioning subscription level includes all features of the Update and Management levels, but adds further features for managing multiple systems. For example, you can create kickstart profiles that allow you to install groups of systems with many features preset (such as time zone, GPG and SSL keys, and specific package sets). If you are installing on similar hardware, you can even preset normally tricky configuration features such as video card configuration. Provisioning subscribers also have the ability to roll back their system software configurations to points in the past. Using snapshots when updates are done, you can go back to previous configuration files, package profiles, and channels.

Besides software management and update features, Red Hat Network offers features for monitoring your registered systems. This can include simple queries (pings) to make sure systems are up and running, as well as responses to alert you to dangerous system states (such as WARNING and CRITICAL log messages). Reports can be generated to provide overviews of your system states.

To find out more about how Red Hat Network works and the features it has available, refer to the Red Hat Network Reference Guide (`http://rhn.redhat.com/help/reference/`).

Using RHEL for high-performance computing clusters

Cluster-based High-Performance Computing (HPC) begins with the concept that you don't need huge, monolithic computers to handle high-demand business and scientific applications. Instead, you can simply put a structure in place that lets you add inexpensive, commodity hardware and open source software to get to the capacity level you need.

Open source software projects such as Ganglia (`http://ganglia.sourceforge.net`) have emerged in recent years to help form the foundation for managing and deploying cluster computing systems. Red Hat offers subscriptions aimed directly at supporting HPC clusters. Contact Red Hat directly for more information.

With HPC clusters, computing that needs to be done within an organization can be spread across multiple *compute nodes* (also called *worker nodes*). All compute nodes are configured identically. Master nodes are set up to direct the work of the compute nodes. Compute nodes run RHEL WS systems, while the master nodes must be an ES or AS system.

Using RHEL Global File System

For organizations with large-scale demands on Web servers, mail servers, file servers, or database servers, Red Hat Global File System (GFS) offers the capability to centralize data storage in a way that is efficient and scalable. The idea is to have all servers that need to access a company's data refer to one namespace that would be lightning-fast to access.

With GFS, RHEL servers are connected to a storage area network (SAN) that acts as a cluster file system. The fact that a GFS file system may reside on multiple disks on multiple storage units is invisible to the people and applications using the data.

Because GFS is a file system type and volume manager, by supporting GFS all Red Hat servers can access GFS volumes as they would any file system. Like file system types such as NFS, GFS can be accessed over a network. Unlike NFS, however, GFS doesn't incur the overhead of using a TCP/IP-based network for communication, but instead relies on iSCSI or Fibre Channel for communications.

Because communication can be done so efficiently using GFS, there is no need to incur the complexity of maintaining multiple versions of data to ensure good performance. Any component of a GFS configuration (storage units, servers, or network interfaces) can be redundant. So any component that goes down can be quickly replaced. If increased capacity is needed, you can add volumes or resize file systems while the GFS is still up.

Because growth of your GFS can be done by scaling *out* (adding machines of the same architecture) instead of scaling *up* (replacing existing machines with better ones), businesses can grow without taking down existing infrastructure. Expansion can be done incrementally.

More Information on RHEL

For more details on RHEL features, subscriptions, and other RHEL topics, refer to the Red Hat Web site (`www.redhat.com/rhel`). The site offers white papers that provide in-depth information on a variety of Red Hat technology topics.

Index

GNU General Public License

Version 2, June 1991

Copyright © 1989, 1991 Free Software Foundation, Inc.

59 Temple Place - Suite 330, Boston, MA 02111-1307, USA

Preamble

The licenses for most software are designed to take away your freedom to share and change it. By contrast, the GNU General Public License is intended to guarantee your freedom to share and change free software — to make sure the software is free for all its users. This General Public License applies to most of the Free Software Foundation's software and to any other program whose authors commit to using it. (Some other Free Software Foundation software is covered by the GNU Library General Public License instead.) You can apply it to your programs, too.

When we speak of free software, we are referring to freedom, not price. Our General Public Licenses are designed to make sure that you have the freedom to distribute copies of free software (and charge for this service if you wish), that you receive source code or can get it if you want it, that you can change the software or use pieces of it in new free programs; and that you know you can do these things.

To protect your rights, we need to make restrictions that forbid anyone to deny you these rights or to ask you to surrender the rights. These restrictions translate to certain responsibilities for you if you distribute copies of the software, or if you modify it.

For example, if you distribute copies of such a program, whether gratis or for a fee, you must give the recipients all the rights that you have. You must make sure that they, too, receive or can get the source code. And you must show them these terms so they know their rights.

We protect your rights with two steps: (1) copyright the software, and (2) offer you this license which gives you legal permission to copy, distribute and/or modify the software.

Also, for each author's protection and ours, we want to make certain that everyone understands that there is no warranty for this free software. If the software is modified by someone else and passed on, we want its recipients to know that what they have is not the original, so that any problems introduced by others will not reflect on the original authors' reputations.

Finally, any free program is threatened constantly by software patents. We wish to avoid the danger that redistributors of a free program will individually obtain patent licenses, in effect making the program proprietary. To prevent this, we have made it clear that any patent must be licensed for everyone's free use or not licensed at all.

The precise terms and conditions for copying, distribution and modification follow.

Terms and Conditions for Copying, Distribution and Modification

0. This License applies to any program or other work which contains a notice placed by the copyright holder saying it may be distributed under the terms of this General Public License. The "Program", below, refers to any such program or work, and a "work based on the Program" means either the Program or any derivative work under copyright law: that is to say, a work containing the Program or a portion of it, either verbatim or with modifications and/or translated into another language. (Hereinafter, translation is included without limitation in the term "modification".) Each licensee is addressed as "you".

   Activities other than copying, distribution and modification are not covered by this License; they are outside its scope. The act of running the Program is not restricted, and the output from the Program is covered only if its contents constitute a work based on the Program (independent of having been made by running the Program). Whether that is true depends on what the Program does.

1. You may copy and distribute verbatim copies of the Program's source code as you receive it, in any medium, provided that you conspicuously and appropriately publish on each copy an appropriate copyright notice and disclaimer of warranty; keep intact all the notices that refer to this License and to the absence of any warranty; and give any other recipients of the Program a copy of this License along with the Program.

   You may charge a fee for the physical act of transferring a copy, and you may at your option offer warranty protection in exchange for a fee.

2. You may modify your copy or copies of the Program or any portion of it, thus forming a work based on the Program, and copy and distribute such modifications or work under the terms of Section 1 above, provided that you also meet all of these conditions:

a) You must cause the modified files to carry prominent notices stating that you changed the files and the date of any change.

b) You must cause any work that you distribute or publish, that in whole or in part contains or is derived from the Program or any part thereof, to be licensed as a whole at no charge to all third parties under the terms of this License.

c) If the modified program normally reads commands interactively when run, you must cause it, when started running for such interactive use in the most ordinary way, to print or display an announcement including an appropriate copyright notice and a notice that there is no warranty (or else, saying that you provide a warranty) and that users may redistribute the program under these conditions, and telling the user how to view a copy of this License. (Exception: if the Program itself is interactive but does not normally print such an announcement, your work based on the Program is not required to print an announcement.)

These requirements apply to the modified work as a whole. If identifiable sections of that work are not derived from the Program, and can be reasonably considered independent and separate works in themselves, then this License, and its terms, do not apply to those sections when you distribute them as separate works. But when you distribute the same sections as part of a whole which is a work based on the Program, the distribution of the whole must be on the terms of this License, whose permissions for other licensees extend to the entire whole, and thus to each and every part regardless of who wrote it.

Thus, it is not the intent of this section to claim rights or contest your rights to work written entirely by you; rather, the intent is to exercise the right to control the distribution of derivative or collective works based on the Program.

In addition, mere aggregation of another work not based on the Program with the Program (or with a work based on the Program) on a volume of a storage or distribution medium does not bring the other work under the scope of this License.

3. You may copy and distribute the Program (or a work based on it, under Section 2) in object code or executable form under the terms of Sections 1 and 2 above provided that you also do one of the following:

a) Accompany it with the complete corresponding machine-readable source code, which must be distributed under the terms of Sections 1 and 2 above on a medium customarily used for software interchange; or,

b) Accompany it with a written offer, valid for at least three years, to give any third party, for a charge no more than your cost of physically performing source distribution, a complete machine-readable copy of the corresponding source code, to be distributed under the terms of Sections 1 and 2 above on a medium customarily used for software interchange; or,

c)   Accompany it with the information you received as to the offer to distribute corresponding source code. (This alternative is allowed only for noncommercial distribution and only if you received the program in object code or executable form with such an offer, in accord with Subsection b above.)

The source code for a work means the preferred form of the work for making modifications to it. For an executable work, complete source code means all the source code for all modules it contains, plus any associated interface definition files, plus the scripts used to control compilation and installation of the executable. However, as a special exception, the source code distributed need not include anything that is normally distributed (in either source or binary form) with the major components (compiler, kernel, and so on) of the operating system on which the executable runs, unless that component itself accompanies the executable.

If distribution of executable or object code is made by offering access to copy from a designated place, then offering equivalent access to copy the source code from the same place counts as distribution of the source code, even though third parties are not compelled to copy the source along with the object code.

4. You may not copy, modify, sublicense, or distribute the Program except as expressly provided under this License. Any attempt otherwise to copy, modify, sublicense or distribute the Program is void, and will automatically terminate your rights under this License. However, parties who have received copies, or rights, from you under this License will not have their licenses terminated so long as such parties remain in full compliance.

5. You are not required to accept this License, since you have not signed it. However, nothing else grants you permission to modify or distribute the Program or its derivative works. These actions are prohibited by law if you do not accept this License. Therefore, by modifying or distributing the Program (or any work based on the Program), you indicate your acceptance of this License to do so, and all its terms and conditions for copying, distributing or modifying the Program or works based on it.

6. Each time you redistribute the Program (or any work based on the Program), the recipient automatically receives a license from the original licensor to copy, distribute or modify the Program subject to these terms and conditions. You may not impose any further restrictions on the recipients' exercise of the rights granted herein. You are not responsible for enforcing compliance by third parties to this License.

7. If, as a consequence of a court judgment or allegation of patent infringement or for any other reason (not limited to patent issues), conditions are imposed on you (whether by court order, agreement or otherwise) that contradict the conditions of this License, they do not excuse you from the conditions of this License. If you cannot distribute so as to satisfy simultaneously your obligations under this License and any other pertinent obligations, then as a consequence you may not distribute the Program at all. For example, if a patent

license would not permit royalty-free redistribution of the Program by all those who receive copies directly or indirectly through you, then the only way you could satisfy both it and this License would be to refrain entirely from distribution of the Program.

If any portion of this section is held invalid or unenforceable under any particular circumstance, the balance of the section is intended to apply and the section as a whole is intended to apply in other circumstances.

It is not the purpose of this section to induce you to infringe any patents or other property right claims or to contest validity of any such claims; this section has the sole purpose of protecting the integrity of the free software distribution system, which is implemented by public license practices. Many people have made generous contributions to the wide range of software distributed through that system in reliance on consistent application of that system; it is up to the author/donor to decide if he or she is willing to distribute software through any other system and a licensee cannot impose that choice.

This section is intended to make thoroughly clear what is believed to be a consequence of the rest of this License.

8. If the distribution and/or use of the Program is restricted in certain countries either by patents or by copyrighted interfaces, the original copyright holder who places the Program under this License may add an explicit geographical distribution limitation excluding those countries, so that distribution is permitted only in or among countries not thus excluded. In such case, this License incorporates the limitation as if written in the body of this License.

9. The Free Software Foundation may publish revised and/or new versions of the General Public License from time to time. Such new versions will be similar in spirit to the present version, but may differ in detail to address new problems or concerns.

Each version is given a distinguishing version number. If the Program specifies a version number of this License which applies to it and "any later version", you have the option of following the terms and conditions either of that version or of any later version published by the Free Software Foundation. If the Program does not specify a version number of this License, you may choose any version ever published by the Free Software Foundation.

10. If you wish to incorporate parts of the Program into other free programs whose distribution conditions are different, write to the author to ask for permission. For software which is copyrighted by the Free Software Foundation, write to the Free Software Foundation; we sometimes make exceptions for this. Our decision will be guided by the two goals of preserving the free status of all derivatives of our free software and of promoting the sharing and reuse of software generally.

NO WARRANTY

11. BECAUSE THE PROGRAM IS LICENSED FREE OF CHARGE, THERE IS NO WARRANTY FOR THE PROGRAM, TO THE EXTENT PERMITTED BY APPLICABLE LAW. EXCEPT WHEN OTHERWISE STATED IN WRITING THE COPYRIGHT HOLDERS AND/OR OTHER PARTIES PROVIDE THE PROGRAM "AS IS" WITHOUT WARRANTY OF ANY KIND, EITHER EXPRESSED OR IMPLIED, INCLUDING, BUT NOT LIMITED TO, THE IMPLIED WARRANTIES OF MERCHANTABILITY AND FITNESS FOR A PARTICULAR PURPOSE. THE ENTIRE RISK AS TO THE QUALITY AND PERFORMANCE OF THE PROGRAM IS WITH YOU. SHOULD THE PROGRAM PROVE DEFECTIVE, YOU ASSUME THE COST OF ALL NECESSARY SERVICING, REPAIR OR CORRECTION.

12. IN NO EVENT UNLESS REQUIRED BY APPLICABLE LAW OR AGREED TO IN WRITING WILL ANY COPYRIGHT HOLDER, OR ANY OTHER PARTY WHO MAY MODIFY AND/OR REDISTRIBUTE THE PROGRAM AS PERMITTED ABOVE, BE LIABLE TO YOU FOR DAMAGES, INCLUDING ANY GENERAL, SPECIAL, INCIDENTAL OR CONSEQUENTIAL DAMAGES ARISING OUT OF THE USE OR INABILITY TO USE THE PROGRAM (INCLUDING BUT NOT LIMITED TO LOSS OF DATA OR DATA BEING RENDERED INACCURATE OR LOSSES SUSTAINED BY YOU OR THIRD PARTIES OR A FAILURE OF THE PROGRAM TO OPERATE WITH ANY OTHER PROGRAMS), EVEN IF SUCH HOLDER OR OTHER PARTY HAS BEEN ADVISED OF THE POSSIBILITY OF SUCH DAMAGES.

END OF TERMS AND CONDITIONS

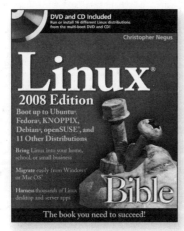